Japan

"When it comes to information on regional history, what to see and do, and shopping, these guides are exhaustive."

—*USAir Magazine*

"Usable, sophisticated restaurant coverage, with an emphasis on good value."

—Andy Birsh, *Gourmet Magazine* columnist

"Valuable because of their comprehensiveness."

—*Minneapolis Star-Tribune*

"Fodor's always delivers high quality...thoughtfully presented...thorough."

—*Houston Post*

"An excellent choice for those who want everything under one cover."

—*Washington Post*

Fodor's Travel Publications, Inc.
New York • Toronto • London • Sydney • Auckland

Fodor's Japan

Editor: Lisa Leventer

Associate Editor: Steven Amsterdam

Copy Editor: Holly Thompson

Contributors: Robert Andrews, Diane Durston, Nigel Fisher, Kiko Itasaka, Dawn Lawson, Jared Lubarsky, Linda K. Schmidt, Mary Ellen Schultz, M.T. Schwartzman (Gold Guide editor), Ian Smith, Dinah Spritzer, Oliver Statler

Creative Director: Fabrizio La Rocca

Cartographer: David Lindroth

Cover Photograph: Brian Lovell/Nawrocki Stock Photo

Text Design: Between the Covers

Copyright

Special Sales

CONTENTS

ON THE ROAD WITH FODOR'S

A GOOD TRAVEL GUIDE is like a wonderful traveling companion. It's charming, it's brimming with sound recommendations and solid ideas, it pulls no punches in describing lodging and dining establishments, and it's consistently full of fascinating facts that make you view what you've traveled to see in a rich new light. In the creation of *Fodor's Japan*, we at Fodor's have gone to great lengths to provide you with the very best of all possible traveling companions—and to make your trip the best of all possible vacations.

About Our Writers

The information in these pages is a collaboration of extraordinary writers.

A resident of Tokyo, **Jared Lubarsky** has lived in Japan since 1973. He has worked for cultural exchange organizations and taught at public and private universities. He still ponders the oddities of Japanese culture and still wonders why the signs that advise you not to ride elevators during an earthquake are posted *inside* the elevators.

Lots of this book is updated by **Nigel Fisher,** the writer and publisher of "Voyager International," a newsletter on world travel. His particular interests are in telling his readers about art, about divine places to stay, and about the most delicious food. He has traveled extensively in Japan for more than 20 years.

Born in Ireland and raised in Ireland and Scotland, **Ian Smith** has lived in Hokkaido for four years. When not lecturing in Hokkai-Gakuen University's Department of American, British and Canadian Studies, Smith writes for local publications and indulges such interests as cartooning, reading gothic literature, pondering Scotland's politics, listening to heavy-metal music, and drinking heavily in Susukino.

We'd also like to thank Mary Beth Maslowski and the New York staff of the Japan National Tourist Oranization (JNTO); the JNTO Tokyo staff, especially Mihoko Suzuki; and Morris Simoncelli of Japan Airlines.

What's New

A New Design

If this is not the first Fodor's guide you've purchased, you'll immediately notice our new look. More readable and easier to use than ever? We think so—and we hope you do, too.

Tavel Updates

In addition, just before your trip, you may want to order a Fodor's Worldview Travel Update. From local publications all over Japan, the lively, cosmopolitan editors at Worldview gather information on concerts, plays, opera, dance performances, gallery and museum shows, sports competitions, and other special events that coincide with your visit. See the order blank at the back of this book, call 800/799–9609, or fax 800/799–9619.

And in Japan

The travel picture looked bleak for Japan in 1995. A devastating earthquake shook the city of Kobe in January, leaving more than 5,000 dead. The value of the yen rose to astronomical heights against other major currencies, making Japan—for a decade now one of the world's most expensive destinations—even more expensive. Members of a fringe religious organization carried out a series of poison gas attacks on the transportation networks in Tokyo and Yokohama, undermining the nation's once-pristine reputation for public safety. The mayor of Tokyo abruptly cancelled an international expo project that had been more than five years in the planning. By midyear, arrivals from overseas were down an estimated 4% from 1994, and at year-end the travel industry was still struggling to break the grip of recession.

The clouds did have a silver lining or two. Hotels awoke at last to the fact that they had been pricing themselves out of the reach of mere mortals, and have begun offering attractive special rates to foreign visitors on package tours; it's even possible these days to walk in off the street and demand a discount at many of the better big-city hotels. Rents for commercial real estate are sharply lower, making it possible for new Western-style restaurants with popular pricing strategies to open in the heart of Tokyo and Osaka. And with their overvalued yen, more and more Japanese are opting to take their vacations abroad; even in holiday seasons, accommodations are easier to find, trains and domestic flights less crowded, and taxis easier to flag down.

Excitement is building toward the **XVIII Winter Olympics,** to be held in Nagano (in the so-called Japan Alps) from February 7 to 22, 1998. An estimated 3,000 athletes and team officials will be participating in seven sports for a total of 64 events. Nagano City, is the center for the Games and the location of the Olympic Village, the main media center, and the ice rinks. It will also be the setting for the opening and closing ceremonies. The Nordic and Alpine events will be held west of Nagano City in the Hakuba area and in the foothills of the Japan Alps.

A **new Shinkansen** (bullet train) line will be operating between Tokyo and Nagano in time for the 1998 Winter Games. Named the Hokuriku Shinkansen, it is scheduled to make its first run from Tokyo in mid-1997 using the Joetsu Shinkansen (the Tokyo–Niigata line) tracks until Takasaki, where it will branch off toward Nagano. Another Shinkansen extension, to begin service in late 1996, will link Morioka (already serviced by Shinkansen trains from Tokyo) with Akita on the northwestern coast of the Tohoku region.

Compared to what they were before the opening of a second terminal building in 1992, arrival and departure prodecures at Tokyo's **Narita International Airport** are pleasant and lightning fast, although using this facility in mid-July through August or in March, when the largest numbers of Japanese take vacations abroad, can still be a harrowing experience. The construction of two new runways at Narita has been held up for years by land acquisition problems; meanwhile, the airport is operating at close to peak capacity, and this can often mean a shortage of berths; arriving passengers—especially on foreign carriers—frequently have to board transfer buses from distant parking spaces to the main building.

The addition of a new West Terminal at Tokyo's **Haneda Airport,** which handles only domestic flights, has done a lot to ease the flow of its 41 million passengers a year. Access via an underground walkway to the main building connects handily to the monorail to the heart of the city.

Finally, after huge cost overruns and extensive delays (building on landfill in Osaka Bay was trickier than contractors anticipated), the new **Kansai International Airport** (KIX) has opened. It is to be used primarily for international flights, though there are connecting domestic flights to Japan's major metropolitan areas. (Osaka's Itami Airport will continue to handle most of the region's domestic flights.) KIX serves the entire Kansai region, alleviating the congestion of Tokyo's airports. However, because of exorbitant landing fees (the highest in the world), the number of carriers flying into KIX is limited.

How to Use This Book

Organization

Up front is the **Gold Guide,** comprising two sections on gold paper that are chock-full of information about traveling within your destination and traveling in general. Both are in alphabetical order by topic. **Important Contacts A to Z** gives addresses and telephone numbers of organizations and companies that offer destination-related services and detailed information or publications. Here's where you'll find information about how to get to Japan from wherever you are. **Smart Travel Tips A to Z,** the Gold Guide's second section, gives specific tips on how to get the most out of your travels, as well as information on how to accomplish what you need to in Japan.

Chapters in *Fodor's Japan* are arranged by region, starting with Tokyo and proceeding west to Kyushu before ending up in the far north, in Tohoku and Hokkaido. Each chapter covers exploring, shopping, sports, dining, lodging, and arts and nightlife, and ends with a section called Essentials, which tells you how to get there and get around and gives you important local addresses and telephone numbers.

At the end of the book you'll find Portraits, a historical timeline and wonderful essays about dining and visiting hot springs in Japan, followed by suggestions for pretrip reading, both fiction and nonfiction.

Stars

Stars in the margin are used to denote highly recommended sights, attractions, hotels, and restaurants.

Restaurant and Hotel Criteria and Price Categories

Restaurants and lodging places are chosen with a view to giving you the cream of the crop in each location and in each price range.

In all restaurant price charts, costs are per person, excluding drinks, tip, and tax. In hotel price charts, rates are for standard double rooms, excluding the 3% federal consumer tax added to all hotel bills and the additional 3% local tax added to the bill if it exceeds ¥15,000.

Hotel Facilities

Note that in general you incur charges when you use many hotel facilities. We wanted to let you know what facilities a hotel has to offer, but we don't always specify whether or not there's a charge, so when planning a vacation that entails a stay of several days, it's wise to ask what's included in the rate.

Dress Code in Restaurants

Look for an overview in the Dining section of Smart Travel Tips A to Z in the Gold Guide pages at the front of this book. The individual chapters' dining sections tell you what's most common in that area. In general, we note a dress code only when men are required to wear a jacket or a jacket and tie.

Credit Cards

The following abbreviations are used: **AE**, American Express; **DC**, Diners Club; **MC**, MasterCard; and **V**, Visa. Discover is not accepted outside the United States.

Please Write to Us

Everyone who has contributed to *Fodor's Japan* has worked hard to make the text accurate. All prices and opening times are based on information supplied to us at press time, and the publisher cannot accept responsibility for any errors that may have occurred. The passage of time will bring changes, so it's always a good idea to call ahead and confirm information when it matters—particularly if you're making a detour to visit specific sights or attractions. When making reservations at a hotel or inn, be sure to speak up if you have a disability or are traveling with children, if you prefer a private bath or a certain type of bed, or if you have specific dietary needs or any other concerns.

Were the restaurants we recommended as described? Did our hotel picks exceed your expectations? Did you find a museum we recommended a waste of time? We would love your feedback, positive and negative. If you have complaints, we'll look into them and revise our entries when the facts warrant it. If you've happened upon a special place that we haven't included, we'll pass the information along to the writers so they can check it out. So please send us a letter or postcard (we're at 201 East 50th Street, New York, New York 10022.) We'll look forward to hearing from you. And in the meantime, have a wonderful trip!

Karen Cure

Karen Cure
Editorial Director

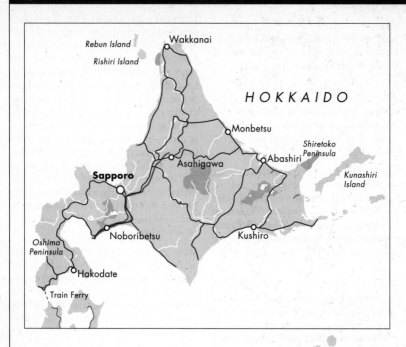

HOKKAIDO
(see inset)

Hakodate

Tsugaru
Peninsula

Shimokita
Peninsula

Sea of Japan

Aomori

Akita   Morioka

Sado
Island

Yamagata

Niigata   Sendai

Noto
Peninsula   Fukushima

Kanazawa   Toyama   Nikko

Fukui   Nagano   Utsunomiya

Takayama   Matsumoto   Oyama

Gifu   Maebashi   Mito

Kofu

Kyoto   Tokyo

Nagoya   Mt. Fuji   Chiba

Nara   Tsu   Yokohama

Shizuoka   Kamakura

Izu
Peninsula

Oshima

HONSHU

PACIFIC OCEAN

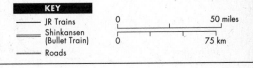

KEY	
——	JR Trains
═══	Shinkansen (Bullet Train)
——	Roads

0   50 miles

0   75 km

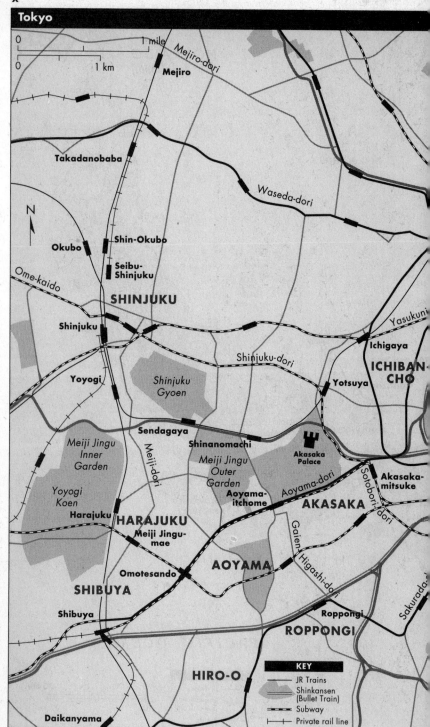

Tokyo

0 — 1 mile
0 — 1 km

N

Mejiro

Mejiro-dori

Takadanobaba

Waseda-dori

Ome-kaido

Okubo

Shin-Okubo

Seibu-Shinjuku

SHINJUKU

Shinjuku

Yoyogi

Shinjuku Gyoen

Shinjuku-dori

Yasukuni

Ichigaya

ICHIBAN-CHO

Yotsuya

Meiji Jingu Inner Garden

Sendagaya

Shinanomachi

Meiji Jingu Outer Garden

Akasaka Palace

Yoyogi Koen

Harajuku

HARAJUKU

Meiji Jingu-mae

Aoyama-itchome

Aoyama-dori

AKASAKA

Akasaka-mitsuke

Sotobori-dori

Meiji-dori

Omotesando

AOYAMA

Gaien-Higashi-dori

SHIBUYA

Shibuya

Roppongi

ROPPONGI

Sakurada

HIRO-O

Daikanyama

KEY

— JR Trains
═ Shinkansen (Bullet Train)
-■-■- Subway
+—+ Private rail line

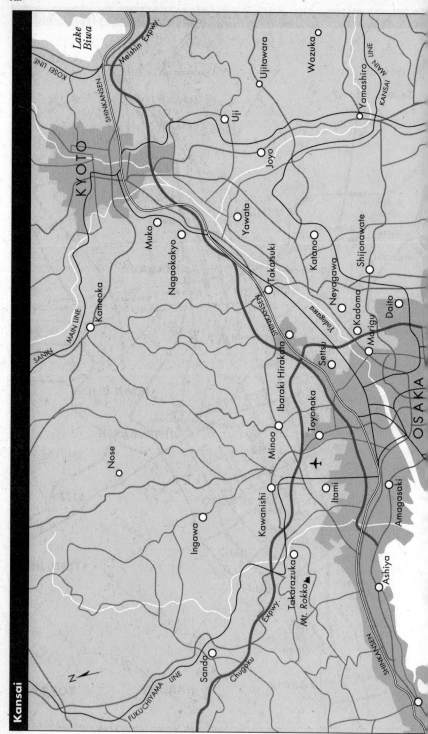

Kansai

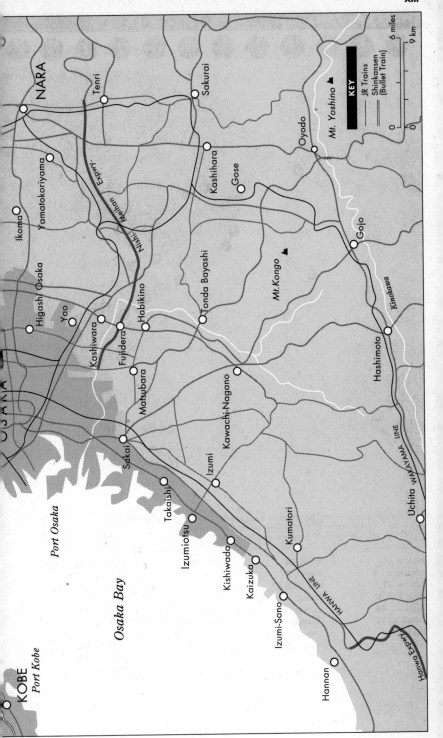

World Time Zones

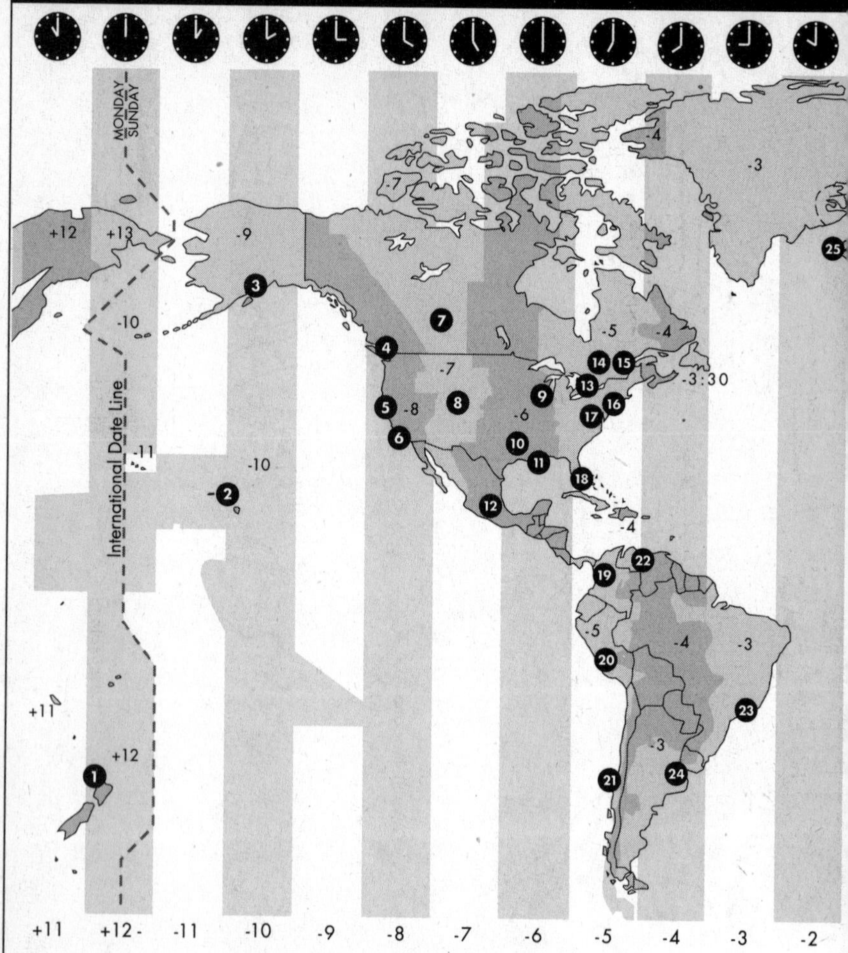

MONDAY
SUNDAY

International Date Line

+12 | +13

-9

-4

-3

25

3

7

-5 | -4

4

14 | 15

-7

-3:30

5 | -8 | 8 | 9 | 13

16

-6 | 17

10

11

12

18

-4

19

22

-5

-4 | -3

20

+11

23

+12

-3

1

21

24

+11 | +12 | -11 | -10 | -9 | -8 | -7 | -6 | -5 | -4 | -3 | -2

Numbers below vertical bands relate each zone to Greenwich Mean Time (0 hrs.).
Local times frequently differ from these general indications,
as indicated by light-face numbers on map.

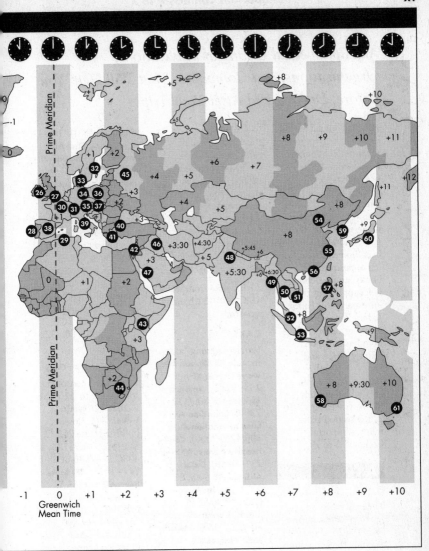

THE GOLD GUIDE / IMPORTANT CONTACTS

IMPORTANT CONTACTS A TO Z

An Alphabetical Listing of Publications, Organizations, and Companies That Will Help You Before, During, and After Your Trip

No single travel resource can give you every detail about every topic that might interest or concern you at the various stages of your journey—when you're planning your trip, while you're on the road, and after you get back home. The following organizations, books, and brochures will supplement the information in *Fodor's Japan*. For related information, including both basic tips on visiting Japan and background information on many of the topics below, study Smart Travel Tips A to Z, the section that follows Important Contacts A to Z.

A

AIR TRAVEL

The major gateway to Japan is **Narita Airport** (☎ 0476/24–5135). To alleviate the congestion at Narita, a new (1994) airport has opened in Osaka: **Kansai International Airport** (☎ 0724/55–2500) serves the Kansai region, which includes Kobe, Kyoto, and Osaka. A few international flights use **Fukuoka Airport** (☎ 092/431–3917), on the island of Kyushu; these include Northwest flights from Honolulu and flights from other Asian destinations. **Chitose Airport** (☎ 0123/23–0111), just

outside Sapporo on the northern island of Hokkaido, handles some international flights, though at present these are mostly nonscheduled flights. Flying time is 13¾ hours from New York, 12¾ hours from Chicago, and 9½ hours from Los Angeles.

Flying time from the U.K. is 11–12 hours nonstop.

CARRIERS

Carriers serving Japan include **All Nippon Airways** (ANA; ☎ 800/235–9262), **American Airlines** (☎ 800/433–7300), **Canadian Airlines International** (☎ 800/426–7000), **Continental Airlines** (☎ 800/231–0856), **Delta Airlines** (☎ 800/221–1212), **Japan Airlines** (JAL; ☎ 800/525–3663), **Korean Air** (☎ 800/223–1155), **Northwest Airlines** (☎ 800/447–4747), **Thai Airways International** (☎ 800/426–5204), and **United Airlines** (☎ 800/538–2929).

The major operators serving Japan from the U.K. are **British Airways** (☎ 0181/897–4000 or 0345/222-111 outside London) and **Japan Airlines** (☎ 0171/408–1000). Others include **All Nippon Airways** (☎ 0171/355–1155); **Korean Air** (☎ 0171/930–6513); **Lufthansa** (☎ 0181/750–3300);

Swissair (☎ 0171/434–7300); and **Thai Airways International** (☎ 0171/499–9113), with one or more transfers.

COMPLAINTS

To register complaints about charter and scheduled airlines, contact the U.S. Department of Transportation's **Office of Consumer Affairs** (400 7th St. NW, Washington, DC 20590, ☎ 202/366–2220 or 800/322–7873).

CONSOLIDATORS

Established consolidators selling to the public include **BET World Travel** (841 Blossom Hill Rd., Suite 212-C, San Jose, CA 95123, ☎ 408/229–7880 or 800/747–1476), **TFI Tours International** (34 W. 32nd St., New York, NY 10001, ☎ 212/736–1140 or 800/745–8000). **FLY–ASAP** (3824 E. Indian School Road, Phoenix, AZ 85018, ☎ 800/359–2727) isn't a discounter, but gets good deals from among published fares, and gets discount tickets from consolidators.

PUBLICATIONS

For general information about charter carriers, ask for the Office of Consumer Affairs' brochure **"Plane Talk: Public Charter Flights."** The Department of Transportation also publishes a 58-page booklet, **"Fly Rights"** ($1.75; Consumer Information Center, Dept. 133B, Pueblo, CO 81009).

For other tips and hints, consult the Consumers Union's monthly **"Consumer Reports Travel Letter"** ($39 a year; Box 53629, Boulder, CO 80322, ☎ 800/234–1970) and the newsletter **"Travel Smart"** ($37 a year; 40 Beechdale Rd., Dobbs Ferry, NY 10522, ☎ 800/327–3633); *The Official Frequent Flyer Guidebook,* by Randy Petersen ($14.99 plus $3 shipping; 4715-C Town Center Dr., Colorado Springs, CO 80916, ☎ 719/597–8899 or 800/487–8893); *Airfare Secrets Exposed,* by Sharon Tyler and Matthew Wonder (Universal Information Publishing; $16.95 plus $3.75 shipping from Sandcastle Publishing, Box 3070-A, South Pasadena, CA 91031, ☎ 213/255–3616 or 800/655–0053); and *202 Tips Even the Best Business Travelers May Not Know,* by Christopher McGinnis ($10 plus $3 shipping; Irwin Professional Publishing, 1333 Burr Ridge Parkway, Burr Ridge, IL 60521, ☎ 800/634–3966).

WITHIN JAPAN

All major Japanese cities have airports connected by domestic flights. (Most internal flights serving Tokyo use Haneda Airport; ☎ 03/3201–7111). The two major services are **All Nippon Airways** (3-6-3 Irifunecho, Chuo-ku, Tokyo, ☎

03/3552--6311) and **Japan Air-lines** (5-37-8 Shiba, Minato-ku, Tokyo, ☎ 03/3456–2111).

B

BETTER BUSINESS BUREAU

For local contacts in the home town of a tour operator you may be considering, consult the **Council of Better Business Bureaus** (4200 Wilson Blvd., Arlington, VA 22203, ☎ 703/276–0100).

BUS TRAVEL

Japanese Railways (☎ 03/3423–0111), which operates domestic bus services, has an English-language information service.

C

CAR RENTAL

Major car-rental companies represented in Japan include **Hertz** (☎ 800/654–3001, 800/263–0600 in Canada, 0181/679–1799 in the U.K.) and **National** (sometimes known as Europcar InterRent outside North America; ☎ 800/227–3876, 0181/950–5050 in the U.K.). Rates in Tokyo begin at $87 a day and $437 a week a for an economy car with unlimited mileage. This does not include tax, which is 3% on car rentals. Reservations in the U.S. should be made at least a week in advance.

CHILDREN AND TRAVEL

FLYING

Look into **"Flying with Baby"** ($5.95 plus $1

shipping; Third Street Press, Box 261250, Littleton, CO 80126, ☎ 303/595–5959), cowritten by a flight attendant. **"Kids and Teens in Flight,"** free from the U.S. Department of Transportation's Office of Consumer Affairs, offers tips for children flying alone. Every two years the February issue of *Family Travel Times* (*see* Know-How, *below*) details children's services on three dozen airlines.

GAMES

The gamemeister Milton Bradley has games to help keep little (and not so little) children from getting fidgety while riding in planes, trains, and automobiles. Try packing the *Travel Battleship* sea battle game ($7), *Travel Connect Four,* a vertical strategy game ($8), the *Travel Yahtzee* dice game ($6), the *Travel Trouble* dice and board game ($7), and the *Travel Guess Who* mystery game ($8).

KNOW-HOW

Family Travel Times, published four times a year by Travel with Your Children (TWYCH, 45 W. 18th St., New York, NY 10011, ☎ 212/206–0688; annual subscription $40), covers destinations, types of vacations, and modes of travel.

The *Family Travel Guides* catalogue ($1 postage; Carousel Press, P.O. Box 6061, Albany, CA 94706; ☎ 510/-527–5849) lists about 200 books and articles on family travel. ***Traveling with Children—And Enjoying It,*** by Arlene K. Butler ($11.95 plus $3 shipping; Globe Pequot Press, Box 833, 6 Business Park Rd., Old Saybrook, CT 06475, ☎ 203/395–0440 or 800/243–0495, 800/962–0973 in CT) helps plan your trip with children, from toddlers to teens. Also check ***Take Your Baby and Go! A Guide for Traveling with Babies, Toddlers and Young Children,*** by Sheri Andrews, Judy Bordeaux, and Vivian Vasquez ($5.95 plus $1.50 shipping; Bear Creek Publications, 2507 Minor Ave., Seattle, WA 98102, ☎ 206/322–7604 or 800/326–6566).

CUSTOMS

U.S. CITIZENS

The **U.S. Customs Service** (Box 7407, Washington, DC 20044, ☎ 202/927–6724) can answer questions on duty-free limits and publishes a helpful brochure, **"Know Before You Go."** For information on registering foreign-made articles, call 202/927–0540.

CANADIANS

Contact **Revenue Canada** (2265 St. Laurent Blvd. S, Ottawa, Ontario K1G 4K3, ☎ 613/993–0534) for a copy of the free brochure **"I Declare/Je Déclare"** and for details on duties that exceed the standard duty-free limit.

U.K. CITIZENS

HM Customs and Excise (Dorset House, Stamford St., London SE1

9NG, ☎ 0171/202–4227) can answer questions about U.K. customs regulations and publishes **"A Guide for Travellers,"** detailing standard procedures and import rules.

D
FOR TRAVELERS WITH DISABILITIES

COMPLAINTS

To register complaints under the provisions of the Americans with Disabilities Act, contact the U.S. Department of Justice's **Public Access Section** (Box 66738, Washington, DC 20035, ☎ 202/514–0301, TTY 202/514–0383, FAX 202/307–1198).

U.S. ORGANIZATIONS

FOR TRAVELERS WITH HEARING IMPAIRMENTS➤ Contact the **American Academy of Otolaryngology** (1 Prince St., Alexandria, VA 22314, ☎ 703/836–4444, FAX 703/683–5100, TTY 703/519–1585).

FOR TRAVELERS WITH MOBILITY PROBLEMS➤ Contact the **Information Center for Individuals with Disabilities** (Fort Point Pl., 27–43 Wormwood St., Boston, MA 02210, ☎ 617/727–5540, 800/462–5015 in MA, TTY 617/345–9743); **Mobility International USA** (Box 10767, Eugene, OR 97440, ☎ and TTY 503/343–1284, FAX 503/343–6812), the U.S. branch of an international organization based in Belgium (*see below*) that has affiliates in 30 countries; **MossRehab Hospital Travel Information Service** (1200 W.

Tabor Rd., Philadelphia, PA 19141, ☎ 215/456–9603, TTY 215/456–9602); the **Society for the Advancement of Travel for the Handicapped** (347 5th Ave., Suite 610, New York, NY 10016, ☎ 212/447–7284, FAX 212/725–8253); the **Travel Industry and Disabled Exchange** (TIDE, 5435 Donna Ave., Tarzana, CA 91356, ☎ 818/344–3640, FAX 818/344–0078); and **Travelin' Talk** (Box 3534, Clarksville, TN 37043, ☎ 615/552–6670, FAX 615/552–1182).

FOR TRAVELERS WITH VISION IMPAIRMENTS➤ Contact the **American Council of the Blind** (1155 15th St. NW, Suite 720, Washington, DC 20005, ☎ 202/467–5081, FAX 202/467–5085) or the **American Foundation for the Blind** (15 W. 16th St., New York, NY 10011, ☎ 212/620–2000, TTY 212/620–2158).

EUROPEAN ORGANIZATIONS

Contact the **Royal Association for Disability and Rehabilitation** (RADAR, 12 City Forum, 250 City Rd., London EC1V 8AF, ☎ 0171/250–3222) or **Mobility International** (Rue de Manchester 25, B-1070 Brussels, Belgium, ☎ 00–322–410–6297), an international clearinghouse of travel information for people with disabilities.

PUBLICATIONS

Several free publications are available from the U.S. Information Center (Box 100, Pueblo, CO

XVIII — Important Contacts A to Z

THE GOLD GUIDE / IMPORTANT CONTACTS

81009, ☎ 719/948–3334): **"New Horizons for the Air Traveler with a Disability"** (address to Dept. 355A), describing legally mandated changes; the pocket-size **"Fly Smart"** (Dept. 575B), good on flight safety; and the Airport Operators Council's worldwide **"Access Travel: Airports"** (Dept. 575A).

The 500-page *Travelin' Talk Directory* ($35; Box 3534, Clarksville, TN 37043, ☎ 615/552–6670) lists people and organizations who help travelers with disabilities. For specialist travel agents worldwide, consult the *Directory of Travel Agencies for the Disabled* ($19.95 plus $2 shipping; Twin Peaks Press, Box 129, Vancouver, WA 98666, ☎ 206/694–2462 or 800/637–2256).

TRAVEL AGENCIES AND TOUR OPERATORS

The Americans with Disabilities Act requires that travel firms serve the needs of all travelers. However, some agencies and operators specialize in making group and individual arrangements for travelers with disabilities, among them **Access Adventures** (206 Chestnut Ridge Rd., Rochester, NY 14624, ☎ 716/889–9096), run by a former physical-rehab counselor.

FOR TRAVELERS WITH MOBILITY IMPAIRMENTS➤ A number of operators specialize in working with travelers with mobility impairments: **Hinsdale Travel Service** (201 E. Ogden Ave.,

Suite 100, Hinsdale, IL 60521, ☎ 708/325–1335 or 800/303–5521), a travel agency that will give you access to the services of wheelchair traveler Janice Perkins; and **Wheelchair Journeys** (16979 Redmond Way, Redmond, WA 98052, ☎ 206/885–2210), which can handle arrangements worldwide.

FOR TRAVELERS WITH DEVELOPMENTAL DISABILITIES➤ Contact the nonprofit **New Directions** (5276 Hollister Ave., Suite 207, Santa Barbara, CA 93111, ☎ 805/967–2841), as well as the general-interest operators above.

Options include **Entertainment Travel Editions** (fee $28–$53, depending on destination; Box 1068, Trumbull, CT 06611, ☎ 800/445–4137), **Great American Traveler** ($49.95 annually; Box 27965, Salt Lake City, UT 84127, ☎ 800/548–2812), **Moment's Notice Discount Travel Club** ($25 annually, single or family; 163 Amsterdam Ave., Suite 137, New York, NY 10023, ☎ 212/486–0500), **Privilege Card** ($74.95 annually; 3391 Peachtree Rd. NE, Suite 110, Atlanta, GA 30326, ☎ 404/262–0222 or 800/236–9732), **Travelers Advantage** ($49 annually, single or family; CUC Travel Service, 49 Music Sq. W, Nashville, TN 37203, ☎ 800/548–1116 or 800/648–4037), and **Worldwide Discount Travel Club** ($50 annually for

family, $40 single; 1674 Meridian Ave., Miami Beach, FL 33139, ☎ 305/534–2082).

E

Send a self-addressed, stamped envelope to the **Franzus Company** (Customer Service, Dept. B50, Murtha Industrial Park, Box 142, Beacon Falls, CT 06403, ☎ 203/723–6664) for a copy of the free brochure "Foreign Electricity Is No Deep Dark Secret."

G

ORGANIZATIONS

The **International Gay Travel Association** (Box 4974, Key West, FL 33041, ☎ 800/448–8550), a consortium of 800 businesses, can supply names of travel agents and tour operators.

PUBLICATIONS

The premier international travel magazine for gays and lesbians is **Our World** ($35 for 10 issues; 1104 N. Nova Rd., Suite 251, Daytona Beach, FL 32117, ☎ 904/441–5367). The 16-page monthly **"Out & About"** ($49 for 10 issues; ☎ 212/645–6922 or 800/929–2268) covers gay-friendly resorts, hotels, cruise lines, and airlines.

TOUR OPERATORS

Toto Tours (1326 W. Albion, Suite 3W, Chicago, IL 60626, ☎ 312/274–8686 or 800/565–1241) offers group tours worldwide.

THE GOLD GUIDE / IMPORTANT CONTACTS

TRAVEL AGENCIES

The largest agencies serving gay travelers are **Advance Travel** (10700 Northwest Freeway, Suite 160, Houston, TX 77092, ☎ 713/682–2002 or 800/695–0880), **Islanders/ Kennedy Travel** (183 W. 10th St., New York, NY 10014, ☎ 212/242–3222 or 800/988–1181), **Now Voyager** (4406 18th St., San Francisco, CA 94114, ☎ 415/626–1169 or 800/255–6951), and **Yellowbrick Road** (1500 W. Balmoral Ave., Chicago, IL 60640, ☎ 312/561–1800 or 800/642–2488). **Skylink Women's Travel** (746 Ashland Ave., Santa Monica, CA 90405, ☎ 310/452–0506 or 800/225–5759) works with lesbians.

H

HEALTH ISSUES

FINDING A DOCTOR

For members, the **International Association for Medical Assistance to Travellers** (IAMAT, 417 Center St., Lewiston, NY 14092, ☎ 716/754–4883; 40 Regal Rd., Guelph, Ontario N1K 1B5, ☎ 519/836–0102; 1287 St. Clair Ave., Toronto, Ontario M6E 1B8, ☎ 416/652–0137; 57 Voirets, 1212 Grand-Lancy, Geneva, Switzerland; membership free) publishes a worldwide directory of English-speaking physicians meeting IAMAT standards.

MEDICAL-ASSISTANCE COMPANIES

Contact **International**

SOS Assistance (Box 11568, Philadelphia, PA 19116, ☎ 215/244–1500 or 800/523–8930; Box 466, Pl. Bonaventure, Montréal, Québec. H5A 1C1, ☎ 514/874–7674 or 800/363–0263), **Medex Assistance Corporation** (Box 10623, Baltimore, MD 21285, ☎ 410/296–2530 or 800/573–2029), **Near Travel Services** (Box 1339, Calumet City, IL 60409, ☎ 708/868–6700 or 800/654–6700), and **Travel Assistance International** (1133 15th St. NW, Suite 400, Washington, DC 20005, ☎ 202/331–1609 or 800/821–2828). Because these companies also sell death-and-dismemberment, trip-cancellation, and other insurance coverage, there is some overlap with the travel-insurance policies sold by the companies listed under Insurance, *below*.

I

INSURANCE

Travel insurance covering baggage, health, and trip cancellation or interruptions is available from **Access America** (Box 90315, Richmond, VA 23286, ☎ 804/285–3300 or 800/284–8300), **Carefree Travel Insurance** (Box 9366, 100 Garden City Plaza, Garden City, NY 11530, ☎ 516/294–0220 or 800/323–3149), **Near Services** (Box 1339, Calumet City, IL 60409, ☎ 708/868–6700 or 800/654–6700), **Tele-Trip** (Mutual of Omaha Plaza, Box 31716, Omaha, NE 68131, ☎ 800/228–9792),

Travel Insured International (Box 280568, East Hartford, CT 06128-0568, ☎ 203/528–7663 or 800/243–3174), **Travel Guard International** (1145 Clark St., Stevens Point, WI 54481, ☎ 715/345–0505 or 800/826–1300), and **Wallach & Company** (107 W. Federal St., Box 480, Middleburg, VA 22117, ☎ 703/687–3166 or 800/237–6615).

IN THE U.K.

The **Association of British Insurers** (51 Gresham St., London EC2V 7HQ, ☎ 0171/600–3333; 30 Gordon St., Glasgow G1 3PU, ☎ 0141/226–3905; Scottish Provident Bldg., Donegall Sq. W, Belfast BT1 6JE, ☎ 01232/249176; and other locations) gives advice by phone and publishes the free **"Holiday Insurance,"** which sets out typical policy provisions and costs.

L

LODGING

INEXPENSIVE ACCOMMODATIONS

Many establishments on the Japanese National Tourist Office's list of reasonably priced accommodations–and many that are not on the list–can be reserved through the nonprofit organization **Welcome Inn Reservation Center** (International Tourism Center of Japan, 2nd. Floor, Kotani Bldg., 1-6-6 Yurakucho, Chiyoda-ku, Tokyo 100, ☎ 03/3580–8353, FAX 03/3580–8256). Reservation forms are available from your nearest JNTO office (*see* Visitor Information, *below*). The Center must receive reservation requests at least one week before your departure to allow processing time. If you are already in Japan, JNTO's Tourist Information Centers (TICs) at Narita Airport, downtown Tokyo, and Kyoto can make immediate reservations for you at these Welcome Inns.

MINSHUKU

For more information on *minshuku* (private homes that accept guests), contact the **Japan Minshuku Association** (1-29-5 Takadan-obaba, Shinjuku-ku, Tokyo, ☎ 03/3232–6561).

RYOKAN

To find the *ryokan* that best suits your needs, contact the **Japan Ryokan Association** (1-8-3 Marunouchi, Chiyoda-ku, Tokyo, ☎ 03/231–5310) or the JNTO (*see* Visitor Information, *below*).

M

MAIL

Have mail sent to **American Express** (Halifax Building, 16-26 Roppongi 3-chome, Minato-ku, Tokyo.

MONEY MATTERS

ATMS

For specific foreign **Cirrus** locations, call 800/424–7787; for foreign **Plus** locations, consult the Plus directory at your local bank.

CURRENCY EXCHANGE

If your bank doesn't exchange currency, contact **Thomas Cook Currency Services** (41 E. 42nd St., New York, NY 10017, or 511 Madison Ave., New York, NY 10022, ☎ 212/757–6915 or 800/223–7373 for locations) or **Ruesch International** (☎ 800/424–2923 for locations).

WIRING FUNDS

You don't have to be a cardholder to send or receive funds through **American Express MoneyGram℠** (☎ 800/866–8800 for transactions, 800/926–9400 for information) from American Express. Just go to a MoneyGram agent, located in retail and convenience stores and in American Express Travel Offices. Pay up to $1,000 with cash or a credit card (MasterCard, Visa, or Discover), anything over that in cash. The money can be picked up within 10 minutes in the form of U.S. dollar traveler's checks or local currency at the nearest MoneyGram agent, or, abroad, the nearest American Express Travel Office (in Tokyo, 1-7-1 Yuraku-cho, Chiyoda-ku; ☎ 03/3214–0280; payment in dollars only). There's no limit, and the recipient need only present photo identification. The cost runs from 3% to 10%, depending on the amount sent, the destination, and how you pay.

You can also send money using **Western Union** (☎ 800/325–6000 for agent locations or to send using MasterCard or Visa, 800/321–2923 in Canada). Money sent from the United States or Canada will be available for pickup at agent locations in 100 countries within 15 minutes. Once the money is in the system, it can be picked up at any one of 25,000 locations. Fees range from 4% to 10%, depending on the amount you send.

P

PASSPORTS AND VISAS

U.S. CITIZENS

For fees, documentation requirements, and other information, call the **Office of Passport Services** information line (☎ 202/647–0518).

CANADIANS

For fees, documentation requirements, and other information, call the Ministry of Foreign Affairs and International Trade's **Passport Office** (☎ 819/994–3500 or 800/567–6868).

U.K. CITIZENS

For fees, documentation requirements, and to get an emergency passport, call the **London Passport Office** (☎ 0171/271–3000).

PHOTO HELP

The **Kodak Information Center** (☎ 800/242–2424) answers consumer questions about film and photography.

THE GOLD GUIDE / IMPORTANT CONTACTS

R
RAIL TRAVEL

Should you need information that is not available at the nearest JR station, there is a **JR hotline English-language information service** (☎ 03/3423–0111.

DISCOUNT PASSES

Japan Rail Passes are available in coach class and first class (Green Car), but most people find that coach class is more than adequate. A one-week adult pass costs ¥27,800 coach class, ¥37,000 first class; a two-week pass costs ¥44,200 coach class, ¥60,000 first class; and a three-week pass costs ¥56,600 coach class, ¥78,000 first class. Travelers under 18 pay lower rates.

To get a rail pass, contact a travel agent or any of the following: **Japan Airlines** (JAL, 655 Fifth Ave., New York, NY 10022, ☎ 212/838–4400), **Japan Travel Bureau** (JTB, 787 Seventh Ave., New York, NY 10019, ☎ 212/246–8030), or **Nippon Travel Agency** (NTA, 120 W. 45th St., New York, NY 10036, ☎ 212/944–8660). JAL, JTB, and NTA also have bureaus in other major U.S. cities. For more information, the **Japan Railways Group** has an office in the United States (One Rockefeller Plaza, Suite 1622, New York, NY 10020, ☎ 212/332–8690) and will answer your questions on the telephone or by fax. Also see Rail Travel *in* Smart Travel Tips A to Z.

S
SENIOR CITIZENS

EDUCATIONAL TRAVEL

The nonprofit **Elderhostel** (75 Federal St., 3rd Floor, Boston, MA 02110, ☎ 617/426–7788), for people 60 and older, has offered inexpensive study programs since 1975. The nearly 2,000 courses cover everything from marine science to Greek myths and cowboy poetry. Fees for two- to three-week international trips—including room, board, and transportation from the United States—range from $1,800 to $4,500.

ORGANIZATIONS

Contact the **American Association of Retired Persons** (AARP, 601 E St. NW, Washington, DC 20049, ☎ 202/434–2277; $8 per person or couple annually). Its Purchase Privilege Program gets members discounts on lodging, car rentals, and sightseeing, and the AARP Motoring Plan furnishes domestic trip-routing information and emergency road-service aid for an annual fee of $39.95 per person or couple ($59.95 for a premium version).

For other discounts on lodgings, car rentals, and other travel products, along with magazines and newsletters, contact the **National Council of Senior Citizens** (membership $12 annually; 1331 F St. NW, Washington, DC 20004, ☎ 202/347–8800) or **Mature Out-**look (membership $9.95 annually; P.O. Box 10448, Des Moines, IA 50306–0448, ☎ 800/336–6330).

PUBLICATIONS

The 50+ Traveler's Guidebook: Where to Go, Where to Stay, What to Do, by Anita Williams and Merrimac Dillon ($12.95; St. Martin's Press, 175 5th Ave., New York, NY 10010, ☎ 212/674–5151 or 800/288–2131), offers many useful tips. **"The Mature Traveler"** ($29.95; Box 50400, Reno, NV 89513, ☎ 702/786–7419), a monthly newsletter, covers travel deals.

STUDENTS

HOSTELING

Contact **Hostelling International–American Youth Hostels** (733 15th St. NW, Suite 840, Washington, DC 20005, ☎ 202/783–6161) in the United States, **Hostelling International–Canada** (205 Catherine St., Suite 400, Ottawa, Ontario K2P 1C3, ☎ 613/237–7884) in Canada, and the **Youth Hostel Association of England and Wales** (Trevelyan House, 8 St. Stephen's Hill, St. Albans, Hertfordshire AL1 2DY, ☎ 01727/855215 or 01727/845047) in the United Kingdom. Membership ($25 in the U.S., C$26.75 in Canada, and £9 in the U.K.) gets you access to 5,000 hostels worldwide that charge $7–$20 nightly per person.

In Japan, contact the **Japan Youth Hostel**

Association, Hoken Kaikan, 1-1, Ichigaya-Sadohara-cho, Shinjuku-ku, Tokyo, ☎ 03/3269–5831.

I.D. CARDS

To be eligible for discounts on transportation and admissions, get the **International Student Identity Card** (ISIC) if you're a bona fide student or the **International Youth Card** (IYC) if you're under 26. In the United States, the ISIC and IYC cards cost $16 each and include basic travel-accident and illness coverage, plus a toll-free travel hot line. Apply through the Council on International Educational Exchange (*see* Organizations, *below*). Cards are available for $15 each in Canada from **Travel Cuts** (187 College St., Toronto, Ontario M5T 1P7, ☎ 416/979–2406 or 800/667–2887) and in the United Kingdom for £5 each at student unions and student travel companies.

ORGANIZATIONS

A major contact is the **Council on International Educational Exchange** (CIEE, 205 E. 42nd St., 16th Floor, New York, NY 10017, ☎ 212/661–1450), with locations in Boston (729 Boylston St., 02116, ☎ 617/266–1926); Miami (9100 S. Dadeland Blvd., 33156, ☎ 305/670–9261); Los Angeles (1093 Broxton Ave., 90024, ☎ 310/208–3551); 43 other college towns nationwide; and the United Kingdom (28A Poland St., London W1V 3DB, ☎ 0171/437–7767). Twice

a year, it publishes *Student Travels* magazine. The CIEE's Council Travel Service is the exclusive U.S. agent for several student-discount cards.

Campus Connections (325 Chestnut St., Suite 1101, Philadelphia, PA 19106, ☎ 215/625–8585 or 800/428–3235) specializes in discounted accommodations and airfares for students. The **Educational Travel Centre** (438 N. Frances St., Madison, WI 53703, ☎ 608/256–5551) offers rail passes and low-cost airline tickets, mostly for flights departing from Chicago. For air travel only, contact **TMI Student Travel** (100 W. 33rd St., Suite 813, New York, NY 10001, ☎ 800/245–3672).

In Canada, also contact **Travel Cuts** (*see above*).

T
TOUR OPERATORS

Among the companies selling tours and packages to Japan, the following have a proven reputation, are nationally known, and offer plenty of options.

GROUP TOURS AND INDEPENDENT PACKAGES

Maupintour (Box 807, Lawrence KS 66044, ☎ 913/843–1211 or 800/255–4266) specializes exclusively in deluxe escorted tours. Other deluxe programs, as well as first-class tours and independent vacation packages, are available from **Interpacific Tours** (111 E. 15th St., New York, NY 10003, ☎ 212/953–

6010 or 800/221–3594), **Japan & Orient Tours** (3131 Camino Del Rio North, No. 1080, San Diego, CA 92108, ☎ 619/282–3131 or 800/377–1080), **Orient Flexi-Pax Tours** (630 Third Avenue, New York, NY 10017, ☎ 212/692–9550 or 800/545–5540), **Pacific Bestour** (228 Rivervale Rd., River Vale, NJ 07675, ☎ 201/664–8778 or 800/688–3288), and **Pacific Delight Tours** (132 Madison Ave., New York, NY 10016, ☎ 212/684–7707 or 800/221–7179). **TBI Tours** (787 Seventh Ave., Suite 1101, New York, NY 10019, ☎ 212/489–1919 or 800/223–0266), the U.S. arm of Japan's largest travel company, has an extensive network of travel partners throughout Japan.

For custom-designed itineraries in Japan, contact **Absolute Asia** (180 Varick St., 16th floor, New York, NY 10014, ☎ 212/627–1950 or 800/736–8187).

In most cities in Japan it is possible to make arrangements for a hired car (usually a taxi) and guide. Cars with drivers cost around ¥10,500 per hour. The cost of an English-speaking guide is approximately ¥20,000–¥30,000 a day, plus expenses. Arrangements can be made through major hotels, or by calling the Japan Guide Association (☎ 03/213–2706) for a list of guides.

Prices are negotiated directly with the guides.

FROM THE U.K.

Contact **British Airways Holidays** (Astral Towers, Betts Way, London Rd., Crawley, West Sussex RH10 2XA, ☎ 01293/518–022), **Creative Tours** (2nd Floor, 1 Tenterden St., London W1R 9AH, ☎ 0171/495–1775), **Japan Travel Bureau** (10 Maltravers St., London WC2R 3EE, ☎ 0171/395–6600), and **Kuoni Travel** (Kuoni House, Dorking, Surrey RH5 4AZ, ☎ 01306/742–222, FAX 01306/744–222).

THEME TRIPS

ADVENTURE ➤ **All Adventure Travel** (5589 Arapahoe No. 208, Boulder, CO 80303, ☎ 800/537–4025), which represents more than 80 tour operators, can satisfy virtually any thirst for adventure in Japan. **Wilderness Travel** (801 Allston Way, Berkeley, CA 94710, ☎ 510/548–0420 or 800/368–2794), another leading adventure operator, also includes Japan in its programs.

ADVENTURE CRUISES ➤ For diving, whale watching, and to join a marine research expedition, contact **Ocean Voyages** (1709 Bridgeway, Sausalito, CA 94965, ☎ 415/332–4681, FAX 415/332–7460).

History ➤ For tours that focus on World War II action in the Pacific theater, contact **World War II Pacific History Tours** (Box 610, Alta Loma, CA 91701,

☎ 909/941–0675 or 800/847–6340).

LEARNING VACATIONS ➤ Anthropology, natural history, and biology are the focus of Asia trips led by **Nature Expeditions International** (Box 11496, Dept. STI, Eugene, OR 97440, ☎ 503/484–6529 or 800/869–0639). Earthwatch (680 Mount Auburn St., Watertown, MA 02272, ☎ 617/926–8200 or 800/776–0188) recruits volunteers to serve in its EarthCorps as short-term assistants to scientists or research expeditions.

TREKKING ➤ Contact **Road Runner International** (6762A Centinela Ave., Culver City, CA 90230, ☎ 310/390–7495 or (800/773–5872), which has had 30 years of experience combining stays at youth hostels and other low-cost accommodations with trekking.

ORGANIZATIONS

The **National Tour Association** (546 E. Main St., Lexington, KY 40508, ☎ 606/226–4444 or 800/755–8687) and **United States Tour Operators Association** (USTOA, 211 E. 51st St., Suite 12B, New York, NY 10022, ☎ 212/750–7371) can provide lists of member operators and information on booking tours.

PUBLICATIONS

Consult the brochure **"On Tour"** and ask for a current list of member operators from the **National Tour Association** (see Organizations, above). Also get a copy of the **"Worldwide Tour**

& Vacation Package Finder" from the USTOA (see Organizations, above) and the Better Business Bureau's **"Tips on Travel Packages"** (publication No. 24-195, $2; 4200 Wilson Blvd., Arlington, VA 22203).

TRAVEL AGENCIES

For names of reputable agencies in your area, contact the **American Society of Travel Agents** (1101 King St., Suite 200, Alexandria, VA 22314, ☎ 703/739–2782).

U

U.S.

GOVERNMENT

TRAVEL BRIEFINGS

The **U.S. Department of State's Overseas Citizens Emergency Center** (Room 4811, Washington, DC 20520; enclose a self-addressed, stamped envelope) issues **Consular Information Sheets,** which cover crime, security, political climate, and health risks as well as embassy locations, entry requirements, currency regulations, and other routine matters. For the latest information, stop in at any U.S. passport office, consulate, or embassy; call the interactive hot line (☎ 202/647–5225 or fax 202/647–3000); or, with your PC's modem, tap into the **Bureau of Consular Affairs'** computer bulletin board (☎ 202/647–9225).

V

VISITOR

INFORMATION

Contact the **Japan**

National Tourist Organization (JNTO) in the U.S. at One Rockefeller Plaza, Suite 1250, New York, NY 10020, ☎ 212/757–5640; 401 North Michigan Ave., Suite 770, Chicago, IL 60601, ☎ 312/222–0874; 360 Post St., Suite 601, San Francisco, CA 94108, ☎ 415/989–7140; 624 South Grand Ave., Suite 1611, Los Angeles, CA 90017, ☎ 213/623–1952; in Canada, 165 University Ave., Toronto M5H 3B8, Ontario, ☎ 416/366–7140; and in the U.K., Heathcourt House, 20 Savile Row, Fifth Floor, London W1X 1AE England, ☎ 071/734–9638.

JNTO has started an on-line information service called Japan Travel Updates (Internet address: http://www.jnto.go.jp).

TOURIST INFORMATION CENTERS

The Japan National Tourist Organization (JNTO) operates **Tourist Information Centers** (TIC) that offer travel information, pamphlets, and suggestions for tour itineraries. Reservations are not handled here. You can either visit or call the TIC offices; all offices are closed on Sundays and national holidays.

Tokyo Office. Kotani Building, 1-6-6 Yuraku-cho, Chiyoda-ku, ☎ 03/3502–1461. Open weekdays 9–5, Saturday 9–noon.

Tokyo International Airport Office. Airport Terminal Building, Narita Airport, Chiba Prefecture, ☎ 0476/32-8711. Open weekdays 9–8, Saturday 9–noon.

Kyoto Office. Kyoto Tower Building, Higashi-Shiokojicho, Shimogyo-ku, ☎ 075/371–5549. ⊙ Weekdays 9–5, Saturday 9–noon.

JAPAN TRAVEL-PHONE➤ If you have travel-related questions or need help in communicating, call the TIC's Travel-Phone service, daily 9–5. In Tokyo and Kyoto, call the TIC offices listed above. Elsewhere, dial toll-free 0120/222–800 for information on eastern Japan and 0120/444–800 for western Japan. The Travel-Phone service is available through yellow, blue, or green public telephones (not red ones), and through private phones. When using a public telephone, insert a ¥10 piece, which will be returned.

TELETOURIST SERVICE➤ A tape-recorded listing in English of cultural events in Tokyo is available by calling ☎ 03/3503–2911; in Kyoto, ☎ 075/361–2911.

W
WEATHER

For current conditions and forecasts, plus the local time and helpful travel tips, call the **Weather Channel Connection** (☎ 900/932–8437; 95¢ per minute) from a touch-tone phone.

SMART TRAVEL TIPS is printed vertically in the left margin, along with **THE GOLD GUIDE / SMART TRAVEL TIPS**.

SMART TRAVEL TIPS A TO Z

Basic Information on Traveling in Japan and Savvy Tips to Make Your Trip a Breeze

The more you travel, the more you know about how to make trips run like clockwork. To help make your travels hassle-free, Fodor's editors have rounded up dozens of tips from our contributors and travel experts all over the world, as well as basic information on visiting Japan. For names of organizations to contact and publications that can give you more information, *see* Important Contacts A to Z, *above*.

A

ADDRESSES

Broken down into single elements, Japanese addresses are very simple. The following is an example of a typical Japanese address: 6-chome 8-19, Chuo-ku, Fukuoka-shi, Fukuoka-ken. In this address the "chome" indicates a precise area, and the numbers following "chome" indicate the location within the area, not necessarily in sequential order—numbers may have been assigned when a building was erected. However, only the postmen in Japan seem to be familiar with the area defined by the chome. Sometimes, instead of a "chome," a "machi" is used. "Ku" refers to a ward, or in other words, a district of a city. "Shi" refers to a

city name, and "ken" indicates a prefecture, which is roughly equivalent to a state in the United States. It is not unusual for the prefecture and the city to have the same name, as in the above address. There are a few geographic areas in Japan that are not called ken. One is Hokkaido. The other exceptions are greater Tokyo, which is called Tokyo-to, and Kyoto and Osaka, which are followed by the suffix "-fu"—Kyoto-fu, Osaka-fu.

Not all addresses will conform exactly to the above format. Rural addresses, for example, do not have "ku," because only urban areas are divided into wards.

It is important to note that often even Japanese people cannot find a building based on the address alone. If you get in a taxi with an address written down, do not assume the driver will be able to find your destination. Usually, people provide very detailed instructions or maps to explain their exact locations. A common method is to give the location of your destination in relation to a major building or department store.

AIR TRAVEL

If time is an issue, always look for nonstop flights, which require no change of plane. If possible, avoid connecting flights, which stop at least once and can involve a change of plane, although the flight number remains the same; if the first leg is late, the second waits.

ALOFT

AIRLINE FOOD➤ If you hate airline food, ask for special meals when booking. These can be vegetarian, low-cholesterol, or kosher, for example; commonly prepared to order in smaller quantities than standard catered fare, they can be tastier.

JET LAG➤ To avoid this syndrome, which occurs when travel disrupts your body's natural cycles, try to maintain a normal routine. At night, get some sleep. By day, move about the cabin to stretch your legs, eat light meals, and drink water—not alcohol.

SMOKING➤ Smoking is banned on all flights within the United States of less than six hours' duration and on all Canadian flights; the ban also applies to domestic segments of international flights aboard U.S. and foreign carriers. On U.S. carriers flying to Japan and other destinations abroad, a seat in a no-smoking section must be provided for every passenger who requests one, and the section must be enlarged to accommodate such passengers if necessary as long as they have complied with the airline's deadline for check-in and seat assignment. If smoking bothers you, request a seat far from the smoking section.

Foreign airlines are exempt from these rules but do provide no-smoking sections. British Airways has banned smoking altogether; some nations have banned smoking on all domestic flights, and others may ban smoking on some flights. Talks continue on the feasibility of broadening no-smoking policies.

CUTTING COSTS

The Sunday travel section of most newspapers is a good source of deals.

CHARTER FLIGHTS➤ Charters usually have the lowest fares and the most restrictions. Departures are limited and seldom on time, and you can lose all or most of your money if you cancel. (The closer to departure you cancel, the more you lose, although sometimes you will be charged only a small fee if you supply a substitute passenger.) The flight may be canceled for any reason up to 10 days before departure (after that, only if it is physically impossible to operate). The charterer may also revise the itinerary or increase the price after you have bought the

ticket, but only if the new arrangement constitutes a "major change" do you have the right to a refund.

Before buying a charter ticket, **read the fine print** about the company's refund policies. Money for charter flights is usually paid into a bank escrow account, the name of which should be on the contract. If you don't pay by credit card, **make your check payable to the carrier's escrow account** (unless you're dealing with a travel agent, in which case, his or her check should be payable to the escrow account). The U.S. Department of Transportation's Office of Consumer Affairs has jurisdiction.

Charter operators may offer flights alone or with ground arrangements that constitute a charter package. You typically must book charters through your travel agent.

CONSOLIDATORS➤ Consolidators buy tickets at reduced rates from scheduled airlines and sell them at prices below the lowest available from the airlines directly—usually without advance restrictions. Sometimes you can even get your money back if you need to return the ticket. Carefully read the fine print detailing penalties for changes and cancellations. If you doubt the reliability of a consolidator, **confirm your reservation with the airline.**

MAJOR AIRLINES➤ The

least-expensive airfares from the major airlines are priced for round-trip travel and are subject to restrictions. You must usually **book in advance and buy the ticket within 24 hours** to get cheaper fares, and you may have to **stay over a Saturday night.** The lowest fare is subject to availability, and only a small percentage of the plane's total seats are sold at that price. **Call a number of airlines, and when you are quoted a good price, book it on the spot**—the same fare on the same flight may not be available the next day. Airlines generally allow you to change your return date for a $25 to $50 fee, but most low-fare tickets are nonrefundable. However, if you don't use it, you can apply the cost toward the purchase price of a new ticket, again for a small charge.

B

BUS TRAVEL

Japan Railways offers a number of overnight long-distance buses that are not very comfortable but are inexpensive. Japan Rail Passes may be used on these buses. City buses are quite convenient, but **be sure of your route and destination,** because the bus driver will probably not speak English. Some buses have a set cost from ¥120 to ¥180, depending on the route and municipality, in which case you board at the front of the bus and pay as you get on. On other buses, cost is determined by the distance you travel. You take a ticket when you board at the rear door of the bus; it will bear the number of the stop at which you boarded. Your fare is indicated by a board with rotating numbers at the front of the bus. Under each boarding point, indicated by a number, the fare will increase the farther the bus travels.

BUSINESS HOURS

General business hours in Japan are 9–5 weekdays. Many offices are also open at least half of the day on Saturday but are generally closed on Sunday.

Banks are open 9–3 weekdays and 9–noon on the first and last Saturdays of the month. They are closed on Sunday.

Department stores are usually open 10–7 but are closed one day a week, which varies from store to store. Other stores are open from 10 or 11 to 7 or 8.

C

CAMERAS, CAMCORDERS, AND COMPUTERS

LAPTOPS

Before you depart, **check your portable computer's battery,** because you may be asked at security to turn on the computer to prove that it is what it appears to be. At the airport, you may prefer to **request a manual inspection,** although security X-rays do not harm hard-disk or floppy-disk storage. Also, **register your**

foreign-made laptop with U.S. Customs. If your laptop is U.S.-made, call the consulate of the country you'll be visiting to find out whether or not it should be registered with local customs upon arrival. You may want to **find out about repair facilities at your destination** in case you need them.

PHOTOGRAPHY

If your camera is new or if you haven't used it for a while, **shoot and develop a few rolls of film** before you leave. Always **store film in a cool, dry place**—never in the car's glove compartment or on the shelf under the rear window.

Every pass of film through an X-ray machine increases the chance of clouding. To protect it, carry it in a clear plastic bag and **ask for hand inspection at security.** Such requests are virtually always honored at U.S. airports, and are usually accommodated abroad. Don't depend on a lead-lined bag to protect film in checked luggage—the airline may increase the radiation to see what's inside.

Fluorescent lighting, which is used a lot in Japan, will give photographs a greenish tint. You can counteract this discoloration with an FL filter.

VIDEO

Before you depart, **register foreign-made camcorders with U.S. Customs.** Also, **test your camcorder, invest in a skylight filter to protect**

the lens, and charge the batteries. (Airport security personnel may ask you to turn on the camcorder to prove that it's what it appears to be.) The batteries of most newer camcorders can be recharged with a universal or worldwide AC adapter charger (or multivoltage converter), usable whether the voltage is 110 or 220. All that's needed is the appropriate plug.

Videotape is not damaged by X-rays, but it may be harmed by the magnetic field of a walk-through metal detector, so **ask that videotapes be hand-checked.** Videotape sold in Japan is based on the NTSC standard, which is different than the one used in the United States. You will not be able to view your tapes through the local TV set or view movies bought there in your home VCR. Blank tapes bought in Japan can be used for camcorder taping, but they are pricey. Some U.S. audiovisual shops convert foreign tapes to U.S. standards; contact an electronics dealer to find the nearest.

CAR RENTAL

CUTTING COSTS

To get the best deal, **book through a travel agent and shop around.** When pricing cars, **ask where the rental lot is located.** Some off-airport locations offer lower rates—even though their lots are only minutes away from the terminal via complimentary shuttle. You may also want to **price local car-rental compa-**

nies, whose rates may be lower still, although service and maintenance standards may not be up to those of a national firm. Also **ask your travel agent about a company's customer-service record.** How has it responded to late plane arrivals and vehicle mishaps? Are there often lines at the rental counter, and, if you're traveling during a holiday period, does a confirmed reservation guarantee you a car?

Always **find out what equipment is standard** at your destination before specifying what you want; **do without automatic transmission or air-conditioning** if they're optional.

INSURANCE

When you drive a rented car, you are generally responsible for any damage or personal injury that you cause as well as damage to the vehicle. Before you rent, **see what coverage you already have** under the terms of your personal auto-insurance policy and credit cards. For about $14 a day, rental companies sell insurance, known as a collision damage waiver (CDW), that eliminates your liability for damage to the car; it's always optional and should never be automatically added to your bill.

REQUIREMENTS

In Japan your own driver's license is not acceptable. An International Driver's Permit, available from the American, Canadian, or U.K. Automobile Association, is necessary.

SURCHARGES

Before picking up the car in one city and leaving it in another, **ask about drop-off charges or one-way service fees,** which can be substantial. Note, too, that some rental agencies charge extra if you return the car before the time specified on your contract. To avoid a hefty refueling fee, fill the tank just before you turn in the car.

CHILDREN AND TRAVEL

BABY-SITTING

Some very expensive Western-style hotels and resort hotels have supervised playrooms where you can drop off children. The baby-sitters, however, are unlikely to speak English. Child-care arrangements can be made through the concierge, but some properties require up to a week's notice.

DRIVING

If you are renting a car, **arrange for a car seat when you reserve.** Sometimes they're free.

FLYING

Always **ask about discounted children's fares.** On international flights, the fare for infants under age 2 not occupying a seat is generally either free or 10% of the accompanying adult's fare; children ages 2 through 11 usually pay half to two-thirds of the adult fare. On domestic flights, children under 2 not occupying a seat travel free, and older children currently travel on the lowest applicable adult fare.

BAGGAGE➤ In general, the adult baggage allowance applies for children paying half or more of the adult fare. Before departure, **ask about carry-on allowances** if you are traveling with an infant. In general, those paying 10% of the adult fare are allowed one carry-on bag, not to exceed 70 pounds or 45 inches (length + width + height), and a collapsible stroller; you may be allowed less if the flight is full.

SAFETY SEATS➤ According to the Federal Aviation Administration (FAA), it's a good idea to **use safety seats aloft.** Airline policy varies. U.S. carriers allow FAA-approved models, but airlines usually require that you buy a ticket, even if your child would otherwise ride free, because the seats must be strapped into regular passenger seats. Japanese and New Zealand carriers do not allow infant seats; other foreign carriers may do so, and may charge the child's rather than the infant's fare for their use, or may require you to hold your baby during takeoff and landing, thus defeating the seat's purpose.

FACILITIES➤ When making your reservation, **ask for children's meals or freestanding bassinets** if you need them; the latter are available only to those with seats at the bulkhead, where there's enough legroom. If you don't need a bassinet, **think twice before requesting bulkhead seats**—the only storage for in-flight necessities is in the inconveniently distant overhead bins.

LODGING

Most hotels allow children under a certain age to stay in their parents' room at no extra charge, while others charge them as extra adults; be sure to **ask about the cut-off age.**

CUSTOMS AND DUTIES

IN JAPAN

Japan is strict about bringing firearms, pornography, and narcotics into the country. Anyone caught with drugs is liable to be detained, deported, and refused re-entry into Japan. Certain fresh fruits, vegetables, plants, and animals are also illegal. Nonresidents are allowed to bring in duty-free: (1) 400 cigarettes or 100 cigars or 500 grams of tobacco; (2) three bottles of alcohol; (3) 2 ounces of perfume; (4) other goods up to ¥200,000 value.

BACK HOME

IN THE U.S.➢ You may bring home $400 worth of foreign goods duty-free if you've been out of the country for at least 48 hours and haven't already used the $400 exemption, or any part of it, in the past 30 days.

Travelers 21 or older may bring back 1 liter

of alcohol duty-free, provided the beverage laws of the state through which they reenter the United States allow it. In addition, 100 non-Cuban cigars and 200 cigarettes are allowed, regardless of your age. Antiques and works of art more than 100 years old are duty-free.

Duty-free, travelers may mail packages valued at up to $200 to themselves and up to $100 to others, with a limit of one parcel per addressee per day (and no alcohol or tobacco products or perfume valued at more than $5); outside, identify the package as being for personal use or an unsolicited gift, specifying the contents and their retail value. Mailed items do not count as part of your exemption.

IN CANADA➢ Once per calendar year, when you've been out of Canada for at least seven days, you may bring in C$300 worth of goods duty-free. If you've been away less than seven days but more than 48 hours, the duty-free exemption drops to C$100 but can be claimed any number of times (as can a C$20 duty-free exemption for absences of 24 hours or more). You cannot combine the yearly and 48-hour exemptions, use the C$300 exemption only partially (to save the balance for a later trip), or pool exemptions with family members. Goods

claimed under the C$300 exemption may follow you by mail; those claimed under the lesser exemptions must accompany you.

Alcohol and tobacco products may be included in the yearly and 48-hour exemptions but not in the 24-hour exemption. If you meet the age requirements of the province through which you reenter Canada, you may bring in, duty-free, 1.14 liters (40 imperial ounces) of wine or liquor *or* 24 12-ounce cans or bottles of beer or ale. If you are 16 or older, you may bring in, duty-free, 200 cigarettes, 50 cigars or cigarillos, and 400 tobacco sticks or 400 grams of manufactured tobacco. Alcohol and tobacco must accompany you on your return.

An unlimited number of gifts valued up to C$60 each may be mailed to Canada duty-free. These do not count as part of your exemption. Label the package "Unsolicited Gift—Value Under $60." Alcohol and tobacco are excluded.

IN THE U.K.➢ From countries outside the EU, including Japan, you may import duty-free 200 cigarettes, 100 cigarillos, 50 cigars or 250 grams of tobacco; 1 liter of spirits or 2 liters of fortified or sparkling wine; 2 liters of still table wine; 60 milliliters of perfume; 250 milliliters of toilet water; plus £136 worth of other goods, including gifts and souvenirs.

Propriety is an important part of Japanese society. Many Japanese expect foreigners to behave differently and are tolerant of faux pas, but are pleasantly surprised when people acknowledge and observe their customs. The easiest way to ingratiate yourself with the Japanese is to **take the time to learn and respect Japanese ways.**

It is customary to **bow upon meeting someone.** The art of bowing is not simple; the depth of your bow depends on your social position in respect to that of the other person. Younger people, or those of lesser status, must bow deeper in order to indicate their respect and acknowledge their position. Foreigners are not expected to understand the complexity of these rules, and a basic nod of the head will suffice. Many Japanese are familiar with Western customs and will offer their hand for a handshake.

Do not be offended if you are not invited to someone's home. In general, most entertaining is done in restaurants or bars. It is an honor when you are invited to a home; this means that your host feels comfortable and close with you. If you do receive an invitation, bring along a small gift—a souvenir from your country is always the best present, but food and liquor are also appreciated. Upon entering a home, **remove your shoes in the foyer and put on the slippers that are provided.** It is important to have socks or stockings that are in good condition.

Japanese restaurants often provide a small hot towel called an *oshibori.* This is to wipe your hands but not your face. You may see some Japanese wiping their faces with their oshibori, but generally this is considered to be bad form. When you are finished with your oshibori, do not just toss it back onto the table, but fold or roll it up. Those who are not accustomed to eating with chopsticks may ask for a fork instead. When eating from a shared dish, do not use the part of the chopsticks that have entered your mouth; instead, use the end that you have been holding in your hand.

DOING BUSINESS

As Japan's role in the global economy expands, the number of business travelers to Japan increases. Although many business practices are universal, certain customs remain unique to Japan. It is not necessary to observe these precepts, but Japanese will always appreciate it if you do.

Business cards are mandatory in Japan. Upon meeting someone for the first time, it is common to bow and to proffer your business card simultaneously. Although English will suffice on your business card, it is better to have one side printed in Japanese (there are outfits in Japan that will provide this service in 24 hours). In a sense, the cards are simply a convenience. Japanese sometimes have difficulty with Western names, and they like to refer to the cards. Also, in a society where hierarchy matters, Japanese like to know job titles and rank, so it is useful if your card indicates your position in your company. Japanese often place the business cards they have received in front of them on a table or desk as they conduct their meetings. Follow suit, and do not simply shove the card in your pocket.

The concept of being fashionably late does not exist in Japan; it is extremely important to **be prompt for both social and business occasions.** Japanese addresses tend to be complicated, and traffic is often heavy, so allow for adequate travel time (see Addresses, above). Most Japanese are not accustomed to using first names in business circumstances. Even workmates of 20 years' standing use surnames. Unless you are sure that the Japanese person is extremely comfortable with Western customs, it is probably better to **stick to last names.** Also, respect the hierarchy, and as much as possible address yourself to the most senior person in the room.

Don't be frustrated if decisions are not made

instantly. Individual businesspeople are rarely empowered to make decisions, and must confer with their colleagues and superiors. Even if you are annoyed, don't express anger or aggression. Losing one's temper is equated with losing face in Japan.

A separation of business and private lives remains sacrosanct in Japan, and it is best not to ask about personal matters. Rather than asking about a person's family, it is better to **stick to neutral subjects in conversation.** This does not mean that you can only comment on the weather, but rather that you should be careful not to be nosy. Because of cramped housing, many Japanese entertain in restaurants or bars. It is not customary for Japanese businessmen to bring wives along. If you are traveling with your spouse, do not assume that an invitation includes both of you. You may ask if it is acceptable to bring your spouse along, but remember that it is awkward for a Japanese person to say no. You should pose the question carefully, or not at all.

Usually, entertaining is done over dinner, followed by an evening on the town. Drinking is something of a national pastime in Japan. If you would rather not suffer from a hangover the next day, do not refuse your drink—sip, but keep your glass at least half full. An empty glass is nearly the equivalent of requesting another drink. You should never pour your own drink or let your companions pour theirs.

A special note to women traveling on business in Japan: Remember that although the situation is gradually changing, most Japanese women do not have careers. Many Japanese businessmen do not yet know how to interact with Western businesswomen. They may be uncomfortable, aloof, or patronizing. Be patient and, if the need arises, gently remind them that, professionally, you expect to be treated as any man would be.

D

DINING

Food, like many things in Japan, is expensive. Eating at hotels and famous restaurants is costly, but by looking for standard restaurants that may not have signs in English, you can eat well at reasonable prices. Many less-expensive restaurants have plastic replicas of the dishes they serve displayed in their front windows, so you can always point to what you want to eat. A good place to look for moderately priced dining spots is in the restaurant concourse of department stores, usually on the bottom floor.

In general, Japanese restaurants are very clean. The water is safe, even when drawn from a tap. Most hotels have Western-style rest rooms, but restaurants may have Japanese-style toilets, with bowls recessed into the floor, over which you must squat.

FOR TRAVELERS WITH DISABILITIES

When discussing accessibility with an operator or reservationist, **ask hard questions.** Are there any stairs, inside or out? Are there grab bars next to the toilet and in the shower/tub? How wide is the doorway to the room? To the bathroom? For the most extensive facilities, meeting the latest legal specifications, **opt for newer properties,** which more often have been designed with access in mind. Older properties or ships must usually be retrofitted and may offer more limited facilities as a result. Be sure to **discuss your needs before booking.**

DISCOUNT CLUBS

Travel clubs offer members unsold space on airplanes, cruise ships, and package tours at as much as 50% below regular prices. Membership may include a regular bulletin or access to a toll-free hot line giving details of available trips departing from three or four days to several months in the future. Most also offer 50% discounts off hotel rack rates. Before booking with a club, **make sure the hotel or other supplier isn't offering a better deal.**

DRIVING

It is possible for foreigners to drive in Japan with an international driver's license, and though few select this option, it is becoming more popular. Major roads are sufficiently marked in the Roman alphabet, and on country roads there is usually someone to ask for help. However, it's a good idea to **have a detailed map with towns written in** *kanji* **(Japanese characters) and** *romaji* **(Romanized Japanese).**

In Japan, people **drive on the left.** Speed limits vary, but generally the limit is 80 kilometers per hour (50 mph) on highways, 40 kph (25 mph) in cities.

Driving along the Tokyo–Kyoto–Hiroshima corridor and in other built-up areas of Japan is not advisable. Trains and subways will get you to your destinations faster and more comfortably. The roads are congested, gas is expensive (about ¥140 per liter or $6.25 per gallon), and highway tolls are exorbitant (tolls between Tokyo and Kyoto amount to ¥9,250). In major cities, parking is a nightmare.

That said, a car can be the best means for exploring the rural parts of Japan. Consider taking a train to those areas where exploring the countryside will be the most interesting and renting a car locally for a day or even half a day.

E

ELECTRICITY

To use your U.S.-purchased electric-powered equipment, **bring a converter and an adapter.** The electrical current in Japan is 100 volts, 50 cycles alternating current (AC) in eastern Japan, and 100 volts, 60 cycles in western Japan; the United States runs on 110-volt, 60-cycle AC current. Wall outlets in Japan accept plugs with two flat prongs, like in the United States, but do not accept U.S. three-prong plugs.

F

FERRY TRAVEL

Ferries connect most of the islands of Japan. Some of the more popular routes are from Tokyo to Tomakomai or Kushiro in Hokkaido; from Tokyo to Shikoku; and from Tokyo or Osaka to Kyushu. You can **purchase ferry tickets in advance** from travel agencies or before boarding. The ferries are inexpensive and are a pleasant if slow way of traveling. Private cabins are available, but it is more fun to travel in the economy class, where everyone sleeps in one large room. Passengers eat, drink, and enjoy themselves, creating a convivial atmosphere.

FESTIVALS

Festivals are very important to the Japanese, and a large number are held throughout the year. Many of these festivals originated in folk and religious rituals and date back hundreds of years. Gala festivals take place annually at Buddhist temples and Shinto shrines. Because festivals offer a unique gimpse into Japanese culture and traditions, you should **consider dates and places for festivals when you are planning your trip.** Contact the nearest branch of the Japan National Tourist Organization (see Visitor Information in Important Contacts A to Z, *above*).

G

GUIDES

JNTO sponsors a Good-Will Guide program in which local citizens volunteer to show visitors around their home towns. These are not professional guides; they usually volunteer both because they enjoy welcoming foreigners to their town and because they want to practice their English. The services of Good-Will Guides are free, but you should pay for their travel costs, their admission fees, and any meals they eat while with you. To participate in this program, **make arrangements for a Good-Will Guide in advance through JNTO** in the United States or through the tourist office in the area where you want the guide to meet you. The program operates in many areas, including Tokyo, Kyoto, Nara, Nagoya, Osaka, and Hiroshima.

I
INSURANCE

Travel insurance can protect your investment, replace your luggage and its contents, or provide for medical coverage should you fall ill during your trip. Most tour operators, travel agents, and insurance agents sell specialized health-and-accident, flight, trip-cancellation, and luggage insurance as well as comprehensive policies with some or all of these features. Before you make any purchase, **review your existing health and homeowner's policies** to find out whether they cover expenses incurred while traveling.

BAGGAGE

Airline liability for your baggage is limited to $1,250 per person on domestic flights. On international flights, the airlines' liability is $9.07 per pound or $20 per kilogram for checked baggage (roughly $640 per 70-pound bag) and $400 per passenger for unchecked baggage. Insurance for losses exceeding the terms of your airline ticket can be bought directly from the airline at check-in for about $10 per $1,000 of coverage; note that it excludes a rather extensive list of items, shown on your airline ticket.

FLIGHT

You should **think twice before buying flight insurance.** Often purchased as a last-minute impulse at the airport, it pays a lump sum when a plane crashes, either to a beneficiary if the insured dies or sometimes to a surviving passenger who loses eyesight or a limb. Supplementing the airlines' coverage described in the limits-of-liability paragraphs on your ticket, it's expensive and basically unnecessary. Charging an airline ticket to a major credit card often automatically entitles you to coverage and may also embrace travel by bus, train, and ship.

HEALTH

If your own health insurance policy does not cover you outside the U.S., **consider buying supplemental medical coverage.** It can cover from $1,000 to $150,000 worth of medical and/or dental expenses incurred as a result of an accident or illness during a trip. These policies also may include a personal-accident, or death-and-dismemberment, provision, which pays a lump sum ranging from $15,000 to $500,000 to your beneficiaries if you die or to you if you lose one or more limbs or your eyesight, and a medical-assistance provision, which may either reimburse you for the cost of referrals, evacuation, or repatriation and other services, or may automatically enroll you as a member of a particular medical-assistance company. (*See* Health Issues *in* Important Contacts A to Z, *above.*)

FOR U.K. TRAVELERS

You can buy an annual travel-insurance policy valid for most vacations during the year in which it's purchased. If you go this route, make sure it covers you if you have a preexisting medical condition or are pregnant.

TRIP

Without insurance, you will lose all or most of your money if you must cancel your trip due to illness or any other reason. Especially if your airline ticket, cruise, or package tour is nonrefundable and cannot be changed, it's essential that you **buy trip-cancellation-and-interruption insurance.** When considering how much coverage you need, look for a policy that will cover the cost of your trip plus the nondiscounted price of a one-way airline ticket should you need to return home early. Read the fine print carefully, especially sections defining "family member" and "preexisting medical conditions." Also **consider default or bankruptcy insurance,** which protects you against a supplier's failure to deliver. However, such policies often do not cover default by a travel agency, tour operator, airline, or cruise line if you bought your tour and the coverage directly from the firm in question.

L
LANGUAGE

Communicating in Japan can be a challenge. This is not because the Japanese don't speak English but because most of us know little, if any, Japanese. It is worthwhile to **take some time before you leave home to learn a few basic words,** such as where (*doko*), what time (*nanji*), bathroom (*benjo*), thanks (*arigato*), excuse me (*sumimasen*), and please (*onegai shimas*).

English is a required subject in Japanese schools, so most Japanese study English for nearly a decade. This does not mean, however, that everyone speaks English. Schools emphasize reading, writing, and grammar; less time is spent on spoken English. As a result, many Japanese can read English but can speak only a few basic phrases. Furthermore, when asked "Do you speak English?" many Japanese will, out of modesty, say no, even if they do understand and speak a fair amount of it. It is usually best to ask what you really want to know slowly, clearly, and as simply as possible. If the person you ask understands, he or she will answer or perhaps take you where you need to go; if that person does not understand, try someone else.

Although a local may understand your simple question, he or she cannot always give you an answer that requires complicated instructions. For example, you may ask someone on the subway how to get to a particular stop, and

he may direct you to the train across the platform and then say something in Japanese that you do not understand. You may discover too late that the train runs express to the suburbs after the third stop; the person who gave you directions was trying to tell you to switch trains at the third stop. To avoid this kind of trouble, **ask more than one person for directions** every step of the way. You could have avoided that trip to the suburbs if you had asked someone *on* the train how to get to your desired destination. Remember that you are communicating on a very basic level, and it is easy to misunderstand. The Japanese are generally very polite and willing to help, but you must ask for assistance.

One of the biggest problems for travelers is that they can't read Japanese. Before you leave home, **buy a phrase book** that shows English, English transliterations of Japanese, and Japanese. You can use the English transliterations to speak Japanese, and you can match the Japanese writing in the phrase book with characters on signs and menus. And if all else fails, you can ask for help by pointing to the Japanese words in your book.

Japanese is not an easy language to learn. Japanese writing consists of three character systems: *kanji*, or Chinese characters, which represent ideas; and two

forms of *kana*—*hiragana* and *katakana*—which represent sounds. Hiragana is used to write Japanese words, verb inflections, and adjectives; katakana is used to represent such things as foreign words, slang expressions, and technical terms. There are 47 kana and more than 6,000 kanji characters, although most Japanese use fewer than 1,000 kanji. This is more than a tourist can learn in a short stay, so you will find yourself scanning your surroundings for Romanized Japanese (*romaji*), which is easier to interpret.

The most common system of writing Japanese words in Roman letters is the Hepburn system, which spells out Japanese words phonetically and is followed in this book. Note that there is no stress on any one syllable in Japanese. For example, most English speakers pronounce the Japanese word for good-bye *sa-yo-NAH-ra*, placing the stress on the second to last syllable as is done in many English words. But the correct pronunciation of this word is *sa-yo-na-ra*, with each syllable getting equal stress.

The vowels of Romanized Japanese words are pronounced the same way in every word and sound a lot like Italian vowels. *A* is pronounced like the "ah" in *father*. *E* is pronounced like the "eh" sound in *men*. *I* is pronounced like the "e" in *eat*. *O* is pronounced

THE GOLD GUIDE / SMART TRAVEL TIPS

like the "oh" sound in *only*. *U* is pronounced like the "oo" sound in *boot*. When you see the "ei" combination in a word, pronounce both vowels, *eh-i*. Also, when a word contains a double consonant, break the word between the consonants and say it as if it were two separate words, hesitating slightly between the syllables. Thus, *Nippon* is pronounced *Nip-pon*.

Also see Vocabulary, at the end of this book.

LODGING

Overnight accommodations in Japan run from luxury hotels to traditional inns to youth hostels and even capsules (*see* Hotels, *below*). Western-style rooms with Western-style bathrooms are widely available in large cities, but in smaller, out-of-the-way towns it may be necessary to stay in a Japanese-style room.

HOME VISITS

Through the Home Visit System, travelers can get a sense of domestic life in Japan by visiting a local family in their home. The program is voluntary on the homeowner's part, and there is no charge for a visit. It is active in many cities throughout the country, including Tokyo, Yokohama, Nagoya, Kyoto, Osaka, Hiroshima, Nagasaki, Sapporo, and others. To make a reservation, **apply in writing for a home visit at least a day in advance** to the local tourist information office of the place you are visiting. Con-

tact the Japan National Tourist Organization (*see* Visitor Information *in* Important Contacts A to Z, *above*) before leaving for Japan for more information on the program.

HOTELS

Full-service, first-class hotels in Japan are similar to their counterparts all over the world, and because many of the staff speak English these are the easiest places for foreigners to stay. They are also among the most expensive.

Business hotels are a reasonable alternative. These are clean, impersonal, and functional. All have Western-style rooms that vary from small to minuscule; service is minimal. However, every room has a private bathroom, albeit cramped, with tub and hand-held shower, television (with Japanese-language channels), telephone, and a hot-water thermos. Business hotels are often conveniently located near the railway station. The staff may not speak English, and there is usually no room service.

Designed to accommodate the modern Japanese urbanite, the capsule hotel is a novel idea. The rooms are a mere 3½ feet wide, 3½ feet high, and 7¼ feet long. They have an alarm clock, television, and phone, and little else. Capsules are often used by commuters who have had an evening of excess and cannot make the long journey home. Although you may want

to try sleeping in a capsule, you probably won't want to spend a week in one.

INEXPENSIVE ACCOMMODATIONS

JNTO publishes a listing of some 200 accommodations that are reasonably priced. To be listed, properties must meet Japanese fire codes and charge less than ¥8,000 per person without meals. For the most part, the properties charge ¥5,000–¥6,000. These properties welcome foreigners (many Japanese hotels and ryokan do not like to have foreign guests). Properties include business hotels, ryokan of very rudimentary nature, minshuku, and pensions. It's the luck of the draw whether you choose a good or less-than-good property. In most cases, the rooms are clean, but very small. Except in business hotels, private baths are not common, and you will be expected to have your room lights out by 10 PM (For information on booking one of these properties, *see* Lodging *in* Important Contacts A to Z, *above*).

MINSHUKU

Minshuku are private homes that accept guests. Usually they cost about ¥5,000 per person, including two meals. Although in a ryokan (*see below*), you need not lift a finger, **don't be surprised if you are expected to lay out and put away your own bedding and bring your own towels in a minshuku.** Meals are often served in communal dining rooms. Minshuku vary in size and atmosphere; some are literally private homes that take in only a few guests, while others are more like no-frill inns. Some of your most memorable stays could be at a minshuku, as they offer a chance to become acquainted with a Japanese family and their hospitality. (*See also* Lodging *in* Important Contacts A to Z, *above*).

RYOKAN

Those who want to sample the Japanese way should **spend at least one night in a ryokan,** or Japanese-style inn. Usually one- or two-story small wood structures with a garden or scenic view, they provide traditional Japanese accommodations: simple rooms in which the bedding is rolled out onto the floor at night.

Ryokan vary in price and quality. Some long-established older inns cost as much as ¥80,000 per person, whereas humbler places that are more like bed-and-breakfasts are as low as ¥5,000. Prices are per person and include the cost of breakfast, dinner, and tax. Some inns allow guests to stay without having dinner and lower the cost accordingly. However, this is not recommend-ed, because the service and meals are part of the ryokan experience. Not all inns are willing to accept foreign guests because of language and cultural barriers, so it is

important to make reservations in advance.

It is important to **follow Japanese customs in all ryokan.** Upon entering, take off your shoes, as you would do in a Japanese household, and put on the slippers that are provided in the entryway. A maid, after bowing to welcome you, will escort you to your room, which will have tatami (straw mats) on the floor and will probably be partitioned off with shoji (sliding paper-paneled walls). Remove your slippers before entering your room; you should not step on the tatami with either shoes or slippers. The room will have little furniture or decoration—perhaps one small low table and cushions on the tatami, with a long simple scroll on the wall. Often the rooms overlook a garden.

Most guests arrive in the late afternoon. After relaxing in their room with a cup of green tea, they have a long, hot bath. In ryokan with thermal pools, you can take to the waters anytime, although the doors to the pool are usually locked from 11 PM to 6 AM. In ryokan without thermal baths or private baths in guest rooms, guests must stagger their visit to the one or two public baths. Typically the maid will ask what time you would like your bath and fit you into a schedule. In Japanese baths, you wash and rinse off entirely before entering the tub. Because other guests will

be using the same bathwater after you, it is important to observe these customs. After your bath, change into a *yukata,* a simple cotton kimono, provided in your room. Do not feel abashed at walking around in what is essentially a robe—all the guests will be doing the same.

Dinner, included in the price of the room, is served in the room. After you are finished, a maid will discreetly come in, clear away the dishes, and lay out your futon. In Japan *futon* means bedding, and this consists of a thin cotton mattress and a heavy, thick comforter. In summer, the comforter is replaced with a thinner quilt. The small, hard pillow is filled with grain. The less expensive ryokan (under ¥7,000 for one) have become slightly lackadaisical in changing the sheet cover over the quilt with each new guest; feel free to complain (in as inoffensive a way as possible, of course, so as not to shame the proprietor). In the morning, a maid will gently wake you, clear away the futon, and bring in your Japanese-style breakfast. If you are not fond of Japanese breakfasts, often consisting of fish, raw egg, and rice, the staff will usually be able to rustle up some coffee and toast.

Because the staffs of most ryokan are small and dedicated, it is important to be considerate and understanding of their somewhat rigid schedules. Guests are expected to arrive in the late afternoon and eat around 6. Usually the doors to the inn are locked at 10, so plan for early evenings. Breakfast is served around 8, and checkout is at 10.

A genuine traditional ryokan with exemplary service is exorbitantly expensive—more than ¥30,000 per person a night with two meals. Many modern hotels with Japanese-style rooms are now referring to themselves as ryokan, and though meals may be served in the guests' rooms, they are a far cry from the traditional ryokan. There are also small inns claiming the status of ryokan, but they are really nothing more than bed-and-breakfast establishments where meals are taken in a communal dining room—for an additional fee—and service is minimal. Prices are around ¥5,000 for a single room, ¥7,000 for a double. JNTO offers a publication listing some of these.

TEMPLES

It is possible to arrange for accommodations in Buddhist temples. JNTO has lists of temples that accept guests. A stay at a temple generally costs ¥3,000–¥9,000 a night, including two meals. Some temples offer instruction in meditation or allow the guests to observe the temple religious practices, while others simply offer a room. The Japanese-style rooms

are very simple and range from beautiful, quiet havens to not-so-comfortable, basic cubicles. Still, temples provide a taste of traditional Japan.

M
MAIL

The Japanese postal service is very efficient. Although numerous post offices exist in any given city, it is probably best to use central post offices located near the main train station, because the workers speak English and can handle foreign mail. Some of the smaller post offices are not equipped to send packages.

Post offices are open weekdays 8–5 and Saturday 8–noon. Some of the central post offices have longer hours, such as the one in Tokyo, located near Tokyo Station, which is open 24 hours, year-round. Most hotels will supply stamps and mail your letters and postcards, usually with no "service fee."

It costs ¥100 to send a letter by air to the United States or Canada, ¥120 to Europe. An airmail postcard costs ¥70 to North America, ¥70 to Europe. Aerograms cost ¥100.

RECEIVING MAIL

To get mail, **have parcels and letters sent poste restante at the central post office in major cities;** unclaimed mail is returned after 30 days. American Express offices, located in all major Japanese cities,

are other good places to have mail sent (*see* Mail *in* Important Contacts A to Z, *above*).

MEDICAL
ASSISTANCE

No one plans to get sick while traveling, but it happens, so **consider signing up with a medical assistance company.** These outfits provide referrals, emergency evacuation or repatriation, 24-hour telephone hot lines for medical consultation, dispatch of medical personnel, relay of medical records, cash for emergencies, and other personal and legal assistance.

MONEY
AND EXPENSES

The unit of currency in Japan is the yen (¥). There are bills of ¥10,000, ¥5,000, and ¥1,000. Coins are ¥500, ¥100, ¥50, ¥10, ¥5, and ¥1. Japanese currency floats on the international monetary exchange, so changes can be dramatic. At press time the exchange rate was about ¥96 to the U.S. dollar, ¥72 to the Canadian dollar, and ¥159 to the pound sterling.

ATMS

Cirrus, Plus, and many other networks connecting automated-teller machines operate internationally. Chances are that you can **use your bank card at ATMs** to withdraw money from an account and get cash advances on a credit-card account if your card has been programmed with a personal identification number, or PIN. Before leaving home, **check on frequency limits** for withdrawals and cash advances. Also **ask whether your card's PIN must be reprogrammed** for use in Japan. Four digits are commonly used overseas. Note that Discover is accepted only in the United States.

On cash advances you are charged interest from the day you receive the money, whether from a teller or an ATM. Although transaction fees for ATM withdrawals abroad may be higher than fees for withdrawals at home, Cirrus and Plus exchange rates are excellent because they are based on wholesale rates only offered by major banks.

COSTS

Japan is expensive, but there are ways to cut costs. This requires, to some extent, an adventurous spirit and the courage to stray from the standard tourist paths. One good way to hold down expenses is to **avoid taxis** (they tend to get stuck in traffic anyway) and **try the inexpensive, efficient subway and bus systems;** instead of going to a restaurant with menus in English and Western-style food, go to places where you can rely on your good old index finger to point to the dish you want, and **try food that the Japanese eat** (*see* Dining, *above*).

A cup of coffee costs ¥350–¥600; a bottle of beer: ¥350–¥1,000; a 2-km taxi ride: ¥600

(¥840 in Tokyo); a McDonald's hamburger: ¥340; a bowl of noodles: ¥700; an average dinner: ¥2,500; a double room in Tokyo: ¥9,000–¥34,000.

EXCHANGING CURRENCY

For the most favorable rates, **change money at banks.** You won't do as well at exchange booths in airports or rail and bus stations, or in hotels, restaurants, and stores, although you may find their hours more convenient. To avoid lines at airport exchange booths, you may want to get a small amount of currency before you leave home.

TAXES

HOTEL➤ A 3% federal consumer tax is added to all hotel bills. Another 3% local tax is added to the bill if it exceeds ¥15,000. You may **save money by paying for your hotel meals separately** rather than charging them to your bill.

At first-class, full-service, and luxury hotels, a 10% service charge will be added to the bill in place of individual tipping. At the more expensive ryokan, where individualized maid service is offered, the service charge will usually be 15%. At business hotels, minshuku, youth hostels, and economy inns, no service charge will be added to the bill.

SALES➤ There is an across-the-board, nonrefundable 3% consumer tax levied on all

sales. Since the tax was introduced in 1989, vendors have either been absorbing the tax in their quoted retail prices or adding it on to the sale. Before you make a major purchase, inquire if tax is extra.

A 3% federal consumer tax is added to all restaurant bills. Another 3% local tax is added to the bill if it exceeds ¥7,500. At the more expensive restaurants, a 10%–15% service charge is added to the bill. Tipping is not the custom.

TRAVELER'S CHECKS

Whether or not to buy traveler's checks depends on where you are headed; **take local currency to rural areas and small towns, traveler's checks to cities.** The most widely recognized are American Express, Citicorp, Thomas Cook, and Visa, which are sold by major commercial banks for 1% to 3% of the checks' face value— it pays to **shop around.** Both American Express and Thomas Cook issue checks that can be countersigned and used by you or your traveling companion, and they both provide checks, at no extra charge, denominated in yen (though traveler's checks in dollars are accepted nearly everywhere). You can cash them in banks without paying a fee (which can be as much as 20%) and use them as readily as cash in many hotels, restaurants, and shops. So you won't be left with excess foreign currency, **buy a few checks in small denominations** to cash toward the end of your trip. Record the numbers of the checks, cross them off as you spend them, and keep this information separate from your checks.

P
PACKAGES AND TOURS

A package or tour to Japan can make your vacation less expensive and more convenient. Firms that sell tours and packages purchase airline seats, hotel rooms, and rental cars in bulk and pass some of the savings on to you. In addition, the best operators have local representatives to help you out at your destination.

A GOOD DEAL?

The more your package or tour includes, the better you can predict the ultimate cost of your vacation. Make sure you know exactly what is included, and **beware of hidden costs.** Are taxes, tips, and service charges included? Transfers and baggage handling? Entertainment and excursions? These can add up.

Most packages and tours are rated deluxe, first-class superior, first class, tourist, and budget. The key difference is usually accommodations. If the package or tour you are considering is priced lower than in your wildest dreams, **be skeptical.** Also, **make sure your travel agent**

knows the hotels and other services. Ask about location, room size, beds, and whether it has a pool, room service, or programs for children, if you care about these. Has your agent been there or sent others you can contact?

BIG VS. SMALL

An operator that handles several hundred thousand travelers annually can use its purchasing power to give you a good price. Its high volume may also indicate financial stability. But some small companies provide more personalized service; because they tend to specialize, they may also be experts on an area.

BUYER BEWARE

Each year consumers are stranded or lose their money when operators go out of business—even very large ones with excellent reputations. If you can't afford a loss, take the time to **check out the operator**—find out how long the company has been in business, and ask several agents about its reputation. Next, **don't book unless the firm has a consumer-protection program.** Members of the United States Tour Operators Association and the National Tour Association are required to set aside funds exclusively to cover your payments and travel arrangements in case of default. Nonmember operators may instead carry insurance; look for the details in the operator's brochure— and the name of an

underwriter with a solid reputation. Note: When it comes to tour operators, **don't trust escrow accounts.** Although there are laws governing those of charter-flight operators, no governmental body prevents tour operators from raiding the till.

Next, **contact your local Better Business Bureau and the attorney general's office** in both your own state and the operator's; have any complaints been filed? Last, **pay with a major credit card.** Then you can cancel payment, provided that you can document your complaint. Always **consider trip-cancellation insurance** (*see* Insurance, *above*).

SINGLE TRAVELERS

Prices are usually quoted per person, based on two sharing a room. If traveling solo, you may be required to pay the full double-occupancy rate. Some operators eliminate this surcharge if you agree to be matched up with a roommate of the same sex, even if one is not found by departure time.

USING AN AGENT

Travel agents are an excellent resource. In fact, large operators accept bookings only through travel agents. But it's good to **collect brochures from several agencies,** because some agents' suggestions may be skewed by promotional relationships with tour and package firms that reward them for volume sales. If you have a special interest,

find an agent with expertise in that area; the American Society of Travel Agents can give you leads in the United States. (Don't rely solely on your agent, though; agents may be unaware of small-niche operators, and some special-interest travel companies only sell direct.)

PACKING
FOR JAPAN

Because porters can be hard to find and baggage restrictions on international flights are tight, **pack light.** What you pack depends more on the time of year than on any dress code. For travel in the cities, pack as you would for an American or European city. At more expensive restaurants and night-clubs, men will usually need to wear a jacket and tie, and women will need a dress or skirt. Conservative-colored clothing is recommended for both men and women to wear at business meetings. Casual clothes are fine for sightseeing. Jeans are as popular in Japan as they are in the United States and are perfectly acceptable for informal dining and sightseeing.

Although there are no strict dress codes for visiting temples and shrines, **you will be out of place in shorts or immodest outfits.** For sightseeing, leave sandals and open-toe shoes behind; you'll need sturdy walking shoes for the gravel pathways that surround the temples and fill the parks. Make sure to bring comfortable

clothing that isn't too tight to wear in tradi-tional Japanese restaurants, where you may need to sit on tatami-matted floors. For beach and mountain resorts, pack informal clothes for both day and evening wear.

Japanese do not wear shoes in private homes or in any temples or traditional inns. Having shoes you can quickly slip in and out of is a decided advantage. Take some wool socks along to help you through those shoeless occasions.

If you're a morning coffee addict, **take along packets of instant coffee.** All lodgings provide a thermos of hot water and bags of green tea in every room, but for coffee you'll have to either call room service (which can be expensive) or buy very sweet coffee in a can from a vending ma-chine. If you're staying in a Japanese inn, they probably won't have coffee, and it may be hard to find in rural areas.

Although sunglasses, sunscreen lotions, and hats are readily avail-able, you're better off buying them at home, because they're much more expensive in Japan. It's a good idea to carry a couple of plastic bags to protect your camera and clothes during sudden cloudbursts.

It's a good idea to take along small gift items, such as scarves or perfume sachets, to thank hosts (on both

business and pleasure trips), whether you've been invited to their home or out to a restau-rant.

Bring an extra pair of eyeglasses or contact lenses in your carry-on luggage, and if you have a health problem, **pack enough medication** to last the trip or have your doctor write a prescription using the drug's generic name, because brand names vary from country to country (you'll then need a prescription from a local doctor). **Don't put prescription drugs or valuables in luggage to be checked,** for it could go astray. To avoid problems with customs officials, carry medications in original packaging. Also don't forget the addresses of offices that handle refunds of lost traveler's checks.

LUGGAGE

Free airline baggage allowances depend on the airline, the route, and the class of your ticket; ask in advance. In general, on domestic flights and on interna-tional flights between the United States and foreign destinations, you are entitled to check two bags— neither exceeding 62 inches, or 158 centime-ters (length + width + height), or weighing more than 70 pounds (32 kilograms). A third piece may be brought aboard; its total dimen-sions are generally limited to less than 45 inches (114 centime-ters), so it will fit easily under the seat in front of you or in the overhead compartment. In the United States, the FAA gives airlines broad latitude to limit carry-on allowances and tailor them to different aircraft and operational conditions. Charges for excess, oversize, or overweight pieces vary.

If you are flying between two foreign destinations, note that baggage allowances may be determined not by piece but by weight—generally 88 pounds (40 kilograms) in first class, 66 pounds (30 kilograms) in business class, and 44 pounds (20 kilograms) in economy. If your flight between two cities abroad *connects* with your transatlantic or transpacific flight, the piece method still applies.

SAFEGUARDING YOUR LUGGAGE➤ Before leaving home, **itemize your bags' contents** and their worth, and label them with your name, address, and phone number. (If you use your home address, cover it so that potential thieves can't see it.) Inside your bag, **pack a copy of your itinerary.** At check-in, **make sure that your bag has been correctly tagged** with the airport's three-letter destination code. If your bags arrive damaged or not at all, file a written report with the airline before leaving the airport.

PASSPORTS AND VISAS

If you don't already have one, **get a passport.** While traveling, **keep one photocopy of the data page** separate from your wallet and leave another copy with someone at home. If you lose your passport, promptly call the nearest embassy or consulate, and the local police; having the data page can speed replacement.

U.S. CITIZENS

All U.S. citizens, even infants, need a valid passport to enter Japan for stays of up to 90 days. New and renewal application forms are available at any of the 13 U.S. Passport Agency offices and at some post offices and courthouses. Passports are usually mailed within four weeks; allow five weeks or more in spring and summer.

CANADIANS

You need a valid passport to enter Japan for stays of up to 90 days. Application forms are available at 28 regional passport offices as well as post offices and travel agencies. Whether for a first or a renewal passport, you must apply in person. Children under 16 may be included on a parent's passport but must have their own to travel alone. Passports are valid for five years and are usually mailed within two to three weeks of application.

U.K. CITIZENS

Citizens of the United Kingdom need a valid passport to enter Japan for stays of up to six months. Applications for new and renewal passports are available from main post offices as well as at the passport offices, located in Belfast, Glasgow, Liverpool, London, Newport, and Peterborough. You may apply in person at all passport offices, or by mail to all except the London office. Children under 16 may travel on an accompanying parent's passport. All passports are valid for 10 years. Allow a month for processing.

R

RAIL TRAVEL

Anyone who plans to travel extensively by rail should **get a Japan Rail Pass,** which offers unlimited travel on Japan Railways (JR) trains. It is possible to purchase one-, two-, or three-week passes. A one-week pass is less expensive than a regular round-trip ticket from Tokyo to Kyoto on the Shinkansen. You must **obtain a rail pass voucher prior to departure for Japan** and the pass must be used within three months of purchase. The pass is available only to people with tourist visas, as opposed to business, student, and diplomatic visas.

When you arrive in Japan, you must exchange your voucher for the Japan Rail Pass. You can do this at the Japan Railways (JR) desk in the Arrivals Hall at Narita Airport or at the JR stations of major cities. When you make this exchange, you determine the day that you want the rail pass to begin—and, accordingly, when it ends. You do not have to begin travel on the day that you make the exchange. Pick the starting date to maximize the pass's use. The Japan Rail Pass allows you to travel on all JR-operated trains (which cover most destinations in Japan), but not lines owned by other companies. It also allows you to use buses operated by Japan Railways. You can make seat reservations without paying a fee on all trains that have reserved-seat coaches, usually the long-distance trains. The Japan Rail Pass does not cover the cost of sleeping compartments on overnight trains (called blue trains).

Japanese trains are efficient and convenient, running frequently and on time. The Shinkansen (bullet train), one of the fastest trains in the world, connects major cities north and south of Tokyo. It is only slightly less expensive than flying but is in many ways more convenient because train stations are more centrally located than airports. Visitors may also purchase a rail pass that permits unlimited travel on all lines operated by Japan Railways—some 26,000 trains daily run over 21,000 kilometers of tracks.

Other trains, though not as fast as the Shinkansen, are just as convenient and substantially cheaper. There are three types of train services: *futsu* (local

service), *tokkyu* (limited express service), and *kyuko* (express service). Both the tokkyu and the kyuko offer a first-class compartment known as the Green Car.

Because there are no porters or carts at train stations, and the flights of stairs connecting train platforms can turn even the lightest bag into a heavy burden, it is a good idea to **travel light when getting around by train.** Savvy travelers often have their main luggage sent ahead to a hotel that they plan to reach later in their wanderings. Good to know as well is that every train station, however small, has luggage lockers (about ¥300 for 24 hours).

PURCHASING TICKETS

Many travelers assume that rail passes guarantee them seats on the trains they wish to ride. Not so. If you are using a rail pass, there is no need to buy individual tickets, but you should **book seats ahead.** This guarantees you a seat and is also a useful reference for the times of train departures and arrivals. You can reserve up to two weeks in advance or just minutes before the train departs. If you fail to make a train, there is no penalty and you can reserve again.

Seat reservations for any JR route may be made at any JR station except those in the tiniest villages. The reservation windows or offices, *midori-no-madoguchi,* have green

signs in English and green-striped windows. For those traveling without a Japan Rail Pass, there is a surcharge of approximately ¥500 (depending upon distance traveled) for seat reservations, and if you miss the train you'll have to pay for another reservation. When making your seat reservation, you may request a no-smoking or smoking car. Your reservation ticket will show the date and departure time of your train as well as your car and seat number. On the platform, you can figure out where to wait for a particular train car. Notice the markings painted on the platform or on little signs above the platform; ask someone which markings correspond to car numbers. If you don't have a reservation, ask which cars are unreserved. Sleeping berths, even with a rail pass, are additional. Nonreserved tickets can be bought at regular ticket windows. There are no reservations made on local service trains. For traveling short distances, tickets are usually sold at vending machines. A platform ticket is required if you go through the wicket gate onto the platform. The charge is ¥140 for an adult and ¥70 for a child. (In Tokyo and Osaka, the tickets are ¥120 adults and ¥60 children.)

Most clerks at train stations know a few basic words of English and can read Roman script. Moreover, they are invariably helpful in plotting your route. The complete railway timetable is a mammoth book written only in Japanese; however, you can **get an English-language train schedule from the Japan National Tourist Organization** (JNTO) that covers the Shinkansen and a few of the major JR Limited Express trains. JNTO's booklet, *The Tourist's Handbook,* provides helpful information about purchasing tickets in Japan.

S

SENIOR-CITIZEN DISCOUNTS

To qualify for age-related discounts, **mention your senior-citizen status up front** when booking hotel reservations, not when checking out, and before you're seated in restaurants, not when paying your bill. Note that discounts may be limited to certain menus, days, or hours. When renting a car, **ask about promotional car-rental discounts**—they may net lower costs than your senior-citizen discount.

SHOPPING

Despite the high value of the yen and the high price of many goods, shopping is one of the great pleasures of a trip to Japan. You may not find terrific bargains here, but if you know where to go and what to look for, you can purchase unusual gifts and souvenirs at reasonable prices. In particular, **don't shop for items that are cheaper at home;** Japan is not the place to buy a Gucci bag (electronics, too, are generally cheaper in the U.S.). Instead, **look for things that are Japanese-made** for Japanese people and sold in stores that do not cater primarily to tourists.

Don't pass up your chance to purchase Japanese handicrafts. Color, balance of form, and superb craftsmanship make these items exquisite and well worth the price you'll pay. That doesn't mean they're all cheap; in fact, some handicrafts are quite expensive. For example, Japanese lacquerware carries a hefty price. But if you like the shiny boxes, bowls, cups, and trays and consider that quality lacquerware is made to last a lifetime, the cost is justified. Be careful, though: Some lacquer items are made from a pressed-wood product rather than solid wood, and only experts can tell the difference. If the price seems low, it probably means the quality is low, too.

STUDENTS ON THE ROAD

To save money, look into deals available through student-oriented travel agencies. To qualify, you'll need to have a bona fide student I.D. card. Members of international student groups also are eligible. *See* Students *in* Important Contacts A to Z, *above.*

T

TAXIS

Taxis are an expensive way of getting around cities in Japan. The first 2 kilometers cost about ¥620 (¥840 in Tokyo), and it is ¥90 for every additional 370 meters (400 yards). If possible, avoid using taxis during rush hours (8 AM–9 AM and 5:30 PM–6:30 PM).

In general, it is easy to hail a cab: Do not shout or wave wildly—simply **raise your hand if you need a taxi.** Japanese taxis have automatic door-opening systems, so **do not try to open the taxi door.** Stand back when the cab comes to a stop—if you are too close, the door may slam into you. When you leave the cab, do not try to close the door; the driver will use the automatic system. Only the curbside rear door opens. A red light on the dashboard indicates an available taxi, and a green light indicates an occupied taxi.

Drivers are for the most part courteous, although sometimes they will balk at the idea of a foreign passenger because they do not speak English. Unless you are going to a well-known destination such as a major hotel, it is advisable to **have a Japanese person write out your destination in Japanese.** Remember, there is no need to tip.

TELEPHONES

LONG-DISTANCE

The country code for dialing Japan is 81.

International calls can be made from the many green phones that have gold plates indicating, in English, that the telephone can be used for these calls. There are three Japanese companies that provide international service: KDD (001), ITJ (0041), and IDC (0061). Dial: company code + country code + city/area code and number of your party. KDD offers the clearest connection, but is also the most expensive. Telephone credit cards are especially convenient for international calls. For operator assistance in English on long-distance calls, dial 0051.

OPERATORS

When calling home from Japan, you can avoid hotel surcharges by using the local access numbers to English-speaking operators provided by AT&T, MCI, and Sprint: **AT&T:** 0039–111; **MCI:** on KDD phones, 0039–121; on IDC phones, 0066–55121; **Sprint:** 0066–55877.

PAY PHONES

Pay phones are one of the great delights of Japan. Not only are they conveniently located in hotels, restaurants, and on street corners, but pay phones, at ¥10 for three minutes, have to be one of the few remaining bargains in Japan.

Telephones come in three styles: pink, red, and green. Pink phones, for local calls, accept only ¥10 coins. Most red phones are only for local use, but some

accept ¥100 coins and can be used for long-distance domestic calls. Domestic long-distance rates are reduced as much as 50% after 9 PM (40% after 7 PM). Green phones take coins and often accept what are known as telephone cards—disposable cards of fixed value that you use up in increments of ¥10. Telephone cards, sold in vending machines, hotels, and a variety of stores, are tremendously convenient, because you will not have to search for the correct change.

TIPPING

Tipping is not common in Japan. It is not necessary to tip taxi drivers, or at beauty parlors, barber shops, bars, and nightclubs. A chauffeur for a hired car will usually receive a tip of ¥500 for a ½-day excursion and ¥1,000 for a full-day trip. Porters charge fees of ¥250–¥300 per bag at railroad stations and ¥200 per piece at airports. It is not customary to tip employees of hotels, even porters, unless a special service has been rendered. In such cases, a gratuity of ¥2,000 or ¥3,000 should be placed in an envelope and handed to the staff member discreetly.

W
WHEN TO GO

The best seasons to travel to Japan are spring and fall, when the weather is at its best. In the spring, the country is warm, with only occasional showers, and flowers grace landscapes in both rural

and urban areas. The first harbingers of spring are plum blossoms in early March; cherry blossoms follow, beginning in Kyushu and usually arriving in Tokyo by mid-April. Summer brings on the rainy season, with particularly heavy rains and mugginess in July. Fall is a welcome relief, with clear blue skies and beautiful foliage. Occasionally a few surprise typhoons occur in early fall, but the storms are usually as quick to leave as they are to arrive. Winter is gray and chilly, with little snow in most areas. Temperatures rarely fall below freezing.

For the most part, the climate of Japan is temperate and resembles the East Coast of the United States. The exceptions are the subtropical southern islands of Okinawa, located south of Kyushu, and the northern island of Hokkaido, where it snows for several months in the winter and is pleasantly cool in the summer.

To avoid crowds, **do not plan a trip for times when most Japanese are vacationing.** For the most part, Japanese cannot select when they want to take their vacations; they tend to do so on the same holiday dates. As a result, airports, planes, trains, and hotels are booked far in advance. Many businesses, shops, and restaurants are closed during these holidays. Holiday periods include the few days before and after New Year's; Golden Week, which follows Greenery Day (April 29); and mid-August at the time of the Obon festivals, when many Japanese return to their hometowns.

CLIMATE

What follows are the average daily maximum and minimum temperatures for major cities in Japan.

TOKYO

Jan.	46F	8C	May	72F	22C	Sept.	78F	26C
	29	– 2		53	12		66	19
Feb.	48F	9C	June	75F	24C	Oct.	70F	21C
	30	– 1		62	17		56	13
Mar.	53F	12C	July	82F	28C	Nov.	60F	16C
	35	2		70	21		42	6
Apr.	62F	17C	Aug.	86F	30C	Dec.	51F	11C
	46	8		72	22		33	1

KYOTO

Jan.	48F	9C	May	75F	24C	Sept.	82F	28C
	35	2		56	13		68	20
Feb.	53F	12C	June	82F	28C	Oct.	74F	23C
	32	0		66	19		53	12
Mar.	59F	15C	July	93F	34C	Nov.	62F	17C
	40	4		72	22		46	8
Apr.	65F	18C	Aug.	89F	32C	Dec.	53F	12C
	44	7		74	23		33	1

FUKUOKA

Jan.	53F	12C	May	74F	23C	Sept.	80F	27C
	35	2		57	14		68	20
Feb.	58F	14C	June	80F	27C	Oct.	74F	23C
	37	3		68	20		53	12
Mar.	60F	16C	July	89F	32C	Nov.	65F	18C
	42	6		75	24		48	9
Apr.	62F	17C	Aug.	89F	32C	Dec.	53F	12C
	48	9		75	24		37	3

SAPPORO

Jan.	29F	– 2C	May	60F	16C	Sept.	72F	22C
	10	–12		40	4		51	11
Feb.	30F	– 1C	June	70F	21C	Oct.	60F	16C
	13	11		50	10		40	4
Mar.	35F	2C	July	75F	24C	Nov.	46F	8C
	20	– 7		57	14		29	– 2
Apr.	51F	11C	Aug.	78F	26C	Dec.	33F	1C
	32	0		60	16		18	– 8

1 Destination: Japan

SEARCHING FOR THE REAL JAPAN

FIRST CAME TO JAPAN after World War II, when it was an occupied country. My most vivid memory is of the industrial area between Yokohama and Tokyo. As far as the eye could see on both sides of the highway, the flat earth was black. The only structures standing were the chimneys of factories the firebombs had consumed.

Like everyone else in the occupying force, I was comfortably housed and amply fed. But for the Japanese, food and clothing were scarce, and housing was at a premium. Faces were gray, and foreign correspondents reported an air of hopelessness. Those close to Prime Minister Shigeru Yoshida have told how, after a day of coping with Japan's problems and occupation officials, he sometimes smoked his postprandial cigar while pacing the garden of his official residence, looking out over ruined Tokyo, and muttering, "Will it ever be rebuilt? Will it ever be rebuilt?"

I came with curiosity about the nation I had been fighting against, but with precious little knowledge of it. I intended to stay only the two years called for by my contract. The two years stretched to 11. My involvement with Japan became lifelong.

Looking back, I can trace three paths that drew me into this fascinating, beautiful, and exasperating country. The first was Japan's contemporary prints. The moment I saw a small exhibition, I fell in love with them. I began collecting, I was able to meet many of the artists, and I formed bonds of friendship that endure to this day. My first book, *Modern Japanese Prints,* grew out of this enthusiasm.

The second path led to the Minaguchi-ya, a *ryokan,* the Japanese inn whose story I eventually set down. Frustrated because I never could get a reservation at any of the Western-style resort hotels the occupation authorities had taken over (they had overlooked none and had declared every other hostelry in the country off-limits to

us), I found, one lucky day, a small advertisement announcing that the Minaguchi-ya had been placed "on-limits" (by the small detachment of American military police stationed in the nearby city, I learned later; they wanted to use the inn). The Minaguchi-ya was a considerable distance from Yokohama, where I was based, and the red tape encountered in getting there was formidable, but I made it, and another love affair began. That was my introduction to the ryokan, and I remain addicted to the special delights of those uniquely Japanese retreats: the quiet elegance of traditional Japanese architecture; the personal service that eschews lobbies and restaurants to coddle you in your rooms, where all attention is focused on you; and the fine food, beautifully served.

The third path took me to the Kabuki theater, which, not at first but at second or third sight, enthralled me and still does. There I found glorious stagecraft put to dramatizing the long and engrossing history of Japan. I had been lured into that history by the story of the Minaguchi-ya; Kabuki quickened my interest by showing me, in action, the princely feudal lords called *daimyo,* their samurai, and commoners of every calling—merchants, farmers, artisans, gamblers, ruffians, and acquiescent waitresses.

I mention my own experiences because I am convinced that pursuing one's personal interests is the best way of meeting Japan. Few of us share with Japan the kind of cultural linkage that bonds us to Europe and the Middle East. For most of us, our ancestors, our language, our heroes, our folklore, and our way of thinking are Western, and it takes some effort to appreciate the equally great civilizations of the East. The handiest bridge is an interest already formed. Whatever it may be— pottery, food, religion, railroads, music, gardens, or marketing—pursuing it can add depth and zest to travel.

The Japanese themselves have always been avid tourists: you must not be surprised to find yourself vastly outnumbered at any popular spot. The Japanese think of travel as education. "If you love your son, let him travel," says one of their proverbs, and there is a corollary: "A traveler is without shame." Travel offers a release from the inhibitions and restraints at home; it's a license to misbehave that is sometimes exercised.

In days past, when travel was difficult—almost entirely on foot and sometimes sharply restricted by feudal regulation—most literate travelers kept a diary (a practice I suggest to you). Most, of course, were personal efforts to waken memories later or to share with family or friends. But some were "public diaries" meant to be published, like the diaries of Samuel Pepys and Daniel Defoe. Among these are some of the masterpieces of Japanese literature. Two favorites of mine are *The Tosa Diary,* about a journey in 935, and *The Narrow Road to the Deep North* (as the title is commonly translated), written 754 years later, in 1689.

The first is by a nobleman and distinguished poet named Tsurayuki, about his journey home to the capital after serving for five years as the governor of the distant province of Tosa (now Kochi Prefecture) on the Pacific side of the island of Shikoku. The second was written by Japan's most famous haiku poet, Basho, the man who raised the 17-syllable verse into art.

Basho shaped and even fictionalized his diary to reflect the landscape of his mind as well as the landscape he journeyed through. Tsurayuki, too, used fictional techniques; he pretended that his diary was written by a woman, perhaps because he considered that a central theme—sorrow over the loss of a little daughter who had died in Tosa—could best be expressed by a mother, and perhaps because he chose to write in colloquial Japanese instead of the elevated style expected of an educated man.

Both are poetic diaries. Both men turned to poetry when their feelings were too intense to be expressed in prose. This was not unusual, for in their times any cultured man was supposed to be able to toss off a poem when the occasion called for it. Even today a great deal of poetry is written by amateurs—shopkeepers, politicians, housewives, businessmen—just for the love of it.

I do not put much faith in analyses that attempt to explain the Japanese character and personality. Of course, in some ways the Japanese are different from us because their history and their culture are different, but human beings are human beings, and we have much more in common than we have differences.

STILL, THE JAPANESE DO HAVE their particular hang-ups and idiosyncrasies. They explain many of these by the fact that they are a homogeneous people. Certainly just about everybody has black hair (unless henna or age has intervened), which, as a friend has remarked, makes for a neat-looking crowd. Because of their homogeneity and because they have lived so closely together for so long, they maintain that they are so attuned to each other that much need not be said: nuance in tone or phrase conveys unspoken meaning. There is truth in this, but if it were totally true there would be no misunderstandings between the Japanese, which is not the case. It is also true that in the West what is unspoken is often more meaningful than what is said, and we, too, have our formulas for avoiding the overt. When casual acquaintances part by saying, "Let's get together sometime," they both understand that they have no intention of planning another meeting.

Because the Japanese have their own nuances, the foreigner would do well to listen carefully; if there is a shadow of a doubt, it's best to probe a bit for the real meaning. The Japanese may consider this gauche, but it is preferable to a misunderstanding. As has been pointed out, the Japanese often say yes to mean that they understand you, not that they agree with you.

Japan is all islands—more than 3,300 of them, of which about 440 are inhabited. The four biggest are Hokkaido, in the north; Honshu, curving south and west; Kyushu, in the west; and Shikoku, smallest of the four, cradled between Honshu and Kyushu across the Inland Sea. The mountaintops that are these islands are themselves very mountainous. Plains are few: The Japanese can cultivate only about 16% of the land they live on. Today that 16% is crowded, but in early centuries it was more than adequate and very attractive to immigrants. And so, long after the land bridge had disappeared, people kept coming in boats. A hundred miles of dangerous sea divide southern Korea and northern Kyushu, but that is the part of Japan closest to the Asian continent, and it was the gateway for both people and culture entering from the continent. Its ports were busy with a continuing flow of settlers and innovations. In that area, metals first replaced stone for making tools and weapons, and hunting and foraging gave way to the cultivation of rice in wet fields. Farming made people stop roaming and settle down in communities—little "kingdoms"—which promptly started to fight each other. As the strong conquered the weak, a few powerful fiefdoms emerged. For a long time, northern Kyushu was the most advanced area of Japan. It is where Japan began.

Legends tell us that the group of clans that produced the imperial family originated in Kyushu and fought their way eastward along the Inland Sea to the inviting plain where eventually rose the cities of Nara, Osaka, and Kyoto. In an area called Yamato, they dug in and asserted their right to rule all Japan.

The early history of Japan is still shrouded in mist that archaeologists and historians are patiently working to disperse, but we know that the Yamato group was not unchallenged. There were other centers of power. Separately, they gave way, some to force of arms, some to persuasion and concession.

What remains for all to see are two great Shinto shrines, which symbolize forces once surely locked in conflict. The Ise Shrine on the Pacific coast is the shrine of the imperial family; one complex of the shrine is dedicated to the family's legendary ancestress, the Sun Goddess, and is the shrine of the victors. The Izumo Shrine on the Sea of Japan, the opposite side of Honshu, is dedicated to the legendary adversary of the Sun Goddess, her unruly brother; it is usually considered the shrine of a people who yielded politically but held on to their gods and their identity. Both shrines are magnificent, but they are different. Ise celebrates light, while Izumo embodies brooding power.

Ise and Izumo are high on my list of important places.

Today, politically, economically, socially, everything in Japan heads up in Tokyo. There is much talk of decentralization and of invigorating the provincial cities, but decentralization seems mostly to end with extending Tokyo's sprawl by pushing some government installations to satellite cities.

Today, Tokyo is more than ever the heart of things; it's the site of government, the financial center, the preeminent headquarters for business, the magnet for intellectuals, the focus of the arts. It is Washington, New York, and Boston rolled into one. It pulses with energy and runs on split-second schedules, yet turn a corner and you find a neighborhood where housewives trade gossip as they shop for the day's groceries in mom-and-pop stores that spill into the street. The city has been called ugly, but I do not agree. It has grand vistas, spacious parks, inviting residential areas, and a giddy mix of architecture that ranges from the cheerfully vulgar and outrageously fantastic to the strong and innovative. It offers more to do than any resident can possibly keep up with, much less a visitor. Above all, Tokyo is exciting; it is never dull.

When people ask me, "Where can I find the *real* Japan?" they usually have in mind the idyllic: thatch-roofed farmhouses set in verdant paddy fields. My answer probably surprises them. "Tokyo," I say. "Today, Tokyo is the real Japan."

—*By Oliver Statler*

WHAT'S WHERE

Hokkaido

Hokkaido, the northernmost of Japan's four main islands, offers a respite from the temples, shrines, and castles that fill the agenda of the tourist to the other, more frequently visited parts of Japan. It is a geological wonderland half-covered in forests, with lava-seared mountains and crystal-clear caldera lakes.

The Japan Alps

The north–south mountain ranges of central Honshu were dubbed the Japan Alps by an English missionary in the late 19th century. Approximately 100 years later, in 1998, the region hopes to come into its own as a major winter resort destination when it hosts the XVIII Winter Olympics.

Kobe

In typical Japanese fashion, this port city on Osaka Bay has made an amazingly quick recovery from the devastating earthquake that struck it in January 1995. A sophisticated and cosmopolitan city that has been an important harbor throughout Japanese history, Kobe has excellent shopping and a wide variety of international cuisines to sample.

Kyoto

A stroll through this city today is a walk through 11 centuries of Japan's history; its 1,600 temples, several hundred shrines, and countless other attractions make it a top tourist destination, even for the Japanese themselves.

Kyushu

The journeys between the major points of interest in Kyushu, the southernmost of Japan's four main islands, afford beautiful views of its rich green fields, mountains, and the ocean. Each of its major tourist destinations—Fukuoka, Nagasaki, Kumamoto, and Beppu—has a different flavor; the last, with its extensive variety of hot mineral springs, is a favorite among Japanese vacationers seeking a restful soak.

Nagoya, Ise-Shima, and the Kii Peninsula

A two-hour train ride from Tokyo, Nagoya is Japan's fourth largest city, an industrial metropolis whose most notable tourist attractions are Nagoya Castle and the shrine known as Atsuta Jingu. South of the city is Ise-Shima National Park, which encompasses the Grand Shrines of Ise, the most venerated shrines in Japan. Although the sightseeing is limited at the shrines, one's reward is in feeling the sanctity surrounding them. Farther south, the Kii Peninsula has magnificent marine scenery, coastal fishing villages and resorts, and Mt. Yoshino, with perhaps the finest display of cherry blossoms in Japan.

Nara

A half-hour south of Kyoto lies Nara, a small, quiet city that is a favorite with many return visitors to Japan, who realized too late the first time around that they had short-changed it timewise because they were, understandably, dazzled by its northern neighbor's cultural riches. In addition to numerous temples and historic sites, Nara has hidden treasures in its backstreets: old wooden shops, merchants' houses, and traditional restaurants.

Osaka

Japan's "Second City" (after Tokyo, of course), in terms of industry, commerce, and technology, Osaka is known for its bunraku (puppet theater) and its superb restaurants. A three-hour train ride from Tokyo, it is a good starting point for trips to Nara, Kyoto, and Kobe.

Shikoku

The smallest of Japan's four main islands, Shikoku lies to the south of Western Honshu, across the Inland Sea and now reachable by road and rail by a remarkable chain of bridges. Rugged east–west mountain ranges halve this island, where travelers are treated more as welcome foreign emissaries than as income-bearing tourists and where Japanese Buddhists still come to make religious pilgrimages to 88 sacred temples, as they have done for centuries.

Tohoku

Tohoku, an area consisting of the six prefectures of northern Honshu, is, undeservedly, one of Japan's least-visited areas. It has some of Japan's greatest attractions, not the least of which is its people, who seem a bit more friendly than their compatriots along the Tokyo–Osaka corridor. The summer here is refreshingly cool, and the sensational August festivals held in Akita, Aomori, Hirosaki, and Sendai offer a convenient excuse to make a stop here then.

Tokyo

A state-of-the-art financial marketplace; a metropolis of exquisite politenesses; a city that is frustratingly large yet has astonishing beauty in its small details—these are just a few of the myriad ways Tokyo can be described, and all contain at least a grain of truth. For the tourist, it is the sum of its districts and neighborhoods—among them Ueno, Asakusa, Ginza, Roppongi, Shibuya, and Shinjuku. Although daunting in its sheer size, Tokyo is, in fact, extremely easy to negotiate: virtually anyplace you're likely to visit is within a five-minute walk of a train or subway station, and all station stops are marked in English.

Tokyo Excursions

Nikko, Kamakura, Mt. Fuji—each of these must-sees is within a couple of hours of the great metropolis. Visitors either love or hate Toshogu, the shrine that is the centerpiece of Nikko, but most agree on the grandeur of that city's natural beauty. Kamakura, capital of Japan for more than a century, has a splendid legacy of historic and cultural sites. And no matter how many photographs or artistic renderings of Mt. Fuji you have seen, the perfect symmetry and supreme majesty of this dormant volcano will fill you with awe when you get a glimpse of the real thing.

Western Honshu

The western side of Japan's main island is home to a number of attractive cities, most notably Kurashiki, a charming town in which old Japan can be truly savored; Hiroshima, where the half-shattered building renamed the A-Bomb Dome stands as a powerful reminder of one of the world's greatest tragedies; and Miyajima, a small island in the Inland Sea that is home to Itsukushima Shrine, with its vermilion gate rising strikingly out of the water.

PLEASURES & PASTIMES

Baseball

Given the labor-management conflicts that have in recent years plagued U.S. major league baseball and diminished its traditional popularity, it is fair to say that baseball is more of a national pastime in Japan than it is Stateside. If you're a fan—and perhaps even if you aren't—you'll probably want to take in a game in Japan: The way the Japanese have adopted and adapted this Western sport constitutes a fascinating and easy-to-grasp microcosm of both their culture and their overall relationship to things Western. The team names alone—the Orix Blue-Wave and the Chiba Lotte Marines, for example—resound amusingly in Western ears accustomed to such monikers as the Yankees and the Indians, and the fans' cheers are different and chanted more in unison than in U.S. ballparks. But a lot is familiar, too. Two non-Japanese players are allowed on each team; past and future American superstars, Kevin Mitchell and Cecil Fielder, to name two, have played *besuboru*. Tokyo Dome at Korakuen is the place to see pro ball in the big city.

Bathing

Partly because of the importance of purification rites in Shinto, Japan's ancient indigenous religion, the art of bathing has been a crucial element of the culture for centuries. But baths in Japan are as much about pleasure and relaxation as they are about washing and cleansing. In traditional Japan, communal bathhouses served as centers for social gatherings, and even though most modern houses and apartments have bathtubs, many Japanese still prefer the pleasures of communal bathing—either at hot springs (see that section below) when they are on vacation or in public bathhouses in their neighborhoods.

Japanese bathtubs themselves are different from those in the West—they're deep enough for bathers to sit in upright with (very hot) water up to their necks—and the procedures for using them are quite different as well. They are only for soaking, not for washing: Soap must not get into the bathwater. How is this accomplished? Before taking the plunge, you sit on a stool in a special area outside the tub that is equipped with faucets or shower hoses and a floor drain. There you wash with soap and rinse thoroughly in preparation for entering the tub. The water in it is as hot as the body can endure, but the reward for the inevitable moment of unease upon entry is the pleasure of a lengthy soak in water that does not become tepid.

Many hotels in major cities offer only Western-style reclining bathtubs, so to indulge in this great pleasure you'll need to stay in a Japanese-style inn or find a public bathhouse. The latter are clean, hygienic, and easy to find, but try to take your own towel: Small ones are available for a fee, but their size is comparable to that of what Americans consider to be merely a hand towel.

Beaches

For a country that consists entirely of islands, Japan has surprisingly few good beaches. Those accessible from Tokyo, in areas such as Kamakura and the Izu Peninsula, are absolutely mobbed all summer long. The beaches of Kyushu and Shikoku are ess crowded, more pleasant, and have clear blue water, and the country's best beaches are found in the subtropical Ryukyu Islands, which include Okinawa. But bear in mind that many Japanese find it less expensive to fly to Hawaii than to go to the Ryukyus.

Bicycling

With its narrow roads and largely mountainous terrain, Japan does not offer ideal conditions for cycling. It can be feasible, inexpensive, and delightful to see the sights in some towns by bicycle, however; these are identifiable by the presence of bicycle-rental shops near their main railway station as in, for example, Kanazawa, Takayama, and Hagi. The best serious cycling can be done on some of the remote islands, such as Sado, on the Sea of Japan, and Iki, off the coast of Kyushu. Wherever you cycle, don't forget that cars drive on the left side of the road in Japan.

Dining

Japanese food is not only delicious and healthy, but also aesthetically pleasing: Even the most humble lunch box (*bento*) procured at a station or on a train will have been created with careful attention to color combination and general presentation. Portions can be smaller than Westerners are accustomed to, however; when eating a restaurant meal that comes with rice, this can be compensated for by requesting an extra portion of that white staple, which is usually either complimentary or very low-priced.

There are many types of restaurants in Japan. In most you are given a warm—or even rather hot—moist washcloth with which to wipe your hands soon after you are first seated. Water or green tea is usually served with the meal (though other beverages may of course be ordered), and green tea is offered after you finish eating as well, frequently along with a complimentary piece of fruit. Standards of hygiene and service are universally high, from the cheapest student-oriented dives to the most exclusive five-star establishments.

Sushiya specialize in sushi and sashimi. Places that do not list their prices can be extremely expensive, especially if you order by the piece. Some of the most inexpensive sushi places have a revolving conveyer belt from which you select what want (generally from a collection of plates laden with two pieces of sushi each) and pay at the end according to the number of empty plates you have accumulated. These can be fun, and going to one is definitely an experience to remember.

Although rice is the staple that most readily comes to mind when one thinks of Japanese cuisine, noodles are also a ubiquitous part of the food scene. *Soba* shops specialize in soba (buckwheat-flour noodles) and usually offer *udon* (thick wheat-flour noodles) as well. In summer, cold noodle dishes such as *zaru soba* (drained chilled noodles served with a cup of dipping sauce) can be very refreshing, while in cold weather, *nabeyaki udon*, in which the thicker noodles are served sizzling in a pan with an array of vegetables and fish, will warm you to the bone. *Domburimono*, dishes consisting of a bowl of rice topped with any of a variety of ingredients (for example, a fried pork cutlet or a piece or two of shrimp tempura), are also often found on the menu at soba shops. Ramen shops specialize in thin wheat-flour noodles of Chinese origin that are served in a highly seasoned broth flavored with either miso or soy sauce. *Gyoza*, delectable fried or steamed dumplings filled with meat and vegetables, are also served at ramen shops.

Ryotei are elegant (and expensive) establishments that specialize in the traditional, elaborate, multicourse cuisine known as *kaiseki ryori*. If you go to one of these, take a camera: Many of the offerings are truly too beautiful to eat (and served on gorgeous ceramics as well), but as you must, at least preserve the masterpieces on film.

Nomiya and *izakaya* are the Japanese equivalents of bars, but in addition to beer, sake, and whiskey they often serve simple, tasty food, including *yakitori* (chicken grilled on skewers), grilled fish, chilled or heated tofu, and Japanese-style pickles (*tsukemono*).

Japanese coffee shops, known as *kissaten*, are always good hangouts for weary tourists. Ask for an "American" cup of coffee if you've found that the Japanese variety is too strong for your tastes. If you don't mind bland white bread, you may want to order a tuna or egg sandwich along with your caffeine.

If you tire of Japanese food, not to worry; just about every cuisine under the sun is available in the major cities, including all varieties of Western and Asian. American chains such as Denny's and McDonald's, and their Japanese imitators, are everywhere.

Hot Springs

Fortunately for the Japanese, a nation of bathing aficionados, their country is dotted with *onsen*, natural hot springs. Many onsen are surrounded by resorts, ranging from large Western-style hotels to small, humble inns; all are extremely popular destinations for Japanese tourists. Traditionally the curative value of hot-spring water was strongly emphasized; added to that today is the need for a place to get away from the frantic pace of modern life and relax. At the resorts, onsen water is usually piped in to hotel rooms or large communal indoor baths, though some feature year-round open-air baths (*rotenburo*) where you can soak outdoors in the midst of a snowy winter landscape. Some of the more well-known spas near Tokyo are at Atami, Hakone, Ito, and Nikko; in Kobe, at Arima; in Kyushu, at Beppu and Unzen; and in Hokkaido, at Noboribetsu.

Shopping

Japan's department stores have to be seen to be believed, from their automaton-like white-gloved elevator operators to their elaborate wrapping of even the most humble purchase. Their stock includes items made by every international designer you can name alongside the best of traditional Japanese arts and crafts items, and most have at least two basement levels devoted entirely to the selling of food, from international groceries to ready-to-eat Japanese delicacies and everyday menu items. Everything mentioned below is likely to be found in at least one major urban department store.

Items made of *washi*—hand-molded paper—are one of the best buys in Japan. Delicate sheets of almost-transparent stationery, greeting cards, money holders, and wrapping paper are available at traditional crafts stores, stationery stores, and department stores. Small washi-covered boxes (suitable for jewelry and other keepsakes) and pencil cases are also strong candidates for gifts and personal souvenirs.

At first glance, the ceramics displayed in Japan seem priced for a prince's table.

Some are, of course, but if you keep shopping you can find reasonably priced functional and decorative items that are generally far superior in design to what is available at home. The best places to shop for these outside stores in pottery villages such as Hagi and Mashiko are—again—the department stores, where the selection is vast and there are items priced for every budget. Sale items often represent amazingly good bargains; among the best gifts are vases, sake sets consisting of one or two small bottles and a number of cups, and chopstick rests.

Printed fabric, whether by the yard or in the form of finished scarves, napkins, tablecloths, or pillow coverings, is another item worth purchasing in Japan. The complexity of the designs and the quality of the printing make the fabric, both silk and cotton, special. *Furoshiki*—square pieces of cloth used for wrapping, storing, and carrying things—make great wall hangings back home.

For a view of how the middle class manages its daily shopping, head to one of the shopping arcades that are often an extension of urban and suburban train or subway stations. Everything—clothes, stationery, books, CDs, electronic goods, food, housewares—is sold in these arcades, which can be madhouses during the evening rush hour.

Skiing

Japan's mountains are beautiful and snowy in the winter season, with very good skiing conditions. Many ski areas are near natural hot springs, so a chilly day on the slopes can conclude with a restorative hot soak. The most popular ski areas are around central Honshu's Nagano, site of the 1998 Winter Olympics; in northern Honshu at Mt. Zao; and in Hokkaido at Jozankei (in Sapporo) and Daisetsuzan National Park (in the central part of the island).

But be forewarned: The major drawback of skiing in Japan is the crowds, especially on weekend and holidays. The slopes can become more packed with people than snow, and the trains and highways leading to the ski areas are also congested. If you must ski in Japan, try to go on a weekday or head for Hokkaido during a nonholiday period.

Sumo

If baseball can be called Japan's modern national pastime, surely sumo is its traditional national pastime, and it remains tremendously popular, even at 2,000 years old. A Shinto-style roof is hung from the ceiling over a circular clay ring in which two enormous wrestlers face off. After various preliminary rites, some of which involve tossing handfuls of salt into the ring to symbolize purification, the actual wrestling begins. The match concludes when any part of a wrestler's body (other than the soles of his feet) touches the ground or he is pushed out of the ring. The wrestlers wear only a loincloth-type garment and have slick topknot hairstyles. Six 15-day tournaments are held each year; they are seen live at sold-out stadiums seating around 10,000 people and on television by millions more. The match-ups are shown on huge screens in major train stations and elsewhere—if a tournament is under way while you're in Japan, you'll know it. Tickets can be difficult to obtain but it's definitely worth a try; if you go, buy the more expensive seats, both because they give you a better view of the action and because they include a bag full of a generous amount of food and fun sumo-themed souvenirs, such as a tea or sake set whose cups feature drawings of the major wrestlers.

FODOR'S CHOICE

Temples and Shrines

★ **Byodoin, Uji.** The Phoenix Hall of this villa-turned-temple southeast of Kyoto is one of Japan's finest religious buildings—it's even memorialized on the back of the 10-yen coin. The hall's main icon is an elegant wood Buddha carved in the 11th century.

★ **Grand Shrines of Ise.** The austere beauty of this shrine complex is especially intriguing in light of the fact that the Inner Shrine is razed and rebuilt every 20 years.

★ **Hasedera, Kamakura.** The main attraction here is Japan's largest carved wooden statue, a 30-foot-tall image of the bodhisattva Kannon; but it is the haunting sight of seemingly endless rows of statues of Jizo—the bodhisattva associated with the souls of miscarried, stillborn, and aborted children—that will remain with visitors to this temple overlooking the sea.

★ **Horyuji, Nara.** Japan's oldest temple compound houses one of the country's best collections of Buddhist art; its 7th-century masterpieces are a vivid testimony to the remarkable variety of artistic traditions that came here from Korea and China at that time.

★ **Itsukushima Jinja, Miyajima.** The vermilion main gate of this shrine is strikingly situated in Hiroshima Bay, between the tiny island of Miyajima and Honshu, one of Japan's four main islands.

★ **Kiyomizudera, Kyoto.** A splendid panorama of the city is afforded by this spacious temple complex's main hall, which is built directly over a cliff.

★ **Sensoji, Tokyo.** A walk through the grounds of this temple in the heart of traditional Tokyo's Asakusa district can feel like a journey back in time to its Edo-period heyday, and great traditional souvenirs can be purchased in the surrounding arcades.

Parks and Gardens

★ **Ginkakuji, Kyoto.** This tranquil temple has two beautiful gardens: One provides changing perspectives on a pond, flowers, and trees as you stroll through it, and the other is a dry garden with two dazzling sand shapes for quiet contemplation.

★ **Villa Katsura Detached Palace, Kyoto.** The loveliness of this vast estate's numerous gardens and rustic teahouses makes the advance planning required to gain permission for a visit worthwhile.

★ **Kenrokuen, Kanazawa.** A remarkable collection of varied miniature landscapes, this garden has been justifiably designated by the Japanese as one of their country's three most beautiful.

★ **Nara Park, Nara.** Don't let the greedy tame deer (they'll eat even paper right out of your hand) deter you from a visit to this sprawling park, which is home to temples, shrines, a national museum, and a historic botanic garden.

★ **Sankeien, Yokohama.** The many varieties of trees and flowers here ensure that something will be blooming—or changing color—at virtually any point in any season of the year; the historic buildings transported here, including a teahouse and a farmhouse, mesh well with the natural beauty.

⭐ **Shinjuku Gyoen, Tokyo.** Renowned for its cherry blossoms in April and its chrysanthemums in November, this 150-acre public park and landscape garden is a virtual oasis of quiet green set in one of Tokyo's most frenetic areas.

Sights

⭐ **Atomic Bomb Dome and Peace Flame, Hiroshima.** The only building left unreconstructed in the city where atomic weaponry was first used against human beings is a poignant and sobering sight, as is the Peace Flame, which will not be extinguished until all of the world's nuclear weapons have been banished.

⭐ **Daibutsu (Great Buddha), Todaiji, Nara.** This colossal gilt-bronze image, built in the eighth century and damaged and restored several times subsequently, is housed in what is thought to be the world's largest wooden structure.

⭐ **Geisha, Gion district, Kyoto.** Although their numbers have dwindled significantly in this century, these traditional female entertainers can still be spotted in the evening as they hurry down the alleys of this Kyoto neighborhood, sparkling white *tabi* (socks) peeking out from under their richly brocaded kimono.

⭐ **Mt. Fuji.** One sighting of the elegant profile of the country's highest mountain and de facto national symbol repays many times over the time and money spent to travel to Japan.

⭐ **Torchlight Noh.** Noh—the world's oldest extant professional theater—is special wherever it is seen, but particularly so when the performance is staged outside, often on shrine or temple grounds, by the light of a bonfire.

⭐ **Tsukiji Market, Tokyo.** Early risers who arrive here in time (i.e., considerably before 6:30 AM) to watch 90 percent of the fish consumed in Tokyo being auctioned off are in for a truly memorable experience, but those who prefer to sleep in shouldn't hesitate to stop by later in the day for the great shopping for tea, pickles, baskets, and crockery.

Restaurants

⭐ **Inakaya, Tokyo.** Sit around a U-shape counter and watch cooks in traditional dress charcoal-grill a delectable array of vegetables, seafood, beef, and chicken. They'll serve your skewered choices direct from the pit on an eight-foot-long paddle. $$$$

⭐ **Attore, Tokyo.** Although some Westerners find it hard to believe—much less accept—some of the world's best Italian food is to be had in Tokyo; the cream of the crop is served here. $$–$$$$

⭐ **Heichinrou, Tokyo.** Sample first-rate Cantonese food while taking in a spectacular view of Hibiya Park and the Imperial Palace at this branch of one of Yokohama Chinatown's oldest and best restaurants. $$$

⭐ **Sasashu, Tokyo.** This *izakaya* (traditional drinking establishment) stocks Japan's finest sake—and serves the best food to accompany it; the house specialty is charcoal-broiled salmon steak brushed with sake and soy sauce. $$$

⭐ **Yagenbori, Kyoto.** The city's best traditional cuisine is attractively presented on beautiful handmade ceramics in this teahouse in the heart of the geisha district. $$$

⭐ **Kanawa Restaurant, Hiroshima.** Hiroshima prides itself on its melt-in-your-mouth oysters; savor them on this restaurant-on-a-barge with river views. $$

⭐ **Sagano, Kyoto.** The subtle, delicate flavor of tofu simmered in savory broth is intensified by the gorgeous natural surroundings of this Arashiyama district retreat. $$

⭐ **Farm Grill, Tokyo.** California-style cuisine meets Tokyo yuppies in this vast, minimally decorated space; the portions are generous, the prices reasonable, and the menu innovative. $–$$

⭐ **Shikairo, Nagasaki.** The specialties of the house are *chanpon*—a tasty noodle dish created in this very restaurant—and Fukien Chinese cuisine, but the menu is nearly as extensive as this restaurant's seating capacity of 1,500. $–$$

Hotels

⭐ **Four Seasons Hotel Chinzan-so, Tokyo.** The million dollars or so that it reputedly cost to complete each guest room here is evident in every inch of the large rooms as well as in the lavish lobby. $$$$

★ **Palace Hotel, Tokyo.** The staff of this stately, deluxe retreat across the moat from the Imperial Palace is particularly helpful and professional. $$$$

★ **Tawaraya, Kyoto.** Subdued traditional beauty and modern comforts blend seamlessly at this lodging of choice of kings, queens, presidents, and dictators. $$$$

★ **Hiroshima Grand Hotel, Hiroshima.** This quietly refined establishment, conveniently located near the city's major tourist attractions, offers fine service and comfort. $$–$$$

★ **Hirota Guest House, Kyoto.** An English-speaking professional guide operates this gem, a restored sake storehouse south of Kyoto's Imperial Palace. $

★ **Sakaya, Beppu, Kyushu.** Meals prepared in a hot-spring–heated backyard oven are included in the reasonable rates charged for accommodations in this beautiful old wooden building. $

★ **Sawanoya Ryokan, Tokyo.** The welcoming owners of this popular low-budget spot make visitors of all nationalities feel at home in the traditional Tokyo neighborhood of Ueno. $

GREAT ITINERARIES

Each chapter in *Fodor's Japan* is described as an itinerary through a particular city or region of Japan. The following are suggestions for other itineraries that cross from one area to another and combine parts of the exploring sections of the various chapters. Keep in mind that if you are planning to do a lot of train travel, it is best to get a Japan Rail Pass, which must be purchased outside of Japan (*see* The Gold Guide, *above*).

Introduction to Traditional Japan (One Week)

Like every nation, Japan has some sights that are more famous than others. These sights tend to be in the major cities. The following itinerary covers the barest minimum, but it does include modern Tokyo; the splendor of Nikko; the temples and shrines of Kamakura, the power center of Japan's first shogunate; the temples of classical Kyoto; and Nara, Japan's first permanent capital. Be warned that this itinerary barely scratches the surface of Japan's heritage.

Day 1: Arrive in Tokyo. Flights from the United States tend to arrive in the late afternoon, which means that by the time you reach your hotel in downtown Tokyo, it is early evening.

Day 2: Visit the major Tokyo sites that appeal to you (*see* Chapter 2). Arrange it so that your evening is spent in one or two of the nighttime districts, such as Roppongi or Shinjuku.

Day 3: Visit Nikko either on your own or with a tour (*see* Chapter 3). Return to Tokyo for evening pleasures.

Day 4: Visit Kamakura on your own, traveling from Tokyo by train (*see* Chapter 3). If there is time left in the day, stop on the way back to Tokyo to visit Yokohama (*see* Chapter 3).

Day 5: Take one of the morning Shinkansen trains from Tokyo to Kyoto (*see* Chapter 6). Visit the sights in the Eastern District (Higashiyama) in the afternoon and enjoy the Gion District in the evening.

Day 6: In the morning visit more of the Eastern District sights and in the afternoon visit the Western District sights.

Day 7: Cover Central Kyoto in the morning and travel to Nara in the afternoon (*see* Chapter 7).

Day 8: Return to Tokyo via Kyoto and go straight to the airport.

An Extended Introduction to Japan (Two Weeks)

Two weeks is obviously better than one week in Japan. Covering the same ground as the one-week itinerary of Japan, this itinerary also includes some of the Japan Alps, Hiroshima, and the Seto Inland Sea.

Day 1–4: Same as above.

Day 5: Take the train to Nagano and visit Zenkoji (temple). Continue by train to Matsumoto and visit Karasujo, the Japan Folklore Museum, and the Japan Ukiyoe Museum (*see* Chapter 5).

Day 6: Travel via Kamikochi to Takayama (*see* Chapter 5).

Day 7: Visit Takayama sights and in the late afternoon travel by train via Toyama to Kanazawa (*see* Chapter 5).

Day 8: Visit the sights of Kanazawa (*see* Chapter 5) and catch the late-afternoon train to Kyoto (*see* Chapter 6).

Day 9: Visit Kyoto's Eastern District (Higashiyama) in the afternoon and enjoy the Gion District in the evening.

Day 10: In the morning visit more of the Eastern District sights and in the afternoon visit the Western District sights.

Day 11: Cover Central Kyoto in the morning and Northern Kyoto in the afternoon.

Day 12: Travel to Nara in the afternoon to see the sights there (*see* Chapter 7).

Day 13: Travel by train to Himeji to visit the castle (*see* Chapter 10). Continue on to Okayama and reach Kurashiki by early afternoon.

Day 14: Leave Kurashiki by train in time to be in Hiroshima for lunch. Visit the Peace Memorial Park and Museum and then take the train and ferry to Miyajima and spend the night there (*see* Chapter 10).

Day 15: Return to Tokyo in the morning and go straight to the airport.

Scenic Japan

Tohoku, in northern Honshu, is a mixture of modern cities and small villages, rustic farmhouses and glorious temples, and high mountain ranges and indented shorelines. Tohoku has yet to be commercialized; there is still the feeling that one is traveling in another era. The chapter on Tohoku (Chapter 13) is an itinerary in itself. Here we have shortened the itinerary so that it can easily be managed in a week and also include a visit to Nikko.

Day 1: Take the Shinkansen train from Tokyo to Sendai. See the sights in Sendai and then take the train to Matsushima.

Day 2: Spend most of the day exploring Matsushima and return to Sendai for the night.

Day 3: Take the train to Hiraizumi and visit the sights. Reboard the train to Morioka.

Day 4: Take the train north as far as Obuke and transfer to a bus to cross the Hachimantai Plateau. At the end of the Aspite Skyline Drive, change buses and head south to Tazawako.

Day 5: Take the train to Kakunodate to visit the samurai houses. Reboard the train to travel to Yamagata to visit Yamadera.

Day 6: Take the train south to Yamagata and on to Fukushima, where you can board the Shinkansen train for Utsunomiya. Here, rather than return to Tokyo, you can take a local train up to Nikko (*see* Chapter 3).

Day 7: Return to Tokyo.

Into the Northern Frontier

Northern Japan is rural Japan, steeped in folklore and natural beauty. Though tourist facilities are available throughout the area of northern Honshu and Hokkaido, the number of tourists is fewer. This itinerary gives the traveler the chance to see the other side of Japan—not the industry that has spawned the country's economic miracle or the aristocratic temples of Imperial Japan—but rustic Japan, with more of what the country looked like before it was swept into 20th-century Western technology.

The itinerary starts in Sapporo in Hokkaido, on the assumption that one arrives there by plane.

Day 1: Explore Sapporo (*see* Chapter 14).

Day 2: Visit the Shakotan Peninsula by rented car, or by a bus/train combination. Return to Sapporo in the evening, perhaps dining at Otaru on the way back (*see* Chapter 14).

Day 3: Take the train to Asahikawa and rent a car for the drive to Sounkyo in the Daisetsuzan National Park. You can also travel by bus (*see* Chapter 14).

Day 4–5: Travel by car or bus to Akan National Park. You may want to spend two nights here exploring (*see* Chapter 14).

Day 6: Travel by car or by bus and train to Abashiri and go north to Monbetsu (*see* Chapter 14).

Day 7: Travel back to Asahikawa, return the car, and take the train back to Sapporo. There is the option of traveling north from Monbetsu to Wakkanai and visiting Rebun and Rishiri islands (*see* Chapter 14).

Day 8: Travel by bus to Lake Toya and on to Noboribetsu Onsen (*see* Chapter 14).

Day 9: By train travel to Hakodate, visit the town (*see* Chapter 14), and then reboard the train for Aomori. Change trains and go on to Hirosaki (*see* Chapter 13).

Day 10: Travel south to Akita by train and then change for a train to Kakunodate to visit the samurai houses. Reboard the train and continue on to Tazawako (*see* Chapter 13).

Day 11: Travel by train to Morioka and farther east to Miyako, with a visit to Jodogahama (beach) (*see* Chapter 13).

Day 12: By train, travel to Kamaishi and then west to Tono (*see* Chapter 13).

Day 13: Continue by train to Hanamaki and change for the train going to Hiraizumi. Visit the temples and before nightfall catch the train on to Sendai (*see* Chapter 13).

Day 14: Visit Matsushima and spend the day exploring. You can either spend the night or return to Tokyo via Sendai (*see* Chapter 13).

Castles

Only 12 donjons from the feudal period have survived intact. The following is a tour designed to cover the best of them, though we have had to omit the one in Hirosaki because it is off by itself in northern Tohoku (northern Honshu). While this six-day tour travels from castle town to castle town, there are plenty of other sights to see in the vicinity of each castle. At certain places you will probably wish to stay longer than the itinerary below suggests, and make it a 10-day trip.

Day 1: Leave Tokyo or Kyoto by Shinkansen train; the first stop is Himeji and its magnificent castle. Then continue on to Okayama to visit its castle, which is the only one on this tour that is a replica. Rather than spend the night at Okayama, take the train to Kurashiki and stay there (*see* Chapter 10).

Day 2: Cross over to Shikoku either by train or ferry, and continue by bus to Kochi and its castle (*see* Chapter 11).

Day 3: Using a combination of train and bus, head for Uwajima and its castle before continuing by train to Matsuyama and its castle (*see* Chapter 11).

Day 4: By ferry, cross over the Inland Sea to Hiroshima and take the train north to Matsue and its castle (*see* Chapter 10).

Day 5: Take the train to Hikone in the direction of Kyoto, visit the castle, and then continue by train via Gifu to Inuyama (*see* Chapter 4).

Day 6: From Inuyama, return to Gifu and then take the train to Matsumoto to visit one of the most attractive feudal castles. From Matsumoto, return to Tokyo (*see* Chapter 5).

In the Shadow of the Mountains

Old traditional Japan is fast disappearing, but the north coast of Western Honshu has largely avoided the eyesore of modern industrialism. This area is ideal for anyone willing to go off the beaten track and take a leisurely trip through small villages, rustic countryside, and medieval castle towns. Minimally this itinerary will take five or six days, but it could easily be extended to a leisurely 10-day exploration (*see* Chapter 10).

Day 1: Head west from Kyoto on the Shinkansen to Ogori. From Ogori (west of Hiroshima), cross from the south coast of Western Honshu to Hagi on the north coast by bus. See Hagi's sights.

Day 2: Travel by bus to Tsuwano and spend the rest of the day here.

Day 3: Take the train to Masuda and begin heading northeast along the coast. If you have the time, you may want to make Matsue your first stop.

Day 4: Make sure that you visit the Izumo Taisha (shrine).

Day 5: Continue northwest along the coast to Tottori and the Tottori Sand Dunes, then on to Kasumi and Kirosaki for the night.

Day 6: The last major sight on the coast is Amanohashidate, one of the Big Three Scenic Wonders in Japan. From here Kyoto is less than three hours away by train.

NATIONAL HOLIDAYS

When a holiday falls on a Sunday, it is celebrated on the following Monday.

JAN. 1➤ **New Year's Day** is the "festival of festivals" for the Japanese. Some women dress in traditional kimonos, and many people visit shrines and hold family reunions. Although the day is solemn, streets are often decorated with pine twigs, plum branches, and bamboo stalks.

JAN. 15➤ **Adults' Day** honors those who have reached the voting age of 20.

FEB. 11➤ **National Foundation Day** celebrates accession to the throne by the first emperor.

MAR. 21 (OR 20)➤ **Vernal Equinox Day** celebrates the start of spring.

APR. 29➤ **Greenery Day.** The first day of **Golden Week,** when many people are taking vacation and hotels, trains, and attractions are crowded. Not a good week to visit Japan.

MAY 3➤ **Constitution Memorial Day.** This day commemorates the adoption of the Japanese constitution.

MAY 5➤ **Children's Day.** Families with little boys display paper or cloth carp on bamboo poles outside the house or a set of warrior dolls inside the home.

AUG. 13–16➤ The **Obon Festival,** a time of Buddhist ceremonies in honor of ancestors. Many Japanese take off the entire week to travel to their home towns. Tourists should avoid this time.

SEPT. 15➤ **Respect for the Aged Day**

SEPT. 23 (OR 24)➤ **Autumnal Equinox Day**

OCT. 10➤ **Health-Sports Day** commemorates the Tokyo Olympics of 1964.

NOV. 3➤ **Culture Day,** a fairly new holiday, encourages the Japanese to cherish peace, freedom, and culture, both old and new.

NOV. 23➤ **Labor Thanksgiving Day** is recognized by harvest celebrations in some parts of the country.

DEC. 23➤ **The Emperor's Birthday**

DEC. 27➤ **Osho-Gatsu,** the first day of the week-long New Year celebrations. Travel not recommended.

2 Tokyo

A state-of-the-art financial marketplace; a metropolis of exquisite politenesses; a city that is frustratingly large yet has astonishing beauty in its small details—these are just a few of the myriad ways Tokyo can be described, and all contain at least a grain of truth. For the tourist, it is the sum of its districts and neighborhoods—among them Ueno, Asakusa, Ginza, Roppongi, Shibuya, and Shinjuku.

By Jared
Lubarsky and
Nigel Fisher

TOKYO: OF ALL THE MAJOR CITIES IN THE WORLD, it is perhaps the hardest to understand, to feel comfortable in, and to see in any single perspective. To begin with, consider the sheer, outrageous size of it. Tokyo incorporates 23 wards, 26 smaller cities, seven towns, and eight villages, together sprawling 55 miles east to west and 15 miles north to south. The wards alone enclose an area of 227 square miles—home to some 8.5 million people. More than 2 million of these residents pass through Shinjuku Station, one of the major hubs in the transportation network, every day.

It's staggering to think what the population density would be if Tokyo went up as well as out. Mile after mile, the houses rise only one or two stories above the ground, that low uniformity broken here and there by the sore thumb of an apartment building. Space, that most precious of commodities, is so scarce that pedestrians have to weave in and out around the utility poles as they walk along the narrow sidewalks—and everywhere, space is wasted. Begin with that observation, and you discover that the very fabric of life in this city is woven of countless, unfathomable contradictions.

Tokyo is a state-of-the-art financial marketplace, where billions of dollars are whisked electronically around the globe every day, in the blink of an eye—and where automatic cash dispensers shut down at 7 PM. (The machines levy a service charge of ¥103 for withdrawals after 6 PM.) It's a metropolis of exquisite politenesses, where uniformed department store staff bow you in and out of the elevators—and where the man in the subway will push an old woman out of the way to get a seat. A city of astonishing beauty in its small details, Tokyo also has some of the ugliest buildings on the planet and generates 20,000 tons of garbage a day. It installed its first electric light in 1833, yet still has hundreds of thousands of households without a bathtub.

Life was simpler here in the 12th century, when Tokyo was a little fishing village called Edo, near the mouth of the Sumida River on the Kanto Plain. The Kanto was a strategic granary, large and fertile; over the next 400 years it was governed by a succession of warlords and other rulers. One of them, named Dokan Ota, built the first castle in Edo in 1457. That act is still officially regarded as the founding of the city, but the honor really belongs to Ieyasu, the first Tokugawa shogun, who arrived in 1590. When the civil wars of the 16th century came to an end, Ieyasu was the vassal of Generalissimo Hideyoshi Toyotomi, who gave him the eight provinces of Kanto in eastern Japan in exchange for three provinces closer to Kyoto—the imperial capital and ostensibly the seat of power. Ieyasu was a farsighted soldier; the swap was fine with him. In place of Ota's stronghold, he built a mighty fortress of his own—from which, 10 years later, he was ruling the whole country.

By 1680, there were more than a million people here, and a great city had grown up out of the reeds in the marshy lowlands of Edo Bay. Tokyo can only really be understood as a *joka-machi*—a castle town. Ieyasu had fought his way to the shogunate, and he had a warrior's concern for the geography of his capital. Edo Castle (Edojo), had the high ground, but that wasn't enough; all around it, at strategic points, he gave large estates to allies and trusted retainers. These lesser lords' villas would also be garrisons, outposts on a perimeter of defense.

Farther out, he kept the barons he trusted least of all. Ieyasu had won the Battle of Sekigahara (1600), which made him shogun, only because someone had switched sides at the last moment; he controlled the barons who might one day turn against him by bleeding their treasuries. They were required to keep large, expensive establishments in Edo; to contribute generously to the temples he endowed; to come and go twice a year in great pomp and ceremony; and, when they returned to their estates, to leave their families—in effect, hostages—behind.

All this, the Edo of feudal estates, of villas and gardens and temples, lay south and west of Edo Castle, but it was called the Yamanote—the Bluff, the "uptown." Here, all was in its proper order, disciplined and ceremonious; every man had his rank and duties. (Within the garrisons were very few women.) Almost from the beginning, those duties were less military than bureaucratic; Ieyasu's precautions worked like a charm, and the Tokugawa dynasty enjoyed some 250 years of unbroken peace, during which nothing very interesting ever happened uptown.

But the Yamanote was only the demand side of the economy: Somebody had to bring in the fish, weed the gardens, weave the mats, and entertain the bureaucrats during their time off. To serve the noble houses, common people flowed into Edo from all over Japan; their allotted quarters of the city were jumbles of narrow streets, alleys, and culs-de-sac, in the low-lying estuarine lands to the north and east. Often enough, the land wasn't even there when it was assigned to them; they had to *make* it by draining and filling the marshes. (The first reclamation project in Edo dates to 1457.) The result was Shitamachi—the "downtown," the part below the castle, which sat on a hill. Bustling, brawling Shitamachi was the supply side: It had the lumberyards, markets, and workshops; the wood-block printers, kimono makers, and moneylenders. The people here gossiped over the back fence in the earthy, colorful Edo dialect. They supported the bathhouses and the Kabuki theaters, had fireworks festivals, and went to Yoshiwara (a walled and moated area on the outskirts of Edo where prostitution was licensed), making it the biggest licensed brothel quarter in the world. The Edokko—the people of Shitamachi—haven't changed much; their city and its spirit have survived, while the great estates uptown are now mostly parks and hotels.

The shogunate was overthrown in 1867. The following year, the Emperor Meiji moved his court to Edo from Kyoto and renamed it Tokyo (Eastern Capital). By now the city was home to nearly 2 million people, and the geography was vastly more complex than before. The broad divisions of Yamanote and Shitamachi remained. The Imperial Palace still provided a point of reference, a locus for the heart of the city, but Tokyo defied such easy organization. As it grew, it became not one but many smaller cities, with different centers of commerce, government, entertainment, and transportation. In Yamanote rose the department stores, the office buildings, and public halls, which made up the architecture of an emerging modern state. The workshops of Shitamachi multiplied, some of them to become small jobbers and family-run factories. Still, there was no planning, no grid. The neighborhoods and subcenters were worlds unto themselves, and the traveler from one was soon hopelessly lost in another.

The firebombings of 1945 left Tokyo, for the most part, in rubble and ashes. Here was an opportunity to start again: to build a planned city, like Kyoto, Barcelona, or Washington, with a rational shape. It never happened. Tokyo reverted to type; it became once again an aggrega-

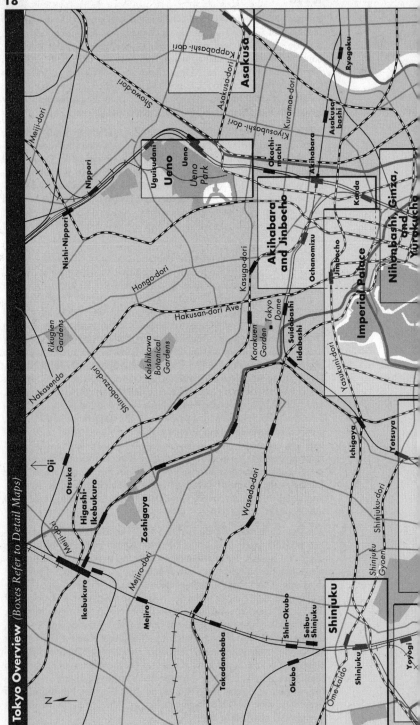

Tokyo Overview *(Boxes Refer to Detail Maps)*

N

Asakusa

Kappabashi-dori

Asakusa-dori

Kuramae-dori

Ryogoku

Kiyosubashi-dori

Asakusa-
bashi

Showa-dori

Meiji-dori

Nippori

Uguisudani

Ueno

Ueno
Park

Okachi-
machi

Akihabara

Kanda

Akihabara
and Jinbocho

Ochanomizu

Jimbocho

Nishi-Nippori

Hongo-dori

Kasuga-dori

Nihonbashi, Ginza,
and Yurakucho

Rikugien
Gardens

Hakusan-dori Ave

Tokyo
Dome

Suidobashi

Iidabashi

Imperial Palace

Nakasendo

Koishikawa
Botanical
Gardens

Korakuen
Garden

Yasukuni-dori

Shinobazu-dori

Oji

Otsuka

Higashi-
Ikebukuro

Zoshigaya

Ichigaya

Yotsuya

Waseda-dori

Shinjuku-dori

Meijiro-dori

Meijiro-dori

Ikebukuro

Mejiro

Shinjuku
Gyoen

Shinjuku

Takadanobaba

Shin-Okubo

Seibu-
Shinjuku

Okubo

Shinjuku

Yoyogi

Ome-kaido

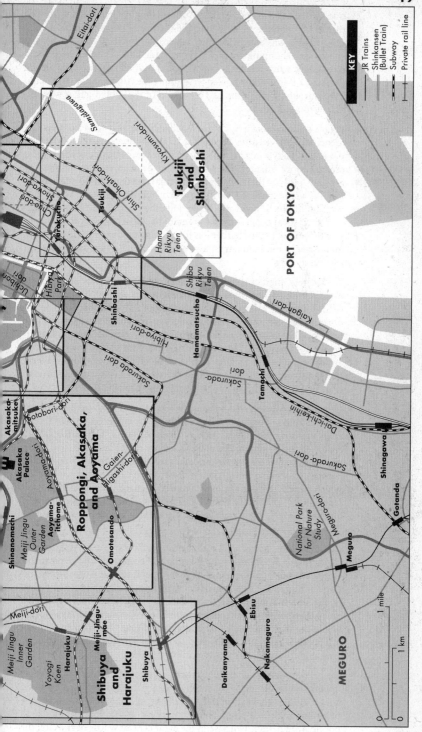

19

KEY

JR Trains
Shinkansen (Bullet Train)
Subway
Private rail line

Eitai-dori

Sumidagawa

Kiyosumi-dori

Chuo-dori

Showa-dori

Shin Ohashi-dori

Yurakucho

Tsukiji

Tsukiji and Shinbashi

Hama Rikyu Teien

Uchibori-dori

Hibiya Park

Shinbashi

Shiba Rikyu Teien

Hibiya-dori

Hamamatsucho

Sakurada-dori

Sakurada-dori

Tamachi

Dai-ichi-keihin

Kaigan-dori

PORT OF TOKYO

Akasaka-mitsuke

Sotobori-dori

Akasaka Palace

Aoyama-dori

Roppongi, Akasaka, and Aoyama

Gaien-Higashi-dori

Shinanomachi

Meiji Jingu Outer Garden

Aoyama-itchome

Omotesando

Meguro-dori

National Park for Nature Study

Shinagawa

Gotanda

Meguro

Sakurada-dori

Meiji-dori

Meiji Jingu Inner Garden

Yoyogi Koen

Harajuku

Meiji Jingu-mae

Shibuya and Harajuku

Shibuya

Daikanyama

Ebisu

Nakameguro

MEGURO

1 mile

1 km

0

tion of small towns and villages. Author Donald Richie once described them as "separate, yet welded to the texture of the metropolis itself." One village was much like any other; the nucleus was always the *shoten-gai* (shopping arcade). Every arcade had a butcher, a grocer, a rice dealer, a mat maker, a barber, and a pinball parlor; every arcade also had a florist and a bookstore—sometimes two of each. You could live your whole life in the neighborhood of the shoten-gai; it was sufficient to your needs.

People seldom moved out of these villages; the vast waves of new residents who arrived after World War II (about three-quarters of the people in the Tokyo metropolitan area today were born elsewhere) just created more villages. Everybody who lived in one knew his way around, and so there was no particular need to name the streets. Houses were numbered not in sequence, but in the order in which they were built; No. 3 might well share a mailbox with No. 12. People still take their local geography for granted; the closer you get to the place you're looking for, the harder it is to get coherent directions. Away from main streets and landmarks, a stranger, or even a taxi driver, can get hopelessly lost.

Fortunately, there are the *koban*: small police boxes, or substations, usually with two or three officers assigned to each of them full time, to look after the affairs of the neighborhood. These koban are one important reason for the legendary safety of Tokyo: On foot or on white bicycles, the police are a visible presence, covering the beat. (Burglaries are not unknown, but street crime is very rare.) You can't go far in any direction without finding a koban. The officer on duty knows where everything is, and is glad to point the way; like the samurai-bureaucrats of Edo, he seldom has anything more pressing to do.

Outsiders, however, seldom venture very far into the labyrinths of residential Tokyo. For the tourist, especially, the city is the sum of its districts and neighborhoods, such as Ueno, Asakusa, Ginza, Roppongi, Shibuya, and Shinjuku. Harajuku is a more recent addition to that list, and soon the waterfront will add another; the *attention* of Tokyo shifts constantly, seeking new patches of astronomically expensive land on which to realize its enormous commercial energy. (Even with the collapse of the speculative bubble in 1992, you can't buy a square yard anywhere in the city's central wards for much less than $35,000.)

Tokyo is still really two areas, Shitamachi and Yamanote. The heart of Shitamachi, proud and stubborn in its Edo ways, is Asakusa; the dividing line is Ginza; to the west lie the boutiques and department stores, the banks and engines of government, the pleasure domes and swell cafés. Today there are 10 subway lines (an 11th is scheduled to open late 1997, and a 12th is also under construction) weaving the two areas together. Another special feature of Tokyo's geography is found where the lines intersect: vast underground malls, with miles of shops in fluorescent-lit, air-conditioned corridors. These stores sell anything you might want to buy between subway rides.

Up on the surface, confusion reigns, or seems to. Tokyo is the most impermanent of cities, constantly tearing itself down and building anew. Whole blocks disappear overnight; the next day, a framework of girders is already rising on the empty lot. It's no longer possible to put up a single-family house in the eight central wards of the city; the plot to put it on costs more than the average person will earn in several lifetimes. Home owners live in the suburbs, usually an hour or more by train from their jobs. Only developers can afford the land closer in;

they build office buildings, condominiums, and commercial complexes. Tokyo has no skyline, no prevailing style of architecture, nothing for a new building to measure itself against. Every new project is an environment unto itself. World-famous architects like Arata Isozaki, Fumihiko Maki, and Kisho Kurokawa revel in this anarchy; so do the designers of neon signs, show windows, and interior spaces. The kind of creative energy you find in Tokyo could flower only in an atmosphere where there are virtually no rules to break.

Not all of that is for the best. Many of the buildings in Tokyo are merely grotesque, and most of them are supremely ugly. In the large scale, Tokyo is not an *attractive* city; neither is it gracious, and it is certainly not serene. The pace of life is wedded to the one stupefying fact of population: Within a 20-mile radius of the Imperial Palace live almost 30 million souls, all of them in a hurry, and all of them ferocious consumers. They live in a city that went from rubble to dazzling affluence in a generation; they are very sure of what they have accomplished, but they are terribly uncertain about who they are. They consume to identify themselves—by what they wear, where they eat, and how they use their leisure time.

Tokyo is a magnet. Its attractive power, of course, is money—enormous amounts of it, looking for new ways of turning itself over. The economy, despite recent setbacks, is still strong, and the Japanese remain among the world's foremost consumers—not merely of things, but of culture and leisure. Everything shows up here, sooner or later: van Gogh's *Sunflowers,* the Berlin Philharmonic, Chinese pandas, Mexican food. Even the Coney Island carousel is here—lovingly restored to the last gilded curlicue on the last prancing unicorn, brought to life again at an amusement park called Toshima-en. And now, because you are reading this guide, the magnet is drawing you. What follows is an attempt to chart a few paths for you through this exasperating, exciting, movable feast of a city.

EXPLORING

Orientation

The distinctions of "downtown" (Shitamachi: north and east) and "uptown" (Yamanote: south and west) have shaped the character of Tokyo since the 17th century and will be your guide, too, as you explore the city. At the risk of an easy generalization, it might be said that downtown offers the visitor more to *see,* and uptown more things to *do;* another way of putting it is that Tokyo north and east of the Imperial Palace embodies more of the city's history, its traditional way of life, whereas the fruit of modernity—the glitzy, ritzy side of Tokyo as an international city—lies generally south and west.

The following exploring section has been divided into 10 tours of major areas of Tokyo. The first six tours follow a downtown loop that starts in central Tokyo at the **Imperial Palace District** and proceeds north to **Akihabara and Jinbocho,** and from there to **Ueno.** From Ueno, the tours turn east to **Asakusa,** then south to **Tsukiji and Shinbashi,** returning to the center of the city by way of **Nihonbashi, Ginza, and Yurakucho.**

The four tours of Tokyo's uptown take you south to **Roppongi** and then north to **Akasaka** (which is west of the Imperial Palace district) and **Aoyama.** The tours continue from Aoyama to the western part of Tokyo, through **Shibuya and Harajuku,** and finally **Shinjuku.**

Fortunately, no point on any of these 10 itineraries is very far from a subway station; you can use Tokyo's efficient subway system to hop from one area to another, to cut a tour short, or to return to a tour the next day. The areas in the 10 tours are not always contiguous—Tokyo is too spread out for that—but they generally border on each other to a useful degree. You will probably want to improvise; you can skip segments of tours according to your fancy, or combine parts of one tour with another in order to end your day exploring the area of your choice.

Let's begin, then, in central Tokyo, with the Imperial Palace District.

Imperial Palace District

Numbers in the margin correspond to points of interest on the Imperial Palace map.

The **Imperial Palace** (Kokyo) occupies what were once the grounds of Edo Castle (in Japanese, Edojo). The first feudal lord here, a local chieftain named Dokan Ota, was assassinated in 1486, and the castle he built was abandoned for more than 100 years. When Ieyasu Tokugawa chose the site for his castle in 1590, he had two goals in mind: First, it would have to be impregnable; second, it would have to reflect the power and glory of his position. He was lord of the Kanto, the richest fief in Japan, and would soon be shogun, the military head of state. The fortifications he devised called for a triple system of moats and canals, incorporating the bay and the Sumida River into a huge network of waterways that enclosed both the castle keep (the stronghold or tower) and the palaces and villas of his court—in all, an area of about 450 acres. The castle had 99 gates (36 in the outer wall), 21 watchtowers (of which three are still standing), and 28 armories. The outer defenses stretched from present-day Shinbashi Station to Kanda. Completed in 1640 and later expanded, it was at the time the largest castle in the world.

The walls of Edo Castle and its moats were made of stone from the Izu Peninsula, about 96 kilometers (60 miles) to the southwest. The great slabs were brought by barge—each of the largest was a cargo in itself—to the port of Edo (then much closer to the castle than the present port of Tokyo is now), and hauled through the streets on sledges by teams of 100 men or more. Thousands of stonemasons were brought from all over the country to finish the work; under the gates and castle buildings, the blocks of stone are said to have been shaped and fitted so precisely that a knife blade could not be slipped between them.

The inner walls divided the castle into four main areas, called *maru*. The *honmaru* (innermost area) contained the shogun's audience halls, his private residence, and, for want of a better word, his seraglio: the *o-oku*, where the shogun kept his wife and concubines, with their ladies-in-waiting, attendants, cooks, and servants. (Concubines came and went; at any given time, as many as 1,000 women might be living in the o-oku. Intrigue, more than sex, was its principal concern, and tales of the seraglio provided a rich source of material for the Japanese literary imagination.) Below the honmaru was the *ninomaru* (second fortress), where the shogun lived when he transferred his power to an heir and retired. Behind it, to the north, was the *kitanomaru*, now a public park; south and west was the *nishinomaru*, a subsidiary fortress.

Not much of the Tokugawa glory remains. The shogunate was abolished in 1868; the Emperor Meiji (1868–1912), restored to power, moved his court from Kyoto to Edo—renaming it Tokyo—and Edo Castle was chosen for the site of the Imperial Palace. Many of the buildings had been destroyed in the turmoil of the Meiji Restoration (1868); others fell victim to fire in 1872; still others were simply torn down. Of the 28 original *tamon* (armories), only two survived. The present-day Imperial Palace is open to the public only twice a year: on January 2 (New Year's) and December 23 (Emperor's Birthday), when many thousands of people assemble under the balcony to offer their good wishes to the imperial family. In 1968, to mark the completion of the current palace, the area that once encompassed the honmaru and ninomaru were opened to the public as the Imperial Palace East Garden. There are three entrance gates—Otemon, Hirakawamon, and Kita-Hanebashimon. Each can easily be reached from the Otemachi or Takebashi subway stations.

❶ A good place to start an exploration of the Imperial Palace area is **Tokyo Station.** The Otemachi subway stop (Chiyoda, Marunouchi, Tozai, and Toei Mita lines) is a closer and handier connection, but the old red-brick Tokyo Station building is a more compelling place. The work of Kingo Tatsuno, one of Japan's first modern architects, it was completed in 1914; Tatsuno modeled his creation on the railway station of Amsterdam. The building lost its original top story in the air raids of 1945, but it was promptly repaired; more recent plans to tear it down entirely were scotched by a protest movement, and the idea now is to have it "remodeled"—which, to judge by the prevailing standards of architecture in Tokyo, can do it very little good. The best thing about the building is the **Tokyo Station Hotel,** which wanders along the west side on the second and third floors; the windows along the corridor look out over the station rotunda. The hotel's frosted glass, flocked wallpaper, and heavy red drapes have seen better days, but it still has enough pride of place—you couldn't ask for a more central location— to charge ¥19,000 to ¥26,000 for a double room. The dining room serves a fairly decent breakfast for ¥1,500. *1-9-1 Marunouchi, Chiyoda-ku,* ☎ *03/3231–2511.*

Leave the station by the Marunouchi Central exit, cross the street in front at the taxi stand, and walk up the broad divided avenue that leads to the Imperial Palace grounds. To your left is Marunouchi, to your right is Otemachi: You are in the heart of Japan, Incorporated—the home of its major banks and investment houses, its insurance and trading companies. Take the second right, at the corner of the New Marunouchi Building; walk two blocks, past the gleaming brown marble fortress of the Industrial Bank of Japan, and turn left. Ahead of you, across Uchibori-dori (Inner Moat Avenue) from the Palace Hotel, ❷ is the **Otemon,** one of three entrances to the Imperial Palace **East Garden.** ☛ *Free.* ☺ *9–3. Closed Mon., Fri., and Dec. 25–Jan. 5.*

The Otemon was in fact the main entrance to the castle itself. The so-called *masu* (box) style was typical of virtually all the approaches to Ieyasu's impregnable fortress: The first portal (*mon* is Japanese for "gate") leads to a narrow enclosure with a second and larger gate beyond, offering the defenders inside a devastating field of fire upon any would-be intruders. Most of the Otemon was destroyed in 1945 but was rebuilt in 1967 on the original plans; the outer part of the gate, however, survived.

Go through the gate, collect a plastic token at the office on the other side (there's no admission fee), and walk up the driveway. The blood-curdling shrieks and howls you may hear on your left are harmless; they come from the National Police Agency *dojo* (martial arts hall).

24

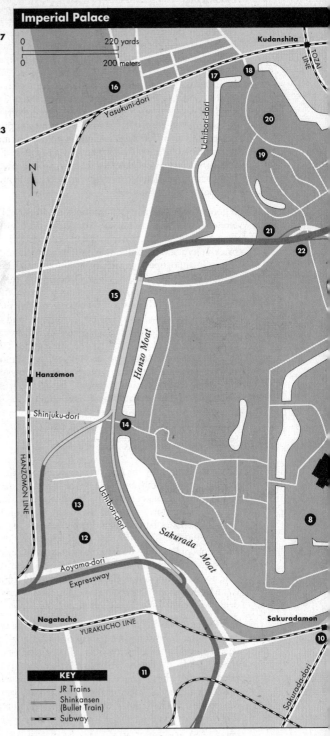

Imperial Palace

0   220 yards
0   200 meters

Kudanshita

TOZAI LINE

N

Yasukuni-dori

Uchibori-dori

Hanzōmon

Shinjuku-dori

HANZOMON LINE

Hanzo Moat

Sakurada Moat

Aoyama-dori

Expressway

Nagatacho

YURAKUCHO LINE

Sakuradamon

Sakurada-dori

KEY
— JR Trains
— Shinkansen (Bullet Train)
-·-·- Subway

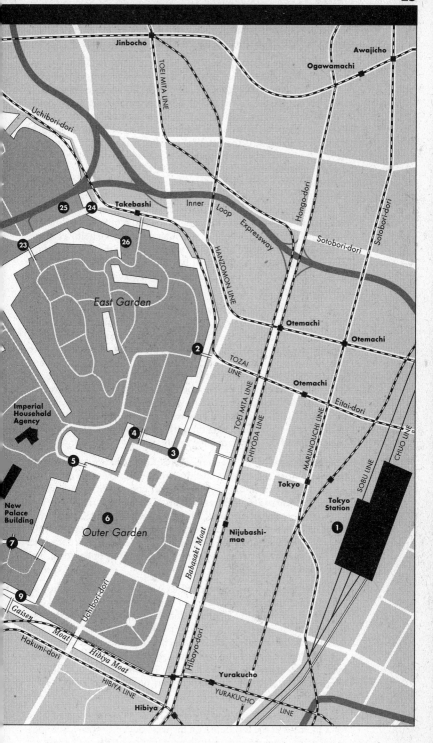

The hall was built in the Taisho period (1912–1925) and is still used for *kendo* (Japanese fencing) practice. On the right is the Ote Rest House, where for ¥100 you can buy a simple map of the garden.

At the top of the drive was once another gate, where feudal lords summoned to the palace would descend from the palanquins and proceed on foot. The gate itself is gone, but two 19th-century guardhouses survive, one outside the massive stone supports on the right, and a longer one inside on the left. The latter was known as the Hundred-Man Guardhouse; this approach was defended by four shifts of 100 soldiers each. Past it, to the right, is the entrance to what was once the ninomaru, now a grove and garden, its pathways defined by rows of rhododendrons manicured to within an inch of their lives, with a pond and a waterfall in the northwest corner. At the far end is the **Suwa Tea Pavilion,** an early 19th-century building relocated here from another part of the castle grounds. Dominating the west side of the garden are the steep stone walls of the honmaru, with the Moat of Swans below (the swans are actually elsewhere, in the outer waterways); halfway along, a steep path leads up to an entrance in the wall to the upper fortress. This is **Shiomi-zaka,** which might be translated as "Briny View Hill," so named because in the Edo period one could see the ocean from this vantage point.

Walk back to the guardhouses, turn right, and follow the road for the main entrance to the honmaru. Nothing remains on the broad expanse of lawn to recall the scores of buildings that once stood here, connected by a network of corridors. The stone foundations of the castle keep may be found at the far end of the grounds. As you enter, turn left and explore the wooded paths that skirt the perimeter. There is shade and quiet, and benches are available where you can sit, rest your weary feet, and listen to bird song. In the southwest corner, through the trees, you can see the back of the **Fujimi Yagura,** the only surviving watchtower of the honmaru; farther along the path, on the west side, is the **Fujimi Tamon,** one of the two remaining armories.

The foundations of the keep make a platform with a fine view of **Kitanomaru Koen** (park) and the city to the north. The view must have been even finer from the keep itself; built and rebuilt three times, it soared more than 250 feet over Edo, five stories high. The other castle buildings were all plastered white; the keep was black, unadorned but for a golden roof. In 1657, a fire destroyed most of the city. Strong winds carried the flames across the moat, where it consumed the keep in a heat so fierce that it melted the gold in the vaults underneath. The keep was never rebuilt.

Now it's time to review your priorities. You can abbreviate your tour of the palace area from here in one of two ways. To the left of the keep, there is an exit from the honmaru that leads to **Kita-Hanebashimon;** to the right, another road leads past the **Toka Music Hall** (an octagonal tower faced in mosaic tile, built in honor of the empress in 1966) down to the ninomaru and out of the gardens by way of **Hirakawamon.** Both these exits will bring you to **Takebashi** (Bamboo Bridge), which you encounter much later in the day on the longer course of this excursion.

To take a longer course, leave the honmaru the way you came in. Stop for a moment at the rest house on the west side of the park, and look at the pairs of before-and-after photographs along the wall; these are the same views of the castle, taken about 100 years apart. In the 1870s, much of the castle was in astonishing disrepair, and the warriors of the Hundred-Man Guardhouse were a trifle ragtag. Hand in your plastic token, turn to the right as you leave the Otemon, and walk along the moat.

(3) Where the wall makes a right angle, you will see the second of the three surviving watchtowers, the **Tatsumi,** or **Niju** (Double-Tiered), **Yagura.** Here the sidewalk opens out to a parking lot for tour buses and the beginning of a broad promenade. In the far corner to your right, where **(4)** the angle of the wall turns again, is the **Kikyomon,** a gate used primarily for deliveries to the palace. (Short and prestigious indeed is the roster of *Go-yotashi*—Purveyors to the Imperial Household.) At the far end **(5)** of the parking lot is **Sakashitamon,** the gate used by the officials of the Imperial Household Agency itself.

(6) From here to **Hibiya Koen** (park), along both sides of Uchiboridori, stretches the concourse of the Imperial Palace **Outer Garden.** This whole area once lay along the edge of Tokyo Bay. Later, the shogun had his most trusted retainers build their estates here; these in turn gave way to the office buildings of the Meiji government. In 1899, the buildings were relocated; the promenade was planted with the wonderful stands of pine trees you see today. Walk along the broad gravel ★ **(7)** path to **Nijubashi** (Two-Tiered Bridge) and the **Seimon** (Main Gate).

This is surely the most photogenic spot on your tour of the Castle, though you can approach it no closer than the head of the short stone bridge called the **Seimon Sekkyo.** Cordoned off on the other side is the gate through which ordinary mortals may pass only on January 2 and December 23; the guards in front of their little octagonal, copper-roof sentry boxes change every hour on the hour—alas, with nothing like the pomp and ceremony of Buckingham Palace. Nijubashi makes its graceful arch over the moat here from the area inside the gate; the building **(8)** in the background, completing the picture, is the **Fushimi Yagura,** built in the 17th century and the last of the three surviving original watchtowers.

(9) Continue on the gravel walk past the Seimon, turn right, and pass through the **Sakuradamon** (Gate of the Field of Cherry Trees). (Before you do, turn and look back down the concourse: You will not see another expanse of open space like this anywhere else in Tokyo.) Sakuradamon is another masu gate; by hallowed use and custom, the little courtyard between the portals is where joggers warm up for their 3-mile run around the palace. Many of them will already have passed you on your exploration; jogging around the palace is a ritual that begins as early as 6 AM and goes on all through the day, no matter what the weather. Almost everybody runs the course counterclockwise; now and then you may spot someone going the opposite way, but rebellious behavior of this sort is frowned upon in Japan.

(10) Across the street as you pass through the gate is the beginning of Sakurada-dori, with the **Metropolitan Police Department** building on the north corner, by world-renowned architect Kenzo Tange; the older brick buildings on the south corner belong to the **Ministry of Justice.** Sakurada-dori runs through the heart of official Japan; between here and Kasumigaseki are the ministries—from Foreign Affairs and Education to International Trade and Industry—that comprise the central government. They inhabit, however, what are surely the most uninteresting buildings, architecturally, of any government center in the world; they should not tempt you from your course. Turn right, and follow the moat as you walk up the hill.

11 Ahead of you, where the road branches to the left, you will see the squat pyramid of the **National Diet Building,** which houses the Japanese Parliament. Completed in 1936 after 17 years of work, it is a building best contemplated from a distance; on a gloomy day, it might well have sprung from the screen of a German Expressionist movie. Bear right as you follow the moat, to the five-point intersection where it curves again to **12** the north. Across the street are the gray stone slabs of the **Supreme Court;** this, and the National Theater (*see below*) next door, are worth a short detour.

The Supreme Court building, by architect Shinichi Okada, was the last in a series of open design competitions sponsored by the various agencies charged with the reconstruction of Tokyo after World War II. Completed in 1968, its fortresslike planes and angles speak volumes for the role of the law in Japanese society; here is the very bastion of the established order. Okada's winning design was one of 217 submitted; before it was finished, the open competition had generated so much controversy that the government did not hold another one for almost 20 years. *4-2 Hayabusacho, Chiyoda-ku (nearest subway station: Hanzomon). Call the Public Relations Office (Kohoka) at 03/3264–8111 for permission to visit inside. Guided tours are normally offered only to Japanese student groups, but can sometimes be arranged for others in May and Oct.*

13 Like the Supreme Court, Hiroyuki Iwamoto's **National Theater** (1966) was also a design-competition winner; the result was a rendition in concrete of the ancient *azekura* (storehouse) style, best exemplified by the 8th-century Shosoin Imperial Repository in Nara. The large hall seats 1,746 and features primarily Kabuki theater, ancient court music, and dance; the small hall seats 630 and is used primarily for Bunraku puppet theater and traditional music. *4-1 Hayabusacho, Chiyoda-ku (nearest subway station: Hanzomon), ☎ 03/3265–7411. Ticket prices vary considerably depending on the performance.*

14 Cross back to the palace side of the street. At the top of the hill, on your right, a police contingent guards the road to the **Hanzomon**—and beyond it, to the new Imperial Palace. At the foot of this small wooden gate was once the house of the legendary Hattori Hanzo, leader of the shogun's private corps of spies and infiltrators (and assassins, if need be)—the black-clad *ninja*, perennial material for historical adventure films and television dramas.

15 North from here, along the Hanzo Moat, is a narrow strip of park; facing it, across the street, is the **British Embassy.** Along this western edge of his fortress, the shogun kept his personal retainers, called *hatamoto,* divided by district (*bancho*) into six regiments. Today these six bancho comprise one of the most sought-after residential areas in Tokyo, where high-rise apartments commonly fetch $1 million or more.

At the next intersection, review your priorities again. You can turn right, and complete your circuit of the palace grounds by way of the **Inuimon,** or you can continue straight north on Uchibori-dori to Kudanzaka and Yasukuni Jinja.

TIME OUT A good, moderately priced place for lunch, if you choose the latter course, is **Tony Roma's**—just past the intersection on the west side of the street. The specialty here, as it is in this chain's umpteen locations, from London to Okinawa, is charcoal-broiled spare ribs. *1 Sambancho, Chi-*

yoda-ku, ☎ *03/3222-3440.* ⊙ *Noon–3 PM for lunch, 5–11 PM for dinner.*

★ ⑯ Where Uchibori-dori comes to an end, cross the street to the grounds of **Yasukuni Jinja** (Shrine of Peace for the Nation). Founded in 1869, Yasukuni enshrines the souls—worshiped as deities—of some 2.5 million people who gave their lives in the defense of the Japanese Empire. Because most of that "defense" took place in the course of what others regard as opportunistic wars abroad, Yasukuni is a very controversial place. It is a memorial out of keeping with the postwar constitution, which commits Japan to the renunciation of militarism forever; on the other hand, hundreds of thousands of Japanese visit the shrine every year, simply to pray for the repose of friends and relatives they have lost. Prime ministers and other high officials try to skirt this controversy, with no great success, by making their visits as private individuals, not in their official capacities.

Pick up a pamphlet and simplified map of the shrine in English from the guard station on the right as you enter. Just ahead of you, in a circle on the main avenue, is a statue of Masujiro Omura, commander of the imperial forces that subdued the Tokugawa loyalist resistance to the new Meiji government in 1868. From here, as you look down the avenue to your right, you see the enormous steel outer *torii* (arch) of the main entrance to the shrine at Kudanshita; to the left, you see the bronze inner torii, erected in 1887. (The arches of Shinto shrines are normally made of wood and are painted red.) Beyond the inner torii is the gate to the shrine itself, with its 12 pillars and chrysanthemums—the imperial crest—embossed on the doors.

The shrine is not one structure but a complex of buildings that includes the **Main Hall** and the **Hall of Worship,** both built in the simple, unadorned style of the ancient shrines at Ise. In the complex are various reception halls, a museum, a Noh theater, and, in the far western corner, a sumo-wrestling ring. Both Noh and sumo have their origins in religious ritual, as performances offered to please and divert the gods; sumo matches are held at Yasukuni April 23, during the first of its three festivals.

Turn right in front of the Hall of Worship, and cross the grounds to the museum, called the **Yushukan.** None of the documents and memorabilia on display here are identified in English, although in some cases the meanings are clear enough; the rooms on the second floor house an especially fine collection of medieval swords and armor. Perhaps the most bizarre exhibit is the *kaiten* (human torpedo) in the main hall on the first floor; this is the submarine equivalent of a kamikaze plane. The kaiten was a black cylinder about 50 feet long and 3 feet in diameter, with 3,400 pounds of high explosives in the nose and a man in the center, squeezed into a seat, who peered into a periscope and worked the directional vanes with his feet. It was carried into battle on the deck of a ship and launched against the enemy; on its one-way journey, it had a maximum range of about 5 miles. *3-1-1 Kudankita, Chiyoda-ku,* ☎ *03/3261–8326.* ☛ *¥200 adults, ¥50 children under 12. Museum open daily, Mar.–Sept. 9–5; Oct.–Feb. 9–4:30. Closed June 22–23, Dec. 28–31. Grounds of the shrine open generally sunrise to sunset.*

If time permits, turn right as you leave the Yushukan and walk past the other implements of war (cannons, ancient and modern; a tank, incongruously bright and gay in its green-and-yellow camouflage paint) arrayed in front of the pond at the rear of the shrine. There is, unfortunately, no admittance to the teahouses on the far side, but the pond is among the most serene and beautiful in Tokyo, especially in spring, when the irises are in bloom. If you are pressed, leave Yasukuni Jinja the way you came in, cross the street, turn left, and walk down the hill. About 50 yards from the intersection, on the right, is the entrance to **Chidorigafuchi Koen,** a pleasant green strip of promenade, high on the edge of the moat, lined with cherry trees. It leads back in the direction of the Imperial Palace; halfway along, it widens, and opposite the **Fairmont Hotel** a path leads down to the **Chidori gafuchi Boathouse.** Long before Edo Castle, there was a lovely little lake here, which Ieyasu Tokugawa incorporated into his system of defenses; now it's possible to rent a rowboat and explore it at your leisure. ☎ *03/3234–1948. Boat rentals: ¥200 for 30 min.* ☺ *Tues.–Sun. 9:30–4:30 (July and Aug. to 5:30). Closed Dec. 16– Feb. 28.*

Leave the park the way you came in, turn right, and continue down the hill to the **Tayasumon,** the entrance to **Kitanomaru Koen** (park). This is one of the largest and finest of the surviving masu gates to the castle; inside, you come first to the **Budokan** (2-3 Kitano-maru Koen, Chiyoda-ku, ☎ 03/3216–5100), built as a martial arts arena for the Tokyo Olympics of 1964. The octagonal design was based on the Hall of Dreams of Horyuji Temple in Nara. Apart from hosting tournaments and exhibitions of judo, karate, and kendo, this arena also serves as a concert hall, especially for visiting super-stars. Tokyo rock promoters are fortunate in their audiences, who don't seem to mind that the ticket prices are exorbitant, the acoustics are unforgivable, and the overselling is downright haz-ardous.

Just opposite the main entrance to the Budokan, past the parking lot, a pedestrian walkway leads off through the park, back in the direc-tion of the palace. Cross the bridge at the other end of the walk, turn right, and right again before you leave the park, on the driveway that leads to the **Kogeikan** (Crafts Gallery of the National Museum of Modern Art). Built in 1910, the Kogeikan was once the headquarters of the Imperial Guard; it is a rambling redbrick building, neo-Gothic in style, with exhibition halls on the second floor. The gallery features work of traditional craftsmanship—primarily lacquerware, textiles, pot-tery, and metalworking—by the modern masters. The exhibits are all too few, but many of the craftspeople represented here have been des-ignated by the government as Living National Treasures—a recogni-tion given only to masters of the finest work in each of these fields. *1-1 Kitanomaru Koen, Chiyoda-ku, ☎ 03/3211–7781. ☛ ¥400 adults, ¥70 children under 12; this ticket includes ☛ to the National Museum of Modern Art. Additional fee for special exhibitions. ☺ Tues.–Sun. 10–4:30.*

Return to the park exit and cross the street to the palace side. Ahead of you is the **Inuimon** (Northwest Gate); a driveway here leads to the Imperial Household Agency and the palace. This gate is used primar-ily by members of the imperial family and by the fortunate few who have managed to obtain special permission to visit the palace itself. A bit farther down the hill is the **Kita-Hanebashimon** (North Drawbridge

Gate), mentioned earlier as one of the entrances to the Imperial Palace East Garden.

㉔ At the foot of the hill is **Takebashi** (Bamboo Bridge); the original bridge material has long since given way to reinforced concrete. Here, depending on how you have organized your tour, you might want to

★ **㉕** cross the street and walk the short distance uphill to the **Tokyo Koku-ritsu Kindai Bijutsukan** (Tokyo National Museum of Modern Art). Founded in 1952 and moved to its present site in 1969, the museum mounts a number of major exhibitions of 20th-century Japanese and Western art throughout the year. The second through fourth floors house the permanent collection (painting, prints, and sculpture), which includes works by Rousseau, Picasso, Tsuguji Fujita, Ryuzaburo Umehara, and Taikan Yokoyama. *3 Kitanomaru Koen, Chiyoda-ku,* ☎ *03/3214–2561.* ☛ *¥400 for adults, ¥70 children under 12; this ticket includes* ☛ *to the Crafts Gallery. Additional fee for special exhibitions.* ☯ *Tues.–Thurs. and weekends 10–5, Fri. 10–8.*

Cross back to the palace side of the street. A short walk from Take-
㉖ bashi is **Hirakawamon,** the third entrance to the Imperial Palace East Garden and the last stop on your tour. The approach to this gate, recently restored, is the only wood bridge that spans the moat; the gate itself is also a reconstruction, but an especially beautiful one—it looks much as it must have when the Hirakawamon was used by the shogun's ladies, on their rare excursions from the seraglio. From here, follow the moat as it turns south again; in a few minutes you will find yourself back at Otemon, tired but triumphant.

Akihabara and Jinbocho

Numbers in the margin correspond to points of interest on the Akihabara and Jinbocho map.

This is it: the greatest sound-and-light show on earth. **Akihabara** is a merchandise mart for anything—and everything—that runs on electricity, block after block of it, with a combined annual turnover well in excess of ¥30 trillion. Here you'll find microprocessors, washing machines, stereo systems, blenders, television sets, and gadgets that beep when your bathwater is hot. Wherever you go in the world, if people know nothing else about Japan, they recognize the country as a cornucopia of electronics equipment and household appliances; about 10% of what Japan's electronics industry makes for the domestic market passes through Akihabara.

Just after World War II there was a black market here, around the railroad station, where the Yamanote Line and the crosstown Sobu Line intersect. In time, most of the stalls were doing a legitimate business in radio parts, and in 1951 they were all relocated in one dense clump under the tracks. Retail and wholesale suppliers prospered there in less-than-peaceful coexistence, as they spread out into the adjacent blocks and made the area famous for cut-rate prices.

No visitor to Tokyo neglects this district; the mistake is to come here merely for shopping. Akihabara may be consumer heaven, but it is also the first stop on a walking tour through the general area known as Kanda (where the true Edokko, the born-and-bred Tokyoites of the old town, claim their roots) to the bookstalls of Jinbocho. In a sense, this tour is a journey through time: It's a morning's walk from satellite-broadcast antennas to the sacred precincts of the printed word.

Start at the west exit of JR Akihabara Station. (There's also a stop nearby on the Hibiya subway line, but the JR provides much easier access.) Come out to the left into the station square, turn right, and walk to the main thoroughfare; ahead of you on the other side of the street you'll

❶ see the **LAOX** building, one of the district's major discount stores. *1-2-9 Soto Kanda, Chiyoda-ku,* ☎ *03/3255–9041.* ☉ *Mon.–Sat. 10–7:30, Sun. 10–7:15.*

Before you get to the corner, on the right, is a little warren of stalls and tiny shops that cannot have changed an iota since the days of the black market—except for their merchandise. Wander through the narrow passageways and see an astonishing array of switches, transformers, resistors, semiconductors, printed circuit cards, plugs, wires, connectors, and tools; this corner of Akihabara is for people who know—or want to know—what the latest in Japanese electronic technology looks like from the inside. (A lot of the foreign browsers here seem to confer in Eastern European languages.)

Turn right at the corner and walk north on Chuo-dori. Music blares at you from hundreds of storefronts as you walk along; this is the heart of the district.

❷ Just past the second intersection, on the right, is **Yamagiwa,** a store that stocks simply everything, from computer software to chandeliers to hearing aids, including a considerable selection of imported goods. There's also an annex for duty-free shopping (bring your passport). *4-1-1 Soto Kanda, Chiyoda-ku,* ☎ *03/3253–2111.* ☉ *Weekdays 10:30–7, weekends 10–7.*

Rival **Minami,** at the far end of the block, offers a similar variety of goods, plus an entire sixth floor devoted to European antiques. *4-3-3 Soto Kanda, Chiyoda-ku,* ☎ *03/3255–3730.* ☉ *Weekdays 10:30–7:30, weekends 10–7.*

Cross the street, continue northward to the Soto Kanda 5-chome intersection (there's an entrance to the Suehirocho subway station on the corner), and turn left on Kuramaebashi-dori. Walk about five minutes—you will cross one more intersection with a traffic light—and in the middle of the next block you will see a flight of steps on the left, between two new brick buildings. Red, green, and blue pennants flut-

❸ ter from the handrails; this is the back entrance to **Kanda Myojin** (shrine).

Kanda Myojin is said to have been founded in 730 in a village called Shibasaki, where the Otemachi financial district stands today. Three principle deities are enshrined here: Daikoku, Ebisu, and Taira no Masakado. Daikoku looks after the well-being of farming and fishing villages and other small communities; one also appeals to him for the cure of various diseases. Ebisu is the god of success in business; he concerns himself as well with the prosperity of families and the happiness of marriages. Taira no Masakado was a 10th-century warrior whose contentious spirit earned him a place in the Shinto pantheon: He led a revolt against the Imperial Court in Kyoto, seized control of the eastern provinces, declared himself emperor—and was beheaded for his rebellious ways in 940.

In 1616 the shrine was relocated, a victim of Ieyasu Tokugawa's ever-expanding system of fortifications; the present site was chosen, in accordance with Chinese geomancy, to afford the best view from Edo Castle and protect it from evil influences. The townspeople of Kanda, contentious souls in their own right, made Taira no Masakado a kind

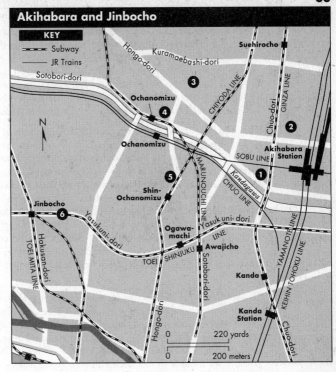

of patron saint, and even today—oblivious somehow to the fact that
he lost—they appeal to him for victory when they face a tough encounter.
The shrine itself was destroyed in the earthquake of 1923; the present
buildings reproduce in concrete the style of 1616. Ieyasu preferred
the jazzier decorative effects of Chinese Buddhism to the simple lines
of traditional Shinto architecture; this is especially evident in the
curved, copper-tile roof of the main shrine and in the two-story front
gate.

Some of the smaller buildings you see as you come up the steps and
walk around the main hall contain the *mikoshi*—portable shrines that
are featured in one of Tokyo's three great blowouts, the **Kanda Festival.** (The other two are the Sanno Festival of the Hie Shrine in Nagatacho, and the Sanja Festival of the Asakusa Shrine.) The essential
shrine festival is a procession in which the gods, housed for the occasion in their mikoshi, pass through the streets and get a breath of
fresh air. The Kanda Festival began in the early Edo period; heading
the procession then were 36 magnificent floats, most of which were
destroyed in the fires that raged through the city after the earthquake
of 1923. The floats that lead the procession today move in stately
measure on wheeled carts, attended by the priests and officials of the
shrine in Heian-period (794–1185) costume; behind them come the
mikoshi, some 70 of them, bobbing and weaving, carried on the shoulders of the townspeople. The spirit of Taira no Masakado is channeled on this day into a determination to shout the loudest, drink
the most beer, and have the best time. *2-16-2 Soto Kanda, Chiyoda-
ku,* ☎ *03/3254–0753. The Kanda Festival takes place in odd-numbered years.*

Leave the shrine by the main gate. The seated figures in the alcoves on either side are its guardian gods; carved in camphor wood, they are depicted in Heian costume, holding long bows. From the gate down to the copper-clad torii (arch) on Hongo-dori is a walk of a few yards; on either side are shops that sell the specialties famous in this neighborhood: pickles, miso (fermented bean paste), and sweet sake (rice wine) laced with ground ginger. On the other side of the avenue you will see the wall and wooded grounds of **Yushima Seido.**

This, too, is a shrine, but one of a very different sort: It was founded in 1632 as a hall for the study of the Chinese Confucian classics. The original building was in Ueno; its headmaster was Razan Hayashi, the official Confucian scholar to the Tokugawa government. The Tokugawas found these Chinese teachings, with their emphasis on obedience and hierarchy, particularly attractive. Confucianism became a kind of state ideology, and the hall (moved to its present site in 1691) turned into an academy for the ruling elite. In a sense, nothing has changed: In 1872 the new Meiji government established the country's first teacher training institute here, and that, in turn, evolved into Tokyo University—the graduates of which still make up much of the ruling elite.

To get to Yushima Seido, cross Hongo-dori and turn left, following the wall downhill. Turn right at the first narrow side street, and right again at the bottom; the entrance to Yushima Seido is a few steps from the corner. Japan's first museum and its first national library were built on these grounds; both were soon relocated. As you walk up the path, you will see a statue of Confucius on your right; where the path ends, a flight of stone steps leads up to the main hall of the shrine—destroyed six times by fire, and each time rebuilt. The last repairs date to 1954. The hall could almost be in China; painted black, weathered and somber, it looks like nothing else you are likely to see in Japan. Confucian scholarship, it seems, did not lend itself to ornamentation. In May of odd-numbered years, when the Kanda Festival passes by, the spirit enshrined here must take a dim view of the frivolities on the other side of the wall. *1-4-25 Yushima, Bunkyo-ku,* ☎ *03/3251–4606.* ☛ *Free.* ⊙ *Fri.–Wed. 9:30–4:30.*

Retrace your steps, turn right as you leave the shrine, and walk along the continuation of the wall on the side street leading up to **Hijiribashi** (Bridge of Sages), which spans the Kandagawa at Ochanomizu Station on the JR Sobu Line. Cross the bridge (you're now back on Hongo-dori); ahead of you, just beyond the station on the right, you'll see the dome of **Nikolai Cathedral,** center of the Orthodox Church in Japan. Formally, this is the Holy Resurrection Cathedral; the more familiar name derives from its founder, St. Nikolai Kassatkin (1836–1912), a Russian missionary who came to Japan in 1861 and spent the rest of his life here propagating the Orthodox faith. The building, planned by a Russian engineer and executed by a British architect, was completed in 1891. Heavily damaged in the earthquake of 1923, the cathedral was restored with a dome much more modest than the original. Even so, it endows this otherwise featureless part of the city with the charm of the unexpected. *4-1 Surugadai, Kanda, Chiyoda-ku,* ☎ *03/3295–6879.* ☛ *Free.* ⊙ *Tues.–Sat. 1–4.*

Continue south on Hongo-dori to the major intersection at Yasukuni-dori. Surugadai, the area to your right as you walk down the hill, is a kind of fountainhead of Japanese higher education: Two of the city's major private universities—Meiji and Nihon—occupy a good part of the hill. Not far from these is a score of elite high schools, public and private. In the 1880s, several other universities were founded in this area. They have since moved away, but the student population here is still enormous; Nihon University alone accepted some 15,000 freshmen this year to its four-year program.

Students are not as serious as they used to be. So saith every generation, but as you turn right on Yasukuni-dori, you encounter palpable proof. Between you and your objective—the **bookstores of Jinbocho**—are three blocks of stores devoted almost exclusively to electric guitars, records, travel bags, skis, and skiwear. The bookstores begin at the intersection called Surugadai-shita, and continue along Yasukuni-dori for about 450 meters (yards), most of them on the south (left) side of the street. This area is to print what Akihabara is to electronics; browse here for art books, catalogs, scholarly monographs, secondhand paperbacks, and dictionaries in most known languages. Jinbocho is home as well to wholesalers, distributors, and many of Japan's most prestigious publishing houses.

A number of the antiquarian booksellers here carry not only rare typeset editions but also wood-block–printed books of the Edo period and individual prints. At shops like **Isseido** (1-7 Kanda Jinbocho, Chiyoda-ku, ☎ 03/3292–0071) and **Ohya Shobo** (1-1 Kanda Jinbocho, Chiyoda-ku, ☎ 03/3291–0062), it is still possible to find a genuine Hiroshige or Toyokuni print (granted, not in the best condition) at an affordable price.

What about that word processor or CD player you didn't buy at the beginning of your walk because you didn't want to carry it all this way? No problem. There's a subway station (Toei Mita Line) right on the Jinbocho main intersection; ride one stop north to Suidobashi, transfer to the JR Sobu Line, and five minutes later you're back in Akihabara.

Ueno

Numbers in the margin correspond to points of interest on the Ueno map.

The JR station at **Ueno** is Tokyo's Gare du Nord: the gateway to (and from) the provinces. The single most important fact of Japanese life since the 17th century has been the pull of the cities, the great migration from the villages in pursuit of a better life; since 1883, when the station was completed, the people of Tohoku—the northeast—have begun that pursuit here.

Ueno was a place of prominence, however, long before the coming of the railroad. When Ieyasu Tokugawa established his capital here in 1603, it was merely a wooded promontory, called Shinobugaoka (The Hill of Endurance), overlooking the bay. The view was a pleasant one, and Ieyasu gave a large tract of land on the hill to one of his most important vassals, Todo Takatora, who designed and built Edo Castle. Ieyasu's heir, Hidetada, later commanded the founding of a temple on the hill. Shinobugaoka was in the northeast corner of the capital; in Chinese geomancy, the northeast approach required a particularly strong defense against evil influences.

That defense was entrusted to Tenkai (1536–1643), a priest of the Tendai sect of Buddhism and an adviser of great influence to the first three Tokugawa shoguns. Tenkai turned for his model to Kyoto, guarded on the northeast by Mt. Hiei and the great temple complex of Enryakuji. The temple he built on Shinobugaoka was called Kaneiji, and he became the first abbot. Mt. Hiei was loftier, but the patronage of the Tokugawas and their vassal barons made Kaneiji a seat of power and glory. By the end of the 17th century, it occupied most of the hill. To the magnificent Main Hall were added scores of other buildings—including a pagoda and a shrine to Ieyasu—and 36 subsidiary temples. The city of Edo itself expanded to the foot of the hill; most of present-day Ueno was once called Monzen-machi (the town in front of the gate).

The power and glory of Kaneiji came to an end in one day: April 11, 1868. An army of clan forces from the western part of Japan, bearing a mandate from Emperor Meiji, had marched on Edo and demanded the surrender of the castle. The shogunate was by then a tottering regime; it capitulated, and with it went everything that had depended on the favor of the Tokugawas. The Meiji Restoration began with a bloodless coup.

A band of some 2,000 Tokugawa loyalists then assembled on Ueno Hill and defied the new government. On May 15, the imperial army attacked; outnumbered and surrounded, the loyalists, known as the Shogitai, soon discovered that right was on the side of modern artillery. A few survivors fled; the rest committed ritual suicide—and took Kaneiji with them; they torched the temple and most of its outbuildings.

The new Meiji government turned Ueno Hill into one of the nation's first public parks. The intention was not merely to provide a bit of greenery, but to make the park an instrument of civic improvement and a showcase for the achievements of an emerging modern state. It would serve as the site of trade and industrial expositions; it would have a national museum, a library, a university of fine arts, and a zoo. That policy continued well into the present era, with the building of further galleries and concert halls—but Ueno is more than its museums. The Shogitai failed to take everything with them; some of the most important buildings in the temple complex have survived or been restored. The "town in front of the gate" is gone, but here and there, in the narrow streets below the hill, the way of life is much the way it was 100 years ago. Exploring Ueno can be one excursion, or two: It can be an afternoon of culture-browsing, or it can be a full day of discoveries in one of the great centers of the city.

The best way to begin, in either case, is to come to Ueno on the JR Yamanote Line, and leave the station by the park exit (*koen-guchi*) on **❶** the upper level. Directly across from the exit is the **Tokyo Metropolitan Festival Hall** (Tokyo Bunka Kaikan), designed by architect Kunio Maekawa and completed in 1961. This is the city's largest and finest facility for classical music, the one most often booked for visiting orchestras and concert soloists. The large auditorium seats 2,327; the smaller one seats 661. *5-45 Ueno Koen, Taito-ku,* ☎ *03/3828–2111.*

❷ Opposite the Festival Hall on the right is the **Seiyo Bijutsukan** (National Museum of Western Art). The building was designed by Le Corbusier and houses what was once the private collection of a wealthy businessman named Kojiro Matsukata. The Rodins in the courtyard—*The Gate of Hell, The Thinker,* and the magnificent *Burghers of Calais*— are genuine; an admirer of French impressionism, Matsukata somehow acquired castings from Rodin's original molds, along with some 850 paintings, sketches, and prints by such masters as Renoir, Monet, and Cézanne. He kept the collection in Europe; it was returned by the French government after World War II, left to the country in Matsukata's will, and opened to the public in 1959. Since then, the museum has diversified a bit; more recent acquisitions include works by Reubens, Tin-

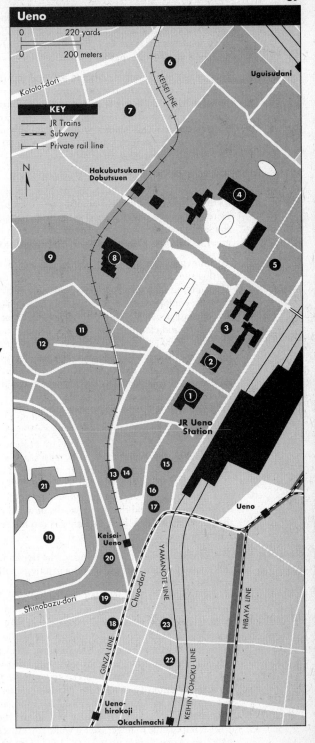

toretto, El Greco, Max Ernst, and Jackson Pollock. *7-7 Ueno Koen, Taito-ku, ☎ 03/3828–5131. ☛ ¥400 adults, ¥70 children under 12. Additional fee for special exhibitions. ⊙ Tues.–Thurs. and weekends 9:30–4:30, Fri. 9:30–6:30.*

❸ Just behind the National Museum of Western Art is the **National Science Museum**—a natural-history museum very much in the conventional mode. That is, it has everything from dinosaurs to moon rocks on display, but it offers relatively little in the way of hands-on learning experiences. This is not a place to linger if your time is short. *7-20 Ueno Koen, Taito-ku, ☎ 03/3822–0111. ☛ ¥400 adults, ¥70 children under 12. ⊙ Tues.–Sun. 9–4.*

Beyond the National Science Museum is a broad street that cuts through the park; turn left on this and you come almost immediately ★ ❹ to the **Tokyo Kokuritsu Hakubutsukan** (Tokyo National Museum). Here you should plan to spend some time, even if you are not overly fond of museums: The Tokyo National Museum is one of the world's great repositories of East Asian art and archaeology.

The museum consists of four buildings grouped around a courtyard; on this site once stood the temple-residence of the abbot of Kaneiji. The building on the left is the **Hyokeikan,** the oldest and smallest of the four; completed in 1909, it has only nine exhibition rooms, all devoted to archaeological objects. Look especially for the flamelike sculptured rims and elaborate markings of Middle Jomon–period pottery (c. 3500–2000 BC), so different from anything produced in Japan before or since. Look also for the terra-cotta figures called *haniwa,* unearthed at burial sites dating from the 4th to the 7th century; these figures are deceptively simple in shape, and mysterious and comical at the same time in their effects.

★ Behind the Hyokeikan is a two-story building called the **Horyuji Homotsukan** (Treasure Hall), which is open only on Thursdays. In 1878, the 7th-century Horyuji Temple in Nara presented 319 works of art in its possession—sculpture, scrolls, masks, and other objects—to the Imperial Household; these were later transferred to the National Museum, and in 1964 the Horyuji Treasure Hall was built to house them. If at all possible, schedule your visit to the museum on Thursday, but bear in mind that these works of wood and paper are more than 1,000 years old; if the weather is too hot or wet, the hall may not be open.

The central building in the complex, the **Honkan,** was built in 1937 and houses Japanese art exclusively: paintings, calligraphy, sculpture, textiles, ceramics, swords, and armor. The more attractive **Toyokan,** on the right, completed in 1968, is devoted to the art of other Asian cultures. Altogether, the museum has some 87,000 objects in its permanent collection, with several thousand more on loan from shrines, temples, and private owners. Among these are 84 objects designated by the government as National Treasures. The Honkan rotates the works on display several times during the year; it also hosts two special exhibitions a year, April–May and October–November, featuring important collections from foreign museums. These, unfortunately, can be an ordeal: The lighting in the Honkan is not particularly good, the explanations in English are sketchy at best, and the hordes of visitors make it impossible to linger over a work you especially want to study. *13-9 Ueno Koen, Taito-ku, ☎ 03/3822–1111. ☛ ¥400 adults, ¥70 children under 12. ⊙ Tues.–Sun. 9–4.*

⑤ Turn to the left as you leave the museum, walk east, and turn left again at the first corner. The building across the road on your right is the **Jigendo,** a memorial hall to Abbot Tenkai, who was given the posthumous title of Jigen Daishi (Great Master of the Merciful Eye). The six bronze lanterns in front, with their dragon faces, are especially fine. At the end of the road that passes the Jigendo, turn left again and walk along the back of the museum; to your right is the **cemetery** of Kaneiji. Several of the Tokugawa shoguns had their mausoleums here; these were destroyed in the air raids of 1945, but you will see the gate that once led to the tomb of the fourth shogun, Ietsuna. At the end of the road, ⑥ in the far northwest corner of the park, is **Kaneiji** itself.

The main hall of Kaneiji, built in 1638, has covered a lot of territory in its day. Abbot Tenkai had it moved to Ueno from a temple in the town of Kawagoe, about 40 kilometers (25 miles) from Tokyo, where he had once been a priest; it was moved again, to its present site, in 1879, and looks a bit weary of its travels. Behind the temple is the ornately carved gate to what was once the mausoleum of Tsunayoshi, the fifth shogun. Tsunayoshi is famous in the annals of Tokugawa history first for his disastrous fiscal mismanagement, and second for his *Shorui Awaremi no Rei (Edicts on Compassion for Living Things),* which, among other things, made it a capital offense for a human being to kill a dog. *1-14-11 Ueno Sakuragi, Taito-ku,* ☎ *03/3821–1259.* ☛ *Free, but contributions welcomed.* ⊘ *8:30–5.*

After you come out again through the main gate of the temple, take the first right turn; this puts you on the road that circles the park. Walk south. If you take the first right turn off this road you will soon come ⑦ to the **Tokyo University of Arts Exhibition Hall,** on the left side. The collection here has some interesting works, some of which are designated National Treasures, but it is not actually a museum. The exhibitions on display are intended primarily as teaching materials for courses in the school curriculum. *12-8 Ueno Koen, Taito-ku,* ☎ *03/3828–6111.* ☛ *Free.* ⊘ *To the public weekdays 10–4 during the school year, mid-Apr.–mid-July, and Sept.–mid-Dec.*

If you'd like to skip the Exhibition Hall, continue walking south on the road that circles the park to the T-intersection; turn left onto the broad street that runs through the center of the park. Return to the entrance of the National Museum, and cross the street to the long esplanade with its reflecting pool. At the opposite end, turn right and ⑧ walk down the path to the **Tokyo Metropolitan Art Museum.**

There are three floors of galleries in the Tokyo Metropolitan; the museum displays its own collection of modern Japanese art on the lower level, and rents out the remaining spaces to various organizations. At any given time, there will be at least five different exhibitions in the building: work by promising young painters, for example, or new forms and materials in sculpture, or modern calligraphy. Completed in 1975, the museum was designed by Kunio Maekawa, who also did the nearby Metropolitan Festival Hall. *8-36 Ueno Koen, Taito-ku,* ☎ *03/3823–6921.* ☛ *Free to the permanent collection; varying fees (usually ¥300 to ¥800) for other exhibitions.* ⊘ *9–4. Closed 3rd Mon. of each month.*

Return to the south end of the esplanade and you will see a sign for ⑨ the entrance to the **Ueno Zoo.** Opened in 1882, the zoo gradually expanded to its present 35 acres; the original section on the hill was con- ⑩ nected to the one below, along the edge of **Shinobazu Pond,** by a bridge and a monorail. The zoo houses some 900 different species, most of which look less than enthusiastic about being there. Ueno is not among the most attractive zoos in the world. On the other hand, it does have three giant pandas (their quarters are near the main entrance). You might decide it's worth a visit on that score alone. On a pleasant Sunday afternoon, however, upwards of 20,000 Japanese are likely to share your opinion; don't expect to have a leisurely view. *9-83 Ueno Koen, Taito-ku,* ☎ *03/3828–5171.* ☛ *¥500 adults.* ☺ *Tues.–Sun. 9:30–4.*

The zoo has one other attraction that makes it unusual: The process **⑪** of expansion somehow left within the zoo's confines the five-story **Kaneiji Pagoda.** Built in 1631 and rebuilt after a fire in 1639, the 120-foot pagoda is painted vermilion and has a copper roof on the top level; most visitors find it a bit out of keeping with the bison cages next door.

A much better view of the pagoda is from the path that leads to ★ **⑫** **Toshogu.** Return to the esplanade and follow the sign to the shrine until you see a small police substation; just beyond it, on a narrow path, the entrance to the shrine is marked by a stone torii (arch), built in 1633. Ieyasu, the first Tokugawa shogun, died in 1616, and the following year was given the posthumous name Tosho-Daigongen (The Great Incarnation Who Illuminates the East). He was declared by the Imperial Court a divinity of the first rank, thenceforth to be worshiped at Nikko, in the mountains north of his city, at a shrine he had commissioned before his death. That shrine is the first and foremost Toshogu. The one here in Ueno dates from 1627; miraculously, it has survived the disasters that destroyed most of the other original buildings on the hill—the fires, the revolt of 1868, the earthquake of 1923, the bombings of 1945—and is thus one of the very few early Edo-period buildings left in Tokyo.

The path from the torii to the shrine is lined with 200 stone lanterns (*ishidoro*); another stone lantern, inside the grounds, is more than 18 feet high—one of the three largest in Japan. (This particular lantern is called *obaketoro,* or "ghost lantern," because of a story connected with it: It seems that one night a samurai on guard duty slashed at the ghost— *obake*—that was believed to haunt the lantern; his sword was so good it left a nick in the stone, which can still be seen.) Beyond these is a double row of bronze lanterns, presented by the feudal lords of the 17th century as expressions of their piety and loyalty to the regime; the lanterns themselves were arrayed in the order of the wealth and ranking of their donors. On the left, before you reach the shrine itself, is the **Peony Garden** (for which you must pay a separate entrance fee), where some 200 varieties are on display. ☎ *03/3822–3575.* ☛ *¥800 adults, ¥400 children under 12.* ☺ *Jan.–Feb. and Apr.–May, daily 9:30–4:30.*

At the end of the path, pay your admission fee and walk around the shrine to the entrance. You'll notice, on the left, a graceful little tea-ceremony pavilion, where Ieyasu Tokugawa's vassal Todo Takatora (who built the shrine itself) is said to have entertained the second and third shoguns. The Toshogu, like its namesake in Nikko, is built in the ornate style called *gongen-zukuri;* it is gilded, painted, and carved with motifs of plants and animals. The carpentry of roof supports and ceilings is especially intricate. The shrine and most of the works of art in it have been designated National Treasures.

The first room inside is the Hall of Worship; the four paintings in gold on wood panels are by Tan'yu, one of the famous Kano family of artists who enjoyed the patronage of emperors and shoguns from the late 15th century to the end of the Edo period. Tan'yu was appointed *goyo eshi* (official court painter) in 1617; his commissions included the Tokugawa castles at Edo and Nagoya, and the Nikko Toshogu. The framed tablet between the walls, with the name of the shrine in gold, is in the calligraphy of Emperor Go-Mizuno-o (1596–1680); other works of calligraphy are by the abbots of Kaneiji. Behind the Hall of Worship, connected by a passage called the *haiden,* is the Sanctuary, where the spirit of Ieyasu is enshrined.

The real glories of Toshogu are its so-called **Chinese Gate,** which you reach at the end of your tour of the building, and the **fence** on either side. Like its counterpart at Nikko, the fence is a kind of natural-history lesson, with carvings of birds, animals, fish, and shells of every description; unlike the one at Nikko, however, this fence was left unpainted. The two long panels of the gate, with their dragons carved in relief, are attributed to Hidari Jingoro—a brilliant sculptor of the early Edo period whose real name is unknown (*hidari* means "left"; Jingoro was reportedly left-handed). The lifelike appearance of his dragons has inspired a legend. Every morning they were found mysteriously dripping with water; finally it was discovered that they were sneaking out at night to drink from the nearby Shinobazu Pond, and wire cages were put up around them to curtail this disquieting habit. *9-88 Ueno Koen, Taito-ku,* ☎ *03/3822–3455.* ☛ *¥200 adults, ¥100 children under 12.* ☉ *Daily 9–5.*

Retrace your steps to the police substation, turn right, and follow the avenue south. Shortly you will see a kind of tunnel of red-lacquer torii, in front of a small shrine to Inari, a Shinto deity of harvests and family prosperity. Shrines of this kind are found all over the downtown part of Tokyo, tucked away in alleys and odd corners, always with their guardian statues of foxes—the mischievous creatures with which the god is associated. A few steps farther, down a small road that branches to the right, is a shrine to Michizane Sugawara (854–903), a Heian-period nobleman and poet worshiped as the Shinto deity Tenjin. Because he is associated with scholarship and literary achievement, Japanese students visit his various shrines by the hundreds of thousands in February and March to pray for success on their entrance exams.

Return to the main road and continue south. You will see on your left ❸ a black gate called the **Kuromon,** a replica of one that once stood at the entrance to the entire Kaneiji complex. The Kuromon, built in the early 17th century, was the main gate of the National Museum until it was moved to this site in 1937; the numerous bullet holes in it were made during the battle for Ueno Hill in 1868. Go through the gate and ❹ up the stone steps to the **Kiyomizu Kannon Hall.**

Kiyomizu was a part of Abbot Tenkai's grand attempt to echo the holiness of Kyoto; the model for it was the magnificent Kiyomizu Temple in that city. The echo is a little weak. Where the original rests on enormous wood pillars over a gorge, the Kiyomizu Hall in Ueno merely perches on the lip of a little hill. The hall is known to afford a grand view of Shinobazu Pond—which itself was landscaped to recall Lake Biwa, near Kyoto—but in fact the trees in front of the terrace are too high and full most of the year to afford any view at all. The Kyoto original is maintained in perfect condition; the copy, much smaller, is a little down-at-the-heels. Another of the few buildings that survived the battle of 1868, Kiyomizu is designated a National Treasure.

The principal Buddhist image of worship here is the Senju Kannon (Thousand-Armed Goddess of Mercy). Another figure, however, receives greater homage; this is the Kosodate Kannon, who is believed to answer the prayers of women having difficulty conceiving children. If their prayers are answered, they return to Kiyomizu and leave a doll, as both an offering of thanks and a prayer for the child's health. In a ceremony held every September 25, the dolls that have accumulated during the year are burned in a bonfire. *1-29 Ueno Koen, Taito-ku.* ☞ *Free.* ☉ *Daily 9–5.*

Leave the hall by the front gate, on the south side. As you look to your left, you will see a new two-story brick services/administration building; on the other side of this is the **Ueno no Mori Royal Museum.** This museum has no permanent collection of its own, but makes its galleries available to various groups, primarily for exhibitions of painting and calligraphy. A more professional museum staff could do some good things here; the Royal Museum has two floors of prime space, but accomplishes very little with it. *1-2 Ueno Koen, Taito-ku,* ☎ *03/3833–4191.* ☞ *Varies, but often free.* ☉ *Daily 10–5.*

If you continue south from the Kiyomizu Kannon Hall, you soon come to where the park narrows to a point, and two flights of steps lead down to the main entrance, on Chuo-dori. Before you reach the steps, on the left, is the **Shogitai Memorial.** Time seems to heal wounds very quickly in Japan; only six years after they had destroyed most of Ueno Hill, the Meiji government permitted the Shogitai to be honored with a gravestone, erected on the spot where their bodies had been cremated. Descendants of one of the survivors still tend the memorial. A few steps away, with its back to the stone, stands the **statue of Takamori Saigo** (1827–1877), chief of staff of the imperial army that took the surrender of Edo and overthrew the shogunate—the army that the Shogitai had died defying. Ironically, Saigo himself fell out with the other leaders of the new Meiji government and was killed in an unsuccessful rebellion of his own. The sculptor Koun Takamura's bronze, made in 1893, sensibly avoids presenting him in uniform.

TIME OUT   Walk down the two flights of steps, leave the park, turn right on Chuo-dori, and right again at the second corner. One block in from the avenue brings you to the authentic part of Shitamachi; off the beaten tourist path here is **Futaba,** an inexpensive *tonkatsu* (fried pork cutlet) restaurant. If you get lost in the narrow streets here, just ask for it by name; this part of Ueno is considered the original home of tonkatsu restaurants, and Futaba is one of the oldest and best. Anyone you stop will know it. Try the *teishoku* (set menu). *2-8-11 Ueno, Taito-ku,* ☎ *03/3831–6483.* ☉ *11:30–2:30 and 5–7. Closed Mon. and Thurs.*

Retrace your steps, keeping on the west side of Chuo-dori, to where Shinobazu-dori comes in on the left. About a block before this corner, you'll see a building hung with banners; this is **Suzumoto,** a theater specializing in a traditional narrative comedy called *rakugo.* In Japan, a monologue comedian does not stand up to ply his trade: He sits on a purple cushion, dressed in a kimono, and tells stories that have been handed down for centuries. The rakugo storyteller has only a fan for a prop; he plays a whole cast of characters, with their different voices and facial expressions, by himself. The audience may have heard his stories 20 times already, and they still laugh in all the right places. Suzumoto dates back to about 1857, making it the oldest theater of its kind in Tokyo. The present building, however (in front of which, incidentally, is a stop on the red double-decker bus for Asakusa), is new. (Note that there are no English interpreters here, and even for Japanese visitors the monologues are difficult to follow as they are filled with dialect and double entendres.) *2-7-12 Ueno, Taito-*

ku, ☎ *03/3834–5906.* ☛ ¥2,500. *Continual performances daily 12–4:30 and 5–8:50.*

⑲ Turn left at the intersection, and walk west on Shinobazu-dori. A few doors from the corner is **Jusanya** (2-12-21 Ueno, Taiko-ku, ☎ 03/3831–3238), a shop selling handmade boxwood combs. The business was started in 1736 by a samurai who couldn't support himself in the martial arts, and it has been in the same family ever since. Directly across the avenue is an entrance to the grounds of Shinobazu Pond; just inside, on the right, is the small black and white building that houses the
★ ⑳ **Shitamachi Museum.**

Shitamachi (Town Below the Castle) lay originally between Ieyasu's fortifications on the west and the Sumida River on the east. As it expanded, it came to include what today constitute the Chuo, Taito, Sumida, and Koto wards. During the Edo period, some 80% of the city was allotted to the warrior class, the temples, and the shrines; in the remaining 20% lived the common people, who made up more than half the population. Well into the modern period, the typical residential units in this part of the city were the *nagaya,* long, single-story tenements, one jammed up against the next along narrow alleys and unplanned streets. The density of Shitamachi shaped the character of the people who lived there: They were gossipy, short-tempered, quick to help a neighbor in trouble, hardworking, and not overly inclined to save for a rainy day. Their way of life will soon be gone completely; the Shitamachi Museum was created to preserve and exhibit what it was still like as late as 1940.

The two main displays on the first floor are a merchant house and a tenement, intact with all their furnishings. Visitors can take their shoes off and step up into the rooms; this is a hands-on museum. On the second floor are displays of toys, tools, and utensils, which were donated, in most cases, by people who had grown up with them and used them all their lives. Photographs of Shitamachi and video documentaries of craftspeople at work may be seen. Occasionally there are demonstrations of various traditional skills, and visitors are welcome to take part. The space in this museum is used with great skill, and there's even a passable brochure in English. Don't miss it. *2-1 Ueno Koen, Taito-ku,* ☎ *03/3823–7451.* ☛ *¥200 adults, ¥100 children under 12.* ⏲ *Tues.–Sun. 9:30–4:30.*

In front of the museum, take the path that follows the eastern shore of Shinobazu Pond. During the first week of June, the path is lined on both sides with the stalls of the annual All-Japan Azalea Fair, a spectacular display of bonsai flowering shrubs and trees; nurserymen in *happi* (workmen's) coats sell a variety of plants, seedlings, bonsai vessels, and ornamental stones.

Shinobazu was once an inlet of Tokyo Bay; reclamation turned it into a freshwater pond, and Abbot Tenkai had an island made in the mid-
㉑ dle of it, on which he built the **Shrine to Benten,** a patron goddess of the arts. Later improvements included a causeway to the island, embankments, and even (1884–1893) a race course. Today the pond is in three sections. The first, with its famous lotus plants, is a sanctuary for about 15 species of birds, including pintail ducks, cormorants, great egrets, and grebes. Some 5,000 wild ducks migrate here from as far away as Siberia, remaining from September to April. The second section, to the north, belongs to the Ueno Zoo; the third, to the west, is a small lake for boating.

Walk up the east side of the embankment to the causeway, and cross to the shrine. The goddess Benten is one of the Seven Gods of Good Luck, a pantheon that emerged sometime in the medieval period from a jumble of Indian, Chinese, and Japanese mythology; she is depicted holding a musical instrument called a *biwa,* and is thus associated with the lake of the same name, near Kyoto—which Abbot Tenkai wanted to recall in his landscaping of Shinobazu Pond. The shrine, with its distinctive octagonal roof, was destroyed in the bombings of 1945; the present version is a faithful copy.

Cross to the other side of the pond, turn left in front of the **boathouse** (⊘ 9–4:30; pedal boats: ¥500 for 30 min., rowboats ¥500 for 1 hr.), and follow the embankment back to Shinobazu-dori. Off to your right as you walk, a few blocks away and out of sight, begin the precincts of Tokyo University, the nation's most prestigious seat of higher learning, alma mater to generations of bureaucrats. Turn left as you leave the park, and walk back in the direction of the Shitamachi Museum. When you reach the intersection, cross Chuo-dori and turn right; walk past the ABAB clothing store and turn left at the second corner: At ★ ㉒ ㉓ the end of this street is **Tokudaiji** and the heart of **Ameya Yokocho Market.**

Tokudaiji (4-6-2 Ueno, Taito-ku) is a curiosity in a neighborhood of curiosities: a temple on the second floor of a supermarket. The principal image of worship is the Indian goddess Marishi, a daughter of Brahma, usually depicted with three faces and four arms; she is believed to help worshipers overcome various sorts of difficulties and to prosper in business. The other image is that of the bodhisattva Jizo; the act of washing this statue is believed to help safeguard one's health. Among the faithful visitors to Tokudaiji are the merchants of Ameya Yokocho.

The history of Ameya Yokocho (often shortened to Ameyoko) begins in the desperate days immediately after World War II. Ueno Station had survived—virtually everything around it was rubble—and anyone who could make his way here from the countryside with rice and other small supplies of food could sell them at exorbitant black-market prices. One thing not to be had in postwar Tokyo at any price was sugar; before long, there were hundreds of stalls in the black market selling various kinds of *ame* (confections), most of them made from sweet potatoes. These stalls gave the market its name: Ameya Yokocho means "Confectioners' Alley."

Shortly before the Korean War, the market was legalized, and soon the stalls were carrying a full array of watches, chocolate, ballpoint pens, blue jeans, and T-shirts that had somehow been "liberated" from American PXs. In the years to follow, the merchants of Ameyoko diversified still further—to fine Swiss timepieces and French designer luggage of dubious authenticity, cosmetics, jewelry, fresh fruit, and fish. The market became especially famous for the traditional prepared foods of the New Year, and during the last few days of December, as many as half a million people crowd into the narrow alleys under the railroad tracks to stock up for the holiday.

There are more than 500 little shops and stalls in the market, stretching from Okachimachi at the south end (the *o-kachi*—"honorable infantry"—were the samurai of lowest rank in the shogun's service; this part of the city was allotted to them for their homes) to the beginning of Showa-dori at the north. Follow the JR tracks as you wander north;

in a few minutes, you will find yourself in front of Ueno Station, your exploring done for the day.

Asakusa

Numbers in the margin correspond to points of interest on the Asakusa map.

In the year 628, so the legend goes, two brothers named Hamanari and Takenari Hinokuma were fishing on the lower reaches of the Sumida River when they dragged up a small gilded statue of Kannon—an aspect of the Buddha worshiped as the Goddess of Mercy. They took the statue to their master, Naji no Nakamoto, who enshrined it in his house.

★ Later, a temple was built for it in nearby **Asakusa.** Now called **Sensoji,** the temple was rebuilt and enlarged several times over the next 10 centuries—but Asakusa itself remained just a village on a river crossing a few hours' walk from Edo. Then Ieyasu Tokugawa made Edo his capital, and Asakusa blossomed. Suddenly, it was the party that never ended, the place where the free-spending townspeople of the new capital came to empty their pockets. Also, for the next 300 years it was the wellspring of almost everything we associate with Japanese popular culture.

The first step in that transformation came in 1657, when Yoshiwara—the licensed brothel quarter not far from Nihonbashi—was moved to the countryside farther north: Asakusa found itself square in the road, more or less halfway between the city and its only nightlife. The village became a suburb and a pleasure quarter in its own right. In the narrow streets and alleys around Sensoji, stalls sold toys, souvenirs, and sweets; there were acrobats, jugglers, and strolling musicians; there were sake shops and teahouses—where the waitresses often provided more than tea. (The Japanese have never worried much about the impropriety of such things; the approach to a temple is still a venue for very secular enterprises of all sorts.) Then, in 1841, the Kabuki theaters—which the government looked upon as a source of dissipation second only to Yoshiwara—were also moved to Asakusa.

Highborn and lowborn, the people of Edo flocked to Kabuki. They loved its extravagant spectacle, its bravado and brilliant language; they cheered its heroes and hissed its villains. They bought woodblock prints, called *ukiyo-e,* of their favorite actors. Asakusa was home to the Kabuki theaters for only a short time, but that was enough to establish it as *the* entertainment quarter of the city—a reputation it held unchallenged until World War II.

When Japan ended its long, self-imposed isolation in 1868, where else would the novelties and amusements of the outside world first take root but in Asakusa? The country's first photography studios appeared here in 1875. Japan's first skyscraper, a 12-story mart called the Junikai, filled with shops selling imported goods, was built in Asakusa in 1890. The area around Sensoji had by this time been designated a public park and was divided into seven sections; the sixth section, called Rokku, was Tokyo's equivalent of 42nd Street and Times Square. The nation's first movie theater opened here in 1903—to be joined by dozens more, and these in turn were followed by music halls, cabarets, and revues. The first drinking establishment in Japan to call itself a "bar" was started in Asakusa in 1880; it still exists.

Most of this area was destroyed in 1945. As an entertainment district, it never really recovered, but Sensoji was rebuilt almost immediately. The people here would never dream of living without it—just as they would never dream of living anywhere else. This is the heart and soul of Shitamachi (downtown), where you can still hear the rich, breezy Tokyo accent of the 17th and 18th centuries. Where if you sneeze in the middle of the night, your neighbor will demand to know the next morning why you aren't taking better care of yourself. Where a carpenter will refuse a well-paid job if he doesn't think the client has the mother wit to appreciate good work when he sees it. Where you can still go out for a good meal and not have to pay through the nose for a lot of uptown pretensions. Even today, the temple precinct embraces an area of narrow streets, arcades, restaurants, shops, stalls, playgrounds, and gardens; it is home to a population of artisans and small entrepreneurs, neighborhood children and their grandmothers, hipsters and hucksters and mendicant priests. In short, if you have any time at all to spend in Tokyo, you really have to devote at least a day of it to Asakusa.

Start your exploration from Asakusa Station, at the end of the Ginza Line. (This was in fact Tokyo's first subway, opened from Asakusa to Ueno in 1927; it became known as the Ginza Line when it was later extended through Ginza to Shinbashi and Shibuya.) Follow the signs (clearly marked in English) to Exit No. 1; when you come up to the street level, turn right and walk west along the broad street called Kam-❶ inarimon-dori. In a few steps you will come to **Kaminarimon** (Thunder God Gate), with its huge, red paper lantern hanging in the center. This is the main entrance to the grounds of Sensoji. ☞ *Free. Temple grounds open 6 AM–sundown.*

Two other means of transportation can take you to Kaminarimon. The "river bus" ferry from Hinode Pier stops in Asakusa at the south corner of **Sumida Koen** (park). Walk out to the three-way intersection, cross two sides of the triangle, and turn right. Kaminarimon is in the middle of the second block. Another way to get here is on the red double-decker bus that runs between Kaminarimon and the Suzumoto Theater in Ueno. The service began in 1981, when the Merchants' Association in Asakusa borrowed a London double-decker for a month to move the overflow crowds they expected for a street fair. The idea proved so popular that it was decided to inaugurate a regular service—but there was an unexpected hitch: By law, a commercial bus could be no higher than 3.8 meters (12½ feet), and the English double-decker was 70 centimeters (28 inches) over the limit. The solution was to order three custom vehicles from a German company; a fourth was added later. The bus runs every ½-hour (every 15–20 minutes on weekends), 10–7, from Ueno, and 10:25–7:25 from Asakusa. The fare is ¥200 for adults, ¥100 for children under 12.

Take note of the Asakusa Tourist Information Center, just opposite Kaminarimon (2-18-9 Kaminarimon, Taito-ku, ☎ 03/3842–5566); a volunteer staff with some knowledge of English is on duty here 9:30–8 daily and will happily load you down with maps and brochures.

Traditionally, two fearsome guardian gods are installed in the alcoves of a temple gate, to protect the temple from evil spirits. The Thunder God (*Kaminari no Kami*) of the Sensoji gate is on the left; he shares his duties with the Wind God (*Kaze no Kami*) on the right. Few Japanese visitors neglect to stop at **Tokiwado** (1-3 Asakusa), the shop on the west side of the gate, to buy some of Tokyo's most famous souvenirs: *kaminari okoshi* (thunder crackers), made of rice, millet, sugar, and beans. The original gate itself was destroyed by fire in 1865; the replica that stands here now was built after World War II.

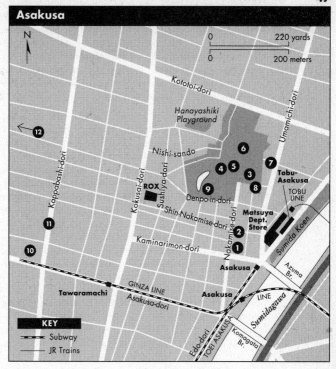

From Kaminarimon to the inner gate of the temple runs a long, narrow avenue called **Nakamise-dori** (The Street of Inside Shops), once composed of stalls that were leased out to the townspeople who cleaned and swept the temple grounds. The rows of redbrick buildings now belong to the municipal government, but the leases are, in effect, hereditary: Some of the shops have been in the same families since the Edo period. One worth stopping at is **Ichiban-ya,** about 100 meters (yards) down on the right, for its handmade toasted *sembei* (rice crackers) and its seven-pepper spices in gourd-shape bottles of zelkova wood. Another recommended shop, on the left, is **Hyotanya,** which carries ivory carvings and utensils. At the end of the street, on the right, is **Sukeroku,** specializing in traditional handmade dolls and models clothed in the costumes of the Edo period.

From here, you enter the courtyard of Sensoji through a two-story gate called the **Hozomon,** which serves as a repository for sutras (Buddhist texts) and other treasures of the temple. This gate, too, has its guardian gods; should either of them decide to leave his post for a stroll, an enormous pair of sandals is hanging on the back wall—the gift of a village famous for its straw-weaving, in Yamagata Prefecture.

At this point, you must take an important detour. To the left of the gate, in the far corner, is a modern two-story building that houses the temple's administrative offices: Walk in, go down the corridor on the right to the third door on the left, and ask for permission to see the **Garden of Denpo-in Temple.** There is no charge; you simply enter your name and address in a register and receive a ticket. Hold on to the ticket; you'll get to Denpo-in later on your excursion.

★ ❹ ❺ Two of the three most important buildings in the compound are the **Five-story Pagoda,** on the left side, and the **Main Hall of Sensoji** (2-3-1 Asakusa, Taito-ku); both are faithful copies in concrete of originals that burned down in 1945. Most visitors stop at the huge bronze incense burner, in front of the Main Hall, to bathe their hands and faces in the smoke—it's a charm to ward off illnesses—before climbing the stairs to offer a prayer to Kannon.

The Main Hall, about 115 feet long and 108 feet wide, is not an especially impressive piece of architecture. Unlike in many temples, however, part of the inside has a concrete floor, so visitors come and go without removing their shoes. In this area hang the Sensoji's chief claims to artistic importance: a collection of votive paintings on wood, from the 18th and 19th centuries. Plaques of this kind, called *ema,* are still offered to the gods at shrines and temples, but they are commonly simpler and smaller; the worshiper buys a little tablet of wood with the picture already painted on one side, and inscribes his prayer on the other. The temple owns more than 50 of these works, which were removed to safety in 1945 and so escaped the air raids; only eight of them, depicting various scenes from Japanese history and mythology, are on display. A catalogue of the collection is on sale in the hall, but the text is in Japanese only. The lighting is poor in the hall, and the actual works are difficult to see. This is also true of the ceiling, done by two contemporary masters of Nihonga (traditional Japanese-style painting); the dragon is by Ryushi Kawabata, and the motif of angels and lotus blossoms is by Insho Domoto. One thing that visitors cannot see at all is the holy image of Kannon itself, which supposedly lies buried somewhere deep under the temple. Not even the priests of Sensoji have ever seen it, and in fact there is no conclusive evidence that it really exists!

That doesn't seem to matter to the people of Shitamachi. It took 13 years, when most of them were still rebuilding their own bombed-out lives, to raise the money for the restoration of their beloved Sensoji. To them—and especially to those involved in the world of entertainment—it is far more than a tourist attraction. Kabuki actors still come here before a new season of performances, and sumo wrestlers come before a tournament, to pay their respects. The large lanterns in the Main Hall were donated by the geisha associations of Asakusa and nearby Yanagibashi.

❻ Several structures in the temple complex survived the bombings of 1945. The largest, to the right of the Main Hall, is **Asakusa Jinja** (2-3-1 Asakusa, Taito-ku)—a Shinto shrine to the Hikonuma brothers and their master Naji no Nakatomo. (In Japan, Buddhism and Shintoism have enjoyed a comfortable coexistence since the former arrived from China in the 6th century; it's the rule, rather than the exception, to find a Shinto shrine on the same grounds as a Buddhist temple.) The shrine, built in 1649, is also known as Sanja Sanma (Shrine of the Three Guardians). The Sanja Festival, held every year on the third weekend in May, is the biggest, loudest, wildest party in Tokyo. Each of the neighborhoods under Sanja Sanma's protection has its own *mikoshi* (portable shrine); on the second day of the festival, these palanquins are paraded through the streets of Asakusa, bouncing and swaying on the shoulders of the participants, to the shrine itself. Many of the "parishioners" take part naked to the waist, or with the sleeves of their tunics rolled up, to expose fantastic red-and-black tattoo patterns that sometimes cover their entire backs and shoulders. These are the tribal markings of the Japanese underworld.

7 Near the entrance to the shrine is another survivor of World War II: the east gate to the temple grounds, called the **Nitenmon,** built in 1618 and designated by the government as an Important Cultural Property. It was made originally for a shrine to Ieyasu Tokugawa, which was also part of Sensoji in the early 17th century.

From the Nitenmon, walk back in the direction of the Kaminarimon to the southeast corner of the grounds. On a small plot of ground stands the shrine to Kume no Heinai, a 17th-century outlaw who repented and became a priest of one of the subsidiary temples of Sensoji. Late in life he carved a stone statue of himself and buried it where many people would walk over it; in his will, he expressed the hope that his image would be trampled upon forever. Somehow, Heinai came to be worshiped as the patron god of lovers—as mystifying an apotheosis as you will ever find in Japanese religion.

8 Just beyond this shrine is the entrance to a narrow street that runs back to Asakusa-dori, parallel to Nakamise-dori. On the left as you enter this street is **Bentenyama** (2-3 Asakusa, Taito-ku), a tiny hillock with a shrine to the Goddess of Good Fortune perched on top. Next to it is the **Toki-no-kane Belfry,** built in the 17th century; the bell used to toll the hours, and it was said that you could hear it anywhere in Shitamachi—a radius of about 4 miles. The bell still sounds at 6 AM every day, when the temple grounds are opened to the faithful, and on New Year's Eve—108 strokes in all, beginning just before midnight, to "ring out" the 108 sins and frailties of mankind and make a clean start for the coming year.

Opposite Bentenyama is a shop called **Nakaya** (2-2-12 Asakusa, Taito-ku, ☎ 03/3841–7877), where they sell all manner of regalia for the Sanja Festival. Best buys at Nakaya are the thick, woven firemen's jackets, called *sashiko hanten,* and *happi* coats (cotton tunics printed in bright colors with Japanese characters or *ukiyo-e* wood-block pictures), available in children's sizes.

Next door is **Kuremutsu** (2-2-13 Asakusa, Taito-ku, ☎ 03/3842–0906; open 4–10 PM), a tiny old teahouse now turned into a fairly expensive *nomiya* (literally, "drinking place," the drink of choice in this case being sake); next to Kuremutsu is **Hyakusuke** (2-2-14 Asakusa, Taito-ku, ☎ 03/3841–7058), the last place in Tokyo to carry government-approved skin cleanser made from powdered nightingale droppings. Ladies of the Edo period—especially the geisha—swore by it; they mixed the powder with water and patted it on gently, as a boon to their complexions. There's only one source left in Japan for this powder—a fellow in the mountains of Aichi Prefecture who collects and dries the droppings from about 2,000 birds. (Nightingale ranching! Japan is a land of many vocations.) Hyakusuke is more than 100 years old and has been in the same family for three generations; it sells relatively little nightingale powder now, but it still does a steady trade in cosmetics and theatrical makeup for Kabuki actors, geisha, and traditional weddings. Interesting things to fetch home from here are seaweed shampoo and camellia oil, as well as handmade wool brushes, bound with cherry wood, for applying cosmetics.

★ Three doors up, on the same side of the street, is **Fujiya** (2-2-15 Asakusa, Taito-ku, ☎ 03/3841–2283), a shop that deals exclusively in printed cotton hand towels called *tenugui.* Owner Keiji Kawakami literally wrote the book on this subject. His *Tenugui fuzoku emaki* (roughly, The Scroll Book of Hand Towel Customs and Usages) is the definitive work on the hundreds of traditional towel motifs that have come down from the Edo period: geometric patterns; scenes from Bunraku puppet theater, Kabuki, and festivals; artifacts from folklore and everyday life; plants and animals. The tenugui in the shop were all designed and dyed by Kawakami himself. They unfold to about 3 feet, and many people buy them to frame. Kawakami towels are in fact collectors' items; when he feels that he has made enough of one, he destroys the stencil.

Turn right at the corner past Fujiya and walk west, until you cross Nakamise-dori. On the other side of the intersection, on the left, is **Yonoya** (1-37-10 Asakusa, Taito-ku, ☎ 03/3844–1755), purveyors of very pricey handmade boxwood combs. The shop itself is postwar, but the family business goes back about 300 years. The present owner/master craftsman is Mitsumasa Minekawa; his grandfather, he observes, was still making combs when he retired at 85. Traditional Japanese coiffures and wigs are very complicated, and they need a lot of different tools; Yonoya sells combs in all sizes, shapes, and serrations, some of them carved with auspicious motifs (peonies, hollyhocks, cranes) and all engraved with the family benchmark.

Now it's time to cash in the ticket you've been carrying around. Walk west another 20 meters (yards) or so, and on the right you will see an old black wood gate; it's the side entrance to **Denpo-in Temple.** The Abbot of Sensoji has his living quarters here. The only part of the grounds you can visit is the garden, believed to have been made in the 17th century by Enshu Kobori, the genius of Zen landscape design. Go through the small door in the gate, cross the courtyard and go through another door, and present your ticket to the caretaker in the house at the end of the alley; the entrance to the **garden** is down a short flight of stone steps to the left.

This is the best-kept secret in Asakusa. The front entrance to Denpo-in Temple can be seen from Nakamise-dori, behind an iron fence in the last block of shops, but the thousands of Japanese visitors passing by seem to have no idea what it is; if they do, it somehow never occurs to them to apply for an admission ticket. The garden of Denpo-in is usually empty and always utterly serene—an island of privacy in a sea of pilgrims. As you walk along the path that circles the pond, a different vista presents itself at every turn. The only sounds are the cries of birds and the splashing of carp. Spring, when the wisteria is in bloom, is the ideal time to be here; in the best of all possible worlds, you come on a Monday, when a tea ceremony is held in the pavilion at the far end of the pond.

Retrace your steps and turn to the right as you leave the black gate; next door is a small Shinto shrine to the *tanuki* (raccoons) who were displaced when Denpo-in was built. Japanese visitors come here more often, however, to leave an offering at the statue of the bodhisattva Jizo, who looks after the well-being of children.

Farther on, in the row of knockdown clothing stalls along the right side of the street, is the booth of calligrapher Koji Matsumaru, who makes *hyosatsu*, the Japanese equivalent of doorplates. A hyosatsu is a block of wood (preferably cypress) hung on a gatepost or an entranceway, with the family name on it in India ink. Enormous reverence still attaches in Japan to penmanship; opinions are drawn about you from the way you write. The hyosatsu is, after all, the first thing people will learn about a home; the characters on it must be well- and felicitously formed, so one comes to Matsumaru. Famous in Asakusa for his fine hand, he also does lanterns, temple signboards, certificates, and other weighty documents. Western names, too, can be rendered in the *katakana* syllabic alphabet, should you decide to take home a hyosatsu of your own.

TIME OUT Opposite the row of clothing stalls mentioned above, on the corner of Orange Street, is the redbrick Asakusa Public Hall; performances of Kabuki and traditional dance are sometimes held here, as well as exhibitions of life in Asakusa before World War II. Across the street is **Nakase,** one of the best of Asakusa's many fine tempura restaurants. Founded about 120 years ago, it was destroyed in the war and rebuilt in the same style. The tatami-mat rooms look out on a perfect little interior garden—hung, in May, with great fragrant bunches of white wisteria. The pond is stocked with carp and goldfish; you can almost lean out from your room and trail your fingers in the water as you listen to the fountain. Nakase is a bit steep: Lunches at the tables inside are ¥2,800; more elaborate meals by the garden start at ¥7,000. *1-39-13 Asakusa, Taito-ku,* ☎ *03/3841–4015.* ☯ *Wed.–Mon. noon–8.*

Now review your options. If you have the time and energy, you may want to explore the streets and covered arcades on the south and west sides of Denpo-in. Where Denpo-in-dori (the avenue you have been following along the south side of the garden) meets Sushiya-dori (the main avenue of Rokku, the entertainment district), there is a small flea market; turn right here, and you are in what remains—alas!—of the old movie-theater district. East of the movie theaters, between Rokku and Sensoji, runs Nishi-Sando (avenue), an arcade where you can find kimonos and yukata fabrics, traditional accessories, fans, and festival costumes at very reasonable prices. If you turn to the left at the flea market, you soon come to the **ROX Building,** a misplaced attempt to endow Asakusa with a glitzy vertical mall. Just beyond it, you can turn left again and stroll along Shin-Nakamise-dori (New Street of Inside Shops). This arcade and the streets that cross it north–south are lined with stores selling clothing and accessories, restaurants and coffee shops, and purveyors of crackers, seaweed, and tea. This area is Asakusa's answer to the suburban shopping center.

When you have browsed to saturation, turn south, away from Denbo-in Temple on any of these side streets, return to Kaminarimon-dori, turn right, and walk to the end. Cross Kokusai-dori, turn left, and then right at the next major intersection; on the corner is the entrance to Tawaramachi Station on the Ginza Subway Line. At the second traffic light, you will see the **Niimi Building** across the street, and atop the Niimi Building is the guardian god of Kappabashi: an enormous chef's head in plastic, 30 feet high, beaming, mustached, and crowned (as every chef in Japan is crowned) with a tall white hat. Turn right.

★ ⑪ **Kappabashi** is Tokyo's wholesale restaurant supply street: nearly a kilometer (about ½-mile) of shops—more than 200 of them—selling everything the city's purveyors of food and drink could possibly need to do business, from paper supplies to bar stools, from signs to soup tureens. In their wildest dreams, the Japanese themselves would never have cast Kappabashi as a tourist attraction, but indeed it is.

For one thing, it is *the* place to buy plastic food. From the humblest noodle shop or sushi bar to neighborhood restaurants of middling price and pretension, it's customary in Japan to stock a window with models of what is to be had inside. The custom began, according to one version of the story, in the early days of the Meiji Restoration, when anatomical models made of wax first came to Japan as teaching aids in the new schools of Western medicine. A businessman from Nara decided that wax models would also make good point-of-purchase advertising for restaurants. He was right: The industry grew in a modest way at first, making models mostly of Japanese food, but in the boom years after 1960, restaurants began to serve all sorts of cookery ordinary people had never seen before, and the models offered much-needed reassurance. ("So *that's* a cheeseburger. It doesn't look as bad as it sounds; let's go in and try one.") By the mid-1970s, the makers of plastic food were turning out creations of astonishing virtuosity and realism, and foreigners had discovered them as pop art.

In the first two blocks of Kappabashi, at least a dozen shops sell plastic food; at the second intersection, on the right, is the main showroom of the **Maizuru Company,** one of the oldest and largest firms in the industry. They are virtuosos in the art of counterfeit cuisine. In 1960, models by Maizuru were included in the "Japan Style" Exhibition at London's Victoria and Albert Museum. Here, one can buy individual pieces of plastic sushi, or splurge on a whole Pacific lobster, perfect in coloration and detail down to the tiniest spines on its legs. *1-5-17 Nishi-Asakusa, Taito-ku,* ☎ *03/3843–1686.* ⏰ *9–6.*

Across the street from Maizuru is **Nishimura,** a shop specializing in *noren*—the short divided curtains that hang from a bamboo rod over the door of a shop or restaurant to announce that it is open for business. The curtain is made of cotton, linen, or silk, and it is usually dyed to order with the name and logo of the shop or what it has for sale. Nishimura also carries ready-made noren with motifs of all sorts, from landscapes in white-on-blue to geisha and sumo wrestlers in polychromatic splendor. Use your imagination; they make wonderful wall hangings and dividers. *1-10-10 Matsugaya, Taito-ku,* ☎ *03/3844–9954.* ⏰ *9–5. Closed Sun.*

In the next block is **Kondo Shoten,** which specializes in all sorts of bamboo trays, baskets, scoops, and containers. *3-1-13 Matsugaya, Taito-ku,* ☎ *03/3841–3372.* ⏰ *Mon.–Sat. 9:30–5:30.*

Generally, however, the exploring is better on the Maizuru side of the street. A few doors down, for example, is **Biken Kogei,** a general supplier of signs, waterwheels, and assorted shop displays; this is a good place to look for the folding red paper lanterns (*aka-chochin*) that grace the front of inexpensive bars and restaurants. *1-5-16 Nishi-Asakusa, Taito-ku,* ☎ *03/3842–1646.* ⏰ *Mon.–Sat. 9–6, Sun. 11–4.*

In the middle of the next block is **Iida Shoten,** which stocks a good selection of embossed cast-iron kettles and casseroles, called *nambu* ware—craftwork certified by the Association for the Promotion of Traditional Craft Products. *2-21-6 Nishi Asakusa, Taito-ku,* ☎ *03/3842–3757.* ⏰ *Mon.–Sat. 9:30–5:30, Sun. 10–5.*

On the next corner is the **Union Company,** which sells everything needed to run a coffee shop: roasters, grinders, beans, flasks and filters of every description, cups, mugs, demitasse, sugar bowls, and creamers. Coffee lovers pronounce the coffee shops of Japan among the best in the world; here's where the professionals come for their apparatus. *2-22-6 Nishi-Asakusa, Taito-ku,* ☎ *03/3842–4041.* ⏰ *Mon.–Sat. 9–6, Sun. 10–5.*

The intersection here is about in the middle of Kappabashi; turn left, and just past the next traffic light, on the right, you come to the temple **Sogenji** (*3-7-2 Matsugaya, Taito-ku,* ☎ *03/3841–2035*)—better known as the Kappa Temple, with its shrine to the imaginary creature that gives this district its name. In the 19th century, so the story goes, there was a river here (and a bridge, back at the intersection where you took the left turn); the surrounding area was poorly drained and was often flooded. A local shopkeeper began a project to improve the drainage, investing all his own money, but met with little success until a troupe of *kappa*—mischievous green water sprites—emerged from the river to help him. The local people still come to the shrine at Sogenji to leave offerings of cucumber and sake—the kappa's favorite food and drink. (A more prosaic explanation for the name of the district points out that the lower-ranking retainers of the local lord used to earn money on the side by making straw raincoats, also called kappa, that they spread to dry on the bridge.)

Retrace your steps to the intersection; there is more of Kappabashi to the north, but you can safely ignore it and continue east, straight past Union Company down the narrow side street. In the next block, on the left, is **Tsubaya Hochoten**. A *hocho* is a knife; Tsubaya Hochoten sells cutlery for professionals—knives of every length and weight and balance, for every imaginable use, from slicing sashimi to making decorative cuts in fruit. The best of these, too, carry the Traditional Craft Association seal: hand-forged tools of tempered blue steel, set in handles banded with deer horn to keep the wood from splitting. *3-7-2 Nishi-Asakusa, Taito-ku,* ☎ *03/3845–2005.* ⊙ *Mon.–Sat. 9–6, Sun. 9–5.*

Continue on this street east to Kokusai-dori, and turn right (south); as you walk you will see several shops selling *butsudan* (Buddhist household altars). The most elaborate of these, hand-carved in ebony and covered with gold leaf, are made in Toyama Prefecture and can cost as much as ¥1 million. No proper Japanese household is without a butsudan, even if it is somewhat more modest; it is the spiritual center of the family, where reverence for one's ancestors and continuity of the family traditions are expressed. In a few moments, you will be back at Tawaramachi Station—the end of your excursion.

Tsukiji and Shinbashi

Numbers in the margin correspond to the points of interest on the Tsukiji and Shinbashi map.

Tsukiji reminds us of the awesome disaster of the great fire of 1657. In the space of two days, it leveled almost 70% of Ieyasu Tokugawa's new capital and killed more than 100,000 people. Ieyasu was not a man to be discouraged by mere catastrophe, however; he took it as an opportunity to plan an even bigger and better city, one that would incorporate the marshes east of his castle. Tsukiji, in fact, means "reclaimed land," and it was a substantial block of land, laboriously drained and filled, from present-day Ginza to the bay.

The common people in tenements and alleys, who had suffered most in the great fire, benefited not at all from this project; the land was first allotted to feudal lords and to temples. After 1853, when Japan opened its doors to the outside world, Tsukiji became Tokyo's first Foreign Settlement—the site of the American legation and an elegant two-story brick hotel, and home to a heroic group of missionaries, teachers, and doctors. Today, this area is best known for its astonishing fish market, the largest in Asia. This is where, if you are prepared to get up early enough, you should begin your exploration.

Take the Hibiya subway line to Tsukiji and exit by the stairs closest to the back of the train. Cross Shin-Ohashi-dori to the Tsukiji Honganji (a temple that looks like a transplant from India), turn right, and walk west on Shin-Ohashi-dori (you'll return to the temple later). Cross Harumi-dori, go over the bridge, and take the first left; walk to the end of the road, and turn right. If you reach this point at precisely 5 AM, you will hear a signal for the start of Tokyo's greatest ongoing open-air spectacle: the fish auction at the **Tokyo Chuo Oroshiuri Ichiba** (Central Wholesale Market).

★ ❶

The city's fish market used to be farther uptown, in Nihonbashi; it was moved to Tsukiji after the Great Kanto Earthquake of 1923, and it occupies the site of what was once Japan's first naval training academy. Today the market sprawls over some 54 acres of reclaimed land. Its warren of buildings houses about 1,200 wholesale shops, supplying 90% of the fish consumed in Tokyo every day and employing some 15,000 people. One would expect to see docks here, and unending streams of fish spilling from the holds of ships, but, in fact, most of the seafood sold in Tsukiji comes in by truck, arriving through the night from fishing ports all over the country.

What makes Tsukiji a great show is the auction system. The catch—more than 100 varieties in all, including whole frozen tuna, Styrofoam cases of shrimp and squid, and crates of crabs—is laid out in the long covered area between the river and the main building; then the bidding begins. Only members of the wholesalers' association may take part. Wearing license numbers fastened to the front of their caps, they register their bids in a kind of sign language, shouting to draw the attention of the auctioneer and making furious combinations in the air with their fingers. The auctioneer keeps the action moving in a hoarse croak that sounds like no known language; spot quotations change too fast for ordinary mortals to follow.

Different fish are auctioned off at different times and locations, but by 6:30 AM or so, this part of the day's business is over, and the wholesalers fetch their purchases back into the market in barrows. The restaurant owners and retailers arrive about 7, making the rounds of favorite suppliers for their requirements. Chaos seems to reign, but everybody here knows everybody else, and they all have it down to a system.

A word to the wise: These people are not running a tourist attraction. They're in the fish business, and this is their busiest time of day. The cheerful banter they use with each other can turn snappish if you get in their way. Also bear in mind that you are not allowed to take photographs while the auctions are underway (flashes are a distraction). The market is kept spotlessly clean, which means the water hoses are running all the time. Boots are helpful, but if you don't want to carry them, bring a pair of heavy-duty trash bags to slip over your shoes and secure them above your ankles with rubberbands.

If you come after 9 AM, there is still plenty to do and see. You'll have missed the auctions, but you may want to explore the maze of alleys between the market and Harumi-dori; there are fishmongers here by the score, of course, but also sushi bars, restaurants, and stores for pickles, tea, crackers, kitchen knives, baskets, and crockery. Markets like these are a vital counterpoint to the museums and monuments of conventional sightseeing; they bring you up close to the way people really live in the cities you visit. If you have time on your itinerary for just one market, this is the one to see.

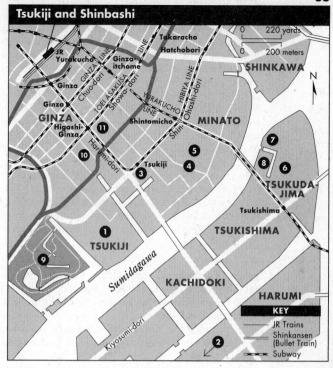

2 Return to Shin-Ohashi-dori, and walk back in the direction of Honganji Temple. When you reach Harumi-dori Avenue, you may want to make a detour. If you walk to the right, cross two bridges, and take the second right, you will eventually (it's a longish walk) reach the **International Trade Center** (5-3-53 Harumi, Chuo-ku, ☎ 03/3533–5314). The expositions presented here during the year—electronics and information systems, imported foods, toys, automobiles, recreation equipment—attract huge throngs of visitors; check the publication *Tour Companion* to see if there's a show running you'll want to catch.

3 If not, return to **Tsukiji Honganji**, the main branch temple in Tokyo of Nishi Honganji in Kyoto. It was located here after the fire of 1657, but disaster seemed to follow it—the temple was destroyed again at least five times, and reconstruction in wood was finally abandoned after the Great Kanto Earthquake. The present stone building dates from 1935. It was designed by Chuta Ito, a pupil of Kingo Tatsuno, who built Tokyo Station. Ito's other credits include the Meiji Jingu (Shrine) in Harajuku; he also lobbied for Japan's first law for the preservation of historic buildings. Ito traveled extensively in the Orient. The evocations of classical Hindu architecture in the domes and ornaments of Honganji were his homage to India for being the cradle of Buddhism.

Turn right on Shin-Ohashi-dori as you leave the main gate of the temple, and right again at the first corner; walk south until you cross a bridge, and turn left on the other side. When you cross another bridge, turn right: In the traffic island at the next intersection are two stone memorials that mark the true importance of Tsukiji in the modern history of Japan.

4 The taller of the two is the **Monument to Ryotaku Maeno and Genpaku Sugita.** With a group of colleagues, these two men translated the first work of European science into Japanese. Maeno and his collaborators were samurai and physicians. Maeno himself was in the service of the Lord Okudaira, whose mansion was one of the most prominent in Tsukiji. In 1770 he acquired a book, a text in Dutch on human anatomy, in Nagasaki. It took his group four years to produce their translation. Remember that at this time Japan was still officially closed to the outside world; the trickle of scientific knowledge accessible through the Dutch trading post at Nagasaki—the only authorized foreign settlement—was enormously frustrating to the eager young scholars who wanted to modernize their country. Also bear in mind that Maeno and his colleagues began with barely a few hundred words of Dutch among them and had no reference works or other resources on which to base their translation, except the diagrams in the book. It must have been an agonizing task, but the publication in 1774 of *Kaitai shinsho,* as it was called in Japanese, in a sense shaped the world we know today. From this time on, Japan would turn away from classical Chinese scholarship and begin to take its lessons in science and technology from the West.

The other stone memorial commemorates the founding of Keio University by Yukichi Fukuzawa (1835–1901), the most influencial educator and social thinker of the Meiji period. Fukuzawa was the son of a low-ranking samurai in the same clan as Maeno. Sent by his lord to start a school of Western learning, he began teaching classes at the Matsudaira residence in Tsukiji in 1858. Later the school was moved west to Mita, where the university is today. Engraved on the stone is Fukuzawa's famous statement: "Heaven created no man above another, nor below." Uttered when the Tokugawa feudal regime was still in power, this was an enormously daring and disturbing thought. It took Japan almost a century to catch up with Fukuzawa's liberal and egalitarian vision.

❺ Across the street to the left is **St. Luke's International Hospital,** founded in 1900 by Dr. Rudolf Teusler, an American medical missionary; the present building dates from 1933. In the several square blocks north of the hospital was the foreign settlement created after the signing of the U.S.–Japan Treaty of Commerce in 1858. (Among the residents here in the latter part of the 19th century was a Scottish surgeon and missionary named Henry Faulds. Intrigued by the Japanese custom of putting their thumbprints on documents for authentication, he began the research that established for the first time that no two person's fingerprints were alike. In 1880 he wrote a paper for *Nature* magazine, suggesting that this fact might be of some use in criminal investigation.)

Review your priorities. From here, you can retrace your steps to the subway, moving on to Higashi-Ginza and Shinbashi, or you can take **❻** a longish but rewarding detour to **Tsukudajima.** If you choose the latter, walk west from the monuments to the next corner, turn right, and walk north for two blocks. Cross the main intersection here, and turn right; the street rises to become the Tsukuda-Ohashi (Bridge), and just before it crosses the river you'll find a flight of steps leading up to the pedestrian walkway.

Built up from mud flats at the mouth of the Sumidagawa (River), Tsukudajima was first created in the early 17th century. Over the years, more and more land has been reclaimed from the bay, more than doubling the size of the island and adding other areas to the south and west. The part to explore is the original section: a few square blocks on your left as you cross the bridge. This neighborhood—its maze of narrow alleys, its profusion of potted plants and bonsai, its old houses with tile roofs—could almost have come straight out of the Edo period.

In 1613 the shogunate ordered a group of fishermen from Tsukuda (a village, now part of Osaka) to relocate on these flats. Officially, they were brought here to provide the castle with whitebait; unofficially, their role was to keep watch and report on any suspicious maritime traffic in the bay. They also developed a method of preserving the fish they caught, by boiling it in soy sauce and salt; this delicacy, called *tsukudani*, is still the island's most famous product. **Tsukugen** (1-3-13 Tsukuda, Chuo-ku, ☎ 03/3531–2649), a shop on the first street along the breakwater as you leave the bridge, has been making tsukudani since the 17th century. ⊙ *Mon.–Sat. 9:30–5:30.*

Go to the end of the breakwater, and turn right; from here it's a short walk to the torii of the **Sumiyoshi Jinja** (1-1 Tsukuda, Chuo-ku), a shrine established by the fishermen from Osaka when they first settled on the island. The god enshrined here is the protector of those who make their livelihoods from the sea; once every three years (1996; 1999), the shrine celebrates its main festival. On the first weekend in August, the god is brought out for his procession in an unusual eight-side palanquin, preceded by huge golden lion heads carried high in the air, their mouths snapping in mock ferocity to drive any evil influences out of the path. As the palanquin passes, the people of the island douse it with water, recalling the custom, before the breakwater was built, of carrying it to the river for a high-spirited ducking.

If you have time, wander through the area bounded by the breakwater and the L-shape canal. It's ramshackle in places (even a little scruffy), but this is an authentic corner of Shitamachi that cannot last much longer. Having survived most of the natural disasters of the past three centuries, it faces a new threat—the huge development project on the north end of the island—that will eventually doom the village to modernity.

TIME OUT Retrace your steps to the Tsukiji subway station, and continue along Shin-Ohashi-dori in the direction of the fish market. Cross Harumi-dori (the broad avenue that runs northwest–southeast from Hibiya to the bay), take the first narrow street on your right, then the first left; just off the corner is **Edo-Gin,** a sushi bar founded in 1924 that is legendary for its generous portions—slices of raw fish that almost hide the balls of rice underneath. Pricey for dinner; ¥1,000 set menu for lunch. *4-5-1 Tsukiji, Chuo-ku,* ☎ *03/3543–4401.* ⊙ *Mon.–Sat. 11–9:30.*

Pass the fish market on your left and the Asahi Newspapers Building on your right. The avenue curves and brings you to an elevated walkway; on the left is the entrance to the **Hama Rikyu Teien** (Detached Palace Garden). The land here was originally owned by the Owari branch of the Tokugawa family from Nagoya, and it extended to part of what is now the fish market. When one of this family became shogun, in 1709, his residence was turned into a shogunal palace—complete with pavilions, ornamental gardens, groves of pine and cherry trees, and duck ponds. The garden became a public park in 1945, although a good portion of it (including the two smaller ponds) is fenced off as a nature preserve. None of the original buildings survives, but on the island in the large pond is a reproduction of the pavilion where former U.S. President Ulysses S. Grant and Mrs. Grant had an audience with the Emperor Meiji in 1879. The building can be rented for parties. (The path to the left as you enter the garden leads to the "river bus" ferry landing, from which you can leave this excursion and begin another: up the Sumida to Asakusa.) *Hama Rikyu Teien, Chuo-ku,* ☎ *03/3541–0200.* ☛ *¥300; children under 6 free.* ☯ *Daily 9–4.*

Retrace your steps, cross the overhead pedestrian bridge, and continue north on Shin-Ohashi-dori. The next major intersection is Showa-dori; if you turned left here, across another elevated walkway, your route would take you past the huge JR Shiodome railroad yards (an "O" marker here and a section of the original tracks commemorate the starting point of Japan's first railway service, between Shinbashi and Yokohama, in 1872) and on to Shinbashi Station.

Shinbashi

Almost nothing remains in Shinbashi to recall its golden age—the period after the Meiji Restoration, when this was one of the most famous geisha districts of the new capital. Its reputation as a pleasure quarter is even older. In the Edo period, when there was a network of canals and waterways here, it was the height of luxury to charter a covered boat (called a *yakata-bune*) from one of the Shinbashi boathouses for a cruise on the river; a local restaurant would cater the excursion, and a local geisha house would provide the companionship. After 1868, the geisha moved indoors. There were many more of them, and the pleasure quarter became much larger and more sophisticated—a reputation it still enjoys among the older (and wealthier) generation of Japanese men. There are perhaps 150 geisha still working in Shinbashi; they entertain at some 30 or 40 *ryotei* (traditional restaurants) tucked away on the back streets of the district, but you are unlikely to encounter any on your exploration. From time to time, the newspapers still delight in the account of some distinguished widower, a politician or captain of industry, who marries a Shinbashi geisha—in the vain expectation that he will be treated at home the way he was treated in the restaurant.

Turn right instead on Showa-dori, away from Shinbashi Station. At the next major intersection, turn right again, and left at the third corner; walk northeast in the direction of Higashi-Ginza Station. In the ❿ second block, on your right, is the **Shinbashi Enbujo** (theater) (*see* The Arts, *below*). On the left is the Nissan Motor Company headquarters. A brisk minute's walk from here will bring you to the intersection of Harumi-dori; turn left, and on the next block, on the right, you will ★ ⓫ see the **Kabuki-za** (theater).

Soon after the Meiji Restoration, Kabuki began to reestablish itself in this part of the city, from its enforced exile in Asakusa. The first Kabuki-za was built in 1889, with a European facade. Here, two of the hereditary theater families, Ichikawa and Onoe, developed a brilliant new repertoire that brought Kabuki into the modern era. In 1912 the Kabuki-za was taken over by the Shochiku theatrical management company, and in 1925 the old theater building was replaced. Designed by architect Shin'ichiro Okada, it was damaged during World War II but was soon restored. (For information on performances, *see* The Arts, *below*). *4-12-15 Ginza, Chuo-ku,* ☎ *03/3541–8597.*

Just in front of the Kabuki-za is the Higashi-Ginza Station of the Hibiya subway line, where you can bring your exploration to a close.

Nihonbashi, Ginza, and Yurakucho

Numbers in the margin correspond to points of interest on the Nihonbashi, Ginza, and Yurakucho map.

Tokyo is a city of many centers. Now that the new City Hall is completed, the administrative center has shifted from Marunouchi to Shinjuku. For almost 350 years, the center of power was Edo Castle, and the great stone ramparts still define—for the visitor, at least—the heart of the city. History, politics, entertainment, fashion, traditional culture: Every tail we want to pin on the donkey goes in a different spot. Geographically speaking, however, there is one and only one center of Tokyo: a tall, black iron pole on the north side of **Nihonbashi** (Bridge of Japan)—and if the tail you were pinning represented high finance, you would also have to pin it right here.

When Ieyasu Tokugawa had the first bridge constructed at Nihonbashi, he designated it the starting point for the five great roads leading out of his city, the point from which all distances were to be measured. His decree is still in force: The black pole on the present bridge, erected in 1911, is the "Zero Kilometer" marker for all the national highways.

In the early days of the Tokugawa Shogunate, Edo had no port. As the city grew, almost everything it needed was shipped from the western part of the country, which was economically more developed. Because the bay shore was marshy and full of tidal flats, the ships would come only as far as Shinagawa, a few miles down the coast, and unload to smaller vessels. These in turn would take the cargo into the city through a network of canals to wharves and warehouses at Nihonbashi. The bridge and the area south and east became a wholesale distribution center, not only for manufactured goods but also for foodstuffs. The city's first fish market, in fact, was established at Nihonbashi in 1628 and remained here until the great earthquake of 1923.

All through the Edo period, this was part of Shitamachi (downtown). Except for a few blocks between Nihonbashi and Kyobashi, where the deputy magistrates of the city had their villas, it belonged to the common people—not all of whom lived elbow-to-elbow in poverty. There were huge fortunes to be made in the markets, and the early millionaires of Edo built their homes in the Nihonbashi area. Some, like the legendary timber magnate Bunzaemon Kinokuniya, spent everything they made in the pleasure quarters of Yoshiwara and died penniless; others founded great trading houses—Mitsui, Mitsubishi, Sumitomo— that exist today and still have warehouses not far from Nihonbashi.

It was appropriate, then, that when Japan's first corporations were created and the Meiji government developed a modern system of capital formation, the Tokyo Stock Exchange (Shoken Torihikijo) would be built on the west bank of the Nihonbashi River. Next to the exchange now are most of the country's major securities companies, which move billions of yen around the world electronically—a far cry from the early years of high finance, when they burned a length of rope on the floor of the exchange; trading was over for the day when it had smoldered down to the end.

A little farther west, money—the problems of making it and moving it around—shaped the area in a somewhat different way. In the Edo period, there were three types of currency in circulation: gold, silver, and copper, each with its various denominations. Determined to unify the system, Ieyasu Tokugawa started minting his own silver coins in 1598, in his home province of Suruga, even before he became shogun. In 1601 he established a gold mint; the building was only a few hundred yards from Nihonbashi, on the site of what is now the Bank of Japan. In 1612 he relocated the Suruga plant to a patch of reclaimed land to the west of his castle; the area soon came to be known informally as the Ginza (Silver Mint).

The value of these various currencies fluctuated. There were profits to be made in the changing of money, and this business eventually came under the control of a few large merchant houses. One of the most successful of these merchants was a man named Takatoshi Mitsui, who had a dry-goods shop in Kyoto and opened a branch in Edo in 1673. The shop, called Echigoya, was just north of Nihonbashi; by the end of the 17th century, it was the base of a commercial empire—in retailing, banking, and trading—known today as the Mitsui Group. Not far from the site of Echigoya stands its direct descendant: the Mitsukoshi Department Store.

Rui wa tomo wo yobu, goes the Japanese expression: "Like calls to like." From Nihonbashi through Ginza to Shinbashi is the domain of all the Noble Houses that trace their ancestry back to the dry-goods and kimono shops of the Edo period: Mitsukoshi, Takashimaya, Matsuzakaya, Matsuya. All are intensely proud of their places at the upper end of the retail business, as purveyors of an astonishing range of goods and services. Together, they are but the latest expression of this area's abiding concern with money. Take some of it with you on your exploration: You may find an opportunity here and there to spend it.

Begin at Tokyo Station. Take the Yaesu Central exit, cross the main avenue in front of you (Sotobori-dori), and turn left. Walk north until you cross a bridge under the Shuto Expressway, and turn right at the second corner, between the Bank of Tokyo and the **Bank of Japan** (2-2 Nihonbashi Hongokucho, Chuo-ku). The older part of the Bank of Japan is the work of Tatsuno Kingo, who also designed Tokyo Station; completed in 1896, the bank is one of the very few surviving Meiji-era Western buildings in the city.

Walk east two blocks to the main intersection at Chuo-dori. To your left is the Mitsui Bank, to your right is **Mitsukoshi Department Store.** The small area around the store, formerly called Surugacho, is the birthplace of the Mitsui conglomerate. *1-41 Nihonbashi Muromachi, Chuo-ku,* ☎ *03/3241–3311.* ☉ *Tues.–Sun. 10–6:30.*

Takatoshi Mitsui made his fortune by revolutionizing the retail system for kimono fabrics. The drapers of his day usually did business on account, taking payment semiannually and adding various surcharges to the price of their goods. Mitsui started the practice of unit pricing, and his customers paid cash on the spot. As time went on, the store was always ready to adapt to changing needs and merchandising styles; these adjustments included garments made to order, home delivery, imported goods, and even—as the 20th century opened and Echigoya had grown, diversified, and changed its name to Mitsukoshi— the hiring of women to the sales force. The emergence of Mitsukoshi as Tokyo's first department store, or *hyakkaten* (hundred-kinds-of-goods emporium), actually dates from 1908, with a three-story Western building modeled on Harrods of London. This was replaced in 1914 by a five-story structure that boasted Japan's first escalator. The present flagship store is vintage 1935.

Turn right on Chuo-dori. As you walk south, you'll see on the left a shop founded in 1849, called **Yamamoto Noriten,** which specializes in *nori,* or dried seaweed, once the most famous product of Tokyo Bay. *1-6-3 Nihonbashi Muromachi, Chuo-ku,* ☎ *03/3241–0261.* ☉ *Daily 9–6:30.*

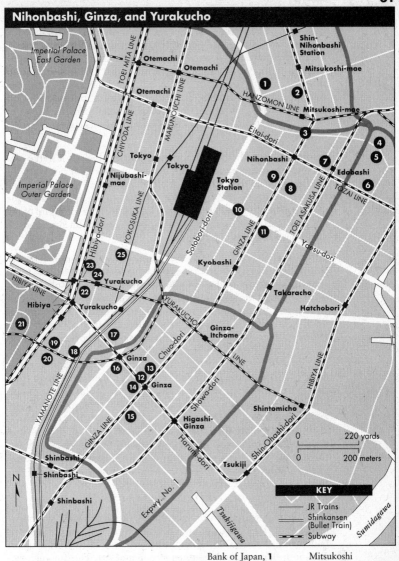

Nihonbashi, Ginza, and Yurakucho

Bank of Japan, **1**

Bridgestone Museum of Art, **11**

Dai-ichi Mutual Life Insurance Company Building, **22**

Hibiya Koen, **21**

Idemitsu Museum of Arts, **24**

Imperial Hotel, **20**

Imperial Theater, **23**

International Shopping Arcade, **18**

Kabuto Jinja, **4**

Kite Museum, **7**

Kyukyodo, **14**

Maruzen, **9**

Matsuzakaya Department Store, **15**

Mikimoto, **13**

Mitsukoshi Department Store, **2**

Mullion Building, **17**

Nihonbashi, **3**

Sukiyabashi, **16**

Takarazuka Theater, **19**

Tokyo International Forum, **25**

Takashimaya Department Store, **8**

Tokyo Stock Exchange, **5**

Wako, **12**

Yaesu Underground Arcade, **10**

Yamatane Museum of Art, **6**

❸ At the end of the next block is the **Nihonbashi.** Why the expressway *had* to be routed directly over this lovely old landmark, back in 1962, is one of the mysteries of Tokyo and its city planning—or lack thereof. There were protests and petitions, but they had no effect. Planners argued the high cost of alternative locations; at that time Tokyo had only two years left to prepare for the Olympics, and the traffic congestion was already out of hand. So the bridge, with its graceful double arch and ornate lamps, its bronze Chinese lions and unicorns, was doomed to bear the perpetual rumble of trucks overhead—its claims overruled by concrete ramps and pillars.

Before you cross the bridge, notice on your left the small statue of a sea princess seated by a pine tree: a monument to the fish market. To the right is the Zero Kilometer marker, from which all the highway distances are measured. On the other side, also to the right, is a plaque depicting the old wood bridge. In the Edo period, the south end of the bridge was set aside for the posting of public announcements—and for displaying the heads of criminals.

Turn left as soon as you cross the bridge, and walk past the Nomura Securities building to where the expressway loops overhead and turns
❹ south. This area is called Kabutocho, after the small **Kabuto Jinja** (shrine) here on the left, under the loop. Legend has it that a noble warrior of the 11th century, sent by the Imperial Court in Kyoto to subdue the barbarians of the north, stopped here and prayed for assistance. His expedition was successful, and on the way back he buried a golden helmet (*kabuto*) on this spot as an offering of thanks. Few Japanese are aware of this legend; "Kabutocho" invokes instead the world of brokers and securities. With good reason: Just across the street from
❺ the shrine is the **Tokyo Stock Exchange** (Shoken Torihikijo). At the exchange's new Exhibition Plaza and Gallery, visitors may watch the fast and furious action on the trading floor. A robot, which resembles a character from *Star Wars,* demonstrates hand signals at the touch of a button. The robot also lectures on the daily trading of securities at the Tokyo Stock Exchange. An array of video exhibits introduces companies and offers worldwide stock news and trading terms. *2-1 Nihonbashi Kabutocho, Chuo-ku,* ☎ *03/3666–0141.* ☛ *Free.* ☼ *Weekdays 9–4. Trading hours: weekdays 9–11 and 12:30–3.*

From the main entrance of the exchange, turn right; walk south two blocks to the intersection at Eitai-dori and turn right again. The black building on the corner is Yamatane Securities Building; on the eighth
❻ and ninth floors is the **Yamatane Museum of Art.** The museum specializes in *nihon-ga,* or painting in the traditional Japanese style, from the Meiji period and later; it was designed with an interior garden by architect Yoshiro Taniguchi, who also did the National Museum of Modern Art in Takebashi. The museum's own private collection includes masterpieces by such painters as Taikan Yokoyama, Gyoshu Hayami, Kokei Kobayashi, and Gyokudo Kawai. The exhibitions, which sometimes include works borrowed from other collections, change every two months. The decor and display at the Yamatane make it an oasis of quiet and elegance in the world of high finance; the chance to buy the lavish catalogue of the collection would be well worth the visit. *7-12 Nihonbashi Kabutocho, Chuo-ku,* ☎ *03/3669–4056.* ☛ *¥600–¥800 adults, ¥200–¥300 children under 12.* ☼ *Tues.–Sun. 10–5.*

TIME OUT Turn right as you leave the Yamatane Building, and continue west on Eitai-dori across the intersection with Showa-dori. Turn right onto Showa-dori, and left on the first small street behind the Bank of Hiroshima; just off the next corner is **Taimeiken,** a restaurant serving Western food at very reasonable prices. (A portion of cabbage salad and vegetable soup, for example, is only ¥50—the same price it was when the restaurant first opened, some 40 years ago.) At lunch, Taimeiken is packed with people from the nearby banks and securities companies; you buy a ticket for the meal you want at the counter to the left of the entrance, and then look for a table to share. *1-12-10 Nihonbashi, Chuo-ku,* ☎ *03/3271–2463.* ☽ *Mon.–Sat. 11–9.*

★ **7** After lunch, take the elevator from the Taimeiken restaurant to the fifth floor, where the late Shingo Motegi, who founded the restaurant, established a wonderful **Kite Museum.** Kite flying is an old tradition in Japan; the Motegi collection includes examples of every shape and variety, from all over the country, hand-painted in brilliant colors with figures of birds, geometric patterns, and motifs from Chinese and Japanese mythology. Call ahead, and the museum will arrange a kite-making workshop (in Japanese) for groups of children. *1-12-10 Nihonbashi, Chuo-ku,* ☎ *03/3275–2704.* ☛ *¥200 adults, ¥100 children under 12.* ☽ *Mon.–Sat. 11–5.*

8 Retrace your steps to Eitai-dori, continue west to Chuo-dori, and turn left. One block south, on the left, is the **Takashimaya Department Store** (2-4-1 Nihonbashi, Chuo-ku, ☎ 03/3211–4111; open weekdays 10–
9 7, weekends 10–6:30); on the right is **Maruzen** (2-3-10 Nihonbashi, Chuo-ku, ☎ 03/3272–7211; open 10–7; closed the 1st and 3rd Sun. of the month, one of Japan's largest booksellers). Maruzen prospers in large part on its imports—at grossly inflated rates of exchange. On the second floor, you can find books in Western languages on any subject from Romanesque art to embryology. There's an extensive collection here of books about Japan, and also a small crafts center.

10 If you look to your right at the next intersection, you will see that you have come back almost to Tokyo Station; below the avenue from here to the station runs the **Yaesu Underground Arcade,** with hundreds of shops and restaurants. The whole area here, west of Chuo-dori, was named after Jan Joosten, a Dutch sailor who was shipwrecked on the coast of Kyushu with William Adams—hero of the contemporary novel *Shogun*—in 1600. Like Adams, Joosten became an adviser to Ieyasu Tokugawa, took a Japanese wife, and was given a villa not far from the castle. "Yaesu" (originally Yayosu) was as close as the Japanese could come to the pronunciation of his name. Adams, an Englishman, lived out his life in Japan; Joosten died at sea, off the coast of Indonesia, in an attempt to return home.

11 On the southeast corner of the intersection is the **Bridgestone Museum of Art,** one of Japan's best private collections of French impressionist art and sculpture and also of post-Meiji Japanese painting in Western styles, by such artists as Shigeru Aoki and Tsuguji Fujita. The collection, assembled by Bridgestone Tire Company founder Shojiro Ishibashi, also includes work by Rembrandt, Picasso, Utrillo, and Modigliani. In addition, the Bridgestone often organizes or co-organizes major exhibitions from private collections and museums abroad. *1-10-1 Kyobashi, Chuo-ku,* ☎ *03/3563–0241.* ☛ *¥500 adults, ¥200 children under 12.* ☽ *Tues.–Sun. 10–5:30.*

Ginza

Consider your feet. By now, they may be telling you that you would really rather not walk to the next point on your exploration; if so, get on the Ginza Line (there's a subway entrance right in front of the Bridgestone Museum) and ride one stop to Ginza. Take any exit directing you to the *4-chome* intersection; when you come up to the surface, you can orient yourself by the Ginza branch of the **Mitsukoshi Department Store** (4-6-16 Ginza) on the northeast corner and the round **Sanai Building** (5-7-2 Ginza) on the southwest.

Ieyasu's silver mint moved out of this area in 1800. The name *Ginza* remained, but it was not until much later that it began to acquire any cachet for wealth and style. The turning point was 1872, when a fire destroyed most of the old houses here. In the same year, the country's first railway line was completed, from nearby Shinbashi to Yokohama. This prompted the city to one of its periodic attempts at large-scale planning: The main street of Ginza, together with a grid of cross streets and parallels, was rebuilt as a Western *quartier.* It had two-story brick houses with balconies; it had the nation's first sidewalks and horse-drawn streetcars; and it had gas lights and, later, telephone poles. Before the turn of the century, Ginza had attracted the great mercantile establishments that still define its character. The **Wako** (4-5-11 Ginza) department store, for example, on the northwest corner of the 4-chome intersection, established itself here as Hattori, purveyors of clocks and watches; the clock on the present building was first installed in the Hattori clock tower, a Ginza landmark, in 1894.

Many of the shops nearby have lineages almost as old, or older. A few steps north of the intersection, on Chuo-dori, is **Mikimoto** (4-5-5 Ginza), selling the famous cultured pearls first developed by Kokichi Mikimoto in 1883; his first shop in Tokyo dates from 1899. South of the intersection, next door to the Sanai Building, is **Kyukyodo** (5-7-4 Ginza), with its wonderful variety of handmade Japanese papers, paper products, incense, brushes, and other materials for calligraphy; Kyukyodo has been in business since 1663, and on the Ginza since 1880. Across the street and one block south is **Matsuzakaya Department Store** (6-10-1 Ginza), which began as a kimono shop in Nagoya in 1611. Exploring this area (there's even a name for browsing: *Gin-bura,* or "Ginza-wandering") is best on Sundays, from noon to 6 or 7 (depending on the season), when Chuo-dori is closed to traffic, from Shinbashi all the way to Ueno, and becomes one long pedestrian mall. On Saturday afternoons, from 3 to 6 or 7, the avenue is closed to traffic between Shinbashi and Kyobashi.

Backtrack and walk west on Harumi-dori in the direction of the Imperial Palace. From Chuo-dori to the intersection called **Sukiyabashi** (named for a bridge that once stood here), your exploration should be free-form: the side streets and parallels north–south are ideal for wandering, particularly if you are interested in art galleries—of which there are 300 or more in this part of the Ginza. The art world works a bit differently here: A few of these establishments, like the venerable **Nichido** (7-4-12 Ginza), **Gekkoso** (6-3-17 Ginza), **Yoseido** (5-5-15 Ginza), **Yayoi** (7-6-61 Ginza), and **Kabutoya** (8-8-7 Ginza), actually function as dealers, representing particular artists, as well as acquiring and selling art. The vast majority, however, are nothing more than rental spaces. The artists or groups pay for the gallery by the week, publicize the show themselves, and in some cases even hang their own work. Not unreasonably, one suspects that a lot of these shows, even in so prestigious a venue as the Ginza, are "vanity" exhibitions by amateurs with money to spare—but that's not always the case. The rental spaces are also the only way for serious professionals, independent of the various art organizations that might otherwise sponsor their work, to get any critical attention; if they're lucky, they can at least recoup their expenses with an occasional sale.

Yurakucho

West of Sukiyabashi, from Sotobori-dori to Hibiya Koen and the Outer Garden of the Imperial Palace, is the district called Yurakucho. The name derives from one Urakusai Oda, younger brother of the warlord who had once been Ieyasu Tokugawa's commander. Urakusai, a Tea Master of some note (he was a student of Sen no Rikyu, who developed the Tea Ceremony), had a town house here, beneath the castle ramparts, on land reclaimed from the tidal flats of the bay. He soon left Edo for the more refined comforts of Kyoto, but his name stayed behind, becoming Yurakucho—the *Quarter (cho)* where one can *Have (yu) Pleasures (raku)*—in the process. Sukiyabashi was the name of the bridge near Urakusai's villa that led over the moat—long gone in the course of modernization—to the Silver Mint.

The "pleasures" associated with this district in the early postwar period stemmed from the fact that a number of the buildings here survived the air raids of 1945 and were requisitioned by the Allied forces. Yurakucho quickly became the haunt of the so-called *pan-pan* girls, who provided the GIs with female company. Because it was so close to the military Post Exchange in Ginza, the area under the railroad tracks became one of the city's largest black markets. Later, the black market gave way to clusters of cheap restaurants, most of them little more than counters and a few stools, serving yakitori (bits of grilled chicken on bamboo skewers) and beer. Office workers on meager budgets, and journalists from the nearby *Mainichi, Asahi,* and *Yomiuri* newspaper headquarters, would gather here at night; Yurakucho-under-the-tracks was smoky, loud, and friendly, a kind of open-air substitute for the local taproom. Alas, the area has long since moved upscale, and no more than a handful of the yakitori stalls survive.

From Sukiyabashi, keep on the left side of the avenue as you cross Sotobori-dori; on the opposite side is the curved facade of the **Mullion Building,** a new shopping and entertainment complex of the sort that is rapidly turning Yurakucho into a high-fashion extension of the Ginza. (The Seibu Department Store, which occupies half the building, is a leader in marketing the fusion of modern and traditional Japanese design.) Take your first left down the narrow side street that runs along the west side of the Hankyu Department Store (the horned monstrosity in the pocket park on your right is by sculptor Taro Okamoto), cross at the corner, take the street that goes under the JR tracks and walk west. On both sides of the street, just under the bridge, you will see entrances for the **International Shopping Arcade,** a collection of stores that feature kimonos and happi coats, pearls and cloisonné, prints, cameras, and consumer electronics—one-stop shopping for presents and souvenirs. In the next block, on the right, you will see the **Takarazuka Theater,** and on the left the **Imperial Hotel;** walk to the end of the street, where it runs into Hibiya-dori, and turn right.

Across the avenue is **Hibiya Koen,** Japan's first Western-style public park, which dates from 1903. With its lawns and fountains, it makes a pretty place for office workers in the nearby buildings to take their lunches on a warm spring afternoon, but there's nothing here to detain you on your exploration. Press on—across the Harumi-dori intersection, past the Marunouchi Police Station, to the **Dai-ichi Mutual Life Insurance Company Building.** Built like a fortress, it survived World War II virtually intact and was taken over by the Supreme Command of the Allied Powers. From his office here, General Douglas MacArthur directed the affairs of Japan for six years (1945–1951). The room is kept exactly as it was then; it can be visited by appointment. *1-1-13*

Yurakucho, Chiyoda-ku, ☎ *03/3216–1211.* ☛ *Free, by appointment, Mon.–Sat. 10–4.*

㉓ On the next corner is the International Building, with the **Imperial Theater** on the first floor. The original Imperial, built in 1911, was Japan's first purely Western-style theater; the present version, by architect Yoshiro Taniguchi, is the venue of choice for big-budget musicals, such as the Japanese productions of *Man of La Mancha* and *Fiddler on the Roof*. Turn right here, and walk halfway down the block to the main entrance of the International Building; on the ninth floor is the

★ ㉔ **Idemitsu Museum of Arts.**

With its four spacious rooms, the Idemitsu is one of the largest private museums in Tokyo, and it is one of the best designed. The strength of the collection is in its Chinese porcelain of the Tang and Song dynasties, and in Japanese ceramics—including works by Ninsei Nonomura and Kenzan Ogata, and masterpieces of Old Seto, Oribe, Old Kutani, Karatsu, and Kakiemon ware. There are also outstanding examples of Zen painting and calligraphy, wood-block prints, and genre paintings of the Edo period. Of special interest to scholars is the resource collection of shards from virtually every pottery-making culture of the ancient world. *3-1-1 Marunouchi, Chiyoda-ku,* ☎ *03/3213–9404.* ☛ *¥500 adults.* ☉ *Tues.–Sun. 10–5.*

Turn left as you leave the International Building and walk to the second corner. Across the street to your left you will see the gleaming white

㉕ expanse of the **Tokyo International Forum,** the work of Uruguay-born American architect Raphael Vinoly. The design of this sumptuous convention and cultural center was selected in a 1989 competition that drew nearly 400 entries from 50 countries. Scheduled to open in January 1997, the Forum has a main hall with seating for 5,000.

Turn right at the corner, away from the Forum, and a minute's walk will bring you to the JR Yurakucho Station, and the end of your exploration.

Roppongi

Numbers in the margin correspond to points of interest on the Roppongi, Akasaka, and Aoyama map.

The best way to arrive in **Roppongi,** in southwestern Tokyo, is to surface from the subway at Roppongi Station on the Hibiya Line. Street traffic, especially from the late afternoon through the evening, can be horrendously congested. Roppongi has two personalities. By day, the area is relatively quiet, with housewives doing their shopping and delivery trucks restocking the bars and restaurants for another evening of revelry. By night, the neighborhood hums with people from all over Tokyo, who come to enjoy the local discos, restaurants, and bars.

Once a sleepy suburban area, Roppongi has become a fashionable high-rent district. Many of the embassies that did not locate in Akasaka, to the north, have settled here, and executives from overseas corporations often select the area for their Tokyo bases. Consequently, Roppongi is Tokyo's international and cosmopolitan neighborhood for both living and partying. Indeed, the district claims to have the best bars and nightclubs at affordable prices, compared with the exceedingly high cost of Ginza's nightlife. As a result, the area appeals to affluent university graduates working their way up the corporate ladder. Roppongi is Yuppieland, with entertainment considerably more sophisticated than that of raunchy Shinjuku and more polished than that of Shibuya.

❶ The first stop on this tour is **Almond,** just across from the Roppongi Station on the southwest corner of Roppongi-dori and Imoarai-zaka (slope). This multistory pink café is used by many as a meeting place despite the inferior coffee and cakes served. Farther down (southwest) Roppongi-dori, on the left-hand side, is a huge outdoor video screen.

❷ That belongs to **Wave** (6-2-27 Roppongi, Minato-ku), one of the best places in Tokyo to shop for music. The first four floors sell tapes and CDs from a stock that exceeds 60,000; through a computer linkup, information on any recorded music is retrieved instantaneously. In the basement of the building is an avant-garde movie theater.

Next, backtrack along Roppongi-dori, under the Shuto Expressway, keeping to the right-hand side of the avenue. If you take a right on the first small street after Gaien-higashi-dori, and then an immediate left,

❸ you will reach the **Square Building** (3-10-3 Roppongi, Minato-ku), which is the home of seven discos. Keep the location in mind when you return in the evening.

If you take the next left, you will soon be back on Roppongi-dori. Take

❹ a right and continue walking northeast to the **Roppongi Prince Hotel** (3-2-7 Roppongi, Minato-ku). In about 200 meters (yards), take a right up a small street, and immediately left up a steep slope is the hotel's entrance. Especially on a summer's afternoon, the café tables around the hotel's courtyard swimming pool are much in demand, perhaps not for refreshing drinks but rather for people-watching. The pool's sides are built with transparent acrylic; the swimmers look like wallowing whales in an aquarium.

From the Roppongi Prince, cut back southwest through the maze of streets to Gaien-higashi-dori. The easiest way is to take a left at the bottom of the Roppongi Prince's ramp. Then, at the first street after Zengakuji (temple), take a right for 50 meters (yards) before going left. This will bring you out on Gaien-higashi-dori just south of the Roppongi Forum Building.

❺ Take a left on Gaien-higashi-dori; the **Axis Building** (5-17-1, Roppongi, Minato-ku), across the avenue, has a well-known collection of stores, with especially fine textiles and high-quality interior-design merchandise. Actually, the wares in Axis are more than just goods for sale; they make up an exhibition of creative design. You do not have to be a shopper to be inspired by a visit here.

Walk back (northwest) up Gaien-higashi-dori and you'll be back at the entrance of the Almond café. Instead of keeping to the main avenue, try to wander down the back streets. Especially after six in the evening, the party mood is everywhere; discos, restaurants, clubs, and bars vie for space, and the streets are packed with trendy Japanese fun-seekers. This is a very safe area and, with its cosmopolitan flavor, is comfortable for the foreigner to explore. However, as the evening wears on, taxis become scarce, so consider leaving the district before the last subway does (soon after 11:30).

(For more information about Roppongi, *see* Nightlife, *below.*)

Akasaka and Aoyama

Though **Akasaka** is only a 15-minute taxi ride west of the Imperial Palace, not much more than a hundred years ago Akasaka grew tea bushes and *akane*, plants that produced a red dye. Indeed, that is how Akasaka, which means "red slope," received its name. Then, in 1936, when the mammoth granite Diet building, which houses the national

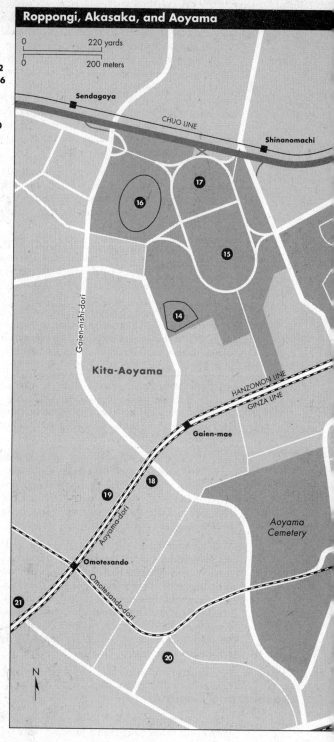

Roppongi, Akasaka, and Aoyama

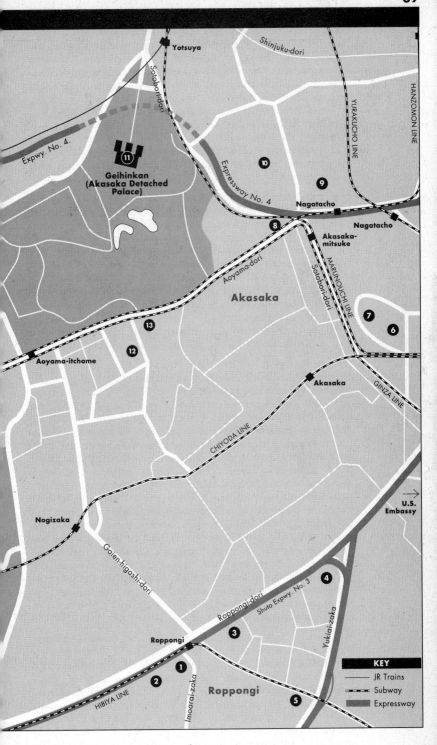

government, moved to Nagatacho (the area north of Akasaka), the neighborhood became an important pleasure quarter for politicos and their lobbyists. Accordingly, the geishas were upgraded, and so was the neighborhood. The geisha houses and *ryotei* (expensive traditional restaurants) with their unobtrusive signs are still to be found—a Mercedes or BMW in the courtyard will help identify them. As the neighborhood improved, it developed an international flair. Many foreign countries, including the United States, established their embassies here to be close to the National Diet. To service visitors, new deluxe hotels sprang up, including the prestigious Hotel Okura. When TBS Television moved to Akasaka in 1960, it brought screen personalities of national fame to the district. In their wake came shops, cabarets, bars, and nightclubs.

Begin your visit to Akasaka at Kokkai Gijido-mae Subway Station (you'll have arrived on either the Chiyoda Line or the Marunouchi Line). If you started from Tokyo Station, you'll be on the Marunouchi Line and will need to walk through the passageways of Kokkai Gijido-mae Station to leave from the Chiyoda exit. When you reach the street, you'll ❻ be opposite the rear entrance of the **Capitol Tokyu Hotel** (2-10-3 Nagatacho, Chiyoda-ku). To save yourself a climb up the hill and around the hotel, enter the building through this rear entrance and take the elevator to the main lobby. The Capitol Tokyu is a good place to start the day with breakfast, either Western or Japanese. In the breakfast room you can look on to a garden surrounding a pond. Then, leave ❼ the hotel by the main entrance, and the **Hie Jinja** will be before you.

As in so much of Tokyo, traditional Japan is hidden among the modern concrete structures. Hie Jinja is an example of this old Japan. The entrance to the shrine is easily spotted by the large torii in front of the steps leading up to the shrine complex. Notice the archway before the shrine; it is distinctive for its unusual triangular roof. The present building was rebuilt in 1959, and the gates in 1962, but its inspiration is from the late 15th century, when a military commander dedicated the building to Oyamakuni-no-Kami, a tutelary deity of Edo. Later, the shrine became a favorite of the Tokugawa Shogunate, and some of the best festivals during the Edo period were held here. Several festivals a year still take place here, but by far the most important is Sanno Matsuri, held June 11–16, with processions of palanquins and marchers that recall the days of the Tokugawa Shogunate, when the event was known as the "Festival Without Equal." For the rest of the year, the shrine has a special appeal to those seeking protection against miscarriages; note the statue in the main courtyard of the female monkey holding her offspring. Recently, people have visited the shrine to protect themselves against traffic accidents; it is not unusual to see a Shinto priest blessing a new car. *2-10-5 Nagatacho, Chiyoda-ku.* ☎ *Free.* ⊙ *Sunrise–sunset.*

To the right of Hie Jinja on Kasumigaseki Hill is the National Diet Building (*see* Imperial Palace District tour, *above*). Instead of climbing up the hill to the Diet, walk back down past the Capitol Tokyu to Akasaka's main avenue, Sotobori-dori, and turn right. Here is Akasaka's shopping area, with stores above and below ground flanking both sides of the street. On the left, running parallel to Sotobori-dori, are two smaller avenues, Tamachi-dori and Hitotsugi-dori. On these two streets, and their cross streets and alleys, are housed Akasaka's evening pleasures: lots of small bars, restaurants, and cafés. Nearby is the Cordon Bleu, a popular cabaret. The few remaining geisha houses are at the southern end of this area. However, unless you have affluent Japanese friends to invite you to a geisha party, you will only be able to note the houses' traditional architecture from the street, or perhaps spot a geisha, dressed in her elaborate kimono as she leaves for an assignment.

At the top end of Sotobori-dori is the Akasaka-mitsuke Station and the intersection with Aoyama-dori. Across the intersection on the left, on the other side of the overpass, is the Suntory Building. On its 11th floor is the **Suntory Museum**, which rotates in exhibition its own substantial collection of traditional art objects, which includes paintings, prints, lacquerware, glassware, and costumes; it also holds special loan exhibitions throughout the year. For the size of the museum, the admission charge is high; but the exhibits are carefully selected, extremely well displayed, and often are the finest of their kind. To one side of the museum is a teahouse. *1-2-3 Moto-Akasaka, Minato-ku,* ☎ *03/3470–1073.* ☛ *¥500 adults, ¥200 children under 12 (Sun. and holidays ¥300/¥100). Tea and traditional Japanese sweets are served for an additional ¥300.* ⊘ *Tues.–Thurs. and weekends 10–5; Fri. 10–7.*

For those wanting something more than tea, Suntory opens a beer garden on its building's rooftop during the summertime (⊘ 5–9). However, the beer garden's views are only of Akasaka-mitsuke's busy intersection, while from across the road, at the **Akasaka Prince Hotel** (1-2 Kioicho, Chiyoda-ku, ☎ 03/3234–1111), the views include all of Tokyo.

The 40-story half-moon structure stands on top of a small hill and dominates the landscape. Designed by Kenzo Tange, the Akasaka Prince meets either with acclaim for its contemporary architecture or with criticism for being cold and sterile. Certainly the building's starkness, with nothing but the sky for its backdrop, stands out as a bold example of 20th-century architecture. Whatever your reaction to the building's design, you will not dispute the views from the hotel's upper floors. It's hard to surpass the view of Tokyo from its penthouse restaurant Blue Gardenia (⊘ 6–11 for dinner; *see* Dining, *below*) or from the cocktail lounge, the Top of Akasaka (⊘ Mon.–Sat. 11 AM–2 AM, Sun. 11 AM–midnight). Indeed, it is worth making a special effort to come here just before twilight to see the sprawl of Tokyo turn into flickering lights against the night's darkening sky.

Across the street from the Akasaka Prince is the **Hotel New Otani Tokyo and Towers** (4-1 Kioicho, Chiyoda-ku), the largest hotel in Asia. Even if you abhor huge hotels, the New Otani holds a certain futuristic fascination as a minicity. Not only does it have 2,100 guest rooms, but there are also banquet facilities for any event, arcades of shops, a minisupermarket in its basement, and numerous bars and restaurants. At times, the New Otani seems more like a crowded subway at rush hour than a hotel, but it does have one area of tranquillity. The hotel's Garden Lounge looks on to a 400-year-old Japanese garden with vermilion bridges over ponds and winding paths—a little of traditional Japan, amid the endless stream of people pacing the hallways of the hotel and browsing through its high-fashion shops. Across the expressway and to the west of the New Otani are the gardens and fountains of **Geihinkan** (also known as the Akasaka Detached Palace; 2-1-1 Moto-Akasaka, Minato-ku). The palace was formerly the home of the crown prince, who was later to become the Taisho emperor (1912–1926); it is now an official state-guest house. The palace is a copy of Buckingham Palace, and the interior, which is not open to the public, imitates the style of Versailles.

Running along the south side of the Geihinkan gardens is Aoyama-dori, which goes all the way through the area to Shibuya. The distance is about 5 kilometers (3 miles), or four subway stops on the Ginza Line if you use the Akasaka-mitsuke Station (opposite the Suntory Building and at the top end of Sotobori-dori). To give your feet a rest, we suggest taking the subway for two stops to Gaien-mae Station. You'll miss walking past the **Canadian Embassy** and **Sogetsu Kaikan,** a famous Ikebana flower arranging school where lessons are given in English on Mondays and Fridays 10–noon. *7-2-21 Akasaka, Minato-ku, ☎ 03/3408–1126. Cost: ¥3,670 for 1st lesson, ¥3,460 thereafter. Reservations must be made a day in advance.*

Aoyama

The Gaien-mae Station on Aoyama-dori takes you to the neighborhood of Aoyama. This is also the subway stop for the **Jingu Baseball Stadium** (13 Kasumigaoka, Shinjuku-ku ☎ 03/3404–8999), home field of the Yakult Swallows. You'll see it across the street from the Chichibunomiya Rugby and Football Ground. Actually, the stadium is in the **Meiji Jingu Outer Garden** (Jingu Gaien); on the other side of this park is the **National Stadium** (10 Kasumigaoka, Shinjuku-ku), the main venue of the 1964 Summer Olympics and Japan's largest stadium, with seating for 75,000 people. Across Gaien-nishi-dori from the stadium is the **Kaigakan** (Meiji Memorial Picture Gallery), which exhibits approximately 80 paintings depicting events in the life of Emperor Meiji. *9 Kasumigaoka, Shinjuku-ku, ☎ 03/3401–5179. ☛ ¥300 adults, ¥100 children under 15. ☯ Daily 9–4:30.*

Now you come to the real reason for getting off the subway at Gaien-mae. If you walk about five minutes along Aoyama-dori toward Shibuya district (west), you'll spot the **Zenkoku Dentoteki Kogeihin Senta** (Japan Traditional Craft Center). Located on the second floor of the Plaza 246 Building, the center exhibits and sells a wide range of traditional craft products from all over Japan, including lacquerware, ceramics, paper products, dolls, and metalwork. Some of the exhibits have English descriptions, others do not, but someone is usually available to answer a question if a particular item takes your fancy. A visit to this center provides a head start to understanding different regional crafts and techniques before one leaves Tokyo to travel Japan's hinterland. *3-1-1 Minami Aoyama, Minato-ku, ☎ 03/3403–2460. ☛ Free. ☯ Fri.–Wed. 10–6.*

If you continue walking down (south) Aoyama-dori toward Shibuya, past a branch of America's **Brooks Brothers** on the right, you'll reach the Omotesando Subway Station. If you take a left at the crossroads on to Omotesando-dori and walk another 10 minutes, you'll find the **Nezu Institute of Fine Arts,** a museum with a priceless collection of East Asian art that includes superb examples of Japanese paintings and scrolls. An extremely attractive aspect of this museum is its extensive garden, with a traditional pond and five tea-ceremony houses. *6-5-1 Minami Aoyama, Minato-ku, ☎ 03/3400–2536. ☛ ¥1,000 adults, ¥700 students. ☯ Tues.–Sun. 9:30–4:30. Closed the day after national holidays.*

The Nezu Institute of Fine Arts is about halfway between Roppongi and Shibuya. If it is still daytime, you might proceed to Shibuya, or even over to the area of Harajuku and the Meiji Shrine. If you do go directly to Shibuya from the Nezu Institute, it's about a 20-minute walk. Return first to Aoyama-dori and take a left. It will lead straight to Shibuya, first passing the **National Children's Castle** (5-53-1 Jingumae, Shibuya-ku, ☎ 03/3797–5666), an emporium designed to constructively entertain the young with its swimming pool, gym, concerts, theater, and audiovisual library.

Shibuya and Harajuku

Numbers in the margin correspond to points of interest on the Shibuya and Harajuku map.

Traffic in **Shibuya** hardly compares to that in Shinjuku, to the north, but it is still a major city center. Two subways, three private railways, the JR Yamanote Line, and the bus terminal move about a million people a day through Shibuya. The commercial character of this hub is shaped by the fierce battle for supremacy between the Seibu and Tokyo department store chains. As fast as one of them puts up a new branch building, vertical mall, or specialty store, its rival counters with another; every new venture incorporates a trendy restaurant or a concert hall or a flashy gallery—something to draw a bigger share of Shibuya's predominantly younger crowd of students and office workers. The result: a consumer paradise, busy, noisy, confusing—and fun.

Shibuya has become a popular area for evening entertainment, such as shopping and going to restaurants and *nomiya* (inexpensive bars). It is not as international or cosmopolitan as Akasaka or Roppongi, but it is less expensive than those districts. Most places in Shibuya, however, are unaccustomed to foreigners, so be prepared to use one or two words of Japanese if you enter a small restaurant.

❶ The flagship store of the Tokyu Department Store, **Tokyu Plaza** (1-2-2 Dogenzaka, Shibuya-ku), dominates the Shibuya Station neighborhood. If you select a window table at one of the two dozen restaurants on the top two floors of the building, you will find yourself gazing in awe at the seething flow of commuters around the station. On the fifth floor of Tokyu Plaza is a branch of **Kinokuniya Bookstore** (☎ 03/3463–3241), with a large selection of books written in English. The selection, however, is not as large as that of the Kinokuniya store in Shinjuku.

Unfortunately, from the restaurants' windows you cannot see the ❷ **statue of Hachiko.** For that, you must return to the station plaza and go to the north exit. You'll spot the statue by the number of people who are standing around it waiting for someone. "Meet you by Hachiko" is an arrangement frequently made by Tokyoites. Hachiko was an Akita, a Japanese breed of dog. Every day he walked his master, a professor at Tokyo University, to Shibuya Station. In the evening, he would return to the station and greet his master off the train. One day in 1925, while at the university, the professor died of a stroke. Every evening for the next seven years, the dog went to the station and waited until the last train had pulled out of the station. Crestfallen, the dog would return to his home to try again the next evening. Then the dog died, too, and his story made the national newspapers. Gifts flooded in. A bronze statue was built, and the dog was stuffed to keep vigil in the Tokyo Museum of Art. The statue seen today is a replica; the original was melted down for its metal in World War II.

TIME OUT Take an ecologically correct and reasonably-priced lunch break at ❸ **Shizenkan II** (3-9-2 Shibuya, Shibuya-ku, ☎ 03/3486–0281), a restaurant in the heart of the district that doubles as a health-food store. The ¥950 "boutique" set menu includes a main dish, brown rice, and an array of small side dishes, with an emphasis on organic veggies. To find this restful little oasis, walk south on Meiji-dori and turn left on the first street past the overhead expressway.

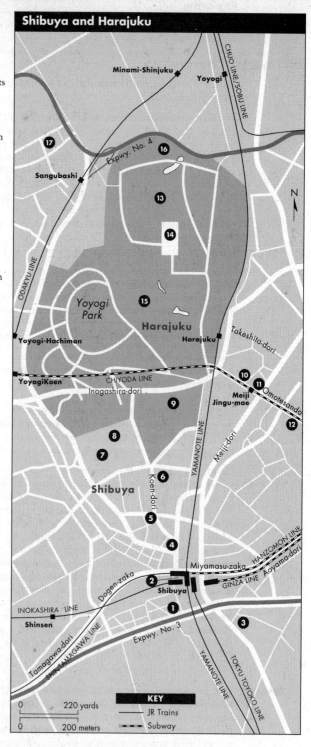

Shibuya and Harajuku

From Shibuya Station, plaza department stores and shops are spread out along Aoyama-dori and Meiji-dori. Tokyu has seven stores, Seibu has six, and Marui has two. For this tour, leave the station plaza in the direction that the Hachiko statue is facing, and cross the major intersection. On your left will be **Seibu Department Store** (21-1 Udagawacho, Shibuya-ku), which has a particularly good selection of European and Japanese designer-label fashions. Equally fascinating is a walk through Seibu's basement, which has one of Tokyo's most extensive food departments.

The street branching left after Seibu is Koen-dori, the smartest street in the neighborhood. A short way uphill, again on the left, is **Parco,** owned by Seibu and said to be Tokyo's leading fashion complex. Parco actually comes in four parts. Parco 1 and Parco 2 (3 Udagawacho, Shibuya-ku) specialize in fashion, and on the top floor of Parco 1 is Parco Theater, for plays and performances. Parco 3 (14 Udagawacho, Shibuya-ku) has interior design merchandise and a floor devoted to visiting cultural exhibitions. Parco 4 (32-13 Udagawacho, Shibuya-ku) features young fashions, and has a performance hall called the Club Quattro on the fifth floor. Across koen-dori, not far from the Parco complex, is the **Tobako to Shio Hakubutsukan** (Tobacco and Salt Museum), which houses every conceivable item associated with tobacco and salt since the days of the Maya. The displays of smoking utensils are fascinating, but the museum is perhaps more interesting to the Japanese, many of whom are inveterate smokers, than to the foreigner, who may have seen similar exhibitions elsewhere. Of more interest is the special exhibit on the fourth floor of *ukiyo-e,* wood-block prints depicting smokers' necessities. *1-16-8 Jinnan, Shibuya-ku,* ☎ *03/3476–2041.* ☛ *¥100 adults, ¥50 children under 12.* ☉ *Tues.–Sun. 10–5:30. Closed 2nd Tues. of June and New Year's.*

Walking farther up Koen-dori leads to **NHK Broadcasting Center** (Nippon Hoso Kyokai) for Japanese National Public Television. This 23-story building was originally built as the Olympic Information Center. Parts of the broadcasting complex are open to visitors. In the main building a tour route is offered, and techniques for sound effects and film are shown. Explanations are given only in Japanese, so foreign tourists may be a little baffled. Perhaps the most exciting part of the tour permits you to watch an actual filming of a television scene and some of the stage sets. *2-2-1 Jinnan, Shibuya-ku,* ☎ *03/3465–1111.* ☛ *¥200 adults.* ☉ *10–6. Closed 2nd Mon. of each month.*

The building next to the NHK Broadcast Center is the **NHK Hall,** which serves as a multipurpose auditorium designed for opera and concert performances. It is quite large, with a seating capacity of 4,000, but its pièce de résistance is its 7,640-piece pipe organ, foremost of its kind in the world (*see* The Arts, *below*).

Across the street from NHK Hall is the ❾ **National Yoyogi Sports Center** (2-1-1 Jinnan, Shibuya-ku), consisting of two ultramodern structures designed by Kenzo Tange. His ability to work with ferro-concrete to evoke a templelike simplicity is impressive. The center was built for the 1964 Olympics, and both the stadium, which can accommodate 15,000 spectators for swimming and diving events, and the annex, which houses a basketball court with a seating capacity of 4,000, are open to visitors when there are no competitions (☛ Free; ☉ daily 10–4). The bronze bust in the center of the Sports Center is of Yoshitoshi Tokugawa, who, in 1910, became Japan's pioneer aviator by staying aloft for four minutes and traveling 230 feet. (His plane is on display at the Transportation Museum in the Koto ward.)

Harajuku

Across from the Sports Center are the green lawns of **Yoyogi Koen.** The park was once the barracks for the Japanese Army; then, after World War II, the U.S. Army took it over, and the area became known as Washington Heights. In 1964 it was used as the Olympic Village. Now it is public parkland lined with paths and, on Sundays, is often the venue for groups of young people to dance, mime, or play their music to the amusement of spectators. This is Harajuku, a minidowntown that attracts the youth of Tokyo.

Perhaps the presence of the U.S. occupation forces stationed in this area after World War II has caused Harajuku to permit a more liberal, Western-type behavior. In the late 1970s and early 1980s, the youth of Tokyo seemed to congregate every Sunday on the wide street between NHK and Harajuku Subway Station. The more exhibitionist youths formed groups that acted out their fantasies in dance, break dancing, skateboard antics, bands, or pantomime. The more inhibited would only watch. The youth were named the "bamboo-shoot children," Japan's counterpart to the flower children of America. Their numbers have since declined, but on Sundays a variety of amusing performances is still offered.

Today's Japanese youth are the product of a new consumerism that is sweeping through the nation after decades of austerity. The young come here on Sundays to be anticorporate and to rebel against the pressure to succeed. They also come to consume. Dressed in the latest fashion fads, they seek out the bargains from the stalls and shops that remain open all day on Sunday.

The JR Harajuku Station is easy to recognize. The 1924 building looks more like an English village station than a metropolitan subway stop. Directly across the road from the station is **Omotesando,** an avenue bustling with pedestrians and shoppers. And, on Sundays, it seems that all the trendy Japanese young people are here, dressed in their finery.

★ ⑩ Up a small street, on the left-hand side before Meiji-dori, is the **Ohta Kinen Bijutsukan** (Ota Memorial Museum of Art). On two floors you'll find a rotating exhibit of *ukiyo-e* (wood-block prints) from the private collection of Seizo Ota. Some of Japan's best-known artists are represented here, including Hiroshige, Sharaku, and Utamaro. *1-10-10 Jingu-mae, Shibuya-ku,* ☎ *03/3403–0880.* ☛ *¥500/¥800 adults, ¥100/¥250 children under 12.* ⊘ *Tues.–Sun. 10:30–5. Closed New Year's and from the 26th to the end of each month for new installations.*

⑪ Across the road from the Ota Memorial Museum, on the corner of Omotesando and Meiji-dori, is **La Foret** (1-11-6 Jingumae, Shibuya-ku), the main fashion building in Harajuku. Inside La Foret are about 110 shops, most of them high-price boutiques. You can rest at one of the coffee shops in the building if you need time to decide on a purchase.

⑫ Lined with ginkgo trees, Omotesando is rich with boutiques and shops, including Paul Stewart from the United States. However, the one store that is really worth looking at for Japanese antiques is the **Oriental Bazaar** (next to Shakey's Pizza). Downstairs in the basement, salesmen set up their stalls and offer a range of old Japanese items, such as kimonos, jewelry, dolls, and wood-block prints. It's like a hands-on museum. *5-9-13 Jingu-mae, Shibuya-ku,* ☎ *03/3400–3933.* ⊘ *Fri.–Wed. 9:30–6:30.*

Backtrack about 100 meters (yards) to Meiji-dori, take a right, and more boutique and fashion stalls will greet you. If you are still not overwhelmed by the mass consumerism, walk a little farther along Meiji-dori and take a left onto **Takeshita-dori,** a short street crammed with fashion vendors, with names like Rap City and Octopus Army, and youthful buyers. Takeshita-dori leads back to Harajuku Station; on the other side of the train tracks is the **Meiji Jingu Inner Garden,** the grounds for **Meiji Jingu.**

⑬
⑭

Meiji Jingu is a welcome contrast of serene solemnity to the youthful consumerism exhibited on the shop-filled streets around Harajuku. The two torii gates, made from 1,700-year-old cypress trees from Mt. Ari in Taiwan, each tower 40 feet high. Indeed, they are the largest (but not the tallest) gates in Japan; here, more than ever, they fulfill their role of symbolizing the separation between the mundane, everyday world and the spiritual world of the Shinto shrine. Legend has it that the shape of the torii derives from the shape of a rooster's perch, and that it was the rooster whose crowing awoke the sun goddess, who thus brought light to the world. (Meiji Jingu's two gates have perches spanning 56 feet.) The shrine was built in memory of Emperor Meiji, who died in 1912, and his wife, Empress Dowager Shoken, who died two years later. He was the emperor who brought Japan out from the isolationist policies of the Tokugawa Shogunate and opened the country's doors to the West. (Incidentally, Emperor Meiji would not be surprised by the behavior of the youth of Harajuku. In 1881, concerned about the influence of Western civilization, he issued a book on public morality.)

Even though the shrine is new (completed in 1920 and rebuilt in 1958 after being badly damaged by fire in 1945), it evokes the traditional asceticism of Japan's past. The buildings (the main hall forms a quadrangle with the outlying structures) are made from Japanese cypress, and the curving green copper roofs seem to symbolize the eternal sweep of time. The shrine—and its surrounding garden, which has some 100,000 shrubs, many of which were donated by the Japanese people—is one of the most popular with the Japanese. At New Year's, about 2½ million people come to pay their ancestral respects. *1-1 Kamizonocho, Yoyogi, Shibuya-ku.* ☛ *Free.* ☉ *Sunrise–sunset.*

Before you reach the shrine, on the left when you walk from Harajuku Station, is the **Jingu Naien** (Iris Garden), in full bloom in late June. Beyond the shrine is the **Treasure House,** a repository for the personal effects and clothes of Emperor and Empress Meiji—perhaps of less interest to the foreigner than to the Japanese. *1-1 Kamizonocho, Yoyogi, Shibuya-ku,* ☎ *03/3379–5511.* ☛ *¥300 adults, ¥200 children under 12.* ☉ *Mar. 1–Oct. 30, weekdays 8–5, weekends 8–6.*

⑮
⑯

If you have walked as far as the Treasure House, consider exiting the Inner Garden on the northwest side, and walk beyond Sangubashi Subway Station to the **Tohken Hakubutsukan** (Japanese Sword Museum), which exhibits the works of noted swordsmiths, both ancient and modern. Sword making is a complex and intricate art in Japan and was perfected during the shogun period. Swords still hold an aura of dignity and honor. Only a few swordsmiths are left in modern Japan; many live and work in the small town of Seki, north of Nagoya. *4-25-10, Yoyogi, Shibuya-ku,* ☎ *03/3379–1386.* ☛ *¥515 adults, ¥310 children under 12.* ☉ *Tues.–Sun. 9–4.*

⑰

From the Sword Museum, if you retrace your steps to Sangubashi Subway Station, it is two stops north on the Odayku Line to Shinjuku, the antithesis of the serenity of the Meiji Jingu. If you did not make it to either the Treasure House or the Sword Museum, then walk back to Harajuku Station and take the JR Yamanote Line two stops north to Shinjuku.

Shinjuku

Numbers in the margin correspond to points of interest on the Shinjuku map.

To experience **Shinjuku,** one should arrive by subway, though we would not recommend using the subway during the morning or evening rush hour. More than 2 million commuters pass through Shinjuku Station twice a day. Nine trains and subway lines converge in Shinjuku to transport human cargo. Broad-shouldered men in white gloves ease commuters into packed trains with a determined shove. The sight of the endless ebb and flow of humanity is worth seeing, but not experiencing.

Shinjuku is a microcosm of Japan, where the ultramodern confronts the past: High-tech industries work alongside the oldest professions; modern, slick, deluxe hotels look down on pink motels, where rooms rent by the hour; and 50-story buildings, complete with plazas and underground parking, tower over one- or two-level buildings crammed into twisting alleys. Shinjuku is a fascinating nightmare, which is alternately off-putting and exciting.

When Ieyasu Tokugawa became shogun and made Edo his capital, Shinjuku was at the junction of two important arteries leading into the city from the west. Here, travelers could rest their horses and freshen up or dally with ladies of pleasure before entering Edo. When the Tokugawa Dynasty collapsed in 1868, the 16-year-old Emperor Meiji moved his capital to Edo, renaming it Tokyo (Eastern Capital). Shinjuku in this modern age was destined to become the connecting railhead to Japan's western provinces. As a playground, its reputation was maintained with its artists, writers, and students, and it became the bohemian section of Tokyo in the 1930s. Shinjuku was virtually leveled during the firebombing of Tokyo at the end of World War II. After the war, Tokyo spread west rather than east, and Shinjuku has now developed into Tokyo's high-tech center. By the 1970s, the property values of the district were the nation's most expensive, far outstripping the Ginza area.

The heart of Shinjuku is still a commuting junction. In the maze of passageways leading to the trains is a vast underground shopping center of more than 130 shops. The large department stores near Shinjuku Station offer everything from bargain basements to musums to restaurants on their upper floors, while the station itself is a bewildering city. One week in the station would not be sufficient time to know half of it, especially with 60 exits from which to choose.

Shinjuku is divided by its train station into its two very different areas, western Shinjuku and eastern Shinjuku.

Western Shinjuku

The west side (Nishi-Shinjuku) of Shinjuku Station is occupied by the new metropolitan center, Tokyo's 21st-century model city, with modern high rises separated by concrete plazas. All of Tokyo is subject to serious earthquakes, except, apparently, Shinjuku. In the 1923 quake that virtually paralyzed Japan's capital, Shinjuku was the only suburb left vertical. On that basis, and because of some sounder scientific evidence, a virtual forest of skyscrapers has been built here in the past two decades, including the new City Hall.

Three of the skyscrapers here are hotels. The first to be built was the
❶ Keio Plaza Inter-Continental Hotel (2-2-1 Nishi- Shinjuku, Shinjuku-
❷ ku). The **Century Hyatt** (2-7-2 Nishi-Shinjuku, Shinjuku-ku) and the
❸ Tokyo Hilton (6-6-2 Nishi-Shinjuku, Shinjuku-ku) followed. The other skyscrapers contain banks, government offices, and showrooms for Japanese computer, optical, and electronics companies.

❹ The skyscraper closest to the railway tracks is the **Yasuda Kasai Kaijo Building** (Yasuda Fire and Marine Insurance Building), on the 42nd floor of which is the **Togo Seiji Museum.** Seiji Togo was a master of putting to canvas the grace and charm of young maidens; more than a hundred of his works are on display at any time. This is also the museum that bought Van Gogh's *Sunflowers* for more than ¥5 billion. The museum's gallery has an obstructed view of the old part of Shinjuku, where clubs and pink hotels abound. *1-26-1 Nishi-Shinjuku, Shinjuku-ku,* ☎ *03/3349–3081.* ☛ *¥800 adults, ¥300 children under 12.* ☺ *Tues.–Sun. 9:30–4:30.*

❺ A few blocks southwest of the Yasuda Building, across from the Century Hyatt, is the **Shinjuku Sumitomo Building** (2-6-1 Nishi-Shinjuku, Shinjuku-ku). Notable for its futuristic architecture, this is actually a 52-story, six-sided building, but because three of its sides are wider, it appears triangular. The center of the building is a long hollow well, and from the ground floor you can look up to see light reflected in by its glass roof. If you are hungry, ride up to the top three floors, where you'll find several restaurants catering to the people who work in the building. Most of the restaurants are open from 10 AM through the evening.

❻ If you walk two blocks south of the Sumitomo Building you'll reach the **Shinjuku NS Building** (2-4-1 Nishi-Shinjuku, Shinjuku-ku), a little dwarfed by the other skyscrapers with only 30 floors; it, too, has a hollow core that directs one's attention to the 24-foot clock in the lobby. Most visitors to this building head directly to the **O.A. Center** on the fifth floor, where around 20 computer companies display their latest wares.

★ **❼** Architect Kenzo Tange's grandiose **Tokyo City Hall** complex, which now dominates this whole area, opened in 1991. Built at a cost of ¥157 billion, it was clearly meant to celebrate the fact that Tokyo's annual budget is bigger than that of the average developing country. Is the intricate lattice facade supposed to invoke a Gothic cathedral or a microchip? Tokyoites either love it or hate it; it's been called everything from "a fitting tribute" to a "forbidding castle." The main building soars 48 stories, splitting on the 33rd floor into two towers; from the observation decks on the 45th floor of both towers you can see—on a clear day—all the way from Mt. Fuji to the Boso Peninsula in Chiba Prefecture. ☺ *Daily 9:30–5. In Aug., the south deck stays open to 9 PM. Both decks closed Dec. 29–Jan. 3.* ☛ *Free.*

❽ Several other buildings in the area have free observation floors: the **Shin-**
juku Center Building (across from the Yasuda Building), on the 53rd
❾ floor; the **Shinjuku Nomura Building** (next to the Yasuda Building), on the 50th floor; and the **Shinjuku Sumitomo Building,** on the 51st floor. However, a more comfortable way of inspecting the horizon is on the Keio Plaza Inter-Continental Hotel's 47th floor; take in the view with some refreshment at the Pole Star Lounge.

Shinjuku

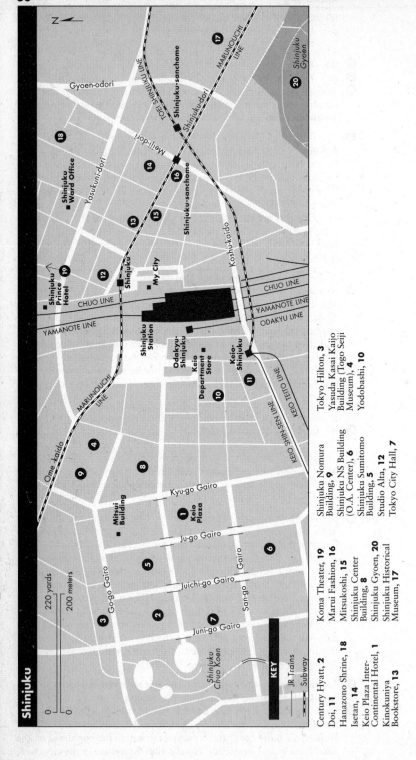

Gyoen-odori

Shinjuku-sanchome

Shinjuku-dori

Meiji-dori

Yasukuni-dori

Shinjuku Ward Office ■

Shinjuku-sanchome

Koshu-kaido

Shinjuku

My City ■

Shinjuku Prince Hotel ■

CHUO LINE

YAMANOTE LINE

CHUO LINE

YAMANOTE LINE

ODAKYU LINE

Shinjuku Station

Odakyu-Shinjuku

Keio Department Store

Keio-Shinjuku

MARUNOUCHI LINE

Ome-kaido

KEIO SHIN-SEN LINE

KEIO TEITO LINE

Kyu-go Gairo

Mitsui Building ■

Keio Plaza

Ju-go Gairo

Juichi-go Gairo

Go-go Gairo

San-go Gairo

Juni-go Gairo

Shinjuku Chuo Koen

220 yards

200 meters

Shinjuku Gyoen

TOEI SHINJUKU LINE

MARUNOUCHI LINE

KEY

—— JR Trains

------ Subway

Century Hyatt, **2**
Doi, **11**
Hanazono Shrine, **18**
Isetan, **14**
Keio Plaza Inter-Continental Hotel, **1**
Kinokuniya Bookstore, **13**

Koma Theater, **19**
Marui Fashion, **16**
Mitsukoshi, **15**
Shinjuku Center Building, **8**
Shinjuku Gyoen, **20**
Shinjuku Historical Museum, **17**

Shinjuku Nomura Building, **9**
Shinjuku NS Building (O.A. Center), **6**
Shinjuku Sumitomo Building, **5**
Studio Alta, **12**
Tokyo City Hall, **7**

Tokyo Hilton, **3**
Yasuda Kasai Kaijo Building (Togo Seiji Museum), **4**
Yodobashi, **10**

As you walk back toward the Shinjuku Station, you may want to stop at a few of Tokyo's leading discount camera stores in the area. Two well-known camera shops are **Yodobashi** (1-11-1 Nishi-Shinjuku, Shinjuku-ku, near Chuo-dori) and **Doi** (1-18-27 Nishi-Shinjuku, Shinjuku-ku, near Kokusai-dori); both shops are about a block from the station. Even if you have no intention of buying, the array of goods on display is a vision in itself.

Eastern Shinjuku

While the west side of Shinjuku is an ambitious expanse of modern high rises, the east side is a labyrinth of streets and alleys packed with department stores, shops, bars, restaurants, theaters, strip shows, and hotels for temporary stays. It starts out as a jumbled mass of shopping stores; as you walk north, the sights become more and more tawdry.

As you leave the station by the east exit (*higashi-guchi*), a huge video screen marks **Studio Alta** (3-24-3 Shinjuku, Shinjuku-ku), a well-known landmark with a crowd usually gathered to look at its flickering images. Beneath the building, which houses a television studio, is the largest subterranean plaza in Japan. Full of shops and restaurants, this is a good place to come during the winter months for something to eat and to watch the melee of people walking around.

Studio Alta is on one end of shop-lined **Shinjuku-dori,** which on Sundays, when the area is closed to traffic, becomes a sea of shoppers. A couple of blocks southeast of Studio Alta is **Kinokuniya Bookstore** (3-17-7 Shinjuku, Shinjuku-ku), its sixth floor devoted to foreign-language books, including 40,000 English titles. Right near Kinokuniya is **Camera no Sakuraya** (3-26-10 Shinjuku, Shinjuku-ku), a discount store for cameras and electronics goods. Farther along on the same side of the street as Kinokuniya is **Isetan** (3-14-1 Shinjuku, Shinjuku-ku), the trendiest of the fashion stores in the neighborhood, with a foreign customer-service counter on the fifth floor. On the opposite side of the street are the two big stores, **Mitsukoshi** (3-29-1 Shinjuku, Shinjuku-ku) and **Marui Fashion** (3-30-16 Shinjuku, Shinjuku-ku).

The **Shinjuku Historical Museum,** still farther southeast along Shinjuku-dori, displays through historical documents, artifacts, and models Shinjuku's growth during the Edo and Showa periods, offering a glimpse of city life in old traditional Japan. *22 San-eicho, Shinjuku-ku,* ☏ *03/3359–2131.* ☞ *¥200 adults, ¥100 children under 18.* ☉ *Tues.–Sun. 9–4:30.*

Retrace your steps and continue a few blocks north of Isetan department store and Yasukuni-dori to **Hanazono Shrine.** Although Hanazono is far from being one of Tokyo's major shrines, it is a tranquil oasis tucked among shops and tall office buildings. Visiting the shrine, which was constructed before Edo Castle, is believed to aid a businessman's commercial prosperity. ☞ *Free.* ☉ *Sunrise–sunset.*

To the north of Yasukuni-dori and west of Hanazono Shrine is the area called **Kabukicho.** After the courtesans were liberated in 1872 and the formalities governing geisha entertainment were dissolved, Kabukicho became Japan's largest center of prostitution until laws against the practice became more strict. In an attempt to change the neighborhood's image after World War II, plans were made to replace the fire-gutted Ginza **Kabuki-za** with a new one in Shinjuku. The plans never came to fruition (the old theater was resurrected), but the area got its name. Today, however, Kabukicho has the **Koma Theater** (1-19-1 Kabukicho, Shinjuku-ku), which houses several discos and bars, as well as a theater with a revolving stage and more than 2,000 seats. The theater serves as a useful central landmark in the district.

Kabukicho is a bewildering maze of bars, discos, strip joints, and theaters. It represents unrefined nightlife at its best, and raunchy seediness at its worst. Neon signs flash the world of various pleasures, and, at the places not to visit, touts try to lure their customers into bars where the ¥18,000 bottle of beer has been made famous. However, if you do not follow these touts, and instead choose a place that looks respectable, there is rarely any problem. Stay away from the cheap *nomiya* (bars) under the railway tracks in Shomben-yokocho. For the Ni-chome (2-chome) area beyond the Koma Theater—where many of the bars are decidedly gay—you might want a knowledgeable guide. But don't be intimidated by the area: It's fun, and one of the least expensive areas of Tokyo in which to engage in nighttime pleasures.

★ ⑳ If you visit Shinjuku during the day and are anxious for some peace of mind, the **Shinjuku Gyoen** (garden) is the place to head for. It's a stiff 20- to 30-minute walk from Shinjuku Station, so you may prefer to hop on the subway (the Marunouchi Line for two stops, to Shinjuku Gyoen-mae Station, which brings you close to the north end of the park). Shinjuku Gyoen was once the estate of the powerful *daimyo* (feudal lord) Naito, but became part of the imperial household after the Meiji Restoration. After World War II it was opened to the public as a national park, and is today a perfect place for leisurely walks, with 150 acres of gardens, artificial hills, ponds with bridges, and thoughtfully placed stone lanterns. The paths wind their way through more than 3,000 different kinds of plants, shrubs, and trees and lead to Japanese-, French-, and English-style gardens, as well as a greenhouse filled with tropical plants. However, the most noted times to visit are during cherry blossom time (early April), when 1,900 trees of 65 different species flower, and in the fall, during the chrysanthemum exhibition. *11 Naitocho, Shinjuku-ku, ☎ 03/3350–0151. ☛ ¥200 adults, ¥50 children. ⊙ 9–4:30. Closed Mon., except in cherry-blossom season.*

WHAT TO SEE AND DO WITH CHILDREN

Amusement Centers

Korakuen. The Korakuen stop on the Marunouchi subway line, about ten minutes from Tokyo, provides access to the Korakuen baseball stadium, now know in its revamped, roofed-over reincarnation as the **Tokyo Dome,** home turf to the Tokyo Giants; a small patch of urban greenery called **Koishikawa Korakuen;** and **Korakuen Yuenchi,** a small amusement center, the chief attractions of which are a giant roller coaster and a "circus train" that does a loop. *1-3-61 Koraku, Bunkyo-ku, ☎ 03/3811–2111. ☛ ¥1,400 adults, ¥700 children under 12. ⊙ Weekdays 10–8, weekends 9:30–8.*

Tokyo Disneyland. Since Tokyo Disneyland opened in 1983, some 10 million visitors a year have been coming to this amusement park, where Mickey-san and his coterie of Disney characters entertain just the way they do in the California and Florida Disney parks.

The easiest way to reach Tokyo Disneyland is by the shuttle bus, which leaves Tokyo Station's Yaesu *kita-guchi* (yaesu north exit) every 30 minutes from 7:30 AM to 7:10 PM (cost: ¥600 adults, ¥300 children under 18). You may also go by subway; from Nihonbashi, take the Tozai Line to Urayasu Station and walk over to the Tokyo Disneyland Bus Terminal for the 15-minute ride (cost: ¥200 adults, ¥100 children). *1-1 Maihama, Urayasu-shi, ☎ 0473/54–0001. There are several types of admission tickets. For example, you can purchase the entrance admission for ¥3,400 (¥3,100 juniors, ¥2,300 children), then buy individual tickets. However, if you plan to see most of the attractions, the Tokyo Disneyland Passport at ¥4,800 (¥4,400 juniors, ¥3,300 children) is the most economical buy. Tickets can be purchased in advance in Tokyo Station, near the Yaesu kita-guchi exit (you'll notice red-jacketed attendants standing outside the booth), or from any travel agent, such as the Japan Travel Bureau. Tokyo Disneyland is open every day 9–7 (Fri. 9–8), except for 6 days in Dec., 6 days in Jan., and 3 days in Feb.*

Toshimaen Amusement Park. This is a large, well-equipped amusement park in the northwest corner of Tokyo. There are four roller coasters, a German carousel, haunted houses, and seven swimming pools. To reach it, take a subway from Tokyo Station to Ikebukuro (Marunouchi Line) and change to a special train that runs frequently on the private Seibu Ikebukuro line to Toshimaen. *3-25-1 Koyama, Nerima-ku, ☎ 03/3990–3131.* ☞ *¥1,600 adults, ¥800 children under 12.* ☞ *Plus amusement tickets are ¥4,000 adults, ¥3,300 children under 12.* ☉ *Daily 10–6.*

Museums

Goto Planetarium. This planetarium, on Aoyama-dori near Shibuya Station, has daily shows displaying the seasonal movements of the constellations, the moons of the universe, and other heavenly bodies projected onto a dome 65 feet in diameter. A special Saturday evening show adds music to the stars. Be warned that the narrative is only in Japanese. *Tokyu Bunka Kaikan, 2-21-12 Shibuya, Shibuya-ku, ☎ 03/3407–7409.* ☞ *¥900 adults, ¥500 children 6–15, ¥300 children under 6.* ☉ *Tues.–Sun. Shows run about an hour continuously from 11:10 AM; the last show begins at 6 PM. No seating after the show begins.*

Nippon Hoso Kyokai (NHK Broadcasting Center). The Japanese National Public Television offers tours around the broadcasting complex where techniques for sound effects and film are displayed. Explanations are given only in Japanese, although there is a pamphlet available in English. Perhaps the most exciting part of the tour is when visitors are permitted to watch an actual filming of a scene and some of the stage sets. An Edo mansion fit for a samurai, for example, seems more authentic than the real thing. *2-2-1 Jinnan, Shibuya-ku, ☎ 03/3465–1111.* ☞ *¥200 adults, ¥150 children under 12.* ☉ *10–6. Closed 2nd Mon. of each month.*

Kotsu Hakubutsukan (Transportation Museum). This is a fun place to take children. Displays explain the early development of the railway system and include a miniature layout of the rail services, as well as Japan's first airplane, which lifted off in 1903. *1-25 Kanda Sudacho, Chiyoda-ku (nearest subway station: Akihabara), ☎ 03/3251–8481.* ☞ *¥300 adults, ¥150 children 4–15.* ☉ *Tues.–Sun. 9:30–4:30.*

Shops

Kiddyland. All the toys and playthings in this toy store (on Omotesando just east of the intersection with Meiji-dori) will surely keep children and teenagers busy. *6-1-9 Jingu-mae, Shibuya-ku (nearest subway* *station: Meiji Jingu-mae),* ☎ *03/3409–3431.* ⊘ *10–8. Closed 3rd Tues. of each month.*

Hakuhinkan (Toy Park). This is reputedly the largest toy shop in Japan. It's right on Chuo-dori. *Hakuhinkan 2F-4F, 8-8-11 Ginza, Chuo-ku (nearest subway station: Shinbashi),* ☎ *03/3571–8008.* ⊘ *Daily 11–8.*

Zoos and Aquariums

Shinagawa Suizokukan. The best feature of Tokyo's small but well-stocked aquarium in southwestern Tokyo is a glass tunnel that you walk through while dozens of species of fish swim around and above you. Alas, there are no guidebooks or explanation panels in English. The aquarium grounds include a park with a saltwater pond and lots of rocks for kids to climb on. Avoid Sundays, when crowds are impossible. Take the local train from Shinagawa to Omorikaigan Station on the Keihin-Kyuko Line. Turn left as you exit the station and follow the ceramic fish on the sidewalk to the first traffic light, then turn right. *Katsushima 3-2-1, Shinagawa-ku,* ☎ *03/3762–3431.* ☛ *¥800 adults, ¥500 children 6–18, ¥300 preschoolers.* ⊘ *Wed.–Mon. 10–5. Dolphin shows four times daily, on a varying schedule. Closed Dec. 29–Jan. 1.*

Tama Dobutsu Koen. Here animals have space to roam, usually with moats to keep them separated from humans. Visitors ride through the Lions Park in a minibus. To reach this zoo, in western Tokyo, take the Keio Line from Shinjuku and transfer at Takahata Fudo Station for the train going to Dobutsu Koen Station. *7-1-1 Hodokubo, Hino-shi,* ☎ *0425/91–1611.* ☛ *¥500 adults, ¥200 children 12–15.* ⊘ *Tues.–Sun. 9:30–4.*

Ueno Dobutsuen. The Ueno Zoo's major attraction is the pair of pandas and their child. However, the zoo is terribly crowded on weekends, and the animals are penned in such small cages it is almost criminal. *9-83 Ueno Koen, Taito-ku,* ☎ *03/3828–5171.* ☛ *¥500 adults, ¥200 children 12–15.* ⊘ *Tues.–Sun. 9:30–4:30 (enter by 4).*

OFF THE BEATEN TRACK

The Arakawa Line. Feeling nostalgic? Take the JR Yamanote Line to Otsuka, cross the street in front of the station, and change to the Arakawa Line—Tokyo's last surviving trolley. West, the line goes to Higashi-Ikebukuro (site of the Sunshine City skyscraper complex, billed as a "complete city within a city" and remarkable only as a complete flop) and Zoshigaya, before turning south to the terminus at Waseda, not far from Waseda University. East, the trolley takes you through the back gardens of old neighborhoods to Oji—once the site of Japan's first Western-style paper mill, built in 1875 by the Oji Paper Manufacturing Company. The mill is long gone, but the memory lingers on at the **Oji Paper Museum,** the only one of its kind in Japan. Some of the exhibits here show the process of milling paper from pulp; others illustrate the astonishing variety of things that can be made from paper itself. *1-1-8 Horifune, Kita-ku,* ☎ *03/3911–3545. Walk south from the trolley stop about 100 meters (yards); the museum is between the Arakawa tracks and those of the JR.* ☛ *¥200 adults, ¥100 children under 12.* ⊘ *Tues.–Sun. 9:30–4:30. Closed national holidays.*

Asakura Sculpture Gallery. In the past two or three years, tourists have begun to "discover" the Nezu and Yanaka areas of Shitamachi (downtown)—much to the dismay of the handful of foreigners who have lived for years in this inexpensive, charming part of the city. To some, the appeal lies in its narrow streets, with their old shops and houses; others are drawn to the fact that many of the greatest figures in the world of modern Japanese culture lived and died in this same area, including novelists Ogai Mori, Soseki Natsume, and Ryunosuke Akutagawa; scholar Tenshin Okakura, who founded the Japan Art Institute; painter Taikan Yokoyama; and sculptors Koun Takamura and Fumio Asakura. If there's one single attraction here, it is probably Asakura's home and studio, converted into a gallery after his death in 1964.

Asakura's work was deeply influenced by Confucian thought, which is expressed symbolically by the arrangement of stones in the extraordinary little pond and rock garden in the central courtyard of the house. The studio is filled with Asakura's works, among them many of his most famous pieces. The tearoom on the opposite side of the courtyard is a haven of quietude from which to contemplate his garden. *7-18-10 Yanaka, Taito-ku, ☎ 03/3821–4549. From the south end of the JR Nippori Station, walk west (Tennoji [temple] will be on the left side of the street) until you reach a police box. Turn right, then right again at the end of the street; the museum is a 3-story black building on the right, a few hundred meters (yards) down. ☛ ¥300 adults, ¥150 children 6–15. ☉ Tues.–Thurs. and weekends 9:30–4:30.*

Asakusabashi and Ryogoku. Sumo, the centuries-old national sport of Japan, is not to be taken lightly—as anyone who has ever seen a sumo wrestler will testify. Indeed, sheer weight is almost a prerequisite to success; one of the current champions tips the scales at a touch under 570 pounds. There are various techniques of pushing, grappling, and throwing in sumo, but the basic rules are exquisitely simple: Except for hitting below the belt (which is all a sumo wrestler wears) and striking with the closed fist, almost anything goes. The contestants square off in a dirt ring about 15 feet in diameter and charge; the first one to step out of the ring, or touch the ground with anything but the soles of his feet, loses.

There are no free agents in sumo. To compete, you must belong to a *heya* (stable) run by a retired wrestler who has purchased that right from the Sumo Association. Sumo is very much a closed world, hierarchical and formal. Youngsters recruited into the sport live in the stable dormitory, doing all the community chores and waiting on their seniors while they learn; when they rise high enough in the tournament rankings, they acquire servant-apprentices of their own.

While tournaments and exhibitions are held in different parts of the country at different times, all the stables in the Sumo Association—now some 30 in number—are in Tokyo. Most of them are clustered on both sides of the Sumida River near the new Kokugikan (National Sumo Arena), with its distinctive green roof, in the areas called Asakusabashi and Ryogoku. One of the easiest to find is the **Tatsunami Stable** (3-26-2 Ryogoku), only a few steps from the west end of the JR Sobu Line Ryogoku Station (turn left when you go through the turnstile and left again as you come out on the street; then walk along the station building to the second street on the right). Another, a few blocks farther south, where the Shuto Expressway passes overhead, is the **Izutsu Stable** (Ryogoku 2-2-7). Wander this area when the wrestlers are in town (Jan., May, and Sept. are best bets), and you are more than likely to see some of them on the streets, cleaving the air like leviathans in their wood clogs and kimonos; come 7–11 AM, and you can peer through the doors and windows of the stable to watch them in practice sessions.

★ **Sengakuji.** One day in the year 1701, a young provincial baron named Asano Takumi no Kami, serving an official term of duty at the shogun's court, attacked and seriously wounded a courtier named Kira Yoshinaka. Kira had demanded the usual tokens of esteem that someone in his high position would expect for his goodwill; Asano refused, and Kira had humiliated him in public to the point where he could no longer contain his rage.

Kira survived the attack. Asano, for daring to draw his sword in the confines of Edo Castle, was ordered to commit suicide; his family line was abolished and his fief confiscated. Headed by Oishi Kuranosuke, the clan steward, 47 of Asano's loyal retainers vowed revenge. Kira was rich and well protected; Asano's retainers were *ronin*—masterless samurai. It took them almost two years of planning, subterfuge, and hardship, but on the night of December 14, 1702, they stormed Kira's villa in Edo, cut off his head, and brought it in triumph to Asano's tomb at Sengakuji, the family temple. Oishi and his followers were also sentenced to commit suicide—which they accepted as the reward, not the price, of their honorable vendetta—and were buried in the temple graveyard with their lord.

The event captured the imagination of the Japanese like nothing else in their history; through the centuries it has become the national epic, the last word on the subject of loyalty and sacrifice, celebrated in every medium from Kabuki to film. The temple still stands and the graves are still there, the air around them filled with the smoke from bundles of incense that visitors still lay reverently on the tombstones.

The story gets even better. There's a small museum on the temple grounds with a collection of weapons and other memorabilia of the event; one of these items dispels forever the myth of Japanese vagueness and indirection in the matter of contracts and formal documents. Kira's family, naturally, also wanted to give him a proper burial, but the law insisted that this could not be done without his head. They asked for it back, and Oishi—mirror of chivalry that he was—agreed. He entrusted it to the temple, and the priests wrote him a receipt, which survives even now in the corner of a dusty glass case. "Item," it begins, "One head." *2-11-1 Takanawa, Minato-ku,* ☎ *03/3441–5560. Take the Toei Asakusa subway line to the Sengakuji stop, turn right as you exit, and walk up the hill. The temple is just past the first traffic light, on the left.* ☛ *To the museum:* ¥200 *adults,* ¥100 *children under 12.* ⊙ *Daily 9–4. Closed Dec. 28–Jan. 3.*

SHOPPING

By Kiko Itasaka   You have doubtless heard horror stories about prices in Japan. Many of them are true. Yes, a cup of coffee can cost $10, a melon can cost $100, and a taxi ride from the airport to central Tokyo costs about $250. The yen has appreciated drastically over the past few years, making the U.S. dollar in Japan seem to have the power of a peso. This does not mean that potential shoppers should get discouraged; shopping in Japan isn't always impossibly expensive, and bargains can still be found. If you need gifts and souvenirs you will still be able to find them, though shopping in Tokyo requires a certain amount of ingenuity and effort.

Some items are better bought at home, such as European designer clothing or imported fruit—but why would anyone go all the way to Tokyo to buy these items? The best shoppers in Japan know that they should concentrate on Japanese goods that are hard to find in America, such as crafts, toys, and kimonos. These are all items that can be found in areas that are easy to reach by public transportation. Try to avoid taxis and instead use Tokyo's convenient subways and trains. Traffic and the byzantine mazes of streets make travel by taxi time-consuming and inordinately expensive. The shopper with only limited time should stick to hotel arcades, department stores, and stores that specifically cater to foreigners. For those with more time and a sense of adventure, Tokyo shopping can be fascinating.

Remember that in some smaller stores and markets prices might be listed with *kanji* (Japanese pictographs derived from Chinese written characters) instead of Arabic numbers. In such cases, just ask, "How much?" It's a phrase that all Japanese will recognize, because it is the name of a popular TV game show in Japan, and someone will either tell you or write down the price for you.

Shopping in Tokyo is generally an extremely pleasant experience, because salespeople are often helpful and polite. In major stores, many people speak at least enough English for you to complete your transactions. There is a saying in Japan that the customer equals God. Upon entering a store, you will be greeted with a bow and the word *irasshaimase* (welcome). The salespeople are definitely there to serve you.

In 1989 Japan instituted an across-the-board 3% value added tax (VAT) in place of past taxes imposed on luxury goods, as well as on restaurant and hotel bills. This tax can be avoided at the duty-free airport shops; however, because these places tend to have higher profit margins, any tax savings is often offset by the higher cost of goods.

Stores in Tokyo generally open around 10 or 11 and close around 7 or 8.

Other shopping options may be found in the Exploring Tokyo section earlier in this chapter.

Shopping Districts

Ginza

Ginza was the first entertainment and shopping district in Tokyo, dating back to the Edo period (1603–1868). Tokyo's first department store, Mitsukoshi, was founded in this area, which once consisted of long, willow-lined avenues. The willows have long since gone, and the streets are now lined with department stores and boutiques. The exclusive stores in this area feature quality and selective merchandise at higher prices. Here it is not unusual to see a well-turned out Japanese woman in a kimono on a shopping spree, accompanied by her daughter, who is exquisitely dressed in a Chanel suit. *Nearest train station: Yurakucho (JR Yamanote Line); nearest subway stations: Ginza (Marunouchi, Ginza, and Hibiya lines), Ginza-itchome (Yurakucho Line).*

Shibuya

This area is primarily an entertainment district filled with movie theaters, restaurants, and bars, mostly geared toward teenagers and young adults. The shopping also caters to these groups, with many reasonably priced smaller shops and a few department stores that are casual

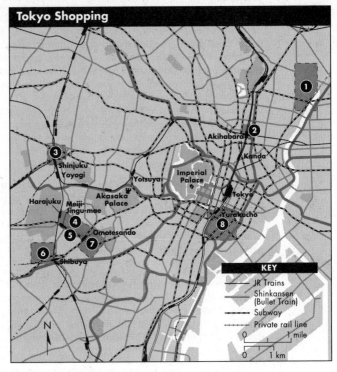

yet chic. *Nearest train station: Harajuku (JR Yamanote Line); nearest subway station: Hanzomon (Ginza Line).*

Shinjuku

Amid the honky-tonk atmosphere of this bustling area, which includes the red-light and gay districts of Tokyo, are some of the city's most fashionable department stores. Shinjuku's merchandise reflects the crowds—young, stylish, and slightly flashy. In addition to clothing, this area features a cluster of electronic-goods stores. *Nearest train station: Shinjuku (JR Yamanote Line); nearest subway stations: Shinjuku (Marunouchi and Toei Shinjuku lines).*

Harajuku

All teenagers seem to congregate in Harajuku (the shopping and residential area that extends southeast from Harajuku station along both sides of Omotesando and Meiji-dori), particularly on the main avenue known as Takeshita-dori. A wild sense of fashion prevails, from '50s greaser looks to '60s mod styles to a variety of assorted looks that are perhaps indicative of what will be the rage in the year 2000. The average age on this street is clearly under 20, and maybe even under 16. Teens all over the world are strapped for cash, so, not surprisingly, everything in this area is moderately priced. The multitude of tiny stores offer not only clothing and accessories but also a lot of kitsch. *Nearest train station: Harajuku (JR Yamanote Line); nearest subway station: Meiji Jingu-mae (Chiyoda Line).*

Omotesando

Known as the Champs-Elysées of Tokyo, this long, wide avenue that runs from Aoyama-dori to Meiji Jingu, is lined with cafés and designer boutiques. Boutiques and cafés, however, are not the only attractions. You'll find a number of antiques and print shops, as well as one of the best toy shops in Tokyo—Kiddyland (*see* What to See and Do with Children, above). Closed to traffic on Sundays, Omotesando is for browsers, strollers, and those who like to relax over café au lait before sauntering into the next store. *Nearest subway station: Omotesando (Chiyoda and Hanzomon lines).*

Aoyama

Shopping in Aoyama is an aesthetically pleasing experience, but it can empty your wallet in no time: This is where many of the leading Japanese and Western designers have boutiques. Although the prices of most European and American designers will be high, Japanese designer clothes are 30%–40% lower than they are in the United States. Even if you do not want to buy anything, you'll have fun simply observing the sense of display: Aoyama tends to be a showcase, not merely of couture, but of the latest concepts in commercial architecture and interior design. In fact, shopping here is like to walking through an art gallery—enjoying the masterpieces, reveling in the atmosphere, and not bothering with the price tags. *Nearest subway station: Omotesando (Chiyoda and Hanzomon lines).*

Akihabara

For the camera and electronic-goods buff who wants to see everything available on the market, Akihabara is high-tech heaven, with its endless multistory buildings. Walkman and portable CD players were on sale here long before they made it across the ocean. The best deals in Japan may be found here, but in general, prices are lower in the United States. *Nearest train station: Akihabara (JR Yamanote Line); nearest subway station: Akihabara (Hibiya Line).*

Asakusa

While sightseeing in this area, take the time to stroll through its arcades. Many of the wares are the kind of souvenirs that you would expect to find on sale at any tourist stop, but if you look a little harder, you will find shops that have tortoiseshell accessories, beautiful wood combs, delicate fans, and other gift items. Venture to some of the back streets, where the small shops have been in business for many generations and offer fine traditional goods. *Nearest subway station: Asakusa (Toei Asakusa and Ginza lines).*

Gifts

The best presents and gifts from Japan are those that are uniquely Japanese. Obviously you do not want to buy a Gucci bag that would cost far less at home. A wide range of interesting things, from traditional crafts to kitsch examples of popular culture, is available at reasonable prices.

Ceramics

Ceramics and pottery in Japan are fragile and cumbersome, but they make wonderful gifts if you are willing to take the trouble of bringing the packages home. In the 16th century, the art of making pottery flourished with the popularity and demand for tea-ceremony utensils. Feudal lords from all over Japan competed to have the finest wares, and as a result, distinctive styles of pottery developed in various regions. Some of the more prominent pottery centers are Arita in Kyushu, where the ceramic ware often features patterns with flowers and birds; Mashiko, outside of Tokyo in Tochigi Prefecture, where the pottery has a simple and rough, dark brown glaze; and Kasama, in Ibaraki Prefecture, with its unique pottery glaze made from ash and ground rocks.

Those who cannot take the time to travel all over Japan can try Tokyo's specialty shops or department stores, which tend to have fairly complete selections of wares.

Tachikichi. Pottery from different localities around the country is sold here. *5-5-8 Ginza, Chuo-ku (nearest subway station: Higashi-Ginza),* ☎ *03/3571–2924.* ☉ *Mon.–Sat. 11–6:30.*

Kisso. This store offers an excellent variety of ceramics in modern design, using traditional glazes, as well as a restaurant and a gift shop. *Axis Bldg. B1, 5-17-1 Roppongi, Minato-ku (nearest subway station: Roppongi),* ☎ *03/3582–4191.* ☉ *Mon.–Sat. 11:30–2 and 5:30–10.*

Dolls

Many types of traditional dolls are available in Japan, each with its own charm. **Kokeshi** dolls are long, cylindrical, painted, and made of wood, with no arms or legs. Fine examples of Japanese folk art, they date back to the Edo period (1603–1868). **Daruma** are papier-mâché dolls with rounded bottoms and faces that are often painted with amusing expressions. They are constructed so that no matter how you push them, they roll and remain upright. Legend has it that they are modeled after a Buddhist priest who maintained his seated lotus position for long periods of time. **Hakata** dolls, made in Hakata City of Kyushu, are clay dolls of traditional Japanese figures, such as geisha or samurai.

Kyugetsu. In business for more than a century, Kyugetsu offers every kind of doll imaginable. *1-20-4 Yanagibashi, Taito-ku (nearest subway station: Asakusabashi),* ☎ *03/3861–5511.* ☉ *Daily 9:15–6.*

Electronics

The best bargains for electronics are found at home, not in Japan. If you're curious to see what's available, go to the area around Akihabara Station, where you'll find more than 200 stores proffering stereos, refrigerators, CD players, and anything else that can be plugged in. If you must buy something, look for shops that sell products that are made for export. These will come with instructions written in English rather than Japanese, and if you have a tourist visa in your passport, you can purchase these export models duty free. One such store is **Yamagiwa** (4-1-1 Soto Kanda, Chiyoda-ku; nearest subway station: Akihabara).

Folk Crafts

Japanese folk crafts, called *mingei*, are simple and sturdy, yet imbued with Japanese aesthetics. They are unique, durable, and reasonably priced. While folk crafts may lack the sophistication of a delicately painted scroll, they do have a basic beauty that speaks for itself. Many objects fall into this category, such as bamboo wares, fabrics, paper boxes, dolls, and toys.

Bingo-ya. A complete selection of crafts from all over Japan can be found here. *10-6 Wakamatsucho, Shinjuku (nearest subway station: Waseda),* ☎ *03/3202–8778.* ☉ *Tues.–Sun. 10–7.*

Japan Traditional Craft Center. This gallery is a good place to familiarize yourself with the wonders of Japanese folk crafts, the creation of which is demonstrated in videos. Many items are for sale. *Plaza 246, 2F: 3-1-1 Minami Aoyama, Minato-ku (nearest subway station: Gaien-mae),* ☎ *03/3403–2460.* ☉ *Fri.–Wed. 10–6.*

Oriental Bazaar. Here are floors of just about everything you want in a traditional Japanese (or Chinese or Korean) handicraft souvenir, from painted screens to pottery to antique chests, at fairly reasonable prices. Kimonos are one flight down. *5-9-13 Jingu-mae (nearest sub-*

way station: Meiji Jingu-mae), Shibuya-
Fri.–Wed. 9:30–6:30.

Kimonos

Kimonos in Japan are usually only worn on special occasio
weddings or graduations, and, like tuxedos in the United State
often rented instead of purchased. They are extremely expensive an
difficult to maintain. A wedding kimono, for example, can cost as much
as ¥1 million.

In general, most foreigners, who are unwilling to pay this much for a
garment that they probably want to use as a bathrobe, settle for a secondhand or antique silk kimono. These vary in price and quality. You
can get one for as low as ¥1,000, but to find one in decent condition,
you should expect to pay about ¥5,000. If you are willing to forgo silk,
new cotton kimonos, known as *yukata,* with attractive geometric blue-
and-white designs, are about ¥5,000. Department stores usually have
good selections of new silk kimonos, but some smaller stores feature
less expensive or secondhand goods.

Hayashi. This store specializes in ready-made kimonos, sashes, and dyed
yukata (cotton summer robes). *1-7-23 Uchisaiwaicho, Chiyoda-ku
(nearest subway station: Hibiya),* ☎ *03/3501–4014.* ☉ *Mon.–Sat.
10–7, Sun. 10–6.*

Lacquerware

For its history, diversity, and fine workmanship, lacquerware rivals ceramics as the traditional Japanese craft nonpareil. One warning: Lacquerware thrives on humidity. Cheaper pieces usually have plastic
rather than wood underneath; because they won't shrink and crack in
dry climates, they make safer—and no less attractive—buys.

Inachu. Specializing in lacquerware from the town of Wajima, a famous
crafts center on the Noto Peninsula, facing the Sea of Japan (*see* Chapter 5, The Japan Alps), this is one of the most elegant (and expensive)
crafts shops in Tokyo. *1-5-2 Akasaka, Minato-ku (nearest subway
station: Kokkai Gijido-mae),* ☎ *03/3582–4451.* ☉ *Mon.–Sat. 10–6.*
Tokyo Lacquerware. A good place to browse for less expensive pieces
in a variety of styles. *2-11-13 Minami-Aoyama, Minato-ku (nearest subway station: Gaien-mae),* ☎ *03/3401–5118.* ☉ *Mon.–Fri. 10–6:30,
Sat. 10–5.*

Paper

What packs light and flat in your suitcase, won't break, doesn't cost
much, and makes great gifts? The answer is traditional handmade
paper, called *washi,* which the Japanese make in thousands of colors,
textures, and designs, and fashion into an astonishing array of useful
and decorative objects.

Ozu Gallery. In business since the 17th century, this shop has one of
the largest washi showrooms in the city and its own gallery of antique
papers. *2-6-3 Nihonbashi-Honcho, Chuo-ku (nearest subway station:
Shin-Nihonbashi),* ☎ *03/3663–8788.* ☉ *Mon.–Sat. 10–6.*
Yushima no Kobayashi. Here you can also tour a papermaking work-
shop, and learn the art of paper-folding, or *origami. 1-7-14 Yushima,
Bunkyo-ku (nearest subway station: Yushima),* ☎ *03/3811–4025.* ☉
Mon.–Sat. 9–5.

Pearls

Japan remains one of the best places in the world to buy pearls. They
will not be inexpensive, but pearls of the same quality cost consider-

tates. It is best to go to a reputable dealer
        will be guaranteed the best in pearls and will

        ...kimoto created his technique for cultured pearls
        ...., the name Mikimoto has become associated with
        ... in pearls. Although the prices at Mikimoto are high,
        ...nore for pearls of this quality in the United States. *4-*
...o-ku (nearest subway station: Ginza), ☎ *03/3535–4611.*
...es. 10:30–6.

... Gallery. Tasaki offers pearls at slightly lower prices than
...moto. The store has several showrooms and offers tours that
dem... .rate the technique of culturing pearls and explain the maintenance and care of these gems. *1-3-3 Akasaka, Minato-ku (nearest subway station: Kokkai Gijido-mae)*, ☎ *03/5561–8881.* ⊙ *Daily 9–6:30.*

Arcades and Shopping Centers

For shoppers who do not have the time or energy to dash about Tokyo in search of the perfect gifts, there are arcades and shopping centers that carry a wide selection of merchandise. Many of these establishments are used to dealing with foreigners.

Axis. On the first floor of this complex, on Gaien-higashi-dori in Roppongi, is **Living Motif,** a home-furnishings shop with high-tech foreign and Japanese goods of exquisite design. On the basement floor is **Nuno,** a fabric shop that sells traditional Japanese materials with modern touches. The fabrics are all creations of Junichi Arai, who once designed fabrics for such famous Japanese designers as Rei Kawakubo of Comme des Garçons and Issey Miyake. Be sure to look at the restaurant called **Kisso,** which sells, along with lacquered chopsticks and fine baskets, an extraordinary selection of unique, modern handmade ceramics in contemporary designs, shapes, and colors. *5-17-1 Roppongi, Minato-ku (nearest subway station: Roppongi).*

International Shopping Arcade. This collection of shops in Hibiya has a range of goods (including cameras, electronics, pearls, and kimonos) and a sales staff with excellent English. Not only is the arcade conveniently located near the Imperial Hotel and TIC (Tourist Information Center), but the shops are all tax-free. *1-7-3 Uchisaiwaicho, Chiyoda-ku (nearest subway station: Hibiya).*

Boutiques

Japanese boutiques can often make you forget you are shopping. Of course, the function of these boutiques is to sell clothes, but in many cases you will not be aware that crass materialism is at work. As much attention is paid to the interior decoration and the lighting as to the clothing, so you have a sense that you are viewing works of art. Although many Japanese designers are represented in department stores for convenient shopping, you'll get a sense of Japanese aesthetics by visiting the simple and elegant boutiques in Aoyama and Omotesando; the stores are conveniently located within walking distance of one another. Even if you don't buy anything, you will be sure to enjoy yourself.

Comme Des Garçons. This is one of the earliest and still most popular "minimalist" design houses, where you can get almost any kind of $70 tank top you want, as long as it's black. *5-11-5 Minami-Aoyama, Minato-ku (nearest subway station: Omotesando)*, ☎ *03/3407–2480.* ⊙ *Daily 11–8.*

From 1st Building (5-3-10 Minami-Aoyama, Minato-ku; nearest subway station: Omotesando). This building houses the boutiques of several of Japan's leading designers, including **Issey Miyake** and **Alpha Cubic,** as well as several smart restaurants. "Produced" by Yasuhiro Hamano, whose atelier designs many of Tokyo's trendiest commercial spaces, From 1st is one of the earliest and best examples of the city's upmarket vertical malls.

Hanae Mori Building. This glass-mirrored structure, designed by Kenzo Tange, houses the designs of the doyenne of Japanese fashion, Hanae Mori, whose clothing has a classic look with a European influence. The café on the first floor is a good place to observe Japan's beautiful people. *3-6-1 Kita-Aoyama, Minato-ku (nearest subway station: Omotesando),* ☎ *03/3406-1021.* ⊗ *Daily 10:30–7.*

Koshino Junko. Available here are upmarket clothes and accessories with a European accent, for the sophisticated shopper. *6-5-36 Minami-Aoyama, Minato-ku (nearest subway station: Omotesando),* ☎ *03/3406-7370.* ⊗ *10–7.*

Department Stores

Today, most Japanese department stores are part of conglomerates that own railways, real estate, and even baseball teams. These stores often include travel agencies, theaters, and art galleries. A shopper can easily spend an afternoon or even an entire day shopping, especially because a cluster of reasonably priced restaurants is usually located on the top or basement floor. Many floors have coffee shops for lighter meals.

Major department stores accept credit cards and provide shipping services. Some staff will speak English. If you are having communication difficulties, someone will eventually come to the rescue. On the first floor of most stores is a general-information booth that has maps of the store in English. Because many of the stores are confusing, these guides are useful.

A trip to a Japanese department store is not merely a shopping excursion; it will also provide insights into Japanese culture. Arrive just before opening hours, and you will witness a ceremony with all of the pomp of the changing of the guard at Buckingham Palace. Right at opening time, two immaculately groomed young women will face the customers from behind the doors and bow ceremoniously, after which they open the doors. As you walk through the store, you will find that everyone is standing at attention, bowing and welcoming you. Notice the uniformity of the angle of the bows—many stores have training sessions in which new employees are taught this art.

For yet another look at Japanese culture, head for the basement floor, which usually houses food halls. Here you will see more clearly than anywhere else just what the average Japanese person eats. Needless to say, the fish section is large, and the meat prices are exorbitant. Many counters have small samples of food for the customers' benefit. If you give the impression that you are planning to make a purchase, you may be given the opportunity to try some of these samples.

Ginza/Nihonbashi

Matsuya. In contrast to the generally refined shopping in the Ginza/Nihonbashi area, this slightly disorganized department store is a welcome change. The merchandise here is geared toward a younger crowd, and shoppers with the patience to comb through the offerings will be rewarded with many good finds, particularly in the sections for young women's clothing. *3-6-1 Ginza, Chuo-ku (nearest subway station: Ginza),* ☎ *03/3567–1211.* ⊙ *10:30–7:30. Closed 2nd and 3rd Tues. of every month.*

Matsuzakaya. Unlike nearby Mistsukoshi, Matsuzakaya was founded in Nagoya and still commands the loyalties of shoppers with origins in western Japan. Style-conscious Tokyoites tend to find the Matsuzaka sense of fashion a bit countrified. *6-10-1 Ginza, Chuo-ku (nearest subway station: Ginza),* ☎ *03/3572–1111.* ⊙ *Thurs.–Tues. 10:30–7:30.*

Mitsukoshi. Founded in 1673 as a dry-goods store, in later years Mitsukoshi became one of the first stores to introduce Western merchandise to Japan. It has retained its image of quality and excellence, with a particularly strong representation of Western fashion designers, such as Chanel, Lanvin, and Givenchy. Mitsukoshi also has a fine selection of traditional Japanese goods. Catering to a distinguished clientele, it is one of Japan's most prestigious department stores. *1-41 Nihonbashi Muromachi, Chuo-ku (nearest subway station: Mitsukoshi-mae),* ☎ *03/3241–3311.* ⊙ *Tues.–Sun. 10–6:30. 4-6-16 Ginza, Chuo-ku,* ☎ *03/3562–1111.* ⊙ *Tues.–Sun. 10–7.*

Takashimaya. The kimono department here, one of the best in Tokyo, draws many brides-to-be shopping for their weddings. In addition to a complete selection of traditional crafts, antiques, and curios, Takashimaya offers both Japanese and Western designer goods, and so has a broad, upscale appeal. *2-4-1 Nihonbashi, Chuo-ku (nearest subway station: Ginza),* ☎ *03/3211–4111.* ⊙ *Weekdays 10–7, weekends 10–6:30. Closed 2 Wednesdays a month, on a varying schedule.*

Wako. This is a specialty store that borders on being a department store. With a reputation for quality at high prices, Wako is particularly known for its glassware. It is also known for its very pretty saleswomen, who tend to marry well-to-do customers. *4-5-11 Ginza, Chuo-ku (nearest subway station: Ginza),* ☎ *03/3562–2111.* ⊙ *Mon.–Sat. 10:30–6.*

Shibuya

Parco. Owned by Seibu (*see below*), Parco is actually not one store but four, all located near one another. Parco Part 1, Part 2, Part 3, and Part 4, as they are called, are in fact vertical malls filled with small retail stores and boutiques. Parts 1 and 4 cater to a very young crowd, Part 2 houses mainly designer fashions, and Part 3 sells a mixture of men's and women's fashions and household goods. *15-1 Udagawacho, Shibuya-ku (nearest subway station: Shibuya),* ☎ *03/3464–5111.* ⊙ *Daily 10–8:30.*

Seibu. The main branch of this department store is rather out of the main shopping course, in Ikebukuro. The Shibuya branch, while smaller, is more manageable than the Ikebukuro branch, where even many Japanese customers get lost. Seibu is a leading member of a group of stores that owns a railway line and a baseball team, the Seibu Lions. When the Lions win the pennant, prepare to go shopping—all of the Seibu stores have major sales on all merchandise the following day. This store has an excellent selection of household goods, from furniture to china and lacquerware. *21-1 Udagawa-cho, Shibuya-ku (nearest subway station: Shibuya),* ☎ *03/3462–0111.* ⊙ *11–8. Closed the 2nd and 3rd Wed. of every month.*

Tokyu. A standard department store, Tokyu offers a good selection of imported clothing, accessories, and home furnishings. *2-24-1 Dogenzaka, Shibuya-ku (nearest subway station: Shibuya),* ☎ *03/3477–3111.* ⊙ *10–7:30. Closed 1st and 3rd Tues. of every month.*

Tokyu Hands. Known commonly as just "Hands," this specialty-hobby store is crowded any day, any time. It offers an excellent selection of carpentry tools, sewing accessories, kitchen goods, plants, and an impressive assortment of other related do-it-yourself merchandise. The toy department is chock-full of kitschy items, such as plastic foods, and the stationery department has a comprehensive selection of Japanese papers. *12-18 Udagawa-cho, Shibuya-ku (nearest subway station: Shibuya),* ☎ *03/5489–5111.* ☺ *10–8. Closed 2nd and 3rd Mon. of each month.*

Shinjuku

Isetan. Often called the Bloomingdale's of Japan—a description that does not quite do this store justice—Isetan has become a favorite with shoppers of all ages, featuring one of the most complete selections of Japanese designers in one place. For those who want distinctive designer looks but not the high prices, the store includes many spin-offs. In addition to European designers, a number of Americans are represented, such as Calvin Klein and Norma Kamali. Don't be surprised if the fit is a little different from that in America—these clothes are made specifically for the Japanese. China, stationery, furniture, you name it—all reflect the general tone of Isetan: high quality and interesting design. Look at the folk-crafts department for a small but good selection of fans, table mats, and other gifts. *3-14-1 Shinjuku, Shinjuku-ku (nearest subway station: Shinjuku),* ☎ *03/3352–1111.* ☺ *10–7:30. Closed Wed., except in Mar.*

Keio. This no-nonsense department store has a standard but complete selection of merchandise. *1-1-4 Nishi-Shinjuku, Shinjuku-ku (nearest subway station: Shinjuku),* ☎ *03/3342–2111.* ☺ *Fri.–Wed. 10–7.*

Marui. More than a department store, Marui is a group of specialty stores that seem to be spawning all over Shinjuku. Of the most interest are the fashion stores—Young Fashion and Men's. Wildly successful for its easy credit policies, Marui attracts a number of younger shoppers simply because it is the only place where they can get credit. The merchandise, too, caters to the young. Twice a year, in February and July, prices are slashed dramatically in major clearance sales, when incredible bargains can be found. If you are in the neighborhood, you will know exactly when the sales are taking place: The lines will extend into the street and around the block. (Let it not be said that Japanese men do not care about fashion. The most enthusiastic customers line up from 6 AM for the men's sales.) *3-30-16 Shinjuku, Shinjuku-ku (nearest subway station: Shinjuku),* ☎ *03/3354–0101.* ☺ *Thurs.–Tues. 11–8.*

Odakyu. Slightly snazzier than neighboring Keio (*see above*), Odakyu is a very family-oriented store, particularly good for children's clothing. Across the street from the main building is Odakyu Halc, with a varied selection of home furnishings and interior goods on its upper floors. *1-1-3 Nishi-Shinjuku, Shinjuku-ku (nearest subway station: Shinjuku),* ☎ *03/3342–1111.* ☺ *Wed.–Mon. 10–7.*

DINING

By Jared Lubarsky

At last count, there were more than 187,000 bars and restaurants in Tokyo; wining and dining is a major component in the local way of life. Japanese companies nationwide spend about $65 million a day (that, at least, is what they report to the tax authorities) on business entertainment, and a good slice of that is spent in Tokyo.

That gives you your first caveat: All that spending on company tabs tends to drive up the bill, and dining out can be hideously expensive.

The other side of that coin, of course, is that Tokyo's 187,000 choices also include a fair number of bargains—good cooking of all sorts, at prices the traveler on a budget can handle. The options, in fact, go all the way down to street food and *yakitori* (Japanese-style chicken kebab) joints under railroad trestles, where the Japanese go when they have to spend their own money. Food and drink, incidentally, are safe wherever you go.

Tokyo is not really an international city yet; in many ways, it is still stubbornly provincial. Whatever the rest of the world has pronounced good, however, eventually makes its way here—sometimes in astonishing variety. (The Highlander Bar in the Hotel Okura, for example, stocks 224 different brands of Scotch whisky, 48 of them single malts.) French, Italian, Chinese, Indian, Middle Eastern, Latin, East European: It's hard to think of a national cuisine of any prominence that goes unrepresented, as Japanese chefs by the thousands go abroad, learn their craft at great restaurants, and bring it home to this city.

Restaurants in Japan naturally expect most of their clients to be Japanese, and the Japanese are the world's champion modifiers. Only the most serious restaurateurs refrain from editing out some of the authenticity of foreign cuisines; in areas like Shibuya, Harajuku, and Shinjuku, all too many of the foreign restaurants cater to students and young office workers, who come for the *fun'iki* (the atmosphere) but can't make much of an informed judgment about the food. Choose your bistro or trattoria carefully, and expect to pay dearly for the real thing—but count also on the fact that Tokyo's best is world-class.

Here are a few general hints and observations. Tokyo's finest hotels also have some of the city's first-rate places to eat and drink. (Alas, this is not always the case elsewhere.) A good number of France's two- and three-star restaurants have established branches and joint ventures in Tokyo, and they regularly send their chefs over to supervise. Some of them stay, find backers, and open restaurants of their own. The style almost everywhere is nouvelle cuisine: small portions, with picture-perfect garnishes and light sauces. More and more, you find interesting fusions of French and Japanese culinary traditions. Meals are served in poetically beautiful presentations, in bowls and dishes of different shapes and patterns; fresh Japanese ingredients, like *shimeji* mushrooms and local wild vegetables, are often used.

Tokyoites know and like French food. They have less of a chance, unfortunately, to experience the real range and virtuosity of Italian cuisine; only a small handful of the city's Italian restaurants would measure up to Italian standards. Indian food here, however, is consistently good and relatively inexpensive. Chinese food is the most consistently modified; it can be quite appetizing, but for repertoire and richness of taste, travelers coming here through Hong Kong will be disappointed. Significantly, Tokyo has no Chinatown.

A few pointers are in order on the geography of food and drink. The farther "downtown" you go—into Shitamachi—the less likely you are to find the real thing in foreign cuisines. There is superb Japanese food all over the city, but aficionados of sushi swear (with excellent reason) by Tsukiji; the sushi bars in the area around the central fish market tend to have the best ingredients, serve the biggest portions, and charge the most reasonable prices. Asakusa takes pride in its tempura restaurants, but tempura is reliable almost everywhere, especially at branches of the well-established, citywide chains. Every department store and skyscraper office building in Tokyo has at least one whole floor devoted to restaurants; none has any great distinction, but all are inexpensive and quite passable places to lunch.

The quintessential Japanese restaurant is the *ryotei*, a large, villalike establishment, usually walled off from the bustle of the outside world and containing a number of small, private dining rooms. The rooms are all in traditional style, with tatami-mat floors, low tables, and a hanging scroll or a flower arrangement in the alcove. One or more of the staff is assigned to each room to serve the many dishes that comprise the meal, pour your sake, and provide light conversation. ("Waitress" is the wrong word; "attendant" is closer, but there really isn't a suitable term in English.) A ryotei is an adventure, an encounter with foods you've never seen before, and with a graceful, almost ritualized style of service that is unique to Japan and centuries old. Many parts of the city are proverbial for their ryotei; the top houses tend to be in Akasaka, Tsukiji, Asakusa, and nearby Yanagibashi, and Shinbashi.

Dining out in Tokyo does not ordinarily demand a great deal in the way of formal attire. It it's a business meal, of course, and your hosts or guests are Japanese, a conservative approach is advisable: for men, a suit and tie; for women, a dress or suit in a basic color, stockings, and a minimum of jewelry. On your own, you'll find that only a very few of the upscale Western venues (mainly the French and Continental restaurants in hotels) will even insist on ties for gentlemen; follow the unspoken dress codes you'd observe at home, and you're unlikely to go wrong. For Japanese-style dining on tatami floors, keep two things in mind: Wear shoes that are easy to slip on and off; and choose clothing you'll be comfortable in for a few hours with your legs gathered under you.

Price-category estimates for the restaurants below are based on the cost of an average meal (three courses, if Western style) per person, exclusive of drinks, taxes, and service charges; thus, a restaurant listed as **$$** can easily slide up a category to **$$$** when it comes time to pay the bill.

A 3% national consumer tax is added to all restaurant bills. Another 3% local tax is added to the bill if it exceeds ¥7,500. At more expensive restaurants, a 10%–15% service charge is also added to the bill. Tipping is not necessary.

Note that business hours indicate when the last order of the evening is accepted, not when the restaurant actually closes.

CATEGORY	COST*
$$$$	over ¥10,000
$$$	¥6,000–¥10,000
$$	¥3,000–¥6,000
$	under ¥3,000

Cost is per person without tax, service, or drinks

Japanese

Aoyama

$$ **Higo Batten.** This restaurant specializes in a style called *kushiyaki,* which refers simply to a variety of ingredients—meat, fish, vegetables—cut into bits and grilled on bamboo skewers. There's nothing ceremonious or elegant about *kushiyaki*; it resembles the more familiar *yakitori*, except there's more variety to it. At Higo Batten you can feast on such dishes as shiitake mushrooms stuffed with minced chicken; scallops wrapped in bacon; and bonito, shrimp, and eggplant with ginger.

The decor here is sort of postmodern traditional, with wood beams painted black, paper lanterns, and sliding paper screens. There's tatami, table, and counter seating. This spot draws a young crowd, among them a lot of the fancy-free Westerners who like the scene in Aoyama—which probably accounts for the helpful English menu. ✕ *AG Bldg. 1F, 3-18-17 Minami-Aoyama, Minato-ku (nearest subway station: Omotesando),* ☎ *03/3423–4462. AE, V.* ☉ *5–11:15* PM.

Asakusa

$$ Tatsumiya. This is a ryotei with at least two delightfully untraditional features: It is neither inaccessible nor outrageously expensive. Most ryotei tend to oppress the first-time visitor a little with the weight of their antiquity and the ceremonious formality of their service. Tatsumiya opened in 1980, and it takes a different attitude to the past: The rooms are almost cluttered—with antique chests, braziers, clocks, lanterns, bowls, utensils, and craftwork (some of which are for sale). The cuisine itself follows the *kaiseki* repertoire, derived from the tradition of the tea-ceremony meal. Seven courses are offered, including something raw, something boiled, something vinegared, something grilled. The atmosphere is relaxed and friendly, in the Shitamachi (downtown) style. ✕ *1-33-5 Asakusa, Taito-ku (nearest subway station: Asakusa),* ☎ *03/3842–7373. Reservations advised. Jacket and tie. No credit cards.* ☉ *Noon–2 and 5–9:30 (enter by 8:30). Closed Mon.*

Ginza

$$ Hakkaku. On the second floor of the Yuraku Food Center building, crammed between other restaurants, this small bar can easily be recognized by its big red lantern hanging outside. At lunchtime, good tempura dishes are offered at very reasonable prices. There is table seating or a counter/bar; you'll be rubbing elbows with local businessmen. ✕ *Ginza Ins 2, 2-2 Nishi-Ginza, Chuo-ku (nearest subway station: Yurakucho),* ☎ *03/3561–0539. No reservations. AE, DC, MC, V.* ☉ *Weekdays 11–9:30, Sat. 11–8.*

Ikebukuro

$$$ Sasashu. Strictly speaking, Sasashu is not a restaurant but an *izakaya*—a tavern that specializes in sake. It's included here for two reasons. First, it stocks only the finest and rarest, the Latours and Mouton-Rothschilds, of sake: These are wines that take gold medals in the annual sake concours year after year. Second, the restaurant serves the best food of any izakaya in town—the Japanese wouldn't dream of drinking well without eating well. Sasashu is a rambling, two-story building in traditional style, with thick beams and step-up tatami floors. The specialty of the house is salmon steak, brushed with sake and soy sauce and broiled over a charcoal hibachi. ✕ *2-2-6 Ikebukuro, Toshima-ku (nearest subway station: Ikebukuro),* ☎ *03/3971–6796. Reservations advised, especially Jan.–Feb. AE, DC, MC, V.* ☉ *5–10:30. Closed Sun. and holidays.*

Meguro

$ Tonki. Meguro, distinguished for almost nothing else culinary, has the numero uno *tonkatsu* (deep-fried pork cutlet) restaurant in Tokyo. It's a family joint, with Formica-top tables and a fellow who comes around to take your order while you're waiting in line. And people do wait in line, every night. Tonki is one of those successful places that never went conglomerate; it kept getting more popular and never got around to putting frills on what it does best: pork cutlets, soup, raw cabbage salad, rice, pickles, and tea. That's the standard course, and almost everybody orders it, with good reason. ✕ *1-1-2 Shimo-Meguro, Meguro-ku (nearest train station: Meguro on the JR Yamanote Line),* ☎

03/3491–9928. No reservations; expect a 10-min. wait. DC, MC, V.
✆ 4–10:45. Closed Tues. and every 3rd Mon.

Nihonbashi

$ Sasashin. No culinary tour of Japan would be complete without a visit to an izakaya, where the food is hearty and close to home cooking. Food at an izakaya, however, is meant—to most of the local clientele, at least—mainly as ballast for the earnest consumption of beer and sake. Arguably one of the two or three best izakaya in Tokyo, Sasashin spurns the notion of decor: There's a counter laden with platters of the evening's fare, and a clutter of rough wooden tables, and not much else. It's noisy, smoky, crowded—and absolutely authentic. Try the sashimi, the grilled fish, or the fried tofu; you really can't go wrong by just pointing your finger to anything on the counter that takes your fancy. ✕ *20-3 Nihonbashi Ningyocho 2-chome, Chuo-ku (nearest subway station: Suitengu-mae),* ✆ *03/3668–2456. No reservations. No credit cards.* ✆ *Mon.–Sat. 5–10:30 PM.*

Roppongi

$$$$ Inakaya. The style here is *robatayaki* (charcoal grill cookery), the
★ ambience pure theater. The centerpiece is a large, U-shape counter. Inside, two cooks in traditional garb sit on cushions behind the grill, with a wonderful cornucopia of food spread out in front of them: fresh vegetables, seafood, skewers of beef and chicken. Point to what you want, or tell your waiter (they all speak a little English); the cook will bring it up out of the pit, prepare it, and hand it across on an 8-foot wooden paddle. ✕ *Reine Bldg. 1F, 5-3-4 Roppongi, Minato-ku (nearest subway station: Roppongi),* ✆ *03/3408–5040. No reservations; expect a ½-hour wait any evening after 7. AE, DC, MC, V.* ✆ *5 PM–5 AM. Closed New Year's Day.*

$$ Ganchan. While the Japanese prefer their sushi bars to be immaculately clean and light, they expect yakitori joints to be smoky, noisy, and cluttered—like Ganchan. There's counter seating only, for about 15; you have to squeeze to get to the chairs in back by the kitchen. The walls are festooned with festival masks, paper kites and lanterns, gimcracks of all sorts, handwritten menus, and greeting cards from celebrity patrons. Behind the counter, the cooks yell at each other, fan the grill, and serve up enormous schooners of beer. Try the *tsukune* (balls of minced chicken) and the fresh asparagus wrapped in bacon. ✕ *6-8-23 Roppongi, Minato-ku (nearest subway station: Roppongi),* ✆ *03/3478–0092. No reservations. V.* ✆ *6 PM–2:30 AM, Sun. and holidays 6–midnight.*

Shibuya

$$–$$$ Tenmatsu. You don't really have to spend a lot of money to enjoy a first-rate tempura restaurant, and Tenmatsu proves the point. The best seats in the house, as in any *tempura-ya,* are at the immaculate wooden counter, where your tidbits of choice are taken straight from the oil and served up immediately. You also get to watch the chef in action. Tenmatsu's brand of good-natured professional hospitality just adds to your enjoyment of the meal. Here you can rely on a set menu or order à la carte from delicacies like lotus root, shrimp, *unagi* (eel), and *kisu* (a small white freshwater fish). ✕ *1-6-1 Dogenzaka, Shibuya-ku (nearest JR/subway station: Shibuya),* ✆ *03/3462–2815. Reservations advised for counter seating. DC, MC, V.* ✆ *11–2 and 5–9. Closed Mon.*

Tsukiji

$$$ Edo-Gin. In an area that teems with sushi bars, Edo-Gin maintains its reputation as one of the best. Portions have shrunk a bit lately, but you would have to visit once every few years to notice. Edo-Gin still serves

N

ASAKUSA

Kappabashi-dori

Asakusa

2

Showa-dori

Inaricho

Asakusa-dori

Tawaramachi

Kuramae-dori

HAMACHO

Asakusa-bashi

15

NIPPONBASHI

Nippori

Ueno

Uguisudani

Ueno

UENO

Ueno Park

Ueno

Kiyosubashi-dori

Ueno

Okachi-machi

Akihabara

Akihabara

Asakusa-bashi

Nihonbashi

Nihonbashi

Tokyo

Kanda

YUSHIMA

Kasuga-dori

Hongo-dori

Hongo-sanchome

JINBOCHO

Ochanomizu

3

Suidobashi

Hakusan-dori

Korakuen

Korakuen Garden

Jinbocho

Iidabashi

4

IMPERIAL PALACE

Uchibori-dori

Koishikawa Botanical Gardens

Shinobazu-dori

Yasukuni-dori

Toranoman

ICHIBAN-CHO

Ichigaya

Shin-Otsuka

Gokokuji

Myogadani

Edogawabashi

Kagurazaka

5

Akasaka-mitsuke

7

Yotsuya

Kojimachi

6

Higashi-Ikebukuro

Waseda-dori

Waseda

Shinjuku-dori

Akasaka Palace

1

Seibu Ikebukuro

Mejiro-dori

Akebonobashi

Shinjuku-dori

Shinanomachi

Shinjuku Gyoen

Meiji Jingu Outer

Ikebukuro

IKEBUKURO

Mejiro

Shin-Okubo

Seibu-Shinjuku

SHINJUKU

Sendagaya

Meiji-j

Takadanobaba

Okubo

Shinjuku

Yoyogi

Meiji Jingu Inner Garden

Ome-kaido

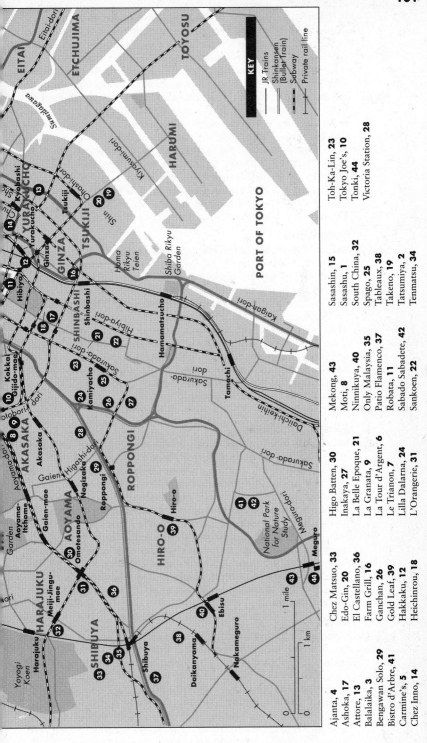

KEY

— JR Trains
= Shinkansen (Bullet Train)
▪▪▪ Subway
—+— Private rail line

PORT OF TOKYO

Ajanta, **4**
Ashoka, **17**
Attore, **13**
Balalaika, **3**
Bengawan Solo, **29**
Bistro d'Arbre, **41**
Carmine's, **5**
Chez Inno, **14**

Chez Matsuo, **33**
Edo-Gin, **20**
El Castellano, **36**
Farm Grill, **16**
Ganchan, **26**
Gold Leaf, **39**
Hakkaku, **12**
Heichinrou, **18**

Higo Batten, **30**
Inakaya, **27**
La Belle Epoque, **21**
La Granata, **9**
La Tour d'Argent, **6**
Le Trianon, **7**
Lilla Dalarna, **24**
L'Orangerie, **31**

Mekong, **43**
Moti, **8**
Ninnikuya, **40**
Only Malaysia, **35**
Patio Flamenco, **37**
Robata, **11**
Sabado Sabadete, **42**
Sankoen, **22**

Sasashin, **15**
Sasashu, **1**
South China, **32**
Spago, **25**
Tableaux, **38**
Takeno, **19**
Tatsumiya, **2**
Tenmatsu, **34**

Toh-Ka-Lin, **23**
Tokyo Joe's, **10**
Tonki, **44**
Victoria Station, **28**

up generous slabs of fish that drape over the vinegared rice rather than perch demurely on top. The centerpiece of the main room is a huge tank, in which the day's ingredients swim about until they are required; it doesn't get any fresher than that! ✕ *4-5-1 Tsukiji, Chuo-ku (nearest subway station: Tsukiji),* ☎ *03/3543–4401. No reservations. AE, MC, V.* ⊘ *10–10. Closed Sun. and some national holidays.*

$$–$$$ **Takeno.** Just a stone's throw from the Tokyo central fish market, Takeno is a rough-cut neighborhood restaurant that tends to fill up at noon with the market's wholesalers and auctioneers and office personnel from the nearby Dentsu ad agency and Asahi Shinbun (newspaper) company. Nothing here but the freshest and the best—big portions of it, at very small tariffs. Sushi, sashimi, and tempura are the staple fare; prices are not posted because they vary with the costs that morning in the market. ✕ *6-21-2 Tsukiji, Chuo-ku (nearest subway station: Tsukiji),* ☎ *03/3541–8698. No reservations. No credit cards.* ⊘ *11–9. Closed Sun. and holidays.*

Yurakucho

$$–$$$ **Robata.** You might find this place a little daunting at first: It's old and funky, impossibly cramped, and always packed. But chef-owner Takao Inoue, who holds forth here with an inspired version of Japanese home cooking, is also a connoisseur of pottery; he serves his own work on pieces acquired at famous kilns all over the country. There's no menu; the best thing you can do is tell Inoue-san (who speaks some English) how hungry you are and how much you want to spend, and leave the rest to him. A meal at Robata—like the pottery—is simple to the eye, but subtle and satisfying. ✕ *3-8 Yurakucho 1-chome, Chiyoda-ku (nearest subway station: Hibiya),* ☎ *03/3591–1905. Reservations advised. No credit cards.* ⊘ *Mon.–Sat. 5:30–9.*

American

Akasaka-mitsuke

$$$$ **Tokyo Joe's.** The very first foreign branch of famed Miami Joe's was in Osaka, a city where volume-for-value really counts in the reputation of a restaurant. The Tokyo branch upholds its reputation the same way—by serving enormous quantities of stone crab, with melted butter and mustard mayonnaise. The turnover here is fierce; waiters in long red aprons scurry to keep up with it, but the service is remarkably smooth. The crabs are flown in fresh from the Florida Keys, their one and only habitat. There are other choices on the menu, but it's midnight madness to order anything else. Top it all off—if you have room—with Key lime pie. ✕ *Akasaka Eight-One Bldg. B1, 2-13-5 Nagatacho, Chiyoda-ku (nearest subway station: Akasaka-mitsuke),* ☎ *03/3508–0325. Reservations advised. AE, DC, MC, V.* ⊘ *11:30 AM–3 PM and 5–11 PM.*

Ginza

$–$$ **Farm Grill.** Here's what hard times have brought us, and not a moment
★ too soon: Tokyo yuppies have finally become budget-conscious about dining out, and restaurants like the Farm Grill are springing up all over town, filling the new market niche with innovative California-style cuisine in generous portions at truly reasonable prices. The Farm Grill, which opened in late 1994, is odds-on the best of the lot, focusing on hearty salads and sandwiches, pasta and rotisserie entrées, and rich desserts. There are more than 90 entries on the wine list, a good percentage of them (gasp!) at ¥1,500 or less. The space is huge by any standard, with seating for 260 at wood-block pedestal tables with rattan chairs. Try the Caesar salad, the Pasta Malibu (penne with chicken,

mushrooms, bacon, mozzarella, and fresh herbs), or the Farm Grill Chili with garlic toast. The carrot cake is pretty good, the linzertorte to die for. What the service lacks in professionalism it makes up for in sheer good will. ✗ *Ginza Nine 3 Gokan 2F, 8-5 Ginza, Chuo-ku (nearest train station: Shinbashi on the JR Yamanote Line),* ☎ *03/5568–6156. Reservations suggested on Thurs. and Fri. eves. AE, DC, MC, V.* ☉ *Daily 11 AM–11 PM.*

Roppongi

$$$–$$$$ **Spago.** So far, this is the only venture overseas by trendsetting Spago of Los Angeles. Owner-chef-celebrity Wolfgang Puck comes periodically to Tokyo to oversee the authenticity of his California cuisine: Will duck sausage pizza with boursin cheese and pearl onions ever be as American as apple pie? Maybe. Meanwhile, Spago is a clean, well-lighted place, painted pink and white and adorned with potted palms. The service is smooth, and the tables on the glassed-in veranda attract a fair sample of Tokyo's gilded youth. ✗ *5-7-8 Roppongi, Minato-ku (nearest subway station: Roppongi),* ☎ *03/3423–4025. Reservations advised. AE, DC, MC, V.* ☉ *6–10:30. Closed Dec. 31 and Jan. 1.*

$$ **Victoria Station.** The style of an American "family" restaurant is instantly recognizable wherever in the world you find it, marked by a certain sense of packaging, a brisk efficiency, and a penchant for themes. Victoria Station's theme is the British railway system, executed with platform signs on the walls, railroad prints, old posters, brass fittings—even a truncated caboose. The space is huge and well laid out in "compartments," with a much-appreciated no-smoking section. The specialty of the house is roast prime rib; the all-you-can-eat salad bar is one of the best in town. ✗ *4-9 Roppongi 2-chome, Minato-ku (nearest subway station: Roppongi),* ☎ *03/3479–4601. No reservations. AE, DC, MC, V.* ☉ *11 AM–midnight, Sun. and holidays 11 AM–11 PM.*

Chinese

Harajuku

$$–$$$ **South China.** A Chinese restaurant for everybody—or at least for everybody you know, and most of their friends. South China occupies the three basement floors of a building near the main entrance to the Meiji Shrine; it can host a reception for a thousand people or a banquet for a hundred, and it also has 13 smaller rooms for private parties. How many tons of red lacquer have gone into the decor is anybody's guess. The menu is on a commensurate scale—more than 20 entries, about half of them Cantonese. South China's 35 cooks can also handle the fiery Szechuan cuisine, as well as the Peking and Shanghai styles. Specialties of the house include shark's fin with crab meat and Peking duck. ✗ *Co-op Olympia Bldg. B1-3, 6-35-3 Jingu-mae, Shibuya-ku (nearest train station: Harajuku on the JR Yamanote Line),* ☎ *03/3400–0031. No reservations. AE, MC, V.* ☉ *11:30–9:30.*

Toranomon

$$$–$$$$ **Toh-Ka-Lin.** Year after year, the Hotel Okura is rated by business travelers as one of the three best hotels in the world. That judgment has relatively little to do with its architecture, which is rather understated. It has to do instead with its polish, its impeccable standards of service—and, to judge by the Toh-Ka-Lin, the quality of its restaurants. The style of the cuisine here is eclectic; two stellar examples are the Peking duck and the sautéed quail wrapped in lettuce leaf. The Toh-Ka-Lin also has one of the most extensive wine lists in town. ✗ *Hotel Okura, 10-4 Toranomon 2-chome, Minato-ku (nearest subway stations: Kamiyacho and*

Toranomon), ☎ 03/3505–6068. *Reservations recommended. AE, DC, MC, V.* ⊙ *11:30–2:30 and 5:30–9:30.*

Uchisaiwaicho

$$$ **Heichinrou.** A branch of one of the oldest and best restaurants in Yoko-
★   hama's Chinatown. On the top floor of a prestigious office building about five minutes' walk from the Imperial Hotel, Heichinrou commands a spectacular view of Hibiya Koen (park) and the Imperial Palace grounds. Much of the clientele comes from the law offices, securities firms, and foreign banks on the floors below. The decor is rich but subdued; the lighting is soft; the linen is impeccable. Heichinrou has a banquet room that will seat a hundred, and a "VIP Room" with separate telephone service for power lunches. The cuisine is Cantonese, and it's first-rate. ✗ *Fukoku Seimei Bldg. 28F, 2-2-2 Uchisaiwaicho, Chiyoda-ku (nearest subway station: Uchisaiwaicho),* ☎ *03/3508–0555. Reservations advised, especially for a table by the window. Jacket and tie. AE, DC, MC, V.* ⊙ *11–9. Closed Sun. and holidays.*

French

Akasaka-mitsuke

$$$$ **La Tour d'Argent.** Pride of the Hotel New Otani Tokyo and Towers since 1984, La Tour d'Argent is a worthy scion of its ritzy Parisian parent. This is a place of grand centerpieces. One of them is in the foyer, enclosed in a glass case—the entire table setting at the Café Anglais (forerunner of the original Tour d'Argent) on June 7, 1867, when Bismarck hosted a dinner for Czar Alexander II of Russia and Emperor William I of Prussia. The other, in the main dining room, is the enormous, drapery-sculpted, marble carving table, with its silver duck press. The specialty of the house, naturally, is *caneton:* As in Paris, you receive a card recording the number of the duck you were served. In 1921, when Crown Prince Hirohito dined at the Tour d'Argent in Paris, he had duck number 53,210; the numbers here in Tokyo began with 53,211 when the restaurant opened. ✗ *4-1 Kioicho, Chiyoda-ku (nearest subway station: Akasaka-mitsuke),* ☎ *03/3239–3111. Reservations required. Jacket and tie. AE, DC, MC, V.* ⊙ *5:30–9. Closed Mon.*

$$$$ **Le Trianon.** Chef Sadao Hotta came over in 1976 from the Tokyo branch of Maxim's to open Le Trianon in the old guest house of the Akasaka Prince Hotel. The house was built for the king of Korea in the style of a French country estate, with parquet floors, lofty wood beams, and stained-glass windows. The restaurant, which takes up the whole second floor, has seven private dining rooms; the largest will hold a party of 12. Many of the regular clientele work in the nearby centers of power: the National Diet, the Liberal-Democratic party headquarters, and the Supreme Court. ✗ *1-2 Kioicho, Chiyoda-ku (nearest subway station: Akasaka-mitsuke),* ☎ *03/3234–1111. Reservations required. Jacket and tie. AE, DC, MC, V.* ⊙ *Noon–2:30 and 6–10:30.*

Kyobashi

$$$$ **Chez Inno.** Chef Noboru Inoue studied his craft at Maxim's in Paris and Les Frères Troisgros in Roanne; the result is brilliant, innovative French food. The main dining room, with seating for 28, has velvet banquettes, white stucco walls, and stained-glass windows; there's also a smaller room for private parties. Across the street is the elegant Seiyo Hotel—making this block the locus of the very best Tokyo has to offer the upscale traveler. Try the fresh lamb in wine sauce with truffles and *fines herbes*, or the lobster with caviar. ✗ *3-2-11 Kyobashi (nearest subway station: Kyobashi),* ☎ *03/3274–2020. Reservations required. Jacket and tie. AE, DC, V.* ⊙ *Noon–2 and 6–9. Closed Sun.*

Omotesando

$$–$$$$ **L'Orangerie.** This very fashion-minded restaurant is on the fifth floor of the Hanae Mori Building, just a minute's walk from the Omotesando subway station on Aoyama-dori. It's a joint venture of the original L'Orangerie in Paris and Mme. Mori's formidable empire in couture. A muted elegance marks the decor, with cream walls, deep brown carpets, and a few good paintings. Mirrors add depth to a room that actually seats only 40. The menu, an ambitious one to begin with, changes every two weeks; the salad of sautéed sweetbreads, when they have it, is excellent. The lunch (**$$–$$$$**) and dinner (**$$$–$$$$**) menus are nouvelle and very pricey. L'Orangerie is best approached on a Sunday between 11 and 2:30, for the buffet brunch, when for ¥3,500 you can graze through to what's arguably the best dessert tray in town. ✕ *Hanae Mori Bldg. 5F, 3-6-1 Kita-Aoyama, Minato-ku (nearest subway station: Omotesando),* ☎ *03/3407–7461. Reservations required. Jacket suggested. AE, DC, MC, V.* ◐ *11:30–2:30 and 5:30–9:30, Sun. 11–2:30.*

Shiroganedai

$$–$$$ **Bistro d'Arbre.** This tiny restaurant (seating for only 12), on what has become one of the more fashionable avenues among Tokyo's affluent young folks, depends on word of mouth for its popularity; it doesn't get many foreign visitors—and more's the pity. Chef Takahiro Taniguchi trained briefly in France, but honed his skills mainly here on the job; his repertoire is not wide, but what he does, he does beautifully. Especially good are the smoked salmon crepes and the fillet of beef in bordelaise sauce. After dinner, climb the narrow, wrought-iron spiral staircase to the lounge on the second floor—an amiable clutter of leather armchairs and footrests made of old wine kegs, stacks of cordwood, antique lamps, and threadbare carpets—and settle in front of the huge, French country-style fireplace for coffee or a liqueur. There's nothing quite like this anywhere in town. ✕ *5-3-1 Shiroganedai, Minato-ku (nearest subway station: Hiro-o),* ☎ *03/3446–4855. Reservations recommended. AE, DC, MC, V.* ◐ *Noon–2 and 6–10 (Sun. 6–9). Closed Mon.*

Shoto

$$$$ **Chez Matsuo.** Shoto is the kind of area you don't expect Tokyo to have— at least not so close to Shibuya Station. It's a neighborhood of stately homes (the governor of Tokyo's, among them) with walls half a block long, a sort of sedate Beverly Hills. Chez Matsuo occupies the first floor of a lovely old two-story house in Western style. The two dining rooms look out on the garden, where you can dine by candlelight on summer evenings. Owner-chef Matsuo studied his craft in Paris, and in London as a sommelier. His food is nouvelle; the specialty of the house is Supreme of Duck. ✕ *1-23-15 Shoto, Shibuya-ku (nearest subway/JR station: Shibuya),* ☎ *03/3465–0610. Reservations advised. Jacket suggested. AE, DC, MC, V.* ◐ *Noon–2:30 (last order at 1) and 6:30–8. Closed Mon.*

Toranomon

$$$$ **La Belle Epoque.** The flagship restaurant of the Hotel Okura, across the street from the American embassy, La Belle Epoque is a monument to the Japanese passion for Art Nouveau, curvilinear and graceful à la Aubrey Beardsley and Gustav Klimt, with panels of stained glass separating the tables into flowered alcoves. A singer holds forth every evening to the strains of a harp and a piano. From the north dining room there's a fine view of the city, with the Eiffel-inspired Tokyo Tower in the foreground. The cuisine is French classique; chef Philippe Mouchel has three-

star credentials, having trained at both the Restaurant Paul Bocuse near Lyon and the Moulin de Mougins on the Riviera. ✗ *10-4 Toranomon 2-chome, Minato-ku (nearest subway stations: Kamiyacho and Tora-nomon),* ☎ *03/3505–6073. Reservations required. Jacket and tie. AE, DC, MC, V.* ۞ *11:30–2:30 and 5:30–9:30.*

Indian

Akasaka

$–$$ Moti. This is the second of three Motis, at last count; the original is in Akasaka-mitsuke, and the newest is in Roppongi. All serve the same good Indian cooking, but the Akasaka branch, right by the Chiyoda Line subway station, is the easiest to get into and the most comfort-able. Moti has the inevitable Indian friezes, copper bowls, and white elephants, but the owners have not gone overboard on decor: The draw-ing card here is the food. They recruit their cooks in India through a member of the family who runs a restaurant in Delhi. The vegetarian dishes here, including lentils, eggplant, and cauliflower, are very good; so is the chicken *masala* style, cooked in butter and spices. ✗ *Kinpa Bldg. 3F, 2-14-31 Akasaka, Minato-ku (nearest subway station: Akasaka),* ☎ *03/3584–6640. Reservations advised. AE, DC, V.* ۞ *11–10.*

Ginza

$–$$ Ashoka. The owners of the Ashoka set out to take the high ground—to provide a decor commensurate with its fashionable address. The room is hushed and spacious; incense perfumes the air; the lighting is recessed, and the carpets thick. Floor-to-ceiling windows overlook Chuo-dori, the main street of the Ginza. The waiters have spiffy uniforms; the *thali* (a selection of curries and other specialties of the house) is served up on a figured brass tray. The *khandari nan,* a flat bread with nuts and raisins, is excellent; so is the chicken *tikka,* boneless chunks marinated and cooked in the *tandoor* (clay oven). All in all, a good show for the raj. ✗ *Pearl Bldg. 2F, 7-9-18 Ginza, Chuo-ku (nearest subway station: Ginza),* ☎ *03/3572–2377. Reservations advised. AE, DC, MC, V.* ۞ *11:30–9:30, Sun. 11:30–8.*

Nibancho

$–$$ Ajanta. The owner of Ajanta came to Tokyo to study electrical engi-neering, and he opened a small coffee shop near the Indian embassy. That was about 35 years ago. He used to cook a little for his friends; the coffee shop is now one of the oldest and best Indian restaurants in town. There's no decor to speak of; the emphasis instead is on the va-riety and intricacy of Indian cooking—and none of its dressier rivals can match Ajanta's menu for sheer depth. The curries are hot to begin with, but you can order them hotter. There's a small boutique in one corner, where saris and imported Indian foodstuffs are for sale. ✗ *3-11 Nibancho, Chiyoda-ku, (nearest subway station: Kojimachi),* ☎ *03/3264–6955. Reservations advised.* ۞ *24 hrs. AE, DC, MC, V.*

Indochinese

Meguro

$ Mekong. The owner of Mekong fled Cambodia and came to Japan al-most two decades ago, and he went to work for a trading company. Later, with the help of some friends, he opened a hole-in-the-wall restaurant near Ebisu, with an eclectic menu of Cambodian, Thai, and Vietnamese cooking. Mekong prospered, and in 1987 it moved to larger quarters in Meguro—but it has remained very much a plastic-tablecloth operation. The selections are few, and the service can be a little disorganized, but at these prices, nobody complains. A menu in English attests to Mekong's popularity with the local foreign community. Try the fried spring rolls and the beef with mustard-leaf pickles. ✕ *Koyo Bldg. 2F, 2-16-4 Kamiosaki, Shinagawa-ku (nearest train station: Meguro on the JR Yamanote Line),* ☎ *03/3442–6664. Reservations advised weekends. MC, V. ☉ Noon–1:30 and 5–12.*

Indonesian/Malaysian

Roppongi

$$ **Bengawan Solo.** The Japanese, whose native aesthetic demands a separate dish and vessel for everything they eat, have to overcome a certain resistance to the idea of *rijsttafel*—a kind of Indonesian smorgasbord of curries, salad, and grilled tidbits that tends to get mixed up on a serving platter. Nevertheless, Bengawan Solo has maintained its popularity with Tokyo residents for about 35 years; this is one of the oldest and most durable restaurants in the city. The parent organization, in Jakarta, supplies the periodic infusion of new staff, as needed. The company also has a thriving import business in Indonesian foodstuffs. Bengawan Solo added a back room some years ago without appreciably reducing the amiable clutter of batik pictures, shadow puppets, carvings, and pennants that make up the decor. The eight-course rijsttafel is spicy-hot and ample; if it doesn't quite stretch for two, order an extra Gado-Gado salad with peanut sauce. ✕ *7-18-13 Roppongi, Minato-ku (nearest subway station: Roppongi),* ☎ *03/3408–5698. Reservations advised. AE, DC, MC, V. ☉ Daily 11:30–3 and 5–11.*

Shibuya

$–$$ **Only Malaysia.** Here's a restaurant with an official seal of approval: The Malaysian Ambassador to Japan hires Only Malaysia to cater his parties. (Haji Raman, who runs the kitchen, was in fact the former ambassador's chef.) This is a small place (seating for only 45), and not easy to book for dinner—especially on weekends. Try the *ayam* (spicy chicken soup), or the *rendang* (chicken or beef with coriander and chili peppers). ✕ *Ikushin Bldg. 3F, 26-5 Udagawacho, Shibuya-ku (nearest subway/JR station: Shibuya),* ☎ *03/3496–1177. Reservations recommended. AE, MC, V. ☉ Daily 11:30–2 and 5:30–9:30.*

International

Ebisu

$–$$ **Ninnikuya.** In Japanese, *ninniku* means "garlic"—an ingredient conspicuously absent from the traditional local cuisine and one that the Japanese were once supposed to dislike. Not so nowadays, if you can believe the crowds that cheerfully line up for hours to eat at this cluttered little place in the Ebisu section. Owner-chef Eiyuki Endo discovered his own passion for the savory bulb in Italy in 1976. Since then, he has traveled the world for interesting garlic dishes. Endo's family owns the building, so he can give free rein to his artistry without charging a lot. There is no decor to speak of, and you may well have to share a table. Good fun. Ninnikuya is a little hard to find, but anybody you ask in the neighborhood can point the way. Try the littleneck clams Italian-style with garlic rice, or the Peruvian garlic chicken. ✕ *1-26-12 Ebisu, Shibuya-ku (nearest subway station: Ebisu),* ☎ *03/3446–5887. No reservations. No credit cards. ☉ Mon.–Sat. 6–10:30.*

Italian

Akasaka

$$–$$$ **La Granata.** Located on the basement level of the Tokyo Broadcasting Systems building, La Granata and its companion restaurant Granata Moderna are both very popular with the media crowd upstairs. Deservedly so: They offer some of the most accomplished, professional Italian food in town. La Granata is decked out in trattoria style, with brickwork arches and red checkered tablecloths; Granata Moderna has the same menu, but reaches for elegance with a polished rosewood bar, Art Deco mirrors, and stained glass. Specialties worth trying include the spaghetti with garlic and red pepper and the batter-fried zucchini flowers filled with mozzarella and asparagus. ✗ *TBS Kaikan B1, 5-3-3 Akasaka, Minato-ku (nearest subway station: Akasaka),* ☎ *03/3582–5891. Reservations advised. AE, MC, V.* ◔ *11–9:30.*

Daikanyama

$$$ **Tableaux.** The mural in the bar depicts the fall of Pompeii, the banquettes in the restaurant are upholstered in red leather, and the walls are papered in antique gold. The waiters glide hither and yon in ponytails and unconstructed Armani knockoffs. Somebody here, one suspects, really *believes* in Los Angeles. Tableaux may lay on more glitz than it really needs, but the service is cordial and professional and the food is superb. Try the *bruschetta* (toasted bread with tomato, basil, and olive oil), the fettuccine with smoked salmon and sun-dried tomatoes, or the grilled pork chop stuffed with chutney, onion, and garlic. The lunch menu is—by Tokyo standards—a bargain. ✗ *Sunroser Daikanyama Bldg. B1, 11-6 Sarugakucho, Shibuya-ku (nearest train station: Daikanyama on the Tokyu Toyoko Line),* ☎ *03/5489–2201. Reservations recommended. AE, DC, MC, V.* ◔ *11:30 AM–2 PM and 5:30–10:30 PM. Bar lounge open to 2 AM.*

Ichigaya

$–$$ **Carmine's.** Everybody pitched in, so the story goes, when Carmine Cozzolino opened this unpretentious little neighborhood restaurant in 1987: Friends designed the logo and the interior, painted the walls (black and white), and hung the graphics, swapping their labor for meals. Good meals, too. For a real Italian gourmet five-course dinner, this could be the best deal in town. Specialties of the house include pasta twists with tomato and caper sauce, and veal scaloppine à la Marsala. Carmine's tiramisu is a serious dessert. Not easy to find, but well worth the effort. ✗ *1-19 Saikucho, Shinjuku-ku (nearest subway station: Kagurazaka),* ☎ *03/3260–5066. Reservations recommended. No credit cards.* ◔ *Mon.–Sat. noon–2 and 6–10.*

Kyobashi

$$–$$$$ ★   **Attore.** The Italian restaurant of the elegant Hotel Seiyo Ginza (*see* Lodging, *below*), Attore is divided into two sections. The "casual" side, with seating for 60, has a bar counter, banquettes, and a see-through glass wall to the kitchen; the comfortable decor is achieved with track lighting, potted plants, marble floors, and Indian-looking print tablecloths. The "formal" side, with seating for 40, has mauve wall panels and carpets, armchairs, and soft, recessed lighting. On either side of the room, you get what is hands-down the best Italian cuisine in Tokyo. Chef Katsuyuki Muroi trained for six years in Tuscany and northern Italy and acquired a wonderful repertoire. Try the pâté of pheasant and porcini mushrooms with white truffle cheese sauce, or the walnut-smoked lamb chops with sun-dried tomatoes. ✗ *1-11-2 Ginza, Chuo-ku (nearest sub-*

way station: Ginza), ☎ *03/3535–1111. Reservations advised. Jacket and tie suggested. AE, DC, MC, V.* ✆ *11–10.*

Korean

Azabu Ju-ban

$$–$$$ **Sankoen.** With the embassy of the Republic of Korea a few blocks away, Sankoen is in a neighborhood thick with barbecue joints; not much seems to distinguish one from another. About 15 years ago, however, Sankoen suddenly caught on, and people started coming in droves. Not just the neighborhood families showed up, but also customers who worked in the media industry. Sankoen opened a branch, then moved the main operation across the street to new, two-story quarters. Korean barbecue is a smoky affair; you cook your own dinner—thin slices of beef and special cuts of meat—on a gas grill at your table. Sankoen also makes a great salad to go with its brisket. ✗ *1-8-7 Azabu Ju-ban, Minato-ku (nearest subway station: Roppongi),* ☎ *03/3585–6306. No reservations. AE, V.* ✆ *11:30 AM–12:30 AM, Sun. 11:30 AM–midnight. Closed Wed.*

Russian

Jinbocho

$$$ **Balalaika.** With all the astonishing, radical changes taking place these days in what used to be the Soviet Union, someone may come up with a nouvelle version of Russian cooking. Until then, this is the place to go when you are truly seriously hungry. The Balalaika is by no means cheap, but it serves an excellent sort of ballast, if you have the room to stow it away. For example: *blinchiki,* small, sweet pancakes with garnishes of red and black caviar; *solyanka,* a savory broth with sausages and vegetables, which is just the thing to sop up with the Balalaika's excellent black bread; chicken Kiev; and *walenicki,* crescent-shaped pastries filled with cheese and topped with sour cream. What atmosphere there is here is provided by the Balalaika Trio, which holds forth every evening from 6 PM. ✗ *1-63 Kanda Jinbocho, Chiyoda-ku (nearest subway station: Jinbocho),* ☎ *03/3291–8363. Reservations advised weekends. AE, DC, MC. V.* ✆ *11–2 and 5–10 (Sun. 5–9:30).*

Spanish

Aoyama

$$ **El Castellano.** Owner Vicente, a native of Toledo who opened El Castellano in the late 1980s, doesn't advertise much; he relies instead on word of mouth. He runs a warm, friendly, cluttered place where Tokyo's Spanish residents come to eat. There's room here for perhaps 30 (elbow to elbow), and word has gotten around well enough to pack it almost every night. No pretensions to elegance here: The once-whitewashed walls are covered with messages of appreciation scrawled with felt-tip pens, accented here and there with the inevitable bullfight posters, painted crockery, and photographs of Spanish soccer teams. Try the paella and a salad, with a jug of Spanish wine: a no-frills, satisfying meal. ✗ *Marusan Aoyama Bldg. 2F, 2-9-11 Shibuya, Shibuya-ku (nearest subway station: Omotesando),* ☎ *03/3407–7197. Reservations advised. No credit cards.* ✆ *6–11. Closed Sun. and holidays.*

Shibuya

$$$ **Patio Flamenco.** This establishment rates less for its cuisine (good but not memorable) than for its dinner show. Owner Yoko Komatsubara, for many years Japan's leading professional flamenco dancer, travels regularly to Spain to find the talented singers, dancers, and guitarists who hold forth here nightly. A small room with seating for perhaps 30, the Patio Flamenco makes you feel as if you have the show to yourself. The specialty of the house is the paella Valenciana, with shrimp, squid, and mussels. Performances begin at 7:30 and 9:30; expect a separate cover charge of ¥1,500 per person for the entertainment. ✕ 2-10-12 Dogenzaka, Shibuya-ku (nearest subway/JR station: Shibuya), ☎ 03/3496–2753. Reservations advised. AE, DC, MC, V. ☉ 5:30–11.

Shiroganedai

$$ **Sabado Sabadete.** Catalonia-born jewelry designer Mañuel Benito loves to cook. For a while, he indulged this passion by renting out a bar on Saturday nights and making an enormous paella for his friends; to keep them happy while they were waiting, he added a few tapas. Word got around: By 8 it was standing room only, and by 9 there wasn't room in the bar to lift a fork. Inspired by this success, Benito found a trendy location and opened his Sabado Sabadete full-time in 1991. The highlight of every evening is still the moment when the chef, in his bright-red Catalan cap, shouts out the Japanese equivalent of "soup's on!" and dishes out his bubbling-hot paella. Don't miss the empanadas (three-cornered pastries stuffed with minced beef and vegetables) or the *escalivada* (a Spanish ratatouille with red peppers, onions, and eggplant). ✕ Genteel Shiroganedai Bldg. 2F, 5-3-2 Shiroganedai, Minato-ku (nearest subway station: Hiro-o), ☎ 03/3445–9353. Reservations advised. No credit cards. ☉ 6–10. Closed Sun. and holidays.

Swedish

Azabu

$$ **Lilla Dalarna.** The original Dalarna, out in the suburbs of Tokyo, was the brainchild of Seiichi Okubo, who, when most of his adventurous contemporaries were wandering through France and Italy, somehow wound up in Sweden. He honed his craft for ten years in a series of Stockholm restaurants, then returned to Tokyo and opened a sort of country inn, with two long wooden tables where his customers could eat family-style. He did so well that he was able to open a branch a few minute's walk from the trendy Roppongi district. The effect here is cozy-cute, achieved mostly with plants, whitewash, and Scandinavian knickknacks. The food is basic and plentiful. Try the meatballs and potatoes, or the sausages with bell peppers. ✕ 5-9-19 Roppongi, Minato-ku (nearest subway station: Roppongi), ☎ 03/3478–4690. Reservations recommended. AE, DC, MC, V. ☉ Noon–3 and 6–9:30. Closed Mon.

Thai

Hiro-o

$$–$$$ **Gold Leaf.** The hottest gastronomic fad in Tokyo now-a-days, literally
★ and figuratively, is "ethnic"; in effect, that's meant a welcome profusion of good new Thai restaurants—among which the Gold Leaf (as the name implies) is probably the most elegant. Gleaming hardwood floors, black-laquered furniture, and fine linen complete the decor. The two chefs, trained in the cooking school of the famed Oriental Hotel in Bangkok, prepare a decidedly upscale version of this spicy yet subtle traditional cuisine. Try the prawn soup and the green curry with chicken. ✕ Taisei-Koki Bldg. B1, 5-4-12 Hiro-o, Shibuya-ku (nearest

subway station: Hiro-o), ☎ *03/3447–1212. Reservations advised.*
AE, DC, MC, V. ☽ *Noon–2 and 6–10:30 (5:30–10:30 Sun.).*

LODGING

When you select a hotel in Tokyo, you should focus on three factors:
the hotel's location, the size of its rooms, and the costliness of the capital city. Three factors of minimal concern are cleanliness, safety, and
helpful service, because these attributes may be found at practically all
Japanese hotels.

The general location of the hotel has a considerable effect on the price
charged for a room. Real estate throughout Tokyo is horrendously expensive, and the more central the location, the more outrageous is the
cost of a square yard. Consequently, hotel prices in the central Imperial Palace and Ginza districts (in Chiyoda-ku) reflect the area's super-
expensive real estate. On a business trip to Tokyo it may make sense
to select a hotel close to where one's business partners are located, but
for the visitor, the hotel's location may be only marginally important.
Bear in mind that, except for rush hour, Tokyo's subway and train system is comfortable and always rapid, inexpensive, safe, and efficient.
The only drawback is that trains stop running around midnight.

As a working estimate, expect to pay about ¥350 for each square foot
of your hotel guest room, with this price decreasing as you move away
from central Tokyo. Because anything less than 65 square feet is small
for a double room, expect to pay around ¥23,000 for what may be
considered an average room. Less expensive hotels offer fewer services
and a more basic decor than do expensive hotels. This affects the cost
of the guest room (on a square-foot basis) less than you might imagine. The larger hotels make more of their profits from the banquet and
dining facilities than from the guest rooms. The cost of the extra services is not part of the room rate. Consequently, even though the
deluxe hotels do charge a high price for the guest rooms, in one sense
they give more for the yen than do the less expensive hotels. Of course,
that's all very well, but you must be willing to pay ¥26,000 and more
to enjoy the bargain!

In other words, rather than selecting an inexpensive hotel in a central
location, consider a better hotel in one of the city subcenters: Roppongi,
Shinjuku, Ikebukuro, Meguro, and Asakusa all offer quite acceptable
choices.

In Tokyo, hotels may be divided into six categories: first-class (full-service) hotel, business hotel, *ryokan,* capsule hotel, youth hostel, and pink
hotel.

First-class (full-service) **hotels** are exactly what you would expect;
most of them tend also to be priced in the $$$ and $$$$ categories.
Virtually all of these full-service hotels have several restaurants offer-
ing different national cuisines, room service, direct-dial telephone and
another phone in the bathroom, minibars, *yukata* (cotton bedroom ki-
monos), concierge service, and porters. Most of the larger full-service
hotels are now equipped with a business center and a physical fitness
center. A few also have swimming pools. At least 90% of the guest rooms
are Western style. Usually a few token Japanese rooms (tatami mats
and futons) are available, and these are offered at a higher price than
the other rooms.

Business hotels are found throughout Japan; Tokyo has an ample supply of them. Business hotels are designed primarily for the traveler who needs a room in which to leave luggage, sleep, and take a quick shower or bath. Guest rooms are never large; some are tiny. A single traveler will often take a small double room rather than suffer claustrophobia in a single room. Each room has a telephone, a small writing desk, a television (sometimes the pay-as-you-watch variety), slippers, a yukata, and a private bathroom. These bathrooms are small, plastic, prefabricated units with tub, shower, and washbasin; they are invariably scrupulously clean. The hotel's facilities are limited usually to one restaurant and a 24-hour receptionist, with no room service or porters. Because the definition of a business hotel is vague, the listing below has not separated them into a special category. However, most of those hotels listed in the $$ price category could be classified as business hotels.

Ryokan have lost their strict meaning as more personal hotels where guests are served dinner and breakfast in their rooms. Some are still like that, but often the term means any hostelry that offers rooms with tatami mats on the floors and futons. They may or may not serve meals in the room. Those listed in the Tokyo section do not. All are of the frugal variety, often family-run. Many of them have rooms with and without bath, and service stems from goodwill, not from professionalism. Because they have few rooms and the owners are usually on hand to answer their guests' questions, these small, relatively inexpensive ryokan are very hospitable places to stay.

Capsule hotels are literally plastic cubicles stacked on top of each other. They are used by very junior business travelers or commuters who have missed their last train home. Guests crawl into their capsule, which has a small bed, an intercom, and a radio. Washing and toilet facilities are shared. (Very rarely, a capsule hotel will have a separate floor for women; otherwise, women are not admitted.) One such place is **Green Plaza Shinjuku** (1-29-2 Kabukicho, Shinjuku-ku, ☏ 03/3207–5411), two minutes from Shinjuku Station. It is the largest of its kind, with 660 sleeping slots. Check-in starts at 3 PM; check-out in the morning is pandemonium. A rush of bleary-eyed businessmen clamor to settle their accounts and scurry sheepishly to their offices. A night's stay in a capsule is about ¥4,100.

Pink hotels are "love" hotels, where rooms are rented by the hour. However, after the peak time (around 9 PM), you can sometimes rent (very inexpensively, about ¥4,000–¥5,000, depending on your negotiating skills) a room for the entire night. Be aware, though, that if you do not leave by the agreed-upon time in the morning, your extra time will be charged at the hourly rate! They are, by the way, spotlessly clean. These pink hotels are easily recognized by their garish facades and are usually located near the entertainment quarters—several may be found in Kabukicho (Shinjuku), Roppongi, and along the suburban highways. In Shinjuku, one such hotel, the **Hotel Perrier** (2-7-12 Kabukicho, Shinjuku-ku, ☏ 03/3207–5921), has rooms with saunas and various scintillating decors—one room, the Galaxy Room, has lights that turn on and off with the sound of your voice.

Separate categories are provided in this section for (1) hotels near Narita Airport and (2) youth hostels and dormitory accommodations. All rooms at the hotels listed below have private baths, unless otherwise specified.

A 3% federal consumer tax is added to all hotel bills. Another 3% local tax is added to the bill if it exceeds ¥15,000. At most hotels, a 10%–15% service charge is added to the total bill. Tipping is not necessary.

CATEGORY	COST*
$$$$	over ¥30,000
$$$	¥21,000–¥30,000
$$	¥10,000–¥21,000
$	under ¥10,000

Cost is for a double room, without tax or service

Akasaka-mitsuke

$$$$ **Akasaka Prince Hotel.** Kenzo Tange completed the ultramodern, 40-story Akasaka Prince in 1983; the simplicity of its half-moon shape may be considered either coldly sterile or classical. It's situated atop a small hill, and all the guest rooms (the higher up, the better) have wide, sweeping views of Tokyo. The decor of white and pastel grays in the guest rooms accentuates the light from the wide windows that run the length of the room. The result is a feeling of spaciousness, though the rooms are no larger in size than those in other deluxe hotels. A welcome feature is the dressing mirror and sink in an alcove before the bathroom. The marble and off-white reception areas on the ground floor are pristine. The hotel's whole atmosphere is crisp, but a little impersonal; it's ideal for the clusters of people at large weddings and convention parties (the Grand Ballroom can accommodate up to 2,500 guests). The Akasaka Prince has no fewer than 12 restaurants and bars, among them the **Blue Gardenia** on the 40th floor, which serves Continental food; the **Top of the Akasaka,** a bar that affords spectacular views of Tokyo's skyline; and a French restaurant, **Le Trianon,** in the old guest house to the side of the hotel (*see also* Dining, *above*). ⌂ *1-2 Kioicho, Chiyoda-ku, Tokyo 102 (nearest subway station: Akasaka-mitsuke),* ☎ *03/3234–1111,* ℻ *03/3205–1956. 761 rooms, most Western style. Restaurants, massage, dry cleaning, 30 meeting rooms, travel services, banquet facilities. AE, DC, MC, V.*

$$$ **Hotel New Otani Tokyo and Towers.** The New Otani is virtually a town in itself. When all the rooms (almost 2,100) are occupied and all the banquet facilities are in use, the traffic flow in and out of the restaurants, lounges, and shopping arcades is like rush hour at a busy railway station. The hotel's redeeming feature is its peaceful, 10-acre manicured garden. Among the many restaurants and bars are **La Tour d'Argent** (*see* Dining, *above*); Japan's first **Trader Vic's;** and the revolving **Sky Lounge,** which completes one revolution every hour. ⌂ *4-1 Kioicho, Chiyoda-ku, Tokyo 102 (nearest subway station: Akasaka-mitsuke),* ☎ *03/3265–1111,* ℻ *03/3221–2619. 2,051 rooms, 30 on the 21st floor for women only. Restaurants, bars, outdoor pool, spa, golf driving range, tennis, rooms for the physically disabled, baby-sitting, Christian chapel, shops, banking services. AE, DC, MC, V.*

Asakusa

$$$ **Asakusa View Hotel.** If you want an elegant place to stay in the heart of Tokyo's old Asakusa area—actually resurrected after the World War II fire bombings—then this hotel is the only choice. The smart marble lobby features a harpist in the tea lounge, and expensive boutiques line the second floor. The standard pastel guest rooms are similar to what you find in all modern Tokyo hotels, but you also have access to communal *hinoki* (Japanese cypress) bathtubs that look onto a sixth-

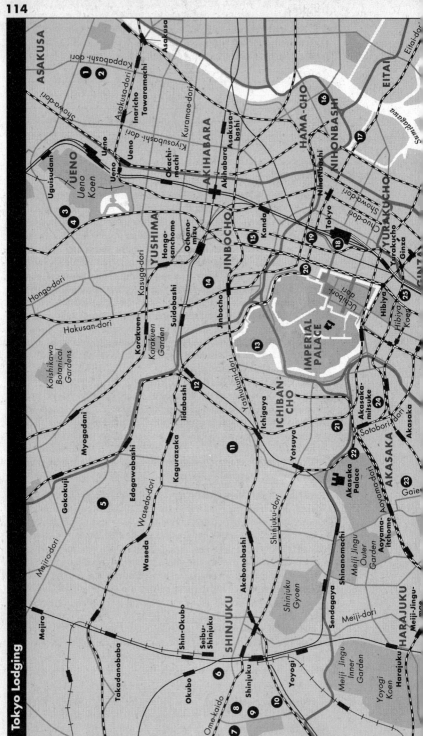

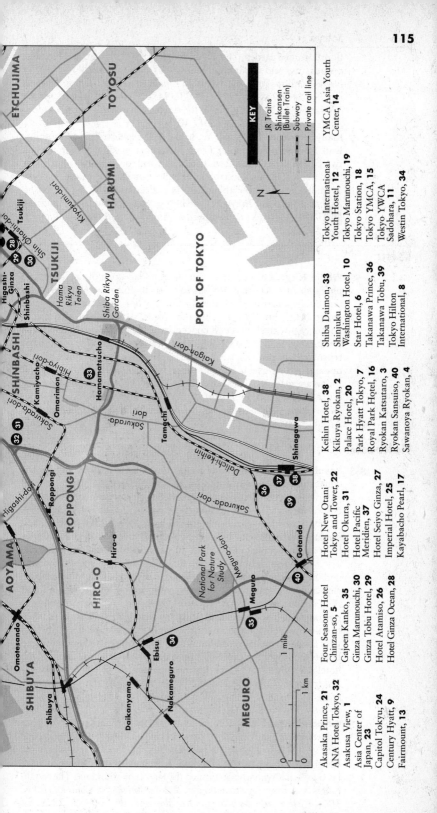

115

floor Japanese garden. There are Chinese, French, Italian, and Japanese restaurants, and a bar that keeps your personal bottle. ☎ *3-17-1 Nishi-Asakusa, Taito-ku, Tokyo 111 (nearest subway station: Tawara-machi),* ☏ *03/3847–1111,* ℻ *03/3845–0530. 350 rooms, mostly Western style. Concierge floor. Restaurants, bar, coffee shop, outdoor pool, health club. AE, DC, MC, V.*

$ Kikuya Ryokan. This small inn in the Asakusa district is a 10-minute walk from Sensoji (temple). From Tawaramachi subway station, walk two blocks up Kokusai-dori, take a left, and the ryokan is on the left-hand side just before Kappabashi-dori. Be warned, the inn locks its doors at midnight, and everything here is midget-sized. ☎ *2-18-9 Nishi-Asakusa, Taito-ku, Tokyo 111 (nearest subway station: Tawaramachi),* ☏ *03/3841–6404. 8 tatami rooms, 4 with private bath. Air-conditioning. AE, MC, V.*

Ebisu

$$ Westin Tokyo. Located in Yebisu Garden Place, one of the last grand pharaonic development projects to go up in Tokyo before the real estate bubble burst in 1994, the Westin provides easy access to a major department store (Mitsukoshi), the Tokyo Metropolitan Museum of Photography, an elegant new concert hall, and the **Taillevent-Robuchon** restaurant ($$$$; ☎ 03/5424–1338), this last housed in a full-scale reproduction of a Louis XV château. The decor of the hotel itself is updated Art Nouveau, with an excess of marble and bronze; standard rooms are spacious, suites huge. ☎ *1-4 Mita 1-chome, Meguro-ku (nearest JR/subway station: Ebisu),* ☏ *03/5423–7000,* ℻ *03/5423–7600. 445 rooms. Restaurants, bar, shops, health club, business services. AE, DC, MC, V.*

Hakozaki

$$$ Royal Park Hotel. This hotel would recommend itself if only for the connecting passageway to the Tokyo City Air Terminal where you can complete all your check-in procedures before you climb on the bus for Narita Airport. There's no luxury—especially at the end of an intensive business trip—like being able to pack, ring for the bellhop, and not have to touch your baggage again until it comes off the conveyor belt back home. Built in 1989, the 20-story Royal Park is well-designed: The large, open lobby has perhaps a bit more marble than it needs, and the inevitable space-age chandelier, but this is offset by wood-paneled columns, brass trim, and lots of comfortable lounge space. Guest rooms, done in coordinated neutral grays and browns, are well-proportioned; deluxe twins have handsome writing tables instead of built-in desktops. Ask for a room on one of the Executive Floors (16F-18F) with a northeast view of the Sumida River; another good option would be a room lower down (6F-8F) on the opposite side, overlooking the hotel's delightful 5th-floor Japanese garden. ☎ *2-1-1 Nihonbashi-Kakigaracho, Chuo-ku, Tokyo 103 (nearest subway station: Suitengu-mae),* ☏ *03/3667–1111,* ℻ *03/3665–7212. 441 rooms, 9 suites. Restaurants, shops. AE, DC, MC, V.*

$$ Kayabacho Pearl Hotel. Rooms here are strictly utilitarian, but the price is low, unless you sleep late; the staff adds a ¥3,000–¥4,000 charge for late check-out (after 10 AM). The hotel is located just across the bridge from Tokyo City Air Terminal, a five-minute walk from exit number 3 or 4 of Kayabacho Station on the Hibiya or Tozai Line. The restaurant is open from 7 AM to midnight. ☎ *1-2-5 Shinkawa, Chuo-ku, Tokyo 104 (nearest subway station: Kayabacho),* ☏ *03/3553–2211,* ℻ *03/3555–1849. 262 rooms. Restaurant. AE, DC, MC, V.*

Hibiya

$$$$ **Imperial Hotel.** The location of this prestigious establishment could not be better—in the heart of central Tokyo, between the Imperial Palace and Ginza. You can exit from the rear of the hotel and be in the center of the city's shopping and restaurant district. If you exit from the front of the hotel and walk five minutes, you can begin jogging around the grounds of the Imperial Palace. The choicest guest rooms, high up (on the 30th floor) in the New Tower, afford views of the Imperial Palace. The lobby has a vast lounge area for watching Tokyo's beautiful people. The shopping arcade has prestigious boutiques, while the restaurants—there are 21 of them—are some of Tokyo's finest and most sophisticated. A particularly memorable place to meet acquaintances before dinner is the **Old Imperial Bar,** with artifacts from the former Imperial building, designed by Frank Lloyd Wright. From its outset (the Imperial opened its doors in 1891), the hotel has been justly proud of its Western-style facilities and Japanese service. Now, with its new tower addition, the hotel is a vast complex, but it still retains its personalized service. ⌕ *1-1-1 Uchisaiwaicho, Chiyoda-ku, Tokyo 100 (nearest subway stations: Hibiya and Yurakucho),* ☎ *03/3504–1111,* FAX *03/3581–9146. 1,058 rooms, which range from standard twin size to suites that are larger than many homes. Restaurants, bars, indoor pool, health club, massage, shops. AE, DC, MC, V.*

Higashi-Ginza

$$$ **Ginza Tobu Hotel.** This hotel's relatively reasonable prices, friendly service, and comfortably sized rooms make it worth considering as a deluxe hotel in the high-rent district of Ginza. The higher price of the concierge floors provides a much larger room; breakfast, afternoon tea, and complimentary cocktails in the concierge lounge; and extras, such as a terry-cloth bathrobe and hair dryers. Especially useful is the hotel's 24-hour coffee shop, and there are French and Japanese (the excellent **Muraki**) restaurants as well. ⌕ *6-13-10 Ginza, Chuo-ku, Tokyo 104 (nearest subway station: Higashi-Ginza),* ☎ *03/3546–0111,* FAX *03/3546–8990. 206 rooms, all Western style. 2 concierge floors. Restaurants, business services. AE, DC, MC, V.*

$$ **Hotel Atamiso.** This hotel is not well known to many Westerners; its location, however, is convenient (near the Ginza area), and the staff's friendliness (marginal English is spoken) makes this place a real find. Formerly a ryokan, the Atamiso was transformed into a Western hotel in 1984 but has kept its Japanese appreciation of hospitality. For the size of the rooms, the hotel is an extremely good value. The hotel is too small to computerize its guests' names, so the receptionist remembers names of guests instead of consulting a computer screen. ⌕ *4-14-3 Ginza, Chuo-ku, Tokyo 104 (nearest subway station: Higashi-Ginza),* ☎ *03/3541–3621,* FAX *03/3541–3263. 74 rooms (singles, doubles, and Japanese-style rooms). Restaurants. AE, DC, MC, V.*

$$ **Hotel Ginza Ocean.** This delightful small hotel is around the corner
★ from the Kabuki-za in the Ginza section. The rooms, though not large, are comfortable. Virtually no English is spoken here, but sign language serves to communicate basic needs. There's an excellent Japanese restaurant, **Matsuryu,** as well. ⌕ *7-18-15 Ginza, Chuo-ku, Tokyo 104 (nearest subway station: Higashi-Ginza),* ☎ *03/3545–1221,* FAX *03/3545–1226. 32 Western-style rooms. Restaurant. AE, DC, V.*

Higashi-Gotanda

$ Ryokan Sansuiso. If you're traveling on a tight budget and want to immerse yourself in Japanese culture, consider this basic ryokan near Gotanda Station on the Yamanote Line. The proprietor will greet you with a warm smile and a bow, and escort you to a small tatami room with a pay TV and a rather noisy heater/air-conditioner mounted in the wall. Some rooms are stuffy (you can't open a window), and only two have private baths, but the Sansuiso is clean, easy-to-find, and only 20 minutes on the subway from Tokyo Station and the Ginza. Although students and young travelers will be most comfortable here, the midnight curfew poses a problem for night owls. This hotel is a member of the Japanese Inn Group; the Japanese National Tourist Organization can help make reservations. ⌂ *2-9-5, Higashi-Gotanda, Shinagawa-ku, Tokyo 141 (nearest train station: Gotanda on the JR Yamanote Line),* ☎ *03/3441–7475,* FAX *03/3449–1944. 2 rooms with bath, 7 rooms share bath. AE, V.*

Kudan-Minami

$$$ Fairmount Hotel. Nostalgia buffs will love the Fairmount; here's a
★ place that underwent a major renovation in 1988 and the water pipes are still exposed. Neatly wrapped and painted, of course, but exposed just the same. In relentlessly high-tech Tokyo, you'd have to look long for a hotel with pull-chain ventilators and real tile in the bathrooms. The Fairmount has all that and furniture (a little chipped) that Sears & Roebuck must have phased out of the catalog in 1955. The hotel isn't seedy, mind you, just old (it was built in 1951) and a bit set in its ways. The best thing about the seven-story Fairmount is its frontage on the park that runs along the east side of the Imperial Palace grounds; rooms facing the park have a wonderful view of the moat and Chidorigafuchi pond, where Tokyo couples take rented rowboats out on summer Sunday afternoons. ⌂ *2-1-17 Kudan-Minami, Chiyoda-ku Tokyo 102 (nearest subway station: Kudanshita),* ☎ *03/3262–1151,* FAX *03/3264–2476. 205 rooms, 3 suites. Restaurant, bar. AE, DC, MC, V.*

Kyobashi

$$$$ Hotel Seiyo Ginza. Location and personalized service are the two reasons to choose this shockingly expensive hotel (double rooms start at ¥50,000). Right in the heart of Ginza, it is designed for those traveling on a generous expense account who want to be close to their Ginza appointments, as well as the shopping and nightlife of the area, and who need a personal secretary to take care of their every need (each room has a direct line to a secretary). Standard rooms and one-bedroom suites are smaller than what Americans might expect for this price, but the modern furnishings and quiet beige-and-peach decor make the rooms seem larger. Although the hallway carpeting is beginning to show signs of wear (the hotel opened in 1989), guest rooms have held up well. White-marble bathrooms are sparkling clean; those in the suites have steam showers. With only 79 rooms, the Seiyo Ginza is quiet and private, almost like a luxury apartment complex but with 220 courteous attendants aiming to make your stay just right. There are four restaurants, including **Attore,** serving Italian food (*see* Dining, *above*), and **Pastorale,** a French/Continental restaurant. ⌂ *1-11-2 Ginza, Chuo-ku, Tokyo 104 (nearest subway station: Ginza),* ☎ *03/3535–1111,* FAX *03/3535–1110. 79 rooms. Restaurants, bar, lounge, health club, banquet hall, cake shop, business services. AE, DC, MC, V.*

Marunouchi

$$$$ **Palace Hotel.** This is a less expensive alternative to the Imperial Hotel
★ for anyone wanting a deluxe hotel near the Imperial Palace. Service is
extremely helpful and professional; half the staff has been with the hotel
for more than 10 years. The location is as close to the Imperial Palace
as one could be; only a water-filled moat separates the hotel from the
palace grounds. On the other hand, it is a taxi or subway ride to the
bright lights of Ginza, or anywhere else, for that matter. The sedate,
calm atmosphere of the hotel reflects its more than 50 years as a leading Tokyo accommodation. The guest rooms are reasonably spacious;
those on the upper floors facing the Imperial Palace are definitely preferred. The hotel's public areas are rectangular and uninspiring. Nevertheless, location and good value make it particularly attractive to
business travelers who want to be close to downtown. ⊡ *1-1-1
Marunouchi, Chiyoda-ku, Tokyo 100 (nearest subway station: Tokyo),*
☎ *03/3211–5211,* ⅨX *03/3211–6987. 405 rooms. Restaurants, bars,
business services. AE, DC, MC, V.*

$$$ **Ginza Marunouchi Hotel.** This establishment opened in 1976 and im-
mediately became popular with foreign visitors because of its price and
its location near Ginza's high-rent district. Recent redecorating has im-
proved this small hotel. Guest rooms are small, compact, and clean.
Except when a large tour group arrives, the lobby/lounge area invites
a shared fellowship among the guests. ⊡ *1-12 Tsukiji 4-chome, Chuo-
ku, Tokyo 104 (nearest subway station: Higashi-Ginza),* ☎ *03/3543–
5431,* ⅨX *03/3543–6006. 114 rooms. Restaurant. AE, DC, MC, V.*

$$$ **Tokyo Marunouchi Hotel.** In business since 1924, the Tokyo Marunouchi
has rooms that were last refurbished in 1987; these have seen a lot of
traffic since then. Guest rooms tend to be a little drab, but they are
(for Tokyo) of reasonable size and have more individuality than the
boxlike rooms in other modern Tokyo hotels. The Tokyo Marunouchi
is very popular with Westerners, and the staff has come to anticipate
their needs. Within two blocks of Tokyo Station, three blocks from the
Imperial Palace, and two subway stops from Ginza, the lodging is in
the prime-rent district. ⊡ *1-6-3 Marunouchi, Chiyoda-ku, Tokyo 100
(nearest subway station: Tokyo),* ☎ *03/3215–2151,* ⅨX *03/3215–
8036. 210 rooms. Restaurant, coffee shop, bar. AE, DC, MC, V.*

$$$ **Tokyo Station Hotel.** Above Tokyo Station, this building is part of
Tokyo's heritage. It was saved in 1990 from the wrecker's ball by preser-
vationists, and an interior renovation included a fresh paint job, a fresh
coat of varnish on the grand old wooden staircase from the lobby to
the second floor, and new carpets for the corridors (which, inciden-
tally, are wider than the rooms of many Tokyo hotels). For the mo-
ment, this hotel should only be recommended for an overnight stay
between trains, though it can be a useful place for breakfast before set-
ting out on a journey. ⊡ *1-9-1 Marunouchi, Chiyodu-ku, Tokyo 100
(nearest subway station: Tokyo),* ☎ *03/3231–2511,* ⅨX *03/3231–
3513. 170 rooms, 56 with bath. AE, DC, MC, V.*

Meguro

$$ **Gajoen Kanko Hotel.** After a major renovation in 1986, this pre–World
War II hotel has made a comeback and offers good value in a residential
area, away from the noise and bustle of Tokyo's traffic. The Gajoen
Kanko is full of old prints, scrolls, and oriental rococo decor. The hotel
has grown since its days as an occupation-era accommodation by the
addition of an annex. This place may not appeal to all, but it is one of
the very few Tokyo accommodations that have character and individ-

uality. ⌖ *1-8-1 Shimo-Meguro, Meguro-ku, Tokyo 153 (nearest train station: Meguro on the JR Yamanote Line),* ☎ *03/3491–0111,* FAX *03/3495–2450. 108 rooms. Restaurants. AE, DC, MC, V.*

Nagatacho

$$$$ **Capitol Tokyu Hotel.** The Capitol Tokyu was once the Hilton, before the latter moved to its new location in Shinjuku in 1984; the lease reverted to the Tokyu chain. It is now Tokyu's flagship hotel. Though it is only 31 years old, it has a feeling of being a grand hotel of a past era, which can be a welcome change to the glitter of Tokyo's newer hotels. The hotel is also relatively small by Tokyo's standards, and, with close to two permanent staff members to every guest, service is excellent. Perhaps that is why the hotel has such a repeat trade among foreign businessmen. Guest-room furnishings (dark wood furniture) have a traditional Western feel, but the shoji screens add a warm lightness to the ambience. As an extra benefit, some of the rooms, No. 1039, for example, look onto the Hie Shrine. To the left of the lobby is a small garden with a pond; two of the hotel's dining rooms (the Origami breakfast café and the Tea Lounge) also afford views of the shrine. ⌖ *10-3 Nagatacho 2-chome, Chiyoda-ku, Tokyo 100 (nearest subway station: Kokkai Gijido-mae),* ☎ *03/3581–4511,* FAX *03/3581–5822. 459 rooms. Restaurants, bars, business center, steam bath, massage, outdoor pool, shops. AE, DC.*

Nishi-Shinjuku

$$$$ **Century Hyatt Hotel.** This member of the Hyatt international hotel chain has the trademark atrium-style lobby—seven stories high, with open-glass elevators soaring upward and three huge chandeliers suspended from above. The larger rooms are arranged to offer the semblance of a separate sitting area, and all rooms are decorated in pastels. The single rooms tend to be small and lack good views from their windows. The Hyatt emphasizes its cuisine (there are 12 restaurants and bars), with special gourmet weeks supervised by visiting international chefs. ⌖ *2-7-2 Nishi-Shinjuku, Shinjuku-ku, Tokyo 160 (nearest subway station: Shinjuku),* ☎ *03/3349–0111,* FAX *03/3344–5575. 774 rooms, including a few luxurious Japanese-style rooms, 1- and 2-bedroom Western-style suites, and 2 concierge floors. Restaurants, bars, indoor pool. AE, DC, MC, V.*

$$$$ **Park Hyatt Tokyo.** The elevator whisks you to the 41st floor, where the hotel begins with an atrium lounge enclosed on three sides by floor-to-ceiling plate-glass windows. The panorama of Shinjuku is laid out before you; the tops of neighboring skyscrapers add to the three-dimensional spectacle. At the other end of the lounge, past the open-plan Girandole restaurant (Continental cuisine), are the check-in desks. Registration forms are put before you already filled with the details and simply awaiting your signature. Service is so efficient and personal, the staff seem to know your name before you introduce yourself! The mood of the hotel is contemporary and understated. Guest rooms, which run from the 42nd to the 50th floors, are vast by any standards, and are furnished with king-size beds (dressed with 100% Egyptian cotton sheets and down-feather duvets), beige, fabric-covered walls, pale olive-green carpets, black lacquer cupboards, and glass-top tables and desk. Even the bathrooms have views: The tub is situated by a window. From the 45th to the 47th floors is a health facility with a Jacuzzi, steam and dry saunas, Shiatsu and Swedish massage, a gym, an aerobic studio, a 20-meter swimming pool, a game room, and fitness trainers. Restaurants, in addition to the Girandole and Peak Lounge, include a two-story space where you can dine on Japanese home-style cooking and, on a clear day, catch a glimpse of Mt. Fuji. On the 52nd floor is the New York Grill and Bar, with an open kitchen that serves steaks, seafood, and poultry. The food is top quality, prepared under the direction of a tiny Irish woman who dominates her team of Japanese cooks. ☎ *3-7-1-2 Nishi-Shinjuku, Shinjuku-ku, Tokyo 163-10 (nearest subway station: Shinjuku),* ☎ *03/5322–1234,* FAX *03/5322–1288. 178 rooms. 4 restaurants, fitness center, indoor pool, banquet and conference rooms. AE, MC, V.*

$$$$ **Tokyo Hilton International.** The newest of the three deluxe Shinjuku skyscraper hotels and the largest Hilton in Asia, the Tokyo Hilton is frequented by Western business travelers. The atmosphere of its public areas is one of impersonal efficiency. The guest rooms, however, afford good views of the other Shinjuku skyscrapers and benefit from using shoji screens instead of curtains. The **Imari Room,** with its displays of museum-quality traditional pottery, is one of Tokyo's more elegant places to dine. ☎ *6-2 Nishi-Shinjuku 6-chome, Shinjuku-ku, Tokyo 160 (nearest subway station: Shinjuku),* ☎ *03/3344–5111,* FAX *03/3342–6094. 807 rooms, including the concierge floor. Restaurants, sauna, indoor and outdoor pools, tennis, business services, shops, dance club, nightclub cabaret. AE, DC, MC, V.*

$$ **Shinjuku Washington Hotel.** This is truly a business hotel, where service is computerized as much as possible. In the third-floor lobby, automated check-in and check-out systems are available; you are assigned a room and provided with a plastic card that allows entry to your small room and access to the minibar. A few staff members in the lobby explain the process, but after that you are on your own. ☎ *3-2-9 Nishi-Shinjuku, Shinjuku-ku, Tokyo 160 (nearest subway station: Shinjuku),* ☎ *03/3343–3111,* FAX *03/3342–2575. 1,650 rooms. Minibars, refrigerators, TV. AE, DC, MC, V.*

$$ **Star Hotel.** This small, friendly hotel has rates more reasonable than
★ many in the area. The staff speaks only Japanese but is sympathetic to sign language. The rooms are clean, though not spacious; a small, pleasant restaurant serves Japanese and Western food. The Star lacks the amenities of doormen, bellhops, and the countless bars of the larger hotels, but the size of the hotel allows the front-desk manager to remember your name without the help of a computer. ☎ *7-10-5 Nishi-Shinjuku, Shinjuku-ku, Tokyo 160 (nearest subway station: Shinjuku),* ☎ *03/3361–1111,* FAX *03/3369–4216. 80 Western-style rooms. Restaurant. AE, DC, MC, V.*

Roppongi

$ **Asia Center of Japan.** This hotel, which seems to host more foreign guests than many other establishments, is popular for its central location, only a 15-minute walk from Roppongi. (Turn left out of the subway up Aoyama-dori and right at the Akasaka Post Office. The hotel is just down the first left-hand side street.) The rooms are basic, clean, small, and not too well soundproofed, but you get a good value for what you pay. ☎ *10-32 Akasaka 2-chome, Minato-ku, Tokyo 107 (nearest subway stations: Roppongi and Aoyama-itchome),* ☎ *03/3402–6111,* FAX *03/3402–0738. 172 Western-style rooms; some with private bath. Cafeteria, bar, garden patio. No credit cards.*

Sekiguchi

$$$$ **Four Seasons Hotel Chinzan-so.** Where else will you have a chance to
★ sleep in a million-dollar room? That's about what it cost to complete each guest room at this Tokyo property, which opened in 1992. Dark-

wood furniture, plush carpeting, ceramic lamps, gold-frame prints, and yards and yards of floral chintz make these some of the most luxurious hotel rooms in the world. Not surprisingly they were decorated by Frank Nicholson, Inc., which also designed rooms for the Chicago Ritz-Carlton. Most of the furnishings are American, complemented by Japanese accessories (lamps, ashtrays, tea sets, and so on). The rooms are large by any standard, and bathrooms are equally grand. These have cream-marble walls and floor, with gold-tone fixtures and a separate toilet room with an electronically controlled toilet/bidet. In the wainscotted lobby there's a green-marble floor from Italy covered by huge wool area rugs woven in Ireland. For some, the best part about the Four Seasons is its setting, in the beautiful Chinzan-so Gardens. The hotel makes it easy to get downtown by offering complimentary shuttle-bus service to the subway station and complimentary limousine service to Tokyo Station. ⌂ *2-10-8 Sekiguchi, Bunkyo-ku, Tokyo 112 (nearest subway station: Waseda),* ☎ *03/3943–2222 or 800/332– 3442,* ☎ *03/3943–2300. 284 rooms, 2 Japanese-style suites. Restaurants, bar, lounge, Japanese baths, massage, Jacuzzi, indoor pool, gym, barbershop, salon, shops, ballroom and meeting rooms, Shinto and Christian chapels. AE, DC, MC, V.*

Shiba Koen

$$ Shiba Daimon Hotel. For a moderately priced hotel that is popular with in-the-know Japanese, try this small establishment located close to Zojoji (temple). The smart, clean rooms are no smaller than what you usually find in Tokyo hotels. Service is politely Japanese—speak a couple of words of the native tongue, and the staff is even friendly. Shiba Daimon does not cater to the foreign tourist, and there are no English-language brochures available, but the staff is willing to help when possible. A good restaurant situated on the ground floor serves breakfast and then Chinese cuisine in the evening. ⌂ *2-3-6 Shiba-koen, Minato-ku, Tokyo 105 (nearest subway station: Daimon),* ☎ *03/3431–3716,* ☎ *03/3434–5177. 96 rooms. Restaurant. AE, DC, MC, V.*

Shinagawa

$$$ Hotel Pacific Meridien. Located on grounds that were once part of the imperial family's estate, the Pacific Meridien is across from the Shinagawa Station and glitters with glass and marble. The hotel markets itself to convention groups and to business travelers who wish to be in this area of Tokyo. Decor is pastel and lilac all the way to the Sky Lounge on the 30th floor, which has views over Tokyo Bay. The coffee lounge on the ground floor looks out onto tranquil gardens. In addition to nine restaurants and bars, there's a good bookstore with English-language books. ⌂ *3-13-3 Takanawa, Minato-ku, Tokyo 108 (nearest train station: Shinagawa on the JR Yamanote, Tokaido, and Keihin Tohoku lines),* ☎ *03/3445–6711,* ☎ *03/3445–5137. 954 rooms. Restaurants, bars, outdoor pool, shops, business services, banquet halls, parking, large Japanese garden. AE, DC, MC, V.*

$$$ Takanawa Prince Hotel. This hotel is separated from its big brother, the New Takanawa Prince, by a beautiful garden that is part Western and part Japanese. This Prince establishment is more geared to the individual traveler than to large groups, though the lobby's design is the large, open plan so favored by the Japanese. Guest rooms are fairly compact; those overlooking the garden are the best. ⌂ *13-1 Takanawa 3-chome, Minato-ku, Tokyo 108 (nearest train station: Shinagawa on the JR Yamanote, Tokaido, and Keihin Tohoku lines),* ☎ *03/3447–*

1111, FAX *03/3446–0849. 416 rooms, each with a balcony, and 18 tatami suites. Restaurants, bars, pools, shops. AE, DC, MC, V.*

$$$ Takanawa Tobu Hotel. Across the street from the monolithic New Takanawa Prince and a five-minute walk from the Shinagawa Station, the Takanawa Tobu offers good value. The guest rooms are on the small side, and no proper lobby sitting area is available, but the virtues are a welcoming staff (who speak modest English) and a friendly bar lounge. There's also a small Western restaurant, the **Boulogne.** ▦ *7-6 Takanawa 4-chome, Minato-ku, Tokyo 108 (nearest train station: Shinagawa on the JR Yamanote, Tokaido, and Keihin Tohoku lines),* ☎ *03/3447-0111,* FAX *03/3447-0117. 190 rooms. Restaurant, bar. AE, DC, MC, V.*

$$ Keihin Hotel. Directly across the street from Shinagawa Station, the Keihin is best described as a business hotel. The building is small, as are the rooms, but the staff is personable and the manager speaks English enthusiastically and enjoys having Westerners stay. For a modest hotel, the Keihin is a good value, given its convenient location. ▦ *4-10-20 Takanawa, Minato-ku, Tokyo 108 (nearest train station: Shinagawa on the JR Yamanote, Tokaido, and Keihin Tohoku lines),* ☎ *03/3449–5711,* FAX *03/3441–7230. 52 Western-style rooms. Restaurant. AE, DC, MC, V.*

Toranomon

$$$$ ANA Hotel Tokyo. In the proximity of the U.S. Embassy, the ANA Hotel arrived on the Tokyo scene in 1986. The first-floor marble lobby covers a large area split by a coffee shop, dining lounge, escalator, and reception desks, with a central fountain as its focal point. Guest rooms are bright and airy; the 34th floor serves as the concierge floor, with a separate breakfast room and evening cocktail lounge for its guests. Throughout the hotel, tasteful vases and artwork help to offset some of the coldness of the marble interior. There are Chinese, French, and Japanese restaurants, three bars, and the Astral Lounge on the top (37th) floor, with superb views. ▦ *12-33 Akasaka 1-chome, Minato-ku, Tokyo 107 (nearest subway stations: Kamiyacho and Toranomon),* ☎ *03/3505-1111,* FAX *03/3505–1155. 900 rooms. Restaurants, bars, exercise room, outdoor pool, men's sauna, business services, shopping arcade, travel services, beauty salon. AE, DC, MC, V.*

$$$$ Hotel Okura. As one of the most prestigious of Tokyo hotels, the ★ Okura is continually striving to maintain a position at the top. The Okura is understated in its sophistication, except for its vast lobby. Ever since it was completed just before the 1964 Olympics, the Okura has been a favorite of the diplomatic and knowledgeable business traveler. The atmosphere is traditional, even old-fashioned to some, and the emphasis is on exemplary service. The spacious guest rooms are tastefully furnished, including sliding frosted shoji screens in front of the windows, which permits a relaxing light to fill the room. Remote-control draperies, hair dryers, and terry-cloth bathrobes are but a few of the extras that come with the room. The odd-numbered rooms, 871-889 inclusive, look onto a small Japanese landscaped garden. On the hotel grounds is the Okura Art Museum, in a traditional Japanese building, with exhibits of antique porcelain, mother-of-pearl, and ceramics. A tea ceremony is held every day 11 am–noon and 1–5 PM. In recent years, the Okura has added the South Wing, which is slightly detached from most of the hotel's facilities; the main building is preferable. (See also Dining, *above.*) ▦ *10-4 Toranomon 2-chome, Minato-ku, Tokyo 105 (nearest subway stations: Kamiyacho and Toranomon),* ☎ *03/3582-0111,* FAX *03/3582–3707. 883 rooms (including 83 suites and 11 su-*

perb Japanese-style rooms). Restaurants, gym, indoor (heated) and outdoor pools, steam bath, massage, business services, banquet facilities. AE, DC, MC, V.

Ueno

$ Ryokan Katsutaro. This small, simple, economical hotel is a five-minute walk from Ueno Park and a 10-minute walk from the National Museum. Leave the Nezu subway station by the Ikenohata exit, cross the road, take the street running northeast, go right at the "T" junction, and the ryokan is 25 meters (yards) on the left-hand side of Dobutsuen-Uramon-dori. The quietest rooms are in the back, away from the main street. ☎ 4-16-8 Ikenohata, Taito-ku, Tokyo 110 (nearest subway station: Nezu), ☎ 03/3821–9808, FAX 03/3891–4789. 7 rooms, 4 with private bath. Breakfast room, pay TV. AE, DC, MC, V.

Yanaka

$ **Sawanoya Ryokan.** Sawanoya is situated in a quiet area to the north-
★ west of Ueno Park; the residential locale and the hospitality of the ryokan make you feel at home in traditional Tokyo. (From Nezu subway station, walk 275 meters (yards) north along Shinobazu-dori, take the street on the right, and the Sawanoya is 165 meters on the right.) The owners truly welcome travelers; they help them plan trips and arrange future accommodations. No dinner is offered, but breakfast (Continental or Japanese) is available at an extra charge. Sawanoya has become very popular with low-budget travelers; make a reservation by fax well before you arrive. ☎ 2-3-11 Yanaka, Taito-ku, Tokyo 110 (nearest subway station: Nezu), ☎ 03/3822–2251, FAX 03/3822–2252. 12 rooms, 2 with private bath. Breakfast room, pay TV, air-conditioning. AE, MC, V.

Hostels and Dormitory Accommodations

$$ **Tokyo YMCA.** Rooms come with and without bath. Both men and women can stay at the hostel, which is a three-minute walk from Awajicho Station on the Marunouchi Line or seven minutes from Kanda Station on the Ginza Line. ☎ 7 Kanda-Mitoshirocho, Chiyoda-ku, Tokyo 101, ☎ 03/3293–1919, FAX 03/3293–1926. 40 rooms.

$$ **Tokyo YWCA Sadohara.** Rooms are available here with bath; as are rooms for married couples. The hostel is a three-minute walk from Ichigaya Station on the Chuo and Toei Shinjuku lines. ☎ 3-1-1 Ichigaya-Sadaharacho, Shinjuku-ku, Tokyo, ☎ 03/3268–7313, FAX 03/3268–4452. 16 rooms.

$ **Tokyo International Youth Hostel.** All residents here are required off the premises 10 AM–3PM. The hostel is very close to Iidabashi Station on the JR, Tozai, and Yurakucho lines. ☎ 18F Central Plaza Bldg., 1-1 Kagura-kashi, Shinjuku-ku, Tokyo, ☎ 03/3235–1107. 138 bunk beds.

$ **YMCA Asia Youth Center.** Both men and women can stay here; all rooms have private baths. The hostel is an eight-minute walk from Suidobashi Station on the JR Mita Line. ☎ 5-5 Saragakucho 2-chome, Chiyoda-ku, Tokyo, ☎ 03/3233–0611, FAX 03/3233–0633. 55 rooms.

Near Narita Airport

$$$ **ANA Hotel Narita.** Opened in 1990, this hotel—like many in the ANA chain—aspires to architecture in the grand style; expect the cost of brass and marble to show up on your bill. The amenities measure up, and the proximity to the airport (about 15 min. by shuttle bus) makes this a good choice for visitors in transit. ☎ 68 Horinouchi, Narita-shi, Chiba-

ken 286-01, ☎ 0476/33–1311, ℻ 0476/33–0244. 422 rooms. Restaurants, bar, pool, shops. AE, DC, MC, V.

$$$ **Holiday Inn Tobu Narita.** A 10-minute ride by shuttle bus from the airport, this establishment offers Western-style accommodations with a full range of amenities. ☎ *320-1 Tokko, Narita-shi, Chiba-ken 286-01, ☎ 0476/32–1234, ℻ 0476/32–0617. 500 soundproof rooms that can also be rented for daytime-only use (¥19,000 for 2 beds). Restaurants, bar, pool, steam bath, massage, barbershop, beauty salon. AE, DC, MC, V.*

$$$ **Narita View Hotel.** Boxy and uninspired, the Narita View offers no view of anything in particular, but can be reached by shuttle bus from the airport in about 15 minutes. Short on charm, it tends to rely on promotional discount "campaigns" to draw a clientele. ☎ *700 Kosuge, Narita-shi, Chiba-ken 286-01, ☎ 0476/32–1111, ℻ 0476/32–1078. 504 rooms that can also be rented for daytime-only use from 7 AM to 9 PM at 50% the normal rate. Restaurants, beauty salon, massage. AE, DC, MC, V.*

$$$ **Radisson Hotel Narita Airport.** This accommodation resembles a resort hotel with spacious grounds. It is new and modern, but it has some greenery on its 72 acres of land—as well as Narita's largest outdoor pool. A shuttle bus runs between the hotel and the airport every 20 minutes or so from 1 to 11 pm; the trip takes about 15 minutes. ☎ *650-35 Nanaei, Tomisato-machi, Inba-gun, Chiba-ken 288-02, ☎ 0476/93–1234, ℻ 0476/93–4834. 500 rooms. Restaurants, air-conditioning, pool, tennis, jogging, shop. AE, DC, MC, V.*

$$ **Narita Winds Hotel.** A regular shuttle bus (at Terminal 1, bus stop No. 11; Terminal 2, bus stop No. 31) makes the 10-minute trip to this modern, efficient, all-purpose hotel, with five restaurants, banquet rooms, and meeting facilities. ☎ *560 Tokko, Narita-shi, Chiba-ken 286-01, ☎ 0476/33–1111, ℻ 0476/33–1108. 321 soundproof rooms. Restaurants, pool, sauna, tennis, shops, meeting rooms. AE, DC, MC, V.*

$$ **Narita Airport Rest House.** A basic business-style hotel without much in the way of frills, the Rest House offers the closest accommodations to the airport itself, less than five minutes away by shuttle bus. ☎ *New Tokyo International Airport, Narita-shi, Chiba-ken 286-11, ☎ 0476/32–1212, ℻ 0476/32–1209. 210 soundproofed rooms that can also be rented for daytime-only use from 8 AM to 6 PM (double: ¥12,000). Restaurant. AE, DC, MC, V.*

THE ARTS

Few cities have as much to offer as Tokyo does in the performing arts. It has Japan's own great stage traditions: Kabuki, Noh, Bunraku puppet drama, music, and dance. It has an astonishing variety of music, classical and popular; Tokyo is a proving ground for local talent and a magnet for orchestras and concert soloists from all over the world. The Rolling Stones, Jean Pierre Rampal, the Berlin Philharmonic, Oscar Peterson: Whenever you visit, the headliners will be here. It has modern theater—in somewhat limited choices, to be sure, unless you can follow dialogue in Japanese; but Western repertory companies can always find receptive audiences here for plays in English. In recent years musicals have found enormous popularity here; it doesn't take long for a hit show in New York or London to open in Tokyo. Film, too, presents a much broader range of possibilities than it used to. The major commercial distributors bring in the movies they expect to draw the biggest receipts—horror films and Oscar nominees—but there are now dozens of small theaters in Tokyo catering to more sophisticated audiences. Japan has yet to develop any serious strength of its own in opera or ballet, but for that reason touring companies like the Metropolitan and the Bolshoi, Sadler's Wells, and the Bayerische Staatsoper find Tokyo a very compelling venue—as well they might, when ¥20,000 seats are sold out even before the box office opens.

Information and Tickets

The best comprehensive guide in English to performance schedules in Tokyo is the "Cityscope" insert in the monthly *Tokyo Journal* magazine. You can probably pick up the *Journal* at one of the newsstands at Narita Airport on your way into the city; if not, it's on sale in the bookstores at all the major international hotels. In addition to reviewing and recommending films, plays, and concerts, "Cityscope" also covers museums and art galleries, television, festivals, and special events. Another source, rather less complete, is the *Tour Companion,* a tabloid visitor's guide published every two weeks that is available free of charge at hotels and at Japan National Tourist Organization offices. For a weekly update, the Monday edition of the English-language *Mainichi Daily News* also carries information on performances.

If your hotel cannot help you with bookings, two of the city's major ticket agencies have numbers to call for assistance in English: **Ticket Pia** (☎ 03/5237–9999) and **Ticket Saison** (☎ 03/5990–9999; closed Wed.). A third possibility is the **Playguide** agency, which has outlets in most of the department stores and in other locations all over the city; you can stop in at the main office (Playguide Bldg., 2-6-4 Ginza, Chuo-ku, ☎ 03/3561–8821) and ask for the nearest counter. Note that agencies normally do not have tickets for same-day performances but only for advanced booking.

Traditional Theater

Kabuki

Kabuki emerged as a popular form of entertainment in the early 17th century; before long, it had been banned by the authorities as a threat to public order. Eventually it cleaned up its act, and by the latter half of the 18th century it had become Everyman's Theater par excellence—especially among the townspeople of bustling, hustling Edo. Kabuki had music, dancing, and spectacle; it had acrobatics and sword fights; it had pathos and tragedy and historical romance and social satire. It didn't have beautiful girls—women have been banned from the Kabuki stage since 1629—but in recompense it developed a professional role for female impersonators, who train for years to project a seductive, dazzling femininity that few real women ever achieve. It had superstars and quick-change artists and legions of fans, who brought their lunch to the theater, stayed all day, and shouted out the names of their favorite actors at the stirring moments in their favorite plays. Edo is now Tokyo, but Kabuki is still here, just as it has been for centuries. The traditions are passed down from generation to generation in a small group of families; the roles and great stage names are hereditary. The Kabuki repertoire does not really grow or change, but stars like Ennosuke Ichikawa and Tamasaburo Bando have put exciting, personal stamps on their performances that continue to draw audiences young and old.

Certainly the best place to see Kabuki is at the **Kabuki-za** (4-12-15 Ginza, Chuo-ku, ☎ 03/5565–6000; call by 6 PM the day preceding performance for reservations; nearest subway station: Higashi-Ginza), built especially for this purpose in 1925, with its hanamichi (runway) passing diagonally through the audience to the revolving stage. The Kabuki-za was rebuilt after the war. The facade of the building recalls the castle architecture of the 16th century; the lanterns and banners and huge theater posters outside identify it unmistakably. Matinees usually begin at 11 AM and end at 3:30 PM; evening performances, at 4:30 pm, end around 9 PM. Reserved seats are expensive and hard to come by on short notice; for a mere ¥600 to ¥1,000, however, you can buy an unreserved ticket that allows you to see one act of a play from the topmost gallery. The gallery is cleared after each act, but there's nothing to prevent you from buying another ticket: The price is low for an hour or so of this fascinating spectacle. Bring binoculars—the gallery is very far from the stage. You might also want to rent an earphone set (¥600) to follow the play in English, but this is really more of an intrusion than a help—and you can't use the set in the upmost galleries, anyway.

Two other theaters in Tokyo specialize in traditional performances and offer Kabuki at various times during the year. The **Shinbashi Enbujo** (6-18-2 Ginza, Chuo-ku, ☎ 03/5565–6000, the same reservation office as the Kabuki-za; nearest subway station: Higashi-Ginza), which dates from 1925, was built originally for the geisha of the Shinbashi quarter to present their spring and autumn performances of traditional music and dance. It's a bigger house than the Kabuki-za, and it still presents a lot of traditional dance as well as conventional drama (in Japanese), but there is no gallery; reserved seats commonly run ¥3,000–¥13,500. The **National Theater of Japan** (4-1 Hayabusacho, Chiyoda-ku, ☎ 03/3265–7411; nearest subway station: Hanzomon), mentioned in our exploring tour of the Imperial Palace area, plays host to Kabuki companies based elsewhere; it also has a training program for young people who may not have one of the hereditary family connections but want to break into this closely guarded profession. Debut performances, called kao-mise, are worth watching to catch the stars of the next generation. ☞ ¥1,400–¥8,200.

Noh

Noh is a dramatic tradition far older than Kabuki; it reached a point of formal perfection in the 14th century and survives virtually unchanged from that period. Where Kabuki was everyman's theater, Noh developed for the most part under the patronage of the warrior class. It is dignified and solemn, ritualized and symbolic; many of the plays in the repertoire are drawn from classical literature or tales of the supernatural, and the texts are richly poetic. Where the Kabuki actor is usually in brightly colored makeup derived from the Chinese opera, the principal character in a Noh play wears a carved wooden mask. Such is the skill of the actor, and the mysterious effect of the play, that the mask seems to express a whole range of emotions. As in Kabuki, the various roles of the Noh repertoire all have specific costumes—robes of silk brocade with intricate patterns that are works of art in themselves. Noh is not a very *accessible* kind of theater: Its language is archaic; its conventions are obscure; and its measured, stately pace can put even Japanese audiences to sleep. More than anything else you will see in Tokyo, however, Noh will provide an experience of Japan as an *ancient* culture.

Somewhat like Kabuki, Noh is divided into a number of schools, the traditions of which developed as the exclusive property of hereditary families. It is occasionally performed in public halls, like the **National Noh Theater** (4-18-1 Sendagaya, Shibuya-ku, ☎ 03/3423–1331; nearest subway station: Sendagaya), but primarily in the theaters of these schools—which also teach their dance and recitation styles to amateurs.

The most important of these are the **Kanze Noh-gakudo** (1-16-4 Shoto, Shibuya-ku, ☎ 03/3469–5241; nearest subway station: Shibuya), the **Kita Roppeita Kinen Noh-gakudo** (4-6-9 Kami-Osaki, Shinagawa-ku, ☎ 03/3491–7773; nearest subway station: Meguro), the **Hosho Noh-gakudo** (1-5-9 Hongo, Bunkyo-ku, ☎ 03/3811–4843; nearest subway station: Suidobashi), and the **Umewaka Noh-gakuin** (2-6-14 Higashi-Nakano, Nakano-ku, ☎ 03/3363–7748; nearest subway station: Nakano-Sakaue). The very best way to see Noh, however, is in the open air, at torchlight performances called Takigi Noh, held in the court-yards of temples. The setting and the aesthetics of the drama combine in an eerie theatrical experience. These performances are given at various times during the year; consult the "Cityscope" or Tour Companion listings. Tickets are normally available only through the temples and are sold out very quickly.

Bunraku

The third major form of traditional Japanese drama is Bunraku, or puppet theater. Itinerant puppeteers were plying their trade in Japan as early as the 10th century; sometime in the late 16th century, a form of narrative ballad called *joruri,* performed to the accompaniment of a three-string banjolike instrument called the *shamisen,* was grafted onto their art, and Bunraku was born. The golden age of Bunraku came some 200 years later, when most of the great Bunraku plays were written and the puppets themselves evolved to their present form—so expressive and intricate in their movements that they require three people at one time to manipulate them. Puppeteers and narrators (who deliver their lines in a kind of high-pitch croak, deep in the throat) train for many years to master this difficult and unusual genre of popular entertainment.

The spiritual center of Bunraku today is Osaka, rather than Tokyo, but performances are given here with some frequency in the small hall of the National Theater (*see above*). In recent years, it has also begun to enjoy a minor vogue with younger audiences, and Bunraku troupes will occasionally perform in trendier locations. Consult the "Cityscope" listings, or check with one of the English-speaking ticket agencies.

Modern Theater

The **Shingeki** (Modern Theater) movement began in Japan at about the turn of the century. The first problem its earnest young actors and directors encountered was the fact that they had no native repertoire. The "conservative" faction at first tended to approach the problem with translations of Shakespeare, the "radicals" with Ibsen, Gorky, and Shaw. It wasn't until around 1915 that Japanese playwrights began writing for the Shingeki stage. Japan of the 1930s and 1940s, in any case, was none too hospitable an environment for modern drama; the movement did not develop any real vitality until after World War II.

The watershed years came around 1965, when experimental theater companies—unable to find commercial space—began taking their work to young audiences in various unusual ways: street plays and "happenings"; dramatic readings in underground malls and rented lofts; tents put up on vacant lots for unannounced performances (miraculously filled to capacity by word of mouth) and taken down the next day. It was in this period that surrealist playwright Kobo Abe found his stride, and director Tadashi Suzuki developed the unique system of training that now draws aspiring actors from all over the world to his "theater community" in the mountains of Toyama Prefecture. Japanese drama today is a lively art indeed; theaters small and large, in unexpected pockets all over Tokyo, attest to its vitality.

The great majority of these performances, however, are in Japanese, for Japanese audiences; you're unlikely to find one with program notes in English to help you follow it. Unless it's a play you already know well, and you're curious to see how it translates (*Fiddler on the Roof*, for example, has been running in Japanese for more than 20 years), you might do well to think of some other way to spend your evenings out.

There is one exception: the **Takarazuka**—the wonderfully goofy all-female review. The troupe was founded in the Osaka suburb of Takarazuka in 1913 and has been going strong ever since; today it has not one but five companies, one of them with a permanent home in Tokyo, right across the street from the Imperial Hotel (1-1-3 Yuraku-cho, Chiyoda-ku, ☎ 03/3591–1711; nearest subway station: Hibiya). A Takarazuka chorine never gives her parents a moment's anxiety about her chosen career; this is show business with a difference—a life chaste and chaperoned, where the yearning admirers waiting with roses by the stage door are mostly teenage girls. Everybody sings; everybody dances; the sets are breathtaking; the costumes are swell. Where else but at the Takarazuka could you see a musical version of *Gone With the Wind*, sung in Japanese, with a young woman in a mustache and a frock coat playing Rhett Butler?

Music

The live music scene in Tokyo keeps getting better and better. Every year, a host of new promoters and booking agencies gets into the act; major corporations, anxious to polish their images as cultural institutions, are building concert halls and unusual performance spaces all over the city, adding to what was already an excellent roster of public auditoriums. It would be impossible to list them all; here are only a few of the most important:

The biggest acts from abroad in **rock** and **popular music** tend to appear at the 56,000-seat **Tokyo Dome sports arena,** which opened in 1988 on the site of the old Korakuen Stadium (1-3-61 Koraku, Bunkyo-ku, ☎ 03/3811–2111; nearest subway station: Korakuen), and at **Nakano Sun Plaza** (4-1-1 Nakano, Nakano-ku, ☎ 03/3388–1151; nearest subway station: Nakano). For **Western classical music,** including **opera,** the major venues are **NHK Hall,** home base for the Japan Broadcasting Corporation's NHK Symphony Orchestra (2-2-1 Jinnan, Shibuya-ku, ☎ 03/3465–1111; nearest subway station: Shibuya); **Tokyo Metropolitan Festival Hall** (Tokyo Bunka Kaikan; 5-45 Ueno Koen, Taito-ku, ☎ 03/3828–2111; nearest JR/subway station: Ueno), which we've mentioned in our exploring tour of Ueno; and **Suntory Hall,** in the Ark Hills complex (1-13-1 Akasaka, Minato-ku, ☎ 03/3505–1001; nearest subway station: Kokkai Gijido-mae). To these should be added three fine places designed especially for **chamber music: Iino Hall** (2-1-1 Uchisaiwaicho, Chiyoda-ku, ☎ 03/3506–3251; nearest subway station: Toranomon), **Ishibashi Memorial Hall** (4-24-12 Higashi Ueno, Taito-ku, ☎ 03/3843–3043; nearest subway station: Ueno), and the new **Casals Hall** (1-6 Kanda Surugadai, Chiyoda-ku, ☎ 03/3294–1229; nearest subway station: Ochanomizu), designed by architect Arata Isozaki, who also did, among other things, the Museum of Contemporary Art in Los Angeles.

Dance

Traditional Japanese dance, like flower arranging and the tea ceremony, is divided into dozens of styles, ancient of lineage and fiercely proud of their differences from each other. In fact, only the aficionado can really tell them apart. They survive not so much as performing arts but as schools, offering dance as a cultured accomplishment to interested amateurs. At least once a year, teachers and their students in each of these schools will hold a recital, so that on any given evening there's very likely to be one somewhere in Tokyo. Truly professional performances are given, as we've mentioned, at the **National Theater** and the **Shinbashi Enbujo** (*see* Traditional Theater, *above*); the most important of the classical schools, however, developed as an aspect of Kabuki, and if you attend a play at the **Kabuki-za** (*see* Traditional Theater, *above*) you are almost guaranteed to see a representative example.

Ballet began to attract a Japanese following in 1920, when Anna Pavlova danced *The Dying Swan* at the old Imperial Theater. The well-known companies that come to Tokyo from abroad perform to full houses, usually at the Tokyo Metropolitan Festival Hall in Ueno (*see* Music, *above*). There are now about 15 professional Japanese ballet companies, several of which have toured abroad, but this has yet to become an art form on which Japan has had much of an impact.

Modern dance is a different story—a story that begins with a visit in 1955 by the Martha Graham Dance Company. The decade that followed was one of great turmoil in Japan; it was a period of dissatisfaction—political, intellectual, artistic—with old forms and conventions. The work of pioneers like Graham inspired a great number of talented dancers and choreographers to explore new avenues of self-expression; one of the fruits of that exploration was **Butoh,** a movement that was at once uniquely Japanese and a major contribution to the world of modern dance.

The father of Butoh was the dancer Tatsumi Hijikata (1928–1986); the watershed work was his *Revolt of the Flesh,* which premiered in 1968. Others soon followed: Kazuo Ono, Min Tanaka, Akaji Maro and the Dai Rakuda Kan troupe, Ushio Amagatsu and the Sankai Juku. To most Japanese, their work was inexplicably grotesque. Dancers performed with shaved heads, dressed in rags or with naked bodies painted completely white, their movements agonized and contorted. The images were dark and demonic, violent and explicitly sexual. Butoh was an exploration of the unconscious: Its gods were the gods of the Japanese village and the gods of prehistory; its literary inspirations came from Mishima, Genet, Artaud. Like many other modern Japanese artists, the Butoh dancers and choreographers were largely ignored by the mainstream until they began to appear abroad—to thunderous critical acclaim. Now they are equally honored at home. Butoh does not lend itself to conventional spaces (a few years ago, for example, the Dai Rakuda Kan premiered one of its new works in a limestone cave in Gunma Prefecture), but if there's a performance in Tokyo, "Cityscope" will have the schedule. Don't miss it.

Film

One of the positive things about the business of foreign film distribution in Japan is that it is extremely profitable—so much so that the distributors can afford to add Japanese subtitles rather than dub their offerings, the way it's done so often elsewhere. The original soundtrack, of course, may not be all that helpful to you if the film is Polish or Italian, but the vast majority of first-run foreign films here are made in the United States. There are, however, other disincentives: The choices are limited; the good films take so long to open in Tokyo that you've probably seen them all already at home; and the tickets are expensive—around ¥1,700 for general admission, and ¥2,200–¥2,500 for a reserved seat, called a *shiteiseki*.

The native Japanese film industry has been in a slump for more than 20 years, and it shows no signs of recovery. It yields, at best, one or two films a year worth seeing, and these are invariably by independent producer/directors. A very small number of theaters will offer one showing a week, with English subtitles, of films that seem to have some international appeal; "Cityscope" will have the listings.

First-run theaters that feature new releases, both Japanese and foreign, are clustered for the most part in three areas: Shinjuku, Shibuya, and Yurakucho/Hibiya/Ginza. The most astonishing thing about them is how early they shut down; in most cases, the last showing of the evening starts at around 7. This is not the case, however, with the best news on the Tokyo film scene: the growing number of small theaters that take a special interest in classics, revivals, and serious imports. Many of them are in the "vertical boutique" buildings that represent the latest Japanese thinking in urban architecture and upscale marketing; somewhere on the premises will also be a chrome-and-marble coffee shop, a fashionable little bar, or even a decent restaurant. Most of them have a midnight show—at least on the weekends. One such is the **Cine Vivant** (Wave Building, 6-2-27 Roppongi, Minato-ku, ☎ 03/3403–6061; nearest subway station: Roppongi); another is the **Cine Saison Shibuya** (Prime Building, 2-29-5 Dogenzaka, Shibuya-ku, ☎ 03/3770–1721; nearest train station: Shibuya on the JR Yamanote Line); still others are the **Haiyu-za Cinema Ten** (4-9-2 Roppongi, Minato-ku, ☎ 03/3401–4073; nearest subway station: Rappongi), and the **Hibiya Chanter Cinema** (1-2-2 Yurakucho, Chiyoda-ku, ☎ 03/3591–1511; nearest train station: Yurakucho on the JR Yamanote Line). **Bunka-mura,** the showcase complex next door to the Tokyu Department Store in Shibuya (2-24-1 Dogenzaka, ☎ 03/3447–9111; nearest train station: Shibuya on the JR Yamanote Line), has two movie theaters, a concert hall, and a performance space; it is the principal venue for many of Tokyo's film festivals.

NIGHTLIFE

Tokyo has more entertainment choices and a greater diversity of nightlife than any other Japanese city. For the tourist to Japan, the structure of Japan's nightlife may be confusing. The neon lights of bars and clubs excite with their glitter, but these places are forbidding to enter for several reasons: An indication of the prices charged for a drink is rarely offered (the charge could be a mere ¥1,000 a drink, or a ¥20,000 cover and another ¥15,000 for a bottle of whiskey); it is often unclear whether the bar has hostesses, and, if it does, whether there is a hostess charge and whether she is there for conversation only; and, finally, you never know whether foreigners will be welcome, let alone whether a word of English will be spoken.

In this section, the establishments listed make foreigners welcome; often, someone will be around who speaks a few words of English. Most of the bars listed are more of the international variety, rather than being bars with hostesses. Hostess bars become like personal clubs, and your appreciation of them depends on how well you enjoy the conversations of the particular hostesses. You are unlikely to appreciate them unless you speak Japanese, especially when the tab will be about ¥20,000 to ¥30,000 a person. At karaoke bars, patrons request a piece of music and accompany it by singing the song into a microphone while reading the words to the song from the bottom of the video screen.

There are five major districts in Tokyo that have an extensive nightlife. While each area offers similar entertainment, the areas have different characters and different price ranges:

Akasaka has an area of two main streets, Tamachi-dori and Hitotsugi-dori, with small alleys connecting them. Cabarets, wine bars, night-clubs, coffee shops, eating and drinking places, as well as a couple of expensive ryotei with geisha entertainment, are all here. It is a so-phisticated neighborhood that is not quite as expensive as Ginza and not as trendy as Roppongi. Also, the area's compactness makes it a comfortable locale for the foreigner to test the waters of Japanese nightlife.

Ginza is probably the city's most well-known entertainment district; however, its heyday is over as an attractive place for foreign visitors to visit at night. The exorbitant price of Ginza's real estate has made its nightlife one of the most, if not *the* most, expensive in the world. Not even foreign businesspeople on expense accounts take their Japanese clients here. Only Japanese corporate expense accounts can afford the prices. There are some affordable places to visit in the evening, but these are not nightclubs as such, but bars and eating and drinking places.

Roppongi, spreading out toward Shibuya, has become Tokyo's main entertainment area for the cosmopolitan, trendy, and fashionable. It is the district where Westerners feel most comfortable; the prices are considerably better here than in Ginza, or even in Akasaka. During the day Roppongi is a quiet, residential area, but after 9 PM it seems that every Tokyo reveler is here making the rounds. More discos and bars of the variety you usually find in any major world capital are located here than in anyplace else in Japan. While Akasaka and Ginza virtually close down by midnight, some of the Roppongi bars stay open until the subways start running in the morning, so, if you have the stamina, this is the area to come for an all-nighter.

Shibuya, less expensive than Roppongi and not raunchy like Shinjuku, attracts students and young professionals to its numerous *nomiya* (inexpensive bars). Not many of the establishments have English-speaking staff, but if you know a little Japanese, this is a pleasant and inexpensive area for a night's entertainment.

Shinjuku's Kabukicho is the wildest of areas in Tokyo for evening revelry, offering a wide range of places, from the sleazy to the respectable. Bars, nightclubs, cabarets, discos, restaurants, and love hotels are all here. Just stay clear of touts speaking English to lure you to their dive, and you'll be fine. We do, however, recommend that unescorted women stay out of Kabukicho after 9 PM, because by then there are bound to be a few drunken males who will make irritating advances.

Bars

Ari's Lamplight. An intimate, comfortable place popular with foreign businesspeople and journalists, Ari's serves some of the best hamburgers in town. A "traditional classic" atmosphere is maintained; there's live music on Thursday nights and the piano tends to turn away the black vinyl crowd. *Odakyu Building, 7-8-1 Minami-Aoyama, Minato-*

ku (nearest train station: Shibuya on the JR Yamanote Line), ☎ *03/3499–1573. Drinks start at ¥800.* ☺ *5:30 PM–2 AM. Closed Sun.*

Charleston. This has been for years the schmoozing-and-hunting bar for Tokyo's single (or putatively single) foreign community, and the young Japanese who want to meet them. Noisy and packed until the wee small hours. *3-8-11 Roppongi, Minato-ku (nearest subway station: Roppongi),* ☎ *03/3402–0372. Drinks are ¥800 and up.* ☺ *Daily 5 PM–5 AM.*

Den. Launched by the mammoth beer and whiskey maker Suntory, Den is partly an exercise in corporate image-making. Meant to express the company's eco-consciousness and its roots in traditional Japanese culture, the motif here is confected of stones, trees, and articles of folkcraft. Den draws a fashionable crowd from the TV production, PR, and design companies thick in this part of town. *DST Building 1F, 4-2-3 Akasaka, Minato-ku (nearest subway station: Akasaka),* ☎ *03/3584– 1899. Drinks start at ¥800.* ☺ *6 PM–2 AM. Closed Sun.*

Garbus Cine Café. Young sophisticates, especially those with latent screen ambitions, come to this smart café for exotic coffees, as well as cocktails. The large plate-glass windows of the café overlook a small square, where palms of famous movie actors are imprinted in stone. The square also flickers with a digital clock flashing the time from under a water fountain. *Hibiya Chanter 1F, 1-2-2 Yurakucho, Chiyoda-ku (nearest subway station: Hibiya),* ☎ *03/3501–3185. Coffees start at ¥600.* ☺ *Daily 10–11.*

Hard Rock Cafe. The Tokyo outpost of this international chain reopened a few years ago with a new decor, similar to that of an American midwestern saloon and offering the same kind of fare for snacks. The building is easy to spot, with a huge sculpted gorilla hanging from the outside wall. *5-4-20 Roppongi, Minato-ku (nearest subway station: Roppongi),* ☎ *03/3408–7018. Drinks start at ¥800. No cover.* ☺ *Mon.–Thurs. 11:30 AM–2 AM, Fri. and Sat. 11:30 AM–4 AM, Sun. 11:30 AM–11:30 PM.*

Henry Africa. Both Japanese and expatriates frequent this Akasaka bar, where the decor is like a movie set used to film an African safari, including the elephant tusks. (There is a similar bar with the same name in Ginza.) *3-15-23 Roppongi, Minato-ku (nearest subway station: Roppongi),* ☎ *03/3403–9751. Drinks begin at ¥600. Snacks are available.* ☺ *Mon.–Thurs. 6 PM–2 AM, Fri.–Sat. 6 PM–5 AM, Sun. 6 PM–midnight.*

Highlander. Should you become tired of Japanese whiskey and want some real Scotch, the Highlander at the Hotel Okura has a selection of more than 200 brands from which to choose. This is a smart place to meet business acquaintances or to have a civilized drink. *Hotel Okura, 2-10-4 Toranomon, Minato-ku (nearest subway station: Toranomon),* ☎ *03/3505–6077. Drinks start at ¥1,100.* ☺ *Mon.–Sat. 11:30 AM–1 AM, Sun. 11:30 AM–midnight.*

The Old Imperial Bar. If you want a place to meet someone for evening drinks, this hotel bar has a comfortable old-world charm with mementos taken from the original Imperial Hotel designed by Frank Lloyd Wright. *Imperial Hotel, 1-1-1 Uchisaiwaicho, Chiyoda-ku (nearest subway station: Hibiya),* ☎ *03/3504–1111. Drinks start at ¥1,000.* ☺ *Daily 11:30 AM–10 PM.*

Stonefield's. A small bar that really wanted to be born a Nashville saloon, Stonefield's surrounds you with down-home hospitality and takes pride in its collection of country-and-western tapes. Now and again, they'll book in a live band; drop by on one of those evenings and discover how surprisingly good Japanese pickers 'n fiddlers can be. *Sunlight Akasaka Building 4F, 3-21-4 Akasaka, Minato-ku (nearest subway station: Akasaka-mitsuke),* ☎ *03/3583–5690. Drinks start at ¥500; a bottle of bourbon is ¥7,000.* ☉ *7 PM–midnight. Closed Sun.*

Wine Bar. Similar to a European wine bar, the cellarlike atmosphere appeals to Japanese and foreigners alike. This is a good place to take a date before hopping on to the Roppongi discos. *3-21-3 Akasaka, Minato-ku (nearest subway station: Akasaka-mitsuke),* ☎ *3586–7186. Drinks start at ¥380.* ☉ *Daily 5 PM–midnight.*

Yuraku Food Center (2-2 Nishi-Ginza, Chuo-ku; nearest subway station: Hibiya). Inside this building and one floor up is a collection of places to eat and drink at reasonable prices—this is where the people who work in the neighborhood go after work. One popular place for drinks, as well as for snacks, is the **Americana** (☎ 03/3564–1971). Drinks start at ¥800. Farther along the hallway is the **Music Pub** (☎ 03/3563–3757), which has live bands playing swing jazz. The cover varies but is usually ¥7,000–¥10,000, and drinks start at ¥700. There are also restaurants in the food center that, along with the bars, start closing at 11 PM. Yuraku Food Center, east of Yurakucho Subway Station, is the next building east of the Kotsu Kaikan Building (where JNTO has its administrative offices). The Kotsu Kaikan Building can be recognized by the circular sky lounge on its rooftop.

Beer Halls

Kirin City. This beer hall is a newer entry and has less of the glass-thumping atmosphere of other brewery-sponsored drinking establishments. (There is also a Kirin beer hall in Shinjuku, on the west side of the station and opposite the Yodobashi Camera store, ☎ 03/3344–6234.) *Bunshodo Bldg. 2F, 3-4-12 Ginza, Chuo-ku (nearest train station: Shinjuku on the JR Yamanote Line),* ☎ *03/3562–2593. Beer is ¥460.* ☉ *11:30 AM–11 PM.*

Levante Beer Hall. This is a favorite spot for the Japanese male to stop in and have some drinks and down a half dozen raw oysters. Over the years, this old-fashioned beer hall has become a well-known landmark, an anachronism in an area known for its marble and flashing lights. Located in the Ginza district, Levante is behind the Imperial Hotel and opposite the Tokyu Kotsu Kakan store. *2-8-7 Yurakucho, Chiyoda-ku (nearest subway station: Hibiya),* ☎ *03/3201–2661. Beer starts at ¥540.* ☉ *Mon.–Sat. 11:30 AM–2 PM and 5–10 PM.*

Sapporo Lion. For a casual evening spent drinking beer and eating snacks—anything from yakitori to spaghetti—the Sapporo Lion offers an inexpensive night out. The beer hall's entrance is off Chuo-dori, near the Matsuzakaya Department Store. *6-10-12 Ginza, Chuo-ku (nearest subway station: Ginza),* ☎ *03/3571–2590. Beer starts at ¥590.* ☉ *Daily 5–9:30 PM.*

Discos

The disco scene is alive in Tokyo, but less well than it was before the uptown crowd started to feel the pinch in its discretionary income. Discos have always been ephemeral ventures, anyhow; they disappear fairly regularly, to open again with stranger names and newer gimmicks: The money behind them is usually the same. Even the ones we've listed here come with no guarantee that they'll still be around when you arrive, but it can't hurt to investigate. Where else can you work out, survey the vinyl miniskirt brigades, and get a drink at 3 AM?

Lexington Queen. From the day it opened in 1980, the Lexington Queen has been patronized by celebrities—from sumo wrestlers to rock stars to media celebrities, such as Sylvester Stallone and Rod Stewart. And they still keep coming. Why? Because the owner is Bill Hersey, society writer for *Tokyo Weekender,* a biweekly local newspaper. A lot of attractive people show up here, from foreign models to those working in the movie industry. *Daisan Goto Bldg., B1, 3-13-14 Roppongi, Minato-ku (nearest subway station: Roppongi),* ☎ *03/3401–1661. Cost: ¥4,000 men, ¥3,000 women, which includes a free drink; a meal ticket to be used at the sushi bar costs ¥1,000. Many waiters speak some English.* ◷ *Nightly 6 PM–5 AM.*

Maharaja. Eclectic is the word here, from the plaster *Venus de Milo* in the display window outside to the quasi-Mogul motifs within. Maharaja survives by being all things to all clients: It's a member's club that doesn't really require a membership; it runs "college nights"; it draws the hip young foreigners from Hiro-o and the spillover crowd from nearby Roppongi. It shuts down, however, unaccountably early. *TBC Azabu Building, 1-3-9 Azabu Ju-ban, Minato-ku (nearest subway station: Roppongi),* ☎ *03/3582–7700. Cost: ¥4,000–¥5,000 for men, ¥3,000–¥4,000 for women, depending on the night of the week.* ◷ *Nightly from 7 PM; closing times vary.*

The Square Building Discos. (Roppongi Square Bldg., 3-10-3 Roppongi, Minato-ku; nearest subway station: Roppongi). Ten floors of assorted nightlife ventures, karaoke clubs, and restaurants that manage, despite the current uncertainties of the trade, to provide a few discos. The most durable of the lot is **Giza,** with its Egyptian motif (☎ 03/3403–6538; cost: ¥4,000 for men, ¥3,000 for women; open 6 PM–6 AM).

Live Music

Blue Note Tokyo. Young entrepreneur Tosuke Ito acquired the Tokyo franchise for this famed New York night spot in 1988 and set about making it the premier jazz club in town. *5-13-3 Minami-Aoyama, Minato-ku (nearest subway station: Omotesando),* ☎ *03/3407–5781. Cover charge varies from ¥8,000 for relative unknowns to as high as ¥17,000 for superstars. Two sets a night, at 7:30 and 10. AE, DC, V.*

Body and Soul. Owner Kyoko Seki has been a jazz fan and an impresario for more than 15 years. There's still nothing fancy about this place— just good, serious jazz. *Senme Bldg. 1F, 3-12-3 Kita-Aoyama, Minato-ku (nearest subway station: Roppongi),* ☎ *03/5466–3525. Cover charge ¥3,000–¥3,500, drinks from ¥600.* ◷ *7 PM–midnight. Closed Sun. AE, MC, V.*

Club Quattro. More of a concert hall than a club, the Quattro does one show nightly, with the accent heavy on "ethnic" music—especially Latin and African—by both Japanese and foreign groups. Audiences tend to be young and enthusiastic. *Parco IV Building, 32-13 Utagawa-cho, Shibuya-ku (nearest train station: Shibuya on the JR Yamanote Line),* ☎ *03/3477–8750. Cover charge from ¥2,500 to ¥6,000. Shows usually start at 7 PM.*

Pit Inn. The shows change nightly, but the emphasis is on Japanese and Western light jazz, attracting such performers as pianist Cecile Taylor. The atmosphere is friendly, with seating shaped in a half-moon facing the stage. It is by no means elegant, more like a well-worn theater than a nightclub. The audience is mostly in their early 20s. *3-16-4 Shinjuku, Shinjuku-ku (nearest train station: Shinjuku on the JR Yamanote Line),* ☎ *03/3354–2024. Cost: ¥3,000 (¥4,000 on occasion, for headliners), 1 drink included.* ◷ *7–11 PM.*

Nightclubs and Cabarets

Cordon Bleu. A full-course meal is served in this dinner theater, with seats to accommodate about 150 people. However, it is more intimate than its size suggests and attracts well-known names. Muhammad Ali's name is in the guest book. There are three shows a night (7:30, 9:30, and 11), with singers and topless dancers bobbing up and down onstage. It is possible to just eat hors d'oeuvres and watch the show. *6-6-4 Akasaka, Minato-ku (nearest subway station: Akasaka),* ☎ *03/3582–7800. Reservations advised. Cost: ¥19,800 or ¥16,500 for full-course dinner and 1 drink; ¥13,200 for hors d'oeuvres and 1 drink.* ☉ *7:30–10 PM. Closed Sun.*

Showboat. Downstairs at the Hilton is this small, cheerful club with international cabaret acts, which attract both hotel guests and non-residents for their leg-kicking dancers and warbling singers. *Tokyo Hilton Hotel, 6-6-2 Nishi-Shinjuku, Shinjuku-ku (nearest train station: Shinjuku on the JR Yamanote Line),* ☎ *03/3344–0510. Cover charge ¥4,500; table charge ¥1,000. Drinks start at ¥1,000.* ☉ *Nightly 6 PM–1 AM; showtimes 7:30, 9:15, and 11:45 PM.*

Skyline Lounges

Pole Star Lounge. For a view of old and new Shinjuku flickering beneath you, this lounge bar on the penthouse floor of the Keio Plaza is hard to beat. *Keio Plaza Inter-Continental, 2-2-1 Nishi-Shinjuku, Shinjuku-ku (nearest train station: Shinjuku on the JR Yamanote Line),* ☎ *03/3344–0111. Drinks start at ¥1,450.* ☉ *Weekdays 5–11:30 PM, weekends 4–11:30 PM.*

Top of the Akasaka. On the 40th floor of the Akasaka Prince Hotel, you can enjoy some of the finest views of Tokyo. If you can time your visit for dusk, the price of one drink gets you two views—the daylight sprawl of buildings and the twinkling lights of evening. *Akasaka Prince, 1-2 Kioicho, Chiyoda-ku (nearest subway station: Akasaka-mitsuke),* ☎ *03/3234–1111. Drinks start at ¥1,100. Table charge: ¥800 per person.* ☉ *Weekdays 11 AM–2 AM, weekends 11 AM–midnight.*

TOKYO ESSENTIALS

Arriving and Departing

By Plane

Tokyo has two airports, Narita and Haneda. **Narita Airport** is 80 kilometers (50 miles) northeast of Tokyo and serves all international flights, except for those operated by (Taiwan's) China Airways, which uses Haneda Airport. Sixteen kilometers (10 miles) southwest of Tokyo, **Haneda Airport** serves all domestic flights. Narita added a new terminal building in 1992, which has somewhat eased the burden on it, but it can still be bottlenecked. Narita is the only Japanese airport that imposes a departure tax (¥2,000, ¥1,000 for children 2–11 years old; no tax for children under 2 or for transit passengers flying out the same day as their arrival).

Narita has more direct flights arriving from around the world than any other Japanese airport. Japan Airlines (JAL) and United Airlines are the major carriers between North America and Narita; Northwest, American Airlines, and All Nippon Airways (ANA) also link North American cities with Tokyo. JAL, Cathay Pacific, Virgin Atlantic Airways, and British Airways fly between Narita and Great Britain; JAL, United Airlines, and Qantas fly between Narita and Australia; and JAL and

Air New Zealand fly between Narita and New Zealand. An extensive network of domestic flights in and out of Haneda is operated by JAL, ANA, and Japan Air System. For information on arrival and departure times, call the individual airlines.

Narita Terminal No. 2 has two wings, north and south, that adjoin each other. When you arrive, your first task should be to convert your money into yen; you'll need it for transport into Tokyo. In both wings, money exchange counters are located in the wall between the customs inspection area and the arrival lobby. Directly across from the customs area exit are the ticket counters for Airport Limousine Buses to Tokyo. (*See* By Bus, *below*.) In between the two wings is the Japan National Tourist Organization's Tourist Information Center, where maps, brochures, and other information can be obtained free of charge. It is well worth visiting this center if you have extra time before your bus departs.

BETWEEN NARITA AIRPORT AND CENTER CITY

By Bus. Two services, the **Airport Limousine Bus** and the **Airport Express Bus,** run from Narita to many of Tokyo's major hotels in the city's different areas, such as Akasaka, Ginza, Ikebukuro, Shiba, and Shinagawa (cost: ¥2,500–¥3,500, depending on your destination). These buses are the best method of reaching your destination; even if you are not staying at one of the hotel drop-off points, take the bus going closest to your hotel, and then use a taxi for the remaining distance. Most of the hotels in the $$$$ category (*see* Lodging, *above*) serve as drop-off points. However, these buses only run every hour, and they do not run after 10 PM. The trip usually takes two hours because of traffic congestion, though the scheduled time is 90 minutes. Tickets for these buses are sold at the large ticket counter in the arrival lobby, directly across from the customs area exit. The buses depart right outside the terminal exit. They leave exactly on time; the departure time is stated on the ticket.

A regularly scheduled bus to the Tokyo City Air Terminal (TCAT) leaves approximately every 10–30 minutes from 6:45 AM to 11 PM (cost: ¥2,700; purchase tickets at same ticket counter as for other airport buses). The problem is that TCAT is located in Nihonbashi in north-central Tokyo, which is far from most desired destinations. From TCAT you can connect directly with the Suitengu station on the Hanzomon subway line, and then to anywhere in the subway network; a taxi from TCAT to most of the major hotels will cost about ¥3,000.

By Train. Trains run every 30–40 minutes between Narita Airport Train Station and the Keisei-Ueno Station on the privately owned Keisei Line; the ride takes approximately an hour. (Cost: ¥1,740 on the Keisei Skyliner, taking 57 minutes; ¥940 on the Keisei limited express, taking 72 minutes). The first limited express departs at 9:02 AM, the first Skyliner at 9:20 AM. It only makes sense to take the Keisei, however, if your final destination is around Ueno; otherwise, you must change to the Tokyo subway system or the Japan Railways loop line at Ueno (the station is adjacent to the Keisei-Ueno Station) or take a cab to your hotel.

Japan Railways (JR East Infoline, ☎ 03/3423–0111) has greatly improved its airport service, with trains that stop at both terminals. The fastest and most comfortable is the **Narita Limited Express** (N'EX) which makes 23 runs a day in each direction. Trains from the airport go directly to Tokyo Station (in central Tokyo) in just under an hour, then continue on to Yokohama and Ofuna; daily departures begin at 7:43

AM; the last train is at 9:43 PM. The one-way fare is ¥2,890 (¥4,890 for the 1st-class "Green Car" and ¥5,280 per person for a private compartment that seats four). All seats are reserved; make reservations in advance, as this train fills quickly. The less elegant **kaisoku** (rapid train) on JR's Narita Line also runs from the airport to Tokyo Station, by way of Chiba; there are 16 departures daily, starting at 7 AM. The fare to Tokyo is ¥1,260 (¥930 more for the Green Car); the ride takes 1 hour and 27 minutes.

By Taxi. Taxis are rarely used between Narita Airport and central Tokyo—the cost of approximately ¥20,000 is prohibitive. Also, because taxis have small trunks, your luggage may have to be placed in the front passenger seat, thus causing cramped conditions if there are three or more passengers. Station wagon taxis do exist, and the meter rates are the same as for the standard sedans, but they are not always available. Limousines are also very expensive; for example, a limousine ride from Narita Airport to the Imperial Hotel costs approximately ¥35,000.

BETWEEN HANEDA AIRPORT AND CENTER CITY
By Monorail. The monorail train from Haneda Airport to Hamamatsucho Station in Tokyo is the best and most frequently used method; the journey takes about 17 minutes and operates approximately every 5 minutes (cost: ¥460). From Hamamatsucho Station, change to the subway or take a taxi.

By Taxi. A taxi to the center of Tokyo takes about 40 minutes (cost: approximately ¥6,000).

By Train
The JR Shinkansen (bullet train) and JR express trains on the Tokaido Line (to Nagoya, Kyoto, Kobe, Osaka, Hiroshima, and the island of Kyushu) use Tokyo Station in central Tokyo. The JR Shinkansen and express trains on the Tohoku Line (to Sendai and Morioka) use Ueno Station, just north of Tokyo Station. The JR Shinkansen and express trains on the Joetsu Line (to Niigata) also use Ueno Station. JR trains to the Japan Alps (Matsumoto) use Shinjuku Station. A new bullet train line is scheduled to open in mid-1997 between Tokyo and Nagano. Named the Hokuriku Shinkansen, it will run on the Joetsu Shinkansen Line to Takasaki, where it will branch off for Nagano, and will use Tokyo Station.

By Bus
Most bus arrivals and departures are at Tokyo (train) Station or Shinjuku Bus Station.

Getting Around

Daunting in its sheer size, Tokyo is, in fact, an extremely easy city to negotiate. If you have any anxieties about getting from place to place, remind yourself first that a transportation system obliged to cope with 4 or 5 million commuters a day simply *has* to be efficient, extensive, and reasonably easy to understand. Remind yourself also that virtually anyplace you're likely to go as a visitor is within a 15-minute walk of a train or subway station—and that station stops are always marked in English. Of course, exceptions to the rule exist; the system has its flaws. In the outline here you'll find a few things to avoid, and also a few pointers that will save you time—and money—as you go.

By Train
Japan Railways (JR) trains are color-coded, making it easy to identify the different lines. The **Yamanote Line** (green or silver, with green

stripes) makes a 35-kilometer (22-mile) loop around the central wards of the city in about an hour. The 29 stops include the major hub stations of Tokyo, Yurakucho, Shinbashi, Shinagawa, Shibuya, Shinjuku, and Ueno. The **Chuo Line** (orange) runs east to west through the loop from Tokyo to the distant suburb of Takao. During the day, however, these are limited express trains that don't stop at most of the stations inside the loop; for local crosstown service, which also extends west to neighboring Chiba Prefecture, you have to take the **Sobu Line** (yellow). The **Keihin Tohoku Line** (blue) goes north to Omiya in Saitama Prefecture and south to Ofuna in Kanagawa, running parallel to the Yamanote Line between Tabata and Shinagawa. Where they share the loop, the two lines usually use the same platform—Yamanote trains on one side, and Keihin Tohoku trains headed in the same direction on the other. This requires a little care. Suppose, for example, you want to take the loop line from Yurakucho around to Shibuya, and you board a blue train instead of a green one; four stops later, where the lines branch, you'll find yourself on an unexpected trip to Yokohama.

JR fares start at ¥120; you can get anywhere on the loop for ¥250 or less. Most stations have a chart in English somewhere above the row of ticket vending machines, so you can check the fare to your destination; if not, you can simply buy the cheapest ticket and pay the difference at the other end. In any case, hold on to your ticket: you'll have to turn it in at the exit. Tickets are valid only on the day you buy them, but if you plan to use the JR a lot, you can save time and trouble with an Orange Card, available at any station office. The card is electronically coded; at vending machines with orange panels, you insert the card, punch the cost of the ticket, and that amount is automatically deducted. ¥1,000 and ¥3,000 Orange Cards are worth their face values; ¥5,000 Orange Cards are coded for ¥5,300 and ¥10,000 for ¥10,700 worth of fares as an incentive to buy them. Your Japan Rail Pass can be used on all JR trains.

Shinjuku, Harajuku, and Shibuya are notorious for the long lines that form at ticket dispensers. If you're using a card, make sure you've lined up at a machine with an orange panel; if you're paying cash, and have no change, make sure you've lined up at a machine that will change a ¥1,000 note—not all of them do!

Yamanote and Sobu trains begin running about 4:30 AM and stop around 12:30 at night. The last departures are indicated at each station—but only in Japanese. Bear in mind that 7–9:30 AM and 5–7 PM trains are packed to bursting with commuters; avoid the trains at these times, if possible. During these hours, smoking is not allowed in JR stations or on platforms.

By Subway

Tokyo is served by 10 subway lines (an 11th is scheduled to open in late 1997, and a 12th is also under construction), seven of them operated by the Rapid Transportation Authority (Eidan) and three by the Tokyo Municipal Authority (Toei). Maps, bilingual signs at entrances, and even the trains are color-coded for easy identification. Subway trains run about every five minutes from about 5 AM to midnight; except during rush hours, the intervals are slightly longer on the newer Toei lines.

The network of interconnections (subway-to-subway and train-to-subway) is particularly good; one transfer—two at most— will take you in less than an hour to any part of the city you're likely to visit. At some stations—such as Otemachi, Ginza, and Iidabashi—long un-

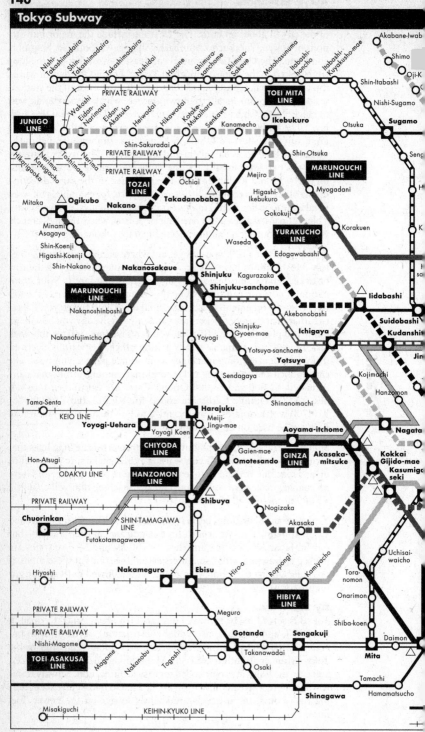

derground passageways connect the various lines, and it does take time to get from one to another. Directions, however, are clearly marked. Less helpful is the system of signs that tell you which of the 15 or 20 exits (exits are often numbered and alphabetized) from a large station will take you aboveground closest to your destination; only a few stations have such signs in English. Try asking the agent when you turn in your ticket; he may understand enough of your question to come back with the exit number and letter (such as A3 or B12), which is all you need.

Subway fares begin at ¥140. Toei trains are generally a bit more expensive than Eidan trains, but both are somewhat cheaper than the JR. From Ueno across town to Shibuya on the old Ginza Line (yellow), for example, is ¥160; the same ride on the Yamanote Line is ¥190. The Eidan (but *not* the Toei) has inaugurated an electronic card of its own, called Metrocard; the denominations are ¥1,000, ¥2,000, and ¥3,000. Automatic card dispensers are installed at some subway stations.

By Bus
Because Tokyo has no rational order—no grid—the bus routes are impossibly complicated. The Tokyo Municipal Government operates some of the lines; private companies run the rest. There is no telephone number even a native Japanese can call for help. The buses all have tiny seats and low ceilings. With one exception, the red double-decker in Asakusa (*see* Exploring Tokyo, *above,* for Asakusa), you should forget the buses.

By Taxi
Tokyo taxi fares are among the highest in the world; the meter starts running at ¥650 and ticks away at the rate of ¥80 every 280 meters (about ¼ mile). There are also smaller cabs, called *kogata,* which charge ¥630 and then ¥80 per 299 meters. If your cab is caught in traffic—hardly an uncommon event—the meter registers another ¥90 for every two minutes and 15 seconds of immobility. Between 11 PM and 5 AM, a 30% surcharge is added to the fare.

You do get very good value for the money, though. Taxis are invariably clean and comfortable. The doors open automatically for you when you get in and out. The driver takes you where you want to go by the shortest route he knows, and he does not expect a tip. Tokyo cabbies are not, in general, a sociable species (you wouldn't be either if you had to drive for 10–12 hours a day in Tokyo traffic), but you can always count on a minimum standard of courtesy. And if you forget something in the cab—a camera, a purse—your chances of getting it back are almost 100%.

Hailing a taxi during the day is seldom a problem; you would have to be in a very remote part of town to wait more than five minutes for one to pass by. In the Ginza, drivers are allowed to stop for passengers only in designated areas; elsewhere, you need only step off the curb and raise your arm. If the cab already has a fare, there will be a green light on the dashboard, visible through the windshield; if not, the light will be red.

Night changes the rules a bit, when everyone's been out drinking and wants a ride home. Don't be astonished if a cab with a red light doesn't stop for you: The driver may have had a radio call, or he may be heading for an area where he can pick up a long, profitable fare to the suburbs. (Or he may simply not feel like coping with a passenger in a foreign language. Refusing a fare is against the law—but it's done all the time.) Between 11 PM and 2 AM on Friday and Saturday nights, you have to be very lucky to get a cab in any of the major entertainment districts; in Ginza, it is almost impossible.

By Ferry

The best ride in Tokyo, hands down, is the suijo basu (river bus), operated by the Tokyo Cruise Ship Company from **Hinode Pier** (2-7-104 Kaigan, Minato-ku, ☎ 03/3457–7830), at the mouth of the Sumidagawa (river), upstream to Asakusa. The pier is a seven-minute walk from the Hamamatsucho Station on the JR Yamanote Line; the glassed-in double-decker boats depart roughly every 30 minutes, 9:50 AM–6:20 PM, daily (extended weekday service to 7:35 PM July–Aug.). The trip takes 35 minutes, and costs ¥560; children ride at half-fare.

The Sumidagawa was once Tokyo's lifeline, a busy highway for travelers and freight alike; the ferry service dates back to 1885. Some people still take it to work, but today the passengers are primarily tourists, most of them Japanese. On its way to Asakusa, the boat passes under 11 bridges; though all are of modern construction, they are deemed worthy of lengthy comment by the guided tour (a recording on the boat's loudspeaker). There are far more interesting things to see: **Tsukiji Market,** the largest wholesale fish and produce market in the world (*see* Exploring, *above,* for Tsukiji); the vast reclamation/construction projects meant to sate the city's insatiable need for high-tech office space; the old lumberyards and warehouses upstream; and the Kokugikan (*see* Off the Beaten Track, *above*), with its distinctive green roof, which is the new arena and headquarters of sumo wrestling.

Another place to catch the ferry is at the **Hama Rikyu Teien** (Detached Palace Garden), a 15-minute walk from Ginza. Once part of the Imperial Detached Palace, the gardens are open to the public, although you will have to pay a separate ¥200 entrance fee; the ferry landing is inside, a short walk to the left as you enter the main gate. Boats depart at 45-minute intervals every weekday 10:15–4:05; the adult fare to Asakusa is ¥520; from Asakusa to Hama Rikyu, the fare is ¥560.

By Hired Car

Large and comfortable cars may be hired (the Japanese call them *haiya*) for about ¥6,000 per hour for a midsize car, up to ¥14,000 per hour for a Cadillac limousine. Call **Hinomaru** (☎ 03/3505–0707). The Imperial, Okura, and Palace hotels also offer limousine services.

By Rental Car

Congestion, lack of road signs in English, and the difficulty of parking make driving in Tokyo impractical for the foreign visitor. That said, should you wish to rent a car, contact **Nippon Interrent** (2-1 Yaesu, Chouku, ☎ 03/3271–6643) or **Toyota Rent-a-Car** (2-3-18 Kudan Minami, Chiyoda-ku, ☎ 03/3263–6321), national car-rental companies with offices all around Tokyo and Japan. The cost is approximately ¥15,000 per day. An international driving license is required.

Maps

Excellent maps of the subway system, with the major JR lines included, are available at any station office, free of charge; you'll find the same map in the monthly *Tour Companion* magazine. Hotel kiosks and English-language bookstores stock a wide variety of pocket maps, some of which have suggested walking tours that also mark the locations of JR and subway stations along the way. A bit bulkier to carry around, but by far the best and most detailed resource, is *Tokyo: A Bilingual Atlas* (Kodansha Publishing, ¥1,850; $14.95 in the United States), which contains subway and rail-system guides and area maps. Because all notations are in both English and Japanese, you can always get help on the street, even from people who do not speak your language, just by pointing at your destination.

Tokyo Addresses

The standard postal system the Japanese themselves use to indicate addresses in Tokyo begins with the ward—designated by the suffix *-ku* (as in Minato-ku)—followed by the name of the district within the ward, such as Roppongi or Nishi-Azabu. The district is usually divided into numbered subsections, sometimes designated by the suffix *-chome;* the subsections can be further divided into units of one or more blocks, each with its own building numbers. Apartment blocks will often have a final set of digits on the address to specify an apartment number. Thus, *Taito-ku 1-4-301 Asakusa 3-chome* will be recognizable to the mailman as "Apartment No. 301 in Bldg. 4 on the first block of Asakusa sub-section No. 3 in Taito Ward"—but don't count on the driver of a taxi you hail on the other side of the city having the faintest idea how to find it. And don't count on the blocks or the building numbers appearing in any rational geographic order, either. The whole system is impossibly complicated, even for the Japanese. People usually direct each other to some landmark or prominent building in a given neighborhood, and muddle on from there. Bear in mind that addresses written in Japanese appear in reverse order, that is, with the postal code, prefecture, and ward first and the name of the person or establishment last; however, Japanese addresses written in English follow Western order, with the name first and the ward, prefecture, and postal code last.

Guided Tours

Orientation Tours

Organized by the Japan Travel Bureau, **Sunrise Tours** (☎ 03/3276–7777) offers guided tours in English around Tokyo. The sights on tours vary according to current popularity, but some recently offered tours are as follows: A morning tour (4 hours) includes the Tokyo Tower Observatory, Asakusa, the Imperial East Garden, and flower arrangement at the Tasaki Pearl Gallery (cost: ¥4,420 adults; ¥3,460 children age 6–11). Incorporating a Sumida river cruise, the afternoon tour includes the Imperial Palace Plaza, the Asakusa Kannon Temple, the Ginza and Kasumigaseki districts, and the Tokyo Tower Observatory (cost: ¥4,850/¥3,720). A full-day tour (7 hours) combines most of what is covered in the morning and afternoon tours, with a tea ceremony at the Happo-en Gardens and lunch at the traditional Chinzan-so (cost: ¥11,820/¥9,240, lunch included). Tours are conducted in large, air-conditioned buses that set out from Hamamatsucho Bus Terminal, but there is also free pickup and return from the major hotels. (If you travel independently and use the subway, we estimate that the full-day tour's itinerary can be accomplished for about ¥2,750, including lunch.) **The Japan Gray Line** (☎ 03/3433–5745) offers tours similar to Sunrise's.

Special-Interest Tours

Sunrise Tours (☎ 03/3276–7777) offers a full-day in Tokyo Disneyland (cost: ¥9,820 adults; ¥9,240 children 12–17, ¥5,990 children 4–11) and a trip to several craft centers (cost: ¥11,170/¥8,890).

Nightlife Tours

Sunrise Tours (☎ 03/3276–7777) offers night tours (6–11 PM) of Tokyo, which, depending on the one selected, include Kabuki drama at the Kabuki-za theater, a geisha show at Matsubaya, or a cabaret/floor show at the Shogun in Roppongi (cost: ¥9,560–¥13,480, depending on which portions of the tour you include). **The Japan Gray Line** (☎ 03/3433–5745) has similar programs.

Tours from Tokyo

To Nikko, **Sunrise Tours** (☎ 03/3276–7777) offers one-day tours (cost: ¥20,000 adults; ¥17,000 children under 12; lunch included) and two-day tours (cost: ¥30,000 adults, ¥24,000 children under 12, one lunch and overnight accommodation included). **Tobu Travel** (☎ 03/3281–6622, a division of Tobu Railways) offers full-day trips to Nikko (with pickup and return to major hotels) including an English-speaking guide, reserved train travel, lunch, and ☛ fees (cost: ¥20,000 adults, ¥17,000 children 6–11). **Sunrise Tours** (☎ 03/3276–7777), **Japan Amenity Travel** (☎ 03/3542–7545), and **The Japan Gray Line** (☎ 03/3433–5745) offer tours to Mt. Fuji and Hakone; one-day tours cost ¥20,000 adults, ¥17,000 children under 12 (lunch included), and two-day tours cost ¥31,000 adults, ¥26,000 children under 12 (meals and accommodation included). Some of these tours include a quick visit to Kamakura. There are also excursions to Kyoto via the Shinkansen that cost from ¥46,500 to ¥76,400.

Personal Guides

The Japan Guide Association (☎ 03/3213–2706) will introduce you to English-speaking guides. However, you will need to establish an itinerary and price with the guide. Assume that the fee will be ¥20,000–¥30,000 for a full eight-hour day.

Important Addresses and Numbers

Emergencies

Ambulance and **Fire,** ☎ 119; **Police,** ☎ 110; **Tokyo English Life Line** (TELL; ☎ 03/5481–4347) is a telephone service available 9 AM–4 PM and 9–11 PM for anyone in distress who cannot communicate in Japanese. The service will relay your emergency to the appropriate Japanese authorities and/or will serve as a counselor. Assistance in English is available 24 hrs. a day on the toll-free **Japan Helpline** (☎ 0120/461–997).

DOCTORS

International Catholic Hospital (Seibo Byoin), 2-5-1 Naka Ochiai, Shinjuku-ku, ☎ 03/3951–1111. Appointments Mon.–Sat. 8–11 AM.
International Clinic, 1-5-9 Azabudai, Roppongi, Minato-ku, ☎ 03/3582–2646 or 03/3583–7831. Accepts emergencies. Appointments weekdays 9 AM–noon and 2:30–5 PM, Sat. 9 AM–noon.
St. Luke's International Hospital (Member of American Hospital Association), 10-1 Akashicho, Chuo-ku, ☎ 03/3541–5151. Accepts emergencies. Appointments Mon.–Sat. 8:30–11 AM.
Tokyo Medical and Surgical Clinic, 32 Mori Building, 3-4-30 Shiba Koen, Minato-ku, ☎ 03/3436–3028. Appointments weekdays 9 AM–5 PM, Sat. 9 AM–1 PM.

DENTISTS

Yamauchi Dental Clinic (member of American Dental Association), Shiroganedai Gloria Heights 1F, 3-16-10 Shiroganedai, Minato-ku, ☎ 03/3441–6377. ☯ Weekdays 9–1 and 3–6; Sat. 9 AM–noon.

PHARMACIES

No drugstores in Tokyo are open 24 hours a day, but grocery stores carry basics such as aspirin. The **American Pharmacy** (Hibiya Park Building, 1-8-1 Yurakucho, Chiyoda-ku, ☎ 03/3271–4034) and **Hill Pharmacy** (4-1-6 Roppongi, Minato-ku, ☎ 03/3583–5044) both stock American products. The American Pharmacy is conveniently located near the Tourist Information Center (*see above*) and is open Mon.–Sat. 9–7 and Sun. 11–7; Hill Pharmacy is open Mon.–Sat. 8–7. **Nagai Yakkyoku** (1-8-10 Azabu Ju-ban, Minato-ku, ☎ 03/3583–3889) will mix a Chinese and/or Japanese herbal medicine for you after a consultation. A little English is spoken.

English-Language Bookstores

Most of the top hotels have a bookstore with a modest selection of English-language books. However, for a wide selection of English and other non-Japanese-language books, the **Kinokuniya Bookstore** (17-7 Shinjuku 3-chome, Shinjuku-ku, ☎ 03/3354–0131) has some 40,000 books and magazine titles (closed 3rd Wed. of each month, except Apr. and Dec.). Kinokuniya also has a branch store in the Tokyu Plaza Building (1-2-2 Dogenzaka, Shibuya-ku, ☎ 03/3463–3241) across from the Shibuya Station. The **Jena Bookstore** (5-6-1 Ginza, Chuo-ku, ☎ 03/3571–2980) also carries a wide range of books and is located near the Ginza and Marunouchi subway line exits in Ginza. **Yaesu Book Center** (2-5-1 Yaesu, Chuo-ku, ☎ 03/3281–1811) is located near the Tokyo Train Station.

Travel Agencies

Japan Travel Bureau (1-13-1 Nihonbashi, Chuo-ku, ☎ 03/3276–7777) has the most extensive network of agencies throughout Tokyo and Japan. This bureau organizes various tours conducted in English, in and around Tokyo; it will make arrangements for your travels throughout Japan and overseas, if you wish.

Other travel agencies include **American Express International** (Yurakucho Denki Bldg., 1-7-1 Yurakucho, Chiyoda-ku, ☎ 03/3214–0280) and **Japan Amenity Travel** (2-3-5 Yurakucho, Chiyoda-ku, ☎ 03/3542–7545).

Lost and Found

The **Central Lost and Found Office** of the Metropolitan Police is located at 1-9-11, Koraku, Bunkyo-ku, Tokyo, ☎ 03/3814–4151. ☻ Weekdays 8:30–5:15, Sat. 8:30–12:30; closed Sun., the second and fourth Sat. of every month, and holidays. If you have lost something on the train, report it to the lost and found office at any station. However, the main lost and found offices for Japan Railways are at the JR Tokyo Station Lost Properties Office (☎ 03/3231–1880) and at Ueno Station (☎ 03/3841–8069).

If you leave something on the subways, contact **Teito Rapid Transit Authority** (TRTA) at its Ueno Lost Properties Office (☎ 03/3834–5577).

If you leave something in a taxi, contact the **Tokyo Taxi Kindaika Center** (7-3-3 Minami-Suna, Koto-ku, ☎ 03/3648–0300). Only Japanese is spoken here.

Currency Exchange and Banks

Most hotels will change both traveler's checks and notes into yen. However, their rates are always lower than banks. Because Japan is so safe and virtually free from street crime, one may consider exchanging large sums of money into yen at banks at any time. Most of the larger banks have a foreign exchange counter. Banking hours: weekdays 9–3.

The major banks can transfer funds to and from overseas. Two banks that may be familiar to you are **Bank of America** (Arc Mori Bldg., 1-12-32 Akasaka, Minato-ku, ☎ 03/3587–3111) and **Citibank** (1-1-3 Otemachi, Chiyoda-ku, toll-free ☎ 0120–322–522). **American Express** has a banking office in its headquarters in the American Express Tower (4-30-16 Ogikubo, Suginami-ku, ☎ 03/3220–6000).

Directory Assistance

For Tokyo telephone numbers, dial 104; for elsewhere in Japan, dial 105.

Post and Telegraph Offices

Most hotels have stamps and will mail your letters and postcards; they will also give you directions to the nearest post office. The main **International Post Office** is on the Imperial Palace side of the JR Tokyo Station (2-3-3 Otemachi, Chiyoda-ku, ☎ 03/3241–4891). For cables, contact the KDD International Telegraph Office (2-3-2 Nishi-Shinjuku, Shinjuku-ku, ☎ 03/3344–5151).

Embassies and Consulates

U.S. Embassy and Consulate, 1-10-5 Akasaka, Minato-ku, ☎ 03/3224–5000. Consulate ⊙ weekdays 8:30–12:30 and 2–4:30.

Australian Embassy, 2-1-14 Mita, Minato-ku, ☎ 03/5232–4111. ⊙ Weekdays 9 AM–noon and 1:30–5.

British Embassy and Consulate, 1 Ichibancho, Chiyoda-ku, ☎ 03/3265–6340. Consulate ⊙ Sun.–Fri. 9–noon and 2–4.

Canadian Embassy, 7-3-38 Akasaka, Minato-ku, ☎ 03/3408–2101. ⊙ Weekdays 9–12:30 and 1:30–5:30.

New Zealand Embassy, 20-40 Kamiyamacho, Shibuya-ku, ☎ 03/3467–2271. ⊙ Weekdays 9–12:30 and 1:30–5:30.

Tourist Information

The **Tourist Information Center** (TIC) (1-6-6 Yurakucho, Chiyoda-ku, ☎ 03/3502–1461; ⊙ weekdays 9–5, Sat. 9–noon) is an extremely useful office for free maps and brochures, as well as for planning any trip in Japan. It is definitely worth visiting this office early in your stay in Tokyo. The closest subway stations to the TIC are Hibiya and Yurakucho. The Hibiya station is on the same avenue, Harumi-dori, as the TIC (take exit A4, walk toward the railway bridge, and the TIC is on the right side of the street); Yurakucho Station is just to the north of the TIC; if you follow the overhead train tracks south one block, the TIC office is across the street.

TRAVEL INFORMATION

Information in English on all domestic travel, buses, and trains can be acquired by phoning the TIC (☎ 03/3502–1461). You may also call **Japan Railways** (☎ 03/3423—0111) or the toll-free **Japan Travel Phone** (0120/222–800 for eastern Japan; 0120/444–800 for western Japan) for information in English.

GENERAL INFORMATION

NTT (Japanese Telephone Corporation, ☎ 03/5295–0101) will help find information (in English), such as telephone numbers, museum openings, and various other facts that it has in its data bases.

CURRENT EVENTS/ EXHIBITIONS

A taped recording in English (☎ 03/3503–2911) gives information on current events in Tokyo and vicinity. **The Tour Companion,** a free weekly newspaper available at hotels, provides some information on events, exhibitions, festivals, plays, etc. **The Tokyo Journal,** however, has a more comprehensive monthly listing of what's happening in Tokyo. It also lists services and stores that may be of special interest to foreigners (cost: ¥600). **The Japan Times,** the country's daily English-language newspaper, is good for national and international news coverage, as well as for entertainment reviews and listings.

3 Tokyo Excursions

Nikko, Kamakura, and Mt. Fuji are each within a couple of hours of the great metropolis. Visitors either love or hate Toshogu, the shrine that is the centerpiece of Nikko, but most agree on the grandeur of that city's natural beauty. Kamakura, capital of Japan for more than a century, has a splendid legacy of historic and cultural sites. And no matter how many pictures of Mt. Fuji you have seen, the perfect symmetry and supreme majesty of this dormant volcano will fill you with awe.

NIKKO

By Jared
Lubarsky

AT NIKKO, A FEW HOURS' JOURNEY to the north of Tokyo, is the monument to a warlord so splendid and powerful that he became a god. In the year 1600, Ieyasu Tokugawa won a battle at a place called Sekigahara, in the mountains of south-central Japan, that left him the undisputed ruler of the archipelago. He died in 1616, but the Tokugawa shogunate would last another 252 years, holding in its sway a peaceful, prosperous, and united country.

A fit resting place would have to be made for the founder of such a dynasty. Ieyasu had provided for one in his will: a mausoleum at Nikko, in a forest of tall cedars, where a religious center had been founded more than eight centuries earlier. The year after his death, in accordance with Buddhist custom, he was given a *kaimyo*—an honorific name to bear in the afterlife; thenceforth, he was Tosho-Daigongen: The Great Incarnation Who Illuminates the East. The Imperial Court at Kyoto declared him a god, and his remains were taken in a procession of great pomp and ceremony to be enshrined at Nikko.

The dynasty he left behind was enormously rich. Ieyasu's personal fief, on the Kanto Plain, was worth 2.5 million *koku* of rice; one koku, in monetary terms, was equivalent to the cost of keeping one retainer in the necessities of life for a year. The shogunate itself, however, was still an uncertainty; it had only recently taken control after more than a century of civil war. The founder's tomb had a political purpose: It was meant to inspire awe and to make manifest the wealth and power of the Tokugawas. It was Ieyasu's legacy, a statement of his family's right to rule.

Toshogu (shrine) was built by his grandson, the third shogun, Iemitsu. (It was Iemitsu who established the policy of national isolation, which closed the doors of Japan to the outside world for more than 200 years.) The mausoleum and shrine required the labor of 15,000 people for two years (1634–1636); craftsmen and artists of the first rank were assembled from all over the country. Every surface was carved and painted and lacquered in the most intricate detail imaginable; Toshogu shimmers in the reflections from 2,489,000 sheets of gold leaf. Roof beams and rafter ends with dragon heads, lions, and elephants in bas-relief; friezes of phoenixes, wild ducks, and monkeys; inlaid pillars and red-lacquer corridors—Toshogu is everything a 17th-century warlord would consider gorgeous, and the inspiration is very Chinese.

Foreign visitors have differed about the effect Iemitsu achieved. Victorian-era traveler Isabella Bird, who came to Nikko in 1878, was unrestrained in her enthusiasm: "To pass from court to court," she writes in her *Unbeaten Tracks in Japan,* "is to pass from splendour to splendour; one is almost glad to feel that this is the last, and that the strain on one's capacity for admiration is nearly over." Fosco Mariani, a more recent visitor, felt somewhat differently: "You are taken aback," he observes in his *Meeting with Japan* (1959). "You ask yourself whether it is a joke, or a nightmare, or a huge wedding cake, a masterpiece of sugar icing made for some extravagant prince with a perverse, rococo taste, who wished to alarm and entertain his guests." Clearly, it is impossible to feel indifferent about Toshogu; perhaps, in the end, that is all Ieyasu could ever really have expected.

Nikko (which means "sunlight") is not simply the site of the Tokugawa shrine, however; it is also a national park—Nikko Kokuritso Koen—of great beauty, about which opinion has never been divided. From above Toshogu, the Irohazaka Driveway coils its way up through maple forests to the park plateau and Chuzenji, a deep lake some 21 kilometers (13 miles) around. To the north, there are hot springs; at the east end of the lake, the spectacular Kegon Falls tumble more than 300 feet to the Daiya River. Towering above this landscape, at 8,149 feet, is the extinct volcanic cone of Mt. Nantai. "Think nothing splendid," asserts an old Japanese proverb, "until you have seen Nikko." Whoever said it first may not even have been thinking of the mausoleum down below.

Arriving and Departing

It's possible, but unwise, to go by car from Tokyo to Nikko. The trip will take at least three hours; getting from central Tokyo to the Tohoku Expressway—an hour of the trip or more—is a nightmare. Coming back, especially on a Saturday or Sunday evening, is even worse. If you must drive, take the expressway north to exit 10 (marked in English), and follow the green toll-road signs from there into Nikko.

Far easier and more comfortable are the Limited Express trains of the Tobu Railway, with 10 direct connections every morning, starting at 7:10 AM (additional trains on weekends and holidays) from the Tobu Asakusa Station, a minute's walk from the last stop on the Ginza subway line in Tokyo. The one-way fare is ¥2,530. All seats are reserved. Bookings are not accepted over the phone; consult your hotel or a travel agent. From Asakusa to the Tobu Nikko Station is 1 hour and 40 minutes. If you are making a day trip, the last return trains are at 5:40 (direct express) and 8:10 PM (with a transfer at Shimo-Imaichi).

If you have a JR Rail Pass, we suggest you use JR service, which connects Tokyo and Nikko, from Ueno. Take the Tohoku Line limited express to Utsunomiya (about 1½ hours) and transfer to the train for JR Nikko Station (45 minutes). The earliest departure from Ueno is at 5:09 AM; the last connection back leaves Nikko at 8:24 PM and brings you into Ueno at 10:45. More expensive but faster is the "yamabiko" train on the north extension of the Shinkansen. The first one leaves Tokyo Station at 6:00 AM (or Ueno at 6:06 AM) and takes about 45 minutes to Utsunomiya; change there to the train to Nikko Station. To return, take the 9:24 PM train from Nikko to Utsunomiya and catch the last "yamabiko" back at 10:40, arriving in Tokyo at 11:24.

Getting Around

In Nikko itself, you won't need much in the way of transportation but your own two feet; nothing is terribly far from anything else. Local buses leave the railway station for Lake Chuzenji, stopping just above the entrance to Toshogu, approximately every 30 minutes from 6:20 AM. The fare to Chuzenji is ¥1,100 for adults, ¥530 for children under 12; the ride takes about 50 minutes. The last return bus from the lake leaves at 8:29 PM. Cabs are readily available; the one-way fare from the Tobu Nikko Station to Chuzenji is about ¥5,800.

Guided Tours

From Tokyo, two companies offer guided tours to Nikko. **Japan Amenity Travel** (☎ 03/3542–7545) operates a one-day motor-coach tour (lunch included) daily March 20–November 30. The tour includes

Toshogu and Lake Chuzenji. Pickup from major hotels begins at 8 AM. Cost: ¥20,000 adults, ¥17,000 children under 12 (lunch included).

Tobu Travel Co., Ltd. (☎ 03/3281–6622) operates an All-Day Nikko Tour that also includes Lake Chuzenji; it departs at 9 AM and returns at 6:45 PM. Cost (breakfast and lunch included): ¥20,000 adults, ¥17,000 children under 12.

Exploring Nikko

Numbers in the margin correspond to points of interest on the Nikko Area map.

Toshogu Area

The town of Nikko is essentially one long avenue (Sugi Namiki or Cryptomeria Avenue), extending for about a mile from the railway stations to Toshogu. This street is lined with tourist inns and shops, and if you have time, you might want to make this a leisurely walk. The antiques shops along the way may turn up interesting—but expensive— pieces (armor fittings, hibachi, pottery, dolls), and the souvenir shops will have ample selections of the local wood carvings. Alternatively, you can save yourself the hike up through town by taking the bus from either railway station (fare: ¥180) to Shinkyo (the Sacred Bridge).

Before the bridge, at the top of the hill, on the left, is the entrance to
❶ the **Kanaya Hotel,** owned and operated by the same family for more than 100 years. The main building is a delightful, rambling Victorian that has played host to royalty and other important personages—as the guest book attests—from all over the world. The road curves to the left and crosses the Daiyagawa (river); on the left is the red-lac-
❷ quer wood **Shinkyo,** a bridge built in 1636 for shoguns and imperial messengers on their visits to the shrine. It is still used for ceremonial occasions. (The original structure was destroyed in a flood; the present version dates from 1907.) Once, ordinary mortals were not permitted on the bridge. Now you may pay ¥300 for the privilege of walking over it.

The main entrances to the Toshogu area are opposite the bridge, on the right, where there is also a **Monument to Masatane Matsudaira,** one of the two feudal lords charged with the actual construction of Toshogu. Matsudaira's great contribution was the planting of the wonderful cryptomerias (Japanese cedars) around the shrine and along all the approaches to it. The project took more than 20 years, from 1628 to 1651; the result was some 64 kilometers (40 miles) of cedar-lined avenues. Fire and attrition have taken their toll, but some 13,000 of these trees still stand—a setting of solemn majesty the buildings themselves could never have achieved.

Take either the ramp or the stone stairway to the grounds of Toshogu. At the top of the stairway, in the corner of the car park, you can purchase a multiple entry ticket (¥1,250 adults, ¥400 children under 12) for Rinnoji (temple), the Daiyuin (the mausoleum of the third shogun, Iemitsu Tokugawa), Toshugu, and the Futaarasan Jinja (shrine); separate fees are charged for admission to other areas.

★ ❸ Turn left from the ticket area to enter the grounds of **Rinnoji.** Rinnoji belongs to the Tendai sect of Buddhism, the head temple of which is Enryakuji, on Mt. Hiei near Kyoto. Behind the Hondo—the abbot's quarters—is an especially fine little Japanese garden, made in 1815, and a museum, which has a good collection of lacquerware, paintings,

Nikko Area

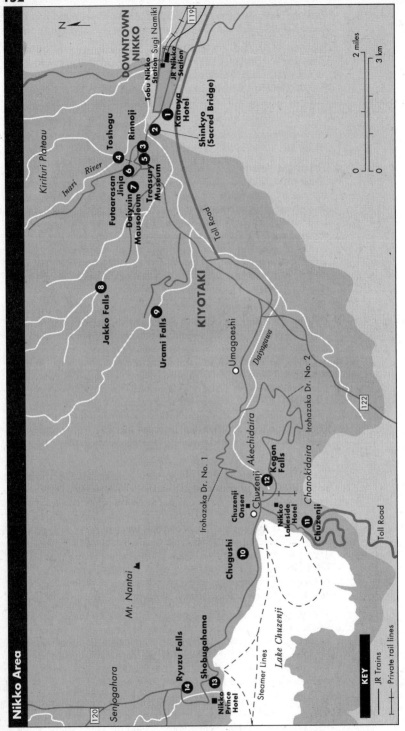

DOWNTOWN NIKKO

Tobu Nikko Station · Sugi Namiki
JR Nikko Station

Kaneya Hotel

Shinkyo (Sacred Bridge)

Kirifuri Plateau

Isari River

Toshogu

Rinnoji

Futaarasan Jinja

Daiyuin Mausoleum

Treasury Museum

Jakko Falls

Urami Falls

KIYOTAKI

Umagaeshi

Daiyagawa

Irohazaka Dr. No. 1

Irohazaka Dr. No. 2

Akechidaira

Chanokidaira

Chuzenji Onsen

Chuzenji

Kegon Falls

Nikko Lakeside Hotel

Chugushi

Mt. Nantai

Ryuzu Falls

Shobugahama

Senjogahara

Nikko Prince Hotel

Lake Chuzenji

Steamer Lines

Toll Road

Toll Road

1
2
3
4
5
6
7
8
9
10
11
12
13
14

119
120
122

2 miles
3 km

KEY

■ JR Trains

── Private rail lines

and Buddhist sculpture. ☞*Museum including the gardens ¥710 adults, ¥280 children under 12. ☯ 8–4 (enter by 3:30).*

The main hall of the temple, called the **Sambutsudo,** is the largest single building at Toshogu; it enshrines an image of Amida Nyorai, the Buddha of the Western Paradise, flanked on the right by a Senju (Thousand-Armed) Kannon, the goddess of mercy, and on the left by a Bato-Kannon, regarded as the protector of animals. These three images are lacquered in gold and date from the early part of the 17th century. The original Sambutsudo is said to have been built in 848 by the priest Ennin (794–864), also known as Jikaku-Daishi; the present building dates from 1648. Opposite, on the north side of the compound, is the **Gohotendo,** a hall that enshrines three of the Seven Gods of Good Fortune. These three are Buddhist deities derived from Chinese folk mythology: Daikoku and Bishamon, who bring wealth and good harvests, and Benten, patroness of music and the arts.

★ ❹ Leave Rinnoji by the west gate, turn right, and walk up the cedar-lined avenue to the stone *torii* (arch) of **Toshogu.** On the left is the five-story **pagoda** of the shrine—a reconstruction dating from 1818 but lately repaired. The first story is decorated with the 12 signs of the zodiac; the black-lacquer doors above each bear the three hollyhock leaves of the Tokugawa family crest.

Walk up the stone steps, and enter the shrine through the Omotemon (Front Gate) or the Niomon (Gate of the Deva Kings), with its two red-painted guardian gods. From here the path turns to the left; in the first group of buildings you reach on the left is the **stable,** decorated with carved panels of pine trees and monkeys. The second panel from the left is the famous group of three monkeys—"Hear no evil, see no evil, speak no evil"—that has become almost the symbol of Nikko, reproduced endlessly on plaques, bags, and souvenirs of every sort. The stable houses a white horse; this animal, either real or represented in a painting or carving, is traditionally found in Shinto shrines. A few steps farther, where the path turns to the right, is a granite font where visitors purify themselves by washing their hands and rinsing their mouths before entering the shrine. Behind the font is the **Kyozo** (Sutra Library), which is a repository for some 7,000 Buddhist scriptures, kept in a huge revolving bookcase nearly 20 feet high. Unfortunately, the Kyozo is not open to the public.

As you pass under the second (bronze) torii and up the steps, you see on the right a belfry and a tall bronze candelabrum; on the left is a drum tower and a bronze revolving lantern. The two works in bronze were presented to the shrine by the Dutch government in the mid-17th century. Under the policy of national seclusion, only the Dutch retained trading privileges with Japan, and even they were confined to the tiny artificial island of Deshima, in the port of Nagasaki; they regularly sent tokens of their esteem to the shogunate to keep their precarious monopoly. Behind the drum tower is the **Yakushido,** which enshrines a manifestation of the Buddha (Yakushi Nyorai) as the healer of illnesses. The original 17th-century building was famous for a huge India-ink painting on the ceiling of the nave, *The Roaring Dragon,* by Yasunobu Kano (1613–1685). The work was so named because when visitors clapped their hands beneath it, the echoes made it seem as though the dragon had roared. The Yakushido was destroyed by fire in 1961, and rebuilt; the dragon on the ceiling is by Nanpu Katayama. (The Kano School, incidentally, was a school of professional artists founded in the late 15th century and patronized by successive military governments until the fall of the Tokugawa shogunate in 1868. The leadership was hereditary; the artists who trained in the Kano ateliers specialized in Chinese-style ink paintings, landscapes, and decorative figures of birds and animals—typically for screens and the paneled sliding doors that comprise the interior "walls" of Japanese villas and temples.)

At the top of the steps is the **Yomeimon,** the Gate of Sunlight, which is the centerpiece of the shrine and is designated a National Treasure. It is also called the Higurashimon (Twilight Gate), implying that one could spend all day until sunset looking at its richness of detail. Rich the gate certainly is; dazzling white and two stories (36 feet) high, it has 12 columns, beams, and roof brackets that are carved with dragons, lions, clouds, peonies, Chinese sages, and immortals. The gate has numerous carvings that are painted red, gold, blue, and green. On one of the central columns, there are two carved tigers; the natural grain of the wood is used to bring out the "fur." To the right and left of the Yomeimon as you enter are galleries running east and west for some 700 feet, their paneled fences also carved and painted with a profusion of motifs from nature: pine and plum branches, pheasants, cranes, and wild ducks.

Inside the gate to the left is the **Mikoshigura,** a storeroom where the portable shrines that appear in the annual Toshogu Festival on May 17–18 are kept. The paintings on the ceiling of *tennin* (Buddhist angels) playing harps are by Ryokaku Kano. To the right is the **Kaguraden,** a hall where ceremonial dances are performed to honor the gods. Directly ahead, across the courtyard, is the **Karamon** (Chinese Gate), the official entrance to the inner shrine—also a National Treasure, and, like the Yomeimon, carved and painted in elaborate detail with dragons and other auspicious figures. Extending right and left from the gate is a wall, which encloses the **Honden** (Main Hall) of the shrine.

The entrance is to the right; here you remove your shoes (lockers are provided) and pass into the outer part of the hall, called the **Haiden** (Oratory), with its lacquered pillars, carved friezes, and coffered ceilings painted with dragons. Over the lintels are paintings of the 36 great poets of the Heian period, by Mitsuoki Tosa (1617–1691), with their poems in the calligraphy of Emperor Go-Mizuno-o. The Haiden is divided into three chambers: At the back of the central chamber is the Sacred Mirror, believed to represent the spirit of the deity enshrined; the room on the right was reserved for visiting shoguns and members of the three principal branches of the Tokugawa family; and the room on the left for the chief abbot of Rinnoji—who was always a prince of the imperial line.

Beyond the Haiden is a passage called the Ishi-no-Ma (Stone Room). This connects in turn with the sanctum, which is divided into three parts: the Haiden (Sanctuary), the Naijin (Inner Chamber), and the Nai-Naijin (Innermost Chamber). No visitors come this far. Here, in the very heart of Toshogu, is the gold-lacquer shrine where the spirit (but not the body) of Ieyasu resides—along with two other deities, whom the Tokugawas later decided were fit companions. One was Hideyoshi Toyotomi, Ieyasu's mentor and liege lord in the long wars of unification at the end of the 16th century; the other was Yoritomo Minamoto, brilliant military tactician and founder of the earlier (12th century) Kamakura Shogunate. (Ieyásu, born Takechiyo Matsudaira, son of a lesser baron in what is today Aichi Prefecture, claimed Yoritomo for an ancestor.)

Return to the courtyard between the Karamon and Yomeimon gates, turn left, walk down the long passage painted in red cinnabar, and then left into an open corridor. Just above the gateway here is another famous symbol of Toshogu, the **Sleeping Cat**—a small panel said to have been carved by the sculptor Hidari Jingoro (Jingoro the Left-handed). A separate admission charge (¥500 adults, ¥350 children under 12) is levied to go beyond this point to the **Sakashitamon** (The Gate at the Foot of the Hill) and to the flight of 200 stone steps, up through the cryptomeria trees to **Ieyasu's Tomb.** The climb is worth making, if only for the view of the Yomeimon and Karamon from above—the tomb itself is unimpressive.

Retrace your steps (it's a lot easier coming down), return to the arch in front of the shrine, and turn right. A few minutes' walk will bring ❺ you to the **Treasury Museum,** on the left, which houses a collection of antiquities from the various shrines and temples. ☞ *¥500 adults, ¥200 children under 12.* ☉ *Apr.–Oct. 8:30–5, Nov.–Mar. 8:30–4.*

★ ❻ At the end of the avenue, bear right for the **Futaarasan Jinja.** To the gods enshrined here, Ieyasu must seem but a callow newcomer: Futarasan was founded in the 8th century to honor the Shinto deity Okuni-nushi-no-Mikoto (god of the rice fields, bestower of prosperity), his consort Tagorihime-no-Mikoto, and their son Ajisukitaka-hikone-no-Mikoto. The shrine is actually in three parts: the Honsha, or main shrine, at Toshogu; the Chugushi, or middle shrine, on Lake Chuzenji; and the Okumiya, or inner shrine, on top of Mt. Nantai.

Walk through the bronze torii to the Karamon (Chinese Gate) and the Honden (sanctum)—the present version of which dates from 1619. To the left, in the corner of the enclosure, is an antique bronze lantern, some 7 feet high, under a canopy. Legend has it that the lantern would assume the shape of a goblin at night; the deep nicks in the bronze were inflicted by swordsmen of the Edo period—on guard duty, perhaps, startled into action by a flickering shape in the dark. This proves, if not the existence of goblins, the incredible cutting power of the Japanese blade. ☞ *Free.* ☉ *Apr.–Nov., 8–5; Dec.–Mar., 9–4.*

Retrace your steps and turn right. The first two buildings you come to, on the left, are the Jogyodo and Hokkedo (popularly called the Futatsudo, or **Twin Halls**) of Rinnoji, founded in 848. Between them, a path leads to the compound of the **Jigendo Hall,** built in honor of Tenkai (1536–1643), the first abbot of the Nikko temples. The Jigendo is at the north end of the compound, to the right. At the west end is the **Go-oden,** shrine to Prince Kitashirakawa (1847–1895), last of the imperial princes to serve as abbot; behind it is his tomb and the tombs of his 13 predecessors.

★ ❼ Return to the Twin Halls and turn left for the **Daiyuin Mausoleum.** (Admission is included in multiple entry ticket to Toshogu area mentioned earlier. ☉ *Apr.–Oct., 8–5; Nov.–Mar., 8-4.*) Iemitsu (1603–1651), one suspects, had it in mind to upstage his illustrious grandfather; he marked the approach to his own tomb with no fewer than six different decorative gates. The first is another Niomon—a Gate of the Deva Kings—like the one at Toshogu. The dragon painted on the ceiling is by Yasunobu Kano (1613–1685). A flight of stone steps leads from here to the second gate, the Nitenmon, a two-story structure protected front and back by carved and painted images of guardian gods. Beyond it, you climb two more flights of steps to the middle courtyard. There is a bell tower on the right and a drum tower on the left, and directly ahead is the third gate, the Yashamon, so named for the figures of Yasha (a demon) in the four niches. This structure is also called the Botanmon (Peony Gate) for the carvings that decorate it.

On the other side of the courtyard is the Karamon (Chinese Gate), gilded and elaborately carved; beyond it is the Haiden, the oratory of the shrine. The Haiden, too, is richly carved and decorated, with the ceiling covered with dragons; the Chinese lions on the panels at the rear are by two distinguished painters of the Kano school. Behind the Haiden is the Ai-no-Ma (anteroom or Connecting Chamber). From here you can see the sanctum (Honden). Designated a National Treasure, it houses a gilded and lacquered Buddhist altar some 9 feet high, decorated with paintings of animals, birds, and flowers, in which resides the object of all this veneration: a seated wooden figure of Iemitsu.

Return to the Karamon Gate, turn left and left again. At the far west end of the wall, on the right, is the fifth gate: the Kokamon, built in the Chinese style of the late Ming Dynasty. From here, another flight of stone steps leads to a small, white-painted oratory. There is one last climb, to the sixth and last gate—the bronze Inukimon—and Iemitsu's tomb.

If you return to the torii in front of Futaarasan Jinja and take the path to the right (south) down Nishisando, you will soon come to an exit from the Toshogu area on the main road. At this point, you may have given Nikko all the time you had to spare. If so, turn left, and a short walk will bring you back to the Sacred Bridge. If not, turn right, and in a minute or so you will come to the Nishisando bus stop, where you can take the local bus to Lake Chuzenji.

To Lake Chuzenji

About 1 kilometer (½-mile) from the shrines (Tamozawa bus stop) is **⑧** a narrow road to the right that leads to the **Jakko Falls**—an uphill walk of some 3 kilometers (2 miles). The falls descend in a series of seven terraced stages, forming a sheet of water about 100 feet high. Another turn to the right off the Chuzenji road, by the Arasawa bus stop, leads **⑨** to the **Urami Falls.** "The water," wrote the great 17th-century poet Basho, "seemed to take a flying leap and drop a hundred feet from the top of a cave into a green pool surrounded by a thousand rocks. One was supposed to inch one's way into the cave and enjoy the falls from behind." It's a steep climb to the cave; the falls and the gorge are striking, but only the visitor with good hiking shoes and a willingness to get wet should try this particular view.

The real climb to Chuzenji Lake begins at **Umagaeshi** (literally: Horse-Return), about 10 kilometers (6 miles) from the Tobu Station, 8 kilometers (5 miles) from Toshogu. Here, in the old days, the road became too rough for riding; the traveler on horseback had to alight and proceed on foot. The lake is 4,165 feet above sea level. From Umagaeshi, the bus climbs a new one-way toll road up the pass; the old road has been widened and is used for the traffic coming down. The two roads are full of steep hairpin turns, and on a clear day the view up and down the valley is magnificent—especially from the halfway point at **Akechidaira** (plain), from which you can see the summit of **Mt. Nantai,** reaching 8,149 feet. From May through mid-October, you'll often see energetic climbers making the ascent in about four hours.

The bus trip ends at Chuzenji village, which was named after the temple established here in 784. The temple was renamed **Chugushi** in the **⑩** 19th century and incorporated into Futarasan Jinja; it lies just outside the village, on the road along the north side of the lake. The treasure house (☛ ¥300 adults, ¥150 children under 12) has an interesting historical collection, including swords, lacquerware and medieval shrine palanquins. ⊙ *Temple, daily, Apr.–Oct. 8–5; Nov.–Mar., 9–4.*

⓫ Chugushi is not to be confused with the present-day temple **Chuzenji** (Tashiki Kannon), which you reach by turning left (south) as you leave the village and walking about 1½ kilometers (1 mile) along the eastern shore of the lake. The temple is part of Rinnoji, at Toshogu. The principal object of worship is a 17-foot-high statue of Kannon, the goddess of mercy, said to have been carved more than 1,000 years ago by the priest Shodo from the living trunk of a single Judas tree. ☛ *¥300 adults, ¥100 children under 18.* ۞ *Daily, Apr.–Oct. 8–5; Nov. 8–4; Dec.–Feb. 8:30–3:30; Mar. 8–4.*

In front of the temple was Utagahama (Singing Beach), so named because an angel was said to have descended from heaven here to sing and dance for Shodo; unfortunately, the "beach" is now a parking lot and a pier.

Just by the bus stop at Chuzenji village is a gondola (round-trip fare: ¥820 adults, ¥410 children under 12) to **Chanokidaira** (plain); about 1,000 feet above the lake, it commands a wonderful view of the whole surrounding area. Just below the gondola, on the outskirts of the village, is the top of **Kegon Falls.** Farther on, as the road starts to descend into the valley, you'll find an elevator (fare: ¥520 adults, ¥310 children under 12) that will take you to an observation platform at the bottom of the gorge. The flow of water over the falls is carefully regulated, but it is especially impressive after a summer rain or a typhoon. In the winter, the falls do not freeze completely, but form a beautiful cascade of icicles.

★ ⓬

If you have budgeted an extra day for Nikko, you might want to consider a walk around the lake. A paved road along the north shore extends for about 8 kilometers (5 miles), or ⅓ of the whole distance, as far as **Shobugahama** (beach); a "nature trail" parallels the road, but it's not very attractive, especially in summer when there are hordes of visitors. It is better to come this far by boat or bus. From here the road branches off to the north for Senjogahara (plain) and Yunoko (lake). Just above the Nikko Prince Hotel at Shobugahama are the **Ryuzu** (Dragon's Head) **Falls.** To the left is a steep footpath that continues around the lake to Senjugahama, and thence to a campsite at Asegata. The path is well marked but can be rough going in places. From Asegata, it's less than an hour's walk back to the temple Chuzenji.

⓭

⓮

Dining

Nikko has no shortage of popular restaurants geared to the tourist trade, though there is nothing special to distinguish one from another. Because they all have display cases outside with price-tagged plastic models of the food they serve, you at least know what you're letting yourself in for. Noodle shops are always safe for lunch; the dishes called *soba* and *udon* are inexpensive, filling, and tasty. In recent years Nikko has also come into its share of Western-style fast-food restaurants.

Dining in Nikko, as in virtually all resort areas in Japan, is informal. Even in hotel restaurants, in winter, men might feel more comfortable in jackets but will not need neckties; women in slacks will not be frowned upon.

For a meal in somewhat more upscale surroundings, try the dining room at one of the hotels listed below. Lunch will cost about ¥3,500 per person. Lunch at the Kanaya, with its air of old-fashioned gentility, is especially pleasant; the Boat House, at the hotel's branch hotel on the shore of Chuzenji, often has fresh trout from the lake.

Lodging

Kanko (tourist) hotels everywhere in Japan do most of their business with tour groups and large private parties. In Nikko and Chuzenji, especially, hotels seem almost relentless in the way they organize their schedules to move these groups in and out. At 7 or 7:30 AM, someone will knock on your door, demanding to remove the bedding; by 8:30, in most cases, no more breakfast service is available. Nothing is leisurely about kanko hotels; they tend to be noisy and relatively expensive for what they provide.

Five Western-style hotels in the area provide a welcome alternative. Be warned that these hotels may add a surcharge to the basic rate at various times: weekends, nights before local festivals, July–August, October—in other words, whenever you are likely to want a room. Call ahead, or check with your travel agent for the prevailing rate at the time.

A 3% federal consumer tax is added to all hotel bills. Another 3% local tax is added to the bill if it exceeds ¥15,000. At most hotels, a 10%–15% service charge is added to the total bill. Tipping is not necessary.

CATEGORY	COST*
$$$$	over ¥25,000
$$$	¥17,000–¥25,000
$$	¥10,000–¥17,000
$	under ¥10,000

Cost is for double room, without tax or service

Nikko

$$$$ **Nikko Kanaya Hotel.** A little worn around the edges after a century of
★ operation, the Kanaya still has the best location in town—literally across the street from the Toshogu area. The hotel is very touristy; daytime visitors, especially Westerners, come to browse through the old building and its gift shops. The staff is very helpful and is better at giving information on the area than the city information office. Rooms vary a great deal, as do their prices—up to ¥25,000 per person on weekends. The more expensive are all spacious and comfortable, with wonderful high ceilings; in the annex, you fall asleep to the sound of the Daiyagawa murmuring below by the Sacred Bridge. ☒ *1300 Kami Hatsuishicho, Nikko, Tochigi 321-14,* ☎ *0288/54–0001 or (Tokyo office) 03/3271–5215. 77 rooms, 62 with bath. Restaurant, pool, nearby golf. AE, DC, MC, V.*

$$ **Pension Turtle.** This member of the Japanese Inn Group offers friendly, modest, and cost-conscious accommodations with or without private bath. To get to the Pension Turtle, take the bus bound for Chuzenji from either railway station and get off at the Sogo Kaiken-mae bus stop. The inn is a minute or so from the bus stop and within walking distance of Toshogu. ☒ *2-16 Takumicho, Nikko, Tochigi 321-14,* ☎ *0288/53–3168. 7 Western- and 5 Japanese-style rooms. Restaurant. AE, MC, V.*

Chuzenji

$$$$ **Chuzenji Kanaya.** On the road from the village to Shobugahama, this branch of the Nikko Kanaya has its own boathouse and restaurant on the lake. The atmosphere here is something like that of a private club. ☒ *2482 Chugushi, Nikko, Tochigi 321-16,* ☎ *0288/51–0001. 60 rooms. Restaurant, boating, fishing, waterskiing. AE, DC, MC, V.*

$$-$$$ **Nikko Lakeside Hotel.** A newish hotel in the village of Chuzenji, at the foot of the lake, the Nikko Lakeside has no particular character, but the views are good, and the transportation connections (to buses and excursion boats) are ideal. Prices vary considerably from weekday to weekend and season to season. Check ahead. ⌨ *2482 Chugushi, Nikko, Tochigi 321-16,* ☏ *0288/55–0321. 100 rooms, all with bath. Restaurant, bicycles, boating, tennis. AE, DC, MC, V.*

Shobugahama

$$$ **Nikko Prince Hotel.** This is a new luxury hotel, within walking distance of the Ryuzu Falls. The Prince chain is one of Japan's largest and most successful leisure conglomerates, with hotels in most major cities and resorts. Minor differences in architecture aside, they are all pretty much the same experience: modern creature comforts and professionalism. ⌨ *Shobugahama Chugushi, Nikko, Tochigi 321-16,* ☏ *0288/55–0661. 60 twin rooms with bath. Restaurant, pool, tennis, water sports. AE, DC, MC, V.*

KAMAKURA

By Nigel Fisher

Updated by
Jared Lubarsky

Visitors are attracted to Kamakura, about 40 kilometers (25 miles) southwest of Tokyo, by its cultural souvenirs of the 141-year period when the city was the seat of Japan's first shoguns. The attraction is even greater because, after the 14th century, the ravages of history occurred elsewhere, and Kamakura's glorious past was unsullied; its history became a romantic blend of fact and fiction. During the 12th century, the Taira and the Minamoto clans were at each other's throats battling for supremacy. The Taira family won a major battle that should have secured their absolute control over Japan, but they made a serious mistake. They killed the Minamoto chief but spared his son, Yoritomo, and sent him to live in a monastery. But Yoritomo Minamoto was not destined for a monk's life; instead he sought to avenge his father. Gathering support against the Taira clan, he chose Kamakura as his base of operations. Surrounded on three sides by hills and with the fourth side guarded by the sea, Kamakura was a natural location for defense against enemy attacks. The battle between the Minamoto and the Taira clans revived. By 1192, under the leadership of Yoritomo's skillful half-brother, Yoshitsune, the Minamoto were victorious, and the Kamakura era (1192–1333) began; Yoritomo established a shogunal government. The emperor was left as a figurehead in Kyoto, and, for the first time in Japan's history, the seat of power was structurally and geographically removed from the imperial capital. The little fishing village of Kamakura became Japan's power center.

Yoritomo kept his antagonists at bay during his lifetime, but his successors were less than successful. His first son was assassinated, even though he had abdicated his position as shogun to become a monk, and the second son had his head sliced off by a disgruntled nephew. Because neither of Yoritomo's two sons had children, the Minamoto dynasty ended. Yoritomo's wife, Masako, who had followed tradition by shaving her head and becoming a nun when her husband died, filled the power vacuum. Upon the murder of her second son, her family, the Hojos, took power. This family remained in control, often acting as regents for nominal child shoguns, for the next hundred years.

The demise of the Kamakura era began as the Hojo resources were drained in the support of armies warding off two invasions (1274 and 1281) by the Mongol armies of China's Yuan dynasty. Although the fortuitous typhoons—the *kamikaze* (divine wind)—may have saved the day against the Mongols, Kamakura still had to reward the various clans who fought alongside the Kamakura army and who had to remain on the alert for further invasions. Displeased with what they received, these clans grew dissatisfied with the Kamakura Shogunate. Emperor Godaigo saw his opportunity and rallied the discontented nobles to successfully defeat the shogunate. Thus ended the Kamakura era. The nation's authority, brought back to Kyoto, was shortly to be wrested away from Emperor Godaigo by the Ashikaga clan.

Kamakura reverted to a sleepy backwater on the edge of the sea. It remained an isolated temple town until the Yokosuka railway line was built in 1889, but not until after World War II did Kamakura develop rapidly as a wealthy residential district for commuters to Yokohama and Tokyo.

Arriving and Departing

By far the best way to reach Kamakura is by train. From Tokyo, trains run from Tokyo Station (and Shinbashi Station) every 10–15 minutes during the day. The trip takes 56 minutes to Kita-Kamakura (North Kamakura), which is where we begin our tour, and one hour to Kamakura. Take the JR Yokosuka Line from track No. 1 downstairs in Tokyo Station. (Track No. 1 upstairs is on a different line and does not go to Kamakura.) The cost is ¥760 to Kita-Kamakura, and ¥880 to Kamakura (or use your JR Rail Pass).

Guided Tours

Unfortunately, no English-speaking tours may be booked in Kamakura. However, you can take one of the Japanese-speaking tours, which depart from Kamakura Station eight times daily, starting at 9:40 AM. Purchase tickets at the bus office to the right of the station. Two itineraries are offered, one lasting about 2 hours, 10 minutes (¥2,500), the other about 2½ hours (¥3,300). The last tours leave at 1:40 PM. Take with you the book *Exploring Kamakura: A Guide for the Curious Traveler,* written in English by Michael Cooper, and you'll have more information at your fingertips than your fellow Japanese tourists on the bus.

On Saturdays and Sundays, a free guide service is offered by the Kanagawa Student Guide Federation. Students show you the city in exchange for the chance to practice their English. Arrangements need to be made in advance through the Japan National Tourist Office in Tokyo (☎ 03/3502–1461). Be at Kamakura Station by 10 AM.

Tours from Tokyo are available every day, often combined with trips to Hakone (*see* Fuji–Hakone–Izu National Park, *below*). All major hotels in Tokyo can make the bookings, and, in most instances, a free pickup service is available from the major hotels. However, before you select a tour, make sure that it covers all of the Kamakura that you wish to see. Many do nothing much more than offer a fleeting glance of the Daibutsu (Great Buddha) in Hase. Our advice is to see Kamakura on your own. It is one of the easiest sightseeing trips to enjoy out of Tokyo.

Exploring Kamakura

Numbers in the margin correspond to points of interest on the Kamakura map.

A tour of Kamakura is a walk through Japan's feudal era that brings back the personalities who lived and fought in the city's glorious age.

The city has 65 Buddhist temples and 19 Shinto shrines. This chapter can include only a small percentage of them, but, hopefully, we can induce you to spend a little longer in Kamakura than the guided tours from Tokyo permit. Furthermore, Kamakura is accustomed to tourists, and most of the sights are either within walking distance of each other or a short hop by bus or train.

For the purpose of seeing Kamakura's major temples and shrines, the following exploring section is divided into three separate areas. Traveling between each area is easily accomplished by short train rides. You could also walk everywhere, but there is certainly enough walking around the shrines and temples to satisfy most visitors.

The first tour explores the Tokyo side of Kamakura. Referred to as Kita-Kamakura (*kita* means north), it features Engakuji (temple). The second tour covers Kamakura, one station stop south of Kita-Kamakura. This is downtown Kamakura, with a multitude of shops, restaurants, and Kamakura's venerated Tsurugaoka Hachimangu (shrine). The third tour visits Hase, to the southwest of Kamakura. It is reached by a 10minute train ride on the Enoden Line. Hase's main attractions are the Daibutsu (Great Buddha) in Kotokuin (temple) and Hasedera (temple). These four sights (Engakuji, Tsurugaoka Hachimangu, Daibutsu, and Hasedera) are Kamakura's most important. It is easy to cover all four in a day and still leave time for lunch, shopping, and even a few more temples. However, a single day would be insufficient to cover all the places discussed in the following excursion, so judicious pruning may be required, and with only one day, you should not take the time to visit Enoshima (island), described at the end of this excursion.

Kita-Kamakura is the first train station to be reached from Tokyo on this excursion. For geographical simplicity, this excursion works its way south through Kamakura and Hase, then west to Enoshima, a resort area along the coast. From there, rather than return through Kamakura, we take a train, using the Odakyu Line, back to Tokyo's Shinjuku. However, most visitors only have the time to go as far south as Hase before returning to Kamakura and Tokyo.

Kita-Kamakura

★ ❶ The first temple of major importance in Kita-Kamakura is **Engakuji.** When you leave Kita-Kamakura Station, keep the train tracks on your right and walk five minutes to the south. On your left will be Engakuji. This is the second most important of Kamakura's five Great Mountain Temples and once contained as many as 50 buildings. It has had more than its fair share of fires, and, though many of the buildings have been restored, Engakuji's former glory has long since passed. However, a simplicity of mood and a feeling of agelessness permeates this temple complex. One would expect it to be so: This Buddhist temple adheres to the Rinzai sect of Zen Buddhism.

Introduced into Japan from China at the beginning of the Kamakura period (1192–1333), Zen Buddhism was quickly accepted by the samurai class. The samurai caste evolved from the stewards and lesser retainers on imperial estates who led lives far from the ease and refinement of the Kyoto court; these new warrior clans were especially attracted to Zen Buddhism, particularly the Rinzai sect, with its asceticism and its spontaneous moments of enlightenment. Rinzai sees the path to enlightenment through the ability to get beyond the immediate reality by understanding, for example, what is meant by the sound of one hand clapping. To reach this understanding is to have

162

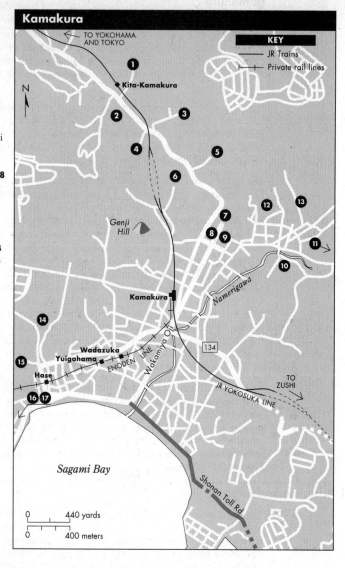

reached a spiritual level where mortal feeling is transcended. Searching for the spiritual among the old Japanese cedars and stone-paved walkways of Engakuji seems natural.

Among the National Treasures within the temple complex is the **Shari-den** (Hall of the Holy Relics of Buddha). It has survived the many fires that have raged through the complex these last seven centuries and is the only temple to have kept its original form since it was built, in 1282. You cannot go beyond its gate, but you can peer through the gate for a fairly good look. The other famous National Treasure at Engakuji is the great **belfry** standing on the hilltop. Cast in 1301, Kamakura's most celebrated bell stands eight feet tall. Only on rare occasions is it used, such as New Year's. If you are fortunate enough to hear its deep resonant tone, you will be one step closer to understanding the sound of one hand clapping. The two structures open to the public are Butsunichian, which has a long tearoom where visitors can enjoy the

Japanese tea ceremony, and the Obai-in. The latter is the mausoleum of Tokimune Hojo, his son, and his grandson, the last three regents before Kamakura fell. Off to the side of the mausoleum is a quiet garden with apricot trees (they bloom in Feb.), where you can contemplate Kamakura's demise. ☛ *¥200 adults, ¥100 children under 12.* ☼ *daily, Nov.–Feb. 8–4; Mar.–Sept. 8–5:30; Oct. 8–4:30.*

★ ❷ Ten minutes away from Engakuji, on the other side of the railway line, is **Tokeiji,** founded in 1285. Its fame, or notoriety, is indicated by its more common name, the "Divorce Temple." In feudal Japan, the husband could obtain a divorce by simply sending his wife packing. Not so for the wife; no matter what cruel and unusual punishments her husband meted out, she had no grounds for securing a divorce. However, in the 13th century, Tokimune Hojo (whose mausoleum you saw at Engakuji) decreed that if a woman ran away and made it to Tokeiji before being caught by her husband, she could receive sanctuary at the temple and stay there as a nun. After three years (later reduced to two), she was officially declared divorced. The temple remained a convent until the end of the Meiji Restoration. The last abbess died in 1902; her headstone is in the cemetery at the back of the temple. The cemetery has the peace of a Japanese garden. The headstones, scattered among the plum trees (they blossom in Feb.), are the symbols of refuge from a male-dominated society. The temple's Treasure Museum (Homotsukan) has a number of Kamakura-period wooden Buddhas, ink paintings, scrolls, and calligraphy on display, some of which has been designated by the government as Important Cultural Objects. ☛ *¥50 (¥300 for the Treasure Museum).* ☼ *Tues.–Sun. 10 AM–3 PM.*

If you have limited time in Kamakura, return from Tokeiji to Kita-Kamakura Station for the train (one stop) to Kamakura. If, however, you have the energy and the time, you can walk to visit four temples en route to Tsurugaoka Hachimangu (shrine), the next major place of interest.

★ ❸ **Meigetsu-in** requires a small detour from the direct route to Tsurugaoka Hachimangu, but if you are in Kamakura in June, the detour may be worthwhile to see the hydrangeas in bloom—a wafting sea of pink, white, and blue. To reach Meigetsu-in from Tokeiji, you must cross back over the railway line, walk down the main road a hundred yards or so, and then turn left. A word of warning, though: This normally quiet and peaceful temple, which is usually so conducive to reflection, becomes a rush of humanity during hydrangea season. ☛ *¥200.* ☼ *Daily 9–4:30, hydrangea season 8–5.*

❹ The next temple to visit is **Jochiji,** located on the same side of the railway lines as Tokeiji. Jochiji's entrance is on the right and over a small bridge. The temple is at the top of a series of moss-covered steps. The buildings are new replacements (about 50 years old) for the originals, which, like so many other temples in Japan, were destroyed by fire. But rather than Jochiji's buildings, it is the garden that makes the temple complex so appealing—standing in the northern sector are statues of the Seven Gods of Fortune. ☛ *¥100 adults, ¥50 children under 12.* ☼ *Daily 9–4:30 (June, 8:30–4:30).*

★ ❺ The next temple on the way to Tsurugaoka Hachimangu is **Kenchoji,** the most important of Kamakura's five main temples. The visitor has only an inkling of how magnificent this temple was when it was completed in 1253. Successive fires destroyed the buildings, and, though many of the buildings have been authentically reconstructed, the complex is half its original size. Near the Sanmon (gate) is a **bronze bell** cast in 1255. It is the most revered treasure of the temple. The other key structures are the **Main Hall** and its **Ceremonial Gate,** a huge structure held together by wood wedges, yet having a light and delicate appearance. Both Kenchoji and Engakuji (the temple we visited first) are still active temples of the Rinzai sect of Zen Buddhism, where novitiates are trained and people come to take sessions in zazen meditation. You will often see groups of lay-people sitting on the grounds while the master, who carries a wooden staff, stands among them, ensuring that their concentration is not wandering. ☛ *¥300 adults, ¥100 children under 14.* ☼ *Daily 8–4:30.*

6 Across the road from Kenchoji is **Ennoji.** While it may not have great aesthetic value, this structure is a macabre change from the others. During the feudal period, a belief was held that souls en route to the afterlife would be judged by the Ten Kings of Heaven. Ennoji houses statues of these judges, and, far from looking compassionate, the judges display the most merciless countenances. To see them is enough to place you on your best behavior until their images fade from your memory. ☛ *¥100 adults, ¥50 children under 12.* ☼ *Daily 9–4.*

If you walk another 200 meters (yards) south from Ennoji, you arrive at the Tsurugaoka Hachimangu. However, for the benefit of those who took the train from Kita-Kamakura to Kamakura, we will begin our visit to Tsurugaoka Hachimangu from the station.

Kamakura

From the east side of Kamakura Station, walk across the plaza and go left on the main broad avenue, Wakamiya Oji—easily recognizable by the golden arch of McDonald's on the left. Straight ahead is the first

★ **7** of three arches leading to **Tsurugaoka Hachimangu** (often abbreviated to "Hachiman"), Kamakura's most important Shinto shrine and the best place to remember the Minamoto family.

When Yoritomo Minamoto became a father-to-be, he decreed that a stately avenue should be built through the center of Kamakura from the sea to the shrine. Such an avenue was to be fitting for a young prince's procession to the shrine. The avenue was completed, a son, Yoriie, was born, and a magnificent procession advanced up the avenue to the shrine for the prince to be blessed. Yoriie's future, though, was limited. At the age of 18, he became shogun. Weak in popularity and unable to master intrigue, Yoriie soon abdicated to become a monk. A year later he was assassinated. Although Yoriie never completed great deeds, his memory lives on with Wakamiya Oji, which translates as "Young Prince Avenue."

At the far end of Wakamiya Oji and at the entrance to the shrine, a small, steeply arched, vermilion bridge (Drum Bridge) crosses over a stream that links two lotus ponds. Yoritomo had requested the creation of these ponds, and his wife, Masako, suggested placing islands in each. In the large pond to the right, filled with white lotus flowers, she placed three islands to represent the Minamoto clan (the Genji Pond); in the smaller pond to the left, she had four islands symbolizing the defeated Taira clan (the Heike Pond). The symbolism is significant. Three is considered a lucky number; four is unlucky.

Once you go over the Drum Bridge, the first structure you see is the **Maiden Hall.** The hall is the setting for the story so often retold in Noh and Kabuki theater, and it bears telling here. Though Yoritomo was the political force in defeating the Taira and establishing the Kamakura Shogunate, it was his dashing half-brother, Yoshitsune, who actually defeated the Taira in battle. In so doing, he won the admiration of many, and Kyoto used this to promote rumors that Yoshitsune had plans to become shogun. Yoritomo started to believe these rumors, and despite Yoshitsune's declaration of allegiance, Yoritomo had him exiled and sent assassins to have him killed. Yoshitsune spent his life fleeing from one place to another until, in his 30th year, his enemies surrounded him and he was left with two options, suicide or capture. He chose the former.

Meanwhile, his lover, Shizuka Gozen, a former dancer, was left behind in Kamakura. Yoritomo and his wife, Masako, commanded Shizuka to perform a dance, expecting her to do penitence. Instead, she danced to the joy of her love for Yoshitsune and her concern for him in exile. Yoritomo was furious, and only Masako's influence kept him from ordering her death. However, when he found out that she was with child by his half brother, he ordered that, if a boy, the child was to be killed. Tension built up as Shizuka came closer to motherhood. A boy was born. Some historians tell how the child was brutally slaughtered down by the sea, while others say the child was placed in a cradle and cast adrift in the reeds, Moses-style. The heart-wrenching drama is enacted once a year during the Spring Festival (early or mid-April, when the cherry trees bloom) on the stage at Maiden Hall.

Behind the Maiden Hall is a flight of steps leading to the shrine's Main Hall. To the left of these steps is a ginkgo tree that was witness to a dastardly deed 700 years ago. From behind this tree, Priest Kugyo lurched out and lopped off the head of his uncle, the 26-year-old Sanetomo Minamoto, the second and last son of Yoritomo. The priest was quickly apprehended, but the head of the second son was never found. Like all Shinto shrines, the Main Hall is relatively bare and not particularly noteworthy. It was originally built in 1191, but the current version dates from 1828.

8 Within the shrine's precincts are two museums. The **Kamakura Shiritsu Kindai Bijutsukan** (Municipal Museum of Modern Art), the ferroconcrete complex near the Heike Pond, contains Japanese oil and watercolor paintings, wood blocks, and sculptures. ☏ *0467/22–5000.* ☞ *¥720 to ¥1,000, depending on the exhibition.* ☉ *Tues.–Sun. 10–4:30. Closed the day following national holidays.*

9 The other museum, the **Kokuhokan** (Treasure Museum), exhibits a fine collection of objects pertaining to the Kamakura period and a display of *ukiyo-e* (wood-block prints). Of the two exhibitions, the latter is more interesting and has more relevance to Japan's early shogunate. ☏ *0467/22–0753.* ☞ *¥150 adults, ¥70 children under 12.* ☉ *Tues.–Sun. 9–4.*

10 While crowds may gather at Tsurugaoka Hachimangu, peace is often found at **Hokokuji,** a little Zen temple of the Rinzai sect that was built in 1334. Over the years, it fell into disrepair and neglect until, recently, an enterprising priest took over. He has since cleaned up the gardens and successfully promotes the temple for sessions in zazen and for calligraphy exhibitions. While some criticize the temple's commercial endeavors, on a quiet day the gardens offer rest and, at the back of the temple, a thick bamboo grove, with a small teahouse. Relaxing here an hour or so makes for a delightful interlude from the endless trail from statue to altar. To reach Hokokuji, walk east along the broad street that forms a T-intersection at the end of Wakamiya Oji in front of Tsurugaoka Hachimangu (that is, turn left when you cross the Drum Bridge and exit the grounds of the shrine). After about 1½ kilometers

(1 mile), there will be a sign on the right-hand side, which leads you to Hokokuji. ☞ *¥200. Tea Ceremony: ¥300.* ⊙ *9–4.*

⑪ Several other temples are in the vicinity of Hokokuji. **Jomyoji,** which was founded in 1188, is across the street and 100 meters (yards) to the right. Some 300 meters back on the road to Kamakura and then **⑫** up a street to the right is **Yoritomo's Tomb.** It is surprisingly plain, but you may want to pay tribute to the man who placed Kamakura on the map. To the right of Yoritomo's Tomb (you must retrace your steps for 100 meters and make virtually a U-turn at the first street on the **⑬** left) is **Kamakuragu,** a Shinto shrine built after the Meiji Restoration as a tribute to Prince Morinaga and as propaganda for the revived imperial regime. Prince Morinaga was the third son of Godaigo. After Godaigo's successful defeat of the Kamakura Shogunate, the imperial family soon came under pressure from the Ashikaga clan. Morinaga was an effective champion of the imperial cause. Naturally, this did not suit the Ashikaga clan's plans for takeover, so they denounced Morinaga as a traitor to the throne of Godaigo. Morinaga was held captive in the cave behind the present site of Kamakuragu, and, before the truth finally dawned on Godaigo, Morinaga was beheaded.

A bus to and from Kamakura Station (bus stop #5) travels the street on which all these temples have their access roads. We recommend walking out from Kamakura and returning by the bus, because it is easier to recognize the stop for downtown Kamakura than the stops for each of the temples and shrines. Or you can take a taxi to Hokokuji; any cab driver knows the way. Downtown Kamakura is a good place to stop for lunch and shop. Restaurants and shops selling locally made products abound on Wakamiya Oji and its parallel street, Komachi-dori.

Hase

★ **⑭** Hase is the next area to explore for reliving Kamakura's past. Here you'll find the **Daibutsu** (Great Buddha) in **Kotokuin** (temple), and also Hasadera (temple). To reach Hase, take the train (the Enoden Line located on the western side of the JR Kamakura Station) three stops to Hase Station. Off to the left of the station is the main street, and this leads, after a 10-minute walk, north to the Daibutsu.

Kotokuin is totally dominated by the 37-foot-tall bronze statue of the Great Buddha. Sitting cross-legged, robed with drapes flowing in the classical lines reminiscent of ancient Greece, the compassionate Amida Buddha serenely smiles down on its audience. The bronze statue was cast in 1292, three centuries before Europeans reached Japan; the concept of the classical Greek lines used in the Buddha's robe must have been transmitted down the Silk Route through China during the time of Alexander the Great. The Daibutsu was probably first conceived, though not completed, in 1180 by Yoritomo Minamoto, who wanted a statue to outshine the enormous Daibutsu in Nara. Until 1495, the statue was housed in a wooden temple, which was washed away in a great tidal wave. Since then, the loving Buddha has stood exposed, facing the cold winters and hot summers for the last five centuries.

To some of us, it seems sacrilegious to walk inside the Great Buddha and inspect the statue's innards. But not to the Japanese. For an extra ¥20, you can enter (until 4 PM) Buddha's right side into his stomach. Not particularly interesting, but it is something that is done by many visitors. ☞ *Kotokuin ¥200 adults, ¥150 children under 12.* ⊙ *Apr.–Sept., 7 AM–6 PM; Oct.–Mar., 7 AM–5:30 PM.*

If you retrace your steps from Kotokuin for about threequarters of the way along the main street (toward Hase Station) and then take a right turn, **Hasedera** will be before you. Hasedera is one of the most enchanting, sad, and beautiful temples in Japan. First, as you enter, is the garden with a small pond formation that inspires serenity despite the many visitors. Then, as you climb the flights of steep stone steps up to the Amida and Kannon Hall, you are astonished by the innumerable small stone images of Jizo Bosatsu. Jizo Bosatsu is one manifestation of the bodhisattva who stands on the border of this life and the next to guide souls to salvation. In its Japanese version, Jizo Bosatsu has many representations. Here at Hasedera, the Jizo Bosatsu is the bodhisattva who guides the souls of stillborn, aborted, and miscarried children. Mothers who have lost or given up their unborn children dedicate small images of this god to pray for their souls. The sight of the stone statues is strangely touching and melancholic.

Walking farther up the steps brings you to the temple's main building; visitors are allowed in the **Amida Hall** (Amida-do) and the **Kannon Hall** (Kannon-do). The Kannon Hall is Hasedera's main attraction. In the center of the hall is Juichimen (11-faced) Kannon; standing 30 feet tall, it is the largest carved wood statue in Japan. The merciful Kannon has 10 smaller faces on top of her head, symbolizing her ability to see and search out in all directions those in need of help. No one knows for sure when Juichimen was carved. Certainly it was before the 12th century. According to the temple records, a monk, Tokudo Shonin, carved two images of the 11-faced Kannon from a huge laurel tree in 721. The image from the main trunk was installed in Hase, located in what is known today as Nara Prefecture. The other image was thrown into the sea to go wherever the sea decided that there were sentient souls in need of the benevolence of Kannon. The statue washed up near Kamakura. (It was not until much later, in 1342, that the statue was covered with gold leaf by Takauji Ashikaga, the first of the 15 Ashikaga shoguns who followed the Kamakura era.)

Amida Hall, the other major building of Hasedera, has the image of a seated Amida. Yoritomo Minamoto ordered the sculpting of this statue in an effort to ward off the dangers of reaching the ripe old age of 42. (This age was considered to be unlucky.) The statue did the trick. Yoritomo made it until he was 52, when he was thrown from a horse and died soon after. Hence, the popular name for this Buddha is the *yakuyoke* (good-luck) Amida, and many visitors take the opportunity to make a special prayer here, especially before graduation exams. To the left of Amida Hall is a small restaurant where you can buy good-luck candy and admire the view over Kamakura Beach and Sagami Bay. Hasedera is the only Kamakura temple looking onto the sea, and this view, accompanied by the benevolent spirit of Hasedera, makes an appropriate end to a day of Kamakura sightseeing. ☞ *¥200 adults, ¥100 children under 12.* ☞ *Homotsukan (Treasure Museum) ¥100 adults, ¥50 children under 12.* ☉ *Daily, Mar.–Nov. 8–5; Dec.–Feb. 28 8–4:30.*

Ryukoji and Enoshima

The Kamakura story would not be complete without Nichiren, the monk who founded the only native Japanese sect of Buddhism. Nichiren spent several years advocating his beliefs and criticizing the Hojo regents, who held power after the Minamoto shoguns. Exasperated, the authorities sent him to exile on the Izu Peninsula, then allowed him to return. But Nichiren still kept on criticizing, and in 1271, the Hojo rulers condemned him to death. Execution was to take place on a hill to the south of Hase. As the executioner swung his sword, a lightning bolt struck the blade and snapped it in two. A little taken aback, the executioner sat down to collect his wits. Meanwhile, a messenger ran back to tell the Hojo regents of the event. On his way, he met another messenger, who was carrying a writ from the Hojo regents commuting Nichiren's sentence to exile on Sado Island.

16 Followers of Nichiren built a temple in 1337 to mark this event on the hill where he was to be executed. The temple is **Ryukoji** and is reached by continuing west on the Enoden Line from Hase. The train cuts through Kamakura's defensive hills to the shoreline en route to Enoshima. The ride is very scenic, running along the coast and trundling along narrow lanes and shopping streets. Get off the train at Enoshima Station and walk about 100 meters (yards) east, keeping the train tracks on your right, and you'll come to Ryukoji.

While there are other Nichiren temples closer to Kamakura—Myohonji and Ankokuronji—for example, Ryukoji not only has the typical Nichiren-style main hall with gold tassels hanging from its roof but also a beautiful pagoda (1904), built as if to embrace the surrounding trees.

The shoreline in this vicinity, by the way, has some of the beaches closest to Tokyo, and, during the hot, humid summer months, it seems that all of the city's teeming millions pour onto these beaches in search of a vacant patch of rather dirty gray sand. It is not a beach resort to be recommended.

17 A more enjoyable place to feel the sea breezes is **Enoshima Island.** (To reach the causeway from Enoshima Station to Enoshima Island, walk south for about 3 kilometers/2 miles, keeping the Katasegawa on your right.) The island is only 4 kilometers (2½ miles) in circumference and peaks with a hill at its center. Partway up the hill is the shrine at which fishermen would pray for a bountiful catch—before it became a tourist attraction. It used to be quite a hike up to the shrine, but now there is a series of moving escalators accompanied by an array of souvenir stalls. Spaced around the island are several cafés and restaurants. On clear days, some of these restaurants have spectacular views of Mt. Fuji and the Izu Peninsula.

The way back to Tokyo from Enoshima is by train to Shinjuku on the Odakyu Line. (From the island, walk back across the causeway and take the second bridge over the Katasegawa, and within five minutes you'll come to the Katase-Enoshima Station on the Odakyu Line.) There are 14 afternoon trains, two each hour on express schedules, between 2:20 and 8:20 (more in the summer); the express takes about 70 minutes to make the trip and costs ¥1,030. Alternatively, you can retrace your steps to Kamakura and take the JR Yokosuka Line to Tokyo Station.

Dining

Kamakura has a multitude of restaurants from which to choose, with places to eat near every sightseeing area. You can literally drop into a restaurant whenever the appetite strikes or a rest is needed. Those mentioned below are especially recommended.

A 3% federal consumer tax is added to all restaurant bills. Another 3% local tax is added to the bill if it exceeds ¥7,500. At more expensive restaurants, a 10%–15% service charge is also added to the bill. Tipping is not necessary.

CATEGORY	COST*
$$$$	over ¥8,000
$$$	¥5,000–¥8,000
$$	¥2,000–¥5,000
$	under ¥2,000

Cost is per person without tax, service, or drinks

$$$–$$$$ **Kaseiro.** In an old Japanese house on the street that leads toward the Daibutsu at Kotokuin, this establishment offers the best Chinese food in the city. The dining room windows look onto a small, restful garden. ✕ *3-1-14 Hase, Kamakura,* ☎ *0467/22–0280. Reservations advised. AE, DC, MC, V.* ☉ *11–9.*

$$–$$$ **Hachinoki Honten.** Traditional *shojin ryori* (the vegetarian cuisine of Zen monasteries) is served here in an old Japanese house adjacent to Kenchoji. There is some table service, but most of the seating is in tatami rooms, with beautiful antique wood furnishings. Allow plenty of time; this is not a meal to be hurried through. ✕ *7 Yamanouchi, Kamakura,* ☎ *0467/22–8719. Reservations suggested. DC, MC, V.* ☉ *Weekdays 11 AM–4 PM, weekends 11 AM–6 PM.*

$$–$$$ **Tori-ichi.** This elegant restaurant serves traditional Japanese fare (*kaiseki*) ★ in tranquil surroundings. In an old country-style building, kimono-dressed waitresses serve sumptuous multi-course meals, including one or more subtle-tasting soups, sushi, tempura, grilled fish, and other delicacies. ✕ *7-13 Onarimachi, Kamakura,* ☎ *0467/22–1818. Reservations advised. No credit cards.* ☉ *noon–2 and 5–9. Closed Tues.*

$ **Kado Restaurant.** This is a small noodle shop on the right side of the main road leading into town from Tokeiji. The owners don't speak English and the menu is in Japanese, but the large portions of noodles with vegetables, meat, and/or fish will supply the energy you'll need to finish touring Kamakura. ✕ *Kamakura-Kaido, no* ☎. *No reservations. No credit cards.*

YOKOHAMA

By Nigel Fisher

Updated by
Jared Lubarsky

For more than 200 years, Japan closed its doors to virtually all foreign contact. Then, in 1853, a flotilla of American ships under Commodore Matthew Perry sailed into the bay of Tokyo (then Edo) and forced the reluctant Tokugawa Shogunate to open Japan to the West. Three years later, Townsend Harris became America's first diplomatic representative to Japan. Once the commercial treaty with the United States was signed, Harris lost no time in setting up his residence in Hangakuji (temple) in Kanagawa, now a part of Yokohama. However, Kanagawa was one of the 53 relay stations on the Tokaido (highway), and the presence of foreigners—perceived as unclean, long-haired barbarians—caused offense to the traditional Japanese. Moreover, many samurai wanted Japan to remain in isolation and were willing to give their lives to rid Japan of the foreign pestilence. Unable to protect the foreigners in Kanagawa, the shogunate required that Harris and all foreigners move from Kanagawa and establish a foreign trading port at nearby Yokohama.

At the time, Yokohama, 20 kilometers (12.5 miles) southwest of Tokyo, was a small fishing village surrounded by ugly mud flats. Foreigners, diplomats, and traders were confined to a compound, guarded with checkpoints. Harris considered, probably correctly, that he and every other Westerner were being placed in isolation. But changes were happening very fast in Japan. Within 30 years, seven centuries of shogunate rule would come to an end, and the period known as the Meiji Restoration would begin, in which, under the authority of Emperor

Meiji, Japan sought Western advice and ideas. By the early 1900s, Yokohama was to become one of the world's busiest ports and Japan's major export and import center.

Yokohama's growth has been as dramatic as the crippling blows it has suffered. As soon as it became a designated international port in 1869, it started to grow rapidly. Most of the foreign traders who came to Japan set up business in Yokohama; as the port grew, so did the international community. An especially large community of British citizens developed from whom the Japanese frequently sought advice, on the grounds that Great Britain was also an island nation. Reminders of their presence can still be seen in the occasional game of cricket at the Yokohama Country and Athletic Club, which, while now open to all nations, used to be where British expatriates would drink their gin and enjoy their refined activities.

Then Yokohama came tumbling down. On September 1, 1923, the Great Kanto Earthquake struck both Tokyo and Yokohama, destroying much of the latter. Some 60,000 homes made of wood and paper burned, and 20,000 lives were lost. After such devastation, Yokohama could not retain its preeminence as Japan's international city and chief trading port. During the six years that it took to restore the city, many foreign businesses took up quarters elsewhere, primarily in Kobe and Osaka, and did not return to Yokohama.

Nevertheless, over the next 20 years Yokohama mushroomed once more; a large industrial zone was built along its shoreline. Then everything came tumbling down again. On May 29, 1945, in a span of four hours, 700 American B-29 bombers leveled nearly half of the city. Destruction was more extensive than that caused by the earthquake. Even so, Yokohama rose once more from the debris, and, boosted by Japan's postwar economic miracle, extended its urban sprawl all the way to Tokyo to the north and to Kamakura in the south.

With the advent of air travel and increased competition from other ports (Nagoya and Kobe, for example), Yokohama's decline as Japan's seaport continued. The glamour of great liners docked at Yokohama's piers has become only a memory, kept alive by a museum ship and the occasional visit by a luxury liner on a Pacific cruise. The only regularly scheduled passenger services are by a Russian and a Chinese vessel. To replace its emphasis on being a port city, Yokahama has concentrated on its industries—shipbuilding, automobiles, and petrochemicals are three of its largest—and its service to Tokyo as a satellite city. Yokohama has always been politically and culturally overshadowed by Tokyo, and that is no more apparent than today, as commuters swarm into Tokyo every morning from their homes in Yokohama.

Is Yokohama worth a visit? Certainly, it should not get top priority. The city has perhaps more interest to the Japanese than to Westerners. Up to World War II, people from Tokyo would come to Yokohama to see the strange *gaijin* (foreigners), their alien ways, and their European-style buildings. That image still persists, despite the destruction of most of the city's late 19th- and early 20th-century buildings. After all, Yokohama had Japan's first bakery (in 1860), operated by an enterprising Japanese, Noda Hyogo, who catered to Westerners. It was also the first city to have public toilets—83 of them were built in 1871. A year later, Japan's first railway, linking Yokohama and Shinbashi in Tokyo, was completed. So Yokohama does have memories of Japan's first encounters with the West; a notable building in the center of the city is the Port Memorial Hall, which commemorates Yokohama's position as the front-runner in opening Japan to the West. Yet, as fun as this trivia may be, Yokohama has less to see than one would expect. Indeed, a visit to Yokohama should only be made if one has an extra day to spare while in Tokyo, or when returning to Tokyo from an excursion to Kamakura, 20 minutes on the train south of Yoko-hama.

Arriving and Departing

Between the Airport and Center City

From Narita Airport, a direct limousine-bus service departs two or three times an hour between 6:45 AM and 10 PM for Yokohama City Air Terminal (YCAT). The fare is ¥3,300. YCAT is a five-minute taxi ride from Yokohama Station. JR Narita Express trains going on from Tokyo to Yokohama leave the airport every hour from 8:13 AM to 9:43 PM. The fare is ¥4,100 (or ¥4,900 for the first-class "Green Car" coaches). Alternatively, you can take the limousine-bus service from Narita to Tokyo Station and continue on to Yokohama by train. With either method, the total journey will take more than two hours, more likely three if the traffic is heavy.

By Train

FROM TOKYO

JR trains from Tokyo Station leave approximately every 10 minutes, depending on the time of day. Take the Yokosuka, the Tokaido, or Keihin Tohoku lines to Yokohama Station. (The Yokosuka and Tokaido lines take 30 min., and the Keihin Tohoku Line takes 40 min.) From there, the Keihin Tohoku Line (platform 3) goes on to Kannai and Ishikawacho, Yokohama's business and downtown areas. If you are going directly to downtown Yokohama from Tokyo, the blue commuter trains of the Keihin Tohoku Line are best. From Shibuya Station in Tokyo, the Tokyu Toyoko Line, a private line, connects directly with Yokohama Station and, hence, is an alternative if you leave from the western part of Tokyo.

FROM NAGOYA AND POINTS SOUTH

The Shinkansen Kodama trains stop at Shin-Yokohama Station, 8 kilometers (5 miles) from the city center. It is then necessary to take the local train for the seven-minute ride into town.

Getting Around

By Train

Yokohama Station is the city transport center, where all train lines link together and connect with the city's subway and bus service. However, Kannai and Ishikawacho are the two train stations for the downtown areas. Use the Keihin Tohoku Line from Yokohama Station to reach these areas. Trains leave every two to five minutes from Platform Three. Once you are at Kannai or Ishikawacho, most of Yokohama's points of interest are within easy walking distance of each other. The one notable exception is Sankeien, a garden that requires a short train and bus ride from downtown.

By Taxi

During the day, ample taxis are available. Taxi stands are outside the train stations, and cabs may also be flagged in the streets. However, often the congested traffic makes walking a faster means of traveling. The basic fare is ¥680 for the first 2 kilometers (1¼ miles), then ¥90 for every additional 350 meters (1,145 feet). Vacant taxis show a red light in the windshield.

By Subway
One line connects Shin-Yokohama, Yokohama, and Totsuka.

By Bus
Buses exist, but their routes confuse even the locals.

By Car
Rental cars are available from Yokohama Station, but the congested traffic and lack of street signs make driving difficult.

Guided Tours

Double-decker buses of the **Blue Line**—not a tour operator, but a municipal bus service—depart every hour from the east exit of Yokohama Station, circle the major tourist route—Chinatown, Motomachi, Harbor View Park, Yamashita Pier, Osanbashi Pier, Bashamichi—and return to the station. These tours, which last just under an hour, operate weekdays 9:40 AM–5:40 PM, weekends and national holidays 9:40 AM–6:10 PM (Dec.–Feb. 10:10–5:25). You may get off on any stop to see the sights and catch a later bus to continue, but you will have to pay the original fare every time you get back on. There are no guides. Fare: ¥270 adults, ¥140 children under 12.

The **Teiki Yuran Bus** is a seven-hour sightseeing bus tour that covers the major sights and includes lunch at a Chinese restaurant in Chinatown. The tour is in Japanese only, though pamphlets written in English are available at most sightseeing stops. Tickets are sold at the bus offices at Yokohama Station (east side) and at Kannai, and the tour departs daily at 10 AM from bus stop 14 on the east side of Yokohama Station. Cost: ¥6,520 adults, ¥4,320 children under 12.

A shuttle boat, the **Sea Bass,** connects Yokohama Station and Yamashita Koen in 15 minutes. The boat leaves every 20 minutes 10–7 from the east side of Yokohama Station and offers another view of Yokohama.

The sightseeing boat **Marine Shuttle** (☎ 045/651–2697) makes 40-, 60-, and 90-minute tours of the harbor and bay for ¥750, ¥1,200, and ¥2,000, respectively. Boarding is at the pier at Yamashita Koen; boats depart roughly every hour between 10:20 AM and 6:30 PM. Another boat, the **Marine Rouge,** offers 90-minute tours departing at 11 AM, 1:30 PM, and 4 PM, and a special two-hour evening tour at 7 PM (¥2,500).

Home-Visit System

The Yokohama International Tourist Association arranges visits to the homes of English-speaking Japanese families. These visits are usually for a few hours and are designed to give foreigners a glimpse into the Japanese way of life. To arrange a visit or for more information, call the Yokohama International Tourist Association (☎ 045/641–5824).

Important Addresses and Numbers

Emergencies
Ambulance or **Fire,** ☎ 119; **Police,** ☎ 110. The **Yokohama Police Station** has a Foreign Affairs Department (☎ 045/623–0110).

DOCTORS
Washinzaka Hospital (169 Yamatecho, Naka-ku, ☎ 045/623–7688).

English-Language Bookstore
Maruzen (2-34 Benten-dori, Naka-ku, ☎ 045/212–2031) has a good selection.

Tourist Information

The **Yokohama Tourist Office** (☎ 045/441–7300; open 10–6; closed Dec. 28–Jan. 3) is in the central passageway of Yokohama Station. A similar office with the same closing times is located at Shin-Yokohama Station (☎ 045/473–2895). The head office of the **Yokohama International Tourist Association** (☎ 045/641–5824; open daily 9–5, closed national holidays) is in the Sangyo Boeki Center Building, 2 Yamashitacho, Naka-ku.

Exploring Yokohama

Numbers in the margin correspond to points of interest on the Yokohama map.

As large as Yokohama is, its central area is quite self-contained. Because Yokohama developed as a port city, much of its activity has always been around its waterfront (the Bund) on the west side of Tokyo Bay. The downtown is called Kannai (literally: "within the checkpoint"), and is where the international community was originally confined by the shogunate. Though downtown has expanded to include the waterfront and Ishikawacho to the south, Kannai has always been Yokohama's heart.

Downtown may be viewed as consisting of two adjacent rectangular areas. One area is the old district of Kannai, bounded by Bashamichi (street) to the northwest and Nippon-odori (avenue) to the southeast, with Kannai Station on the southwestern side and the waterfront on the northeastern. This area contains the business offices of modern Yokohama. Another main area extends southeast from Nippon-odori to the Motomachi shopping street and the International Cemetery. This rectangle is flanked by Ishikawacho Station to the west, and Yamashita Koen (park) and the waterfront to the east. The middle of this part of the city is dominated by Chinatown.

Notwithstanding the lure of Bashamichi's shops and its reconstructed 19th-century appearance, the southeastern area holds the most interest if you are short of time, and is where the following walking tour of Yokohama begins.

Whether you are coming from Tokyo, Nagoya, or Kamakura, the best place to begin a tour of Yokohama is from **Ishikawacho Station.** Take the south exit from the station and head in the direction of the waterfront. Within a block of the station is the beginning of **Motomachi shopping street,** which follows Nakamuragawa (river) toward the harbor. This is where the Japanese set up shop 100 years ago to serve the strange foreigners living within Kannai. Now the same street is lined with smart boutiques, jewelry stores, and coffee shops, and it attracts a fashionable younger crowd.

At the far end of Motomachi and up to the right is a small hill. Here is the **International Cemetery,** a Yokohama landmark as a preserve for foreigners and a reminder of the port city's heritage. The cemetery was started in 1854 when an American sailor chose this spot for his final resting place. Since then the burial ground has been restricted to non-Japanese. About 4,000 graves are on this hillside, and the inscriptions on the crosses and headstones attest to some 40 different nationalities who lived and died in Yokohama.

Behind the cemetery is the **Yamate Shiryokan** (museum), which preserves mementos of the late-19th-century lifestyle of Westerners who lived in Yokohama. It is perhaps more interesting to the Japanese than

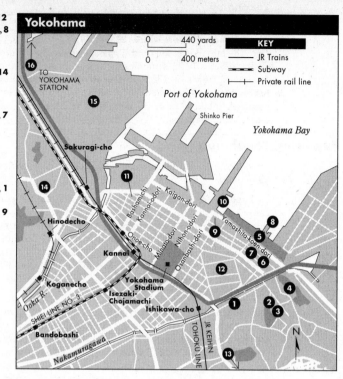

it is to foreigners. *247 Yamate, Naka-ku,* ☎ *045/622–1188.* ☛ *¥200 adults, ¥150 children under 12.* ⊘ *Daily 11–4. Closed Dec. 30– Jan. 1.*

❹ One hundred meters (yards) beyond the museum is **Minato-no-Mieru-Oka Koen** (Harbor View Park). Once the barracks of the British forces in Yokohama, the hilltop park affords fine views of Yamashita Koen and the harbor beyond. The view at night, when the gardens of Yamashita are floodlit and the harbor lights shine is enchanting.

❺ **Yamashita Koen,** an urban oasis just down from Minato-no-Mieru-Oka and running along the waterfront, is a park for strolling or a place to rest—if you can find an empty bench free of young Japanese couples. Its existence is perhaps the only redeeming factor of the Great Kanto Earthquake in 1923. The debris of collapsed buildings left by the earthquake was swept away, and the area was made into a 17-acre park with lawns, trees, and flowers. The park's fountain, by the way, is a statue of the Guardian of the Water, presented to Yokohama by San Diego, one of Yokohama's sister cities.

❻ Near the park is the **Yokohama Doll Museum,** which houses 4,000 dolls from Japan and the rest of the world. The fairy-tale quality of the museum is a pleasant diversion from Yokohama's rather mundane sights with or without a child in tow. *18 Yamashitacho, Naka-ku,* ☎ *045/671– 9361.* ☛ *¥300 adults, ¥150 children under 15.* ⊘ *10–5, July–Aug. 10– 6:30. Closed Mon. (Tues. after a national holiday), Dec. 29–Jan. 1.*

❼ At the entrance to Yamashita Koen is the rather ugly **Marine Tower** (☎ 045/641–7838), a decagonal building standing 348 feet high. It has a navigational beacon at the 338-foot mark and purports to be the tallest lighthouse in the world. At the 328-foot level, an observation gallery offers 360-degree views of the harbor and city. It is the best place to acquire an aerial appreciation of the area, and on clear days, in autumn or winter, it is possible to see Mt. Fuji in the distance. Also in the Marine Tower is a bird museum (Birdpia) and the Yokohama Science Museum. *Marine Tower Observation Room* ☛ *¥700 adults, ¥350 children 6–15, ¥250 children 3–6.* ⊘ *10–9:30 (Sat. 10), winter 10–6. (If sunny on winter holidays, open until 8:30.)*

⑧ Moored on the waterfront halfway down the park is the *Hikawa-maru,* which for 30 years shuttled passengers between Yokohama and Seattle, making a total of 238 trips. Though the ship recalls the time when Yokohama was a great passenger port of oceangoing liners, it is not worth touring, as brochures suggest. The Hikawa-maru does have a public restaurant, and in summer, the upper deck becomes a beer garden.

At the northwestern end of the park is the Silk Center Building; on its **⑨** second floor is the **Silk Museum,** which pays tribute to the days when, at the turn of the century, all of the Japanese silk for export was shipped out of Yokohama. As well as a display of a variety of silk fabrics, the museum has an informative exhibit on the silk-making process. The attendants are very happy to answer questions. Also in the Silk Center Building, on the first floor, is the head office of the Yokohama International Tourist Association and the Kanagawa Prefecture Tourist Information Office. *1 Yamashitacho, Naka-ku,* ☎ *045/641–0841.* ☛ *¥300 adults, ¥100 children under 15.* ⊘ *9–4:30. Closed Mon., day after a national holiday, and Dec. 29–Jan. 1.*

⑩ Across the street from the Silk Building is the **Yokohama Archives of History.** Once the British Consulate, the building now houses some 140,000 items recording the history of Yokohama since the port's opening. On the other side of the street is the monument to the U.S.–Japanese Friendship Treaty. *3 Nihon-odori, Naka-ku,* ☎ *045/201–2100.* ☛ *¥200 adults, ¥100 children under 15.* ⊘ *9:30–4:30. Closed Mon., day after a national holiday, and Dec. 29–Jan. 1.*

If you continue along the street running parallel to the waterfront you'll reach **Bashamichi,** the street that runs between Kannai Station and Shinko Pier. Literally, Bashamichi means "horse-carriage street," so named after it was widened to allow Westerners' carriages to pass. Now this redbrick road has become a nostalgic symbol of the city's 19th-century international past, with antique-looking telephone booths and imita-**⑪** tion gas lamps. Halfway up the street is the **Kanagawa Prefectural Museum.** This Western-style structure with a domed roof was built in 1904 and is one of the few buildings in Yokohama to have survived both the Great Kanto Earthquake and World War II. Alas, the exhibits inside the museum—archaeological and natural-history artifacts from the region—have only marginal interest for the tourist. *5-60 Minami Naka-dori, Naka-ku,* ☎ *045/201–0926.* ☛ *¥300.* ⊘ *9–5. Closed Mon., the last Tues. of each month, and the day after national holidays.*

★ **⑫** At the top end (away from the waterfront) of Bashamichi is Kannai Station; Yokohama's **Chinatown** (Chuka-gai) is a 10-minute walk from here. Walk southeast from the station and, just before you reach Yokohama Stadium, turn left to cut through Yokohama Koen to reach the top of Nihon-odori. Then take a right, and you'll enter Chinatown through the North Gate, which leads to the vermilion, 50-foot-high Hairomon (gate).

Yokohama's Chinatown is the largest settlement of Chinese in Japan. Its small alleys are full of shops selling Chinese goods, biscuits, and medicines, and wonderful exotic aromas waft from the shops selling spices. The area offers a good opportunity to dine on authentic Chinese food and is the choice place for lunch in Yokohama. You'll find more than a hundred restaurants from which to choose. If you prefer a good Western meal, continue walking along the main street through Chinatown; you'll exit at the East Gate leading to Yamashita Koen and the New Grand Hotel.

Additional Attractions

What has been left out of this walking tour through Yokohama are Sankeien (garden), Iseyama Kodai Jingu (shrine), *Nippon-maru* Memorial Park, and Sojiji (temple). Let's first go to Sankeien, of which the *hamakko* (the name the locals give each other) are justly proud.

★ ⑬ **Sankeien** was once the garden of Tomitaro Hara, one of Yokohama's wealthiest men, who made his money as a silk merchant before becoming a patron of the arts. His garden was opened to the public in 1906. Amid its rolling hills, valleys, and ponds are traditional Japanese buildings, some of which have been transported from Kamakura and the Kansai area of western Honshu. Especially noteworthy is Rinshunkaku, a villa built for the Tokugawa clan in 1649. There is also a tea-ceremony house, Choshukaku, built by the third Tokugawa shogun, Iemitsu Tokugawa. Other noteworthy buildings include the small temple transported from Kyoto's famed Daitokuji (temple) and the farmhouse brought from the Gifu district in the Japan Alps.

Walks through Sankeien are especially rewarding for its flowering trees in the spring: plum blossoms in February, and cherry blossoms in early April. Then, in June, come the irises, followed by the water lilies. With the coming of autumn, the trees come back into their own with their tinted golden leaves. To reach Sankeien, take the JR Keihin Tohoku Line to Negishi Station, from where buses make the 10-minute trip to the garden. *293 Honmoku Sannotani, Naka-ku,* ☎ *045/621–0635.* ☛ *General ¥300 adults, ¥60 children; inner garden containing Rinshunkaku ¥300 adults, ¥120 children.* ☺ *Inner garden 9–4, outer garden 9–4:30. Both gardens closed Dec. 29–31.*

⑭ **Iseyama Kodai Jingu,** a branch of the nation's revered Grand Shrines of Ise, is the most important shrine in Yokohama (☛ Free; ☺ dawn–dusk). A 10-minute walk from Sakuragicho Station, the shrine is perhaps only worth the time if you have seen most everything else in Yokohama.

⑮ **Minato Mirai 21,** on the other hand, is a must. The aim of this project, which was launched in the mid-1980s, was to turn some ¾ of a square mile of waterfront, lying east of the JR Negishi Line railroad tracks between Yokohama and Sakuragicho stations, into a model city of the future. In addition to an amusement park and an international exhibition and conference center, Minato Mirai 21 is now the site of the **Yokohama Bijutsukan** (Yokohama Museum of Art), designed by Kenzo Tange and housing works by both Western and Japanese artists, including Cézanne, Picasso, Braque, Klee, Kandinsky, Kishida, and Taikan Yokoyama. *4-1 Minato Mirai 3-chome, Nishi-ku,* ☎ *045/221–0300.* ☛ *¥500.* ☺ *Mon.–Wed. and Fri.–Sun. 10–6.*

Also here is the **Nippon-maru Memorial Park,** *Nippon-maru* being a 1930 fully rigged sailing ship known as the "Swan of the Pacific." It is open to visitors on guided tours. *1-1 Minato Mirai 2-chome, Nishi-ku, ☎ 045/221–0280. ☛ ¥600. ⊘ Tues.–Sun. 10–5.*

The 70-story **Landmark Tower** here, Japan's tallest building, has an observation deck that affords spectacular views of the city, especially at night. On the tower's first level is the Mitsubishi Heavy Industry Corporation's **Minato Mirai Museum,** with rocket engines, power plants, a submarine, and simulation displays that allow visitors to experience piloting helicopters and other gadgets—great fun for kids. *3-1 Minato Mirai 3-chome, Nishi-ku, ☎ 045/224–9031. ☛ ¥500. ⊘ Mon.–Wed. and Fri.–Sun. 10–5:30.*

⑯ The last notable sight to visit before leaving Yokohama is **Sojiji,** a worthwhile stop en route back to Tokyo. Take the JR Keihin Tohoku Line two stops to Tsurumi Station. Upon exiting the station, walk five minutes south (back toward Yokohama), passing Tsurumi University on your right. You'll soon reach the temple complex, which you may enter at the stone lanterns.

The Soto Buddhist sect, founded in 1321, was headquartered at Ishikawa on the Noto Peninsula (on the north coast of Japan, near Kanazawa). However, when the complex at Ishikawa was destroyed by fire in the 19th century, the sect erected its Yokohama temple complex. (Another Sojiji is located at Eiheiji in Fukui Prefecture.) The Yokohama Sojiji is, therefore, relatively new, but it is a good example of Zen architecture; it is a very busy temple, with more than 200 monks and novitiates in residence. Visitors are not allowed to enter Emperor Godaigo's mausoleum (he was the emperor who defeated the Kamakura Shogunate), but you can visit the Buddha Hall and Main Hall. Both are large concrete structures. The Treasure House contains a wide variety of Buddhas. ☛ *¥300. ⊘ 10–4:30.*

Dining

Yokohama is a large, international city. The number and variety of restaurants are great, including more than 100 Chinese restaurants in Chinatown. The number of Japanese restaurants is uncountable; in the Mitsukoshi Department Store alone there are at least 32 tearooms and restaurants. The following thus represents a small selection of what Yokohama offers and includes restaurants familiar with the needs of foreign guests.

A 3% federal consumer tax is added to all restaurant bills. Another 3% local tax is added to the bill if it exceeds ¥7,500. At more expensive restaurants, a 10%–15% service charge is also added to the bill. Tipping is not necessary.

CATEGORY	COST
$$$$	over ¥8,000
$$$	¥5,000–¥8,000
$$	¥2,000–¥5,000
$	under ¥2,000

Cost is per person without tax, service, or drinks

$$$$ **Rinka-en.** If you visit Sankeien, drop in at this traditional country restaurant serving *kaiseki*-style (traditional Japanese) cuisine. The owner, by the way, is the granddaughter of Mr. Hara, the founder of the Sankeien. ✕ *Honmoku Sannotani, Naka-ku, ☎ 045/621–0318. Reservations recommended. Jacket and tie. No credit cards. ⊘ Noon–5. Closed Wed. and midsummer.*

$$$$ **Scandia.** Known for its smorgasbord, Scandia is located near the Silk Center and the business district. It is popular for business lunches as well as for dinner, and stays open later (midnight) than many other restaurants. ✕ *1-1 Kaigan-dori, Naka-ku,* ☎ *045/201–2262. Reservations advised. No credit cards.* ⊘ *11 AM–midnight; Sun. 5–midnight.*

$$$–$$$$ **Miroir.** One of the most elegant venues in town, Miroir is on the sec-
★ ond floor of a seven-story banquet facility called Excellent Coast, be- tween the Motomachi and Chinatown districts. The facade of the building evokes the Paris Opera House; the restaurant itself is a bit more casual and understated than its surroundings. The food (French classic) is superb, the service is exceptional. ✕ *105 Yamashitacho, Naka-ku,* ☎ *045/211–2252. Reservations recommended, especially on weekdays. Jacket and tie. AE, DC, MC, V.* ⊘ *Tues.–Sun. 11:30–2:30 and 6–8:30.*

$$$ **Aichiya.** Should you wish to try *fugu* (blowfish), the only chef in Yoko-
★ hama licensed to prepare this delicacy is at this seafood restaurant. The crabs here—as expensive as the fugu—are also a treat. ✕ *7-156-1 Seza-kicho, Naka-ku,* ☎ *045/251–4163. Jacket and tie. No credit cards.* ⊘ *3–10. Closed Mon.*

$$$ **Kaseiro.** A smart Chinese restaurant with red carpets and gold-tone walls, Kaseiro serves Beijing cuisine and is the best of its kind in the city. ✕ *164 Yamashitacho, Naka-ku,* ☎ *045/681–2918. Reservations recommended. Jacket and tie in the evening. AE, DC, V.* ⊘ *11:30– 9:30.*

$$$ **Seryna.** This establishment is famous for its *ishiyaki* steak, which is grilled on a hot stone, as well as for its *shabu-shabu.* ✕ *Shin-Kannai Bldg., 1 floor down, Sumiyoshicho, Naka-ku,* ☎ *045/681–2727. Reservations advised. AE, DC, MC, V.* ⊘ *11:30–9:30.*

$$–$$$ **Chongking.** This is the city's best restaurant for Szechuan cooking. The focus of attention here is on the food rather than decor. ✕ *164 Ya-mashitacho, Naka-ku,* ☎ *045/641–8288. AE, DC, MC, V.* ⊘ *Noon–9.*

$$ **Rome Station.** Located between Chinatown and Yamashita Koen (just down from the Holiday Inn), this restaurant is popular for Italian food. ✕ *26 Yamashita-cho, Naka-ku,* ☎ *045/681–1818. Reservations suggested. No credit cards.* ⊘ *11:30–10, holidays noon–9.*

$$ **Saronikos.** The Akebonocho district of Yokohama, east of China-town, has long been home to a small cluster of Greek restaurants; sailors off the Greek ships in port still drift over this way to bring gifts of feta cheese, spices, and *sirtaki* music tapes to friends and relatives of the owners. Saronikos is among the best of these restaurants, not the least because it invests more effort in the food than in tarted-up reproductions of the Parthenon and other pretensions to decor. Try the eggplant with garlic, the Greek salad—and, of course, the moussaka. ✕ *3-30 Akebono-cho, Naka-ku,* ☎ *045/251–8980. MC, V.* ⊘ *6 PM–1 AM. Closed 1st and 3rd Mon. of every month.*

FUJI-HAKONE-IZU NATIONAL PARK

By Nigel Fisher

Updated by Jared Lubarsky

The Fuji-Hakone-Izu National Park, southwest of Tokyo between Su-ruga and Sagami bays, is one of Japan's most popular resort areas. The park's proximity to Tokyo has encouraged several tour operators to promote the region to foreign visitors. However, while the area offers certain pleasures, perhaps other excursions from Tokyo, for example to Nikko and Kamakura, should take precedence for those with limited time in Japan.

The park's chief attraction is, of course, Mt. Fuji, a dormant volcano (last erupted in 1707) that rises to an altitude of 12,388 feet. It is undoubtedly beautiful and, in changing light and from different perspectives, spellbinding; its perfect symmetry and supreme majesty have been immortalized by poets and artists alike. Some have even assigned spiritual qualities to the mountain. Unfortunately, during spring and summer, Mt. Fuji often hides behind a blanket of clouds, to the disappointment of the crowds of tourists who travel to Hakone or the Fuji Five Lakes for a glimpse of Japan's most revered mountain.

Aside from Mt. Fuji, the Fuji-Hakone-Izu National Park offers an escape from the urban pace and congestion of Tokyo. Each of the three areas of the park—the Izu Peninsula, the town of Hakone, and the Fuji Five Lakes—has its own special attractions. The Izu Peninsula has a craggy coastline with beaches and numerous hot-spring resorts, both along the shore and among the mountains. The Hakone region has aerial cable cars traversing the mountains, boiling hot springs, and lake cruises. The Fuji Five Lakes is a recreational area with some of the best views of Mt. Fuji's cone. In each of these areas are monuments to Japan's past.

Though it is possible to make a grand tour of all three areas at one time, most travelers make each of them a separate excursion from Tokyo. For those interested in climbing Mt. Fuji, a popular activity in July and August, *see* Mt. Fuji section, *below.*

Routes to the different areas of the national park are given at the beginning of each section. Because these are tourist attractions accustomed to foreign visitors, there is always someone to help out in English should you want to explore off the beaten track.

Guided Tours

Several different tours from Tokyo cover Hakone and the Fuji Five Lakes, either as separate tours or combined with other destinations. For example, **Japan Amenity Travel**'s (☎ 03/3542–7200) Imperial Coachman Tour is a full-day excursion: first to the Fuji Lakes district; then to Hakone with a ride on the gondola over Owakudani, a cruise on Lake Ashi to Hakonemachi and the Hakone Barrier; and then the Shinkansen back to Tokyo. (Offered daily Mar.–Nov.; cost: ¥20,000 with lunch; ¥17,000 children under 12.)

Sunrise Tours, a division of the **Japan Travel Bureau** (☎ 03/3276–7777), offers a tour to Hakone, crossing Lake Ashi on the cruise boat, and traveling the gondola over Owakudani (cost: ¥20,000 adults, ¥17,000 children 6–11, including return to Tokyo Station from Odawara by Shinkansen). The Sunrise Tours depart daily (Mon.–Fri., Mar. 22–Nov. 26) from the Hamamatsucho Bus Terminal; there are also pick-ups at some major hotels.

You may also consider including Hakone on a tour that continues on to Kyoto. For example, through Japan Amenity Travel, you may take a three-day tour that includes the Fuji Lakes area, Hakone, Kyoto, and Nara. The standard tour is ¥71,800; the deluxe version, which includes most meals and upgraded rail and overnight accommodations, is ¥88,000. However, read the print carefully. This tour, billed as three days, is only 2½ days, and it ends back at Tokyo Station.

There are no guided tours of the Izu Peninsula, though the Japan Travel Bureau can make arrangements for all your hotel and travel needs.

Izu Peninsula

South of Mt. Fuji, the Izu Peninsula projects out into the Pacific, with Suruga Bay to the west and Sagami Bay to the east (Kamakura is on the opposite side of Sagami Bay). The central part consists of the Amagi Highlands, a continuation of the Hakone Mountains. The shores are a combination of rugged headlands and beautiful bays. The whole area is covered with woods, highland grasses, and some 2,300 hot springs (*izu* means "springs"). In fact, the Izu Peninsula has one-fifth of all the hot-spring baths in Japan, and, with its mild climate, the region is a favorite resort area for the Japanese, especially for honeymooners.

A few words on hot springs: Japan being mostly volcanic, there are lots of places on the archipelago where you can drill for—or tap naturally into springs of—hot water rich in all sorts of restorative minerals. Any place where this happens is called, generically, an *onsen* ("hot springs"); any place where lots of establishments have tapped the sources to cash in on the Japanese passion for immersing themselves to the neck in hot water is an *onsen chiiki* (hot-springs resort area) like Shuzenji or Yugashima. These establishments take many forms. The ne plus ultra is the small, secluded Japanese inn, up in the mountains somewhere, where you sleep on futons on tatami floors and meals—drop-dead presentations of local cuisine—are served in your room. Such an inn will have its own open-air mineral springs pool, called a *rotemburo*, in a screened-off nook with a panoramic view of the mountains, for the exclusive use of its guests. These inns must be booked at least six months in advance.

More typical is the large resort hotel, geared mainly to groups, with one or more large indoor mineral baths of its own. Where whole towns and villages have developed to cash in on a local supply of hot water there will be several of these large hotels, as well as an assortment of smaller inns, and probably a few modest public bathhouses, with no accommodations, where you just pay an entrance fee for the privilege to soak for as long as you wish.

There's nothing in particular to know about *how* to visit a hot spring: As with any Japanese bath, you soap up and rinse off *before* you get in the tub. The atmosphere at onsen resorts is quite informal, with people walking about in the hotels and on the streets in the kimono-like cotton robes called *nemaki*. Perhaps the only thing to bear in mind is that the hotels and bathhouses almost never have full-size bath towels; you must bring your own if you don't want to make do with the skimpy hand towels provided.

Arriving and Departing
BY TRAIN

The best way to start a tour of the Izu Peninsula is to take the Kodama Shinkansen from Tokyo to Atami (48 min.), then travel by local train to Ito (25 min.) and on to Shimoda (another hour). Atami is also served by the JR Odoriko Super Express (not the Shinkansen), which continues beyond Atami to Ito (1 hr., 52 min.) and on to Shimoda (2 hrs., 44 min.). South of Atami, the railroad tracks are privately owned by Izu Railways, and so the JR Rail Pass is not valid after Atami.

To continue around the Izu Peninsula from Shimoda or up through its center you must use buses, which run frequently during the day. However, you should always check the time of the last bus to make sure that you are not left stranded.

Shuzenji, the spa resort in the north-central part of the Izu Peninsula, can be reached from Tokyo via Mishima on the Izu-Hakone Railway Line (2 hrs., 20 min.). Mishima is on the JR Tokaido Line, with direct train service to Tokyo.

BY CAR

From Tokyo, take the Tomei expressway as far as Oi-Matsuda (about 84 kilometers/52 miles), then pick up Routes 255 and 135 to Atami (approximately 28 kilometers/17 miles). From Atami you'll drive another 55 kilometers (34 miles) or so down the east coast of the Izu Peninsula to Shimoda. It takes some effort—but exploring the peninsula *is* a lot easier by car than by public transportation. The best solution is to call either the Nissan or Toyota rental agencies in Tokyo and book a car to be picked up at their Shimoda branch, and go to Shimoda by train. To get to Shuzenji from Shimoda, drive back up the coast to Kawazu (35 min.), on to Yugashima (1 hr.), and then to the hot-spring resort (30 min.).

Exploring

Numbers in the margin correspond to points of interest on the Fuji-Hakone-Izu National Park map.

❶ The gateway to the Izu Peninsula is **Atami.** Often, honeymooners make it no farther into the peninsula, so Atami has numerous hotels, ryokan, and souvenir shops. When you arrive, collect a map from the Atami Tourist Information Office (☎ 0557/81–6002) located at the train station.

★ The most worthwhile attraction in the area is the **MOA Art Museum,** named after its founder, Mokichi Okada. While establishing one of Japan's new religions, the Church of Messianity, Okada was able to collect more than 3,000 works of art, dating from the Asuka period (6th and 7th centuries) to the present day, including a most notable exhibit of *ukiyo-e* (wood-block prints) and ceramics. Located on a hill above the station and set in a garden full of old plum trees and azaleas, the museum also offers a sweeping view over Atami and the bay. *To find out about special exhibitions,* ☎ *0557/84–2511.* ☛ *¥1,500 adults, ¥600 children under 15.* ⊙ *Fri.–Wed. 9:30–6.*

At the opposite end of the ratings spectrum, barely worth the 15-minute walk from Atami Station, is the **Oya Geyser.** It used to gush at a fixed time every 24 hours, but it stopped after the Great Kanto Earthquake. Not happy with this, the local chamber of commerce now makes it gush for four minutes every five minutes and gives it top billing in the tourist brochures.

Fifteen minutes by bus from Atami, or an eight-minute walk from Kinomiya Station (the next stop south of Atami and serviced only by local trains), is **Atami Baien** (plum garden). The time to visit here is in late January or early February, when the 850 trees come into bloom. At other times, it is simply a pleasant, relaxed garden. If you do come here, also stop by the small shrine, dedicated to the god of Temperance, to see the huge and ancient camphor tree on its grounds. The tree has been designated a national monument.

Another excursion from Atami, but only if you have the time and the inclination for a beach picnic, is to take the 40-minute high-speed ferry from the pier over to **Hatsushima.** The island, only 4 kilometers (2½ miles) in circumference, can easily be walked around in less than two hours.

Fuji-Hakone-Izu National Park

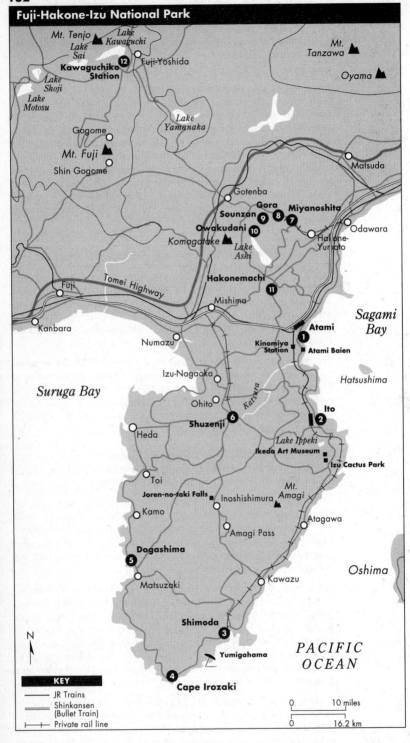

Mt. Tenjo
Lake Kawaguchi
Lake Sai
Lake Shoji
Lake Motosu
Kawaguchiko Station ⑫ Fuji-Yoshida

Mt. Tanzawa
Oyama

Lake Yamanaka

Gogome
Mt. Fuji
Shin Gogome

Matsuda

Gotenba
Gora ⑧ **Miyanoshita** ⑦
Sounzan ⑨
Owakudani ⑩
Komagatake
Lake Ashi
Hakone-Yumoto
Odawara

Tomei Highway

Hakonemachi ⑪

Fuji
Mishima

Sagami Bay

Kanbara

Numazu
Atami ①
Kinomiya Station ■ **Atami Baien**

Hatsushima

Izu-Nagaoka

Suruga Bay

Ohito
Shuzenji ⑥
Katsura
Ito ②

Lake Ippeki
Ikeda Art Museum ■
Izu Cactus Park

Heda

Toi
Joren-no-taki Falls ■ Inoshishimura
Mt. Amagi

Kamo

Amagi Pass
Atagawa

Dogashima ⑤
Oshima

Matsuzaki
Kawazu

Shimoda
③
Yumigahama

PACIFIC OCEAN

④
Cape Irozaki

N

KEY
— JR Trains
═ Shinkansen (Bullet Train)
╫ Private rail line

0 ———— 10 miles
0 ———— 16.2 km

2 Sixteen kilometers (10 miles) south of Atami is **Ito,** a full-fledged spa resort town that can trace its history with the West to 1604, to the arrival of William Adams (1564–1620), the Englishman whose adventures served as the basis for James Clavell's novel *Shogun.*

Four years earlier, Adams beached his Dutch vessel, *De Liefde,* on the shores of Kyushu and became the first Englishman to set foot on Japan. He was first taken to Osaka Castle for interrogation by Shogun Ieyasu Tokugawa and was temporarily imprisoned on the basis of the rumor that he and his men were Portuguese pirates. However, Ieyasu was won over by Adams's personality and, as shogun, provided him with a house in Nihonbashi, Edo (present-day Tokyo), and appointed him adviser on foreign affairs and teacher of mathematics, geography, gunnery, and navigation to shogunate officials. In 1604, Adams was ordered to build an 80-ton Western-style vessel. Pleased with this venture, the shogun ordered the construction of a larger oceangoing vessel. These two ships were built at Ito, and Adams lived there from 1605 to 1610. All this history was temporarily forgotten until the British Commonwealth occupation forces used Ito as a health resort after World War II. Adams's memory was revived, and since then, the Anjin Festival has been held in his honor every August. A monument to the Englishman stands at the mouth of the river.

One reason that the British Commonwealth occupation forces chose Ito is that there are 800 thermal springs in the area. These springs— along with Ito's location on a beautiful, rocky, indented coastline— remain the resort's major attractions. Some 150 hotels and inns serve the area.

In addition to the hot springs, the Ito area has a number of other attractions. The **Izu Saboten Koen** (Izu Cactus Park), 20 minutes by bus from Ito Station, consists of a series of pyramidal greenhouses set up at the base of Mt. Omuro that contain 5,000 kinds of cacti from around the world. ☎ *0557/51–1111.* ☛ *¥1,800 adults, ¥300 children under 6.* ☉ *Daily 8:40–4:30. Closed Dec. 26–28.*

Five minutes by bus, or a 15-minute walk beyond the Izu Cactus Park, is the **Ikeda Kinen Bijutsukan** (Ikeda Memorial Art Museum) at Lake Ippeki, with works by Picasso, Dalí, Chagall, and Matisse, and a number of wood-block prints. ☎ *0557/45–2211.* ☛ *¥800 adults, ¥400 children under 15.* ☉ *July–Aug. 10–5:30, Sept.–June 10–4:30.*

Finally, there is **Mount Omura Koen** (park), which has, on its east side, 3,000 cherry trees of 35 different varieties that bloom at different times throughout the year. The park is a 20-minute bus ride south from Ito Station.

South of Ito, the coastal scenery is more of the same—each sweep around a headland gives another picturesque sight of a rocky indented shoreline. There are several spa towns en route to Shimoda. Higashi-Izu is a collection of hot-spring towns, of which **Atagawa** is the most fashionable. Farther south is **Kawazu,** which offers quiet solitude, with pools in the forested mountainside and waterfalls plunging through lush greenery. However, for history, none of these resort towns has the distinction of **Shimoda.**

3

Shimoda's meeting with the West occurred when Commodore Perry anchored his ships off the coast in 1854. To commemorate the event, the Kurofune Matsuri (Black Ship Festival) is held annually May 16– 18. It was here, too, that the first American Consulate was located before being transferred to Yokohama in 1857. Townsend Harris was the consul, and Tojin Okichi was his consort. There are several versions about the Harris-Okichi relationship. With the Japanese penchant for sad romance, the heroine is Okichi. One version has Okichi being ordered by the authorities to leave her lover and comfort Harris so that he may feel at home. Another version suggests that Harris picked Okichi out of a line of prostitutes. In either case, when Harris returned to America, he abandoned her. (Harris's version is that he forthrightly declined her advances.) Whatever is the truth, apparently when Harris left poor Okichi, she tried for a reconciliation with her former lover, Tsurumatsu. When that failed, she opened a restaurant, took to drink, and eventually took a final plunge into the river.

The easiest itinerary in English to follow is the one given by the **Shimoda Tourist Office** (☎ 0558/22–1531), located in front of the station. The 2½-kilometer (1½-mile) itinerary covers most of the major sites, and all of those concerning Okichi. Also, on request, the tourist office will find travelers accommodations in Shimoda.

Hofukuji was the family temple of Tojin Okichi and serves as a memorial-museum. The adjoining annex displays a life-size image of the woman. Just behind the temple is her grave; you'll notice that incense is still kept burning in her memory. (The grave of her lover, Tsurumatsu, is at Todenji, a temple about midway between Hofukuji and the station.) ☛ *¥300 adults.* ✸ *8–5.*

The major site on this Shimoda walk is **Ryosenji,** the temple at which the talks were concluded in the Japan–U.S. Friendship Treaty that forced the Tokugawa Shogunate to open Japan to the West. The temple's treasury hall also contains personal artifacts of Tojin Okichi. In the adjoining temple, **Chorakuji,** the U.S.–Japan treaty was actually signed, as was the trade agreement with the Russians. ☛ *Ryosenji, ¥500 adults, ¥150 children;* ✸ *8:30–5.* ☛ *Chorakuji, ¥200 adults;* ✸ *9–5.*

Slightly farther down the road is a monument to Perry and Harris, built to celebrate the establishment of U.S.–Japanese relations. Still farther along, overlooking Shimoda Harbor, is another monument to Perry. Finally, you come to the Sushikane restaurant, said to be the one opened by Tojin Okichi a few years before she committed suicide. On display here are Okichi's belongings.

❹ The southernmost point of the Izu Peninsula is **Cape Irozaki,** reached either by bus from Shimoda Station or by a sightseeing boat from Shimoda. If you visit Cape Irozaki in January, you are in for a special treat: a blanket of yellow daffodils to greet you. To reach the cape, whatever the season, the best plan is to take the boat one way and the bus the other. Both take about 40 minutes. The bus stops at **Yumigahama,** one of the best sandy beaches on the whole peninsula, and then continues on to Cape Irozaki, the last stop on the route. From where the bus stops there is a walk past the **Irozaki Jungle Park,** with huge hothouses containing 3,000 varied and colorful tropical plants, to the lighthouse at the edge of the cliff facing the breadth of the Pacific Ocean. *Park* ☎ *0558/65–0050.* ☛ *¥900 adults, ¥450 children.* ✸ *8–5.*

Just as Shimoda is the end of the line for the trains, so it is for most visitors, who take the two-hour, 45-minute express train ride back to Tokyo. However, for the more adventurous, a bus from Shimoda con-
❺ tinues around the Izu Peninsula to the seaside town of **Dogashima.** There is little to do here but walk the sandy beaches and watch the fishermen at work. The tourist office (☎ 05585/2–1268) is in the small building behind the bus station and near the pier.

Dogashima is famous for its sedimentary rock formations, shaped by erosion, jutting out from the coast into the sea. The best way to see them is on the sightseeing boat that leaves from the pier. The names of the rocks are called out from the loudspeaker on the cruise boat, which makes 20-minute runs to see the rocks (cost: ¥850 adults, ¥430 children). If you don't understand Japanese, close your ears to the incessant loudspeaker and take the boat anyway. It is the best (and virtually only) way to appreciate the varied shapes of these rocks.

⑥ From Dogashima, another bus travels up the coast as far as Heda and then turns inland to **Shuzenji,** a traditional spa town in the center of the peninsula. For a more relaxing return trip take the boat from Dogashima to Numazu and catch the train back to Tokyo from there.

An alternative, and easier, way of reaching Shuzenji is to take one of the five daily buses from Shimoda via the Amagi Mountains. The scenery is attractive and the trip only takes about two hours (cost: ¥2,070 adults, ¥1,040 children). You may wish to stretch your legs at **Inoshishimura,** where trained boars and badgers put on a show. The show is not particularly worthwhile, but a pleasant 15-minute walk from town brings you to **Joren-no-taki** (waterfall), from where you can rejoin the bus. By the way, the specialty dish at the local ryokan is roasted boar meat.

Shuzenji is a lavish inland spa town along the valley of the Katsuragawa. Don't judge the town by the area around the station; most of the hotels and springs are a mile to the west of the station. Though Shuzenji has the notoriety of being the place where the second Kamakura shogun was assassinated (though he had abdicated his office) early in the 13th century, there is little to interest the foreign visitor. However, we recommend returning to Tokyo through the mountainous center of the Izu Peninsula via Shuzenji and Mishima for a contrast to the coastal route. There are numerous hotels in Shuzenji, and 24 kilometers (15 miles) farther north is **Izu-Nagaoka,** with several deluxe ryokan (*see* Lodging, *below*).

From Shuzenji, you can catch the private railway line (cost: ¥470) to Mishima and change for the Shinkansen to Tokyo or Kyoto. Frequent buses make the 40-minute trip from Mishima Station to Hakonemachi (cost: ¥980).

Hakone

Hakone, a national park and resort area, is a popular day trip from Tokyo and a good place for a close-up view of Mt. Fuji. A word of caution, though, before you dash off to Hakone with plans to see Mt. Fuji: It is often cloud covered, especially during the summer months. Also, the excursion to Hakone has become so popular that sometimes it seems that all of Tokyo has come with you. You can expect to stand in line at the cable cars and be stuck in traffic on the roads.

Arriving and Departing
BY TRAIN
The privately owned Odakyu Line has trains departing from Tokyo's Shinjuku Station to Odawara. Odakyu's commuter trains leave every half hour. However, Odakyu also has a special train, the "Romance Car," which offers comfortable seating and large viewing windows. These Romance Cars go one stop beyond Odawara to Hakone-Yumoto. Reservations are required for the Romance Car, and tickets can be purchased from any Odakyu railway station or Odakyu Travel Service

agency (cost: ¥1,820). Beyond Odawara and Hakone-Yumoto, travel is on the privately owned Hakone Tozan Tetsudo Line or by bus.

If you are using a JR Rail Pass, it is more economical to take the Kodama Shinkansen from Tokyo Station to Odawara. (The faster Hikari does not stop at Odawara.) From Odawara, change to the private railway.

The most economical way of traveling to and within Hakone is to purchase the Hakone Free Pass. Sold by Odakyu Railways, this coupon ticket allows you to use any mode of transportation in the Hakone area, such as the Hakone Tozan Railway, the Hakone Tozan Bus, the Hakone Ropeway, the Hakone Cruise Boat, the Sounzan Cable Car, and so on (cost: ¥5,400 from Shinjuku, with an additional surcharge of ¥800 to travel on the Romance Car). If you hold a JR Rail Pass, then purchase the Hakone Free Pass just for the travel within the Hakone region and use JR Railways to reach Odawara (cost: ¥4,500). The coupon is valid for four days and is sold at any station serving the Odakyu Railways. With the exception of a detour up the east side of Lake Ashi to the Prince Hotel, all of the itinerary described below is covered by the Hakone Free Pass.

Getting Around

Hakone has a network of public transportation from cable cars to buses and from railways to cruise boats. Because traffic on the narrow mountain roads is a slow-moving jam, rental cars are not advised. Indeed, part of the pleasure of exploring Hakone is traveling one way on the cruise boats and aerial gondolas, which you would miss when driving your own car.

Exploring

The following itinerary covers the best of Hakone in a one-day trip out of Tokyo. If you want to enjoy the curative powers of the thermal waters or do some hiking, then an overnight stay will be necessary. The two areas we recommend are around Miyanoshita, an old-fashioned spa town, and the Prince Hotel resort area, on the slopes of Mt. Komagatake facing Lake Ashi.

Though the itinerary described below sounds complex, it is not. In fact, though many companies offer guided tours of the region, this is one excursion from Tokyo that is so well defined that there is no risk of becoming lost. Indeed, except in the coldest winter months, thousands of Japanese visitors take this same itinerary. The route is a procession of tourists. However, if you wish to take a guided tour, *see* Guided Tours, *above.*

From Odawara or Hakone-Yumoto we take you by train and cable car to Togendai on the north shore of Lake Ashi. Our route traverses the mountains, though an easier option is simply to catch a bus from Odawara Station. Taking the bus, however, defeats much of the purpose of a visit to Hakone. Still, if any members of your group cannot stand heights, we recommend putting them on the bus at Odawara, Hakone-Yumoto, or Miyanoshita for Togendai and joining them on the pier at Togendai in about 2½ hours. The bus is scheduled to do the journey in 60 minutes, though traffic usually increases travel time to 90 minutes. Your trip over the mountains will take about two hours.

To go over the mountains, either from Odawara or Hakone-Yumoto, take the Hakone Tozan Tetsudo Line for Gora. The train may be accused and excused for being possibly the slowest train you've ever taken. It takes 50 minutes to travel the 16 kilometers (10 miles) from Odawara to Gora (35 min. from Hakone-Yumoto). How the train climbs the mountain is a wonder. But, by using three switchbacks, it steps up the cliff side, and the views become grander as the plunges down the mountain grow steeper.

The train makes several stops on the way; though trains do not stop at any station for any length of time, they do run frequently enough to allow you to disembark, visit a sight, and catch another train. The **7** first of note is **Miyanoshita.** True, Hakone-Yumoto is a bigger resort center, with some 60 inns, but Miyanoshita has a more sophisticated air and elegant approach. There is one old Western-style hotel, the **Fujiya,** that is full of 19th-century charm. Even if you're not staying there, drop in for a morning coffee on the first floor overlooking the garden and, on the way out, take a peek at the library for its vintage collection of old books and magazines. (*See* Lodging, *below.*)

The next interesting stop is **Chokoku-no-mori.** Within a minute's walk ★ of the station is the **Hakone Open-Air Museum** (Chokoku-no-mori Bijutsukan) one of Japan's more attractive museums, where the building is designed to work with the environment. Outside are displayed numerous sculptures by such masters as Rodin and Moore; inside are works by Picasso, Léger, and Kotaro Takamura, among others. The collection of art exhibits may have more novelty interest to the Japanese, but the setting of the sculpture gardens set into the cliff side has universal appeal. *To find out about special exhibitions,* ☎ *0460/2–1161.* ☛ *¥1,500 adults, ¥800 children under 15.* ⊙ *Daily, Mar.–Oct. 9–5; Nov.–Feb. 9–4.*

8 The final stop on the line is **Gora,** a small town that services both those who have chosen the village as a base for hiking and exploring, and those passing through on their way up to Sounzan. Shops and small restaurants abound. However, if you can be first out of the train, forget the souvenir stands and make a dash for the cable car located in the same building as the train station. If you let the rest of the passengers arrive there before you, and perhaps a tour bus or two, you may stand 45 minutes in line.

9 The cable car up to **Sounzan** departs every 20 minutes and takes nine minutes (cost: ¥400; free with the Hakone Free Pass). There are four stops en route, and you may get off and reboard the cable car if you've purchased the full fare up to the top. The one stop in particular where you may consider disembarking is **Koen-kami,** the second stop up, to visit the **Hakone Bijutsukan** (Hakone Art Museum) for its collection of porcelain and ceramics from China, Korea, and Japan. ☎ *0460/2– 2623.* ☛ *¥800 adults, ¥300 children under 15.* ⊙ *Fri.–Wed. 9–4.*

At Sounzan, the gondola begins a 28-minute journey down to **Togendai.** The gondola is in the same building as the cable-car terminus. With your ticket (cost: ¥1,300) or your Hakone Free Pass, stand in line to get a boarding-pass number. This will determine when you can stand in the line for clambering into a car. The gondola seats about eight adults and departs every minute.

Less than 10 minutes out of Sounzan, the gondola swings over a ridge ★ and crosses over **Owakudani.** Suspended hundreds of feet above the "boiling valley," you may observe volcanic activity on the ground below, with sulfurous steam escaping through holes from some inferno deep within the earth.

Having swung safely over the valley the gondola comes to the top of **10** the far ridge and **Owakudani,** one of the two stations on the gondola route. If you disembark here, however, keep in mind that you—and the others in front of you—must wait for someone to disembark before you can board again. It can be at least a 15-minute wait.

Below Owakudani Station is a restaurant. The reputation for its food is terrible, but, on a clear day, the view of Mt. Fuji is perfect, and that view should tempt you to suffer the food. Next to the station is the **Owakudani Shizen Hakubutsukan** (Owakudani National Science Museum), which has exhibits relating to the ecosystems and volcanic history of the area. ☎ 0460/4–9149. ☛ *¥400 adults, ¥250 children under 12.* ☉ *Daily 9–4:30.*

There is also a ¾-kilometer-long (½-mile-long) walking course that passes by some "hellholes" with steam pouring out. You may see someone who boils eggs in the holes and sells them at exorbitant prices.

From Owakudani the descent to Togendai on the shore of **Lake Ashi** takes 25 minutes. There is no reason to linger at Togendai. It is an arrival and departure point. Buses leave from here for Hakone-Yumoto and Odawara, as well as the resort villages in the northern area of Hakone. For us, it is the departure point for the cruise boat to **⑪ Hakonemachi.** The boat is free with your Hakone Free Pass; otherwise you must purchase your ticket (cost: ¥950) at the office in the terminal. The pier is 100 meters (yards) away, and, if the boat is in, you'll recognize it by its gaudy design. (One boat is made to look like a 17th-century warship.) Boats depart every 30 minutes, and the cruise to Hakonemachi takes about 30 minutes, giving you the opportunity to appreciate the bow-shape Lake Ashi. Because the mountains plunge to the lake, one of the attractions of the boat ride is the reflection of the mountains in the lake's waters.

★ The key sight in Hakonemachi is **Hakone Sekisho** (Hakone Barrier), a few minutes' walk from the pier in the direction of Moto-Hakone, if you keep as close to the lakeshore as is possible. Hakone was on the Tokaido, the main highway between the imperial capital of Kyoto and the administrative center of the shogunate at Edo (present-day Tokyo). Because of the steep mountains, travelers could scarcely avoid passing through Hakone. It was thus a strategic checkpoint where travelers to and from Edo could be stopped. The Tokugawa Shogunate erected a barrier in 1618 and required travelers to be rigorously searched. Especially important for the security of the shogunate was the examination of each *daimyo* (feudal lord) and his retainers, making their required visit to Edo. Every procession was checked for its number of warriors and their weaponry.

To fully understand the significance of the Hakone Sekisho, remember that the Tokugawa Shogunate required that each daimyo make a visit to Edo once every two years. This served two purposes. It reaffirmed the shogun's authority and diminished the authority of the daimyo, who had to be absent from his lands for a considerable time in order to make the trip. Second, because the daimyo had to travel with a large number of retainers, the expense to the daimyo was great and kept him poor. The less trustworthy daimyo were given lands far from Edo, so their expenses and their time away from their power base were even more crippling. One other method to control the obeisance of the daimyo was used: The wives of the daimyo were required to live in Edo all the time. They were, in fact, hostages; if a daimyo stepped out of line, he did so at the risk of his wife's head. The Hakone Sekisho was, therefore, also a barrier to prevent wives from returning to their husbands.

For two and a half centuries, travelers were stopped at the Hakone Barrier. Then, in 1869, with the Meiji Restoration, it was demolished. However, for the delight of tourists, an exact replica, including an exhibition hall displaying costumes and arms used during Japan's feudal period, was rebuilt in 1965. ☛ ¥200 *adults,* ¥100 *children under 12.* ⊙ *daily 9–4:30.*

From Hakonemachi and the Hakone Sekisho, buses run every 15–30 minutes to Hakone-Yumoto (40 min.) and Odawara (1 hr.) for either the Romance Car back to Shinjuku Station or the JR Shinkansen to Tokyo Station. The fare is ¥880 to Yumoto, ¥1,100 to Odawara—or free with the Hakone Free Pass.

Fuji Five Lakes

Whereas Hakone is the region south of Mt. Fuji, Fuji-Goko (literally, "Fuji-five-lakes") is the area to the north of Mt. Fuji. Needless to say, the star attractions of this area are the view of the mountain and the base from which you can climb to its summit. However, the area also has five lakes that add to the scenic beauty and offer the chance to see Mt. Fuji reflected in the waters. The Fuji Lakes are a popular resort for families and business seminars. Numerous outdoor activities, ranging from skating and fishing in the winter to boating and hiking in the summer, are organized to accommodate the increasing numbers who visit here each year.

Of the five lakes, Lake Kawaguchi and Lake Yamanaka are the two most developed resort areas. Lake Yamanaka, to the southeast of Lake Kawaguchi, is the largest lake, but Lake Kawaguchi is considered the focus of Fuji-Goko. The area can be visited in a day trip from Tokyo, but because the main reason for coming to this region is relaxation, more than one day is really necessary unless you want to spend most of the day on buses or trains.

Arriving and Departing

The transportation hub, as well as one of the major resort areas in Fuji-Goko, is Kawaguchiko. Getting there from Tokyo requires a change of trains at Otsuki. The JR Chuo Line "Kaiji" and "Azusa" express trains depart from Shinjuku Station to Otsuki on the half-hour throughout the morning (less frequently in the afternoon) and take approximately one hour. At Otsuki, change to the private Fujikyuko Line for Kawaguchiko, which takes another 50 minutes. The total traveling time is about two hours, and you can use your JR Pass as far as Otsuki. The fare from Otsuki to Kawaguchiko is ¥1,110. There are about seven trains a day (more in the summer) from Shinjuku that make convenient connections at Otsuki. There are also one or two trains on Sundays and national holidays (Mar.–Nov.) that operate directly between Shinjuku and Kawaguchiko Station. On weekends (Mar.–June 28), an express train departs from Shinjuku early in the morning and arrives at Kawaguchiko about 1½ hours later; a train making the return trip departs Kawaguchiko in the late afternoon and arrives at Shinjuku in the early evening. (Times should be verified before your departure; only coaches 1, 2, and 3 make the through run.)

A direct bus service from Shinjuku to Kawaguchiko operates hourly between 7:30 AM and 6 PM (cost: ¥1,700).

For a different route back to Tokyo, you may want to consider taking the two-hour bus ride from Kawaguchiko to Mishima (cost: ¥2,130). Approximately three buses a day make the trip, skirting the western lakes and circling Mt. Fuji before descending the mountains to Mishima. At Mishima, transfer to the JR Shinkansen Line for Tokyo or Kyoto. A shorter bus ride (70 min., cost: ¥1,740) goes from Kawaguchiko to Gotenba with a transfer to the JR local line.

If you want to go to Hakone rather than Tokyo from Fuji-Goko, take the bus from Kawaguchiko first to Gotenba, then change to another bus to Sengoku. From Sengoku, there are frequent buses to Hakone-Yumoto, Togendai, and elsewhere in the Hakone region. If you want to go to the Izu Peninsula, take the bus to Mishima and, from there, go by train either to Shuzenji or Atami.

Buses depart from Kawaguchiko Station to all parts of the area and to all five lakes. On a single day's visit, you will probably only have the time to visit Lake Kawaguchi and, if you don't take a break, possibly one other lake.

Exploring

⑫ Arriving from Tokyo at **Kawaguchiko Station,** you'll have a five- to 10-minute walk to the lakeshore. If you take a right along the shore, another five minutes will bring you to the gondola for a quick ride up to **Mt. Tenjo.** At the top of Mt. Tenjo (3,622 feet), there is an observatory from which you can get a look at the lay of the land. Lake Kawaguchi is before you, and beyond the lake is a classic view of Mt. Fuji. Back down the gondola and across the road is the pier for the Kawaguchi's cruise boat. The boat offers 30-minute tours of the lake. The promise, not always fulfilled, is to have two views of Mt. Fuji: one in its natural form, and another inverted in the reflection from the water.

On the north shore of the lake next to the Fuji Lake Hotel is **Fuji-Hakubut-sukan** (Fuji Museum; ☎ 0555/73–2266), where on the first floor there are displays related to the geology and history of the area. The kids view these academic exhibits while adults (only those aged 18 and older are permitted) visit the second floor. Here are exhibits of erotic paraphernalia used, apparently, by Japanese families until relatively recently. ☛ ¥100 adults, ¥50 children under 12; second floor ¥400. ۞ Wed.–Mon. 9–4.

Kawaguchi is the most developed of the five lakes; all around its shores are villas owned by companies and universities, where weekend retreats are held. There are also a number of recreational facilities, the largest of which is **Fujikyu Highland.** It is not particularly recommended for the day visitor, but it does have everything to amuse children, from a scream-engendering loop-the-loop to a more genteel carousel. The amusement park stays open all year and in the winter offers superb skating, with Mt. Fuji for its backdrop. To reach Fujikyu Highland, take the train back (in the direction of Odawara) one stop, or walk the 15 minutes from Lake Kawaguchi.

Buses from Kawaguchiko Station go to all the other lakes. The farthest lake is **Motosu,** which takes about 50 minutes to reach by bus. It is also the deepest lake of the Fuji-Goko, and has the clearest waters. **Shoji,** the smallest of the lakes, is regarded by many to be the prettiest. It has the added pleasure of not being built up with vacation homes. The Shoji Trail leads from the lake to Mt. Fuji through Aokigahara (Sea of Trees), a forest under which is a magnetic lava field that makes compasses go haywire. For that reason, people planning to climb Mt. Fuji are advised to take this route with a guide.

Between Shoji and Kawaguchi is **Sai,** the third largest lake of the region and only modestly developed. From its western side there is a good view of Mt. Fuji. The largest of the five lakes is **Yamanaka,** 35 minutes by bus to the southeast of Kawaguchi. A cruise-boat makes 30-minute excursions of the lake. Because Yamanaka is the closest lake to the popular trail up Mt. Fuji that starts at Gogome, many climbers use the resort for their base.

Mt. Fuji

★ There are six possible routes to the summit of **Mt. Fuji,** but only two are recommended: Gogome (fifth station) on the north side, and Shin-Gogome (new fifth station) on the south side. From Gogome it is a five-hour climb to the summit, and a three-hour descent if you return the same way. From Shin-Gogome the ascent to the summit is slightly longer and stonier than from Gogome, but the descent is faster. Hence, we recommend climbing Mt. Fuji from Gogome and descending to Shin-Gogome, via the Sunabashiri—more about that in a moment.

Arriving and Departing

Buses take about one hour from Kawaguchiko Station to Gogome, and there are 3 to 15 runs a day, depending on the season (cost: ¥1,620). There are also daily buses from Tokyo (July through August, from Hamamatsucho or Shinjuku stations) that go directly to Gogome, departing from Hamamatsucho at 8:15 AM, and from Shinjuku at 7:45 AM, 8:45 AM, and 7:30 PM. The last bus allows sufficient time for the tireless to make it to Mt. Fuji's summit before sunrise. The journey takes about three hours from Hamamatsucho and two hours, 30 minutes from Shinjuku (cost: ¥2,800 from Hamamatsucho, ¥2,600 from Shinjuku). Reservations are required, through the Fuji Kyuko Railway (☎ 03/3374–2221), the Japan Travel Bureau (☎ 03/3284–7026), or other major travel agents.

A bus makes the 70-minute trip from Shin-Gogome to Gotenba (cost: ¥1,500). From Gotenba take the JR Tokaido and Gotenba lines to Tokyo Station, or the JR Line to Matsuda and change to the Odakyu Line for Shinjuku (cost: ¥1,120).

The Climb

It has become increasingly popular to make the climb at night in order to reach the summit just before sunrise. Sunrises, wherever you are, are beautiful, but the sunrise from the top of Mt. Fuji is exceptional. *Goraiko,* as the sunrise is named, takes on a mystical quality as the reflection of the light shimmers across the sky just before the sun itself appears over the horizon. Mind you, there is no guarantee of seeing it: Mt. Fuji attracts clouds, especially in the early morning.

The climb is taxing, but not as arduous as you might imagine it to be to scale Japan's highest mountain, 12,388 feet above sea level. However, it is humiliating to struggle to find the oxygen for another step ahead when 83-year-old grandmothers stride past you; on occasion, they do. Have no fear in getting off the trail on either of the two main routes. Some 196,000 people make the climb during the official season, July 1–August 31, and en route there are vendors selling food and drinks. (Consider taking your own nourishment and some water rather than paying their high prices.) In all, there are 10 stations to the top—you start at the fifth. However, the stations are located at unequal distances. Also, along the route at each station are huts where, dormitory-style, you can catch some sleep. A popular one is at the Hachigome (eighth station), from which it is about a 90-minute climb to the top. However, these huts are often overcrowded and are none too clean, so more and more people leave Gogome (the fifth station) at midnight and plan to be at the summit 4½ hours later for sunrise. The mountain huts are open from the end of April to Nov. 23. Lodging costs approximately ¥6,000 with two meals, ¥4,000 without food (Saturday surcharge: ¥1,000). Camping on the mountain is prohibited.

Coming back down is easy. Instead of returning to Gogome, descend to Shin-Gogome, using the volcanic sand slide called *sunabashiri*—you take a giant step and slide. It's fun, but not so much fun that you will want to climb Mt. Fuji again.

Be prepared for fickle weather around and up Mt. Fuji. Summer days can be warm (very hot when climbing), and nights can be freezing cold. Wear strong hiking shoes. The sun really burns at high altitude, so take protective clothing and a hat. Gloves are a good idea; they protect the hands while climbing and when sliding down the volcanic sand during the descent. Use a backpack so that your hands are free.

Lodging

Because the region covered in this chapter is a resort area, most hotels quote prices on a per-person basis with two meals, exclusive of service and tax. If you do not want dinner at your hotel, it is usually possible to renegotiate the price. Stipulate, too, whether you wish to have Japanese or Western breakfasts, if any. For the purposes here, the categories assigned to all hotels reflect the cost of a double room with private bath and no meals. However, if you make reservations at any of the noncity hotels, you will be expected to take breakfast and dinner at the hotel—that will be the rate quoted to you, unless you specify otherwise. During the peak season, July 15–August 31, prices can increase by 40%.

A 3% federal consumer tax is added to all hotel bills. Another 3% local tax is added to the bill if it exceeds ¥15,000. At most hotels, a 10%–15% service charge is added to the total bill. Tipping is not necessary.

CATEGORY	COST*
$$$$	over ¥25,000
$$$	¥17,000–¥25,000
$$	¥10,000–¥17,000
$	under ¥10,000

Cost is for double room, without tax or service

Izu Peninsula

ATAMI

$$$$ **New Fujiya Hotel.** A modern resort hotel with large public areas, this is a useful hotel to use simply as a base for sightseeing. It is located inland (five minutes by taxi from the station), and only the top rooms have a view of the sea. The impersonal, but professional, service only gets flustered when a group arrives. ☎ 1-16 Ginzacho, Atami, Shizuoka 413, ☎ 0557/81–0111. 316 rooms, half Western-style. Japanese and Western restaurants, indoor pool, hot springs, sauna. AE, DC, MC, V.

$$$$ **Taikanso Ryokan.** A Japanese inn of the old style with beautiful fur-
★   nishings and individualized service, the villa was once owned by the Japanese artist Taikan. The views over the sea must have been his inspiration. The inn is a 10-minute walk from the station. ☎ 7-1 Hayashigaokacho, Atami, Shizuoka 413, ☎ 0557/81–8137. 44 Japanese-style rooms. Breakfast and dinner served in your room. AE, DC, V.

DOGASHIMA

\$\$\$ **Ginsuiso.** This is the smartest luxury resort on Izu's west coast. Service is first class, despite its popularity with tour groups. The location along the top of the cliff, with every room overlooking the sea, is superb. ☎ *2977-1 Nishina, Nishi-Izucho, Dogashima, Shizuoka,* ☎ *0558/52–1211. 90 Japanese-style rooms. Restaurant, pool, nightclub with cabaret, shops. AE, DC, MC, V.*

ITO

\$\$\$\$ **Ryokan Nagoya.** This is a small, very charming establishment with un-
★ derstated elegance and sophistication; antiques have been placed around the inn with simplicity and harmony. English is not spoken, but smiles and a few words in Japanese seem to go a long way. Breakfast and dinner are served in your room. ☎ *1-1-18 Sakuragaoka, Ito, Shizuoka,* ☎ *0557/37–4316. 14 rooms. No credit cards.*

IZU-NAGAOKA

\$\$\$\$ **Ryokan Sanyoso.** Elegant and beautiful, the Sanyoso is decorated with
★ antiques and luxurious furniture—as you would expect from the former villa of the Iwasaki family of the Mitsubishi conglomerate. Meals cannot be excluded from the room fee. The Sanyoso is a five-minute taxi ride from the station. ☎ *270 Domanoue, Izu-Nagaoka, Tagata-gun, Shizuoka 410,* ☎ *05594/8–0123. 21 rooms. Restaurant. AE, DC, MC, V.*

\$\$ **Matsushiro-kan.** This small ryokan, five minutes by bus or taxi from
★ the station, is nothing fancy, yet because it is a family operation, it feels like a friendly home. Some English is spoken. Japanese meals are served in a common dining room. Room-only reservations (no meals) are accepted only on weekdays. ☎ *55 Kona, Izu-Nagaoka, Tagata-gun, Shizuoka 410-22,* ☎ *05594/8–0072. 16 rooms. Restaurant. AE, V.*

SHIMODA

\$\$\$-\$\$\$\$ **Shimoda Prince Hotel.** This modern, V-shape resort hotel faces the Pacific, steps away from a white sandy beach. (It's just out of Shimoda, 10 minutes by taxi from the station.) The building and rooms are more functional than aesthetic in design and are geared to those seeking a holiday by the sea. However, the broad expanse of picture windows from the dining room, offering a panorama of the Pacific Ocean, does make this establishment the best in town. ☎ *1547-1 Shirahama, Shimoda, Shizuoka 415,* ☎ *05582/2–7575. 134 rooms, mostly Western-style. Continental main dining room, Japanese restaurant, terrace lounge, bar, nightclub, outdoor pool, sauna, tennis courts. AE, DC, MC, V.*

\$\$\$-\$\$\$\$ **Shimoda Tokyu Hotel.** Perched just above the bay, the Shimoda Tokyu has impressive views of the Pacific from one side (where the rooms cost about 10% more) and mountains from the other. The public areas are large and lack character and warmth, but that is typical of Japanese resort hotels. Prices run significantly higher in the midsummer months. ☎ *5-12-1 Shimoda, Shimoda, Shizuoka 415,* ☎ *05582/2–2411. 117 rooms, mostly Western-style. Western dining room, Japanese restaurant, sushi bar, summer garden restaurant, pool, hot springs, tennis courts, shops. AE, DC, MC, V.*

Hakone

LAKE ASHI

\$\$\$\$ **Hakone Prince Hotel.** This is a completely self-contained resort com-
★ plex on the edge of the lake at Hakone-en. The hotel attracts tours, the individual traveler, and business meetings. The location is superb, with the lake on one side and Komagatake (mountain) on the other. You can escape the largeness of the hotel by staying in one of two

Japanese-style annexes. Request the *ryuguden,* which overlooks the lake and has its own hot-spring bath; it is absolutely superb, despite having the most expensive rooms in the hotel. ☏ *144 Moto-Hakone, Hakonemachi, Ashigarashimo-gun, Kanagawa 250-05,* ☎ *0460/3–7111. 455 rooms; the main building has 96 rooms; the chalet has 12 rooms; the lakeside lodge has 77 rooms; the 2 annexes have a total of 73 rooms. Formal Western dining room, steak and seafood restaurant, Chinese restaurant, Japanese restaurants, coffeehouse, bar/lounge, tennis courts, pools, shops. AE, MC, V.*

<u>MIYANOSHITA</u>

$$$$ **Fujiya Hotel.** Though this Western-style building is showing signs of
★ age (built in 1878, but with modern additions), that simply increases the hotel's charm, which is especially felt in the library, with its stacks of old books. In the delightful gardens in the back is an old imperial villa used for dining. With the exceptional service and hospitality of a fine Japanese inn, this is the best traditional Western hotel in town. ☏ *359 Miyanoshita, Hakonemachi, Kanagawa 250-04,* ☎ *0460/2–2211. 149 Western-style rooms. Western and Japanese restaurants, indoor and outdoor pools, thermal pool, golf. AE, DC, MC, V.*

$$$$ **Ryokan Naraya.** A traditional inn, the Naraya retains a simple, even
★ mystical, understated elegance and an exquisite formal hospitality. The same family has owned the inn for generations. The main building has more atmosphere than does the annex. You are expected to have breakfast and dinner, which are served in your room. ☏ *162 Miyanoshita, Hakonemachi, Kanagawa 250-04,* ☎ *0460/2–2411. 19 rooms, some with private bath. AE, DC, MC, V.*

$$ **Hotel Kowakien.** This hotel attracts busloads of tourists. It's far from ideal, but its prices are reasonable for the fair-size rooms, and you can usually get a reservation. (The hotel also owns the adjacent **Hakone Kowakien,** which is equally large and with little character, but has Japanese-style rooms.) ☏ *1297 Ninotaira, Hakonemachi, Kanagawa 250-04,* ☎ *0460/2–4111. 237 Western-style rooms. Western and Japanese restaurants, indoor and outdoor pools, thermal pool, sauna, golf, tennis, gym. AE, DC, MC, V.*

<u>SENGOKU</u>

$$ **Fuji-Hakone Guest House.** A small, family-run Japanese inn, this guest house has simple tatami rooms with the bare essentials. The owners, Mr. and Mrs. Takahashi, speak English and are a great help in planning off-the-beaten-path excursions. The inn is between Odawara Station and Togendai; take a bus from the Odawara Station terminal (bus lane 4), get off at the Senkyoro-mae bus stop, and walk one block. The family also operates the nearby Moto-Hakone Guest House (103 Moto-Hakone, Kanagawa 250-05; ☎ 0460/3–7880), which has five Japanese-style rooms, none with private bath. ☏ *912 Sengokuhara, Hakone, Kanagawa 250-06,* ☎ *0460/4–6577. 12 Japanese-style rooms, none with private bath. Hot springs. AE, MC, V.*

Fuji Five Lakes

<u>LAKE KAWAGUCHI</u>

$$$–$$$$ **Fuji View Hotel.** Conveniently located on Lake Kawaguchi, the Fuji View is a little threadbare, but it does provide comfort. Its terraced lounge offers fine views of the lake and of Mt. Fuji beyond. The staff also speak English and are helpful in planning your excursions. Rates are significantly higher on weekends and in August. ☏ *511 Katsuyamamura, Minami-Tsuru-gun, Yamanashi 401-04,* ☎ *05558/3–2211. 78 rooms, mostly Western-style (twins only). Western restaurant; hotel will arrange golf, boating, tennis. AE, DC, MC, V.*

$$ **Hotel Ashiwada.** This Japanese-style hotel on Lake Kawaguchi has been designed as a utilitarian base for those interested in seeking the recreational facilities in the area rather than sitting around the hotel. The staff are helpful and, though Japanese food is served in the small dining room, they will make English breakfasts. ☎ *395 Nagahama, Ashiwadamura, Minami-Tsuru-gun, Yamanashi 401-04, ☎ 05558/2–2321. 40 Japanese-style and 4 Western-style rooms, some with private bath. Japanese dining room, laundry room. AE, DC, MC, V.*

LAKE YAMANAKA

$$$ **Hotel Mount Fuji.** The best resort hotel on Lake Yamanaka, the Mount Fuji offers all the facilities needed for a recreational holiday, and its guest rooms are larger than those at the other hotels on the lake. The lounges are spacious, rather like waiting rooms, but they do offer fine views of the lake and mountain. Rates are about 20% higher on weekends. ☎ *Yamanaka, Yamanakakomura, Yamanashi 401-05, ☎ 0555/62–2111. 88 Western-style rooms, 4 Japanese-style. Western and Japanese restaurants, pool, tennis, golf, skating. AE, DC, MC, V.*

$$–$$$ **New Yamanakako Hotel.** Though the rooms are slightly smaller than those at Hotel Mount Fuji, the New Yamanakako has its own thermal pool, especially pleasant after summer hiking or winter skating. Rates go up dramatically on weekends and in August. ☎ *Yamanaka, Yamanakakomura, Yamanashi 401-05, ☎ 05556/2–2311. 63 rooms, mostly Western-style. Western and Japanese restaurants, thermal pool, tennis. AE, DC, V.*

4 Nagoya, Ise-Shima, and the Kii Peninsula

A two-hour train ride from Tokyo, Nagoya is Japan's fourth largest city, an industrial metropolis whose most notable tourist attractions are Nagoya Castle and the shrine known as Atsuta Jingu. South of the city is Ise-Shima National Park, which encompasses the Grand Shrines of Ise, the most venerated shrines in Japan. Farther south, the Kii Peninsula has magnificent marine scenery, coastal fishing villages and resorts, and Mt. Yoshino, with perhaps the finest display of cherry blossoms in Japan.

GAZING OUT THE WINDOW OF the Shinkansen as it speeds out of Tokyo, you will see one continuous strip of factories and concrete office blocks.

By Nigel Fisher This is the industrial quarter of Honshu, which stretches all the way to Hiroshima—to some, an economic miracle. The sight is most likely to make travelers want to stay on the train in the vain hope of reaching the greenery of travel-brochure Japan. But there are reasons to disembark: Kyoto, Japan's capital for more than 10 centuries, is located along this route, and to the north and south of this corridor lie lush countryside and small towns still rich in traditional culture. Consider stopping first in Nagoya to explore areas to the city's north and southwest.

Nagoya, Japan's fourth largest city, has only a few major national treasures. The two most important are Nagoyajo (Nagoya Castle) and Atsuta Jingu (shrine). The city is not among Japan's most attractive, but it is a convenient base from which to set out into the countryside. After visiting the major sights of Nagoya, the first recommended excursion takes you on a trip of one or two days to the north of the city to see cormorant fishing, sword making, fertility shrines, and much more. Heading south from Nagoya, the second and longer excursion covers the Grand Shrines of Ise, the Shima Peninsula and its pearl industry, and proceeds to the Kii Peninsula, including Mt. Koya and Mt. Yoshino. This second excursion ends at Nara.

NAGOYA

A visit to Nagoya today gives little indication of the city's role in the Tokugawa period (1603–1868), when Nagoya was an important stop between Kyoto and Edo (Tokyo). In 1612, Ieyasu Tokugawa established Nagoya town by permitting his ninth son to build a castle. In the shadow of this magnificent castle, industry and merchant houses sprang up, as did pleasure quarters for the samurai. A town was born, and because of its location between Kyoto and Edo, the seat of the shogunate, it quickly grew in strategic importance. Supported by taxing the rich harvests of the vast surrounding Nobi plain, the Tokugawa family used the castle as its power center for the next 250 years. By the early 1800s, Nagoya's population had grown to around 100,000. Although it was smaller than Edo, where the million-plus population surpassed even Paris, Nagoya had become as large as the more established cities of Kanazawa and Sendai.

Only with the Meiji Restoration in 1868, however, when Japan embraced Western ideas and technology, did Nagoya develop as a port city. Once its harbor was open to international shipping (1907), Nagoya's industrial growth accelerated, so that by the 1930s it was supporting Japanese expansionism in China with munitions and aircraft. That particular choice of industry caused Nagoya's ruin. American bombers virtually razed the city to the ground during World War II. Very little was left standing by the time the Japanese surrendered unconditionally, on August 14, 1945.

Nagoya came back as an industrial metropolis. Except for the fact that every building is of recent vintage, there is no evidence of its war-blitzed past. Now the fourth largest city in Japan, Nagoya bustles with 2.2 million people living in its 126.5-square-mile area. Industry is booming, with shipbuilding, food processing, and the manufacturing of ceramics, railway rolling stock, automobiles, textiles, machine tools, and even aircraft. Nagoya has become prosperous: a comfortable cosmopolitan town for its 36,000 foreign residents, but with only a few sites to interest the visitor.

In rebuilding this city, urban planners created the new Nagoya on the grid system, with wide avenues intersecting at right angles. Hisaya-odori, a broad avenue with a park in its meridian (328 feet wide) bisects the town. At its center is Nagoya's symbol of modernity, an imposing 590-foot-high television tower; it is ugly to look at but useful for visitors to establish their bearings. To the north of the tower is Nagoyajo, to the west are the botanical gardens and zoo, to the south is Atsuta Jingu, and to the east is the Japan Railways (JR) station. The main downtown commercial area is centered around the Sakae subway station, and a secondary commercial area has developed next to the JR station.

Exploring

Numbers in the margin correspond to points of interest on the Nagoya map.

❶ With its rectangular layout, Nagoya is simple to navigate. JR trains arrive at the **Nagoya Railway Station,** where this tour of the city begins. First, stop at the Visitor's Information Office in the middle of the station's central mall, identified by a big red question mark. Even if the tourist section, with its English-speaking attendant, is closed, you can collect an English-language map from the other officials behind the counter. In Japanese or sign language, they can also give directions and obtain hotel reservations for you.

Four subway lines run under the city's main avenues. To get to the first attraction on this tour, Nagoyajo, take the Higashiyama Line, located in front of the railway station, to the center of town (walking takes about 15 minutes) or take bus No. 8 directly to Nagoyajo. The subway is easy to manage, because all subway signs are written in both Japanese and English. Get off at Sakae, the second stop, where you can either change for the Meijo subway line and ride one stop to Shiyakusho Station, or exit in the middle of downtown Nagoya and walk up Hisaya-odori (avenue) past the 590-foot-tall TV tower to Nagoyajo.

❷ Your Nagoya tourist brochure will suggest taking the elevator up the **TV tower** to its observation platform for the view. Certainly, if there is no smog, haze, or clouds, you will get a wide panorama that reaches the Japan Alps to the north and Ise Bay to the south. However, what you mostly see is the city, and, if you have seen urban sprawls before, the view will simply add to that tiresome list. ☛ ¥700. ☼ *Mon.–Fri. 10–5:20, Sat. and Sun. 10–8.*

❸ Continuing up Hisaya-odori, past the Prefectural Government Office and Shiyakusho subway station, you catch your first glimpse of **Nagoyajo.** The castle was originally built in 1612, severely damaged in 1945, and rebuilt with ferro-concrete in 1959. It is famous for its impressive size and the pair of golden dolphins, male and female, mounted on the roof of the donjon (stronghold). The donjon and the dolphins are replicas, but they are faithful to their originals. In contrast to the castle's exterior, however, the interior makes no attempt to replicate the original residential quarters of the Tokugawa family. Instead, you'll find a museum containing artifacts—toys, armor, swords, and so forth—from the original castle. Completely incongruous to this re-created 17th-century castle is an elevator that takes visitors between floors; yet

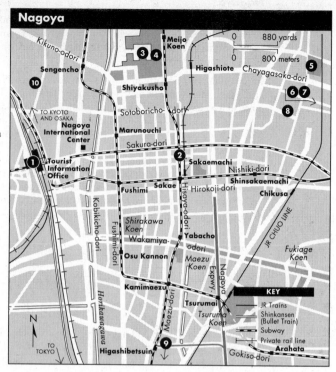

without it, you might miss the fourth floor of the castle. Here is a collection of paper dolls representing the people who take part in the city's Chrysanthemum Exhibition, held in October.

4 To the east of the castle, but within the castle complex, is **Ninomaru Teien.** The refined simplicity of these gardens makes them a place to restore one's inner harmony, which Nagoya's traffic does its best to undermine. However, during the October festival, the display of chrysanthemum bushes can be disconcerting. Each bush is shaped so that its flowers form faces and hands. Then, the bush is dressed in costumes and arranged to represent a legend or historic event. The effect is extremely surrealistic, resembling a fantasy filled with flower children. ☛ *Castle and gardens ¥500.* ⊙ *9:30–4:30. Closed Dec. 29–Jan. 1.*

★ **5** After the castle, the next Nagoya attraction worth visiting is the **Tokugawa Bijutsukan** (art museum). Walk back to Shiyakusho Station and take the Meitetsu Seto train line two stops to Ozone Station, or take bus No. 16 from "Stop 6" (near Shiyakusho Station) to Shindekamachi. Because the museum is on a back street, you may need to ask directions.

Some 7,000 historical treasures are stored in the Tokugawa Bijutsukan, but only a fraction of the collection is displayed at any one time. All that you can be sure of seeing are ancient armor, swords, paintings, and assorted artifacts from the Tokugawa family. For many, the main reason for visiting the museum is the various picture scrolls, including one illustrating the *Tale of Genji.* If you'd like to see the scrolls, ask someone at your hotel to telephone the museum to make sure they are on display. ☎ *052/935–6262.* ☛ *¥1,000.* ⊙ *10–4:30. Closed Mon.*

From the Tokugawa Museum, take a 15-minute brisk walk east along Chayagasaka-dori. After passing Nagoya Women's College, take a

6 right down Tenma-dori. This will lead to **Nittaiji,** a temple given to Japan by the king of Siam in 1904. Supposedly, its function is to serve as a repository for Buddha's ashes, but all you can see is a magnificent gilded Buddha. In fact, the actual temple is less noteworthy than the nearby

7 **Gohyaku Rakan Hall** (Hall of the 500 Disciples), with rows of Buddha's 500 disciples carved in wood, each statue in a slightly different

8 pose from the others. Back toward the city center is **Kenchuji,** a temple famous for its original two-story gate (1651), and one of the few Nagoya structures to survive the bombing of World War II.

9 If Nagoyajo is the number one tourist attraction in Nagoya, **Atsuta Jingu,** in the southern part of the city, is number two. To get to the shrine from either the Tokugawa Bijutsukan or the castle and downtown, take the Meijo subway line south to Jingunishi Station. Take a right as you leave the station and walk down the main avenue.

For 1,700 years, a shrine has been at the site of Atsuta Jingu. The current one is, like Nagoyajo, a concrete replica of the one destroyed in World War II. That diminishes neither its importance nor the reverence in which it is held by the Japanese. Atsuta Jingu remains one of the three most important shrines in the country and has the distinction of serving as the repository of one of the emperor's three imperial regalia, the Kusanagi-no-Tsurugi (Grass Mowing Sword). The shrine is located on thickly wooded grounds, with a 15th-century bridge (Nijugochobashi). The attraction is an oasis of tradition in the midst of bustling, modern industrialism. When you witness Shinto priests blessing newborn children held in the arms of their kimono-clad mothers, you will easily recognize the reverence Atsuta Jingu is still accorded. Some 60 traditional festivals, albeit many small ones, are held here each year—check with the tourist office so that you may schedule your trip to the shrine to coincide with an event of old Japan. ☛ *Free.* ☾ *Sunrise–sunset.*

A little farther to the south of the shrine is **Nagoyako Port,** now Japan's third largest port, after Kobe and Tokyo. From here, Honda, whose factories are in Nagoya's suburbs, ships its automobiles around the world.

10 The last place of major interest in Nagoya is the **Noritake China Factory,** a 15-minute walk north of Nagoya Railway Station or five minutes from the Kamajima subway station (one stop north of Nagoya Station on the Higashiyama Line). Noritake is the world's largest manufacturer of porcelain. A free, one-hour tour of the factory is offered, with an English-speaking guide and a short film. ☏ *052/562–5072.* ☾ *Weekdays 10–4. 1-hr. factory tours at 10 and 1. Reservations required for the tour.*

Rather than making purchases at the factory, you may want to browse through the downtown shops. To return downtown, get on the Higashiyama Line at Kamajima Station, traveling toward Nagoya Station and on to Sakae (the third stop). **Sakae** is not only Nagoya's shopping center but also the entertainment center, with hundreds of bars and small restaurants. Many of these restaurants display their dishes with prices in the windows, so you may decide what you want and how much it will cost before you enter. Furthermore, because Nagoya strives to be an international city, Westerners are usually welcomed without the fluster of embarrassment that sometimes greets them in less cosmopolitan areas.

EXCURSIONS FROM NAGOYA

While Nagoya is modern Japan hurtling into the 21st century, traditional Japan is still visible to the north and south of the city. The two
excursions described below take in most of these sights. The first covers a circular route to the north of Nagoya. The second goes southwest to the Shima Peninsula, from which you can either return to
Nagoya or, better yet, continue on to Nara and Kyoto—either directly
or, as we have done in this excursion, via the Kii Peninsula.

Gifu and North of Nagoya

*Numbers in the margin correspond to points of interest on the Nagoya
Excursions map.*

To the north of Nagoya, and not more than an hour or so by train,
are several places of interest whose origins for the most part are centuries old. The general area is the southern part of the Gifu Prefecture,
an area that also includes the mountains of the Japan Alps around
Takayama. However, this tour does not go that far north and instead
keeps within the foothills of the mountains.

❶ Begin this excursion at **Gifu** and work your way back down to Nagoya.
Gifu is a half-hour's journey on the Tokaido Line train from Nagoya
and can easily be visited in a day. During the summer, however, if you
want to watch the evening event of cormorant fishing in the rivers, it's
a good idea to make this an overnight excursion.

Bombing during World War II destroyed the attractiveness of Gifu, but
the city still draws visitors for several reasons, although you may wish
to skip it and go straight to Inuyama. Gifu is famous for making paper
lanterns and umbrellas, for cormorant fishing, and for its bathhouses,
which have been described as "sex spas." The last may not interest most
foreigners, but they do seem to raise the local hotel prices. Gifu is also
a major manufacturer of apparel, and you'll see some 2,000 wholesale shops crammed on a couple of city blocks as you leave the station. A **city tourist office** is located at the train station (☎ 0582/62–4415).

Umbrellas are made by certain families in small shops. Though these
umbrellas are available in Gifu's downtown stores, there are one or
two umbrella-making shops a 15-minute walk to the southeast of the
JR station. If you speak a little Japanese, the shop owner may invite
you back to watch the process. The easiest store to visit is **Sakaida's**
(☎ 0582/63–0111).

Lantern making is easier to observe. The major factory, **Ozeki** (☎
0582/63–0111), welcomes visitors. To reach Ozeki, take the tram toward downtown Gifu and disembark at the Daigaku Byoin-mae stop,
the fifth from Gifu Station. It's at the junction of the main road, which
leads to the Kinkazan Tunnel. The factory is up this road on the left.
Visitors are led through the process of winding bamboo or wire around
several pieces of wood to give the lantern shape. The tour then pro-
gresses to where the paper is pasted onto the bamboo. Once the paste
has dried, the pieces of wood that have given the lantern its shape are
removed from one end of the lantern. The actual design on the lantern
may either be stenciled on the paper at the beginning of the process or
painted on by hand after the lantern has been made. To arrange to see
the lantern-making process, consult the information desk at your hotel.

Ukai (cormorant fishing) is the major summer evening event for locals
and visitors. It is an organized spectator attraction and an occasion for

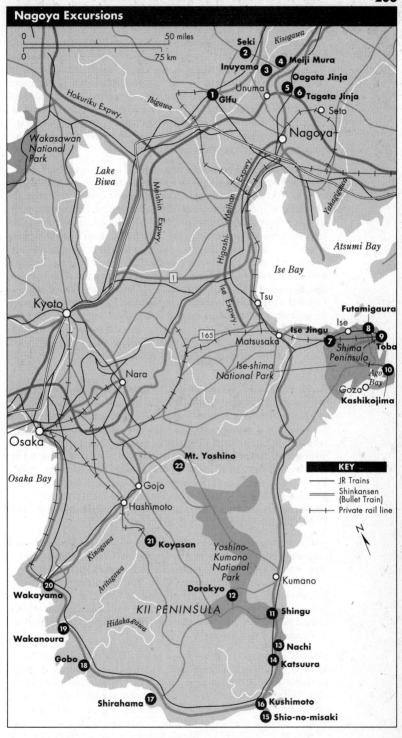

Nagoya Excursions

Seki ②
Inuyama ③
④ **Meiji Mura**
⑤ ⑥ **Tagata Jinja**
Oagata Jinja
① **Gifu**
Unuma
Seto
Nagoya

50 miles
75 km

Kisogawa

Hokuriku Expwy.

Ibigawa

Wakasawan National Park

Lake Biwa

Meishin Expwy.

Higashi-Meihan Expwy.

Yahagigawa

Atsumi Bay

Ise Bay

Kyoto

1

Ise Expwy.

Tsu

Futamigaura

Ise ⑧
⑨ **Toba**
Ise Jingu ⑦

165

Matsusaka

Shima Peninsula

Ise-shima National Park

⑩

Ago Bay

Goza

Kashikojima

Nara

Osaka

Osaka Bay

Mt. Yoshino
㉒

Gojo

Hashimoto

㉑ **Koyasan**

Yoshino-Kumano National Park

Kumano

Kinogawa

Dorokyo
⑫

⑪ **Shingu**

Aritagawa

KII PENINSULA

Hidakagawa

⑬ **Nachi**

⑭ **Katsuura**

㉔
Wakayama

⑲
Wakanoura

Gobo ⑱

Shirahama ⑰

⑯ **Kushimoto**

⑮ **Shio-no-misaki**

KEY

— JR Trains
══ Shinkansen (Bullet Train)
┼─┼ Private rail line

N

partying while watching a centuries-old way of catching fish. Fishermen, dressed in the traditional costume of reed skirts, glide down the river in their boats. Suspended in front of each boat is a wood brazier burning bright to attract *ayu* (river smelt or sweet fish) to the surface. *U* (cormorants), several to a boat, are slipped overboard on leashes to snap up the fish. Because of a small ring around each of the birds' necks, the fish never quite reach the cormorants' stomachs. Instead, their long necks expand to hold five wiggling fish. When a bird can't take in another fish, the fisherman hauls the bird back to the boat, where it is made to regurgitate its neckful. The actual fishing takes less than a half-hour, but the partying lasts much longer.

Approximately 130 boats, carrying 10 to 30 spectators in each, heave-to in the Nagaragawa (river) about two hours before the fishing commences. This is party time, given to eating and drinking. A boat, full of singing and dancing maidens dressed as geisha, drifts through the spectator boats. Other boats ply the river, selling food and drink. Because the ayu are attracted by the light from a boat's wood-burning braziers, no fishing occurs when the river is muddy from heavy rains or on nights when there is a full moon. Tickets for the spectator boats are sold in most of Gifu's hotels and also at the main ticket office downstream from the Nagarabashi (bridge). *Cost: about ¥2,650 (more in July and Aug., less in June and Sept.) without food or drink. However, because the spectacle lasts several hours, most people buy the ticket with food, for ¥3,500. The ticket office opens at 6, but you may make advance reservations through the Gifu City Spectators Office,* ☎ *0582/62–0104, or at the Gifu City Tourist Agency at the station,* ☎ *0582/62–4415.*

Architectural sights in Gifu are worth visiting only if you have the spare time to wander around waiting for ukai. An unusual statue of Buddha (45 feet tall), with a 6-foot-long ear as a symbol of omnipotent wisdom, is housed in an orange and white building, **Shoji.** This building is easy to recognize from the street as you ride the bus from the train station into downtown Gifu and toward the river. It is about a five-minute walk from its entrance to the cable car that takes you to Mt. Kinka. The statue, one of the three largest Buddhas in Japan, was completed in 1832 after 38 years of pasting together 2,000 pounds of paper *sutra* (prayers); this was then coated with clay and stucco before being lacquered and gilded.

The other major feature of Gifu is **Gifujo** (Gifu Castle), which houses a museum and stands before Mt. Kinka (Mt. Gold). The castle is relatively new (1951), having replaced a 16th-century structure that was destroyed by an earthquake in 1891. You can either climb up the mountainside or take the aerial gondola (called a "ropeway" in Japanese-borrowed English), but the castle really looks its best at night from down below, when it is illuminated. ☛ *¥400.* ⊙ *Spring and fall, 9–6; summer, 9–7; winter, 9–4:30.*

❷ **Seki,** 15 kilometers (9 miles) north of Gifu via a tramcar/train, is one of the most famous traditional centers of sword production, and a must to visit if you can time your trip to coincide with a (free) demonstration. This show will help you understand the artistry and mystique of the traditional Japanese sword, which may cost around ¥6 million. *Demonstrations are held at the Sangyo Shinko (Industry Promotion) Center,* ☎ *05752/2–3131. The show is given 5 times a day on the 1st Sun. of the month; in Oct. it's held on the 2nd Sun.; in Jan. it is held on Jan. 2.*

❸ The next stop is **Inuyama.** Though the JR line can be used from Gifu, the privately operated Meitetsu Line is more convenient. If you want to make use of a JR Rail Pass, take the JR train to Unuma and change to the Meitetsu Line for a three-minute ride to Inuyama. If you are coming straight from Seki, the JR line goes to Inuyama. Coming to Inuyama directly from Nagoya, take the Meitetsu Line, which continues on to Gifu.

★ Inuyama is known for having Japan's oldest existing castle, **Inuyama-jo,** built in 1440. It is not a grand structure, but it is pleasant to see the real thing rather than another concrete replica. The top floor of this quaint four-story castle is a lookout room that offers a commanding view of the river below. ☛ ¥300. ⊘ 9–5. Closed Dec. 29–Jan. 1.

Even better is Inuyamajo's location on a cliff above a pretty stretch of the **Kisogawa** (river), which has been dubbed "Nihon Rhine" (the Japanese Rhine); a large rock rises dramatically out of the water here. A pleasant way to see the river is by raft (completely safe). To take this 13-kilometer (8-mile) river trip, take the train on the Meitetsu Hirome Line from Inuyama to Nihon-Rhine-Imawatri. Once there, check out several companies before selecting the type of boat you prefer. A well-established company is the Nippon Rhine Kanko (☎ 0574/26–2231). The trip downstream takes about one hour and costs ¥3,400.

Inuyama also offers another opportunity to watch cormorant fishing, and, as in Gifu, tickets are available from the major hotels. Because there is no difference between cormorant fishing in Gifu and Inuyama, the choice is best decided by where you will be at nightfall, bearing in mind that Inuyama is the more attractive town. Ticket prices for the spectator boats are the same. (Trips also run from Nagoya to watch cormorant fishing; the cost, which includes round-trip transportation, is ¥7,680; Nagoya Yuran Bus, ☎ 052/541–4036.)

In Urakuen (garden) of the Meitetsu Inuyama Hotel and 350 meters (yards) from the castle is the **Jo-an Teahouse.** Registered as a national treasure, the building was constructed by Grand Master Urakusai Oda in 1618 and moved to its present site only recently. ☛ ¥800 for teahouse and gardens; additional ¥500 for tea. ⊘ Daily 9–5. You may also hire the tea house for your own private ceremony at ¥20,000.

❹ A short distance to the east and south of Inuyama, accessible by a direct bus that takes 20 minutes from Inuyama or by the Meitetsu-Komaki Line, is **Meiji Mura** (park); get off at the Meiji Mura-guchi Station and take a bus for 5 kilometers (3 miles) to the park. More than 50 buildings from the Meiji Restoration (1868–1912) have been transplanted here. Emperor Meiji, who regained his imperial power from the Tokugawa Shogun dynasty, opened the doors of Japan to the West and began Japan's rapid transformation into a modern economy. This transformation is illustrated by Meiji Mura's exhibits. Traditional buildings, such as a Kabuki theater and a bathhouse, exist alongside Christian places of worship and Western-style mansions. The 19th-century buildings and Western architecture make this park more appealing to the Japanese than to Westerners. An exception may be the lobby taken from the old Imperial Hotel, which was designed by Frank Lloyd Wright. ☎ 0568/67–0314. ☛ ¥1,550. ⊘ Mar.–Oct., 10–5; Nov.–Feb., 10–4. To reach Meiji Mura directly from Nagoya, take the 1-hour bus *journey (fare: ¥1,120) from the Meitetsu Bus Center, a 5-min. walk from JR Nagoya Station.*

More fascinating for the foreign tourist are two of Japan's most accessible fertility shrines, **Oagata Jinja** (the first stop southeast of Meiji Mura) and **Tagata Jinja** (two stops southeast of Meiji Mura). Both stops are on the Komaki Line. Oagata Jinja, the female shrine, attracts women who are about to marry and wives who want children. Most of the objects in the shrine are symbols to that end, such as a cleft rock resembling female genitalia. Tagata Jinja is the male shrine, with a bewildering collection of phalluses, ranging in size from a few inches to 6 feet, left as offerings by thankful mothers.

The big event at Tagata Jinja is on March 15, when a splendid festival is held; sake flows liberally from morning to night. The festival's focal point is a 9-foot phallus, carried by a woman who is accompanied by a Shinto priest (with an elongated nose) and by several other women carrying more modest-size male accoutrements. The procession, which starts from a minor shrine on the other side of town, makes frequent stops to imbibe from sake casks set up at the side of the road. The participants become progressively drunker; when they finally reach Tagata Jinja in the late afternoon, the entire village is seeing double.

TIME OUT   If you have to wait for a train in Takata Jinja, drop into **Terukumni** (☎ 0508/ 77–9647), a small *nomiya* (informal bar) located on the main street not far from the station. There is sushi if you are hungry, but you can also order just a beer.

From Tagata Jinja, you can hop on board a train at the Tagata Station and be back in Nagoya in 30 minutes, but you will need to transfer to the Miejo subway line at Kamijida. It may be easier to return to Inuyama and take the direct train to Nagoya.

Ise-Shima National Park and the Kii Peninsula

Southwest of Nagoya are the Shima and Kii peninsulas. On the Shima Peninsula are the most venerated shrines in Japan, Ise Jingu. The shrines are part of Ise-Shima National Park, which extends from the city of Ise to Toba, the center of the pearl industry, and south to Kashikojima, with its indented coastline studded with pine-clad islands. The Kii Peninsula, southwest of the Shima Peninsula, boasts magnificent marine scenery, coastal fishing villages and resorts, and Yoshino-Kumano National Park. The latter features pristine gorges, holy mountains, and two large, ancient Buddhist community complexes, one of which, Mt. Yoshino, has perhaps the finest display of cherry blossoms in Japan.

A traveler may visit the Ise Jingu in a day or all of the Shima Peninsula in two. To cover both the Shima Peninsula and the Kii Peninsula requires a minimum of five days. You can also take a full-day tour to Ise and the Mikimoto Pearl Island at Toba from Kyoto or Osaka for ¥24,800, through **Sunrise Tours** (☎ 075/361–7241).

★ ❼   **Ise Jingu** (also called the Grand Shrines of Ise) in Ise are the most recommended attractions to visit outside Nagoya. You may travel to the shrines from Nagoya on a JR train, but the trip requires a train change, usually at Taki, and each train is a local. The fastest and most direct route is the Limited Express on the privately owned Kintetsu Line (fare: ¥2,280; taking the Kintetsu train all the way to Kashikojima costs

¥3,100). Even if you have a JR Rail Pass, the time saved on the Kintetsu may be worth the extra cost.

The journey out of Nagoya takes you through depressing industrial suburbs, but don't despair. Thirty minutes before Ise, the polluting factories end and the farmlands begin. Ise is a small town whose major business comes from the pilgrims who pay respects to the Outer Shrine and the Inner Shrine. From either the Kintetsu or the JR train station it is only a 10-minute walk through town to the Outer Shrine. A frequent shuttle bus makes the 6-kilometer (4-mile) trip between the Outer and Inner Shrines; a bus also goes directly from the Inner Shrine to Ise Station. The most crowded times to visit the shrines are during the Grand Festival held October 15–17 every year, when thousands come to see the pageantry, and on New Year's Eve and Day when Shinto believers pray for a good new year.

Astounding as it may be, the main halls at both the Outer and Inner Shrines are, in accord with Shinto tradition, torn down every 20 years. New constructions are then built, as exact replicas of the previous halls, using the same centuries-old method, on adjacent sites. The main halls you see now were completed in 1993 at a cost estimated to be over ¥4.5 billion.

Deep in a park full of ancient cryptomeria (Japanese cedar), the **Outer Shrine** (Geku), which dates from AD 478, is dedicated to Toyouke-Omikami, goddess of grain and agriculture. Its buildings are simple, predating the surge of Chinese influence that swept through the country in the 6th century. Its plain design makes it seem part of the magnificent grounds; it is made from unpainted *hinoki* (cypress wood), with a fine, closely shaven thatch roof. Unfortunately, the visitor can see very little of the exterior of the Geku and none of its interior. Four fences surround the shrine, and only the imperial family and its envoys may enter it.

The same is true for the even more venerated **Inner Shrine** (Naiku), southwest of Geku. Naiku is where the Yata-no-Kagami (Sacred Mirror) is kept, one of the three sacred treasures of the imperial regalia. This shrine is also the home to Amaterasu, the sun goddess and the highest deity in the Shinto pantheon. (The name "Japan" in Japanese is *Nihon,* meaning "the origin of the sun.") Amaterasu, born of the left eye of Izanagi (in Japanese mythology, the first god to inhabit earth), was the great-great-grandmother of the first mortal emperor of Japan, Jinmu. Seventy generations later, Hirohito, who led Japan through World War II and into prosperous peacetime, became the 123rd divine emperor. Hirohito, however, renounced his divine relationship at the insistence of the U.S. occupation forces.

The Grand Shrines both have more of a natural harmony with nature than the more controlled, even contrived, buildings in later Japanese architecture. The Inner Shrine's architecture is simple. If one did not know its origin, one would term it classically modern. Again, the use of unpainted cypress causes the shrine to blend into the ancient forest that circles it and covers the grounds of the 63-acre park. As with Geku, the visitor can see very little through the wooden fences surrounding the shrine. Although the sightseeing is limited at the Grand Shrines, one's reward is in feeling the sanctity surrounding both sights. This experience is totally Japanese, one that Westerners can only begin to understand. ☞ *Grounds of both shrines free. Grounds open sunrise–sunset.*

Two routes may be followed onward to Toba, the resort town made famous by Mikimoto pearls. You can take a 45-minute bus ride from near the Inner Shrine for ¥910. There is one bus every hour, with the last bus at 3:56 PM. The bus goes along the **Ise-Shima Skyline Drive,** which offers fine mountainous and wooded scenery. The other alternative, and perhaps the more memorable, is to take the JR train (it follows the coast road) from Ise to Toba (fare: ¥560) with a stop at **8** **Futamigaura,** a popular spot for Japanese lovers. Two rocks, one said to be male and the other female, rise out of the water. Because they are of the opposite sex, the Japanese married them, linking the two together with a straw rope (replaced every Jan. 5 as part of a cheerful festival). These rocks, known as the **Meoto-Iwa** (wedded rocks), represent Izanagi and Izanami, Japan's Adam and Eve.

9 Back on the train, it is less than 10 minutes to **Toba,** where the cultivation of pearls was perfected. Before Kokichi Mikimoto completed his technique for harvesting pearl-bearing oysters at the turn of the century, pearls were a rare freak of nature. *Ama* (female divers—women were believed to have bigger lungs) could dive all day long; even after bringing up a thousand oysters, they might not find one with a valuable pearl. Thanks to Mikimoto, the odds have changed. Nevertheless, even after the considerable effort of injecting an irritating substance—muscarine, from Iowa—into two-year-old oysters, only one in two bears pearls, and no more than 5% are of gem quality. Because the two-year-old oyster takes three more years to secrete layer after layer of nacre over his irritating implant to form the pearl, these gems remain expensive.

Before pearl-oyster farming, women dove for pearls with more frequency than now. Such a hit-or-miss operation can no longer support them in face of the larger quantities (and cheaper prices) possible through Mikimoto's research and farming. However, on the outlying islands, women do still dive for abalone, octopus, and edible seaweed.

On **Pearl Island,** 500 meters (yards) from Toba Station, **Mikimoto's Museum** (he died in 1954) gives a fascinating, if a little long-winded, account of pearl cultivation. (The tours are in Japanese, but the guides usually speak some English and the accompanying film has an English voice-over.) A demonstration is also given by female pearl divers. ☛ ¥850. ☉ 8:30–5 (9–4 in winter).

Toba is a resort town with resort hotels and activities. An aquarium displays native and exotic marine life, such as rare Alaskan sea otters and Baikal seals (☛ ¥2,000; ☉ 8–5). The ship **Brazil Maru,** which transported many Japanese rice farmers to Brazil, is now a floating entertainment center with restaurants and souvenir shops (☛ ¥1,050; ☉ Daily 8:30–4:30). Cruise boats make 50-minute tours of Toba Bay (cost: ¥1,460), and ferries go to the outer islands. Because the town has a couple of reasonable hotels (Toba International offers the best views; *see* Dining and Lodging, *below*), Toba is a possible overnight stop. Alternatively, Kashikojima is 40 minutes away by rail.

★ **10** The Kintetsu Line continues from Toba to **Kashikojima** (fare: about ¥900), in the center of Ago Bay, but the tracks cut inland. (There are also two buses a day at 9:40 and 2:25; fare is ¥1,300.) To appreciate the spectacular coastline, disembark the train at Ugata and take the bus to Nakiri. Then change buses for the one going along the headland to Goza, a small fishing village that faces Kashikojima from across Ago Bay. From Goza, frequent ferries navigate past hundreds of rafts, from which pearl-bearing oysters are suspended, to Kashikojima. The jagged coastline at Ago Bay presents a dramatic final view of the Ise Peninsula. The town of Kashikojima is now the pearl center and has a few reasonable hotels for an overnight stay; the most sophisticated is the Shima Kanko Hotel (*see* Dining and Lodging, *below*). Consider, however, one of the smaller guest houses, such as the Asanaro, where you will have the opportunity to meet the local community. Be sure to visit Daio, the fishing village tucked behind a promontory. Standing above the village is a grand lighthouse (☛ ¥80; ⊘ Daily 9–5). To reach this towering structure, walk up the narrow street lined with fish stalls at the back of the harbor. From this lighthouse, you can see Anori, the oldest (1870) stone lighthouse in Japan, 11 kilometers (7 miles) to the east. Between the two lighthouses on the curving bay are small fishing villages, coffee shops, and restaurants. And there are three golf courses here. The Hamajima Country Club (Hamajima 517-04, ☎ 05995/2–1141; greens fees ¥8,750 weekdays, ¥18,000 weekends, caddy ¥3,750) has especially fine views of Ago Bay, dotted with numerous small islands and oyster beds.

It is possible to follow the coast from Kashikojima to the Kii Peninsula, but there is no train and in many places the road cuts inland, making the journey long and tedious. You are far better off taking the Kintetsu Line back from Kashikojima to Ise, where you must change to the JR Sangu Line and travel to Taki, at which point you must change to another JR train, heading south to the peninsula. If you prefer to skip the Kii Peninsula, you can take the Kintetsu Line directly to Nagoya or to Matsusaka, where connections to Nara and Kyoto may be made.

To go to the Kii Peninsula, transfer at Taki to the JR Kisei main line for Shingu and Kushimoto. Take your nap at the beginning of the train ride, for within hours the scenery becomes more and more picturesque as the train runs along the coastline. The first major town is Kumano, not a particularly attractive place, but often used by hikers as a gateway to the Yoshino-Kumano National Park.

⑪ If you have limited time it is better to continue on the train to **Shingu.** This town is home to an important shrine, Kumano-Hayatama-Taisha, but the thrill for the adventurous is to take a four-hour trip (fare: ¥4,750) up the Kumano River on a flat-bottom, air propeller–driven boat to ⑫ **Dorokyo** (Doro Gorge). The trip up the valley is gently attractive, with hills rising on either side of emerald green water. From late May to early June, with azaleas and rhododendrons lining the banks, the valley is a beautiful introduction to the gorge that lies farther upstream. Dorokyo is considered by many to be Japan's finest gorge. Sheer 150-foot cliffs tower above the Kumano River, which alternates between gushing rapids and calm waters. You may also travel up through the valley by taking a 45-minute bus ride from Shingu Station (fare: ¥1,250) or a 30-minute bus ride from Kumano Hongu (fare: ¥1,120).

The boat trip ends at **Doro-hatcho,** the first of the three gorges and rapids that extend for several miles upstream and may also be explored by boat. Long fiberglass boats continue up the gorge for a two-hour round-trip (cost is ¥3,280). A less expensive alternative is a bus up to Kitayamakyo, where there are good glimpses of Doro-hatcho Gorge.

From Doro-hatcho, you can take a bus back to Shingu. If you do not want to continue around the Kii Peninsula, an alternative is to backtrack by bus as far as Shiko and pick up the Shingu-Nara bus. The bus takes seven hours from Shingu (6 hrs. from Shiko) to reach Nara and passes through the heart of Yoshino-Kumano National Park. (The bus stops at Gojo, from where you can make your way to Mt. Koya and Yoshino.)

Back in Shingu, if you have the time, take a quick look at Kumano Hayatama Jinja, one of the three main shrines of Kii Peninsula. Though it is a bright and cheerful place, it is not worth missing your train, unless you are there on October 15 for its festival. The other two main shrines are at Hongu, near Doro-hatcho, and at Nachi, the next stop around the Kii Peninsula.

⑬ To get to **Nachi,** take the local JR train 14 kilometers (9 miles) south. A 20-minute bus ride from the Nachi train station will bring you to the next major attraction, **Nachi-no-taki,** the highest waterfall in Japan, with a drop of 430 feet. At the bus stop near the falls, you'll see a torii at the top of several stone steps, which lead down to a paved clearing near the foot of the falls. For a view from the top, climb up the path from the bus stop to 1,400-year-old **Nachi Taisha,** which, aside from being one of the three great shrines of the Kii area, is perched just above the waterfall. Next to the shrine is the Buddhist temple Seigantoji, a popular stop for pilgrims.

⑭ A couple of miles farther down the coast from Nachi, and the halfway point (6 hrs. either way by rail) between Osaka and Nagoya, is **Katsuura,** located on a pleasant bay surrounding pine-covered islands. Sightseeing boats cruise the bay (cost: ¥1,690), promoting it as Kiino-Matsushima. The bay is named after one of the three big scenic draws in Japan, Matsushima Bay near Sendai, and if you've seen that, taking the cruise is not worth the money.

⑮ Another 48 kilometers (30 miles) down the coast at the bottom of the Kii Peninsula is **Shio-no-misaki,** Honshu's southernmost point, marked by a white lighthouse high above its rocky cliffs. Nearby is the resort **⑯** town of **Kushimoto,** which, with its direct flights to Nagoya and Osaka, has become popular with residents from those cities. Stretching out to sea toward Oshima (the island a mile offshore) is a notable and odd formation of 30 large rocks, spaced evenly as they jut out to sea. They resemble what their name suggests, Hashi-kui-iwa (Rock Pillars), though the more imaginative have seen them as a procession of hooded monks trying to reach Oshima.

⑰ Rounding the peninsula, 54 kilometers (34 miles) to the north, is **Shirahama,** rated (by the Japanese) as one of the three best hot-spring resorts in the country. (The other two are Beppu on Kyushu and Atami on the Izu Peninsula. We would add Noboribetsu Onsen in Hokkaido to these.) Unfortunately, the Japanese have a penchant for building mammoth, drab hotels around their spa waters, and this town fits that mold. But it does have some attractive coastal scenery, so Shirahama can be a pleasant place for an overnight stay. The town itself is a 17-minute bus ride from the train station.

⑱ Between Shirahama and Wakanoura is the famous **Dojoji** (temple) in **Gobo.** According to legend, Kiyohime, a farmer's daughter, became enamored of a young priest, Anchin, who often passed by her house. One day she blurted out her feelings to him. He, in turn, promised to return that night to see her. However, during the course of the day, the priest had second thoughts and returned to Dojoji. Spurned, Kiyohime became enraged. She turned herself into a dragon and set in pursuit of Anchin, who, scared out of his wits, hid under the temple bell that had not yet been suspended. Kiyohime sensed his presence and wrapped her dragon body around the bell. Her fiery breath heated the bell until it became red-hot. The next morning, only the charred remains of Anchin's body were found under the bell.

⑲ Equally as good as Shirahama for an overnight stay is **Wakanoura,** 48 kilometers (30 miles) farther north. This resort makes the rather ambitious claim of having the most beautiful coastal scenery in Japan. A **⑳** few miles north of Wakanoura is **Wakayama,** the largest town on this route since Nagoya. Ferries (from Wakayamako Port) depart for Tokushima on the island of Shikoku. As a city, Wakayama has little of historic interest, but it has become a resort destination, especially for residents of Osaka who live only an hour away. A new mini-city, Wakayama Marina City, built on a man-made island, has developed a theme park called **Porto Europa.** Here the buildings have been given the look of a Mediterranean port town with modern technological amusements that include an underwater safari, a water ride that climaxes in a 72–foot drop, and a high-tech maze that you have to walk and shoot your way through. You don't even have to leave the indoors to enjoy the sea. Just don a head set and then head to VR, a virtual reality interactive game where you find treasure and adventure under the computer ocean. (☛ ¥1,900; ⊙ Daily 9–9.) If this is not your bailiwick, use Wakayama to replenish your supply of camera film, yen, and other needs before traveling inland to visit sacred Koyasan (Mt. Koya) and Mt. Yoshino before ending this itinerary in Nara.

To get to Koyasan, take the JR line to Hashimoto and change to the Nankai Line for the final 19 kilometers (12 miles) to Gokurakubashi Station. From there, a cable car runs up to the top of sacred Mt. Koya. (If you have cut across the Yoshino-Kumano National Park by bus from Shingu or Hongu on Rte. 168, instead of circling the Kii Peninsula, get off the bus at Gojo and backtrack one station on the JR line to Hashimoto for the Nankai Line.)

To reach Koyasan directly from Tokyo or Kyoto, go first to Osaka and take the private Nankai Line that departs for Koyasan every 30 minutes from Namba Station. (To reach Namba Station from Shin-Osaka Shinkansen Station, use the Midosuji subway.) The Osaka-Koyasan journey takes just under two hours, including the five-minute cable car ride up to Koyasan Station, and costs around ¥2,000 (you may want to reserve a seat if you're traveling on a weekend).

★ **㉑** On a mesa amid the mountains is **Koyasan,** a great complex of 120 temples, monasteries, schools, and graves and the seat of the Shingon sect of Buddhism founded by Kobo Daishi in 816. Every year about a million visitors pass through the **Daimon,** a huge wooden gate typical of many entrances to Japanese temples.

The cable car will deposit you at Koyasan Station, at the top of 3,000-foot Mt. Koya, where you can pick up a map. You will need to take a bus to the main attractions, which are about 2½ kilometers (1½ miles) from the station and about 5½ kilometers (3½ miles) from each other, on opposite sides of town.

Two buses leave the station every 20 or 30 minutes, when the cable car arrives. One goes to Okunoin Cemetery, on the eastern side of the main road, and the other goes to the Daimon, on the west side of town. Both buses start out following the same route to the center of town, to a "T" junction, where the tourist office is located (600 Koyasan, Koyacho, Ito-gun, Wakayama-ken, ☎ 07365/6–2616). The bus fare is ¥300 to the tourist office. En route from the station, you will pass the mausoleums of the first and second Tokugawa shoguns. You may want to walk back and visit these two gilded structures later (⊙ 9–5).

If your time is limited, head for **Okunoin Cemetery** first. Take the bus to the Okunoin-mae bus stop, where you can pick up a wide, well-worn path that provides a shortcut to the cemetery's Lantern Hall (you can take the long route out). Many of your fellow visitors will be Japanese, who are making pilgrimages to the mausoleum of Kobo Daishi or paying their respects to their ancestors buried here. The pilgrims often travel in groups; they dress in white and carry wooden staffs. Make sure you arrive very early in the morning, before the groups take over.

Entering this cemetery is like entering Alice's Wonderland. Magnificent 300-year-old cedar trees stretch skyward, some of their dark, textured trunks forming columns 12-feet around. This old-growth forest is a rarity in most places, including Japan. Among the trees are buried some of the country's most illustrious families, their graves marked by moss-covered pagodas and red- and white-robed buddhas carved from black stone. You will feel small here, but contemplative; the holiness of Koyasan is strongly sensed.

The path from Okunoin-mae leads into the main avenue of mausoleums, a cobblestone lane that ends at the **Lantern Hall,** named after its 11,000 lanterns. Two fires burn in this hall: One has been alight since 1016, the other since 1088. Behind the hall is the mausoleum of Kobo Daishi (774–835). *Lantern Hall.* ☉ *Apr.–Oct., 8–5; Nov.–Mar., 8:30–4:30.*

You may be tempted to spend the day wandering through the cemetery, but be careful—it is easy to get lost if you stray from the main avenue. Some people prefer to visit the cemetery at dusk, when the cobbled lane is lit by lanterns, setting an eerie mood. In any case, you should exit Okunoin by way of the 2½-kilometer (1½-miles) main avenue, lined with tombs, monuments, and statues. More than 100,000 historical figures are honored here. The lane exits the cemetery at Ichinohashi-guchi; follow the main street straight ahead to return to the center of town (a 20-min. walk) or wait for the bus that is headed for Kongo-buji.

On the southwestern side of Mt. Koya, **Kongobuji** (Temple of the Diamond Seat) is the chief temple of Shingon Buddhism, a sect that is closest to Tibetan Buddhism. Kongobuji was built in 1592 as the family temple of Hideyoshi Toyotomi, but it was rebuilt in 1861 and is now the main temple of the Koyasan community. ☞ *¥500.* ☉ *8–5; in winter, 8–4:30.*

Walk down the main stairs of the temple and take the road to the right of the parking lot in front of you; in less than five minutes you will reach **Danjogaran,** a complex consisting of many halls as well as the **Daito** (Great Central Pagoda). This red pagoda, with its interior of brilliantly colored beams, is home to five sacred images of Buddha. Built in 1937, the two-story structure stands out in part because of its unusual style, but also because of its rich vermilion color. It's worth taking a look inside. ☞ *¥100 each building.* ☉ *Apr.–Oct., 8–5; Nov.–Mar., 8:30–4:30.*

South and across a small path from the Danjogaran is the **Reihokan,** a museum with a total of 5,000 art treasures. The exhibits are continually changing, but at least some of the 180 pieces that have been designated as national treasures are always on display. The most notable of these are the scroll of Reclining Image of Sakyamuni Buddha on His Last Day (Shaka-nehan-zo) and the exotic images of the Eight Guardian Deities (Hachi-dai-doji-zo). ☞ *¥500.* ☉ *9–5 (9–4 in winter).*

Although you can easily visit Koyasan's major sites in a day trip from Kyoto or Osaka, it is best to spend the night in a Buddhist temple here (*see* Dining and Lodging, *below*).

② The next and final stop before Nara is **Mt. Yoshino,** the other major religious and historic site of the region. To get to Yoshino from Koyasan, rejoin the train at Hashimoto for Yoshino-guchi, and change to the Kintetsu Line for Yoshino. (This Kintetsu Line is the Osaka–Yoshino route, which departs from Abenobashi Station in Osaka. Yoshino may also be reached directly from Kashikojima on the Kintetsu Line.)

Though the community of temples at Mt. Yoshino is less impressive than that of Koyasan, Mt. Yoshino is one of the most beautiful places in Japan to visit during cherry-blossom season. The Cherry Blossom Festival, which attracts thousands of visitors each year, is April 11–12. Because the 100,000 trees in four groves are staggered down the mountainside, and because the temperature changes with the elevation, the wafting sea of pink petals lasts at least two weeks. When you look upon this vision of color, thank En-no-Ozunu, the 7th-century Buddhist priest who planted the trees and put a curse on anyone who tampered with them.

In the middle of the cherry groves is **Kimpusenji,** the main temple of the area. Make a point of seeing the main hall, Zaodo, which is not only the second largest wooden structure in Japan, but also has two superb sculptures of Deva kings at the main gate. The other important temple is **Nyoirinji,** founded in the 10th century and located just to the south of Kimpusenji. Here the last remaining 143 warriors prayed before going into their final battle for the imperial cause in the 14th century. Behind the temple is the mausoleum of Emperor Godaigo (1288–1339), who brought down the Kamakura Shogunate. ☞ *¥350.* ⊘ *9–5.*

Built into the surrounding mountains, Yoshino is a quaint town where the shops—and there are many to serve the thousands of visitors—are on the third floor of the house, the first and second floors being below the road. All around Yoshino are superb mountain vistas and isolated temples. For the pilgrim, Mt. Sanjo is considered the holiest mountain, with two temples at the summit, one of which is dedicated to En-no-Ozunu, the cherry-tree priest. Lodgings are available at both temples May 8–September 27. The **tourist office** (Yoshinoyama, Yoshinomachi, Yoshino-gun, Nara-ken, ☎ 07463/2–3014) can arrange accommodations at local minshuku. From Yoshino, Nara is an hour away (on the Kintetsu Line, with a change either at Kashihara Jingu Station or to the JR line at Yoshino-guchi), and Kyoto is 50 minutes farther north.

DINING AND LODGING

Dining

Nagoya is known for only a few special dishes: **kishimen,** white, flat noodles of the *udon* variety, with a velvety smoothness against the palate; **misonikomi udon,** a thick noodle boiled with chicken and Welsh onion; **moriguchizuke** (Japanese pickle), made from a special radish, pickled either with or without sweet sake; and **uiro,** a sweet cake made of rice powder and sugar, most often eaten during the tea ceremony. The most highly prized food product is the **Nagoya-tori,** a type of chicken similar to the famous French *poulet Bresse*. These chickens are given special feed just before their execution, said to improve the texture and taste of their white meat.

Other than these items, Nagoya's cuisine is mostly Kyoto-style (see Dining in Chapter 6, Kyoto), but every type of Japanese and international food may be found in this cosmopolitan city. For Western cuisine, the best choices in the city are the French restaurants at the Nagoya Castle Hotel, the Nagoya Kanko Hotel, and the International Hotel Nagoya. The one good Western restaurant outside the hotels is the Okura Restaurant.

On the Ise Peninsula, the **lobster** is especially fine. On the Kii Peninsula, farmers raise cattle for **Matsuzaka beef** (the town of Matsuzaka is 90 minutes by train from Nagoya). However, the best beef is typically shipped to Tokyo, Kyoto, and Osaka.

Outside Nagoya, if you want to eat Western food, you should go to the dining rooms of the larger hotels. However, we strongly recommend that you eat out at local Japanese restaurants. Most reasonably priced restaurants have a visual display of their menu in the window. On this basis, you can decide what you want before you enter. If you cannot order in Japanese, and no English is spoken, after securing a table, lead the waiter to the window display and point.

A 3% federal consumer tax is added to all restaurant bills. Another 3% is added to the bill if it exceeds ¥7,500. At more expensive restaurants, a 10%–15% service charge is also added to the bill. Tipping is not the custom.

CATEGORY	COST*
$$$$	over ¥6,000
$$$	¥4,000–¥6,000
$$	¥2,000–¥4,000
$	under ¥2,000

Cost is per person without tax, service, or drinks

Lodging

Nagoya offers a range of lodging, from clean, efficient business hotels offering the basics to large luxury hotels with additional amenities. Nagoya has three major areas in which to stay: the district around the JR Nagoya Station, the downtown area, and Nagoya Castle area. Though ryokan are listed below, international-style hotels are often more convenient for the Nagoya visitor who wants flexible dining hours.

Outside Nagoya, most hotels quote prices on a per-person basis with two meals, exclusive of service and tax. If you do not want dinner at your hotel, it is usually possible to renegotiate the price. Stipulate, too, whether you wish to have Japanese or Western breakfast, if any. The categories assigned to all hotels below reflect the cost of a double room with private bath but no meals. However, if you make reservations at any of the noncity hotels, you will be expected to take breakfast and dinner at the hotel; the rate quoted to you will include these meals unless you specify otherwise.

A 3% federal consumer tax is added to all hotel bills. Another 3% is added to the bill if it exceeds ¥15,000. At most hotels, a 10%–15% service charge is added to the total bill. Tipping is not the custom.

CATEGORY	COST*
$$$$	over ¥20,000
$$$	¥15,000–¥20,000
$$	¥10,000–¥15,000
$	under ¥10,000

Cost is for double room, without tax or service

Nagoya

Dining

$$$$ ★ Koraku. One of the most exclusive restaurants in Nagoya, Koraku is nationally known for its chicken dishes. The restaurant is in an old samurai mansion, with formal service by women dressed in beautiful kimonos. The setting is traditional and refined; guests feel as if they are stepping back into Japan's more noble past. ✕ *3-3 Chikaramachi, Higashi-ku, Nagoya,* ☎ *052/931–3472. Reservations essential, preferably with an introduction. Jacket and tie. AE. No lunch.*

$$$ Kamone. The innovative Japanese menu here adds Chinese and/or French touches to the dishes, and, as if to enhance the foreign culinary influences on the Japanese dishes, the decor is more Western than Japanese—window drapes instead of *shoji* screens, for example. Since the restaurant is on the 15th floor of the Meiji Seimei Building, try for a table with a view. ✕ *1-1 Shin-Sakaemachi, Naka-ku, Nagoya (located across from the Sakaecho subway station exit),* ☎ *052/951–7787. Reservations advised. Jacket and tie. DC, MC, V.* ⊙ *Noon–3 and 5–9. Closed Mon.*

$$$ ★ Okura Restaurant. The Okura has the best French cuisine in Nagoya, outside of the hotels. This is the place where Western businessmen often entertain their Japanese partners. Some recommended dishes include the veal slices with mushrooms in madeira sauce and the steamed salmon. Another good choice is Matsuzaka beef (a Nagoya specialty) served with béarnaise sauce. ✕ *Tokyo Kaijo Bldg., 23rd floor, Naka-ku, Nagoya,* ☎ *052/201–3201. Reservations required. Jacket and tie. AE, DC, V.*

$$$ Torikyu. This traditionally decorated restaurant in a Meiji-period building specializes in chicken dishes—raw, grilled, in a casserole, or as a very formal meal. The restaurant is next to a river, and in the old days, patrons used to arrive by boat. ✕ *1-15 Naiyacho, Nakamura-ku, Nagoya,* ☎ *052/541–1888. Reservations advised. Jacket and tie. AE.* ⊙ *11–9:30. Closed Sun.*

$$$ ★ Yaegaki. This is the best tempura restaurant in town; the fish and vegetables are cooked in front of you. One of the few wood structures among a sea of concrete, Yaegaki has its own small garden. An English-language menu is offered. ✕ *3-7 Nishiki, Naka-ku, Nagoya,* ☎ *052/951–3250. Reservations advised. Jacket and tie. AE, V.* ⊙ *Noon–9. Closed Sun.*

$$ Kani Doraku. The specialty here is crab, either boiled or steamed, elegantly served by waitresses dressed in kimonos. The restaurant, which is located opposite the Nagoya Tokyu Hotel's entrance, may be identified by its small sign of a crab. ✕ *4-chome, Sakae, Naka-ku, Nagoya,* ☎ *052/242–1234. Reservations advised. Jacket and tie. AE, V.*

$$ Kisoji. Not far from the International Hotel Nagoya, Kisoji has a reasonably priced (¥4,000) *shabu-shabu* beef dinner, but if you take the shabu-shabu special with tempura and sashimi, the price increases dramatically. The decor is rustic, but the kimono-clad waitresses give it a touch of tradition and smartness. ✕ *Nishiki 3-chome, Naka-ku, Nagoya,* ☎ *052/951–3755.* ⊙ *11–10. V.*

$$ **Usquebaugh.** This bar/restaurant with a polished wood decor takes its name from the Gaelic word for "water of life"—whiskey. Nautical paintings and gear hang on the walls, and there are some impressive glass-enclosed wine racks. Modern *kaiseki* cuisine is served at reasonable prices; you can also have a light meal at the bar. The restaurant is on Hirokuji-dori, one block east of the Rich Hotel. ✕ *2-4-1 Sakae, Naka-ku, Nagoya,* ☎ *052/201–5811. No reservations. Jacket and tie. AE, DC, MC, V.*

$ **Yamamotoya.** For Nagoya's local dish, misonikomi, you can't beat this no-frills eatery, which serves a steaming bowl of *udon* for ¥1,500. The superb misonikomi is especially welcome during the colder months. Yamamotoya is also a block east of the Rich Hotel. ✕ *2-4-5 Sakae, Naka-ku, Nagoya,* ☎ *052/471–5547. No reservations. No credit cards.*

Lodging

$$$$ **Century Hyatt.** The distinct advantage of the newest (1993) and small-
★ est of the city's leading hotels is its personal service. Stay here a day and the staff know you and you know the staff, most of whom speak some English. Even the television has five of its 30 satellite dedicated to English-language programs, which, outside Tokyo, is unusual. Besides this boutique-hotel approach, another advantage is the Century Hyatt's location, just a five-minute walk from the JR Nagoya Station. Unlike at most Hyatts there is no Regency floor. Instead, free coffee is served all day in the ground-floor lounge. In the evening, guests gather in the restaurant-bar called the Whizz, a comfortable, wood-paneled room where you may choose from a variety of Asian fare—from cheese spring rolls to pizza to such main dishes as Thai-style chicken with shallots and leeks, and *tataki* (lightly blanched bonito). There is also a formal dining room serving Continental cooking and a lounge for afternoon tea. Rooms are pleasantly decorated with dark wood furniture. Space is at a premium, and an extra ¥3,000 buys a much-appreciated extra three square meters to the deluxe rooms. Bathrooms are cozy, but have all the modern necessities, including high-tech toilets. 🏢 *2-43-6 Meiki, Nakamura-ku, Nagoya, Aichi-ken 450,* ☎ *052/541–1234,* 📠 *052/569–1717. U.S. reservations, 800/233–1234. UK reservations, 0171/580–8197. 115 rooms. Restaurants, bar, lounge, business services. AE, DC, MC, V.*

$$$$ **Nagoya Hilton.** Rooms on the upper floors of this late-80s skyscraper have a panoramic view of Nagoya. The light-pastel furnishings and the shoji window screens add to the bright, airy feel of the rooms. The plastic polyurethane covering on the tables and chairs should be eliminated, but the king-size beds are a pleasure. Single travelers do especially well because the hotel has none of the closet-size rooms found in most Japanese hotels. You'll appreciate the attentive, enthusiastic staff. 🏢 *1-3-3 Sakae, Naka-ku, Nagoya, Aichi-ken 460,* ☎ *052/212–1111,* 📠 *052/212–1225. 453 rooms, including 26 suites, and 2 concierge floors. Chinese, Continental, and Japanese restaurants, coffee shop, health club, sauna, indoor pool, massage, tennis court, business services, wedding and conference facilities, and shops. AE, DC, MC, V.*

$$$–$$$$ **Nagoya Castle Hotel.** Its location next to Nagoya Castle makes this
★ the choice sightseer's hotel in Nagoya. A room with a view onto the castle shows Nagoya at its best—especially at night, when the castle is floodlit. The bedrooms are spacious and pleasantly furnished, with original oil paintings. Even the lobby is attractively and hospitably decorated, with plenty of wood paneling. The establishment is efficiently run, with a range of restaurants and bars; at the Rosen Bar, Western and Japanese businessmen meet for a drink after work. The hotel has a new, vast annex of 6,400 square feet of convention halls. 🏢 *3-19*

Hinokuchicho, Nishi-ku, Nagoya, Aichi-ken 451, ☎ 052/521–2121, FAX 052/531–3313. 274 rooms, including 5 suites. Western, Chinese, and Japanese restaurants, indoor pool, beauty salon, health club, shops, business services, and an hourly shuttle bus to the JR station. AE, DC, MC, V.

$$$ **International Hotel Nagoya.** With the best location in the city, the International Hotel has been a longtime favorite with business travelers. It is not the newest accommodation in town, but it maintains a high standard. The lobby resembles that of a European hotel, with gold and dark brown tones and antique furnishings. Some of the rooms are small for the price, but they are comfortably furnished. ⌖ *3-23-3 Nishiki, Naka-ku, Nagoya, Aichi-ken 460, ☎ 052/961–3111, FAX 052/962–5937. 265 Western-style rooms. Western, Chinese, and Japanese restaurants, penthouse bar with live music, business services. AE, DC, MC, V.*

$$$ **Ryokan Suihoen.** A large concrete city, Nagoya is not the ideal setting for old-style ryokan, but this one, in the thick of downtown chaos, is the most traditional, luxurious, and expensive of its kind in Nagoya. The tatami rooms are furnished with good reproductions of traditional furniture. Meals may be served in your room. ⌖ *1-19-20 Sakae, Naka-ku, Nagoya, Aichi-ken 460, ☎ and FAX 052/241–3521. 25 rooms, most with bath. AE.*

$$ **Castle Plaza Hotel.** A five-minute walk from the main railway station, the Castle Plaza is an efficient and top-notch business person's hotel, with more amenities than most. The few Japanese rooms are larger in size than the others. ⌖ *4-3-25 Meieki, Nakamura-ku, Nagoya, Aichi-ken 450, ☎ 052/582–2121, FAX 052/582–8666. 258 Western-style rooms, 4 Japanese-style rooms. Western and Japanese restaurants, indoor pool, sauna, exercise room. AE, V.*

$–$$ **Fitness Hotel 330.** This new business hotel is considerably smarter than neighboring business-category hotels. Rooms, albeit typically small, are done in gay, cheerful fabrics, and there's the ubiquitous wooden cabinet to serve as desk and table top for the TV. The fitness center is high tech, and the business center has a computer work station. A friendly, intimate café and bar is on the ground level next to the lobby. The welcoming staff are good with gesturing, if your Japanese fails you. The hotel is a five-minute walk from the JR Nagoya Station. ⌖ *1-2-7 Sakae, Nakamura-ku, Nagoya, Aichi-ken 450, ☎ 052/562–0330, FAX 052/562–0331. 120 Western rooms. Japanese restaurant, café/bar, health club, business services. AE, DC, MC, V.*

$ **Oyone Ryokan.** In a small wood building, Oyone is a friendly inn resembling a B&B, with small, sparsely furnished rooms. ⌖ *2-2-12 Aoi, Higashi-ku, Nagoya, Aichi-ken 460, ☎ 052/936–8788, FAX 052/936–8883. 18 rooms, all without bath, but with air-conditioning. AE, MC, V.*

$ **Ryokan Meiryu.** Economy is the biggest draw to this four-story concrete building and its two-story annex. There is no particular charm here, just a small tatami room with a table and a futon. Meals (optional) are served in a small dining room. ⌖ *2-24-21 Kamimaezu, Naka-ku, Nagoya, Aichi-ken 460, ☎ 052/331–8686, FAX 052/321–6119. 23 rooms, none with bath. AE, V.*

Outside Nagoya

Futaminoura

LODGING

$$$ **Ryokan Futamikan.** This traditional Japanese inn is on the coast near
★ the wedded rocks off the Ise Peninsula, about 10 kilometers (6 miles) north of Toba (and a three-minute taxi ride from Futaminoura Station).

This is an extremely quiet place; guests spend much of their time in their rooms, which overlook a small garden. ☎ *569-1 Futamimachi, Mie-ken 519,* ☎ *05964/3–2003. 43 rooms. AE.*

Gifu

LODGING

$$$ **Ryokan Sugiyama.** Close to the Nagara River, Sugiyama is Gifu City's best Japanese inn. The presence of the river adds to the mood of peace and quiet. Very good food, including *ayu* (river smelt), is usually served in the rooms. ☎ *73-1 Nagara, Gifu City 502,* ☎ *0582/31–0161,* 𝗙𝗔𝗫 *0582/33–5250. 49 Japanese-style rooms. AE.*

$$ **Gifu Grand Hotel.** This large resort hotel is efficiently run and slightly impersonal, but it is popular with the Japanese who come for its thermal baths. ☎ *648 Nagara, Gifu City 502,* ☎ *0582/33–1111,* 𝗙𝗔𝗫 *0582/33–1122. 147 rooms, about half Western-style. Western and Japanese restaurants, pool, sauna, hot springs. AE, V.*

Inuyama

LODGING

$$ **Mietetsu Inuyama Hotel.** This resort hotel's location on the Kiso River makes it a good base for shooting the rapids. Guest rooms are on the small side, but the lobby is large, with a sitting area where guests mingle and chat. ☎ *107 Kita-Koken, Inuyama, Aichi-ken 484,* ☎ *0568/61– 2211,* 𝗙𝗔𝗫 *0568/67–5750. 99 rooms, mostly Western-style, but Japanese-style rooms in the annex. Western and Japanese restaurants, pool. AE, V.*

Ise

LODGING

$ **Hoshide Ryokan.** A small Japanese inn in a traditional-style wood building a short walk from the Ise Outer Shrine and Kintetsu Station, the Hoshide is bare and simple, but it has clean tatami rooms and congenial hosts. The food served follows a macrobiotic diet, though instant coffee is available at breakfast. ☎ *2-15-2 Kawasaki, Ise, Mie-ken 516,* ☎ *0596/28–2377,* 𝗙𝗔𝗫 *059/627–2830. 13 Japanese-style rooms, none with bath. Laundry room, Japanese bath. AE, MC, V.*

Kashikojima

LODGING

$$–$$$ **Shima Kanko Hotel.** This large and established resort hotel has grand
★ views over Ago Bay, especially at sunset. Certainly for its location, it's a choice hotel. The staff are friendly and efficient, willing to advise you in your touring, even willing to make arrangements for golf. Some English is spoken. The hotel's smart French restaurant offers the best Western cuisine on the Shima Peninsula, creatively using the delicious local lobster to its best advantage. Guest rooms are spacious and well furnished, though in a rather dreary pale yellow/beige color. All rooms have views of the bay. A shuttle bus picks up guests from Kashikojima Station. ☎ *731 Shimmei Ago-cho, Shima-gun, Mie-ken 517,* ☎ *05994/3–1211,* 𝗙𝗔𝗫 *05994/3–3538. 147 Western-style rooms, 51 Japanese-style rooms. French and Japanese restaurants, beauty salon, pool, arrangements for golf, boating, and fishing, shops. AE, DC, V.*

$ **Asanaro Minshuku.** Owner Yuzo Matsmura is boisterously friendly.
★ In broken English, he welcomes his guests with enthusiastic abandon. The inn is in a small fishing village facing the Pacific between Daio and Anori lighthouses. Rooms are large, spotless, and come with air-conditioning and heating. Bathrooms, also spotless, are just down the hall. Breakfast and dinner are served in your room. Dinner is absolutely superb—fresh broiled lobsters, sashimi, fried oysters, fish cooked in soy sauce or grilled, and fresh fruit. Matsmura-san will insist you use his

bicycles to explore and will take you in his car to all the places you missed. He also owns a snack bar (pub), similarly called Asanaro (☎ 05994/3–4197) in Ugata, where he will no doubt take you after dinner. ⊡ *3578 Kooka Ago-chiyo, Shima-gun, Mie-ken 517-05, ☎ 05994/5–3963, ℻ 05994/5–3393. 8 rooms. 2 meals included. Owner will meet guests at Ugata Station; telephone on arrival. No credit cards.*

$ **Ryokan Ishiyama-so.** On tiny Yokoyamajima (island) in Ago Bay, this
★   small concrete inn is just a two-minute ferry ride from Kashikojima. Phone ahead, and your hosts will meet you at the quay. The inn is nothing fancy, but it has warmth and hospitality. The meals are good, too, but don't let the hosts try pleasing you with Western-style food. ⊡ *Yokoyamajima, Kashikojima, Agocho, Shima-gun, Mie-ken 517-05, ☎ 05995/2–1527, ℻ 059/952–1240. 12 Japanese-style rooms, 3 with private bath. AE, MC, V.*

Koyasan (Mt. Koya)
LODGING

Mt. Koya has no actual hotels. Fifty-three of the temples offer Japanese-style accommodations—tatami floors and futon mattresses—although only a handful accept foreign guests. The temples do not have private baths, and the two meals served are vegetarian, the same as those eaten by the priests. The price is either side of ¥10,000 per person, including the two meals. These prices are higher than those at other temples in Japan. This may be because this is the only Buddhist sect in which wealth is necessary for advancement in the religious hierarchy. If possible, reservations should be made in advance through **Koyasan Kanko Kyokai,** Koyasan, Koyamachi, Itsu-gun, Wakayama-ken, ☎ 07365/6–2616. Reservations can also be booked through the Nankai Railway Company office in Osaka, and the Japan Travel Bureau in most Japanese cities. One especially lovely temple that is open to foreigners is **Rengejoin** (☎ 07365/6–2231). Both the head priest and his mother speak English. Be sure to ask where the morning service takes place and rise before 6 to see and hear it.

Matsuzaka
DINING

$$$ **Restaurant Wadakin.** This establishment claims to be the originator
★   of Matsuzaka beef; it raises cattle with loving care on its farm. Sukiyaki or the chef's steak dinner will satisfy both your taste buds and any craving for red meat. ✗ *1878 Nakamachi, Matsuzaka 515, Mie-ken, ☎ 0598/21–3291. Reservations suggested. Jacket and tie. ⊙ 10:30–9. Closed 4th Tues. of each month. No credit cards.*

Shirahama
LODGING

$$$ **Shirasso Grand Hotel.** This resort-spa hotel seems to be more appealing to the Japanese than to Westerners. Though it has little architectural merit as a modern, rectangular cement block structure, it does have bathing pools fed by thermal water for adults. ⊡ *Shirahama, Wakayama-ken 649, ☎ 0739/42–2566, ℻ 073/942–2438. 125 Japanese-style rooms with bath. Western and Japanese restaurants, shops, electronic games for children, hot springs. AE, DC, V.*

Toba
LODGING

$$ **Toba International Hotel.** Toba's chief resort hotel sits up on a bluff overlooking the town and bay. Take a room facing the sea, and be sure to be up for the marvelous sunrises. ⊡ *1-23-1 Toba, Mie-ken 517, ☎ 0599/25–3121, ℻ 0599/25–3139. 147 rooms, mostly Western, but*

Japanese-style rooms in the annex. Pool, golf, boating, fishing. AE, DC, V.

NAGOYA ESSENTIALS

Arriving and Departing

By Plane

There are direct overseas flights to Nagoya on Japan Airlines (JAL) from Honolulu, Hong Kong, and Seoul. The major airlines that have routes to Japan have offices in downtown Nagoya. For domestic travel, Japan Airlines (JAL), All Nippon Airways (ANA), and Japan Air System offer flights between Nagoya and most major Japanese cities.

BETWEEN THE AIRPORT AND CENTER CITY

The Meitetsu Airport bus makes the 50-minute run from the airport to the Meitetsu Bus Center, near the Nagoya Railway Station for ¥690.

By Train

Nagoya is on the Shinkansen Line, with frequent bullet trains between Nagoya and Tokyo (1 hr., 52 min. on the fast Hikari; 2½ hrs. on the slower Kodama); Nagoya and Kyoto (43 mins.); and Nagoya and Shin-Osaka (1 hr.). You can also take the less expensive Limited Express trains. In addition, Limited Express trains proceed from Nagoya into and across the Japan Alps (to Takayama and Toyama, and to Matsumoto and Nagano).

By Bus

Buses connect Nagoya with Tokyo and Kyoto. The bus fare is half that of the Shinkansen trains, but the journey by bus takes three times as long.

By Car

The journey on the expressway to Nagoya from Tokyo takes about five hours; from Kyoto, allow two hours.

Getting Around

By Subway

Several main subway lines run under Nagoya's major avenues. The Higashiyama Line runs from the north down to the JR station and then due east, cutting through the city center at Sakae. The Meijo Line runs north–south, passing through the city center at downtown Sakae. The Tsurumai Line also runs north–south through the city, but between the JR station and Sakae, at the city center. A fourth subway line, the Sakuradori, cuts through the city center from the JR station, paralleling the east–west section of the Higashiyama Line. The basic fare, good for three stops, is ¥180. A one-day pass, good for Nagoya's buses and subways, is ¥820.

By Bus

Buses crisscross the city, running either north to south or east to west. The basic fare is ¥200.

By Taxi

Metered taxis are plentiful, with an initial fare of ¥580.

Guided Tours

The **Nagoya Yuran Bus Company** (☎ 052/561–4036) operates five different bus tours of the city. The three-hour "panoramic course" tour (¥2,610) includes Nagoyajo and Atsuta Jingu and has scheduled morning and afternoon departures. A full-day tour (¥6,270) takes travelers out of Nagoya to visit Meiji Mura and Tagata Jinja. These tours have only a Japanese-speaking guide.

Important Addresses and Numbers

Emergencies
DOCTORS
Police, ☎ 110; **Ambulance,** ☎ 119. **National Nagoya Hospital,** ☎ 0521/951–1111; **Kokusai Central Clinic,** Nagoya International Center Building, ☎ 0521/201–5311.

Tourist Information
Nagoya International Center (3rd floor, Nagoya Kokusai Center Bldg., 1-47 Nakono 1-chome, Nakamura-ku, Nagoya, ☎ 052/581–5679) is quite possibly the best-equipped information center in Japan for assisting foreign visitors and residents. Not only is there an information desk to provide answers to your questions, but there are also audiovisual presentations and an extensive library of English-language newspapers (both Japanese and foreign), magazines, and books. The center also provides an English language telephone hotline service (☎ 052/581–0100) from 9–8:30. **City Tourist Information Office** (1-4 Meieki 1-chome, Nakamura-ku, Nagoya, ☎ 052/541–4301) will give you city maps and make your hotel reservations. There is another branch of the tourist office in the center of the Nagoya Railway Station (☎ 052/541–4301, ☉ 9–5).

Japan Travel-Phone
This toll-free service will answer travel-related questions and help with communication, daily 9–5. Dial 0120/444–800 for information on western Japan.

Travel Agencies
Japan Travel Bureau (☎ 0521/563–1501) has several locations, including the JR station and in the Matsuzakaya Department Store downtown. The major domestic airlines (JAL, ☎ 052/563–4141; JAS, ☎ 052/201–8111; and ANA, ☎ 052/962–6211) have offices in Nagoya, as do major international carriers.

English-Language Bookstore
Maruzen (☎ 0521/261–2251) is downtown behind the International Hotel Nagoya, at 3-23-3 Nishiki, Naka-ku.

5 The Japan Alps

The north–south mountain ranges of central Honshu were dubbed the Japan Alps by an English missionary in the late 19th century. Approximately 100 years later, in 1998, the region hopes to come into its own as a major winter resort destination when it hosts the XVIII Winter Olympics.

By Nigel Fisher

ALTHOUGH 80% OF ALL OF JAPAN is categorized as mountainous, it took a Briton, the Reverend Walter Weston, to call the north–south mountain ranges of Honshu's central region the Japan Alps. Through his writings, the Reverend Weston helped to change the Japanese attitudes to the mountains from one of reverence and superstition—a place where gods alight from the heavens—to one of physical appreciation. Mountain climbing is now a popular national sport, and the Japan Alps are a training ground for the Japanese. Another Englishman, Archdeacon A. C. Shaw, who served as his church's prelate in Tokyo, gave prestige to the mountains by building his summer villa on the lower slopes of Mt. Asama to escape the muggy summers of the capital. Since then, and over the course of the past hundred years, the Japan Alps have been "discovered" by the Japanese, not only for their grandeur but also for the rural traditional culture, architecture, and folkcraft, which have been bulldozed away by the industrial progress sweeping the coastal plains. Of all the regions of Japan, the Alps have perhaps the most to offer the first-time visitor: forested mountains, snowy peaks, rushing rivers, fortified castles, temples, folklore, festivals, and food.

In the winter, the Japan Alps attract skiers to their northern slopes—those facing the Sea of Japan—where the snow is deepest. (In February 1998, Nagano will host the XVIII Winter Olympics, which, it is hoped, will help establish the Japan Alps as a major winter resort destination.) The southern slopes, those facing the Pacific, get very little snow. In spring the trees start blossoming, and by summer alpine flowers are out. The temperatures are warm and crisp compared with the hot humidity of the lowland areas of the Chubu region (the central part of Honshu). In autumn, the changing colors of the trees turn the Japan Alps into a kaleidoscope of hues. Then winter comes again, with the sweetest shrimps to be plucked from the cold waters of the Sea of Japan. The Japan Alps offer particular seasonal delights, but it is in the summer that they are the most crowded with both Japanese and foreign tourists.

The name "Japan Alps" refers to the mountains within the Chubu region of Honshu (Chubu is the relatively fat section of Japan's main island, bracketed by Niigata and Tokyo to the north and east and Kyoto and Fukui on the south and west). In addition to the Japan Alps, this chapter focuses on the north coast of Chubu along with Japan's fifth largest island, Sado, which is situated in the Sea of Japan slightly north of Niigata.

EXPLORING

Although several routes, by train and road, are available into the Japan Alps from either the Sea of Japan or the Pacific coastal regions, we begin our itinerary from Tokyo and enter the eastern edge of the Japan Alps at Karuizawa. From there we stay up in the mountains to work our way first to Nagano, then west to Matsumoto. A tour has been included from Matsumoto that visits the old post towns, Tsumago and Magome, along the Kiso Valley, where the trunk road between Kyoto and Tokyo used to pass during the Edo period (1603–1868). (This excursion may also be managed from Nagoya.) From Matsumoto we cross the mountains via Kamikochi to one of Japan's most attractive and preserved towns, Takayama. Then we descend to the Sea of Japan to Kanazawa and the Noto Peninsula. You may want to end your journey here, and take the train from Kanazawa to Kyoto. But we make the final leg of our journey north along the Sea of Japan to Niigata, where we take a short ferry ride to Sado Island.

To cover and enjoy the whole itinerary would take a week, or five days if you did not go up to Niigata and over to Sado Island. However, there is no need to cover all the destinations in the itinerary. For example, if you were traveling to Tokyo from Kyoto, you could go up to Kanazawa and cross the Japan Alps via Takayama en route to Nagoya, where you could catch the Shinkansen for Tokyo. Such a trip could easily be managed in 48 hours.

Karuizawa

Numbers in the margin correspond to points of interest on the Japan Alps map.

❶ Karuizawa, two hours on the JR Shinetsu Line from Tokyo's Ueno Station, is a fashionable entrance to the Japan Alps. The best way to travel around Karuizawa is by bicycle, plenty of which are available for hire (about ¥500 an hr., ¥1,500 a day) at the Karuizawa train station, about 1½ kilometers (1 mile) south of the downtown area.

Karuizawa's popularity began when Archdeacon A. C. Shaw, an English prelate, built his summer villa here in 1888. His example was soon followed by other foreigners living in Tokyo, and Karuizawa's popularity continues today among affluent Tokyoites, who transfer their urban lifestyle in the summer to this small town located 3,000 feet above sea level. The camp followers come as well; every summer, branches of more than 500 trendy boutiques open their doors here to sell the same goods as their main stores in Tokyo. Karuizawa becomes a little Ginza. In addition to shopping, activities to pursue here include archery in summer, skating, tennis, and horseback riding, all of which can be arranged through your hotel.

Nature, though, still prevails over Karuizawa. **Mt. Asama,** a triple-cratered active volcano, soars 8,399 feet above and to the northwest of town. Lately, Mt. Asama has been making grumbling sounds, possibly threatening to erupt; these noises certainly provide a sufficient reason to prohibit climbing up to the volcano's crater. For the time being, you must be satisfied with a panoramic view of Mt. Asama and its neighbor, **Mt. Myogi,** as well as the whole **Yatsugatake Mountain Range,** from the observation platform at **Usui Pass.** The view justifies the 90-minute uphill walk from Nite Bridge, located at the end of Karuizawa Ginza, the boutique-filled street.

Outside Karuizawa are the **Shiraito Falls,** only about 10 feet high, but 220 feet across. The falls are at their best in the autumn, when the maples are crimson and the sun glints in the streaks of white water that tumble over the rocks. The falls can be reached by a 30-minute bus ride from Karuizawa Station. Another option is to take the 25-minute bus ride to Mine-no-chaya (mountain-top teahouse) and then hike for an hour down through the forests of birch and larch to the falls. You can then return to Karuizawa by bus or continue the walk, via more falls at **Ryugaeshi,** and return through the small spa village of **Kose Onsen** to the old **Mikasa Hotel,** the oldest wood Western-style hotel in Japan. From the Mikasa it is a 30-minute walk back to Karuizawa. The total course from Mine-no-chaya to town is about 11 kilometers (7 miles) and takes 4½ hours.

Also a short distance by bus from Karuizawa and close to **Hoshino Onsen,** another spa, is **Yacho-no-mori** (Wild Bird Forest), where about 120 species of birds have taken up residence. Along the 2½-kilometer (1½-mile) forestal course are two observation huts from which the birds' habitat may be observed.

The same JR train that brought you here from Tokyo climbs steeply from Karuizawa through the mountains to a plateau before making a quick descent into Nagano. This is the easiest route to take, but an alternative is through the mountains by road (bus or car) via **Kusatsu,** one of Japan's best-known *onsen* (hot-spring spa) resorts. More than 130 ryokan cluster around the *yuba* (hot-spring field) that supplies the gushing, boiling, sulfur-laden water. **Netsunoyu** (☉ 7 AM–10 PM) is the main public bath; its water is unbearably hot, even for some Japanese.

The Shiga-Kusatsukogen Highway (a toll road, closed in winter) continues across the Kusatsu Pass and at times climbs as high as 6,550 feet to Yudanaka, the base from which skiers set out to the **Shiga Kogen Ski-jo** (Shiga Heights Ski Resort). This is Nagano's largest ski area, with 22 slopes and a combination of 81 lifts, gondolas, and ropeways. Nearby **Yudanaka Onsen,** by the way, is a hot-spring resort made famous by photographs of monkeys covered with snow sitting in open-air thermal pools to keep warm. From here, both the road and train line descend for the 24-kilometer (15-mile) run to Nagano.

Nagano

In 1998 **Nagano** (pop. 300,000) will host the XVIII Winter Olympics, from February 7 to 22. Construction and preparations for this major event are already underway within the city and in the surrounding mountain resorts: Hotels and athletic structures are being built, and there are rumors of plans for several golf courses and an amusement park. A Shinkansen line direct from Tokyo is also being constructed and will be ready in time for the Olympics. It will cut travel time from Tokyo considerably, making Nagano as closely connected to the capital as it is to its surrounding mountains.

★ In the meantime, Nagano's only major attraction is **Zenkoji,** a temple that draws thousands of pilgrims each year. Founded in the 7th century by Yoshimitsu Honda, this temple is unique to Japan for two reasons: It belongs to no particular Buddhist sect, and it has never closed its doors to women. Zenkoji's most venerated statue, a bronze dating from 552, is displayed only once every seven years—the next time will be in 1999.

You can pick up a free map at the City Tourist Office (☎ 0262/26–5626) to the left (as you exit) of the station entrance before hopping on one of the frequent buses that makes the 10-minute journey through the center of Nagano to the temple. After getting off at the temple bus stop, walk down the 200-meter (yard) pedestrian avenue lined with food, souvenir shops, and smaller temples. Then, up two flights of steps and through a magnificent roofed gate, Zenkoji is laid out before you.

In the courtyard before the Main Hall are six magnificent Buddhas, which represent various aspects of life. To the left and right are several small shrines; in the center of the courtyard each pilgrim deposits a smoldering stick of incense into a giant brass burner. The temple has burned to the ground many times; each time it has been resurrected with donations from all over Japan. The most recent version was finished in 1707, and the present Main Hall is the largest thatch-roof building in Japan. The fishnets covering the inside of the roof dissuade pigeons from resting and dropping "good fortune" on the pilgrims' heads or

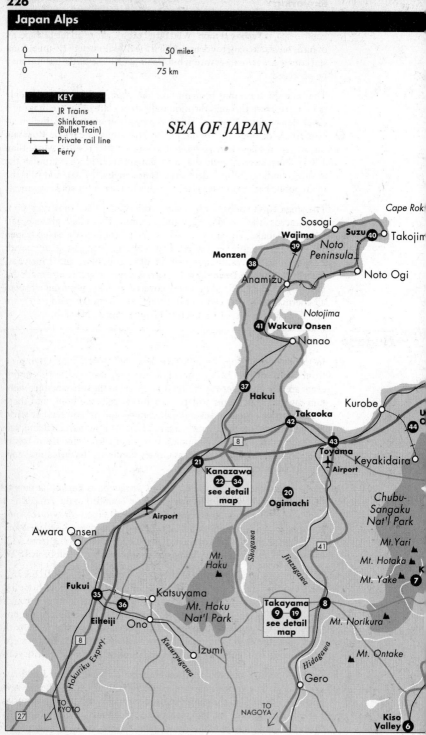

KEY
JR Trains
Shinkansen (Bullet Train)
Private rail line
Ferry

SEA OF JAPAN

0   50 miles
0   75 km

Cape Rok

Sosogi
Wajima 39
Suzu 40 Takojim
Noto Peninsula
Monzen 38
Anamizu
Noto Ogi
Notojima
41 **Wakura Onsen**
Nanao

37 **Hakui**

Kurobe
Takaoka
42
43
U
44
Toyama
Keyakidaira
Airport

21
Kanazawa
22 34
see detail map

20
Ogimachi

Chubu-Sangaku Nat'l Park

Airport

Awara Onsen

Mt. Haku

Shogawa

Jinzugawa

41

Mt. Yari
Mt. Hotaka
Mt. Yake 7

Fukui
35
Katsuyama
36
Mt. Haku Nat'l Park

Takayama
9 19
see detail map

8

Mt. Norikura

Eiheiji
Ono

Kuzuryugawa

Izumi

Mt. Ontake

Hidagawa

Gero

Hokuriku Expwy.

TO
KYOTO

27

TO
NAGOYA

Kiso Valley 6

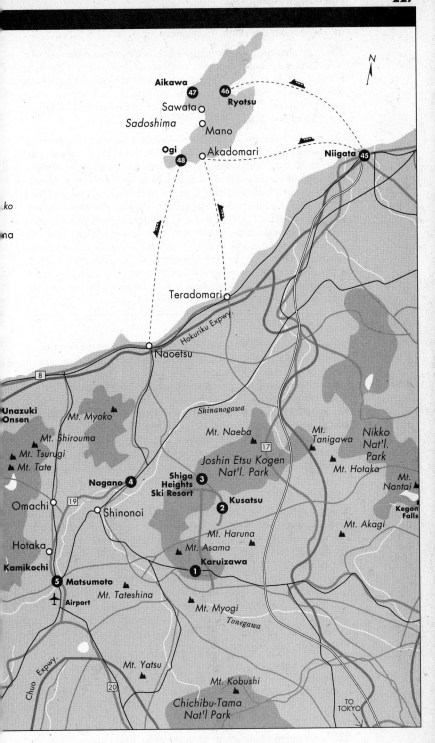

N

Aikawa

47

46

Sawata

Sadoshima

Ryotsu

Mano

Ogi

48

Akadomari

Niigata

45

ko

na

Teradomari

Hokuriku Expwy.

Naoetsu

8

Unazuki
Onsen

Mt. Myoko

Shinanogawa

Mt. Shirouma

Mt. Naeba

Mt.
Tanigawa

Nikko
Nat'l.
Park

Mt. Tsurugi

Mt. Tate

17

Joshin Etsu Kogen
Nat'l. Park

Mt. Hotaka

Mt.
Nantai

Omachi

Nagano

4

Shiga
Heights
Ski Resort

3

Kusatsu

2

19

Shinonoi

Kegon
Falls

Hotaka

Mt. Haruna

Mt. Akagi

Kamikochi

Mt. Asama

5

Matsumoto

1

Karuizawa

Airport

Mt. Tateshina

Mt. Myogi

Tonegawa

Chuo Expwy.

Mt. Yatsu

20

Mt. Kobushi

Chichibu-Tama
Nat'l Park

TO
TOKYO

on the scribe who sits on the temple floor writing short inscriptions in the small books carried by the pilgrims.

The main attraction for the pilgrims is a lock located on the wall of a tunnel under the Inner Sanctuary. You'll notice the entrance to the right of the altar. The goal of each pilgrim is to walk through the pitch-dark tunnel and touch the lock, a specific stone in the wall known as the "Key to Paradise," and thus be assured of an easy path to salvation. *Inner Sanctuary ☉ daily 5:30 AM–4:30 PM.*

Nagano has little else to interest the visitor. Behind the temple is an **amusement park** for small kids, and at Mt. Jizuki there is a **zoo,** but, aside from that, Nagano remains a pilgrims' town and a gateway into the surrounding mountains. However, should you find yourself staying overnight in Nagano, there is an ancient traditional ryokan, Hotel Fujiya, just before the pedestrian avenue to Zenkoji. The ryokan's pride is its *daimyo* (feudal lord) suite; for ¥25,000 per person, you can enjoy the suite's several rooms decorated with ancient scrolls and look into a garden that is magnetic in its contrasting complexity and simplicity (*see* Nagano Lodging, *below*). Nagano Prefecture, of which Nagano is the capital, is famous in Japan for its delicious *soba* (buckwheat noodles), which you can see being made in the window at a couple of restaurants near the walkway that leads to Zenkoji.

Matsumoto

From Nagano the JR Shinonoi Line climbs steeply into the mountains; at the town of Shinonoi it begins to follow switchbacks to the high plateau on which **Matsumoto** is situated. (The train ride from Tokyo's Shinjuku station takes two hours and 40 minutes; from Nagano, the train takes just under an hour.) In a basin surrounded by the high peaks of the mountain ranges, the town of Matsumoto has one of Japan's finest castles, set in grounds of cherry trees and open spaces, about a 20-minute walk to the north and east from the train station (pick up a map from the tourist office at the front of the station). En route you will pass through the old section, with many stone *kura* (warehouses), typical of the early Meiji period, which are unusual in their use of irregular stones held in place by mortar.

★ Known as **Karasujo** (Crow Castle) for its unusual black protective walls, the castle was built in 1504, during the turbulence of civil wars. The surrounding moats and walls remain, and the imposing five-tier, six-story donjon is the oldest surviving keep in Japan. While it is an exercise in agility to climb and walk through all six stories, the effort adds to the feeling of what life as a samurai was like during feudal Japan. The views from the sixth story are inspiring, with a broad panorama of the surrounding alpine peaks. Karasujo is a very popular attraction; be there when it opens to avoid the overwhelming crowds. You will have to wear the slippers provided while walking through the castle.

In front of Karasujo is the **Nihon Minzoku Shiryokan** (Japan Folklore Museum), whose 70,000 artifacts display the folklore, history, and everyday life of preshogun days and of the Edo period. *☛ ¥500, covering castle and museum. Castle and museum ☉ daily 8:30–4:30. Closed Dec. 29–Jan. 3.*

The other points of interest in town are minor in comparison with the castle. Directly across town to the east of the JR station is the **Matsumoto Mingeikan** (Folkcraft Museum), which displays some 600 local domestic utensils of wood, bamboo, and glass. To get there, either take a taxi or a 15-minute bus ride and get out at the Shimoganai Mingeikan-guchi bus stop. ☛ ¥300. ⊙ *Tues.–Sun. 9–5. Closed Dec. 29–Jan. 3.*

★ More worthwhile is the **Japan Ukiyo-e Museum,** west of the JR station. Unfortunately, it is too far to walk, and there is no bus, so you must invest in a ¥1,250 taxi ride. (You can also take the Kamikochi train on the Matsumoto Dentesu Line from Matsumoto Station to Oniwa Station, from which it is a 10-minute walk to the museum.) Located next to the **Shiho Butsukan** (Japan Judicature Museum; ☛ ¥500), the oldest extant Japanese palatial court building, the Ukiyo-e Museum every month rotates its collection of 100,000 *ukiyo-e* wood-block prints from the Edo period. The collection has some of Japan's finest prints and is the largest of its kind in the world. ☛ ¥750. ⊙ *Tues.–Sun. 10–4:30.*

One stop from Matsumoto Station on the Oito Line is **Hotaka.** From the station it is a 10-minute walk to the **Hakubutsukan Rokuzan** (art museum), which displays the work of Rokuzan Ogiwara, a master sculptor often referred to as the "Rodin of the Orient," who died at the age of 32. Aside from the appeal of Rokuzan's works, the gallery is in a beautiful setting of greenery against a backdrop of the Northern Alps. ☛ ¥500. ⊙ *Tues.–Sun. 9–5 (9–4 Nov.–Mar.). Closed days following national holidays.*

Also near Hotaka is the **Gohoden Wasabien,** the largest *wasabi* (Japanese horseradish) farm in the country. To reach it you must rent a bike or take a 40-minute walk along a path from the train station. (The station attendant will give you directions.) Wasabi is cultivated in the clean water beds built in a shallow, curving valley. Surrounded by rows of acacia and poplar trees on the embankments, the fields of fresh green wasabi leaves bloom with white flowers in the late spring. Be sure to try some of the farm's unique foods, which range from wasabi cheese and chocolate to green wasabi ice cream.

Kiso Valley

★ ❻ Another trip from Matsumoto is to the **Kiso Valley,** located half-way between Matsumoto and Nagoya. Called Kisoji by the Japanese, this deep valley, formed by the Kiso River, is surrounded by the Central Alps to the east and the Northern Alps to the west. It was through this valley that the old Nakasendo (highway) connected Kyoto and Edo (present-day Tokyo) between 1603 and 1867. For 250 years, daimyos and their retinue used this highway when they made their annual trip to Edo to pay their respects to the Shogunate. This part of the highway was the most difficult section for travelers. The valley's thick forests and steep slopes required three days to pass through, while today the new road allows the same trip to be done in a few hours.

With the building of the new Tokaido route from Kyoto to Tokyo along the Pacific coast and the Chuo train line from Nagoya to Niigata, the 11 old post villages where travelers had stopped to refresh themselves became deserted backwaters (sometimes referred to as Minami-Kiso). Two of the villages, **Tsumago** and **Magome,** are easy to reach. Take the JR train from Matsumoto to Nagiso, about 60 minutes away, and then take a 10-minute bus ride (fare: ¥240) from the Nagiso JR station to Tsumago. Buses from the JR station leave every hour for the 30-minute trip. From Tsumago you can take either the footpath to Magome or another bus. Still another bus travels from Magome to Nakatsugawa on the JR line. Then, it is back to Matsumoto or on to Nagoya by train, or over the mountains to Takayama. This trip to Kiso Valley could be accomplished with equal ease as a day trip from Nagoya.

Both Tsumago and Magome have retained much of their old character. Indeed, more than in most places in Japan, walking along the main street of Tsumago is like stepping back in time to the shogun era (except for the souvenir shops). If you have time, it's a pleasant three-hour walk along the old post trail between Tsumago and Magome. (Be sure to go from Tsumago to Magome, as walking in the other direction is almost completely uphill.) Both are served by buses from Nakatsugawa and Nagiso stations, so you can bus to one village and return from the other. There are ryokan and minshukus throughout the valley should you wish to stay overnight, and both Tsumago and Magome have tourist information offices that will help find accommodations and provide free maps.

Takayama

Getting There

There are two routes to Takayama from Matsumoto. One is by JR trains all the way, but this requires descending to the coastal plain and changing trains at Nagoya for the two-hour run up the Hida River Valley to Takayama. This is the least interesting route and can take up to four hours' traveling time, but it is the only way in the winter. If you wish to go straight from Kiso Valley to Takayama, take a one-hour, 50-minute bus ride from Magome to Gero and transfer to the JR train for a 45-minute run to Takayama. Buses leave three times daily (7:21 AM and 12:05 with a change at Sakashita, and a direct bus at 4 PM; cost: ¥2,150).

❼ The other route is straight over the mountains through Chubu-Sangaku National Park via **Kamikochi.** This is one of the most scenic routes through the Japan Alps and should not be missed. You should even consider spending the night at Kamikochi to fully enjoy the scenery. Getting here does require a bus/train combination, but it is straightforward and poses no problem. However, this can only be accomplished in the summer (May–Oct.), because winter snows close the road.

First, take the Matsumoto Electric Railway from Matsumoto Station to Shin-Shimashima; the journey takes 30 minutes (fare: ¥650). (Do not make the mistake of getting off the train at Shimojima, three stops before Shin-Shimashima.) Once off the train, cross the road at Shin-Shimashima Station for the bus going to Naka-no-yu and Kamikochi. The total bus journey takes about one hour and 20 minutes (fare: ¥1,840). The most scenic part is the 20 minutes from Naka-no-yu to Kamikochi, and you'll quickly understand why the road is closed by the winter snows. Just before you reach Kamikochi, the valley opens onto a plain with a backdrop of mountains. **Mt. Oku-Hotaka** is the highest, at 10,466 feet. To the left is **Mt. Mae-Hotaka,** 10,138 feet, and to the right is **Mt. Nishi-Hotaka,** 9,544 feet. Through the narrow basin flow the icy waters of the Azusagawa, which form a small pond, **Taisho-ike,** at the entrance to the basin, where lodges and inns are located (see Kamikochi Lodging, below). The bus terminal is a few hundred meters (yards) beyond.

There are trails in and around Kamikochi to please every level of hiker and climber. One easy three-hour walk follows the river past the rock sculpture of the Reverend Walter Weston, the Briton who was the first to explore and climb these mountains, to Kappabashi, a small suspension bridge over the crystal-clear waters of the Azusagawa. Continuing on the south side of the river, the trail cuts through the pasture to rejoin the river at Myoshinbashi. The little Hotaka Shrine is on the other side at the edge of Myoshin-ike (pond), from where another bridge leads to the trail back on the opposite side of the river to Kappabashi.

From Kamikochi, buses (six a day, only between early May and early Nov.) take an hour and 15 minutes to **Hirayu Onsen** (fare: ¥1,510), where you must change to another bus (operates all year) for the 70-minute ride to Takayama (fare: ¥1,430; total transportation cost from Matsumoto: ¥5,430).

Coming from either Tokyo or Kyoto, take the Shinkansen to Nagoya and change for the JR Limited Express to Takayama. The train leaves every hour during the day and takes two hours and 20 minutes.

Exploring

❽ One of the most attractive towns in the Japan Alps, **Takayama,** is often left off foreign tourists' itineraries; it is their loss. In the heart of the Hida Mountains, this tranquil town has retained its old-fashioned charm. No wonder so many artists have made their homes here. The city is laid out in a grid pattern; it's compact and easy to explore on foot or by rented bicycle (there's a rental shop south of the station building; cost: ¥300 per hour). An exotic option is a 30-minute ricksha tour of the old town for ¥1,000 per person. You'll find the rickshas based in Sanmachi-Suji. If you just want to pose in one for a photograph, be ready to hand over ¥200.

Make a point of collecting maps and information from the tourist office (open 8:30–6:30, 1:30–5 Nov.–Mar.) just in front of the JR station. Also, throughout Takayama you can get help at businesses that are designated as Travel Information Desks (look for the "?" sign in the window). In most cases, the person at the cash register in these establishments will speak English or will find someone else who does to assist you. Although sightseeing bus tours are available, they are unnecessary and expensive (about ¥3,510 for 3 hours).

Numbers in the margin correspond to points of interest on the Takayama map.

Walk (or ride) east on Hirokoji-dori for a few blocks and you'll come to the old section of town, with its small shops, houses, and tearooms. Before the bridge, which crosses the small Miyagawa (river), go right, ❾ past another bridge, and the **Takayama Jinya** will be on your right. Though perhaps not worth the admission charge to enter, this imposing structure was the manor house of the governor, with samurai barracks and a garden behind the house. In front of the manor house, from 7 AM to noon each morning, the **Jinyamae Asa-ichi** (morning market) sells vegetables, fruits, and local handicrafts. ☛ *House* ¥360. ☉ *Daily 8:45–4:30.*

Across the river from the market area and up the hill, a small street ❿ leads to Shiroyama Koen (park) and **Shorenji**. The Main Hall of this temple was built in 1504 and was moved in 1961 from its original site in Shirakawago before the area was flooded by the Miboro Dam. Now, positioned on the hill looking down on Takayama, the sweep of its curved roof, its superb drum tower, and the surrounding gardens give an earthy tranquillity that symbolizes the atmosphere of all of Takayama. ☛ *¥200.* ☉ *Daily 8–4:30. (Shiroyama Koen is always open; no ☛ charge.)*

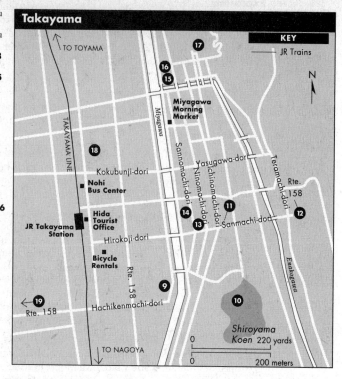

Down from Shiroyama Park, follow the main street north to Sanmachi-dori. Across Sanmachi-dori is the **Kyodo Gangukan** (Folk Toy
Museum) and the **Takayama-shi Kyodokan** (history museum), which
exhibits various antiques and folklore materials of the Hida people.
☛ *¥300.* ⏱ *Tues.–Sun. 8:30–5. Closed Dec. 29–31.*

Turn left on Sanmachi-dori upon exiting the history museum and you'll
come to the temple and youth hostel **Tenshoji**—a magnificent building, though the rooms are sure to be bitterly cold in the winter. Retrace your steps on Sanmachi-dori past the history museum (toward
the river) and you'll come to the **Hida Minzoku Kokokan** (archaeology museum), in an old house that once belonged to a physician who
served the local lord. The unique structure of the mansion—with its
hanging ceilings, secret windows, and hidden passages—hints of
spies, so prevalent in the Edo period. Now the house displays wall
hangings, weaving machines, and sundry items, both archaeological
and folkloric, collected from the Hida region. ☛ *¥350.* ⏱ *Daily 7–*
7 (8–5 Dec.–Feb.).

North of the archaeology museum you enter the **Sanmachi-suji** section,
which includes Ichinomachi, Ninomachi, and Sannomachi streets, all
parallel to the Miyagawa. This was the merchant area during the feudal days. Most of the old teahouses, inns, dye houses, and sake breweries with latticed windows and doors are preserved in their original
state, making Sanmachi-suji a rare vestige of old Japan before the
Meiji Restoration. Down along the river is the **Miyagawa Asa-ichi** (morning market), where flowers and vegetables are sold until noon each day.

Across a small tributary of the Miyagawa and on the west side of Ni-
nomachi-dori is the **Kusakabe Mingeikan** (folkcraft museum), in the
old Kusakabe (wealthy merchant) family home of the 1880s. The in-

terior, with heavy beams of polished wood that emphasize the refined taste of that period, is an appropriate setting for a display of Hida folkcrafts. ☞ ¥500. ⊙ *Daily 9–5 (9–4:30 and closed Fri. Dec.–Feb.). Closed Dec. 27–Jan. 4.*

⑯ On the next corner is another elegant merchant house, the **Yoshijima-ke.** It was rebuilt in 1908, but it retains the distinctive characteristics of the Hida architectural style. ☞ *¥300.* ⊙ *Daily 9–5 (9–4:30 and closed Tues. Dec.–Feb.). Closed Dec. 28–Jan. 1.*

★ **⑰** Up the street to the right of the Yoshijima House and next to the Hachiman Shrine is the **Takayama Yatai Kaikan,** a hall that displays four of the 11 Takayama festival floats (*yatai*), which are used in Takayama's famous Spring Sanno Matsuri (Apr. 14–15) and Autumn Yahata Matsuri (Oct. 9–10) festivals. (Some 160,000 visitors come each year for the festivals, nearly tripling Takayama's population of 68,000. Hotels are booked solid, so if you plan to visit during this time, make your reservation months in advance.) These floats have many figurines representing people in the parade, as well as elaborately carved wooden lion heads used for dances in the parade. ☞ ¥800. ⊙ 8:30–5 (9–4:30 Dec.–Feb.).

More than two centuries ago, when the country was ravaged by the plague, the building of yatai and parading them through the streets was a way of appeasing the gods. Because these actions seemed to work in Takayama, they continued building bigger and more elaborate yatai as preventive medicine. The yatai are gigantic (the cost to build one today would exceed ¥1 million), and the embellishments of wood-carved panels and tapestries are works of art. Technical wizardry is also involved. Each yatai has puppets, controlled by rods and wires, that perform amazing feats, including gymnastics that you would expect only Olympian athletes to perform.

⑱ As you walk toward the train station you'll see, just off to the right side of the main modern shopping street (Kokubunji-dori), **Kokubunji,** the oldest temple in the city. Founded in 1588, it preserves many objects of art, including the precious sword used by the Heike clan. In the Main Hall (built in 1615) there is a seated figure of Yakushinyorai (Healing Buddha), and before the three-story pagoda is a statue of Kannon. The ginkgo tree standing beside the pagoda is said to be more than 1,200 years old. ☞ *To Main Hall: ¥300.* ⊙ *Daily 9–4. Closed Dec. 31 and Jan. 1.*

The delight of Takayama is that the entire town resembles a museum piece; there is also a "Folk Village" less than 3 kilometers (2 miles) away that is a real museum, though it's so well done that it looks like a working village you would expect to have found in medieval Japan. To get to this village, called Hida Minzoku Mura, either walk the 20 minutes or take the bus at platform #2 from the bus terminal located in a bay on the left side (same side as the tourist information booth) of the JR station. (If you walk, go right from JR Takayama Station and take a right over the first bridge onto Highway 158. Continue walking straight for 20 minutes.)

⑲ Set against a mountain backdrop, **Hida Minzoku Mura** (Hida Folk Village) is a collection of traditional farmhouses moved to a park from several areas within the Hida region. Because the traditional Hida farmhouse is held together by ropes rather than nails, the dismantling and reassembling of the buildings posed few problems. Many of them have high-pitch thatch roofs, called *gassho-zukuri* (hands in prayer); others are shingle-roofed. Twelve of the houses are "private houses" that display such folk materials as tableware and spinning and weaving tools. Another five houses are folkcraft workshops, with demonstrations of *ichii ittobori* (wood carving), Hidanuri (Hida lacquering), and other traditional arts of the region. ☞ ¥700. ⊙ *Daily 8:30–5 (8:30–4:30 Nov.–Mar.). Closed Dec. 30– Jan. 2.*

Numbers in the margin correspond to points of interest on the Japan Alps map.

❷⓪ From Takayama there are frequent trains out of the mountains to Toyama and on to Kanazawa (an absolute must to visit) and the Noto Peninsula. Kanazawa, with a change of trains at Toyama, is about a two-hour trip from Takayama, but consider taking a side trip to **Ogimachi,** a traditional town in Shirakawago Valley.

Surrounded by mountains and dotted with terraced rice fields and gardens, Ogimachi is one of the most beautiful old-style towns in Japan. The majority of the residents in this quiet little village still live in *gassho-zukuri*–style farmhouses, many of which serve as minshuku (private homes that accept guests). Inside, cooking is still done over an *irori,* or open hearth, with guests seated around the fire as the smoke rises and escapes through the thatched roof. Among the local specialties served are mountain vegetables cooked in dark miso over a small burner. Reservations can be made through the Ogimachi tourist office (☎ 0576/96–1751). It's best to ask a Japanese-speaking person to do this for you before you arrive, but stop at the tourist office in the square at the center of town for a map. Most of the buildings here look pretty much the same and none of the minshukus have signs, so get someone to circle the location of your minshuku on your map. Once you've checked in, go out and stroll, and make sure you have a camera. Find your way to the hill that looks out over the town. In the evening, try to locate the local bar, which from the outside looks like all the other structures; the noise of people partying will give it away.

Opposite Ogimachi, on the banks of the Shogawa (river), is **Shirakawa Gassho Mura,** a restored village where you can learn how the farmers of the Japan Alps region used to live. The gassho-zukuri–style houses here were actually transplanted from four villages that fell prey to progress—the building of the Miboro Dam in 1972. There are demonstrations of local craftmaking in some of the 25 buildings. ☞ ¥500. *Village ⊙ daily 8:30–5; Dec.–Mar. 9–4.*

To reach the village from Takayama, take the Nohi bus to Makido for an hour and 35 minutes (fare: ¥1,840) and then the JR bus to Ogimachi for one hour (fare: ¥1,270). There are only six buses a day (four a day Dec.–Mar.) from Takayama, so before leaving Takayama, plan your schedule with the help of the tourist office in front of Takayama Station.

❷① From Shirakawago, instead of returning to Takayama, you may want to take a bus that leaves Ogimachi for **Kanazawa;** the trip takes just under three hours (departs Ogimachi 2:40 PM; arrives Kanazawa 5:27 PM). On this route you will see more of the Hida Mountains than you can from the JR train out of Takayama, which passes through many tunnels and narrow valleys.

If you are not arriving from Takayama, Kanazawa can easily be reached by JR Limited Express trains from Kyoto (2 hrs., 30 min.) and Nagoya (3 hrs.). A new city and prefecture tourist office in the JR Station dispenses maps and can help you find accommodations. The terminal for buses to downtown is at the front of the station.

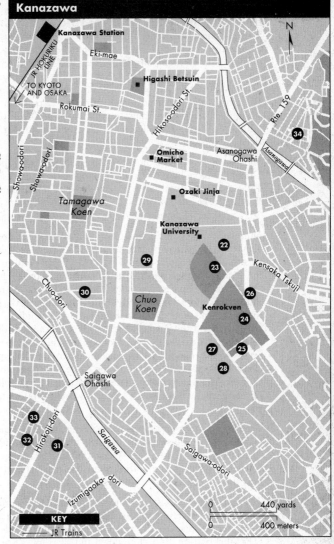

Kanazawa

Numbers in the margin correspond to points of interest on the Kanazawa map.

Many sizable Japanese cities were destroyed by the bombs of World War II; Kanazawa is an exception. Many of its old neighborhoods have remained intact for the past two or three centuries, despite modern Japan's tendency to bulldoze the old and replace it with concrete.

㉒ ㉓ **Kanazawajo** (castle), though, has fallen victim to seven fires in all, and only the **Ishikawamon** (gate) remains intact (rebuilt in 1788). Note the gate's lead tiles: The *daimyo* (feudal lords) never knew when they might be under siege and require more munitions, which could be made from the tiles.

Because Kanazawa was a fortress town centered on its castle, this is the best point from which to start appreciating Kanazawa and its past. To reach the castle from the train station, take any bus (fare: ¥200) from gate 11 at the bus terminal outside the JR station. You can also purchase, for ¥900, an intracity "Free Pass" from the Hokutetsu Bus Ticket Office, in front of the JR station. The pass permits unlimited day travel on the city's buses. Beneath the recently rebuilt Kanazawa JR Station there are arcades with numerous restaurants and shops. A station branch of the Kanazawa Information Office (☎ 0762/32–6200, ☉ daily, 9–5) is adjacent to the JR Reserved Seat Ticketing office.

Should you want to go directly downtown, to Oyama Jinja, the New Grand or Tokyu hotels, or the City Information Center (☎ 0762/22–1500; ☉ 10–6; closed Wed.) on the ground floor of the Korinbo 190 Building, take bus No. 30, No. 31, or No. 32 from gate 8, or bus No. 20, 21, 22, or 41 from gate 9.

During the Tokugawa period (1603–1868), the fertile region around Kanazawa (Kaga region) was dominated by the Maeda daimyo. Their wealth was tremendous, based on the 1 million koku rice harvests of the region. With this wealth came power and distrust. They distrusted the shogun in Edo, and the shogun distrusted them. The manifestation of this distrust was a mighty castle that had not only the protection of high walls and moats but also the intentionally winding, narrow town streets around the castle, which made attacks more difficult. Two other security measures were taken. A Buddhist temple complex was set up on the road to Edo as a delaying tactic; it also supplied an underground escape route back to the castle. Then, at another two approaches to the city, entertainment quarters were established so that invaders might be waylaid by amorous pursuits rather than by fighting.

These security measures appear to have been successful. Kanazawa maintained its independence and prospered for three centuries. Moreover, throughout its dynasty, the Maeda clan encouraged education and cultural pursuits. It seems fitting, therefore, that the castle grounds are now the site of Kanazawa University.

★ ㉔ The best-known tourist attraction in Kanazawa is **Kenrokuen,** a garden across from Kanazawa Castle's Ishikawa Gate. For many Japanese, Kenrokuen is one of the three finest landscaped gardens in Japan. (The other two are Mito's Kairakuen and Okayama's Korakuen.) Kenrokuen began as the outer garden of Kanazawajo in 1676 under the fifth daimyo. Two hundred years and eight generations of daimyos later, Kenrokuen reached its final form. It received its name—which means Garden of Six Qualities—because it possessed the six superior qualities required for the perfect garden: extensiveness, factitiousness, antiquity, abundant water, wide prospect, and quiet seclusion. Today, the last quality seems in question. The gardens are near bedlam in the holiday season, with Japanese tourists being told the names of the trees through their group leader's megaphone. Either arrive at the garden first thing in the morning or risk losing its intended solemnity. ☛ ¥300. ☉ Daily 6:30–6 (Oct. 16–Mar. 15, 8–4:30).

㉕ In the southeast of Kenrokuen is **Seisonkaku,** a two-story villa built in 1863 by one of the Maeda lords for his mother's retirement. Now it houses the family heirlooms and a collection of art objects that have been handed down through the generations of the Maeda clan. ☛ ¥500. ☉ Thurs.–Tues. 8:30–4:30.

★ 26 A much quieter garden, and one preferred by those who desire tranquillity, is **Gyokusenen** (☛ ¥500; ⊙ daily 9–4; closed mid-Dec.–mid-Mar.), northeast of Kenrokuen and before the **Kanko Bussankan**, a building that demonstrates Yuzan dyeing, pottery, and lacquerware production. Gyokusenen has an intimacy created by an owner (a wealthy merchant) seeking calm and contemplative peace rather than accolades for his green thumb. The moss, maple trees, and small steppingstones by the pond afford more serenity than do the bold strokes of Kenrokuen.

27 On the other side of Kenrokuen is the **Ishikawa Kenritso Bijutsukan** (Ishikawa Prefectural Art Museum), which displays the country's best permanent collection of Kutani pottery, dyed fabrics, old Japanese paintings, and various other art objects. ☛ ¥350. ⊙ Daily 9:30–4:30.

28 A narrow path at the back of the art museum leads to the **Honda Museum.** The Honda family members were the key political advisers to the Maeda daimyos, and the museum contains 700 art objects, armor, and household utensils used by the Hondas during their tenure. Don't miss the uniforms of the family's personal firefighters and the trousseau of the Maeda brides marrying into the Honda family. ☛ ¥500. ⊙ Fri.–Wed. 9–5. Nov.–Feb. and Dec. 29–Jan. 1.

29 Retrace your steps and keep south of Kanazawajo and you'll come to **Oyama Jinja.** Built in 1599, the shrine is dedicated to Lord Toshiie Maeda, the founder of the Maeda clan. It's noted for its three-story gate, Shinmon, designed in 1875 with the assistance of two Dutch instructors. At the top of the gate's squared arch is a stained-glass window that originally beamed a light to guide ships in from the Sea of Japan to the Kanaiwa port, 4 miles to the northwest. ☛ Free.

30 A few blocks southwest of Oyama Jinja is the **Nagamachi Samurai District**, where the Maeda clan's samurai lived. Narrow, crooked streets are lined with tile-roof mud walls designed to protect the quarters from curious eyes. One of the houses has been carefully restored and turned into a museum, **Buke Yashiki.** Another old house is now the **Saihitsuan Yuzen Silk Center**, which demonstrates the art of painting intricate designs on yuzen silk used for kimonos. ☛ ¥500. ⊙ Fri.–Wed. 9–12 and 1–4:30. Closed Dec. 28–Jan. 4.

TIME OUT While in this area of samurai houses, you can take green tea and Japanese cookies at **Nikore** (☎ 0762/61–0056). Mrs. Mori and her son converted a samurai house in order to serve tea on a veranda facing a small garden. To find Nikore, walk straight ahead from Saihitsuan Yuzen Silk Center and cross the street. It's on your right, marked by three Japanese *kanji* characters in yellow. ⊙ 10–5.

After your green tea, go left from Nikore to the corner and take another left. On the next corner across the street is the **Nomura House.** Though most of the samurai houses were demolished with the Meiji Restoration, this abode was rebuilt by an industrialist at the turn of the century and furnished in that period's traditional style. Visit the Jyodan-no-ma drawing room made of cypress wood, with elaborate designs in rosewood and ebony. Each of the sliding *shoji* (paper) doors has a great landscape drawn by Sasaki Senkai of the Kano school. Facing the living room is a small garden with a winding stream and a bridge made of cherry granite. ☎ 0762/21–3553. ☛ ¥400. ⊙ Daily 10–5.

★ 31 Cross over to the south side of the Saigawa (river); a five-minute walk beyond is **Myoryuji**, a temple famous for its complicated structure. Its popular name, **Ninjadera** (Temple of the Ninja—ninja are warriors and experts in the art of concealment), tells all. The innocent-looking temple is a complex of labyrinthine corridors, trapdoors, hidden chambers, secret tunnels, and 29 staircases to 22 of its 23 rooms. An exaggerated case of paranoia, perhaps, but it was designed to hold off invaders until the daimyo could make good his escape. In high tourist season, visitors wait in line for a tour (in Japanese). Reservations are essential, though late in the afternoon you may be able to slip in with a small group. ☎ *0762/41–0888 (operator speaks adequate English).* ☛ *¥700.* ☉ *Daily 9–4:30 (Dec.–Feb., 9–4).*

The small housed *jizo* figure (representation of bodhisattva, an altruist Buddhist deity) in the temple grounds is not on the tour, but he does have a story to tell. His facial features are almost rubbed away. In days before penicillin, syphilitics would rub the little jizo's nose in the hope that their disease would go away. Today Japanese come to ritually scrub him with a nail brush and take photographs of themselves with the little figure. Why the little jizo is here at the temple is a mystery, but its presence may be related to the belief that the daimyo used the secret passages of Ninjadera as a way of reaching the Western Pleasure Quarter undetected. There's no fee to rub the jizo, although donations are accepted.

One street to the west and one block to the south from Myoryuji is
㉜ the **Kosen Kutani Pottery Kiln,** where you can watch the entire process of making local Kutani pottery. ☛ *Free.* ☉ *8:30–noon and 1–5. Closed Sun. afternoon.*

From the Kosen Kutani Pottery Kiln you can catch a bus or make a brisk walk back along Hirokoji-dori and over the Saigawa Ohashi (bridge) to the downtown shopping center and Kanazawajo. If you are
㉝ walking, pass through **Nishi-no-Kuruwa (Western Pleasure Quarter)** en route. The geishas are no longer walled in, but the checkpoint that kept the ladies from escaping has been preserved. The area lacks the bustle of intrigue that existed 200 years ago; however, in the maze of narrow, crooked streets, perhaps you'll see a geisha or two. They are
㉞ said to be younger and more beautiful in this quarter than those in **Higashi-no-Kuruwa (Eastern Pleasure Quarter),** on the other side of town and across the Asanogawa, Kanazawa's other river.

The Eastern Pleasure Quarter was set aside as a high-class area of entertainment. Now, the pleasures of visiting here are the old buildings with wood-slat facades in the narrow, winding streets. Most of the old geisha houses have been turned into tearooms or minshukus, but occasionally you see a scurrying geisha traveling to her appointment. One elegant former geisha house, **Shima-ke,** is open to the public and gives visitors a chance to see the inside and its relaxing garden. ☛ *¥200.* ☉ *Tues.–Sun. 8:30–4:30.*

The easiest way to reach the Eastern Pleasure Quarter is to take the JR bus from the JR station using a Japan Rail Pass (¥160 without the pass). The bus stops at Hachiracho, just before the Asanogawa Ohashi (bridge). You can also take this bus to get to the **Omicho Market,** and, if you don't mind a 10-minute walk, you can take it to Kanazawa Castle and Kenrokuen.

Only Kanazawa's major sights have been touched upon here. It is a city full of little surprises, such as a small temple that does an amazing business reading *sutra* (Buddhist precepts) and dispensing herbs to cure hemorrhoids. Anyone staying for more than a day should obtain a copy of Ruth Stevens's detailed English-language guide, *Kanazawa,* written with a love for the city and leading the visitor to all the discoveries Ms. Stevens has made during her many years of living here.

The book can be purchased in English-language bookstores in Tokyo; sometimes it is available in the lobby book stand of the Holiday Inn Hotel across from the JR Kanazawa Station and at the Kanazawa Information Office at the station.

Numbers in the margin correspond to points of interest on the Japan Alps map.

35 From Kanazawa you can take a train southwest to **Fukui.** The town itself is not very interesting, but 19 kilometers (12 miles) southeast of **36** Fukui is **Eiheiji,** one of the two main temples of the Soto sect of Zen Buddhism (the other is now in Yokohama). Founded in 1244, the complex of 70 temple buildings sits on a hillside surrounded by trees, some of which are as old as the original temple buildings. The temple is still very active, and there are 200 novitiates in training at any given time. Visitors are welcome, and an English-language pamphlet is given at the gate to mark out the key buildings, once visitors have had a long-winded introductory lesson to the Soto sect. Foreigners are also welcome to stay at the temple, though arrangements should be made by writing in advance. (Write to: Eiheiji Kokusaibu International, Eiheijicho, Yoshida-gun, Fukui 920, ☎ 0776/63–3102. Cost: ¥7,000, including two meals. Arrive by 4 PM, prepare to rise at 3 AM, and check out at 8 AM.) ☛ ¥300. ⊗ 5–5.

Eiheiji is most easily reached by train from Fukui. If you do not want to return to Fukui and reboard the train for Kyoto and Osaka, there is a bus that runs down to the JR line that allows you to travel up to Ono and two beautiful gorges, Kuzuryu and Managawa.

There are several hotels in Fukui, but consider spending the night at **Awara Onsen,** just northwest of Fukui. To get there, get off at JR Awara Onsen and take a bus from gate 2 to Awaracho Onsen. The area is close to the rocky shore of the Sea of Japan, and off the beaten track for foreigners. It is, however, a popular resort for Japanese families. There are attractive and expensive ryokan as well as less expensive minshuku (*see* Lodging, *below*).

Noto Peninsula

The **Noto Peninsula** is rolling countryside with paddies, divided by steep hills, and a coastline that is mild and peaceful. On the eastern side, the inner (*uchi*) shore, there are many indentations and sea-bathing opportunities, while the western, outer (*soto*) coast is rugged and rock-strewn. It's best to work your way around the peninsula by car or, because it is relatively flat, by bicycle; however, the peninsula also can be explored through a combination of train and bus. Daylong bus tours of the area set out every day from Kanazawa (*see* Guided Tours, *below*).

Wajima is the terminal for the JR line from Kanazawa and is reached in a two-hour, 15-minute train ride; however, the line turns inland and misses some of Noto Peninsula's best sights. Hence, the best plan is to **37** take the 40-minute train ride from Kanazawa as far as **Hakui.** Chirihama (beach), a 20-minute walk from the station, is a good stretch of coast for taking in the summer sun and for swimming, as well as being one of the noted scenic spots along the Noto coast. The Japanese like this area because they can drive their cars along the sand and bring *bento* picnic lunches.

A few kilometers north by bus from Hakui (buses leave outside the train station) is 17th-century **Myojoji,** a five-story pagoda that stands out from the surrounding plain. It was originally built in the 13th century, though the present structure dates to the 1600s.

Instead of following the inland bus route north to Monzen, take the longer (70-minute) bus ride that runs to Monzen along the coast. This way you'll experience the 13-kilometer (8-mile) stretch known as **38** Noto-Kongo, noted for fantastic formations of eroded rock. **Monzen** is where the Zen temple **Sojiji** stands. Sojiji was once the headquarters of the Soto sect, but a fire destroyed most of the buildings in 1818 and the sect moved its headquarters to Yokohama.

The next stop on the bus, only 16 kilometers (10 miles) up the road, **39** is **Wajima,** a fishing town that is known not for its fish but for its lacquerware. (Stop in at the tourist office at the station for maps of the area; ☎ 0768/22–1503; ⊙ daily 10–6.) Every shop in town seems to sell this craft, though before you buy, visit the **Wajima Shikki Kaikan** (Lacquerware Hall). It's easy to find; ask the ticket-booth conductor at the bus station for directions. Here the painstaking process of lacquerware production is shown: It involves about 18 different steps, from wood preparation to coating of numerous layers of lacquer, with careful polishing in between each coat. ☞ ¥300. ⊙ *Daily 8:30–5:30.*

Once familiar with the product, walk to the *asa-ichi* (morning market), held every day between 8 and 11:30, except the 10th and 25th of each month. Here, among the fruit, vegetables, and seafood, the local crafts and lacquerware are sold to tourists. There is also a *yu-ichi* (evening market), a smaller version of the asa-ichi, which starts around 3:30 PM.

From Wajima, a bus travels 20 minutes northeast to Sosogi, a small village, passing terraced rice fields that descend from the hills to the edge of the sea. At Sosogi the road forks inland. Soon after the fork (five minutes) are two traditional farm manor houses. The **Shimo-Tokikuni House** is more than 300 years old and is furnished with antiques. Rent the tape recorder at the entrance for an English explanation of each room. Close by is **Kami-Tokikuni House,** which took 28 years to rebuild in the last century and remains in near-perfect condition. Each room has a special purpose, and, by following the English leaflet, you become very conscious of the strict adherence to the class ranking system of medieval Japan. *Both houses charge a small admission.* ⊙ *Daily 9–4:30.*

40 The same bus route (hourly service) continues to **Suzu,** on the *uchi* coast (inner, or eastern, shore), serviced by the Noto Railway Line. It is, in fact, possible to travel around the northern tip of the Noto Peninsula by bus (continue on from Sosogi to **Cape Rokko** and down to the northern terminus of the Noto Railway Line at Takojima), but the views and scenery do not justify the infrequency of public transport.

From Suzu, take the train line south to Tsukumowan Ogi Station. **Tsukumowan** means "a bay with 99 indentations." To appreciate this part of the rocky coastline, take a ride on one of the glass-bottom boats **41** that circle the bay. Farther south and on the train line is **Wakura Onsen,** a smart resort town with many hotels and ryokan. It is especially popular among Japanese families, who take their children across the bridge to Notojima (Noto Island), where there is an elaborate marine park. Wakura Onsen is a direct two-hour train ride from Kanazawa, but you may want to take a bus south and east along the coastal road **42** (Rte. 160) to the city of **Takaoka.**

Takaoka, the southern gateway to the Noto Peninsula, is not worth lingering in, though it does claim to have Japan's third largest Daibutsu

(Great Buddha Statue), after those at Nara and Kamakura. It is made of bronze and stands 53 feet high. Also in Tahaoka, a 10-minute walk from the station, is **Zuiryuji,** a delightful Zen temple of the Soto sect that doubles as the local youth hostel. However, the city is mostly known for its craft traditions of copper, lacquerware, and ironware, especially its cast-iron bells.

㊸ Southeast of Takaoka is **Toyama,** a busy industrial center. Its only redeeming virtue is the Toyamajoshi (castle park), a spread of greenery with a reconstructed version of the original (1532) castle in the center of town. Forty minutes to Toyama's northeast, one stop after Kurobe **㊹** on the Toyama Chiho Tetsudo Line, is **Unazuki Onsen,** located at the mouth of a mountain valley. A tramcarlike train (the Kurobe Kyokoku Railway—operates May–mid-Nov.) runs through this picturesque valley for 19 kilometers (12 miles), past gushing springs and plunging waterfalls and through the Kurobe Gorge to Keyakidaira (cost: ¥1,350).

From Toyama (or Kurobe, if you have visited Unazuki Onsen), our **㊺** itinerary takes the express train up to **Niigata** to board the ferry to Sado Island. Niigata, Japan's major port and industrial city on the Japan Sea coast, is linked to Tokyo's Ueno Station by a two-hour trip on the Joetsu Shinkansen. It's a good place for replenishing supplies and changing money; however, the city has limited attractions for the sightseer. The tourist information office (☎ 025/241–7914) to the left of the station can help you find a hotel as well as supply city maps and ferry schedules for Sado Island.

Sadoshima (Sado Island)

Sado has always been a melancholy island. Its role in history has been as a place where antigovernment intellectuals, such as the Buddhist monk Nichiren, were banished to endure the harshest exile. Then, when gold was discovered during the Edo period (1603–1868), the homeless, especially those from Edo (now Tokyo), were sent to Sado to work as forced laborers in the gold mines. This heritage of hardship has left behind a tradition of soulful ballads and folk dances. Even the bamboo grown on the island is said to be the best for making *takohochi,* the plaintive flutes that accompany the ballads.

May through September is the best time to visit Sado. During the other months the weather can prevent sea and air crossings, and in January and February Sado is also bitterly cold. Though the island is Japan's fifth largest, it is comparatively small (331 sq mi). Two parallel mountain chains, running along the north and south coasts, are split by an extensive plain containing small rice farms and the island's principal cities. Despite the fact that more than a million tourists visit the island each year (more than 10 times the number of island inhabitants), the pace of life is slow, even preindustrial. That is Sado's attraction.

Getting There
By Boat. There are two main ferry routes across to Sadoshima, with each route having both a regular ferry and a hydrofoil service. The bus from bay No. 6 at the terminal in front of the JR Niigata Station takes 15 minutes (¥160) to reach the dock for the Sado Kisen ferries (☎ 025/245–1234) sailing to Ryotsu on Sado. The same company has ferries going to Ogi, leaving from Naoetsu (☎ 0225/43–3791), south of Niigata. From Niigata to Ryotsu the ferry crossing takes 2½ hours, with six or seven crossings a day (cost: ¥1,780 for ordinary second class, ¥2,600 for a seat reservation, ¥3,560 for first class, and ¥5,340 for special class). The hydrofoil takes one hour, with seven to 10 cross-

ings in the summer, two in the winter, and anywhere between three and eight at other seasons depending on the weather. In February, the hydrofoil service is down to one crossing per day (cost: ¥5,460 one way, ¥10,590 round trip). To Ogi from Naoetsu the hydrofoil cost is the same as the Niigata–Ryotsu crossing, while the regular ferry is ¥1,960 for ordinary second class, ¥2,780 for a seat reservation, ¥3,930 for first class, and ¥5,890 for special class). The ferry terminal is a ¥150 bus ride or ¥900 taxi ride from the JR Naoetsu Station.

There is also one ferry a day from Niigata to Akadomari in winter; two more are added in summer. The route takes two hours (cost: ¥1,550). Depending on the season, one to three ferries sail between Teradomari (between Niigata and Naoetsu) and Akadomari, taking two hours (cost: ¥1,220 for second class and ¥2,450 for first class).

By Plane. The small plane takes 25 minutes from Niigata; there are six flights a day in the summer and three in the winter (☎ 025/275–4352; cost: ¥7,360).

Getting Around

Frequent bus service is available between the major towns, making travel around the island simple. There are also four- and eight-hour tours of the island that depart from both Ryotsu and Ogi (not available Dec.–Apr.). However, these tour buses do tend to patronize the souvenir shops. The best combination is to use the tour bus for the mountain skyline drive (¥3,720) or the two-day Skyline and Historic Site combined tour (¥5,210) and then rent a bike to explore on your own. Inquiries and reservations may be made directly with the Niigata Kotsu Regular Sightseeing Bus Center, ☎ 0259/52–3200.

Exploring

46 Sado's usual port of entry is **Ryotsu,** the island's largest township. The center of town is the strip of land that runs between Lake Kamo and the Sea of Japan, with most of the hotels and ryokan on the shore of the lake. Lake Kamo is actually connected to the Sea of Japan by a small inlet running through the middle of town. Ryotsu's Ebisu quarter has the island's concentration of restaurants and bars. Every evening (8:30–9:30) from April to early November, the Ryotsu Kaikan here stages a performance of *Okesa,* melancholic folk dances and songs performed by women, and the *Ondeko,* a lion dance to drum beats. (☛ ¥600; ¥100 discount if the ticket is bought at any ryokan in Ryotsu.) Similar performances during the summer season are given elsewhere on Sado: the Sado Kaikan in Aikawa; the Niigata Kotsu, 2nd floor, in Ogi; and the Sado Chuo Kaikan in Sawata.

47 The simplest way to begin exploring Sado is to take the bus from Ryotsu west to **Aikawa.** Buses leave every 30 minutes and take about 90 minutes (fare: ¥630). Once Aikawa was a small town of 10,000 people. Then, in 1601, gold was discovered, and the rush was on. The population swelled to 100,000 until the ore was exhausted. Now it is back to 10,000 inhabitants, and the tourists coming to see the old gold mine are a major source of the town's income.

Though some 10,000 tons of silver and gold ore are still mined annually, Aikawa's **Sodayu-ku** (mine) is more of a tourist attraction than anything else. There are about 250 miles of underground tunnels, some running as deep as 1,969 feet beneath sea level; some of this extensive digging is open to the public. Instead of the slave labor that was used throughout the Edo period, there are now robots serving in its place. These robots are, in fact, quite lifelike, and they demonstrate the appalling conditions that were endured by the miners. Sound effects of shovels and pick axes add to the sobering reality. ☞ ¥700. ☉ 8–5:30 *(until sunset in autumn and winter)*.

To reach the mine from the bus terminal, it is a tough 40-minute up-hill walk or a five-minute taxi ride (about ¥800). The walk back from Sado Kinzan is easier.

★ North of Aikawa is **Senkakuwan** (Senkaku Bay), the most dramatic stretch of coastline and a must-see on Sado Island. To reach the bay, take a 15-minute bus ride from Aikawa to Tassha and then the 40-minute sightseeing cruise boat (Apr.–Oct.) to see fantastic, sea-eroded rock formations and cliffs rising 60 feet out of the water. Passengers disembark at Senkakuwan Yuen, a park where you can picnic, stroll, and gaze upon the varied rock formations offshore. From the park, you can return by bus to Aikawa. *One-way cruise-boat fare: ¥600; includes ☞ to the park.*

The most scenic drive on Sado is the **Osado Skyline.** However, no public buses follow this route. You must either take a tour bus from Ryotsu or a taxi from Aikawa across the skyline drive to Chikuse (cost: ¥3,770), where you connect with a public bus either to Ryotsu or back to Aikawa.

To reach the southwestern tip of Sado, first make your way on a bus to Sawata either from Aikawa or Ryotsu, then transfer to the bus for Ogi. En route you may want to stop at the town of **Mano,** where the emperor Juntoku (1197–1242) is buried. The mausoleum (Mano Goryo) and the museum that exhibits some of the emperor's personal effects are in **Toki-no-Sato** (park), a half-hour walk from the center of town. There is a sadness to this mausoleum built for a man who at 24 was exiled for life to Sado by the Kamakura shogunate for his unsuccessful attempt to regain power. ☞ ¥500. ☉ *Daily Apr.–mid-Nov.*

At Mano, incidentally, the *tsuburosashi* dance is given nightly at the Sado New Hotel. The unique dance is performed by a man holding a *tsuburo* (phallic symbol) with the goddesses Shagri and Zeni Daiko. The trip from Sawata to Ogi takes 50 minutes, with the journey's highlight being the beautiful Benten-iwa (rock formations), just past Tazawaki. Be sure to take a window seat on the right-hand side of the bus.

48 **Ogi** can be used as a port for returning to Honshu by the ferry (2½ hours to Naoetsu) or on the jetfoil (1 hour). Other than that, Ogi's chief attraction is the *taraibune,* round, tublike boats used in the past for fishing. Available to tourists for rent (¥450 for a 30-min. paddle), they accommodate up to three people, and with a single oar you wend your way around the harbor. The taraibune can also be rented at Shukunegi, a more attractive town on the Sawasaki Coast, where the water is dotted with rocky islets and the shore is covered with rock lilies in summer. Shukunegi has become a sleepy backwater since it stopped building small wood ships to ply the waters between Sado and Honshu, and has retained its traditional atmosphere and buildings. You can reach Shukunegi from Ogi by a sightseeing boat or by bus; both take about 20 minutes, so consider using the boat at least one way for the view of the cliffs, which were created by an earthquake 250 years ago.

Rather than return to Ryotsu for the ferry to Niigata, it's nice to take the bus along the coast from Ogi to **Akadomari** and catch the ferry for Niigata from there.

DINING AND LODGING

Dining

Virtually all regions in Japan have their own way of cooking, and none more so than the regions within the Japan Alps and the coastal areas of the Sea of Japan. In the area called Hokuriku, which consists of the Ishikawa, Fukui, and Toyama prefectures, fish from the cold, salty waters of the Sea of Japan is superb.

Toyama has **beni-zuwaigani,** a long-leg red crab that is a special delicacy during the November–March season. **Amaebi,** a sweet prawn that, when eaten raw with **wasabi** (Japanese horseradish), literally melts in the mouth, is available from Toyama Bay. Another local treat is **masu-zushi,** salmon trout pressed onto shallow, round cakes of vinegared rice.

In Ishikawa, the cuisine is called **Kaga,** in which the harvest from the sea is prepared with Kyoto-style elegance. **Tai** (sea bream), cooked in a style called **karamushi,** is certainly one dish to try. **Kaga-ryori** is a kind of cooking in which the mountain vegetables of mushrooms and ferns are used. Fish and shellfish are frequently included in regional dishes. **Miso** soup, for example, often contains tiny clams still in their shells; sweet crab legs are a mouth-watering delicacy.

In Fukui, the **echizen-gani** crabs stretch 28 inches on the average. These crabs are pure heaven when boiled with a little salt and eaten with the fingers after being dipped in a little rice vinegar. **Wakasa-karei** is a fresh sole that is dried briefly before being lightly grilled. In both Fukui and Ishikawa, there is **echizen-soba,** buckwheat noodles, handmade and served with mountain vegetables. Echizen-soba is also served with dips of sesame oil and bean paste, a reflection of the Buddhist vegetarian tradition.

In the Niigata Prefecture, try **noppei,** a hot or cold soup with **sato-imo** (a kind of sweet potato) as its base, and mushrooms, salmon, and other local ingredients. It goes with hot rice and grilled fish. **Wappameshi** is a hot dish of steamed rice garnished with local ingredients. In the autumn, try **kiku-no-ohitashi,** a side dish of chrysanthemum petals marinated in vinegar. Like other prefectures on the Sea of Japan coast, Niigata has outstanding fish in winter—yellowtail, flatfish, sole, oysters, abalone, and shrimp. A local specialty is **nanban ebi,** raw shrimp dipped in soy sauce and wasabi. It is especially sweet and butter-tender on Sado Island. Also on Sado Island, take advantage of the excellent **wakame** (seaweed) dishes and **sazae-no-tsuboyaki** (wreath shellfish) broiled in their shells with soy or miso sauce.

In the landlocked Hida Prefecture around Takayama, the cuisine looks to the mountains and rivers for its produce. The typical cuisine of the district is called **sansai,** in which mountain vegetables, such as edible ferns and wild plants, are cooked with the rich local miso. **Sansai ryori** includes fresh river fish, such as **ayu,** which are grilled with salt or soy sauce. The local specialty is **hoba-miso,** where miso, mixed with vegetables, is roasted on a magnolia leaf. Other local foods are **mitarashi-dango,** grilled rice balls flavored with soy sauce, and **shio-senbei,** salty rice crackers.

Nagano Prefecture is famous for its handmade buckwheat noodles; more esoteric dishes in the area include raw horsemeat and sweet-boiled baby bees. Matsumoto is known for its wasabi and its **sakura-nabe,** horsemeat cooked and served in an earthenware pot.

At all times, the Japanese take pains to dress smartly and neatly. In casual restaurants, slacks and a sweater will suffice for men and women, but in more elegant establishments, men are expected to don jacket and tie.

A 3% federal consumer tax is added to all restaurant bills. Another 3% local tax is added to the bill if it exceeds ¥7,500. At more expensive restaurants, a 10%–15% service charge is also added to the bill. Tipping is not the custom.

CATEGORY	COST*
$$$$	over ¥6,000
$$$	¥4,000–¥6,000
$$	¥2,000–¥4,000
$	under ¥2,000

Cost is per person without tax, service, or drinks

Lodging

Accommodations cover the wide spectrum from Japanese-style inns to large, modern resort hotels that have little character but offer all the facilities of an international hotel. All of the large city and resort hotels offer Western and Japanese dining. During the summer season, hotel reservations are advised.

Youth hostels, which are in all the major areas, have not been listed. Their names and addresses can easily be obtained by requesting the Japan National Tourist Organization's free booklet *Youth Hostels in Japan*.

Outside the cities or major towns, most hotels quote prices on a per-person basis with two meals, exclusive of service and tax. If you do not want dinner at your hotel, it is usually possible to renegotiate the price. Stipulate, too, whether you wish to have Japanese or Western breakfasts, if any. The categories assigned below to all hotels reflect the cost of a double room with private bath and no meals. However, if you make reservations at any of the noncity hotels, you will be expected to take breakfast and dinner at the hotel—that will be the rate quoted to you unless you specify otherwise.

A 3% federal consumer tax is added to all hotel bills. Another 3% local tax is added to the bill if it exceeds ¥15,000. At most hotels, a 10%–15% service charge is added to the total bill. Tipping is not the custom.

CATEGORY	COST*
$$$$	over ¥20,000
$$$	¥15,000–¥20,000
$$	¥10,000–¥15,000
$	under ¥10,000

Cost is for double room, without tax or service

Awara Onsen

Lodging

$ **Minshuku Kimuraya.** This quiet minshuku, located in the center of the spa town, is a welcome alternative to staying in a plain hotel in Fukui. A few words of Japanese help here, but the family that runs the place will do their best to understand your sign language. The rooms are large—eight or ten tatami mats—and heated by kerosene stoves. A table with a blanket heater is the sole furnishing. The home-style Japanese fare for breakfast and dinner is average. Awaracho Onsen is close to the Japan Sea coast and west of Fukui. To reach the minshuku from the JR station, take a bus from gate 2 (fare ¥270) to the Awarayu-no-machi bus stop in Awaracho Onsen. The minshuku is a five-minute walk from the bus stop. ⌂ *Awaracho Onsen 910-41,* ☎ *0776/77–2229. 10 rooms. No credit cards.*

Fukui

Lodging

$ Hotel Akebono Bekkan. This small, two-story wooden building is a simple and convenient Japanese inn for those who want to stay in Fukui. The owners can arrange training sessions in Zen meditation and classes in pottery and papermaking. All the small tatami rooms share the communal bath. Both Japanese and Western breakfasts are offered, but only Japanese dinners are available. The inn, a member of the Welcome Inn group, is 10 minutes by foot from the JR Fukui Station and next to the Sakura Bridge. ⌂ *3-9-26, Chuo, Fukui City, Fukui-ken 910,* ☎ *0776/22–0506,* FAX *0776/22–8023. 10 Japanese-style rooms, all without bath. Restaurant. AE, V.*

Kamikochi

All hotels and ryokan in Kamikochi close down mid-November–late April.

Lodging

$$$–$$$$ Imperial Hotel. Refurbishment of this hotel, which resembles an Alpine
★ lodge with high ceilings, wood paneling, and verandas, has made it the most desirable place to stay in the Japan Alps between Matsumoto and Takayama. It is owned by Tokyo's Imperial Hotel, with many of the staff borrowed from that establishment for the summer, bringing the service to an international level. You'll see the hotel right near the bus terminal. ⌂ *Kamikochi, Azumimura, Nagano-ken,* ☎ *0263/95–2006,* FAX *0263/95–2412. 75 rooms. Western and Japanese restaurants. AE, V.*

$$ Gosenjuku Ryokan. This standard Japanese inn is reasonably priced and located just beyond the bus terminal en route to Kappabashi (bridge). ⌂ *4468 Kamikochi, Azumimura, Nagano-ken,* ☎ *0263/95–2131. 31 Japanese-style rooms. AE, V.*

Kanazawa

Dining

$$$$ Goriya. The specialty here is river fish, including *gori.* One of Kanazawa's oldest restaurants (more than 200 years old), Goriya is justly famous, with its lovely garden on the banks of the Asano River. The dining areas consist of several small rooms, and the setting is unusual, even if the cooking may not be Kanazawa's finest. Prices at lunch are considerably more modest (around ¥7,000) than at dinner. ✕ *60 Tokiwacho,* ☎ *0762/52–5596. Reservations advised. Jacket and tie. AE, V, MC.* ◷ *11–9:30.*

$$$$ Tsubajin. One of Kanazawa's best restaurants for Kaga cooking, Tsub-
★ ajin is actually part of a small, traditional, and expensive ryokan. Try the crab, and also the house specialty, a chicken stew called *jibuni.* Be forewarned that dinner for one will exceed ¥20,000. Lunch is less elaborate and less expensive than dinner. ✕ *5-1-8 Teramachi,* ☎ *0762/41–2181. Reservations required. AE.* ◷ *11–9.*

$$$ Kincharyo. This restaurant, associated with the famous Kincharyo
★ ryokan, recently moved to the Tokyu Hotel (*see* Lodging, *below*) and is now that establishment's showpiece. The private dining room's Go-

tenyo ceiling is an impressive piece of delicate craftsmanship. Equally compelling is the lacquered, curved countertop of the sushi bar. The main dining room's decor is less noteworthy but the chef's culinary skill is superb. The menu here features seasonal specialties. In the spring, for example, your seven or eight dishes may include *hotaru-ika* (baby squid that by law may be taken from Toyama Bay only in the spring) and *i-doko* (baby octopus) no larger than a thumbnail. ✕ *3F, Kanazawa Tokyu Hotel, 1-1 Korinbo, 2-chome,* ☎ *0762/31–2411. Reservations advised. Jacket and tie. AE, DC, MC, V.* ☉ *11–2 and 5–10.*

$$ **Miyoshian.** Excellent *bento* (box lunches), at approximately ¥2,000
★ apiece, and fish and vegetable dinners have been served here for about 100 years in the renowned Kenrokuen (garden). ✕ *11 Kenrokucho,* ☎ *0762/21–0127. Reservations advised. Jacket and tie at dinner. AE, MC, V.* ☉ *11:30–9:30. Closed Tues.*

$$ **Sennin.** For a restaurant near the station, the Sennin is a lively, friendly *izakaya* (tavern) with counter service or tatami-mat seating (you sit on the floor, but there is a well for your feet). An array of Kaga cooking is offered from succulent sweet shrimp to *kani* (crab) and vegetables served in steaming broth. The restaurant is located beyond the right side of Miyako Hotel in the basement of the Live One building—look for a plaque above the stairs reading "Kirin," because the restaurant's name is written in kanji. ✕ *2-13-4 Katamachi,* ☎ *0762/21–1700. No reservations. No credit cards.* ☉ *Noon–2:30 and 5–10.*

Lodging

$$$$ **Ryokan Asadaya.** This new, small, luxury ryokan is designed in a
★ grand style that combines the luxury of modernity with classical simplicity. The antique furnishings and the carefully positioned scrolls and paintings establish a pleasing harmony. There is no ferro-concrete or plastic here. Superb regional cuisine is served in the room or in the restaurant. ⊞ *23 Jukkenmachi, Kanazawa, Ishikawa-ken 920,* ☎ *0762/32–2228,* ℻ *0762/52–4444. 5 rooms. Restaurant. AE.*

$$$$ **Ryokan Kincharyo.** This small, picture-postcard Japanese inn with six
★ small houses on an incline overlooks the Saigawa (river). Prime ministers and princes have slept here, and guests need references in order to stay here. The Kaga cooking is superb, featuring regional fresh fish and vegetables. ⊞ *1 Teramachi, Kanazawa, Ishikawa-ken 920,* ☎ *0762/43–2121. AE.*

$$$–$$$$ **ANA Kanazawa.** This member of the ANA chain within a block of the JR station and a 10-minute taxi ride from Kanazawa's center, has established itself as the swankiest and most expensive hotel in the proximity of JR Kanazawa Station. The building has a moon-shaped tower, an expansive lobby with a waterfall and pond, and more than its share of marble glitter. Guest rooms are remarkably soothing. Soft beige wallpaper, fabrics, and furnishings give a restful ambience, and the L-shape rooms are a pleasant change from the usual boxiness of most Japanese hotel rooms. The staff, most of whom speak English, go out of their way to help foreign guests. Of the several restaurants, the penthouse Teppanyaki offers succulent grills with a panoramic view of the city, while the Unkai restaurant offers kaiseki dinners with excellent sashimi and a view of a miniature version of Kanazawa's renowned Kenrokuen (garden). ⊞ *16-3, Showacho, Kanazawa, Ishikawa-ken 920,* ☎ *0762/24–6111,* ℻ *0762/24–6100. 255 rooms. Chinese, Japanese, and Western restaurants, coffee shop, shops, fitness center, parking. AE, DC, MC, V.*

$$$ **Holiday Inn Kanazawa.** Standing in the shadow of the ANA hotel on the other side of the station plaza, this modern redbrick facility lacks the character of the city, as do most of the contemporary hotels. On the other hand, it has a fresh, smart lobby with a book stand, and the guest rooms have good-size American beds, a rare find, especially in single rooms. As an added benefit, coffee refills are free in the coffee lounge, instead of the usual ¥400 plus per cup. Many of the staff speak some English. ⊞ *1-10 Horikawacho, Kanazawa, Ishikawa-ken 920,* ☎ *0762/23–1111,* ℻ *0792/23–1110. 169 Western-style rooms. Japanese and Western restaurants, lounge, coffee shop, shops. AE, DC, MC, V.*

$$$ **Kanazawa New Grand Hotel.** English is spoken at this large, estab-
★ lished, international hotel in the center of the city. The service is ex-
cellent, and its location across from the Oyama Shrine is another plus. Watching the sunset is especially pleasant from the hotel's sky lounge or from the adjacent Sky Restaurant Roi, which features French nouvelle cuisine, possibly the best of its kind in Kanazawa. Guest rooms are done in soft colors and are reasonably spacious. ⊞ *1-50, Takaoka-
machi, Kanazawa, Ishikawa-ken 920,* ☎ *0762/33–1311,* ℻ *0762/33–
1591. 109 rooms, mostly Western style. Continental, Japanese, and Chinese restaurants, coffee shop, sky lounge shops. AE, DC, MC, V.*

$$$ **Kanazawa Tokyu Hotel.** Conveniently located in the heart of town, this modern hotel has a spacious lobby on the second floor and a pleasant coffee shop. Guest rooms are standard and efficient, with pale cream walls. Kincharyo is a superb Japanese restaurant here; the Schloss Restaurant on the 16th floor serves French cuisine and offers a sky-
line view. ⊞ *1-1 Korinbo 2-chome, Kanazawa, Ishikawa-ken 920,* ☎ *0762/31–2411,* ℻ *0762/63–0154. 120 rooms. 3 restaurants, coffee shop, shops, meeting rooms. AE, DC, MC, V.*

$$$ **Ryokan Miyabo.** Once the teahouse of Kanazawa's first mayor, this traditional Japanese inn is peaceful, authentic, and charming, though it could use some sprucing up. Guest rooms open onto beautiful gar-
dens, and some of the cheerful tatami rooms have little sitting areas that also overlook the gardens. ⊞ *3 Shimo-Kakinokibatake, Kanazawa, Ishikawa-ken 920,* ☎ *0762/31–4228,* ℻ *0762/32–0608. 39 Japanese-
style rooms. Meals usually included. AE, V.*

$ **Kanazawa Station Hotel.** Rooms here are not as coffinlike as they often are at inexpensive business hotels; hence, we rate it Kanazawa's best in this category. A three-minute walk from the station and across from the Holiday Inn, it is also convenient for the bus stop to downtown. There is a small comfortable lounge for tea, coffee, and drinks, a Japanese restaurant, and a room for breakfast. ⊞ *18-8 Horikawacho, Kanazawa, Ishikawa-ken 920,* ☎ *0762/23–2600,* ℻ *0762/23–2607. 62 rooms. Restaurant, coffee lounge. AE, DC, MC, V.*

$ **Minshuku Toyo.** This very small, private house is just across the wooden pedestrian bridge, Ume-no-hashi, in the Eastern Pleasure Quarter. (Take the JR bus from the station to Higashi-hashi [bridge].) Rooms are small, but the price is only ¥3,800 for a single and ¥4,800 for a double, and guests are not required to take their meals at the inn. There is a small restaurant next door and an excellent traditional Japanese restaurant, the Seifuso, across the street, but a kaiseki dinner there will exceed ¥10,000 per person. ⊞ *1-18-19, Higashiyama, Kanazawa, Ishikawa-ken 920,* ☎ *0762/52–9020. 5 rooms, none with private bath. No credit cards.*

$ **Yogetsu.** This small minshuku is in a 100-year-old geisha house in the Eastern Pleasure Quarter. With aged wood and beams, it's a delight-
ful home. The guest rooms are small, but owner Temeko Ishitata is a welcoming hostess and offers rooms without meals (¥4,500), with

breakfast (¥5,000), and with breakfast and dinner (¥6,000). ⊡ *1-13-22 Higashiyama, Kanazawa, Ishikawa-ken 920, ☎ 0762/52–0497. 5 rooms. Dining room.*

Karuizawa

Lodging

$$$$ **Hotel Kayu Kajima-no-Mori.** An exclusive resort, this hotel is tastefully furnished with Japanese handicrafts and antiques. The buildings are surrounded by forest, which heightens the mood of tranquillity. ⊡ *Hanareyama, Karuizawamachi, Nagano-ken 389-01, ☎ 0267/42–3535. 50 rooms. Western/Japanese restaurant, golf course, tennis courts. AE, DC, V.*

$$$–$$$$ **Karuizawa Prince Hotel.** Though the Prince is a large resort hotel, it is
★ quiet and relaxing. Because of its popularity, reservations need to be made well in advance for the summer season. In winter, the neighboring mountain serves as a modest ski slope for the hotel. ⊡ *Karuizawa, Karuizawamachi, Kitasaku-gun, Nagano-ken 389-01, ☎ 0267/42–8111, FAX 0267/42–7139. 240 rooms, mostly Western style. Western and Japanese restaurants, golf, pool, horseback riding. AE, MC, V.*

$ **Pensione Grasshopper.** This guest house has friendly hospitality, Western beds (great views of Mount Asama from room 208), and a mix of Japanese and Western fare. The owner, Mrs. Kayo Iwasaki, speaks English. The house is in the suburbs, but the management will transport you to and from the station. ⊡ *5410 Karyada, Karuizawa, Kitasaku-gun, Nagano-ken 389-01, ☎ 0267/46–1333. 10 rooms, none with private bath. Dining room. MC, V.*

Kiso Valley

Lodging

There are many small Japanese inns in the area, though reservations are strongly advised, especially during weekends. The **Magome Tourist Information Office** (☎ 0264/59–2336) and the **Tsumago Tourist Information Office** (☎ 0264/57–3123) will make these reservations for you. Telephone between 9 and 5. Magome's office is closed Sundays December–March; Tsumago's office closes January 1–3.

One particularly good minshuku is the **Onyado Daikichi,** (Tsumago, Minami Kisomachi Kiso-gun Nagano-ken 399-54, ☎ 0264/57–2595, FAX 0274/57–2209; ¥6,500 per person). All six tatami rooms face the valley; the wood bath is shared; the dinners, making good use of the local exotic specialties (horse sashimi, fried grasshoppers, and mountain vegetables), are excellent; and Nobaka-san (the lady of the house), in her limited English, makes foreigners feel very welcome. For surroundings and service that match Tsumago's traditional atmosphere, check in at **Matsushiro Ryokan** (Tsumago, Nagisomachi, Kiso-gun, Nagano-ken, ☎ 0264/57–3022; ¥9,000–¥12,000 per person), which has been operating as a guest house for 140 years. Ten large tatami rooms share a single bath and four pit toilets that are immaculately clean. Dinner is a delicious feast served in your room. The Japanese breakfast is also satisfying. No one speaks English here, but the tourist office will make you a reservation.

Matsumoto

Dining

$$ **Kura.** For an informal evening dining on feathery tempura or sushi from
★ the Sea of Japan, Kura is well priced. In an old moated house—the moat

smells a bit—in the center of town, husband and wife run the cashier's desk while the two waitresses bring trays of food from the kitchen to a high-ceilinged, tavernlike dining room. There are tables and counter service and *shabu shabu* for those who like to cook their food. ✗ *Ko Kudesai (behind the Parco department store),* ☎ *0263/33–6444. No reservations. No credit cards.*

$ **Hachimen.** Named after a local resistance hero of the Shogunate era, this bar is for the young or young at heart. Diners sit on stools at three counter areas, eating, talking, and drinking. Most of the Japanese food is grilled, but noodles and a hotpot are offered as well. It is in the central shopping area, down a small alley that has a Mister Donut on the corner. ✗ *Isemachi-dori,* ☎ *0263/35–3832. No reservations. No credit cards.*

Lodging

$$$ **Hotel Buena Vista.** One of Matsumoto's newest and most expensive hotels, the Buena Vista has a large, spartan marble lobby; a coffee lounge; and Chinese, sushi, kaiseki, and teppanaki restaurants as well as a French restaurant with a sky lounge bar. The rooms are decorated in pastels. Singles snugly fit a small double bed; standard double and twin-bedded rooms have enough space for a table and easy chairs. Corner rooms are the choice at ¥20,000. ☎ *1-2-1, Honjyo, Matsumoto, Nagano-ken 390,* ☎ *0263/37–0111,* ℻ *0263/37–0666. 127 Western-style rooms. 5 restaurants, coffee lounge, business services, disco, banquet and meeting rooms, parking. AE, DC, MC, V.*

$$–$$$ **Matsumoto Tokyu.** The location of this hotel across from the JR train station makes it a good choice as a functional base in Matsumoto. The rooms are not much larger than those of a typical business hotel, so you may want to upgrade yours. But beware, while the small doubles fall in the **$$** price range, the deluxe twin-bed rooms with a separate mirror and sink outside the bathroom climb to the **$$$** category. ☎ *1-2-37 Fukashi, Matsumoto, Nagano-ken 390,* ☎ *0263/36–0109,* ℻ *0263/36–0883. 99 Western-style rooms. Dining rooms serving Japanese and Western food. AE, V.*

$–$$ **Hotel New Station.** As at all business-class hotels, the single rooms here are tiny, but the furniture that can fit into the rooms is worn wood rather than plastic. The hotel offers good value and has at least some character. The smallest singles are ¥5,000; the deluxe twin for ¥12,000 is actually a full-size room. The staff is friendly and cheerful. The location is a minute from the station in the direction of the castle and close to many restaurants, but you should be sure to have one meal in the hotel. In the rock pool just inside the door are *iwana,* a freshwater fish special to the region with a taste akin to smoked salmon, which quickly become sashimi or are grilled or boiled in sake. (If this hotel is fully booked, the Mount Hotel is an adequate, slightly more expensive hotel at the back of the JR station, ☎ *0263/35-6480.)* ☎ *1-1-11 Chuo, Matsumoto, Nagano-ken 390,* ☎ *0263/35–3850,* ℻ *02361/83–6301. 103 rooms. Japanese restaurant, conference rooms. AE, V.*

$ **Enjyo Bekkan.** This small, concrete inn is just outside Matsumoto in the spa village of Utsukushigahara Onsen, reached by a 20-minute bus ride from the JR Matsumoto Station to the Utsukushigahara bus terminal. The tatami rooms don't leave much room after your futon is laid out, but the inn is neat and clean. Some English is spoken. Only half the rooms have a private bath, but no matter—the village is a hot-spring resort, and you can take to the thermal waters 24 hours a day. ☎ *110 Utsukushigahara Onsen, Satoyamabe-ku, Matsumoto, Nagano-ken 390-02,* ☎ *0263/33–7233,* ℻ *0263/36–2084. 19 rooms (11 with bath). Japanese dining room. AE, MC, V.*

Nagano

Lodging

$$–$$$$ **Hotel Fujiya.** This establishment appears the same today as it did 300
★ years ago. The age-darkened wood and creaking floors transport guests
back to the days when feudal lords stayed here while making pilgrim-
ages to Zenkoji. The tatami guest rooms vary from small (¥15,000 for
two, including meals) to large. Consider the royal suite (¥30,000 for two,
including meals); it has three rooms with sliding doors onto an old, slightly
overgrown garden. The furnishings are priceless antiques and scrolls. The
hotel also has a deep, indulgent Japanese bath. This inn is not smart or
sophisticated, but it is wonderfully old-fashioned. No English is spoken,
but the management loves its inn and will respect foreigners who show
their appreciation. ☎ *Central Avenue, Nagano City 380,* ☎ *0262/32–
1241,* 𝔽𝔸𝕏 *0262/32–1243. 30 rooms. AE.*

$$ **Nagano Royal Hotel.** Across from the JR station, this new hotel sparkles
with crisp efficiency. Guests enter the marble lobby at street level and
take the escalator up to the first floor reception area and tea lounge.
On the 10th floor, the Sky Bar offers seats with a view out to the city
below. A similar view is enjoyed by the Lambert restaurant, which serves
Continental French fare. A Japanese restaurant is on the second floor.
A coffee table and two easy chairs are squeezed into the compact, neat
guest rooms, which are decorated with subdued colors. ☎ *1-28-3 Mi-
nami-Chitose, Nagano City 380,* ☎ *0262/28–2222,* 𝔽𝔸𝕏 *0262/28–
2244. 114 rooms. Japanese and French restaurants, coffee shop, bar.
AE, DC, MC, V.*

Niigata

Dining

$–$$ **Ishihawa.** Located only two blocks from the station (on the left just
before the second traffic light as you head downtown), this restaurant
is run by a charming woman, who will guide you through the menu
in her best English. You can settle for tempura or try the more interesting local dishes, such as *wappaneshi* (steamed rice with fish and vegetables), or fresh fish caught in the Sea of Japan. Seating is either at
the counter or in a raised alcove on tatami matting. Ishihawa is one
flight down from the street—look for the signs for a barber shop, which
is also in the building's basement. ✕ *1B, 4-19 Kawabatacho,* ☎
0252/45–2602. No reservations. DC, V.

Lodging

$$$$ **Onaya Ryokan.** This is a classic ryokan, a joy to stay in, with excel-
★ lent food and service. The guest rooms look over a tranquil Japanese
garden. All rooms have a private toilet, but the Japanese bath is separate and prepared for guests individually. Recent refurbishings have
made this the most fashionable ryokan in the city. No English is spoken, and guests should know a few words of Japanese. ☎ *981 Fura-
machi-dori, Niigata City, Niigata-ken 951,* ☎ *0252/29–2951,* 𝔽𝔸𝕏
025/229–3199. 24 Japanese-style rooms. AE.

$$–$$$ **Okura Hotel Niigata.** A modern, sparkling hotel on the Shinano River,
across the bridge from the station, the Okura is the newest addition
to Niigata's international hotels. The service is first-class, and the
rooms are tastefully decorated, with rich-colored bedspreads contrasting with the pastel walls. For those who like to read or work at the
hotel, the Okura is one of few places that has ample lighting in its rooms.
Because of the view, rooms overlooking the Shinano River are the best.
The formal French restaurant in the penthouse looks down on the city
lights, and over the Japan Sea to Sado Island. The Japanese restaurant

has superb kaiseki dinners, though the Chinese restaurant is nothing special. Breakfast and lighter meals are served in the Grill Room. (If you cannot get reservations here, the next choice is the Hotel Niigata, ☎ 0252/45–3331, a 15-min. walk from the station.) ⌂ *6-53 Kawabatacho, Niigata City, Niigata 951,* ☎ *0252/24–6111,* FAX *025/225–7060. 300 rooms, mostly Western style. Restaurants, business services, shops. AE, DC, MC, V.*

$$ **Niigata Toei Hotel.** For an inexpensive business hotel conveniently located a block and a half from the station, this ranks the best. The 9th floor has two restaurants and a bar for evening entertainment. ⌂ *1-6, 2 Benten, Niigata 950,* ☎ *025/244–7101,* FAX *025/241–8485. 90 rooms. Restaurants, banquet/conference rooms. AE, D, MC, V.*

Sadoshima (Sado Island)

Lodging
Hotel reservations can be made at the information counters of Sado Kisen ship company at Niigata Port or Ryotsu Port.

$$$ **Sado Royal Hotel Mancho.** This is the best hotel on Sado's west coast. The establishment caters mostly to Japanese tourists, but the staff makes the few Westerners who come by feel welcome; however, English is not spoken. ⌂ *58 Shimoto, Aikawa, Sadoshima, Niigata-ken,* ☎ *0259/74–3221. 87 rooms. Japanese restaurant, but a few Western dishes are offered. DC, V.*

$ **Sado Seaside Hotel.** Located 20 minutes by foot from the Ryotsu Port,
★ this is more a friendly inn than a hotel. If you telephone before you catch the ferry from Niigata, the owner will meet you at the dock. He'll be carrying a green Seaside Hotel flag. ⌂ *80 Sumiyoshi, Ryotsu City, Niigata-ken 952,* ☎ *0259/27–7211. 12 Japanese-style rooms, 5 with private bath. Japanese meals available, laundry room, Japanese baths. AE, V.*

Takayama

Dining
$$$ **Suzaki.** This is Takayama's number one restaurant for *kaiseki* cuisine
★ served in traditional style with kimono-clad waitresses. Make a point of trying a meal prepared with wild plants from the Hida mountains and salted river fish. Each dish is exquisitely presented on delicate china. ✕ *4-14 Shinmei,* ☎ *0577/32–0023. Reservations advised. Jacket and tie. AE, V.* ◷ *Lunch and dinner.*

$$–$$$ **Kakusho.** The most established restaurant for Takayama's well-known
★ *shojin-ryori,* a vegetarian meal that consists of various mountain plants, Kakusho is located on the far side of the Miya River from the railway station and near Tenshoji (temple). There is no restaurant sign in English; look for a small building with a courtyard patio diagonally across from a parking lot. Meals here are both nourishing and tasty—often a local bean paste is used in the cooking to add extra flavor. If the freshwater fish *ayu* is on the menu, be sure to try it. Owner Sumitake-san will happily help you with the menu; her English is delightful. ✕ *2 Babacho-dori,* ☎ *0577/32–0174. Reservations advised. Jacket and tie. AE, V.* ◷ *Lunch and dinner.*

$$ **Susuya.** Across Kokobunji-dori from the Sogo Palace hotel is this delightful small Japanese restaurant in a traditional Hida-style house. Owned by the same family for generations, the timbered restaurant is small and intimate. The traditional specialty is *sansai-ryori,* with mountain plants and freshly caught river fish, such as ayu, grilled with soy

sauce. It's superb. ✕ *24 Hanakawa,* ☎ *0577/32–2484. Reservations advised. AE, V.* ⊙ *Lunch and dinner.*

Lodging

The **Hida Tourist Information Office** (☎ 0577/32–5328), just in front of the train station, will help you find accommodations, both in town and in the surrounding mountains. This is one of the most helpful information offices in Japan.

$$$$ **Ryokan Kinkikan.** This splendid traditional Japanese inn is Takayama's ★ top place to stay. It is also very small, and reservations are essential. Antique Hida furniture is used throughout the inn. ▥ *48 Asahicho, Takayama, Gifu-ken 506 (located in the center of town, left off Kokobunji-dori and 2 blocks from the river),* ☎ *0577/32–3131,* ℻ *0577/31–3130. 9 Japanese-style rooms. AE.*

$$$ **Ryokan Hishuya.** For the genuine atmosphere of a Japanese inn, of- ★ fering kaiseki-style meals and refined furnishings, stay at this ryokan. Quiet and contemplative, it is away from Takayama and close to Hida Minzoku Mura. ▥ *2581 Kami-Okamotocho, Takayama, Gifu-ken 506,* ☎ *0577/33–4001,* ℻ *0577/34–5065. 16 Japanese-style rooms. AE, MC.*

$$–$$$ **Hida Plaza Hotel.** This is the best international-style hotel in town. Al- ★ though its newer, modern wing is not attractive, the rooms in that part of the hotel are larger. In terms of value, all the rooms are a cut above most Japanese hotels. In the older structure, the traditional Hida ambience is present, particularly in the old, exposed beams and wide-plank floors of the Japanese restaurant. The Hida Plaza is a three-minute walk from the train station and a 10-minute walk from downtown. ▥ *2- 60 Hanaokacho, Takayama, Gifu-ken 506,* ☎ *0577/33–4600,* ℻ *0577/33–4602. 152 Western-style rooms. Japanese and Continental restaurants, coffee shop, disco, karaoke bar, indoor pool, health club, sauna, mineral baths, shops. AE, DC, MC, V.*

$$ **Honjin Hiranoya.** There are two parts to this hotel, Honkan (old) Hiranoya and Shinkan (new) Hiranoya, in two buildings on the same street, across from one another. Though both have the same name and ownership, they were built three centuries apart. Years ago the old structure was a samurai house; now it is a friendly ryokan with lots of aged charm, though short on elegance. The rooms vary from Western-style to tatami-style. The Shinkan Hiranoya has modern tatami rooms and a superb multiperson bath on the seventh floor with huge windows overlooking the Hida Mountains. Meals are included. ▥ *1-chome, Honmachi, Takayama, Gifu-ken 506,* ☎ *0577/34–1234,* ℻ *0577/34–7721. 19 rooms in the old building, 27 rooms in the new. Restaurant. AE, DC, MC, V.*

$$ **Sogo Palace.** Conveniently located in the center of Takayama, this is a fairly modern Japanese inn. It may not have the charm of the older, traditional inns, but it caters to and understands the international traveler. Service is extremely friendly and helpful, which adds to the pleasure of this hotel. ▥ *54 Suehirocho, Takayama, Gifu-ken 506,* ☎ *0577/33–5000. 20 Japanese-style and 7 Western-style rooms. V.*

$–$$ **Yamaku.** This inn offers one of the best values in town. Though listed ★ as a minshuku, Yanaku is more like a small, privately run Japanese-style hotel. The building is old, and cozy nooks in the lobby with chairs and coffee tables serve as small lounges. The tatami guest rooms are typically small, but the ample closets help add space. Room No. 33 is the quietest. The public baths are large and are given the kind of social importance found in an onsen—in the men's bath, a water wheel slowly turns to hypnotize you as you soak. Dinner hours are more flexible than those at the typical minshuku: The food is good, though not extraordinary. The inn is on the other side of town from the JR Takayama Station (a 20-min. walk). ☎ *58, Tenshojimachi, Takayama, Gifu-ken 506, ☎ 0577/32−3756, FAX 0577/35−2350. 22 rooms, none with private bath. Japanese meals served in dining room, souvenir shop. No credit cards.*

$ **Minshuku Sosuke.** Although this concrete building is a private home, it feels more like a boarding house for travelers, both Japanese and Western. Mama-san rules with a firm hand and speaks essential English. Only after dinner has been served does she loosen up for a chat. Rooms are small, either four tatami or six tatami mats, and have electric (rather than kerosene) heaters. The shared toilets are kept spotless. The food here is average, but because meals are taken at long tables (tatami seating), guests have the opportunity to meet each other. Although this minshuku is 15 minutes from the town's center, the room rate makes it a good value. To get there, turn right from the JR Takayama Station, then right at the first bridge, and walk seven minutes. The minshuku is opposite the huge and ugly Green Hotel. ☎ *1-64, Okamotocho, Takayama, Gifu-ken 506, ☎ 0577/32−0818, FAX 0577/33−5570. 14 rooms, none with private bath. Meals included. Dining room. No credit cards.*

Yudanaka Onsen

Lodging

$$ **Uotoshi Ryokan.** This small Japanese inn has only eight tatami rooms, which share a delightful *hinoki* (cypress) bath tub filled with hot thermal spring waters to ease your weary traveler muscles. Western food is not served, but don't miss the dinners: They are a treat of mountain vegetables and fresh seafood from the Japan Sea. The owners can arrange for you to try Japanese archery. To reach Yudanaka Onsen, take the 40-minute train ride on the Nagano Dentetsu Railway from Nagano. The inn is a seven-minute walk from Yudanaka Station. The owners will also collect you, for a fee, from the JR Nagano Station. ☎ *2563, Sano, Yamanouchimachi, Shimo-Takai-gun, Nagano-ken 381-04, ☎ 0269/33−1215, FAX 0269/33−0074. 8 Japanese-style rooms. Restaurant. AE, V.*

JAPAN ALPS ESSENTIALS

Arriving and Departing

Several major routes access the Japan Alps. Below are several train routes arranged by destination. For Kanazawa and Matsumoto, flight information is also given.

By Train

Kanazawa. From Osaka, the JR Hokuriku to Kanazawa takes just under three hours; the same train from Kyoto takes two hours and 20 minutes. From Niigata, the JR Hokuriku takes four hours. From Tokyo, take the Tokaido Shinkansen to Maibara, then the Hokuriku Honsen Express to Kanazawa; the journey takes four hours and 40 minutes.

Karuizawa. From Tokyo's Ueno Station on the JR Shinetsu Line, the train to Karuizawa takes two hours. From Niigata, use the Shinkansen to Takasaki and change to the JR Shinetsu Line to Karuizawa. The total traveling time is approximately two hours.

Matsumoto. From Tokyo's Shinjuku Station on the JR Chuo Line, the journey to Matsumoto takes three hours. From Nagoya, the JR Chuo Line takes two hours and 15 minutes.

Nagano. From Tokyo's Ueno Station on the JR Shinetsu Line, the same train that goes to Karuizawa continues on to Nagano; the total journey takes just under three hours. From Nagoya, the same train that stops in Matsumoto, continues on to Nagano; the total journey takes just over three hours. A new Shinkansen will be in operation in time for the XVIII Winter Olympics in February 1998, reducing the travel time between Nagano and Tokyo to approximately two hours.

Niigata. From Tokyo's Ueno Station, the Joetsu Shinkansen to Niigata makes the journey in two hours, seven minutes.

Takayama. From Nagoya, the JR Takayama Line takes a little over two hours. From Toyama, the JR Takayama Line takes just under two hours. There are eight trains a day.

Toyama. From Nagoya via Takayama, the JR Takayama takes approximately four hours; there are four trains a day in each direction. From Nagoya via Kanazawa, the journey takes just under four hours; there are seven trains a day in each direction. Numerous daily trains run from Osaka and Kyoto; the journey takes three and a half and three hours, respectively.

By Plane

Kanazawa. From Tokyo's Haneda to Komatsu Airport is a one-hour flight on Japan Airlines (JAL) or All Nippon Airlines (ANA); allow 55 minutes for the airport bus connection to downtown Kanazawa.

Matsumoto. Matsumoto Airport opened in 1994; JAS offers daily flights to and from Fukuoka, Osaka, and Sapporo.

Toyama. ANA offers five flights daily between Tokyo and Toyama.

Getting Around

Roads and railways through the Japan Alps follow the valleys. All major stations have someone who speaks sufficient English to plan your schedule. Each major town described in the following excursion section has a tourist office at the railway station that will supply free maps and, if necessary, find you accommodations. Remember that the last train or bus in the evening can be quite early.

Rental cars are available at the major stations, but it is best to reserve the car before you leave Tokyo, Nagoya, or Kyoto. The Nippon-Hertz company has the greatest number of locations in this region.

During the winter months, certain roads through the central Japan Alps are closed. In particular, the direct route between Matsumoto and Takayama via Kamikochi cannot be taken between November and April.

Guided Tours

The **Japan Travel Bureau** has offices at every JR station in each major city and town and can assist in local tours, hotel reservations, and travel ticketing. Though you should not assume that any English will be spoken, you can usually find someone whose knowledge is sufficient for your basic needs. Most of the travel through this region is very straightforward, using public transport. In the two places where public transportation is infrequent—the Noto Peninsula and Sado Island—local tours are available, though the guides speak only Japanese.

Noto Peninsula

The **Hokuriku-Tetsudo Co.** (☎ 0762/37–8111) has a 6½-hour tour that covers much of the peninsula for ¥6,200, with a Japanese-speaking guide. It operates year-round and departs from Kanazawa Station.

Sadoshima (Sado Island)

A tour of Sado Island is useful only because it covers Skyline Drive, which public buses do not travel. The price for this tour, which departs from Ryotsu, May–November, is ¥3,600. Contact the **Niigata Kotsu Information Center** at the Ryotsu Bus Terminal (☎ 0259/27–3141).

Regional Tour

The **Japan Travel Bureau** operates a five-day tour from Tokyo that departs every Tuesday, April 1–October 26. The tour goes via Lake Shirakaba to Matsumoto (overnight), to Tsumago and Takayama (overnight), to Kanazawa (overnight), to Awara Onsen (overnight), and ends in Kyoto. Cost: ¥150,000, including four breakfasts and two dinners.

Important Addresses and Numbers

Emergencies

Police, dial 110; **ambulance,** dial 119.

Tourist Information

JR Travel Information Centers and **Japan Travel Bureaus** have offices at all the train stations at the major cities and towns.

KANAZAWA

The **Kanazawa Tourist Information Service** is in front of the JR station (☎ 0762/31–6311).

KARUIZAWA

The **Karuizawa Station Tourist Office** is at the JR station (☎ 0267/42–2491).

KISO VALLEY

The **Magome Tourist Information Office** (☎ 0264/59–2336) is open 8:30–5; closed Sunday December–March. The **Tsumago Tourist Information Office** (☎ 0264/57–3123) is open 9–5; closed January 1–3. Both offices will make reservations at local inns for you.

MATSUMOTO

The **Matsumoto City Tourist Information Office** is on the street level to the right as you exit the JR station (☎ 0263/32–2814).

NIIGATA

The **Niigata City Tourist Information Center** is in front of the JR station (☎ 0252/41–7914).

TAKAYAMA

The **Hida Tourist Information Office,** in front of the JR station (☎ 0577/32–5328), is open April–October, 8:30–6:30; November 1–March, 8:30–5.

Japan Travel-Phone

The nationwide service for English language assistance or travel information is available 9–5 daily. Dial toll-free 0120/444-800 for information on western Japan. When using a yellow, blue, or green public phone (do not use the red phones), insert a ¥10 coin, which will be returned.

6 Kyoto

A stroll through this city today is a walk through 11 centuries of Japan's history; its 1,600 temples, several hundred shrines, and countless other attractions make it a top tourist destination, even for the Japanese themselves.

KYOTO'S HISTORY IS FULL OF CONTRADICTIONS: famine and prosperity, war and peace, calamity and tranquillity. Although the city was Japan's capital for more than 10 centuries, the real center of political power was often somewhere else, such as in Kamakura (1192–1333) and in Edo (1603–1868). Such was Kyoto's decline in the 17th and 18th centuries that, when the power of the government was returned from the shoguns to the emperor, he moved his capital and imperial court to Edo, renaming it Tokyo. Though that move may have pained the Kyoto residents, it actually saved the city from destruction. While most major cities in Japan were flattened by World War II bombs, Kyoto survived; it is now the sixth largest city in Japan.

By Nigel Fisher

Until 710, Japan's capital was moved to a new location with the succession of each new emperor. This continuous movement started to become rather expensive as the size of the court and the number of administrators grew, so Nara was chosen as the permanent capital. It did not last long as the capital. Buddhists rallied for, and achieved, tremendous political power. In the effort to thwart them, Emperor Kanmu moved the capital in 784 to Nagaoka; the Buddhists were left behind in their elaborate temples. Within 10 years, however, Kanmu decided that Kyoto (then called Uda) was better suited for his capital. Poets were asked to compose verse about Uda and invariably they included the phrase Heian-kyo, meaning "Capital of Peace," which no doubt reflected the hope and desire of the time.

For 1,074 years, Kyoto remained the capital, though at times only in name. From 794 to the end of the 12th century, the city flourished under imperial rule. It might be said that this was the time when Japan's culture started to become independent of Chinese influences and began to develop its unique characteristics. Unfortunately, the use of wood for construction, coupled with Japan's two primordial enemies, fire and earthquakes, have destroyed all the buildings from this era, except Byodoin (temple) in Uji. The short life span of a building in the 11th century is exemplified by the Imperial Palace, which burned down 14 times in a 122-year period. As if natural disasters were not enough, imperial power waned in the 12th century. Then came a period of rule by the shoguns, but each shogun's rule was tenuous; by the 15th century, civil wars tore the country apart. Many of Kyoto's buildings were destroyed or looted, especially during the Onin Civil War.

The Onin Civil War (1467–1477) was a dispute between two feudal lords, Yamana and Hosokawa, over who should be the shogun's successor. The dispute was devastating for Kyoto. Yamana camped in the western part of the city with 90,000 troops, and Hosokawa settled in the eastern part with 100,000 troops; central Kyoto was the battlefield.

Not until the end of the 16th century, when Japan was welded by the might of Nobunaga Oda and Hideyoshi Toyotomi, did Japan settle down. This period was soon followed by the usurpation of power by Ieyasu Tokugawa, who began the dynasty of the Tokugawa Shogunate that lasted for the next 264 years, during which time the government's power was in Edo. However, Kyoto did remain the imperial capital, and the first three Tokugawa shoguns paid homage to it. Old temples were restored, and new villas were built. Much of what you see in Kyoto was built or rebuilt at this time (the first half of the 17th century) to legitimize the rule of the Tokugawa Shogunate.

Steeped in history and tradition, Kyoto has in many ways been the cradle of Japanese culture, especially with its courtly aesthetic pastimes, such as moon-viewing parties, and tea ceremonies. A stroll through Kyoto today is a walk through 11 centuries of Japanese history. Yet this city has been swept into the modern industrialized world with the rest of Japan. Glass-plate windows, held in place by girders and ferroconcrete, dominate central Kyoto. Elderly women, however, continue to wear kimonos as they make their way slowly along the canal walkways. Geishas still entertain, albeit at prices out of reach for most of us. Sixteen hundred temples and several hundred shrines surround central Kyoto. Rather a lot to see, to say the least. Our exploration of Kyoto will be selective. Even so, the exploration will be expensive. With attractions charging ¥400 to ¥500 for admission, in three days of visiting temples and museums you can easily spend $100 per person.

EXPLORING

Most of what interests the visitor is on the north side of Kyoto Station. Let's think of this northern sector as three rectangular areas abutting each other. The middle rectangular area fronts the exit of Kyoto Station. This is **central Kyoto.** Here are the hotels, the business district, the Pontocho geisha district, and the Kiyamachi entertainment district. Central Kyoto also contains one of the oldest city temples (Toji), the rebuilt Imperial Palace, and Nijojo (Nijo Castle), former Kyoto abode of the Tokugawa shoguns.

Eastern Kyoto (Higashiyama) is home to many of the city's renowned tourist attractions, including Ginkakuji (Temple of the Silver Pavilion), Heian Jingu (shrine), and Kiyomizudera (temple). Also in this part of Kyoto is Gion, a traditional shopping neighborhood by day and a geisha entertainment district by night. You could easily fill two days visiting eastern Kyoto.

Western Kyoto includes the temples Ryoanji and Kinkakuji (Temple of the Golden Pavilion).

An exploration of these three areas will take up most of a three-day visit to Kyoto. However, two other areas have major sights. West of the western district is **Arashiyama,** which is home to the temple Tenryuji. To the north of central Kyoto is the northern district of **Mt. Hiei** and Kyoto's suburb, **Ohara,** where the poignant story of Kenreimonin takes place at Jakkoin (temple).

Kyoto's attractions do cover a wide area. However, many of the sights are clustered together, so you may walk from one to another. Where the sights are not near each other, you can use Kyoto's bus system, which works on a grid pattern, and is easy to follow. Maps of the bus routes are supplied by the JNTO office. The following exploring sections keep to the divisions described above so as to allow walking from one sight to another. However, notwithstanding the traffic, if armed with a bus-route map, you could cross and recross Kyoto without too much difficulty should you wish to choose sights to suit your special interests.

Our exploration begins in Higashiyama (the eastern district); if you have time to visit only one district, this is the one we would recommend. This area has a lot to see, more than you could cover comfortably in one day, so you may want to judiciously prune some of the following itinerary according to your interests.

Kyoto *(Boxes Refer to Detail Maps)*

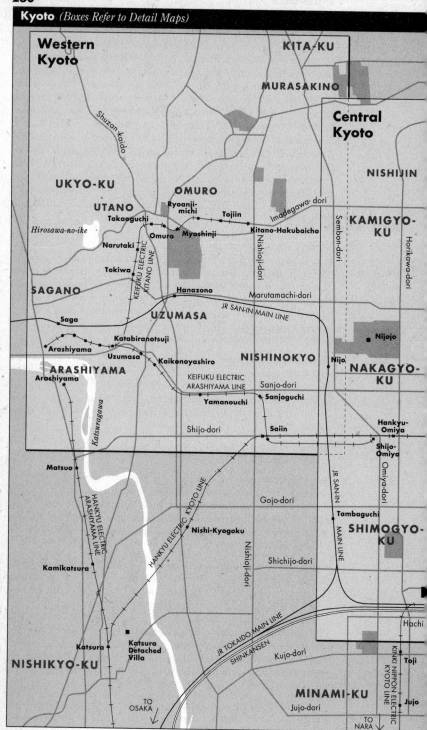

Western Kyoto

KITA-KU

MURASAKINO

Central Kyoto

UKYO-KU

NISHIJIN

OMURO

Ryoanji-michi

Tojiin

Imadegawa-dori

KAMIGYO-KU

UTANO

Takaoguchi

Kitano-Hakubaicho

Hirosawa-no-ike

Omuro

Myoshinji

Narutaki

Tokiwa

SAGANO

Hanazono

Marutamachi-dori

Saga

UZUMASA

JR SAN-IN MAIN LINE

Katabiranotsuji

Nijojo

ARASHIYAMA

Uzumasa

Kaikonoyashiro

NISHINOKYO

Nijo

NAKAGYO-KU

Arashiyama

KEIFUKU ELECTRIC
ARASHIYAMA LINE

Sanjo-dori

Yamanouchi

Sanjoguchi

Matsuo

Shijo-dori

Saiin

Hankyu-Omiya

Shijo-Omiya

Gojo-dori

Nishi-Kyogoku

Tambaguchi

SHIMOGYO-KU

Kamikatsura

Shichijo-dori

Hachi

Katsura

Katsura
Detached
Villa

NISHIKYO-KU

JR TOKAIDO MAIN LINE

SHINKANSEN

Kujo-dori

Toji

MINAMI-KU

TO
OSAKA

Jujo-dori

Jujo

TO
NARA

Botanical Garden

Kitaoji-dori

Kitaoji

Kamogawa

SHIMOGAMO

Takanogawa

EIZAN ELECT. KURAMA LINE

EIZAN ELECT. EIZAN LINE

Ichijoji

KITA-SHIRAKAWA

Kuramaguchi

TAKANO

Chayama

Mt. Uryu

SUBWAY

Eastern Kyoto

Mototanaka

SAKYO-KU

Imadegawa

Demachi-Yanagi

Imadegawa-dori

N

Karasuma-dori

Kawaramachi-dori

Demachi-Yanagi Keihan

Kyoto Imperial Palace

Shirakawa-dori

Maruta-machi

Marutamachi

Marutamachi-dori

Higashioji-dori

Heian Jingu

Nyoigatake

Oike

Oike-dori

OKAZAKI

Kamogawa

Higashiyama-Sanjo

Sanjo-dori

Keage

Keihan-Sanjo

Keishin-Sanjo

KEIHAN ELECTRIC KEISHIN LINE

AWATAGUCHI

Shijo-dori

Karasuma Shijo

Kawara-machi

Shijo Keihan

Kujoyama

GION

Gojo

Gojo

HIGASHIYAMA-KU

Hino-oka

YAMASHINA-KU

TO TOKYO

Misasagi

Yamashina

Mt. Kiyomizu

Mt. Kazan

Keihan-Yamashina

Shinomiya

Shichijo

KEY

JR Trains

Shinkansen (Bullet Train)

Subway

Private rail line

1 mile

1 km

JR TOKAIDO MAIN LINE

Mt. Rokujo

Kyoto Station

SHINKANSEN

JR NARA LINE

hijo-dori

Kujo-dori

Tofukuji

KEIHAN ELECTRIC MAIN LINE

Jujo-dori

Tobakaido

Eastern Kyoto

Numbers in the margin correspond to points of interest on the Eastern Kyoto map.

Let's start at one of Kyoto's most famous sights, Ginkakuji, a wonderful villa-turned-temple. To reach Ginkakuji, take Bus 5 from Kyoto Station to Ginkakuji-michi bus stop. Walk on the street along the canal, going east. Just after the street crosses another canal flowing north–south, you'll see **Hakusasonso Garden,** the quiet villa of the late painter Hashimoto Kansetsu, with an exquisite garden and teahouse open to the public. ☛ *¥700; with tea and sweets, an extra ¥800.* ☺ *daily 10–5 (enter by 4:30).*

Ginkaku means "silver pavilion," but the temple is not silver. It was only intended to be. Shogun Yoshimasa Ashikaga (1435–1490) had this villa built for his retirement. He started building it as early as the 1460s, but it was not until 1474 that, disillusioned with politics, he gave his full attention to the construction of his villa and to the arts of romance, moon-gazing, and the tea ceremony, which he helped develop into a high art. Though he never had time to complete the coating of the pavilion with silver foil, he constructed a dozen or so buildings. Many of them were designed for cultural pursuits such as incense and tea ceremonies. On his death, the villa was converted into a Buddhist temple, as was often the custom during the feudal era. However, with the decline of the Ashikaga family, Ginkakuji fell into decline, and many buildings were destroyed.

★ ❶ What we see today are the two remaining original buildings, **Togudo** (East Request Hall) and **Ginkakuji** (Temple of the Silver Pavilion). The four other structures on the grounds were built in the 17th and 19th centuries. The front room of Togudo is where Yoshimasa is thought to have lived, and the statue of the priest is probably of Yoshimasa himself. The back room, called Dojinsai (Comradely Abstinence), became the prototype for the traditional tea-ceremony room that is still used today.

Ginkakuji is a simple and unadorned two-story building. On the upper floor it contains a gilt image of Kannon (the Goddess of Mercy) said to have been carved by Unkei, a famous Kamakura-period sculptor, though it is not ordinarily open to public view. Mostly it is the exterior shape of the structure that is so appealing and restful, as it combines Chinese elements with the developing Japanese Muromachi
★ (1333–1568) architecture. Ginkakuji overlooks the complex **gardens** attributed to architect and artist Soami. They are in two sections and serve to contrast each other to establish a balance. Adjacent to the pavilion is the pond, with a composition of rocks and plants designed to offer different perspectives from each viewpoint; the other garden has two sculptured mounds of sand, with the higher one perhaps symbolizing Mt. Fuji. The garden sparkles in the moonlight and has been aptly named "Sea of Silver Sand." *Ginkakuji-machi, Sakyo-ku.* ☛ *¥400 adults, ¥200 children 6–15.* ☺ *Daily Mar. 15–Nov. 30, 8:30–5; winter, 9–4:30.*

❷ If you can tear yourself away from Ginkakuji, retrace your steps on the entrance road until you reach, on your left, the **Path of Philosophy,** or, as the Japanese say, "Tetsugaku-no-michi." This walkway along the canal, lined with cherry trees, has been a place for contemplative strolls since a famous scholar, Ikutaro Nishida, took his constitutional here. Now professors and students have to push their way through tourists who take the same stroll and whose interest lies mainly with the path's specialty shops.

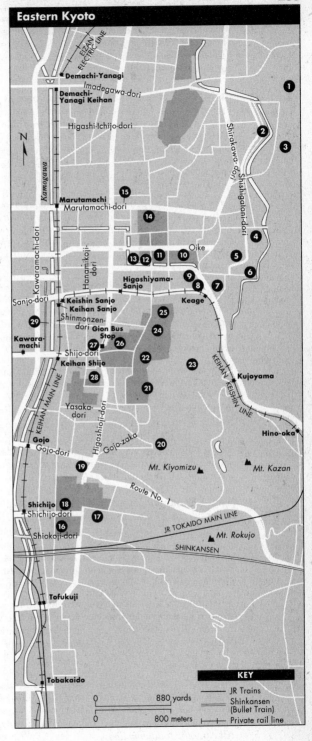

Eastern Kyoto

TIME OUT The Path of Philosophy has several coffee shops and small restaurants at which to stop and relax along the way. **Omen** restaurant, one block west of the Path of Philosophy, is an inexpensive, popular place, known for its homemade white noodles. If you are desperate for Western food, you can try **Bobby Soxer** for pizza.

❸ At the fourth bridge (larger than the first three, as you walk south) off the path, cross over the canal and take the road east to **Honenin** (temple), a modest structure with a thatch roof. Not too many people come here, and the walk through the trees leading to the temple is mercifully quiet and comforting. The temple was built in 1680, on a site that in the 13th century simply consisted of an open-air Amida statue. Honenin honors Priest Honen (1133–1212), who brought Buddhism down from its lofty peak to the common folk by making the radical claim that all were equal in the eyes of Buddha. Honen focused on faith in the Amida Buddha; he believed that *nenbutsu* ("Namu Amida Butsu," the invocation of Amida Buddha), which he is said to have repeated up to 60,000 times a day, and reliance on Amida, the All-Merciful, were the path of salvation. Because his ideas threatened other sects, especially the Tendai sect, Honen's teachings of Jodo-shu, "the Pure Land Sect," were accused of advocating that the masses seduce the ladies of noble classes. At the insistence of the established Buddhist powers, Emperor Gotoba had several of Honen's followers executed and Honen sent into exile. Eventually, in 1211, Honen was pardoned and permitted to return to Kyoto, where a year later, at Chionin, he fasted to death at the age of 79. ☛ *Free.* ⊙ *Daily 7–4.*

❹ From Honenin, walk back to the Path of Philosophy and continue in a southerly direction. In 15 minutes or so you'll reach **Eikando** on your left. Eikando is the temple's popular name. Officially it is Zenrinji, founded in 856 by Priest Shinsho, but it honors the memory of an 11th-century priest, Priest Eikan, which explains the popular name. He was a man of the people and would lead them in a dance in celebration of Amida Buddha. On one such occasion, the Amida statue came to life and stepped down from his pedastal to join the dancers. Taken aback, Eikan slowed his dancing feet. Amida looked back over his shoulder to reprimand Eikan for slowing his pace. This is the legend that explains why the unusual statue in the Amidado (hall) has its face turned to the side, as if glancing backward. For the energetic, a climb to the top of the pagoda offers superb views of the grounds below and Kyoto beyond. In autumn, the grounds are especially magnificent with the turning leaves of the maple trees. The buildings are 16th-century reconstructions made after the originals were destroyed in the Onin Civil War (1467–1477). ☛ *¥400.* ⊙ *Daily 9–5 (enter by 4:30).*

❺ If you cross the street from Eikando and continue south, you'll see the **Nomura Bijutsukan** (art museum) on the right. Instead of bequeathing their villas to Buddhist sects, the modern wealthy Japanese tend to donate their art collections to museums. Such is the case here. Founder of the Daiwa Bank and a host of other companies, Tokushichi Nomura gave his collection of scrolls, paintings, tea-ceremony utensils, ceramics, and other art objects to establish his namesake museum. *61 Shimogawaracho, Nanzenji, Sakyo-ku,* ☎ *075/751–0374.* ☛ *¥600.* ⊙ *Tues.–Sun. 10–4:30 (enter by 4) late-Mar.–mid-June and mid-Sept.–early Dec. When national holidays fall on Mon., the museum is open and will close the following day.*

(If the day is close to an end, walk from the Nomura Art Museum to the Heian Shrine and the Kyoto Handicraft Center on Marutamachi-dori behind it. If not, continue this tour, which returns shortly to the Heian Shrine.)

6 Next, walk south from the Nomura Art Museum and follow the main path; on your left will be **Nanzenji,** another one of those retirement villas that was turned into a temple on the death of its owner. This donor was Emperor Kameyama (1249–1305). The Onin Civil War (1467–1477) demolished the buildings, but some were resurrected during the 16th century, and Nanzenji has become one of Kyoto's most important temples, in part because it is the headquarters of the Rinzai sect of Zen Buddhism. As you enter the temple, you'll pass through the **San-mon** (Triple Gate), built in 1628. This is the classic "gateless" gate of Zen Buddhism serving as a symbol of entrance into the most sacred part of the temple precincts. From the top floor of the gate there is a view of Kyoto spread out below. The steps are pretty steep, and you might decide to forgo the pleasure, but give a moment to Goemon Ishikawa, a Robin Hood–style outlaw of Japan who hid in this gate until his eventual capture.

On through the gate is **Hojo Hall,** a National Treasure. Inside, the chambers are divided by screens with impressive 16th-century paintings. These wall panels of the *Twenty-four Paragons of Filial Piety and Hermits* are by Eitoku Kano (1543–1590) of the Kano school (really the Kano family, because the school consists of eight generations—Eitoku being from the fifth—of one bloodline). The Zen-style garden attached to the Hojo Hall has stones amid the sculpted trees and sand. This garden has been assigned several names, but the one that stands out is "Leaping Tiger Garden."

Within Nanzenji's 27 pine tree–covered acres are several other temples, known more for their gardens than for their buildings. Two are worth visiting if you have time. The first is **Nanzenin,** once the temporary abode of the Kameyama (1249–1305), who founded the temple. Nanzenin holds a mausoleum and has a garden that dates to the 14th century; a small creek passes through it. Only recently open to the public, Nanzenin is not as famous as other temples, making it a peaceful place to visit. ☛ *¥350.* ○ *Daily, Nov.–Mar. 8:30–4:30; Apr.–Oct. 8:20–5.*

7 The other temple worth visiting is outside the main gate of Nanzenji but still part of it. As you leave Nanzenji, take the side street to the left and you will come to **Konchiin,** with its pair of gardens, one with a pond in the shape of the Chinese character *kokoro,* or heart, and the other a dry garden with a "sea of sand" and a backdrop of greenery borrowed from the mountains behind. The garden was designed by the famous tea master and landscape designer Enshu Kobori in 1632. The two rock groupings in front of a plant-filled mound are in the crane-and-tortoise style. Since ancient times these creatures have been associated with longevity, beauty, and eternal youth. In the feudal eras, the symbolism of the crane and the tortoise became very popular with the samurai class, whose profession often left them with only the hope of immortality. *86 Fukuchi-cho, Nanzenji, Sakyo-ku.* ☛ *¥400 adults, ¥300 high school students, ¥200 children under 12.* ○ *Daily 8:30–5 (8:30–4:30 in winter).*

8 At the intersection at the foot of the road to Nanzenji, you'll see the expansive grounds of the **Kyoto International Community House** across the street to the left. The center offers library and information facilities and rental halls for public performances. The bulletin board by the entry way is full of tips on housing, study, and events in Kyoto. The

KICH also offers weekly lessons in tea ceremony, koto, calligraphy, and Japanese language at reasonable prices. The book *Easy Living in Kyoto* (available free) gives helpful information for a lengthy stay. *2-1 Awataguchi, Toriicho, Sakyo-ku,* ☎ *075/752–3010.* ☛ *Free.* ☉ *Tues.–Sun. 9 AM–9 PM. When Mon. is a national holiday, the House closes the following day instead.*

Walk back to the main road to Nanzenji and turn left. Cross at the traffic light to **Murin-an Garden,** whose entrance is on a side road half a block east. The property was once part of Nanzenji, but it was sold to Prince Yamagata, a former prime minister and advocate of the reforms that followed the Meiji Restoration (1868). The garden incorporates new ideas into Japanese thinking, just as the Meiji Restoration did. There is more freedom of movement in this garden than in the rigid, perfected harmony of more traditional gardens. ☛ *¥300.* ☉ *9–4:30. Closed Dec. 29–Jan. 3.*

Walk back north toward the canal and turn left. If you were to cross the canal at the first right, you would be at the **Dobutsu-en** (Kyoto Zoo). There is no pressing reason to visit it, unless you have children in tow. The zoo has a Children's Corner, where your youngsters can feed the farm animals. *Hoshojicho, Okazaki, Sakyo-ku,* ☎ *075/771–0210.* ☛ *¥400 adults, free for elementary-school children and younger.* ☉ *Tues.–Sun. 9–5 (winter 9–4:30). When Mon. is a national holiday, it closes the following day instead.*

Unless you turn off for the zoo, continue to the next right and cross the bridge over the canal. You'll see an immense vermilion *torii* (gate), because this is the road that leads to the Heian Shrine. Immediately after the torii, the **Kyoto-shi Bijutsukan** (Municipal Art Museum) will be on your right, and the **Kindai Bijutsukan** (National Museum of Modern Art) will be on your left.

The Municipal Art Museum is primarily an exhibition hall for traveling shows and those of local art societies. It owns a collection of Japanese paintings of the Kyoto school, a selection of which goes on exhibit once a year. *Enshojicho, Okazaki, Sakyo-ku,* ☎ *075/771–4107.* ☛ *Depends on exhibition, but usually around ¥800.* ☉ *Tues.–Sun. 9–5 (enter by 4:30).*

The National Museum of Modern Art, established in 1903, reopened in 1986 in a new building designed by Fumihiko Maki, one of the top contemporary architects in Japan. The museum is known for its collection of 20th-century Japanese paintings, as well as for its ceramic treasures by Kanjiro Kawai, Rosanji Kitaoji, Shoji Hamada, and others. *Enshojicho, Okazaki, Sakyo-ku,* ☎ *075/761–4111.* ☛ *¥400 (more for special exhibitions).* ☉ *Tues.–Sun. 9:30–5.*

The **Dento Sangyo Kaikan** (Kyoto Museum of Traditional Industry) houses a wide array of traditional Kyoto crafts and gives craftsmaking demonstrations that are both educational and useful, should you wish to collect some—a shop on the premises will help fulfill this temptation. In the basement is a model interior of a traditional town house. *9-2 Seishojicho, Okazaki, Sakyo-ku,* ☎ *075/761–3421.* ☛ *Free.* ☉ *Tues.–Sun. 9–5 (enter by 4:30).*

The street between the Municipal Art Museum and the National Museum of Modern Art leads directly to **Heian Jingu,** one of Kyoto's newest historical sites. Built in 1895 to mark the 1,100th anniversary of the founding of Kyoto, the shrine is dedicated to two emperors: Kanmu (737–806), who founded the city in 794, and Komei (1831–1866), the last emperor to live out his reign in Kyoto. The new buildings are for the most part replicas of the old Imperial Palace, but only two-thirds the original size. In fact, because the original palace (rebuilt many times) was finally destroyed in 1227, and only scattered pieces of information are available relating to its construction, Heian Jingu should be taken as a Meiji interpretation of the old palace. Still, the dignity and the relative spacing of the **East Honden, West Honden** (Main Halls), and the **Daigokuden** (Great Hall of State), where the Heian emperor would issue decrees, conjure up an image of the magnificence that the Heian court must have presented.

During New Year, the imposing gravel forecourt leading to Daigoku-den is trampled by kimono-clad and gray-suited Japanese who come to pay homage; the most wonderful time to visit is in the spring, during cherry-blossom time. The gardens are also a modern interpretation of a Heian garden, but they follow the Heian aesthetic of focusing on a large pond whose shores are gracefully linked by the arched Taibei-kaku Chinese-style bridge. An even better time to visit the shrine is during the Jidai Festival, held on October 22, which celebrates the founding of Kyoto. The pageant, featuring a procession of 2,000 people attired in costumes from every period of Kyoto history, winds its way from the original site of the Imperial Palace and ends at the Heian Shrine. *Okazakinishi Tennocho, Sakyo-ku.* ☛ *To the garden: ¥500 adults, ¥400 teenagers 15–18, ¥250 children 6–14, children under 6 free.* ⊗ *Mar. 15–Aug. 31, 8:30–5:30; Sept.–Oct. and Mar. 1–Mar. 14, 8:30– 5; Nov.–Feb., 8:30–4:30.*

Another choice time to be at the shrine is on June 1–2 for Takigi Noh performances, so-named because it is performed at night in the open air and the lighting is provided by burning firewood (*takigi*); the performances are presented on a stage built before the shrine's Daigoku-den (*see above*). ☛ *For Takigi Noh is ¥3,000 at the gate, ¥2,000 in advance. Call the TIC for advance ticket outlets (☏ 075/371–5649).*

⑮ If the urge comes on to do some shopping, cross Marutamachi-dori and turn left, and you'll come to the **Kyoto Handicraft Center,** where there are seven floors of everything Japanese, from dolls to cassette recorders. The center caters to tourists. (*See* Shopping, *below.*) *Kumano Jinja Higashi, Sakyo-ku, ☏ 075/761–5080.* ⊗ *9:30–6 (9:30–5:30 in winter). Closed Dec. 31–Jan. 3.*

At the crossroads of Marutamachi-dori and Higashioji-dori (west of the Kyoto Handicraft Center) is the Kumano Jinja-mae bus stop. If you've had enough sightseeing for one day, take Bus 202 or 206 five stops south on Higashioji-dori to the Gion bus stop; here, the world of restaurants and bars is at your disposal. Gion will be discussed later. If you are going to continue sightseeing, stay on Bus 202 for five more stops (Hi-gashiyama-Shichijo) to explore the southern part of Higashiyama. If you have taken Bus 206, stay on it for one more stop (it makes a right turn onto Shichijo-dori and heads for the station) and get off at the Sanjusangendo-mae bus stop. You may want to join this tour here to-morrow. If that is the case, you may also reach Sanjusangendo-mae bus stop by taking Bus 206 or 208 from Kyoto Station.

If you disembarked from the bus at Sanjusangendo-mae bus stop, Sanjusangendo will be to the south, just beyond the Kyoto Park Hotel. If you disembarked from Bus 202 at Higashiyama-Shichijo bus stop, you need to walk down Shichijo-dori and take the first major street to the left. However, you may want to visit Chishakuin first; that will allow you to avoid doubling back.

⑯ **Sanjusangendo** is the popular name for Rengeoin (temple). Sanjusan means "33"; that is the number of spaces between the 35 pillars that lead down the narrow, 394-foot-long hall of the temple. Enthroned in the middle of the hall is the six-foot-tall, 1,000-handed Kannon (National Treasure), carved by Tankei, a sculptor of the Kamakura period (1192–1333). Surrounding the statue are 1,000 smaller statues of Kannon, and in the corridor behind are 28 guardian deities who are protectors of the Buddhist universe. Notice the frivolous-faced Garuda, a bird that feeds on dragons. If you are wondering about the 33 spaces mentioned earlier, Kannon can assume 33 different shapes on her missions of mercy. Because there are 1,001 statues of Kannon in the hall, 33,033 shapes are possible. People come to the hall to see if they can find the likeness of a loved one (a deceased relative) among the 1,001 statues. *657 Sanjusangendo-Mawaricho, Higashiyama-ku.* ☛ *¥500 adults, ¥300 high-school and junior-high-school students, ¥200 grade-school children.* ☽ *8–5 (9–4 in winter).*

From Sanjusangendo, retrace your steps back to Shichijo-dori and take a right. Chishakuin will be facing you on the other side of Higashioji-dori.

⑰ The major reason for visiting the temple **Chishakuin** is for its famous paintings, which were executed by Tohaku Hasegawa and his son Kyuzo (known as the Hasegawa school, rivals of the Kano school) and are some of the best examples of Momoyama art. These paintings were originally created for the sliding screens at Shounin, a temple built in 1591 on the same site but no longer in existence. Shounin was commissioned by Hideyoshi Toyotomi. When his concubine, Yodogimi, bore him an heir in 1589, Hideyoshi named his son Tsurumatsu (Crane-pine), two symbols of longevity. Ironically, the child died when he was two, and Shounin was built for Tsurumatsu's enshrinement. The Hasegawas were then commissioned to do the paintings. Saved from the fires that destroyed Shounin, the paintings are now on display in the Exhibition Hall of Chishakuin. These paintings, rich in detail and using strong colors on a gold ground, splendidly display the seasons by using the symbols of cherry, maple, pine, and plum trees and autumn grasses.

You may also want to take a few moments in the pond-viewing garden. It is only a vestige of its former glory, but from the temple's veranda, you'll have a pleasing view of the pond and garden. ☛ *¥350.* ☽ *9–4:30.*

⑱ Back across Higashioji-dori is the prestigious **Kokuritsu Hakubutsukan** (Kyoto National Museum), with a collection of more than 8,000 works of art housed in two buildings. Exhibitions are continually changing, but you can count on an excellent display of paintings, sculpture, textiles, calligraphy, ceramics, lacquerware, metalwork, and archaeological artifacts from its permanent collection. *Yamato-oji-dori, Higashiyama-ku,* ☎ *075/541–1151.* ☛ *¥400 (more for special exhibitions).* ☽ *Tues.–Sun. 9–4:30.*

Just north, less than a five-minute walk along Higashioji-dori from the
⑲ Kyoto National Museum, is **Kawai Kanjiro Kinenkan** (memorial house). Now a museum, this was the home and studio of one of Japan's most renowned potters. The house was designed by Kanjiro Kawai, who took for his inspiration a traditional rural Japanese cottage. He was one of the leaders of the Mingei (Folk Art) Movement, which sought to promote a revival of interest in traditional folk arts during the 1920s and '30s, when all things Western were in vogue in Japan. On display are some of the artist's personal memorabilia and, of more interest, some

of his exquisite works. An admirer of Western, Chinese, and Korean ceramic techniques, Kawai won many awards, including the Grand Prix at the 1937 Paris World Exposition. *Gojo-zaka, Higashiyama-ku,* ☎ *075/561–3585.* ☞ *¥700 adults, ¥500 college and high-school students, ¥300 junior-high-school students and younger.* ☉ *Tues.–Sun. 10–5. Closed Aug. 10–20, Dec. 24–Jan. 7. When Mon. is a national holiday, museum closes following day instead.*

★ ❷⓪ The next place to visit is a very special temple, **Kiyomizudera,** which may be reached by crossing the major avenue Gojo-dori and walking up Higashioji-dori. The street to the right, Gojo-zaka, leads into Kiyomizu-zaka, which you'll take to the temple.

Kiyomizu-zaka is lined with shops selling souvenirs, religious articles, and ceramics. There are also tea shops where you can sample *yatsuhashi,* a doughy, triangular sweet filled with cinnamon-flavored bean paste—a Kyoto specialty. Because of the immense popularity of the temple above it on the hill, this narrow slope is often crowded with sightseers and bus tour groups, but the magnificent temple is worth the struggle.

Kiyomizudera is a 1633 reconstruction of the temple that was built here in 798, four years after Kyoto was founded. It is a unique temple in more ways than one. It does not belong to one of the local Kyoto Buddhist sects but rather to the Hosso sect that developed in Nara. Kiyomizudera is one of the most visited temples in Kyoto and is closely associated with the city's skyline. In the past, people would come here to escape the open political intrigue of Kyoto and to scheme in secrecy. Visually, Kiyomizudera is unique because it is built on a steep hillside. Part of its Main Hall is held up by 139 giant pillars. Finally, it is one of the few temples where you can walk around the veranda without taking your shoes off.

The temple's location is marvelous. Indeed, one reason for coming here is the view. From the wood veranda you have both a fine view of the city and a breathtaking look at the valley below. "Have you the courage to jump from the veranda of Kiyomizu?" is a saying asked when someone sets out on a daring new venture.

The temple is dedicated to the popular 11-faced Kannon (Goddess of Mercy), who can bring about easy childbirth. Over time, Kiyomizudera has become "everyone's temple"; you'll see evidence of this throughout the grounds, from the little Jizo Bosatsu statues (representing the god of travel and children) stacked in rows to the many *koma-inu* (mythical guard dogs) marking the pathways, which have been given by the temple's grateful patrons. *Kiyomizu 1-chome, Higashiyama-ku, Kyoto-shi.* ☞ *¥300 adults, ¥200 junior-high-school students and younger.* ☉ *Daily 8–6.*

If you take a right halfway down the road leading from Kiyomizudera, you can walk along the Sannen-zaka and Ninen-zaka (slopes). These two lovely winding streets are an example of old Kyoto with their cobbled paths and delightful wooden buildings. This area is one of four historic preservation districts in Kyoto, and the shops along the way offer local crafts and wares such as *Kiyomizu-yaki* (Kiyomizu-style pottery), Kyoto dolls, bamboo basketry, rice crackers, and antiques.

❷① Take a left after Ninen-zaka and then an immediate right, as you keep going in a northerly direction. After walking another five minutes you will see, on the right, **Kodaiji,** a quiet nunnery established in the early 17th century and only recently opened to the public. This temple was built as a memorial to Hideyoshi Toyotomi by his wife Kita-no-Mandokoro, who lived out her remaining days in the nunnery there. Ko-daiji has gardens designed by Kobori Enshu, and the Kaisando (Founder's Hall) has ceilings decorated in raised lacquer and paintings by artists of the Tosa school. The teahouse above on the hill, designed by tea master Sen-no-Rikyu, has a unique umbrella-shape bamboo ceiling and a thatch roof. ☛ ¥500. ⊙ *Daily 9–4:30 (9–4 in winter).*

Continue northward: By doing a right–left zigzag at the Maruyama Music **㉒** Hall, you reach **Maruyama Koen** (park). The road to the right (east) **㉓** leads to **Chorakuji,** a temple famous today for the stone lanterns that lead to it. Although it's a pleasant temple, it may not be worth the hard climb up the mountainside.

★ **㉔** Proceed north through Maruyama Koen and you'll find **Chionin,** head-quarters of the Jodo sect of Buddhism, the second largest Buddhist sect in Japan. The entrance to the temple is through a 79-foot, two-story Sanmon Gate. In many people's minds, this is the most daunting temple gate in all of Japan, and it leads to one of Japan's largest temples. On the site of Chion-in, Honen, the founder of the Jodo sect, fasted and died in 1212. The temple was built in 1234; because of fires and earthquakes, the oldest standing buildings are the Main Hall (1633) and the Daihojo (Abbots' Quarters; 1639). The temple's belfry houses the largest bell in Japan, which was cast in 1633 and requires 17 monks to ring. The corridor behind the Main Hall, which leads to the Assembly Hall, is called *uguisu-bari* (nightingale floor). It was constructed to "sing" at every footstep to warn the monks of intruders. Walk underneath the corridor to examine the way the boards and nails are placed to create this inventive burglar alarm. *400 Hayashishitacho 3-chome, Yamato-oji, Higashi-Hairu, Shinbashi-dori, Higashiyama-ku, Kyoto-shi.* ☛ *¥400 adults, ¥200 junior-high-school students and younger.* ⊙ *Daily 9–4:30 (9–4 in winter). Not all buildings are open to the public.*

㉕ More paintings by the Kano school are on view at **Shorenin,** a five-minute walk to the north of Chionin. Though the temple's present building dates only from 1895, the sliding screens of the Main Hall have the works of Motonobu Kano, second-generation Kano, and Mitsunobu Kano of the sixth generation. The gardens of this temple are pleasant—with an immense camphor tree at the entrance gate and azaleas surrounding a balanced grouping of rocks and plants. It was no doubt more grandiose when Soami designed it in the 16th century, but with the addition of paths through the garden, it's a pleasant place to stroll. Another garden on the east side of the temple is sometimes attributed, probably incorrectly, to Kobori Enshu. Occasionally, koto concerts are held in the evening in the Soami garden. (Check with a Japan Travel Bureau office for concert schedules.) ☛ *¥400.* ⊙ *Daily 9–5. Closed one day in Oct. or Nov. for a special Buddhist ceremony (no specific date is set).*

Should you have missed visiting the Heian Shrine, the National Museum of Modern Art, and the Municipal Museum of Art described earlier, note that these are just 10 minutes by foot north of Shorenin, on the other side of Sanjo-dori. If you take a right (east) from Shorenin on Sanjo-dori, you'll eventually reach the Miyako Hotel; left (west) on Sanjo-dori leads across Higashioji-dori to the downtown area and covered mall. If you turn left on Higashioji-dori, you will reach Shijo-dori and the Gion district.

At the Gion bus stop, Shijo-dori goes off to the west. Before going down this street, consider taking a short walk east (back into Maruyama Koen) **26** to **Yasaka Jinja.** Because its location is close to the shopping districts, worshipers drop by for some quick salvation. This is a good shrine to come to if you have business or health problems; leave a message for the God of Prosperity and Good Health, to whom the shrine is dedicated. Especially at New Year, Kyoto residents flock here to ask for good fortune in the coming year. *625 Gionmachi, Kitagawa, Higashi-yama-ku.* ☛ *Free.* ⊙ *24 hours.*

27 Walk back from Yasaka Jinja, cross Higashioji-dori, and you are in Kyoto's Gion district, on Shijo-dori. On the right-hand corner is the **Kyoto Craft Center,** where Kyoto residents shop for fine contemporary and traditional crafts—ceramics, lacquerware, prints, and textiles. You can also find moderately priced souvenirs, such as dolls, coasters, bookmarks, and paper products. *Higashi-Kitagawa, Hanami-koji, Gion-Shijo-dori, Higashiyama-ku,* ☎ *075/561–9660.* ⊙ *Thurs.–Tues. 10–6.*

Parallel to Shijo-dori and to the north is Shinmonzen-dori, a street famous for its antiques shops and art galleries. Here you'll find collectors' items—at collectors' prices, too—but there is no harm in just browsing. The shops on Shijo-dori have slightly more affordable products, from handcrafted hair ornaments to incense to parasols—all articles that are part of the geisha world.

Off Shijo-dori, halfway between Higashioji-dori and the Kamogawa, is Hanamikoji-dori. The section of this street that runs south of Shijo-dori (on the right, if you are walking back from the river) will bring ★ you into the heart of the **Gion** district. Here is where the top geisha live and work; they can be seen scurrying in the evening en route to their assignments, trailed by young apprentice geisha (*maiko*), who can be distinguished from their mistresses by the longer sleeve lengths of their kimonos. Because Westerners have little opportunity to enjoy a geisha's performance in a private party setting, a popular entertainment during the month of April is the Miyako Odori (cherry blossom ★ **28** dance) held at the **Gion Kaburenjo Theater** (Gion Hanamikoji, Higashiyama-ku, ☎ 075/561–1115). Miyako Odori features musical presentations by geisha, who are dressed in their elaborate traditional kimonos and makeup. Next door to the theater is **Gion Corner,** where demonstrations of traditional performing arts are held nightly from March through November (*see* The Arts and Nightlife, *below*).

If you continue west along Shijo-dori you'll cross over the Kamogawa (river); on your right will be Pontocho-dori. Like Gion, this area is known for its nightlife and geisha entertainment. At the top (north) end of Pon-**29** tocho-dori, the **Pontocho Kaburenjo Theater** presents geisha song-and-dance performances in the spring (May 1–May 24) and autumn (Oct. 15–Nov. 7). *Pontocho, Sanjo-sagaru, Nakagyo-ku,* ☎ *075/221–2025.*

Western Kyoto

Numbers in the margin correspond to points of interest on the Western Kyoto map.

Our exploration of western Kyoto starts in the north where the major attractions are located. Then, if you become tired or run out of time, you can cut short the tour and return to your hotel. We begin at Kitano Tenmangu (shrine) but if you are short of time, you may want to start at Daitokuji.

To reach Kitano Tenmangu from downtown, take either Bus 50 or 52 from downtown Kyoto and Kyoto Station. The rides take a little more than ½ hour. **Kitano Tenmangu** made history in about 942, when Michizane Sugawara was enshrined here. Previously the shrine had been dedicated to Tenjin, the god of thunder. Michizane had been a noted poet and politician, but when Emperor Godaigo ascended to the throne, Michizane was accused of treason and sent to exile on Kyushu, where he died. For decades afterward, Kyoto suffered inexplicable calamities. Then the answer came in a dream. The problem was Michizane's spirit; he would not rest until he had been pardoned. Because the dream identified Michizane with the god of thunder, Kitano Tenmangu was dedicated to him. Furthermore, Michizane's rank as minister of the right was posthumously restored. When that was not enough, he was promoted to the higher position of minister of the left, and later to prime minister. The shrine was also the place where Hideyoshi Toyotomi held an elaborate tea party, inviting the whole of Kyoto to join him. Apart from unifying the warring clans of Japan and attempting to conquer Korea, Toyotomi is remembered in Kyoto as the man responsible for restoring many of the city's temples and shrines during the late 16th century. The shrine's present structure, by the way, dates from 1607. A large flea market is held on the grounds on the 25th of each month; there are food stalls and an array of antiques, old kimonos, and other collectibles. *Bakuro-cho, Kamigyo-ku.* ☞ *Free. The plum garden is* ☉ *in Feb. and Mar.* ☞ *¥400 (includes green tea). Shrine* ☉ *daily 5:30 AM–6 PM; plum garden* ☉ *daily 10 AM–4 PM.*

About a five-minute walk north of Kitano is **Hirano Jinja,** which actually consists of four shrine buildings dating from the 17th century. However, the shrine has a much older history. It was brought from Nagaoka (the previous capital) as one of the many shrines used to protect Kyoto (Heian-kyo) during its formative days. The buildings are less the reason to visit here than the gardens, with their 80 varieties of cherry trees. *Miyamotocho 1, Hirano, Kita-ku.* ☞ *Free.* ☉ *Daily 6 AM–5 PM.*

Now head for Daitokuji. Go east from Hirano Jinja, to the bus stop on Sembon-dori, and take Bus 206 north for about 10 minutes.

There are several ways to get to the temple from downtown Kyoto. Take the subway north from Kyoto Station to Kitaoji Eki-mae Station, and take any bus going west along Kitaoji-dori to the Daitokuji-mae bus stop. You can also take Bus 12 north up Horikawa-dori and disembark soon after the bus makes a left on Kitaoji-dori.

Daitokuji is a large temple of the Rinzai sect of Zen Buddhism. The name refers to a complex of 24 temples in all, several of which are open to the public. The original temple was founded in 1319 by Priest Daito Kokushi (1282–1337), but fires during the Onin Civil War destroyed it in 1468. Most of the buildings you see today were built under the patronage of Hideyoshi Toyotomi. However, it is thought that Priest Ikkyu oversaw its development. Ikkyu, both a poet and a priest, is reported to have said, "Brothels are more suitable settings for meditation than temples."

The layout of the temple is straightforward. Running from north to south are the Chokushimon (gate), the Sanmon (gate), Butsuden (Buddha Hall), Hatto (Lecture Hall), and the Hojo (Abbots' Quarters). The 23 subtemples are located on the west side of these main buildings and were donated mainly by the wealthy vassals of Toyotomi.

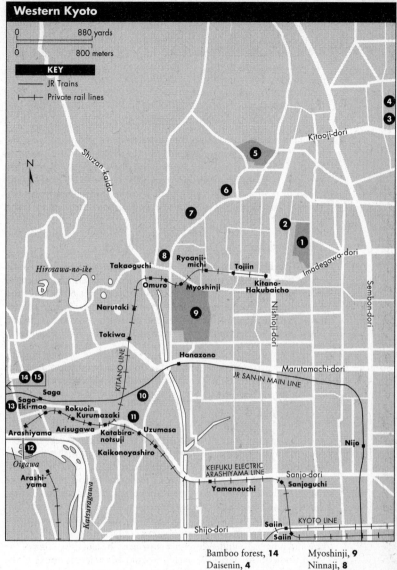

Western Kyoto

KEY
— JR Trains
╠═╬═╬═ Private rail lines

0 ——— 880 yards
0 ——— 800 meters

N

Shuzan-kaido

Kitaoji-dori

Hirosawa-no-ike

Takaoguchi
Ryoanji-michi
Tojiin
Kitano-
Hakubaicho

Omuro
Myoshinji

Narutaki

Tokiwa

Hanazono

Marutamachi-dori

Saga
JR SAN-IN MAIN LINE

Saga-
Eki-mae
Rokuoin
Kurumazaki

Arashiyama
Arisugawa
Katabira-
notsuji
Uzumasa

Kaikonoyashiro
Nijo

Oigawa

Arashi-
yama
KEIFUKU ELECTRIC
ARASHIYAMA LINE
Sanjo-dori
Sanjoguchi

Yamanouchi

Katsuragawa

Shijo-dori
Saiin
KYOTO LINE
Saiin

KITANO LINE

Nishioji-dori

Imadegawa-dori

Sembon-dori

The **Chokushimon** (Gate of Imperial Messengers) originally served as the south gate of Kyoto's Imperial Palace when it was constructed in 1590. Then, Empress Meisho in the mid-17th century bequeathed it to Daitokuji. It is appreciated today for its curved-gable style, typical of the Momoyama period. The Sanmon triple gate is noteworthy for the addition of its third story, designed by tea master Sen-no-Rikyu (1521–1591), who is, by the way, buried in the temple grounds. *Daitokujicho, Murasakino, Kita-ku.* ☛ *To different temples averages ¥500. Temple hours vary between 9 and 4.*

❹ Of all the subtemples at this complex, **Daisenin** is perhaps the most well known, especially for its excellent landscape paintings by the renowned Soami (1465–1523) and for its *karesansui* (dry-style) garden that some attribute to Soami and others to Kogaku Soko (1465–1548). The sand and stone represent the eternal aspects of nature, while the streams suggest the course of life. The single rock, once owned by Shogun Yoshimasa Ashikaga, may be seen as a ship. Be aware though, that Daisenin has become commercialized. ☛ *¥400 adults, ¥270 junior-high-school students and younger.* ☼ *Daily 9–5 (9–4:30 in winter).*

Another subtemple open to the public is **Kotoin,** famous for its long, maple tree–lined approach and the single stone lantern that is central to the main garden. Not as popular as Daisenin, it is often quiet and peaceful, as is **Ryogenin,** still another sub-temple. Ryogenin has five small gardens of moss and stone, one of which (on the north side) is the oldest in Daitokuji. ☛ *To each: ¥350.* ☼ *Daily 9–4:30 (enter by 4).*

The best way to our next stop, Kinkakuji, is to hop on Bus 12 going west on Kitaoji-dori for a 10-minute ride to the Kinkakuji-mae bus stop.

★ ❺ For a retirement home, **Kinkakuji** (Temple of the Golden Pavilion) is pretty magnificent. Shogun Yoshimitsu Ashikaga (1358–1409) had it constructed in 1393 for the time when he quit politics (in 1394) to manage the affairs of state through the new shogun, his 10-year-old son. On Yoshimitsu's death, his son followed his father's wishes and converted the villa into a temple named Rokuonji. The structure is positioned, following the Shinden style of the Heian period, at the edge of the lake. The three-story pavilion is supported on pillars, extends over the pond, and is reflected in the calm waters. It is a beautiful sight, but it also was designed to convey its existence somewhere between heaven and earth. The pavilion was the shogun's political statement of his prestige and power. To underscore that statement, he had the ceiling of the third floor of the pavilion covered in gold leaf. Hence, not only the harmony and balance of the pavilion and its reflection, but also the richness of color shimmering in the light and in the water, make Kinkakuji one of Kyoto's most powerful visions.

In 1950, a student-monk with metaphysical aspirations torched Kinkakuji and burned it to the ground. It was rebuilt in 1955 following the original design, except that all three stories were covered with gold leaf (as had been the shogun's intention) instead of only the third-floor ceiling. Marveling at this pavilion, you may find it difficult to imagine the historical perspective of the time when Shogun Yoshimitsu Ashikaga lived out his golden years. The country was in turmoil, and Kyoto residents suffered severe famines and plagues that sometimes reached death tolls of 1,000 souls a day. *1 Kinkakujicho, Kita-ku.* ☛ *¥400 adults and older students, ¥200 junior-high-school students and younger.* ☼ *Daily 9–5:30 (9–5, Oct.–Mar.).*

From Kinkakuji, walk back to the Kinkakuji-mae bus stop and take Bus 12 or 59 south for 10 minutes to the Ritsumeikan-Daigaku-mae bus stop for the **Domoto Bijutsukan** (Domoto Insho Art Museum), which exhibits paintings and sculpture by Insho Domoto, the 20th-century abstract artist. *Kami-Yanagicho, Hirano, Kita-ku,* ☎ *075/463–1348.* ☞ *¥500 adults, ¥400 college and high-school students, ¥200 junior-high and younger students.* ☉ *Tues.–Sun. 10–5. Closed Dec. 28–Jan. 4.*

When you leave the Domoto Art Museum, either hop on Bus 12 or 59, or walk for about 10 minutes going south; **Ryoanji** will be on your right.

The garden at Ryoanji, rather than the temple, attracts visitors from all over the world. Knowing that the temple belongs to the Rinzai sect of Zen Buddhism will help you appreciate the austere aesthetics of the garden. It is a dry (*kare sansui*) garden: just 15 rocks arranged in three groupings of seven, five, and three in gravel. From the temple's veranda, the proper viewing place, only 14 rocks can be seen at one time. Move slightly and another rock appears and one of the original 14 disappears. In the Buddhist world, the number 15 denotes completeness. You must have a total view of the garden to make it a whole and meaningful experience.

If possible, visit Ryoanji in the morning before the crowds come, disturbing the contemplative scene. If you do need a moment or two to yourself, there is a small restaurant on the temple grounds near an ancient pond, where you can rest awhile with an expensive beer. *13 Goryoshitamachi, Ryoanji, Ukyo-ku.* ☞ *¥400 adults, ¥200 junior-high-school students.* ☉ *Daily 8–5 (8:30–4:30 Dec.–Feb.)*

From Ryoanji, it is about 1½ kilometers (1 mile) farther south on Bus 26 to Myoshinji. En route you'll pass **Ninnaji** on the right, a temple that was once the palace of Emperor Omuro, who started the building's construction in 896. Needless to say, nothing of that remains. The complex of buildings that stands today was rebuilt in the 17th century. There is an attractive five-story pagoda (built 1637), and the Main Hall, which was moved from the Imperial Palace, is also worth noting as a National Treasure, with its focus of worship, the Amida Buddha. ☞ *¥350.* ☉ *Daily 9–5.*

From Ninnaji, take the street veering to the left (southwest); within ¾ kilometer (½ mile) you'll reach Myoshinji. Another option from Ryoanji is to take Bus 12 or 59 three stops south to Ninnaji and then change to Bus 8 or 10.

Japan's oldest bell (cast in 698) hangs in the belfry near the South Gate of **Myoshinji,** a temple founded in the 14th century. When Emperor Hanazono died, his villa was converted into a temple; the work required so many laborers that a complex of buildings was built to house them. In all, there are some 40 structures here, though only four are open to the public. Beware of the dragon on the ceiling of Myoshinji's Hatto (Lecture Hall). Known as the "Dragon Glaring in Eight Directions," it will be looking at you wherever you stand. ☞ *¥400.* ☉ *Daily 9–4.*

The other temple to visit here is **Taizoin,** which was built in 1404; like the rest of the Myoshinji complex, it suffered in the Onin War and had to be rebuilt. Taizoin has a famous painting by Sanraku Kano called *Four Sages of Mt. Shang,* recalling the four wise men who lived in isolation on a mountain to avoid the reign of destruction. The garden of Taizoin is gentle and quiet—a good place to rest. ☞ *¥400.* ☉ *Daily 9–5.*

Leave the temple complex by the south side and you can pick up Bus 61 or 62; both go southwest to Uzumasa Eiga Mura (Movie Village). If, however, you have no interest in stopping off here—a visit will take at least two or three hours—continue on the bus to Koryuji.

⑩ **Uzumasa Eiga Mura** is Japan's equivalent of the United States' Hollywood. Had Kyoto been severely damaged in World War II, this would have been the place to see old Japan. Traditional country villages, ancient temples, and old-fashioned houses make up the stage sets, and if you are lucky, a couple of actors dressed as samurai will be snarling at each other, ready to draw their swords. It is a fine place to bring children. For adults, whether it is worth the time touring the facilities and visiting the museum depends on your interest in Japanese movies. *10 Higashi-Hachigaokacho, Uzumasa,* ☎ *075/881–7716.* ☛ *¥2,000 adults, ¥1,100 students under 18.* ☉ *Daily 9–5 (9:30–4 in winter). Closed Dec. 21–Jan. 1.*

⑪ **Koryuji** is a short walk south of Uzumasa Eiga Mura. One of Kyoto's oldest temples, it was founded in 622 by Kawakatsu Hata in memory of Prince Shotoku (572–621). Shotoku, known for issuing the Seventeen-Article Constitution, was the first powerful advocate of Buddhism after it was introduced to Japan in 552. In the Hatto (Lecture Hall) of the main temple stand three statues, each a National Treasure. The center of worship is the seated figure of Buddha, flanked by the figures of the Thousand-Handed Kannon and Fukukenjaku-Kannon. In the rear hall (Taishido) is a wood statue of Prince Shotoku, which is thought to have been carved by him personally. Another statue of Shotoku in this hall was probably made when he was 16 years old.

In the temple's Treasure House (Reihoden) are numerous works of art, many of which are National Treasures, including the most famous of all, the **Miroku Bosatsu.** The statue has been declared Japan's number one National Treasure. This image of Buddha is the epitome of serene calmness, and of all the Buddhas that you see in Kyoto, this is likely to be the one that will most captivate your heart. No one knows when it was made, but it is thought to be from the 6th or 7th century, perhaps even carved by Shotoku himself. *Hachigaokacho, Uzumasa, Ukyo-ku.* ☛ *¥500.* ☉ *Daily, Mar.–Nov. 9–5; Dec.–Feb. 9–4:30.*

From Koryuji, it is easy to head back into downtown Kyoto. Either take the bus (60–64) back past the Movie Village to JR Hanazono Station, where the JR San-in Line will take you into Kyoto Station, or take the privately owned railway, the Keifuku Electric Railway Arashiyama Line, and go east to its last stop at Shijo-Omiya. This stop is on Shijo-dori, from where Buses 201 or 203 will take you to Gion, or Bus 26 will take you to Kyoto Station.

However, because we are so close to the area known as Arashiyama, we are going to take the Keifuku Electric Railway Arashiyama Line west to Tenryuji and the bamboo forests just to the north, a pleasant end to the day. You may get the chance to watch some cormorant fishing. If you decide to postpone this excursion until tomorrow, use the JR San-in Line from Kyoto Station to Saga Station, or use the Keifuku Electric Railway Arashiyama Station.

Arashiyama

The pleasure of Arashiyama, the westernmost part of Kyoto, is the same as it was a millennium ago. The gentle foothills of the mountains, covered with cherry and maple trees, are splendid, but it is the bamboo forests that really create the atmosphere of untroubled peace. It is no wonder that the aristocracy of feudal Japan liked to come here and leave behind the famine, riots, and political intrigue that plagued Kyoto with the decline of the Ashikaga Shogunate.

⑫ To the south of Arashiyama Station is the Oigawa (river) and the **To-getsukyo Bridge,** from where you can watch *ukai* (cormorant fishing) during the evening in July and August. Fishermen use cormorants to scoop up small sweetfish, which are attracted to the light from the flaming torches hung over the fishermen's boats. The cormorants would love to swallow the fish, but small rings around their necks prevent their appetites from being assuaged. After about five fish, the cormorant has more than his gullet can hold. Then the fisherman pulls the bird back on a string, makes the bird regurgitate his catch, and sends him back for more. The best way to watch this spectacle is to join one of the charter passenger boats. *Cost: ¥1,960 adults, ¥1,120 children. Reservations: Arashiyama Tsusen, 14-4 Nakaoshitacho, Arashiyama, Nishikyo-ku, ☎ 075/861–0223 or 861–0302. You may also contact the Japan Travel Bureau (075/361–7241) or your hotel information desk.*

The temple to head for is Tenryuji. If you have arrived at Arashiyama Station, walk north; if you have arrived on the JR line at Saga Station, walk west.

⑬ **Tenryuji** is for good reason known as the Temple of the Heavenly Dragon. Emperor Godaigo, who had successfully brought an end to the Kamakura Shogunate, was unable to hold on to his power. He was forced from his throne by Takauji Ashikaga. After Godaigo died, Takauji had twinges of conscience. That is when Priest Muso Kokushi had a dream in which a golden dragon rose from the nearby Oigawa. He told the shogun about his dream and interpreted it to mean the spirit of Godaigo was not at peace. Worried that this was an ill omen, Takauji built Tenryuji in 1339 on the same spot where Godaigo had his favorite villa. Apparently that appeased the spirit of the late emperor. In the Hatto (Lecture Hall), where today's monks meditate, a huge "Cloud Dragon" is painted on the ceiling. Now for the bad news. The temple was often ravaged by fire, and the current buildings are as recent as 1900; the painting of the dragon was rendered by 20th-century artist Shonen Suzuki. The garden of Tenryuji, which dates from the 14th century, is noted for the arrangement of vertical stones in the large pond and for being one of the first to use "borrowed scenery," incorporating the mountains in the distance into the design of the garden. *68 Susuki-no-banba-cho, Saga-Tenryuji, Ukyo-ku. Garden ☛ ¥500 adults, ¥300 junior-high-school students and younger. (An additional ¥100 is required to enter the temple building.) ☉ Daily, Apr.–Oct. 8:30–5:30; Nov.–Mar. 8:30–5.*

One of the best ways to enjoy some contemplative peace is to walk the estate grounds of one of Japan's new elite—Denjiro Okochi, a renowned silent movie actor of samurai films. To reach his estate, you must either walk through the temple garden or leave Tenryuji ⑭ and walk north on a narrow street through a **bamboo forest,** one of the best you'll see in the Kyoto region. Bamboo forests offer a unique ⑮ composure and tranquillity. The **Okochi Sanso** (mountain villa) will soon be in front of you, with its superb location. The views of Arashiyama and Kyoto are splendid, and on the grounds you are offered tea and cake while you absorb nature's pleasures. *8 Tabuchiyama-cho, Ogurayama, Saga, Ukyo-ku, ☎ 075/872–2233. ☛ ¥800. ☉ Daily 9–5.*

Central Kyoto

Numbers in the margin correspond to points of interest on the Central Kyoto map.

Our exploration of central Kyoto follows tours of eastern and western Kyoto, because the sights here are likely to be convenient to your hotel and you can visit each sight individually rather than combining them into a single itinerary.

The two major places in this area to see are Nijojo (Nijo Castle) and the Imperial Palace. Let's go to the Imperial Palace first, because that is one of the sights that requires permission. The easiest ways to reach the **Imperial Palace** are to take the subway to Imadegawa or to take the bus to the Karasuma-Imadegawa stop. You will join the tour at the Seishomon entrance.

The present palace is a third-generation construction. The original, built for Emperor Kanmu to the west of the present site, burned down in 1788. A new palace, modeled after the original, was then built on the present site, but that, too, ended in flames. The present structure was completed in 1855, and, in fact, was home to only two emperors, including the young Emperor Meiji before he moved his Imperial Household to Tokyo. On the 30-minute tour, you will only have a chance for a brief glimpse of the Shishinden (the hall where the inauguration of emperors and other important imperial ceremonies take place) and a visit to the gardens. Though a trip to the Imperial Palace is on most people's agenda, and despite the space it fills in downtown Kyoto, it perhaps holds less interest than do some of the older historic buildings in the city. ☛ *Free. To visit the Imperial Palace, arrive before 9:40 AM for the 50-minute 10 AM guided tour in English. Present yourself, along with your passport, at the office of the Imperial Household Agency in the palace grounds. For the 2 PM guided tour in English, arrive by 1:40 PM. Sat. afternoon tours only on 1st and 3rd Sat. of the month; no tours Sun. Imperial Household Agency, Kyoto Gyoen-nai, Kamigyo-ku, Kyoto, ☎ 075/211–1211. Office ⊘ weekdays 8:45–noon and 1–4, Sat. 8:45–noon; no tours 2nd and 4th Sat. of month.*

★ ❷ If you have chosen to visit the Imperial Palace, **Nijojo** is easily combined on the same trip. Take the bus going west along Marutamachi-dori for a couple of stops to Horikawa-dori, and then walk two blocks south along Horikawa-dori to Nijo Castle.

Nijo Castle was the local Kyoto address for the Tokugawa Shogunate. Dominating central Kyoto, it is an intrusion, both politically and artistically. The man who built the castle in 1603, Ieyasu Tokugawa, did so to emphasize that political power had been completely removed from the emperor and that he alone determined the destiny of Japan. As if to emphasize that statement, he built and decorated his castle with blatant ostentation in order to cower the populace with his wealth and power. Such overt displays were antithetical to the refined restraint of Kyoto's aristocracy.

Ieyasu Tokugawa had risen to power through skillful politics and treachery. His military might was unassailable, and that is probably why his Kyoto castle had relatively modest exterior defenses. However, as he well knew, defense against treachery is never certain. The interior of the castle was built with that in mind. Each building had concealed rooms where bodyguards could maintain a watchful eye for potential assassins, and the corridors had a built-in squeaking system, so no one could walk in the building without announcing his presence.

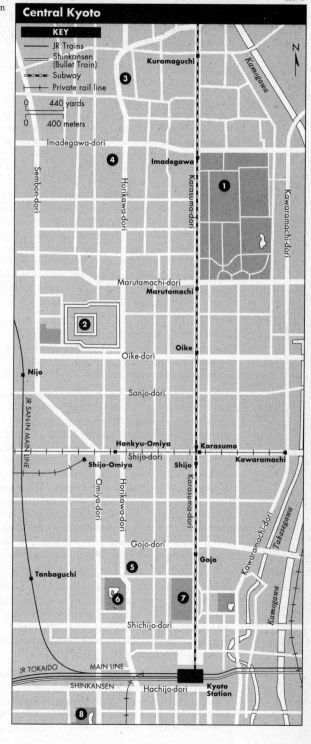

Central Kyoto

KEY
— JR Trains
Shinkansen
(Bullet Train)
Subway
Private rail line

0 ___ 440 yards
0 ___ 400 meters

N

Kuramaguchi

③

Imadegawa-dori

④

Imadegawa

①

Kamogawa

Semban-dori

Horikawa-dori

Karasuma-dori

Kawaramachi-dori

Marutamachi-dori

Marutamachi

②

Oike-dori

Oike

Nijo

Sanjo-dori

JR SANIN MAIN LINE

Hankyu-Omiya   **Karasuma**

Shijo-dori

Shijo-Omiya   **Shijo**   **Kawaramachi**

Omiya-dori

Horikawa-dori

Karasuma-dori

Kawaramachi-dori

Takasegawa

Gojo-dori

⑤

Gojo

Tanbaguchi

⑥   ⑦

Kamogawa

Shichijo-dori

JR TOKAIDO   MAIN LINE

SHINKANSEN   **Kyoto
Station**

Hachijo-dori

⑧

Rooms were locked only from the inside, so no one from the outer rooms could gain access to the inner rooms without admittance. The outer rooms were kept for visitors of low rank and were adorned with garish paintings that would impress them. The inner rooms were for the important lords, whom the shogun would impress with the refined, tasteful paintings of the Kano school.

The opulence and grandeur of the castle was, in many ways, a snub to the emperor. It relegated the emperor and his palace to insignificance, and the Tokugawa family even appointed a governor to manage the emperor and the imperial family. The Tokugawa shoguns were rarely in Kyoto. Ieyasu stayed in the castle three times, the second shogun twice, including the time in 1626 when the emperor, Emperor Gomizuno-o, was granted an audience. After that, for the next 224 years, no Tokugawa shogun came to Kyoto. The castle started to fall into disrepair and neglect. Only when the Tokugawa Shogunate was under pressure from a failing economy, and international pressure developed to open Japan to trade, did the 14th shogun, Iemochi Tokugawa (1846–1866), come to Kyoto to confer with the emperor. The emperor told the shogun to rid Japan of foreigners, but Iemochi did not have the strength. As the shogun's power continued to wane, the 15th and last shogun, Keiki Tokugawa (1837–1913), spent most of his time in Nijo Castle. Here he resigned, and the imperial decree was issued that abolished the shogunate after 264 years of rule.

After the Meiji Restoration (1868), Nijo Castle became the Kyoto Prefectural Office until 1884; during that time, it suffered from acts of vandalism. Since 1939, the castle has belonged to the city of Kyoto, and considerable restoration work has been completed.

Entrance to the castle is through the impressive **Karamon** (Chinese Gate). Notice that you must turn right and left at sharp angles to make this entrance—a common attribute of Japanese castles designed to slow the advance of any attacker. From the Karamon, the carriageway leads to the **Ninomaru** (Second Inner) **Palace,** the five buildings of which are divided into many chambers. The outer buildings were for visits by men of lowly rank, the inner ones for higher ranks. The most notable room, the **Ohiroma** (hall), is easy to recognize. In the room, figures in costume reconstruct the occasion when Keiki Tokugawa returned the power of government to the emperor. This spacious hall was where, in the early 17th century, the shogun would sit on a raised throne to greet important visitors seated below him. The sliding screens of this room have magnificent paintings of forest scenes.

As impressive as the Ninomaru Palace is the garden designed by the landscaper Kobori Enshu shortly before Emperor Gomizuno-o's visit in 1626. Notice the crane and tortoise islands flanking the center island (the land of paradise). The symbolic meaning is clear: strength and longevity. The garden was originally designed with no deciduous trees, for the shogun did not wish to be reminded of the transitory nature of life by autumn's falling leaves.

The other major building on the grounds is the **Honmaru Palace,** but, because it is a replacement for the original that burned down in the 18th century, Honmaru holds less interest than Ninomaru. *Horikawa Nishi-Iru, Nijo-dori, Nakagyo-ku,* ☎ *075/841–0096.* ☛ *¥500 adults, ¥190 children under 12.* ☉ *Daily 8:45–5 (enter by 4). Closed Dec. 26– Jan. 4.*

If, after the overt opulence and blatant use of wealth demonstrated by Nijo Castle, you feel in need of some refinement, make your way north to the **Raku Bijutsukan,** a museum that displays tea bowls made by members of the Raku family, whose roots can be traced back to the 16th century. As a potter's term in the West, *raku* refers to a low-temperature firing technique, but the word originated with this family, who made tea bowls for use in the Shogun's tea ceremonies. *Aburakoji, Nakadachuri-agaru, Kamigyo-ku,* ☎ *075/414–0304.* ☞ *¥800 adults, ¥600 students, ¥300 children (additional charge for special exhibitions).* ⊙ *Tues.–Sun. 10–4. Closed Aug. 14–17 and Dec. 27–Jan. 5.*

For another change of pace, if you have interest in traditional Japanese silk weaving, visit the Nishijin silk weaving district south from the Raku Museum on Horikawa-dori at the corner of Imadegawa-dori. To get here, take Bus 9. At the **Nishijin Orimono** (Textile Center) here, demonstrations are given of age-old weaving techniques, and fashion shows and special exhibitions are presented. On the mezzanine, you can buy kimonos and gift items, such as *happi* (workmen's) coats and silk purses. *Horikawa-dori, Imadegawa-Minami-Iru, Kamigyo-ku,* ☎ *075/451–9231.* ☞ *Free.* ⊙ *9–5.*

From the Raku Museum, the Nishijin Textile Center, or Nijojo, take Bus 9 south on Horikawa-dori. Disembark at the Kyoto Tokyu Hotel. Across from the Tokyu Hotel, on the fifth floor of the Izutsu Building at the intersection of Horikawa and Shin-Hanayacho, is the **Fuzoku Hakubutsukan** (Kyoto Costume Museum). You may want to pop in here to see the range of fashion that starts in the pre-Nara era and works up through the historical eras to the Meiji period. It is one of the best of its kind and, in its own way, gives an account of the history of Japan. Exhibitions change twice a year, with each exhibition highlighting a specific period in Japanese history. *Izutsu Building, Shimogyo-ku,* ☎ *075/361–8388.* ☞ *¥400 adults, ¥300 college and high-school students, ¥200 junior-high-school students and younger.* ⊙ *Mon.–Sat. 9–5. Closed June 1–19 and Dec. 16–Jan. 6.*

The last major attractions in central Kyoto are **Nishi-Honganji** and **Higashi-Honganji,** which were one temple until the early 17th century. Then Ieyasu Tokugawa took advantage of a rift among the Jodo Shinshu sect of Buddhism and, to diminish its power, split them apart into two different factions. The original faction has the west temple, Nishi-Honganji, and the latter faction the eastern temple, Higashi-Honganji. To reach the two temples, walk south on Horikawa-dori from the Kyoto Costume Museum; Nishi-Honganji will be on the right, and Higashi-Honganji will be a few blocks east (left).

Though the rebuilt (1895) structure of Higashi-Honganji is the largest wood structure in Japan, it contains fewer historical objects of interest than does its rival temple, Nishi-Honganji, many of whose buildings were brought from Hideyoshi Toyotomi's Jurakudai Palace in Kyoto and from Fushimi Castle, which Ieyasu Tokugawa had dismantled outside of Kyoto in an attempt to erase the memory of his predecessor.

Hideyoshi Toyotomi was quite a man. Though most of the work in unifying Japan was accomplished by the warrior Nobunaga Oda (he was ambushed a year after defeating the monks on Mt. Hiei), it was Hideyoshi who completed the job. Not only did he stop civil strife, but he also restored the arts. For a brief period (1582–1598), Japan entered one of the most colorful periods of its history. How Hideyoshi achieved his feats is not exactly known. One legend relates that he was the son of the emperor's concubine. She had been much admired by a man to whom the emperor owed a favor, so the emperor gave the concubine to him. Unknown to either of the men, she was soon with child, namely, Hideyoshi. In fact, Hideyoshi was brought up as a farmer's son. His nickname was Saru-san (Mr. Monkey), because he was small and ugly. Whatever his origins (he changed his names frequently), he brought peace to Japan.

Because much of what was dear to Hideyoshi Toyotomi was destroyed by the Tokugawas, it is only at Nishi-Honganji that you can see the artistic works closely associated with his personal life, including the great **Karamon** (Chinese Gate) brought from Fushimi Castle, the **Daishoin Hall** (also from Fushimijo), and the **Noh stage** from Juraku-dai Palace.

Nishi-Honganji. Visits to some of the buildings are permitted four times a day on application from the temple office. Prior to leaving home, write to the temple (enclosing a selfaddressed envelope with an international postage coupon) at Shichijo-agaru, Horikawa-dori, Shimogyo-ku. Give your name, the number of people in your party, and the day and time you would like to visit. You can also phone for an appointment after you arrive in Kyoto: ☎ 075/371–5181; because you'll probably experience language problems, ask your hotel to make the arrangements for you.

Tours of Daishoin Hall (in Japanese) are given occasionally throughout the year. Call for information. Reservations required. Shichijo-agaru, Horikawa-dori, Shimogyo-ku. ☛ Free. ☉ Daily Mar., Apr., Sept., Oct. 5:30 AM–5:30 PM; May, June, July, Aug. 5:30 AM–6:00 PM; Nov., Dec., Jan., Feb. 6 AM–5 PM.

Higashi-Honganji: Shichijo-agaru, Karasuma-dori, Shimogyo-ku. ☛ Free. ☉ Daily 9–4.

⑧ From Nishi-Honganji it is a 10-minute walk southeast to Kyoto Station. However, if you have the time, visit **Toji,** one of Kyoto's oldest temples. Leave Nishi-Honganji by the west exit and take Bus 207 south on Omiya-dori. Get off at the Toji-Higashimon-mae bus stop, and Toji will be across the street.

Toji, established by imperial edict in 796 and called Kyo-o-gokokuji, was built to guard the city. It was one of the two temples that Emperor Kanmu permitted to be built in the city. He had had enough of the powerful Buddhists during his days in Nara. The temple was later given to Priest Kukai (Kobo Daishi), who began the Shingon sect of Buddhism; Toji became one of Kyoto's most important temples.

Fires and battles during the 16th century destroyed the temple's buildings, but many were rebuilt, including the Kondo (Main Hall) in 1603. However, the Kodo (Lecture Hall) has managed to survive the ravages of war since it was built in 1491. Inside this hall are 15 original statues of Buddhist gods that were carved in the 8th and 9th centuries. Perhaps Toji's most eye-catching building is the 180-foot, five-story pagoda, reconstructed in 1695.

An interesting time to visit the temple is on the 21st of each month, when a flea market, known locally as Kobo-san, is held. Antique kimonos, fans, and other memorabilia can sometimes be found at bargain prices, if you know your way around the savvy dealers. Many elderly people flock to the temple on this day to pray to Kobo Daishi, the temple's founder, and to shop. *1 Kujocho, Minami-ku. ☛ (to the main buildings): ¥500 adults, ¥400 high-school students, ¥350 children under 15. ☉ Daily 9–4:30.*

This concludes the exploration of central Kyoto. From Toji it is about a 10-minute walk east to the central exit of JR Kyoto Station; you can also take the Kinki Nippon Electric train at Toji Station for the one-stop ride to Kyoto Station.

Northern Kyoto

Ohara

In the northern suburbs of Kyoto are Mt. Hiei and Ohara. Our first destination is Ohara, for several centuries a sleepy Kyoto backwater surrounded by mountains. Although it is now catching up with modernity, it still has a feeling of old Japan, with several temples that deserve visiting. To reach this area, take either Kyoto Bus 17 or 18 (not city bus) from Kyoto Station and get out at the Ohara bus stop. This is a long bus ride, about 90 minutes, that costs ¥480.

From the bus station, walk northeast for about seven minutes along the signposted road to **Sanzenin,** a small temple of the Tendai sect founded by a renowned priest, Dengyo-Daishi (767–822). The Main Hall was built by Priest Eshin (942–1017), who probably carved the temple's Amida Buddha (though some say it was carved 100 years after Eshin's death). Flanked by the two disciples, Daiseishi and Kannon, the statue is a remarkable piece of work, because rather than being the bountiful Amida, it displays much more the omnipotence of Amida. Although Eshin was not really a master sculptor, this statue possibly reflects Eshin's belief that, contrary to the prevailing belief of the Heian aristocracy that salvation could be achieved through one's own actions, salvation could be achieved only through Amida's limitless mercy. The statue is in the Hondo (Main Hall), itself an ancient building from the 12th century. Unusual for a Buddhist temple, it faces east and not south. Note its ceiling. The painting depicts the descent of Amida accompanied by 25 bodhisattvas to welcome the believer.

Not only is the temple worth visiting, but the grounds are also delightful. Full of maple trees, the gardens are serene in any season. During autumn, the colors are magnificent, and the approach to the temple up a gentle slope enhances the anticipation for the burned gold trees guarding the old, weathered temple. *Raigoincho, Ohara, Sakyo-ku.* ☛ *¥500 adults, ¥300 high-school and junior-high-school students.* ☯ *Daily 8:30–5 (8:30–4 in winter).*

★ Two hundred yards from Sanzenin is the small, little-frequented **Jikkoin,** where you can sit, relax, and drink powdered green tea. To enter, ring the gong on the outside of the gate, and then wander through the carefully cultivated garden. ☛ *¥500.* ☯ *Daily 9–5.*

★ On the other side of Ohara and the Takanogawa (river) is **Jakkoin,** a temple to touch the heart. To get there, walk back to the Ohara bus stop and continue another 20 minutes or so along the road leading to the northwest. In April 1185, the Taira clan met its end in a naval battle against the Minamoto clan. For two years, Yoshitsune Minamoto had been gaining the upper hand in the battles, and this battle was final. The Minamotos slaughtered the clan, making the Inland Sea run red with Taira blood. Recognizing that all was lost, the Taira women drowned themselves, taking with them the young infant Emperor Antoku. His mother, Kenreimonin, too, leapt into the sea, but Minamoto soldiers snagged her hair with a grappling hook and hauled her back on board their ship. She was the sole surviving member of the Taira clan, and at 29, she was beautiful.

Taken back to Kyoto, Kenreimonin shaved her beautiful head and became a nun. First, she had a small hut at Chorakuji (*see* Exploring Eastern Kyoto, *above*), and when that collapsed in an earthquake, she was accepted at Jakkoin. She was given a 10-foot-square cell made of brushwood and thatch, and was left with images of her drowning son and her massacred relatives. Here she lived in solitude and sadness until, 27 years later, death ended her memories and took away the last of the Taira. Her mausoleum is in the temple grounds.

When Kenreimonin came to Jakkoin, it was far removed from Kyoto. Now Kyoto's sprawl reaches this far out, but the temple, hidden in trees, is still a place of solitude and peace, and a sanctuary for nuns. It is easy to relive the experience eight centuries ago, when Kenreimonin walked up the tree-shrouded path to the temple with the autumn drizzle falling and reflecting her tears. ☛ ¥500. ☻ *Daily 9–5 (10–4:30 in winter).*

Mt. Hiei

The next stop is Mt. Hiei. Take the Kyoto Bus (16, 17, or 18) down the main highway, Route 367, to the Yase Yuenchi bus stop, next to the Yase Yuen Train Station. You'll see the entrance to the cable car on your left. It departs every 30 minutes, and you can transfer to the ropeway at Hiei for the remaining distance to the top. At the summit is an observatory affording panoramic views of the mountains and of Lake Biwa. ☛ ¥500 *mid-Mar.–Nov.,* ¥300 *Dec.–mid-Mar.* ☻ *Daily, Apr.–Sept. 9–6; Oct.–Mar. 9–5 (Mid-July–late-Aug., observatory stays open until 9.)*

From the observatory, a serpentine mountain path leads to **Enryakuji,** which remains a most important center of Buddhism. At one time it consisted of 3,000 buildings and had its own standing army. That was its downfall. Enryakuji really began in 788. Emperor Kanmu, the founding father of Kyoto, requested Priest Saicho (767–822) to establish a temple on Mt. Hiei to protect the area (including Nagaoka, which was the current capital) from the evil spirits. Demons and evil spirits were thought to come from the northeast, and Mt. Hiei was a natural barrier between the fledgling city and the northeastern Kinmon (Devil's Gate), where devils would pass. The temple's monks were to serve as lookouts and, through their faith, keep evil at bay.

The temple grew, and, because neither women nor police were allowed on its mountaintop sanctuary, criminals also flocked there, ostensibly to seek salvation. By the 11th century, the temple had formed its own army to secure order on its estate. In time, this army grew and became stronger than that of most feudal lords. The power of Enryakuji threatened Kyoto. No imperial army could manage a war without the support of Enryakuji, and when there was no war, Enryakuji's armies would burn and slaughter monks of rival Buddhist sects. Not until the 16th century was there a force strong enough to assault the temple, though many had tried. With accusations that the monks had concubines and never read the sutras, Nobunaga Oda (1534–1582), the general who unified Japan by ending the Onin Civil Wars, attacked the monastery in 1571 to rid it of its evil. In the battle, monks were killed, and most of the buildings were destroyed. What structures we see today were built in the 17th century.

Enryakuji is divided into three precincts: the Eastern Precinct, where the main building in the complex, the Konponchudo, stands; the Western Precinct, with the oldest building, the Shakado; and the Yokawa district, a few miles north. The Konponchudo dates from 1642, and its dark, cavernous interior quickly conveys the sense of mysticism for which the esoteric Tendai sect is known. Giant pillars and a coffered ceiling give shelter to the central altar, surrounded by religious images and sacred objects. The ornate lanterns that hang before the altar are said to have been lit by Saicho himself and have never been extinguished throughout the centuries.

The Western precinct is where Saicho founded his temple and where he is buried. An incense burner wafts smoke before his tomb, which lies in a small hollow. The peaceful atmosphere of the cedar trees surrounding the main structures (Jodoin, Ninaido, and Shakado) offers an imitation of the essence of the life of a Tendai Buddhist monk, who has devoted his life to the esoteric. Enryakuji is still an important training ground for Buddhism, on a par with the temples at Koyasan. Visitors come here because of the feeling of profound religious significance, rather than for the particular buildings. It is experiential, and, though the temple complex is only a twentieth of its original size, the magnitude of the place and the commitment to esoterica pursued here are awesome. *4220 Sakamoto-hon-machi, Otsu-shi.* ☛ *¥400 adults, ¥250 high-school students, ¥220 junior high students.* ⊘ *Daily, Mar.–Nov. 8:30–4:30; Dec.–Feb. 9–4.*

ADDITIONAL ATTRACTIONS

Historical Buildings and Sights

The following lists include additional places of interest in Kyoto that were not covered in the preceding exploring tours:

★ **Katsura Detached Villa.** Katsura Detached Villa is considered the epitome of cultivated Shoin architecture and garden design. Built in the 17th century for Prince Toshihito, brother of Emperor Goyozei, it is charmingly located in southwestern Kyoto on the banks of the Katsuragawa (river), with peaceful views of Arashiyama and the Kameyama Hills. Perhaps more than anywhere else in the area, the setting is the most perfect example of Japanese integration of nature and architecture. The villa is fairly remote from other historical sites—allow an entire morning for your visit.

Although the villa was built over several decades, beginning in 1620, with new additions over time, the overall architectural effect is one of elegant harmony, thanks to the faultless craftsmanship and the meticulous structural details. The main building includes the Nakashoin, with three apartments containing nature paintings by the Kano family of artists, and the Hall for Imperial Visits, with decorations made from different kinds of rare wood, including sandalwood and ebony.

The garden has several rustic teahouses alongside a central pond. The names of these teahouses—such as the Tower of Moonlit Waves and the Hut of Smiling Thoughts—conjure up the physical control and delicate aesthetics of the tea ceremony.

Katsura Detached Villa requires special permission for a visit. To obtain this permission, applications must be made by mail or in person, preferably at least a week in advance. (In the off-season, Nov.–early Apr., you may be lucky enough to obtain same-day permission.) Indicate which of the tour times listed below you prefer. Application forms are available at JNTO offices throughout the world. You will need to enclose a selfaddressed envelope with an international postage coupon. Send the application to the Imperial Household Agency (Kyoto Gyoennai, Kamigyo-ku, Kyoto, ☎ 075/211–1215). To apply in person, (the

Imperial Household Agency, at the Imperial Palace, is open Monday–Friday, 8:45–noon and 1–4), take the subway in the direction of Kitayama. Stay in the last car of the subway train; get off at the fifth stop, Imadegawa Station, and use the No. 6 exit. Walk a short distance south on Karasuma-dori and go through the Inui Gomon into the Imperial Palace. You will need your passport to pick up your permit, and you must be at least 20 years of age. The time of your tour will be stated, and you must not be late. The tour is in Japanese only, although a videotape introducing various aspects of the garden in English is shown in the waiting room before each tour begins. *Katsura Shimizucho, Ukyo-ku,* ☎ *075/381–2029.* ☛ *Free. Tours at 10, 11, 2, 3. Closed Sat. (except in May, Oct., and Nov.), Sun., national holidays, Dec. 25–Jan. 25, and when special ceremonies are held (call the Imperial Household Agency to check).*

To reach the villa, take the Hankyu Railway Line from Kyoto's Hankyu Kawaramachi Station to Katsura Station, and then walk 10 minutes to the villa. Or take a taxi from the station for ¥530.

Shugakuin Imperial Villa. Located in northeastern Kyoto, this villa consists of a complex of three palaces. The Upper and Lower Villa were built in the 17th century by the Tokugawa family to entertain the emperor. The Middle Villa was added later as a palace home for Princess Ake, daughter of the emperor. When she decided that a nun's life was her calling, the villa was transformed into a temple. The most pleasant aspects of a visit here are the grounds and the panoramic views from the Upper Villa.

Special permission is required to visit the villa. Follow the same instructions for permission as for the Katsura Detached Villa (*see above.*) *Shugakuin Muromachi, Sakyo-ku.* ☛ *Free. Tours (in Japanese only) at 9, 10, 11, 1:30, 3. Closed Sat. (except in May, Oct., and Nov.), Sun., national holidays, and Dec. 25– Jan. 5.*

This villa may be visited on the way back from Mt. Hiei by taking the Eizan Railway from Yase Yuen Station to Shugakuin Station; the villa is a 15-minute walk from the station. If you come from downtown Kyoto, the trip takes an hour on Bus 5 from Kyoto Station, or 20 minutes by Keifuku Eizan train from Demachi-Yanagi Station, just north of Imadegawa-dori beside the Kamogawa.

Temples and Shrines

★ **Byodoin.** South of Kyoto in Uji City, this temple was originally the private villa of a 10th-century "prime minister" who was a member of the influential Fujiwara family. The Amidado, also known as the Phoenix Hall, was built in the 11th century by the Fujiwaras and is still considered one of Japan's most beautiful religious buildings, where heaven is brought close to earth. There is also a magnificent statue of a seated Buddha by one of Japan's most famous 11th-century sculptors, Jocho. To reach the temple, take the JR train to Uji Station; from there, the temple is a 12-minute walk. Uji is a famous tea-producing district, and the slope up the temple is lined with tea shops where you can sample the finest green tea and perhaps pick up a small package to take home. *Ujirenge, Uji-shi,* ☎ *0774/21–2861.* ☛ *¥400 adults, ¥200 children 12–15, ¥150 children 6–12.* ☉ *Daily, Mar.–Nov. 8:30–5. (9–4 in winter).*

Daigoji. In Yamashina, a suburb southeast of Kyoto, Daigoji was founded in 874. Over the succeeding centuries, other buildings were added, and its gardens expanded. Its five-story pagoda, which dates from 951, is reputed to be the oldest existing structure in Kyoto. By the late 16th century, the temple had begun to decline in importance and showed signs of neglect. Then Hideyoshi Toyotomi paid a visit one April, when the temple's famous cherry trees were in blossom. Hideyoshi ordered the temple restored. Be sure also to see the paintings by the Kano school in the smaller Sanboin (temple). To reach Daigoji, take the Kyoto City Bus Higashi 9 or the Keihan Bus 12 from Keihan Sanjo, and disembark at the Daigo-Sanboin stop. The ride takes about 40 minutes. *22 Higashi Ujicho, Fushimi-ku.* ☛ *¥700 adults, ¥350 children under 12 years.* ☼ *Daily 9–5 (9–4 in winter).*

Fushimi-Inari Taisha. One of Kyoto's oldest and most revered shrines, the Fushimi-Inari is dedicated to the goddesses of agriculture (rice and rice wine) and prosperity. It also serves as the headquarters for all the 40,000 shrines representing Inari. The shrine is noted for its bronze foxes and for some 10,000 small *torii* (arches), donated by the thankful, which stand on the hill behind the structure. To reach the shrine, take the JR Nara Line to Inari Station, from which it is a three-minute walk to the shrine. If you are coming from Tofukuji, join the JR train at Tofukuji Station and journey for one stop to the south (toward Nara). *68 Fukakusa Yabunouchicho, Fushimi-ku.* ☛ *Free.* ☼ *Sunrise–sunset.*

Kamigamo Jinja. Along with its sister shrine, the Shimogamo Jinja (farther south on the Kamogawa), Kamigamo (about 1½ km/1 mile north of Kitayama Station) was built by a legendary warrior named Kamo. Such is Kamo's fame that even the river that flows by the shrine and through the center of Kyoto bears his name. However, Kamigamo has always been associated with Wakeikazuchi, a god of thunder, rain, and fertility. Indeed, until 1212, a virgin from the imperial household was always in residence at the shrine. Now the shrine is famous for its Aoi (Hollyhock) Festival, which started in the 6th century when people thought that the Kamigamo deities were angry at being neglected. Now held every May 15, the festival consists of 500 people wearing Heian-period costumes riding on horseback or in ox-drawn carriages from the Imperial Palace to Shimogamo and then to Kamigamo. *339 Motoyama, Fushimi-ku.* ☛ *Free.* ☼ *Daily 9–4:30.*

Tofukuji. Southeast of Kyoto Station, this Zen temple of the Rinzai sect was established in 1236. In all, two dozen subtemples and the main temple comprise the complex, which ranks as one of the most important Zen temples in Kyoto, along with the Myoshinji and Daitokuji. The autumn is an especially fine time for visiting, when the burnished colors of the maple trees add to the pleasure of the gardens. To reach Tofukuji, either take Bus 208 from Kyoto Station to the temple or take either the JR train on the Nara Line or the Keihan train to Tofukuji Station; from either it is a 15-minute walk to the temple. You may want to combine a visit here with the Fushimi-Inari Taisha farther south (*see* above). *Honmachi 15-chome, Higashiyama-ku.* ☛ *¥300 adults, ¥200 junior-high and elementary-school students.* ☼ *Daily 9–4.*

FESTIVALS AND SEASONAL EVENTS

Many of the special celebrations of Kyoto are associated with the changing of the seasons. Most are free of charge and attract thousands of visitors as well as locals. Double-check with your hotel concierge or the Kyoto Tourist Information Center for current dates and times. For the big three festivals of Kyoto, the Gion, Jidai, and Aoi festivals, hotel bookings should be made well in advance.

May 15. The **Aoi Festival,** also known as the Hollyhock Festival, is the first of Kyoto's three most popular celebrations. Dating back to the 6th century, an "imperial" procession of 300 courtiers starts from the Imperial Palace and makes its way to Shimogamo Shrine to pray for the prosperity of the city. Today's participants are local Kyotoites.

July 16–17. The **Gion Festival,** which dates back to the 9th century, is perhaps Kyoto's most popular festival. Twenty-nine huge floats sail along downtown streets and make their way to Yasaka Shrine to thank the gods for protection from a pestilence that once ravaged the city.

Aug. 16. Daimonji Gozan Okuribi features huge bonfires that form Chinese characters on five of the mountains that surround Kyoto. The most famous is the "Dai," meaning big, on the side of Mt. Daimonji in the eastern district of Kyoto. Dress in a cool *yukata* (cotton robe) and walk down to the banks of the Kamogawa to view this spectacular summer sight, or catch all five fires from the rooftop of your hotel downtown.

Oct. 22. The **Jidai Festival,** the Festival of Eras, features a colorful costume procession of fashions from the 8th through 19th centuries. The procession begins at the Imperial Palace and winds up at Heian Shrine. More than 2,000 Kyotoites voluntarily participate in this festival, which dates back to 1895.

Oct. 22. For the **Kurama Fire Festival** at the Kurama Shrine, a roaring bonfire and rowdy portable shrine procession makes its way through the narrow streets of the small village in the northern suburbs of Kyoto. If you catch a spark, it is believed to bring good luck.

SHOPPING

Most shops slide their doors open at 10. Most shopkeepers partake of the morning ritual of sweeping and watering the entrance to welcome the morning's first customers. Shops lock up at 6 or 7 in the evening. Usually, once a week shops remain closed. As Sunday is a big shopping day for the Japanese, most stores remain open on this day.

The traditional greeting of a shopkeeper to a customer is *oideyasu,* voiced in a lilting Kyoto dialect with the required bowing of the head. When a customer makes a purchase, the shopkeeper will respond with *ookini,* a smile, and a bow. Take notice of the careful effort and adroitness with which purchases are wrapped; it is an art in itself. Also, the clicking of the abacus rather than the clanging of a cash register can still be heard in many Kyoto shops.

American Express, MasterCard, and Visa are widely accepted, as are traveler's checks.

The Crafts of Kyoto

Temples, shrines, gardens, and the quintessential elements of Japanese culture are all part of Kyoto's attractions, but none of these can be brought home, except in photographs. What can be taken back, however, are mementos (*omiyage*)—tangible gifts for which this city is famous. The ancient craftsmen of Kyoto served the imperial court for more than 1,000 years. In Japan, the prefix *kyo-* before a craft is synonymous with fine craftsmanship. The crafts of Kyoto are known throughout the world for their superb artistry and refinement.

Kyo-ningyo are the exquisite display dolls that have been made in Kyoto since the 9th century. Constructed of wood coated with white shell paste and clothed in elaborate miniature patterned silk brocades, Kyoto dolls are considered the finest in Japan. Kyoto is also known for fine ceramic dolls.

Kyo-sensu are embellished folding fans used as accoutrements in the Noh play, the tea ceremony, and Japanese dance. They also have a practical use—to ward off heat. Unlike other Japanese crafts, which have their origin in Tang Dynasty China, the folding fan originated in Kyoto.

Kyo-shikki refers to Kyoto lacquerware, which also has its roots in the 9th century. The making of lacquerware, adopted from the Chinese, is a delicate process requiring patience and skill. Finished lacquerware products range from furniture to spoons and bowls, which are carved from cypress, cedar, or horse-chestnut wood. These products have a brilliant luster, and some designs are decorated with gold leaf and inlaid mother-of-pearl.

Kyo-yaki is the general term used for ceramics made in local kilns; the most popular ware is from Kyoto's Kiyomizu district. Often colorfully hand-painted in blue, red, and green on white, these elegantly shaped teacups, bowls, and vases are thrown on potters' wheels located in the Kiyomizu district and in Kiyomizu-danchi in Yamashina. Streets leading up to Kiyomizudera—Chawan-zaka, Sannen-zaka, and Ninnen-zaka—are sprinkled with kyo-yaki shops.

Kyo-yuzen is a paste-resistant silk-dyeing technique developed by 17th-century dyer Yuzen Miyazaki. Fantastic designs are created on plain white silk pieces through the process of either *tegaki yuzen* (hand-painting) or *kata yuzen* (stencil).

Nishijin-ori is the weaving of silk. Nishijin refers to a Kyoto district producing the best silk textiles in all of Japan, used to make kimonos. Walk along the narrow back streets of Nishijin and hear the persistently rhythmic sound of looms.

Crafts Centers

The **Kyoto Craft Center** on Shijo in Gion offers two floors of both contemporary and traditional crafts for sale in a modern setting. More than 100 craft studios are represented, giving a diversity to the products for sale. *Shijo-dori, Gionmachi, Higashiyama-ku, Kyoto-shi,* ☎ *075/561–9660.* ☉ *Thurs.–Tues. 10–6.*

The **Kyoto Handicraft Center** is a seven-story shopping emporium offering everything from tape decks and pearl necklaces to porcelains and lacquerware designed to appeal to tourists. It's a good place to compare prices and grab last-minute souvenirs. *Kumano Jinja Higashi, Sakyo-ku,* ☎ *075/761–5080.* ☉ *Daily, Feb.–Dec.; Jan. 9:30–6, 9:30–5:30. Closed Dec. 31–Jan. 3.*

Shopping Districts

Compared with sprawling Tokyo, Kyoto is compact and relatively easy to navigate. Major shops for tourists and natives alike line both sides of **Shijo-dori,** which runs east–west, and **Kawaramachi-dori,** which runs north–south. Concentrate on Shijo-dori, between Yasaka Jinja and Karasuma Station, and Kawaramachi-dori between Sanjo-dori and Shijo-dori.

Shin-Kyogoku, a covered arcade running parallel to Kawaramachi-dori, is another general-purpose shopping area with many souvenir shops.

Roads leading to Kiyomizudera are steep inclines, yet the steepness is hardly noticed because of the alluring shops that line the entire way to the temple. Be sure to peek into these shops for unique gifts. Food shops offer sample morsels, and tea shops offer complimentary cups of tea.

Whereas the shopping districts above are traditional in atmosphere, Kyoto's latest shopping "district" is the modern underground arcade, **Porta,** at Kyoto Station. More than 200 shops and restaurants can be found in this sprawling, subterranean arcade.

Gift Ideas

Art and Antiques

Shinmonzen-dori holds the key to shopping for art and antiques in Kyoto. It is an unpretentious little street of two-story wood buildings that is lined with telephone and electricity poles between Higashioji-dori and Hanamikoji-dori, just north of Gion. What gives the street away as a treasure trove are the large credit-card signs jutting out from the shops. There are no fewer than 17 shops specializing in scrolls, *netsuke* (small carved figures to be attached to Japanese clothing), lacquerware, bronze, wood-block prints, paintings, and antiques. Shop with confidence, because shopkeepers are trustworthy and goods are authentic. Pick up a copy of the pamphlet *Shinmonzen Street Shopping Guide* from your hotel or from the Tourist Information Center.

Nawate-dori, between Shijo-dori and Sanjo-dori, is noted for fine antique textiles, ceramics, and paintings.

Teramachi-dori, between Oike-dori and Marutamachi, is known for antiques of all kinds, and tea-ceremony utensils.

Bamboo

The Japanese hope for their sons and daughters to be as strong and flexible as bamboo. Around many Japanese homes are small bamboo groves, for the deep-rooted plant has the ability to withstand earthquakes. On the other hand, bamboo is so flexible that it bends into innumerable shapes. The entire city of Kyoto is surrounded by vast bamboo groves. Bamboo is carefully cut and dried for several months before being stripped and woven into baskets and vases.

Kagoshin is a historic shop that has made bamboo baskets since 1862. Only the best varieties of bamboo are used in this fiercely proud little shop. *Ohashi-higashi, Sanjo-dori, Higashiyama-ku,* ☎ *075/771–0209.* ⊘ *Mon.–Sat. 9–6. Closed holidays.*

Ceramics

Tachikichi, on Shijo-dori west of Kawaramachi, has four floors of contemporary and traditional ceramics and the best reputation in town. *Shijo-Tominokoji, Nakagyo-ku,* ☎ *075/211–3143.* ⊘ *Thurs.–Tues. 10–7.*

Asahi-do, located in the heart of the pottery district near Kiyomizudera, specializes in Kyoto-style hand-painted porcelains, and a variety of other ceramics. *1-280 Kiyomizu, Higashiyama-ku,* ☎ *075/531–2181.* ⊘ *Mon.–Sat. 8:30–6, Sun. 9–6.*

Dolls

Dolls were first used in Japan in the purification rites associated with the Doll Festival, an annual family oriented event on March 3. Kyoto *ningyo* (dolls) are made with fine detail and embellishment.

Nakanishi Toku Shoten has old museum-quality dolls. The owner, Mr. Nakanishi, turned his extensive doll collection into the shop two decades ago and has since been educating customers with his vast knowledge of the doll trade. *359 Motocho, Yamato-oji Higashi-Iru, Furumonzen-dori, Higashiyama-ku,* ☎ *075/561–7309.* ☉ *Daily 10–5.*

Folk Crafts

Yamato Mingei-ten, next to Maruzen Book Store downtown, has the best selection of Japanese folk crafts, including ceramics, metal work, paper, lacquerware, and textiles. *Kawaramachi, Takoyakushi-agaru, Nakagyo-ku,* ☎ *075/221–2641.* ☉ *Wed.–Mon. 10 am–8:30 pm.*

At **Ryushido** you can stock up on your calligraphy and sumie supplies, including writing brushes, ink sticks, ink stones, Japanese paper, paperweights, and water stoppers. *Nijo-agaru, Terramachi-dori (north of Nijo), Kamigyo-ku,* ☎ *075/252–4120.* ☉ *Daily 10–7.*

Kuraya Hashimoto has one of the best collections of antique and newly forged swords, as well as reproductions. *Nishihorikawa-dori, Oike-agaru (southeast corner of Nijo Castle), Nakagyo-ku,* ☎ *075/821–2791.* ☉ *Thurs.–Tues. 10–6.*

Kimonos and Accessories

Shimmering new silk kimonos can cost more than U.S. $10,000, while equally stunning old silk kimonos can cost less than U.S. $30. Unless you have a lot of money to spend, it is wiser to look upon new silk kimonos as art objects.

The **Nishijin Orimono** (Textile Center), in Central Kyoto, will provide an orientation on silk-weaving techniques. *Horikawa-dori, Imadegawa-Minami-Iru, Kamigyo-ku,* ☎ *075/451–9231.* ☛ *Free.* ☉ *Daily 9–5.*

Two blocks east of the textile center on Imadegawa-dori and a block south is **Aizen Kobo,** which specializes in the finest handwoven indigo-dyed textiles. The shop is in a traditional weaving family's home, and the friendly owners will show you a wide variety of dyed and woven goods, including garments designed by Hisako Utsuki, the owner's wife. *Omiya Nishi-Iru, Nakasuji-dori, Kamigyo-ku,* ☎ *075/441–0355.* ☉ *Daily 9–5:30.*

Authentic silk kimonos are very heavy; this factor may dissuade some of you from making that special purchase. If smaller objects are your fancy, try a fan or comb. The most famous fan shop in all of Kyoto is **Miyawaki Baisen-an,** in business since 1823. It delights customers not only with its fine collection of lacquered, scented, painted, and paper fans but also with the old-world atmosphere that emanates from the building that houses the shop. *Tominokoji Nishi-Iru, Rokkaku-dori, Nakagyo-ku,* ☎ *075/221–0181.* ☉ *Daily 9–5.*

Umbrellas are used to protect kimonos from the scorching sun or pelting rain. Head for **Kasagen** to purchase authentic oiled paper umbrellas. The shop has been in existence since 1861, and its umbrellas are guaranteed to last years. *284 Gionmachi Kitagawa, Higashiyama-ku,* ☎ *075/561–2832.* ☉ *Daily 9:30–9.*

Department Stores

Kyoto department stores are small by comparison with their mammoth counterparts in Tokyo and Osaka. One department store looks just like the other, as they have similar floor plans. Scarves, shoes, jewelry, and handbags can be always found on the ground floor. The basement floor is devoted to foodstuffs, and the top floor is reserved for pets and pet-care goods, gardening, and restaurants.

Daimaru, on the main Shijo-dori shopping avenue, is the most conveniently located of these one-stop shopping emporiums. *Shijo-Karasuma, Shimogyo-ku,* ☎ *075/211–8111.* ☉ *Thurs.–Tues. 10–7.*

Hankyu, directly across from Takashimaya on Kawaramachi-dori, has two restaurant floors. Window displays show the type of food served, and prices are clearly marked. *Shijo-Kawaramachi, Shimogyo-ku,* ☎ *075/223–2288.* ☉ *Fri.–Wed. 10–7.*

Kintetsu is on Karasuma-dori, the main avenue leading north from Kyoto Station. *Karasuma-dori, Shimogyo-ku,* ☎ *075/361–1111.* ☉ *Fri.–Wed. 10–7.*

Takashimaya, on Kawaramachi-dori, has a well-trained English-speaking staff at its information desk, as well as a convenient money-exchange counter on its premises. *Shijo-Kawaramachi, Shimogyo-ku,* ☎ *075/221–8811.* ☉ *Thurs.–Tues. 10–7.*

Food and Flea Markets

Kyoto has a wonderful food market, **Nishiki-koji,** which branches off from the Shin-Kyogoku covered arcade (across from Daimaru department store in Central Kyoto). Try to avoid the market in late afternoon, for this is the time housewives come to do their daily shopping. The market is long and narrow; when a sizable crowd is present, there is always the possibility of being pushed into the display of fresh fish.

Two renowned flea markets take place monthly in Kyoto. Reserve the 21st of the month for the famous **Toji market** (*see* Central Kyoto, *above*) and the 25th of the month for the **Kitano Tenmangu market** (*see* Western Kyoto, *above*). Both are open from dawn to dusk. Among the old kimonos, antiques, and bric-a-brac may be an unusual souvenir.

Unusual Shopping

Shops dedicated to incense, wood tubs and casks, Buddhist objects, and chopsticks indeed offer unusual experiences. But the prized souvenir of a visit to Kyoto should be the **shuinshu,** a booklet usually no larger than 4-by-6 inches. It is most often covered with brocade, and the blank sheets of heavyweight paper inside continuously fold out. The booklet can be purchased at stationery stores or at temples for as little as ¥1,000 and serves as a "passport" to collect ink stamps from places visited while in Japan. Stamps and stamp pads are ubiquitous in Japan; they may be found at attractions, train stations, and some restaurants. Most ink stamping will be done for free, but at temples you can ask a monk to write calligraphy over the stamp for a small fee.

DINING

By Diane Durston

"Paris East" is a difficult epithet to live up to, but in many ways the elegant sister cities do seem to be of the same flesh and blood—both are the homes of their nation's haute cuisine.

Although Tokyo has been the capital since 1868, Kyoto—which wore the crown for the 10 centuries before—is still the classic Japanese city. The traditional arts, crafts, customs, language, and literature were all born, raised, and refined here. Kyoto has the matchless villas, the incomparable gardens, the magnificent temples and shrines—2,000 of them. And it is to Kyoto that you travel for the most artful Japanese cuisine.

The presence of the imperial court was the original inspiration for Kyoto's exclusive **yusoku ryori.** Once served on lacquered pedestals to the emperor himself, it is now offered at but one restaurant in the city, Mankamero.

The dining experience not to be missed in Kyoto, however, is **kaiseki ryori,** the elegant full-course meal that was originally intended to be served with the tea ceremony. All the senses are involved in this culinary event: the scent and flavor of the freshest ingredients at the peak of season; the visual delight of a continuous procession of porcelain dishes and lacquered bowls (each a different shape and size) gracefully adorned with an appropriately shaped morsel of fish or vegetable to match; the textures of foods unknown and exotic, presented in sequence to banish boredom; the sound of water in a stone basin outside in the garden; and finally, that other necessity—the atmosphere of the room itself, complete with a hanging scroll displayed in the alcove and a flower arrangement, both to evoke the season and to accent the restrained appointments of the tatami room. Kaiseki ryori is often costly, yet always unforgettable.

For those seeking initiation (or a reasonably priced sample), the **kaiseki bento** (box lunch) offered by many *ryotei* (as high-class Japanese restaurants are known) is a good place to start; box lunches are so popular in Kyoto that the restaurants that serve them compete to make their bento unique, exquisite, and delicious.

Located a two-day journey from the sea, Kyoto is historically more famous for ingenious ways of serving preserved fish—dried, salted, or pickled—than for its raw fish dishes (though with modern transportation, there are now several decent sushi shops in town). Compared with the style of cooking elsewhere in Japan, *Kyo-ryori* (Kyoto cuisine) is lighter and more delicate than most. The natural flavor of the ingredients is stressed over the enhancement of heavy sauces and broths. **Tsukemono** (pickled vegetables) and **wagashi** (traditional sweets) are two other specialties of Kyoto; they make excellent souvenirs. The food shops are often kept just as they were a century ago—well worth the trip just to browse.

Kyoto is also the home of **shojin ryori,** the Zen vegetarian-style cooking, best sampled right on the grounds of one of the city's Zen temples. Local delicacies like **fu** (glutinous wheat cakes) and **yuba** (soy milk skimmings) have found their way into the mainstream of Kyoto-style cuisine but were originally devised as protein substitutes in the traditional Buddhist diet.

A few practical notes on dining in Kyoto need to be mentioned. Many of the city's finest traditional restaurants have done business in the old style for generations and do not believe in modern nuisances like credit cards. Though several establishments are changing their ways, it's wise to check in advance. Also, people generally dine early in Kyoto (7–8 PM), so most places (apart from hotel restaurants and drinking places) close relatively early. Make sure to check the listings below before you go. Concerning appropriate attire, the average Japanese businessman wears a suit and tie to dinner—anywhere. Young people, though, tend to dress more informally. Although many Kyoto restaurants do have someone who speaks English, call the Kyoto Tourist Information Center (TIC) at 075/371–5649 if you need assistance in making reservations.

Famous throughout Japan for the best in traditional Japanese cuisine, Kyoto, unfortunately, has never been the place to go for Western food. Recently, however, some fine French, American, Indian, and Chinese restaurants have opened in the city—a welcome surprise to foreign residents (and visitors who've had enough of raw fish and squiggly foods). Apart from the restaurants listed below, Kyoto does have its share of the sort of budget quasi-Western–style chain restaurants found all over Japan, serving things like sandwiches and salads, gratins, curried rice, and spaghetti. These are easy to locate along Kawaramachi-dori downtown, and they usually come complete with plastic models in the window to which you can point if other methods of communication fail.

Kyoto is not without an impressive (depending on how you look at it) array of American fast-food chains, including McDonald's, Kentucky Fried Chicken, Mr. Donut, Tony Roma's, and both Shakey's and Chicago Pizza in case you get homesick. Many have branches in the downtown area, as well as throughout the city. For specific locations, call the TIC. An additional source of information is the *Kyoto Visitors' Guide,* available free at most hotels.

A 3% federal consumer tax is added to all restaurant bills. Another 3% local tax is added to the bill if it exceeds ¥7,500. At more expensive restaurants, a 10%–15% service charge is also added to the bill. Tipping is not necessary.

CATEGORY	COST*
$$$$	over ¥15,000
$$$	¥7,000–¥15,000
$$	¥3,000–¥7,000
$	under ¥3,000

Cost is per person without tax, service, or drinks

Eastern Kyoto

Japanese

$$$$ **Ashiya Steak House.** A short walk from the Gion district, famous for its teahouses and geisha, Ashiya Steak House is the best place in Kyoto to enjoy "a good steak . . . a real martini . . . and the essence of traditional Japan," in the words of 30-year-resident and owner, Bob Strickland, and his wife, Tokiko. While you are seated at a *kotatsu* (recessed hearth), your *teppanyaki* dinner of the finest Omi beefsteak, grilled and sliced in style, will be prepared as you watch. Cocktails, domestic and imported wines, and beer are available, as well as the best Japanese sake. Cocktails can be had in the art gallery upstairs, which has a display of traditional and contemporary arts and crafts. You'll be impressed by the service and the $160 price tag for a 12-ounce steak. ✕ *172-13 Yonchome, Kiyomizu, Higashiyama-ku,* ☎ *075/541–7961. Reservations required. AE, DC, V.* ◷ *5:30–11:30 (last order at 10). Closed Mon. and national holidays.*

$$$ **Yagenbori.** North of Shijo-dori in the heart of Kyoto's still-thriving geisha ★   district, this restaurant is in a teahouse just a few steps down a cobbled path from the romantic Shira River (a small tributary of the Kamogawa) in Gion. The *o-makase* full-course meal is an elegant sampler of Kyoto's finest kaiseki cuisine, with local delicacies beautifully presented on fine handmade ceramics. The *shabu-shabu* (thinly sliced beef, dipped briefly into hot stock) and *suppon* (turtle dishes) are excellent. Don't miss the *hoba miso* (bean paste with *kinoko* mushrooms and green onions, which are wrapped in a giant oak leaf and grilled at your table over a charcoal hibachi) on the à la carte menu. ✗ *Sueyoshicho, Kiridoshi-kado, Gion, Higashiyama-ku,* ☎ *075/551–3331. Reservations advised. AE, DC, V. Lunch noon–2, dinner 4–11.*

$$ **Rokusei Nishimise.** Few restaurants in Kyoto have matched Rokusei Nishimise's magical combination of traditional cuisine served in a contemporary setting. Polished marble floors and manicured interior garden niches offset the popular *te-oke bento* lunch, a collage of flavors and colors presented in a handmade cypress-wood bucket/serving tray. With an 80-year history as caterers of formal kaiseki cuisine, Rokusei also offers a different exquisite full-course meal each month at reasonable prices. A three-minute walk west of the turn-of-the-century gardens of Heian Shrine, the restaurant itself overlooks a tree-lined canal and is famous for its colorful azaleas in May. ✗ *71 Nishitennocho, Okazaki, Sakyo-ku,* ☎ *075/751–6171. Dinner reservations advised. DC, V.* ⊗ *11:30–9. Closed Mon.*

$–$$ **Kappa Nawate.** Lively (noisy to some ears) and fun, Kappa Nawate has all the boisterous local atmosphere, grilled goodies, and *nama* (draft) beer a dozen people crammed around a counter could possibly ever hope for. The head cook vacillates between edgy and jovial—he has fish to grill and little patience with the indecisive eater. The English menu helps, but the choices are next to limitless: *oden* (vegetables and other foods simmered in broth), *yakitori* (grilled skewers of chicken), sashimi, you name it. A favorite after-work watering hole in the middle of the Gion entertainment district, Kappa stays open later than most such grills in Kyoto. ✗ *Sueyoshicho, Higashi-Kitakado, Nawate-dori, Shoji 2-sujime-agaru, Higashiyama-ku,* ☎ *075/531– 4048. No reservations. No credit cards.* ⊗ *6 PM–2 AM. Closed 1st, 2nd, and 3rd Mon. every month; first Mon. and Dec. 24.*

$ **Nishimura.** You do the cooking at this casual eatery, where the specialty is *okonomiyaki,* a kind of Japanese frittata made with a batter of egg and flour mixed with vegetables and your choice of meat or seafood. It's all smothered with green onions and ginger and topped with a special sauce, and then you grill it at your table. Nishimura is a stone's throw from Kyoto University, down a path beside the Asahi Shinbun Building, and is surrounded with shrubbery. The food is good, the garden view is wonderful, and the prices are very reasonable. ✗ *Hyakumanben Kosaten-agaru, Nishi-Iru, Sakyo-ku,* ☎ *075/721–5880. No reservations. No credit cards.* ⊗ *Noon–2 and 5–9. Closed Fri.*

$ **Omen.** Just south of Ginkakuji (Temple of the Silver Pavilion), this is
★ one of the best places to stop for an inexpensive homestyle lunch before proceeding down the old canal (a walkway beneath the cherry trees known as the Path of Philosophy) on the way to Nanzenji. Omen is not only the name of the shop but also the name of the house specialty: thick white noodles brought to your table in a basket with a bowl of hot broth and a platter of seven different vegetables. The noodles are added to the broth a little at a time, along with the vegetables (spinach, cabbage, green onions, mushrooms, burdock, eggplant, radishes, and others, depending on the season). Sprinkle the top with roasted sesame seeds and you have a dish so popular that you can expect a few minutes' wait before you're seated. Like the food, the restaurant itself is country-style, with a choice of counter stools, tables and chairs, or tatami mat seating. The waiters dress in *happi* (workmen's) coats and headbands; the atmosphere is lively and comfortable. ✗ *74 Ishibashicho, Jodoji, Sakyo-ku,* ☎ *075/771–8994. No reservations on Sat., Sun., and national holidays. No credit cards.* ⊗ *11–10. Closed Thurs.*

296

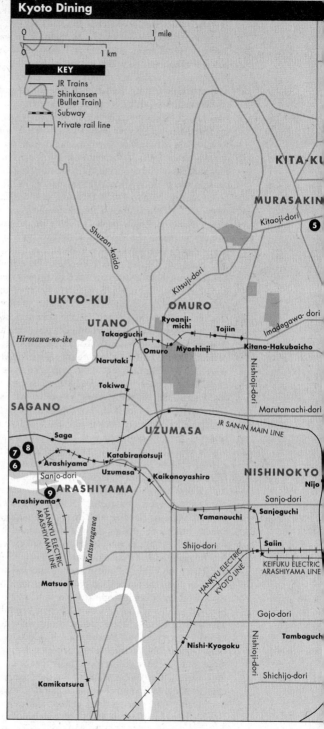

Kyoto Dining

Miyake-hachiman

Takaragaike

② ①

❸ Shugakuin

Kitayama-dori

Kitayama

Botanical
Garden

Shimogamo-hondori

Kitaoji

Kitaoji-dori

④

SHIMOGAMO

EIZAN ELECT. KURAMA LINE

EIZAN ELECT. EIZAN LINE

Ichijoji

KITA-
SHIRAKAWA

Chayama

Kuramaguchi

TAKANO

SAKYO-KU

Kamogawa

Teramachi-dori

NISHIJIN

Takanogawa

Mototanaka

Imadegawa

⑪

Demachi-Yanagi

⑬

KAMIGYO-
KU

⑫

Karasuma-dori

Kawaramachi-dori

Imadegawa-dori

Demachi-
Yanagi Keihan

Shirakawa-dori

Sembon-dori

Nakadachiuri-dori

Kyoto
Imperial
Palace

⑭

⑩

Horikawa-dori

⑮

Marutamachi

Marutamachi-dori

Marutamachi

OKAZAKI

Nijo-dori

Nijo
Castle

Oike

⑰

⑱
⑲

Higashioji-dori

⑯

NAKAGYO-
KU

Oike-dori

⑳

Higashiyama-
Sanjo

Keage

Sanjo-dori

㉒ ㉑

㉓ Keihan-
Sanjo

KEIHAN ELECTRIC KEISHIN LINE

㉕

㉔

㉘ ㉚

Keishin-Sanjo

AWATAGUCHI

㉖ ㉗

㉛

㉝

Hankyu-
Omiya

Karasuma

㉙

㉜ ㉞

Kujoyama

Shijo-
Omiya

Omiya-dori

Shijo

Kawaramachi

Keihan-
Shijo

Shijo-dori

Hinooka

JR SANIN MAIN LINE

㉟

SHIMOGYO-
KU

Gojo

Gojo

Kamogawa

Gojo-zaka

HIGASHIYAMA-
KU

Mt. Kazan

㊱

Mt.
Kiyomizu

Shichijo

JR TOKAIDO MAIN LINE

Kyoto
Station

㊲

SHINKANSEN

Mt.
Rokujo

N

$ **Rakusho.** Along the path between Maruyama Koen and Kiyomizu-
★ dera, this tea shop in a former villa is a pleasant place to stop for morning coffee or afternoon tea. A table beside the sliding glass doors looks
out on an elaborately landscaped garden that features a pond in which
the owner's colorful array of prize-winning *koi* (carp), hoping it's
feeding time again, lurk just beneath the surface. Flowering plum trees,
azaleas, irises, camellias, and maple trees take turns anointing the four
seasons while you sip your bowl of *matcha* (frothy tea-ceremony tea)
or freshly brewed coffee. The tea shop is just minutes on foot from Sannen-zaka, one of Kyoto's historic preservation districts—a cobblestone path lined with shops on the way to Kiyomizudera. ✗ *Kodaiji
Kitamon-mae-dori, Washiocho, Higashiyama-ku,* ☎ *075/561–6892.
No reservations. No credit cards.* ⊙ *Daily 9:30–6. Closed 4 times a
month (call first).*

American

$ **Time Paradox.** The Japanese owner-chef here learned most of the great
things he knows in California. The tantalizing menu offers homemade
gratins, thick-crust pizza, spinach omelets, scallops in garlic and wine
sauce, bread sticks baked fresh while you wait, and crispy spinach, bacon,
and avocado salads. Beer and wine are also served. Located a few blocks
south of Kyoto University (just north of Heian Shrine), it is a popular
student haunt, heavy on the foreign element. ✗ *Yoshida-hon-dori,
Marutamachi-agaru, Sakyo-ku,* ☎ *075/751–6903. Reservations advised weekends. MC, V.* ⊙ *5 PM–1 AM (last order at midnight). Closed
Thurs.*

Western Kyoto

Japanese

$$$$ **Kitcho.** What Maxim's is to Paris, Kitcho is to Kyoto—classic cuisine,
unparalleled traditional atmosphere, exclusive elegance. Lunches start
at ¥45,000, dinners at ¥50,000, making this perhaps the world's most
expensive restaurant. Although the original restaurant is in Osaka, the
Kyoto branch has the advantage of a stunning location beside the Oi
River, nestled at the foothills of Arashiyama. Here you can experience
the full sensory delight of formal kaiseki cuisine. Only the finest ingredients are used, prepared by master chefs and served on priceless
lacquered trays in exquisite antique porcelain ware—all in an elegant
private room sparsely decorated with a hanging scroll painted by a famous master, whose message sets the seasonal theme for the evening.
The ability to identify the vessels used, an appreciation of the literary
allusions made in the combination of objects and foods served, and
knowledge of the arts of Japan all add depth to the experience. Expect
to spend at least two hours here. ✗ *58 Susuki-no-banba-cho, Tenryuji,
Saga, Ukyo-ku,* ☎ *075/881–1101. Reservations required. Jacket and
tie. AE. Lunch 11:30–1, dinner 4–7. Closed 1st and 3rd Wed.*

$$ **Nishiki.** Tucked inside a rustic bamboo fence, Nishiki sits on an island
★ in the middle of the Oi River (the local name for the Katsuragawa as
it passes through Arashiyama), surrounded by the densely forested
Arashiyama mountains. The *oshukuzen-bento* lunch is the best sam-
pler of formal, Kyoto-style kaiseki cuisine available at such a reason-
able price. Unlike most bento lunches, it is served in seven courses and
is so beautifully presented in a tiered lacquer box, with meticulous at-
tention to the finest foods in season, that it rivals meals at three times
the price. A summer lunch might include a course of *kamo-nasu,* the
prized Kyoto eggplant, served *dengaku*-style, smothered in sweet miso
sauce in a silver serving dish the shape of an eggplant itself. The top
layer of the lacquered box might be covered with a miniature bamboo

trellis in which are nestled tiny porcelain cups the shape of morning glories, a favorite summer flower in Kyoto, each one filled with a different appetizer—a touch of sea urchin or a few sprigs of spinach in sesame sauce. ✕ *Nakanoshima Koen-uchi, Arashiyama, Ukyo-ku,* ☎ *075/871–8888. Call for reservations, or expect a 30-min. wait. DC, MC, V.* ☺ *11–9 (last order at 7). Closed Tues.*

$$ **Sagano.** Amid the lush green bamboo forests of the Arashiyama dis-
★ trict, this quiet retreat serves one of the finest *yudofu* meals (cubes of bean curd simmered in a broth at your table) in Kyoto. The full course includes such local delicacies as tempura and *aburage* (deep-fried tofu) with black sesame seeds and a gingko-nut center garnished with a sprig of *kinome* leaves from the Japanese pepper tree. Take a seat at the sunken counter, and waitresses in kimonos will prepare the meal in front of you—with a backdrop of antique wood-block prints on folding screens, surrounded by walls lined with delicately hand-painted antique porcelain bowls—or walk out through the garden to private, Japanese-style rooms in the back. If weather permits, dine on low tables in the courtyard garden beneath the towering bamboo. It's reasonably priced for this superb combination of atmosphere and good food. Reservations are a good idea year-round, particularly during the fall tourist season when the maple trees of Arashiyama are at their brilliant-red best. ✕ *45 Susuki-no-banbacho, Saga, Tenryuji, Ukyo-ku,* ☎ *075/861–0277. No credit cards.* ☺ *11–8.*

Spanish

$$ **Bodegon.** A white-walled, tile-floored, wrought-iron and blown-glass Spanish restaurant in Arashiyama is about as rare (and as welcome) as decent paella in a neighborhood famous for its tofu. Bodegon sits unobtrusively along the main street that runs through the center of this scenic district, offering guests Spanish wines and Kyoto hospitality. A wildly popular tourist area in daylight, Arashiyama rolls up its sidewalks after dark, so Bodegon is a good place to escape the crowds downtown in the evening. ✕ *1 Susuki-no-banbacho, Tenryuji, Saga,* ☎ *075/872–9652. Reservations suggested on weekends. MC, V. Lunch noon–2, dinner 5–10. Closed Thurs.*

Central Kyoto

Japanese

$$$$ **Daimonjiya.** One of Kyoto's many famous *ryori-ryokan* (restaurant/inns), Daimonjiya is noted for its superb formal kaiseki cuisine. Located on the Sanjo Arcade in the downtown shopping district, its inconspicuous traditional entrance is easy to miss among the boutiques and record shops that now line the street. A narrow stone path leads down a bamboo-fence corridor to the doorway of this classic 80-year-old inn, a popular haunt of literary men such as the late Eiji Yoshikawa, author of *Musashi*. The evening kaiseki meal is exquisitely presented; the *kaiseki bento* (box lunch) offered at lunchtime is one of Kyoto's finest and is moderately priced. ✕ *19 Ishibashicho, Sanjo-Teramachi Higashi-Iru, Nakagyo-ku,* ☎ *075/221–0603. Dinner reservations required. Jacket and tie. AE, DC, V. Lunch 11:30–1, dinner 5–7 (last seating).*

$$–$$$ **Ebisugawa-tei.** Annexed to the Fujita Hotel, this is the Meiji-period villa of former industrialist Baron Fujita. It contains two excellent steak restaurants, both serving the celebrated, beer-fed, massaged Omi beef. The **Omi** is the more expensive and formal of the two (men should wear jacket and tie), serving slightly higher quality beef. The **Chidori** is a bit less formal, but also serves superb beef and has a better view of the garden. Stop in at the bar in the basement of the Fujita Hotel for a drink beside the beautiful duck pond and waterfall. ✕ *Fu-*

jita Hotel, Nijo-dori, Kiyamachi Kado, Nakagyo-ku, ☎ *075/222–1511. Reservations advised for both. AE, DC, MC, V. Omi* ✆ *4–9:30. Chidori* ✆ *noon–9:30.*

\$\$–\$\$\$ Mankamero. Established in 1716, Mankamero is the only restaurant in Kyoto that serves formal *yusoku ryori,* the type of cuisine once served to members of the imperial court. The preparation of foods is carried out by a specially appointed imperial chef, using unique utensils made only for the preparation of this type of cuisine. Dressed in ceremonial robes, the chef "dismembers" the fish into elaborately arranged sections brought to the guest on pedestal trays. Prices are also quite elaborate, though in recent years an incomparable *take-kago bento* lunch (served in a bamboo basket) is offered at prices within reach of the rest of us commoners. ✗ *Inokuma-dori, Demizu-agaru, Kamigyo-ku,* ☎ *075/441–5020. Reservations required. Jacket and tie. AE, DC, MC, V. No credit cards for take-kago bento at lunch.* ✆ *Noon–8. Closed once a month.*

\$\$–\$\$\$ Mishima-tei. There is really only one choice for sukiyaki in Kyoto, and that is Mishima-tei. Located conveniently in the heart of the downtown shopping district, it is also one of the best restaurants in the area. Kyoto housewives line up out front to pay premium prices for Mishima-tei's famous high-quality beef, sold by the 100-gram over the counter at the meat shop downstairs. Mishima-tei was established in 1904, and climbing the staircase of this three-story, traditional wood-frame restaurant is like journeying into the past. Down the long, dark corridors, with polished wood floors, maids in kimonos bustle about with trays of beef and refills of sake to dozens of private tatami-mat rooms. Ask for a room that faces the central courtyard garden for the best view, and enjoy your meal in privacy. Mishima-tei has not yet undergone any extensive remodeling, so it retains an authentic, turn-of-the-century atmosphere. (Plan on dining by 7:00 or so, as the service—and the preparation of your food—can be rushed toward the end of the evening.) ✗ *Teramachi, Sanjo-sagaru, Higashi-Iru, Nakagyo-ku,* ☎ *075/221–0003. Reservations advised. AE, DC, MC, V.* ✆ *11:30–10. Closed Wed.*

\$\$–\$\$\$ Yoshikawa. This quiet, traditional inn with its beautiful landscaped gardens is within walking distance of the downtown shopping area. The specialty of the house is tempura, either a full-course kaiseki dinner served in a tatami room or a lunch at the counter in its cozy "tempura corner," where the chef fries each vegetable and shrimp in front of you while you wait. Tempura should be light and crisp—best right from the pot—and for this Yoshikawa is famous. English is spoken. ✗ *Tominokoji, Oike-sagaru, Nakagyo-ku,* ☎ *075/221–5544 or 075/221–0052. Reservations advised. Jacket and tie at dinner. AE, DC, MC, V. Lunch 11–2, dinner 5–8:30. Closed Sun.*

\$\$ Agatha. This restaurant offers a "mystery" twist on the Japanese *robatayaki* (charcoal grill). The decor is period Agatha Christie—'40s book covers and movie posters, chic polished marble walls, potted palms, decent jazz, black-and-white checkerboard floors, and counter or table seating. Watch the chef grill interesting variations of traditional Japanese delicacies, such as white, long-stem *enoki* mushrooms wrapped in strips of thinly sliced beef, scallops in bacon, or pork in *shiso* (a red or green mintlike herb). Both the A-course and the B-course combine these treats with unadorned standards such as *tebasaki* (grilled chicken wings). Salad and appetizers are included, and a wide selection of drinks are available—everything from sake to a gin fizz. Popular with the *juppie* (Japanese yuppie) crowd, this restaurant has two other branches in Kyoto, and one each in Osaka, Tokyo, and . . . Boston. ✗ *2nd floor, Yurika Bldg., Kiyamachi-dori, Sanjo-agaru, Nakagyo-ku,* ☎

075/223–2379. Reservations advised weekends. AE, DC, MC, V. ✪ *5–midnight.*

$$ Oiwa. At the head of the Takasegawa Canal, south of the Fujita Hotel, Oiwa serves *kushikatsu,* which are skewered meats and vegetables battered, deep-fried, and then dipped in a variety of sauces. The building itself is actually a *kura* (treasure house) that belongs to a kimono merchant family, and it is one of the first to have been turned into a restaurant in Kyoto, where restorations of this type are still a new idea. The Japanese chef was trained in one of the finest French restaurants in Tokyo, and his version of kushikatsu (usually considered a working man's snack with beer) might be called unpretentiously elegant. Order by the skewer or ask for the *o-makase* course. Oiwa is a fine place to spend a relaxing evening. ✘ *Kiyamachi-dori, Nijo-sagaru, Nakagyo-ku,* ☎ *075/231–7667. Reservations advised weekends. No credit cards.* ✪ *5–10, Sun. 4–10. Closed Wed.*

$–$$ Daikokuya. If you're shopping downtown and want a quick meal, stop in at Daikokuya for a *soba* (buckwheat) noodle dish or *donburi,* a bowl of rice with your choice of toppings. The *oyako donburi,* rice with egg and chicken, is the best choice (*oyako* means "parent and child"). The restaurant also serves sushi in a beautiful Japanese-style setting, with both tatami and table-and-chair seating. ✘ *Kiyamachi, Takoyakushi Nishi-Iru, Nakagyo-ku,* ☎ *075/221–2818. No reservations. No credit cards.* ✪ *11:30–10. Closed Tues.*

$–$$ Yamatomi. The geisha district that runs along the west bank of the Kamogawa is known as Pontocho. Many of the places along the narrow street are teahouses, and you must be formally introduced by a regular patron to enter. There are a few reasonably priced restaurants in Pontocho, and Yamatomi is among the best. The specialty of the house is called *teppin-age,* a tempura-style meal of battered vegetables, seafood, and meat that you cook yourself in a small iron kettle at your table. In the winter, the feature item is *oden,* a combination of vegetables and local specialties simmered in copper vats behind the counter from which you choose. But it's really the hot, humid summers that make Kyoto-ites flock to Yamatomi. Summer is the season when all the restaurants and teahouses along Pontocho set up temporary verandas out over the river bank so their guests can enjoy both their meals and the cool river breeze under the stars. You may catch sight of guests being entertained by geisha on the veranda of the teahouse next door—paying 10 times the price you'll pay at Yamatomi. ✘ *Pontocho, Shijo-agaru, Nakagyo-ku,* ☎ *075/221–3268. No reservations. No credit cards.* ✪ *Noon–11. Closed Tues.*

$ Porta. Under Kyoto Station is Porta, a shopping arcade with a mall called Restaurant Alley, where a dozen or more restaurants offer a range of Japanese food at reasonable prices. While none warrants a special visit, if you are waiting for a train and need sustenance, then come here and take your pick. We recommend **Fujiya** (☎ *075/343–2641*), which has noodle and rice dishes with different toppings. ✘ *No reservations. No credit cards.*

$ Suzu. Don't trek across town just for a meal here, but if you find yourself in the area (Pontocho) and are staggered by the prices at most restaurants, this little place will come as a relief. A cheerful crowd crams in either at the counter or at one of the closely packed tables, and you are sure to start up one or more conversations. The food is a Japanese rendition of American-style snacks, from pizza with bacon to batter-fried shrimp and vegetables, prices average around ¥650 a dish. ✘ *Pontocho, Shijo-agaru, Nakagyo-ku,* ☎ *075/252–1760. No reservations. No credit cards.* ✪ *6:30–11 PM.*

$ **Tagoto.** One of the best noodle shops in which to stop for lunch in the downtown area, Tagoto is located on the north side of the covered Sanjo Arcade, half a block west of the avenue Kawaramachi-dori. Tagoto has been serving homemade *soba* (buckwheat noodle) soup for more than a hundred years in the same location on a shopping street that is now almost completely modernized. Tagoto, too, has remodeled, and the result is a pleasant surprise—modern, yet in traditional Japanese style. Natural woods, *shoji* paper windows, tatami mats, and an interior garden integrated with slate floors, tables and chairs, and air-conditioned comfort. Tagoto serves both thin soba and thick white *udon* noodle dishes with a variety of toppings (such as shrimp tempura), hot or cold to suit the season. ✕ *Sanjo-dori, Teramachi Higashi-Iru, Nakagyo-ku,* ☎ *075/221–3030. No reservations. No credit cards.* ⊘ *11–9. Closed Tues.*

Coffee Shop

$ **Inoda.** Hidden down a side street in the center of town, this 100-year-old establishment is one of Kyoto's oldest and best-loved coffee shops. The turn-of-the-century, Western-style brick buildings along Sanjo-dori nearby are part of a historic preservation district, and Inoda's original old shop blends well with its surroundings. Floor-to-ceiling glass windows overlook an interior garden; a spacious room seats nearly 100 people. And the coffee is excellent: for breakfast, toast and coffee; for lunch, sandwiches and coffee; for a break from sightseeing, coffee and coffee. It even has some stained-glass windows and a pair of witty parrots. ✕ *Sakaimachi-dori, Sanjo-sagaru, Nakagyo-ku,* ☎ *075/221–0505. No reservations. No credit cards.* ⊘ *Daily 7–6.*

French

$$–$$$ **Ogawa.** Down a narrow passageway across from the Takasegawa
★   (canal), this is the place to sample the best in Kyoto-style nouvelle cuisine. Finding a seat at the counter of this intimate French restaurant is like getting tickets for opening night at the opera—one you've never seen. With particularly Japanese sensitivity to the best ingredients only in the peak of the season, proprietor Ogawa promises never to bore his guests by serving them the same meal twice. *Ayu* (a popular local river fish) is offered in the summer (or perhaps abalone), salmon in the fall, crab in the winter, shrimp in the spring. Ogawa features marvelous sauces, puddings, and, yes, even fresh papaya sherbet and mango mousse with mint sauce. The full-course meal at lunch and dinner is spectacular, but some prefer to order hors d'oeuvres with wine over which to languish ecstatically for hours. Counter seating is available for only 16. ✕ *Kiyamachi Oike-agaru Higashi-Iru, Nakagyo-ku,* ☎ *075/256–2203. Reservations required. Jacket and tie. AE, DC, MC, V. Lunch 11:30–2, dinner 5–10 (last order at 9:30). Closed Tues.*

$$ **Natsuka.** This fine French restaurant overlooks the Kamogawa. The
★   Japanese couple who manage the place lived and learned their trade in Paris for several years. Natsuka has the most reasonably priced French lunch menu in town (¥1,750 fixed menu). The dessert tray here is sumptuous, with a choice of two freshly baked delights from about eight possibilities. ✕ *Pontocho, Shijo-agaru, Higashigawa, Nakagyo-ku,* ☎ *075/255–2105. Dinner reservations advised. MC. Lunch 11:30–2, dinner 5–10. Last order at 9 (at 8 on Sun.). Closed Wed.*

Indian

$–$$ **Ashoka.** Unlike cosmopolitan Tokyo, Kyoto, with all its fine Japanese restaurants, suffers from a serious lack of international options—particularly when it comes to cuisine. That was true until the owners of

Ashoka brought their tandoori chicken (and their wonderful Indian chefs) to town. Marinated for hours and baked on long skewers in a clay oven while you watch, this chicken dish is the closest you'll get to downright spiciness in the capital of the culinary dainty. Ashoka's atmosphere is evoked by red carpets, carved screens, brass lanterns, and tuxedoed waiters, though the dress code for guests ranges from denim to silk. The dazzling *Thali* course dinner offers half a dozen curries in little bowls on a brass tray with rice and tandoori—order this only if you're very hungry. ✕ *Kikusui Bldg., 3rd floor, Teramachi-dori, Shijo-agaru, Nakagyo-ku,* ☎ *075/241–1318. Reservations advised weekends. AE, DC, MC, V. Lunch 11:30–2:30, dinner 5–9. Closed 2nd Tues. of each month.*

Italian

$–$$ **divo-diva.** In the relatively short time divo-diva has been in business, it
★ has become one of the most popular restaurants in Kyoto. You'll dine here on authentic Italian food prepared by chefs trained in Italy but with a Japanese flair for color and design. The long narrow room has a counter, three small tables, and one long table for parties and large groups; tasteful lighting sets off the contemporary decor. The wine list is interesting (and not prohibitively expensive), the pasta and breads homemade. ✕ *Nishikikoji, Takakura-Nishi-Iru, Nakagyo-ku,* ☎ *075/256–1326. Reservations advised. AE, DC, MC, V.* ☉ *Lunch 11:30–2, dinner 6–10. Closed Wed. and 2nd and 3rd Tues. of each month.*

Mixed Menu

$ **Tinguely.** Located in the same basement as a Chinese restaurant, Mr. Chow's Tinguely overlooks a mini-terrace and has a black interior. This dining spot may be described as ethnic (the menu covers a lot of bases—East and West), eclectic (not the place you'd think the local banking district would frequent—but it does), and kinetic (the flashing, jangling work of artist Jean Tinguely hangs from every rafter). It's a "mysterious space for city adults" in the evening, as the restaurant's slogan says. ✕ *Basement of the Karasuma Plaza 21, Karasuma-dori, Rokkaku-sagaru, Nakagyo-ku,* ☎ *075/255–6810. Reservations advised weekends. No credit cards.* ☉ *11–10. Closed Sun.*

Northern Kyoto

To get to these Northern Kyoto establishments, you might take the Eizan Electric Railway on the Kurama Line to Shugakuin Station and then proceed by taxi.

Japanese

$$ **Heihachi-Jaya.** A bit off the beaten path in the northeastern corner of
★ Kyoto, along the old road to the Sea of Japan, this roadside inn has offered comfort to many a weary traveler in its 400-year history. Heihachi-Jaya hugs the levee of the Takano River and is surrounded by maple trees in a quiet garden with a stream. Apart from the excellent bento lunch and full-course kaiseki dinner, what makes this restaurant special is its clay sauna, the *kamaburo*, a mound-shaped clay steam bath heated from beneath the floor by a pinewood fire. Have a bath and sauna, change into a cotton kimono if you wish, and retire to the dining room (or to a private room) for a *very* relaxing meal—an experience not to be missed. ✕ *8-1 Kawagishi-cho, Yamabana, Sakyo-ku,* ☎ *075/781–5008. Reservations advised. DC, MC, V (no credit cards at lunch).* ☉ *11–9. Closed Wed.*

$$ **Izusen.** In the garden of Daijiin, a sub-temple of Daitokuji, a revered center of Zen Buddhism in Japan, this restaurant specializes in *shojin ryori* (Zen vegetarian cuisine). Lunches are presented in sets of red-lac-

quer bowls of diminishing sizes, each one fitting inside the next when the meal is completed. Two Kyoto specialties, *fu* (glutinous wheat cake) and *yuba* (curd from steamed soy milk), are served in a multitude of inventive forms—in soups and sauces that prove vegetarianism to be as exciting a culinary experience as any meaty dish can hope to be. Meals are served in tatami-mat rooms, Japanese-style, and in warm weather on low tables outside beneath the trees in the temple garden. ✕ *4 Daitokujicho, Murasakino, Kita-ku,* ☎ *075/491–6665. Reservations advised in spring and fall. No credit cards.* ⊙ *11–5. Closed Thurs.*

$–$$ **Sagenta.** Discovering the town of Kibune is one of the best parts of
★ summer in Kyoto. A short, bump'n'rumble train ride into the mountains north of Kyoto on the nostalgic little Keifuku train lets you off on a mountain path that leads farther up into the forest beside a cool stream. (Take the Eizan Electric Railway on the Kurama Line to Kibuneguchi Station and then transfer to the Keifuku train to Kibune. Allow a good 45 minutes from Central Kyoto.) The path is lined on both sides with restaurants that place tables near the stream during the summer months; you can dine beneath a canopy of trees, with the water flowing at your feet. Most of the restaurants along the river are excellent, but some are quite expensive. Sagenta is the last restaurant, at the very top of the slope, serving kaiseki lunches year-round, as well as one-pot *nabe* dishes in fall and winter. It is reasonably priced, particularly for its popular summertime specialty *nagashi-somen,* chilled noodles that flow down a bamboo spout from the kitchen to a boat-shape trough; you catch the noodles from the trough as they float past, dip them in a sauce, and eat them with mushrooms, seasonal green vegetables, and shrimp. ✕ *76 Kibunecho, Kurama, Sakyo-ku,* ☎ *075/741– 2244. Reservations advised in summer. AE, DC, MC, V.* ⊙ *11–10. Closed periodically during winter.*

$ **Azekura.** On the northern outskirts of Kyoto, not far from Kamig-
★ amo Shrine, Azekura serves home-style buckwheat noodles under the giant wood beams of a 300-year-old sake warehouse. Originally built in Nara, the warehouse was moved here more than 20 years ago by a kimono merchant named Mikio Ichida, who also maintains a textile exhibition hall, a small museum, and a weavers' workshop within the walls of this former samurai estate. Have lunch on low stools around a small charcoal brazier or on tatami next to a window overlooking the garden and waterwheel outside. The soba noodles at Azekura have a heartier country flavor than you'll find in most of the other noodle shops in town. A perfect place to stop while exploring the *shakemachi* district around the shrine, an area in which shrine priests and farmers have lived for more than 10 centuries. ✕ *30 Okamotocho, Kamigamo, Kita-ku,* ☎ *075/701–0161. No reservations. No credit cards.* ⊙ *9–5. Closed Mon.*

American

$ **Knuckle's.** In search of a taste of the Big Apple in the Ancient Capital
★ of Japan? What could be better after a visit to Daitokuji, a center of Zen Buddhism, than a Reuben sandwich, some nachos, and a margarita, or the house specialty, Knuckle Sandwich (with homemade Italian sausage), washed down with a cold Corona beer? And don't forget the fresh-baked blueberry cheesecake for dessert. Knuckle's has good espresso and a comfortable atmosphere. The Big Apple without the bite. ✕ *Kitaoji-dori, Senbon Higashi-Iru, Kita-ku,* ☎ *075/441–5849. No reservations. No credit cards.* ⊙ *Noon–10. Closed Mon.*

Coffee Shop

$ **Honyarado.** Kyoto has always been a university town, and Doshisha
★ University, on the north side of the old Imperial Palace, is one of the
oldest and most respected in the city. Honyarado is a "home-away-
from-dormitory" for many of its students. During the student movement of the '60s and '70s, Kyoto had its share of "incidents." What's
left of the spirit of the peace movement—the environmentalists, the poets,
and the musicians of that era—eat their lunches at Honyarado. The
notices on the bulletin are of a less incendiary nature these days (rooms
for rent, poetry readings, used stereos for sale), but the sandwiches are
still on homemade wheat bread, the stew is still good, and the company still real. Take along a good book (this guide, perhaps?), order
lunch, and relax. ✗ *Imadegawa-dori, Teramachi Nishi-Iru, Kamigyo-
ku,* ☎ *075/222–1574. No reservations. No credit cards.* ⊗ *9:30–9:30.
Closed 1st Wed. of each month.*

$ **Papa Jon's.** Just north of Doshisha University, this American-owned
café serves a light quiche lunch and the finest home-style cakes and
espresso in town. Owner-chef Charles Roche features the work of
local artists on the walls of his elegant little shop. This, plus the antique European decor and sunlit coziness, provides a welcome place
to rest after a visit to the nearby Imperial Palace. ✗ *642-2 Shokokuji
Monzen, Karasuma Kamidachiuri Higashi-Iru, Kamigyo-ku,* ☎
075/415–2655. No reservations. No credit cards. ⊗ *11–10. Closed
Mon.*

LODGING

Kyoto is a tourist city, and its hotel rooms are often designed merely
as places to rest at night. Most rooms are small by international standards, but they are adequate for relaxing after a busy day of sightseeing. As it is throughout Japan, service in this city is impeccable; the
information desks are well stocked with maps and pamphlets about
the sights. The assistant manager, concierge, or guest-relations manager is always available in the lobby to respond to guests' needs, although English may or may not be spoken.

Each room in expensively (**$$$**) and moderately (**$$**) priced lodgings
comes equipped with a hot-water thermos and tea bags or instant coffee. Stocked refrigerators, television featuring English-language CNN
news, and radio are standard, as are *yukata* (cotton kimonos), intended
for use in the rooms.

Kyoto offers a choice of both Western- and Japanese-style accommodations, including traditional ryokan. If you choose a ryokan, be sure
to read the section on lodging in The Gold Guide, at the front of this
book. Not all ryokan offer private toilets and baths, so check in advance if you don't like to share facilities.

Obviously, higher priced inns offer the most personalized service. Be
aware that they can be very, very expensive. Prices quoted are usually
per person (including two meals) and not per room. Make sure to check
carefully, because some ryokan cost as much as U.S. $1,000 per per-
son per night.

Moderately (**$$**) and inexpensively (**$**) priced inns offer only a fraction
of the total ryokan experience. Tubs may be plastic rather than cedar-
wood. Meals may be served in the dining area rather than elaborately
prepared and presented in your room. Rooms, which may not be much
larger than a prison cell, may overlook a street rather than a garden.

The room, however, will have tatami straw mat floors, futon bedding, and a scroll and/or flower arrangement in its rightful place.

Most accommodations in the **$$$$**, **$$$**, and **$$** categories have representation abroad, so ask at the nearest Japan National Tourist Organization (JNTO) office for information on booking. If there is no representation, bookings must be made by writing directly to the establishment. Book at least a month in advance, or as early as three months ahead, if you are traveling during peak spring and autumn seasons or around important Japanese holidays and festivals.

A 3% federal consumer tax is added to all hotel bills. Another 3% local tax is added to the bill if it exceeds ¥15,000. At most hotels, a 10%–15% service charge is added to the total bill. Tipping is not necessary.

CATEGORY	COST*
$$$$	over ¥30,000
$$$	¥20,000–¥30,000
$$	¥8,000–¥20,000
$	under ¥8,000

Cost is for double room, without tax or service

Central Kyoto

$$$$ Hiiragiya. Hiiragiya is on par with the Tawaraya (*see below*) as the preferred ryokan among dignitaries and celebrities. The inn was founded in 1818 to accommodate provincial lords and their parties who were visiting the capital. The founder himself was a metalsmith whose artful sword guards were commissioned by powerful samurai. Luxurious elegance combined with strength is the pervasive style of this lodging place, which echoes with memories of the samurai visitors during the 19th century. Charlie Chaplin and Yukio Mishima have been among its noted past fans. As the motto of the inn implies: "A guest arrives . . . back home to comfort." Some baths feature stained-glass windows. The cheapest rooms are in the newer annex. ☎ *Fuyacho-Oike-kado, Nakagyo-ku, Kyoto-shi,* ☎ *075/221–1136,* FAX *075/221–1139. 33 rooms, 28 with bath. AE, DC, MC, V.*

$$$$ Tawaraya. The most famous of Kyoto's inns, this is the abode of kings
★ and queens, princes and princesses, and presidents and dictators when they visit Kyoto. Tawaraya was founded more than 300 years ago and is currently run by the 11th generation of the Okazaki family. For all its subdued beauty and sense of tradition, the inn does have modern comforts such as heat and air-conditioning, but they are introduced so inconspicuously that they hardly detract from the venerable atmosphere of yesteryear. Rooms feature superb antiques from the Okazaki family collection. The service and food here might be disappointing, however, if you have not been recommended to the ryokan by a respected Japanese. Indeed, there appear to have been occasions lately of taking the unwary foreigner for a few quick dollars: Guests are given the option of staying on a European Plan basis and, if they wish, of ordering a selection of dinners from ¥12,000 to ¥60,000, the former option being rather meager. ☎ *Fuyacho-Aneyakoji-agaru, Nakagyo-ku, Kyoto-shi,* ☎ *075/211–5566,* FAX *075/211–2204. 18 rooms with bath. AE, DC, V.*

$$$ ANA Hotel Kyoto. The best thing about this hotel is its location, directly across from Nijojo. If your room faces the castle rather than another high-rise, you can be assured that you are indeed in Kyoto. Now for the less-good news: Off the long, narrow, rather depressing corridors are long, narrow guest rooms that could use refurbishing—espe-

Reality check. Call home.

—— *AT&T USADirect® and World Connect®. The fast, easy way to call most anywhere.* ——

Take out AT&T Calling Card or your local calling card.** Lift phone. Dial AT&T Access Number for country you're calling from. Connect to English-speaking operator or voice prompt. Reach the States or over 200 countries. Talk. Say goodbye. Hang up. Resume vacation.

American Samoa 633 2-USA	Korea 009-11	Taiwan* 0080-10288-0
Australia 1800-881-011	Macao ■ 0800-111	Thailand♦ 0019-991-1111
Cambodia ■ 1800-881-001	Malaysia* 800-0011	
China, PRC♦♦♦ 10811	Micronesia ■.................................288	
Cook Islands ■ 09-111	New Zealand 000-911	
Fiji ■ 004-890-1001	Palau ■ 02288	
Guam...................................018-872	Philippines* 105-11	
Hong Kong 800-1111	Saipan† 235-2872	
India♦ 000-117	Singapore............................800-0111-111	
Indonesia† 001-801-10	South Africa 0-800-99-0123	
Japan*■ 0039-111	Sri Lanka....................................430-430	

AT&T
Your True Choice

For a free wallet sized card of all AT&T Access Numbers, call: 1-800-241-5555.

All the best trips start with **Fodor's**.

EXPLORING GUIDES
At last, the color of an art book combined with the usefulness of a complete guide.

"As stylish and attractive as any guide published." —*The New York Times*

"Worth reading before, during, and after a trip." —*The Philadelphia Inquirer*

More than 30 destinations available worldwide. $19.95 each.

BERKELEY GUIDES

The budget traveler's handbook

"Berkeley's scribes put the funk back in travel."
—*Time*

"Fresh, funny, and funky as well as useful."
—*The Boston Globe*

"Well-organized, clear and very easy to read."
—*America Online*

14 destinations worldwide. Priced between $13.00 - $19.50. ($17.95 - $27.00 Canada)

AFFORDABLES

"All the maps and itinerary ideas of Fodor's established gold guides with a bonus—shortcuts to savings." —*USA Today*

"Travelers with champagne tastes and beer budgets will welcome this series from Fodor's." —*Hartfort Courant*

"It's obvious these Fodor's folk have secrets we civilians don't." —*New York Daily News*

Also available: Florida, Europe, France, London, Paris. Priced between $11.00 - $18.00 ($14.50 - $24.00 Canada)

At bookstores, or call **1-800-533-6478**

Fodor's
The name that means smart travel.™

Kyoto Lodging

cially considering the rates charged. ☎ *Nijojo-mae, Horikawa-dori, Nakagyo-ku, Kyoto 604,* ☎ *075/231–1155,* FAX *075/231–5333. 303 rooms. 7 restaurants (including French, Chinese, and Japanese), bars, health spa, indoor pool, shops. AE, DC, MC, V.*

$$$ **Daimonjiya.** Just off the busy shopping area of Sanjo-dori, this tiny inn is as famous for its guest rooms as for the food served (in the guest rooms). Each room, with fine wood interiors, overlooks a small garden. *Kaiseki* (formal Japanese meal with tea ceremony) is the specialty of the house; the chef was trained at the best Kyoto culinary establishment. You do not need to be a guest to use one of the rooms for a meal, but then you would be missing out on the quintessential ryokan experience. (A branch of the restaurant Daimonjiya is located in the Tokyo Hilton International Hotel.) ☎ *Nishi-Iru, Kawaramachi-Sanjo, Nakagyo-ku, Kyoto-shi,* ☎ *075/221–0603. 7 rooms. AE, DC.*

$$$ **Hotel Fujita Kyoto.** This pleasant hotel is situated along the famed Kamo-
★ gawa, not far from the nightlife center of Gion. In the light of a full moon, the waterfall in its garden sparkles while waterfowl play. The lobby is narrow and long, with comfortable gray armchairs playing nicely against deep red carpeting. The Fujita features Japanese and Scandinavian decor throughout, and 18 rooms have Japanese-style furnishings. The two main restaurants are a kaiseki dining room and a steak house with counter- and table service. ☎ *Nishizume, Nijo-Ohashi, Kamogawa, Nakagyo-ku, Kyoto-shi 604,* ☎ *075/222–1511,* FAX *075/256–4561. 195 rooms. 6 restaurants and bars, beauty salon, shops. AE, DC, MC, V.*

$$$ **Kyoto Brighton Hotel.** Opened in 1987, the Brighton is still unques-
★ tionably the city's best hotel in this price range (and the most expensive). The cream-color central atrium is accented with chrome and brass trim and decorated with sage green furnishings. Hallways circle the atrium, and plants hang from the banisters of every floor. Glass elevators carry guests up the atrium to their rooms. On the whole, the Brighton has a simple, clean design that gives it an airy and spacious quality lacking in most Kyoto hotels. Large by Japanese standards, rooms have separate seating areas with a couch and TV. No need to worry about big-city noise: The Brighton is on a quiet side street close to the Imperial Palace (although not within walking distance of most of Kyoto's main attractions). ☎ *Nakadachiuri, Shinmachi-dori, Kamigyo-ku, Kyoto-shi,* ☎ *075/441–4411,* FAX *075/431–2360; in the U.S.,* ☎ *800/223–6800; in the U.K.,* ☎ *0800/181–123. 181 rooms, 2 suites. Restaurants, bars, outdoor pool, beauty salon, shops. AE, DC, MC, V.*

$$$ **Kyoto Grand Hotel.** The Grand's lobby can sometimes be crowded because the hotel is popular with tour groups. The green concrete building, which is on the drab side, has a circular attachment on the roof—a revolving restaurant. Terrycloth bathrobes, CNN TV, and remote-control toilet gadgetry are all part of the hotel's effort to keep up-to-date. If your room faces the street, make sure to draw the curtains or slide the shoji screens before undressing, because office buildings are right across the way. The Grand is famous for its cheerful and friendly staff. A free bus continuously shuttles guests to and from the Shinkansen central exit of Kyoto Station. The Grand's neighbors include Nishi-Honganji and Toji. ☎ *Shiokoji-Horikawa, Shimogyo-ku, Kyoto-shi 600,* ☎ *075/341–2311,* FAX *075/341–3073. 554 rooms. 12 restaurants (including Western, Japanese, and Chinese) and bars, bakery, indoor pool, sauna, barber shop, beauty salon, shops, travel services. AE, DC, MC, V.*

$$$ **Kyoto Tokyu Hotel.** This seven-story hotel is part of Japan's largest hotel chain. The pillared main entrance, the entrance hall, and lobby are expansive and airy, while the courtyard, with its reflecting pool and waterfall, creates a dramatic atmosphere. The well-appointed rooms, predominantly decorated in off-white tones, are comfortable and spacious. ⌧ *580 Kakimotocho, Gojo-sagaru, Horikawa-dori, Shimogyo-ku, Kyoto-shi 600,* ☎ *075/341–2411,* ⓕⓐⓧ *075/341–2488. 437 rooms. 5 restaurants (including French, Chinese, and Japanese) and bars, wedding hall, meeting and banquet rooms, pool, beauty salon, shops, travel services. AE, DC, MC, V.*

$$ **New Miyako Hotel.** This large hotel situated directly in front of Kyoto Station is under the same management as the Miyako Hotel (*see above*); it is used widely by groups and tours. The 10-story white edifice has two protruding wings with landscaping and street lamps reminiscent of a hotel in the United States. Its location makes it attractive for those planning train trips from the city. ⌧ *17 Nishi-Kujoincho, Minami-ku, Kyoto-shi 601,* ☎ *075/661–7111,* ⓕⓐⓧ *075/661–7135. 714 rooms, 4 Japanese-style. Japanese, Chinese, and Continental restaurants, bar and tea lounge, barber shop, shops. AE, DC, MC, V.*

$ **Hiraiwa.** Imagine the ambience of a friendly, Western-style youth hostel with tatami-mat rooms, and you have the Hiraiwa ryokan, a member of the Hospitable and Economical Japanese Inn Group. To be a member, inns must have English-speaking staff and offer clean, comfortable accommodations. Hiraiwa is the most popular of these inns in Kyoto; it's a great place to meet fellow travelers from around the world. Rules and regulations during your stay are posted on the walls. Guests are welcome to eat with the family owners around the dining table in the small kitchen. No private facilities and no baths; only showers are available. ⌧ *314 Hayaocho, Kaminoguchi-agaru, Ninomiya-cho-dori, Shimogyo-ku, Kyoto-shi,* ☎ *075/351–6748. 21 rooms. AE, MC, V.*

$ **Hirota Guest House.** This hidden treasure of an inn, south of the Im-
★ perial Palace, is run by a professional English-speaking guide. A long passageway behind the family's accounting office leads to a lush garden that surrounds a beautifully restored sake storehouse. The Japanese-style rooms have a great view of the secluded, quiet garden. Reserve well in advance. ⌧ *665 Nijo-dori, Tominokoji Nishi-Iru, Nakagyo-ku, Kyoto-shi,* ☎ *075/221–2474. 3 rooms, 1 with bath and kitchen. No credit cards.*

$ **Myokenji.** This temple lodging is an alternative accommodation that affords the guest a firsthand look at the activities of monks. Be ready to share a room with several fellow travelers. If you are modest, write ahead for a private room. The reasonable room rate includes breakfast. ⌧ *Teranouchi, Higashi-Iru, Horikawa-dori, Kamigyo-ku, Kyoto-shi,* ☎ *075/414–0808. 12 rooms. No credit cards.*

Eastern Kyoto

$$$ **Miyako Hotel.** The Miyako, the grand old dame of Kyoto's Western-
★ style hotels, has been around for close to 100 years. The hotel sits dramatically on the western hills of Kyoto, near the temples and shrines of Higashiyama (Eastern Kyoto). Every soundproof guest room offers beautiful panoramic views of the city and the surrounding hills. ⌧ *Sanjo-Keage, Higashiyama-ku, Kyoto-shi 605,* ☎ *075/771–7111,* ⓕⓐⓧ *075/751–2490. 320 rooms, 20 Japanese-style. 5 restaurants, coffee shop, lounges, bars, health facilities, outdoor pool, shops, meeting and banquet facilities. AE, DC, MC, V.*

$$$ **Seikoro.** This lovely inn is just a stone's throw away from busy Gojo
★ Station, a convenience that makes it popular among both foreigners
and Japanese. Established in 1831, the ryokan is managed by a native
resident who is fluent in English. Among the interesting decor are
Western antiques that mysteriously blend in quite well with the oth-
erwise traditional Japanese setting. When you return to Seikoro after
a day of sightseeing, you get the distinct feeling that you are returning
to your Japanese home. ☷ *Toiyamachi-dori, Gojo-sagaru, Higashiyama-
ku, Kyoto-shi,* ☎ *075/561–0771,* ⁣ⅎ⁣ⅈ⁣ⅈ *075/541–5481. 23 rooms with
bath. AE, DC, MC, V.*

$$$ **Yachiyo.** The special entrance to Yachiyo has low-hanging tiled eaves
★ and woodwork surrounded by carefully shaped bushes, pine trees, and
rocks. The sidewalk from the gate to the ryokan curves snakelike into
the doorway. Yachiyo is less expensive than its brethren in the deluxe
category but nevertheless provides fine, attentive care. You can reduce
the cost of staying at this ryokan by choosing not to dine here. Perhaps the biggest draw of Yachiyo is its proximity to Nanzenji, one of
the most appealing temples in Kyoto. ☷ *34 Nanzenji-fukuchicho,
Sakyo-ku, Kyoto-shi,* ☎ *075/771–4148,* ⁣ⅎⅈ *075/771–4140. 25 rooms,
20 with bath. AE, DC, MC, V.*

$$ **Holiday Inn Kyoto.** This member of the famous American chain (a
15-min. taxi ride from Kyoto's downtown area) boasts the best
sports facilities of any Kyoto hotel, including a bowling alley and ice-
skating rink. The hotel is located in a residential area with small, mod-
ern houses, occasionally interrupted by large, traditional Japanese
estates. To compensate for its location away from most of the action,
a shuttle bus makes the 30-minute run to and from Kyoto Station
every 90 minutes. Rooms for the disabled are available. ☷ *36 Nishi-
hirakicho, Takano, Sakyo-ku, Kyoto-shi 606,* ☎ *075/721–3131,* ⁣ⅎⅈ
*075/781–6178. 270 rooms. Restaurants, bar, coffee shop, outdoor
pool, indoor pool, gym, sauna, bowling alley, ice-skating rink, ten-
nis court, driving range, shops, banquet and meeting rooms. AE, DC,
MC, V.*

$$ **Iwanami.** Amid the antiques shops of Shinmonzen-dori is this priceless little inn, whose loyal clientele, including many foreigners, would
like to keep its existence a secret. The inn has gained such a reputation, in fact, that rooms must be booked well in advance. When booking, be sure to ask for a room with a view of the garden or canal. ☷
Higashioji, Nishi-Iru, Shinmonzen-dori, Higashiyama-ku, Kyoto-shi,
☎ *075/561–7135. 7 rooms. No credit cards.*

$$ **Kyoto Gion Hotel.** This hotel sits right in the heart of the Gion geisha
district, just west of Yasaka Shrine. It is modest, clean, and the loca-
tion is excellent—across from the Kyoto Craft Center, a five-minute
walk from downtown, and a 10-minute bus ride from Kyoto Station.
☷ *555 Gionmachi, Minamigawa, Higashiyama-ku, Kyoto-shi,* ☎
075/551–2111, ⁣ⅎⅈ *075/551–2200. Coffee shop, rooftop beer garden,
bar. 130 rooms. AE, DC, MC, V.*

$$ **Three Sisters Inn Annex** (Rakutoso Bekkan). A traditional inn popular with foreign guests for decades, the annex sits on the northeast edge
of Heian Shrine, down a trellised path that hides it from the street (the
annex is nicer than the main branch). This is a quiet and friendly
place, and a good introduction to inn customs because the management is accustomed to foreign guests. On the down side, the rooms
could use refurbishment, and the doors close at 11:30 PM sharp. ☷
Heian Jingu, Higashi-Kita-Kado, Sakyo-ku, Kyoto-shi, ☎ *075/761–
6333,* ⁣ⅎⅈ *075/761–6335. 12 rooms. AE, DC.*

$ **Kyoto Traveler's Inn.** This no-frills modern inn is located in the per-
fect spot for sightseeing, with Heian Shrine, Nanzenji, and the muse-

ums in Okazaki Park just minutes away on foot. Its 40 Western-style and 38 Japanese-style rooms are plain and small, but clean and practical, all with private bath and toilet. Ask for a room with a view if possible (most don't have one). Because of its location, size, and price, it is often used for group travel as well as for individuals. Head for the coffee shop on the first floor to look out over the river and plot your course for the day. ☷ *Heian Jingu Torii-mae, Okazaki, Sakyo-ku, Kyoto-shi,* ☎ *075/771–0225. 78 rooms with bath. Coffee shop, meeting and party rooms. AE, MC, V.*

$ **Pension Higashiyama.** A 10-minute walk from downtown and the major temples along the eastern foothills, this relatively new, small pension overlooks the lovely Shirakawa canal south of Sanjo-dori. The pension has created a friendly atmosphere for families on a budget, and is accustomed to foreign guests. ☷ *474-23 Umemiyacho, Shirakawa-suji, Sanjo-sagaru, Higashiyama-ku, Kyoto-shi,* ☎ *075/882–1181. 15 rooms, some with toilet; all share bath. Dining room. AE.*

$ **Ryokan Yuhara.** A 15-minute walk from the old quarters of Gion and Pontocho, Yuhara is popular among repeat visitors wishing to save a few yen while exploring Kyoto. The friendliness of the staff more than compensates for the spartan amenities. Especially rewarding is a springtime stay, when the cherry trees are in full bloom along the Takasegawa, which the inn overlooks. ☷ *188 Kagiyacho, Shomen-agaru, Kiyamachi-dori, Higashiyama-ku, Kyoto-shi,* ☎ *075/371–9583. 8 rooms. No credit cards.*

Northern Kyoto

$$$$ **Takaragaike Prince Hotel.** Kyoto's only deluxe hotel is located on the northern outskirts of the city, across from the International Conference Hall and Takaraga-ike (pond). Although useful for those attending an event at the conference hall, the hotel is a good 30 minutes from the city center and not convenient for tourists. Nevertheless, its unusual doughnut-shape architectural design provides each room with a view of the surrounding mountains and forests. Corridors along the inside overlook the landscaped inner garden. The fine touches include the huge floral arrangements in the lobby, the impressive chandeliers all around the building, and the original Miró prints, which hang in every suite. The spacious rooms have beds that are probably the largest you'll find in Japan. All rooms are tastefully decorated in pastel colors that complement the natural green of the outside views. This is one of the only hotels in Kyoto with its own authentic teahouse, which overlooks the pond. Demonstrations of the tea ceremony can be arranged upon request. ☷ *Takaragaike, Sakyo-ku, Kyoto-shi 606,* ☎ *075/712–1111,* 𝔽𝔸𝕏 *075/712-7677. 322 rooms. 6 restaurants (including French, Chinese, and Japanese), bars, shop, meeting and conference rooms, teahouse. AE, DC, MC, V.*

THE ARTS AND NIGHTLIFE

The Arts

Kyoto is quickly following Tokyo and Osaka as a must stop for both domestic and international artists. Kyoto has played host to the likes of Bruce Springsteen, but it is famous for the traditional arts—Kabuki, Noh, and traditional dances. All dialogue at theaters, however, is in

Japanese; the infrequent visitor may find that time is better spent visiting shrines, temples, and gardens.

Information on performances is available from a number of sources, the most convenient being your hotel concierge or guest-relations manager. He or she may even have a few tickets on hand, so don't hesitate to ask.

Kyoto boasts a 24-hour recording of the week's tourist events, including festivals, sporting events, and performances. Call 075/361–2911 for a recording in English. Another good source of information is **JNTO's Tourist Information Center (TIC),** which is located directly across from Kyoto Station. It is strongly suggested that you make a trip to TIC to pick up the latest information on Kyoto's arts scene and other tourist matters. Available here is a monthly newspaper for tourists called *Kyoto Visitor's Guide,* which devotes a few pages to "This Month's Theater." If you don't have time to go to TIC, you can call 075/371–5649 to speak to an English-speaking information officer.

Gion Corner

If there is one performance that should not be missed in Kyoto, it is the quick but comprehensive overview of Kyoto's performing arts at the Gion Corner. The one-hour show features court music and dance, ancient comic plays, Kyoto-style dancing performed by apprentice geisha called *maiko,* and puppet drama. Segments are also offered on the tea ceremony, flower arrangement, and koto music.

To obtain tickets, contact your hotel concierge or call **Gion Corner** (1st floor, Yasaka Hall, Gion, ☎ 075/561–1119). The show is quite a bargain at ¥2,500. Two performances nightly are given at 7:40 and 8:40 March 1–November 29. No performances are offered August 16 and December–February.

Before attending the show, walk around the Gion and Pontocho areas. Most likely you will see beautifully adorned geisha and maiko making their way to work. It is permissible to take their picture, but as they have strict appointments, don't delay them.

Seasonal Dances

If you are in Kyoto in April, be sure to take in the **Miyako Odori;** or, in May and October, the **Kamogawa Odori.** These dances are performed by geisha and apprentices and pay tribute to the seasonal splendor of spring and fall. The stage setting is spectacular, with festive singing and dancing.

Performances are held at the **Gion Kaburenjo Theater** (Gion Hanamikoji, Higashiyama-ku, ☎ 075/561–1115; tickets: ¥1,650, ¥3,300, and ¥3,800) and the **Pontocho Kaburenjo Theater** (Pontocho, Sanjo-sagaru, Nakagyo-ku, ☎ 075/221–2025; tickets: ¥1,650, ¥3,300, and ¥3,800).

Kabuki

Kabuki has found quite a following in the United States due to recent tours by Japan's Kabuki troupes in Washington, D.C., New York, and a few other cities. Kabuki is faster paced than Noh, but a single performance can easily take half a day. Devoted followers pack their box lunches and sit patiently through the entire performance, mesmerized by each movement of the performers.

For a first-timer, however, this all may be too exotic. Unless you are captured by the Kabuki spirit, don't spend more than an hour or two at Kyoto's famed **Minamiza Theater** (Shijo Kamogawa, Higashiyama-ku, ☎ 075/561–1155), the oldest theater in Japan. It was beautifully renovated and now hosts a variety of performances year-round. Top Kabuki stars from around the country make guest appearances during the annual, month-long **Kaomise** (Face Showing) Kabuki festival in December. Performance and ticket information can be obtained through the Tourist Information Center (*see* Important Addresses and Numbers, *below*). Tickets range from ¥2,000 to ¥9,000.

Noh

Noh is another form of traditional theater, more ritualistic and sophisticated than Kabuki. Some understanding of the plot of each play is necessary to enjoy a performance, which is generally slow-moving and solemnly chanted. The major Noh theaters often provide synopses of the plays in English. The masks used by the main actors are carved to express a whole range of emotions, though the mask itself may appear expressionless until the actor "brings it to life." Particularly memorable are the outdoor performances of Noh, especially **Takigi Noh,** held outdoors by firelight on the nights of June 1–2 in the precincts of the Heian Shrine.

Performances are given throughout the year at these two theaters: **Kanze Kaikan Noh Theater,** 44 Enshojicho, Okazaki, Sakyo-ku, ☎ 075/771–6114; and **Kongo Noh Theater,** Muromachi, Shijo-agaru, Nakagyo-ku, ☎ 075/221–3049. ☛ Prices vary according to each performance and range from ¥4,000 to ¥6,000.

Nightlife

Kyoto's nightlife is much more sedate than Tokyo's, but the areas around the old geisha quarters downtown are still thriving with nightclubs and bars. The Kiyamachi area along the small canal near Pontocho is as close to a consolidated nightlife area as you'll get in Kyoto. It is full of small drinking establishments with red lanterns (indicating inexpensive places) or small neon signs in front. It is also fun to walk around the Gion and Pontocho areas to try to catch a glimpse of a geisha or apprentice geisha going to or coming from work.

In the city center, check out the disco scene at **Gaia,** located in the Pleasure Dome Imagium Building (Nishikiyamachi-dori north of Shijo, Nakagyo-ku, ☎ 075/231–6600). This five-floor "labyrinth," as the owners call it, also has a bar, restaurant, club, and saloon. Another casual evening possibility is the **Pig & Whistle Pub** (across from the Keihan Sanjo Station, in the Shobi Bldg., ☎ 075/761–6022). Every weekend the Pig & Whistle is bulging at the seams with U.K. refugees and Japanese, who come for the draft beer, the fish and chips, and the dart board. The music is too loud, but no one seems to mind; the place is open till midnight during the week and 1 AM on weekends. For jazz, blues, and soul, try the **Live Spot Rag** (5F Kyoto Empire Bldg., Kiyamachi, ☎ 075/241–0446), north of Sanjo, which has a reasonable cover charge of about ¥1,200 for its live sessions between 7 and 11 PM. If you're looking for a light dinner or a late-night snack, head for **Kongolo** (Furukawacho, Niomon-dori-sagaru, Sakyo-ku, ☎ 075/751–9276), tucked in a half-basement on a quiet side street south of Heian Shrine. The sleek café/bar serves salads, spaghetti, and fried chicken, along with beer, mixed drinks, and Italian wine. It's open until 2 AM on Saturday and until midnight the rest of the week (closed Tues.).

KYOTO ESSENTIALS

Arriving and Departing

By Plane

The closest international airport to Kyoto is the new **Kansai International Airport** (code-named KIX). Though KIX also has domestic flights, particularly to Japan's major cities, the majority of internal air traffic still uses the old Osaka International Airport, now called **Itami.** Flight time between Tokyo and Osaka is about 70 minutes.

BETWEEN THE AIRPORTS AND CENTER CITY
Transport between KIX and Kyoto Station is by the Haruka Limited Express, which departs every 30 minutes to make the 75-minute run at ¥3,340. From Itami Airport, buses depart for Kyoto approximately every 20 minutes, 7:45 AM–9:30 PM, and drop passengers at nine hotels, as well as at Kyoto Station. The bus trip takes 55 to 90 minutes and costs ¥890 or ¥950, depending on the Kyoto destination. If you consider the distance involved and the high cost, it does not make sense to take a taxi from the airport to Kyoto as it can run well over ¥10,000.

By Train

Frequent daily Shinkansen express trains run between Tokyo and Kyoto (2 hrs., 40 min.). The one-way fare, including express charges for a reserved seat, is ¥12,970. JR train service between Osaka and Kyoto (30 min.) costs ¥530, one way. From the Shin-Osaka Station, you can take the Shinkansen and be in Kyoto in 15 minutes; tickets cost ¥2,250. You may use a Japan Rail Pass on both these trains. Two private lines, the Keihan and the Hankyu trains (40 min. each), are less expensive than the JR. The one-way fare between Osaka and Kyoto is ¥360 on the Keihan and ¥350 on the Hankyu train. Kyoto Station was recently rebuilt, and has been greatly modernized.

Getting Around

By Train

Kyoto has a 13-station subway line that runs between Takeda Station in the south and Kitayama Station in the north. The entire run takes 20 minutes. Tickets must be purchased before boarding at the station's automatic vending machines. Fares depend on the destination and begin at ¥180. Service runs 5:30 AM–11:30 PM. In Kyoto, the Keihan train from Osaka is now partly underground (from Shichijo to Demachi-Yanagi) and extends all the way up the east bank of the Kamogawa to Imadegawa-dori (street). From there a passage connects it with the Eizan Railway at Demachi-Yanagi Station. The Eizan has two lines, the Kurama Line running north to Kurama, and the Eizan Line running northeast to Yase. The Hankyu train connects with the subway at Karasuma Station.

By Bus

A network of bus routes covers the entire city. Most of the city buses operate 7 AM–9 PM daily, but a few start as early as 5:30 AM and run until 11 PM. The main bus terminals are Kyoto Station, Keihan Sanjo Station, Karasuma-Kitaoji, and at the Shijo–Karasuma intersection. Many city buses do not have signs in English, so you will need to know the bus number. Because you will probably ride the bus at least once in Kyoto, try to pick up a bus map early in your stay from the Tourist Information Center (☎ 075/371–5649) at the Kyoto Tower Building, across from the JR Kyoto Station.

At each bus stop, a guidepost indicates the stop name, the bus route, and the bus-route number. Because the information at most guideposts is only in Japanese (except for the route number, which is given as an Arabic numeral), you are advised to ask your hotel clerk beforehand to write down your destination and route number to show to the bus driver and fellow passengers; this will allow the driver and others to help you if you get lost. You might also ask your hotel clerk beforehand how many stops your ride will take.

Within the city, the standard fare is ¥200, which you pay before leaving the bus; outside the city limits, the fare varies according to distance. Special one-day passes are valid for unlimited rides on the subway, city buses, and private Kyoto bus lines, with restrictions on some routes. The passes, which cost ¥1,200 for adults and ¥600 for children under 12, are sold at travel agencies, main bus terminals, and information centers in Kyoto Station.

You may use the JR Pass on the local bus that travels between Kyoto Station and Takao (in northwestern Kyoto), passing close to Nijo Station.

By Taxi
Taxis are readily available in Kyoto. Fares for smaller-size cabs start at ¥580 for the first 2 km, with a cost of ¥90 for each additional 540 meters.

Guided Tours

Orientation Tours
Half-day morning and afternoon deluxe motor-coach tours featuring different city highlights are offered daily by **Sunrise Tours,** which is run by the **Japan Travel Bureau** (Kyoto Eki-mae, Shiokoji Karasuma Higashi-Iru, Shimogyo-ku, ☎ 075/361–7241). Tours are also given daily March–November by **Kintetsu Gray Line Tours** (New Miyako Hotel, Minami-ku, ☎ 075/691–0903) and **Japan Amenity Travel** (International Hotel Kyoto lobby, ☎ 075/222–0121, or the Kyoto Grand Hotel lobby, ☎ 075/343–2304). Pickup service is provided at major hotels, and reservations can be made through travel agents or by calling the numbers above. A morning tour, which commonly covers Nijojo (castle), Kinkakuji (the Temple of the Golden Pavilion), Kyoto Imperial Palace, Higashi-Honganji (temple), and the Kyoto Handicraft Center, costs ¥5,000. A ¥5,200 afternoon tour includes the Heian Shrine, Sanjusangendo, and Kyomizu Temple. A ¥10,800 full-day tour covers all the above sights and includes lunch.

Special-Interest Tours
Joe Okada Travel Service (3F Masugata Bldg., Teramachi-agaru Imadegawa, Kamigyo-ku, ☎ 075/241–3716) conducts special tours of Kyoto and arranges home visits for individuals and groups. Call Joe and he will tailor your tour to fit your interests and budget. Private tours are more expensive, so it's best to get together a group. Home visits are also arranged by the **Tourist Section, Department of Cultural Affairs and Tourism** (Kyoto City Government, Kyoto Kaikan, Okazaki, Sakyo-ku, Kyoto, ☎ 075/752–0215).

Walking Tours
The **Japan National Tourist Organization** publishes suggested walking routes, which offer maps and brief descriptions for five tours (ranging in length from about 40 min. to 80 min.). The walking-tour brochures are available from the JNTO's Tourist Information Center office at the

Kyoto Tower Building in front of Kyoto Station (☎ 075/371–5649). For its guests, the **Kyoto Grand Hotel** suggests three jogging and walking courses around the famous temples near that hotel.

Excursions

Full- and half-day tours to Nara are offered by **Japan Travel Bureau** (☎ 075/361–7241), **Fujita Travel Service** (☎ 075/222–0121), and **Kintetsu Gray Line Tours** (☎ 075/691–0903). Pickup service is available at principal hotels. An afternoon tour to Nara costs about ¥6,500. Morning and afternoon trips to Osaka, for ¥7,900 and ¥5,000, respectively, are not worth the cost, especially if you have a JR Pass. **Sunrise Tours** (*see* Orientation Tours, *above*) organizes excursions down an 8-mile stretch (about 90 minutes) of the Hozu Rapids in flat-bottom boats, from Kameoka to Arashiyama, for ¥9,800.

Personal Guides

Contact **Japan Amenity Travel** (☎ 075/222–0121), **Joe Okada Travel Service** (☎ 075/241–3716), and **Inter Kyoto** (☎ 075/256–3685). **Volunteer guides** are available free of charge through the Tourist Information Center (TIC), but arrangements must be made by visiting the TIC in person one day in advance (*see* Important Addresses and Numbers, *below*).

Important Addresses and Numbers

Emergencies

Police, ☎ 110; **Ambulance,** ☎ 119.

DOCTORS
Japan Baptist Hospital, Kita-Shirakawa, Yamanomotocho, Sakyo-ku, ☎ 075/781–5191.
Daini Sekijuji Byoin (2nd Red Cross Hospital) at Kamanza-dori, Marutamachi-agaru, Kamigyo-ku, ☎ 075/231–5171; and **Daiichi Sekijuji** (Red Cross Hospital) at Higashiyama Honmachi, Higashiyama-ku, ☎ 075/561–1121.
Sakabe Clinic (435 Yamamotocho, Gokomachi, Nijo Sagaru, Nakagyo-ku, ☎ 075/231–1624) has 24-hour emergency facilities.

English-Language Bookstores

Maruzen Kyoto (296 Kawaramachi-dori, Nakagyo-ku, ☎ 075/241–2161).
Izumiya Book Center (Avanti Bldg., 6F, south of Kyoto Station, Minami-ku, ☎ 075/671–8987).
Kyoto Shoin (3F Kawaramachi, north of Shijo, Nakagyo-ku, ☎ 075/221–1062).

Travel Agencies

Japan Travel Bureau (Kyoto Eki-mae, Shiokoji Karasuma Higashi-Iru, Shimogyo-ku, ☎ 075/361–7241).
Japan Amenity Travel (International Hotel Kyoto lobby, ☎ 075/222–0121).
Kintetsu Gray Line Tours Reservation Center (New Miyako Hotel, Minami-ku, ☎ 075/691–0903).
Joe Okada Travel Service (Masugata Bldg., Teramachi-agaru Imadegawa, Kamigyo-ku, ☎ 075/241–3716).

Tourist Information

The Japan National Tourist Organization (JNTO) **Tourist Information Center** (TIC) is located in the Kyoto Tower Building, in front of the JR Kyoto Station (take the Karasuma exit, on the side opposite the Shinkansen tracks). *Karasuma-dori Higashi-Shiokojicho, Shimogyo-*

ku, ☎ *075/371–5649.* ☉ *9–5 weekdays; 9–noon Sat. Closed national holidays.*

The JNTO Teletourist Service (☎ 075/361–2911) offers taped information on events in and around the city.

The **Kyoto City Government** operates a tourist information office. *Kyoto Kaikan, Okazaki, Sakyo-ku,* ☎ *075/752–0215.* ☉ *8:30–5 weekdays, 8:30–noon Sat. Closed 2nd and 4th Sat. of the month and national holidays.*

The Japan Travel Phone, a nationwide telephone information system in English for visitors, is available 9–5 daily, year-round. It is run out of the same office as the TIC (*see above*). In Kyoto, ☎ 075/371–5649. A three-minute call costs ¥10.

Consulates

The nearest U.S., Canadian, and British consulates are located in Osaka (*see* Osaka Essentials *in* Chapter 8).

7 Nara

A half-hour south of Kyoto lies Nara, a small, quiet city that is a favorite with many return visitors to Japan, who realized too late the first time around that they had short-changed it timewise because they were, understandably, dazzled by its northern neighbor's cultural riches. In addition to numerous temples and historic sites, Nara has hidden treasures in its backstreets: old wooden shops, merchants' houses, and traditional restaurants.

THE ANCIENT CITY OF NARA WAS FOUNDED in 710 by Emperor Kanmu and predated Kyoto as the capital of Japan. Nara was the first capital to remain in one place over a long period of time. Until then, the capital had been established in a new location with each successive ruler. The founding of Nara, then known as Heijo-Kyo, occurred during a period when Japan's politics, arts, architecture, and religion had been heavily influenced by China. Even the Japanese writing system, which was developed at this time, utilized Chinese written characters.

By Kiko Itasaka

Updated by
Nigel Fisher

Introduced by China beginning in the 6th century, Buddhism flourished in Nara and enjoyed the official favor of the rulers and aristocracy, as it coexisted with the indigenous religion of Shintoism. Many of Nara's Buddhist temples and monasteries were built by emperors and noble families, while other temples were transferred to Nara from former capitals. At its peak during the 8th century, Nara was said to have had as many as 50 pagodas. Emperor Shomu built Todaiji, a grand temple complex that was to serve as a central monastery for other Buddhist monasteries constructed in each province of Japan. Todaiji's construction began in 745 and was completed in 752. It was established not only for spiritual purposes but also to serve as a symbol of a united Japan. Emperor Shomu, who saw much to emulate in Chinese culture, astutely realized that religion could play a strong role in consolidating Japan.

In 784, the capital of Japan was transferred to Kyoto, and Nara was no longer a city of political consequence. As a result, the many buildings of Nara, including Todaiji, remained essentially untouched by the ravages of war. Kofukuji recalls the power of the Fujiwara clan in the 7th century. Its close connection with Kasuga Taisha, the Fujiwara family shrine, demonstrates the peaceful coexistence between Buddhism and Shintoism. Both Todaiji and Toshodaiji reflect the pervasive influence of Buddhism on the Japanese way of life over the centuries.

For many years, Nara, a small and quiet city, has been a favorite with many travelers in Japan. Apart from many temples and historical sites of interest in Nara, the narrow backstreets of Naramachi, just south of Sarusawa Pond in Nara Koen (park), have hidden treasures: old wooden shops, merchants' houses, and traditional restaurants. Here you'll find shops selling the crafts for which Nara is famous: *fude* (handmade brushes) and *sumi* (ink sticks) for calligraphy and ink painting, Nara dolls carved in wood, and Nara *sarashi-jofu*—fine, handwoven, sun-bleached linen.

★ Most of Nara's sights are within walking distance of the centrally located and picturesque **Nara Koen,** inhabited by approximately 1,000 very tame (and sometimes aggressive) deer, which roam freely around the various temples and shrines. The deer are considered to be divine messengers; they are particularly friendly when you feed them deer crackers, which can be purchased at stalls in the park. It is a singular pleasure to wander around the lush green park, dotted with numerous ponds, as you stroll from temple to temple.

Most day-trippers tend to visit only Nara Koen, but we recommend skipping some of its sights and taking the time to visit Horyuji, the oldest remaining temple complex in all of Japan, in the outskirts of Nara.

It is impossible to see all of the temples and shrines of Nara in one day. The Exploring section of this chapter has a two-day itinerary. If you have only one day to spend in Nara, you may prefer to visit the less-congested Horyuji complex, and forgo the other temples near it; then you can proceed to explore more of Nara Koen district.

EXPLORING

Numbers in the margin correspond to points of interest on the Nara map.

At its founding in the 8th century, Nara was planned as a rectangular city with checkerboard streets based on the model of the Chinese city of Ch'ang-an. The city still maintains this highly organized pattern, and it is therefore extremely easy to navigate. Many sights are located within or near Nara Koen. Other major temples, such as Horyuji, Yakushiji, and Toshodaiji, are located west and southwest of Nara, and all can be reached by the same bus.

★ ❶ Begin your tour of Nara at the resplendent **Todaiji,** in Nara Koen. Get there by boarding Bus 2, which departs from the front of the JR and Kintetsu stations, and get off at the Daibutsuden stop. Cross the street and you will be at the path that leads to the Todaiji complex. You can also walk from Kintetsu Nara Station to Todaiji in about 15 minutes. Exit the east end of the station and walk east along Noborioji-dori, the avenue that runs parallel to the station building. Walk past the Nara Prefectural Office Building and under Highway 369, continuing east to the next large intersection. Turn left onto the pedestrians-only street that leads to Todaiji. It is lined with souvenir stalls and small restaurants. You may also walk from the JR station but this route is longer and passes through the less attractive modern sections of town.

❷ As you walk along the path leading to the temple complex, you will pass through the impressive dark wood front gate known as **Nandaimon** (Great Southern Gate); the original was destroyed in a typhoon in 962 and rebuilt in 1199. The gate is supported by 18 large wood pillars, each 62 feet high and 39 inches in diameter. In the two outer niches on either side of the gate are wood figures of Deva Kings, who guard the great Buddha within. They are the work of master sculptor Unkei, of the Kamakura period (1185–1335). In the inner niches are a pair of stone *koma-inu* (Korean dogs); these creatures are mythical guardians placed beside the gates to ward off evil.

❸ Continue straight along the path leading to the main buildings of the Todaiji complex. In front of you is the entrance of the Daibutsuden, but before entering this building, first go to the small temple on the left, **Kaidanin.** Inside are clay statues of the Four Heavenly Guardians. The images are depicted in full armor, wielding weapons and displaying fierce expressions. *Kaidan* is a Buddhist word for the terrace on which priests are ordained; the Chinese Buddhist priest Ganjin (688–763) ordained many Japanese Buddhist priests here. The original temple was destroyed repeatedly by fire, and the current structure was built in 1731. ☞ ¥400. ⊗ *Daily 8–5 (8–4:30 in winter).*

321

Daibutsuden, **4**
Kaidanin, **3**
Kasuga Taisha, **8**
Kofukuji, **11**
Mt. Wakakusa, **7**
Nandaimon, **2**
Nara Kokuritsu Bijutsukan (Nara National Museum), **10**
Naramachi, **12**
Nigatsudo, **5**
Sangatsudo, **6**
Shin-Yakushiji, **9**
Todaiji, **1**

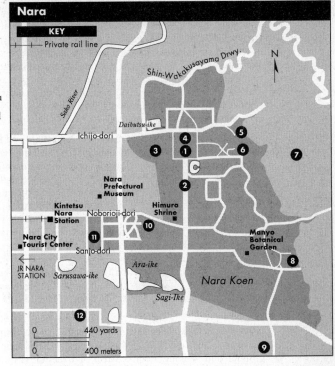

4 From Kaidanin, return to the entrance of the **Daibutsuden** (Hall of the Great Buddha), purportedly the largest wooden structure in the world (157 ft. high and 187 ft. long). The elegant and austere white building, with its wood beams darkened from age, is an impressive sight. Note a pair of gilt ornaments decorating the roof ridge. These are called *kutsugata* (shoe-shape) because they resemble footwear, and in ancient times they were not only ornamental but were believed to ward off fire. They unfortunately did not work. The current Daibutsuden was restored in 1709, at only two-thirds the scale of the original structure. Inside the Daibutsuden is the **Daibutsu**, a 53-foot bronze statue of Buddha that is perhaps the most famous sight in all of Nara. The Daibutsu was originally commissioned by Emperor Shomu in 743. After numerous unsuccessful castings, the figure was finally made in 749. A statue of this scale had never before been built in Japan, and it was hoped that it would serve as a symbol to unite the country. The statue was dedicated in 752 in a grand ceremony attended by the then-retired Emperor Shomu, the imperial court members, and 10,000 priests and nuns.

Behind the Daibutsu to the right, you'll see a large wooden pillar with a hole at its base. You will also observe many Japanese tourists attempting to crawl through the opening, which is barely large enough for a petite adult. Local superstition has it that those who pass through the opening will eventually go to paradise. Children, in particular, love easing through and watching adults suffer the indignity of barely making it through the opening. In the back of the Daibutsu, to the left, is a model of the original Todaiji. ☞ ¥400. ☉ *Daily, Jan.–Feb. 8–4:30; Mar. 8–5; Apr.–Sept. 7:30–5:30; Oct. 7:30–5; Nov.–Dec. 8–4:30.*

As you exit the Daibutsuden, turn left and walk up a winding path. Turn right, go up a stone staircase, and then veer left on the slope lined with stone lanterns. On your left, on top of the slope, you will come **5** to **Nigatsudo** (Second Month Temple), named because of a religious rite that used to be performed here every February. The temple was founded in 752 and houses some important images that are not on display to the public. However, because of the hilltop location, the temple's veranda offers a breathtaking, panoramic view of Nara Koen. ☞ *Free.* ☉ *Daily 8–5:30.*

Return along the same incline that led to Nigatsudo and turn left. The **6** wood structure on your left is **Sangatsudo** (Third Month Temple), named after a rite that was performed each March. The entrance is on the right side as you face the building. Founded in 733, this temple is the original structure and the oldest building in the Todaiji complex. As you enter, to your left are some benches covered with tatami mats, where you can sit and contemplate the 1,200-year-old National Treasures that crowd the small room. The principal image is the dry lacquer statue of Fukukenjaku Kannon, the Goddess of Mercy, whose diadem is encrusted with thousands of pearls and gemstones. The two clay statues on either side of her, the Gakko (Moonlight) and the Nikko (Sunlight) bodhisattvas, are considered fine examples of the Nara (or Tenpyo) period, the height of classic Japanese sculpture. ☞ *¥400.* ☉ *Daily 7:30– 5:30 (8–4:30 in winter).*

Leave the entrance of Sangatsudo, and walk straight ahead, following the signs in English for Mt. Wakakusa. You will be leaving the temple **7** grounds and walking along a street. On the left is the base of **Mt. Wakakusa,** which is actually more a hill covered with grass than a mountain. Once a year, on January 15, 15 priests set the hill's dry grass on fire. The blazes on the entire hill create a grand spectacle.

TIME OUT   Because there are few areas to grab a bite in Nara Koen, this street near Mt. Wakakusa is a good place to have a cup of coffee, a snack, or even lunch. Most of the restaurants along here are similar, but a few offer a better selection than the others. **Shiroganeya** (☎ 0742/22- 2607) has noodles for ¥650–¥750 and lunches for ¥1,000–¥2,500. **Asahiken** (☎ 0742/22-2384) has a tasty tempura lunch for ¥1,500 and eel for ¥1,200. In both places, you pay when served.

If you continue past all of the restaurants and shops, at the end of the street you will see some stone steps. Go down these and cross a small bridge over a stream, then walk along the path that leads into shady and peaceful woods. At the end of the path, turn left up the staircase ★ **8** before you, and you will be in front of **Kasuga Taisha.** Kasuga was founded in 768 as a tutelary shrine for the Fujiwaras, a prominent feudal family. It is famous for the more than 2,000 stone lanterns that line the major pathways to the shrine, all of which are lit three times a year on special festival days (Feb. 2, Aug. 14–15). For many years after its founding, the shrine was reconstructed, following the original design, exactly every 20 years according to Shinto custom, as is the case with the famous Ise Jingu in Mie Prefecture. (Kasuga, however, has not been rebuilt in 100 years.) The reason that many Shinto shrines are rebuilt is not only to renew the materials, but also to purify the site. It is said that Kasuga Taisha has been rebuilt more than 50 times, the last time in 1893. After you pass through the *torii* (gate), the first wooden structure you'll see is the Haiden (Offering Hall), and to its left is the Naoraiden (Entertainment Hall). In back of the latter hall are the four Honden (Main Shrines). They are National Treasures, all built in the same Kasuga style, and painted vermilion and green—a striking contrast to the dark wooden exterior of most of the temples in Nara. The sacred deer of this shrine are protected, and they roam freely about the grounds. ☞ *Kasuga Shrine Museum ¥400, shrine's outer courtyard free, inner precincts with 4 Honden structures and gardens ¥500.* ⊗ *Museum daily 9–4, inner precincts daily, Apr.–Oct. 8:30–5; Nov.–Mar. 9–4:30.*

Leaving Kasuga Taisha, walk south, down the path lined with stone lanterns and past the Kasuga-Wakamiya Shrine. Continue down this wooded path until you reach a paved road. Cross the road and take the first right, onto a residential street with many traditional Japanese houses. Take the first left and follow it south about 100 meters (yards), till it curves to the right and leads to the entrance of **Shin-Yakushiji.** (If time is limited and you want to skip Shin-Yakushiji, take the path straight down from Kasuga Taisha to the Nara National Museum and Kofukuji.) This temple was founded in 747 by Empress Komyo (701–760) as a prayer requesting the recovery of her sick husband, Emperor Shomu. Most of the temple buildings were destroyed over the years; only the Main Hall, which houses many fine objects of the Nara period, still exists. In the center of the hall is a wood statue of Yakushi Nyorai, the Physician of the Soul. Surrounding this statue are 12 clay images of the Twelve Divine Generals who protected Yakushi. Eleven of these figures are originals. The generals stand in threatening poses, bearing spears, swords, and other weapons, and display terrifying expressions. ☞ *¥500.* ⊗ *8:30–sunset.*

Leaving Shin-Yakushiji, retrace your steps to the residential street you walked down earlier. Turn left down this street and walk to the major intersection at the end of it. Across the street you will see a bus stop, where you can board Bus 1 back to the Daibutsuden stop. **Nara Koku-ritsu Bijutsukan** (Nara National Museum) specializes in Buddhist art. The East Wing, built in 1973, has many examples of calligraphy, paintings, and sculpture. The West Wing, built in 1895, features objects of archaeological interest. Each fall during the driest days of November, when the Shosoin Repository, located behind Todaiji, opens its doors to air its magnificent collection, some of its ancient treasures are displayed at the National Museum. *10-6 Noboriojicho,* ☎ *0742/22–7771.* ☞ *¥400 adults, ¥130 college and high-school students, ¥70 junior-high and grade-school students (more for special exhibitions).* ⊗ *Tues.–Sun. 9–4:30 (enter by 4). When national holidays fall on Mon., closed on Tues.*

Leaving the west exit of the East Wing of the Museum, walk west for about five minutes, and you will find yourself at the **Kofukuji** complex. This temple was originally founded in 669 in Kyoto by the Fujiwara family; with the establishment of the new capital of Nara, it was transferred to its current location in 710. At its peak in the 8th century, Kofukuji (Happiness Producing Temple) was a powerful temple that had 175 buildings, of which fewer than a dozen remain.

The history of Kofukuji reflects the intense relationship between Buddhism and Shintoism in Japan. In 937, a Kofukuji monk had a dream in which the Shinto deity of Kasuga appeared in the form of a Buddha, asking to become a protector of the temple; in 947, some Kofukuji monks held a Buddhist ceremony at the Shinto Kasuga Taisha to mark the merging of the Buddhist temple with the Shinto shrine. Although you can enter many buildings in this temple complex, perhaps the most interesting is the **Kokuhokan** (National Treasure House). This unattractive, modern concrete building holds a fabulous collection of National Treasure sculpture and other works of art from the Nara period.

Also of interest at the Kofukuji complex are the two pagodas. The **Five-Story Pagoda,** at 164 feet, is the second tallest pagoda in all Japan. The original pagoda in this spot was built in 730 by Empress Komyo, and several succeeding pagodas were destroyed by fire, but the current pagoda is an exact replica of the original and was built in 1426. The **Three-Story Pagoda** was built in 1114 and is renowned for its graceful lines and fine proportions. ☞ *¥500 adults, ¥400 high-school and junior-high students, ¥150 grade-school students.* ☉ *Daily 9–5 (enter by 4:30).*

There are several fine restaurants within minutes of the Kofukuji Pagoda (*see* Dining, *below*).

⑫ Before continuing on to the Western district and Horyuji, take some time out from temple-viewing to walk through **Naramachi,** just south of Sarusawa-ike (pond). This neighborhood is a maze of narrow residential streets lined with traditional houses and old shops, many of which deal in Nara's renowned arts and crafts. Gangoji (temple) lies at the heart of Naramachi, and near it the little town museum known as the Naramachi Shiryokan (Historical Library). Maps to the area are available through the city's tourist information centers and the Shiryokan: A signboard map on the southwest edge of Sarusawa-ike shows the way to all the important shops, museums, and galleries.

Look for **"Yu" Nakagawa** (☎ 0742/22–1322), which specializes in handwoven, sunbleached linen textiles, a Nara specialty known as *sarashi-jofu.* From October to April, make an appointment to watch the making of ink sticks at **Kobaien** (☎ 0742/23–2965), for 400 years the makers of fine Nara ink sticks for calligraphy and ink painting. Visit the Silk Road folk-craft shop **Kikuoka** (0742/26–3889) near the Historical Library. On foot or by bicycle, Naramachi can offer a change of pace from ordinary sightseeing, and local residents are friendly and eager to help.

Numbers in the margin correspond to points of interest on the Western Nara Temples map.

From the JR Nara or Kintetsu Nara stations, it is quite simple to visit the four major temples located on the outskirts of Nara. From the Kintetsu and JR stations, take Bus 52, which stops at Toshodaiji, Yakushiji, and Horyuji and Chuguji, and returns along the same route. The bus to Horyuji, the farthest temple, takes about 50 minutes and costs ¥640. You can also take the JR train on the Kansai Main Line to Horyuji Station, from where it is a 15-minute walk to the temple.

★ ❶ **Horyuji** is the most captivating of these temples, and should be visited before any of the others. Get off the bus at the Horyuji-mae stop and walk down the path leading to the temple complex. Horyuji was founded in 607 by Prince Shotoku (573–621); some of the temple buildings are among the oldest wood structures in the world. The first gate you pass through at Horyuji is the **Nandaimon,** rebuilt in 1438. The second gate is the **Chumon** (Middle Gate), which is the original, built in 607. Unlike most Japanese gates, which are supported by two pillars at the ends, this gate is supported by pillars in the center. Note the unusual shape of the pillars, which are entastic (curved outward in the center), an architectural technique used in ancient Greece that traveled as far as Japan. Entastic pillars in Japan exist only in the 7th-century structures of Nara.

As you pass through the gate you enter the western precincts of the temple. The first building you see on your right is the **Kondo** (Main

Hall). On its left is a five-story pagoda. The entire pagoda was disassembled in World War II; after the war, it was reconstructed in its original form, using the same materials that were first used to build it in 607. In back of the pagoda is the **Daikodo** (Lecture Hall), which was destroyed by fire and rebuilt in 990. Inside the hall is an image of Yakushi Nyorai (Physician of the Soul).

From the Daikodo, walk back past the Kondo and Chumon, then turn left and walk past the pond on your right. You will come to two concrete buildings known as the **Daihozoden** (Great Treasure Hall). On display in these buildings are statues, sculptures, ancient Buddhist religious articles, and brocades. Of particular interest is a miniature shrine that belonged to Lady Tachibana, mother of the Empress Komyo. The shrine is only a little over 9 feet in height, and the Buddha image inside is about 20 inches tall.

As you leave the exit of the Daihozoden, turn left, walk a short distance until the path ends, and turn left again. You will be at the **Todaimon** (Great East Gate), which leads to the eastern precincts of the temple complex. The octagonal building is the **Yumedono** (Hall of Dreams), so named because Prince Shotoku used to meditate here. ☛ ¥1,000. ☉ *Daily 8–5 (8–4:30 in winter); enter 1 hr. before closing.*

In the rear of the eastern precinct of Horyuji is an exit that leads to
② **Chuguji**. As you enter the temple, notice the carefully raked pebbles on which you must walk to approach the entrance. Chuguji was originally the home of Prince Shotoku's mother. After she passed away, it became a temple dedicated to her memory. This quiet nunnery houses a graceful wooden image of the Miroku Bodhisattva, the Buddha of the Future. This statue dates from the Asuka period (552–645), and its gentle countenance has made it famous, as an ageless view of hope for the future. Also of interest is the oldest example of embroidery in Japan, which dates from the Asuka period (552–645). The framed cloth depicts Tenjukoku (Land of Heavenly Longevity). In front of the temple is a small, carefully tended pond with a rock garden emerging from just below the surface. Although this nunnery is a peaceful spot for wandering, it is not worth seeing if you are pressed for time. ☛ ¥400. ☉ *Daily 9–4:30 (9–4 in winter).*

★ **③** Get back on Bus 52 (going in the direction from which you came) and get off at the Yakushiji-mae stop. **Yakushiji** was originally founded in 680 and was transferred to its current location in 718. As you enter the temple grounds, on your right you will see the **East Tower**, a pagoda that dates from 1285. The pagoda has an interesting asymmetrical shape, so startling that it inspired American scholar Ernest Fenollosa (1853–1908) to remark that it was as beautiful as "frozen music." Although it appears to have six stories, in fact it only has three; it consists of three roofs with smaller ones attached underneath. The **West Tower**, to your left, was built in 1981. The new building in the center is the **Kondo** (Main Hall), which was rebuilt in 1976 and is painted in garish vermilion. These newer buildings are not nearly as attractive as the older structures, and they look out of place in the otherwise appealing temple complex. ☛ ¥500. ☉ *Daily 8:30–5.*

④ From the rear gate of Yakushiji it is a 10-minute walk to the temple **Toshodaiji** down the "Path of History," trod by important dignitaries and priests for centuries. The path is lined with clay-wall houses, gardens, and small shops selling antiques, crafts, and *narazuke* (vegetables pickled in sake), a popular local specialty. There are also several good restaurants here (*see* Van Kio *in* Dining, *below*). Toshodaiji was

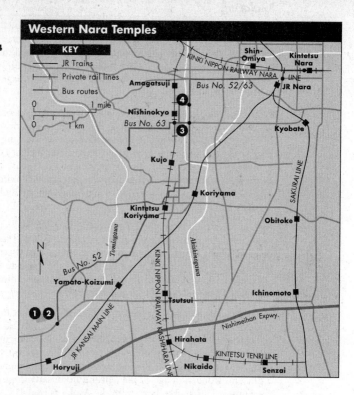

Western Nara Temples

KEY
— JR Trains
—|— Private rail lines
— Bus routes

0 — 1 mile
0 — 1 km

Shin-Omiya
Kintetsu Nara
KINKI NIPPON RAILWAY NARA LINE
JR Nara
Amagatsuji
Bus No. 52/63
4
Nishinokyo
Bus No. 63
3
Kyobate
Kujo
Koriyama
Kintetsu Koriyama
Obitoke
SAKURAI LINE
Tomiogawa
Akishinogawa
N
Bus No. 52
KINKI NIPPON RAILWAY KASHIHARA LINE
Yamato-Koizumi
Ichinomoto
Tsutsui
1 **2**
Nishimeihan Expwy.
JR KANSAI MAIN LINE
Hirahata
KINTETSU TENRI LINE
Horyuji
Nikaido
Senzai

founded in 751 by Ganjin, a Chinese priest who traveled to Japan at the invitation of Emperor Shomu. At this time, Japanese priests had never received formal instruction from a Buddhist priest. The invitation was extended by two Japanese priests who had traveled to China in search of a Buddhist priest willing to undertake the arduous and perilous journey to Japan. Ganjin agreed to go but was unsuccessful in his first attempts to reach Japan.

On Ganjin's first journey, some of his disciples betrayed him. His second journey resulted in a shipwreck. During the third trip, his ship was blown off course, and on his fourth trip, he was refused permission to leave China by government officials. Before his next attempt, he contracted an eye disease that left him blind. Nevertheless, he persevered in his goal of reaching Japan and finally arrived in 750. Ganjin shared his knowledge of Buddhism with his adopted country and served as a teacher to many Japanese priests as well as Emperor Shomu; he is also remembered for bringing the first sugar to Japan.

In order to enter the temple complex, you pass through the **Nandai-mon** (Great South Gate), which is supported by entastic pillars (like those seen in the gate of Horyuji). The first building you see is the **Kondo** (Main Hall), which is considered to be one of the finest remaining examples of Nara architecture. Inside the hall is a lacquer statue of Vairo-cana Buddha, the same incarnation of Buddha that is enshrined at Todaiji. The halo surrounding this figure originally was covered with 1,000 Buddhas, though only 864 remain. In back of the Kondo is the **Dai-Kodo** (Lecture Hall), which was originally an assembly hall of the Nara Imperial Court and was moved to its current location when Toshodaiji was founded. Because all the other buildings of the Nara imperial court have been destroyed, the Kodo is the only remaining example of Nara palace architecture. In the back of the temple grounds is the **Mieido,** in which there is a lacquer statue of Ganjin that dates from 763. This image is on public display only once a year, on June 6, in commemoration of the birthday of the illustrious priest. ☞ *¥500.* ⊘ *Daily 8:30–5.*

When you leave Toshodaiji, you can take Bus 63 back to Kintetsu Nara or JR Nara station; pick it up right in front of the temple.

DINING

Nara cuisine resembles that of its neighboring city, Kyoto. The specialty of this region is **kaiseki,** carefully prepared and aesthetically pleasing Japanese full-course meals (usually 7–12 courses). One local dish is **chagayu,** rice porridge flavored with green tea and served with vegetables in season. Nara boasts the lowest rate of stomach cancer in Japan, and local wisdom attributes this to the healthfulness of chagayu. An unforgettable gourmet experience is your first bite of **narazuke,** tangy vegetables pickled in sake, often served as a side dish with traditional meals in Nara.

Most visitors here are day-trippers who do not plan to dine in town, but an elegant Japanese meal in a traditional Nara restaurant is an appropriate and enjoyable way to conclude a day of temple viewing. Those who do not have time for dinner should at least try for a leisurely lunch. One word of warning: Many Nara restaurants are small and offer limited menus with set courses and no à la carte dishes, so it is a good idea to make reservations in advance. Restaurants tend to close early in Nara, so plan accordingly. Because some places do not have English-speaking staff or menus in English, it's best to ask someone from your hotel to help make your arrangements. This may seem a lot of trouble for the sake of eating, but the quiet atmosphere and the hospitality of the local residents make Nara a memorable place to enjoy a fine traditional meal.

A 3% federal consumer tax is added to all restaurant bills. Another 3% local tax is added to the bill if it exceeds ¥7,500. At more expensive restaurants, a 10%–15% service charge is added to the bill. Tipping is not necessary.

CATEGORY	COST*
$$$$	over ¥7,000
$$$	¥5,000–¥7,000
$$	¥3,500–¥5,000
$	under ¥3,500

Cost is per person without tax, service, or drinks

$$$$ **Onjaku.** Not far from Nara Koen, this restaurant offers exquisitely pre-
★ sented kaiseki meals in a serene Japanese-style room with gentle lighting. The exterior, with its faded wood walls, is in keeping with the architectural style of Nara. The menu consists only of kaiseki meals of varying prices. ✕ *1043 Kita-Tenmacho,* ☎ *0742/26–4762. Reservations required. No credit cards.* ⊘ *Lunch 12–1, dinner 5–7:30. Closed Tues.*

$$$$ **Tsukihitei.** A quiet restaurant set in the hills behind Kasuga Taisha, Tsukihitei serves formal kaiseki feasts. Your dining experience begins when you walk up the shaded, wooded path leading to the restaurant. When you make your reservation, ask for a kaiseki set meal. As you dine on delicate morsels of fish, vegetables, and rice, and sip on sweet plum wine, you can gaze out on the forests surrounding the restau-

rant. ✕ *158 Kasuganocho,* ☎ *0742/26–2021. Reservations required. Jacket and tie. DC, V.* ⊘ *Daily 11:30–7.*

$$$ **Bekkan Kikusuiro.** For those who want to try kaiseki, but do not want a formal and complicated meal, Bekkan Kikusuiro offers what it calls "mini kaiseki," an abridged version with fewer courses. Unlike standard kaiseki, where each course is served separately, your whole meal will be served on one tray. You can either sit at a table, which is less expensive, or in a Japanese-style room with a tatami. ✕ *1130 Takahatatacho,* ☎ *0742/23–2001. Reservations advised. No credit cards.* ⊘ *Daily 11–8:30. Closed Dec. 31.*

$$ **Tempura Asuka.** Directly south of Sarusawa Pond in Naramachi, Asuka offers full-course tempura meals and reasonably priced *bento* or tempura soba noodle lunches. Sit at the counter, reserve a tatami room, or sit at a table overlooking the garden. ✕ *11 Chonanincho,* ☎ *0742/26–4308. No reservations. MC, V.* ⊘ *11:30–2 and 4:30–9 (last order at 8:30); Sun. and holidays 11:30–9. Closed Tues.*

$$ **Uma no Me.** Kaiseki is not the only Japanese food available in Nara.
★ Uma no Me prides itself on home cooking, featuring roast fish, tofu, and other home-style Japanese dishes. The atmosphere is friendly and informal, with dark wood walls decorated with attractive pottery. This restaurant is within a few minutes' walk of Nara Koen. ✕ *1158 Takahatacho,* ☎ *0742/23–7784. Reservations required. No credit cards. Lunch 11:30–3, dinner 5:30–8:30. Closed Thurs.*

$$ **Van Kio.** The deer of Nara are sacred, but still available for a price: Located outside the south gate of Yakushiji, this traditional restaurant is famous for its hot stone steam cookery, which includes costly Nara venison. Sushi and vegetarian dishes are also available. The resident landscape gardener, Kawatake-san, sells a selection of stone lanterns, basins, and other garden ornaments, as well as a variety of Nara antiques on the premises. ✕ *410 Rokujocho,* ☎ *0742/33–8942. Reservations advised. AE, MC, V.* ⊘ *11–10. Closed Mon.*

$$ **Yanagi-chaya.** Yanagi-chaya specializes in excellent bento meals, served
★ in basic black-lacquer boxes. The food is Nara style: elegantly simple, with sashimi, stewed vegetables, and tofu. There are two branches of this revered old teahouse: (the elder) Yanagi-chaya is on the north bank and overlooks Sarusawa Pond. ✕ *49 Noboriojicho,* ☎ *0742/22–7460.* The younger sister is just east of Kofukuji. ✕ *48 Teraojicho,* ☎ *0742/22–7560. Reservations required. No credit cards.* ⊘ *11:30–7:30. Noborioji-cho location is closed Wed., Teraojicho branch is closed Mon.*

$ **Ginsho.** Across from the Nara Shiryokan (Historical Library) on a tiny side street in Naramachi, this soba noodle shop has a strikingly contemporary Japanese-style interior in a traditional building that harmonizes with the old neighborhood around it. Great *ten-zaru* soba (cold noodles and tempura) or tempura soba (hot tempura noodle soup) make a fabulous (and cheap) lunch stop. ✕ *18 Nishishinyacho,* ☎ *0742/23–1355. No reservations. No credit cards.* ⊘ *11–2. Closed Mon.*

$ **Harishin.** Old, unassuming, and small, this lunch place is easy to miss in the maze of Naramachi; you can find it by looking for its red *noren* (short curtain hanging in the doorway) decorated with a crest of crossed arrows. Open for lunch only, Harishin serves a Katsumichi bento that comes in a double-layer lacquer box and often includes almond fried chicken, shrimp, seasonal pilaf, vegetables, soup, fruit, and an aperitif of homemade strawberry wine. It's an excellent bargain. ✕ *15 Chushinyacho,* ☎ *0742/22–2669. No reservations. No credit cards.* ⊘ *11:30–3:30. Closed Mon.*

$ To-no-chaya. One distinctive Nara meal is chagayu. To-no-chaya offers a light meal of this special dish, combined with some sashimi and vegetables, plus a few sweetened rice cakes for dessert. From the restaurant you can see the Five-Story Pagoda of Kofukuji. Appropriately, the name of this restaurant means the "tearoom of the pagoda." ✕ 47 Noboriojicho, ☎ 0742/22–4348. *Reservations required for chagayu kaiseki. No credit cards.* ☻ *Chagayu 11:30–9, for bento 11:30–4. Closed Wed. and national holidays.*

LODGING

There is much to see and do in Nara, but surprisingly few people plan to stay overnight. The city has fine accommodations in every style and price range, and because most people think of Nara as a day-trip destination, the streets are deserted at night, allowing those wise enough to tarry a chance to stroll undisturbed beside the ponds and in temple grounds. A 3% federal consumer tax is added to all hotel bills. Another 3% local tax is added if the bill exceeds ¥15,000. At most hotels, a 10%–15% service charge is added to the total bill. Tipping is not necessary. The postal code for Nara is 630.

CATEGORY	COST*
$$$$	over ¥30,000
$$$	¥20,000–¥30,000
$$	¥10,000–¥20,000
$	under ¥10,000

Cost is for double room, without tax or service

$$$ Edo-San. A night in this ryokan envelops the guest in Japanese tradi-
★ tion. The accommodations here consist of small cottages with complete privacy. The cottages, old-fashioned Japanese structures with thatch roofs, are all surrounded by lovely trees, flowers, and greenery. Deer from Nara Koen occasionally wander onto the grounds of the inn. The excellent food, served in your private cottage, is included in the cost of your stay and consists of a variety of seafood dishes. ☎ 1167 Takahatakecho, Nara-shi, Nara-ken, ☎ 0742/26–2662, FAX 0742/26–2663. 11 rooms. AE, DC, V.

$$$ Hotel Fujita Nara. This hotel, on the main street running from the JR Nara Station to Nara Koen, offers attractive, simply decorated rooms. The Japanese restaurant serves excellent food, and succulent Kobe steaks are available in the steak house. ☎ 47-1 Shimo Sanjo-cho, Nara-shi, Nara-ken, ☎ 0742/23–8111, FAX 0742/22–0255. 118 rooms. Japanese and Western restaurants, coffee shop. AE, DC, MC, V.

$$$ Kankaso. Elegance reigns at this ryokan, right in the heart of
★ Nara Koen. The rooms have all been exquisitely decorated with Japanese scrolls, pottery, and other artwork. Great care is taken with the flower arrangements set in the alcove of each room. The communal baths look out on a lovely garden. ☎ 10 Kasuganocho, Nara-shi, Nara-ken, ☎ 0742/26–1128, FAX 0742/26–1301. 10 rooms. V.

$$$ Nara Garden Hotel. This small hotel on a hillside above Todaiji is within walking distance of all the sites in central Nara. Rooms here are furnished in light woods with green carpeting and floral bedspreads and curtains. Each has a view of the hillside cherry trees. The restaurant serves excellent Japanese and French food. ☎ Wakakusa, Sanrokucho, Nara-shi, Nara-ken, ☎ 0742/27–0555, FAX 0742/27–0203. 21 rooms. Restaurant, banquet rooms, coffee shop. AE, DC, MC, V.

$$$ **Nara Hotel.** Set right in the heart of Nara Koen, this establishment is
★   itself a site of historical interest. Built in the Meiji period (1868–
1912), the architectually delightful Nara Hotel has a graceful Japanese
tiled roof and a magnificent lobby with high wood ceilings. Although
most rooms have a good view of the surrounding temples, those in the
new wing are not as interesting as the turn-of-the-century–style rooms
in the old wing. ☎ *1096 Takabatakecho, Nara-shi, Nara-ken,* ☎
0742/26–3300, FAX *0742/23–5252. 132 rooms. Western restaurant, tea-
room. AE, DC, MC, V.*

$$ **Hotel Sun Route Nara.** With clean and comfortable rooms, this
hotel is a cut above business hotels. Its location near the Kintetsu
Nara Station makes it a convenient place to stay. ☎ *1110 Taka-
batake Bodaicho, Nara-shi, Nara-ken,* ☎ *0742/22–5151,* FAX
*0742/27–3759. 95 rooms. French restaurant, coffee shop. AE, DC,
MC, V.*

$$ **Japan Pension (Nara Club).** With only traces of Japanese influence, this
family-run pension resembles a small European hotel. Some of its
modest-size rooms have skylights, and all are decorated in delicate pink
printed fabrics with simple, dark wood furniture. Each room has a pri-
vate bath and toilet. The restaurant's dining room overlooks a little
garden; Western food is served. You may book a room here with or
without meals included. ☎ *21 Gomoncho, Nara-shi, Nara-ken,* ☎
0742/22–3450, FAX *0742/22–3490. 10 rooms. Restaurant. AE, V.*

$$ **Kotton Hyakupasento.** The name of this pleasant little hotel is a play
on words written with Chinese characters that mean 100% Old Cap-
ital (rather than 100% Cotton). Popular with young Japanese, it is on
a side street near Sarusawa Pond, a short walk south of Nara Koen.
☎ *1122-21 Bodaijicho, Nara-shi, Nara-ken,* ☎ *0742/22–7117,* FAX
0742/26–2771. 14 rooms. No credit cards.

$$ **People's Inn Hanakomichi.** This attractive, slightly overpriced estab-
lishment is near Kintetsu Nara Station; it is also close to shops and within
walking distance of Nara Koen. A drawback to its central locale—its
finest feature—is the street noise, which is especially annoying in the
summer when you need to keep your bedroom window open for fresh
air. The first and second floors feature boutiques, a gallery, and a café.
☎ *23 Konishicho, Nara-shi, Nara-ken,* ☎ *0742/26–2646,* FAX *0742/26–
2771. 20 Western-style rooms, 8 Japanese-style rooms. AE, DC, MC,
V.*

$ **Ryokan Hakuhoh.** This member of the low-priced Japanese Inn Group
chain has the advantage of being in the center of town, one traffic light
up the main street (Sanjo-dori) from the JR Station on the right hand
side. It's a three-story concrete building with no particular charm.
However, set back from the road, it is quiet and the tatami rooms (ig-
nore the scuff marks on the walls) are clean. There are also two very
small Western-style rooms, neither of which has a bath (half of the
Japanese-style rooms do). No food is served but there are many restau-
rants along the street. The owners don't speak English, but cheerfully
communicate in sign language. ☎ *4-1 Kamisanjocho, Nara-shi, Nara-
ken,* ☎ *0742/26–7891. 21 rooms, 10 with bath. AE, V.*

$ **Naramachi Seikanso.** This family-run inn has a relaxed atmosphere,
with most rooms in the wood structure overlooking a central garden.
It's a 15-minute walk from the Kintetsu Nara Station and a 25-minute
walk from the JR Nara Station to the inn; most of the walk is under
arcades. This place is extremely popular with foreigners, so try to
make advance reservations. ☎ *29 Higashikitsujicho, Nara-shi, Nara-
ken,* ☎ *0742/22–2670,* FAX *0742/22–2670. 13 rooms, none with pri-
vate bath. AE, MC, V.*

NARA ESSENTIALS

Arriving and Departing

By Plane

The nearest airports are in Osaka. International flights (as well as a few domestic) use the new Kansai International Airport; most domestic flights use Osaka's Itami Airport.

BETWEEN THE AIRPORTS AND CITY CENTER

There is no direct transportation from the airports to Nara. Bus service is available to central Osaka or Kyoto, from which you can take a train to Nara.

By Train

From Kyoto, the Kinki Nippon (*Kintetsu*) Railway's Limited Express trains take 33 minutes to reach Nara. They leave every half hour and cost ¥980. Three JR trains from Kyoto make the journey to Nara every hour. The express takes 45 minutes (cost ¥680), while the two locals take 70 minutes.

From Osaka's Kintetsu Nanba Station, Nara is a 30-minute ride on the Kinki Nippon Railway's Limited Express. Trains leave every hour, and the fare is ¥920. The Ordinary Express to Nara takes 40 minutes, leaves every 20 minutes, and costs ¥480. From Osaka, the JR train on the Yamatoji Line to Nara takes 50 minutes. The train leaves every 20 minutes and costs ¥760, free with the JR Rail Pass.

From Kobe, take the JR Tokaido Line rapid train from Sannomiya Station to Osaka and transfer to one of the trains described above.

Getting Around

By Train

Because Nara's main attractions are concentrated in one area in the western part of the city, you will do much of your sightseeing on foot. However, the JR Kansai Main Line and the Kinki Nippon Railway's Nara Line slice through the city and bring you close to major attractions. Rates depend upon the distance you travel. From downtown to Horyuji, the ride costs about ¥250.

By Bus

The most economical way to explore Nara is by bus. Two local bus routes circle the main sites (Todaiji, Kasuga Taisha, and Shin-Yakushiji) in the central and eastern parts of the city: Bus 1 runs counterclockwise and Bus 2 runs clockwise. This urban loop line costs ¥160 for a ride of any distance. Both stop at the JR Nara and Kintetsu Nara stations. Bus 52 westward to Horyuji (with stops at Toshodaiji and Yakushiji) takes about 50 minutes and costs ¥680; it can be caught in front of either the Kintetsu Nara Station or the JR Nara Station. Pick up a bus map at the Nara City Tourist center (*see below*).

By Taxi

The rate is ¥510 for the first 1½ kilometers and ¥90 for each additional 360 meters. From Kintetsu Nara Station to Kasuga Taisha by taxi runs about ¥900 one-way; to Horyuji, about ¥5,000 one-way.

By Bicycle

Because Nara is a small city with relatively flat roads, it is a good place for cycling. Bicycles can be rented from **Kintetsu Sunflower** (☎ 0742/24–3528), on Konishi-dori near the Kintetsu Nara Station (cost: ¥800 for

4 hours; ¥1,150 for 8 hours). Ask the Nara City Tourist Information Office on the first floor of this station for further information or directions. Some hotels also rent bicycles.

Guided Tours

Orientation Tours

Tours of Nara in English must be arranged in advance through the Kyoto or Osaka offices of the **Kintetsu Gray Line Bus Company.** Arrangements can also be made at the travel office in the basement of the New Miyako Hotel in Kyoto (☎ 075/691–0903), or by calling 06/313–6868 in Osaka. The fare for the afternoon tour is ¥7,200 adults, ¥5,200 children 6–11, children under 6 free.

Walking Tours

The Japan National Tourist Organization (JNTO) publishes the leaflet *Walking Tour Courses in Nara,* which gives brief descriptions of highlights along the way. One two-hour tour includes Nara Koen and several nearby temples and shrines; other tours start with a bus ride from the center of the city. Because Nara has no JNTO office, ask for the leaflet at JNTO offices in Tokyo (6-6 Yurakucho 1-chome, Chiyoda-ku, ☎ 03/502–1461) or in Kyoto (Kyoto Tower Bldg., Higashi-Shiokojicho, Shimogyo-ku, ☎ 075/371–5649).

Personal Guides

The **Student Guide Service** (Sarusawa Tourist Information Center, 4 Nobori Ojicho, north side of Sarusawa Pond, ☎ 0742/26–4753) and the **YMCA Guide Service** (at Kasuga Taisha, ☎ 0742/44–2207) are available for free at the JR Nara Station information center and the Kintetsu Nara Station. Because these services use volunteer guides, it is best to call in advance to determine availability. Unfortunately, the guides' ability to speak English is extremely limited; many serve as guides to practice their English and to meet foreigners.

Important Addresses and Numbers

Emergencies

Police, ☎ 110; **Ambulance,** ☎ 119.

Tourist Information

Nara City Tourist Information Office is on the first floor of the Kintetsu Nara Station, ☎ 0742/24–4858. ⊘ Daily 9–5.

A **City Information Window** (☎ 0742/22–9821) can be found at the JR Nara Station. ⊘ Daily 9–5.

Nara City Tourist Center is located at 23-4 Kami-Sanjocho, Nara-shi, ☎ 0742/22–3900. The office is open 9–9, but the English-language staff are on duty only until 5. This center, a 10-minute walk from both the Kintetsu Nara and JR Nara stations, has free maps, information on sightseeing in English, local crafts, a souvenir corner, and a lounge where you can rest and plan your day.

The **Japan Travel Phone** (☎ 0120/444–800) will give you toll-free English-language tourist information.

Consulates

The nearest U.S., Canadian, and British consulates are located in Osaka (*see* Chapter 8).

8 Osaka

Japan's "Second City" (after Tokyo, of course), in terms of industry, commerce, and technology, Osaka is known for its bunraku (puppet theater) and its superb restaurants. A three-hour train ride from Tokyo, it is a good starting point for trips to Nara, Kyoto, and Kobe.

By Nigel Fisher

IN TERMS OF INDUSTRY, COMMERCE, and technology, Osaka is definitely Japan's "Second City," after Tokyo. Until the Meiji Restoration (1868), the merchant class was at the bottom of the social hierarchy, even though many of this class were financially among the richest people in Japan. Osaka expanded as a trading center at the end of the 16th century. Denied the usual aristocratic cultural pursuits, merchants sought and developed their pleasures in the theater and in dining. Even today, Osaka is known for its Bunraku (puppet theater) and its superb restaurants. Indeed, it is often said that many a successful Osaka businessman has eventually gone bankrupt by spending so much on eating.

In the 4th and 5th centuries, the Osaka-Nara region was the center of the developing Japanese (Yamato) nation. It was through Osaka that knowledge and culture from mainland Asia filtered into the fledgling Japanese society. During the 5th and 6th centuries, several emperors maintained an imperial court in Osaka, but the city lost its political importance after a permanent capital was set up in Nara in 694.

For the next several hundred years, Osaka, then known as Naniwa, was just another backwater port on the Inland Sea. Then, at the end of the 16th century, Hideyoshi Toyotomi (1536–1598), a great warrior and statesman, had one of Japan's most majestic castles built in Osaka as part of his successful unification of Japan. The castle took three years to build and was completed in 1586. Hideyoshi encouraged merchants from around the country to set up their businesses in the city, which soon prospered.

After Hideyoshi died, Ieyasu Tokugawa usurped power from the Toyotomi clan in 1603. However, the Toyotomi clan still maintained Osaka as their base. In 1614, Ieyasu sent his troops from Kyoto to Osaka to oppose rebellious movements in support of the Toyotomis. Ieyasu's army defeated the Toyotomi clan and their followers, and destroyed the castle in 1615. Even though the Tokugawa Shogunate eventually rebuilt the castle, Osaka was once again apart from Japan's political scene. Nevertheless, the Osakan merchants, left to themselves and far from the shogun's administrative center in Edo (Tokyo), continued to prosper, and they sent products from the hinterland through the city to Kyoto and Edo. During this time of economic growth, some of Japan's business dynasties were founded, whose names we still hear of today— Sumitomo, Marubeni, Sanwa, and Daiwa. Their growing wealth also gave them the means to pursue pleasure, and, by the end of the 17th century (the Genroku Era), Osaka's residents were giving patronage to such literary giants as the dramatist Chikamatsu (1653–1724), often referred to as the Shakespeare of Japan, and the novelist Saikaku Ihara (1642–1693). Chikamatsu's genius as a playwright elevated the Bunraku to a dignified dramatic art. Also at this time, Kabuki was patronized and developed by the Osakan merchants.

With the opening of Japan to Western commerce in 1853 and the end of the Tokugawa Shogunate in 1868, Osaka stepped into the forefront of Japan's commerce. At first Yokohama was the major port for Japan's foreign trade, but when the Great Kanto earthquake leveled that city in 1923, foreigners looked to Kobe and Osaka as alternative gateways for their import and export business. Osaka's merchant heritage placed the city in a good position for industrial growth—iron, steel, fabrics, ships, heavy and light machinery, and chemicals all became part of Osaka's output. Today, the region accounts for 25% of the country's industrial product and 40% of the nation's exports. Since the building of its new harbor facilities, Osaka has become a major port in its own right, as it relies less on the facilities in Kobe.

Osaka is also still a merchant city, with many streets devoted to wholesale business activity. For example, medical and pharmaceutical companies congregate in Doshomachi, and fireworks and toys are found in Matchamachi-suji. The city is also famous for shopping. Head to Umeda, Shin-Saibashi, or Nanba for the greatest concentration of department stores, movie theaters, and restaurants.

Anyone over 50 in Japan remembers Osaka as an exotic maze of crisscrossing waterways that provided transportation for the booming merchant trade. All but a few of the canals were destroyed, along with most of the traditional wood buildings, during the bombings of World War II. With all the present-day high-rise buildings and broad avenues, it is hard to visualize what the vivacious city must have been like at that time. Today, however, the city is working hard to restore some of the beauty that was lost, with a movement for the greening of Osaka running strong.

Although Osaka may not have many sites of historical interest, it is a good starting point for trips to Nara, Kyoto, and Kobe. As a visitor, you can also participate in one of Osaka's leading pleasures: the pursuit of fine dining. In addition, the city's nightlife is legendary. Be sure to stroll through the Dotonbori district, beside the Dotonbori River, which has more nightclubs and bars per square foot than any other place in town.

EXPLORING

Numbers in the margin correspond to points of interest on the Osaka map.

Visitors often arrive in Osaka at Shin-Osaka Station, which is the terminal for the Shinkansen Super Express trains. Located 3 kilometers (2 miles) north of Osaka's main railway station amid some of Osaka's most modern architecture, it is also close to the Expo Memorial Park. If you arrive at Shin-Osaka, take either the Mido-suji subway to Umeda or, if you have a Japan Rail Pass, the JR Kobe Line to Osaka Station. Umeda and Osaka stations are right next to each other, on the edge of central Osaka.

Osaka is divided into 26 wards, and, though the official city population is only 2.6 million, if one were to include the suburbs, this number would be around 6 million. Central Osaka is predominantly a business district, but there is shopping and entertainment.

Central Osaka is encircled by the JR Kanjo (Loop) Line. The main railway station, Osaka Station, is at the northern part of this loop. In front of this station and to the east of the Hankyu Umeda Station is the center of the Kita (north) district. While ultramodern skyscrapers soar above the streets, underground is a maze of malls (Umeda Chika Center), crowded with shops that sell the latest fashions, dozens of restaurants, and department stores that offer every modern gadget. This district is one of the two major shopping areas in Osaka.

If you continue south, you come to two rivers, the Dojimagawa and the Tosaborigawa, with Nakanoshima (island) separating them. Here is Osaka's oldest park, which is home to many of the city's cultural and administrative institutions, including the Bank of Japan and the Museum of Oriental Ceramics.

Beyond these rivers and south of Nakanoshima are the Minami (south) and Shin-Saibashi districts. They are very close together and are surrounded by the JR Kanjo Line. Shin-Saibashi is Osaka's expensive shopping street. The nearby America Mura, with American-style boutiques, and the Europe Mura, with Continental fashion shops, appeal to the hip Osaka young. Minami has a wonderful assortment of bars and restaurants, especially on Dotonbori-dori. The Bunraku National Theater is also close by, a few blocks to the southeast, near the Nipponbashi Subway Station. The city's tourist attractions are limited and can easily be visited in one full day.

★ ❶ The most famed sight in Osaka is **Osakajo** (Osaka Castle), in the eastern part of the city. Osakajo was one of Hideyoshi Toyotomi's finest buildings. The first stones were laid in 1583, and for the next three years as many as 100,000 workmen labored to build a majestic and impregnable castle. Note the thickness and the height of the walls. In order to demonstrate their loyalty, the feudal lords from the provinces were requested to contribute immense granite rocks. The largest piece of stone is said to have been donated by Hideyoshi's general, Kiyomasa Kato (1562–1611), and brought from Shodo Island. Known as Higo-Ishi, the rock measured a gigantic 19 feet high and 47 feet wide.

Hideyoshi was showing off with this castle. He had united Japan after a period of devastating civil wars, and he wanted to secure his western flanks. He also wanted to establish Osaka as a vibrant merchant town that could distribute the produce from the surrounding wealthy territories. The castle was intended to demonstrate Hideyoshi's power and commitment to Osaka, in order to attract merchants from all over Japan.

Hideyoshi's plan succeeded, but within two years of his death in 1598, Ieyasu Tokugawa, an executor of Hideyoshi's will, took power and got rid of the guardians of Hideyoshi's son. However, it was not until 1614 that Ieyasu sent his armies to defeat the Toyotomi family and their allies. In 1615, the castle was destroyed, and Ieyasu Tokugawa was victorious.

Over a 10-year period, the Tokugawa Shogunate rebuilt the castle, according to original plans, and this version stood from 1629 until 1868, when the Tokugawa Shogunate's power was at an end. Rather than let the castle fall into the hands of the forces of the Meiji Restoration, the Tokugawa troops burned it. In 1931, the present five-story (eight stories inside) donjon was built in ferro-concrete for the prestige of the city. An exact replica of the original, though marginally smaller in scale, it stands 189 feet high (including 46-foot-high stone walls). At night, when it is illuminated, it becomes a brilliant backdrop to the city.

Inside the castle is a museum with artifacts of the Toyotomi family and historical objects relating to Osaka prior to the Tokugawa Shogunate's reign. Unless you are a Hideyoshi fan, these exhibits are of marginal interest. The castle's magnificent exterior and the impressive view from the eighth floor of the donjon are the reasons to see Osakajo. If you are really fortunate, your visit may coincide with cherry-blossom time, when the Nishinomaru Teien (garden) is at its best (to enter costs another ¥200). The easiest way to reach the castle from Osaka Station is to take the Tanimachi Subway Line from Higashi-Umeda Station (just to the southeast of Osaka Station) to Tanimachi 4-Chome Station. From there it is a 15-minute walk up the hill to Osakajo. An

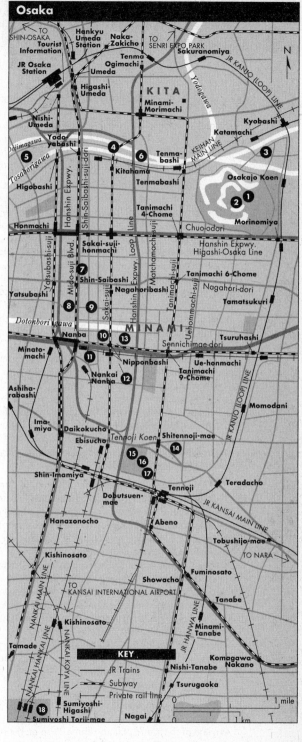

Osaka

alternative route, and one that is slightly easier, is to take the JR Kanjo Line from Osaka Station to Osakajo Koen-mae Station. You'll still have a walk up the hill from the other side. *1-1 Osakajo, Chuo-ku, Osaka,* ☎ *06/941–3044.* ☛ *¥500 adults, ¥50 children 5–15.* ⊘ *Daily 9–5 (enter by 4:30); July 15–Aug. 31, 9–8:30 (enter by 8). Closed Dec. 28–Jan. 1.*

❷ The **Osaka City Museum** also on the castle grounds, is a storehouse of municipal memorabilia. On display are books, photographs, and other records of the city's history. *1-1 Osakajo, Chuo-ku, Osaka,* ☎ *06/941–7177.* ☛ *Permanent collection ¥300 adults, ¥200 college and high-school students, ¥100 younger students (special exhibitions vary).* ⊘ *9:15–4:45 (enter by 4:15). Closed 2nd and 4th Mon. of each month.*

Leave the castle and, facing north, walk down the hill past Osakajo Hall (a center used for sports competitions and concerts), and cross the overpass near the Aqua Liner (water bus) pier. On the other side of Hiranogawa (river) is the New Otani Hotel and, just behind it, the ❸ Twin 21 towers of **Osaka Business Park. Panasonic Square,** on the second floor of one of the Twin 21 structures, the National Tower Building, features displays of the Matsushita Electric Group's high-tech developments. Both fun and educational, the exhibits are divided into four zones: Knowing, Learning, Experiencing, and Creating with Electronics. On any given day, you'll see crowds of Japanese schoolchildren absorbed in testing the TV telephone that allows them to see the person they're talking to on a monitor screen, or donning Superman costumes to star in and direct their own mini-TV shows. Other displays allow you to check your golf, baseball, or tennis skills on a video camera at the Swing Check Corner; have your portrait drawn by a robot; and test what you've learned via a computerized question-and-answer session—a computer will even calculate your score. Moderately priced food shops serve sushi and other light fare, and there is also a souvenir shop. *Twin 21, National Tower Bldg., 2nd floor, 1-61 Shiromi 2-chome, Chuo-ku, Osaka,* ☎ *06/949–2122.* ☛ *¥300 adults and high-school students, ¥200 junior-high and elementary-school students.* ⊘ *Daily 10–6 (enter by 5:30).*

❹ The **Shiritsu Toyo Jiki Bijutsukan** (Museum of Oriental Ceramics) is in ❺ Nakanoshima Koen (park), on **Nakanoshima** (island), between Dojimagawa and Tosaborigawa. (From Osaka Business Park, take the JR train from Katamichi Station to the Kyobashi stop and transfer to the Keihan Line, which you take to the Yodoyabashi stop. It's a five-minute walk from that station.) The museum houses about 1,000 pieces of Chinese and Korean ceramics. The artworks come from the priceless Ataka Collection, which belonged to a wealthy Japanese industrialist, and were donated to the museum by the giant Sumitomo Group conglomerate. The ceramic collection, rated as one of the finest in the world, includes 14 works that have been designated as National Treasures or Important Cultural Properties. *1-1 Nakanoshima, Kita-ku,* ☎ *06/223–0055.* ☛ *¥500 adults, ¥300 college and high-school students, ¥150 junior-high and elementary-school students (special exhibitions vary).* ⊘ *Tues.–Sun. 9:30–5 (enter by 4:30). Closed Tues. if Mon. is a national holiday.*

After your visit to the museum, take some time for a stroll in Osaka's ❻ oldest park, **Nakanoshima Koen,** which opened in 1891; it's at the eastern end of the island Nakanoshima. Also on the island are **Osaka University** and **Osaka Festival Hall,** which is considered the city's best concert hall. Major Japanese and international musicians regularly appear here. The **Royal Hotel** is at the far end of the island. If you linger till after dark, you'll be able to enjoy the illuminated view of **Osaka City Hall,** near the ceramics museum, and of the bridges that link the island with the mainland.

7 Take the Mido-suji Subway Line from Yodoyabashi to Shin-Saibashi Station. When you emerge you'll be on **Mido-suji Boulevard.** Shin-Saibashi and Ebisubashi, which run parallel to Mido-suji, are two of Osaka's best shopping and entertainment streets. West of Mido-suji **8** Boulevard is **America Mura** (American Village), a group of streets that feature stores with youth-oriented American clothes. Bright neon signs with the Japanese version of American names hang over the shop doors as the sound of rock music booms from inside. The stores carry an assortment of U.S.–made jeans and sportswear, and are tended by punkishly coiffed Japanese youth.

9 East of Mido-suji Boulevard is **Europe Mura** (European Village), with its boutiques of fashionable clothes from European capitals. The sidewalks in this area, which are made of cobblestones, attempt to re-create the feeling of a traditional Continental city. Here are Parco, Sogo, and Daimaru department stores, some of Japan's top chain stores.

★ **10** If you continue walking south on Mido-suji Boulevard and cross the river you'll come to **Dotonbori-dori,** a broad cross street that runs alongside the river of the same name. The street and the area around it are filled with restaurants and nightclubs. A virtual feast for neon connoisseurs, this is the place to stroll in the evening for a glimpse of nightlife, Osaka-style. Locate the giant, undulating Kani Doraku crab sign, a local landmark.

11 Two blocks south of Dotonbori-dori is the **Niji-no-machi** (Rainbow Town) underground shopping mall, which extends six blocks east to west. About two blocks from Rainbow Town is **Nan Nan Town,** another underground mall, which runs eight blocks south from the southern end of Mido-suji Boulevard. Both malls offer a good selection of clothes, appliances, and unpretentious restaurants. At the far southern end of Mido-suji Boulevard are the Kabukiza Theater and the Takashimaya department store. East of the southern terminus of Nanba **12** Station is **Den Den Town,** where, amid its nearly 300 specialty shops, you can purchase discounted electrical appliances. About a block south of Nankai Nanba Station is **Osaka Stadium,** where the local baseball teams square off.

★ **13** From Nanba Station (the subway station, not the Nankai rail station), if you take the Sennichi-mae Subway Line, it is just one stop east to the Nipponbashi Station and the **National Bunraku Theater.** Take Exit 7, and you will be right outside the theater. Osakans have helped make Bunraku a sophisticated art form. You should try to see a show while you're here. This puppet form of drama began during the Heian period (794–1192), but it was not until the late 17th and early 18th century that the genius of playwright Chikamatsu elevated Bunraku to a dignified dramatic art. A typical Bunraku play deals with themes of tragic love or stories based on historical events. The story is chanted in song by a *joruri* singer who is accompanied by ballad music played on a three-stringed *shamisen.* Although you may not understand the words, the tone of the music certainly sets a mood of pathos.

Bunraku actors are puppets, about two-thirds human size. Elaborately dressed in period costume, each puppet is made up of interchangeable parts—a head, shoulder piece, trunk, legs, and arms. For example, various puppet heads are used for roles of different sex, age, and character, and a certain hairstyle will indicate a puppet's position in life. Each puppet is operated by three puppeteers, who must act in complete unison. The *omozukai* controls the expression on the puppet's face and its right arm and hand. The *hidarizukai* controls the puppet's left arm and hand, and any props that it is carrying. The *ashizukai* moves the puppet's legs. This last task is the easiest. The most difficult task belongs to the omozukai. It takes about 30 years to become an accomplished expert. A puppeteer must spend 10 years as ashizukai, a further 10 as hidarizukai, and then 10 years as omozukai. These master puppeteers not only skillfully manipulate the puppets' arms and legs, but also roll the eyes and move the lips so that the puppets express fear, joy, and sadness. *12-10 Nipponbashi 1-chome, Chuo-ku, Osaka,* ☎ *06/212–2531, for reservations,* ☎ *06/212–122.* ☛ *¥4,000 and ¥5,200. Bunraku performances are scheduled 6 times a year (Jan., Mar., Apr., June, July, Aug., Nov.). Each run starts on the 3rd of the month and lasts about 3 wks.*

After you leave the Bunraku Theater, walk east for about 10 minutes to the Tanimachi 9-Chome Subway Station. If you take the Tanimachi Subway Line going south, it is only one stop to the Shitennoji-mae Station and from there only a few minutes' walk to Shitennoji. If you wish to come directly here from Osakajo, take the JR Kanjo Line from Osakajo Koen Station or Kyobashi Station going south. If you exit at Tennoji Station, you'll see the street going north up to Shitennoji; Tennoji Koen will be on the left.

⓮ **Shitennoji,** popularly known as Tennoji, is one of the most important historical sights in Osaka. Architecturally, the temple has suffered. The ravages of fire have destroyed it many times. Maintaining the original design and adhering to the traditional mathematical alignment, the last reconstruction of the Kondo (Main Hall), Kodo Taishiden Hall, and the five-story pagoda was in 1965. What has managed to survive is the stone *torii* (arch) that was built in 1294 and stands at the main entrance. One does not often see a torii at a Buddhist temple. Shitennoji claims that it is the oldest Buddhist temple in Japan. Outdating Horyuji in Nara (607), Shitennoji was founded by Prince Shotoku in 593.

Umayado no Mikoto (573–621), who is posthumously known as Prince Shotoku or Shotoku Taishi, was one of early Japan's most enlightened rulers. He was made regent over his aunt, Suiko, and set about instituting reforms and establishing Buddhism as the state religion. Buddhism had been introduced to Japan from China and Korea in the early 500s, but it had been seen as a threat to the aristocracy, who claimed prestige and power based upon their godlike ancestry. Prince Shotoku recognized both the power of Buddhism and how it could be used as a tool for the state. His swords and a copy of his Hokkekyo Lotus Sutra, made during the Heian period (897–1192), were stored at Shitennoji, though today they are kept in the National Museum of Tokyo. On the 21st of every month, the temple has a flea market that sells antiques and baubles; it shouldn't be missed if you're in town at this time. *1-11-18 Shitennoji, Tennoji-ku, Osaka,* ☎ *06/771–0066.* ☛ *¥200 adults, ¥120 children.* ◷ *Daily, Apr.–Sept. 8:30–4:30; in winter 8:30–4.*

⓯ ⓰ To the southwest of Shitennoji is **Tennoji Koen,** where the **Shiritsu Bijutsuhan** (Municipal Museum of Fine Arts) is located. This museum is best known for its collection of classical art from the 12th to the 14th century. An exception to this are the special exhibitions that feature the works of an Edo period artist, Ogata Korin. Some modern art is also included in its permanent collection (though this seems to appeal more to the Japanese than to foreigners), as well as a collection of Chinese paintings and archaeological artifacts. *1-82 Chausuyamacho,*

Tennoji-ku, ☎ *06/771–4874.* ☛ *Permanent collection: ¥300 adults, ¥200 college and high-school students, ¥100 younger students (special exhibitions vary).* ⊘ *Tues.–Sun. 9:30–5 (enter by 4:30).*

⑰ Adjacent to the art museum is **Keitakuen,** a garden with flowers, trees, and a pond. The garden, originally constructed in 1908, was given to the city by the late Baron Sumitomo. An example of the Japanese circular garden, its cherry trees and azaleas are lovely to behold when in bloom. The garden offers a welcome respite from the rest of the city. ☛ *¥150 adults, free for children under 12.* ⊘ *Tues.–Sun. 9:30–4:30 (enter by 4).*

The park also contains the **Tennoji Shokubutsuen** (Botanical Gardens; ⊘ 9:30–5). Next to Keitakuen is the **Municipal Zoological Gardens,** one of the largest in Japan, with some 22,000 caged animals. *6-74 Chausuyamacho, Tennoji-ku, Osaka,* ☎ *06/771–8401.* ☛ *¥500 adults, free for senior citizens and children under 16.* ⊘ *Tues.–Sun. 9:30–4:30 (enter by 4). Closed national holidays and Dec. 29–Jan. 1.*

Before you leave Tennoji Koen you may also notice **Chausuyama Kofun,** a prehistoric burial mound and the site of Ieyasu Tokugawa's camp during the siege of Osakajo in 1614–1615.

⑱ The final site on this exploring tour is **Sumiyoshi Taisha** (Grand Shrine). Most of the Shinto shrines in Japan today were built after the 8th century and were heavily influenced by Buddhist architecture. The three shrines that were built prior to the arrival of Buddhism in Japan are the Ise Jingu (Grand Shrines at Ise), Izumo Taisha near Matsue, and the Sumiyoshi Taisha in Osaka. To reach this last shrine, take the 20-minute ride on the Nankai Main Line to the southern suburbs of Osaka.

Sumiyoshi Taisha is dedicated to the goddess of sea voyages, Sumiyoshi, and, according to legend, was founded by Empress Jingu in 211 to express her gratitude for her safe return from a sea voyage to Korea. In those days, the shrine faced the sea rather than the concrete urban sprawl that now surrounds it. On the shrine's grounds are many stone lanterns donated by sailors and shipowners as dedications to Sumiyoshi and other Shinto deities that also guard the voyages of seafarers. Note the arched bridge on the grounds, said to have been given by Yodogimi, the consort of Hideyoshi Toyotomi who bore him a son. Of the three ancient shrines (Ise Jingu, Izumo Taisha, and Sumiyoshi Taisha), only Sumiyoshi has a Japanese cypress structure that is painted vermilion; the other two are left unpainted with their natural wood showing. According to the Shinto custom, shrines were torn down and rebuilt periodically to the exact specifications of the original. Sumiyoshi, which, incidentally, is also the name given to the style of architecture of this shrine, was last replaced in 1810. Sumiyoshi Matsuri, one of the city's largest and liveliest festivals, is held from July 30 to August 1. A crowd of rowdy young men carries a two-ton portable shrine from the Sumiyoshi Taisha to the Yamato River and back; this event is followed by an all-night street bazaar. *2-9-89 Sumiyoshi, Sumiyoshi-ku, Osaka,* ☎ *06/672–0753.* ☛ *Free.* ⊘ *Daily, Apr.–Oct. 6–5; Nov.–Mar. 6:30–5.*

ADDITIONAL ATTRACTIONS

The following lists additional places of interest that were not covered in the preceding exploring tour:

Historical Buildings and Sights

Nintoku Mausoleum. The 4th-century mausoleum of Emperor Nintoku is in Sakai City, southeast of Osaka. Archaeologists calculate that the central mound of this site is 1.3 million square feet; the mausoleum was built on an even larger scale than that of the pyramids of Egypt. Its construction took more than 20 years and required a total work force of about 800,000 laborers. Surrounding the emperor's burial place are three moats and pine, cedar, and cypress trees. Visitors may walk around the outer moat to get an idea of the size of the mausoleum and the grounds. However, entry into the mausoleum is not allowed. To get to the mausoleum, take the JR train on the Hanwa Line from Tennoji Station to Mozu Station (a ½-hr. ride). From there, the mausoleum is a five-minute walk away. *7 Daisencho, Sakai-shi,* ☎ *0722/41–0002.*

Temples and Shrines

Fujiidera. An 8th-century 1,000-handed seated statue of Kannon, the Goddess of Mercy, is the main object of worship at this temple. The statue, a National Treasure, is the oldest Buddhist sculpture of its type. To reach the temple, take the Mido-suji Subway Line from Umeda Station to Tennoji Station, then transfer to the Kintetsu Minami–Osaka Line and take it to Fujiidera Station. The temple is a few minutes' walk from the station. *1-16-21 Fujiidera, Fujiidera-shi,* ☎ *0729/38–0005. The statue is on view the 18th of each month, 9–5.*

Tenmangu Shrine. A short walk from the Minami-Morimachi Station on the Tanimachi Line, this 10th-century shrine is the main site of the annual **Tenjin Festival,** held July 24–25, one of the three biggest and most enthusiastically celebrated festivals in Japan. During the festival, dozens of floats are paraded through the streets, and more than 100 vessels, lighted by lanterns, sail along the canals amid a dazzling display of fireworks. A renowned scholar of the 9th century, Michizane Sugawara, is enshrined at Tenmangu; he is now considered the God of Academics. *2-1-8 Tenjinbashi, Kita-ku, Osaka,* ☎ *06/353–0025.* ☛ *Free.* ⊙ *Daily, Apr.–Sept. 5:30 AM–sunset; Oct.–Mar. 6 AM–sunset.*

Museums and Galleries

Nihon Mingeikan (Japan Folk Art Museum). Located in Expo Park, this museum contains outstanding examples of traditional regional handicrafts. On view are ceramics, textiles, wood crafts, bamboo ware, and other items. To get to the museum, *see* directions to Expo Park, *below.* *10-5 Banpaku Koen, Senri, Suita-shi,* ☎ *06/877–1971.* ☛ *¥400 adults, ¥310 college and high-school students, ¥100 junior-high and elementary-school students (special exhibitions vary).* ⊙ *Thurs.–Tues. 10–5 (enter by 4:30).*

Zohei (Mint Museum). This money museum displays about 16,000 examples of Japanese and foreign currencies. It also exhibits Olympic medals, prehistoric currency, and ancient Japanese gold coins. Near the museum is the Mint Garden, part of which is open to the public for a short period during the cherry-blossom season (usually April); visitors can stroll on a pathway, shaded by blossoms, along the Yodogawa. The museum is a 15-minute walk from Minami-Morimachi or Tenmabashi station on the Tanimachi Subway Line. *1-1-79 Tenma, Kita-ku, Osaka,* ☎ *06/351–8509.* ☛ *Free.* ⊙ *Mon.–Sat. 9–4 (enter by 3:30). Closed holidays and 2nd and 4th Sat. of each month.*

Kokuritsu Minzokugaku Hakubutsukan (National Museum of Ethnology). This building, also in Expo Park, offers a range of exhibits on comparative cultures of the world, with displays arranged according to regions. Automatic audiovisual equipment, called Videotheque, provides close-up views of the customs of the peoples of the world. To reach the museum, *see* directions to Expo Park, *below. Senri Expo Park, Senri, Suita-shi,* ☎ *06/876–2151.* ☛ *¥400 adults, ¥250 high-school and college students, ¥110 junior-high and elementary-school students.* ⊘ *Thurs.–Tues. 10–5 (enter by 4:30). Closed Dec. 28–Jan. 4.*

Parks and Gardens

Senri Expo Park. On the former site of Expo '70, this 647-acre park houses the two museums listed above, an amusement park called Expo Land (☎ 06/877–0560 ☛ ¥1,200, children ¥600; closed Wed.), sports facilities, and several gardens, including a Japanese garden with two teahouses. To reach the park, take the Mido-suji Subway Line to Senri-Chuo Station (30 min. from Umeda Station), then take the Expo Land bus to Nihon Teien-mae Station (30 min.) or monorail to Banpaku Koen-mae (20 min.). *Senri Expo Park, Senri, Suita-shi.* ☛ *Natural garden ¥150, to the Japanese garden ¥300, individual facilities within the park impose additional entrance fees, which vary.* ⊘ *Thurs.–Tues. 9–5. Closed Dec. 28–Jan. 1.*

Hattori Ryokuchi Park. This recreation park has facilities for horseback riding and tennis, a youth hostel, and a museum of old farmhouses. To reach the park, take the Mido-suji Subway Line from Umeda to Esaka Station, then the Kita-Osaka Kyuko Line to Ryokuchi Koen Station. The park is a 10-minute walk from the station. ☛ *Park is free; Farmhouse Museum ¥410 adults, ¥300 high-school students. Nonmembers can take a 30-min. riding lesson for ¥5,000. The cost is ¥610–¥710 for 1 hr. of tennis. Have your hotel make a reservation for you a day in advance for horseback riding; no reservation necessary for tennis during the week; if you're going on a weekend, you may need as much as a week's advance reservation.* ⊘ *Daily, Apr.–Oct. 9:30–5 (enter by 4:30); Nov.–Mar. 9:30–4 (enter by 3:30).*

Mino Park. Osakans come here in autumn to admire the dazzling fall foliage, especially the maple trees, whose leaves turn to brilliant crimson. The path along the river leads to the Mino Waterfall. Monkeys reside in a protected habitat. The park is 30 minutes from Hankyu Umeda Station on the Mino Line, north of the Mino Station. ☛ *Free.*

SHOPPING

Osaka's role as a transportation hub for more than 1,500 years has enabled it to prosper first as a merchant town and today as a center of business and commerce. Osakans are known for driving hard bargains, but at the same time, they are practical in their approach to life. Osaka has two main shopping areas: One is centered on Nanba Station in the Minami (southern) district, the other on Osaka and Umeda stations in the Kita (northern) district. Minami is the older of the two, but the merchandise sold here is a mixture of traditional and modern goods.

To the northeast of Nanba Station are the **Ebisubashi Street** shopping area and the **Niji-no-machi** (Rainbow Town) underground shopping mall. To the southeast are **Nanba City** and **Nan Nan Town** underground shopping malls. Farther east of Nanba Station, but still within walking distance, is **Den Den Town** (*see* Electronics, *below*).

Near Osaka and Umeda stations, which connect with underground con-
courses, are the **Umeda Chika Center** and the **Hankyu Sanbangai** and
Hankyu Higashidori malls. This complex of stores is the largest underground shopping area in all of Japan and perhaps the world, complete with man-made streams and its own version of Rome's Trevi
Fountain.

Over Osaka Station is the **Acty Osaka Building,** a 27-story shopping
and office building. To the west of this complex, near Nishi-Umeda
Station on the Yotsubashi Subway Line, are the **Dojima** and
Nakanoshima underground malls.

Osaka's most elegant shopping arcade, however, is **Shin-Saibashi-suji.**
This covered arcade with marble pavement is near Shin-Saibashi Station on the Mido-suji Line, halfway between the Minami and Kita districts. To the east of the arcade is yet another shopping arcade, called
Europe Mura (European Village), with trendy, European-influenced clothing. Across Mido-suji Boulevard to the west is **America Mura** (American Village), with clothing styles inspired by U.S. designers, for both
the young and old.

Specialized wholesale areas can be found throughout the city. A few
retail shops are located in these areas so it is worth a visit. **Dobuike** is
the wholesale area for clothing and accessories (located near Honmachi
Station on the Chuo, Tanimachi, and Yotsubashi subway lines, or
Sakai-suji-honmachi Station on the Sakai-suji Subway Line).
Matchamachi-suji is famous for its rows of toy and doll shops.

Department Stores

All major Japanese department stores are represented in this ultramodern
city. Many of them, such as Hankyu, Hanshin, and Kintetsu, are headquartered here. All the department stores are open 10–7 except for
Matsuzakaya, which closes at 6:30 (its food hall is open until 7). The
following are some of Osaka's leading department stores: **Hankyu,** 8-
7 Kakutacho, Kita-ku, ☎ 06/361–1381, closed Thurs.; **Hanshin,** 1-13-
13 Umeda, Kitaku, ☎ 06/345–1201, closed Wed.; **Matsuzakaya,** 1-1
Tenmabashi Kyomachi, Chuo-ku, ☎ 06/943–1111, closed Wed.; **Mitsukoshi,** 7-5 Koraibashi 1-chome, Chuo-ku, ☎ 06/203–1331, closed
Tues.; **Daimaru,** 1-7-1 Shin-Saibashi-suji, Chuo-ku, ☎ 06/343–1231,
closed Wed.; **Sogo,** 1-8-3 Shin-Saibashi-suji, Chuo-ku, ☎ 06/281–
3111, closed Tues.; **Takashimaya,** 5-1-5 Nanba, Chuo-ku, ☎ 06/631–
1101, closed Wed.; **Kintetsu,** 1-1-43 Abeno-suji, Abeno-ku, ☎
06/624–1111; closed Thurs. There is also a Kintetsu branch at 6-1-
55 Ue-honmachi, Tennoji-ku, ☎ 06/775–1111, closed Thurs.

Gifts

At one time famous for its traditional crafts, particularly its ornately
carved *karaki-sashimono* furniture, its fine Naniwa Suzuki pewter
ware, and its Sakai *uchihamono* cutlery, Osaka lost much of its fine
traditional industry during World War II. The simplest way to find a
wide selection of Osaka crafts is to visit one of the major department
stores, many of which carry a selection of locally made crafts.

For folk crafts from all over the country, including ceramics, basketry,
paper goods, folk toys, and textiles, visit the **Nihon Kogeikan Mingei
Fukyubu** (Japan Folkcraft Collection), near the Umeshin East Hotel in
the popular gallery district, within walking distance of the U.S. Consulate. *4-7-15 Nishi-Tenma, Kita-ku,* ☎ *06/362–9501.* ☺ *Mon.–Sat.*
10–6. Closed 2nd Sat. of each month and national holidays.

Electronics

Den Den Town has about 300 retail shops that specialize in electronic products (Den Den is a take-off on the word *denki,* which means electricity) as well as stores for cameras and watches. The area is located near Ebisucho Station on the Sakai-suji Subway Line (Exit 1 or 2), and Nipponbashi Station on the Sakai-suji and Sennichi-mae subway lines (Exit 5 or 10). Shops are open 10–7 daily. Take your passport, and make your purchases in stores with signs that say "Tax Free." (Note: Even without the tax, prices are still considerably higher than the same goods purchased in the U.S. as Japanese discount the goods sold to America.)

DINING

Not only are the residents of Osaka known to be passionate about food, but they also insist on eating well. Osakans expect the restaurants they frequent to use the freshest ingredients available from the area. This assumption developed over the centuries because of the city's proximity to the Inland Sea, which allowed all classes (not just the aristocracy) easy access to fresh seafood. Today Osakans have discriminating palates and demand their money's worth. In fact, Osakans are famous for their gourmet appetites. *"Osaka wa kuidaore,"* the old saying goes—Osaka people squander their money on food.

Osaka cuisine is flavored with soy sauce that is lighter in color, milder in flavor, and saltier than the soy sauce used in Tokyo. One local delicacy is **okonomiyaki,** a pancake made to order on an iron grill that may be filled with cabbage, mountain yam, pork, shrimp, and other ingredients.

Osaka-zushi (Osaka-style sushi), which is made in wood molds, has a distinctive square shape, with pieces of fish placed on top of rice and then pressed together. Another variation of Osaka-zushi is wrapped around an omelet and filled with pickles and other delights. **Eel,** prepared in several different styles, remains a popular local dish; grilled eels are often eaten during the summer months for quick energy. **Fugu** (blowfish), served boiled or raw, is a gourmet fish that is less expensive in Osaka than in other Japanese cities.

Another Osaka invention is **takoyaki,** griddle-cooked dumplings with bits of octopus, green onions, and ginger smothered in a delicious sauce. Sold by street vendors in Dotonbori, these tasty snacks and their lively makers are also in evidence at every festival and street market in the Kansai district.

Surrounding Osaka Umeda Station are a number of "gourmet palaces" with several floors of restaurants of every type imaginable. Exploring them is always fun. Head for restaurants in the Hankyu Grand Building, the Hankyu Sanban-gai (in the basement below Hankyu Station), and Acty Osaka (in front of the JR Osaka Station). Most of the big department stores also house scores of good restaurants, notably the Daimaru Department Store in front of the JR Osaka Station.

Osaka's shopping arcades and underground shopping areas abound in affordable restaurants and coffee shops, but when in doubt, head to Dotonbori and Soemoncho, two areas along the Dotonbori River that specialize in restaurants, nightclubs, and bars. If money is not a problem, walk to the northern part of Osaka to Kita-Shinchi, the city's most exclusive dining quarter, but be prepared to pay a stiff price for an elegant meal. This area is similar to Tokyo's Ginza district.

A 3% federal consumer tax is added to all restaurant bills. Another 3% local tax is added to the bill if it exceeds ¥7,500. At more expensive restaurants, a 10%–15% service charge is also added to the bill.

CATEGORY	COST*
$$$$	over ¥6,000
$$$	¥4,000–¥6,000
$$	¥2,500–¥4,000
$	under ¥2,500

Cost is per person without tax, service, or drinks

Japanese

$$$$ **Benkay.** For those who appreciate Japanese-style red snapper (served with stewed plums), Benkay is the place to go. Sea urchin, squid, and prawns are staples on the menu here; tempura and sushi are popular as well. The restaurant utilizes the traditional Japanese decor of blond wood paneling, and there's a sushi bar on one side. ✕ *Hotel Nikko Osaka, 1-3-3 Nishi-Shin-Saibashi, Chuo-ku,* ☎ *06/244–1111. Reservations advised. Jacket and tie. AE, DC, MC, V.* ☽ *Lunch 11:30–2:30, dinner 5:30–10.*

$$ **Fuguhisa.** This no-nonsense little restaurant specializes in *fugu ryori,* the blowfish delicacy for which Osaka is famous. Extremely expensive almost everywhere else, Chef Kato's *tessa* (raw blowfish) and *techiri* (one-pot blowfish stew) are the most reasonable and delicious around. What the place lacks in glamour, it makes up for in good, down-to-earth, Osaka-style food. It's across from the west exit of Tsuruhashi Station on the JR Kanjo (Loop) Line. ✕ *3-14-24 Higashi-Ohashi, Higashinari-ku,* ☎ *06/972–5029. Reservations suggested. No credit cards.* ☽ *Noon–10:30 (last order at 9:30). Closed Mon.*

$$ **Kani Doraku.** The most famous restaurant on Dotonbori-dori, Kani Doraku is noted for its fine crab dishes at reasonable prices. The giant mechanical crab above the door is a local landmark. As you sit at tables or on tatami mats overlooking the Dotonbori Canal, you have a perfect view of the ultramodern Kirin Plaza Building glittering across the water. For lunch, a crab dish will run you around ¥4,000 while dinner will be above ¥6,000. Other less expensive dishes include delicious *nabe* (one-pot stews). There is an English language menu. ✕ *1-6-18 Dotonbori, Chuo-ku,* ☎ *06/211–8975. Reservations advised weekends. AE, DC, MC, V.* ☽ *11–11.*

$$ **Kanki.** *Akachochin,* or red lanterns, are the symbol of inexpensive eating in Japan, but the wonderful combination of Western and Japanese dishes offered at this friendly place makes it different from most *nomiya,* as these inexpensive drinking places are called. Order *"Kyo no osusume,"* the daily special. You might end up with Florentine-style scallops. Table seating is available on the second and third floors. ✕ *1-3-11 Shibatacho Kita-ku (on the northeast end of Hankyu Umeda Station),* ☎ *06/374–0057. Reservations advised. No credit cards.* ☽ *6–11. Closed Sun. and national holidays.*

$$ **Mimiu.** *Udon-suki* was born here. The thick, white noodle stew simmered in a pot over a burner at your table—with Chinese cabbage, clams, eel, yams, *shiitake* mushrooms, *mitsuba* greens, and other seasonal ingredients—is an old favorite in Osaka, particularly when served in this traditional restaurant. ✕ *6-18, Hiranomachi 4-chome, Chuo-ku (near Honmachi Station on the Dojima-suji Subway Line),* ☎ *06/231–5770. No reservations. V.* ☽ *11:30–8:30. Closed Sun.*

$$ **Tako-ume.** Take a rest from the glitter of Dotonbori nightlife at this
★ 200-year-old traditional dining spot, which specializes in *oden,* a mix-

ture of vegetables, fish cakes, hard-boiled eggs, and fried tofu, cooked in a broth they say has been simmering here in the same pot for the past 30 years (just add liquid . . .). Sake is poured from pewter jugs, handmade in Osaka. The hot Chinese mustard dip is mixed with sweet miso—a house recipe. This is one of Osaka's most famous establishments. ✕ *1-1-8 Dotonbori, Chuo-ku,* ☎ *06/211–0321. Reservations advised weekends. No credit cards.* ⊘ *5–11. Closed Wed.*

$–$$ **Kushitaru.** Specializing in dinners served up piping hot on skewers, Kushi-
★ taru is an Osaka favorite. Your possible selections include *tsukune* (chicken meatballs), celery with sea eel, quail egg with half beak, Chinese mushrooms, pineapple with sliced pork, and oysters with bacon. The restaurant is informal and has two dining rooms; the one upstairs is a throwback to the 1970s, with furniture and music of that period. Kushitaru is behind the Nikko Hotel. ✕ *Sander Bldg., 13-5 Nishi-Shin-Saibashi 1-chome, Unagidani, Chuo-ku,* ☎ *06/281–0365. Reservations advised for upstairs, open seating on 1st floor. AE, DC, MC, V. Lunch 11:30–1:30, dinner 5–11 (last order at 10:30), upstairs opens at 6. Closed national holidays.*

French/Continental

$$$$ **Chambord.** Named for a castle in France's Loire Valley, the Chambord
★ restaurant is French in every way, from the crystal chandeliers to the chef's innovative cuisine. Specialties served by tuxedoed waiters include tenderloin with chestnuts and mushrooms, boiled lobster with tomato and cream sauce, and roast lamb with green peppers. Situated on the 29th floor of the Royal Hotel, the restaurant treats guests to a panoramic view of Osaka's flickering night lights and river activities. ✕ *Royal Hotel, 5-3 Nakanoshima, Kita-ku,* ☎ *06/448– 1121. Reservations required. Jacket and tie. AE, DC, MC, V. Lunch 11:30–2:30, dinner 5:30–10.*

$$$$ **Le Rendezvous.** Atop the Plaza Hotel, Le Rendezvous offers guests not only an elegant meal but also expansive views of the city. A regal French restaurant with lovely wood paneling and formal place settings, it features French nouvelle cuisine and a fine selection of wines. Chef Paul Bocuse, who advises the kitchen here, has an established reputation in Japan for presenting eye-pleasing gourmet dishes ranging from beef cuts to choice salmon. ✕ *2-2-49 Oyodo-minami, Oyodo-ku,* ☎ *06/453–1111. Reservations advised. Jacket and tie. AE, DC, MC, V. No lunch. Dinner 5:30–10.*

$$$$ **Les Célébrites.** On the menu at Les Célébrites are French items identified by their association with such painters as Cézanne, Degas, Renoir, and Toulouse-Lautrec. The gourmet selections include such dishes as terrine of eel and spinach, dodine of stuffed wild duck with foie gras, chilled consommé flavored with tomato, and tenderloin steak with morels, as well as French cheeses, green and mixed salads, and, of course, espresso. The two intimate dining rooms (only 33 seats total) are decorated in lavender and pink, and they feature fresh flowers and beautiful chandeliers. You can also come here for breakfast. Les Célébrites is in the Hotel Nikko, which also has the distinction of hosting another class act: Benkay, a gourmet Japanese restaurant (*see above*). ✕ *Hotel Nikko Osaka, 1-3-3 Nishi-Shin-Saibashi, Chuo-ku,* ☎ *06/244–1111. Reservations advised. Jacket and tie. AE, DC, MC, V. Lunch 11:30–2:30, dinner 5:30–10.*

$$$$ **Rose Room.** Yet another elegant hotel restaurant, this one is dressed
★ up in green marble and has color-coordinated furnishings. The Rose Room features a formal atmosphere, enhanced by candlelit tables, fresh flowers, and a mirrored ceiling. This intimate establishment seats only 59 guests and serves Continental cuisine. Fish and beef dishes are

the specialties, which include grilled sea bass with onion-flavored vinegar, steamed turbot with ravioli, grilled sirloin steak, and Châteaubriand. ✗ *ANA Sheraton Hotel Osaka, 1-3-1 Dojimahama, Kita-ku,* ☎ *06/347–1112. Reservations required. Jacket and tie. AE, DC, MC, V. Lunch 11:30–2:30, dinner 5:30–10.*

$$$$ **The Seasons.** This grand, elegant dining room in the Hilton Interna-
★ tional is in the bustling restaurant and retail sector around Osaka Station. Subtle colors, lustrous marble, and shining chandeliers blend together in The Seasons to create a lovely, warm ambience. The Continental menu offers selections you'll recognize from home: Maine lobster, fine wines, and the local favorite, Kobe beef. Seating less than 100 guests, the restaurant's formality assures patrons a dining event. Specialties include duckling terrine with goose liver, sliced beef in red wine sauce, and fillet of beef with goose liver in a puff pastry. The quick, lower priced lunch menu is ideal for a sampling of what the Hilton chef has to offer; at night, a pianist entertains. ✗ *Osaka Hilton International, 8-8 Umeda 1-chome, Kita-ku,* ☎ *06/347–7111. Reservations advised. Jacket required. AE, DC, MC, V. Lunch 11:30–2:30, dinner 5:30–10:30.*

Steak Restaurants

$$$$ **Ron.** This establishment bills itself as having the best steak in the world; if its bustling business on three floors is any indication, the kudos are not off base. A five-minute walk from Osaka Station, Ron is housed in a five-story brick building. On the menu you'll find fried prawns, fried vegetables, boiled rice, tossed salad, and, of course, prime Kobe-beef steak. The setting is casual and homey, with only 13 tables on three floors. Your beef and other delectables will be prepared on the iron grill table around which you sit—the preparation is half the experience. ✗ *1-10-2 Sonezakishinchi, Kita-ku,* ☎ *06/344–6664. Reservations advised. AE, DC, MC, V.* ☺ *Mon.–Sat. lunch 11:30–2, dinner 5–10, Sun. and holidays dinner only 4–10.*

$$$–$$$$ **Kobe Misono.** This dining spot is a branch of a restaurant in Kobe, and the chefs have managed to transfer the successful Kobe-beef recipe to Osaka. Amid dozens of other less distinguished restaurants, Kobe Misono stands out for its attentive service and casual ambience. Besides the Kobe-beef dinners with all the fixings, other dishes include a chef salad, scallops, and fried vegetables. One family or couple is seated at each iron grill table; there are only six tables, which seat a maximum of 43 persons. ✗ *Near Osaka Station, Star Bldg., 3F, 11-19 Sonezakishinchi, Kita-ku,* ☎ *06/341–4471. Reservations advised. AE, DC, MC, V.* ☺ *Mon.–Sat. lunch 11:30–2, dinner 5–10; Sun. noon–9.*

$$$–$$$$ **Osaka Joe's.** First came Miami Joe's, then Tokyo Joe's; now here is the third version of that formidable institution for stone crabs. The obvious specials are the crabs (with melted butter and mustard mayonnaise) flown in from Florida and, for dessert, Key lime pie. Also on the menu are baked prawns, T-bone steak, and lamb chops. The setting is casual, with a distinctive American flair—even the music is from the States. A cozy, rustic bar at the entry seats only eight people; the two dining rooms seat a total of 99. Lunch is served until 3 PM and is relatively inexpensive at about ¥1,500. Dinner with choicer items can be considerably higher—around ¥6,000 for crab claws. Ex-pats are the regular clientele, but it is a good opportunity to make the comparison between American crab meat and the *kani* (crab) found in Japanese waters. ✗ *IM Excellence Bldg., 2nd floor, 1-11-20 Sonezakishinchi, Kita-ku,* ☎ *06/344–0124. Reservations advised. AE, DC, MC, V.* ☺ *11–11:30 (last order at 10:30).*

Seafood

$–$$ Little Carnival. You'll find Little Carnival tucked away on the lower
★ level of the Umeda Center Building, where singing waiters serve up lobster, salmon, crab, and raw fish. The restaurant's library theme and multiwood paneling combine with dining areas on different levels to create a casual, friendly atmosphere. Little Carnival also features a big buffet and salad bar, and from 6 to 10 in the evening, a piano player accompanies the singing servers. This place is very popular with young people. ✗ *Umeda Center Bldg., B1F, 2-4-12 Nakazaki-Nishi, Kita-ku,* ☎ *06/373–9828. No reservations. AE, DC, MC, V.* ⊙ *Weekdays 11:45–11:30 (lunch menu 11:45–3); weekends 11:45–11:30.*

Mexican

$$ La Bamba. The owner/chef learned his craft in Mexico and learned it
★ so well that success has caused him to change location for larger premises in Umeda and to open a branch in Dotonburi-Minami (☎ 06/213–9612). The same superior quality of the tacos, guacamole, burritos, quesadillas, and magnificent pitchers of margaritas persists. Decor is typically Mexican (sombreros and posters), so for a time you will forget you are in the land of raw fish and chopsticks! ✗ *Shiko Crown Bldg., 10-7 Doyamacho, Kita-ku,* ☎ *06/367–0192. Reservations advised weekends. No credit cards.* ⊙ *5–11. Closed Mon.*

Vegetarian

$ Country Life. The current health boom has at last started to dispel the notion left over from less prosperous days in Japan that brown rice is something only poor people eat. Country Life, with its inexpensive yet gourmet vegetarian meals, has Early American decor; the food (no meat, fish, eggs, or milk) is served buffet-style—all you can eat, and all delicious at very reasonable prices. The restaurant is across the river to the southeast of the Museum of Oriental Ceramics. ✗ *3-11 Kyobashi, Chuo-ku,* ☎ *06/943–9597. No reservations. No credit cards.* ⊙ *11–3. Closed Sat.*

Night Spots with Food

$$ Kirin City. This beer hall is on the second floor of the fantastic Kirin Plaza Building designed by architect Shin Takamatsu, one of Japan's most controversial new architects. This hypertechno postmodern extravaganza presides over the old Narubashi (bridge) on the Dotonbori Canal. Stop here for a cold draft beer and a bite to eat in the Shin-Saibashi district. The menu features fried chicken, "city potatoes" (french fries), and chorizo, among many delights. ✗ *2F Kirin Plaza Bldg., 7-2 Soemoncho, Chuo-ku,* ☎ *06/212–6572. No reservations.* ⊙ *Weekdays 11:30–1; weekends 11–11. V.*

$–$$ Yasubei. This small *izakaya* (pub) has both a fun atmosphere and good food. Sit at the counter, where you can watch the chefs at work, or at a table and select from an extensive menu that includes grilled fish, hibachi-grilled chicken, and scallops wrapped in bacon. ✗ *Dai-ichi Blvd., BF2, 1-3 Umeda, Kita-ku (close to Umeda Station),* ☎ *06/344–4545. No reservations. No credit cards.* ⊙ *Daily until 10:30 PM.*

$ Karma. A reasonably priced night spot and gathering place, Karma has a full-service bar, snacks and complete menus, audiovisual entertainment, and Friday- and Saturday-night dancing to tunes spun by local DJs (cover charge: ¥1,500). Drinks average ¥800, and a BLT on a bagel costs ¥800. Karma is across Route 2 from the Osaka Dai-ichi Biru. ✕ *Eiraku Biru, Sonezaki Shinchi, Chuo-ku,* ☎ *06/344–6181. No reservations. No credit cards.* ☉ *5 PM–midnight (to 2 AM Fri. and Sat.).*

$ **Pig & Whistle.** Both branches of this establishment (one in Umeda and one in Shin-Saibashi) offer a publike atmosphere with a standup bar and tables, a variety of imported beers, a dart board, and an informal ambience conducive to conversation. ✕ *2F IS Bldg., 1-32 Shin-Saibashi-suji 2 chome, Chuo-ku,* ☎ *06/213–6911; B1 Ohatsutenjin Bldg., 2-5 Sonezaki, Kita-ku,* ☎ *06/361–3198. No reservations. No credit cards.* ☉ *4:30 PM–midnight (to 1 AM Fri. and Sat.).*

LODGING

Osaka is known more as a business than as a tourist destination. Although the trend for tourists is still to stay in nearby Kyoto and visit Osaka on a day trip, Osakans would like to see this pattern reversed. Among the city's assets are sparkling new Western-style hotels constructed with comfort and luxury in mind. Osaka bills itself as the premier city of the 21st century; each new building appears to resemble a prototype for future architecture.

Osaka has accommodations for almost every taste, from first-class hotels to more modest business hotels, which unfortunately aren't very distinctive. You may be somewhat disappointed if you expect guest quarters to be along the same lines as the better hotels in the United States. The Japanese hotel designers are often concerned with being efficient and functional rather than elegant and flamboyant. However, discriminating travelers will appreciate the individual attention provided by the solicitous staff at most hotels. Because Osaka hotels offer much the same both in decor and room size within a given price range, choose your accommodation in terms of location rather than amenities.

You'll be relieved to discover that a hotel room in Osaka costs less than one of comparative size in Tokyo. And Osaka has more hotels to choose from than Kyoto, which is especially important to keep in mind during the peak tourist seasons.

A 3% federal consumer tax is added to all hotel bills. Another 3% local tax is added to the bill if it exceeds ¥15,000. At most hotels, a 10%–15% service charge is added to the total bill. Tipping is not necessary.

CATEGORY	COST*
$$$$	over ¥20,000
$$$	¥15,000–¥20,000
$$	¥10,000–¥15,000
$	under ¥10,000

Cost is for double room, without tax or service

$$$$ **ANA Sheraton Hotel Osaka.** One of only a half-dozen Osaka hotels to be classified as deluxe, the ANA Sheraton overlooks the city's picturesque Nakanoshima. A handsome 24-story white-tile structure, it has some unusual architectural features, including a six-story rock sculpture behind its main stairway and huge fluted columns in its lobby. There is also an enclosed courtyard with trees. Guest rooms are done in pastel shades and have travertine-marble baths with phone extensions. Each room is furnished with twin or double beds; some rooms have extra sofa beds. The hotel's fine restaurants include the elegant Rose Room (*see* Dining, *above*). ☎ *1-3-1 Dojimahama, Kita-ku, Osaka 530,* ☎ *06/347–1112,* 🆑 *06/347–9208. U.S. reservations,* ☎ *800/262–4683;*

UK reservations, ☎ *071/995–8211. 500 rooms. 5 restaurants, coffee shop, indoor pool, sauna, business services, parking. AE, DC, MC, V.*

$$$$ **Hotel New Otani Osaka.** The New Otani is ideally situated next to
★ Osakajo Koen on the JR line. Popular with Japanese and Westerners alike, it offers such amenities as indoor and outdoor pools, tennis, superior rooms, and a sparkling marble atrium lobby. The rooms, large by Japanese standards, afford handsome views of Osakajo and the Neyagawa (river). The room decor is modern, with twin or double beds, light color schemes, dining tables, lined draperies, and excellent bathrooms with decent counter space. A large selection of bars and restaurants offers enough diversity to suit almost any taste. Indeed, the New Otani is like a minicity within the Osaka Business Park. Its drawback is that anytime you need to go to midtown Osaka, you need to board the Aqua Liner water bus, which stops right in front of the hotel. ⊡ *4-1 Shiromi 1-chome, Chuo-ku, Osaka 540,* ☎ *06/941–1111,* FAX *06/941–9769. 559 rooms. 18 restaurants and bars, health club. AE, DC, MC, V.*

$$$$ **Hotel Nikko Osaka.** An impressive and rather striking white tower in the colorful Shin-Saibashi Station area, the Nikko Osaka is within easy reach of Osaka's nightlife. The hotel's atmosphere is lively and even exciting: As you enter, you'll probably be greeted by a doorman in top hat and tails. Some rooms offer contemporary furnishings with Japanese touches and traditional light decor. Higher price rooms have expensive furniture, thick carpets, bedside controls, and cable TV featuring the CNN news station. On the executive floors, the tile baths come complete with hair dryers and phones. The drinking and dining establishments (*see* Benkay *and* Les Célébrites *in* Dining, *above*) are numerous and varied, and the hotel's management has elevated service to an art. ⊡ *1-3-3 Nishi-Shin-Saibashi, Chuo-ku, Osaka 542,* ☎ *06/244–1111,* FAX *06/245–2432. 640 rooms. French, Japanese, Chinese, and Western restaurants, 3 bars, coffee shop, shops. AE, DC, MC, V.*

$$$$ **Hyatt Regency Osaka.** This most recent (1994) luxury hotel to be built in Osaka is in the city's newest development area, Nanko Cosmosquare. Though this Hyatt bills itself as a city/resort hotel, it is a good 40 minutes by shuttle bus or subway from Osaka Station, which makes it an unlikely choice for the tourist keen on sightseeing. For a business traveler, though, with meetings in the area, or who wants a hotel close to the new Kansai International Airport (a 45-minute bus ride away), this Hyatt offers Osaka's best in modern comfort. Guest rooms are spacious even by American standards, especially the deluxe doubles. Choose one on the upper floors for sweeping views of Osaka Bay. Modern conveniences are everywhere, including a fax/modem dataport in each room. The marble bathrooms have a separate shower stall and the bath towels are huge. For entertainment and dining there are 15 restaurants and bars ranging from haute Cantonese cuisine (with Shanghainese appetizers) at the Ten Kuh on the 28th floor to a basement complex of small bistro-style eating shops that includes patisseries, snack bars, Italian and Japanese restaurants, and a bar with live music. Across the street at the Asia and Pacific Trade Center is a host of other restaurants, most with a Japanese flavor. ⊡ *1-13 Nanko-Kita, Suminoe-ku, Osaka 559,* ☎ *06/612–1234,* FAX *06/614–7800. U.S. reservations,* ☎ *800/233–1234. UK reservations,* ☎ *071/580–8197. 500 rooms. 15 restaurants and bars, health club, pool, wedding and banquet facilities, meeting rooms, business services, Kansai International Airport limousine. AE, DC, MC, V.*

$$$$ Nankai South Tower Hotel. One of the best features of this three-year-old hotel is its location, right inside the Nankai Nanba Station, where travelers can connect with a number of rail lines, including the Nankai train to Koyasan and Wakayama, the subway to Umeda and Shin-Osaka stations, and the Nankai train to the new Kansai International Airport. This modern tower has 36 floors, but because public spaces are on the lower levels, all of the guest rooms have views of the city. Rooms are decorated in three color schemes—light shades of blue, brown, and purple—with low-pile rugs, electronically controlled curtains, and brass fixtures. Suites have kitchenettes and Jacuzzis as well as showers and two toilets. Bathrobes are supplied for those staying on the Executive floors. This is a bright, Western-style hotel, akin to what you'd expect in a Hilton: first-rate comfort but little character. Some will find this a welcome escape from the noise of the city and the challenge of traveling in a foreign land. Be sure to have a drink in the Sky Lounge. ☎ *1-60 Nanba 5-chome, Chuo-ku, Osaka 542, ☎ 06/646–1111, FAX 06/648–0331. 548 rooms, including 11 Western suites and 2 Japanese suites. 12 restaurants, 18 ballrooms, 2 private dining rooms, health club, indoor pool, hot tubs, sauna, massage, business services with English-speaking staff, Christian and Shinto chapels.*

$$$$ Osaka Hilton International. Glitz and glitter draw both tourists and
★ expense accounters to the Hilton International, Osaka's leading hotel. Located across from Osaka Station in the heart of Osaka's business district, it is a typical Western-style hotel, replete with marble and brass. The high-ceiling lobby is dramatically luxurious, and the hotel's arcade boasts several designer boutiques. Standard rooms are first-rate, with almost all the extras, and the three executive floors offer higher price rooms if you desire even more comfort, plus the convenience of a lounge for complimentary Continental breakfasts and evening cocktails. The staff are very helpful. (*See also* The Seasons *in* Dining, *above.*) ☎ *8-8 Umeda 1-chome, Kita-ku, Osaka 530, ☎ 06/347–7111, FAX 06/347–7001. 526 rooms. Restaurants, café, coffee shop, health club, outdoor tennis, indoor pool, gym, sauna, massage, business services, shops. AE, DC, MC, V.*

$$$$ Royal Hotel. With a host of restaurants (*see* Chambord *in* Dining, *above*) and bars from the basement to the top floor of its tower, the Royal is a self-contained city—which it needs to be as there is nothing of interest in easy walking distance. The lobby is the perfect spot for people-watching, with crowds going in and out of the hotel's many lounges. Guests staying in the VIP tower have access to the swimming club with two sunroofed pools. Standard rooms, either with twin beds or a queen-size bed, are reasonably spacious and have a coffee table, two chairs, and big picture windows (views improve with the higher floors). A shuttle runs from the hotel to the Grand Hotel (nearby) and to the Yodoyabashi Subway Station. ☎ *5-3-68 Nakanoshima, Kita-ku, Osaka 530, ☎ 06/448–1121, FAX 06/448–4414. 1,167 rooms. 15 restaurants, health club, 2 swimming pools, tanning beds, sauna, steam room, massage room, lounges. AE, DC, MC, V.*

$$$–$$$$ Holiday Inn Nankai Osaka. Americans will recognize the familiar Holiday Inn touches—the rooms are a bit bland, with twin or double beds, modern baths, and a television with standard Japanese stations. Despite the proximity to nightlife and Nankai Station, the rooms are fairly quiet. The best rooms are found on the 10th floor. Restaurants range from a grill room to a coffee shop with a garden promenade. This is not the best value in the city. ☎ *5-15 Shin-Saibashi-suji 2-chome, Chuo-ku, Osaka 542, ☎ 06/213–8281, FAX 06/213–8640. 229 rooms. Chinese and Japanese restaurants, pub, coffee shop, grill, rooftop pool, three floors of shops. AE, DC, MC, V.*

$$$–$$$$ ★ **Hotel Osaka Grand.** A sister to the Royal Hotel, the Grand is a lively first-class commercial hotel with free shuttle service every few minutes to the Royal and to Yodoyabashi Subway Station. Everything is neat and clean; the staff is large and hardworking. Housekeeping is very good, and the rooms bigger than average for Japan. The decor is somewhat dated but in good repair. ☎ *2-3-18 Nakanoshima, Kita-ku, Osaka 530,* ☎ *06/202–1212,* ℻ *06/227–5054. 350 rooms. Western and Japanese restaurants, shops. AE, DC, MC, V.*

$$$–$$$$ **Miyako Hotel Osaka.** A 21-story high rise, the Miyako is filled with expansive public rooms such as the lobby, which rises two stories and is decorated with marble columns and attractive pastel color schemes. The rooms are also pastel; they are modern and inviting, with such extras as bedside television controls, and dining tables. Executive rooms occupy two floors and have plusher appointments. The Miyako is near the Ue-honmachi Subway Station, and trains for Kyoto on the Kintetsu Line leave from an adjacent building, which makes the hotel convenient for travelers. The National Bunraku Theater is also fairly close. ☎ *6-1-55 Ue-honmachi, Tennoji-ku, Osaka 543,* ☎ *06/773–1111,* ℻ *06/773–3322. 608 rooms. Restaurants, grill, coffee shop, shops, roof lounge, bars, health club with indoor pool and retractable roof, Japanese bath, racquetball. AE, DC, MC, V.*

$$$–$$$$ **Osaka Terminal Hotel.** Across from Osaka Station (not to be confused with Shin-Osaka Station, where Shinkansen trains arrive and depart), the Osaka Terminal is housed in a skyscraper and shares floors with offices and shops. It ranks as a minimally first-class hotel but has many restaurants, including a grill and coffee shop. Rooms have minibars, bedside TV controls, and small, plastic bathrooms. ☎ *3-1-1 Umeda, Kita-ku, Osaka 530,* ☎ *06/344–1235,* ℻ *06/344–1130. 644 rooms. 4 restaurants, 2 lounges, shops. AE, DC, MC, V.*

$$–$$$ **Hotel Do Sports Plaza.** Situated in the heart of Osaka's colorful nightlife district, the Do Sports Plaza earned its reputation by catering to sports enthusiasts and athletic teams. Most of the rooms are small, but fairly bright, singles; doubles are not much larger. Fitness activities are the main attraction here. The hotel adjoins a members-only sports club that is open to hotel guests for an additional ¥2,500 per person. Facilities at the club include a heated pool, running track, gym, sauna, and aerobics studio. ☎ *3-3-17 Minami-Senba, Chuo-ku, Osaka 542,* ☎ *06/245–3311,* ℻ *06/245–5803. 208 rooms. Restaurant, pub, coffee shop, health club. AE, DC, MC, V.*

$$–$$$ **Hotel Hanshin.** Popular mostly with Japanese businessmen, the 15-story Hotel Hanshin does manage to attract a few tourists. The moderately priced rooms are found between the 10th and 15th floors. Furnishings are mostly Scandinavian; the tile baths are so small you might say they are claustrophobic. Waterbeds are available. The hotel is located near the underground shopping center at Umeda and Osaka Station. ☎ *2-3-30 Umeda, Kita-ku, Osaka 530,* ☎ *06/344–1661,* ℻ *06/344–9860. 243 rooms. Japanese-Western restaurant, coffee shop, 2 bars, sauna, shops. AE, DC, MC, V.*

$$–$$$ **International Hotel Osaka.** This massive L-shape hotel may be a bit hard to reach in traffic, but it's a reliable choice. The best rooms are in an annex; if you're on a budget, ask for a room in the back. The color scheme can best be described as reserved and uninspiring. Popular mostly with Japanese clientele, the International's lobby and public areas are often busy with groups coming or going. ☎ *2-3-3 Honmachibashi, Chuo-ku, Osaka 540,* ☎ *06/941–2661,* ℻ *06/941–5362. 393 rooms. 5 restaurants, coffee shop, grill, lounge. AE, DC, MC, V.*

$$–$$$ **Mitsui Urban Hotel.** The decor in the rooms of this hotel are the ever-popular pastels; autumn-colored rooms have coffee makers and other extras. Some of the carpeting in the rooms is new, and the baths are fairly modern, though a bit small. There's also a 17th-floor restaurant. The staff's English is fairly good, considering the hotel receives mostly Japanese guests. The Mitsui Urban is accessible to the Midosuji Subway Line at Nakatsu Station. ⌖ *18-8 Toyosaki, Oyodo-ku, Osaka 531,* ☎ *06/374–1111,* FAX *06/374–1085. 406 rooms. Restaurant, lounge, bar. AE, DC, MC, V.*

$$–$$$ **New Hankyu Hotel and New Hankyu Annex.** This busy hotel complex is located in the popular area around Osaka Station, with its restaurants and shopping. The 17-story Annex, a block from the main hotel, houses the newest, largest, and best rooms; it also offers a café, three other eateries, and an indoor pool. The single rooms in the main hotel, however, are about as roomy as telephone booths. Guests are permitted the use of facilities in both buildings. ⌖ *1-1-35 Shibata, Kita-ku, Osaka 530,* ☎ *06/372–5101,* FAX *06/374–6885. 1,249 rooms. 5 restaurants in main building, 2 in annex, health club, indoor pool, bars. AE, DC, MC, V.*

$$–$$$ **Osaka Airport Hotel.** This place is for those with an early flight out of Osaka Airport: It's right inside the airport terminal building. These are not the most luxurious rooms for the price, but the location saves time and trouble for the busy traveler. ⌖ *3F Osaka Airport Bldg., Toyonaka, Osaka-ku.* ☎ *06/855–4621,* FAX *06/855–4620. 105 rooms. Japanese and Western restaurants, shops, and bars serving the airport and hotel. AE, DC, MC, V.*

$$–$$$ **Osaka Dai Ichi Hotel.** As Japan's first cylinder-shape skyscraper, known as the Maru-Biru (Round Building), the Dai Ichi is easy to locate amid the Osaka cityscape. Now somewhat overshadowed by the Hilton, it still receives many groups. The rooms are wedge-shape, and half are small singles that are usually taken on weekdays by Japanese businessmen. The hotel has a coffee shop, which is open around the clock, and an underground shopping arcade. The Dai Ichi is conveniently located across from Osaka Station. ⌖ *1-9-20 Umeda, Kita-ku, Osaka 530,* ☎ *06/341–4411,* FAX *06/341–4930. 478 rooms. Chinese, Japanese, and Western restaurants, bar, shops. AE, DC, MC, V.*

$$ **Hotel Echo Osaka.** This hotel is recommended for those seeking good, moderately priced accommodations. Though near the JR station, the Echo Osaka is far from other major parts of the city. The 83 plain rooms offer air-conditioning and routine furnishings, including double or twin beds, uncoordinated carpeting, and small baths. The hotel is neat and clean, if nothing more, and has an accommodating young staff. ⌖ *1-4-7 Abeno-suji, Abeno-ku, Osaka 545 (near Tennoji Station),* ☎ *06/633–1141,* FAX *06/633–3849. 84 rooms. Chinese and French restaurants, coffee shop, bar. AE, DC, MC, V.*

$$ **Osaka Castle Hotel.** This square mid-rise building is unexceptional and receives its name for its location near Osakajo, not for any majestic manner. It has a rooftop beer garden in summer and a subway stop in the basement. Rooms are small and not very bright; the furniture is uninspired. Some rooms in front have good views, but all have dwarf-size baths. You may have to bone up on your Japanese to communicate with the front desk. ⌖ *2-35-7 Kyobashi, Chuo-ku, Osaka 540 (at Tenmabashi Station on Tanimachi Line),* ☎ *06/942–2401,* FAX *06/946–9043. 120 rooms. Japanese, Chinese, and French restaurants, café, beer garden, shops. AE, DC, MC, V.*

$$ **Osaka International Community Center Hotel.** The city community center has a hotel with pleasant, well-furnished rooms at reasonable rates. The center hosts lectures and cultural events and offers simultaneous interpreting services. ☎ *8-2-6 Kamimotocho, Tennoji-ku, Osaka 543,* ☎ *06/773–8181,* FAX *06/772–7600. 50 rooms with bath. Restaurant, café, bar, library, conference rooms. AE, DC, MC, V.*

$$ Umeshin East Hotel. In the antiques shop and art gallery neighborhood near the U.S. Consulate, this small brick hotel has an attractive modern design, with a lush green interior garden café, a restaurant, and a bar in its tiled lobby. Rooms are small, but comfortably furnished. ☎ *4-11-5 Nishi-Tenma, Kita-ku (a 10-min. walk from Midosuji Subway Line and Umeda Station),* ☎ *06/364–1151,* FAX *06/364–1150. 144 rooms. AE, DC, MC, V.*

$ Ebisu-so Royan. This, Osaka's only member of the inexpensive Japanese Inn Group, is a partly wood structure with 15 Japanese-style rooms. It's a very basic, no-frills operation, without a restaurant (though there are plenty nearby). Close to the electrical appliance and computer center of Den Den Town and the National Theater, the Ebisu-so Royan is a five-minute walk from the Ebisucho Station on the Sakai Suji-sen Line. ☎ *1-7-33 Nipponbashi-nishi, Naniwa-ku, Osaka 556,* ☎ *06/643–4861. 15 rooms, none with private bath. AE, MC, V.*

OSAKA ESSENTIALS

Arriving and Departing

By Plane

All international flights arrive at the new Kansai International Airport (KIX). There are also connecting domestic flights to the major Japanese cities. The airport, built on reclaimed land in Osaka Bay, is laid out vertically. The first floor is for international arrivals; the second floor is for domestic departures and arrivals; the third floor has shops and restaurants; and the fourth floor is for international departures. A small Tourist Information Center on the first floor of the passenger terminal building is open from 9 to 5.

The majority of domestic flights use the Osaka's old airport, Itami Airport, about 30 minutes from Osaka. Flights from Tokyo, which operate frequently throughout the day, take 70 minutes. Regular domestic flights from major Japanese cities to Osaka are handled by Japan Airlines (JAL), All Nippon Airways (ANA), and Japan Air System (JAS).

BETWEEN THE AIRPORT AND CENTER CITY

Kansai International Airport is designed to serve the entire Kansai region, not just Osaka, so there are many ways to access it. There are three main access routes from Osaka: From Shin-Osaka, take the JR Kansai Airport Express "Haruka" for the 45-minute run at ¥2,900; from Tennoji Station, the same train will get you to the airport in 29 minutes for ¥2,230; and from JR Kyobashi Station, take the Kansai Airport Rapid Trains for a 70-minute run at ¥1,140; and, finally, from Nankai Nanba Station, take the Nankai Rapid Limited Express for a 29-minute trip at ¥1,250. Access to and from Kyoto is by the Haruka Limited Express, which departs from Kyoto Station every 30 minutes to make the 75-minute run at ¥3,340. For Kobe, take the JR Kansai Airport Express "Haruka" to Shin-Osaka and change to the JR Tokaido Line for Kobe's JR Sannomiya Station, 70 minutes away, for ¥1,800; or ride the boat from the airport ferry terminal to Kobe City Air Terminal (K-CAT), which takes 30 minutes and costs ¥2,650.

Airport buses from Itami Airport operate at intervals of 15 minutes to one hour, 6 AM–9 PM, and take passengers to seven locations in Osaka: Shin-Osaka Station, Umeda, Nanba (near the Nikko and Holiday Inn hotels), Ue-honmachi, Abeno, Sakai-higashi, and Osaka Business Park (near the New Otani Hotel). Buses take 25–50 minutes, depending on destination, and cost ¥340–¥680. Schedules, with exact times and fares, are available at the information counter at the airport.

Taxis to the city from Kansai International Airport are prohibitively expensive; between the Itami Airport and hotels in central Osaka, taxis cost approximately ¥5,500 and take about 30 minutes.

By Train

The Tokaido Shinkansen Super Express trains from Tokyo to Osaka's Shin-Osaka Station take just under three hours and cost ¥13,480 for reserved seats, or ¥12,980 for nonreserved. The Shin-Osaka Station, on the north side of the Shin-Yodo River, is linked to the center of the city by the JR Kobe Line and the Mido-suji Subway Line. The ride, which takes 6–20 minutes, depending on your midcity destination, costs ¥180–¥230. Train schedule and fare information can be obtained at the Travel Service Center in the Shin-Osaka Station. A taxi from the Shin-Osaka Station to central Osaka costs ¥1,500–¥2,700.

Getting Around

By Subway

Osaka's fast, efficient subway system offers the most convenient means of exploring the city, because the complicated bus routes display no signs in English, and taxis, while plentiful, are costly. The six subway lines converge at Osaka Station, at Umeda, where they are linked underground. The main line is the Mido-suji, which runs between Shin-Osaka and Umeda in six minutes; Shin-Osaka and Shin-Saibashi in 12 minutes; Shin-Osaka and Nanba in 14 minutes; and Shin-Osaka and Tennoji in 20 minutes.

Subways run from early morning until nearly midnight at intervals of three to five minutes. Fares begin at ¥180 and are determined by the distance traveled. A one-day pass for unlimited municipal transportation on subways, the New Tram (a new train line that runs to the docks area), and city buses, can be obtained at the commuter ticket windows in major subway stations and at the Japan Travel Bureau office in Osaka Station (cost: ¥850 adults, ¥450 children). A subway network map of Osaka is available from the Japan National Tourist Organization, the city tourist offices and most hotels, and at the Japan Travel Bureau office in Osaka Station.

Adding to the efficiency of the subway system is the JR Kanjo (Loop) Line, which circles the city above ground and intersects all subway lines. Fares range from ¥160 to ¥390, but you can use a JR Rail Pass on this train.

By Bus

Economical one-day transportation passes (*see* By Subway, *above*) for Osaka are valid on bus lines as well as subway routes, and the service operates throughout the day and evening, but bus travel is a challenge best left to local residents or those fluent in Japanese.

By Taxi

You'll have no problem hailing taxis on the street or at specified taxi stands. (A red light in the lower left corner of the windshield indicates availability.) The problem is moving in Osaka's heavy traffic. Fares are metered at ¥560 for the first 2 kilometers, plus ¥80 for each additional 460 meters. It is not customary to tip the driver.

Guided Tours

Orientation Tours

The **Municipal Bus System** (☎ 06/311–2995) operates regular sight-seeing tours of the city on its double-deck "Rainbow" bus. The tours are in Japanese. The five different tour routes start at the Umeda Sightseeing Information Center. They vary in length from three to four hours and cost from ¥2,810 to ¥4,230.

The **Aqua Liner** (☎ 06/942–5511) operates a 60-minute tour through Osaka's waterways, departing every hour 10–4 from April through September; there are also evening tours from 6 to 7 PM on Friday, Saturday, Sunday, and national holidays from three piers at Osakajo, Tenmabashi, and Yodoyabashi. This is the only tour of Osaka conducted in both Japanese and English (cost: ¥1,800 adults, ¥900 children).

Special-Interest Tours

Japan's **Home Visit System,** which enables foreign visitors to meet local people in their homes for a few hours and learn more about the Japanese lifestyle, is available in Osaka. Visitors should apply in advance through the **Osaka Tourist Information Center** (☎ 06/305–3311) at the JR Shin-Osaka Station; at the **Osaka Tourist Association** (☎ 06/208–8955) at the Sumitomo Seimei Yodoyabashi Building.; or at the Osaka **City Tourist Information Office** (☎ 06/345–2189) at the JR Osaka Station.

Excursions

Japan Travel Bureau (☎ 06/343–0617) operates daily afternoon tours to Kyoto and Nara. Pickup is available at several hotels. **Japan Amenity Travel** (075/222–0121) offers two full-day tours: one to Kyoto only (¥12,000), and one to Kyoto and Nara (¥13,500). They depart from the Osaka Hilton International and include train fare to Kyoto.

Important Addresses and Numbers

Emergencies

Police, ☎ 110; ambulance, ☎ 119.

DOCTORS

Tane General Hospital, 1-2-31 Sakaigawa, Nishi-ku, ☎ 06/581–1071; **Sumitomo Hospital,** 2-2 Nakanoshima 5-chome, Kita-ku, ☎ 06/443–1261; **Yodogawa Christian Hospital,** 9-26 Awaji 2-chome, Higashi Yodogawa-ku, ☎ 06/322–2250; **Osaka University Hospital** (accepts emergency patients by ambulance only), 1-50 Fukushima 1-chome, Fukushima, ☎ 06/451–0051. For medical advice, call the **International Medical Information Center,** ☎ 06/213–2393.

Tourist Information

Osaka Tourist Information Center (☎ 06/305–3311), on the east side of the main exit of the JR Shin-Osaka Station, is open daily 8–8; closed December 29–January 3. Another branch (☎ 06/345–2189) at the Mido-suji gate of the JR Osaka Station operates daily 8–8; closed December 31–January 4.

The **Information Center** in Osakajo (06/941–0546) is open daily 9–5.

Tourist Information Service, Osaka Prefectural Government (☎ 06/941–9200), is in the lobby of the International Hotel (58 Hashizumecho, Uchi-honmachi, Chuo-ku), a five-minute walk from Sakai-suji-honmachi Subway Station ⊘ 9–5 Mon.–Sat.; closed national holidays).

Japan Travel Phone (☎ 0120/444–800) provides free information service in English daily 9–5.

Consulates

U.S., 2-11-5 Nishi-Tenma, Kita-ku, ☎ 06/315–5900.
Canadian, 2-2-3 Nishi-Shin-Saibashi, Chuo-ku, ☎ 06/212–4910.
U.K., Seiko Osaka Bldg., 19 F, 35-1 Bakuromachi, Chuo-ku, ☎ 06/281–1616.

English-Language Bookstore

Kinokuniya Book Store Co., Ltd. (Hankyu Sanban-gai 1-1-3, Shibata, Kita-ku, ☎ 06/372–5821) is open 10–9, except for the third Wednesday of the month. It is across the street from the Midosuji entrance of Osaka Station in the Hankyu Station building complex.

Travel Agencies

Japan Travel Bureau, Foreign Tourist Division, Sakai-suji-honmachi Center Bldg., 7F, 2-1-6 Honmachi, Chuo-ku, ☎ 06/271–6195; **Hankyu Express International,** 8-47 Kakutacho, Kita-ku, ☎ 06/373–5471; **Tokyu Tourist Corp.,** Kansai Foreign Tourist Center, Wakasugi Osaka Eki-mae Bldg. 10F, 2-3-13, Sonezakishinchi, Kita-ku, ☎ 06/344–5488.

Business Assistance

Contact **Information Service System Co., Ltd.** (Hotel Nikko Osaka, 1-3-5 Nishi-Shin-Saibashi, Chuo-ku, ☎ 06/245–4015) for business-related assistance, including quick-print business cards and interpreting.

9 Kobe

In typical Japanese fashion, this port city on Osaka Bay has made an amazingly quick recovery from the devastating earthquake that struck it in January 1995. A sophisticated and cosmopolitan city that has been an important harbor throughout Japanese history, Kobe has excellent shopping and a wide variety of international cuisines to sample.

By Kiko Itasaka

Updated by
Nigel Fisher

KOBE HAS BEEN A PROMINENT HARBOR CITY throughout Japanese history. In the 12th century, the Taira family moved the capital from Kyoto to Fukuhara, the western part of modern Kobe, with the hope of increasing Japan's international trade. Fukuhara remained the capital for a mere six months, but its port, known as Hyogo, continued to flourish. Japan opened her ports to foreign trade in 1868 after a long period of isolationism. In order to prevent foreigners from using the profitable and active port of Hyogo, the more remote port of Kobe, located slightly northeast of Hyogo, was opened to international trade. Within a few years, Kobe eclipsed Hyogo in importance as a port.

Now a major industrial city, Kobe has an active port that serves as many as 10,000 ships a year. A century of exposure to international cultures has left its mark on Kobe, a sophisticated and cosmopolitan city. In the hills above the port area is a residential area where foreign merchants and traders have settled over the years. Many Western-style houses built in the late 19th century are still inhabited by Kobe's large foreign population, while others have been open to the public as buildings of historical interest. Many sailors passing through Kobe, beguiled by the charm of this city, have settled here. As a result, Kobe boasts remarkable diversity in its shops and restaurants.

Travelers searching for exotic or traditional Japan will be disappointed by the very modern Kobe, but visitors will be satisfied by the city if they are eager to relax in a cosmopolitan setting with excellent places to shop and a variety of international cuisines to sample. Though the damage wreaked by the January 1995 earthquake was indeed tremendous in Kobe, the process of recovery has been speedy, especially in the city proper. From a tourist's perspective, by the middle of 1996 Kobe probably will not look like a war-torn, bombed-out town. However, many of the cultural attractions may not be open, and the sake breweries, which were damaged beyond repair, never will be.

EXPLORING

Numbers in the margin correspond to points of interest on the Kobe map.

The downtown section of Kobe, where most businesses are located, is near the harbor area. The rest of Kobe is built on slopes that extend as far as the base of Mt. Rokko. In the middle of the harbor is the man-made Port Island, which has conference centers, an amusement park, and the Portopia Hotel. The island is linked with the downtown area by a fully computerized monorail that is without a human conductor. The major nightlife area, Ikuta (a subsection of the Kitano area), is just north of Sannomiya Station.

In January 1995, a massive earthquake hit Kobe; approximately 5,000 people were killed and some 100,000 buildings destroyed. At press time, Kobe was still in the process of cleaning up, with many of the tourist attractions closed and under repair. Conservative estimates, however, predict that most of the major attractions will be fully operational by the middle of 1996. What cannot be replaced or repaired are the wonderful old sake breweries that had been converted into museums. The most famous of these, Kikumasamune Shiryokan, along with the others, was completely demolished.

★ ❶ A good place to start your trip to Kobe is the **Kobe Shiritsu Hakubutsukan** (Kobe City Museum), where you'll find out about the history of this international port town. Alongside earlier artifacts, the museum has an interesting collection of memorabilia from the heyday of the old foreign settlement, including a scale model of the foreign concession. Three entire rooms from a turn-of-the-century Western house are on display. You'll also discover selections from the museum's famous *nanban* collection of prints, screens, and paintings by Japanese artists of the late 16th to 17th century that depict foreigners in Japanese settings from that period. The 1995 earthquake caused severe damage to the museum, especially to the ground floor. At press time, the museum was scheduled to reopen in spring 1996.

To get to the museum, walk south down Flower Road from Sannomiya Station, past the Flower Clock and City Hall to Higashi-Yuenchi Koen (park). Walk through the park to the Kobe Minato Post Office, across the street on the west side. Walk east on the road in front of the post office toward the Oriental Hotel. Turn left at the corner in front of the hotel and you'll find the City Museum in the old Bank of Tokyo building, at the end of the block. *24 Kyomachi, Chuo-ku, Kobe-shi,* ☎ *078/391-0035.* ☛ *¥200 (more for special exhibitions).* ☉ *Tues.–Sun. 10–5.*

Return to Sannomiya Station, browsing through Nankinmachi (Chinatown) and the Motomachi and Sannomiya shopping arcades (*see* Shopping, *below*) if time permits. Once back at Sannomiya Station, begin your tour of the northern district by crossing the street that runs along the tracks and turning left at the first main intersection. Before the earthquake, you would have seen the orange *torii* (arch)
❷ of **Ikuta Jinja.** According to legend, the shrine was founded by Empress Jingu in the 3rd century. Unfortunately, the earthquake completely shattered the torii and severely damaged the shrine. Plans, probably not to be executed until 1996 or 1997, are to build a replica of the original.

The road that runs up the right side of the shrine leads up the slope to Nakayamate-dori. Cross the avenue and continue up the slope.

Turn right at the corner of Yamamoto-dori, a road lined with high-fashion boutiques and restaurants. Turn left at Kitano-zaka, which leads
★ ❸ to **Kitano,** an area where Western traders and businessmen have been living since the late 19th century. The district is extremely popular with young Japanese tourists, who enjoy the rare opportunity of seeing old-fashioned Western houses (referred to in Kobe as *ijinkan),* which are rare in Japan. Many of the residences are still inhabited by Westerners, but some have been turned into museums. More than a dozen 19th-century Kitano residences are open to the public, and seeing all of them can get repetitious. A few are recommended here for those who are interested. Otherwise, you may simply enjoy a walk around the hills of this area while you admire the Victorian and Gothic architecture. Most of this area survived with only minor damage from the 1995 earthquake.

362

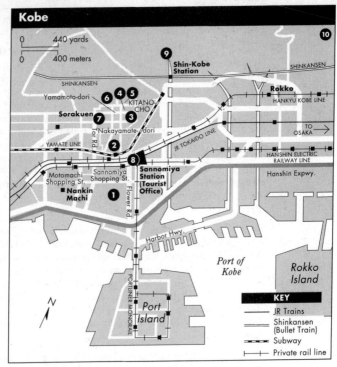

Those who want to see the interior of some of the buildings should continue up the slope from Nakayamate-dori. At the first intersection after Yamamoto-dori (nicknamed Ijinkan-dori), just past Rin's Gallery (filled with boutiques of Japan's top designers), turn right and walk

4 east to the **Eikokukan** (English House), constructed in 1907 by an English architect and then inhabited by another Englishman, one J.E. Baker. A private residence until 1979, Eikokukan is now open to the public. *2-3-16 Kitanomachi, Chuo-ku, Kobe-shi,* ☎ *078/241-2338.* ☞ *¥600.* ⊙ *Weekdays 9–5, weekends 9–5:15.*

5 Three of the ijinkan in the Kitano area are publicly owned and free of charge. The **Rhein-no-Yakata** (Rhine House), opposite the English House, has a pleasant German-style coffee shop inside. Near

6 Kitano Tenman Jinja at the top of the hill is the **Kazami-dori-no-Yakata** (Weathercock House), made famous on a national TV series some years ago. It is the most elaborate of Kobe's ijinkan, listed as an Important Cultural Property. Continue back down the slope via Kitano-zaka toward Sannomiya Station. One ijinkan house not to miss

7 is the **Chouéké Yashiki** (Chouéké Mansion), built in 1889. The only house still inhabited, it is filled to the rafters with turn-of-the-century memorabilia from East and West. Until the 1995 earthquake, Mrs. Chouéké was on hand to show you her treasures, which include a large number of *nanban* wood-block prints, and to share her vast knowledge of Kobe. At press time, however, Mrs. Chouéké was uncertain whether it was feasible to repair the structural damages to her home.

8 Return to Sannomiya Station and walk to the **Portliner** platform. This automatic monorail leaves every six minutes on its loop line around Port Island, with eight stops along the way. From the Portliner you get a close-up view of Kobe Harbor. Get off at Shimin Hiroba Station, right in the heart of a futuristic complex, with parks, hotels, restaurants, and fashion boutiques to explore. (Portliner round-trip fare: ¥480 adults, ¥240 children).

EXCURSIONS

Nunobiki Falls

⑨ A quiet side trip from the city is the 20-minute walk up the hill behind Shin-Kobe Station to **Nunobiki Falls,** whose beauty has been referred to in Japanese literature since the 10th century. It is actually a series of four cascades of varying heights, together described as one of the three greatest falls in Japan.

Mt. Rokko

⑩ **Mt. Rokko,** the highest peak of the Rokko Mountains, offers a magnificent view of the city and the Inland Sea. On top of the mountain are various recreational areas, including the oldest golf course in Japan (designed in 1903 by Englishman Arthur H. Gloom) and the summer homes of some of Kobe's wealthier residents. The most exciting view is probably from the cable car that runs up the mountain.

To get to Mt. Rokko, take the Hankyu Kobe Line from the JR Sannomiya Station to Rokko Station (cost: ¥160). From there, take either a taxi or a bus to Rokko Cableshita Station; a cable car travels from there up the mountain to Rokko-sanjo Station (cost: ¥560).

SHOPPING

Kobe is a shopper's paradise. Unlike Tokyo, Osaka, and other places in Japan where individual shops are scattered all over the city, most of the shopping districts in Kobe are in clusters, so you can visit numerous shops with great ease. The historic shopping area of Kobe is known as **Motomachi,** which extends for one mile between JR Motomachi Station and Daimaru department store. Most of the district is under a covered arcade, so even if the weather is inclement, you can wander around from shop to shop. You can purchase nearly anything in Motomachi, ranging from antiques to cameras to electronics. A favorite stop for many tourists is **Maruzen** (1-4-12 Motomachi-dori, Chuo-ku, tel. 078/391–6003) bookstore, right at the entrance on the Motomachi Station side of the arcade. This store has an excellent selection of books in English. At the opposite end of the arcade are two small shops that sell traditional Japanese goods. **Sakaeya** (8-5 Motomachi-dori 5-chome, Chuo-ku, ☎ 078/341–1307) specializes in Japanese dolls. **Naniwaya** (3-8 Motomachi-dori 4-chome, Chuo-ku, ☎ 078/341–6367) has an excellent selection of Japanese lacquerware at reasonable prices. Also try **Harishin** (3-10-3 Motomachi-dori, Chuo-ku, ☎ 078/331–2516) on the west end of the arcade for antiques.

Nearly connected to the Motomachi shopping arcade, and extending from the Sogo department store to the Motomachi area for half a mile, is **Sannomiya Center Gai** shopping arcade. This mall has fewer shops and more restaurants than the neighboring Motomachi. Because of its extremely convenient location right next to Sannomiya Station, this is a good place to have a quick bite to eat.

The famous pearl company **Tasaki Shinju** (Tasaki Bldg. 6-3-2 Minatojima Nakamachi, Chuo-ku, ☎ 078/302–3321), in Center Plaza across from Sannomiya Station, has a museum and demonstration hall along with its retail pearl shop.

The new **Santica Town** underground shopping mall, which runs for several blocks beneath Flower Road south from Sannomiya Station, has 120 shops and 30 restaurants. (Closed third Wed. of each month.)

Kobe's trendy crowd tends to shop in the many exclusive shops lining **Tor Road,** which extends from the north to the south of the city on a slope lined with trees. Fashionable boutiques featuring Japanese designers and imported goods alternate with chic cafés and restaurants.

DINING

Kobe beef is considered a delicacy all over Japan. Tender, tasty, and extremely expensive, it is a must for beef lovers. The beef is raised in the nearby Tajima area of Hyogo Prefecture. The cows are fed beer and are massaged to improve the quality of the meat and to give it its marbled texture. As a result, Kobe beef is rather high in fat content, which may disappoint lean-meat lovers.

Ethnic food fans will also appreciate the many international cuisines available in Kobe. Sailors passing through often stay on in Kobe, and some of them open restaurants that are popular not only with the large foreign community, but also with resident and visiting Japanese. The number of international restaurants is perhaps fewer than in Tokyo, but the quality and authenticity are unsurpassed. Simply walking around north of Sannomiya Station in the Kitano area, you are bound to come across restaurants representing nearly every cuisine imaginable. From the corner of Hanta-dori and Yamamoto-dori (also known as Ijinkan-dori), there are at least a dozen fine restaurants of every different cuisine imaginable—Italian, German, French, Swiss, Middle Eastern, Thai, American, and, of course, Japanese. Port Island has also begun to gain a reputation for its variety of good restaurants (look for these in the vicinity of the Portopia Hotel).

A 3% federal consumer tax is added to all restaurant bills. Another 3% local tax is added to the bill if it exceeds ¥7,500. At more expensive restaurants, a 10%–15% service charge is also added to the bill. Tipping is not necessary.

CATEGORY	COST*
$$$$	over ¥10,000
$$$	¥6,000–¥10,000
$$	¥3,500–¥6,000
$	under ¥3,500

Cost is per person without tax, service, or drinks

Kobe Beef

$$$$ **Aragawa.** Japan's first steak house is famed for its superb hand-fed
★ Kobe beef. The wood-paneled, chandeliered dining room has an old-country atmosphere. Aragawa serves melt-in-your-mouth *sumiyaki*

(charcoal broiled) steak that is worth its weight in yen—an evening here is the ultimate splurge, but this is considered *the* place for Kobe beef as it should be, at ¥20,000. ✗ *2-15-18 Nakayamate-dori, Chuo-ku,* ☎ *078/221–8547. Reservations advised. Jacket and tie. AE, DC, MC, V.* ✆ *Noon–3 and 5–10.*

$$$ **Highway.** This small and exclusive restaurant has a reputation for serving fine Kobe beef. The quality of the meat is extraordinary. ✗ *13-7 Shimoyamate-dori 2-chome, Chuo-ku,* ☎ *078/331–7622. Reservations advised.* ✆ *11–9. No credit cards. Closed Mon.*

$$ **A-1.** This is one of the only steak restaurants among many in the neighborhood north of Hankyu Sannomiya Station that serve prime Kobe beef at anywhere near affordable prices. The *teppan*-style steak is served on a hot grill with a special spice and wine marinade that is as memorable as the garlic and crisp fried potatoes. Right across from the Washington Hotel, A-1 has a relaxed and friendly atmosphere. ✗ *Amashi-biru 2F, 2-2-9 Shimoyamate-dori, Chuo-ku,* ☎ *078/331– 8676. Reservations advised. No credit cards.* ✆ *3–11 pm. Closed Tues.*

International

$$$ **Totenkaku.** This establishment has been famous among Kobe residents since 1945 for its Peking duck, flown in fresh from China. The building itself is worth the splurge—built at the turn of the century, it is one of Kobe's ijinkan, the F. Bishop House. You can keep the price down by ordering one of the Chinese noodle specialties to fill yourself up. ✗ *3-14-18 Yamamoto-dori, Chuo-ku,* ☎ *078/231– 1351. Reservations advised. DC, V.* ✆ *11:30–9, closed weekdays 2–5.*

$$ **Gaylord.** Just a few minutes' walk from Sannomiya Station, this Indian restaurant, with a flashy decor, is a favorite with Kobe's foreign residents. The curries are on the mild side but are very tasty. ✗ *Meiji Seimei Bldg. B1, 8-3-7 Isogami-dori, Chuo-ku,* ☎ *078/251–4359. AE, DC, MC, V.* ✆ *Lunch 11:30–2:30, dinner 5–9:30.*

$$ **King's Arms.** Famous for its excellent platter of roast beef and its traditional British atmosphere, the old King's Arms pub has become a Kobe landmark. A portrait of Sir Winston Churchill still presides over the old wooden bar that some 40 years ago was the exclusive territory of some of Kobe's thirstiest Englishmen. The clientele have increased in number and kind, but the flavor of the legendary roast beef, the finest Scotch whiskey, and the seriousness of the annual dart tournament haven't changed. ✗ *4-2-15 Isobe-dori, Chuo-ku,* ☎ *078/221–3774. Dinner reservations advised. AE, DC, MC, V.* ✆ *11:30–9.*

$$ **Marrakech.** Elmaleh Simon, a former sailor and the Moroccan chef/owner of this restaurant, and his wife serve excellent Middle Eastern food. In this cozy little basement dining spot, it is easy to forget that you are in Japan. The couscous and kabobs are particularly delicious, and portions are generous. ✗ *Maison de Yamate B1, 1-20- 15 Nakayamate-dori, Chuo-ku, Kobe-shi,* ☎ *078/241–3440. Reservations advised. AE, V.* ✆ *5–11 (last order at 10:30). Closed Mon.*

$$ **Rote Rose.** A block east of the Kobe Club on the west end of Kitano, this restaurant is owned by a wine importer and is most famous for its wine list, with over 180 selections of fine German wines. To sample them, order the six-glass flight. Although Rote Rose has long been known as a family-style German pub, it now serves a range of European dishes, including French sausage and *tournedos aux*

champignon. ✕ *9-14 Yonchome, Kitanocho, Chuo-ku,* ☎ *078/222–3200.Reservations advised on weekends. AE, V.* ◷ *11–2:30 and 5–9:30. Closed Wed.*

$$ **Salaam.** A light and airy restaurant with potted palms and white walls,
★ Salaam credits itself with being the first Middle Eastern restaurant in Japan. It has a very complete menu with a variety of pickles, desserts, and main courses, such as kabobs, grilled seafood, and lamb. If you find the selection overwhelming, try the special dinners, in which you get a little of everything. Finish off your meal with refreshing hot mint tea and a piece of baklava. ✕ *Ijin Plaza Bldg., 2F, 12-21 Yamamoto-dori 2-chome, Chuo-ku,* ☎ *078/222–1780. Reservations advised. AE, V.* ◷ *Lunch 11:30–2:30 (Sat. and Sun. only), dinner 5–10.*

$$ **Wakkoku.** If you want to try the world-famous Kobe beef without spending a bundle, come to this smart but plain restaurant on the third floor of the shopping plaza adjacent to the Oriental Hotel and across from the Shinkansen station. Don't be distracted by the other restaurants on this floor; Wakkoku is the best choice. Lunchtime prices are lower than dinner—count on ¥3,000 for Kobe beef. ✕ *Shin-Kobe Oriental Park Avenue, Shin-Kobe,* ☎ *078/262–2838. AE, DC, V.* ◷ *11–11.*

$ **Attic.** Several years ago, former U.S. baseball player Marty Kuehnert opened this little haven for ballpark refugees and beer lovers of all sorts. Along with the Budweiser, Marty brought pizza, fried chicken, roast beef, and American-style fun to Kobe—complete with jukeboxes and peanut shells. ✕ *Ijinkan Club Bldg. 3F, 4-1-12 Kitanocho, Chuo-ku,* ☎ *078/222–1586 or 222–5368. AE, DC, MC, V.* ◷ *6–2. Closed Tues.*

$ **Raja.** A former chef of Gaylord (*see above*) opened this small, unas-
★ suming place near Motomachi Station. Raja features home-style Indian cooking, with spicy and tasty curries and excellent saffron rice. ✕ *Sanonatsu Bldg. B1, Sakaemachi 2-chome, Chuo-ku,* ☎ *078/332–5253. AE, D, V.* ◷ *Lunch 11:30–2:30, dinner 5–9.*

$ **Wang Thai.** This is one of the few Thai restaurants in the area; it fea-
★ tures a menu with hot Thai and slightly less spicy Chinese dishes. ✕ *Chuo-ku, President Arcade 2F, 14-22 Yamamoto-dori 2-chome,* ☎ *078/222–2507. No credit cards.* ◷ *Lunch 11–2:30, dinner 5:30–9:30. Closed Wed.*

LODGING

Kobe has a wide range of hotels varying in price and quality. Because it is a heavily industrialized city, Kobe caters to a lot of business travelers. As a result, the business hotels are conveniently located, and most are quite comfortable.

A 3% federal consumer tax is added to all hotel bills. Another 3% local tax is added to the bill if it exceeds ¥15,000. At most hotels, a 10%–15% service charge is added to the total bill. Tipping is not necessary. The postal code for Kobe is 650.

CATEGORY	COST*
$$$$	over ¥20,000
$$$	¥15,000–¥20,000
$$	¥10,000–¥15,000
$	under ¥10,000

*Cost is for double room, without tax or service

$$$$ **Hotel Okura Kobe.** This 35-story hotel on the wharf in Meriken Park
★ is Kobe's finest. Beautifully furnished and fully equipped for the
business traveler, the Okura Kobe lives up to the Okura Hotel chain's
worldwide reputation for excellence. Room interiors were done by
British designer David Hicks, who designs for the royal family. The
hotel has a well-equipped health club with pool and gym, stunning
views of the bay from the Emerald Restaurant, and a hotel shuttle
bus to Sannomiya Station. ☎ *Meriken Koen, 2-1 Hatobacho, Chuo-
ku, Kobe-shi,* ☎ *078/333–0111,* ℻ *078/333–6673. 472 rooms. 5
restaurants, 2 bars, coffee shop, health club, business services. AE,
DC, MC, V.*

$$$$ **Kobe Portopia Hotel.** Situated on Port Island, the Portopia is a dazzling modern hotel with every facility imaginable. The spacious
rooms look over the port. The restaurants and lounges on the top
floors of the hotel have spectacular panoramic views of Mt. Rokko
and Osaka Bay. Because of its location, this hotel can only be reached
by the Portliner monorail or by taxi. This inconvenience is counter-
balanced by the fact that everything from food to clothing is available inside the hotel. ☎ *6-10-1 Minatojima Nakamachi, Chuo-ku,
Kobe-shi,* ☎ *078/302–0111,* ℻ *078/302–6877. 761 rooms. Chinese,
Japanese, and French restaurants, coffee shops, beauty salon, indoor
and outdoor pools, gym, sauna, tennis courts, shops. AE, DC,
MC, V.*

$$$$ **Shin-Kobe Oriental Hotel.** The tallest building in western Japan, this
luxury hotel faces the JR Shin-Kobe Station, where the Shinkansen arrives, three minutes from downtown by subway. Guest rooms, with
marble-tile bathrooms, are relatively small but neatly decorated in
pastel fabrics and furnished with a desk, a coffee table, and two easy
chairs. ☎ *Kitanocho 1-chome, Chuo-ku, Kobe-shi,* ☎ *078/291–1121,*
℻ *078/291–1154. 600 rooms. French, Chinese, Japanese, steak, and
sushi restaurants, beauty salon, indoor pool, sauna, gym, shops. AE,
DC, MC, V.*

$$$ **Hotel Monterey.** Not far from Sannomiya Station, this little hotel
takes you off the busy streets and into old Italy, with its marvelous
Mediterranean-style courtyard fountains and European furnishings.
Despite being modeled after a monastery in Florence, the Monterey
has modern features that most hotels in Japan lack, such as a fitness
room, Jacuzzi, and pool (available to guests at a slight additional charge).
Though the twin rooms are standard, the duplex (maisonette) rooms
with the carpeted bedroom upstairs also have a small lounge area with
a tiled floor. Both the Italian and Japanese restaurants on the premises
are charming. ☎ *2-11-13 Shimoyamate-dori, Chuo-ku, Kobe-shi,* ☎
*078/392–7111. 164 rooms. Restaurants, bar, gym, pool. AE, DC,
MC, V.*

$$$ **Sannomiya Terminal Hotel.** Located in the terminal building above the
★ JR Sannomiya Station, this hotel is extremely convenient, particularly
for anyone who has to catch an early train. The rooms are large for
this price range, and are clean and pleasant. Damages incurred during
the 1995 earthquake should be fully repaired by the beginning of
1996. ☎ *8 Kumoi-dori, Chuo-ku, Kobe-shi,* ☎ *078/291–0001,* ℻
*078/291–0020. 190 rooms. French, Japanese, and Chinese restau-
rants. AE, DC, MC, V.*

$$ **Arcons.** You'll need a taxi to get here from Sannomiya Station, because
it's up on the hill in Kitanocho, in the heart of the Ijinkan district. Many
of the immaculate rooms at this little white hotel have a view out over
the city to the sea. There's patio dining at the first-floor café when the
weather is good. At press time the hotel was closed for renovation in
the wake of the earthquake but was expected to reopen by early 1996.

⌂ *3-7-1 Kitanocho, Chuo-ku,* ☎ *078/231–1538. 22 rooms. Café. AE, DC, V.*

$$ **Kobe Gajoen Hotel.** This delightful hotel is a change from the modern, impersonal hotels that flourish in Japan. Although it is distinctly Japanese, with delicate cuisine served in a dining room paneled with decorated screens and a staff that bows to guests, the hotel has European furnishings, reminders of the time when Kobe was a major port for Western traders. Close to downtown, it is a couple of minutes' walk from the west exit of the Hanaku-mae Station on the Hankyu Line. ⌂ *8-4-23 Shimoyamate-dori, Chuo-ku, Kobe-shi,* ☎ *078/341–0301,* FAX *078/341–0353. 52 Western-style rooms. Restaurant. AE, DC, MC, V.*

$ **Union Hotel.** The most attractive feature of this business hotel, a short walk from Sannomiya Station, is its low rates. A 24-hour convenience store is right next door, which comes in handy for midnight snacks. ⌂ *1-9 Nunobikicho 2-chome, Chuo-ku, Kobe-shi,* ☎ *078/222–6500. 167 rooms. Western restaurant. AE, DC, MC, V.*

KOBE ESSENTIALS

Arriving and Departing

By Plane

The airport for Kobe is the new Kansai International Airport (KIX— *see* Osaka Essentials *in* Chapter 8), which handles the region's international flights as well as some domestic flights to Japan's larger cities. The majority of domestic flights, however, still fly out of Osaka's Itami Airport, approximately 40 minutes away.

BETWEEN THE AIRPORTS AND CENTER CITY
KIX is accessible either by train from Kobe's JR Sannomiya Station for a 70-minute run (cost: ¥1,800) or by boat from Kobe City Air Terminal (K-CAT), which takes 30 minutes (cost: ¥2,650). From Itami Airport, an airport bus to Kobe Sannomiya Station (Kobe's main train station) leaves from the domestic terminal's main entrance and from a stop between the domestic and international terminals approximately every 20 minutes, 7 AM–10 PM. The trip takes about 40 minutes and costs ¥940.

Because public transportation is excellent, a taxi is not a practical alternative for getting into Kobe from the airport.

By Train

Japan Railways offers frequent Shinkansen Super Express service between Tokyo and Shin-Kobe Station. From Tokyo, the trip to Kobe takes about three hours, 30 minutes (cost: ¥14,000). The trip between Osaka Station and Kobe's Sannomiya Station takes 30 minutes on the JR Tokaido Line Rapid Train, which leaves at 15-minute intervals throughout the day (cost: ¥390). Japan Rail Passes may be used for these trains.

Two other private lines, the Hankyu and Hanshin lines, offer service between Osaka and Kobe for ¥280.

Getting Around

By Train

Within Kobe, Japan Railways and the Hankyu and Hanshin lines run parallel from east to west and are easy to negotiate. Sannomiya and Motomachi are the principal downtown stations. Tickets are purchased from a vending machine and surrendered upon leaving the train. Fares depend upon your destination.

The city's subway system runs from Shin-Kobe Station west to the outskirts of town. Fares start at ¥160 and are determined by destination. A ride between Sannomiya Station and Shin-Kobe Station costs ¥180.

By Bus

The city bus service is frequent and efficient, though it might be somewhat confusing to a first-time visitor. At each bus stop, you will find a pole that displays a route chart of official stops. Enter at the rear or center of the bus; pay your fare as you leave at the front (cost: ¥180 adults; ¥90 children, regardless of the distance). Exact change is needed. A special city loop bus stops at 15 major sights on its 12½-kilometer (7½-mile), 80-minute run between Nakatottei Pier and Shin-Kobe. The buses operate at 16- to 20-minute intervals and cost ¥250 per ride or ¥650 for a day pass, which may be purchased on the bus. (There are signs along the route that read, in English, "Loop Bus," indicating stops.)

By Taxi

Taxis are plentiful and can be hailed on the street or at taxi stands. The fare starts at ¥580 for the first 2 kilometers and goes up ¥90 for each additional 380 meters.

By Portliner

The Portliner is a computerized monorail that services Port Island. The monorail central station is connected to the JR Sannomiya Station; the ride from the station to Port Island takes about 10 minutes (round-trip cost: ¥480 adults, ¥240 children).

Guided Tours

Between March 21 and November 30, the City Transport Bureau offers several half-day tours of major attractions in the city and surrounding areas. Although the tours are conducted in Japanese, they do give you a satisfactory overview of Kobe. Itineraries vary, depending upon the day of the week. The buses depart from the south side of the Kobe Kotsu Center Building, near Sannomiya Station (cost: ¥2,500–¥3,000 adults, ¥1,200–¥1,500 children). Tickets and information can be obtained at the **Shinai Teiki Kanko Annaisho** (Sightseeing Bus Tour Information Office) on the second floor of the Kobe Kotsu Center Building (☎ 078/391–4755).

A series of sightseeing tours is also offered by authorized taxi services. The tours cover 11 different routes and range in time from two to five hours (cost: ¥4,200 per hour). The taxi tours can be reserved at the Kobe Tourist Information Center (☎ 078/271–2401).

Important Addresses and Numbers

Emergencies

Police, ☎ 110; **Ambulance,** ☎ 119.

DOCTORS

Kobe Adventist Hospital (4-1 Arinodai 8-chome, Kita-ku, ☎ 078/981–0161); **Kobe Kaisei Hospital** (3-11-15 Shinohara-Kitamachi, Nada-ku, ☎ 078/871–5201).

PHARMACIES

The **Daimaru Department Store** (40 Akashicho, Chuo-ku, ☎ 078/331–8121), a three-minute walk from the JR Motomachi Station, has a pharmacy.

Tourist Information

The **Kobe Information Center** (078/322–0220), on the west side of the JR Sannomiya Station, is open daily 9–5:30. Here you can pick up a free detailed map of the city in English. The Tourist Information Center has branches at the JR Kobe Station (☎ 078/341–5277) and Shin-Kobe Station (☎ 078/241–9550), both open daily 10–6.

The **Japan Travel Phone** (☎ 0120/444–800) provides free information in English on Kobe and other points in western Japan daily 9–5.

Consulates

The closest U.S., U.K., and Canadian consulates are in Osaka (*see* Chapter 8).

English-Language Bookstores

Bunyodo (Kobe Kokusai Kaikan 1st fl., 1-6 Goko-dori 8-chome, Chuo-ku, ☎ 078/221–0557); **Maruzen** (1-4-12 Motomachi-dori, Chuo-ku, ☎ 078/391–6003).

Travel Agencies

Japan Travel Bureau, JR Sannomiya Station (☎ 078/231–4118).

10 Western Honshu

The western side of Japan's main island is home to a number of attractive cities, most notably Kurashiki, a charming town in which old Japan can be truly savored; Hiroshima, where the half-shattered building renamed the A-bomb Dome stands as a powerful reminder of one of the world's greatest tragedies; and Miyajima, a small island in the Inland Sea that is home to Itsukushima Shrine, with its vermilion gate rising strikingly out of the water.

WESTERN HONSHU IS SPLIT through the center by mountains that run east to west. On either side of this split are two distinct regions. The south side of the mountains, facing the Inland Sea, is referred to as the Sanyo region (Mountains in the Sun). The north side of Western Honshu, which faces the Sea of Japan, is called San'in (In the Shadow of the Mountains). From these descriptive names you might think that Sanyo is the more attractive of the two regions, but the southern coast, the route that the JR Shinkansen travels from Osaka to Hakata (on Kyushu), is heavily industrialized and visually, if not environmentally, polluted. The San'in coast, on the other hand, has so far escaped the onslaught of fabricated buildings of Japan's economic miracle and retains its identity as a more traditional Japan.

By Nigel Fisher

This chapter sketches an itinerary from Osaka down the Sanyo coast, stopping at Himeji, Okayama, Kurashiki, Hiroshima, and Miyajima before reaching Honshu's westernmost point, Shimonoseki. Then we return to Kyoto (or Osaka) by traveling through San'in. Only a few places are mentioned in San'in, namely, Hagi, Tsuwano, Matsue, Tottori Dunes, and Ama-no-hashidate, but, for the intrepid traveler, much more is left to explore.

THE SANYO REGION

Though the Sanyo region faces the Seto Inland Sea (Setonaikai), only glimpses of water are seen from the train traveling from Osaka to Shimonoseki. Most of the coastal plain is heavily industrialized all the way to Hiroshima. Only from there, until the outskirts of Shimonoseki, does the postwar grayness diminish and open country begin. Furthermore, because the main Sanyo railway line is away from the coast, you must take a cruise or visit the islands to fully absorb the serenity of the Inland Sea. There are, for example, several day-cruises from Hiroshima, and you can travel the length of the Inland Sea by ferries that ply the waters between Osaka and Beppu, on Kyushu. In this chapter we'll take you on one short trip to Miyajima, one of the most beautiful (though unfortunately tourist-filled) islands. (In the following chapter, on Shikoku, we suggest an excursion from Takamatsu to Shodo Island, the second-largest island in the Inland Sea.)

Getting Around

Except for crossing over to Miyajima island, a 22-minute ferry ride from near Hiroshima, all of the following itineraries through the Sanyo region use JR trains, either the Shinkansen or the local commuter and express trains. Explanations of which trains to take between destinations are given throughout the Exploring section. Essentially, though, the itinerary follows the main trunk railway line along the southern shore of Western Honshu, and it is simply a matter of hopping on and off the trains plying between Osaka and Hakata. Local buses or streetcars are used in the major cities. Driving your own rented car is not recommended. The roads are congested in urban areas, tolls are costly, and travel by train is usually not only faster but also less expensive.

Himeji

Numbers in the margin correspond to points of interest on the Western Honshu map.

The sight of Himeji's castle commands the visitor's attention from the moment the train pulls into the town's station. Himejijo is the grandest and most attractive of Japan's 12 surviving feudal castles. Also known as Shirasagijo (White Egret Castle), it stands on a 150-foot-high bluff and dominates the city.

Arriving and Departing

The city of Himeji is on the JR Shinkansen Line, with trains arriving and departing every 15 minutes during the day. The train journey to Himeji is three hours, 52 minutes from Tokyo; 59 minutes from Kyoto; and 42 minutes from Shin-Osaka. The Shinkansen to Okayama (the next destination to the west on this itinerary) arrives and departs every hour during the day.

Exploring

➊ Himeji was severely damaged in World War II and retains little to interest the foreigner. However, the castle miraculously escaped the air attacks, and, because of the frequent train service, it is easy to disembark one train, visit the castle, and reboard another train two hours later. From the central exit (north) of the JR Himeji Station, the castle is a 15-minute walk or a five-minute bus ride (fare: ¥160); the bus departs from the station plaza, on your left as you exit. There is a Tourist Information Office (☎ 0792/85–3792) to the right of the station's north exit.

★ The present structure of **Himejijo** took eight years to build and was completed in 1609. Ieyasu Tokugawa had given his son-in-law the surrounding province as a reward for his victory at the Battle of Sekigahara, and this magnificent castle was built to isolate the Osaka *daimyo* (lord) from his friends in the Western provinces. So, the castle was built not only as a military stronghold but also as an expression of Tokugawa power.

The five-story, six-floor, main donjon (stronghold) stands 102 feet high and is built into a 50-foot-high stone foundation. Surrounding this main donjon are three lesser ones; all four are connected by covered passageways. This area was the central compound of the castle complex. There were also other compounds to the south and west. Enemies would therefore have to scale the bluff, cross three moats, breach the outer compounds, and then be raked by fire from the four donjons. The castle existed not only to maintain military control over the Hyogo province but was also meant to impress. Note the aesthetic qualities of the donjon's dormerlike windows, cusped gables, and walls finished with white plaster, displaying a stark power that still inspires awe. From a distance, this white vision has the grace and steadiness of an egret—hence the castle's nickname, White Egret. Japanese filmmaker Akira Kurosawa used Himejijo's exterior and the castle's grounds in his 1985 movie *Ran* (interior shots were filmed in a studio set). ☛ *¥500.* ☉ *Daily 9–5 (grounds open to 6).*

The next stop along the Shinkansen Line is Okayama, a stop for garden lovers. (For anyone anxious to experience the Inland Sea, five ferries a day leave Himeji Port for Shodo Island. The one-hour, 40-minute trip costs ¥1,170; however, there are shorter sea crossings to the island from Okayama.)

Okayama

The three most famous gardens in Japan are Kenrokuen in Kanazawa, **➋** Kairakuen in Mito, and Korakuen in **Okayama.** Recently, Okayama has become quite cosmopolitan, attracting students from overseas. It

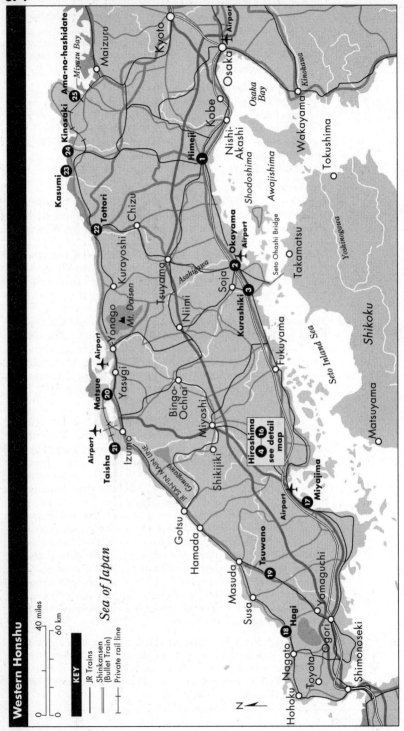

Western Honshu

KEY

— JR Trains
═ Shinkansen (Bullet Train)
┼ Private rail line

0 ────── 40 miles
0 ────── 60 km

Sea of Japan

Santo-in Main Line

Hohoku
Toyota
Nagato
Susa
Masuda
Hamada
Gotsu
Shikiiki
Miyoshi
Bingo-Ochiai
Yasugi
Matsue
Izumo
Taisha
Shimonoseki
Ogori
Yamaguchi
Tsuwano
Miyajima
Hiroshima
see detail map
Fukuyama
Kurashiki
Soja
Niimi
Tsuyama
Yonago
Mt. Daisen
Kurayoshi
Chizu
Tottori
Kasumi
Kinosaki
Ama-no-hashidate
Maizuru
Miyazu Bay
Kyoto
Osaka
Kobe
Himeji
Nishi-Akashi
Okayama
Airport
Seto Ohashi Bridge
Takamatsu
Shodoshima
Awajishima
Osaka Bay
Wakayama
Tokushima
Yoshinogawa
Shikoku
Matsuyama
Matsuyama
Seto Inland Sea
Kinokawa
Asahigawa
Gonogawa

18 Hagi
19 Tsuwano
20 Matsue
21 Izumo
22 Tottori
23 Kasumi
24 Kinosaki
25 Ama-no-hashidate
1 Himeji
2 Okayama
3 Kurashiki
4 to **16** Hiroshima
17 Miyajima

Airport

N

is also the best departure point for Shodo Island for anyone coming from Osaka or Hiroshima. Twenty-three ferries a day make the 40-minute run from Okayama Port to the island. To make the 45-minute trip to Okayama Port from the JR Okayama train station, take Bus 12. Because Okayama is only 35 minutes down the Shinkansen Line from Himeji, and because you will need to change from the Shinkansen to a local train at Okayama in order to travel to Kurashiki, the next destination on our itinerary, it is convenient to stop and visit the gardens as well as Okayama castle, which you can compare with Hime-jijo. If your time is limited, it is best to skip Okayama and go directly to Kurashiki.

Exploring

Should you need a map or information on the city, there is a **Tourist Information Office** (☎ 0862/22–2912; ⊙ 8:30–8) in the JR station. However, the layout of the city is easy to follow. Just hop on board the streetcar (fare: ¥150) bound for Higashiyama in front of the JR station and go directly north for 10 minutes. Get out at the **Orient Bijutsukan** (Museum of Near Eastern Art), recognizable by its resemblance to Athens's Parthenon. If you have the time, you may want to go inside to see the 2,000 items of Asian art on display. It was one of the first museums in Japan to devote its collection to Asian art and has special exhibits showing how Middle Eastern art reached Japan via the Silk Route. ☛ ¥300. ⊙ Daily 9–5.

At the Orient Bijutsukan, the streetcar turns right. Korakuen, however, is straight ahead on the other side of the Asahigawa (about a 10-min. walk). If you do not want to visit the museum, you may choose to take a bus for ¥150 from Platform 2 in front of the station; this bus goes directly to Korakuen.

Laid out three centuries ago on the banks of the Asahigawa, **Korakuen** is a stroller's garden, with rustic tea arbors, extensive lawns, ponds, and artificial hills. The maple trees, apricot trees, and cherry trees give the 28 acres a seasonal contrast. Despite the garden's emphasis on the harmony of its elements, it is not astounding in its beauty (and it can get quite crowded). The garden is appreciated for its wide expanse of lawns, a rare commodity in Japan but less of a novelty to Westerners. What is attractive, though, is the garden's setting along the banks of the Asahigawa, against the backdrop of Okayama Castle, which seems to float above the garden. ☛ ¥300. ⊙ Daily, Apr.–Sept., 7:30–6; Oct.–Mar. 8–5.

It takes less than five minutes to walk from the south exit of Korakuen to **Okayamajo.** Painted black, the four-story castle is known as Ujo (Crow Castle). Okayama's castle was first built in 1573, but, except for the turrets, it fell victim to the bombs of World War II. A ferro-concrete replica was constructed in 1966 and now houses objects of the region's history, including the usual collection of armor and swords. There is also, as behooves its modern construction, an elevator to take you between floors. ☛ ¥250. ⊙ Daily 9–5.

Aside from visiting Korakuen, the castle, and, perhaps, the Orient Bijutsukan, the other reason for disembarking from the Shinkansen at Okayama is to change to the local JR train for Kurashiki.

Kurashiki

★ ❸ **Kurashiki** is a town in which to savor old Japan. During feudal times, merchants shipped rice and cotton from its port to Osaka. No longer a granary or textile town, Kurashiki has become a living museum of the past, surviving on the income produced by some 4 million visitors a year. Miraculously, Kurashiki escaped war damage and the wrecker's ball that has so often preceded Japan's industrial growth.

Arriving and Departing

Commuter trains depart frequently from JR Okayama Station and take approximately 15 minutes to reach Kurashiki Station (not Shin-Kurashiki, where the Shinkansen trains stop). If you are coming directly from Tokyo, Kyoto, or Osaka, you may wish to stay on the Shinkansen until Shin-Kurashiki and take the local train back to the Kurashiki Station. For those arriving at the Shin-Kurashiki Station, there is a small and friendly tourist office (☎ 084/546–8446, ◷ daily 9–6) with maps, advice, and the offer to make accommodation reservations. At the JR Kurashiki Station there is a **Tourist Information Office** (☎ 086/426–8681) opposite the entrance to the train platforms. The main tourist office (Kurashikikan, Bikan Historical Area, ☎ 086/422–0542) is in the center of the old town. Both offices are open daily 9–5. If you telephone the day before, the main office can arrange for a volunteer guide to show you the city. The center of the old town is a 10-minute walk from the station and can be reached by going down the main avenue extending perpendicular (southeast) from the station; turn left at the street before the Kurashiki Kokusai Hotel.

Exploring

Though you can tour Kurashiki in half a day, the ideal way to enjoy this traditional town is to arrive in the late afternoon and stay the night in a ryokan. Being in Kurashiki on a Monday has an advantage and disadvantage; most of the museums are closed, but for that reason, there are fewer visitors in town.

Amid the industrialized Sanyo coastal plains, Kurashiki is an oasis of traditional Japanese culture. There are several museums to visit, but, in fact, all of the old town resembles a museum. The curving tiled roofs of the houses, the swaying willows lining the canal, and the stone half-circle bridges from which to watch the white swans float by transport the visitor back in time.

The major museum is the **Ohara Bijutsukan** (art museum), in the old town. Magosaburo Ohara built this Greek pantheon-type building to house a collection of art that includes works by El Greco, including the Annunciation, Corot, Rodin, Gauguin, Picasso, Toulouse-Lautrec, and many other Western artists. To counter this preponderance of Western art, an additional wing was constructed in 1961 for modern Japanese paintings and, more recently, tapestries, wood-block prints, pottery, and antiques. ☛ ¥800. ◷ *Tues.–Sun. 9–4:30. Closed Dec. 28–Jan. 3. When Mon. falls on a public holiday, the museum stays open.*

More Western art, this time Greek and Roman sculpture, may be seen two minutes away at the **Kurashiki Ninagawa Bijutsukan** (☛ ¥800; ◷ daily 8:30–5). Around the corner from this museum (next to the tourist office) and of more interest to the foreign visitor is the **Kurashiki Mingeikan** (Kurashiki Folkcraft Museum). In four converted granaries, still with their white walls and black-tile roofs of the Edo period, are some 4,000 folkcraft objects including ceramics, rugs, wooden carvings, and bamboo wares from all over the world. This museum can be disappointing to some; the displays are dusty and not very well lit, and the descriptions of objects are in Japanese. Still, the experience of taking off your shoes and walking in slippers on the wooden floors gives the willing viewer the appropriate context for this art. ☛ ¥500. ◷

Tues.–Sun. 9–4. Closed Dec. 28–Jan. 3. When Mon. falls on a public holiday, the museum stays open.

Next door to the Folkcraft Museum is the **Nihon Kyodo Gangukan** (Japan Rural Toy Museum), one of the two top toy museums in Japan, and a pure delight. It exhibits some 5,000 toys from all regions of the country and has one room devoted to foreign toys. ☛ ¥310. ☻ *Daily 8–5. Closed Jan. 1.*

TIME OUT Before leaving this cluster of museums, you may care to drop into the famous **El Greco** coffeehouse (next to the Ohara Bijutsukan). It has scrumptious ice cream, milk shakes, cakes, and other Western temptations.

All of these museums are clustered together on the north bank of the Kurashiki River. Now cross over the bridge, and in less than five minutes you will reach **Ivy Square,** an ivy-covered complex that used to be a weaving mill. With artful renovation, it now contains a hotel (aptly named Ivy Hotel), several boutiques, a restaurant, and, in the central courtyard, a summer beer garden. The courtyard and beer garden are popular rendezvous points in the early evening, when locals and tourists gather for refreshment. Be sure to browse through the shop that sells Japanese textiles, pottery, and other crafts.

Three museums can be found in the complex, though only one is of any real interest: **Kurabo Memorial Hall** retells the history of spinning and textiles, an industry that, along with the shipping of rice and cotton, was a major source of income for Kurashiki. In many ways it is a museum of Japan's industrial revolution, and it includes a video of the factory workshop floor, the dormitory that housed its unmarried female employees (☛ ¥300; ☻ Daily 9–5). The other two museums are the **Torajiro Kajima Memorial Museum,** which has Western and Asian art, and the **Ivy Gakkan,** which is an educational museum using reproductions to explain Western art to the Japanese. ☛ *¥500 covers all 3 museums.* ☻ *Tues.–Sun. 8:30–5.*

For many of us, the real pleasure of Kurashiki is not the museums, but rather the ambience of the old town. Even the tourist hordes don't destroy it, but you should try to rise early in the morning to stroll through the old neighborhood and catch the pink glow of the early-morning light dancing off the buildings, the waterways crossed by arched bridges, and the willows lining the streets.

The next stop down the Sanyo Line is Hiroshima, a city destroyed in the deepest sense and energetically rebuilt—a world away from Kurashiki.

Hiroshima

❹ **Hiroshima** will forever be etched in the collective conscience as the first city to suffer atomic destruction. No visitor can fail to be acutely aware of the event, which took place at 8:15 AM, August 6, 1945. On that morning, three B-29s flew toward Hiroshima; two planes were decoys, but one flew directly over the city and cut loose a single four-ton bomb, code-named Little Boy. The bomb exploded at 1,900 feet above the Industrial Promotion Hall, in the center of the city. Two hundred thousand people died, including 10,000 Korean prisoners forced to serve the Japanese empire as slave laborers. The only bomb to land on Hiroshima during World War II, it wiped out half the city.

Only one obvious reminder remains from the havoc and death wrought by the atomic bomb. Miraculously, the Industrial Promotion Hall did not completely collapse; its charred structure remains untouched since that fated morning. It has been renamed the A-Bomb Dome and stands surrounded by the rebuilt city of ferro-concrete buildings.

Arriving and Departing

By Plane. Seven daily flights run between Hiroshima and Tokyo's Haneda Airport, and there are flights to Kagoshima, on Kyushu, and Sapporo, on Hokkaido.

By Train. Hiroshima is the major city in Western Honshu and a major terminal for the JR Shinkansen trains; several Shinkansen trains end their runs at Hiroshima rather than continue to Hakata, on Kyushu. During the day, Shinkansen trains arrive and depart for Okayama, Osaka, Kyoto, and Tokyo approximately every 30 minutes and about every hour for Hakata, on Kyushu. From Tokyo, train time is four hours and 37 minutes and, unless you have a Japan Rail Pass, the fare is ¥17,700. The Hiroshima train station also serves as the hub for JR express and local trains traveling along the Sanyo Line. The train ride from Kurashiki is only an hour if you take the local JR train to Shin-Kurashiki (2 stops) and transfer onto the Shinkansen rather than double back to Okayama. There are also two trains a day that link Hiroshima to Matsue on the northern shore (the Sea of Japan coast) of Western Honshu.

By Ferry. Hiroshima is serviced by many ferries. Two important ones are: to and from Matsuyama, on Shikoku (16 hydrofoil ferries a day that take 1 hr. at ¥5,700 and 11 regular ferries a day that take 3 hrs. at ¥4,260 for 1st class and ¥2,130 for 2nd class); and to and from Beppu, on Kyushu (departs Hiroshima at 10:30 PM to arrive in Beppu at 6 AM and departs Beppu at 4 PM to arrive in Hiroshima at 10 PM at ¥4,200 to ¥11,020). *Contact the Setonaikai Kisen Co., 12–23, Ujinakaigan 1-chome, Minami-ku, Hiroshima City,* ☎ *082/253–1212,* ℻ *082/22–4178.*

Getting Around

There are two **Tourist Information offices** at JR Hiroshima Station: one at the south exit (☎ 082/261–1877), the exit for downtown, and one at the north exit (☎ 082/263–6822), the exit for the Shinkansen. Both provide free maps and brochures as well as help in securing accommodations. There is also the main office, **Hiroshima City Tourist Information,** in the Peace Memorial Park (☎ 082/247–6738).

The streetcar (tram) is the easiest form of transport in Hiroshima. Enter the tram from its middle door and take a ticket. Pay the driver at the front door when you leave. All fares within the city limits are ¥130. A one-day pass is ¥600, available for purchase at the platform outside the JR Hiroshima Station. There are seven streetcar lines, and four of them either depart from Hiroshima Station or make it their terminus. Stops are announced by a tape recording, and each stop has a *romaji* sign (spelled with roman letters) posted on the platform. Buses also ply Hiroshima's streets; the basic fare is ¥170.

Taxis are available throughout the city. The initial fare for small taxis is ¥560 for the first 1½ kilometers (¥620 for larger taxis), then ¥70 for every 365 meters. There are also sightseeing taxis; for a three-hour tour, the charge is approximately ¥14,200. Because the taxi driver is not a guide, you should rent a taped recording describing the key sights in English. These special taxis depart from a special depot in front of Hiroshima Station at the Shinkansen entrance. If you want to arrange for one of these taxis ahead of time, telephone the **Hiroshima Station Tourist Information Center** (☎ 082/261–1877).

Guided Tours

Hiroshima International Relations has recently established a **Home Visit Program.** To make arrangements, go the day before to the International Center on the ground floor of the International Conference Center in Peace Memorial Park (1-5 Nakajimacho, Naku-ku, Hiroshima 730, ☎ 082/247–8007).

A number of sightseeing tours are available, including tours of Hiroshima and cruises on the Inland Sea, in particular to Miyajima (island). A four-hour, 40-minute tour (Japanese-speaking guide only) to the city's major sights costs ¥6,190. An eight-hour tour of both the city and Miyajima costs ¥8,970. These tours are operated by the **Hiroshima Bus Company** (☎ 082/261–7104) and depart from in front of Hiroshima Station at the Shinkansen entrance.

The **Setonaikai Kisen Company** (☎ 082/253–1212) operates several cruises on the Inland Sea. Its cruise boat, the *Southern Cross,* operates a 5½-hour trip (9:30–3:10) every Sunday, Monday, Friday, and Saturday, March–November, which includes visits to Etajima, Ondo-no-Seto, Kure Bay, and Enoshima (cost: ¥12,000, includes lunch and soft drinks). For a shorter cruise, you can take the boat (10:10 and 12:20) to Miyajima (cost: ¥1,060 one way, ¥1,980 round-trip). There is also the Sunset Cruise, which leaves Hiroshima Bay at 6:45 PM and returns at 8:40 PM (cost: ¥2,600, with dinner on board as an optional extra, for a total of ¥9,056).

Exploring

Numbers in the margin correspond to points of interest on the Hiroshima map.

Entirely rebuilt after World War II, Hiroshima is a modern city. The atomic bomb is its living history. The monuments and the museum dedicated to "No More Hiroshimas" in the **Peace Memorial Park** are the key sights to visit. To reach the park from the station, take either Streetcar 2 or 6 from Hiroshima Station Plaza to the Genbaku-Domu-mae stop. On disembarking from the streetcar, your first sight will be the **A-Bomb Dome**—a powerful and poignant symbol. The old Industrial Promotion Hall, with its half-shattered structure, stands in sharp contrast to the vitality and wealth of the new Hiroshima. The A-Bomb Dome is the only structural ruin of the war left erect in Hiroshima, and, for that, its impact is even stronger.

From the Genbaku-Domu-mae bus stop, walk onto Aichi Bridge, the double bridge that crosses the rivers Otagawa (also called Honkawa) and Motoyasugawa. In the middle of the bridge is the entrance to the Peace Memorial Park. The Peace Memorial Museum is at the far end of the park. En route are statues and monuments, but, because you'll probably be returning through the park, head straight for the museum, about a 10-minute walk from the bridge. If you require more tourist information, there is a city tourist information center in the rest house located on the left-hand side of the park near another bridge crossing the Motoyasugawa. A less dramatic approach from Hiroshima Station is to take the Hiroshima Bus Company's red-and-white Bus 24 to Kokaido-mae, which is only a two-minute walk from the museum, or take Streetcar 1 to Chuden-mae for a five-minute walk to the museum.

The **Peace Memorial Museum** is as disturbing as it is educational. Through exhibits of models, charred fragments of clothing, melted tiles, and photographs of devastation and contorted bodies, the story of havoc and agonizing death unfolds. Nothing can capture the reality of 7,000°C (12,632°F), the surface heat of the atomic fireball, but the remains of the melted statue of Buddha or the imprinted human shadow on granite steps is enough to unnerve our confidence in man's future existence. Most of the exhibits have brief explanations in English. However, more detailed information is given on tape cassettes, which may be rented for ¥150. ☛ ¥50. ⊙ *Daily, May–Nov., 9–6; Dec.–Apr. 9–5. Closed Dec. 29–Jan. 2.*

8 On the east side of the museum is the **Peace Memorial Hall,** where documentaries on the effects of the atomic explosion are given in English. (Times are posted at the museum's entrance.) On the west side is the International Conference Center. In front of the museum on its north

9 side is the **Memorial Cenotaph.** Designed by Japanese architect Kenzo Tange, the cenotaph resembles the primitive A-frame houses of Japan's earliest inhabitants. Buried inside the vaults of the cenotaph is a chest containing the names of those who died in the holocaust. On the exterior of the cenotaph is the inscription (in Japanese), "Repose ye in Peace, for the error shall not be repeated." In front of the cenotaph,

★ **10** the **Peace Flame** burns. The flame will be extinguished only when all atomic weapons in the world are banished. In the meantime, every August 6, there is a solemn commemoration in which the citizens of Hiroshima float paper lanterns on the city's rivers for the repose of the souls of the atomic-bomb victims.

11 Before you leave the park, pause before the **Statue for the A-Bomb Children.** The figure is of a young girl who died of leukemia caused by the atomic radiation. Her will to live was strong. She believed that if she could fold 1,000 paper cranes (cranes are a symbol of good fortune and long life), her illness would be cured. She died after making her 954th crane.

The Peace Memorial Park is disquieting. It does not engender hope. However, if you cross the Aichi Bridge at the park's northern entrance and walk 200 meters (yards) north and east, keeping the river on your left and the baseball stadium where the Hiroshima Carps play on your

12 right, you'll come to the **Hiroshima Science and Cultural Center for Children** (Kodomo Bunka Kagakukan), a wonderfully laid out hands-on museum. The joy and enthusiasm of the youngsters here dispels some of the depression that the Peace Memorial Park is bound to have caused. Next door is a planetarium. ⊙ *Tues.–Sun. 9–5. Closed the day following public holidays.* ☛ *Center free, planetarium ¥410.*

13 A ten-minute walk farther north is the resurrected **Hiroshimajo** (Broad Island Castle), which gave the city of Hiroshima its name when Terumoto Mori built it in 1589. A Japanese Army headquarters in World War II, it was (intentionally) destroyed by the bomb. In 1958, the five-story donjon (stronghold) was rebuilt to its original specifications. Its interior has been used as a local museum, but since 1989 it has served as Hiroshima's historical museum, with exhibits from Japan's feudal period. ☛ *Castle grounds free, museum ¥300.* ⊙ *Daily, Apr.–Sept. 9–6; Oct.–Mar. 9–5.*

14 The other place worth visiting in Hiroshima is **Shukkeien,** slightly to the east of the castle on the banks of the Kyobashigawa. This garden was laid out in 1630 by Lord Nagaakira Asano in a design resembling that of a famed scenic lake in Hangzhou, China. The beauty of the garden stems from the streams and islets winding their way between the sculpted pine trees. Small bridges cross the streams, which are filled with exotic-colored carp, so praised for their long lives. It is a fitting end for a visit to Hiroshima—though all the ancient plantings and structures were destroyed by the bomb, so what you see here are young plants

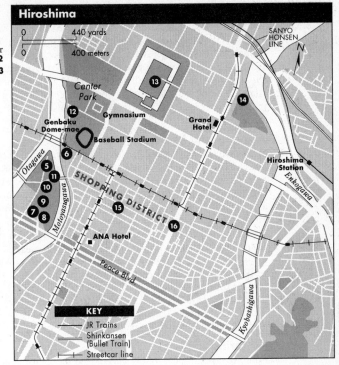

Hiroshima

and new construction. You can return to the JR Station by taking Streetcar 9 to the end of the line and then transferring to Streetcar 1, 2, or 6. ☞ ¥250. ⊙ *Daily, Apr.–Sept. 9–6; Oct.–Mar. 9–5.*

If you like big cities and want an urban base to explore the Inland Sea, Hiroshima combines international and Japanese urban pleasures with 4,000 bars. In its central district, around **Hondori,** there are the major department stores and masses of smaller shops. The major stores, Fukuya (closed Wed.), Tenmaya (closed Tues.), Mitsukoshi (closed Mon.), and Sogo (closed Thurs.), are open 10–6. Restaurants abound, and oysters are the specialty of the region, best washed down with sake, of which Hiroshima produces some of Japan's finest. There is, of course, a range of modern hotels from which to choose *(see* Dining and Lodging, *below),* located in the city center to the east of the Peace Memorial Park and around the JR station. To the east of the Hondori Shopping District is **Shintenchi,** an entertainment district.

Miyajima

Numbers in the margin correspond to points of interest on the Western Honshu map.

★ **⑰ Miyajima.** The most enjoyable part of any visit to Hiroshima is the excursion to **Miyajima.** The Japanese have what are known as the "Big Three Scenic Attractions." Matsushima, in Tohoku, is one; Ama-no-hashidate, on the San'in coast, is another; and the third is Miyajima, a small island just off the coast in the Inland Sea. Here is the famous Itsukushima Jinja, a shrine, built on wooden supports that extend the buildings into the sea; this shrine is known for its much-photographed *torii* (arch) rising out of the waters.

The island of Miyajima is only 30 kilometers (19 miles) in circumfer-ence, but its center peaks at 1,740 feet with Mt. Misen. With forested slopes on the mountain and the surrounding Inland Sea, it is a pretty, though touristy, village; Miyajima, with history and tradition every-where, is delightful either as a day trip or for an overnight stay. All of the island is sacred. You will note that there are no cemeteries on the island. No one is allowed to die here, or even to be born here. When either time comes, the concerned party must be taken over to the mainland.

Arriving and Departing

Sightseeing boats bound for Miyajima leave from Hiroshima (*see* Guided Tours, *below*). However, the easiest, least expensive way to get there is to take the commuter train on the JR Sanyo Line from Hiroshima Station to Miyajima-guchi Station. From Miyajima-guchi Station, it is a three-minute walk down to the shore and the pier from which the ferries scoot over to Miyajima. The train takes about 25 minutes and departs from Hiroshima every 15–20 minutes. The first train departs from Hiroshima at 5:55 AM and, for the return, the last ferry leaves Miyajima at 9:20 PM. There are two ferry boats, one of which belongs to JR—your Japan Rail Pass is valid on this boat only. The one-way cost for the train and ferry, without a JR Pass, is ¥560. There are also direct ferries from Hiroshima Ujina Port that leave seven times a day and take 22 minutes to make the trip (cost: ¥1,250). Allow a minimum of three hours to cover the major sights of Miyajima.

Exploring

From Miyajima's pier, follow the coast to the right (west). This leads to the village, which is crowded with restaurants, hotels, and souvenir shops. At the far end of the village is the park, which leads past the torii and on to Itsukushima Jinja. Expect to be greeted by deer as you walk through the park. The deer are protected, and they take full ad-vantage of their status, demanding edibles and nudging you if you are not forthcoming.

★ The **torii,** 500 feet from the shore at an entrance to the cove where the shrine stands, rises 53 feet out of the water, making it one of the tallest in Japan. Built in 1875, it has become a symbol not only of Miyajima but also of Japan. Especially as the sun sets over the Inland Sea, the vermilion structure and its reflection in the rippling water is an un-forgettable sight. Past the torii stands the shrine. Poets write of how the shrine's building seems to float on the water, but they omit the fact that it "floats" only at high tide. Photographers take note: At other times, the shrine stands on wooden stilts above less photogenic mud flats.

Itsukushima Jinja was created in 593 and dedicated to the three daugh-ters of Susano-o-no-Mikoto, the Shinto god of the moon and the oceans. The structure has had to be continually repaired and rebuilt, and the present structure is thought to be a 16th-century copy of the 12th-century buildings. Most of the shrine is closed to the public, but you can walk around its deck, which gives some idea of the size of the building complex as well as gorgeous views of the torii. ☛ *¥300 (or a combined ticket with the Treasure House for ¥500).* ⊙ *Daily 6:30–6 (6:30–5 in winter).*

Across from the shrine's exit is the **Treasure House** (Homotsukan). Be-cause every victor of battles that took place on the Inland Sea saw fit to offer their gratitude to the gods by giving gifts to Itsukushima Jinja, the Treasure House is rich with art objects, 246 of which have been designated as either National Treasures or Important Cultural Properties. ☛ ¥300 (*or a combined ticket with Itsukushima Jinja for ¥500*). ☉ *Daily 9–5.*

Adding to the uniquely Japanese scene of the "floating" torii and shrine are the **Five-Story Pagoda** and **Senjokaku.** Senjokaku (Hall of One Thousand Mats), dedicated by Hideyoshi Toyotomi in 1587, has rice scoops attached to the walls, symbols of the soldiers who died fighting for Japan's expansionism. The Goju-no-to (Five-Story Pagoda) dates from 1407. Both are situated on top of a small hill overlooking the shrine. If you climb up the steps to these two buildings for a closer look, a small street on the other side (away from the shrine) serves as a shortcut back to the village.

Though many visitors spend only a half day on the island, those with more time to enjoy its beauty may enter **Momijidani Koen,** inland from the shrine. Here in the park is the start of the mile-long gondola that takes you virtually up to the summit of **Mt. Misen.** A short hike past the gondola's terminus takes you to the very top. It's worth it; the views of the Inland Sea and Hiroshima beyond are splendid. You may choose to walk back down. *Cost: ¥900 one-way, ¥1,500 round-trip.*

Miyajima has become a vacation spot for Japanese families; hence, there are many hotels and ryokan in and around the village. One of these ryokan is worth remembering. It is the famous **Iwaso Ryokan** (☎ 08294/4–2233), which has been a host to pilgrims and vacationers for 130 years. Even if you are not staying in town overnight, Iwaso makes an ideal spot for lunch (*see* Dining and Lodging, *below*). Also, be aware that the most exciting (and the most congested) time to visit Miyajima is in June (lunar calendar) for the annual **Kangen-sai Festival,** when three stately barges bearing a portable shrine, priests, and musicians cross the bay, flanked by a squadron of festooned boats.

From Hiroshima the westbound Shinkansen heads for Shimonoseki, an hour away, before crossing to Kyushu and terminating in Hakata. But instead of crossing over to Kyushu with the Shinkansen, this itinerary does practically a 180-degree turn to travel east along Western Honshu's northern region, the San'in.

THE SAN'IN REGION

San'in officially stretches along Western Honshu from Shimonoseki all the way to Kyoto. However, the special atmosphere of San'in ends on the Sea of Japan (Nihonkai) coast at Maizuru, just inside the border of Kyoto Prefecture. Whereas the coastline that faces the Inland Sea receives the direct light of the sun, San'in has a misty, eerie light that diffuses to cause an ever-changing mood of flirting shadows. San'in means "In the Shadow of the Mountains." San'in has also been in the shadow of Japan's economic miracle. The presence of the mountains makes transport expensive between the north and south coasts and has staved off the pollution of sprawling factories and the modern urbanization that have destroyed so much of the Sanyo coast. The influx of tourists, both Japanese and foreign, has also been less; San'in is off the beaten track, which adds to its appeal.

San'in moves at a slower pace. Trains and buses are less frequent. There is an austerity in the architecture, the crafts, and in the attitude of the people—a reflection of the cold winters and the isolation from mainstream Japan. An example of their art may help illustrate this: To the San'in people, a chipped tea bowl has more aesthetic appeal than the perfected symmetry used by Kyoto's craftspeople. San'in potters will create a crack in a bowl and artfully glaze it. The imagination must make the leap to what ultimate perfection could be. This is San'in—inspiring, restrained, forever conceiving perfection but never harnessing it.

Getting Around

By Train

Along the Sea of Japan coast, the JR San'in Main Line runs from Shimonoseki to Kyoto. The line is the second longest in Japan, 680 kilometers (422 miles), and has the most stations of any line, which means lots of stops and longer traveling times. In addition, there are only two Limited Express trains a day to cover the Shimonoseki–Kyoto route in either direction. There are, however, local trains that go back and forth between the major cities along the San'in coast.

At several points along the San'in coast are routes through the mountains to cities on the Inland Sea. A few of the major connecting routes are:

Between Hagi and Ogori: one hour, 30 minutes on the JR or Bocho bus lines. It is advisable to make seat reservations for these buses at JR train stations' seat reservation counters. Despite what some JR booking offices say, the JR bus is covered by the JR Pass.

Between Tsuwano and Ogori: one hour on the JR Yamaguchi Line.

Between Masuda and Ogori: two hours on the JR Yamaguchi Line.

Between Yonago and Okayama: three hours on the JR Hakubi Line.

Between Matsue and Hiroshima: five hours on the JR Geibi and Kitsugi Line (one train a day, departing from Hiroshima at 8:45 AM).

Between Matsue and Okayama: two hours and 25 minutes on the JR Yakumo Limited Express (four Limited Express and five local trains a day). From Kyoto, the train to Matsue takes six hours. There are also two night trains from Tokyo to Matsue; the trip takes 13 hours.

Unless you do not mind waiting around stations or being stranded overnight, research the train schedule for your route in advance. Trains run so infrequently that you will need to plan your time to fit their schedule, unlike in many other regions in Japan, where the next train is never too far off.

Indeed, there are not many trains that set out each day from Shimonoseki to Hagi, so plan ahead. The Limited Express takes two hours; the local takes four hours. Try not to find yourself stranded in Shimonoseki overnight. Shimonoseki is an industrial port town from which ferries leave for various ports on Kyushu, the Inland Sea, and Pusan, across the Sea of Japan in Korea. Even the first hour on the JR train heading for Hagi shows landscape heavily built up with factories, but gradually the scenery becomes more natural, and the views of the coastline start setting the tone of San'in and its first major city, Hagi.

Hagi

★ ⑱   Although its castle was dismantled in 1874 as a relic of feudalism, **Hagi** retains the atmosphere of a traditional castle town. Hagi is rich with history, one that is closely linked to the Mori family. Even though they had opposed the Tokugawa Shogunate and were defeated by Ieyasu

Tokugawa in 1600 at the Battle of Sekigahara, the Mori were able to keep their fiefdom for 13 generations. The Tokugawa Shogunate had tried to isolate the Mori as much as possible, but in so doing, the Mori, who had never forgotten their defeat, became the forerunners of the movement to restore power to the emperor. It was the army from Hagi and the surrounding Nagato Province that, on the second attempt, captured Kyoto and turned the tide against the shogunate. Hagi's fame lies not simply in defeating the shogunate but also in supplying the intellectual ideas for the new Japan. Indeed, Japan's first prime minister, Hirobumi Ito (1841–1909), was born and educated in Hagi.

Hagi has another claim to fame: Hagi-yaki, a pottery that has been cherished for 375 years for its subtle pastel colors and its milky, translucent glazes. Mind you, the tradition of Hagi-yaki has less than noble beginnings. Returning from Japan's aborted attempt to invade Korea in the late 16th century, a Mori general brought home two Korean potters as "souvenirs." With techniques that were probably used during the Silla Kingdom, these Korean brothers, Sukkweng Yi and Kyung Yi, created Hagi-yaki for their masters. Hagi-yaki has since become second to Raku-yaki as the most praised pottery in Japan. Unfortunately, the two most famous kilns, Rikei's Saka Kiln and Miwa Kiln, do not accept visitors, but several others do, including Shizuki Kiln, conveniently located on the way to the castle grounds.

Arriving and Departing

Though the second part of this chapter's itinerary begins at Hagi as if we were coming from Kyushu or Shimonoseki, it is possible to cross over the mountains from the Inland Sea town of Ogori, served by the Hiroshima–Hakata Shinkansen, to Tsuwano by train, and then to Hagi by bus; or you may travel directly to Hagi from Ogori by JR bus, which is the quicker way. Without a JR Pass, the one-way bus fare is about ¥2,000. Remember, the bus is covered by the JR Pass even if some JR seat reservation clerks seem to think otherwise.

Getting Around

The ideal way to explore Hagi is by bicycle, and there are many outlets where bikes can be rented for approximately ¥1,000 per day. Try the bicycle shop across from the Rainbow Building, left of the station plaza. Alternatively, you can hire a "sightseeing taxi" for about ¥4,300 per hour; it takes about three hours to complete a hurried city tour.

A four-hour sightseeing bus tour (Japanese-speaking guides only) operated by the **Bocho Bus Company** departs from the Bocho Bus Station, located on the eastern edge of the central city (cost: ¥3,250, plus ¥1,200 for lunch.).

Exploring

Hagi, surrounded by mountains on three sides and by the Sea of Japan on the fourth, is set in the V formed by two rivers, Matsumotogawa on the east side and the Hashimotogawa on the west. The major train station is Higashi-Hagi (not Hagi), on the eastern side of town. For tourist information at the station try **Hagi Ryokan Kyodo-kumiai** (☎ 0838/22–7599, FAX 0838/22–7517), whose main business is booking accommodations but whose English-speaking owner, Mr. Oki, serves as a helpful adviser to tourists and dispenses official guide maps. The agency is located in the Rainbow Building to the left of the station, in the first office on the left side of the shopping arcade. The **City Tourist Office** is downtown (☎ 0838/25–3131 and 0838/25–1750).

To get to the Hagi downtown area from the Higashi-Hagi Station, cross the bridge over the Matsumotogawa and, bearing right, continue on the street until you reach the Hagi Grand Hotel. Then, take a left, and six blocks up on the right-hand side is the beginning of Tamachi Mall. Just on the corner is the **Ishii Chawan Museum,** a small, second-floor museum with a rare collection of antique tea bowls produced in Hagi, including some by the Korean potter whose creations first captured the attention of the Japanese. Also in this prized collection are Korean tea bowls made during the Koryo Dynasty (916–1392). For aficionados this museum is a pleasure, but if you are short of time you may want to skip this to be sure of visiting the Kumaya Art Museum (*see below*). ☛ *¥350.* ⊘ *Daily 9–5. Closed Dec.–Mar.*

Tamachi Mall is the busiest street in Hagi, with some 130 shops offering both the latest fashions from Tokyo and the more interesting local products from Yamaguchi Prefecture. You may well wish to return to purchase Hagi-yaki after touring the sights and the kilns where the pottery is made. Two stores worth noting are **Harada Chojuan** and **Miwa Seigado.** The latter is at the top end of Tamachi, past the San Marco restaurant. Another gallery and store is **Saito-an,** in which both the masters and "unknown" potters display their works for sale. If you search through the wares, you may be able to find a small sake cup for less than ¥500, or, if you have your gold credit card ready, you may choose a tea bowl by such living master potters as Miwa Kyusetsu for ¥250,000.

At the top of Tamachi Mall, a right turn toward Hagi Bay will lead you through the Teramachi section of town. Numerous temples here cry out for someone to pay heed to them. The locals just take them for granted. Each one of these temples has something to offer and all have a tranquillity rarely transgressed by tourists. There are about 10 from which to choose and explore, from the old wooden temple of **Hofukuji,** with its bibbed statues of Jizo (guardian deity of children), to **Kaichoji,** with its two-story gate and veranda around the Main Hall's second floor.

Instead of walking all the way to Hagi Bay, take a left after Kaichoji to the **Kumaya Art Museum,** which will be on the left—look for a big metal gate. The complex was once the home of a wealthy merchant, and the warehouse has been made into a museum, which houses art objects and antiques. Of special note are the scrolls, paintings, a screen of the Kano school, and a collection of ceramics, which includes some of the first Hagi-yaki produced. ☛ *¥500.* ⊘ *Daily 9–5.*

From the Kumaya Art Museum, take the next left (south and away from the sea) to visit the **Kikuya House,** once the home of the chief merchant family to the Mori clan. Though the Kikuya were only merchants, they held a special relationship with the Mori. (After the Mori defeat at Sekigahara, the Kikuya family sent their daimyo money to return to Hagi.) As a result, this house has more extravagance than merchants were normally allowed to display. *Keyaki* (Japanese zelkova wood) was, for example, forbidden to merchants, yet notice its extensive use in this home. This is not your typical Edo-period family home, but it does indicate the good life of the few. ☛ *¥370.* ⊘ *Daily 9–5.*

The next stop is **Shizuki Koen,** the park that contains the ruins of Hagijo. Head west from Kikuya House past the NHK broadcasting building, and keep Sosuien (park) on your left. After the next major cross street on the left, you will find the **Shizuki Kiln.** You may want to stop in here and browse over its Hagi-yaki pottery and, if the wallet can bear it, purchase some of the magnificent work. Also, most of the time, you will be welcome to enter the adjoining building where the kilns are fired.

At the next major intersection after Shizuki Kiln, take a left and walk or bicycle along the street between the **Toida Masuda House Walls.** These are the longest mud walls of the Horiuchi samurai section of town, and, for a moment, one is thrust back into feudal times. Follow the walls around and head west to the grand wooden **Fukuhara Gate.** A right turn here leads directly to the **Tomb of Tenjuin,** a memorial to Terumoto Mori, who founded the clan giving rise to 13 generations of Mori rule.

At the memorial, take a left turn and head toward the park grounds. On the left, past the Shizuki Youth Hostel, is the **Mori House,** a long (170 ft.) and wide (17 ft.) building that was once home to the samurai foot soldiers. ☞ ¥200 *(also covers entrance to Shizuki Koen and castle grounds).* ☽ *Daily 8–6:30 (8–4:30 in winter).*

On the way to the castle you will pass two pottery kilns, **Shogetsu Kiln** and **Hagijo Kiln,** both of which offer the opportunity for browsing, watching the potters at work, and, of course, purchasing the products. Once inside the actual castle grounds, there is **Shizukiyama Jinja,** built as recently as 1879; the wood used has weathered to give the shrine a comfortable, reassuring presence. Beyond the shrine is a highly recommended place to visit, the **Hananoe Teahouse.** Set in delightful gardens, this thatch teahouse exudes peace and tranquillity. The attendants will make tea for you while you savor the quiet of the gardens. ☞ *Free, but the tea is ¥450.*

The actual **Hagi Castle** is no more. Its demise, though, was unusual. Neither warfare nor fire destroyed it. Instead, the castle was dismantled as a gesture of support for the Meiji Restoration. Also, with the arrival of Western gunboats 15 years before the Meiji Restoration, the castle became vulnerable to attack.

In fact, the Mori family had moved from the castle in 1863 to create a new home and provincial capital at landlocked Yamaguchi. All that remains of the castle are its high walls and wide moats. (It will cost you ¥200 to inspect these ruins.) But the real pleasure of Shizuki Koen is its space and setting.

The castle walls and moat are a few steps beyond the Hananoe Teahouse. From the top of the walls, there is a panoramic view of Hagi, the bay, and the surrounding mountains inland. However, the best view is from **Mt. Shizuki,** which rises 145 meters (475 feet) behind the castle. It takes about 20 minutes to hike up the path to the top. On one side of Mt. Shizuki there is a new amusement park (☞ ¥1,110; ☽ 9 AM–10 PM) that attracts Japanese families but has little to offer the foreign visitor, except for a monorail that climbs up Mt. Shizuki.

On the way back down Mt. Shizuki you may want to stop at the **Hagi Shiryokan,** the local history museum. (☞ ¥300; ☽ Daily 9–5, in winter 9–4). If your time is limited, forgo a visit to the museum and leave the park to head for Daishoin (temple). It is a lengthy hike, so unless you have a bicycle, in which case it is about a 20-minute pedal, a taxi is advised. To reach Daishoin, cross over the canal that marks the boundary of Shizuki Koen and follow it south to the Tokiwabashi. Once over the Hashimotogawa, take the main road that follows the river upstream. Daishoin is on the right, on the other side of the JR San'in Main Line tracks.

Daishoin is the counterpart to the more frequented Tokoji (*see below*). Screened by the surrounding mountains, Daishoin is the final resting place for half of the Mori family: The first two Mori generations are buried at Daishoin, the third generation at Tokoji. Thereafter, even-numbered generations of the Mori generations are buried at Daishoin, odd-numbered generations at Tokoji. What is unusual about both Daishoin and Tokoji are the lanterns and the placement of the daimyo's wife next to her husband's tomb. Such a close affiliation, or recognition of the wife, in death was not the custom in feudal Japan. The lanterns tell another story.

When Hidehari Mori, the first Mori daimyo to be buried at Daishoin, died, seven of his principal retainers followed, dutifully committing ritual suicide. Extending this custom further, one of the retainers to one of the daimyo's retainers also killed himself. The eight graves are lined up in a row of descending rank. The Tokugawa Shogunate realized that this custom could decimate the aristocracy and decreed that such ritual suicide upon the death of one's lord was illegal. Future generations of retainers gave up their suicidal rights and, instead, donated lanterns. The path leading to the main hall of Daishoin is lined with 603 lanterns. The temple is a special place to visit at any time, but in May the temple grounds burst into a purple haze with the wisteria in full bloom. Another special time to visit is from August 13 to 15, when all the lanterns are lit for Bon, the Buddhist festival of the dead. ☛ ¥150. ☼ Daily 9–4:30.

Daishoin is in the southern outskirts of Hagi, but we now head to the eastern sector of town, the same sector as JR Higashi-Hagi Station. If you are without a bicycle, then walk five minutes to the east of Daishoin, take the train from Hagi Station to Higashi-Hagi Station, and walk south to Matsumoto Bridge. If you are on a bicycle, return to Hashimoto River, follow it upstream to Hashimoto Bridge, and head into central Hagi. At the Bocho Bus Center, go right and cross over Matsumoto Bridge.

Directly east of Matsumotobashi, the road leads to **Tokoji,** containing the other cemetery of the Mori family. The temple was founded by the Zen priest Domio in 1691 under the auspices of Yoshinari Mori, the third lord of Hagi. It is here that he (and every succeeding odd-numbered generation of the Mori family) is buried. You enter the temple grounds through the three-story Sanmon (gate) to reach the Main Hall, which contains rather garish images of Buddha. Behind this building are the monuments of the Mori lords and their wives. Needless to say, it is easy to point to the husbands' graves. They are the grandest of all. Surrounding the monuments, amid the pine trees, are 500 lanterns donated by the lords' retainers. On August 15, during the Bon festival, all of these lanterns are lit—an impressive sight, indeed. ☛ ¥150. ☼ Daily 8:30–5:30.

Instead of returning directly to the Matsumotogawa, keep to the left as you leave the shrine and, after a steep climb, you'll reach the **Monument to Shoin Yoshida** (1830–1859). Yoshida was a revolutionary. With the coming of Commodore Matthew Perry's Black Ships in 1853, Shoin recognized the need for Japan to step out of feudalism and accept certain Western practices. In his quest to understand the West, he attempted to slip aboard an American ship. He was caught by the shogunate, imprisoned, and later sent home to Hagi to be kept under house arrest. During his arrest, he started expounding a liberal philosophy that suggested both adapting to Western practices and introducing democratic elements into government. In the eyes of the shogunate, these preachings were outright sedition. At age 29, Shoin was executed. His execution inflamed and united the antishogunate elements of Hagi and the Namoto Province (now Yamaguchi Prefecture).

Coming down the hill from Yoshida's monument, take a left turn and you will pass the house of one of Shoin's students, Hirobumi Ito, the first prime minister of Japan. Across the street from the **Ito House** is **Shoin Jinja,** with the Shoka-Sonjuku, the private school that Shoin founded to teach his students his revolutionary philosophy. At the shrine's exit there is a museum that recounts Shoin's life depicted in three-dimensional scenes with model figures. There are, however, no English explanations of their meaning. ☞ *¥550.* ◷ *Daily 8:30–5.*

From Shoin Jinja you can cross the Matsumotobashi and go straight to Tamachi Mall, or take a right before the bridge and return to the JR Higashi-Hagi Station to journey onward through San'in. The next stop in San'in is Tsuwano, situated inland and nestled in the mountains. En route between Hagi and Masuda is the small fishing village of **Susa,** on an attractive bay. Few foreigners ever come here, and it has one of Japan's best minshuku (*see* Lodging, *below*). You may prefer to spend a quiet night here rather than at Hagi.

Tsuwano

★ ⑲ The castle town of **Tsuwano** is much smaller than Hagi; because of that, it has a more intimate atmosphere. One can quickly feel part of the town and its 700-year history. Indeed, Tsuwano is occasionally referred to as a "little Kyoto" for its genteel qualities and the river that flows through town. However, aside from these similarities, Tsuwano is not Kyoto. Tsuwano is a mountain town, small and compact, and often shrouded in mists drifting through the valley to give a surreal effect.

Arriving and Departing

To reach Tsuwano, you can take the JR train on the San'in Main Line to Masuda, where you must change trains for a 30-minute run up to Tsuwano. You can also take a bus from Hagi's Bocho Bus Center directly to Tsuwano, a trip that takes two hours (fare: ¥1,950). Unfortunately, it is not covered by the JR Pass, but, since travel time is a good hour less than the train, it may be worth the expense. To reach Tsuwano directly from Ogori take the JR train, which takes one hour. Ogori is 40 minutes by Shinkansen from Hiroshima.

Getting Around

All the sights are within easy walking distance, or you can rent a bicycle (cost: ¥800 for 3 hours, ¥1,050 for a full day). Four bicycle rental shops are located around the station plaza. A taxi may also be used at ¥9,400 for two hours and ¥14,100 for three hours; it takes about two to three hours to visit the sights. There is a **Tourist Information Office** (☎ 08567/2–1144) at the railway station that has free brochures and will help in securing accommodations.

Exploring

Except for the stone walls, nothing is left of the mountaintop castle, but Tsuwano's other attraction, the multicolored carp that fill the waters of the Tsuwanogawa and the water-filled ditches, is still much in evidence. Indeed, the carp outnumber Tsuwano's residents by 10 to 1. Carp were originally introduced into the river and sewers as a ready source of food should the town ever be under siege. There was no siege, and because carp live about 60 years, they have had a rather privileged existence. Life is still good for them. If you make your way from the JR station to Tonomachi Street (a 5-min. walk), you can feed these exotic-colored fish (swimming in the ditches along the street) with "carp snacks" bought at the coffee shop across from the Catholic church.

(Gourmands may like to dine on carp at the Yuki Restaurant on Honcho-dori, close to the post office.)

The **Catholic church,** though built in 1931, is a reminder of the time when Christianity was outlawed in Japan. In 1865, in an effort to disperse Christian strongholds and cause them extreme hardship, with the hope that they would recant their faith, the Tokugawa Shogunate transported 153 Christians from Nagasaki to Tsuwano. By the time the Meiji government lifted the ban on Christianity, 53 Christians remained in Tsuwano. Thirty-six had been martyred, and the remainder had either recanted or died of natural causes. It's worth stopping at the church: Where but in Japan can one find a Catholic church with floors covered with tatami matting?

A few steps farther up Tonomachi Street, on the left-hand side, is the **Yorakan,** originally a feudal school where the sons of samurai would train in the arts of manhood. Today, in its fencing hall, there is a folk-craft museum. ☞ *¥150.* ⊗ *Daily 8:30–5:30.*

At the top of Tonomachi Street, the road crosses the Tsuwanogawa at the Ohashi (bridge). Just on the other side is the **Kyodokan,** a museum with a collection of exhibits that recount regional history. ☞ *¥400.* ⊗ *Daily 8:30–5.*

However, you may want to save the time and, instead of crossing the bridge, fork to the right under the torii, cross the railway tracks of the JR Yamaguchi Line, and follow the river for approximately 250 meters (yards). Indicative of the million visitors who make the pilgrimage each year, the number of souvenir stands and teahouses increases until you reach **Yasaka Jinja,** a shrine where, every July 20 and July 27, the festival of the Heron Dance is held. Behind this shrine is the stepway to the **Taikodani Inari Jinja,** one of the five most important Inari shrines in Japan. The approach resembles a tunnel, because you pass under numerous red torii—1,174 of them—to reach the shrine high on the cliffside. (Nowadays, the weak of spirit may reach the shrine by bus along another road.)

From the shrine you can either hike a hard 20 minutes up to the site of **Tsuwanojo,** or take the road down the other side of the shrine to the chairlift, which takes five minutes to reach the base of the castle grounds. To ascend the summit from the top of the chairlift requires a further eight-minute walk. Whichever way you make it to the top, it is worth every effort. The view from where this mountaintop castle once stood sweeps over the tile-roof town of Tsuwano and the valley below. What a marvelous castle it must have been! The original castle was built in the 13th century and took 30 years to build. Its demise took a lot less time. Like Hagijo, as a sign of good faith this castle was dismantled during the Meiji Restoration.

You can walk back down from the castle grounds to the main street or use the chairlift for ¥450. Because the views from the chairlift are so superb, you may prefer the latter. At the bottom of the chairlift, turn left and then right to cross over the Tsuwanogawa. Immediately on crossing the river, take the right-hand street and follow it around to the left, where you will pass by the **Old House of Ogai Mori.** Ogai Mori (1862–1922) was one of the prominent literary figures in the Meiji Restoration. He spent only his first 11 years in Tsuwano (he went to the Yorokan school), but his hometown never forgot him, nor he his hometown. His success as a doctor led him to travel overseas, and, in so doing, he tried to reconcile the differences between Western and

Japanese cultures. His tomb is at **Yomeiji,** a temple located to the east of the JR Tsuwano Station. ☛ *Temple: ¥300.* ⊗ *Daily 8:30–5.*

Next door to the Mori House is **Sekishukan,** a museum displaying *washi* (Japanese handmade paper). Demonstrations of papermaking are given, and there is a display of Iwami-style paper. On the second floor there are displays of washi made from other regions of Japan. If you have not seen the process of creating handmade paper or wish to compare different regional types, this is a good museum to visit. ☛ *Free.* ⊗ *Daily 9–5.*

From this museum, continue along the street until the main road and take a left, which will lead you back to town over the Ohashi. If there is time before your train, and you did not see the exhibition of papermaking at Sekishukan, you may want to stop in at the **Tsuwano Industry Museum,** in front of the station. Demonstrations are given of the town's traditional industries, and most of the space is devoted to the craft of papermaking. There is also a section on sake brewing (☛ *¥100;* ⊗ *Daily 8:30–5*). Also, five minutes to the east of the JR station and up the hill through the Pass of the Virgin is **St. Maria's Church,** built in 1951 to commemorate the Christian martyrs, whose plight is portrayed in the stained-glass windows. The Pass of the Virgin (in Japanese, *otometoge*) is the site of the graveyard where 36 martyrs have their crosses. If you still have time, visit the Tsuwano **Katsushika Hokusai Museum,** just a block from the train station. Katsushika Hokusai (1760–1849) was a famous painter from the end of the Tokugawa era who influenced future generations of painters both in Japan and overseas. This museum exhibits his wood-block prints, illustrated books, and paintings. ☛ *¥450.* ⊗ *Daily 9:30–5. Closed Dec. 31–Jan. 2.*

The next stop east along the San'in coast is Matsue, a three-hour, 30-minute ride from Tsuwano on the JR Limited Express. However, you may want to break your journey an hour before Matsue and visit Izumo Taisha. If so, disembark from the train at Izumo (*see* Izumo Taisha, *below*).

Matsue

❷⓿ Of all the towns in the San'in district, the city of **Matsue** is the one best known as a summer vacation destination. Like the rest of San'in, though, Matsue sees few foreigners, yet it is rich in beauty and heritage. Only scattered archaeological remains exist from the days when the people of "The Eightfold-Towering-Thunderhead Land of Izumo" lived here in the 2nd and 3rd centuries, and only ruins have been left behind of Matsue's early days, when the town became the capital of the Izumo in the 8th century. However, many of today's existing shrines originate from that time, and the more recent past is still visible. Matsue is the only town along the San'in coast with part of its castle intact. In fact, Matsue's castle is one of the dozen castles in Japan that are originals and not ferro-concrete replicas.

Matsue's location, inland from the Sea of Japan at the conjunction of two small lagoons, is unique. Known as the City of Water, Matsue lies at a point where the lagoon Nakaumi, to the east, connects with Lake Shinji, to the west. This makes Matsue a gourmet heaven, with not only fresh fish taken from the cold waters of the Sea of Japan but also the seven delicacies—eel, shrimp, shellfish, carp, sea bass, pond smelt, and whitebait—from Lake Shinji. The narrow isthmus between Nakaumi and Lake Shinji divides the city. However, except for the JR station and the bus terminal, most of Matsue's points of interest lie on the northern side of the isthmus.

Getting Around

An added delight of Matsue is that even though its population is 140,000, most of its sights are within walking distance of each other; when they are not, Matsue has a comprehensive bus system. For those who would like to be accompanied on their tour of Matsue, the city has a Goodwill Guide Program, which offers an English-speaking volunteer to show you around the city and also escort you to Izumo Taisha. There is no charge for this, though you should pay your guide's expenses, including lunch. To arrange for a Goodwill Guide, contact the **Matsue Tourist Information Office,** Asahimachi, Matsue (☎ 0852/27–2598), a day in advance. The office is located in the JR Matsue Station and is open daily 9:30–6. You can also use this office to collect free maps and brochures.

Exploring

★ The first place to head for is **Matsuejo** and environs, diagonally across town from the JR station. Take the bus (cost: ¥200) to Kencho-mae from either stop No. 1 or stop No. 2, both in front of the JR station. (The same buses continue on to Matsue Onsen, should you want to go there first to check into a hotel.) It is about a 10-minute ride, and the Kencho-mae stop is near the Prefectural Government Office. When you leave the bus, walk a little farther to the north; the castle, in Jozen Koen (park), is on the left.

Made entirely out of pine, Matsuejo was built in 1611, and, with a partial reconstruction in 1642, it was never ransacked or burned during the Tokugawa Shogunate. Amazingly, soon after the Meiji Restoration, the castle was put on the auction block. Sentimental locals, whose ancestors had been living under its shadow for 345 years, pooled their resources and purchased the castle for posterity.

Yoshiharu Horio built the castle for protection. The donjon is, incidentally, the tallest (98 ft.) left in Japan. Camouflaged among the surrounding trees, the castle seems to move with the shadows of San'in's opaque light. Note the overhanging eaves above the top floor, designed to cut down glare that might have prevented the spotting of an attacking force. Inside, the five-story facade contains six levels; the lower floors now exhibit a collection of samurai swords and armor. The climb to the uppermost floor is worth it—the view encompasses the city, Lake Shinji, and the distant mountains. ☛ ¥400. ۞ Daily 8:30–5.

In a Western-style building close to the castle is the **Matsue Kyodokan** (Matsue Cultural Museum), which displays arts, folkcrafts, and implements, including such items as *bento* (box lunch) boxes and hairpins, used during the first three eras after the fall of the Tokugawa Shogunate. ☛ ¥250. ۞ Daily 8:30–5.

If you leave Jozen Koen at its east exit and follow the moat going north, at the top of the park will be a road leading to the right. A little way up this road, no more than a five-minute walk, is the **Meimei-an Teahouse.** Lord Fumai Matsudaira of the Matsue clan built this teahouse in 1779, and it is one of the best preserved teahouses of the period. You must walk up a long flight of stairs to this thatch-roof teahouse, but your effort will be rewarded by both a fine view of Matsuejo and, if you request, tea. ☛ ¥200; ¥300 for green tea. ۞ Daily 9–5.

If you return down the side street on which Meimei-an is located to the main road, and take a right (keeping the castle moat on your left), you will reach four historical sights next door to each other. The first is **Buke Yashiki,** a samurai house built in 1730. Samurai at this time lived fairly well, depending on their rank. This house belonged to the Shiomi family, a chief retainer to the daimyo, and you'll notice the separate servant quarters, a shed for the palanquin, and the slats in the walls to allow the cooling breezes to flow through the rooms. ☞ *¥250.* ☉ *Daily 8:30–5.*

Next door to the Buke Yashiki is the **Tanabe Art Museum,** dedicated mainly to objects of the tea ceremony and ceramics from the region. The museum also exhibits works of wood-block prints by local artists. ☞ *¥500 (though it varies according to the exhibition).* ☉ *Tues.–Sun. 9–4:30. Closed Dec. 28–Jan. 3.*

The next house is the **Koizumi Yakumo Kyukyo** (Lafcadio Hearn Residence), unchanged since Koizumi left Matsue in 1891. Koizumi (1850–1904) was born of an Irish father and a Greek mother, and was christened Lafcadio Hearn. His early years were spent in Greece, but he left there to study in Britain before traveling to the United States, where he became a journalist. In 1890, he traveled to Japan and soon became a teacher in Matsue. During his tenure he met a samurai's daughter, who nursed him when he fell sick. Recovered, he married her and later became a Japanese citizen, taking the name Yakumo Koizumi. He spent only 15 months in Matsue, but it was here that he became enthralled with Japan, and, in his writings—*Japan: An Interpretation* and *In Ghostly Japan,* among others—he helped introduce Japan to the West. He died at the age of 54, while working as a professor at Waseda University in Tokyo. ☞ *¥250.* ☉ *Daily 8:30–5.*

Adjacent to Koizumi Yakumo's former home is the **Koizumi Yakumo Kinenkan** (Lafcadio Hearn Memorial Hall), which contains a good collection of Koizumi's manuscripts and other items, including his desk, that reflect his life in Japan. If it is at all possible, you should read his essay "In a Japanese Garden," contained in the volume *Glimpses of Unfamiliar Japan,* in which he writes his impressions of Matsue. You will surely be asked by every local resident whether you are familiar with his work. ☞ *¥250.* ☉ *Daily 8:30–5.*

Two minutes from the Memorial Hall is the Hearn Kyukyo bus stop, where you can catch a bus back to Matsue's center and the JR station. The main shopping street, Kyomise Shopping Arcade, is just before the bridge to the JR station. However, you may prefer to shop for crafts at the **Matsue Meisan Center** (☉ Daily 9–9), next to the smartest hotel in town, the Ichibata. (You can also shop on the north shore of Lake Shinji in the area known as Matsue Onsen.) At the center, products from all over Shimane Prefecture are on display and for sale, and, on its fourth floor, performances of folk dances are given four times a day. The Tourist Information Office at the JR station has the current schedule. ☞ *Performances ¥500 (tourist office).*

Should dusk soon be falling, position yourself to see the sun set over Lake Shinji. You can watch from the Matsue Meisan Center or from Shinjiko Ohashi, the first bridge over to the south side of Matsue (the same side as the JR station).

The railway station at Matsue Onsen is the most convenient setting-off point for Izumo Taisha, the second (after the Grand Shrines at Ise) most venerated shrine in Japan.

Izumo Taisha

Arriving and Departing

㉑ To go from Matsue Onsen to **Taisha,** the location of Izumo Taisha, it takes only 55 minutes on the Ichibata Electric Railway (fare: ¥750). You will need to change trains at Kanato Station for the Izumo Taisha-mae Station. The shrine is just a five-minute walk from there.

You can also get there by taking the JR train from Matsue Station back to Izumo, then transferring to the JR Taisha Line and taking that to Taisha Station, where you can either take a five-minute bus ride to Taisha-mae Station or walk directly to the shrine in about 20 minutes. The only two advantages of using the JR trains are the savings of using the JR Rail Pass and arriving at the ornate, palace-style JR Taisha Station—it is quite an oddity.

Exploring

Izumo Taisha claims the oldest site for a shrine in Japan, though the contemporary structure was built in 1874. Entrance to the shrine is under a giant torii followed by a 15-minute walk along a pine-shaded path. At the end stands the impressive Main Hall, shielded by a double fence so that one can only have glimpses of the architectural style, representative of Japan's oldest shrine construction. The shrine is dedicated to a male god, O-Kuni-Nushi, known as the creator of the land. Over time, his role has broadened to include managing fruitful relationships such as marriage and, even more recently, corporate mergers.

Notice the very steep, gabled roof of compressed bark descending from the ridge line, which runs from front to back rather than from side to side. Notice, too, that the ornately carved beams at the roof peak have their ends beveled perpendicular to the ground, an indication that the shrine is dedicated to a male god. (Shrines dedicated to female gods have their crossed beams beveled parallel to the ground.)

On either side of the compound are two rectangular buildings that are said to be the home of the Shinto gods, who meet annually at the shrine in October (the lunar month, which often falls in our Nov.). That is why in the rest of Japan, the lunar October is referred to as Kannazuki (Month Without Gods), while in Izumo, October is called Kamiarizuki (Month With Gods). This is where Japan was born, where her mythology was founded, and where the invading and successful Yamato and Izumo peoples accommodated each other's gods during the 2nd and 3rd centuries.

If you would like to go out to Hinomisaki (cape), exit the temple grounds to the west and take the bus (they go every hour) from the Ichibata Bus Terminal for the 25-minute ride (fare: ¥1,150). The seascape contains more of the beauty you see all along the San'in coast when traveling between Hagi and Matsue. The lighthouse on the cape is open to the public, and you may climb up the 127 feet to the top (remove your shoes first). Built in 1903, **Hinomisaki Lighthouse** is Japan's tallest and beams its light 21 nautical miles out to sea. And for climbing to its top, you will receive a certificate of ascent. ☛ *¥80.* ⊙ *Daily 8:30–4.*

The next destination up the San'in coast is the Tottori Sand Dunes, two hours by JR train from Matsue. En route you will pass by the town of **Yasugi,** best known for the Adachi Museum of Art (320 Furukawa-cho, Yasugi Shimane-ken, ☎ 0854/28–7111), which exhibits the works of both past and contemporary Japanese artists and has an inspiring series of gardens (☞ ¥2,300, half price if you show your passport; ☉ Tues.–Sun. 9–4:30). From **Yonago,** the next major town, buses leave every hour for the 50-minute ride to **Daisen** (fare: ¥590). Mount Daisen, a volcanic cone that locals liken to Mt. Fuji, is popular with hikers. But only during the autumn is the beauty of the region worth a detour. On the slopes above the town of Daisen is the ancient Tendai sect temple, Daisenji. A few sub-temples offer lodgings, such as Domyo-in (☎ 0859/52–2038) and Renjoin (☎ 0859/52–2506), where novelist Shiga Naoya stayed and used the setting for the ending of his *A Dark Night's Passing;* these cost about ¥6,300 per person with two meals. There are also several overpriced minshuku, such as the well-worn and dormitorylike Hakuun-so (25 Daisen, Daisencho, Saihaku-gun, Tottori-ken, ☎ 0859/52–2331) for around ¥8,000 per person, including two meals. After Yonago comes **Kurayoshi,** from where a 25-minute bus ride takes you to nearby **Misasa Onsen,** a revered 1,000-year-old hot-spring resort claiming the hottest, highest radium waters in the country. Then comes Tottori.

Tottori Dunes

Exploring

㉒ The reason for stepping off the train at **Tottori** is to visit the *hamasaka* (dunes). To reach them, take Bus 20, 24, 25, or 26 from gate 3 at the bus terminal in front of the JR station for the 15-minute ride (fare: ¥320) north. (The City Tourist Information Office is at the station; ☎ 0857/22–3318.) The dunes, a unique feature of the San'in coast, stretch along the shore for 16 kilometers (10 miles) and are 1½ kilometers (1 mile) wide. Some of the crests rise up to 300 feet, and they are always in motion. Endlessly, the sands shift and the shadows change. Each dune has wavy rivulets that seem to flow in the wind. The Tottori Dunes are an unexpected phenomenon, and therein lies their interest for the Japanese, though world travelers are likely to be disappointed. The dunes have appealed to the Japanese for making humans seem so temporal and insignificant. Literary figures would come to be mesmerized by the continually changing patterns of the dunes and the isolation they offered. Now tourists come in droves during the summertime. Camel rides are for hire, and there is a "kiddieland" to appeal to families. You must walk farther to escape the crowds and find your solitude. Better yet, rent a bicycle from the Cycling Terminal (Kodomo-no-kuni—near the entrance to the dunes), and work your way east to the Uradome Seashore. At the pier near the Iwamo-tobashi, you can board the San'in Matsushima Yuran sightseeing boat for a 50-minute trip along the coast to see the twisted pines and eroded rocks of the many islands that stand offshore (cost: ¥1,100).

Though Tottori is the prefectural capital, it has only marginal points of interest, so rather than stay in Tottori, continue on the JR San'in Main Line up the coast to either Kasumi or Kinosaki. The train parallels the shoreline, offering glimpses of the beautiful seascapes. One particular attraction is **Kasumi Bay,** where, on the east side, the sleepy **㉓** fishing village of **Kasumi** is located. Be sure to get up early, around 6 AM, to go down to the quay to watch the offloading of the night's catch and visit the fish market. The boats go out in the late evening and trawl during the night with a string of lights running fore and aft to attract the fish. The boats return to harbor at about 4 AM, but the market action doesn't begin until after the sun has come up.

To the left of the harbor is a small headland, **Okami Koen,** a park that used to be popular for lovers' suicides. Now there is a small restaurant in which to slurp noodles while contemplating the cliffs. Various sightseeing boats also leave from the quay. If you have time while you are in Kasumi, be sure to visit **Daijoji,** directly inland from the JR Kasumi Station. This temple's history began in 746, but it didn't become well known until the 18th century, when Okyo Maruyama, a leading artist of the time, came from Kyoto on a field trip with his students. Apparently Maruyama felt inspired, and he assigned his students to paint various themes in several rooms of the temple. Some of these themes took a long time to paint, especially the Gilded Peacock; the field trip lasted eight years. ☛ *¥500.* ☻ *Daily 8:30–4:30.*

An even more picturesque village is **Kundani,** two stations farther down the track on the local train from Kasumi (get off at Satsu Station). This small town of 300 people and two bars is a quiet haven on a horseshoe-shaped bay. There is nothing to do here but relax. You can stay at a hospitable minshuku (*see* Dining and Lodging *below*).

The alternative to spending the night at Kasumi or Kundani is to visit ㉔ **Kinosaki.** There are a couple of small temples in Kinosaki, **Onsenji** and **Gokurakuji,** to interest the visitor, but the real reason for staying here is the thermal baths. Virtually every inn and hotel has its own springs, but join in the traditional custom of visiting the seven public baths. Don't bother about dressing up: It is perfectly correct simply to wear your yakuta and join the procession from one bath to another. Each of these public baths charges about ¥300 and closes at 11:30 PM (two close at midnight, the Mandata-yu and the Sato-no-yu). Before taking the baths, you may want to visit the **Mugisen Folkcraft Shop,** at the top of the village's main street, to look at the wickerwork baskets and cases for which the area is known.

Ama-no-hashidate

㉕ The next and final major attraction on the San'in coast is **Ama-no-hashidate,** one of the Japanese "Big Three" scenic wonders. Most Westerners are slightly disappointed by it, and, indeed, the younger Japanese are, too. However, in the past, Japanese literati have waxed poetic about Ama-no-hashidate, so you may want to disembark from the train at Ama-no-hashidate Station, rent a bicycle from one of the stores in front of the station, and go and see what all the fuss is about.

Ama-no-hashidate is a 3-kilometer-long (2-mile-long) sandbar that stretches across **Miyazu Bay.** Its width varies from 100 to 350 meters, and it is lined with those contorted pine trees that so stir the Japanese imagination. For the best vantage point take the cable car from the northwest side of the **Kasamatsu Koen** (cost: ¥200); to get there, take the 15-minute bus ride from Ama-no-hashidate Station to Ichinomiya, or the ferry boat from Ama-no-hashidate Pier. (There are also bicycles for rent at the stores in front of the JR station.) When you have finally reached the top of Kasamatsu Koen, don't be surprised to see masses of people standing on stone benches with heads between their legs. This is the "proper" viewing stance to see Ama-no-hashidate (Bridge of Heaven), as the sandbar becomes a bridge in the sky. It is even more amusing to watch people taking photographs.

The San'in coast continues north as far as Maizuru, and though this tour ends at JR Ama-no-hashidate Station (from where there are trains to Kyoto), there are other sights to see. Any traveler seeking the traditional Japan should continue to leisurely explore the area.

DINING AND LODGING

Dining

When touring this region, we strongly recommend that you eat out at local Japanese restaurants. Most reasonably priced establishments will have a visual display of the menu in the window. On this basis, you can decide what you want before you enter. If you cannot order in Japanese and no English is spoken, after you secure a table, lead the waiter to the window display and point.

Unless the establishment is a *ryotei* (high-class, traditional Japanese restaurant), reservations are usually not required. Whenever reservations are advised or required at any of the restaurants listed, this is indicated.

A 3% federal consumer tax is added to all restaurant bills. Another 3% local tax is added to the bill if it exceeds ¥7,500. At more expensive restaurants, a 10%–15% service charge is added to the bill. Tipping is not the custom.

CATEGORY	COST*
$$$$	over ¥6,000
$$$	¥4,000–¥6,000
$$	¥2,000–¥4,000
$	under ¥2,000

Cost is per person without tax, service, or drinks

Lodging

Accommodations cover a broad spectrum, from pensions and *minshuku* to large, modern resort hotels that have little character but offer all the facilities of an international hotel. All of the large city and resort hotels offer Western as well as Japanese food. During the summer season, hotel reservations are advised.

Outside the cities or major towns, most hotels quote prices on a per-person basis with two meals, exclusive of service and tax. If you do not want dinner at your hotel, it is usually possible to renegotiate the price. Stipulate, too, whether you wish to have Japanese or Western breakfasts, if any. For the purposes here, the categories assigned to all hotels reflect the cost of a double room with private bath but no meals. However, if you make reservations at any of the noncity hotels, you will be expected to take breakfast and dinner at the hotel—that will be the rate quoted to you unless you specify otherwise.

A 3% federal consumer tax is added to all hotel bills. Another 3% local tax is added to the bill if it exceeds ¥15,000. At most hotels, a 10%–15% service charge is added to the total bill. Tipping is not the custom.

CATEGORY	COST*
$$$$	over ¥20,000
$$$	¥15,000–¥20,000
$$	¥10,000–¥15,000
$	under ¥10,000

Cost is for double room, without tax or service

Hagi

Dining

$$ Higaku-Mangoku. One of the delights of traveling along the San'in coast is enjoying the seafood. For each season the cold waters of the Japan Sea produce some of the sweetest delicacies, and there is no finer place in Hagi than Higaku-Mangoku to try them. Most of the fish is served as sashimi, but a few items are lightly grilled, and the crabs are boiled. ✕ *Shimo Gokenmachi, Hagi,* ☎ *0838/22–2136. Jacket and tie.* ☉ *Daily 11–8. V.*

$$ Nakon-mu. This is one of Hagi's better reasonably priced restaurants. The set menu (¥2,500) may include sashimi, baked fish, fish grilled in soy sauce, mountain vegetables, miso soup, and steamed rice. The restaurant has tatami and Western seating available but no English menu (select your food from the window display). ✕ *Huru-Hagi,* ☎ *0838/22–6619. No reservations. No credit cards.*

$ Fujita-ya. This is a casual restaurant, full of color, where locals delight
★ in handmade *soba* (buckwheat noodles) and hot tempura served on handmade Japanese cypress trays. ✕ *Kumagaicho, Hagi,* ☎ *0838/22–1086. No credit cards.* ☉ *11–7; closed 2nd and 4th Wed. of each month.*

Lodging

$$$$ Hokumon Yashiki. This elegant ryokan with luxurious rooms overlooks a garden. The gracious and refined service makes you feel pampered in the style to which the ancient Mori clan were surely accustomed. Japanese meals are served in your room. The inn is in the samurai section, near the castle grounds. ☎ *210 Horiuchi, Hagi, Yamaguchi-ken 758,* ☎ *FAX 0838/22–7521. 21 Japanese-style rooms. AE.*

$$–$$$ Hagi Grand Hotel. Convenience to the JR Higashi-Hagi Station makes this the number one choice for an international-style hotel in Hagi. The staff here are helpful and friendly, and the guest rooms are relatively spacious. ☎ *25 Furuhagicho, Hagi, Yamaguchi-ken 758,* ☎ *0838/25–1211,* FAX *0838/25–4422. 190 rooms, half Western-style. Japanese and Western restaurants, shops, travel services. AE, DC, MC, V.*

$$ Hotel Royal. Located in the Rainbow Building above JR Higashi-Hagi Station, this business hotel is friendly and efficient. The guest rooms are on the small size, but they are clean and comfortable. Business travelers and tourists stay here, and the front desk can arrange bicycle rentals for you. ☎ *3000-5 Chinto, Hagi, Yamaguchi-ken 758,* ☎ *0838/25–9595,* FAX *0838/25–8434. MC, V.*

$–$$ Hifumi Ryokan. Although the carpets in the ground-floor lounge and along the corridors are stained, the tatami rooms here are clean and well kept. Many have a private bath and a separate alcove with two easy chairs and a table. Ask for a quiet room; those facing the main street suffer from traffic noise. The food, served in your room, is above average but not as interesting as it should be with the Japan Sea so close. The common bath is small and can be congested just before dinner, so time yourself accordingly. Just across the bridge from the JR Higashi-Hagi station, on your right, Hifumi is 1½ kilometers (1 mile) from the center of Hagi. Bicycles can be rented nearby. ☎ *613 Tsuchihara, Hagi, Yamaguchi-ken 758,* ☎ *038/22–0123,* FAX *038/25–5937. 25 Japanese rooms, some with private bath. No credit cards.*

$ Fujita Ryokan. Across the river from downtown and a five-minute walk from JR Higashi-Hagi Station, this two-story concrete building is the best choice for inexpensive accommodations. The tatami rooms are standard but better kept than at the nearby Higashi-Hagi Minshiku, and the common bath is clean. There is a small lounge for relaxing. Ask for a room facing the river and with luck you'll see fishermen at work when you wake up. The owners do like their guests to take two meals (Japanese breakfast and dinner) here, but if you stay a night you may be able to persuade them not to enforce this. ☎ *Shinkawa Nishi-ku, Hagi, Yamaguchi-ken 758,* ☎ *0838/22–0603,* FAX *0838/26–1240. 13 Japanese-style rooms. Dining room. No credit cards.*

Hiroshima

Dining

$$$ **Mitakiso Ryokan.** For a kaiseki lunch or an elaborate kaiseki dinner
★ in a private tatami room, the Mitakiso Ryokan is superb. One of the
most respected ryokan in Hiroshima, it makes an excellent place to en-
tertain Japanese guests. It is not necessary to stay at the ryokan in order
to enjoy its cuisine. If you do stay, it is worth splurging and choosing
a room with sliding doors onto the private garden. ✕ *1-7 Mitakimachi,
Nishi-ku, Hiroshima 733,* ☎ *082/237–1402. Reservations required.
Jacket and tie. AE.*

$$ **Kanawa Restaurant.** Hiroshima is known for its oysters, especially in
★ the winter, when they are fresh and sweet. Kanawa, on a barge moored
on the Motoyasu River, near the Peace Memorial Park, is Hiroshima's
most famous oyster restaurant. Dining is on tatami matting, with river
views. Only oysters are served here, in at least 10 different ways. ✕
Moored on the river at Heiwa Bridge, Naka-ku, Hiroshima, ☎ *082/241–
7416. Jacket and tie. AE, V.* ◷ *11–10:30. Closed 1st and 3rd Sun. of
each month except Dec.*

$$ **Suishin Restaurant.** Famous for its sashimi and sushi, this restaurant
offers the freshest fish from the Inland Sea—globefish, oysters, and eel,
to name but a few. Order à la carte or from a set selection. If you do
not like raw fish, try the rockfish grilled with soy sauce. Suishin now
has an English-language menu. Ambience is plain and simple; there's
a counter bar and four tables. ✕ *6-7 Tatemachi, Naka-ku, Hiroshima,*
☎ *082/247–4411. AE, DC, V.* ◷ *11–10. Closed national holidays.*

$$ **Ten Ko.** The specialty in this small restaurant is seafood tempura. Part
of the secret to good tempura is the continual changing of the oil (after
every 4th or 5th order) so that a delicate crispness can be achieved.
This shop changes the oil frequently (probably selling the old oil to
the lesser tempura shops in the city). Other dishes are on the menu,
but come for the tempura. ✕ *2nd floor, Nakamachi 5-1, Naka-ku, Hiroshima,* ☎ *082/247–6088. AE, V.* ◷ *11–9:30.*

$ **Okonomi Mura.** In this modern, three-story building there are two dozen
small shops serving *okonomiyaki,* sometimes called Japanese pizza but
more like a Japanese frittata. ("Mura" means village.) A bed of noodles is topped with heaps of onions and green and red peppers, as well
as your choice of shrimp, pork, mussels, or chicken. Different areas in
Japan have their own style of creating okonomiyaki; in Hiroshima, the
ingredients are layered rather than mixed as is done in Osaka. Seating
in these shops is either at a wide counter in front of a grill or at tables
with their own grills. The chef-waiter prepares the ingredients and starts
the grilling; you complete the task. Choosing one shop over the other
is a dilemma, only partially solved by looking at the displays. Consider
trying Chii-Chau, which is owned by the man who conceived the idea
of creating a mall of okonomiyaki shops. The complex is close to the
Hondori shopping area, just west of Chuo-dori. ✕ *Okonomi Mura Bldg.,
Showamachi, Naka-ku, Hiroshima,* ☎ *082/241–8758. No credit cards.*
◷ *11–10.*

Lodging

$$$ **ANA Hotel Hiroshima.** In the business district on Peace Boulevard, the
★ hotel is within walking distance of the Peace Museum. With glittering
chandeliers, the pink-carpeted lobby looks onto a small garden with
a waterfall. The tea lounge facing the garden is an excellent place to
rest after visiting the Peace Memorial Park. The furnishings of the guest
rooms are uninspired, but the rooms have all the extras of a first-class
hotel, including English-speaking channels on the television. The Unkai

restaurant on the fifth floor has not only good Japanese food but also a view onto a Japanese garden of dwarf trees, rocks, and a pond of colorful carp. Many second-time visitors, as well as the local tourist office, consider the Hiroshima Grand the city's top hotel. ⌕ *7-20 Naka-machi, Naka-ku, Hiroshima 730,* ☎ *082/241–1111,* ℻ *082/241–9123. 431 rooms, all but 4 Western-style. Chinese, Japanese, and Western restaurants, summer rooftop beer garden, indoor pool, health club, sauna, shops. AE, DC, MC, V.*

$$$ **Hiroshima Prince.** The newest hotel (1994) in Hiroshima is a sparkling triangular complex down by Hiroshima Port. Its advantages are its newness and its views of the Inland Sea. Its disadvantage is its location, a 15-minute taxi ride from downtown and the Peace Park. Because of its isolation, the Prince bills itself as a resort hotel, with a swimming pool, a gallery of shops, an amusement hall, bowling alleys, a Burger King, and a marina for small boats. The mammoth scale is echoed in the hotel's expansive marble lobby with a fountain and pool the size of a small lake. Add to this the lobby's circular staircase and you have the paradigm of new Japan's ostentatiousness. The rooms, on the other hand, are quite ordinary, furnished with mass-produced products, characterless but extremely functional. The hotel has several restaurants (the Boston Steak House, a Chinese restaurant, the Hagoromo Japanese restaurant, and a coffee shop). The best spot is the bar and lounge at the top of the building, the 23rd floor, which offers a rare view over the Inland Sea. ⌕ *23-1 Moto-ujinamachi, Minami-ku, Hiroshima 734,* ☎ *082/256–1111,* ℻ *082/256–1134. 550 rooms. 4 restaurants, bar, lounge, pool, shops, banquet rooms. AE, DC, MC, V.*

$$–$$$ **Hiroshima Grand Hotel.** Operated by Japan Airlines, the Hiroshima
★ Grand is slightly more affordable in price than the newer ANA Hotel. Downtown, four blocks from the Peace Memorial Park and between Hiroshima Castle and Shukkeien, the Grand has established a reputation for fine service and comfort. It has less glitter than the ANA Hotel and appeals to the traveler who is looking for quiet refinement. The guest rooms are pleasantly furnished, though the views from their windows onto the street below are unappealing. ⌕ *4-4 Kami-Hatcho-bori, Naka-ku, Hiroshima 730,* ☎ *082/227–1313,* ℻ *082/227–6462. 381 rooms, all but 6 Western style. Chinese, Japanese, and Western restaurants, beauty salon, shops. AE, DC, V.*

$$–$$$ **Hiroshima Terminal Hotel.** This is the smartest and largest hotel near the station (located at the back, not the front); an expansive vaulted marble lobby greets you as you enter. The guest rooms, spacious by Japanese standards, are furnished in subdued pastels and ochers. The staff are briskly efficient, and many employees speak English. On the penthouse (21st) floor, the Japanese, Chinese, and French restaurants offer panoramic vistas, and there are cafés and a coffee shop on the second floor. Downtown Hiroshima and the Peace Park are only eight minutes away by streetcar. ⌕ *1-5 Matsubaracho, Minami-ku, Hiroshima 732,* ☎ *082/262–1111,* ℻ *082/262–4050. 440 rooms, mostly Western style. 4 restaurants, coffee shop, 2 bars, travel services, business services, meeting rooms. AE, DC, V.*

$ **Kenmin Bunka Center.** For a no-nonsense place to stay close to the Peace Memorial Park, this accommodation offers the best value for money in Hiroshima. It is strictly a business hotel, with small rooms and tiny bathrooms, but the decor is cheerful and refreshing, and the bathtubs are deep enough for a good soak. The Kenmin Bunka Center has neither lobby space nor lounges, but it does have an inexpensive cafeteria. Check-in is at 4 PM, and advance reservations are recommended.

⌨ *1-5-3 Otemachi-ku, Hiroshima 730,* ☎ *082/245–2322. 200 rooms. Cafeteria with Western and Japanese food. V.*

$ **Mikawa Ryokan.** This simple wooden ryokan offers the basics—tatami rooms, coin-operated television, air-conditioning, but no rooms with private baths. There are too many guests for the limited toilet facilities—indeed, they can get rather grubby. However, the inn has a good location seven minutes on foot south of the JR station; turn right on the street before Aori-dori. Advance reservations are advised. ⌨ *9-6 Kyobashicho, Minami-ku, Hiroshima 730,* ☎ *082/261–2719,* ⌨ *082/263–2706. 13 Japanese-style rooms. Breakfast only. AE.*

Kasumi

Dining

$–$$ **Hyotan.** You'll probably encounter someone here who knows ten words of English, which, combined with your ten words of Japanese, will be enough for an evening of conviviality. Hyotan is small, with counter seating for about ten people and space on tatami matting for only a small group. Tatsumi Nishimoto, his wife, and mother work behind the counter fulfilling requests for beer, sake, sashimi, and grilled fish. Some sashimi is likely to be presented with your drink order, so you may want to order the *hata-hata,* a small fish that is dusted with salt and grilled—an order is usually three fish that taste like they were just caught. ✕ *340-1 Nonokaichi, Kasumicho,* ☎ *0796/36–4047. No reservations. Evenings only. No cards.*

Lodging

$$ **Marusei Ryokan.** This small, quiet inn is in a concrete two-story building between the JR station and the harbor. The tatami rooms are quite spacious, made larger by the minimal furnishings. The scuff marks on the lower parts of the wall need to be removed; otherwise, everything is spotlessly clean. Bathrooms are cramped, but do have deep, narrow tubs. Meals are served in your room on request, but unless *kani-suki* (succulent crab casserole) is being offered you may want to venture out to the small pub named Hyotan (*see above*). ⌨ *Kasumicho, Kinosaki-gun, Hyogo-ken, 669,* ☎ *07963/6–0028,* ⌨ *0796/362–018. 11 Japanese-style rooms, 4 with private bath. Restaurant. No credit cards.*

Kinosaki

Lodging

$$$ **Mikaya Ryokan.** This three-story wood inn is delightfully old-fashioned,
★   with creaking timbers and spacious tatami rooms. It has its own thermal baths, which look out onto the garden. ⌨ *Kinosaki-gun, Hyogo-ken,* ☎ *07963/2–2031. 35 Japanese-style rooms. Japanese restaurant, thermal baths. AE, DC, V.*

Kundani

Lodging

$ **Minshuku Genroku Bekkan.** This private guest house is a true find. The
★   eight tatami guest rooms are spacious and freshly decorated, though none has a private bath. Excellent Japanese dinners are served. The husband speaks English—his wife tries—and he will likely invite you to the local bar after dinner. The house is in the center of the quiet fishing village, two streets from the sea. The closest JR station is Satsu; call on arrival and the owners will meet you at the station. ⌨ *Kundani Kasumi, Kinosaki-gun, Hyogo-ken,* ☎ *07963/8–0018. 8 rooms. Dinner and breakfast served. No credit cards.*

Kurashiki

Dining

$$ Hamayoshi. Only three tables (tatami seating with a well for your legs beneath the table) and a counter bar make up this personable restaurant specializing in fish from the Inland Sea. Sushi is just one option; another is *mamakari,* a kind of sashimi sliced from a live (very ugly) fish. A less adventurous dish is filleted fish lightly grilled. Another delicacy is *shako,* chilled boiled prawns. No English is spoken, but the owner will help you order and instruct you on how to enjoy the chefs' delicacies. Hamayoshi is on the main street leading from the station just before the Kurashiki Kokusai Hotel. ✘ *Chuo-dori,* ☎ *086/422–3420. No credit cards.* ◷ *11–2 and 5–10.*

$$ Kiyutei. For the best grilled steak in town, come to this attractive restaurant, where chefs work over the fires grilling your steak to order. The entrance to the restaurant is through a courtyard just across from the entrance to the Ohara Museum. ✘ *1-2-20 Chuo, Kurashiki,* ☎ *086/422–5141. No credit cards.* ◷ *11–9. Closed Mon.*

Lodging

$$$ Ryokan Kurashiki. In the atmosphere of the Edo period, this delight-
★ ful ryokan is made up of a merchant's mansion and three converted rice and sugar storehouses. Close to the Ohara Museum, with the Kurashikigawa flowing gently before it, this elegant ryokan maintains its serenity, no matter how many visitors are walking the streets in town. The cuisine is famous for its regional dishes, making the most of the oysters in the winter, fish straight from the Inland Sea in spring and autumn, and freshwater fish in the summer. There is a wonderful inner garden on which to gaze while sipping green tea in the afternoons. Here is Japanese hospitality at its best. Even if you are not staying here, you can still experience the ryokan by having lunch (¥10,000 per person) or dinner (¥14,000 per person). ☒ *4-1 Honmachi, Kurashiki, Okayama-ken 710,* ☎ *086/422–0730,* ℻ *086/422–0990. 20 rooms, some with private bath. Japanese restaurant, teahouse. AE, DC.*

$$–$$$ Kurashiki Kokusai Hotel. Owned by Japan Airlines, this is the best Western hotel in town, although it caters mostly to Japanese. The staff don't speak much English, and room TVs have no English channel. The lobby has a black tile floor and dramatic woodblock prints by Japanese artist Shiko Munakata. Corridors in the older part of the hotel are dark and somewhat worn, and the rooms in this section are small and in need of redecorating. Ask for a room in the newer annex, which is bright and cheery; those in the back of the building overlook a garden. The location of the Kokusai is ideal—a 10-minute walk on the main road leading from the station and just around the corner from the old town and the Ohara Museum. There is a 24-hour store nearby. The Achi Japanese restaurant serves good seafood from the Inland Sea; tempura is prepared at the table. ☒ *1-1-44 Chuo, Kurashiki, Okayama-ken 710,* ☎ *086/422–5141,* ℻ *086/422–5192. 106 rooms, 4 Japanese style. Western and Japanese restaurants, bar, banquet rooms, beauty salon, parking. AE, DC, MC, V.*

$$ Hotel Kurashiki. Just above the station, this is an efficient business hotel that is useful if you have an early morning train to catch. Even after refurbishing it is a little dreary, but at least the bathrooms are custommade, and not the usual plastic cubicles. Certainly, now with a new coat of paint, this Japan Railways hotel is better than the adjacent Kurashiki Terminal hotel, where the rooms are downright shabby. ☒ *1-1-1 Achi, Kurashiki, Okayama-ken 710,* ☎ *086/426–6111,* ℻

068/426–6163. 139 Western-style rooms. Japanese/Western restaurant. AE, DC, MC, V.

$ **Kamoi.** This hostelry is the best bargain in Kurashiki. The rooms are simple—tatami style. The food is good, as it should be; the owner is also the owner and chef of Kamoi Restaurant, across from the Ohara Museum. A visual display in the window shows what is offered, and the walls are decorated with artifacts such as cast-iron kettles and ancient rifles. An eight-minute walk from the Ohara Museum, this minshuku is close to Tsurugatayama Park and Achi Jinja. ☎ *6-21 Honmachi, Kurashiki, Okayama-ken 710, ☎ 086/422–4898, ℻ 086/427–7615. 17 Japanese-style rooms, none with bath. Japanese breakfast (Western breakfast on request) and dinner served. No credit cards. Closed Mon.*

Matsue

Dining

$$ **Ginsen Restaurant.** Close to the Tokyu Inn and not far from the north exit of JR Matsue Station, this restaurant is popular with the locals for its fresh seafood casseroles. The season determines what these are, and with Lake Shinji on hand, the fish is superb and the prices are reasonable. ✕ *Asahimachi, Matsue, ☎ 0852/21–2381. No credit cards. ⊙ 11–10.*

$–$$ **Kawabata Sushi.** Take sweet, succulent fish from the Sea of Japan, ★ combine them with top-rate sushi chefs, and you have Kawabata. No English is spoken, but the chefs will make you feel comfortable, and you can point to the fish that take your fancy. The long counter bar is a good place to sit and watch the action, but there are also tables with tatami seating. This sushi bar has more atmosphere than many, with Japanese drums hanging from the walls. The restaurant is upstairs from a spacious entrance hall—models of the dishes are displayed in a window downstairs—three short blocks from the Matsue Washington Hotel. Walk left from the hotel's entrance to where the street becomes a pedestrian-only mall and then take a right. The restaurant is at the next corner on your right. ✕ *Off Kyomise Arcade, Matsue, ☎ 0852/21–0689. No reservations. No credit cards.*

$ **Hi-daka-toshi-yuki.** For fun and socializing with the locals, this yakitori bar with counter service offers a delightful evening's entertainment, good grilled chicken, and flowing sake. Two doors from Ginsen restaurant, it's easily recognized by its red lanterns outside. ✕ *Asahimachi, Matsue, ☎ 0852/31–8308. No credit cards. ⊙ 11–11.*

Lodging

$$$ **Minamikan.** This is Matsue's most elegant and prestigious ryokan, taste- ★ fully furnished and with refined service. It also has the best restaurant in Matsue for kaiseki haute cuisine and *tai-meshi* (sea bream with rice). Even if you do not stay here, make reservations for dinner. ☎ *Ohashi, Matsue, Shimane-ken 690, ☎ 0852/21–5131, ℻ 0852/26–0351. 27 Japanese-style rooms. Japanese restaurant. AE.*

$$–$$$ **Hotel Ichibata.** Located in the spa section of town, next to Lake Shinji, the Ichibata appeals to those on a restful vacation who want to enjoy the thermal waters. For a long time, the hotel has been the leading place to stay in central San'in and, consequently, shows signs of wear. The guest rooms facing the lake are the nicest but are also the most expensive. All of the Japanese-style rooms face the lake; not so the Western ones. Still, if you do not mind the 20-minute walk from the station or downtown (or a ¥1,750 taxi ride), the Ichibata is Matsue's first choice, if only to watch the sunsets from its vermilion lounge on the penthouse floor. ☎ *30 Chidoricho, Matsue, Shimane-ken 690,* ☎ *0852/22–0188,* FAX *0852/22–0230. 137 rooms, half Western-style. Japanese/Western restaurant, summer beer garden, hot-springs baths. AE, DC, MC, V.*

$$ **Matsue Washington Hotel.** The rooms here are modern but very small; take a more expensive room if you don't want to trip over your suitcase. The coffee shop on the ground floor serves both as a lounge and a place for light meals. There is also a formal restaurant serving *shabu-shabu* and other Japanese meals. The big advantage of this upmarket business hotel is its location in the old downtown section of Matsue, where restaurants abound. There's a pedestrian mall lined with shops nearby, the castle is a ten-minute walk away, and the lake is even closer. ☎ *Hagashi Honmachi 2-22, Matsue, Shimane-ken,* ☎ *0852/22–4111,* FAX *0852/22–4120. 158 rooms. Japanese and Western restaurants, coffee shop. AE, DC, MC, V.*

Less expensive (about ¥4,200) accommodations close to the JR station are the business hotels—the **Green Hotel** (☎ 0852/27–3000) and the **Business Yamamoto** (☎ 0852/21–6121)—or two small, 10-room lodging houses, the **Business Ishida** (☎ 0852/21–5931) and the popular **Ryokan Terazuya** (☎ 0852/21–3480), both of which have only Japanese-style rooms.

Miyajima

Lodging

$$$–$$$$ **Iwaso Ryokan.** For tradition and elegance, this is the Japanese inn
★ at which to stay or dine on the island. The inn has a newer wing, but the older rooms have more character. Two cottages on the grounds have Japanese suites that are superbly decorated with antiques. The prices at the inn vary according to the size of the guest room, its view, and the dinner that you select. Be sure, when you make reservations in advance, to specify what you want and fix the price. Breakfast and dinner are usually included. ☎ *345 Miyajimacho, Hiroshima-ken 739,* ☎ *0829/44–2233,* FAX *0829/44–2287. 45 Japanese-style rooms. Japanese restaurant, but Western breakfast served on request. AE.*

$$ **Jyukeiso Ryokan.** For a more modest place to stay, this family ryokan (the owner speaks English) makes a pleasant home. However, it is to the east of the ferry pier (away from the town and shrine), which may not be what you want. Breakfast and dinner are usually included. ☎ *Miyajimacho, Hiroshima-ken 739,* ☎ *0829/44–0300,* FAX *0829/44–0388. 20 Japanese-style rooms, 2 with private bath. Japanese restaurant, but Western breakfast served on request. AE, MC, V.*

Shimonoseki

Lodging

$ **Bizenya Ryokan.** Should you have to spend the night in this town waiting for a ferry to Pusan or the morning train up the San'in coast, this small ryokan has clean tatami rooms and offers either Continental or Japanese breakfasts before you leave in the morning. To reach the ryokan, take the bus at bus stop No. 2 from the JR station to Nishinohashi bus stop. The ryokan is a two-minute walk from there. ☎ *3-11-7 Kamitanakamachi, Shimonoseki, Yamaguchi-ken 750,* ☎ *0832/22–6228. 13 rooms, not all with bath. Japanese food served, as well as Continental breakfast. AE, V.*

Susa

Lodging

$–$$ **Minshuku Susa.** Rooms at this minshuku are huge, at least 10-tatami,
★ and have an alcove for a coffee table and two chairs. The best look
onto the harbor of this picturesque fishing village between Hagi and
Masuda on the Japan Sea. The bathroom is splendid, with an iron Goemon tub (Goemon Ishikawa, a Japanese version of Robin Hood, was
boiled alive). Service is more in the style of a traditional ryokan and
such niceties as an orange in the bath to scent the water are not overlooked. No English is spoken, but the staff's friendliness overcomes
any language barrier. Dinner served in a tatami-floor dining room is
an occasion to try the region's delicacies from the sea. ⌂ *Irie, Susa-
cho, Abu-gun, Yamaguchi-ken, 690,* ☎ *08387/6–2408. 6 rooms, 2 with
private toilet. Japanese meals served in the dining room. No credit cards.*

Tottori

Lodging

$$–$$$ **New Otani.** This multistory red-concrete building across from the JR
station is the most modern hotel in town. The guest rooms are compact and are smartly decorated in cream and red. ⌂ *2-153 Imamachi,
Tottori-shi 650,* ☎ *0857/23–1111,* ℻ *0857/23–0979. 150 rooms. Western and Japanese restaurants, meeting rooms. AE, DC, MC, V.*

Tsuwano

Dining

$$ **Yu-uki.** This restaurant is famous for its carp dishes (such as carp
sashimi and carp miso soup) and mountain vegetables. The decor in-
cludes traditional beams, a sunken pit for your feet under the table,
and a stream running through the center of the dining room. ✗ *Hon-
cho-dori, Tsuwano,* ☎ *0856/2–0162. No credit cards.* ◷ *Noon–2
and 6–8.*

$ **Hibaya.** A pub could get no tinier than this. There are only six stools
at the counter, and Mama-san behind has barely enough room to turn.
Somehow, though, she is able to make up *yakisoba,* fried dumplings,
hotpots, and horsemeat sashimi for her clients and keep the beer and
sake flowing. Although she speaks no more than 20 words of English,
she'll make you feel welcome, and what may have begun as a quick
drink will end up as a full evening of food and amiable company. ✗
Higashi-dori, Isuwano, ☎ *0856/2–2288. No reservations. No credit
cards.*

Lodging

$$ **Sunroute Tsuwano.** This is the only place in town that has Western-
style accommodations. Rooms, as in other Sunroute hotels, are com-
pact: The mass-produced furniture is crammed in. Bathrooms are
plastic modules with tiny bathtubs. Still, all is clean, and the staff,
though unable to speak English, are friendly. There is a restaurant
and bar, but it is better to eat in and then drink in town. The down
side is that the hotel is a stiff, ten-minute walk from town and the
station. ⌂ *Terada, Tsuwanocho, Kanoashi-gun 699,* ☎ *0856/2–
3232,* ℻ *0856/2–2805. 50 Western rooms. Restaurant, bar. AE,
MC, V.*

$$ **Tsuwano Kanko Hotel.** This pleasant establishment is the most centrally
located hotel in town, with fair-size guest rooms and a friendly staff.
The furnishings have become worn and drab, however, and the Japanese
restaurant is only passable. ⌂ *Ushiroda, Tsuwanomachi, Kanoashi-*

gun 699, ☎ *0856/2–0333,* FAX *0856/2–1543. 39 Japanese-style rooms, 31 with bath. Japanese restaurant, Western breakfast on request. AE, V.*

$ **Wakasagi-no-Yado.** This is a small minshuku run by a friendly fam-
★ ily who speak very limited English. They are, however, eager to help overseas tourists and will meet guests at Tsuwano Station, an eight-minute walk away. ⊞ *Mori, Tsuwanocho, Kanoashi-gun 699-56,* ☎ *08567/2–1146. 8 rooms, none with bath. Japanese and Western break-fasts. No credit cards.*

WESTERN HONSHU ESSENTIALS

Arriving and Departing

By Plane

Domestic airports at Hiroshima, Izumo, Tottori, and Yonago connect these cities to Tokyo with daily flights. However, Hiroshima is the major airport for this region, with seven daily flights to Tokyo's Haneda Airport (1 hr., 15 mins.) as well as direct daily flights to the city of Kagoshima (1 hr., 10 mins.), on Kyushu, and the city of Sapporo (1 hr., 55 mins.), on Hokkaido.

By Train

By far the easiest way to travel to Western Honshu and all along its southern shore is by the Shinkansen trains that run from Tokyo and Kyoto through southern Western Honshu to Hakata, on the island of Kyushu. The major stops on the Shinkansen line are Himeji, Okayama, and Hiroshima. It takes four hours and 37 minutes on the Shinkansen to travel to Hiroshima from Tokyo, one hour and 39 minutes from Osaka. To cover the length of southern Western Honshu from Osaka to Shimonoseki (the last city on Honshu before Kyushu) takes only three hours.

JR express trains cover both the southern and northern shores of Western Honshu, making, as it were, an elliptical loop around the shoreline, beginning and ending in Kyoto. Crossing from one coast to the other in Western Honshu requires traveling through the mountains (slow going), but there are several train lines that link the cities on the northern Sea of Japan coast to Okayama, Hiroshima, and Ogori. These are discussed above in the San'in section.

Guided Tours

The **Japan Travel Bureau** (JTB) has offices at every JR station in each of the major cities and can assist in local tours, hotel reservations, and ticketing. Except for JTB's Hiroshima office (☎ 082/261–4131), one should not assume that any English will be spoken beyond the essentials.

Japan Travel Bureau, operating through Sunshine Tours, has one-, two-, and three-day tours from Kyoto and Osaka to Hiroshima. The one-day tour (¥52,720 per person) covers Hiroshima and Miyajima. The two-day tour (¥105,000 per person) also includes a hydrofoil trip on the Inland Sea to visit the islands Omishima and Ikuchijima. The three-day tour (¥147,250 per person) adds a visit to Kurashiki and Okayama.

No guided tours of the San'in region are conducted in English, though the Japan Travel Bureau will arrange your individual travel plans.

Important Addresses and Numbers

Emergencies
Police, ☏ 110; **Ambulance,** ☏ 119.

Tourist Information Centers
Most major towns or sightseeing destinations have tourist information centers that offer free maps and brochures. They will also help in securing accommodations. The following telephone numbers are for the tourist information centers located at the major tourist destinations in Western Honshu: **Hagi City Information Office,** ☏ 08382/5–3145; **Hagi City Tourist Association** at Emukai, ☏ 08382/5–1750; **Himeji Tourist Information Office,** ☏ 0792/85–3792; **Hiroshima City Tourist Office,** ☏ 082/245–2111; **Hiroshima Prefectural Tourist Office,** ☏ 082/221–6516; **Hiroshima Tourist Information Office,** ☏ 082/249–9329; **Kurashiki Tourist Information Office,** ☏ 086/426–8681; **Matsue Tourist Information Office,** ☏ 0852/21–4034; **Miyajima Tourist Association,** ☏ 0829/44–2011; **Okayama Prefectural Tourist Office,** ☏ 0862/24–2111; **Okayama Tourist Information Office,** ☏ 0862/22–2912; **Tsuwano Tourist Association Information Office,** ☏ 08567/2–1144.

Japan Travel Phone
The nationwide service for English-language assistance or travel information is available seven days a week, 9–5. Dial toll-free 0120/444–800 for information on western Japan. When using a yellow, blue, or green public phone (do not use the red phones), insert a ¥10 coin, which will be returned.

11 Shikoku

The smallest of Japan's four main islands, Shikoku lies to the south of Western Honshu, across the Inland Sea and now reachable by road and rail by a remarkable chain of bridges. Rugged east-west mountain ranges halve this island, where travelers are treated more as welcome foreign emissaries than as income-bearing tourists and where Japanese Buddhists still come to make religious pilgrimages to 88 sacred temples, as they have done for centuries.

THE SMALLEST OF JAPAN'S FOUR MAJOR ISLANDS, Shikoku is often omitted from tourist plans by both Japanese and foreigners. This is due in part to the fact

By Nigel Fisher that, until rather recently, travelers had to take a ferry across the Inland Sea. But with the 1989 opening of the Seto Ohashi (bridge), which links Shikoku by both road and rail to Honshu at Kojima (south of Okayama), the island is attracting more visitors. Many come to see the 12-kilometer-long (7 1/2-mile-long) bridge that seems to leap from island to island as it arches across the water, high above the ships passing beneath. The bridge is composed of several shorter expanses, making it possible to get off on the small islands between Honshu and Shikoku, with their lookout areas and souvenir shops. Those who make it all the way across the bridge head for Takamatsu to visit Ritsurin Koen (park) and then go on to Kotohira and its much revered Kotohiragu (shrine). Far fewer travelers venture beyond Kotohira into the heart of Shikoku and down to its southern shores. This, however, is also likely to change with the Japanese people's growing appreciation of warm days on the beach.

Shikoku's isolation may also be attributed to the rugged mountain ranges that run east to west and divide Shikoku into two halves, each with a different climate. The northern half, which faces the Inland Sea, has a dry climate, with only modest rains in the autumn during typhoon season. The southern half, which faces the Pacific, is more likely to have ocean storms sweep in, bringing rain throughout the year. With its shores washed by the warm waters of the Kuroshio (Black Current), it has a warmer climate and especially mild winters. The mountain ranges of the interior are formidable, achieving heights up to 6,400 feet, and are cut by wondrous gorges and valleys. Nestled in these valleys are small farming villages that appear unchanged since the Edo period (1603–1868). Shikoku is an island worth exploring, where travelers are greeted more as welcome foreign emissaries than as income-bearing tourists.

Despite the fact that Shikoku has been part of Japan's political and cultural development since the Heian period (794–1192), the island has retained an independence from mainstream Japan. Some factories litter the northern coast, but, to a great extent, Shikoku has been spared the ugliness of Japan's industrialization. The island is still considered by many Japanese as a rural backwater where pilgrims trek to the 88 sacred temples.

The Buddhist saint Kobo Daishi was born on Shikoku in 774, and it was he who founded the Shingon sect of Buddhism that became popular in the shogun eras. (During the reign of the Tokugawa Shogunate, travel was restricted, except for pilgrimages.) Pilgrims visit 88 temples to honor Kobo Daishi, and by doing so, they can be released from having to go through the cycle of rebirth. Many Japanese wait until they have retired to make this pilgrimage, in part because the time is right and in part because it used to take two months on foot to visit all the temples. In modern times, however, most pilgrims now scoot around by bus in 13 days.

EXPLORING

Numbers in the margin correspond to points of interest on the Shikoku map.

There are three major cities on Shikoku: Takamatsu in the north, Kochi in the south, and Matsuyama in the northwest. To these three you may possibly add Tokushima, on the island's east coast. Few overseas visitors travel to Tokushima, but if you can visit there during August 12–15, you will witness one of the liveliest, most humor-filled festivals in Japan. The Awa Odori (dance) is an occasion for the Japanese to let all their reserves fall away and act out their fantasies. Prizes are even given to the "Biggest Fool" in the parades, and foreigners are welcome to compete for these awards. Also, near Tokushima are the Naruto Straits, with giant whirlpools. At each ebb and flow of the tide, the currents rush through this narrow passage to form hundreds of foaming whirlpools of various sizes. To reach the whirlpools, take yellow bus No. 1 from JR Tokushima Station plaza (fare: ¥690) to Seto Inland Sea National Park, of which the Naruto whirlpools are part. From the station it's a 15-minute walk to the new Onaruto Suspension Bridge, which crosses the straits to Awajishima (island). (By the year 2000, another bridge will link Awajishima to Honshu.) The Naruto whirlpools can be seen below the beginning of the bridge.

A short and popular itinerary for the overseas visitor to Shikoku is to arrive at Takamatsu and travel west along the north coast to Matsuyama, with one short detour to Kotohiragu (shrine). Such an itinerary could be accomplished in two nights and two days. However, we recommend continuing on from Kotohiragu, crossing through the mountains to Kochi on the Pacific Coast, and traveling around the island's west coast to approach Matsuyama from the south. From Matsuyama, there is a hydrofoil to Hiroshima.

Takamatsu

❶ The JR station and the pier at **Takamatsu** share the same location at the north end of Chuo-dori, Takamatsu's main avenue, where most of the large hotels are located. The Takamatsu Information Office (☎ 0878/51–2009) has a small office just outside the JR Station. The maps and brochures are limited to Kagawa Prefecture, of which Takamatsu is the capital. If you need information on the entire island, make sure that you visit the Tourist Information Center in Tokyo or Kyoto before you set out for Shikoku. A bus tour (Japanese-speaking guide only) departs at 8:45 AM from Takamatsu-Chikko Bus Station (near the JR station) and covers Takamatsu's Ritsurin Koen (park), Kotoshira, and other sights. The tour takes about eight hours, 45 minutes.

Three hundred meters down Chuo-dori, on the left-hand side, begin the shopping arcades, within which are department stores, shops, and restaurants. The east–west arcade is intersected by another arcade running north–south (parallel to Chuo-dori). The small streets off the arcades are crowded with bars, cabarets, and smaller restaurants.

★ The number one attraction in Takamatsu is **Ritsurin Koen,** once the summer retreat of the Matsudaira clan. To reach the garden, which is at the far end of Chuo-dori, take a 10-minute ride (cost: ¥220) on any bus that leaves from in front of the Grand Hotel from stop No. 2. (The bus makes a short detour from the main avenue to include a bus depot on its route. Don't disembark from the bus until it rejoins the main avenue—Chuo-dori—and travels two more stops.) Alternatively, take the JR train bound for Tokushima and disembark five minutes later at the second stop, Ritsurin Koen.

Ritsurin Koen, completed in the late 17th century after 100 years of careful planning, landscaping, and cultivation, is actually two gardens.

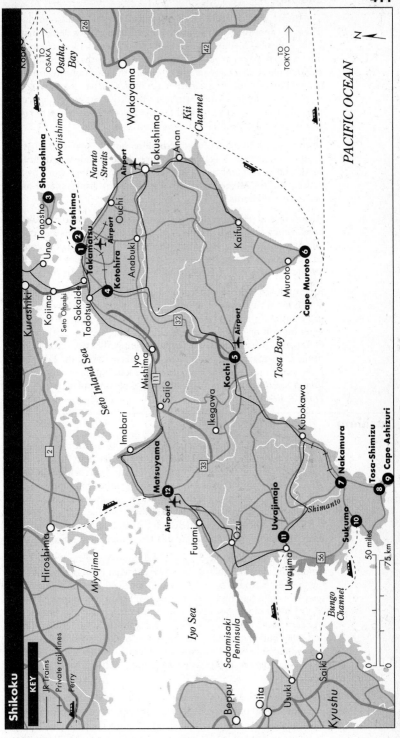

Shikoku

KEY

— JR Trains

—|— Private rail lines

--- Ferry

TO
KOBE

26

TO
OSAKA

Osaka
Bay

42

TO
TOKYO

N

PACIFIC OCEAN

Kii
Channel

Wakayama

Awajishima

Naruto
Straits

Tonosho

Shodoshima

3

Uno

Yashima

Airport

Tokushima

Anan

1 2

Takamatsu

Airport

Ouchi

Kurashiki

Kojima

Seto Ohashi

Sakaide

Tadotsu

Anabuki

Kotohira

4

Kaifu

Muroto

Cape Muroto 6

32

Iyo-
Mishima

11

Saijo

Airport

5

Kochi

Tosa Bay

Seto Inland Sea

Imabari

Ikegawa

Kubokawa

2

33

Nakamura

Tosa-Shimizu

Cape Ashizuri

Matsuyama

12

Airport

7

8 9

Hiroshima

Futami

zu

Uwajimajo

11

Shimanto

Sukumo

10

Miyajima

Uwajima

56

Iyo Sea

Sadamisaki
Peninsula

Bungo
Channel

Saiki

50 miles

75 km

Beppu

Oita

Usuki

Kyushu

0

The north garden is more modern and has wide expanses of lawns. The more appealing south garden is traditional, with a design that follows a classical layout. The garden's 6 ponds and 13 scenic mounds are arranged so that as you walk the intersecting paths, at virtually every step there is a new view or angle to hold the focus of attention. You cannot hurry through this garden: Each rock, each tree shape, each pond rippling with multicolored carp has a fluidity of motion enhanced by the reflections of the water and the shadows of the trees. ☛ ¥310. ⊙ *Daily 5:30 AM–7 PM (5:30–5 in winter).*

Within the north garden is an **exhibition hall,** displaying and selling local products from Kagawa Prefecture; these include wood carvings, masks, kites, and umbrellas. Another museum exhibits work by local artists, and the **Mingeikan** (Folk Art Museum) displays local handicrafts and folkcrafts.

Ritsurin's real gem is in the south garden. It is the teahouse, **Kikugetsutei,** which looks as if it is floating on water. Here, you may enjoy a cup of green tea and muse on the serene harmony of the occasion, just as the lords of Matsudaira did in previous centuries. ☛ ¥310; *tea is an additional ¥310, or you can get a combination ticket for ¥590.*

Ritsurin Koen is the reason to visit Takamatsu; the bombings of World War II left the city with few other visible attractions. However, if you are waiting for a train or ferry, there's one more sight to see: Across from the station and behind the Grand Hotel are the castle grounds of Tamamo Koen. **Tamamojo Castle,** built in 1588, was once the home of the Matsudaira clan, who ruled Takamatsu during the Edo period. Now, only a few turrets of the castle are left, but its setting, with the Inland Sea in the background, makes it a pleasant place. ☛ ¥100. ⊙ *Daily 8:30–6.*

Yashima

JR trains from Takamatsu Station make the 20-minute run every hour east to **Yashima,** or you can take the commuter tram Kotoden from the Chikko terminal (across from the JR station and behind the Grand Hotel). These run 10 times a day; the tourist office can supply a schedule. When you arrive at Yashima Station, simply walk up the hill to the reconstructed village of **Shikoku Mura** and the battle site where, in 1185, the Minamoto clan defeated the Taira family, allowing Yoritomo Minamoto to establish Japan's first shogunate, in Kamakura.

In this open-air museum village, 21 houses have been relocated from around the island of Shikoku to represent what rural life was like during the Edo period. The village may be artificial, but in this age where ferro-concrete has replaced so much of traditional Japan, Shikoku Mura provides an opportunity to see traditional thatch-roof farmhouses, a papermaking workshop, a ceremonial teahouse, a rural Kabuki stage, and other buildings used in the feudal age. Similar to Hida Village near Takayama, Shikoku Mura presents a picture of what life was like 200 to 300 years ago. ☛ ¥800. ⊙ *Daily, Apr.–Oct. 8:30–5; Nov.–Mar. 8:30–4:30.*

Close to Shikoku Mura's entrance is a cable car, which takes five minutes (fare: ¥600 one-way, ¥1,010 round-trip) to travel up to **Yashima Plateau.** Yashima was once an island (it's now connected to Shikoku by a narrow strip of land), and on its summit, nearly 1,000 feet above the Inland Sea, the Minamoto and Taira clans clashed. Relics from the battle are on view in the Treasure House at Yashimaji (originally constructed in 754, it is the 84th of the 88 sacred temples), but the major reasons for ascending this plateau are the expansive vistas over the Inland Sea and views of Shodoshima.

Shodoshima

★ ❸   A longer excursion from Takamatsu is to **Shodoshima,** the second largest island in the Inland Sea. The ferry (fare: ¥520) takes an hour from Takamatsu Pier to reach Tonosho, the island's major town and port. A hydrofoil makes the same run in 35 minutes (fare: ¥1,100). Tonosho may also be reached by a 40-minute hydrofoil ride (fare: ¥1,660) from Okayama Port (take Bus 12 from JR Okayama Station to Okayama Port) or on a regular ferry from Himeji Port (1 hr., 40 mins.; fare: ¥1,170). Sightseeing bus tours depart from Tonosho to cover all the island sights, or you can simply use the public buses—they cover the island efficiently and thoroughly. Motorized bicycles may also be rented for ¥3,000 a day, including insurance, from Ryobi Rent-a-Bike (☎ 62–6578, open 8:30–5) near Tonosho's pier.

The major attraction on Shodo is **Kankakei Gorge,** an hour's bus ride (fare: ¥610) from Tonosho. The gorge is about 3½ miles long and 2½ miles wide, hemmed in by a wall of mountainous peaks with weather-eroded rocks. The thick maple and pine forest lining the gorge creates a splash of color in the autumn; in the spring, the profusion of azaleas makes for an equally colorful spectacle. If the grandeur of the gorge is not thrilling enough, you can take an aerial tramway to the summit that travels frighteningly close to the cliffs' walls. Then take a bus back to Tonosho via Kusakabe.

The other principal attractions on Shodo are **Kujukuen** (15 mins. by bus from Tonosho), where 3,000 peacocks roam; **Choshikei Gorge** (25 mins. by bus from Tonosho), which extends along the upper stream of the Denpo River; and the nearby **monkey park,** where 700 wild monkeys cavort.

Several minshuku offer accommodation on the island. Try **Churchi** (☎ 0879/62–3679), with 10 rooms, or **Maruse** (☎ 0879/62–2385), with six rooms, both in Tonosho.

Kotohira

❹   From Takamatsu, the JR train takes 55 minutes to reach **Kotohira** Station, from which it is an eight-minute walk to the steps that lead up

★   to **Kotohiraguo.** (If the JR train is not convenient, you can take the 70-minute tram ride that departs from the other side of the Takamatsu Station plaza.) Note: While occasionally there is an open cloakroom to the left of the station, there are no lockers. If you are only visiting for the day, travel light—even small packs become very heavy while you are mounting the 785 stairs to the shrine. This shrine may not rank quite as high in importance as do the Grand Shrines at Ise or Izumo Taisha near Matsue, but it is one of Japan's oldest and grandest. It is also one of the most popular shrines in Japan: Four million visitors come to pay their respects each year.

Founded in the 11th century and built on the slopes of Mt. Zozu, Kotohiragu is dedicated to Omono-nushi-no-Mikoto (Konpira, as he is fondly known), the guardian god of the sea and patron of seafarers. Traditionally, fishermen and sailors would come to visit the shrine and solicit godly help for their safe passage at sea. However, their monopoly on seeking the aid of Konpira has ended. His role has expanded to include all travelers, including tourists, though it is uncertain whether messages written in English will be understood.

To reach the main gate of the shrine, you must first mount 365 granite steps. On either side of the steps are souvenir and refreshment stands. However, don't dawdle. There are another 420 steps to the main shrine. Beyond the main gate, the souvenir stands are replaced by stone lanterns. The climb becomes more of a solemn, spiritual exercise. Just before the second torii (arch) is the shrine's **Homotsukan** (Treasure House), with an impressive display of sculpture, scrolls, and, despite their Buddhist origins, Noh masks. ☛ ¥250. ☺ Daily 9–4.

The next important building, on your right, is **Shoin** (1659), its interior covered in paintings by the famous 18th-century landscape artist Okyo Maruyama (1733–1795). Maruyama came from a family of farmers and, not surprisingly, looked to the beauty of nature for his paintings. Such was his talent that a new style—the Maruyama school—of painting developed, which may be best termed "Return to Nature."

Onward and forever upward, you'll see the intricate carvings of animals on the facade of **Asahino Yashiro,** and, at the next landing, you'll finally be at the main shrine, a complex of buildings that were rebuilt 100 years ago. Aside from the sense of accomplishment in making the climb, the views over Takamatsu and the Inland Sea to the north and the mountain ranges of Shikoku to the south justify the climb of 785 steps, even more perhaps than a visit to the shrine itself. That is, unless you ask Konpira for good fortune, and, after climbing 785 steps, you may want to.

Allow a total of an hour from the time you start your ascent up the granite stairs until you return. Just as the feudal lords once did, you may hire a palanquin to porter you up and down (cost: ¥4,500 one-way, ¥6,000 round-trip). Riding in a palanquin has a certain appeal, and it most certainly saves the calf muscles, but the motion and narrow confines are not especially comfortable.

It is worth making the time to visit the oldest Kabuki theater in Japan. Located in Kotohira Koen, it is only a 10-minute walk from Kotohira Station and is near the first flight of steps leading to Kotohiragu. The theater, called **Konpira O-Shibai,** is exceptionally large and was moved from the overcrowded center of Kotohira in 1975. At the same time, the theater was completely restored to its original grandeur. Kabuki plays are now performed only once a year, in April, but throughout the year the theater is open for viewing. Because the theater was built in 1835, one of the interesting aspects is how the theater managed its special effects without electricity. Eight men in harness, for example, rotate the stage. Within the revolving stage are two trap lifts. The larger one is used for quick changes in stage props, the smaller one for lifting actors up to floor level. Equally fascinating are the sets of sliding *shoji* screens used to adjust the amount of daylight filtering onto the stage. ☛ ¥500. ☺ Wed.–Mon. 9–4.

From Kotohira Station, the JR Limited Express train continues south to Kochi, the principal city of Shikoku's southern coast. (Or you can return to the north coast of Shikoku and travel west to Matsuyama.)

Kochi

⑤ The views from the train en route from Kotohira to **Kochi** are stunning, though the tunnels through which the train passes sometimes become frustrating. The train goes up the inclines to follow the valleys, cut deep by swift-flowing rivers. The earth is red and rich, and the foliage is lush and verdant. It is an area of scenic beauty that could happily lend itself to exploration by car, though once you are off the main roads, a little knowledge of Japanese will help your navigation.

From Kotohira, the train takes about two hours to reach Kochi; Kochi's **Tourist Information Office** (☎ 0888/82–7777) is to the left of the station's exit. Should you need language assistance while in Kochi, you may telephone the Nichibei School (☎ 0888/23–8118; ✆ weekdays 9–5, Sat. noon–5), which has bilingual volunteers who will assist foreigners. The JR bus terminal for direct JR buses to Matsuyama (there is no train line) is in the left wing (as you exit the station) of the station plaza.

The train station is a 20-minute walk from the city center. A taxi ride from the station to downtown is about ¥550. There are also buses.

Half- and full-day sightseeing tours (☎ 0888/82–3561) of Kochi and the surrounding environs leave from the area around the JR bus terminal at Kochi Station at 8:30 AM and 1:50 PM. Full-day sightseeing tours (☎ 0880/35–3856) travel down to Cape Ashizuri from Nakamura Station; these are not available throughout the whole year, so be sure to call ahead.

★ For residents of Kochi, fishing and agriculture are the mainstays. For the tourist, the major attraction is **Kochijo,** one of Japan's 12 feudal castles to have survived the course of time.

Kochi's castle, which dominates the town, is the only one in Japan to have kept both its donjon (stronghold) and its daimyo's (feudal lord's) residence intact. The donjon, admittedly, was rebuilt in 1753, but it faithfully reflects the original (1601–1603). The stone foundation of the donjon seems to merge into the cliff face of the bluff on which the structure is built. The donjon has the old style of watchtower design, and, by climbing up to its top floor, you can appreciate its purpose. The view is splendid. The daimyo's residence, **Kaitokukan,** is southwest of the donjon. Its formal main room is laid out in the Shoin style, a style known for its decorative alcove, staggered shelves, decorative doors, tatami-covered floors, and shoji screens reinforced with wooden lattices. Also on the castle grounds, beneath the donjon, is Kochi University. ☛ ¥350. ✆ Daily 9–5 (enter before 4:30).

Except for the castle, Kochi is not architecturally the most exciting of towns. However, perhaps because of its warm climate, the people of Kochi are full of humor. Even their local folk songs poke fun at life, such as, "On Harimayabashi, people saw a Buddhist priest buy a hairpin. . . ." Priests in those days were forbidden to love women, and they shaved their heads—some naughty business was afoot. Kochi is friendly and fun-loving; people congregate every evening in the compact downtown area. Several streets in the heart of downtown are closed off from traffic to form shopping arcades. Every day of the week seems to be a market day; however, should you be in Kochi on a Sunday morning, be sure to visit the thriving **sunday open-air market** on Ote-suji-dori, just north of Harimayabashi in downtown Kochi, where farmers bring their produce to sell at some 650 stalls. It is a tradition that has been maintained for 300 years. As an added bonus, you may also see the incredibly long-tailed (more than 20 ft.) roosters for which Kochi is known.

During the summer, residents of Kochi flock to **Katsurahama** (beach), 13 kilometers (8 miles) southeast of town. Buses depart from the Kochi Station plaza and the Harimayabashi stop and take 35 minutes (fare: ¥530). The beach consists of gravelly white sand, but the swimming is good, and there are scenic rock formations offshore. Also here is the **Tosa Token** (Fighting Dog) **Center** (☎ 0888/42–3315), where the victor of a bout is paraded around the ring dressed in a sumo wrestler's apron, and given the same ranking title as his human counterpart. ☞ ¥1,000.

If you prefer to spend an afternoon amid lawns, greenery, and an old temple, take the bus to Mt. Godai and **Godaisan Koen.** The 20-minute bus ride departs from the Toden bus stop, next to the Seibu department store on Harimayabashi (fare: ¥300). First visit **Chikurinji,** a temple with an impressive five-story pagoda that, despite beliefs to the contrary, is fairly uncommon in Japan. This one can stand up to those of Kyoto; the people from Kochi say it's more magnificent. The temple belongs to the Shingon sect of Buddhism and, founded in 724, is the 31st temple in the sequence of the 88 sacred temples. Down from the temple is the **Makino Shokubutsuen** (botanical garden), built to honor the botanist Dr. Tomitaro Makino (1862–1957). The greenhouse has an exotic collection of more than 1,000 plants, and the gardens are full of flowers, which have been planned so that in all seasons something is in bloom. ☞ ¥350. ☼ Daily 9–5.

East along the coast from Kochi the road follows a rugged shoreline marked by frequent inlets and indentations. Most of the coast consists of a series of 100- to 300-foot terraces. Continuous wave action, generated by the Black Current, has eroded these terraces. The result is a surreal coastline of rocks, surf, and steep precipices. It is about a 2½-hour drive along the coast road out to **Cape Muroto,** a popular sightseeing tour destination where the sea crashes against the cliffs.

If you'd like to proceed directly to Matsuyama from Kochi, take the JR bus from the JR Kochi Station. The fare is ¥3,600, but is covered by the JR Pass—though you may have to argue the matter with JR officials if you make your seat reservations from elsewhere than Kochi. The trip takes three hours.

Our tour takes us west and south from Kochi to Ashizuri National Park, in the southwestern tip of Shikoku. The JR Dosan Line goes to Kubokawa Station, where, if you were going straight to Uwajima, you'd change trains. For Nakamura, our destination, there is usually no change. This last leg of the journey is on the Kuroshio Tetsudo Line, and JR Pass holders will be charged an additional ¥210. At **Nakamura** you continue by JR bus to **Tosa-Shimizu,** where you can catch another bus out to **Cape Ashizuri.** (Sightseeing buses also depart from JR Nakamura Station to Cape Ashizuri; ☎ 0880/35–3856.) It is wonderfully wild country, with a skyline-drive road running down the center of the cape. At the end of the cape is a lighthouse and Kongofukuji, 38th of the 88 sacred temples, whose origins trace back 1,100 years, though what you see was rebuilt 300 years ago.

Returning from Cape Ashizuri, you can reboard the bus at Tosa-Shimizu and follow the coastline west to **Sukumo,** from where four ferries a day sail for Saiki, on Kyushu (fare: ¥1,650). Sukumo can also be reached directly by an hour's bus ride from Nakamura (fare: ¥1,100). With a change of bus, continue north to **Uwajima,** the terminal for JR lines arriving from Matsuyama and Kochi. Ferries depart from Uwajima for Usuki, on Kyushu (fare: about ¥2,200), which is two JR train stops from Beppu.

Another of Japan's extant feudal castles (*see also* Kochi, *above*) is **Uwajimajo,** though the first castle was torn down and replaced with an updated version in 1665. It's a friendly castle, without the usual defensive structures such as a stone drop. This suggests that by the end of the 17th century, war (at least those fought around castles) was a thing of the past. Most people, however, do not come to Uwajima to see the castle. They come for the **togyu** (bullfights). Though there are very similar bouts in the Ogi Islands, Uwajima claims these bullfights are a unique tradition dating back 400 years (good for tourism). Tournaments are held five times a year (dates vary, except for the Wareisai (festival) on July 23–24, but usually they are Jan. 2, the first Sun. in Mar. and Apr., the third Sun. in May, July 24, Aug. 14, and the first Sun. in Nov.). In these tournaments, two bulls lock horns and, like sumo wrestlers, try to push each other out of the ring. The Togyujo, where the contests are held, is at the foot of Mt. Tenman, about a 30-minute walk from the JR station.

From Uwajima, it is a one-hour 45-minute ride on the JR train to Matsuyama. There is frequent JR train service to Matsuyama from Takamatsu (3 hrs.), and also hourly hydrofoil (60 mins. at ¥5,700) and ferry (3 hrs. at ¥4,260 for 1st class and ¥2,130 for 2nd class) service from Hiroshima.

Matsuyama

⑫   The two most popular attractions of **Matsuyama** are its castle and the nearby hot-spring spa of Dogo Onsen.

Matsuyama, Shikoku's largest city, bristles with industries ranging from chemicals to wood pulp and from textiles to porcelain. It's a useful town for replenishing supplies—to change traveler's checks, for example—but with the exception of the castle, it lacks character. Stop in at the **City Tourist Information Office** (☎ 0899/31–3914), just inside the JR station, for a map and brochures. Downtown Matsuyama, often defined as the Okaido Shopping Center, which is at the foot of the castle grounds, is best reached by taking Streetcar 5, which departs from the plaza in front of the train station (cost: ¥170).

Matsuyamajo is on top of Matsuyama Hill, right in the center of the city. Originally built in 1603, the castle is the third feudal castle in Shikoku to have survived—though barely. It burned down in 1784 but was rebuilt in 1854, with a complex consisting of a major three-story donjon and three lesser donjons. The lesser ones succumbed to fire during this century, but all have been reconstructed. Unlike other postwar reconstructions, these smaller donjons were rebuilt with original materials, not with ferro-concrete. The main donjon now serves as a museum for feudal armor and swords owned by the Matsudaira clan, the daimyo family that lorded over Matsuyama (and Takamatsu) during the entire Edo period. The castle is perched high on the hill; unless you are very energetic, take the cable car that shuttles visitors up and down every 10 minutes. ☛ *Cable car ¥400, castle ¥350.* ☉ *Daily 9–4:30.*

★   Because Matsuyama has no special character of its own, rather than stay in town, many visitors spend the night at **Dogo Onsen** (tourist office: 5-6 Yunomachi, ☎ 0899/21–5141). It is only 18 minutes away by streetcar, which you can take from the JR Matsuyama Station or catch from downtown—there is a stop before the ANA Hotel. In either case, take Streetcar 5. With a history that is said to stretch back for more than two millennia, Dogo Onsen is one of Japan's oldest hot-spring spas. It hasn't outlived its popularity, either. There are more than 60 ryokan and hotels, old and new. Most of these now have their own thermal waters, but at the turn of the last century, visitors used to go to the public bathhouses; the grandest of them all was, and still is, the municipal bathhouse (*shinrokaku*), **Dogo Onsen Honkan.**

Indeed, even if your hotel has the fanciest of baths, to stay at Dogo Onsen or even downtown Matsuyama and not socialize at the shinrokaku is to miss the delight of this spa town. The grand old three-story, castlelike wood building was built in 1894 and, with its sliding panels, tatami floors, and shoji screens, looks like an old-fashioned pleasure palace. It is, in many ways. Two thousand bathers or more come by each day to pay their ¥280 and take the waters. Some of them pay a little more and lounge around after their bath, drinking tea in the communal room. Bathing is a social pastime, and the bath has the added benefit of scalding water that has medicinal qualities, especially for skin diseases.

There are different price levels of enjoyment. A basic bath is ¥280; a bath, a rented *yukata* (cotton robe), and access to the communal tatami lounge is ¥780; access to a smaller lounge and bath area away from hoi polloi is ¥980; and a private tatami room is ¥1,240. A separate wing was built in 1899 for imperial soaking. Most of the time it is not used, but for ¥210 visitors are allowed to wander through this royal bathhouse, which is open daily 6:30 AM–9 PM. The baths are open 6:30 AM–11 PM.

Matsuyama has eight of the 88 sacred temples. The best known of these is **Ishiteji,** 10 minutes on foot from Dogo Onsen Honkan. Representative of Kamakura-style architecture, the temple has its origins early in the 14th century. It may not be that grand, but its simple three-story pagoda is a pleasant contrast to the public bathhouse. Note the two statues of Deva kings at the gate. One has his mouth open, representing life, and the other has his mouth closed, representing death. Praying at Ishiteji is said to cure one's aching legs and crippled feet. The elderly, in fact, hang up their sandals in the temple as an offering of hope.

DINING

The delight of Shikoku is the number of small Japanese restaurants that serve the freshest fish, either caught in the Inland Sea or in the Pacific. Noodle restaurants abound, too. We have not singled out particular restaurants because they rarely differ in terms of ambience or quality of food. You may want to control your adventure in eating by choosing those restaurants that offer visual displays of their menus in the windows. However, if you have been in Japan for a week, you'll probably feel comfortable going into a small restaurant and ordering what the chef recommends. That dish is always the best. Just tell them that you wish to keep the price within certain limits.

In each of the three major cities—Takamatsu, Kochi, and Matsuyama—the entertainment districts have innumerable Japanese restaurants, and the fun of these areas is selecting your own restaurant. However, if you are staying at the Grand Hotel in Takamatsu or are waiting for the train or the next ferry at the JR station and have time enough for a good meal, there are nine excellent Japanese restaurants from which to choose on the second floor of the Grand Hotel's building. All the restaurants have their menus visually displayed in the windows, so you can select the dish and price your meal before you enter. If you are feeling more ambitious, there are dozens of good, small restaurants on and around Nakahonmachi—an arcade that runs parallel to the main boulevard, Chuo-dori. A particularly good restaurant in Takamatsu is

Maimaitei (☎ 0878/33–3360, closed Sun.), which serves excellent Sanuki cuisine—based upon the produce of the Seto Inland Sea—at approximately ¥4,700 for two.

In Matsuyama, the Okaido shopping arcade near the ANA Hotel has numerous good restaurants serving Western and Japanese food in all price ranges—the local specialty is **ikezukuri,** a live fish with its meat cut into strips. Off to either side of the arcade are many small restaurants and club bars. Here the adventuresome take their pick, but if you do not want any surprises, try **Dan Dan Jaya** (in Dan Dan Square, behind the Mitsukoshi department store, ☎ 0899/45–7101), a large *izakaya* with counter seating around the cooking area and small, semi-enclosed areas with tatami seating to the sides. The menu has pictures, and there are dozens of dishes that range in price from ¥500 to ¥1,000.

For Western-style cuisine, you are better off eating at the top hotels. The Hankyu, in Kochi, for example, has an excellent French restaurant, as does the ANA Hotel in Matsuyama. If you're on a budget, these hotels have Western-style coffee shops, and the ANA Hotel in Matsuyama also has a delightful rooftop beer garden, open in the summer, where you can also eat well and inexpensively.

LODGING

Accommodations on Shikoku cover a broad spectrum, from pensions and minshukus to large, modern resort hotels that have little character but offer all the facilities of an international hotel. All of the large city and resort hotels offer Western as well as Japanese food. During the summer, reservations are advised.

Outside the cities or major towns, most hotels quote prices on a per-person basis with two meals, exclusive of service and tax. If you do not want dinner at your hotel, it is usually possible to renegotiate the price. Stipulate, too, whether you wish to have Japanese or Western breakfasts, if any. For the purposes here, the categories assigned to all hotels reflect the cost of a double room with private bath and no meals. However, if you make reservations at any of the noncity hotels, you will be expected to take breakfast and dinner at the hotel—that will be the rate quoted to you unless you specify otherwise. A 3% federal consumer tax is added to all hotel bills. Another 3% local tax is added to the bill if it exceeds ¥15,000. At most hotels, a 10%–15% service charge is added to the hotel bill. Tipping is not the custom.

CATEGORY	COST*
$$$$	over ¥20,000
$$$	¥15,000–¥20,000
$$	¥10,000–¥15,000
$	under ¥10,000

Cost is for double room, without tax or service

Kochi

$$$ **Hotel Shin-Hankyu.** Right in the center of town, within sight of Kochijo,
★ the Shin-Hankyu is indisputably the best hotel in Kochi. On the ground floor is the modern, open-plan lobby, with a lounge away from the reception area and a small cake/tea shop to the side. On the second floor are several excellent restaurants, serving Japanese, Chinese, and French cuisine. The spacious guest rooms, decorated with light pastel furnishings,

create a sense of well-being, and the staff are extremely helpful to foreign guests. ⌂ *4-2-50 Honmachi, Kochi-shi, Kochi-ken 780,* ☎ *0888/73–1111,* ℻ *0888/73–1145. 201 rooms, mostly Western style. Restaurants, health club. AE, DC, MC, V.*

$$$ **Ikawa Ryokan.** English is not spoken here, but the genteel hospitality and sophistication of this inn make a stay relaxing and comfortable. Elegant simplicity achieves harmony. Even the few Western guest rooms are simply adorned. Dinner is *kaiseki*-style (served in the room) and uses the produce of the sea to full advantage. ⌂ *5-1 Nichudai-cho, Kochi-shi, Kochi-ken 780,* ☎ *0888/22–1317,* ℻ *0888/24–7401. 40 rooms, most Japanese style. Small banquet room, Japanese garden. AE, DC, V.*

$$ **Washington Hotel.** On the street leading to Kochijo and a 20-minute walk from the station, this is a small, friendly business hotel in downtown Kochi. It has a small restaurant, and the rooms are a good size for this kind of lodging. ⌂ *1-8-25 Otesuji, Kochi-shi, Kochi-ken 780,* ☎ *0888/23–6111,* ℻ *0888/25–2737. 62 Western-style rooms. Restaurant. AE, V.*

$ **Hotel Sunroute Kochi.** This business hotel has slightly larger rooms than the average of its kind, but should be considered only if you need to be within walking distance of the station. ⌂ *1-1-28 Kita-honcho, Kochi-shi, Kochi-ken 780,* ☎ *0888/23–1311,* ℻ *0888/23–1383. 64 rooms. Breakfast room. AE, DC, V.*

Matsuyama

$$$ **ANA Hotel Matsuyama.** The best international hotel downtown, the ANA caters to the business executive. The location is excellent, within five minutes on foot to the cable car to Matsuyamajo. Streetcar 5 that goes out to Dogo Onsen, which stops right out in front. The hotel has banquet rooms, shopping arcades, and a summer beer garden on its roof. The guest rooms are well maintained, reasonably spacious, and fully equipped, with everything from bathrobes to hair dryers. Ask for a room on the 11th or 12th floor that overlooks Bansuise Mansion, an imitation French château that is floodlit at night. ⌂ *3-2-1 Ichiban-cho, Matsuyama, Ehime-ken 790,* ☎ *0899/33–5511,* ℻ *0899/21–6053. 334 rooms. Restaurants, rooftop beer garden (open May–Sept). AE, DC, V.*

$$$ **Funaya Ryokan.** The best Japanese inn in Dogo Onsen, this is where the imperial family stays when it comes to take the waters. The ryokan has a long history, but the present building was built in 1963. The best rooms look out on the garden. Breakfast and dinner are included in the tariff. ⌂ *1-33 Godo Yumomachi, Matsuyama, Ehime-ken 790,* ☎ *0899/47–0278,* ℻ *0899/49–2139. 43 rooms, most Japanese style, some with private bath. Thermal baths. AE, V.*

$ **Hotel Sunroute.** This business hotel has no particular charm, but its rooms are not too small, and it is just a five-minute walk from the JR station. The best part of the hotel is its rooftop beer garden (open summer only), from which you can catch a glimpse of the castle. ⌂ *Miyatacho, Matsuyama, Ehime-ken 790,* ☎ *0899/33–2811,* ℻ *0899/33–2763. 110 Western-style rooms. AE, V.*

Takamatsu

$$–$$$ **Kawaroku Ryokan.** The original Kawaroku was bombed out in World
★ War II; this replacement—the best hotel in the center of town—is unappealing from the outside but is pleasantly furnished on the inside. The rooms have a light, refreshing decor, and all have private bath. The restaurant serves French food, but Japanese food can be served in

your room. ☎ *1-2 Hyakkencho, Takamatsu, Kagawa-ken 760,* ☎ *0878/21–5666,* FAX *0878/21–7301. 70 rooms, 21 Western style. Restaurant. AE, V.*

$$–$$$ **Keio Plaza Hotel.** This efficient hotel is at the far end of Chuo-dori near Ritsurin Koen, a good 10 minutes by taxi from the JR station. Guest rooms are reasonably spacious and comfortable, though the rooms facing Chuo-dori do suffer slightly from traffic noise. ☎ *11-5 Chuocho, Takamatsu, Kagawa-ken 760,* ☎ *0878/34–5511,* FAX *0878/34–0800. 180 rooms, 2 Japanese style. Japanese and Western restaurants.*

$$ **Takamatsu Grand Hotel.** Right on the city's main avenue, Chuo-dori, the Grand is within a five-minute walk from the JR station. The lobby is on the third floor (there are nine independently owned restaurants on the second floor), and the main restaurant is on the seventh floor. Tamamo Koen and Tamamojo are behind the hotel, so the views on that side of the building are quite splendid. All the guest rooms could use refurbishing, but they are clean. ☎ *1-5-10 Kotobukicho, Takamatsu, Kagawa-ken 760,* ☎ *0878/51–5757,* FAX *0878/21–9422. 136 Western-style rooms. Restaurants. AE, DC, MC, V.*

SHIKOKU ESSENTIALS

Arriving and Departing

By Plane

Takamatsu is serviced by seven daily flights from Tokyo and by 10 daily flights from Osaka. Tokushima receives five daily flights from Tokyo and 10 daily flights from Osaka. Kochi is serviced by five daily flights from Tokyo and by 23 daily flights from Osaka. Matsuyama receives six daily flights from Tokyo and six daily flights from Osaka.

By Train

Shikoku can be reached by taking the JR Shinkansen to Okayama (3 hrs., 50 mins. from Tokyo; 1 hr., 20 mins. from Kyoto), then transferring onto the JR Limited Express bound either for Takamatsu (1 hr.), Matsuyama (3 hrs.), or Kochi (3 hrs.).

Matsuyama can also be reached by taking the JR Shinkansen to Hiroshima (5 hrs., 10 mins. from Tokyo; 2 hrs., 20 mins. from Kyoto). From Hiroshima's Ujina Port, the ferry takes three hours to cross the Inland Sea to Matsuyama; the hydrofoil takes one hour.

By Ship

Takamatsu can also be reached by the Kansai Kisen (steamship), which takes five hours, 30 minutes from Osaka's Bentenfuto (pier), and four hours, 30 minutes from Kobe's Naka-Tottei Pier. The boat leaves Osaka at 8:30 AM and 2:20 PM, Kobe at 9:50 AM and 3:40 PM; it arrives at Takamatsu at 2 PM and 8:10 PM. The cost is approximately ¥2,500 and up from Osaka, slightly less from Kobe. Passenger ships travel to Kochi from Osaka (depart at 9:20 PM and arrive in Kochi at 6:40 AM, returning to Osaka with departures at 9:20 PM and arriving in Osaka at 7 AM). Kochi can also be reached from Tokyo by a ship that departs at 7:40 PM, stops in Katsuura, Wakayama Prefecture, at 8:50 AM, and arrives in Kochi at 5 AM.

Getting Around

By Train and Bus

All the major towns of Shikoku are connected either by JR express and local trains or by bus. Because of the lower population density on

Shikoku, transportation is not so frequent as on the southern coast of Honshu. So before you step off a train or bus, find out how long it will be before the next one departs for your next destination.

The main routes are from Takamatsu to Matsuyama by train (2 hrs., 45 mins.); from Takamatsu to Kochi by train (3 hrs.), from Takamatsu to Tokushima (90 mins.); from Matsuyama to Kochi by JR bus (approximately 3 hrs., 15 mins.); from Matsuyama to Uwajima by train (2 hrs.); and from Kochi to Nakamura by train (2 hrs.).

By Car

Because traffic is light, the scenery marvelous, and the distances relatively short, Shikoku is one region in Japan where renting a car makes sense. (Remember that an international driving license is required.) **Budget Rent-a-Car** has rental offices in Matsuyama, Takamatsu, and Kochi, as do other car-rental agencies.

Guided Tours

No guided tours covering the island of Shikoku are conducted in English, though the **Japan Travel Bureau** will make individual travel arrangements. The Japan Travel Bureau has offices at every JR station in each of the prefectural capitals and can assist in local tours, hotel reservations, and ticketing onward travel. Local city tours, conducted in Japanese, cover the surrounding areas of each of the four major cities in Shikoku. These may be arranged through your hotel.

Important Addresses and Numbers

Emergencies
Police, ☎ 110. **Ambulance,** ☎ 119.

Tourist Information Centers
Major tourist information centers are located at each of Shikoku's main cities: **Takamatsu,** ☎ 0878/51–2009; **Kochi,** ☎ 0888/23–1434; **Matsuyama,** ☎ 0899/31–3914; and **Tokushima,** ☎ 0886/52–8777.

Japan Travel Phone
A nationwide service for English-language assistance or travel information is available seven days a week, 9 to 5. Throughout Shikoku, dial toll-free 0120/444–800 for information on western Japan. When using a yellow, blue, or green public phone (do not use the red phones), insert a ¥10 coin, which will be returned.

12 Kyushu

The journeys beween the major points of interest in Kyushu, the southernmost of Japan's four main islands, afford beautiful views of its rich green fields, mountains, and the ocean. Each of its major tourist destinations—Fukuoka, Nagasaki, Kumamoto, and Beppu— has a different flavor; the last, with its extensive variety of hot mineral springs, is a favorite among Japanese vacationers seeking a restful soak.

By Kiko Itasaka

Updated by
Nigel Fisher

KYUSHU, THE RELATIVELY QUIET ISLAND southwest of the main island of Honshu, offers a mild climate, lush green countryside, hot springs, and eerie volcanic formations. However peaceful it may be now, this island was for centuries the most active and international island in all of Japan. To this day, it is considered to be the birthplace of Japanese civilization. Far from Tokyo, the cities of Kyushu are mostly free of skyscrapers and filled with sights of historical and cultural significance.

Legend has it that the grandson of Amaterasu, the sun goddess, first ruled Japan from Kyushu. Another tale relates that Jinmu, Japan's first emperor, traveled from Kyushu to Honshu, consolidated Japan, and established the imperial line that exists to this day.

As a result of its geographic proximity to Korea and China, from the 4th century on Kyushu was the first area of Japan to be culturally influenced by its more sophisticated neighbors. Through the gateway of Kyushu, Japan was first introduced to pottery techniques, Buddhism, the Chinese writing system, and other aspects of Chinese and Korean culture.

Not all outside influence, however, was welcome. In 1274, Kublai Khan led a fleet of Mongol warriors in an unsuccessful attempt to invade Japan. The Japanese, in preparation for further attacks, built a stone wall along the coast of Kyushu; remnants of it can still be seen today outside Fukuoka. When the Mongols returned in 1281 with a force 100,000 strong, they were repelled by the stone wall and by the fierce fighting of the Kyushu natives; the fighters were aided by a huge storm, known as *kamikaze* (divine wind), which blew the Mongol fleet out to sea. (This term may be more familiar in its revived form, used in World War II to describe suicide pilots.)

In the mid-16th century, Kyushu was once again the first point of contact with the outside world, when Portuguese ships first landed on the shores of Japan. The arrival of these ships signaled Japan's initial introduction to the West and its knowledge of medicine, firearms, and Christianity. The Portuguese were followed by the Dutch and the Spanish. The Tokugawa Shogunate was not entirely pleased with the intrusion of the Westerners and feared political interference. In 1635, the shogunate established a closed-door policy that permitted foreigners to land only on a small island, Dejima, in the harbor of Nagasaki. As a result, until 1859, when Japan opened its doors to the West, the small port town of Nagasaki became the most important center for both trade and Western learning for Kyushu and the entire nation. To this day, the historical influence of Europe is apparent in Nagasaki, with its 19th-century Western-style buildings and the lasting presence of Christianity.

A visit to Kyushu's major attractions requires travel around the island. Fortunately, the journeys between the points of interest in Kyushu afford beautiful views of Kyushu's rich green rice fields, mountains, and the ocean. The starting point of most visits to Kyushu is Fukuoka, where there is a major airport and a JR Shinkansen train station. Of course, it is possible to travel to the different sights of Kyushu in any order, but in this chapter, we take a circular route that starts in Fukuoka, proceeds to Nagasaki on the western coast, goes east to Kumamoto and Mt. Aso, and concludes at the Inland Sea hot-spring resort of Beppu (from which you can return to Fukuoka).

FUKUOKA

Numbers in the margin correspond to points of interest on the Kyushu map.

Fukuoka is the second-largest city in Kyushu and the most logical starting point for travel around the island. Many people visiting Kyushu spend at least a day or two here.

Arriving and Departing

By Plane

Japan Airlines (JAL), All Nippon Airways (ANA), and Japan Air System (JAS) have 1½-hour flights between Haneda Airport in Tokyo and Fukuoka Airport (Fukuoka-huho). Twenty flights are offered daily. JAL provides service (1 hr. 45 mins.) between Narita International Airport and Fukuoka Airport daily. JAL and ANA also offer a total of eight direct flights between Osaka and Fukuoka (1 hr. 45 mins.), making it convenient for travelers to begin or end their Japan travels in Kyushu. Northwest Airlines operates direct flights from Hawaii.

BETWEEN THE AIRPORT AND CENTER CITY

Fukuoka Airport is very near the center of the city. A subway line links the airport with the JR Hakata Station; tickets cost ¥220.

By Train

JR Shinkansen Hikari trains travel between Tokyo and Hakata Station in Fukuoka (time: 6 hrs. 26 mins. to 7 hrs. 24 mins.). There are 15 daily runs. Shinkansen trains travel between Osaka and Hakata Station, and also between Hiroshima and Hakata. Regular JR express trains travel these routes but take twice as long.

Getting Around

The easiest way to get around Fukuoka is by bus or by one of the two subway lines (minimum fare: ¥180). The two major transportation centers of Fukuoka are located around Hakata Station and in the downtown area known as Tenjin, the terminal station for both of the subway lines. Buses leave from the Kotsu Bus Center just across the street from Hakata Station, and from the Fukuoka Bus Center at Tenjin.

Guided Tours

You can take sightseeing bus tours of the major historic sights of Fukuoka City from the **Tenjin Bus Center** (☎ 092/771–2961) or the **Kotsu Bus Center** (☎ 092/431–1171). Not all tours are in English, so it is better to have your hotel call for further information or to ask at the tourist information office. A three-hour tour costs approximately ¥1,950.

Important Addresses and Numbers

Tourist Information

The **Fukuoka City Tourist Information Office** (☎ 092/431–3003) is in Hakata Station. Some of the office staff speak English, and excellent maps of the city and neighboring areas are available. The office is open daily 9–7. If you plan on staying in Fukuoka for more than a day or two, you may wish to contact **The Fukuoka International Association** (Rainbow Plaza, IMS 5F, 1-7-11 Tanjin, Chuo-ku, Fukuoka 810, ☎ 092/733–2220, ℻ 092/733–2215), which serves as an information resource and center for networking.

Kyushu

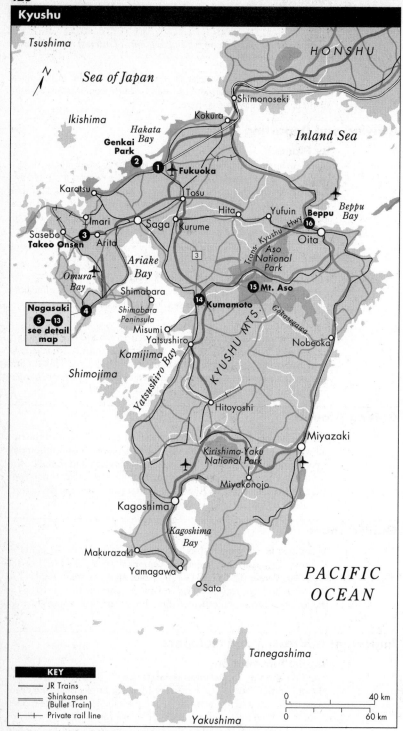

Tsushima

Sea of Japan

HONSHU

Ikishima

Shimonoseki

Kokura

Hakata Bay

Genkai Park
2

1 ✈ **Fukuoka**

Inland Sea

Karatsu

Tosu

Imari

Saga

Hita

Yufuin

✈ **Beppu** *Beppu Bay*

Sasebo
Takeo Onsen
3

Arita

Kurume

Oita

Ariake Bay

3

Aso National Park

Trans-Kyushu Hwy

Omura-Bay

Shimabara

16 Mt. Aso

Nagasaki
5 – 13
see detail map

4

Shimabara Peninsula

14 **Kumamoto**

Gokasegawa

Misumi

Yatsushiro

KYUSHU MTS.

Kamijima

Nobeoka

Shimojima

Yatsushiro Bay

Hitoyoshi

Miyazaki

Kirishima-Yaku National Park

Miyakonojo

Kagoshima

Kagoshima Bay

Makurazaki

PACIFIC OCEAN

Yamagawa

Sata

Tanegashima

KEY
— JR Trains
═ Shinkansen (Bullet Train)
├—├ Private rail line

0   40 km
0   60 km

Yakushima

U.S. Consulate (5-26 Ohori 2-chome, Chuo-ku, Fukuoka ☎ 092/751–9331).

Travel Agencies
Japan Travel Bureau (Daiwa Seimei Kaikan Bldg., 1-14-4 Tenjin, Chuo-ku, Fukuoka ☎ 092/771–5211).

Exploring

Fukuoka is the commercial, political, and cultural center of Kyushu and the island's largest city. With 1.2 million inhabitants, it is the eighth largest city in Japan. Virtually flattened by bombing in World War II, it was rebuilt on a grid plan and is considered to be a fine example of postwar city planning. It is small and provincial in comparison to Tokyo, but there is a dynamic quality to Fukuoka, whose city council is determined to position the city as Japan's gateway to Asia. Most activities and entertainment events happen around the two city centers, Hakata Station and the downtown Tenjin district. (Use the subway—fare: ¥180—to travel between them.) Most of the places you visit in Fukuoka, whether they are restaurants, shops, or sights, are near these two centers, or can be reached easily from them. The city is divided in two parts by the Nakagawa (Naka River). All areas west of the river are known as Fukuoka, and everything east of the river is known as Hakata. Along the Naka and Hakata rivers is Nakasu, the largest nightlife district in western Japan, with 3,000 bars, restaurants, and street vendors. Fukuoka was originally a castle town founded at the end of the 16th century, and Hakata was the place for commerce. In 1889 the two districts were officially merged as Fukuoka, but the historical names are still used.

Start your tour of Fukuoka at **Shofukuji,** which can be reached by a 15-minute walk from Hakata Station, or a five-minute Nishitetsu bus ride from the adjacent Hakata Kotsu Bus Center to the Okunodo stop. This temple was founded in 1195 by Eisai (1141–1215) upon his return to Kyushu after years of study in China. He was one of the first Japanese priests to introduce Zen Buddhism to Japan—the claim is often made that this is the site of Japan's first Zen temple. Eisai is also said to have brought the first tea seeds from China to Japan. Note the Korean-style bronze bell in the belfry, designated an Important Cultural Property by the Japanese government. ☛ Free. ⊙ Daily 9–5.

From Shofukuji, return to Hakata Station and walk or take a bus from the adjacent Hakata Kotsu Bus Center to Sumiyoshi Station and visit **Sumiyoshi Jinja.** This is the oldest Shinto shrine in Kyushu, founded in 1623 and dedicated to the guardian gods of seafarers. An annual festival is held at this shrine October 12–14, complete with sumo wrestling. The temple sits on top of a hill with a lovely view of both the Nakagawa and the city, and the grounds are dotted with camphor and cedar trees. ☛ Free. ⊙ 9–5.

For a recreational break, take the subway from Hakata Station to Ohori Koen Station, about a 20-minute ride. **Ohori Koen** is a spacious park built around a lake that was once part of a moat surrounding Fukuokajo. Bridges connect three small islands in the center of the lake. In early April, the northern portion of the park is graced with the blossoms of 2,600 cherry trees. On weekends you will see many Fukuoka residents taking advantage of this oasis in the middle of an otherwise grim and gray industrial city. Bring a picnic and enjoy a leisurely walk, or boat and fish on the lake.

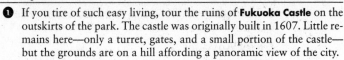

❶ If you tire of such easy living, tour the ruins of **Fukuoka Castle** on the outskirts of the park. The castle was originally built in 1607. Little remains here—only a turret, gates, and a small portion of the castle—but the grounds are on a hill affording a panoramic view of the city.

Shopping

Fukuoka is famous for two local products—**Hakata ningyo** (dolls) and **Hakata *obi*** (kimono sashes).

Hakata dolls, popular throughout Japan, are made with fired clay and are hand painted with bright colors and distinctive expressions. These dolls are mostly ornamental and depict such figures as children, women, samurai, and geisha.

Hakata obi are made of an interesting local silk that has a rougher texture than most Japanese silk, which is usually perfectly even and smooth. For local young girls, the purchase of their first Hakata obi is an initiation into adulthood. Other products, such as bags and purses, are made of this Hakata silk.

The main area for shopping is the downtown district of Tenjin, which can be reached by subway from Hakata Station (third stop). Here you will find many boutiques, department stores, and restaurants along Tenjin Nishi-dori. Underground at Tenjin subway station is an arcade of small shops and restaurants that offer both high fashion and affordable merchandise from clothes to souvenirs.

Iwataya Department Store (2-11-1 Tenjin, Chuo-ku, ☎ 092/721-1111) carries the most complete selection of merchandise in the area, including Hakata dolls, Hakata silk, and an excellent china department that features some of the distinctive pottery of Kyushu. The store is in the center of the Tenjin shopping area.

Hakusen (Tenjin 2-chome, Shirai, Chuo-ku, ☎ 092/712–8900. ☼ Daily 9–8:30), also in the Tenjin shopping district, is a specialty shop with an extensive selection of Hakata dolls.

A store that specializes in Hakata silk is **Hakata Ori Kaikan** (Hakata Eki-minami, Hakata-ku, ☎ 092/472–0761), the best place to get obi and bags.

Excursions from Fukuoka

Genkai Park

❷ **Genkai Park,** which extends from Hakata Bay along the coasts of Fukuoka and Saga prefectures, has long beaches with white sands and eerie Japanese black pines. The waters of Hakata Bay facing the Genkai Sea (Genkainada) are surprisingly clean and relatively uncrowded. You can combine a swim in the bay with a visit to the *boheki,* the ruins of stone walls (next to a beach) that were built in the 13th century to stave off the invasions of the Mongols. From Hakata Kotsu Center, take the Nishi-Tetsu bus to Karatsu-Oteguchi (90 mins., ¥1,050), then transfer to the Showa bus for Yobiko (40 mins., ¥700).

Takeo Onsen and Arita

❸ As an alternative to a two-hour JR train ride, consider going to Nagasaki via **Takeo Onsen,** a small town known for its hot springs. Surrounded by mountains, the spa became famous when, according to legend, approximately 1,700 years ago, Empress Jingu on her way home from invading Korea stopped in Takeo Onsen to recover from childbirth. Since that time, the Japanese have been coming here to take its waters. The town's other claim to fame is its pottery, which was introduced by Korean potters brought to Kyushu by Hideyoshi Toyotomi's armies 400 years ago. The pottery is noted for its simple designs and subdued natural colors. Takeo Onsen is also home to three lofty camphor trees, all of them more than 3,000 years old and designated as National Natural Monuments. Though Takeo Onsen may not be all charm, because it's only a fraction the size of Fukuoka, it has an intimate atmosphere not found in big-city Japan. Thus, it makes an intriguing and convenient overnight alternative to Fukuoka or Nagasaki. All of the ryokan and *izakaya* (casual drinking and eating establishments) are within walking distance from the station.

The JR train to Takeo Onsen takes just over an hour from Hakata, and though it is not the main route to Nagasaki, you can continue for another two hours on the same line to reach Nagasaki.

The next town after Takeo Onsen is **Arita,** a small village with one main street that is entirely lined with pottery shops, each with their own kilns and run by the same families for generations. Prices depend on quality, but you can get a beautiful handmade teacup for around ¥2,000, or a set of five cups and a teapot for ¥10,000. Once a year, at the end of April or early May (contact the tourist office), there is a large pottery fair, when everything in all the shops goes on sale. At these times, many of the ceramic pieces are priced as low as ¥500.

Continuing east, the train will take you to the Huis Ten Bosch and Holland Village (*see* Off the Beaten Track from Nagasaki, *below*). From Huis Ten Bosch, it is a 90-minute run down to Nagasaki.

NAGASAKI

④ Nagasaki, a quiet city of hills with a peaceful harbor, is often called the San Francisco of Japan. The harbor, now serenely dotted with a few fishing boats, was once the most important trading port in the country. In 1639, when Japan decided to close its ports to all foreigners, it appointed the small island of Dejima in Nagasaki Harbor as the one place where foreigners were allowed to land. The only Japanese allowed to have contact with the foreigners were merchants and prostitutes. The Tokugawa Shogunate established this isolationist policy to prevent Western powers from having political influence in Japan. With Nagasaki as the focal point, however, knowledge of the West, particularly in fields such as medicine and weaponry, began to spread throughout Japan. Japan reopened its doors to the West in 1859, thus ending Nagasaki's heyday as the sole international port. Many of the original buildings and churches from the 19th century still stand as testaments to this unique period in Japanese history.

After more than two centuries of prominence, Nagasaki became a relatively obscure Japanese city until the atomic bomb was dropped on it in 1945. Although the bomb destroyed one-third of the city, enough remained standing so that, to this day, Nagasaki has an atmosphere that mixes both Eastern and Western traditions from the last century.

Travelers to Nagasaki will want to pick up a copy of *Harbor Light,* a monthly publication in English that provides detailed information on various activities in the city.

Arriving and Departing

By Plane

Omura Airport is approximately one hour by bus or car from Nagasaki. ANA and Japan Air System offer five daily direct flights from Haneda Airport in Tokyo to Omura Airport (1 hr. 45 mins.). From Osaka the flights are 1 hour and 10 minutes.

BETWEEN THE AIRPORT AND CENTER CITY

A regular shuttle bus travels between Omura Airport and Nagasaki Station in 55 minutes. The cost is ¥1,150.

By Train

Take the JR Nagasaki Line Limited Express train from Fukuoka (2 hrs. 30 mins.). To get to Kumamoto from Nagasaki by train, take the Kamone Line from Nagasaki to Tosu Station (2 hrs.). From Tosu, board the Kagoshima Main Line and get off at Kumamoto (1 hr.).

By Bus

The Kyushu Kyuko Bus Company offers bus service between Fukuoka and Nagasaki (3 hrs. 20 mins.; the bus leaves from the Fukuoka Bus Center in the Tenjin downtown district). A bus service also runs between Nagasaki and Kumamoto (4 hrs.; *see* Kumamoto, *below*).

Getting Around

By Streetcar

Streetcars are the most convenient way of getting around Nagasaki. Although slow, they appropriately reflect the relaxed atmosphere of Nagasaki and evoke another century. The streetcars stop at most of the major sights, and many stops have signs in English. You can purchase a one-day pass for unlimited streetcar travel for ¥550 at the City Tourist Information Center or at major hotels. Otherwise, you pay ¥120 as you get off the streetcar. If you wish to transfer from one streetcar to another, take a *norikai kippu* (transfer ticket) from the driver of the first streetcar as you alight and drop your ¥120 in the box.

By Bus

Bus routes exist in Nagasaki, but they are complicated and not very convenient.

Guided Tours

By Boat

A 50-minute port cruise of Nagasaki Harbor departs at 11:40 and 3:15. Fare: ¥900. Take a streetcar to Ohato Station, then go to Pier No. 1.

By Ricksha

Rickshas, once ubiquitous, are now a rare sight in Japan. Prices vary according to the course you take, but the minimum is ¥2,000 per person. Ask your hotel or the tourist information office to call in Japanese to arrange your tour (☎ 0958/24–4367).

City Tours

Japan Travel Bureau (☎ 0958/24-3200) offers a few city tours with English-speaking guides. A three-hour tour of the city's major sights costs ¥2,950.

Important Addresses and Numbers

Tourist Information

The **City Tourist Information Center** (1-88 Onouecho, ☎ 0958/23–3631) is on the left-hand corner (as you leave the station) of the station plaza. There is no sign written in English, so it takes perseverance to find, but the office is useful for maps and directions. The office is open Monday–Saturday 9–6. **The Nagasaki Prefecture Tourist Office** (2nd floor, Nagasaki Kotsu Sangyo Bldg., 3-1 Daikokumachi, ☎ 0958/23-4041) is across the street from the JR station one floor above street level in a department store. To reach it from the station, use the pedestrian bridge. The staff are not very helpful, but maps and bus schedules to various areas within the prefecture are available. The office is open weekdays 9–5:30, Saturday 9–12:45.

Exploring

Numbers in the margin correspond to points of interest on the Nagasaki map.

Nagasaki is a beautiful harbor city that is small enough to cover on foot if you have the energy to face some of the steep inclines, which veer and meander, drawing comparison to the hills of San Francisco. Most of the sights of interest and restaurant and shopping areas are located south of Nagasaki Station. The Peace Park, the memorial and ruins left in memory of the victims of the second atomic bomb in 1945, and Nishi-zaka, the last two stops on our itinerary, are to the north.

★ ❺ **Glover Gardens,** which affords panoramic views of Nagasaki and the harbor, is a good place to begin your tour of Nagasaki. To get here, board Streetcar 1 from the JR station to the downtown stop, Tsuki-machi, and transfer (don't forget to collect a transfer ticket) to Streetcar 5. Get off at the Oura-Tenshudo-shita stop (the second-to-last stop on the line). Take the side street to the right, cross the bridge over a small canal, and then take the second street on your left up the hill. On your left is the Tokyu Hotel, a place to keep in mind for afternoon tea, and on the right is an array of souvenir shops. Facing you as you turn one corner on the hill is Oura Catholic Church, a later stop on this itinerary.

The gardens feature Western-style houses built in the late 19th century. The main attraction is the Glover Mansion (1863), former home of Thomas Glover, a British merchant who married a Japanese woman and settled in Nagasaki. Glover introduced the first steam locomotive and established the first mint in Japan. The house remains as it was in Glover's time, and his furniture and possessions are on display. The story for Puccini's opera Madame Butterfly is said to have been set here. Escalators going up the slopes toward the Glover Mansion seem out of place, but they do provide a rest for the weary as well as a panorama of Nagasaki harbor. The gardens are unspoiled and distinctly Western in design, providing a sense of what Glover's little colonial sanctuary was like when Japan opened up to the West. ☎ 0958/22–8223. ☛ ¥600. ☺ *Daily Mar.–Nov. 8–6; Dec.–Feb. 8:30–5.*

❻ Just outside the exit of the Glover Gardens is **Jurokuban-kan,** a mansion built in 1860 as accommodations for the American consular staff. It is now a museum that displays Dutch and Portuguese objects related to the history of early trade between these countries and Japan. ☎ 0958/23–4260. ☛ ¥400. ☺ *Daily Mar.–Nov. 8:30–6; Dec.–Feb. 8:30–5.*

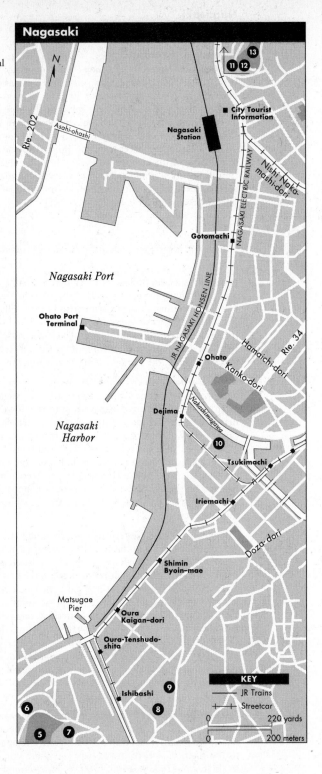

Nagasaki

N

Rte. 202

Asahi-ohashi

City Tourist
Information

Nagasaki
Station

Nishi Naka-
mashi-dori

NAGASAKI ELECTRIC RAILWAY

Gotomachi

Nagasaki Port

JR NAGASAKI HONSEN LINE

Rte. 34

Hamaichi-dori

Ohato Port
Terminal

Ohato

Kanko-dori

Nakashimagawa

Dejima

10

Nagasaki
Harbor

Tsukimachi

Iriemachi

Doza-dori

Shimin
Byoin-mae

Matsugae
Pier

Oura
Kaigan-dori

Oura-Tenshudo-
shita

9

Ishibashi

8

6

5   **7**

KEY

—— JR Trains

++ Streetcar

0 _____ 220 yards

0 _____ 200 meters

11 **12**

13

❼ After you leave Jurokuban-kan, continue down the same street past the Glover Mansion for a few minutes and you will come to another 19th-century European-style structure: **Oura Catholic Church,** which is the oldest Gothic-style building in Japan. The church was constructed in 1865 by a French missionary and was dedicated to the memory of the 26 Christians who were crucified in 1597 after Christianity was outlawed. The church features beautiful stained-glass windows. ☛ ¥250. ⊘ Daily 8:30–6.

❽ As you leave the church, walk down the hill, across the canal, and past the Ishibashi streetcar stop. Nearby is **Tojinkan** (Chinese Mansion), built in 1893 by the Chinese residents of Nagasaki. The hall now houses a gallery of Chinese crafts and souvenir shops. Although this is a favorite with many Japanese tourists, it is probably more popular for its many little shops than for its historic interest. ☛ ¥515. ⊘ Daily 8:30–5.

❾ After seeing the interiors of these 19th-century buildings, you may want to see some quaint old facades. Follow the street to the side of Tojinkan and after about 100 meters (yards), on your left, will be a cobblestone incline known as **Oranda-zaka** (Holland Slope), a pleasant walk alongside wood houses built by 19th-century Dutch residents.

❿ The walk up Oranda-zaka will lead you to the Shimin Byoin-mae streetcar stop, just in front of Nagasaki View Hospital. Board the streetcar and go to the Tsukimachi stop, where you can see the original site of **Dejima,** the man-made island where the Dutch were allowed to land in the years when Japan maintained its isolationist policy. It is no longer an island, because the area has been land-filled, but there is a miniature reconstruction of the entire village and community of Dejima, as part of the **Dejima Historical Museum.** ☛ Free. ⊘ Tues.–Sun. 9–5.

⓫ After you view all of these picturesque sights, Nagasaki may seem to be a quaint port town that time and progress have somehow passed by—but it is important to remember that Nagasaki suffered the devastation of an atomic bomb. So that the memory of this tragedy endures, a **Peace Park** was built at the exact site of the epicenter of the August 9, 1945, atomic blast. In a blinding flash, 2.59 square miles were obliterated and 74,884 people were killed, with another 74,909 injured out of an estimated population of 204,000. (And it was only a small bomb compared to present-day atomic weapons.) At one end of the park is a black pillar, grimly denoting the exact center of the blast. At the other end is a graceless 32-foot statue of a male figure with one arm pointing horizontally (symbolizing world peace), the other pointing toward the sky (indicating the harm of nuclear power). Despite the park's small size (a fraction of Hiroshima's Peace Park), an appropriate somber gloom pervades this memorial. Every year on August 9 there is an anti–nuclear war demonstration here. To get to this park, return to the Tsukimachi stop and take Streetcar 1 to the Matsuyamachi stop. (If you are going to the Peace Park directly from the JR Station, take either Streetcar 1 or 3 to the Matsuyamachi stop, about a 10-min. ride.) ☛ Free.

⓬ Standing on the hill above the Peace Park is the **Nagasaki International Cultural Hall.** To reach it, climb the steps at the southern end of the park, past the Flame of Peace. Inside the hall, which looks like a prefabricated building from early postwar days, are displays of photos and objects demonstrating the devastation caused by the atomic bomb. The museum is far more grim and informative than the Peace Park itself. Walking through the hall is a sobering experience. Note the tiny corner on the third floor given to the foreign victims of the bomb dropped by the American B-29 Bockstar. It notes that there were 500 Allied POWs interned in the middle of a factory site that was decimated, although 200 of them had died of disease, malnutrition, and torture before the bomb was dropped. ☛ ¥50. ☾ *Daily 9–5.*

⑬ One last place to visit in Nagasaki is **Nishi-zaka** (West Slope), a short walk from the Nagasaki train station. As you leave the front of the station, turn left and walk along the road next to the train tracks for a few minutes. Turn right on the first major road and you will be at Nishi-zaka. In the early 16th century, Christian missionaries successfully converted many Japanese to Christianity. Japanese leaders feared the potential influence of Christianity and banned its practice in 1587. Ten years later, 20 Japanese and six foreigners were crucified on this hill for refusing to renounce their religious beliefs. A monument was built in 1962 dedicated to the memory of the 26 martyrs, and a small museum documents the history of Christianity in Japan. ☛ ¥250. ☾ *Daily 9–5.*

Off the Beaten Track

An hour by bus (fare: ¥1,300) to the north of Nagasaki and near Sasebo is the new **Nagasaki Holland Village Huis Ten Bosch** (1-1 Huis Ten Boschmachi, Sasebo, ☎ 0956/27–0001, ℻ 0956/27–0912). You can also take the JR train from Nagasaki (or Takeo Onsen), which takes 90 minutes to reach the Huis Ten Bosch station. Opened in 1992 at a cost of $1.75 billion, this is Japan's largest theme park (375 acres). The attractions are modeled after 17th-century Holland, with replicas of a Dutch village and the Cathedral of Horn (Dom Horn). Though there are scheduled activities such as horse parades, many of the Japanese tourists spend their time choosing among the many restaurants available and shopping at the numerous souvenir outlets. With an admission cost of ¥3,900, plus additional fees for specific attractions, it can become an expensive day's outing and one that foreign visitors may find only marginally interesting. The complex includes the 330-room Hotel Europa. ☾ *9 AM–11 PM.*

Shopping

Hamanomachi, located not far from Dejima, is the major shopping district in downtown Nagasaki. In this area you can find traditional crafts, antiques, and restaurants. Keep in mind that it is illegal to bring tortoiseshell products into the United States.

Gift Ideas

Castella cake. Based on a Dutch cake, this dessert resembles a pound cake with a moist top. It has long been the most commonly known Nagasaki product, and was popular here when baked goods were still unknown in the rest of Japan. **Fukusaya** is a bakery that has been in business since the beginning of the Meiji period (1868-1912). When you say "castella," most people think of this famous shop and its distinctive yellow packaging of the cake. Tokyoites would never return from a trip to Nagasaki without their Fukusaya castella. *3-1 Funadaikumachi,* ☎ *0958/21-2938.* ☾ *8:30–8. Closed every 2nd Thurs.*

Glassware. Biidoro Bijutsukan, near the Peace Park, is a museum featuring exhibits documenting the history of Nagasaki glassware, an art that was introduced by the Dutch during the Tokugawa period. The museum has a small gift shop; the museum annex has a more extensive selection of items for sale. *16-10 Hashiguchimachi,* ☎

0958/43–0100; annex: 5-19 Hamanomachi, ☎ *0958/27–0100.* ☉
Daily 9–5.

KUMAMOTO

*Numbers in the margin correspond to points of interest on the Kyushu
map.*

⑭ In the years of the Tokugawa Shogunate (1603–1868), **Kumamoto** was
one of Japan's major centers of power. The main attractions in Kumamoto—the castle and the landscaped gardens of Suizenji Koen—
date from this period and are among the most famous in Japan.
Kumamoto may no longer be a major political center, but, with its broad
and lush tree-lined avenues, it is an extremely attractive city. Despite
having no real political importance since the Meiji Restoration, the city
is currently enjoying a commercial boom.

Arriving and Departing

By Plane

Five daily flights on All Nippon Airways (ANA) and Japan Air System connect Haneda Airport (Tokyo) with Kumamoto Airport (1 hr.
40 mins.). From Osaka Airport, ANA has four flights daily (1 hr.).

BETWEEN THE AIRPORT AND CENTER CITY
A regular bus service connects the airport with the JR Kumamoto Station. The bus takes 55 minutes and costs ¥720.

By Train

Japan Railways offers a Limited Express train from Hakata that stops
in Kumamoto (1½ hrs.) en route to Kagoshima. From Nagasaki, take
the train to Shimabara, board a one-hour ferry across Ariake Bay to
Misumi, then take the train to Kumamoto. Japan Rail Pass holders can
save the ferry fare by taking the train to Tosu and changing to the train
to Kumamoto (3 hrs. total).

By Bus

From Nagasaki Bus Terminal you can take a four-hour bus trip to Kumamoto. The bus goes as far as Shimabara, after which you board a
one-hour ferry across Ariake Bay to Misumi, then take the bus directly
to Kumamoto Kotsu Center. The cost of this journey, which takes you
through some of Kyushu's most beautiful scenery, is ¥2,860 including
the ferry ride.

Getting Around

By Streetcar

The easiest way to get around Kumamoto is by the two streetcar lines
that connect the major areas of the city. When you board the streetcar, take a ticket. When you get off, you will pay a fare that depends
on the distance traveled. The chart of the fares is displayed at the front
to the left of the driver. (On the ticket that you take is the number of
the zone in which you boarded the bus; on the chart, the current fare
flashes for each numbered zone, based on the distance traveled from
the respective zones.) From the Kumamoto Eki-mae streetcar stop, in
front of the JR Kumamoto Station, it is a good 10-minute ride into
downtown (fare: ¥160). One-day travel passes good for use on streetcars and municipal buses are available for ¥500 from the Kumamoto
Station Travel Information Bureau (☎ 096/352–3743).

By Bus

The main bus terminal is the Kotsu Center, a few minutes' walk from Kumamotojo. Although the buses travel all over the city, the routes are more complicated than those of the streetcars.

Important Addresses and Numbers

Tourist Information

City Information Office, 3-15-1 Kasuga, ☎ 096/352–3743, is inside JR Kumamoto Station complex to the left as you exit the platforms. ☉ Daily 9–5.

Exploring

Unlike in many other Japanese cities, there is very little activity around the JR station. Shops, restaurants, and hotels are clustered downtown under the shadow of the castle instead. The heart of the town is a broad shopping arcade from which small streets branch off. This area comes alive at night with neon lights advertising restaurants and bars.

Kumamotojo, in the heart of downtown Kumamoto, is where most people begin their tour of Kumamoto City. To get to this castle, board Streetcar 2, get off at the Kumamotojo-mae stop, and walk up a tree-lined slope toward the castle. Kumamotojo was first built in 1607 under the auspices of Kiyomasa Kato, feudal lord of this region. It is especially famous for its unique and massive concave defensive walls, known as *mushagaeshi,* which made it exceedingly difficult for attackers to scale. It is often referred to as Ginkojo, after a giant ginko tree that was supposedly planted by Lord Kato. Much of the original castle was destroyed in 1877, after it lay under siege for 57 continuous days by an army from Kagoshima led by Takamori Saigo. It was rebuilt in 1960.

Often reconstructed buildings are of little interest, but this castle of concrete is an excellent example of reconstruction that manages to evoke the magnificence of the original. By walking around the expansive grounds, you can get a true sense of the grandeur of feudal Japan. Few castles in Japan today, reconstructed or not, can boast of 49 turrets, 18 turret gates, and 29 castle gates. Inside Kumamotojo is a museum exhibiting relics like samurai armor and palanquins for those who are interested in feudal history. As you look at the displays, you cannot help but imagine samurai in full regalia, fiercely protecting their lord. From the top floor there is an excellent view of Kumamoto. If time permits further exploration of the grounds, go to the Higo Gardens, filled with lovely flowers and a peaceful place to conclude your visit. ☛ ¥200 (grounds), ¥300 (castle). ☉ Daily Apr.–Sept. 8:30–5:30; Oct.–Mar. 8:30–4:30.

To the west of the castle in a modern, redbrick building is the **Kumamoto Kenritsu Bijutsukan** (Prefectual Art Museum), which in the spring and autumn exhibits the famous Hosokawa collection of antiques from the Tokugawa Shogunate era. Be sure to see the full-scale models of the burial chambers with Kumamoto's design of painted geometrical shapes. ☛ ¥300. ☉ Tues.–Sun. 9:30-4:30.

Next take either Streetcar 2 or 3 east from the castle to the Suizenji Koen-mae stop and **Suizenji Koen,** a 300-year-old garden that is a tribute to the art of landscaping. The garden was originally created in 1632 by the Hosokawa clan as part of the grounds of their villa. Although the park is often crowded with tour groups and lacks a certain serenity, there are still elements of beauty where artistry has worked with nature. A part of the garden with ponds and small artificial mounds re-creates the 53 stations of the Tokaido (the route between Edo and Kyoto) and its prominent features such as Lake Biwa and Mt. Fuji. ☛ ¥200. ☉ Daily 7–6.

TIME OUT Take a break in the park at the small, old-fashioned teahouse by the garden's pond. Here, for a small fee, you can sip green tea as you sit on tatami mats and appreciate the exquisite view.

On the hill to the west of town is **Honmyoji,** a Nichiren temple built by daimyo Kiyomasa Kato. It is reached by streetcar from the JR Kumamoto Station or by Bus 12 from the Kotsu Center. Kato is buried here in the tomb at the top of a flight of stairs so that his spirit may look across at eye level to the donjon of his castle, Kumamotojo. The temple's museum contains Kato's personal effects, including the helmet that he wore while campaigning in Korea for his master, Hideyoshi Toyotomi. ☛ Museum ¥300. ☉ Tues.–Sun. 9-4:30.

Off the Beaten Track

If you have time, you may want to go south from Kumamoto to the modern city of **Kagoshima.** The scenic three-hour train ride to Nishi-Kagoshima passes mountains on the left and the sea on the right. Downtown is a five-minute walk from the JR station, and there is a tourist information office to the left as you leave the JR Nishi-Kagoshima Station.

Though Kagoshima has few sightseeing attractions, there are other reasons to take a break here. Kagoshima's mild climate gives this city a tropical feel, and getting around is easy and inexpensive. Two lines of streetcars cover the city and ¥160 takes you any distance. (There is ¥500 one-day pass for unlimited rides.)

Kagoshima serves for many as a jumping-off point to the surrounding country and Okinawa islands, or as a stopover on the train ride across to Kyushu's east coast. The **Park Hotel** (15-24 Chuomachi, Kagoshima 890, ☎ 0992/51-1100), two minutes from Nishi-Kagoshima Station, has reasonable rates, clean rooms, a pleasant coffee lounge, a Japanese restaurant, and helpful staff. There is also the more expensive (¥14,000 for a twin) and slightly smarter **Kagoshima Tokyu Inn** (Chuo-chome 5-1, Kagoshima 590, ☎ 0992/56–0109, FAX 0992/53–3692), with 182 rooms. In the downtown entertainment district you'll find **Edoko Sushi** (Bunka St., 2-16 Sannichicho, ☎ 0992/25–1890), an excellent sushi bar (counter seating and two tables with tatami seating) with a very hospitable owner. Take the first right off Yubudo (the wide shopping-arcade street), and Edoko is the last restaurant on the left. Prices are moderate.

Shopping

One of Kumamoto's most famous products is **higo zogan,** a form of metalwork consisting of black steel inlaid with silver and gold, creating a delicate yet striking pattern. Originally an ornamentation technique for samurai swords, scabbards, and gun stocks of the Hosokawa clan, it is now used mostly in jewelry and other accessories. (The more higo zogan is worn, the glossier it becomes.) Another popular local product is the **Yamaga doro,** a lantern of gold paper. On August 16, as part of the annual Bon festival, young women carry these gold lanterns through the streets of Kumamoto.

Shimatori Shopping Arcade, near Kumamotojo, is a good place to find everything from toothpaste to local crafts. One of the best places for higo zogan, Yamaga doro, and other local crafts is the **Kumamoto Traditional Crafts Center** (3-35 Chigajo, ☎ 096/324–4930; ⊙ Tues.–Sun. 9–5), a combination gallery and shop that displays crafts from all over Kumamoto Prefecture. It is next to the Kumamoto Castle Hotel. The **Tsuraya Department Store** (Tericho-dori, ☎ 094/356–2111) is a good source for Yamaga doro as well as a host of other items.

MT. ASO

★ ⑮ On the way to **Mt. Aso** you pass through Kyushu's radiant green countryside. As you look upon farmers bent over their rice fields, bamboo groves, and other idyllic sights, you have a sense of the peaceful relationship that people of this region have with nature. This serene image quickly fades when you arrive at the smoking and rumbling volcano of Mt. Aso; here you become aware of the violent potential of nature.

Mt. Aso is, in fact, a series of five volcanic peaks, one of which, Nakadake, is still active. The five peaks, along with lakes and fields at its base, form a beautiful national park. Mt. Aso can be seen either on a day trip from Kumamoto or on a stop on the way from Kumamoto to Beppu. If you are interested in spending more time relaxing in this park, you can stay in one of the many mountain pensions on the south side of Mt. Aso (*see* Dining and Lodging, *below*).

Arriving and Departing

By Train
The JR Hohi Line runs between Kumamoto Station and Aso Station (1 hr.). From Aso Station to Beppu there are three JR express trains daily (2½ hrs.). From the JR Aso Station, you must board a bus (40 mins.; fare: ¥620) to get to the Aso Nishi Ropeway Station. The ropeway leads you to the top of the crater in four minutes (fare: ¥940). It is better to begin your trip well before noon, because the last buses for the ropeway station leave mid-afternoon.

By Bus
Buses leaving from the Kumamoto Kotsu Bus terminal go directly to the Aso Nishi Ropeway Station (1½ hrs.).

Exploring

Although Mt. Aso National Park is very pleasant, the main reason to come here is to see the one active volcano, **Nakadake.** From the inside of the largest crater of Nakadake, which is 1,968 feet across and 525 feet deep, you hear the rumblings of the volcano and see billowing smoke. Sometimes the volcano is deemed dangerous, and visitors can't view it up close, so check at Kumamoto or Beppu before you make this excursion. After viewing the volcano you can descend via the ropeway or walk along a path that leads you back to the ropeway station. If you are up for a hike of several hours, you can skip the ropeway altogether and follow the path up to Nakadake and down to the Sensuikyo (gorge). From there you must walk to the JR Miyaji Station, the next stop after Aso Station. Because most visitors to the mountain do not choose to take this arduous route, the paths are delightfully uncrowded, and the views of the live crater and the gorge are awe-inspiring.

BEPPU

After all your travels, an enjoyable way to rest your weary body is by soaking in an *onsen* (hot spring). One of the most popular resorts in all of Japan, **Beppu** provides more than 3,000 sources of hot water not only to the hotels and inns but also to private homes. Its location—the sea in the foreground and mountains to its rear—and the variety of hot mineral springs make it a favorite vacation spot for the Japanese. As a result, Beppu is a garish town with neon lights, amusement parks, Pachinko halls by the dozen, and souvenir shops. Many tourists come here and do not leave their hotel or inn to see any of the local sights. The leisurely pace of this resort is indicated by the many Japanese tourists walking around the streets in their *yukata* (cotton kimonos), casually strolling and looking as though they have not a care in the world.

Arriving and Departing

By Plane

The closest airport to Beppu is Oita Airport, which is served by ANA and JAS domestic flights from Tokyo's Haneda Airport (1 hr. 40 mins.) and from Osaka Airport (1 hr.).

BETWEEN THE AIRPORT AND CENTER CITY

Buses leave regularly from the airport for Beppu City. The one-hour trip costs ¥1,300 and terminates at Kitahama bus stop on the bay side of Beppu's main street.

By Train

The Hohi Main Line travels between Kumamoto and Beppu (3 hrs. 20 mins.), stopping at Mt. Aso. The Nichirin Limited Express Train runs more than 10 times daily (2½ hrs.) between Beppu and Hakata Station in Fukuoka.

By Bus

Buses travel between Kumamoto and Beppu (3½ hrs.) and between Mt. Aso and Beppu on the Trans-Kyushu Highway (3 hrs.). Sightseeing buses operated by the Kyushu Kokusai Kanko Bus Company travel regularly between Beppu and Kumamoto, stopping at Mt. Aso.

By Boat

Three ferries (two of which call at Matsuyama and Imabari or Takamatsu and Sakaide, all on Shikoku) connect Beppu with Osaka and Kobe on the Kansai Kisen Line (in Tokyo, ☎ 03/274–4271; in Osaka, ☎ 06/572–5181; in Beppu, ☎ 0977/22–1311). These overnight ferries leave in the early evening (the direct ferry for Osaka leaves Beppu at 7:20 PM and arrives at 8:20 AM; fare: ¥5,870, 2nd class). Reservations are necessary for first class. A ferry to Hiroshima leaves Beppu at 2 PM and arrives at Hiroshima at 7 PM and leaves Hiroshima at 9:30 PM, arriving in Beppu at 6 AM. (fare: ¥3,600–¥5,550).

Getting Around

By Bus

Regular buses travel to most places of interest in Beppu. The main bus terminal, Kitahama Bus Station, is just down the road from the JR Beppu Station. The minipass for one day's travel within the city limits (¥800) is a good buy. The cost of travel between the station and the hot springs with single tickets adds up to ¥1,540.

By Taxi

Because most of the sights in Beppu are relatively close to one another but too far to walk, this is one of the few places in Japan that it may be worthwhile simply to hop in a taxi. Fares range from ¥1,000 to ¥3,000. Hiring a taxi for two hours to visit the major thermal pools would run approximately ¥5,000, after negotiation.

Guided Tours

A regular sightseeing bus service, leaving from Kitahama Bus Station, located just east of the JR Beppu station, covers most of the major sights in the area. The tour lasts about 2½ hours. Although an English-speaking guide is not always available, most of the sights are self-explanatory.

Important Addresses and Numbers

Beppu City Information Office (12-13 Eki-maecho, ☎ 0977/24–2838) in Beppu Station has, as long as you persevere in asking for them, several useful maps and brochures in English. The office is open daily 9–5. **Foreign Tourist Information Service** (Furosen 2F, 7-16 Chuomachi, Beppu City, Oita-gun 874, ☎ 0977/23–1119) is four minutes from the station—use the map posted on the City Information Booth in the JR station. This office has an enthusiastic volunteer staff. The office is open Monday–Saturday 10–4.

Exploring

Beppu is a resort area; the main attractions are the hot springs. A few sights in Beppu are worth seeing, though many people choose to bypass them, and just recline and relax.

★ If you grow tired of inactivity, visit the **Eight Hells,** the Kannawa section of Beppu, with eight distinctive hot springs. Take Bus 15, 16, 17, 41, or 43 from the stop across from the JR station for the 30-minute trip to Kamenoi Bus Station (fare: ¥310). One of the springs, **Chi-no-ike Jigoku** (Blood Pond Hell), is a boiling spring with red gurgling water, the vapors of which are purported to have curative powers for skin diseases. **Umi Jigoku** (Sea Hell) features not only water the color of the ocean, but also tropical plants. **Oniyama Jigoku** (Devil Mountain Hell) is a place where crocodiles are bred. An entertaining aspect of the Eight Hells are the many vendors nearby who try to sell their wares, such as eggs placed in baskets and boiled in the water. Although it is fascinating to see just how *hot* hot springs can be, keep in mind that this very popular attraction is crowded year-round. Each hot spring charges ¥400 admission, but a combined ticket for ¥2,000 will admit you to all except Jigoku Meguri.

After your tour of the springs, take a bath at **Hyotan Onsen,** one of the more interesting thermal baths, across the road from Kamenoi Bus Terminal. The pool is outdoors, with waterfalls, hot stones, and sand. ☛ *¥500.* ⊘ *Daily 7 AM–9 PM.*

The other main sight near Beppu is **Takasakiyama Monkey Park,** home to 1,900 monkeys. To get there, take a 10-minute bus ride from Kitahama Bus Station. These once-wild monkeys were a problem for local farmers, but now they are domesticated. The monkeys are divided into three groups, each carefully guarding their territory. Observation of the hierarchy within each group is fascinating for adults and endlessly diverting for children. ☎ *0975/32–5010.* ☛ *¥500.* ☉ *Daily 8–5.*

All hotels and inns in Beppu have baths, but if you want to spend a day in a veritable amusement park of hot springs, the **Suginoi Palace** (☎ 0977/24–1141), a part of the Suginoi Hotel, is quite a spectacle. This indoor complex has a variety of hot springs including a sand bath and a saltwater bath. There is also live cabaret in the evening as well as a vast souvenir-shopping complex, with electronic games—quite ghastly, but a place to visit once. ☛ *¥2,000 (see* Lodging, *below).* ☉ *Daily 9–11.*

Other attractions in Beppu include the **Beppu Ropeway** up to Mount Tsunumi for views over the city and bay (take Bus 2, 34, 36, or 37 from Beppu Station and then the 10-min. ropeway to the top; cost: ¥1,400; ☉ Daily 9–5) and the **Marine Palace Aquarium** (☛ ¥1,050; ☉ Daily 8–5). Both seem to have more appeal for Japanese vacationers than for foreign tourists. The small **Take-no Museum** in the center of town exhibits Beppu's celebrated crafts made from bamboo (☎ 0977/25–7776; ☛ ¥500; ☉ Daily 8:30–6). You can purchase bamboo objects in Kishi-mae, the adjoining shop.

Off the Beaten Track

★ Those who find the glitz of Beppu distasteful often choose the relative peace and serenity of **Yufuin,** situated on a plateau an hour's bus ride inland from Beppu (or a 90-min. ride on a JR train from Beppu via Oita). The air here (1,400 feet above sea level) is intoxicatingly fresh, and the pace, slow and leisurely. A helpful tourist office (☎ 0977/84–2446; ☉ Daily 9–7) at the station will supply a map and make hotel reservations for you. Because Yufuin is spread out, you may want to rent a bicycle (cost: ¥300 per hour) to get around. The town has become the artsy alternative to Beppu, with clusters of galleries showing and selling crafts. A popular cluster is Kusonomori, but beware of the prices both for admission (ranging from ¥250 to ¥600) and of the items for sale. Yufuin is also home to a film festival, a music festival, and outdoor summer concerts. There are a few historic monuments in Yufuin—Rokushogu, Bussanji, Kozenji—but it's the Yunotsubo public onsen alongside the lake that is the most evocative of traditional Japan.

For those who find Yufuin too commercial—and its popularity is increasing—quaint **Yunohira Onsen,** with cobblestone streets, traditional inns, and a history of 270 years of people coming to take its waters, is even farther off the beaten track. At least three buses a day make the 36-minute trip from Yufuin to Yunohira Onsen.

DINING AND LODGING

Dining

Until the 20th century, Kyushu was the international center of Japan. Certain Kyushu dishes, not surprisingly, show the influence of China and Europe. Tempura, for example, is often thought of as a standard Japanese dish; in fact, it was introduced by Europeans to Kyushu in the 17th century. Particularly in Nagasaki, the influence of foreign cuisines is still apparent. In addition to international flavors, many regions in Kyushu have special dishes that incorporate the food available in that locale.

Beppu is famous for its delicious seafood. Because it is primarily a resort town, most people tend to remain in their hotels or inns even for meals, so many of the hotels have fresh, locally caught fish. One particularly popular local dish is **fugu** (blowfish).

Fukuoka, Kyushu's largest city, has a wide range of excellent Japanese and Western restaurants. Many of the best Western restaurants are located in hotels. Fukuoka is well known for its **Hakata ramen,** noodles with a strongly flavored soup with *negi* (scallions) and strips of roast pork. It is also known for its **ikesu** restaurants, places that have a fish tank from which you can select your entree, guaranteeing its freshness.

Adventurous eaters will enjoy the challenge of the regional specialty of Kumamoto, **horse meat,** which is served roasted, fried, or raw. Another Kumamoto delicacy is **dengaku,** tofu or fish covered by a strong bean paste and grilled. Dengaku is a good example of Kyushu cuisine's strong flavors—unlike the very delicate taste of food from Kyoto, for example.

Nagasaki is really the place where you get a sense of the many cuisines that have influenced Kyushu dining. One dish, available only in Nagasaki, and with distinct Chinese, European, and Japanese influences, is **shippoku.** Shippoku is actually a variety of dishes that, when combined, make a full meal. Dinners center on a fish-soup base with European flavorings, to which many foods are added, including stewed chunks of pork cubes prepared Chinese-style, marinated in ginger and soy sauce; rice cakes; and a variety of vegetables. Shippoku usually is served as one large communal dish, which is uncommon in Japan. (In the traditional way of serving and eating Japanese food, individual portions are prepared.) Another distinctive Nagasaki dish is **chanpon,** heavy Chinese-style noodles in a soup. Not surprisingly, Nagasaki also has some of the best Western restaurants in Kyushu.

A 3% federal consumer tax is added to all restaurant bills. Another 3% local tax is added to the bill if it exceeds ¥7,500. At more expensive restaurants, a 10%–15% service charge is also added to the bill. Tipping is not the custom.

CATEGORY	COST*
$$$$	over ¥9,000
$$$	¥6,000–¥9,000
$$	¥3,000–¥6,000
$	under ¥3,000

Cost is per person without tax, service, or drinks

Lodging

Accommodations in Kyushu are plentiful, and because the number of tourist and business travelers is limited, it is nearly always possible to get reservations. Fukuoka has major hotels with excellent facilities. Nagasaki features grand old hotels and ryokan that, like the city itself, seem to be frozen in the 19th century.

Travelers looking for a more active vacation may choose to spend a few days in the Mt. Aso region at a pension. Pensions are similar to bed-and-breakfasts, with supper served as well. The pensions near Aso are set in the mountains and are located near trails for hiking. Some also have tennis courts.

A 3% federal consumer tax is added to all hotel bills. Another 3% local tax is added to the bill if it exceeds ¥15,000. At most hotels, a

10%–15% service charge is added to the total bill. Tipping is not the custom.

CATEGORY	COST*
$$$$	over ¥20,000
$$$	¥15,000–¥20,000
$$	¥10,000–¥15,000
$	under ¥10,000

Cost is for a double room, without tax or service

Beppu

Dining

$$–$$$ Fugumatsu. This small, popular restaurant, with a simple, Japanese-style interior, has counters, tables, and private rooms. Its specialty is *fugu* (blowfish), which is a favorite in the area. Fugu is a potentially poisonous fish that restaurants must be licensed to serve. In the summer Fugumatsu serves a type of *karei* (flatfish) that can only be caught in Beppu Bay. Courses start at ¥5,000. Upon your request you can have less- or more-expensive food; the restaurant will adjust to your budget. It is one block north of the Tokiwa department store and one block from the bay. ✗ *3-6-14 Kitahama,* ☎ *0977/21–1717. No credit cards.*

$ Jin. For an inexpensive evening of beer, sake, and *izakaya* (pub) cuisine that includes *yakitori* (skewered chicken) and grilled seafood, Jin is popular with Japanese and foreign visitors. Seating is either at wooden tables and chairs or at the bar looking over displays of fish resting on crushed ice and waiting to be selected by the next diner. The mood is jovial, and you are sure to start up a conversation with your neighbors. Jin is easy to find: Walk from JR Beppu Station on the right side of Eki-mae-dori and toward the bay; it is just before the "T" junction and across from Tokiwa department store. ✗ *422 Eki-mae-dori,* ☎ *0977/21–1768. No credit cards.*

Lodging

$$$$ Suginoi Hotel. More than just a hotel, this is a miniresort. Once you arrive and check in, you may not feel any need to go anywhere else. The hotel is situated on a hill with a panoramic view of the city and the ocean. Connected to the hotel is the Suginoi Palace, which features a variety of hot springs, such as the "Dream Public Bath" and the "Flower Public Bath." Once you've washed and rinsed off, you proceed into a room full of plants and trees. You can soak in a standard hot spring, bury yourself in warm sand, or, if you get bored with hot water, move to the swimming pool. Breakfast and dinner are included in the price of the accommodations, and there are both Western- and Japanese-style buffets. Guests tend to wander around the hotel and attend meals in their yukata. The rooms—rather austere in decor—are a welcome break from the opulence of the rest of the hotel. If a quiet and refined experience is what you seek, this is not the right choice. It feels a little bit like a Japanese Las Vegas. Nevertheless, this is the most popular hotel in all of Beppu. ▦ *Kankaiji Onsen, Beppu, Oita-ken 874,* ☎ *0977/24–1141,* ℻ *0977/21–0010. 600 rooms, 80 Western style. Restaurant, pool, beauty salon, bowling, playground, shops, Japanese banquet hall. AE, DC, MC, V.*

$$$ Beppu Kankaiso. This ryokan used to be a hotel with many Japanese-style rooms. It now serves two meals, which are included in the price of accommodations. The rooms are large and clean; the Japanese rooms can sleep as many as five, which cuts down on the cost per head. Although the baths here are nothing special, the ryokan is close enough to the Suginoi Hotel that it is easy to pay the daily admission of around

¥2,000 and take advantage of their facilities. The food in the Japanese restaurant Orion is excellent. ☷ *Kankaiji Onsen, Beppu, Oita-ken 874,* ☎ *0977/23–1221,* ☒ *0977/21–6285. 51 rooms, 9 Western style. Japanese restaurant. AE, DC, V.*

$ **Sakaeya.** Many minshuku are drab concrete buildings that are different
★ from youth hostels only in that they have private rooms. This minshuku is a rare gem in a beautiful old wooden building with surprisingly low rates, which include meals. The meals consist of straightforward Japanese food with fish and rice, but they are prepared in the oven in the backyard, which is heated from the hot springs. Only one public bath is available, but as you relax in it with your fellow guests, you have a sense that this is how the Japanese have been enjoying the wonders of hot springs for centuries. This minshuku is small and gaining popularity quickly, so make reservations. To reach the inn, take Bus 16, 17, 24, or 25 from Beppu Station. ☷ *Idonikumi, Ida, Kannawa, Beppu, Oita-ken 874,* ☎ *0977/66–6234. 10 rooms. No credit cards.*

If you cannot get in at Sakaeya, the Tourist Information Center at Beppu Station has a listing of several other inexpensive minshuku. One to try is **Minshuku Kokage** (8-9 Eki-maecho, Beppu, Oita-ken ☎ 0977/23–1753, ☒ 0977/23–3895), just two minutes by foot from the station in the direction of the bay. The three-story concrete building has 16 rooms, ten of which have private baths, for approximately ¥7,000 for two people. Japanese breakfast (¥825) and dinner (¥1,860) are available.

Fukuoka

Dining

$$$$ **Ikesu Kawataro.** A large tank full of fish—potential dinner—sits in the middle of this large establishment, which offers counters, Japanese-style rooms with tatami mats, and regular tables. If you don't mind sitting on the floor for the duration of the meal, the tatami section is the most pleasant, because the other areas of the restaurant tend to be rather noisy. Try any of the remarkably fresh sashimi dishes. If you order certain kinds of fish and shrimp, they will still be wriggling on your plate when served. ✕ *1-6-6 Nakasu, Hakata-ku,* ☎ *092/271–2133. DC, MC, V.*

$$ **Gyosai.** The humble atmosphere of Gyosai belies the quality of the food. Order any of the sashimi dishes or steamed fish. Although the staff do not speak much English, they are very helpful, and gestures and a smile will go a long way. This restaurant has the added advantage of being within walking distance of Hakata Station. ✕ *2-2-12 Eki-mae, Hakata-ku,* ☎ *092/441–9780. No credit cards.*

$ **Deko.** A cheerful izakaya just a three-minute walk from the New Otani
★ hotel, this is a delightful place to while away an evening over good food. Seating is Japanese-style at the counter and at shared tables, but there is a well for your legs. The Western-style seating in the back is outside the fraternity of communal dining. Deko has no English menu, but the staff will do their best to make suggestions. Usually the special of the day is a good choice; it might be an egg roll stuffed with spinach for ¥750. The mackerel lightly grilled in soy sauce and salt is superb. From the New Otani go diagonally across the intersection, pass the Pachinko parlor on the left-hand side of the street, and you'll come to a tall, new building outside of which there is a big sign that says "Lhasa"; Deko is down one flight of stairs. ✕ *1-24-22 Jonansen-dori, 1 BF, Chuo-ku,* ☎ *092/526–7070. No credit cards.*

$ **Ichiki.** If you are interested in checking out Japanese nightlife but are not sure where to go, try this bar/restaurant and see how many Japanese spend their recreational evenings. The atmosphere is relaxed and friendly, and as the evening wears on, it is more likely than not that one of your Japanese neighbors will attempt to make your acquaintance. Try the *kushiyaki*, a sort of Japanese shish kabob with fish, meat, and vegetables, fried on a hot, flat grill and served on a wood skewer. This is not a restaurant where you just sit down and order your meal, but rather a place where you relax for the evening, have a few beers, and order a few small dishes at a time. The price range for each dish is ¥400–¥1,000. ✕ *1-2-10 Maizara, Chuo-ku,* ☎ *092/751–5591. No credit cards.*

Lodging

$$$$ **Hotel Il Palazzo.** Fukuoka's most chic lodging is a boutique hotel created by art director Shigeru Uchida and architect Aldo Rossi. It's a showpiece of contemporary design and has won an award from the American Institute of Architects for its innovations. The interior is classically simple, yet dramatic. The glow of muted lights in the Italian restaurant reflects off the walls, and the ceiling lights sparkle as if they were stars. The Western-style guest rooms have simple furnishings, rich, deep-pile carpets, and soft colors. The Japanese rooms are basically traditional, except for semi-partitions that give a feeling of increased space. 🏨 *3-13 Haruyoshi, Chuo-ku, Fukuoka, Fukuoka-ken 810,* ☎ *092/716–3333,* FAX *092/724–3330. 62 rooms, mostly Western-stlye. Italian restaurant, café, 3 bars, nightclub. AE, DC, MC, V.*

$$$$ **Hotel New Otani Hakata.** This member of the New Otani hotel group is typical of modern Japanese comfort—smart, characterless, and efficient, with sparkling surrounds. Within those parameters, this is Fukuoka's top hotel and a quick taxi ride from the station. The rooms, decorated in muted tones, are spacious and have a writing table and easy chair. This is one of the few hotels in all of Kyushu where you can expect most of the staff to speak English. One very unusual feature is that it offers free baby-sitting services. The large lobby reception area has a coffee lounge and adjoins a complex of upmarket boutiques whose merchandise is the height of fashion and price. 🏨 *1-1-2 Watanabe-dori, Chuo-ku, Fukuoka, Fukuoka-ken 810,* ☎ *092/714–1111,* FAX *092/715–5658. 423 rooms. Chinese, Japanese, and French restaurants, bars, barbershop, beauty salon, massage, shops, travel services, tea-ceremony room, indoor pool. AE, DC, MC, V.*

$$$ **Hyatt Regency.** Obviously gambling on the future growth of Fukuoka, Hyatt will have two hotels in the city when the Century Hyatt opens in autumn 1996. In the meantime, the Hyatt Regency, eight minutes from Hakata Station (Shinkansen side), serves primarily the business traveler looking for polite, efficient service with comfortable, if innocuously furnished, guest rooms filled with plastic-veneer furniture. The two pluses are the size of the rooms and the futon-style coverlets for the bedding. A negative is the low water pressure of the showers. Guests on the Regency Floor (the sixth) are served good complimentary breakfasts, afternoon tea, and evening cocktails. On the ground floor off the atrium lobby are several outlets. Le Café offers light snacks with a Spanish flavor; the Boston bar is for cocktails; and the Bansai restaurant serves Japanese fare. 🏨 *2-14-1 Hakata-eki-higashi, Hakata-ku, Fukuoka, Fukuoka-ken 812,* ☎ *092/412–1234,* FAX *092/414–2490. U.K. reservations,* ☎ *071/580–8197; U.S. reservations,* ☎ *800/233–1234. 248 rooms. 2 restaurants, bar, conference rooms.*

$$$ **Fukuoka Yamanoue Hotel.** The name of this hotel means "on a mountain," and it is on a hill above Fukuoka, with excellent views of the

ocean on one side and the city on the other. The service is quietly polite and extremely helpful. The rooms are on the small side, but not uncomfortably so. The hotel is a little out of the way—10 minutes from Hakata Station by taxi or bus (catch the Nishitetsu Bus 56 or 57)—but the spectacular views make the travel time worthwhile. ☎ *1-1-33 Terakuni, Chuo-ku, Fukuoka, Fukuoka-ken 810, ☎ 092/771–2131, FAX 092/771–8888. 55 rooms. Japanese and Western restaurants, tennis courts, large public bath. AE, DC, MC, V.*

$$ **★** **Clio Court Hotel.** This hotel is the best value in Fukuoka. Conveniently located across the street from Hakata Station (Shinkansen side), it has remarkably attractive rooms furnished with great care. They are decorated in a variety of styles, such as Art Deco and early American. You can request the type of room decor you prefer when you make your reservations. Request a room in the front—rooms No. 1202 and No. 1203 are good choices. One whole floor contains tea-ceremony rooms modeled on designs by Kamiya Sotan and Hosakawa-Sansai, both disciples of the founder of the tea ceremony, Sen-no-Rikyu. Another tea-ceremony room is designed with benches and tables for foreigners. One of the hotel's most pleasant features is the courtyard on the 13th floor, which serves as a beer garden in the summer. One floor higher is the hotel's revolving restaurant, which serves grilled steak and seafood cooked Western and Japanese style; in 60 minutes, you've seen all of Fukuoka! ☎ *5-3 Hakata Eki Chuo-gai, Hakata-ku, Fukuoka, Fukuoka-ken 812, ☎ 092/472–1111, FAX 092/474–3222. 194 rooms (some for the handicapped). French, Chinese, and Japanese restaurants, bar, café. AE, DC, MC, V.*

$–$$ **Sun Life Hotels.** Across the station plaza from the Shinkansen exit there are actually three Sun Life Hotels within 100 yards of each other. All three are business hotels. Rooms at Sun Life 1 are approximately 20% less expensive than those at Sun Life 2 and 3; they are also not as new and spacious. In addition, Sun Life 2 and 3 have Japanese restaurants that are open all day, and computer work-stations for the tireless business traveler. ☎ *Hakata-ku, Fukuoka, Fukuoka-ken 812 (across from JR Hakata Station on the Shinkansen side), ☎ 092/473–7112, FAX 092/471–5075. 234 Western rooms. Japanese restaurants, coffee shop, business services. AE, DC, MC, V.*

Kumamoto

Dining

$$$$ **Loire.** If you are tired of Japanese food and want a good French meal, try this elegant, spacious restaurant on the 11th floor of the Kumamoto Castle Hotel with an excellent view of the castle. The set-course meals, which feature fish or meat dishes, change every month. During some months, special all-you-can-eat buffets are available. The desserts are varied and recommended. Those who do not feel like paying so much for the view can instead sample the reasonably priced lunches. ✕ *4-2 Jotomachi, ☎ 096/326–3311. Reservations advised. AE, DC, MC, V.*

$$$–$$$$ **★** **Togasaku Honten.** Formal Japanese cuisine is at its best in this restaurant, which serves a set menu. The dinners, served at low, Japanese-style tables, consist of several small courses of fish, meat, tofu, and vegetables, which add up to a very filling meal. The prices are high, but your yen are well spent, because the meals not only are tasty but are presented with exquisite beauty. Togasaku Honten overlooks a peaceful garden, and the staff are formal and polite without being stiff. Ask for a table with a view when you make your reservations. ✕ *1-15-3 Hamazuno, ☎ 096/353–4171. Reservations required. Jacket and tie. DC, MC, V. No lunch.*

A branch of Togasaku Honten with good food at slightly lower prices is located right by Suizenji Koen. This restaurant is more informal and has Western-style tables. ✕ *Togasaku Suizenji Koen, Tsuchiyama Bldg., 2F. 3-4 Suizenji Koen,* ☎ *096/385–5151. Reservations recommended. DC, MC, V. No lunch.*

$$ **Mutsugoro.** This casual dining spot, with pale paper-and-wood walls, is located in the basement of the Green Hotel. Curious, adventurous eaters will note that this restaurant serves horse meat in 40 different ways, including raw horse-meat sashimi and fried horse meat. If you go and decide that these specialties are not to your taste, you can choose from a variety of seafood dishes. As is the case with many informal Japanese restaurants, you order many small dishes. Each dish is about ¥800–¥1,000; for a full meal, you will probably want four or five dishes. ✕ *12-11 Hanabatacho,* ☎ *096/356–3256. No credit cards. No lunch.*

$$ **Senri.** Couple a visit to beautiful Suizenji Koen with lunch or dinner at Senri, situated right in the gardens. Senri serves a wide variety of dishes, including seafood, eel, and horse-meat sashimi. Although Western-style tables and chairs are available, the tatami rooms and low tables are really more in keeping with the ambience of the gardens. Even if you do not choose to have a meal here, you can get a light snack or an appetizer. ✕ *7-17 Suizenji,* ☎ *096/384–1824. No credit cards.*

Lodging

$$ **Fujie.** On the main street leading directly away from the station, this is a smart business hotel with Western single rooms and attractive Japanese double rooms. The lobby lounge faces a Japanese garden, and the restaurant serves well-presented Japanese food. Service is personable and friendly, though the English language is not the staff's strong point. ▥ *2-2 Kasuga, Kumamoto, Kumamoto-ken 860,* ☎ *096/353–1101,* FAX *096/322–2671. 47 rooms. Restaurant. AE, V.*

$$ **Kumamoto Castle Hotel.** This hotel is conveniently situated near Kumamoto Castle and the downtown district. Request a room with a view of the castle, if possible. The rooms here are quiet, a cut above those of business hotels. However, not many of the staff speak English. ▥ *4-2 Jotomachi, Kumamoto, Kumamoto-ken 860,* ☎ *096/326–3311,* FAX *096/326–3324. 208 rooms. Chinese, Japanese, and French restaurants, coffee shop. AE, DC, V.*

$$ **New Sky Hotel.** Managed by the ANA group, in many ways the New Sky is the best lodging Kumamoto has to offer. In addition to several good restaurants, the hotel maintains a relationship with a health club down the street so that its guests can use the pool for ¥700, or all facilities for ¥1,500. The rooms are small, but they are bright and cheerful. ▥ *2 Amidajicho, Kumamoto, Kumamoto-ken 860,* ☎ *096/354–2111,* FAX *096/354–8973. 358 rooms. Chinese, Japanese, and French restaurants, beauty salon, barbershop. AE, DC, MC, V.*

$ **Kumamoto Station Hotel.** A three-minute walk from the station, this hotel is marginally less expensive than the others listed here and strictly utilitarian. ▥ *1-16-14 Kumamoto, Kumamoto-ken 860,* ☎ *096/325–907,* FAX *096/325–2001. 55 rooms. Restaurant. AE, DC, V.*

$ **Minshuku-ryokan Kajita.** This two-story Japanese wooden house has been made into a friendly inn (part of the Japanese Inn Group). The (small) public room has some Western trappings, but the (also small) tatami rooms are typically Japanese—none comes with a private bath. Breakfast (¥700) and dinner (¥1,500) are offered. To reach the inn, take the city bus from the JR Kumamoto Station to Shinmachi bus stop, then cross the street and walk two minutes up the side street. ▥ *1-2-7, Shinmachi, Kumamoto, Kumamoto-ken 860,* ☎ *096/353–1546. 10 Japanese-style rooms without bath. AE.*

Mt. Aso

Lodging

$$ Flower Garden. This small, Western-style lodging is surrounded by gardens. The owners also fill the rooms with blossoms of the season. This cheerful place serves bountiful meals and attracts a young crowd. The nearest station is Takamori, and someone from the pension will come and pick you up if you call. ☎ *Takamorimachi, Ozu, Takamori, Kumamoto-ken 3096-4,* ☎ *09676/2–3021. 9 rooms, a few with private bath. No credit cards.*

$$ Pension Cream House. The rooms at this pension are on the small side, but they are light and airy. The owners do not object to squeezing a group of people into one room, and lowering the costs per head accordingly. ☎ *Takamorimachi, Ozu, Takamori, Kumamoto-ken 3096-1,* ☎ *0976/2–3090. 9 rooms. No credit cards.*

Nagasaki

Dining

$$$$ Harbin. This establishment serves Continental cuisine in a dark, romantic setting. The sauces are a bit heavy, and the food is slightly overcooked, but perhaps the chef is only trying to re-create the dishes as they would be served in Europe. It is not hard to imagine the residents of the 19th-century Western-style houses of Nagasaki eating at this restaurant. ✕ *2-27 Kozenmachi,* ☎ *0958/22–7433. Reservations advised. Jacket required. AE.*

$$$$ Kagetsu. This quiet establishment, set on top of a hill, is Nagasaki's most prestigious restaurant. Dishes are served in the kaiseki manner, but the menu combines Japanese and Chinese cuisine. The building that houses Kagetsu was visited long ago by the Meiji Restoration leader, Ryoma Sakamoto. According to local legend, Sakamoto, while involved in a fight, slashed his sword into a wood pillar and left a gash that is still visible in the restaurant today. ✕ *2-1 Maruyamacho,* ☎ *0958/22–0191. Reservations advised. Jacket and tie. AE, DC, MC, V.*

$$$ Fukiro. Some of the best *shippoku* (meals composed of several dishes) in Nagasaki is served in this roomy Japanese restaurant with tatami mats and shoji screens. Shippoku combines tasty morsels of Chinese and Japanese food, all presented in an aesthetically pleasing way. To get to Fukiro, you must first walk up a steep set of stone steps. The restaurant is an old Japanese-style building, with a tiled roof and long wooden beams. ✕ *146 Kami-nishiyama-machi,* ☎ *0958/22–0253. Reservations advised. Jacket required. DC. Closed Sun.*

$–$$ Shikairo. This large restaurant—1,500 can be seated in various-sized
★ rooms—with garish decor is the birthplace of the well-known Nagasaki *chanpon* noodles, which are the house specialty, though Shikairo has an extensive menu. The seafood dishes are particularly good, and the beef with bamboo shoots is recommended; the menu features many excellent Chinese dishes from the Fukien region—a surprise, because most Chinese food in Japan is rather bland. The service is somewhat brusque by Japanese standards. ✕ *4-5 Matsugae-machi,* ☎ *0958/822–1296. DC.*

$ Hamakatsu. Fans of the Japanese dish *tonkatsu* (fried pork cutlets) will enjoy the Nagasaki version, which uses ground pork mixed with scallions. Hamakatsu specializes in this local treat. Other dishes are available, but most diners stick with the tonkatsu, especially because it is one of the lower-priced dishes on the menu. ✕ *1-14 Kajiyamachi,* ☎ *0958/23–2316. No credit cards.*

$ **Kosanko.** Within Nagasaki's compact Chinatown district are a dozen or so Chinese restaurants. Most famous of these is Kosanko. Dining is on the second floor, though you'll probably have to wait in the ground floor lobby for a table. Dishes cost approximately ¥800–¥1,000 each and run the gamut from chanpon noodles to egg rolls and sweet-and-sour pork. Even though its reputation is grander than its cooking, it is a fun, lively restaurant, especially enjoyable if you are with a group. ✕ *12-2 Sakuramachi,* ☎ *0958/21–3735. No credit cards.*

Lodging

$$$$ **Hotel New Nagasaki.** Losing its preeminence to the new Prince Hotel, ★ this hotel still has the advantage of being just a two-minute walk from Nagasaki Station. The standard twin guest rooms, the largest in the city, have enough space for a couple of easy chairs and a table. The lobby lounge is sparkling fresh, and the French restaurant, Hydrangea, has the airy, light ambience of a conservatory. On the 13th floor are a Chinese restaurant and the Moonlight Lounge for evening drinks; the Steak House serves beef from Goto Island. Many staff members are fluent in English. ☎ *14-5 Daikokumachi, Nagasaki, Nagasaki-ken 850,* ☎ *0958/26-8000,* ℻ *0958/26–6162. 149 Western-style rooms. 5 restaurants, indoor pool, gym, sauna, shops, business services. AE, DC, MC, V.*

$$$$ **Nagasaki Prince Hotel.** This is the city's newest, grandest, and most expensive hotel. Despite its ugly block-tower exterior, the inside is relaxing even if it slightly overdoes the "opulent look" so common in new Japanese hotels. The long, rectangular lobby shimmers with glass, marble, and ponds, but the warm red carpet softens the glare. Guest rooms are decorated in the ubiquitous pastels and have natural-colored processed wood furniture. Each room has bedside panels and is equipped with the amenities of a first class hotel. Restaurants run the gamut from the New York Steak and Seafood dining room to a Japanese sushi bar. Note: The Prince is a 10-minute walk from Nagasaki Station in the opposite direction from downtown, though the streetcar passes by the front entrance and taxis are plentiful. ☎ *2-26 Takaramachi, Nagasakicho, Nagasaki, Nagasaki-ken 850,* ☎ *0958/21–1111,* ℻ *0958/23–4309. 183 rooms. 5 restaurants, room service, beauty salon, parking. AE, DC, MC, V.*

$$$$ **Sakamoto-ya.** This ryokan, started in 1895, seems to have changed ★ very little from its founding days. Cedar baths are offered, and the wood building is a testament to the beauty of the simple lines of Japanese architecture. The restaurant specializes in *shippoku* (meals composed of several dishes), and the cost per night includes breakfast and dinner. The inn is very small and has extremely personalized service. The cost of the rooms varies depending on size and location. ☎ *2-13 Kanayamachi, Nagasaki, Nagasaki-ken 850,* ☎ *0958/26–8211,* ℻ *0958/25–5944. 15 rooms. AE.*

$$$ **Nagasaki Grand Hotel.** This hotel is small and quiet, with a dignified atmosphere. Best of all is the outdoor beer garden. The rooms are compact, but are pleasantly decorated in pastels. ☎ *5-3 Manzaimachi, Nagasaki, Nagasaki-ken,* ☎ *0958/23–1234,* ℻ *0958/22–1793. 126 rooms (3 Japanese style). Japanese and Western restaurants. AE, DC, MC, V.*

$$–$$$ **Nagasaki View Hotel.** This is one notch above a business-category hotel. The large tatami guest rooms, most of which face Nagasaki Bay, also have twin beds in a separate alcove permitting ample space for four guests. The Western-style rooms are half the price, but are modest in size (two twin beds, table and two chairs) and face inland. All rooms have private baths. The large common bath is on the 10th floor with

a huge window looking onto Nagasaki Harbor. The location is convenient for sightseeing, shopping, and evening entertainment. ⌂ *Oura Kaigan-dori, Ouramachi, Nagasaki, Nagasaki-ken 850,* ☎ *0958/24–2211,* FAX *0958/27–1891. 113 rooms. Restaurant, coffee shop, parking (fee). AE, DC, MC, V.*

$$ **Yataro.** On top of a mountain, about 20 minutes by taxi from the center of Nagasaki, is this ryokan and its hotel annex. Yataro has an excellent view of all of Nagasaki, and the meals at the ryokan are plentiful and presented with great care. The view from the shared bath is particularly good. You'll probably enjoy staying in the ryokan, where meals are served in your room, more than staying in the hotel annex. Request a room with a view when you make your reservation. The hotel is less expensive than the inn. ⌂ *2-1 Kazagoshiramachi, Nagasaki, Nagasaki-ken 850,* ☎ *0958/22–8166,* FAX *0958/28–1122. Ryokan: 56 rooms. Hotel: 169 rooms. Restaurant. AE, DC, MC, V.*

$ **Ajisai Inn One.** Rooms are small but clean at this small establishment near the station, opposite the Hotel New Nagasaki. The staff are friendly, and speak a few words of English. ⌂ *11-4 Daikoku, Nagasaki, Nagasaki-ken 850,* ☎ *0958/27–3110. 42 rooms. Breakfast room. V.*

Takeo Onsen

Dining

$ **Muraichi-ban.** This cheerful izakaya is for the young or young-at-heart. Locals meet here to while away the evening eating an array of foods from grilled fish to sashimi, and yakitori to omelettes. The centerpiece of the restaurant is a large, square kitchen where cooks energetically fillet fish, stir-fry noodles, and generally put on a show for the diners sitting at the counter. For those not desirous of these distractions, there are booths around the edge of the dining room. Bric-a-brac hang from the wood-beamed ceilings and posters on the walls give a light ambience to this local joint. ✕ *Takeo-ku,* ☎ *0954/23–4995. No credit cards.*

Lodging

$$ **Kyoto-ya.** There are some 20 ryokan in this small spa town. Kyoto-ya, a comfortable choice in the middle price range, genuinely welcomes foreign guests. The tatami guest rooms are reasonably spacious and include a separate alcove with a table and two chairs by the window. If you reserve room No. 405, you'll have a view of the hotel's open-air thermal pools. These, with their forced air jets to create a whirlpool effect, are wonderfully massaging. Those with tender skin will be pleased to know that the thermal waters here are not as hot as in some onsen. Meals are brought to your room, though you can opt to pay for just the room and eat at one of the local restaurants. ⌂ *34 rooms, most with private bath. Thermal baths, shop. MC. V.*

Yufuin

Lodging

$–$$ **Pension Momotaro.** The owners of this modern pension go out of their way to make guests feel at home; they'll even take you to the station when you depart. For dinner you can choose from the regional specialty of *gi-tori* (wild chicken), pork, *ayu* (sweet river fish), and shiitake cooked in a pot at the table, or the standard meal, which may be grilled beef over a charcoal brazier and mountain vegetables. Momotaro has three thermal baths, one of which is a *rotenburo* (open-air bath) where you can soak in 60° Celsius water and view the inspiring mountains. There are both Western- and Japanese-style rooms in the main building and Japanese-style rooms in the four A-frame chalets. ☎ *Yufuin, Oita-gun 879,* ☎ *0977/85–2187,* ☎ *0977/85–4002. 6 Western rooms, 3 Japanese rooms, 4 chalets. Dining room, hot springs. No credit cards.*

KYUSHU ESSENTIALS

Arriving and Departing

By Plane

The only international airport in Kyushu is Fukuoka Airport (*see* Arriving and Departing in Fukuoka, *above*). Nagasaki, Kagoshima, Oita, Miyazaki, and Kita-Kyushu have airports that are serviced by domestic airlines.

By Train

The JR Shinkansen trains travel only as far as Fukuoka (*see* Arriving and Departing in Fukuoka, *above*). JR trains connect all major destinations in Kyushu.

By Ferry

The Kansai Kisen Line operates ferries connecting the cities of Kobe and Osaka with Beppu (*see* Arriving and Departing in Beppu, *above*) and Kita-Kyushu. There are also ferries that cross the Japan Sea to Pusan, Korea.

Ferries have scheduled runs between the Hakata Pier Ferry Terminal at Fukuoka and Yosu and Pusan, both in Korea. There is also a hydrofoil service to Pusan.

13 Tohoku

Tohoku is, undeservedly, one of Japan's least-visited areas. It has some of Japan's greatest attractions, not the least of which is its people, who seem a bit more friendly than their compatriots along the Tokyo-Osaka corridor. The summer here is refreshingly cool, and the sensational August festivals held in Akita, Aomori, Hirosaki, and Sendai offer a convenient excuse to make a stop here then.

By Nigel Fisher

FEW FOREIGN TOURISTS make it farther north from Tokyo than Nikko. It is their loss. Tohoku, the name given to the six prefectures of northern Honshu, has country charm, rugged mountains, small villages, its share of temples, and some glorious coastline. For a long time the area was known as Michinoku, which, translated, means the "end of the line" or "back-country." That image of remote rusticity is still held by many Japanese, and the result has been that Tohoku is one of the areas least visited in Japan. Yet the image does not tell all. Tohoku has some of the country's greatest attractions, not the least of which is its people.

In a land where politeness is paramount, it seems that the people in Tohoku are actually more friendly than their fellow citizens who live in the industrial Tokyo–Osaka corridor. With the exception of Sendai, Tohoku's cities are small, and the fast pace of urban living is foreign to their inhabitants. Also, because of the lack of high-speed trains and the rugged terrain, Tohoku's residents live their lives with fewer of the urban conveniences that industrialism has brought to the southern two-thirds of Honshu.

The consequence has been that many of the traditional ways and folk arts have been maintained here, as well as an independence of spirit, much like you find in Hokkaido farther north. Visiting Tohoku gives a glimpse into old Japan. All of the large cities are prefectural capitals (prefectures are similar to states in the United States or counties in Great Britain) and have all the amenities of any international community. Though these six cities (with the possible exception of Sendai) aren't particularly well endowed with sightseeing spots, they have been trying hard in recent years to attract and accommodate tourists—as evidenced by the appearance of such modern complexes as the Atorion Building in Akita and the ASPAM Building in Aomori, serving as giant souvenir shops, museums, and information centers rolled into one.

Tohoku's climate is similar to New England's. The winters are cold; in the mountains, snow blocks off some of the minor roads. However, in Sendai and Matsushima, and along the Pacific coast, snow is rarely seen, and temperatures rarely fall to freezing. Spring and autumn are the most colorful seasons. Summer is refreshingly cool and, consequently, attracts Japanese tourists escaping the heat and humidity of Tokyo and points south. August is the month for big festivals in Akita, Aomori, Hirosaki, and Sendai, all of which draw huge crowds.

Tohoku, like all of the island of Honshu, has mountain ranges running along its spine. Most of the island's trains and highways run north–south on either side of the mountains. Hence, when traveling the major roads or railway trunk lines, you tend to miss some of the grandest mountain scenery. This chapter, laid out as an itinerary up the Pacific side of Tohoku's spine and down the Sea of Japan side, embraces the best of Tohoku using the JR trains as much as is possible, but it also takes the traveler to more remote areas.

In brief, the itinerary starts with Tohoku's unofficial capital, Sendai. It then continues on to Matsushima and travels north to Aomori, with detours to Hiraizumi, the Tono Basin, the Pacific coast, Morioka, and Towada-Hachimantai National Park. Those wishing to continue on to Hokkaido from Aomori should jump to the chapter devoted to that island, and then return to this chapter for the journey south. Our itinerary takes us south to Akita and Tsuruoka, where it then turns inland to Yamagata and Fukushima prefectures; from here you can return to Tokyo, continue south to Nikko, or go west to Niigata and the Japan Alps.

SENDAI

Numbers in the margin correspond to points of interest on the Tohoku map.

❶ With a population of nearly 900,000, **Sendai** is the largest city between Tokyo and Sapporo, on the northern island of Hokkaido. The city is very modern, because American firebombs left virtually nothing unscorched by the end of World War II. The buildings that replaced the old ones are not particularly attractive, but Sendai is an open city with a generous planting of trees that justifies its nickname *mori-no-miyako,* "the city of trees." With eight colleges and universities, including the prestigious Tohoku University, the city has intentionally developed an international outlook and appeal. This has attracted many foreigners to take up residency. For the visitor, the blend of old customs and modern attitudes makes Sendai a comfortable southern base from which to explore Tohoku.

Sendai is easy to navigate, and even the major streets have signs in romaji (Japanese words rendered in roman script). The downtown area of Sendai is compact, with modern hotels, department stores with the latest international fashions, numerous Japanese and Western restaurants, and hundreds of small specialty shops. Three broad avenues, Aoba-dori, Hirose-dori, and Jozenji-dori, head out from the station area toward Sendai Castle and cut through the heart of downtown, where they are bisected by two wide shopping arcades, Ichibancho and Chuo-dori. Between these two malls and extending farther east are narrow streets, packing in the 3,000 to 4,000 bars, tea shops, and restaurants that make up Sendai's entertainment area.

While it is easy to get your bearings in Sendai, public transport is not so convenient. Most awkwardly, the subway runs north to south only, and its stations are far from most of the tourist attractions. (A new east–west subway line is being planned, which may improve the situation.) Fortunately, the center of the city is within easy walking distance from the train station, and all hotels are between the center and the station. For sightseeing, the city's buses may be used, though it's advisable to consult the bus and subway information office (located near the subway station in front of the JR station) beforehand. Here you can pick up English-language brochures that tell you about bus departure points, stops, and fares necessary for getting to each of the main tourist attractions. Otherwise, taxis are a convenient way of covering the (generally) short distances between the sights.

Like all the urban centers of Tohoku, Sendai has a limited number of sights worth visiting, and these can easily be covered in a morning's tour. The tour is made easier, too, because Sendai's history focuses almost entirely on a fantastic historic figure, Masamune Date (1567–1636). Affectionately called the "one-eyed dragon" for his valor in battle and the loss of an eye from smallpox when he was a child, Masamune Date established a dynasty that maintained its position as one of the three most powerful *daimyo* (feudal lord) families during the shogun period. But aside from his military skills and progressive administration (he constructed a canal linking two rivers, thus improving the transport of rice), he was also an artist and a scholar who did not close his eye to new ideas.

Tohoku

0 — 50 miles
0 — 75 km

Tsugaru Straits

Fukushima

TO HAKODATE

Mt. Osorezan

Minmaya

Mutsu Bay

Tsugaru Peninsula

Shimokita Peninsula

20 Aomori

19 Sukayu Onsen

Misawa

Hachinohe

18 Hirosaki

Mt. Iwaki

Lake Towada

15

17 Yasumiya

Oyu Onsen

16

4

Kuji

Odate

7

14 Towada-minami

Noshiro

Yoneshirogawa

13

4

Hachimantai

Towada-Hachimantai National Park

12 Obuke

Taro

Oga Peninsula **22**

Oga Onsen

Komaga-take

25 Nyuto Onsen

26

11 Morioka

Jodogahama **9**

Miyako **8**

Oga

21

Akita

24 Tazawako

Shiwa

10 Take

6 Tono

Sea of Japan

23 Kakunodate

Omagari

Hanamaki

7

7 Kamaishi

Omonogawa

Tohoku Expwy

Hiraizumi **5**

4

13

398

Ichinoseki

Tsuruoka **27**

28

Mt. Haguro

Atsumi Onsen

Mogamigawa

Hojusan Risshakuji

Nobiru

3 Matsushima

31

2 Hon-Shiogama

29 Yamagata

1 Sendai

30 Mt. Zao

4

Niigata

Yonezawa

Abukuma

PACIFIC OCEAN

49

Lake Hibara

Kitakata

32

Aganogawa

34

Fukushima

Inawashiro

33

Aizu-Wakamatsu **35**

TO TOKYO

Koriyama

6

Exploring

The tourist information office on the second floor of Sendai's JR station is not particularly big; it's a better idea to visit the local International Center, (*see below*), where much more information can be obtained in English. The center also operates an English-language hotline—☎ 022/224–1919—to answer questions about the city and its prefecture. While you are in the station, however, be sure to explore the tempting arrays of prepared foods and numerous restaurants in the underground mall aptly named Restaurant Avenue. Then take a bus from stand 9 outside the station for a 15-minute ride to **Aobayama Koen** (park), where the International Center and several places of interest lie within close proximity. Get off in front of **Sendai-ishi Hakubutsukan** (Sendai Municipal Museum), at the foot of the hill (the International Center will be on the other side of the road). Those interested in the history of the Date family, whose rule over the region lasted 266 years, should visit the museum, which contains several thousand artifacts connected with the clan, including a collection of armor. From there, it's a short hike up the hillside to the park. ✒ ¥400. ☉ *Tues.–Sun. 9–4:45 (enter by 4:15). Closed the day following a national holiday, and Dec. 28–Jan. 4.*

Masamune Date's presence is everywhere. His statue dominates Aobayama, on which his mighty castle, Aobajo, stood and served as the Date clan's residence for 266 years. The hill rises 433 feet above the city and is guarded by the high rock walls of the Hirosegawa (river) to the east and the deep Tatsunokuchi Valley to the south. No wonder Date's castle was considered impregnable when it was built in 1602.

The castle was destroyed during the Meiji Restoration, though the outer gates survived an additional 70 years, until firebombs destroyed them in 1945. Now the **Gokoku Shrine** is the main feature of the area where the castle stood. The shrine is a rather grandiose building, heavy and cumbersome. To the rear of the castle grounds, a 360-foot-long bridge over the deep Tatsunokuchi Valley leads to the **Yagiyama Zoo,** which is not worth visiting.

Near Masamune Date's statue is an observation terrace from which you can look down over the city and plan your next route, a 20-minute walk to Zuihoden (hall), the Date family's mausoleum.

Cross over the Hirosegawa, take a right, walk along the river past the sports grounds, cross back over the river, and walk up the hill. Zuihoden is to the left. From JR Sendai Station, Bus 11 will take you to the Otamayabashi bus stop. The mausoleum is a short walk up the hill.

★ **Zuihoden** was also bombed in 1945, but a five-year reconstruction project was begun in 1974. During the excavation, Masamune Date's well-preserved remains were found and are now reinterred in what appears to be a perfect replica of the original hall. Two other mausoleums for the remains of the second (Tadamune Date) and third (Tsunamune Date) lords of Sendai were also reconstructed. These mausoleums, which cost in excess of ¥800 million to rebuild, are astounding in their craftsmanship and authenticity in the architectural style of the Momoyama period (16th century). Each mausoleum is the size of a small temple, and the exterior is inlaid with figures of people, birds, and flowers in natural colors, which are sheltered by elaborate curving roofs. Gold leaf is used extravagantly on the pillars and in the eaves of the roofs, creating a glinting golden aura. ✒ ¥515. ☉ *Daily 9–4.*

Next, visit **Osaki Hachimangu,** in the northwest section of the city, about 10 minutes by taxi, either from downtown or Aobayama. You can also take Bus 15 from JR Sendai Station for ¥220. This is the main historic building in Sendai to have survived the war. It was actually built in 1527 in Yonezawa, and was later moved to Toda-gun. Masamune Date liked it, and, in 1607, had it moved from its second site to be rebuilt in Sendai. Its free-flowing architectural form has a naturalness similar to the architectural style in Nikko, and its rich, black-lacquered main building more than justifies its designation as a National Treasure. ☞ *Free.* ⊙ *Daily sunrise to sunset.*

★ A 20-minute walk from Osaki Hachimangu and to the northwest of the city center is the **Rinnoji garden.** Use Bus 24 if you are going directly there from the JR Sendai Station. Of the several gardens in the neighborhood, this Zen-type garden is the most peaceful. A small stream leads the eye to the lotus-filled pond, the garden's focal point. Flowing around the pond and creating a balance are the waving, undulating hummocks covered with clusters of bamboo. In June the garden is a blaze of color, with irises everywhere, but there are so many visitors that much of the tranquillity is lost. ☞ *¥300.* ⊙ *Daily 8–5.*

Bustling downtown Sendai is a shopper's paradise; the area is compact, and many of the stores and small shops are in or connected to the two main shopping arcades, **Ichibancho** and **Chuo-dori.** Sendai is the unofficial capital of the Tohoku region, and you can find many of the regional crafts made outside of Miyagi Prefecture here. Also along the arcades are many Japanese and Western restaurants, which begin to fill up at around 7 PM as the shops start closing.

Sendai's big festival is **Tanabata** (Aug. 6–8), and, while similar festivals are held throughout Japan (usually on July 7), Sendai's is the largest, swelling the city to three times its normal size with Japanese tourists. The celebration stems from a poignant Chinese legend of a weaver girl and her boyfriend, a herdsman, represented by the stars Vega and Altair. Their excessive love for each other caused them to become idle, and the irate king of heaven exiled the two lovers to opposite sides of heaven. However, he permitted them to meet one day a year—that day is now celebrated as Tanabata, highlighted with a theatrical onstage performance of the young lovers' anguish. For the festival, houses and streets are decorated with colorful paper and bamboo streamers fluttering from poles.

If you want a bird's-eye view of the city, the **SS 30 Building,** 30 stories high, is the tallest building in town. The top three floors are reserved for restaurants and viewing galleries. At night, riding up in the outside elevator, with the city lights descending below, is quite a thrill.

EXCURSIONS AROUND TOHOKU

From Sendai to Matsushima

Matsushima and its bay are the most popular coastal resort destinations in Tohoku and are only about 25 minutes by train from Sendai. Therefore, you can easily visit Matsushima as a day trip from Sendai or, because there are many hotels and ryokan, stay on the coast rather than return to Sendai. The Japanese have named three places as their Three Big Scenic Wonders—Ama-no-hashidate on the Sea of Japan in Western Honshu, Miyajima in Hiroshima Bay, and Matsushima Bay. Matsushima made it into the big three because the Japanese are infatuated with oddly shaped rocks, which are featured at Matsushima. Counts differ, but there are about 250 small, pine-clad islands scattered in the bay. Some are mere rocks with barely room for a couple of trees, while others are large enough to shelter a few families. Each of the islets has a distinctive shape; several have tunnels through them large enough for a rowboat to pass through. It is indeed a beautiful bay and a pleasant day's excursion from Sendai.

Getting There

BY TRAIN TO SHIOGAMA

Though you can go directly by train, the prettiest way to arrive at Matsushima is by sea. First, however, we suggest you take the JR train (Senseki Line), whose platforms are reached from the Sendai Station basement, for a 30-minute trip to **Hon-Shiogama** Station. (The same train goes on to the Matsushima Kaigan Station, so this itinerary may be done in reverse.)

Shiogama, the port city of Sendai, has little appeal—except for one shrine, **Shiogama Jinja,** supposedly the home of guardian deities who look after mariners and expectant mothers. Its buildings, with bright orange-red exteriors and simple, natural wood interiors, are well worth the climb up the hill before you catch the boat to Matsushima. To reach Shiogama Jinja, on a wooded hill overlooking the town, turn left from the station, and walk for about 10 minutes. Be warned that after passing through the main entrance, you have to clamber up 202 stone steps to get to the buildings. There are actually two shrines, Shiogama Jinja and the **Shiwahiko Jinja.** The former is the second one you'll reach and is the main building of the complex; (☛ Free).

Two other reasons for the climb up to Shiogama Jinja are the view of Shiogama Bay and a 500-year-old Japanese holly tree on the grounds. You'll usually be able to recognize the tree by the crowds of Japanese taking photographs of themselves standing before it. Near Shiwahiko Jinja is a modern building that houses swords, armor, and religious articles on its first floor and exhibits about fishing and salt manufacturing on its second. ☛ ¥309. ☺ Daily, Apr.–Nov. 8–5; Dec.–Mar. 9–4.

BY FERRY TO MATSUSHIMA

From April to November, between 9 AM and 3 PM, sightseeing ferries leave from Shiogama every 30 minutes (every hour from December to March) for Matsushima. Whether you catch the gaudy "Chinese dragon" ferry or one that is less ostentatious, the route through the bay will be the same. So will the incessant and distracting loudspeaker naming (in Japanese) the islands. The first 10 minutes of the hour-long trip are dismal. Don't fret! Shiogama's ugly port and the oil refinery on the promontory soon give way to the beauty of Matsushima Bay and its islands. *Cost: ¥1,400 one-way, second class; ¥2,600 for the upper deck in first class. The dock is to the right (seaward side) of the Hon-Shiogama train station.*

Exploring

Once you are in **Matsushima,** the key sights are within easy walking distance of each other. For maps and brochures, visit the tourist office at the end of the Matsushite Kaigan pier. The first sight, **Godaido,** is just to the right as you step off the boat on the pier. Constructed at the behest of Masamune Date in 1609, this temple is on a tiny islet connected to the shore by two small arched bridges. Weathered by the sea and salt air, the small building's paint has peeled off, giving it an intimacy often lacking in other temples. Animals are carved in the timbers beneath the temple roof and among the complex supporting beams. Anyone hoping to inspect the temple's interior has a long wait, however: It is open to the public only during special ceremonies held once every 33 years, and the next opening is scheduled for 2006.

★ Along the street from Godaido, across Route 45 and the central park, is the main temple, **Zuiganji.** Its origins date from 828, but the present structure was built on Masamune Date's orders in 1609. Designated as a National Treasure, Zuiganji is the most representative Zen temple in the Tohoku region. The Main Hall is a large wood structure with ornately carved wood panels and paintings (faded with age) from the 17th century. Surrounding the temple are natural caves filled with Buddhist statues and memorial tablets that novices carved from the rock face as part of their training. The grounds surrounding the temple are full of trees, two of which are plum trees brought back from Korea in 1592 by Masamune Date after an unsuccessful military foray. ☛ *¥500.* ⊙ *8–5; shorter hrs. Oct.–Mar.*

For a glimpse at how people looked and dressed during Masamune Date's time, visit the wax museum, **Michinoku Date Masamune Rekishikan** (Masamune Date Historical Museum), on Route 45 (turn left when you walk back toward the bay from Zuiganji). With life-size figures, the museum displays scenes from the feudal period—battles, tea ceremonies, and processions. ☛ *¥1,000.* ⊙ *Daily 8:30–5.*

★ On the opposite (south) side of the harbor from Godaido is **Kanrantei,** translated as "Water Viewing Pavilion." Originally, the structure was part of Fushimi-Momoyamajo in Kyoto, but when that castle was demolished, it was moved to Edo (Tokyo), before being shifted again to its present location in Matsushima by Tadamune Date. Here, the Date family held their tea parties for the next 270 years. Next to Kanrantei is the **Matsushima Hakubutsukan,** a museum with a full collection of the Date family's armor, swords, pikes, and more genteel items, including an array of lacquerware. ☛ *¥200 for both Kanrantei and the museum.* ⊙ *Daily, Apr.–Oct. 8:30–5; Nov.–Mar. 8:30–4:30.*

From Matsushima Kaigan Station it is a 40-minute ride by local train on the JR line back to Sendai. East from Sendai the train goes to **Nobiru,** six stops down the line. A 10-minute walk from the station brings you to the beach where, on weekends, the young cruise in their cars trying to attract the attention of the opposite sex. It's a good place to go for youthful company if you know a few words of Japanese. The road follows the shore, and it is a 30-minute hike to Ogatani Peninsula for spectacular views of Matsushima.

North of Sendai to Hiraizumi

Another day's excursion from Sendai is north to **Hiraizumi,** which in the 12th century came close to mirroring Kyoto as a cultural center. Hiraizumi was the family seat of the Fujiwara clan, who for three generations dedicated themselves to promoting peace and the arts. The fourth-generation lord became power hungry, and his ambition wiped out the Fujiwara dynasty. Not too much remains of the great age under the first three generations of the Fujiwara clan, but what does, in particular, Chusonji, is a tribute to Japan's past.

Getting There

To reach Hiraizumi, take the JR local train (95 min.) or the Shinkansen
❹ (35 min.) on the main Tohoku Line going north to **Ichinoseki** (there is no express train service). At Ichinoseki, there are two options. You can use a taxi or bus to get from the JR station to the Genbikei and Geibikei
❺ gorges, then return to the station and continue by rail to **Hiraizumi** Station. From Hiraizumi you can walk to the two major temples. Alter-

natively, you can skip the Ichinoseki–Hiraizumi train journey and travel directly from the gorges to the temples by taxi.

If your time is short and you wish to limit your sightseeing to the temples, Motsuji and Chusonji, simply take the local train from Sendai for the 100-minute run to Hiraizumi. You can obtain maps at the tourist office (☎ 0191/46–2110) on the right as you go out of the JR station (◷ Daily, Apr. 1–Oct. 31 8:30–5; Nov. 1–Mar. 31 8:30–4:30; closed Dec. 29–Dec. 31). To reach Motsuji, walk 1,000 meters (yards) up the street leading directly away from the JR station. For Chusonji, you can either walk along a narrow road from Motsuji (30 minutes), take a taxi (¥950), or return to the JR station and walk or take a short bus ride.

Exploring

★ By taxi from Ichinoseki, it's less than 10 minutes to **Genbikei,** at a thousand yards long and less than 20 feet deep a miniature gorge, but with all the features of the world's best gorges. Once, rushing water carved its path into solid rock; now it is quiet. Because of its small scale, you can walk its entire length and appreciate every detail of its web of sculptured patterns; the circular holes (Jacob Wells) scoured into the rock side become personal discoveries.

From Genbikei, either by bus or by taxi, it is 1½ kilometers (1 mile) to Motsuji. En route is **Takkoku-no-Iwaya,** a cave with a small temple dedicated to Bishamonten, the Buddhist deity of warriors, at its entrance. To the side of the cave and etched into the rock face are faint traces of an imposing image of Dainichi-Nyorai, a pose of Buddha said to have been carved in the 11th century. The temple is a 1961 rendition of the 17th-century temple. ☛ ¥200. ◷ *Daily 8:30–5.*

During the 12th-century dynasty of the Fujiwara clan, **Motsuji** was the most venerated temple in northern Honshu. The complex consisted of 40 temples and some 500 lodgings. Eight centuries later, only the foundations remain. The current buildings are of more recent vintage, including the local youth hostel. However, what have survived in good condition are the Heian period Jodo-style (paradise-style) gardens, laid out according to the Buddhist principle some 700 years ago. Off to the side of the gardens is the Hiraizumi Museum, with artifacts of the Fujiwara family. ☛ ¥800. *Gardens and museum* ◷ *Daily 8–5.*

★ Now for the major sight, **Chusonji.** Set amid thick woods, Chusonji was founded by the Fujiwara family in 1105. At that time, there were more than 40 buildings; by the temple's heyday the number reached 300. War and a tremendous fire in 1337 destroyed all but two halls, **Kyozo** and **Konjikido.** The other buildings in the complex are reconstructions from the Edo period.

Of the two original buildings, Kyozo is the less interesting. It once housed the greatest collection of Buddhist sutras (precepts), but fire destroyed many of them, and the remainder have been removed to the **Sankozo Museum** next door. Konjikido, on the other hand, may be considered one of Japan's most historic temples. Indeed, it was the first of Japan's National Treasures to be so designated.

Konjikido (Golden Hall) is small but magnificent. The exterior is black lacquer, the interior paneled with mother-of-pearl and gold leaf. In the Naijin (Inner Chamber) are three altars, each with 11 statues of Buddhist deities. Beneath the central altar are the remains of the three rulers of the Fujiwara family—Kiyohira, Motohira, and Hidehira. ☛ ¥500 *(includes Sankozo Museum).* ⊙ *Daily, Apr. 1–Oct. 31 8–5; Nov. 1–Mar. 31 8:30–4:30. Enter 30 mins. before closing time.*

★ The other major attraction of the area is **Geibikei** (Geibi Gorge). To get to the gorge from Chusonji by rail, you must return to the center of Hiraizumi, take a train back to Ichinoseki, and then change to the Ofunato Line for a 30-minute ride to Higashiyama. However, the direct route is only about 21 kilometers (13 miles), so a taxi (about ¥2,000) is much more convenient.

Geibikei Gorge is Genbikei Gorge's big brother. Flat-bottom boats, poled by two boatmen, ply the river for a 90-minute round-trip through the gorge. The waters are peaceful and slow moving, relentlessly washing their way through silver-streaked cliffs. The high point of the trip is reaching the depths of the gorge, faced with 300-foot cliffs. Coming back downstream would be an anticlimax if it were not for the boatmen, who, with little to do but steer the boat, sing traditional songs. The boat trip makes a marvelous rest from the temples (cost: ¥1,030).

From Hiraizumi, you can return to Sendai and Tokyo, continue on the train north to Morioka, or, as we do, go east to the Pacific coast before returning inland to reach Morioka.

To the Tono Basin and the Pacific

This itinerary to the Pacific coast requires approximately two days for you to enjoy traditional pastoral Japan and the southern coastline. Tono is rich in traditional ways and folklore, and the coast is an ever-changing landscape of cliffs, rock formations, and small coves.

Getting There

From Hiraizumi, take the train north in the direction of Morioka to Hanamaki. If you take the Shinkansen from Ichinoseki, disembark at Shin-Hanamaki. Then take the JR train to Tono for a 60-minute ride. The same train continues to Kamaishi and Miyako. From there, take the train up to Morioka.

Exploring

❻ The people of **Tono** like their old ways. The town itself is not particularly remarkable, but in the Tono Basin are old buildings and historical remains that take us back to old Japan and allow the ugliness of modern offices and factories to be temporarily forgotten. The Tono Basin is surrounded by forest-clad mountains, so the setting for this enclave of rusticity is picture- perfect. Along the valley on either side of Tono are several L-shaped *magariya* (thatch-roof Nanbu-style farmhouses). Families live in the long side of the L, and animals are kept off to the side. One of these has been made into a family-run hotel, the **Minshuku Magariya** (without the animals; Niisato 30-58-3, Ayaoicho, Tono-shi, Iwate-ken, ☎ 0198/62–4564; no credit cards; ¥9,800 per person). To the southeast of Tono is a *suisha* (waterwheel), one of the few working ones left in Japan. In a peaceful, wooded area above the Atago Shrine are the *gohyaku rakan* (500 disciples of Buddha) images carved by a priest on boulders in a shallow ravine. The priest wanted to appease the spirits of the quarter of Tono's inhabitants who starved to death in the two-year famine of 1754–55.

The Tono Basin has much more—temples, including Fukusenji, with Japan's tallest wood Kannon (Goddess of Mercy), which was built by priest Yuzen Suriishi to boost morale after World War II; an abundance of shrines; the Tsuzuki Stone, a huge boulder mysteriously balanced on two smaller ones; and a *kappa* pool (kappa are supernatural amphibious creatures that are said to drag people, horses, and cows into the water and to impregnate young girls, who then give birth to demikappas). There is also a redbrick **museum** and a **folk village** exhibiting Tono's heritage. All sites are listed on two maps given out by the Tono Tourist Office in the village. *Joint* ☛ *¥500.* ⊙ *Daily 9–5 (no entry after 4:30). Closed last day of each month, Mar. 1–4, Nov. 24–30, and Mon. Nov.–Mar.*

Distances between points of interest are too far to walk; unless you have a car, a rented bicycle is necessary. (Many places, including hotels, bicycle shops, and the Tono Tourist Office, rent bikes.) Finally, to make the most of the Tono experience, you should read Kunio Yanagita's *Tono Monogatari,* translated into English by Robert Morse as the *Legends of Tono.*

➐ From Tono the train runs down (60 min.) to the Pacific seaport and iron-making town of **Kamaishi.** Note the 160-foot statue of Buddha **(Kamaishi Daikannon)** built in 1970 that stands on Kamazaki Point. To visit the **Fukusenji,** take the 15-minute bus ride from JR Kamaishi Station. It costs a steep ¥850 to enter and see the 33 small wood statues of Kannon. Then, with a change of trains, the journey turns north

➑ to run along the coast (another 80 min.) to **Miyako,** a busy, prosperous town that is pleasantly compact and has several reasonable places

★ ➒ to stay. However, the reason for staying over is to enjoy **Jodogahama** (Paradise Beach), a 15-minute bus ride (from bus stop 6 at Miyako Station) up the coast. Jodogahama was given its name by a priest who thought it was what the hereafter must look like. The combination of glinting white-quartz beach, the peculiarly shaped rock formations, and the pine trees on the cliffs bending to the wind makes Jodogahama a special place. Two rock formations to spot are **Rosoku Iwa** (Candle Rock) and **Shiofuki Ana** (Salt Spraying Hole).

The best way to appreciate Jodogahama is from the water. Rowboats are for hire, but the easier way to get around is to take a 40-minute cruise of the bay. The boats leave from Jodogahama Pier and are operated by the Iwate Kenpoku Jidosha Company. ☎ *0193/62–3350. Cost: ¥1,000. 9 trips a day mid-Mar.–mid-Nov.*

Alternatively, you may want to use **Taro** as your base (16 min. up the coast from Miyako by the Sanriku Railway. Fare: ¥390). There are several minshuku and hotels offering hospitality in this small fishing village. Walk along the north side of the harbor and you will find a marked, paved nature trail that curves around the jagged, rock-strewn shore. Notice the marks some 50 feet above your head on the side of the cliff at the harbor entrance. These indicate the highest waves recorded. The trail leads to a series of steps that climb to a parking area outside the Sannokaku Hotel. From there it's a downhill walk along the road back to the village.

Further up the Sanriku Railway Line is **Kuji** (fare from Miyako: ¥1,600), where, in the summer, the *ama* (women divers) search for sea urchins. At Kuji the JR line starts again, heading north to Hachinohe, where it connects with the JR Aomori-Morioka route. It is a slow ride up the coast from Miyako to Hachinohe, and much of the beautiful shoreline is missed owing to frequent tunnels.

A Special Detour

If you do not go down to the Rikuchi coast from Tono, consider rent-

★ ➓ ing a car or hiring a taxi to get to **Take** (which on some maps is indicated only by the name of its local shrine, Hayachine Jinja). It is especially worth considering if you are traveling at the end of July, when there is a delightful Shinto festival. The road from Tono winds through picturesque hills to reach the village of Take, situated on the slopes of Mt. Hayachine. For centuries Mt. Hayachine has been regarded as a sacred mountain, and every July 31 to August 1 there is the festival of Hayachine Jinja. For two days folkloric stories known collectively as *yamabushi-kagura* are acted out in masked dance performances. However, the most colorful part of the festival is on August 1, when a procession of townspeople, wearing lion costumes and wood lion masks, parade through the village en route from the main shrine to a lesser shrine nearby. Because the festival has grown in popularity, it is advisable to telephone the local festival authorities (☎ 0198/48–5864) to secure accommodations.

From Take, the road goes to Shiwa, a stop on the Tohoku Line. Morioka is 20 minutes up the line.

Morioka

⑪ **Morioka** is a busy commercial and industrial city ringed by mountains. Because it is at the northernmost end of the Shinkansen Line, it has become a transfer point for destinations to northern Honshu and Hokkaido. Recently, the city has been trying to increase its appeal for tourists, and it managed to attract nearly 4 million visitors in 1994. Westerners will be pleased by the generous amount of information written in English—for example on street signs and on the destination boards in the bus terminal. Once Morioka had a fine castle built by the 26th Lord of Nanbu in 1597, but it was destroyed in the Meiji Restoration and all that remains are its ruins. Its site is now **Iwate Koen** (park), the focus of town and the place to escape the congestion of traffic and people in downtown Morioka.

Getting There
Morioka is the last stop on the Tohoku Shinkansen Line. From here, all trains going north are "regular" JR trains. So while it can take less than one hour to travel between Sendai and Morioka, the same distance to Aomori (north Honshu) takes two hours and 20 minutes. Morioka also has a JR line, via Tazawako, to Akita on the Sea of Japan coast, as well as the line down to the Pacific coast at Miyako.

Exploring
The tourist office, Kanko Center, in the Train Square lounge on the second floor of the JR Morioka Station, has useful maps and other information on Morioka and Iwate prefectures. It can also help arrange accommodations. To reach downtown take Bus 5 or 6 from the terminal in front of the JR station. ☎ *0196/25–2090.* ☉ *Daily 8:30–7:30.*

Should you wish to take a tour of the city, the Iwate Kanko Bus Company offers full-day, half-day, and evening "night-view" tours with Japanese-speaking guides. *Cost: full-day tour ¥5,400, departs 10 AM from Morioka Station, returns at 4:30; half-day tour ¥2,300, departs 9:30 and 1:30 from Morioka Station, returns 3 hrs. later; night-view tour ¥4,000, departs 5 PM from Morioka Station, returns 3 hrs. later. Tours operate Apr. 20–Nov. 23; night-view tour July 1– Aug. 31 only.*

The major attraction of Morioka is its special craft, *nanbutetsu* (ironware). The range of articles, from small wind-bells to elaborate statues, is vast, but the most popular items are the *nanbutetsubin* (heavy iron kettles), which come in all shapes, weights, and sizes. Hundreds of shops throughout the city sell nanbutetsu, but the main shopping streets are Saien-dori and O-dori, which run by Iwate Koen. Across the river from the park is **Gozaku,** an area of small shops that look much as they did a century ago—a more interesting place in which to browse for nanbutetsu. On the other hand, if you are just changing trains at Morioka with little time to spare, a shop in the middle of the basement shopping area under the JR station has a wide selection of nanbutetsu.

To reach Gozaku from the park, use the Nakanohashi (bridge) and take the first main street on the left. A short way down, just past the Hotel Saito, you will find the large Nanbu Iron shop and the narrow streets of the Gozaku section on your left. Beyond Gozaku is another bridge, Yonojibashi. At the street corner you'll see a very Western-looking firehouse, built in the 1920s and still in operation. The next bridge, Morioka's pride, is Kaminohashi, one of the few decorated bridges in Japan. Eight specially crafted bronze railings were commissioned in 1609 and ten bronze posts added two years later.

★ If there is time to spare in Morioka, visit the **Hashimoto Bijutsukan** (museum), a 25-minute bus ride from the station. (Buses run infrequently, especially during the winter, so verify the time of the return bus before you set out.) From mid-April to the end of November, Bus 8 (fare: ¥330) goes up to the observation tower on Mt. Iwayama; the museum is halfway up the small mountain. In winter, Bus 12 will drop you off within 10 minutes' walk of the museum if you tell the driver beforehand. The museum was created by Yaoji Hashimoto, himself an artist, from a traditional Nanbu *magariya* (L-shape thatch-roof farmhouse) rescued from a valley drowned by a dam. The building itself is worth a visit, and the works of Hashimoto and other Iwate artists are an added pleasure, but you could skip the room exhibiting 19th-century paintings by French naturalists of the Barbizon school. There is also one room devoted to ironware and pottery in case you have not had your fill. ☛ *¥700. ✆ Daily 10–5. Closed Dec. 29–Jan. 3.*

An alternative place to visit on the city's outskirts is the **Morioka Handiworks Square,** a tourist center that promotes the region's crafts (including, of course, the ubiquitous local ironware). Fourteen workshops allow you to watch Iwate craftsmen at work in such varied fields as pottery, fabric dyeing, doll-making, and bamboo work, and lessons are offered should you wish to participate. There are also a large shop, an exhibition hall, and yet another magariya farmhouse. Take Bus 10 from the JR station for a 30-minute ride to the square. ☛ *To the exhibition hall: ¥100. ✆ Daily 8:40–5. Closed Dec. 29–Jan. 3.*

Back at the JR station on the Shinkansen platforms, a special *bento* (box lunch) is sold. The content (mostly tuna sushi) is less interesting than the container, which is made of pottery in the shape of a *kokeshi,* the folk-craft doll that is so popular throughout Tohoku.

From Morioka through Towada-Hachimantai Park to Aomori

From Morioka, the main railway line runs north to Aomori via Hachinohe, circumventing Tohoku's rugged interior, the Hachimantai Plateau.

★ In **Towada-Hachimantai National Park** are rugged mountains affording sweeping panoramas over the gorges and valleys (forming wrinkles in which natives shelter during the region's harsh winters), gnarled and windswept trees, volcanic mountain cones, and crystal-clear lakes.

Needless to say, winter weather conditions here are not conducive to extensive traveling. If you plan to visit the area during the winter months, be sure to check beforehand which bus services are running and which roads are open.

Getting There

From Morioka, you take the JR Hanawa Line for a 43-minute ride to Obuke, just 19 kilometers (12 miles) from the plateau. From there, it is best to travel on by bus. After exploring that area you can rejoin the train at Towada-minami to travel on to Hirosaki and Aomori. The travel time is less than a day, but you should plan on spending at least one night en route.

Exploring

Obuke is at the southern entrance to Towada-Hachimantai National Park. A bus leaves from Obuke Station for the 50-minute trip to **Higashi-Hachimantai,** the resort town where hikers and skiers begin their ascent into the upper reaches of the mountains. Nearby is a village complex called the **Putaro Mura,** which consists of log cabins with private thermal pools. A few miles farther on is **Gozaisho Onsen,** a popular spa resort that can be a useful overnight stop. Aside from a large hotel called the **Hachimantai Kanko** (Midorigaoka 5-2-1, Matsu Mura, Iwate-ken 028-73, ☎ 0195/78–2211, FAX 0195/78–2165), there is a huge youth hostel that accommodates skiers in the winter and hikers in the summer.

The left-hand fork of the road from Higashi-Hachimantai leads to **Matsukawa Onsen** (noted for its pure waters), which has Kyoun-so Inn (*see* Hachimantai Lodging, *below*). This spa town is on the backside of Mt. Iwate, amid the eerie barrenness left by the volcano's eruption in 1719. A faster way of reaching Hachimantai and Matsukawa is to take a bus direct from Morioka (1 hour and 50 minutes; fare: ¥1,060). The last stop of this bus is the Hachimantai Kanko Hotel. For Matsukawa, change buses at the stop before in Higashi-Hachimantai.

Past Gozaisho is the entrance to the **Aspite Line,** a 27-kilometer (17-mile) scenic toll road (closed Nov.–Apr.) that skirts Mt. Chausu (5,177 feet) and Mt. Hachimantai (5,295 feet). With every turn there is another view of evergreen-clad slopes and alpine flowers. From the Hachimantai-chojo (bus stop) it is a 20-minute walk up a path to **Hachiman-numa** (pond), originally a crater lake of a volcano. There is a paved esplanade around the crater, and in July and August the alpine flowers bloom at their best.

The road turning left after Hachimantai-chojo leads to **Toshichi Onsen,** which, at a height of 4,593 feet and a location at the foot of Mt. Mokko, is a popular spring skiing resort and a year-round spa town. On the northern side of Toshichi is **Horaikyo,** a natural garden with dwarf pine trees and alpine plants scattered among strange rock formations. In early October, the autumn colors are resplendent.

Just before the end of the Aspite Line toll road is another spa town, **Goshogake Onsen,** noted for its abundance of hot water. This spa and Toshichi are the best spas for overnight stays, especially Goshogake if you want to try *ondoru* (Korean-style) steam baths and box-type steam baths where only your head protrudes. Just outside of Goshogake is a mile-long nature trail highlighting the volcanic phenomena of the area, including *doro-kazan* (muddy volcanoes) and *oyu-numa* (hot-water swamps).

After Goshogake Onsen, the toll road joins Route 341. A left turn here leads south to Lake Tazawa, discussed later in this chapter. A right turn at the junction heads north for an hour's bus journey to the town of ⑬ **Hachimantai,** where you can rejoin the JR Hanawa Line either to return to Obuke and Morioka or to travel north toward Aomori.

Twenty minutes north of Hachimantai on the JR Hanawa Line is ⑭ **Towada-minami.** From here, buses leave to make the 60-minute trip ⑮ to **Towadako** (Lake Towada) (fare: ¥980). The area around Lake Towada is one of the most popular resorts in northern Tohoku. The main feature is the caldera lake, which fills a volcanic cone with depths of up to 1,096 feet, the third deepest in Japan and which, strangely enough, had no fish in it until Sadayuki Wainai stocked it with trout in 1903. Since buses frequently travel between Towada-minami and ⑯ Towadako, you may want to get off the bus at **Oyu Onsen** and travel the 4 kilometers (2½ miles) to Japan's Stonehenge, **Oyu Iseki**—a circle of stones with another center ring of upright stones, one of them shaped like a sundial. Oyu Iseki was discovered only in the 1930s, but studies have estimated that the ring is 4,000 years old. Local buses leave Oyu Onsen four times a day to visit the circle, though the trip can also be made on foot.

After Oyu Onsen, the road snakes over **Hakka-toge** (pass)—which affords some of the best views of the lake—and, via a series of switchbacks, descends to circle the lakeshore (though the bus from Towada-minami goes only part of the way around it). If you take a ⑰ right at the lake you'll come to the village resort of **Yasumiya,** from which pleasure boats depart (from mid-Apr. to early Nov.) every 30 minutes for a run across the lake to **Nenokuchi** (the boats operate less frequently from early Nov. until Jan. 31, and then not at all until mid-April). The one-hour trip on the boat (fare: ¥1,300) covers the most scenic parts of the lake, and at Nenokuchi there are bicycles to rent for further exploration. (Rental bicycles are also available in Yasumiya.) From Nenokuchi there is a bus that continues around the lake's northern shore to **Taki-no-sawa**—more superb views of the lake—and then goes on to Hirosaki.

★ ⑱ **Hirosaki** is one of northern Tohoku's friendliest and most attractive cities, said to be the home of Japan's most beautiful women. Its major (and really only) sight is Hirosaki Castle, but the town has an intimacy that makes it appealing. There is a tourist information office on the right side of the station as you go out (☎ 0172/32–0524. ◷ 8:45–6; closed Dec. 29–Jan. 3).

Though Hirosaki is compact and walkable, finding your bearings in this ancient castle town may be difficult: Hirosaki's streets were laid out as confusingly as possible to disorient invaders before they could get to the battlements (it's a good idea to pick up a map at the tourist information office). If you want to sample Hirosaki's nightlife, look for the small entertainment area just beyond the river as you head toward the castle, south of the two main streets, Chuo-dori and Dotemachi; or, if you're still baffled by the town's geography, simply say the area's name, **Kajimachi,** to any citizen and you'll be directed to its clutter of narrow streets. Here are numerous choices for dining, from *izakaya* (small bars) to restaurants with picture menus in their windows; and for after dinner there are coffeehouses, *nomiya* (pubs), and more expensive clubs for further pleasure. Perhaps because of the large resident foreign population in Hirosaki, foreigners are accepted, understood, and welcomed, seemingly more so than in other Tohoku small towns. You'll even find a bookshop, **Kinokuniya** (☎ 0172/36–4511), next door to the Hotel Hokke Club on Dotemachi, with a selection of English-language books.

Located at the northwestern end of town and across the river is **Hirosakijo** (Hirosaki Castle), an original—a pleasant change from admirable replicas. Completed in 1611, it is relatively small but perfectly proportioned, and it is guarded by moats. The gates in the outlying grounds are also original, and when the more than 5,000 *someiyoshino* (cherry trees) blossom (festival, Apr. 25–May 6) or the maples turn red in autumn (festival, late Oct.–mid-Nov.), the setting is marvelous. In winter snows mirror the castle's whiteness and give the grounds a sense of stillness and peace (snow lantern festival with illuminated ice sculptures, early Feb). ☛ ¥200. ⊘ *Daily 9–5. Closed Nov. 23–Mar. 31.*

The **Hirosaki Sightseeing Information Center,** south of the castle grounds, displays local industry, crafts, and regional art as well as providing tourist information. ⊘ *Daily 9–6.* ☛ *Free.*

Also, don't miss the five-story pagoda, **Saishoin,** by the river on the southwest edge of town. Built in 1672, it has the distinction of being the tallest pagoda in Japan supported by a single center beam.

At any time, Hirosaki makes for a pleasant overnight stay, but during the first week of August the city comes even more alive with its famous **Neputa Festival.** Each night different routes are followed through the town, with floats displaying scenes from Japanese and Chinese mythology represented by huge fanlike paintings that have faces painted on both sides. With lights inside the faces, the streets become an illuminated dreamscape.

From Hirosaki it is a 40-minute local train ride to Aomori.

★ ⑲ Unfortunately, Aomori's attractions are rather limited; when it comes to accommodation, you may prefer to overnight at **Sukayu Onsen,** near the Hakkoda Ropeway. The bus journey from JR Aomori Station takes 1 hour and 10 minutes; get off at Sukayu Onsen-mae. One snag is that the last bus sets off at 3:50 PM, but if you can catch it, it's worth it.

It is known that more than 300 years ago a hunter shot and wounded a deer near here. Three days later he saw the deer again, miraculously healed. He realized that the deer had cured itself in the sulfur springs. Since then, people have been coming to Sukayu for the water's curative powers. The inn—and there is nothing but the inn—is a sprawling wooden building with highly polished creaking floors. The main bath, known as Sen Nin Buro (Thousand People Bath), is made of *hiba* (Japanese cypress), a very strong wood. It is not segregated—men and women bathe together. Two big tubs fill the bathhouse: One pool called Netsu-no-yu is 42° C, while the other, Shibu rokubu, is one degree hotter. The other two bathtubs, called Hie-no-yu, are for cooling off by pouring water only on your head so you don't wash the minerals off your body. (*See* Lodging, *under* Hachimantai, *below.*)

Aomori

⑳ **Aomori** is another of Tohoku's prefectural capitals that have more appeal to their residents than to travelers. There is a tourist information center at the station (☏ 0177/22–7781; ⊘ Daily 8:30–8), but most of their brochures are in Japanese. Foreign visitors used to stop here while waiting for the ferry to cross over to Hokkaido. Now, the traveler can transfer to the express train and ride through the Seikan Undersea Tunnel (33.66 miles long, with 14.5 miles of it deep under the Tsugaru Straits) to Hokkaido. The Seikan tunnel was the world's longest tunnel under the sea until the 1994 debut of the Channel Tunnel linking Britain and France.

EXPLORING

Aomori has only marginal interest unless you can be there for its **Nebuta Festival** (Aug. 3–7), which should not be confused with Hirosaki's Neputa Festival (and residents of both places are greatly irritated when they are). Though both are held in early August; both consist of large, illuminated floats being paraded through the streets at night; and both have an ancient mythology to do with a battle fought by the Tsugaru clan, there are important differences: Hirosaki's festival is rooted in the period before the battle and has a somber atmosphere with slowly beating drums; Aomori's celebrates the postbattle victory and is thus noisier and livelier. And while visitors at the festivities in Hirosaki are able only to spectate, at Aomori they can participate themselves if they are willing to jump, yell, and generally lose their inhibitions.

If you are in Aomori at another time, you might take the JR bus from gate 8 or 9 (cost ¥440; 35 minutes) to **Nebuta-no-Sato** (Nebuta Museum) in the southeast of town, where 10 of the figures used in Aomori's festival are stored and displayed. (The same JR bus continues on from Nebuta-no-Sato to Sukayu Onsen and the Hachimantai Plateau, so if you are coming from that spa, you may wish to get off and visit this museum before continuing into downtown Aomori.) ☛ ¥620. ☺ *Daily, July–Sept. 9–8, except during the Nebuta Festival, beginning of Aug.; mid-Apr.–June 30 and Oct. 1–Nov. 30, 9–6. Closed Dec.–mid-Apr.*

Munakata Shiko Kinenkan, a museum dedicated to native son Shiko Munakata (1903–1975), displays the prints, paintings, and calligraphy of this internationally known artist. The building itself is constructed in the attractive azekura style. To reach the Munakata Shiko Kinenkan requires taking a bus from the JR station in the direction of Tsutsumi and getting off at Shimin Bunka Senta-mae. Then walk back to the crossing and take a left. You will see the museum on the left. ☛ ¥300. ☺ *Tues.–Sun., Apr.–Oct. 9:30–4:30; Nov.–Mar. 9:30–4. Closed on the last day of the month (except Sat. and Sun.), national holidays, and Dec. 27–Jan. 4. From Apr.–Oct., if a national holiday falls on Sun. or Mon., museum is closed on Tues.*

You may also wish to visit the **Kyodokan** (Prefectural Museum), a ten-minute bus ride from the station), which displays folkcrafts and archaeological material. ☛ ¥310. ☺ *Tues.–Sun. Apr.–Sept. 9:30–4:30; Oct.–Mar. 9:30–4. Closed Dec. 28–Jan. 4.*

The **Keikokan** (Museum of Folk Art), 20 minutes away from the station by bus (board at gate 9), has a larger display of local crafts, including fine examples of Tsugaru-nuri (lacquerware), which achieves its hardness through 48 coats of lacquer. Dolls representing the Haneto dancing girls of the Nebuta Festival are also on display. Incidentally, the Museum of Folk Art is located on a busy highway of malls, arcades, and giant pachinko parlors, and is easily missed: Watch for the Sanwa complex on your right, get off the bus three sets of traffic lights later, and you'll find the museum tucked away on the right side. ☛ ¥600. ☺ *9:30–4:30 (enter by 4). Closed Thurs. Nov.–Apr.*

For a quick overview of Aomori there is the ASPAM (Asupamu) Building down by the waterfront, where the ferryboats once docked. The 15-story ultramodern eyesore is easy to recognize by its pyramid shape.

Though the staff there speak little English, a tourist information desk in the entrance lobby is very helpful in supplying details of the prefecture's attractions. An outside elevator whisks you 13 floors up to an enclosed observation deck. Inside the building are a number of restaurants and exhibits on Aomori's tourist attractions and crafts. ☛ ¥400. ⊙ *Daily 9 AM–10 PM.*

Although Aomori city has its shortcomings, it should be stressed that Aomori prefecture possesses a great deal of natural beauty. If you have ★ a day to spare, a worthwhile trip would be to **Osorezan** in the center of the Shimokita Peninsula, the ax-shaped piece of land that juts from Aomori's northeastern corner. Osorezan's temple, Entsuji, is dedicated to the spirits of dead children. The atmosphere of otherworldliness is heightened by the setting: the surrounding peaks, the neighboring dead lake, the steam from the hot springs, and the desolate grounds that have been whitened by sulfuric rock. Even eerier are some of the visitors: Crows often come to feed on the crackers and candles left at the shrines by mourning parents, and several blind old women frequent the site to offer their services as mediums for contacting the dead. Buses make the 35-minute trip between Osorezan and Mutsu Bus Terminal (Mutsu is the main town of Shimokita Peninsula) from the end of April until the end of October (¥690). Mutsu itself can be reached by bus from Aomori city in 2 hours and 40 minutes (cost: ¥2,230).

Aomori ends this excursion north through Tohoku. Now, we go south down Tohoku's Sea of Japan coast. For those of you going first to Hokkaido, either take the train under, or the ferry across, the Tsugaru Straits to Hakodate.

South from Aomori to Akita on the Sea of Japan

So far, our travels have been on the central and Pacific sides of Tohoku. The return journey travels south down the Sea of Japan side to Akita before moving back into Tohoku's mountainous central spine at Tazawako. From there, staying within the mountains, our excursion continues on to Yamagata. Then comes the final leg through the southern Tohoku prefecture of Fukushima.

Exploring

Leaving Aomori for Akita (a 3-hour ride), the train goes back through Hirosaki and past **Mt. Iwaki** (5,331 feet high), which dominates the countryside. A bus (40 minutes) from Hirosaki travels to the foot of this mountain, from where you can take the sightseeing bus up the Iwaki Skyline toll road (open late Apr.–late Oct.) to the eighth station. The final ascent, with the reward of a 360-degree view, is by a five-minute ropeway, followed by a 30-minute walk to the summit.

South of Mt. Iwaki, straddling Aomori Prefecture's border with Akita, are the Shirakami Mountains, home of the world's largest virgin beechwood forest and one of only two Japanese entries on UNESCO's list of World Heritage Sites. Access to the mountains is provided by just a few minor roads on their Aomori and Akita flanks, but they make a rewarding destination for adventurous hikers. Back on the train at Hirosaki, however, and soon after Mt. Iwaki, the mountains give way to the rice fields and flat plains that surround Akita.

㉑ **Akita,** the prefectural capital (pop. 300,000), is a relaxing and friendly city, though not one loaded with sightseeing attractions. Indeed, the tourist information office at the station is a tiny affair, under the escalator in front of the ticket wickets. Essentially, Akita is a built-up and commercial city whose major attraction for tourists is its famous

Kanto Festival (Aug. 5–7), when young men balance a 30-foot-long bamboo pole that supports as many as 50 lit paper lanterns on its eight crossbars. The area around Akita is said to grow the best rice and have the purest water in Japan—the combination produces excellent dry sake.

If you have time between trains, walk west from the station for 10 minutes on Hirokoji-dori to **Senshu Park,** once the site of the now-ruined Kubota Castle and today a pleasant spot of greenery, with cherry blossoms and azaleas adding color in season. Aside from the prefectural art museum, the park includes the **Hirano Masakichi Bijutsukan** (art museum), with a noted collection of paintings by Tsuguji Fujita (1886–1968), as well as works by van Gogh and Cézanne. The most eye-catching exhibit is Fujita's *Events in Akita,* in which three of the local festivals are merged together to form a single scene: painted on one, monstrous piece of canvas measuring 3.65 by 20.5 meters, Fujita did it in just 15 days and bragged that the feat would never be bettered. The building itself is architecturally interesting for its Japanese palace-style roof covered with copper, which slopes down and rolls outside at the edge. ☛ ¥410. ✆ *May–Sept., Tues.–Sun. 10–5:30; Oct.–Apr., Tues.–Sun. 10–5 (enter 30 mins. before closing). Closed Dec. 28–Jan. 3.*

For regional arts and crafts and more information about the prefecture, visit the 12-story **Atorion Building,** a two-minute walk south from the park, on the other side of Hirokoji. In the basement is a large shop selling local crafts and souvenirs (✆ Daily 10–7); elsewhere on the premises are a prefectural tourist center; an art gallery (✆ Daily 10–6) showing the work of local artists as well as oil paintings by Okada Kenzo, who achieved some fame in New York after World War II; and a concert hall. Six blocks west of the Atorion, across the Asahigawa and slightly to the south, is Kawabata-dori. This is where everyone comes in the evening to sample the regional hot-pot dishes *shottsuru-nabe* (made with pickled sand fish) and *kiritanpo-nabe* (made with rice cakes and chicken), to drink the local jizake, and to be entertained at one of the many bars.

㉒ Only 30 kilometers (19 miles) to the north and west of Akita is **Oga Peninsula,** its coastline indented by strange rock formations and reefs, its mountains clad with Akita cedar, its hills carpeted in green grass. At the neck of the peninsula is Mt. Kanpu, whose summit affords a panoramic view extending as far as Akita city. Nearby, the town of Oga plays host to a strange custom every December 31: Men dressed in ferocious demon masks and coats of straw, carrying buckets and huge knives, go from home to home issuing dire warnings against any loafers and good-for-nothings in the households. This ritual is re-enacted for the public at the **Namahage Sedo Festival** on February 13–15 on the grounds of the local Shinzan Shrine.

Though roads trace Oga's coastline, public transport is infrequent. The easiest way to tour the peninsula is by using the services of the Akita Chuo Kotsu bus lines (☎ 0188/23–4411). Tour buses leave daily from Akita Station, Oga Station, and Oga Onsen from late-April to early November. However, the tour is conducted in Japanese.

Instead of continuing south along the Sea of Japan coast from Akita and going directly to Tsuruoka, this excursion detours inland up to Tazawako, or Lake Tazawa. From there we turn south, offering the detour to Tsuruoka en route to Yamagata. (Trains run directly from Akita to Yamagata on the Ou Honsen—Ou Main Line—in just over 3 hours.)

★ **㉓** On the way to Tazawako, via Omagari, is the small and delightful town of **Kakunodate.** Founded in 1620 by the local lord, the town has remained an outpost of traditional Japan that, with cause, boasts of being Tohoku's little Kyoto. Within a 15-minute walk northwest from the station are several samurai houses that date back to the founding of the town, all well preserved and maintained. The most renowned of the samurai houses is Aoyagi, with its sod-turf roof. The cherry tree in Aoyagi's garden is nearly three centuries old. The whole town is full of weeping cherry trees, more than 400, which are direct descendants of those imported from Kyoto three centuries ago. A number of them form a 2-kilometer-long (1¼-mile-long) "tunnel" along the banks of Hinokinai River. ☛ *To houses: ¥500.* ۞ *Apr.–Nov., daily 8:30–5; Dec.–Mar., daily 9–4.*

If there is time before the next train to Tazawako, visit **Denshoken,** a hall in front of a cluster of samurai houses that serves as a museum and a workshop for cherry-bark handicrafts. ☛ *¥300.* ۞ *Apr.–Nov., daily 9–5; Dec.–Mar., Fri.–Wed. 9–4:30. Closed Dec. 28–Jan. 4.*

Should you wish to overnight in Kakunodate, your choice is limited to one business hotel, six ryokan where the owners would like their guests to know some Japanese, and a small minshuku, Hyakusuien, that has been converted from a 19th century warehouse (*see* Lodging, *below*).

★ **㉔** From Kakunodate it is a 16-minute ride on the train to **Tazawako.** (The total journey from Akita to Tazawako takes 1 hour and 10 minutes. The train then continues on to Morioka, another hour away.) You will need to take a 15-minute bus ride (fare: ¥340) from the JR station to Tazawako Kohan on the lake shore, but first drop in at the tourist information office to the left of the JR station for maps and bus schedules. ☎ *0187/34–0307.* ۞ *Daily 8:30–5:15. Closed Jan. 1.*

Tazawa is Japan's deepest lake (1,390 feet), though its blue waters are too alkaline to support any fish. Like most of Japan's lakes, Tazawa is in a volcanic cone, but its shape is a more classic caldera than most. With its clear waters and forested slopes, it captures a mystical quality that appeals so much to the Japanese. In winter, the Tazawako area is a popular and picturesque skiing destination, the lake being visible from the ski slopes. According to legend, the great beauty from Akita, Takko Hime, sleeps in the water's deep as a dragon. Apparently, that is why the lake never freezes over in winter. Takko Hime and her dragon husband churn the water with their passionate lovemaking. Or, perhaps, as scientists say, the water doesn't freeze because of a freshwater source that enters the bottom of the lake.

An excursion boat makes 40-minute cruises on the lake from late April to November (cost: ¥1,150). There is also regular bus service around the lake (halfway around in winter), and bicycles are available for rent at the Tazawa Kohan bus terminal as an alternative to the cruise boat. If you go by bike, more time can be spent appreciating the beauty of Takko Hime, whose bronze statue is on the western shore.

A 30-minute bus ride (fare: ¥580) from the JR Tazawako Station via Tazawa Kohan takes you up to **Tazawako Kogen** (plateau) northeast of Lake Tazawa. The journey offers spectacular views of the lake, showing off the full dimensions of its caldera shape. The same bus then **㉕** continues on for another 15 minutes to **Nyuto Onsen,** a collection of small, unspoiled, mountain hot-spring spas in some of the few traditional spa villages left in Tohoku. Most of these villages have only one inn, so it is advisable to arrange accommodations before you arrive if you wish to stay the night. *(See* Lodging, *below.)*

㉖ A few miles east of Lake Tazawa stands **Komagatake.** At 5,370 feet, it is the highest mountain in the area, yet it is one of the easiest to climb. Between June and October, a bus from Tazawako Station runs up to the eighth station, from which it takes an hour to reach the summit; you'll walk through clusters of alpine flowers if you choose June or July for your hike.

★ Another old traditional spa town, **Tamagawa Onsen,** is to the north of Tazawako on Route 341. There is frequent bus service between the two towns (90 minutes; fare: ¥1,340). The spa is quaint and delightfully old-fashioned, with mainly wood buildings surrounding the thermal springs. The elderly who come to take the waters are very serious about the curative qualities of the mineral waters. However, think twice before staying here overnight; the inn is a little ramshackle. Beyond Tamagawa Onsen, the road joins the Aspite Line toll road described earlier in the Hachimantai excursion. Because there is direct JR train service between Morioka and Tazawako, an alternative itinerary to the one described above is to go first to Tazawako from Morioka and travel up Route 341 to Hachimantai.

Heading south from Tazawako, you can either travel directly down the middle of Tohoku to Yamagata or make a detour to visit Tsuruoka and Mt. Haguro by returning to the Sea of Japan coast. Then turn inland again to Yamagata.

South of Akita and along the Sea of Japan coast toward Niigata are small fishing villages, noteworthy only for the fact that few tourists stop over en route. (There are five trains a day between Akita and Niigata; the trip takes 3 hours and 40–50 minutes.) The one exception

㉗ is **Tsuruoka,** the religious center of Shugendo, an esoteric religious sect that combines Buddhism with Shintoism. It's famous for its temple,

★ **Zenpoji,** which has a pagoda containing images of Buddha in every pose that could possibly be attributed to him. The city also serves as the gate-

㉘ way for visiting **Mt. Haguro,** the most accessible of the three mountains in the Dewa-san range. All three mountains are sacred to the *yamabushi,* the popular name given to members of the Shugendo sect, but it is the thatch-roof shrine Dewa Sanzan Jinja, on the summit of Mt. Haguro, that attracts pilgrims throughout the year.

Nowadays most pilgrims take the easy way up to the summit—a direct bus from Tsuruoka Station along the toll road. The old way, the one that the more devout or energetic tourists take, is by bus from the JR station or the Shoko Mall in Tsuruoka to Haguro's central bus stop; from there, they walk to the Zaishin Gate and then up the 2,446 stone steps to the summit. The climb is not for the faint at heart, but the route along avenues of 300-year-old cedar trees—with shafts of sunlight filtering through, the occasional waterfall, the tiny shrines, and the tea shop halfway up—is the reason for reaching the summit. Running alongside the steps is a trail of rock carvings, depicting such things as sake cups, gourds, lotus cups, and so on. According to legend, the lucky pilgrim who locates all 33 of the carvings will have a wish granted. The actual shrine, **Dewa Sanzan Jinja,** is not so impressive; you'll be glad to get on the bus to return to Tsuruoka, leaving behind on the slopes of Mt. Haguro the numerous small huts used by yamabushi pilgrims engaged in their penance. Once back in Tsuruoka, it is a two-hour, 20-minute train ride to Yamagata.

Should you wish to spend the night in the Tsuruoka area, take the JR express train 20 minutes south to **Atsumi Onsen,** a spa town where the curative waters are good for your skin as well as your digestive system. Facing the stormy Japan Sea and backed by mountains, the small village exists in isolation. Unfortunately, it lost its old buildings in a fire that swept the valley in 1951, so virtually all the buildings are new. One particularly hospitable ryokan is Tachibana-ya (*see* Lodging, *below*). To reach the village use the bus (fare: ¥190) from the JR Atsumi Onsen Station; it's a 10-minute journey to town.

Yamagata

㉙ **Yamagata,** with a population of 240,000, is the capital of the prefecture of the same name. For visitors to Japan, Yamagata is more a transportation hub than a destination in itself, but it is a friendly town and anxious to become more of a tourist destination. (Yamagata Prefecture, incidentally, has at least one onsen in each of its 44 municipalities—the only Japanese prefecture that can boast a 100% record.) Pick up free maps and brochures from the tourist information office opposite the ticket turnstiles inside the JR station. ☎ *0236/31–7865.* ⊘ *Weekdays 10–6, weekends 10–5.*

Getting There

To reach Yamagata directly from Tokyo it's best to take the Shinkansen, which takes just under three hours. There is also direct train service on the JR Senzan Line from Sendai (about 1 hour). A train on the JR Yonesaka Line running between Niigata and Yamagata takes 3½ hours; the train from Tsuruoka, following the Uetsu and Riku-u Sai lines, takes two hours and 20 minutes. From Akita, a trip via the Ou Line takes just over three hours, while the Tazawako Line, connecting with the Ou Line at Omagari, provides access from Morioka.

Yamagata is also serviced by All Nippon Airways (ANA) flights from Tokyo's Haneda Airport (50 minutes) and by Japan Air System (JAS) from Osaka (75 minutes). Yamagata's airport is 40 minutes by bus from the city center.

Exploring

Yamagata is a small, country town whose major attractions are summer hiking and winter skiing in the nearby mountains. The main event is the **Hanagasa Festival** (Aug. 5–7), in which some 10,000 dancers from the entire area dance their way through the streets in traditional costume and *hanagasa,* hats so named for the safflowers used to decorate them. Floats are interspersed among the dancers, and stalls provide food and refreshments. For anyone interested in pottery a trip to **Hirashimizu** on the outskirts of the city is recommended. This small enclave of traditional buildings and farmhouses is a step back in time and a sharp contrast to the modern urban sprawl of Yamagata. About six pottery families live here, each with its own kiln, each specializing in a particular style. Two of them, the Shichiemon and Hirayashi, offer pottery lessons, and participants can have the results fired and then mailed to their homes. The pottery of the Seiryugama family is the best known, and, with exhibitions of their wares in America and Europe, their prices are high. (Until now, the bus route to Hirashimizu has been a very confusing one for non-Japanese speakers, and taxis have been recommended as an easier means of getting there. However, at the time of writing, Yamagata's prefectural government is preparing a new sightseeing guide with detailed instructions on reaching Hirashimizu by bus.)

30 Most visitors come to Yamagata, though, to make their way to the prefecture's largest draw, **Mt. Zao,** where nearly 1.4 million alpine enthusiasts come from December to April to ski its 14 slopes and 11 runs. (During the winter, there are direct buses from Tokyo to Zao Onsen and back.) The mountain's resort town, **Zao Onsen,** is only 19 kilometers (12 miles) from Yamagata Station (45 minutes by bus). From Zao Onsen, the first cable car leaves from the base lodge (2,805 feet above sea level) to climb 1,562 feet, and the second one makes the final ascent of an additional 1,083 feet. Even nonskiers make the round trip to see the *juhyo,* a phenomenon caused by heavy snow on the conifers. Layer after layer of snow covers the fir trees, creating weird, cylindrical figures that look like fairy-tale monsters. In the summer hikers come, though in fewer numbers than the winter skiers, to walk among the colored rocks and visit Zao Okama, a caldera lake with a diameter of nearly 1,200 feet.

★ **31** Another attraction, 16 kilometers (10 miles) outside Yamagata (20 minutes on the JR Senzan Line toward Sendai), is **Hojusan Risshakuji,** more commonly known as Yamadera. Built 1,100 years ago, Yamadera's complex of temples with steeply pitched slate roofs on the slopes of Mt. Hoju is the largest of the Tendai sect in northern Japan and attracts some 700,000 pilgrims a year. The small town at the base of the hill has become very touristy with hotels and souvenir shops, but beyond the entrance to the temple grounds, a modicum of serenity prevails. Just inside the entrance and to the right is Konpon Chudo, the temple where a sacred flame called the Flame of Belief has been burning constantly for 1,000 years (with, admittedly, one interruption: In 1521, a local lord called Tendo Yorinaga ransacked the complex and extinguished the flame, so that a replacement had to be brought from the original sacred fire at Mt. Hiei in Kyoto). Near the Konpon Chudo is a statue of the Japanese poet Matsuo Basho (1644–1694), who wrote extensively of his wanderings throughout Japan in 17-syllable haiku. The path continues on and up. Its 1,115-odd steps have recently been repaired, and the ascent is relatively easy, but the path can be crowded during the summer and treacherous with snow in winter. (The best views are from Nio Mon, part of the way up.) Finally, after a steep ascent, there is Kaizando, a hall at the summit dedicated to the temple founder, Jikaku Daishi.

Into Fukushima Prefecture and out of Tohoku

From Yamagata, there are three possible routes: directly across the mountains by JR trains to Sendai; south and west to Niigata, Sado Island, and the Japan Alps *(see* Chapter 5); or continuing down Tohoku's mountainous spine to the fifth prefecture of the region, Fukushima, from where you can cross over to Nikko *(see* Nikko *in* Chapter 3).

Fukushima Prefecture is tamer both in scenery and in attitudes than the rest of Tohoku; it was the first region in northern Honshu to become a popular resort area for Japanese families, especially around the plateau known as Bandai Kogen. Mt. Bandai erupted in 1888, and in 15 short minutes wiped out more than 40 small villages, killing 477 people and resculpturing the landscape. The result was nature's damming of several streams to form hundreds of lakes, the largest of
32 which is **Lake Hibara,** with its crooked shoreline and numerous islets.

Getting There
From Yamagata, Bandai Kogen is reached by taking the Shinkansen to Fukushima City. A direct bus to Bandai Kogen from the city of Fukushima departs from near the Shinkansen station each day between

April 22 and November 5 and travels over the Bandai-Azuma Skyline Drive, offering splendid views of mountains by climbing up through **Jododaira Pass** at 5,214 feet. The whole mountain resort is, in fact, crisscrossed by five scenic toll roads.

All the sightseeing buses from Fukushima City, Koriyama, and Aizu-Wakamatsu, as well as the local bus from Inawashiro, arrive at **Bandai Kogen** bus stop, the tourist center on Lake Hibara, where the Japanese vacationers disperse to their campgrounds, bungalows, or modern ryokan.

Exploring

Though the Bandai Kogen area is somewhat spoiled by hordes of tourists, a particularly pleasant walk, the Goshiki-numa Trail, meanders past the dozen or more tiny lakes (ponds, really) that are collectively called **Goshiki-numa** (Five-color Lakes), because each throws off a different color. The trail begins across from the Bandai Kogen bus station and runs in the opposite direction from Lake Hibara; the round-trip takes two hours.

A bus that departs from Bandai Kogen goes straight to Aizu-Wakamatsu, taking 90 minutes. En route, the bus makes a stop at **Inawashiro,** the town on the northern edge of Lake Inawashiro, Japan's third largest. Unlike Tohoku's other large lakes, Towada and Tazawa, Inawashiro is not a caldera lake but instead is formed by streams. Hence, its flat surrounding shore is not particularly spectacular, though the scenery is pretty enough as far as Japanese beaches go. The Japanese like the lake for the gaudy sightseeing swan-shape cruise boats that circle on the water. Of more cultural interest (only 10 minutes by bus from Inawashiro Station) is **Hideo Noguchi's birthplace** and a memorial museum in honor of his extraordinary life and his research of yellow fever, which eventually killed him in Africa in 1928.

An alternative route to Aizu-Wakamatsu is via **Kitakata** (though the bus connecting Bandai Kogen and Kitakata operates only during the summer). Mud-wall *kura* (storehouses) are to be seen all over Japan, but for some reason Kitakata has more than 2,600 of them. Kura are not only simple places to store rice, miso, soy sauce, sake, fertilizer, and charcoal, however; they are also status symbols of the local merchants. The kura fascination spread in the past so that shops, homes, and inns were built in this architectural style, as each citizen tried to outdo his neighbor. One can quickly use up a couple of rolls of film taking photographs of the many different kura—some are black-and-white plaster, some simply of mud, some with bricks, and some with thatch roofs; still others have tiles.

Aside from Kitakata's major architectural attraction—**Kai-no-Kura,** an elaborate mansion that took seven years to build (☛ ¥200; ۞ Mid-Mar.–early Dec., daily 9–5, and the **Aizu Lacquer Museum** (☛ ¥300; ۞ Daily 9–5)—your final goal should be the **Yamatogawa Sake Brewery** (☎ 0241/22–2233), across the center of town from the Lacquer Museum. The brewery consists of seven kura, one of which serves as a small museum to display old methods of sake production. The other buildings are still used for making sake. After a dutiful tour, you are offered the pleasurable reward of tasting different types of sake. ☛ *Free.* ۞ *Daily 9–5. Closed Dec. 31–Jan. 5.*

The tourist office (☎ 0241/32–0688; ۞ Mon.–Sat. 9:30–5:30, Sun. and national holidays 10–5) at the local station has a kura walking-tour map for the city, but, if you are short on time, the area northeast of the JR station has a selection of storehouses, including **Kai Shoten,** a black kura storefront of an old miso and soy sauce factory. Incidentally, Kitakata is also famous for its variety of delicious ramen noodles; several tourism-conscious entrepreneurs have combined the two attractions by converting storehouses into ramen shops. The town even has a kura-shaped carriage, towed by a brawny carthorse, in which tourists can be shown around.

㉟ The train from Kitakata to **Aizu-Wakamatsu** takes 20 minutes. (From Sendai the JR train ride is 90 minutes and from Nikko just over 2 hours if you take the Shinkansen part of the way; the ride by local train takes 3 hours.) The city tourist office is in the center of town (☎ 0242/32–0688), but the JR information and reservation office at the station distributes a free English-language map and leaflets about the area.

Aizu-Wakamatsu's **Tsurugajo** was the most powerful stronghold of the northeast during the shogun period. Because the castle is located on the opposite—southeast—side of the JR station, take the bus from the station plaza (gate 14 or 15, but check with the information booth first) that loops around the city to include the castle and the Byakkotai monument. The Aizu clan was closely linked to the ruling family in Edo and remained loyal until the end. When the imperial forces of the Meiji Restoration pressed home their successful attack in 1868, that loyalty caused the castle, which had stood for five centuries, to be partly burned down, along with most of the city's buildings; the new government destroyed the castle completely in 1874. The five-story castle was rebuilt in 1965 as a museum (☞ ¥400; open daily 8:30–5; enter by 4:30) and is said to look like its original, but without the presence it must have had in 1868, when 19 teenage warriors committed ritual suicide. Every Japanese knows this story, so it bears telling: These young warriors, known as Byakkotai (White Tigers), had been fighting pro-Restoration forces outside the city, when they were sent back to Tsurugajo to aid in its defense. The 20 boys arrived on a nearby hillside, Iimoriyama. Then, to their horror, they saw smoke rise from the castle and mistakenly believed the castle to be overrun by the enemy. As good samurai, all 20 boys began a mass suicide ritual. One boy was saved before he bled to death and spent the rest of his life with a livid scar and the shame of having failed to live up to the samurai code. Ironically, the castle had not at that point fallen into enemy hands and the fighting continued for another month—indeed, had they lived, the Byakkotai might have helped to turn the battle in their side's favor. There is now a monument to the 19 on the hill next to their graves. The **Byakkotai monument**, a small memorial museum, and a strange hexagonal Buddhist temple, Sazaedo, are reached by a 10-minute bus ride from the station. You may want to visit Iimoriyama September 22–24, when a special festival is held in memory of the Boshin civil war and the Byakkotai. ☞ ¥400. ☉ Daily, Apr.–Nov., 8–5; Dec.–Mar. 8:30–4. Closed first Mon.–Thurs. of July, and first Tues.–Thurs. of Dec.

★ To the east of the castle is **Aizu Buke Yashiki,** an excellent reproduction of a wealthy samurai's manor house. The 38-room house gives some idea how well one could live during the shogun period. A museum on the grounds displays Aizu craft, culture, and history, and there are several other old or reconstructed buildings in addition to the manor house. Access to Aizu Buke Yashiki is by Higashiyama bus from the JR station. ☞ ¥800. ☉ Daily, Apr.–Nov. 8:30–5; Dec.–Mar. 9–4:30.

Higashiyama Onsen, a spa town 20 minutes beyond Aizu Buke Yashiki with several modern ryokan, is, an alternative layover to Aizu-Wakamatsu, especially for those who enjoy hot mineral baths. Take the bus from platform 4 at the JR Aizu-Wakamatsu Station for the 20-minute ride (fare: ¥300). The village is in a gorge, and the bus route terminates at the bottom end of the village. Most ryokan will send a car to collect you so that you don't have to hike up the narrow village street. The tourist information booth at Higashiyama bus stop will telephone the ryokan for you, if you give the attendant the ¥10 for the pay phone. The village's scenic location and its shamble of older houses deserves better than the new and monstrous looking ryokan that have supplanted most of the old. Nevertheless, Hiagashiyama is a Japanese spa town and a pleasant alternative to staying in Aizu-Wakamatsu (*see* Lodging, *below*).

The unfortunate aspect of Aizu-Wakamatsu is that, for our excursions throughout Tohoku, it is the end of the line. Routes south, by train and bus, go to Nikko. Traveling east by train to Koriyama puts you on the Tohoku Shinkansen for Sendai to the north and Tokyo to the south. The train going west leads you to Niigata and the Sea of Japan.

DINING AND LODGING

Dining

When traveling in Tohoku, we strongly recommend that you eat out at local Japanese restaurants. Most restaurants that are reasonably priced will have a visual display of their menu in the window. On this basis, you can decide what you want before you enter. If you cannot order in Japanese, and no English is spoken, after you secure a table, lead the waiter to the window display and point.

Unless the establishment is a *ryotei* (high-class, traditional Japanese restaurant), reservations are usually not required except for formal restaurants at a hotel or a ryokan. Whenever reservations are recommended or required at any of the restaurants listed, this is indicated.

Some of the regional Japanese dishes of Tohoku are special, and you should make a point of enjoying them:

Akita is famous for its clean water and its rice, and these two ingredients make good sake, be sure to try the **kara-kuchi** (dry) sake. Akita's **kiritanpo** is made from boiled rice that is pounded into cakes and molded on sticks of **sugi** (Japanese cedar), which is then simmered in broth with chicken and vegetables.

Sendai miso is a red and salty version of fermented soybeans, famed for its longevity: In the 1590s, when Japanese forces were fighting in Korea, only the miso brought along by soldiers of Sendai's Date clan retained its freshness over a long period of time. **Kokonoe,** found in Sendai, is a delicious drink that receives its flavor from many tiny, floating rice balls, themselves flavored with *yuzu* (Japanese citron). Sendai's **dagashi** are traditional candies and cakes, usually made with rice, soybean flour, and sugar.

Sansai ryori, from Yamagata Prefecture, refers to a variety of dishes made from mountain vegetables and river fish (mostly carp and sweet fish).

In any reasonably smart venue you can be sure that the Japanese diners will be in formal attire—that is, men will be wearing a jacket and tie. So unless you want to feel conspicuous, avoid jeans and dress neatly. Remember to wear a decent pair of socks to any traditional, tatami-matted restaurant where shoes must be removed.

A 3% federal consumer tax is added to all restaurant bills. Another 3% local tax is added if the bill exceeds ¥7,500. At more expensive restaurants, a 10%–15% service charge is added to the bill. Tipping is not the custom.

CATEGORY	COST*
$$$$	over ¥6,000
$$$	¥ 4,000–¥6,000
$$	¥ 2,000–¥4,000
$	under ¥2,000

Cost is per person without tax, service, or drinks

Lodging

Tohoku has a broad spectrum of accommodations, from inns and minshuku to large, modern resort hotels. However, because the region has only recently opened itself up to tourists, many of the accommodations are of recent vintage. That means the hotels are often utilitarian and functional. The difference between them is that the more expensive the tariff, the larger the lobby area and the guest rooms. Do not expect to easily find a hotel with character. Moreover, because the Japanese are renowned for their service, politeness, and cleanliness, these characteristics do not differ significantly between hotels. Hence, the hotels listed below are chosen because their locations have certain advantages, their prices are in line for what they offer, and they welcome foreign visitors (some Japanese hotels are timorous of accepting foreign guests because of the differences in language and customs). As the region becomes more vigorous in trying to attract tourists, however, the situation improves. Hotels that are more appealing and imaginative in design are starting to appear.

All of the large city and resort hotels offer Western and Japanese food. During the summer season, hotel reservations are advised.

Outside the cities or major towns, most accommodations quote prices on a per-person basis with two meals, exclusive of service and tax. If you do not want dinner at your hotel, it is usually possible to renegotiate the price. Stipulate, too, whether you wish to have Japanese or Western breakfasts, if any. For the purposes here, the categories assigned to all hotels reflect the cost of a double room, with private bath but no meals. However, if you make reservations at any of the hot-spring hotels, you will be expected to take breakfast and dinner at the hotel—that will be the rate quoted to you, unless you specify otherwise.

A 3% federal consumer tax is added to all hotel bills. Another 3% local tax is added if the bill exceeds ¥15,000. At most hotels, a 10%–15% service charge is added to the total bill. Tipping is not the custom.

CATEGORY	COST*
$$$$	over ¥20,000
$$$	¥15,000–¥20,000
$$	¥10,000–¥15,000
$	under ¥10,000

Cost is for double room, without tax or service

Akita

Dining

$$ **Restaurant Bekkan Hamanoya.** This establishment is the local favorite for *hata-hata* (sand fish), a regional specialty that is especially good in the wintertime. ✕ *4-2-11 Omachi,* ☎ *0188/23–7481. Jacket and tie. MC, V.* ☺ *Lunch and dinner.*

Lodging

$$$ **Akita View Hotel.** This hotel has clean, fresh rooms and is the largest of the hotels in Akita. Located on the right side of a Seibu department store and seven minutes by foot from the JR station, it is convenient to shopping but a 10-minute walk from downtown Akita. The staff will give you advice on what to see and do in the city and prefecture. An indoor pool adds to the hotel's appeal. ▣ *2-6 Nakadori, Akita-shi, Akita-ken 010,* ☎ *0188/32–1111,* ℻ *0188/33–6957. 115 Western-style rooms. Western and Japanese restaurants, coffee shop, bar, indoor pool, health center, shops. AE, DC, MC, V.*

$$–$$$ **Akita Castle Hotel.** With the best location (opposite the moat and a 15-
★ minute walk from the station) and the most professional service in Akita, the Castle Hotel has well-maintained rooms, but be aware that the larger double rooms (normal American size) fall in the $$$ category. The more commodious Japanese-style rooms (only three in the hotel) are the same price as the Western-style ones. The bar and the French restaurant offer a park view. ▣ *1-3-5 Nakadori, Akita-shi, Akita-ken 010,* ☎ *0188/34–ᐧ 1141,* ℻ *0188/34–5588. 182 rooms, mostly Western style. Western, Japanese, and Chinese restaurants. AE, DC, MC, V.*

$ **Kohama Ryokan.** Though none of the rooms in this small inn has a private bath, the Kohama is friendly, homey, and priced right. Moreover, it is conveniently located to the left of the square in front of the JR Akita Station. The Japanese-style dinner using local fresh seafood is a bargain at ¥1,500. The owners also provide a photography service, whereby foreign guests can don traditional Japanese costumes and have their picture taken in front of a scenic mural. ▣ *6-19-6 Nakadori, Akita-shi, Akita-ken 010,* ☎ *0188/32–5739. 10 rooms without bath. Japanese dining, but Continental breakfast is offered. AE, V.*

Aomori

Lodging

$$ **Aomori Grand Hotel.** Close to the station, this establishment is the best in town for an overnight stay. A refurbishing has made the lobby personable. The lounge for morning coffee has superbly comfortable armchairs, and the Continental Bellevue restaurant on the 12th floor is an enjoyable place to spend an evening. Guest rooms tend to be small. ▣ *1-1-23 Shinmachi, Aomori-shi, Aomori-ken 030,* ☎ *0177/23–1011,* ℻ *0177/34–0505. 139 rooms, mostly Western style. Restaurant. AE, DC, MC, V.*

Atsumi Onsen

Lodging

$$$$ **Tachibana-ya.** Many traditional ryokan are reluctant to take reservations from foreigners, especially if they do not speak Japanese. Not so with Tachibana-ya. This resort ryokan in the center of the spa town of Atsumi Onsen welcomes foreign visitors, and its accommodations are excellent. Guest rooms are spacious (12 tatami mats), with a separate dressing room that is large enough to serve as a second sleeping room, a small kitchen for the maid to prepare meals, a washroom, and a separate toilet with heated seat. Should you wish to bathe privately, there is also a *hinoki* (Japanese cypress-wood) bathtub with faucets tapped into the thermal springs. But best of all is a small terrace alcove off the main room with two large leather armchairs and a table. The sliding glass doors overlook a landscaped garden that surrounds

a large pond filled with carp. The best rooms are on the ground floor—room Tokiwa 137 is especially nice. The hotel's buildings are angled so that rooms do not directly face each other, thus ensuring privacy. Service is extremely efficient and friendly. Meals, served in your room, are a delight to the eye and palate. The common baths have been splendidly refurbished using natural stone and are filled with steaming water from the thermal springs. ⊞ *Yatsumimachi-tei 3, Atsumimachi Yamagata-ken, 999-72,* ☎ *0235/43–2211,* FAX *0235/43–3681. 67 Japanese rooms. Coffee shop, bar, mineral baths. AE, DC, MC, V.*

Hachimantai

Lodging

$$$ **Sukayu Onsen.** In a vast, rambling wood building in the mountains,
★ this traditional japanese inn is one of the few left in the country where men and women are not separated in the main baths. (There are smaller baths that are segregated.) The sulfur mineral waters have been used for their curative powers for three centuries. The guest rooms are small and only thinly partitioned from each other, so light sleepers may find it hard to fall asleep. A fixed, multidish dinner is served in your room. Japanese breakfasts are served in a large dining room. There is no village nearby, but ski slopes and hiking trails are close. You can get to Sukayu Onsen by bus (1 hour, 10 mins.) from JR Aomori Station (get off at Sukayu Onsen-mae) or by car or taxi (45 mins.) from the city center. No English is spoken by the staff. ⊞ *Sukayu Onsen, Hakkoda-Sunchu, Aomori-ken 030-01,* ☎ *0177/38– 6400;* FAX *0177/38–6677. 134 rooms. Thermal baths. AE, DC, MC, V.*

$–$$ **Matsukawa-so.** This ryokan is popular for its rustic flair and the rejuvenating spa waters. It is simple, clean, and traditional, with highly polished wooden floors. Two meals are included, and all rooms are Japanese style. ⊞ *Matsukawa Onsen, Matsuomura, Iwate-gun, Iwate-ken 028-73,* ☎ *01957/8–2255. 35 rooms. Dining room, thermal baths. No credit cards.*

$ **Kyoun-so Inn.** Just the basic essentials are offered at this little two-story wooden inn: small tatami rooms and shared bathroom facilities. Meals (optional) are served in a communal room. The owners are always delighted to have a Westerner stay. Open-air hot springs are nearby. To reach the inn, you can either take the 50-minute bus ride from JR Obuke Station or a 110-minute bus ride from JR Morioka Station. ⊞ *Matsukawa Onsen, Matsuomura, Iwate-gun, Iwate-ken 028-73,* ☎ *01957/8–2256. 18 rooms. Dining room. AE, V.*

Higashiyama Onsen (Near Aizu-Wakamatsu)

Lodging

$$$ **Mukaitaki Ryokan.** The Mukaitaki is one ryokan in this spa town that retains a traditional ambience, thanks to its plank floors, shoji screens, and screen prints. English is spoken, and rooms can be reserved until 9:30 PM, though the place is open 24 hours a day. ⊞ *200 Kawamukou, Yumoto, Higashiyamamachi, Fukushima-ken 965,* ☎ *0242/27– 7501. 25 Japanese-style rooms. Japanese dining only, thermal (public) baths. AE, DC, MC, V.*

$$ **Hotel Koyo.** Although the Koyo is located in the upper part of this spa village, the buildings across the street block its view of the gorge. A modest hotel with large (10-tatami-mat) Japanese-style rooms, each equipped with a computerized dice game to keep its occupants entertained, it could use some sprucing up, but the room rate is low. The owner also has a fish market, so the meals, served in your room and included in the price, are prepared with good, fresh seafood. Meat can be provided, however, if requested in advance. Two staff members speak some English. A driver will pick you up at the bus stop. ⌂ *Higashiyama Onsen, Fukushima-ken 965,* ☎ *0242/26–9000 (or, toll-free, 0120/26– 4504),* FAX *0242/26–9166. 18 Japanese-style rooms. Mineral baths, snack bar, karaoke room. AE, V.*

Hirosaki

Dining

$$ **Yamauta.** Hirosaki's most interesting venue, a minute's walk from the station, Yamauta offers tasty Japanese food and live *shamisen* (a three-string banjo-like instrument) music every hour. The restaurant gets its musical character from its owner, who was once national shamisen champion and now uses the premises as a school for aspiring shamisen artists. Yamauta is closed one day a month, though the day varies. ✕ *2-7 Omachi 1-chome,* ☎ *0172/36–1835,* FAX *0172/36–6115. No credit cards.* ☾ *5–11.*

Lodging

$$–$$$$ **Hotel New Castle.** A smart business hotel on a par with the Hokke Club (*see below*), the New Castle is fractionally more expensive, though no better. It is, however, a good alternative if the Hokke is full. The restaurant here offers formal and elegant Japanese meals. ⌂ *24-1 Kamisayashimachi, Hirosaki, Aomori-ken 036 (located on the castle side of downtown Hirosaki),* ☎ *0172/36–1211,* FAX *0172/36–1210. 59 rooms, mostly Western style. Restaurant. AE, DC, MC, V.*

$$ ★ **Hokke Club Hotel.** This modern, efficient hotel in the center of town uses sparkling marble in its public rooms, which seem larger than they are due to an open design. Bedrooms tend to be small as well, so you may want to upgrade your room. Surrounded by shops and restaurants, the Hokke Club begins two flights up a moving escalator. The Kasen Japanese restaurant has excellent formal dining. ⌂ *126 Dotemachi, Hirosaki, Aomori-ken 036,* ☎ *0172/34–3811,* FAX *0172/32–0589. 65 rooms, mostly Western style. Restaurants, tearoom, American-style bar (The Jolly Dog). AE, DC, MC, V.*

Kakunodate

Lodging

$ **Hyakusuien.** This minshuku is in a 19th-century converted warehouse, and during the winter, the drafts constantly remind you of this heritage. Hospitality is limited despite a brochure that welcomes guests enthusiastically. Meals are served in a large, cluttered room that holds a small charcoal open fire, a library of old books, and a shrine. Food, included in the price, is average. The tatami rooms are larger than those at some minshukus, but be prepared to hear the coughs and splutters of your neighbors through the thin walls. The bathroom facilities are clean but primitive, and like many residences in rural Japan, they are not connected to a sewage or septic system. The minshuku is in the center of Kakunodate, a 10-minute walk from the JR station, south of the post office. ⌂ *31 Shimina Kamachi, Kakunodate, Akita-ken 014-03,* ☎ *0187/55–5715,* FAX *0187/55–2767. 12 rooms without bath. No credit cards.*

Matsushima

Lodging

$$ **Koganesano.** The advantage of this minshuku, which is in Nobiru, a village situated on the far (north) side of Matsushima Bay, is its loca-

tion—an easy five-minute walk from the JR Nobiru Station and a block from the beach. Otherwise, the rooms are tiny (six tatami mats), and the paper-thin walls permit you to hear every guest's footfall. Avoid the room next to the toilet! Food is served in your room in a perfunctory manner, but the fresh Pacific seafood—mussels, crab, oyster, and shrimp—especially in the colder months, is a redeeming feature. ☎ 68-46 Aza-minami-yogei, Nobiru, Oku-Matsushima, Narusemachi, Monoo-gun, Miyagi-ken 981-04, ☎ 0225/88–2183. 13 rooms, none with private bath. No credit cards.

Miyako

Lodging

$ **Minshuku Obata.** Sixteen minutes on the Senniku Railway from Miyako is Taro, a small village well located for sightseeing. This large minshuku provides fair-size (eight-tatami-mat) rooms, two meals a day, and clean public bath and toilet facilities. The food is adequate, not special, but you will usually have the opportunity to taste the local specialties—scallops and abalone. Unfortunately, the owner of this minshuku doesn't seem to understand the concept of politeness, which may explain why it's been doing little business recently. ☎ 60-2 Nokara, Tarocho, Shimohei-gun, Iwate-ken 027-03 (15-min. walk from Taro railway station), ☎ 0193/87–2631. 16 rooms, none with private bath. No credit cards.

Morioka

Dining

$$$ **Restaurant Nanbu Robata.** Recognized for its regional specialties cooked over charcoal, the Nanbu Robata is like an old country farmhouse with a traditional hearth. Try the grilled fish, which is first filleted and then reassembled. The restaurant is near the Hachiman Firewatch Tower, a five-minute walk from the bus center. Its popularity has grown since we first mentioned it; prices now run close to ¥7,000 per person. ✕ Hachimancho, ☎ 0196/22–5082. No credit cards. ☉ 11:30–9:30.

$$ **Azumaya.** For wanko soba (buckwheat noodles), there are at least 16 restaurants in the city, some directly across the road from the JR station plaza. However, you should try Azumaya, 10 minutes from the station by taxi. ✕ 1-8-3 Nakanohashi-dori, ☎ 0196/22–2252. No credit cards. ☉ 11–3 and 5–8. Closed the 1st and 3rd Tues. of each month.

$$ **Restaurant Wakana.** This dining spot is within an eight-minute walk from the station—cross the river, fork left, and take another left after the Kawatoku department store. The Wakana offers good teppanyaki (food cooked on a flat grill) and claims the best beef in the city. The fish and steaks are grilled in front of the customers. Some English is spoken. ✕ 1-3-33 Osawakawara, ☎ 0196/53–3333. Jacket and tie. AE, DC, MC, V. ☉ 11:30–2 and 5–10:30 (for last orders). Closed Tues.

Lodging

$$$ **Morioka Grand Hotel.** The most personable and smartest modern hotel
★ in town, the Grand is situated on a small hill on the edge of the city, 10 minutes by taxi from the station. Its views are broader, the air is cleaner, and its rooms are slightly larger than most hotels in the area, but this is reflected in the price of the rooms, the most expensive in Morioka. Do not confuse this hotel with the cheaper Morioka Grand Hotel Annex. ☎ 1-10 Atagoshita, Morioka, Iwate-ken 020, ☎ 0196/25–2111, FAX 0196/22–4804. 36 rooms, 21 Western style. Japanese and Continental restaurants. AE, DC, MC, V.

$$–$$$ **Hotel Higashi-Nihon.** The largest hotel in town, the Higashi-Nihon bustles with groups, wedding parties, and banquets. It has all the amenities of an international, but impersonal, hotel, including three restaurants (Japanese, Chinese, and French). The two Japanese-style rooms are slightly larger and no more expensive than the Western-style ones. ▦ *3-3-18 Odori, Morioka, Iwate-ken 020,* ☎ *0196/25–2131,* ℻ *0196/26– 9092. 209 rooms, 207 Western-style. Restaurants, bar, coffee shop, tennis, beauty salon, photography studio. AE, DC, MC, V.*

$–$$ **Metropolitan Morioka.** Just to the left of the station plaza, this hotel has clean and utilitarian rooms. The combination Japanese and Western buffet at breakfast is the best value in town. The staff are extremely helpful, despite the language barrier. Though the hotel has a good Chinese restaurant on the fourth floor, ask the reception clerk to take you across the street and introduce you at Umakko, a tiny *nomiya*, or pub. No English is spoken here, so point to what you want or have the clerk order for you. The Kin Kin, a slowly grilled fish, is delicate and succulent. ▦ *1-44 Morioka Eki-mae-dori, Morioka, Iwate-ken 020,* ☎ *0196/25–1211,* ℻ *0196/25–1210. 134 rooms. Restaurants. AE, DC, MC, V.*

$ **Ryokan Kumagai.** In a two-story wooden building, this simple hostelry is a member of the inexpensive Japanese Inn Group, offering basic tatami rooms. None of the rooms has a private bath, but there is a small dining area where Japanese and Western breakfasts and Japanese dinners are optional. Located between the station and center city, it is a 10-minute walk from the JR Morioka Station—cross the river and walk along Kawinbashi-dori two blocks and turn right (a gas station is on the left and a bank on the right). Cross over one block and the ryokan is on the left. ▦ *3-2-5 Oosawakawara, Morioka, Iwate-ken 020,* ☎ *0196/51– 3020. 11 rooms, none with private bath. Dining room. No credit cards.*

Nyuto Onsen

Lodging

Nyuto consists of six small spa villages, each with an inn, generally in the **$$$–$$$$** range. Only Japanese rooms are available, and you must take your meals there. No Western credit cards are accepted. Following are the telephone numbers to be called for reservations at each of the villages' inns: **Tsurono Onsen,** *closed in winter,* ☎ *0187/46–2139.* **Taeno-yu Onsen,** ☎ *0187/46–2740.* **Ogama Onsen,** ☎ *0187/46– 2438.* **Kaniba Onsen,** ☎ *0187/46–2021.* **Magoroku Onsen,** ☎ *0187/46– 2224.* **Kuro-yu Onsen,** *closed in winter,* ☎ *0187/46–2214.*

Sendai

Dining

Restaurants abound in Sendai. Many of the Japanese restaurants are along Chuo-dori, and most display their menus in their windows, along with the prices for each dish. The following is a sampling of the many restaurants from which to choose:

$$$–$$$$ **Chisoutei.** This restaurant, a member of the Iwashiya chain, is famous for its fresh sashimi. The specialty is slivers of meat taken from the back of the fish while it is still alive. The slivers and the tail-twitching fish are then presented on a plate before you. Grilled-fish dishes are also available and perfectly done. Service is either at the counter or at tables placed on tatami matting. To find Chisoutei, take the alley left just before the Gateaux Boutique on Ichibancho, and then the first right. The restaurant is on the right, with a fish tank in the window. ✕ *4-5- 42 Ichibancho,* ☎ *022/222–6645. Jacket and tie suggested. AE, DC.* ☽ *5–midnight.*

$$ Izaka. This ground-floor restaurant offers yakitori-style cuisine (grilled skewers of chicken) and beef dishes, including sukiyaki. It's on Chuo-dori, just north of Hirose-dori. ✗ *4-3-7 Ichibancho,* ☎ *022/222–7080. No credit cards.* ☉ *5–11.*

SS 30 Building. The restaurants on the top three floors of the tallest building in town do a brisk trade. There are plenty to choose from: **Saboten** (☎ 022/267–4083), on the 28th floor, serves inexpensive fried fish and salads; and **Toh-Ten-Koh** (☎ 022/267–8841), on the 29th floor, serves Chinese cuisine. If you prefer just a cocktail with your view, drop into **Ermitage,** on the 30th floor, (☎ 022/261–4777), a cozy, Western-style bar.

For serious French cuisine you're best off at either the **Sendai Hotel** or the **Koyo Grand Hotel** (*see below*).

Lodging

$$$–$$$$ Hotel Metropolitan Sendai. Adjacent to the railway station, this upscale business traveler's hotel has reasonably large guest rooms decorated in light colors. The 21st-floor Sky Lounge restaurant offers the best city view—and French food to go with it. Simpler fare at more reasonable prices is found in the coffee shop. ⌖ *1-1-1 Chuo-dori, Sendai, Miyagi-ken 980,* ☎ *022/268–2525,* FAX *022/268–2521. 300 rooms, including 3 suites and 4 Japanese-style rooms. Restaurants, coffee shop, indoor pool, gym, small business center, banquet rooms. AE, DC, MC, V.*

$$$–$$$$ **Sendai Kokusai Hotel.** The newest of Sendai's hotels (completed in 1990,
★ next to the new SS 30 complex) immediately won attention as the town's leading hotel. The lobby glistens with marble and stainless steel; guest rooms are furnished in light pastels, and larger rooms have stucco arches to exaggerate their size. Fresh flowers add a touch of color. Lighting is subdued—not so good for late-night reading. Competing with the dozen restaurants in the SS 30 Building, the hotel offers French, Chinese, and Japanese fare and a bar. ⌖ *4-6-1 Chuo, Aoba-ku, Sendai, Miyagi-ken 980,* ☎ *022/268–1112,* FAX *022/268–1113. 234 rooms. Restaurants, sushi bar, bar, coffee shop, children's room, banquet/conference rooms, shop. AE, DC, MC, V.*

$$–$$$ Sendai Hotel. Pale colors and cheerful prints make up the decor at this modern hotel, popular with business travelers wishing to stay near the station. Foreign guests enjoy attentive service and get the English-language newspaper the *Japan Times* every morning. ⌖ *1-10-25 Chuo, Sendai, Miyagi-ken 980,* ☎ *022/225–5171,* FAX *022/268–9325. 113 rooms, mostly Japanese style. Chinese, Japanese, Italian, and French restaurants, shops. AE, DC, MC, V.*

$$ Koyo Grand Hotel. The Koyo Grand must be the most weirdly furnished hotel in Japan: It has objects of art from China and Europe mixed with Louis XV reproductions. The total assemblage is a mismatch of statues, mounted deer heads, Regency upholstered furniture, gold painted chandeliers, and ceiling murals. Thankfully, the guest rooms have more simple and standard furniture (though with turn-of-the-century French reproductions); otherwise you might have horrendous nightmares. The hotel has a small but good French restaurant, and also a Chinese restaurant, offering Szechuan and Cantonese cooking. ⌖ *1-3-2 Honcho Aoba-ku, Sendai, Miyagi-ken 980,* ☎ *022/267–5111,* FAX *022/265–2252. 149 Western-style rooms. Japanese, French, and Chinese restaurants. AE, DC, MC, V.*

$$ **Ryokan Aisaki.** This inn has been run by the same family since 1868,
★ but the present building is post–World War II. Only two rooms have private bathrooms, but the public bath has the added benefit of a sauna. Still, the hostelry is enjoyable for friendly companionship with other

guests, and the owner welcomes foreigners. He speaks fluent English and often will take guests on sightseeing trips. Open until midnight, Ryokan Aisaki is behind Sendai Central Post Office, a 15-minute walk from JR Sendai Station (five minutes by taxi). Meals, which are compulsory, are served in a dining room; room rates include the cost of two meals. ⌂ *5-6 Kitamemachi, Sendai, Miyagi-ken 980,* ☎ *022/264–0700,* ℻ *022/227–6067. 15 rooms. Dining room, sauna. AE, V.*

Tazawako

Lodging

$$ **Tazawako Prince.** A modern white hotel on the edge of Lake Tazawa, the Tazawako Prince has views of Komagatake. Choose from rooms that are large with a lake view, small with a lake view, or small with a mountain view. Aside from the main dining room, there is a garden room down near the lake. ⌂ *Katajiri, Saimyoji, Nishikimura, Senboku-gun, Akita-ken 014-05,* ☎ *0187/47–2211,* ℻ *0187/47–2104. Dining room, shops, game room, boating. AE, DC, MC, V.*

Tono

Lodging

$$$
★ **Fukuzanso Inn.** Highly polished, creaky floors characterize this friendly, old-fashioned ryokan, which is a five-minute walk from JR Tono Station and boasts of being open 24 hours a day, 365 days a year. Rooms have a dressing room/closet area and a small enclosed balcony with table and chairs. Dinner, served in your room, consists mainly of seafood and Japanese vegetables. No English is spoken, but the hospitality is all smiles; the staff lends bikes for sightseeing. ⌂ *5-30 Chuo-dori, Tono, Iwate-ken 028,* ☎ *01986/2–4120 or, toll-free, 0120/48–8588. 18 rooms. Japanese public baths. V.*

Yamagata

Lodging

$$–$$$ **Hotel Castle.** A seven-minute walk from the station, the Castle is a modern, utilitarian hotel with small rooms. Guests mill around the lobby area, where there is a coffee/tea lounge (refills on coffee are free). ⌂ *2-7 Tokamachi 4-chome, Yamagata, Yamagata-ken, 990,* ☎ *0236/31–3311,* ℻ *0236/31–3373. 160 Western-style rooms. Restaurants, pub. AE, DC, MC, V.*

$$ **Yamagata Washington Hotel.** This downtown hotel is smart and efficient and has a friendly staff. The coffee shop is on the ground floor; reception and the Japanese restaurant are on the next floor; and the guest rooms are up above, from the third to eighth floors. Rooms are compact, with merely functional furnishings that are at least new. Bathrooms are the typical prefabricated plastic units. ⌂ *1-4-31 Nanokamachi, Yamagata, Yamagata-ken 990,* ☎ *0236/25–1111,* ℻ *0236/24–1512. 227 rooms. Restaurant. AE, DC, MC, V.*

TOHOKU ESSENTIALS

Arriving and Departing

By Plane

Akita has four daily flights from Tokyo's Haneda Airport by ANA (All Nippon Airways), which also operates flights from Nagoya.

Three flights from Osaka International Airport are provided by JAS (Japan Air System).

Aomori has four daily flights from Tokyo's Haneda Airport by JAS and one by ANA. Aomori also has flights from Nagoya and Osaka, and to Sapporo's Chitose Airport.

Morioka (whose Hanamaki Airport is 50 minutes by bus from downtown) has four flights from Osaka International Airport by JAS. Morioka also has flights to Nagoya and to Sapporo's Chitose Airport and to Nagoya Airport.

Sendai has seven daily flights from Osaka International Airport by ANA. Sendai also has flights to Fukuoka, Nagoya, Hiroshima, and to Sapporo's Chitose Airport.

Yamagata has three daily flights from Tokyo's Haneda Airport by ANA and four flights from Osaka International Airport by JAS. Flights also arrive from Nagoya and depart for Sapporo.

By Train

The most efficient method to reach Tohoku from Tokyo is on the Tohoku Shinkansen trains, which run as far north as Morioka. The Shinkansen makes a total of 63 runs a day from Tokyo to destinations in Tohoku: Fukushima (1½ to slightly more than 2 hours), Sendai (2 hours to 2 hours and 40 minutes), and Morioka (2 hours and 45 minutes to 3½ hours) North of Morioka, conventional trains continue on to Aomori (2 hours and 10 minutes). To reach Akita, the Limited Express from Morioka takes 1 hour and 40 minutes. Yamagata is now connected to Tokyo by a Shinkansen line that branches off at Fukushima; travel time is only 2½ hours. Alternatively, Yamagata may be reached by JR Limited Express trains from Sendai in 1 hour.

On Tohoku's western side (facing the Sea of Japan), the train from Niigata takes 3 hours and 40–50 minutes to travel along the Sea of Japan coast to Akita, and an additional 3 hours to reach Aomori. From Niigata inland to Yamagata, the train takes 3½ hours. (Niigata is connected to Tokyo's Ueno Station by the Joetsu Shinkansen, which at its fastest makes the run in 2 hours.)

Any extensive traveling through Tohoku justifies use of the Japan Rail Pass, which costs ¥27,800 for a week's unlimited travel. For example, the one-way economy fare on the Shinkansen train (with a seat reservation) from Tokyo to Sendai is ¥10,390; to Morioka, ¥13,570.

By Bus

While the Tohoku Kyuko Express Night Bus from Tokyo to Sendai is inexpensive (¥6,100), it takes 7 hours and 40 minutes. It leaves Tokyo Station (Yaesu-guchi side, on the left as you walk along Yaesu-dori, just before you get to the Matsuoka men's wear shop) at 10 PM and arrives in Sendai at 5:40 AM. The bus from Sendai departs at 10 PM and arrives in Tokyo at 5:40 AM.

By Car

The Tohoku Expressway now links Tokyo with Aomori, but the cost of gas, tolls, and car rental makes driving an expensive form of travel. It is also considerably slower to drive than to ride on the Shinkansen. Assuming you can clear metropolitan Tokyo in 2 hours, the approximate driving time is 5 hours to Fukushima, 6 hours to Sendai, 8–10 hours to Morioka, and 10–11 hours to Aomori.

Getting Around

Transportation in the rural areas of Tohoku was, until recently, limited, which is why Tohoku still has been undiscovered by modern progress and tourists. However, that is changing rapidly. Now, using a combination of trains and buses, most of Tohoku's hinterland is easily accessible, except during the heavy winter snows.

By Train

Trains are fast and frequent on the north–south runs. They are slower and less frequent (more like every 2 hours rather than every hour during the day) when they cross Tohoku's mountainous spine. Most of the railways are owned by Japan Railways, so Rail Passes are accepted. Be aware that most trains stop running before midnight.

By Bus

Buses take over where trains do not run, and, in most instances, they depart from the JR train stations. Though English may not be widely spoken in Tohoku, there is never any difficulty at train stations in finding someone to direct you to the appropriate bus.

During the summer tourist season, there are also scenic bus tours operating from the major tourist areas. The local Japan Travel Bureau at the train station in each area, or the major hotels, will make the arrangements.

By Boat

Three sightseeing boats are especially recommended: at Matsushima Bay, near Sendai; at Jodogahama on the Pacific coast, near Miyako; and at Lake Towada. Keep in mind that these boats offer constant commentary in Japanese over the loudspeaker; this can be particularly annoying if you do not understand what's being said. (*See* appropriate Exploring sections for details.)

By Car

Once in the locale you wish to explore, a rented car is ideal for getting around. All major towns have car-rental agencies. The Nippon-Hertz agency is the one most frequently represented. Bear in mind, though, that except on the Tohoku Expressway, few road signs are in *romaji* (Japanese words rendered in English). However, major roads have route numbers. With a road map in which the towns are spelled in romaji and *kanji*, (the Chinese characters used in Japanese writing), it becomes relatively easy to decipher the directional signs. Maps are not provided by car-rental agencies. Be sure to obtain your bilingual maps in Tokyo or Sendai.

Guided Tours

The **Japan Travel Bureau** has offices at every JR station in each of the prefectural capitals and can assist in local tours, hotel reservations, and ticketing onward travel. There is usually someone whose English is sufficient for your basic needs. In Tokyo, ☎ 03/3276–7777; in Kyoto, ☎ 075/341–1413; in Sendai, ☎ 022/221–4422.

The Japan Travel Bureau also arranges a two-day tour of Tohoku out of Tokyo. For ¥195,000, the tour includes Chusonji, Motsuji, Naruoka spa (overnight), Matsushima (including a cruise), and Sendai. Only one breakfast and one dinner are included, and there is a ¥20,000 single supplement. These tours operate daily April 1–October 31.

Important Addresses and Numbers

Emergencies
Police, ☎ 110. **Ambulance,** ☎ 119.

Tourist Information

There are tourist information centers at all the train stations at the prefectural capitals. The largest and most helpful tourist center that gives information on all of Tohoku and not just the local area is at Morioka's train station (☎ 0196/25–2090). In Sendai, it might be a better idea to consult the International Center at the bottom of Aobayama Koen. The telephone numbers of each prefectural government tourist section are: Akita, ☎ 0188/60–2266; Aomori, ☎ 0177/22–5080; Fukushima, ☎ 0245/21–3811; Iwate, ☎ 0196/51–3111; Miyagi, ☎ 022/211–2743; and Yamagata, ☎ 0236/30–2373.

Each prefecture also has an information center near Tokyo Station with a few English brochures and maps. The centers for Akita (☎ 03/3211–1775), Iwate (☎ 03/3231–2613), Miyagi (☎ 03/3231–0944), and Yamagata (☎ 03/3215–2222) are on the 9th floor of Tetsudo Kaikan (above Daiman department store at the station's Yaesu exit), 1-9-1 Marunouchi, Chiyoda-ku. The Aomori center (☎ 03/3216–6010) is on the 2nd floor of the nearby Kokusai Kanko Kaikan, 1-8-3 Marunouchi, Chiyoda-ku, while Fukushima's center (☎ 03/3214–2789) is one floor higher in the same building.

Japan Travel Phone

This nationwide service for English-language assistance or travel information is available seven days a week, 9–5. Dial toll-free 0088/22–2800 or 0120/222–800 for information on eastern Japan. When using a yellow, blue, or green public phone (do not use the red phones), insert a ¥10 coin, which will be returned. There are different numbers for callers in Tokyo (3503–4400) and Kyoto (371–5649), and in those cities the service costs ¥10 per 3 minutes.

14 Hokkaido

This northernmost of Japan's four main islands offers a respite from the temples, shrines, and castles that fill the agenda of the tourist to the other, more frequently visited parts of Japan. It is a geological wonderland half-covered in forests, with lava-seared mountains and crystal-clear caldera lakes.

By Nigel Fisher

HOKKAIDO IS UNTAMED JAPAN. In the rest of the country it may be said that the cities dominate the countryside—not so in Hokkaido. Its cities and towns are modern outposts of urban humanity that are surrounded by wild, untamed mountains, virgin forests, crystal-clear lakes, and surf-beaten shores. Hokkaido is Japan's last frontier, and the attitudes of the inhabitants are akin to those of the pioneers of the American West.

Hokkaido was not even mentioned in books until the 7th century; even then, for the next millennium, it was discounted as the place where the "hairy Ainu" lived. The Ainu, the original inhabitants of Japan (and probably related to ethnic groups that populated Siberia), were always thought of as the inferior race by the Yamato Japanese, who arrived in Japan from the south (Kyushu) and founded Japan's imperial house. As the Yamato spread and expanded their empire up from Kyushu through Honshu, the peace-loving Ainu retreated north to Hokkaido. There they lived, supporting themselves with their traditional pursuits of hunting and fishing. By the 16th century the Yamato had established themselves in the southern tip of Hokkaido, and they soon began to make incursions into the island's interior. Finally, in the middle of the 19th century, Hokkaido's Ainu lost the last of their territory to the Yamato.

With the Meiji Restoration in 1868, Japan changed its policy toward Hokkaido and opened it up as the new frontier to be colonized by the Yamato Japanese. The Tokyo government encouraged immigration from the rest of Japan to Hokkaido but made no provision for the Ainu peoples. Indeed, the Ainu were given no choice but to assimilate themselves into the life and culture of the colonizers. Consequently, the Ainu's culture went into a sudden and near-terminal decline. It has been fashionable for academics in the 20th century to write them off as a "doomed" or even "extinct" race.

It should be noted, though, that in recent years there has been something of a revival in Ainu culture and activism. The number of full-blooded Ainu might be very small, but 24,000 people believe themselves to possess enough of the bloodline to have officially declared themselves "Ainu." Similarly, though the Ainu language has virtually disappeared as a native tongue, many people have begun to study it in a burgeoning number of college and evening courses. Ainu activism, meanwhile, received a boost when the United Nations made 1993 a Year of Indigenous Peoples; and though they still aren't recognized as a distinct ethnic group by the Japanese government, the Ainu scored a propaganda victory in 1994 when their leading activist, Shigeru Kayano, was elected to Japan's House of Councillors—the first Ainu to reach such a prominent position. Sadly, little of this may be obvious to tourists who head for Hokkaido's (reconstructed) Ainu villages, many of which are tourist traps making money for Japanese entrepreneurs rather than for the Ainu themselves, and they can be depressing places.

The Ainu are not the only Japanese aborigines. There was also another race, the Moyoro, that lived before the Ainu, but little is known about these mysterious peoples. Anthropological evidence found on Hokkaido's east coast in the Moyoro Shell Mound, now displayed in the Abashiri Museum, supports the belief that Moyoro civilization ended in the 9th century.

With little visible past and with newly born cities, Hokkaido offers a respite from temples, shrines, and castles. For the tourist, Hokkaido is a geological wonderland: Lava-seared mountains hide deeply carved ravines; hot springs, gushers, and steaming mud pools boil out of the ground, and crystal-clear caldera lakes fill the seemingly bottomless cones of volcanoes. Half of Hokkaido is covered in forests. Wild, rugged coastlines hold back the sea, and all around Hokkaido, islands surface offshore. Some are volcanic peaks poking their cones out of the ocean, and others were formed eons ago by the crunching of the earth's crust. The remnants of Hokkaido's bear population, believed to number about 2,000, still roams the forests, snagging rabbits and scooping up fish from mountain streams, and deer wander the pastures, stealing fodder from cows. The crane (*tsuru*), which connotes long life and happiness, is often used as Hokkaido's symbol; Hokkaido's native crane, *tancho,* is especially magnificent, with a red-cap head and white body trimmed with black feathers.

May and early summer bring the blossoming of alpine flowers and lilacs. The cherry trees in Hokkaido are the last to bloom in Japan—in late-April and early May. Summers are drier and cooler than in the rest of Japan, and thus a trip to Hokkaido allows an escape from humidity. Hotel accommodations become relatively difficult to find in summer, and the scenic areas become crowded with tour groups and Japanese families. September brings autumn, and the turning leaves offer spectacular golden colors, reaching their peak in early October. November and April are the least desirable months; the first falls of snow in November just dirty the roads, and in April the snow melts into a brown mess. The winter makes travel more difficult (some minor roads are closed), and, especially on the east coast, the weather is frigid. Yet it is also a beautiful time of year, with crisp white snow lying everywhere.

One of the delights of traveling through Hokkaido is meeting the people, who are known as the Dosanko. Since virtually all of the Japanese in Hokkaido are "immigrants to a new frontier," there is less emphasis placed on tradition and more on accomplishing the matter at hand. The Dosanko are still very Japanese, sharing the same culture as the rest of Japan, but they are also open to new customs and other cultures. Furthermore, they have a great attachment to their island. In a survey conducted by the *Yomiuri Shinbun* (newspaper) in 1993, to find out how positively the Japanese felt about their home prefectures, Hokkaido received the most impressive score.

Hokkaido was born during the Meiji Restoration, a time when the Japanese government turned to the West for new ideas. Hokkaido, especially, sought advice from America and Europe for its development. In the 1870s, some 63 foreign experts came to this island, including an American architect who designed Hokkaido's principal city, Sapporo. Around the same time, agricultural experts from abroad were brought in to introduce dry-farming as a substitute for rice, which could not grow in the severe winter climate. This has left the Dosanko with a peculiar fondness for Europeans. In Sapporo, Westerners are warmly received. In the countryside, the Dosanko are shy but not timid in coming to the aid of Westerners.

Because Hokkaido consists of more countryside than cities, the number of foreign tourists it has traditionally attracted has been small, compared to the many Japanese who have chosen Hokkaido for winter skiing and summer hiking. However, recent refurbishments at Sapporo's Chitose Airport have opened up the island to more international flights (from such places as Hong Kong and Honolulu), and the number of international travelers coming in and out of Hokkaido has increased (278,000 in 1993)—an indication that foreign visitors are likely to be even more abundant in the future. Because Hokkaido is Japan's northernmost and least developed island, there is a strong sense shared by resident and visitor alike of discovering uncharted territory. It's untrue, of course. Hokkaido has a road and rail network that crisscrosses the island, but the feeling of newness still remains.

HAKODATE

When traveling by train from Honshu, the first town you'll come to in Hokkaido is **Hakodate.** Prior to 1988, crossing over to Hokkaido required taking the four-hour ferry trip from Aomori to Hakodate; now the Seikan Tunnel lets trains make the passage in two hours and ten minutes. En route through the tunnel is a railway station 400 feet beneath the sea, where there is a museum dedicated to the construction of the tunnel. You can get off the train here and stretch your legs, take in the museum, and catch the next train 90 minutes later. However, because the first stop in Hokkaido proper is Hakodate, with 3½ hours still to go on the train before reaching Sapporo, Hakodate may be a better place to stretch your legs. Stop at the Information Office (☎ 0138/23–5440; ⊘ Daily, Apr.–Oct. 9–7; Nov.–Mar. 9–5) just to the right as you exit the JR Hakodate Station to collect maps in English. If you arrive in the morning and only want a short stopover, visit the **asa-ichi,** a morning fish and vegetable market just a three-minute walk south of the station (open Mon.–Sat. from about 6 AM to noon, peaking at 8; the market takes place only occasionally on Sundays). Recently, it has grown to be more than just a market, with 400 shops selling anything from *kegani* (a type of crab) to sea urchins, asparagus to cherries. The neighboring **Hakodate Seaport Plaza** is a shopping and restaurant complex that stays open until 6 PM (the Restaurant Seaport upstairs until 9 PM). The Hokuto Kotsu Bus Company (☎ 0138/57–7555) runs four-hour sightseeing tours of the city, leaving from JR Hakodate Station and covering most of the city sights for ¥4,400. Travel on the streetcars ranges from ¥200 to ¥240, and on the municipal buses from ¥200 to ¥270. A one-day bus-and-streetcar pass is available from the tourist office at ¥1,000.

Exploring

In 1859 Hakodate was one of only three Japanese ports opened to trade with the West. This heritage supplies the attractions for visitors today. Old (sometimes rather decrepit) buildings with definite European- and American-style architecture cluster around the section of town known as **Motomachi.** To get there from the JR station, take Streetcar 5 to the Suehirocho stop and walk 10 minutes toward Mt. Hakodate, which rises above the city. No particular building stands out, though a useful spot to start is the **Orthodox Church of the Resurrection,** which dates from 1859, when it served the first Russian consulate in the city. After a fire in 1907, it was rebuilt in Byzantine style in 1916. A large-scale restoration project was completed here in 1989, and the church has become an important tourist attraction for the city.

Below the church, by the streetcar line, are the **Bungakukan** (Literature Museum) and the **Hoppo Minzoku Shiryokan** (Museum of

Northern Peoples; ☉ Both daily, Apr.–Oct. 9–7; Nov.–Mar. 9–5). The former provides information, some of it in English, about the city's most noted writers. Needless to say, none of these are household names in the West, but the museum is pleasant and also has a photographic display of the "eight most beautiful scenes in Hakodate"—evidence yet again of the Japanese mania for cataloging and ranking everything. (Quite how it was determined that there were eight such scenes is anyone's guess!) The Museum of Northern Peoples gives a straightforward introduction to Hokkaido's Ainu culture, though it's not nearly as detailed as other museums farther north, and the decor is rather spartan. For ¥840, a ticket gives you access to both these museums and also to the **Kyu Igirisu Ryojikan** (British Consulate Building; ☉ Daily, Apr.–Oct. 9–7, Nov.–Mar 9–5) farther up the hillside, now a museum devoted to the opening of the port in the 19th century. Architecturally, the consulate is picturesque, but the exhibits are spoiled for Western tourists by the lack of information in English. Finally, slightly above the consulate (entry afforded by same ¥840 ticket), is the building that served as the city's public hall, now referred to as the **Kyu Hakodate-ku Kokaido** (Old Hakodate Public Hall), but with its classical columns and antebellum architecture, it looks as if it should be a manor house in America's Deep South.

In the center of the city is **Goryokaku,** a Western-style fort completed in 1864. You can reach the fort from JR Hakodate Station either by bus (12 or 27) from gate B on the side of the terminal nearest the JR station, to the Goryokaku Koen-mae bus stop or by streetcar (2 or 5) to the Goryokaku Koen-mae streetcar stop. From either stop, it is about a 10-minute walk to the fort. The fort's design is unusual for Japan, especially with its five-pointed-star shape, which enabled its defenders to rake any attackers with murderous cross fire. However, the Tokugawa shogunate's defenders were unable to hold out against the forces of the Meiji Restoration, and its walls were breached. Nothing of the interior of the castle remains today, though there is a small museum with relics from the battle. Now the fort area is a park with some 4,000 cherry trees, which, when they bloom in late April, make the stopover in Hakodate worthwhile. There is also an observation tower in the park, but at ¥520 admission, it is not worth the climb for the view. ☉ *Daily, May–Oct. 8–8; Nov.–Apr. 9–6.*

★ Behind, as if guarding the city, is **Mt. Hakodate,** a volcanic hill rising 1,100 feet. The panoramic views of the city from the top are good at any time, but especially at night, with the lights of the buildings and street lamps below. A 20-minute bus ride takes you to the top of Mt. Hakodate from the JR station. For a more interesting trip, take Streetcar 2 or 5 to Jujigai stop and then walk about seven minutes to the cable car for the three-minute ride up the mountain. The city claims that this cable car, with its capacity of 125 passengers, is the largest in Asia. A restaurant at the top is particularly appealing for its nighttime view. ☛ *Cable car ¥620, one-way; ¥1,130, round-trip.* ☉ *Daily Apr. 26–Oct. 31, 10–10; Nov. 1–Apr. 25, 10–9. (From Apr. 26 to May 5 and from July 25 to Aug. 20 it begins operation at 9 AM). The road is closed late-Nov.–late-Apr.*

A number of buildings are being restored around the harbor, close to the Jujigai streetcar stop. One is the **Hakodate Factory** (☎ 0138/22–5656), open every day from 9 to 9. It's a cross between a fish market, gourmet supermarket, bar, and restaurant. There are plenty of souvenirs for sale, while the sight of the dozens of crabs and other marine life crammed into the display tanks may put you off visiting the seafood restaurant upstairs. Also in this area are a number of Western-style bars and cafés with such names as The Very Beast (*sic*), California Baby, and the Happy Octopus.

Finally, should you need a bath before leaving Hakodate, take Streetcar 2 from the JR station for a 15-minute ride followed by a five-minute walk to **Yachigashira Onsen,** where a large public bathhouse accommodates 380 people. ☛ ¥320. ⊘ *Apr.–Oct., 6 AM–9:30 PM; Nov.–Mar. 7 AM–9:30 PM. Closed Jan. 1 and the 2nd and 4th Friday of each month.*

From Hakodate there are two train routes to Sapporo. The slow way cuts through the west side of Shikotsu Toya National Park and heads up to the north coast of Hokkaido to Otaru before veering east for Sapporo. The fast way travels along the southern coast before turning north to Sapporo. On this route, you may disembark from the train to visit Lake Toya and/or Noboribetsu Onsen before continuing on to Sapporo. For the purposes of this book, both Lake Toya and Noboribetsu Onsen are covered as excursions out of Sapporo (*see* Toyako Onsen, *below*).

At the Hakodate train station, you can purchase something to eat. Try the local *eki-ben* (station box lunch), the *nishin-migaki-bento,* which consists of *nishin* (herring) boiled in a sweet, spicy sauce until the bones are soft enough to eat. Then, when your appetite returns at Mori station, an hour's distance from Hakodate en route to Sapporo, you can have another well-known eki-ben, *ika-meshi,* a box lunch made by stuffing a whole *ika* (squid) with rice and cooking it in a sweet, spicy sauce. Each meal includes two or three ika.

SAPPORO

Sapporo is not just Hokkaido's capital; it is also the island's premier city. With 1.7 million inhabitants, it is four times larger than Hokkaido's second largest city (Asahikawa). And it continues to expand, as Hokkaido's unemployed from the economically depressed shipbuilding towns in the southwest and the farms in the central plains migrate to Sapporo for work. Though it is a large city, it is not confusing or congested; this can be explained by its origins: In 1870, the governor of Hokkaido visited President Grant in the United States and requested that American advisers come to Hokkaido to help design the capital on the site of an Ainu village. As a result, Sapporo was built on a 100-meter (330-foot) grid system with wide avenues and parks. This is not, then, the exotic and cultured city you expect to find in Japan: It is distinctly lacking in pre-Meiji historic sights. On the other hand, you can walk the sidewalks without being swept away in a surge of humanity; and though the city is architecturally boring, it is easily navigated.

By hosting the 1972 Winter Olympics, Sapporo made itself an international city and developed a cosmopolitan attitude. Numerous international-style hotels and restaurants came into being at that time and have stayed. Banks here are used to traveler's checks, and there is always someone on hand to help you out in English. Ultimately, though, Sapporo is best considered a base from which to make excursions into the wild, dramatic countryside. The actual time spent exploring the city can be minimal—a day, perhaps two at the most.

Arriving and Departing

By Plane

Sapporo's airport, in Chitose, 40 kilometers (25 miles) south of Sapporo, is Hokkaido's main airport. More than 30 domestic routes link it to the rest of Japan, while flights from Chitose to other parts of Asia have been increasing. Japan Airlines (JAL) (☎ 011/231–4411 international; ☎ 011/231–0231 domestic), All Nippon Airways (ANA) (☎ 011/281–1212 international; 011/726–8800 domestic), and Japan Air System (JAS) (☎ 011/222–8111) use this airport. For information on arrival and departure times, call the individual airlines. For the airport itself (Hokkaido Airport Terminal Co.), dial 0123/23–0111.

BETWEEN THE AIRPORT AND CENTER CITY

Japan Railways (JR) has frequent train service between the airport terminal (Chitose Airport Station—Shin-Chitose Kuko—not Chitose City Station) and downtown Sapporo. The trip is usually made by "rapid transit" trains, costing ¥940 and taking about 40 minutes. ANA runs a shuttle bus (¥750) that connects with its flights at Chitose and its hotel, the ANA Zenniku, in Sapporo. The Chuo Bus (¥750) runs a shuttle between the airport and Sapporo's Grand Hotel. Taxis are available, but the distance between Sapporo and the airport makes them ridiculously expensive, so they are rarely used.

By Train

All JR trains come into the central station, located on the north side of downtown Sapporo. Trains arrive and depart for Honshu (sometimes involving a change of trains in Hakodate) about every two hours. As many as half a dozen trains run to and from Otaru every hour, while every half hour from 7 AM to 10 PM there are trains for Asahikawa, in central Hokkaido.

By Car

Sapporo has two expressways: the Doo Expressway, which heads southeast to Chitose and then veers southwest, to hug Hokkaido's underside as far as Muroran; and the Sasson Expressway, linking Otaru in the west with Asahikawa in the northeast.

Getting Around

Sapporo is a walking city with wide sidewalks; it's easy to find your way around. The **International Information Corner** (*see* Important Addresses and Numbers, *below*) at the Sapporo railway station has a city map, and most hotels have a smaller map marking their hotels and the major points of interest.

By Subway

Sapporo's subway is a pleasure. As in Toronto and Moscow, the trains have rubber wheels and run quietly. There are three lines: One (the Nanboku Line) runs south from the station past Susukino to Nakajima; a second (the Tozai Line) bisects the city from east to west. These two cross at Odori Station. A third subway line (Toho Line) opened at the end of 1988. It enters central Sapporo from the southeast of the city, then parallels the Nanboku Line from Odori Station to the JR station before branching off into the northeastern suburbs. The last trains set off around 11:30 and stop running at midnight. The basic fare covering about three stations is ¥180. There is a one-day open ticket for ¥950 that gives unlimited trips on the subway, bus, and streetcar, while a ¥600 "eco" ticket (encouraging citizens to leave their cars at home for the day) covers the same three types of public transport on the 5th and 20th of every month. These tickets are available at any subway station, though the most central ticket counters are at the Odori Station Underground Commuter's Ticket Office (⊙ Daily 10–6; closed Dec. 30–Jan. 3).

By Bus
Bus fares begin at ¥190. Buses follow the grid system and stop running at midnight.

By Streetcar
Sapporo also has a streetcar service with a flat fare of ¥170. However, it is confined to a single line connecting the Susukino entertainment area with Mt. Moiwa in the city's southwest (well away from the tourist attractions mentioned in this section), and has kept in business because of public affection rather than any profitability. In an effort to scrape a little more money out of the service, the city has made its streetcars available for party-hire, and it is not uncommon to see the vehicles trundling across town with a crowd of eating, drinking, merrymaking revelers on board.

By Taxi
Taxi meters start at ¥550; an average fare, such as from the train station to Susukino, runs about ¥730.

Important Addresses and Numbers

Emergencies
Police (☎ 110). **Ambulance** (☎ 119).

DOCTORS
City General Hospital (☎ 011/261–2281). **Hokkaido University Hospital** (☎ 011/716–1161).

DENTISTS
The Emergency Dental Clinic (☎ 011/511–7774); open evenings only, 7–11.

English-Language Bookstores
Outside Sapporo, finding English-language books is difficult, so you may want to browse in Sapporo's two largest bookstores with (limited) books in English: **Kinokuniya** (Daini Yuraku Bldg., 2F, S1, W1, ☎ 011/231–2131), on the south side of the TV Tower and accessible from Aurora Town, and **Maruzen** (4F, S1, W3, ☎ 011/241–7251), one block south of Odori Park, adjoining the Mitsukoshi Building above Odori subway station. The latter also sells small, interesting, Japanese-style gifts in its basement that, by the standards of the neighboring large stores, are fairly well priced. Smaller selections of books can be found in **Asamiya Bookstore** (Arche Bldg., B2, M3, W4, ☎ 011/241–3007), on the east side of Pole Town, and **Art Logos** (Parco Bldg., 7F, S1, W3, ☎ 011/214–2301), across the street from the Mitsukoshi Building.

Road Travel
For road-condition information during the winter, call 011/281–6511.

Tourist Information
The most helpful and informative places for information on Sapporo and on Hokkaido in general are the **International Information Corner** (Kokusai Joho Corner, ☎ 011/213–5062; ⊙ Daily 9–5, closed the 2nd and 4th Wed. of each month, 2nd Wed. only Jan., Feb., July–Sep.), in

the western Lilac Paseo of JR Sapporo Station, and the **Sapporo International Communication Plaza's** tourist office, **Plaza i** (ground floor, MN Building, Kita 1, Nishi 3, Chuo-ku, ☎ 011/211–3678; ⊘ Daily 9–5:30, closed Dec. 29–Jan. 3). Other offices that supply information include: **Sapporo City Tourism Dept. Office,** Nishi-2-chome, Kita 1, Chuo-ku, ☎ 011/211–2376; ⊘ Weekdays 8:45–5:15; closed holidays and Dec. 29–Jan. 3. **Hokkaido Tourist Association,** Keizai Center Building, Nishi-1-chome, Kita 2, Chuo-ku, ☎ 011/231–0941; ⊘ Weekdays 9–5; closed holidays.

Travel Agencies
The **Japan Travel Bureau** (☎ 011/241–6201).

U.S. Consulate
Kita 1, Nishi 28, Chuo-ku, ☎ 011/641–1115.

Exploring

The comforting fact about Sapporo is the simplicity of the city's layout. Streets running east to west are called *jo,* and those running north to south are called *chome.* These streets are numbered consecutively, and one block consists of about 100 meters square (approximately 100 yards by 100 yards).

Numbers in the margin correspond to points of interest on the Sapporo map.

Sapporo's few major sites of interest can easily be seen in a day. A **❶** good place to start your visit is at Sapporo's landmark, the **Tokeidai** (Clock Tower). Built in 1878 in the Russian style, with a clock from Boston added three years later, the Clock Tower is where Japanese tourists take photographs of one another to prove that they were in Sapporo. However, other than being on every Sapporo travel brochure, it is very ordinary to a Westerner's eye and has little architectural value. Inside the building, a small museum recounts the local history of Sapporo and includes such items as horse-drawn trams, but it lacks information about the Ainu village that preceded present-day Sapporo and from which the city takes its name. ("Sapporo" is derived from a combination of Ainu words meaning "a river running along a reed-filled plain.") ☞ *Free.* ⊘ *Tues.–Sun. 9–4. Closed the day after national holidays and Dec. 29–Jan. 3. (At press time, the Clock Tower was closed for repairs and was expected to reopen in July 1997.)*

Across the street from the Clock Tower, on the third floor of an office **❷** building fronted by the Royal Host restaurant, is the **Sapporo Kokusai Puraza** (International Communication Plaza). Established to facilitate commercial and cultural relations with the world beyond Japan, the center is the best place—far better than the tourist office—for suggestions on travel in Hokkaido and for meeting people who speak English. It is also a useful place to have something translated from Japanese into English. The center has a reading room with books, newspapers, and brochures in English. *Kita 1, Nishi 3, Chuo-ku,* ☎ *011/221–2105.* ⊘ *Weekdays 9–5:30. Closed national holidays and Dec. 29–Jan. 3.*

On the ground of the building is **Plaza i,** a tourist information service for Sapporo that is staffed by volunteers. They are extremely helpful and distribute free brochures, maps, and flyers on current happenings in town, and if they can't help you, they'll send you upstairs. The office will also send and receive faxes for travelers. You may want to

Sapporo

browse through its English-language books on Hokkaido and other islands of Japan and take a look at the display of local crafts. ☎ *011/211–3678,* FAX *011/219–0020.* ⊘ *Daily 9–5:30. Closed Dec. 29–Jan. 3.*

❸ On the other side of the Clock Tower is the **Hokkaido Tourist Association Office.** Little English is spoken here, and the staff are limited in the amount of useful advice they have to offer, but maps and brochures in English are available. A collection of products, including crafts, made in Hokkaido is for sale. *Keizai, Center Bldg., Nishi-2-chome, Kita 1, Chuo-ku,* ☎ *011/231–0941.* ⊘ *Weekdays 9–5. Closed holidays and Dec. 29–Jan. 3.*

★ **❹** Two blocks south of the Clock Tower is **Odori Koen,** a park in the median of a broad, 345-foot-wide avenue that runs east and west, bisecting the city center. Here, in the summer, office workers buy lunch from various food vendors and take in the sun, so long absent during the winter months. For the out-of-towner, it is a place to people-watch and to try Hokkaido corn on the cob—an overpriced yet delicious area speciality. It's first boiled, then roasted over charcoal and, just before it is handed to you, given a dash of soy sauce. In February the park displays large, lifelike snow sculptures made for the Sapporo Snow Festival, which has made the city famous. *(See* Nightlife, *below, and* Festivals and Seasonal Events *in* The Gold Guide, *above.)*

❺ At the east end of Odori Koen is the **TV Tower,** which stands at 470 feet. It's ugly, but the Sapporo Tourist Association promotes it for the view from its observation platform (⊘ Daily, hours vary; closed Dec. 30–Jan. 2). Don't be persuaded. It costs ¥600 for a view of the city that is better, and free, from any of the high-rise hotels.

Odori Koen is actually at the heart of Sapporo's downtown shopping center, where many of the shops are underground rather than lining the park. The shopping center is located at the intersection where Eki-mae-dori heads south from JR Sapporo Station and where the two subway lines intersect at the Odori Subway Station. Aboveground are large department stores. Two underground shopping malls (especially welcome during the five-month winters) attract shoppers and diners who come to browse as much as to buy or to eat. Underneath Odori Koen, from the TV Tower to Odori Station,

6 is **Aurora Town,** an arcade of shops and restaurants. At Odori Sta-
7 tion, Aurora Town turns south to **Pole Town,** a long mall that continues all the way to Susukino.

Running parallel to Odori Koen 2½ blocks to the south is a covered
8 arcade called **Tanuki Koji,** which many years ago was the city's main shopping street. (A *tanuki* is a raccoon-dog, which in Japanese mythology is known for its cunning and shiftiness; the arcade got its name because it used to be frequented by prostitutes, who displayed similar characteristics when it came to relieving their clients of their cash.) Stretching across several blocks, its sides crowded with many small shops selling clothing, footwear, electrical goods, records, and, inevitably, Ainu-style souvenirs of Hokkaido, Tanuki Koji offers considerably lower prices than the area's department stores. It also provides welcome shelter from the snow during the lengthy winter. Adding some variety to the arcade is the presence of several coffee and ramen shops, four cinemas, and a novelty shop specializing in magic tricks.

9 **Susukino,** Sapporo's entertainment district, is a nighttime reveler's paradise, with more than 5,000 bars and restaurants offering the Japanese equivalent to bacchanalian delights. (*See* Nightlife, *below.*) Because Susukino is for the night (until 5 AM, if you have the yen and stamina), let's return to Odori Station and walk up the main street, Eki-mae-dori, toward the JR station. Along this street are the major banks and airline offices. Here you can change your traveler's checks and confirm plane reservations. Once out of Sapporo, such matters are more difficult to accomplish.

As you walk toward the train station, on your left (west side) will be
10 the side entrance of the **Sapporo Grand Hotel,** a traditional European-style building with substantial pillars and majestic lobbies. Because it appears so out of place in Japan, especially in modern Sapporo, it seems even more of a landmark than the Clock Tower. The hotel has a bustling café looking out to the street, making it a convenient tea or coffee stop.

If you leave the Grand Hotel by its front entrance and go left, you will come to a complex of municipal buildings, on the right. Among them
11 is a large, redbrick building, the grandest structure in Sapporo: the **Docho Kyu Chosha** (Old Hokkaido Government Building), a pleasing Western-style building built in 1888 and now containing exhibits displaying the early development of Hokkaido. (☉ Weekdays 9–5; closed
12 national holidays and Dec. 29–Jan. 1.) Beyond are the **Shokubutsuen** (Botanical Gardens), with more than 5,000 plant varieties—a cool retreat in the summer, both for its green space and its shade from the sun. ☛ ¥400, plus ¥110 to visit the greenhouse. ☉ Tues.–Sun., Apr. 29–Sep. 30, 9–4; Oct. 1–Nov. 3, 9–3:30. Only the greenhouse is open Nov. 4–Apr. 28, weekdays 10–3, Sat. 10–noon. Closed national holidays and Dec. 28–Jan. 4.

⓭ Farther west is the **Hokkaido Migishi Kotaro Museum** (☛ ¥250), which was opened in 1983 for the sole purpose of housing 235 oil and water-color paintings, drawings, and prints by native son Migishi, who died in 1934 at the age of 31. The museum was designed to reflect the many changes of style that characterize the artist's career. On the next block **⓮** is the attractive **Hokkaidoritsu Kindai Bijutsukan** (Hokkaido Museum of Modern Art), with local and foreign exhibits (☛ ¥250 for the permanent exhibits only). Both museums, though not holding priceless works of art, enable foreigners to see what in Japanese art is appreciated by the Japanese and, in that sense, are worth visiting. ⊙ *Both museums Tues.–Sun. 10–5. Closed national holidays Nov.–Apr., on specially designated holidays, and Dec. 28–Apr. 1.*

Retrace your steps to the Botanical Gardens and then head north for ¾ kilometer (½ mile), and you'll come to the spacious grounds of **⓯** **Hokkaido Daigaku** (Hokkaido University), Japan's largest campus, with more than 12,000 students. The beautifully designed grounds make the campus another summer escape from the concrete to greenery and blossoming flowers. During the warmer months, the numerous green and open spaces connected by wide, lilac-lined avenues make Sapporo a particularly pleasant city.

Cut back southeast from the university campus and return to the **⓰** downtown area at the **JR Sapporo Station.** Underneath the station is another shopping mall with one mouth-watering section devoted to food stalls and restaurants. Recent expansion of the station has created a smart new shopping and restaurant complex known as **Paseo.** The restaurants are good, personable, and reasonably priced, while the shops tend to carry expensive designer merchandise. A post office is conveniently located on the East Concourse near the entrance for the train platforms.

★ **⓱** About a 15-minute walk east from the station and past the local ward office (about a ¥1,000 taxi ride from downtown) is the **Sapporo Beer Garden and Museum.** During the day, free tours around the redbrick museum are offered, acquainting visitors with the history and the modern brewing technology of Hokkaido's most famous product. However, the fun of coming here is the huge beer garden and the cavernous, three-tier beer hall. The beer hall, where most of the action occurs in the evening until closing at 9 PM, is similar in atmosphere to a German beer hall (it was a German, after all, who, when finding wild hops growing on Hokkaido, taught the local Japanese how to make beer), but instead of bratwurst, *genghis khan* (strips of mutton and vegetables cooked on a hot iron grill) is the favored meal. It's Sapporo's favorite dish, and the beer hall is the perfect place to try it. In the summer, the beer garden is both a day and evening gathering place for locals and visitors. Mugs of beer are downed with gusto amidst exclamations of "Kampai!" In the winter, around February, igloos and snow sculptures adorn the site. ⊙ *Museum daily 9–5 (9–6 in June, July, Aug.) Enter 80 minutes before closing time. Closed Dec. 29–Jan. 5. Reservations necessary. Request a guide who speaks some English.* ☎ *011/731–4368. Beer garden and beer halls 11:30–9 (see* Dining, *below).*

⓲ If you make the 20-minute walk from the Beer Garden and Museum to Odori Koen, you'll likely come across **Sapporo Factory** en route. This is one of the city's newest (opened in 1993) and most-vaunted attractions: Indeed, for the tourist more interested in shopping, eating, and drinking than in trekking around the sightseeing spots, Sapporo Factory offers enough boutiques, restaurants, and entertainment to fill an entire day. Small wonder it boasts of being a "town within a city." The complex occupies several buildings (including an old Sapporo Beer brewery, which retains its distinctive red brick and chimney), all but one linked by a second-floor passageway. Among the venues inside are a 1,500-seat beer restaurant, a wine cellar containing some 2,000 varieties of wine, a gigantic-screened IMAX theater, and a space museum. Most striking of all, however, is the 275-foot-high atrium, with an arching glass roof that shields an indoor garden and terrace from the worst that Hokkaido's climate can offer. It's the largest structure of its type in Japan. *Kita 2 Higashi 4, Chuo-ku.* ☉ *Stores 10–8; restaurants open 11–10 (although the American-style Nutberry Club doesn't close until 3 am).*

⑲ The last place to visit is **Nakajima Koen,** a park about 3 kilometers (2 miles) from the railway station. The easiest way to get there is by the Nanboku subway from the JR station to the Nakajima Koen stop; from here it's a couple minutes' walk to the park. Nakajima Koen has a playground with a small lake for boating, a beautiful rose garden, and the Nakajima Sports Center. The park also features two national cultural treasures, one Japanese and one Western. The **Hasso-an Teahouse,** harmoniously surrounded by a Japanese garden, is virtually the only traditional Japanese structure in Hokkaido and is in stark contrast to the new frontier style of architecture on the rest of the island (☉ May–Nov. 9–4). The other national treasure is **Hoheikan,** a Western-style building originally constructed as an imperial guest house (☉ 9–5; closed Dec. 29–Jan. 3). It is symbolic of an age when Hokkaido was colonized by Japan and the Meiji government looked to the West for the country's modern transformation.

Nightlife

★ **Susukino** is Sapporo's entertainment area and the largest of its kind north of Tokyo. More than 5,000 bars, restaurants, and nightclubs, all lit by lanterns and flashing signs, crowd into a compact area. It is mind-boggling and, in itself, justifies an overnight stay in Sapporo. Most of the bars stay open until the wee hours, as late as 5 AM, though the restaurants often close before midnight. Just make sure you know the type of bar before you enter. Aside from all kinds of restaurants, from the relatively inexpensive to expensive, there are several kinds of bars: the clubs with many conversational hostesses (¥10,000 and up); the snack bars, with a few conversational hostesses (they don't offer food, as their name suggests, only expensive *odoburu*—hors d'oeuvres); *izakaya,* for different kinds of food and drink; bars with entertainment, either taped video music you can sing along with (*karaoke* bars) or live bands; and "soaplands," which is the new name for Turkish baths or houses of pleasure. If at all possible, go to the clubs and snack bars with a Japanese acquaintance.

For agreeably mellow surroundings and a fine selection of cocktails and whiskies, try the popular **Blues Alley** in the basement of the Miyako Building (Minami 3 Nishi 3). It's worth paying the ¥1000 seating charge, for the atmosphere, the background blues music (plus sporadic live performances from a saxophonist-cum-pianist), and the generous hours: You can stay here until 5 AM (6 on weekends) if you want. Other Susukino bars that reflect the eclectic Japanese taste for foreign music and styles include **Gee** (Arc 36 Bldg., 2F, Minami 3 Nishi 6), a jazz-tinged venue that offers both British beer and Brazilian food; and the tiny-but-cozy **Anyway** (Mimatsu Muraoka Bldg., 6F, Minami 5 Nishi

2), whose affable, Stetson-wearing owner is besotted with country and western.

Izakaya are well-represented in Susukino, though one that offers a menu with a distinctly Hokkaido flavor is **Irohanihoheto,** on the second floor of the Bacchus Building (Minami 5 Nishi 4). Wine lovers might prefer the **Wine Bar** (New Hokusei Bldg., 9F, Minami 4 Nishi 3), which is reputed to be Sapporo's number one spot for young courting couples. Be warned, though, that you'll be hit by both a seating charge and a 10% service fee added to your bill.

Finally, for the adventurous, there is the district's strangest bar, the **Susukino Reien** (Green Bldg. No. 2, 8F, Minami 4 Nishi 3), which has been furnished to resemble an Asian cemetery. Despite the awful-sounding concept, it is surprisingly comfortable. The genial atmosphere is helped by the floor-staff, who'll entertain you with conjuring tricks when not serving drinks. Vulgarity does make an appearance around 2 AM, when, in a haunted house–style finale to the evening, the waiters don Halloween masks and unconvincing shrunken "heads" drop from the ceiling.

★ Though not nightlife per se, mention should be made here of Sapporo's best-known annual event. In the first week of February, the **Sapporo Snow Festival** is held, and it is the greatest of its kind. More than 300 lifelike sculptures, as large as 130 feet high, 50 feet deep, and 80 feet wide, are created each year. The history of the festival began in 1950 with six statues that were created to entertain the local citizens, depressed by the aftermath of the war and the long winter nights. Now the event is so large that sculptures may be seen in three sections of the city—Odori Koen, Makomanai, and Susukino. The festival attracts more than 2 million visitors each year.

EXCURSIONS AROUND HOKKAIDO

Because Sapporo is such a comfortable and reassuring city, it serves as a convenient base for making excursions into Hokkaido's interior. Following are three that cover the best of Hokkaido:

The first excursion, to Otaru and the Shakotan Peninsula northwest of Sapporo, requires a minimum of a day to complete with a rented car, or two days by public transport.

The second excursion travels southwest of Sapporo through the Shikotsu-Toya National Park and includes crystal-clear caldera lakes surrounded by mountains and hot-spring resorts. This excursion takes a minimum of two days by car, three by public transport, though you can shorten the itinerary to make it a day trip out of Sapporo.

The third and final excursion, which requires at least one week, heads into central Hokkaido through Daisetsuzan National Park, Akan National Park to the east coast, and the Sea of Okhotsk. From there, the itinerary follows the coast to Hokkaido's northernmost point at Cape Soya and over to the islands of Rebun and Rishiri before returning to Hokkaido.

Otaru and the Shakotan Peninsula

This first excursion goes northwest of Sapporo to Otaru on the coast. West of Otaru is the Shakotan Peninsula, which offers a taste of Hokkaido's rugged coastal scenery.

Getting There

Otaru is 48 minutes by train from Sapporo. By car on the expressway, Otaru is only 38 kilometers (24 miles) from Sapporo. Thirty minutes by local train beyond Otaru, the Shakotan Peninsula begins at Yoichi.

You can take the train as far as Yoichi. From there, buses travel around the peninsula as far as Yobetsu, where, unfortunately, the road then ends. Cars need to backtrack as far as Furubira and cross the center of the Shakotan Peninsula to Kamoenai via Tomaru Pass, a route that is closed in winter. (Perversely, motorists in this area face a different problem in summer, when the roads along the northern coast of the peninsula are often beset with traffic congestion.)

Numbers in the margin correspond to points of interest on the Hokkaido map.

Exploring

❶ **Otaru** is described as "famous for its canals and old Westernstyle buildings" by the Hokkaido Tourist Office. In truth, Otaru is a commercial city in the shadow of Sapporo. Very few of its 19th-century, wood-frame houses are left standing, and those are sandwiched between modern concrete structures. Instead, what you find is a traffic-congested center city with shops and office buildings, a busy port area from which ferries depart for Niigata to the south, and some ramshackle suburbs.

The major attractions in Otaru are available only in the evening. Otaru has two of Hokkaido's best sashimi restaurants, **Uoisshin** (1-11-1 Hanazono, ☎ 0134/32–5202) and **Isshintasuke** (1-5-3 Hanazono, ☎ 0134/34–1790). Connoisseurs of sashimi from Sapporo will make a special trip to these two restaurants, and, because there is frequent train service to and from Sapporo, you can do the same. Your Sapporo hotel will be happy to make reservations at either restaurant; reservations are essential. Should you find yourself with a couple of hours to spare, take a 10-minute walk from the JR Otaru Station to the Otaru Canal section of town, which has undergone considerable restoration. Even the gas lanterns are now in working order. The area has numerous restaurants and cafés and many restored turn-of-the century buildings, including the **Otaru Hakubutsukan** (City Museum; ☛ ¥100, though extra may be charged for special exhibitions; ☉ Tues.–Sun. 9:30–5, closed the day after national holidays), in a former warehouse, which combines a natural history section with displays about the town's development since the 19th century. Also by the canal are an arts and crafts gallery, a glassware shop, and a toy museum. You can first collect a map from the Otaru Tourist Office (☎ 0134/29–1333; ☉ Daily 9–6), secreted away in a small wooden building to the left of the JR station.

❷ We recommend not dallying in Otaru but continuing west along the coast road leading to **Yoichi.** Before Yoichi are some of Hokkaido's best sandy beaches; once through Yoichi, these beaches soon give way to
★ cliffs rising out of the sea. This is the beginning of the **Shakotan Peninsula.** Two mountain peaks, Yobetsu (4,019 feet) and Shakotan (4,258 feet), dominate the peninsula's interior. On the north coast are two capes, Shakotan and Kamui, on its eastern and western tips. Sentimental Japanese go to Kamui for the sunsets over the Sea of Japan.

The Shakotan is a sample of the real Hokkaido. Cliffs stave off the endless surging sea, while volcanic mountains dominate the interior. Thick forests blanket the slopes with dark, rich greens, and ravines crease the mountainsides. The Shakotan Peninsula is nature in full drama.

Cape Soya

Wakkanai

Rebun Island
Kafuka
Oshidomari
Kutsugata
Rishiri Island

Lake Kutcharo

Hama Tonbetsu

Esashi

Horonobe

238

KITAMI MTNS.

Ok

Monbetsu

Sea of Japan

Tomamae

Nayoro

Taking

Mt. Teshio

Rumoi

Mashike

Asahikawa

Sounkye

Mt. Asahi

Asahidake Onsen
Shirogane Onsen

Lake Da
Daiset
Nation

Cape Shakotan
Yobetsu
Cape Kamui
Tomaru Pass
Kamoenai
Iwanai

Furubira
Yoichi
Otaru

Ishikari Bay

Furano

Mt. Tokachi

Lake Shiko

Mt. Tengu

Jozankei Onsen

Sapporo

Mt. Yubari

Obi

Iwamizawa

Mt. Niseko-annupuri

Nakayama Pass

Chitose

Shikotsu-Toya National Park

HIDAKA RANGE

Mt. Yotei

Toyako Onsen

Lake Shikotsu

Noboribetsu Onsen

Tomakomai
Shiraoi

Nibutani

Tomikawa

Hiro-o

Mt. Apoi

Uchiura Bay

Muroran

Oshima Peninsula

5

Komagadake

Esashi

Hakodate

Fukushima

Tsugaru Straits

N

Seikan Tunnel

TO AOMORI

Minmaya

HONSHU

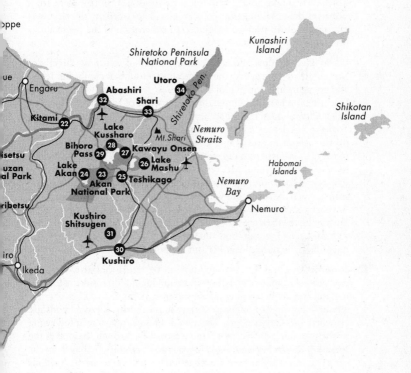

❸ The road from Yoichi circles the peninsula, keeping to the coast as much as the cliffs allow. At **Yobetsu,** near Cape Kamui, the corniche road is even more spectacular as it heads south to Iwanai. Unfortunately, soon after Yobetsu the road becomes a track, unsuitable for cars at the time this book goes to print. Unless you can pass this stretch of road, you ❹ have to drive back to **Furubira** and cross the peninsula by taking the ❺ hairpin road (closed in winter) through **Tomaru Pass** for a thrilling drive ❻ ❼ that skirts Mt. Yobetsu to **Kamoenai** and then goes down to **Iwanai.**

From Iwanai a road cuts across the base of the peninsula back to Otaru. There is also the alternative, at Iwanai, to go south and combine this excursion with one through Shikotsu-Toya National Park (*see below*).

If you want to tour the northern coast of the peninsula by public transport, start by taking the train from Sapporo through Otaru to Yoichi. Then take a bus from Yoichi to Yobetsu. Unfortunately, from Yobetsu, the only direction you can go is backward, as the ferry service that used to transport sightseers farther around the peninsula is no longer in operation.

★ ❽ If you have the time and use of a car, instead of returning directly to Sapporo from Otaru, take the picturesque detour that climbs **Mt. Tengu** and goes through one of Hokkaido's most scenic mountain passes before reaching Jozankei Onsen, on the outskirts of Sapporo. The detour will add two hours, but the scenery up through the mountains is lovely. To make this detour, take the Otaru–Jozankei Highway, which branches off the Sasson Expressway 5 kilometers (3 miles) east of Otaru. The road heads straight into the mountains and follows a ravine that winds its way up and around Mt. Tengu before descending to Jozankei. The forests and rock outcroppings make this trip especially beautiful in late spring, when the patches of white snow are melting into crystal streams. Another good time for this journey is autumn, when golden leaves stand out among the dark green of the conifers. It is possible to go from Otaru to Jozankei by bus, but these run infrequently. There are, however, frequent buses between Jozankei and Sapporo.

❾ **Jozankei Onsen** is a year-round hot-spring resort that attracts skiers from all over Japan during the winter and Hokkaido residents for hiking and weekend camping in the summer. Because Jozankei is virtually an extension of Sapporo's sprawling suburbs, the weekends are crowded with day-trippers. The actual ski area, which is in full swing by the beginning of December (the season lasts through May), is at the **Jozankei Kogen International Skiground,** 25 minutes by bus from the spa. The resort town itself is wedged in a small valley in the foothills beneath the mountains of Shikotsu-Toya National Park. Were it not for the modern, square-block hotels, the village would be beautiful. Unfortunately, while it has all the creature comforts of a resort, plus the hot springs, the hotels' architects have managed to deface nature's beauty. Still, refreshment at a hot spring will be rewarding before heading back to Sapporo.

Shikotsu-Toya National Park

The second excursion loops around the Shikotsu-Toya National Park and includes traveling through Jozankei Onsen, up through Nakayama Pass, down to Toyako (Lake Toya), and on to the hot-spring spa resorts of Toyako Onsen and Noboribetsu Onsen before returning to Sapporo via the Ainu village at Shiraoi and Lake Shikotsu. The area of Shikotsu-Toya National Park, about 100 kilometers (60 miles) southwest of Sapporo, is full of old and young volcanoes, mountains, forests, lakes, hot springs, and several hotels.

Getting There

Although the itinerary described below is by road from Sapporo, it can be accomplished by bus and train. It is also possible to do only part of this excursion, as there are direct buses from Sapporo to Toyako Onsen, Noboribetsu Onsen, and Lake Shikotsu, as well as from Toyako Onsen to Noboribetsu Onsen.

BY TRAIN

Toyako Onsen and Noboribetsu Onsen are easily accessible by train from Sapporo on the JR Sapporo–Hakodate Line. For Toyako Onsen, disembark from the train at the JR Toya station for a 15-minute bus ride to the lake. For Noboribetsu Onsen, disembark from the train at Noboribetsu and then take the Donan bus (a 13-minute ride) to Noboribetsu Onsen.

BY BUS

The direct bus service from Sapporo to Toyako Onsen via Nakayama Pass takes two hours and 50 minutes. Fare: ¥2,550; reservations necessary.

Direct bus coaches, the Chuo and the Donan lines, also run from Sapporo to Noboribetsu Onsen; this trip takes two hours and 45 minutes. Fare: ¥1,700; reservations necessary.

Between Toyako Onsen and Noboribetsu via the Orofure Pass, a one-hour-and-40-minute bus ride operates five times daily from June 1 to October 31; only one bus a day makes this journey during the rest of the year. Fare: ¥1,450; reservations necessary.

Exploring

Leaving Sapporo by car to the first destination, Jozankei, is easy. Take the road running along the west side of the Botanical Gardens; it is a straight run to Jozankei, less than an hour's drive south of the city. All along this itinerary are sufficient signs in *romaji* (Japanese written in Roman script) to give you directional confidence, and the road number (Route 230) is frequently displayed.

Once through Jozankei Onsen (*see above*), the twisting, winding road up through the ravine warns of the high drama of the mountains ahead. The final ascent to 2,742 feet is through a tunnel that opens out at **Nakayama Pass,** where the traveler discovers wide, sweeping panoramas of lonely mountains and peopled plains. In the distance, beyond the surrounding mountain peaks, stands **Mt. Yotei,** rising out of the plains. Mt. Yotei's near-perfect conical shape leads to automatic comparisons to Mt. Fuji, but any native worth his salt would say his Mt. Yotei has no competition.

There is a souvenir shop to the side of the road at Nakayama Pass, with a restaurant called Potato Daishaku on its second floor where you can buy food and refreshments to help you get your breath back after the drive up and before the descent.

Toyako

The road descends from the pass to Kimobetsu and Rusutsu, where soon after a flat stretch **Toyako** (Lake Toya) suddenly appears. The lake, in a collapsed volcanic cone, is almost circular. Just after the first glimpse of the lake, the inevitable crowd of small shops appears on either side of the road, though at least one of them is to be commended for the quality of the ice cream it sells. From here you get views that embrace the northern circumference of the lake and its small islands, which are the peaks of smaller volcanoes that pop up in the lake's middle.

⑪ The road from the ice cream shop descends to the lake and follows the shore to **Toyako Onsen,** at the southwestern edge of the lake. This spa town is the chief holiday center for this part of the Shikotsu-Toya Park and, consequently, is loaded with hotels, inns, and souvenir shops. The hotels are open all year, but the busiest time is the summer (June through August), when Japanese families come by the droves for trout fishing, hiking, boating, visiting Nakajima (the largest of the cluster of islands in the center of the lake), and, of course, taking the curative waters of the hot springs.

Indeed, Toyako Onsen is famous for its curative waters, but the geographical wonder is **Showa Shinzan,** Japan's newest volcano, which made its first appearance in 1943. Showa Shinzan surprised everyone, but no one more than the farmer who witnessed the volcano's emergence from his wheat field. The volcano grew steadily during the next two years, until it reached its final height of 1,312 feet. Now the nearby **Abuta Kazan Kagakukan** (Volcanic Science Museum) chronicles both Showa Shinzan's development and the volcanic activity of the entire area.

Perhaps not to be outdone, one mountain over from Showa Shinzan, **Mt. Usu,** erupted in 1977. It did so with flair, sending out 200 tremors an hour before blowing its top. This advance notice allowed local residents to flee and photographers to set up their cameras. Their photographs are shown amid sound effects of thunder and lightning at the Abuta Kazan Kagakukan, located between the lakeside and the foot of Mt. Usu. The presentation is dramatically realistic and better seen after, rather than before, taking the cable car to the top of Mt. Usu for the superb views of Lake Toya.

From Toyako Onsen, the road continues around the lake through Sobetsu Onsen, a quieter version of Toyako Onsen. Here we take Route 453 away from the lake; a little farther on, the road forks, with the right-hand branch (the one we take, as does the Donan bus line; closed in the winter) heading southeast over the mountains to **Noboribetsu.** The 90-minute trip brings you to **Orofure Pass** (3,051 feet) and offers tremendous views of soaring mountains, hidden valleys, and, in the distance, Lake Toya, Mt. Yotei, Lake Kuttara, and the Pacific Ocean.

(Do not confuse Noboribetsu Onsen with Noboribetsu, a city on the coast that is 13 minutes away by bus from its namesake spa town. Noboribetsu is an ugly industrial city at which the JR trains stop. From the station, a shuttle bus runs up to Noboribetsu Onsen. Indeed, the whole coastal area from Date to Tomakomai is an industrial eyesore, made worse by a sagging regional economy.)

Noboribetsu Onsen

★ ⑫ **Noboribetsu Onsen** is the most famous spa in Hokkaido, perhaps even in all of Japan. It's said that some 34,300 gallons of water are pumped out every hour, making it the most prodigious hot spring in Asia. Its 11 types of hot-spring waters are said to cure ailments ranging from rheumatism to diabetes to menopausal problems. Most hotels have their own baths, and the grandest of them all are the baths at the **Dai-ichi Takimotokan.** This hotel is a monstrosity with 401 rooms, video game halls, buffet dining rooms, and evening cabarets, but its baths are the best. The 12 pools in each area (men's and women's) have seven different waters at varying temperatures. Signs above each pool are in

Japanese, so which minerals are in the waters and what they do to one's body remain mysteries to most foreigners. The solution is just to try them. Even for non-hot-spring fanatics, these baths are worth the ¥2,000 nonresident fee to attend, if only for the view beyond the bathhouse's plate-glass window: It looks upon the steaming, volcanic gases of Jigokudani (*see below*). On the floor beneath the baths is a swimming pool with a slide for those who like their water straight. The baths are open to nonresidents only from 9 to 3, though once in you can stay until 5 PM.

★ A couple hundred yards from the village is **Jigokudani** (The Valley of Hell), a volcanic crater that looks like a bow-shape valley. Boiling water spurts out of thousands of holes, sounding like the heartbeat of the earth itself, though, because of its strong sulfur smell, others have described it differently. Apparently, the Dante-like inferno is a popular place for suicides. Entire families have been known to make their last leaps from here.

Nearby on the slopes of Mt. Shirohei, are the **Bear Ranch** and **Ukara-no-Sato,** the latter a commercial replica of an Ainu village; access is via the cable car from Noboribetsu Onsen. The few elderly Ainu who perform a dance or two every couple of hours at Ukara-no-Sato look bored to tears. The bears, all 180 of them, are tame and lethargic. The ranch and the four replica Ainu houses are solely for the tourists, but, perhaps because of its location and because the bears are not in minuscule cages, the area is less depressing than the Ainu village at Shiraoi (*see below*). ☛ *¥2,300 (including gondola).* ⊙ *Ukara-no Sato: daily June–Oct., 6 AM–7 PM June–Aug., 7 AM–6 PM Sept.–Oct. (closed in winter).* ⊙ *Bear Ranch daily.*

Five kilometers (3 miles) south of Noboribetsu Onsen is **Date Jidai Mura,** a reconstructed Edo village named for the members of the Date clan who migrated here from Sendai after the fall of the Shogunate. The complex includes samurai houses and geisha pleasure palaces watched over by actors attired in traditional garb. A visit here is probably not worth the hefty fee. ☎ *0143/83–3311.* ☛ *¥500 parking, ¥2,500 to enter the grounds only, ¥3,000 to enter grounds and buildings.* ⊙ *Daily, Apr.–Nov. 9–5; Dec.–Mar. 9–4.*

The village of Noboribetsu Onsen is a tourist town, so expect masses of hotels and souvenir shops. However, though the modern hotel architecture could be far more aesthetic and in tune with its surroundings of mountains and forests, the village is not without charm. Its main street still has cobblestones, and a stream runs through the village. More important, the buildings do not block out the presence of the mountains.

Traveling along Route 36 from Noboribetsu toward Tomakomai, you pass through the coastal town of Shiraoi, where there's yet another Ainu museum and reconstructed Ainu village, Shiraoi Porota Kotan. However, because of the dispirited-looking Ainu participants and the miserable conditions of the bear cages, the atmosphere is even grimmer than at Ukara-no-Sato. If you have a few hours to spare, rather than stopping here a better idea might be to continue along the coast from Tomakomai as far as the village of Tomikawa, where you can turn north

★ ⓭ along Route 237 to reach the village of **Nibutani** and the Ainu heartland. (A small railway line provides transport between Tomakomai and Tomikawa. To the right of JR Tomikawa Station you can catch a bus to take you the rest of the way. Don't make the mistake of getting off the bus too early, at the village of Biratori. Though it is described on brochures as a "village," Nibutani scarcely even qualifies as that, and is a handful of buildings tucked away into the countryside a few miles beyond Birator.)

Nibutani is one of the very last places in Hokkaido with a sizeable Ainu population (or rather, part-Ainu—the number of pure-blooded Ainu is very small now). Consequently, though the usual souvenir shops are much in evidence, there's some comfort in knowing your money has a better chance of finding its way into the pockets of proper Ainu. Besides, the village has an excellent museum, the **Nibutani Ainu Bunka Hakubutsukan** (Nibutani Ainu Culture Museum; ☛ ¥300; ☯ Tues.–Sun. 9:30–4:30; closed Dec. 16–Jan. 15), on the left side of the road. No information is given in English, but a selection of videos lets you sample the eerie sound of traditional Ainu chants and songs. On the other side of the road is a smaller museum, the **Kayano Shigeru Ainu Memorial Museum** (☛ ¥300; ☯ Apr.–Nov., daily 9–5), that displays artifacts collected by Shigeru Kayano, the most prominent Ainu activist and now a member of Japan's House of Councillors. Despite Kayano's high public profile and busy schedule, it is not unheard of to find him manning the ticket counter of his own museum. The surrounding rolling hills and spacious horse ranches make Nibutani a beguiling place to visit in summer, though it has been spoiled somewhat by the building of a new dam that put part of the area underwater (much of the lost land being of sacred or economic value to the local Ainu; even in the 1990s, the Japanese authorities have not treated them sympathetically).

★ ⑭ Your last stop before returning to Sapporo should be **Lake Shikotsu.** To reach the lake, travel to Tomakomai on the freeway and follow Route 276 to Shikotsu Onsen (or by train to Tomakomai from either Noboribetsu or Tomikawa; then it's a 40-minute bus ride from Tomakomai Station).

Lake Shikotsu is the deepest lake in Hokkaido (outfathomed only by Honshu's Lake Tazawa as the deepest in all of Japan). Swimmers should remember that although the beach shelves gently for 33 feet, it drops suddenly to an eventual depth of 1,191 feet. The lake's shape is a classic caldera except for the two volcanoes, which have risen to crumble its periphery on both the north and south shores. The southern volcano, Mt. Tarumae, is now dead, though its northern counterpart, Mt. Eniwa, remains active. At the base of Mt. Eniwa is **Marukoma Onsen,** whose *rotenburo* (outdoor thermal springs) along the lakeshore were, until recently, among the last places in Japan to offer mixed bathing.

Rental boats are available for leisurely drifting around the lake, and sightseeing boats offer tours. *½-hr. trips halfway around the lake cost ¥930.*

From Lake Shikotsu, the quickest route back to Sapporo (by car or bus) is via Chitose and up the expressway. You could also return to Tomakomai by bus and take the JR train back westward in the direction of Hakodate, or take the bus to Chitose Kuko (Chitose Airport) and get the JR train to Sapporo.

Central Hokkaido, the Sea of Okhotsk, and the Northern Cape

The third excursion goes east from Sapporo to Daisetsuzan National Park, on to Akan National Park, and then to the Sea of Okhotsk on the east coast. From there the route quickly goes to Hokkaido's northernmost cape and to the islands of Rebun and Rishiri before returning to Sapporo.

Getting Around

This journey may be accomplished entirely by train and bus. But because traveling between Daisetsuzan and Akan requires several bus changes, a rented car is more convenient and more enjoyable for this part of the excursion. However, we do recommend taking the train to Asahikawa and renting a car from there. Also, it is a long drive north of Monbetsu along the coast of the Sea of Okhotsk to Hokkaido's north cape. Therefore, we recommend returning the car to Asahikawa, or dropping it off at Monbetsu, for travels north to Wakkanai and Rebun and Rishiri islands. Then, either take the train or fly back to Sapporo.

Exploring

⑮ The main gateway to Daisetsuzan National Park is **Asahikawa,** Hokkaido's second largest city. Asahikawa is vast and sprawling, even though it was only in 1885 that the first pioneers established their base here. Now 365,000 people reside in an area of 750 square kilometers (300 square miles). The endless suburbs are depressing, but the center of town is small, easy to navigate, and friendly. Several international hotels, including the sparkling Palace Hotel (*see* Lodging, *below*), are in the center of downtown, close to the pedestrian shopping mall (the first such car-free mall in Japan) and the nightly scene of restaurants, izakaya, and bars.

Asahikawa's major attractions are the **Ainu Kinenkan** (memorial hall) and the **Ice Festival** in February. The Ainu Kinenkan is a reasonably good Ainu museum, though slightly ramshackle and certainly not as slick as that in Noboribetsu. However, like the Kayano Shigeru Ainu Memorial Museum, it does have the moral advantage of being run by a genuine Ainu, a man called Kaneto Kawamura, whose family has lived in the Asahikawa area for seven generations. There's a feeling that the museum really does exist to educate people about Ainu culture, rather than to cynically exploit it for money. Don't confuse this museum with the "Traditional Ainu Village" in Arashiyama Park (☎ 0166/51– 2461, ☛ ¥300, ☉ Daily 9–5, closed in winter, though it can be opened on request). The Ice Festival is a smaller version of Sapporo's Snow Festival (200 sculptures, compared with the 300 at Sapporo), but Asahikawa's has more of a country-fair feel.

Several routes lead from Asahikawa into Daisetsuzan National Park, but only one runs completely through the park, from north to south: Asahikawa to Sounkyo, through the park and on to Obihiro. Other roads, mainly from the west, make stabs into the mountains here and there but come to a dead end.

⑯ On the west side of the park, the spa towns of **Asahidake Onsen** and ⑰ **Shirogane Onsen** serve as hiking centers in the summer and ski resorts in the winter. Shirogane, at 2,461 feet, has had especially good skiing since its mountain, Mt. Tokachi, erupted in 1962 to form a blanket of lava, making a superb ski bowl. (Since then, Mt. Tokachi erupted again, in 1988.) At Asahidake Onsen, you can take a cable car up Mt. Asahidake (Hokkaido's highest mountain) to a height of 5,250 feet, and hike for two hours to the 7,513-foot summit. In the late spring and early summer, the slopes are blanketed with alpine flowers. In winter, this area offers both the earliest and latest skiing in Japan.

Daisetsuzan National Park

The geographical center of Hokkaido and the largest of Japan's national parks, **Daisetsuzan** (Great Snow Mountains) contains the very ⑱ essence of rugged Hokkaido: vast plains, soaring mountain peaks, hidden gorges, cascading waterfalls, forests, wildflowers, a spa resort, hiking trails, and wilderness. Daisetsuzan refers to the park's five major peaks, all of them towering more than 6,500 feet. Their presence dominates the area and controls human entry into the park.

★ **⑲** For an excursion through the park, the first place to head for is **Sounkyo,** less than two hours southeast by car from Asahikawa. Or you can take the bus from in front of Asahikawa's JR station, which goes directly to Sounkyo Onsen. If you are using a Japan Rail Pass, you can save some money by taking the JR train to Kamikawa Station and transfering onto the Dohoku bus for the 30-minute run to Sounkyo.

Sounkyo (*kyo* means "gorge") is the park's most scenic attraction, a 15-mile ravine extending into the park from its northeast entrance. For a 5-mile stretch, sheer cliff walls rise on both sides of the canyon as the road winds up into the mountains. Halfway up is the Sounkyo Onsen spa resort. How the Japanese are able to abuse scenic splendors with their ugly resort hotels is beyond belief. But they do, and Sounkyo Onsen is yet another example. One hotel in particular, the Choyotei Hotel, sticks out as an eyesore of concrete. Sitting on a bluff, the hotel dominates what otherwise would be a dramatic view of the gorge. Instead, guests of the hotel do have a magnificent view but also a view of other concrete hotels down the gorge. Still, you have no option but to stay in Sounkyo Onsen if you choose to stay in this area of the park. Drop by the **Sounkyo Tourist Information Center** (☏ 01658/2–1811) for maps. For assistance in finding lodging, contact the **Sounkyo Tourist Accommodation Office** (☏ 01658/5–3350). You can also try the small youth hostel (☏ 01658/5–3418.)

Resting precariously on the side of the gorge are a couple of grocery stores, some houses, and a couple of inns and restaurants, plus the inevitable souvenir shops that make up the village of Sounkyo. There is also the small **Sounkyo Museum** (☏ 01658/5–3427, ◷ 9–5), which has exhibits on the formation of Mt. Daisetsu. Activities take place in the resort hotels, not in the village, and during the day most people are out on the trails hiking through the park. One popular trip is to use the combination of a seven-minute gondola, or ropeway, ride (cost: ¥800 one-way) and a 15-minute ride on a chair lift (cost: ¥280 one-way) from Sounkyo up Kurodake for panoramic views over the Daisetsuzan range. For the best views, including one looking over Sounkyo, take the hour's walk to the very top. In July or August the mountain is bedecked in alpine flowers. Another activity is to rent a bicycle from Sounkyo's bus terminal (cost: ¥1,500 a day) and pedal through the gorge. A bicycle has the advantage over a car because the road goes through dark tunnels, blocking out the views, whereas the bike path skirts the gorge. The area's bicycle paths are also good for walking along.

Three kilometers (2 miles) up the road from Sounkyo Onsen are two picturesque waterfalls, **Ryusei-no-taki** (Shooting Star) and **Ginga-no-taki** (Milky Way). Neither is dramatic, but because they are like twins, separated only by a protruding cliff face called Buddhist Rock, they form a balanced beauty. The road continues past the falls, following the Ishikawa (river) through perpendicular cliffs and fluted columns of rock until it reaches the dammed-up **Lake Daisetsu.** The dam is a feat of engineering, its walls constructed only of earth and rubble. In itself, the dam has no particular visual merit, but the lake behind has islands that appear to float and a surrounding backdrop of mountains clad with conifers.

At the lake the road divides. The right fork, Route 273, goes south and traverses the rough wilderness and least visited part of the park. The road has been upgraded to avoid closure in winter, but there are no public buses. If you do not have a car, you must hitchhike as far as **Nukabira,** where you can catch buses and trains. This dramatic route climbs up through **Mikuni Pass** and drops down to lush valleys and through small ghost towns. In one such ghost town, **Mitsumata,** stop in at the only restaurant, where you will be enthusiastically welcomed with a dish of *shika* (deer) soba—noodles with deer meat. So fortified, it is an easy 18-kilometer (11-mile) run into **Nukabira** and civilization.

㉑ Nukabira is a quiet spa town close to **Lake Shikaribetsu,** the park's only natural lake. In the winter, toward the end of December, the lake freezes over and an igloo village is established on the ice, where several weddings with white-clad brides are performed with great ceremony. In early March, the igloo village becomes the site of the local festival, the Shikaribetsu Kotan Festival.

㉒ Back at Lake Daisetsu: The left fork, Route 39, veers east to **Kitami** and Abashiri on the Sea of Okhotsk. The road is well paved, and buses make frequent trips between Sounkyo Onsen and Kitami. As spectacular as the route south, this road to Kitami climbs over the forested mountains and breaks through the peaks at Sekihoku Pass. However, the distance is short, and within 19 kilometers (12 miles) from the lake the road has left Daisetsuzan National Park to descend among flat fields of peppermint that sparkle white and purple in summer.

The road continues to Kitami and Abashiri on Hokkaido's east coast; however, south of Kitami is Akan National Park.

Akan National Park

㉓ **Akan National Park** rivals Shikotsu-Toya National Park for its scenic combination of lakes and mountains. And while the mountains are not as high as those in Daisetsuzan, they are no less imposing. In addition, Akan has three major lakes, each of which has a unique character. And, crucial to the success of any resort in Japan, the park has an abundance of thermal springs.

GETTING AROUND

There is virtually no train service through the park except for the JR Kunmo Line from Kushiro on the Pacific coast north to Shari and Abashiri. Trains on this line stop at Mashu and Kawayu Onsen.

There are buses to Lake Akan from Kushiro and Kitami. It is also possible to travel by bus from Lake Akan to Abashiri, if you change buses in the town of Bihiro.

★ **㉔** From Kitami a road heads south to the small town of Tsubetsu, where it joins Route 240, entering Akan National Park shortly before **Lake Akan.** From the southern part of Daisetsuzan National Park at Nukabira, a road to Kamishihoro continues to Ashoro, which connects with Route 241; this runs directly to Akan. A small number of bicycles are available for rent at the Akan Bus Terminal and at Akan View Hotel.

EXPLORING

The resort on the western side of Lake Akan is watched over by the smoking volcanoes **Me-Akan** and **O-Akan** (Mr. and Mrs. Akan). The lake itself is famous for *marimo*—green balls of algae that may be as small as a Ping-Pong ball or as large as a soccer ball (the latter taking up to 500 years to form). Marimo are rare, and the only other areas they can be found are in Lake Yamanaka near Mt. Fuji, and in a few lakes in North America, Siberia, and Switzerland. These strange plants act much like submarines, photosynthesizing by absorbing carbon dioxide from the water and then rising to the surface, where they exhale oxygen and sink. They also serve as weather forecasters, rising closer to the surface when bright sunshine increases photosynthesis than they do when inclement weather portends and light levels drop. Lake Akan is especially beautiful in the winter when it is frozen over and surrounded by snow-covered mountains. A popular sport from January to March is skating between the *wakasagi* (smelt) fishermen. The wakasagi are hooked from ice holes and laid on the ice to immediately freeze. Their freshness makes them popular minced and eaten raw, though some eat them fried.

The town of **Akan-kohan** is the major resort area. This small village has expanded around the lake as new hotels are built. As is true in so much of Hokkaido, the hotels are not very attractive. The key is to obtain a room over the lake so that you are looking at nature's and not man's creation. The village center is kitschily dressed up for tourists and cluttered with souvenir shops with endless rows of carved bears. The bears are great in number here because a small Ainu population lives in the village.

From Akan the road to Teshikaga runs along the Akan Traverse. The distance is only 51 kilometers (32 miles), but it has more than its share of scenery. The road winds past O-Akan, and at one point you can look over the drop-off to the right and its volcanic cone almost seems at eye level. It's not a road to be driven at night; not only are the views obscured, but there is also the possibility of encountering a bear! However, there is a greater risk of smashing into a deer, mesmerized by the glare of your headlights. The local bus between Akan and Teshikaga takes this road and stops at the Sokodai, an observational lookout, though only to collect and drop off passengers.

㉕ Teshikaga is a small resort town with a few Japanese inns; its JR station goes under the name of "Mashu." The Mashu Onsen is nearby. Lake Mashu itself is a 20-minute drive (35 minutes by bus to the nearest observation point) from Teshikaga.

★ **㉖ Lake Mashu** is ringed by 656-foot-high rock walls. Curiously, no water has been found to either enter or leave the lake, so what goes on in its 695-foot depths is anybody's guess. Perhaps that mystery and the dark blue water combine to exert a strange hypnotic effect and cause tourists to stare endlessly down from the cliffs into the lake. These cliff sides are incredibly steep and have few or no footholds. You may live longer if you forgo the pleasure of inspecting the water's clarity, said to be clear to a depth of 115 feet. Instead, appreciate the lake from its two observation spots on the west rim. You'll recognize them by the parking lots and the buildings housing souvenir and food stands.

The road continues past Lake Mashu for 14 kilometers (9 miles) to **㉗ Kawayu Onsen,** lined with relatively expensive hotels (with mostly Japanese-style rooms) for those who believe in its curative hot springs. Kawayu is not particularly attractive. However, just before Kawayu is **Io-san,** an active volcano that emits sulfurous steam from vents in two ravines. There is a parking lot and souvenir/grocery store just off the road. Buy a couple of fresh eggs from the store, then walk up to one of the saucepan-size pools and boil them.

㉘ The road from Kawayu hugs the eastern side of **Lake Kussharo,** and connects with Route 243 to the south. There are various hotels and campgrounds along the shore. Lake Kussharo (sometimes spelled Kutcharo) is Akan National Park's largest lake. Once it had a nearly perfect caldera shape, but other volcanoes have since sprung up and caused its shores to become flat and less dramatic. It is, however, an ideal area for camping and is popular with families who come for boating and paddling in the water. There are also a couple of natural hot-springs that can be used free of charge. One other tourist attraction has been enthusiastically promoted in recent years—perhaps with an eye on the profits being made on the shores of Scotland's Loch Ness: "Kusshie," a creature said to inhabit the lake's depths. The lake is at its finest in the autumn, when the different shades of golds and greens on the trees extend from the lake shore into the higher mountain altitudes.

29 At the northwest end of the lake, the road climbs up **Bihoro Pass,** affording the last great view of Akan National Park's mountains and the green waters of Lake Kussh021 below. At Bihoro the road swings west back toward Asahikawa or northeast to Abashiri.

An alternative exit from Akan National Park is to return from the lake to Kawayu Hot Springs and continue 3 kilometers (2 miles) to a "T" junction and the JR Kawayu Station. There, take either Route 391 north-**30** east or the train to Abashiri, or make a side trip south to **Kushiro,** either by train or car.

A word or two about Kushiro before discussing Abashiri and the Sea of Okhotsk: Kushiro is a port city of no great appeal that used to be known for its rather seedy entertainment area for sailors and the tourists coming in off the Tokyo ferry. But the city is getting a new lease on life. Part of the old waterfront has been restored and now has a complex called, mysteriously, MOO-EGG, which contains many souvenir shops and food stalls, cafés, a small botanical garden, and a popular ice cream stand. Even the entertainment district has some revamped bars with traditional fireplaces where fish is cooked to order. Just to **★ 31** the north and west of Kushiro (35 minutes by bus) is **Kushiro Shitsugen** (Great Marsh), constituting 60% of Japan's marshland and home to the red-crested *tancho* (crane). These birds were ruthlessly hunted at the beginning of this century and were even believed to be extinct, until a handful of survivors were discovered in 1924; they have slowly come back and now number about 650. The crane—long-legged, pointy-billed, with a white body trimmed in black and a scarlet cap on its head—is a symbol of long life and happiness. Although said to live a thousand years, the birds have actually lived about 80 in zoos and pair for life (which has also made them the symbol of an ideal couple—they are frequently cited in Japanese wedding speeches). Each March or April, the female lays two eggs. The male and female play an equal role in looking after the eggs and, later, the chicks. Despite the fact that the birds have made something of a comeback under government protection, there are fears that not enough is being done to preserve their habitat.

It is difficult to recommend a trip to see the cranes in the summer: The birds are busy rearing their chicks and go deep into the swamps where they can only be viewed through binoculars. Only a few are on view at an artificial breeding park, and these are kept behind a fence. In the winter, when they come for food handouts (especially near the village of Tsurui), they are easier to spot.

Sea of Okhotsk north to Rebun and Rishiri Islands

From Akan the northeast coast is only two hours away. This coast in the outer reaches of Japan, abutting the icy waters of the Sea of Okhotsk (Ohotsukukai), has a feeling of being at the end of the world.

The people make their living catching fish in the summer; in the winter the sea is frozen, and their livelihood depends on how successful the summer catch has been. The icy cold waters produce the sweetest shrimp you'll ever taste, and the *kegani* (hairy crab—best in June or July) may look ugly but its meat is so delicate that you forgive it. Except for the Shiretoko Peninsula, which the Ainu named the "World's End," the coastline is relatively flat, and the drama is in the isolation rather than the scenery. The major town on the coast, Abashiri, is not large, and the distances between points of interest become farther apart. However, most of the points mentioned in this excursion can easily be reached by public transportation.

After a short detour to the Shiretoko Peninsula, the itinerary sketched below travels up the coast from Abashiri to Cape Soya, Hokkaido's (and Japan's) most northerly point, and crosses by ferry from Wakkanai to Rebun and Rishiri islands.

GETTING THERE

By Train. On the JR railway system, a line connects Abashiri to Kushiro; the train passes through Akan National Park at Mashu and Kawayu. The same line connects Abashiri with Shari, east along the coast (toward the Shiretoko Peninsula). Traveling west from Abashiri, the JR train goes to Asahikawa and to Sapporo, some 5¼ hours away. To reach Wakkanai, the rail traveler has to change to the Soya Line at Asahikawa. Meanwhile, for Monbetsu, the only public transport from Abashiri is a bus service.

By Bus. A bus leaves Lake Akan and, with a transfer at Bihoro, goes to Abashiri.

EXPLORING

③² **Abashiri** is the main town on the Sea of Okhotsk, but it is quite small. In winter, ice floes, known in Japanese as *ryuho,* jam up on its shores and stretch out to sea as far as the eye can see. Two pleasure boats, *Aurora 1* and *Aurora 2,* give sightseers a chance to inspect the *ryuho* at close quarters from mid-January to mid-April, for a ¥3,000 charge (☎ 0152/41–6000 or 6200 for details). A museum at Mt. Tento— **Okhotsk Ryu-hyo Hakubutsukan**—explains the role of ice floes in nature. ☞ *¥500.* ☉ *Daily, Apr.–Oct. 8–6; Nov.–Mar. 9–5. Closed mid-Dec.–mid-Jan.*

A little farther inland, on the southeastern side of Mt. Tento, is the **Hoppo Minzoku Hakubutsukan** (Hokkaido Museum of Northern Peoples), containing artifacts belonging not only to the Ainu, but also to indigenous cultures on the neighboring island of Sakhalin and in northern areas of America and Eurasia, such as the Inuit and the Lapps. If the museum's layout seems a little bizarre, it's because the building was designed to resemble the outline of a flying swan. The nodule housing the entrance lobby is fashioned like a conical tent. ☞ *¥250.* ☉ *Tues.–Sun. 9:30–4:30. Closed some national holidays and Dec. 29–Jan. 3.*

★ Down the hill from Mt. Tento, toward Lake Abashiri and a little closer to town, is the **Abashiri Kangoku Hakubutsukan** (Abashiri Prison Museum), which recalls the days when convict labor was used to develop the region. (☞ *¥1,030.* ☉ *Daily, Apr.–Oct. 8–6; Nov.–Mar. 9–5.*) The **Abashiri Kyodo Hakubutsukan** (Municipal Museum) houses a good collection of Ainu artifacts and anthropological findings taken from the nearby Moyoro Shell Mound that are believed to be relics from aboriginal people who predate the Ainu. It is located across the railroad tracks to the south of downtown and in the local park. ☞ *¥100.*

⊘ *May–Nov. 9–5, Nov.–Apr. 9–4; closed Dec. 31–Jan. 1 and some Mondays.*

Another place worth visiting is **Lake Tofutsu,** just south of Abashiri (take the train as far as Kitahama Station and walk south for 10 minutes). In the winter, swans come down from Siberia to hole up here. In summertime (late June to late July), between the lake and the Sea of Okhotsk, the main attraction is the **Koshimizu Flower Gardens.** Spread over 7 miles of sand dunes, containing 50 species of flowers, this is where the locals take their afternoon promenades.

If you continue traveling southeast of Abashiri on the Kanno Line beyond Hama-Koshimizu, you will reach **Shari**—the end of the line and the jumping-off point for the **Shiretoko Peninsula.** Most proper roads end about halfway along the peninsula. The final one terminates at Aidomari, with 30 kilometers (19 miles) remaining before Shiretoko's tip. Bus service is erratic and winter closes most of the area off to wheeled vehicles. Add to this the changeable weather and the local bear population—neither of which are conducive to hiking—and you have a place that discourages all but the most adventurous of Japanese tourists. As a result, Shiretoko is the most remarkable of Japan's national parks, an untouched pocket of wilderness in this most industrialized and technologically advanced nation in Asia. To get there by public transport (summer only), take a 55-minute bus ride from Shari to **Utoro.** There is a sightseeing boat out of Utoro that goes out to the cape between April 28 and October 31. As the boat skirts the shore and rounds the cape's tip, the views are impressive, with 600-foot cliffs coming straight out of the sea and rugged mountains inland. In summer, you can also drive along the north shore to **Kamuiwakka Onsen** under Mt. Io. Along the shore are hot-spring rotenburo. They are free; just take off your clothes and hop in.

Returning to Abashiri and going north, the traveler finds that the road runs along the coast of the Sea of Okhotsk to Monbetsu. Small summer resort hotels dot the coast, especially along the shores of Lake Saroma, a seawater lagoon almost locked in by two sand pits. However, all you can look at here are the sea to the right and distant mountains to the left.

Monbetsu is a small port whose main industry is fishing the Sea of Okhotsk in the summer. In the winter the sea freezes, and Monbetsu is bitterly cold and surrounded by ice floes. Yet Monbetsu receives many tourists in the winter, who come to see the ice floes and board a special boat, the *Garinko Go,* which acts as an icebreaker, moving through the floes. *Reservations and tickets,* ☎ *01582/4–8000. Cost: ¥2,030.*

Monbetsu's **Okhotsk Ryu-hyo Kagaku Senta** (Okhotsk Sea Ice Museum) opened in 1991 as a multifunctional facility to promote understanding of ice floes. Its main feature is the Astrovision Hall, where spectacular views of sea ice are projected on a 360° dome re-creating the experience of flying over the Okhotsk Sea when the ice floes are most impressive. There is also a low-temperature simulation room, where visitors, clad in Eskimo-type clothing, experience the severe cold and wander around blocks of sea ice. ☛ *¥250, with extra charges for the Exhibition and Astrovision halls.* ⊘ *Tues.–Sun. 9:30–4:30.*

Monbetsu's municipal museum, **Monbetsu Kyodo Hakubutsukan,** has examples of Hokkaido's flora and fauna, some stone arrowheads, and ancient pottery. ☛ *Free.* ⊘ *Tues.–Sun. 9–5:30.*

That's it, aside from a small, friendly entertainment section, a few shops on the main street, and a couple of hotels. But Monbetsu is the last settlement fit to be called a town until Wakkanai, 300 kilometers (190 miles) to the north, the ferry port for Rebun and Rishiri islands.

If you want to head straight back to Sapporo from Monbetsu, follow the new, well-paved highway that cuts through the wooded mountain range to Asahikawa; the journey takes a little more than three hours by car or bus. Then, from Asahikawa, the train makes the 90-minute run to Sapporo.

The journey north from Monbetsu to Wakkanai is a long one if you go by road (Route 238), but there are some redeeming features. Thirty minutes southwest of Monbetsu (via Route 273) is the town of **Taki-noue,** famous for its Shiba-sakura Festival in June, when the surrounding hills are covered in purple flowers. Many of the villages on the coast between Monbetsu and Wakkanai host smaller versions of the same festival. The small coastal town of **Esashi** (north along Route 238) also hosts a *kani* (crab) festival in July, when the seafood available is particularly delicious. Farther north on Route 238, **Lake Kutcharo** is home in winter to large numbers of swans, who congregate around the unfrozen patches of water at its edges. And of course, any winter traveler along this coast has a splendid chance to view the drift-ice covering the sea.

36 Fifty kilometers (30 miles) before **Cape Soya,** the mountains move out toward the sea. Out across the cold sea stands the Soviet Union's Sakhalin Island. Cape Soya is at the northernmost limits of Japan; this lonely but significant spot is the site of several monuments marking the end of Japan's territory, and also a memorial to the Korean airliner downed by the Soviet military a little farther north of here in 1982. (A public bus makes the hour-long run up from Wakkanai to Cape Soya six times a day.) Soon after rounding the cape and heading west, you get your first glimpse of Rishiri Island and its volcanic cone standing on the horizon. But first, you must go through the town of Wakkanai.

37 **Wakkanai** is a working-class town that subsists on farming the scrubland and fishing the cold waters for Alaskan pollack and Atka mackerel when the sea is not packed with ice floes. Wakkanai is an isolated outpost of man. In the winter, the nights are long, and in the summer there is a feeling of poetic solitude that comes from the eerie quality of the northern lights. From Wakkanai Park, on a ridge to the west of the city, is a commanding view of Sakhalin, an island taken over by the Russians at the end of World War II. Several monuments in this park are dedicated to the days when Sakhalin was part of Japan. One commemorates nine female telephone operators who committed suicide at their post office in Maoka (on Sakhalin) when the island changed hands. Few visitors come to Wakkanai other than to wait for one of the three ferries that daily make the two hour crossing to Rebun-to and Rishiri-to (islands). (Higashi-Nihon Ferry, ☎ 0162/23–3780; fares: ¥3,710 [1st class] and ¥2,060 [2nd class] to Rebun, ¥3,300 [1st class] and ¥1,850 [2nd class] to Rishiri). By the way, there is also a ferry between Kafuka on Rebun Island and Oshidomari and Kutsugata on Rishiri Island (fare: ¥1,240 [1st class] or ¥720 [2nd class]).

★ **38** **Rebun Island** is the older of the two, created by an upward thrust of the earth's crust. The island is long and fairly skinny, running from north to south. Along the east coast are numerous small fishing villages where men bring their catch, usually *nukaboke* (a fish that is baked in rice-bran paste), while women rake in the edible yellowish-green sea-weed (*konbu*) from the shore. On the west coast, cliffs stave off the waves coming in from the Japan Sea. Inland during the short summer months wild alpine flowers, 300 species in all, blanket the mountain meadows. In Momoiwa, the wildflowers are in such profusion in mid-June that one fears to walk, for each step seems to crush a dozen delicate flowers, including the white-pointed *usuyo-kiso,* a flower found only on Rebun.

★ ③⑨ **Rishiri Island** is the result of a submarine volcano whose cone now protrudes 5,640 feet out of the water. The scenery is wilder than on Rebun, and, though a larger island, Rishiri has fewer inhabitants. The ruggedness of the terrain makes it harder to support life, and it's less suitable for hiking than is Rebun. To see this island, it is better to take one of the regularly scheduled buses, which make a complete circle of the island in two hours. From May 1 to November 30, there are six a day, starting at 6 AM, both clockwise and counterclockwise. During the colder part of the year, one bus less makes the circuit. Get off at any of the several tourist stops along the way, and take the hiking routes laid out to the major scenic spots. With the tree line at about 3,000 feet, views are alpine panoramas of wildflowers, a cone-shape mountain, and wide expanses of sea. Tokyo and the industry of Honshu are not part of this Japan. These two islands remain beautiful refuges from modern industrialism.

From Oshidomari, the ferry to Wakkanai takes one hour and 40 minutes. From there the train takes just under six hours to return to Sapporo, 335 kilometers (210 miles) away. There are also direct flights back to Sapporo (Chitose).

DINING AND LODGING

Dining

Western food is served in all the major Sapporo hotels. Invariably, it is French-accented Continental cuisine and always fairly expensive. Sapporo also has a number of ethnic restaurants, from Italian to Russian to Indian, and there are even American fast-food chains. In the hinterlands, Western food is less common. However, almost all the large resort hotels offer a Western menu.

The joy of Hokkaido, however, is its regional food. We strongly recommend that you eat out whenever possible at local Japanese restaurants. Most restaurants that are reasonably priced will have a visual display of their menu in the window. On this basis, you can decide what you want before you enter. If you cannot order in Japanese and no English is spoken, lead the waiter to the window display and point.

Hokkaido is known for its seafood. **Salmon** (*sake*), **squid** (*ika*), **sea urchin** (*uni*), **herring** (*nishin*), and **shellfish** are abundant, but the real treat are fat, sweet scallops (*kaibashira*) collected from Wakkanai. Ramen (a Chinese-noodle soup) is the staple, and it is extremely popular and inexpensive.

The other great favorite is **kegani** (*hairy crabs*). Supposedly, it is forbidden to catch them, but not to eat them—the local people enjoy them too much for that rule to be enforced!

Genghis khan (also spelled *jingisukan*) are thin strips of mutton cooked in an iron skillet. Added to the sizzling mutton are seasoned vegetables—usually onions, green peppers, and cabbage.

Hokkaido people pride themselves on their broadmindedness, so it's not such a great crime if you wear informal clothes in high-class restaurants. However, Japanese diners in such places will probably look immaculate, so if you don't want to feel conspicuous, avoid jeans and wear a shirt and tie. Despite its modernity, Hokkaido has its share of traditional tatami-matted restaurants, so wear a decent pair of socks in case you have to remove your shoes. Anyone planning to tackle Ghengis khan barbecue should be warned that it's messy (though restaurants usually supply plastic aprons) and smelly enough to taint your clothes for days—don't wear your Sunday best.

A 3% federal consumer tax is added to all restaurant bills. Another 3% local tax is added if the bill exceeds ¥7,500. Tipping is not the custom. At more expensive restaurants, a 10%–15% service charge is also added to the bill.

CATEGORY	COST *
$$$$	over ¥6,000
$$$	¥4,000–¥6,000
$$	¥2,000–¥4,000
$	under ¥2,000

Cost is per person without tax, service, or drinks

Lodging

In the 1970s and 1980s, accommodations in Hokkaido consisted of modern, characterless hotels built for Japanese tour groups. Large, unattractively furnished sitting areas and spacious lobbies were the norm, the view being the redeeming factor. Invariably, hotel prices correlate with the views offered and with the size of the public areas and guest rooms. It should be noted, though, that as the tourist industry in Hokkaido grows more important, more attractive and comfortable hotels have begun to appear.

Outside Sapporo and Hokkaido's industrial and/or commercial cities, hot-spring hotels quote prices on a per-person basis with two meals, exclusive of service and tax. If you do not want dinner at your hotel, it is usually possible to renegotiate the price. The hotel categories below reflect the cost of a double room with private bath and no meals. Bear in mind, then, that you will be expected to take breakfast and dinner at hot-spring hotels, and that will be the rate quoted unless you specify otherwise. On the average, the food charges are 50%, per person, of the room cost. So, for example, if the double room is in the **$$$** category (¥15,000–¥20,000), then add ¥15,000 to ¥20,000 for two meals for two people.

A 3% federal consumer tax is added to all hotel bills. Another 3% local tax is added if the bill exceeds ¥15,000. At most hotels, a 10%–15% service charge is added to the total bill. Tipping is not necessary.

CATEGORY	COST *
$$$$	over ¥20,000
$$$	¥15,000–¥20,000
$$	¥10,000–¥15,000
$	under ¥10,000

Cost is for double room, without tax or service

Akan

Lodging

$$$$ **New Akan Hotel.** In Japanese eyes, this establishment is the most pres-
★ tigious in the area. It does have an ideal location on Lake Akan, but
it tends toward sterility and vastness. It has expanded rapidly, with the
opening in 1995 of a new annex called Shangri-La, and now boasts a
total of 370 rooms. Despite its size, there are no English speakers
among its staff. Western- and Japanese-style food are offered. ⊠ *Akan-
kohan, Akan, Hokkaido 085,* ☎ *0154/67–2121,* FAX *0154/67–3339.
370 rooms, 100 Western style. Restaurant, thermal baths, shops, boating. AE, DC, MC, V.*

$$$–$$$$ **Hotel Yamoura.** At the south end of the village and still on the lake
front, the Yamoura has recently acquired a new *onsen* with sauna and
Jacuzzi, and upped its number of rooms to 92, of which 47 are
Japanese style; nearly all the others are a hybrid Western/Japanese style.
All are equipped with bathrooms. Prices vary, with the most expen-
sive rooms going well above the ¥20,000 mark, but include two
Japanese-style meals. There are some English-speaking staff. ⊠ *Akan-
kohan, Akan, Hokkaido 085,* ☎ *0154/67–2311. 92 rooms. Conti-
nental and Japanese restaurants, thermal baths, sauna, Jacuzzi, boating.
AE, DC, V.*

$$ **Hotel Parkuin.** Because this small hotel is not on the lake (it's just off
★ the main road that skirts the village), you must request a room on the
top floor to get a view of the lake and mountains. There are Japanese-
and Western-style rooms; the Japanese restaurant, which attracts a local
clientele, is especially good with its grilled fish. The owners are very
friendly. ⊠ *Akan-kohan, Akan, Hokkaido 085,* ☎ *0154/67–3211. 34
rooms. AE, MC, V.*

Asahikawa

Dining

$$$ **Haut Point.** At the Palace Hotel, this is the best restaurant in town for
French cuisine. Its rooftop setting is attractive and formal, though the
views are only of the tops of other nearby buildings. ✕ *7-jo 6-chome,
Asahikawa, Hokkaido 070,* ☎ *0166/25–8811. Reservations advised.
Jacket and tie. AE, DC, MC, V.* ◷ *11 AM–10 PM.*

Lodging

$$$ **Palace Hotel.** Decorated with mock marble, the public spaces here are
★ brightly lit and airy, with potted plants separating the registration area
from the lounge. The Polestar lounge on the 15th floor affords a skyline view; the Haut Point restaurant (*see* Dining, *above*) is on the same
floor. The Palace is located downtown, one block from the New
Hokkai. Some English is spoken. ⊠ *7-jo 6-chome, Asahikawa, Hokkaido
070,* ☎ *0166/25–8811,* FAX *0116/25–8200. 265 rooms, mostly Western style. Japanese, Chinese, and French restaurants, coffee lounge. AE,
DC, MC, V.*

$$ **Toyo Hotel.** Opposite the Palace Hotel on the main street, this small
hotel has recently refurbished its rooms with white-and-gray de-
cor. The Toyo is used to serving Japanese guests but is friendly
and helpful to Westerners. No English spoken. ⊠ *7-jo 7-chome,
Asahikawa, Hokkaido 070,* ☎ *0166/22–7575,* FAX *0116/23–1733.
104 rooms, mostly Western style. Japanese restaurant. AE, DC,
MC, V.*

Chitose

Lodging

$$$ **Hotel Nikko Chitose.** This is the best hotel in the Chitose area if you wish to be near Sapporo airport, about 3 kilometers (2 miles) away. It is owned by Japan Airlines and is used by its flight crews. ⌂ *4-4-4 Honcho, Chitose-shi, Hokkaido 066,* ☎ *0123/22–1121,* ℻ *0123/22–1153. 258 rooms, mostly Western style. Continental, Chinese, and Japanese restaurants. AE, DC, MC, V.*

Hakodate

Lodging

$$ **Harborview Hotel.** Next to the JR Hakodate Station and near buses to destinations within town, this hotel is very conveniently located. It maintains a fresh, cheerful ambience and a friendly staff. There is a pleasant coffee/tea lounge and a sociable bar in the lobby. Guest rooms are standard Western style, furnished in light blue or peach—not particularly attractive but comfortable enough for an overnight. ⌂ *14-10 Wakamatsucho, Hakodate, Hokkaido 040,* ☎ *0138/22–0111,* ℻ *0138/23–0154. 190 rooms. Japanese and Western restaurants, coffee shop, bar, banquet rooms. AE, DC, MC, V.*

$ **Hakodate Ryokan.** This small house with tatami rooms is 10 minutes by foot from the JR station. ⌂ *28-7 Omoricho, Hakodate, Hokkaido 040,* ☎ *0138/26–1255,* ℻ *0138/26–1256. 15 rooms, 4 with bath. Japanese and Continental breakfasts only. No credit cards.*

$ **Pension Kokian.** The reason for selecting this lodging is its central, waterfront location, close to the historic sights. On the next street are several cafés and bars. The small tatami rooms are nothing special, with smudged walls and cracked plaster. The shared toilet facilities are basic, and for your bath you are told to hop on a tram for the 15-minute ride to the public baths at Yashigashira Onsen. Better than the accommodations is the restaurant, which has been spruced up so that even locals come in to dine (two meals are included in the room rate). ⌂ *13-2 Suehirocho, Hakodate, Hokkaido 040,* ☎ *0138/26–5753,* ℻ *0138/22–2710. 17 rooms. Restaurant. AE, MC, V.*

Kushiro

Lodging

$$ **Kushiro Pacific Hotel.** This hotel is recommended mainly for its central location (five minutes by taxi from the train station). The staff are efficient, some English is spoken, and the rather small rooms are clean. Chinese and Western food is served in the restaurant. ⌂ *2-6 Sakaecho, Kushiro, Hokkaido 085,* ☎ *0154/24–8811,* ℻ *0154/23–9192. 132 rooms, mostly Western style. Restaurant. AE, MC, V.*

Lake Shikotsu

Lodging

$$ **Marukoma Onsen Ryokan.** Neither the building nor its interior furnishings have any aesthetic value, but the lobby, lounges, and restaurant face the northwest shore of Lake Shikotsu. The tatami-style guest rooms have plain, modern, light wood furnishings. If you have a room facing the lake and mountain, the view is splendid. Service is attentive and tolerant of foreigners, and dinner—served in your room—is above average. However, the real benefit of this ryokan is that besides the indoor thermal pool facing the water, there is a public *rotenburo* (outside thermal pool) on the lake shore, within yards of the hotel. ⌂

*Morapunai, Bangaichi, Chitose-shi, Hokkaido 066-02, ☎ 0123/25–
2341. 60 Japanese-style rooms. Restaurant, coffee shop, bar, game room,
thermal pool and private beach on lakefront. AE, DC, V.*

Monbetsu Area

Dining

Monbetsu's entertainment area, three streets up from the Harbor View
Hotel (*see* Lodging, *below*), is small, but there are plenty of bars that
serve food and one or two modest discotheques (try the **New Jazz Club**).
There are fewer restaurants than bars. While many of the restaurants
have visual displays in their windows to indicate prices and the type
of food served, the bars do not. Count on about ¥5,000 per person if
you go into one of the bars that have hostesses with whom to talk, though
that will be in Japanese, not English. Prices can climb steeply, so establish the costs before you gulp too much whiskey.

Lodging

$$ Togiya Ryokan. This ryokan is an extremely friendly, old-fashioned inn.
It's not elegant, but it has the warmth of rural Japan. The inn is lo-
cated on a small street, one block up from the harbor road. No En-
glish is spoken, but mama-san does wonders with your use of a
dictionary. Good Japanese family fare (fish—raw and grilled) is served
in your room. There are no private baths, but good, deep, Japanese
baths are offered. ☎ *Monbetsu, Hokkaido 094, ☎ 01582/3–3048. 15
rooms. No credit cards.*

$ Harbor View Hotel. This is the best Western-style hotel in town. Even
★ though the Harbor View is modest, it is clean and comfortable. Re-
quest a room overlooking the harbor. Japanese and Western breakfasts
are provided, while lunch or dinner might include grilled fish or shell-
fish. No English is spoken. The hotel is a half-hour's drive from Ohot-
suku-Monbetsu Airport; the trip from Memanbetsu Airport takes one
hour and 45 minutes. ☎ *Monbetsu, Hokkaido 094, ☎ 01582/4–
6171. 35 Western-style rooms, 1 Japanese-style room. Restaurant,
party rooms. V.*

Noboribetsu Onsen

Lodging

$$$$ Dai-ichi Takimotokan. This huge, famous spa hotel may have as many
as 1,200 guests at one time. They come to enjoy its thermal pools, the
best and most famous throughout Japan. The hotel is very expensive,
yet it has zero ambience. It is like a giant youth hostel and, invariably,
fully booked. Service is efficiently impersonal, and you must hike from
your bedroom to the lobby and to the thermal baths. One indication
of the place's size is the English-language map available at reception
to help you negotiate the labyrinth of buildings and passageways. The
hotel's new extension has only increased the traffic to and from the
baths. A vast dining room, the Food Plaza, serves average Japanese and
Western food and features nightclub variety acts. ☎ *55 Noboribetsu
Onsen, Noboribetsu, Hokkaido 059-05, ☎ 0143/84–2111, FAX
0143/84–2202. 401 rooms. Dining room, game room, shops, thermal
baths (nonguests pay ¥2,000 to use the baths). AE, DC, MC, V.*

$$$–$$$$ Akiyoshi Hotel. This is a friendly, hospitable, modern ryokan in the cen-
★ ter of the village. Antiques and paintings are judiciously placed to give
a balance between traditional hospitality and modern amenities. If you
enjoy sleeping on tatami with a futon, this is recommended as the most
personable hotel in town. Japanese food is served in the room. ☎ *No-*

boribetsu Onsen, Noboribetsu, Hokkaido 059-05, ☎ 0143/84–2261, ℻ 0143/84–2263. 43 Japanese-style rooms. Thermal bath. V.

$$$ **Noboribetsu Grand Hotel.** This is another huge hotel with large, barren public rooms. Since it is at the bottom of the village and off to the side, its modern ugliness is well hidden. ⌶ 154 Noboribetsu Onsen, Noboribetsu, Hokkaido 059-05, ☎ 0143/84–2101, ℻ 0143/84–2543. 261 rooms, 87 Western style and 174 Japanese style. Japanese restaurant, thermal baths, shops. AE, DC, V.

$ ★ **Ryokan Hanaya.** A member of the Japanese Inn Group, this small inn is less than 10 minutes on foot from the center of Noboribetsu. (Coming from JR Noboribetsu Station, take the bus to Noboribetsu Onsen and get off at the Hanaya-mae bus stop.) It has been very highly rated in the past, though at the time of writing it is being refurbished and will have an entirely different style and appearance in future. English is spoken. Among the meals provided in your room is kaiseki, aesthetically pleasing full-course meals. (Dinner is also served in your room). ⌶ 134 Noboribetsu Onsenmachi, Noboribetsu, Hokkaido 059-05, ☎ 0143/84–2521, ℻ 0143/84–2240. 21 rooms. AE, V.

Otaru

Lodging

$$$ **Hasegawa Minshuku.** This is a popular but slightly overrated ryokan just outside Otaru, on the way to the aquarium. The furnishings are worn, and the staff do not seem to be overjoyed at having foreigners stay. Japanese food is served in your room. ⌶ 2-15 Inaho 3-chome, Otaru, Hokkaido 047, ☎ 0134/22–5276. 10 rooms. No credit cards.

$$ **Otaru International Hotel.** Above a shopping arcade, this modern hotel is reached by an escalator from the main street. The lobby area is rather bare and uncomfortable, but the guest rooms are cheerful, though small. The staff speak a little English. ⌶ 3-9-1 Inaho, Otaru, Hokkaido 047, ☎ 0134/33–2161, ℻ 0134/33–7744. 76 Western- plus 4 Japanese-style rooms. Japanese, Chinese, and Western restaurants. AE, MC, V.

Sapporo

Dining

Continental food is served in all the major hotels in either a formal dining room and/or coffee shop. Invariably, the formal dining room looks to French cuisine for inspiration, and the food is always expensive. In addition to their Japanese restaurants, most large hotels have a Chinese restaurant. Most of Sapporo's restaurants, whatever their culinary origin, use visual displays for their menus. The greatest concentration of restaurants is in the entertainment district of Susukino. Hokkaido is known for its ramen, a Chinese noodle served in broth. There are more than 1,000 ramen shops in Sapporo, but do try to make it to **Ramen Yokocho,** in a small alley that runs perpendicular to the southern side of Susukino-dori (Minami 4). In the same area there are as many as three dozen tiny shops with counter service. If you prefer to eat in less cramped surroundings—but still cheaply and with quick and unfussy service—you might try one of the larger izakaya in Susukino: perhaps **Potato Circus,** on the fourth floor of the Urban Sapporo Building (Minami 3, Nishi 4), or a member of the ubiquitous **Tsubahachi** chain. Their picture menus make life easy for even the most determinedly monoglot English speaker.

$$$$ **Ambrosia Room.** On the penthouse floor of the Keio Plaza Hotel, this restaurant offers ambitious French fare served by extremely attentive

and personable staff. Perhaps more memorable than the cooking, though, is the view over the botanical gardens. ✕ *Keio Plaza Hotel, 7-2 Nishi, Kita 5, Chuo-ku, Sapporo 060 (downtown),* ☎ *011/271–0111. Reservations advised. Jacket and tie. AE, DC, MC, V.* ⊙ *Lunch 11:30–2:30, dinner 5–9:30.*

$$$ Big Jug. In the Grand Hotel, this casual, beer hall–type brasserie is good for lunch, with a limited Continental menu and an opportunity to talk. It's popular with businessmen. ✕ *Sapporo Grand Hotel, 4 Nishi, Kita 1, Chuo-ku (downtown),* ☎ *011/261–3311. AE, DC, MC, V.* ⊙ *Lunch noon–3, dinner 6–10.*

$$$ Yamatoya. Excellent sushi and sashimi is served here, with counter ser-
★ vice on the left and tatami seating on the right. Yamatoya is across the street from the JAL office downtown. ✕ *Koshiyama Bldg. B1, 3 Nishi, Kita 2, Chuo-ku (downtown),* ☎ *011/251–5667. No reservations. V.* ⊙ *11–10 Mon.–Sat., 11–9:30 Sun. and national holidays.*

$$ Izakaya Kurumaya. Downstairs in Plaza 109 (on the south side of the
★ main east–west street in Susukino), this local bar has the best *yakitori* (chicken on skewers) in town. The elegant atmosphere makes it pop-
ular with Japanese and foreigners. (There is an English-language menu.) Aside from yakitori, Karumaya also serves *oden* (diced vegetables boiled in a soup with fish bones) as one of its specialties. ✕ *4 Minami, 5 Nishi Chuo-ku (Susukino),* ☎ *011/512–9157. No reservations. AE, DC, MC, V.* ⊙ *5 PM–midnight.*

$$ Sapporo Beer Brewery. Genghis khan is popular here, though other Japanese dishes are offered. You'll find a festive atmosphere in either the garden or the cavernous halls of the old brewery (east of the station). ✕ *Nishi 9, Kita 7, Higashi-ku,* ☎ *011/742–1531. Reservations necessary for party rooms. AE, DC, MC, V.* ⊙ *11:30–9.*

$$ Sasa Sushi. This small restaurant has a wide variety of sushi and is ex-
tremely popular with the local businessmen. Sit at the counter and you'll likely strike up a conversation with fellow patrons. ✕ *2 Nishi, Kita 2, Chuo-ku (downtown),* ☎ *011/222–2897 (close to the Hokkaido Tourist Office). No reservations.* ⊙ *11–10. Closed Sun. No credit cards.*

$$ Shoya. In the Plaza 109 building, this popular restaurant serves grilled fish, but the side orders of sashimi and yakitori are also delicious. Seating is either at the counter or at tables. It's a casual place where talk-
ing to fellow diners is a likely possibility. No English is spoken, but sign language suffices, and the prices are not too high. ✕ *4 Minami, 5 Nishi Chuo-ku (Susukino),* ☎ *011/512–1241. No reservations. AE, DC, MC, V.*

$$ Silo. This has a countrylike decor and a menu to match. The restau-
rant serves only Hokkaido foods, including bear and deer. Some En-
glish is spoken. ✕ *5 Minami, 3 Nishi, Chuo-ku (in the Hokusen Bldg., Susukino),* ☎ *011/531–5837. AE, DC, MC, V.* ⊙ *Dinner 5–11. Closed Sun.*

$$ Yoyotei. If you can't make it to the Sapporo Beer Brewery (*see above*), try the Genghis khan dinner here. Young waitresses in Bavarian dresses and a large open space combine to re-create a German beer hall. ✕ *5 Minami, 4 Nishi, Chuo-ku, on the 5th floor of the Matsuoka Bldg. (Susukino),* ☎ *011/241–8831. AE, DC, MC, V.* ⊙ *4–10.*

$ Ajinotokeidai. Uptown and across from the Grand Hotel, Ajinotokei-
dai is one of the more well-known ramen shops. You enter from the street level (there's a picture of a ramen bowl hanging outside) and go downstairs into the cellar restaurant. Choose either the counter or a table, which you might share with other diners if the restaurant is crowded. Though there are one or two other items available, ramen is the specialty, and the steaming noodles will only set you back ¥650–

¥2,000. ✕ *3 Nishi, Kita 1, Sanwa Ginko (Bank) Building,* ☎ *011/232–8171. No reservations. No credit cards.* ⊘ *10 AM–3 AM.*

Lodging

$$$$ **ANA Zennikku Hotel.** In the heart of the business center, three blocks from the JR station, this is Sapporo's tallest high-rise hotel (26 floors). Shops and a coffee/pastry restaurant are on the ground floor, and up the escalator is an open lobby area with lounges and bars. The rooms are spacious and brightly decorated. Good views are available from the Sky Restaurant and Sky Lounge. The hotel is convenient for ANA passengers, because it runs buses to and from Chitose Airport. ▣ *1 Nishi, Kita 3, Chuo-ku, Sapporo, Hokkaido 060,* ☎ *011/221–4411,* ⅢX *011/222–7624. 412 rooms, mostly Western style. French and Japanese restaurants. AE, DC, MC, V.*

$$$$ **Grand Hotel.** This is Sapporo's oldest established Western hotel, cen-
★   trally located on the main commercial street. Built in 1934 and reno-
vated in 1984, the Grand is in the tradition of a great European hotel. It has a range of restaurants—Japanese, Chinese, French, and a pub (The Big Jug), popular for business lunches. The service is first-rate. The rooms in the new annex have a fresher, more modern tone than those in the older wing. The hotel's numerous facilities, from a cake and coffee shop to elegant restaurants, create a more lively atmo-sphere than you may expect from Sapporo's oldest hotel. ▣ *4 Nishi, Kita 1, Chuo-ku, Sapporo, Hokkaido 060,* ☎ *011/261–3311,* ⅢX *011/231–0388. 585 rooms, mostly Western style. Restaurants, shops. AE, DC, MC, V.*

$$$$ **Hotel Alpha Sapporo.** This hotel has the best location for tourists who want to walk to the shopping and downtown area of the city and be close to the evening action in Susukino. The service is excellent and the decor of warm rust-browns and reds makes it an inviting place to return to after a day of sightseeing. Though its copious facilities in-clude a Japanese tea ceremony room and a cinema called the Mitsukoshi Movie Theater, it is smaller than most of the other top hotels and the hotel's staff soon know you by name. Guest rooms tend to be a little ordinary, but the rooms are larger than most standard hotel rooms in Japan. Western rock bands playing the very sporadic gig in Sapporo usually stay here. The French restaurant, Alsienne, an elegant wood-paneled dining room, imports many of its ingredients from France. ▣ *Nishi 5, Minami 1, Chuo-ku, Sapporo, Hokkaido 060,* ☎ *011/221–2333,* ⅢX *011/221–0819. 146 rooms. Restaurants, bar, banquet rooms, indoor pool, beauty salon. AE, DC, MC, V.*

$$$$ **Hotel Arthur.** Located south of Susukino and at the top of Nakajima Park, this hotel opened in 1989, and although the guest room carpet-ing needs to be replaced, the hotel has been well maintained. The rooms are reasonably large for Japan, and the dark-stained furniture gives them a European feel. Bathrooms have a hand-held shower, and the toilet is in a separate room that adjoins the alcove dressing area. The spacious lobby area has an open lounge where you may dine with views of the park. There are restaurants on the fourth, fifth, and 24th floors, while the 25th floor has a bar and, confusingly, a club called the 21 Club. The staff's English is limited, but their willingness to help foreign guests is not. ▣ *S 10, W 6, Chuo-ku, Sapporo, Hokkaido 064,* ☎ *011/561–1000,* ⅢX *011/521–5522. 229 Western-style rooms. Restaurants, bar, nightclub, beauty salon, gift shop. AE, DC, MC, V.*

$$$$ **Keio Plaza Hotel.** A five-minute walk to the right of the JR station, the Keio is a large, modern hotel with a vast, open-plan lobby. Because it stands between the botanical gardens and the Hokkaido University cam-pus, the views from the guest rooms on the upper floors are the best

in town. The rooms are very spacious for a Japanese hotel. If you are not staying here, the views may be enjoyed from the Ambrosia (French) and Miyama (Japanese) restaurants on the hotel's 22nd floor. The 24-hour Jurin coffee shop, one of the few all-night restaurants in town, can be a welcome respite for the insomniac suffering from jet lag. There are also an izakaya and sushi bar, a tea lounge, and a delicatessen. The enthusiastic, helpful staff will always find someone to help out in English, if required. ⊞ *7-2 Nishi, Kita 5, Chuo-ku, Sapporo, Hokkaido 060,* ☎ *011/271–0111,* ℻ *011/221–5450. 525 rooms, mostly Western style. Restaurants, coffee shop, health club, car rental, travel services. AE, DC, MC, V.*

$$$$ **Sapporo Renaissance Hotel.** This upscale Ramada hotel, which opened in late 1991, has slightly larger rooms than other high-priced hotels in town for the same price. Its drawback is its location, a short taxi ride from most places you'll want to visit—five minutes to Susukino, 10 minutes to the JR station. The hotel's lobby area and public facilities are rarely crowded, and the fitness club, with a large swimming pool and baths, is excellent (although guests not staying on the Renaissance Club floor must pay ¥5,000 to use the club). Guest rooms are indistinguishable from those at other modern hotels; they have light color schemes and cheap-looking furniture. The hotel's one touch of humor is the mural painted on the arched ceiling of the reception lobby depicting the Japanese islands supported by Western cherubs and Roman-looking gods. Many of the staff speak English. ⊞ *1-1, Toyohira 4-jo 1-chome, Toyohira-ku, Sapporo, Hokkaido 062,* ☎ *011/821–1111,* ℻ *011/842–6191. 323 Western-style rooms, 6 Japanese-style suites. Restaurants, bars, fitness center with indoor pool and sauna, shops, business services, banquet rooms. AE, DC, MC, V.*

$$–$$$ **Fujiya Santus Hotel.** Although more than 15 years old, the Fujiya San-
★ tus has kept up a fresh appearance. The staff is wonderfully friendly, and the smallness of the hotel adds to the personal warmth. Though they depend on the type of room you want and the time of year, the prices tend toward the low end of this category. The hotel is next to the botanical gardens, a pleasant location but one that requires a 10-minute walk to the JR station and downtown. ⊞ *7 Nishi, Kita 3, Chuo-ku, Sapporo, Hokkaido 060,* ☎ *011/271–3344,* ℻ *011/241–4182. 40 rooms, 32 Western style. Restaurant. V.*

$$ **Nakamuraya.** This ryokan near the Botanical Park dates from 1898—ancient for Sapporo—though the current building is more recent. The six-tatami-mat rooms seem larger because of the spacious cupboards, built-in minibar, and wide window shelf. Most rooms have private (tiny) bathrooms. The staff are diffident with foreign guests, but warm up after you've managed a few words in Japanese. The large communal bath is most appreciated in winter. When making reservations, explain that you saw a listing in the Japanese Inn Group brochure; otherwise you may be charged a higher rate. The Japanese dinner (¥3,000) is expansive, with a selection of fresh seafood from Hokkaido's waters. ⊞ *7 Nishi, Kita 3, Chuo-ku, Sapporo, Hokkaido 060,* ☎ *011/241–2111,* ℻ *011/241–2118. 29 rooms, mostly Japanese style. Restaurant (open 11:30–2 and 5–9). AE, DC, MC, V.*

$ **Hotel Public.** The best and swankiest (lots of marble) business hotel in
★ town, the Public has a friendly staff and Western-size beds, instead of the normal narrow ones found in business hotels. The Public also has a reasonable restaurant-cum-coffee lounge, and a new izakaya (bar) that opened in 1995. Though considerably to the west of the main attractions of central Sapporo, the hotel is next to the streetcar line, which can take you into town. ⊞ *1 Minami, 15 Nishi, Chuo-ku, Sapporo,*

Hokkaido 060, ☎ *011/644–7711. 105 Western-style rooms. Restaurant, izakaya. AE, DC, MC, V.*

Sounkyo Onsen

Note: Rates tend to be 20% lower during the winter season. The **Tourist Office Hotel Association** (☎ 01658/5–3350) can help you find accommodations.

Lodging

$$$ **Choyotei.** Perched on a bluff halfway up the side of the gorge, this hotel has the best views (and, because of this, spoils some of the natural beauty). Its corner window in the huge foyer lounge looks straight down the gorge; however, the hotel itself is an ugly and mammoth building, cold and sterile in the modern Japanese style. While rooms that face the gorge may merit the hotel's price, a room at the back looks onto a parking lot, another ugly building, and cliff walls. ⊞ *Sounkyo Onsen, Kamikawa-cho, Kamikawa, Hokkaido 078-17,* ☎ *01658/5–3241. 272 rooms, mostly Japanese style. Bar, thermal baths, shops, game room. AE, DC, MC, V.*

$$ **Mount View Hotel.** This hotel has the nicest design around and an
★ air of freshness to it. Built as a modern interpretation of an alpine inn, the decor is in cheerful, warm pastels. Unfortunately, as a recent newcomer to Sounkyo, it is situated down by the road and has limited views. Nevertheless it has taste, which the other hotels lack. Western- and Japanese-style meals are available. ⊞ *Sounkyo Onsen, Hokkaido,* ☎ *01658/5–3011. 97 rooms, 69 Western style. Thermal baths. V.*

$$ **Kumoi.** This small new ryokan offers simple but clean tatami rooms. ⊞ *Sounkyo Onsen, Hokkaido,* ☎ *01658/5–3553. 35 rooms, 20 with private bath. Continental breakfast on request, thermal bath. V.*

$ **Pension Yukara.** This small inn is better priced than many in Sounkyo Onsen, and though no English is spoken, the owners are hospitable to foreigners. There's air-conditioning in the summer and hot springs to soak in year-round. Western-style meals are available and are included in the price. ⊞ *Sounkyo Onsen, Hokkaido 078,* ☎ *0165/85–3216. (Reservations may be made through the Welcome Inn association.) 3 Japanese and 8 Western rooms without bath. Dining room, thermal baths. AE, V.*

Toyako Onsen

Lodging

$$ **Toya Park Hotel.** This is a sister hotel to the Toya Park Sun Palace, but it's smaller and more personal, though not quite as deluxe. The manager enjoys speaking English. Located at the head of the town and on a slight bluff, it has an unrestricted view of the lake. However, only the Japanese-style guest rooms face the lake. ⊞ *Toyako Onsen, Hokkaido* ☎ *01427/5–2445,* 𝔽𝔸𝕏 *01427/5–3918. 167 rooms, about half Western-style. Continental and Japanese restaurants, thermal baths, tennis courts, game room. AE, DC, MC, V.*

$ **Nakanoshima.** This is a small hotel around the lake 3 kilometers (2 miles) west of Toyako Onsen. No English is spoken, but the owners are happy to use sign language. There is a restaurant on the premises. ⊞ *Sobetsu Onsen, Hokkaido,* ☎ *0142/75–4115. 26 rooms, mostly Japanese style. No credit cards.*

HOKKAIDO ESSENTIALS

Arriving and Departing

For most visitors to Hokkaido, the points of entry are either Sapporo (by plane) or Hakodate (by train).

By Plane

Japan Airlines (JAL), Japan Air System (JAS), and All Nippon Airways (ANA) link Hokkaido to the island of Honshu by direct flights from Tokyo's Haneda airport to Hakodate, Sapporo (Chitose), Asahikawa, Memanbetsu (Abashiri), Nakashibetsu (Nemuro), and Kushiro. Many other major cities on Honshu (including Sendai, Aomori, Akita, Niigata, Nagoya, Osaka, and Hiroshima) have flights to Sapporo, as do five places in the Asian and Pacific neighborhood (Seoul, Hong Kong, Guam, Saipan, and Honolulu). Sapporo's airport is Chitose, 40 kilometers (25 miles) south of Sapporo. Frequent trains and buses connect the city with the airport (*see* Sapporo, *above*). The cost by air from Tokyo to Sapporo is ¥23,850, compared with ¥21,380 by train. Some air travelers arriving in Japan on European flights can, with a change of planes at Tokyo, fly at no extra charge to Sapporo.

By Train

With the 55-kilometer (34-mile) Seikan Tunnel permitting train travel between Hokkaido and Honshu, the train journey from Tokyo to Sapporo can take as little as 10 hours, 41 minutes, allowing for a changing time of 17 minutes; this trip involves a combination of the Shinkansen train to Morioka (2 hours, 36 minutes), the northernmost point on the Tohoku Shinkansen line, and a change to an express train for the remaining journey to Hakodate (4 hours, 8 minutes) and then to Sapporo (3 hours, 45 minutes). Alternatively, there is the Blue Train (the blue-colored long-distance sleeper) from Tokyo to Sapporo, which takes about 15 hours. The Japan Rail Pass covers the train fare in either case, but an additional charge is made for a sleeping compartment (¥13,000) or a bunk (¥6,180) on the Blue Train. (To both sums you must add the extra express train fee, so that the overall charges are ¥16,040 and ¥9,220 respectively.)

By Ferry

The least expensive form of travel to Hokkaido is by ferry from Honshu. From Tokyo to Kushiro (32 hours), there is the luxury ferryboat *Marimo,* which sails three or four times weekly and is operated by the Kinkai Yusen Company (cost: ¥19,050 first class, ¥14,420 second class). From Tokyo to Tomakomai (32½ hours), another large ferry, the *Shiretoko,* is operated by the Blue Highway Line (cost ¥29,660 first class, ¥11,840 second class). The same company also operates an overnight ferry (15 hours) from Sendai to Tomakomai. The ferry between Aomori and Hakodate (4 hours), which was the only way to cross from northern Honshu to Hokkaido before the Seikan Tunnel, plans to stay in operation for those not wishing to take the train through the tunnel.

Getting Around

By Plane

The two domestic airlines that connect Sapporo with Hakodate, Kushiro, Wakkanai, and the smaller Memanbetsu, Naka-Shibetsu, and Ohotsuku-Monbetsu airports in eastern Hokkaido are Japan Air System (JAS) and Nippon Kinkyori Airways. There is also a daily air service between Wakkanai and both Rebun and Rishiri islands, although its schedule suffers occasional interruptions; travelers should check flights beforehand.

By Train and Bus

Japan Railways (JR) has routes connecting most of the major cities. For the most part, the trains travel the unscenic routes and are simply efficient means to reach the areas that you want to explore. Buses cover most of the major routes through the scenic areas, and all the excursions in this chapter may be accomplished by bus.

By Car

Cars are easy to rent; the Nippon-Hertz agency has offices at Minami 5 Nishi 1, Chuo-ku, in central Sapporo; at Chitose airport; and at Hakodate and JR Asahikawa stations. An international driving permit, obtainable from any AAA office in the United States, is required for driving in Japan. Driving is on the left-hand side of the road, and speed limits are frustratingly low. For the most part, the Japanese are cautious drivers and obey the rules of the road, though a combination of wide, straight roads and light traffic has bred a certain recklessness in Hokkaido's motorists: The prefecture has the worst accident figures in Japan. International traffic signs are used and are easy to understand. Directional signs are often sufficiently given in *romaji* (Japanese written in Roman script) to enable non-Japanese readers to navigate, and all major roads have route numbers. Also, the Dosanko are extremely helpful in giving instructions and directions to the Western tourist. The limitation to renting a car is the expense. A day's rental is about ¥14,500 (not including tax), including 220 free kilometers, after which you are charged ¥20 per kilometer. Gas and tolls on the few expressways are three times as costly as in the United States. The best plan is, wherever possible, to travel long distances by public transport and then rent a car for local trips.

Guided Tours

The **Japan Travel Bureau** (03/3276–7777) operates three- and four-day tours of Hokkaido from Tokyo. For ¥170,000, the three-day tour includes Sapporo (overnight), Nakayama Pass, Lake Toya, Noboribetsu (overnight), and Shiraoi, before going back to Chitose. Two breakfasts and one dinner are included, and there is a ¥32,000 single supplement. The four-day tour costs ¥280,000 and includes Sapporo (overnight), Asahikawa, Sounkyo (gorge), Abashiri (overnight), Bihoro Pass, Lake Kusaharo, Lake Mashu, and Lake Akan (overnight), before returning to Chitose. Three breakfasts and two dinners are included, and there is a single supplement of ¥41,000. For both tours, bookings should be made at least 10 days in advance. These tours operate daily from April 1 through October 31.

Important Addresses and Numbers

Emergencies
Police, ☎ 110; **ambulance,** ☎ 119.

Tourist Information
The Japan National Tourist Organization's **Tourist Information Center (TIC)** in Tokyo (Kotani Bldg., 1-6-6 Yurakucho, Chiyoda-ku) has free maps and brochures on Hokkaido. Also, the **Hokkaido Tourism Association** has an office on the second floor of the Kokusai Kanko Kaikan building in Tokyo (near the Yaesu exit of Tokyo Station), Marunouchi 1-8-3, Chiyoda-ku. Within Hokkaido, the best place for travel information is in Sapporo (*see* Sapporo, *above*).

Other important regional tourist information centers are: **Akan Lake** (☎ 0154/67–2254); **Noboribetsu Onsen** (☎ 0143/84–2068); **Sounkyo Onsen** (☎ 01658/5–1811); and **Lake Toya** (☎ 01427/5–2446).

There are bus and train travel information centers at all the major train stations. The main Hokkaido office of the **Japan Travel Bureau,** in Sapporo, is where you are most likely to find English spoken (☎ 011/241–6201).

The **Japan Travel Phone** (the nationwide service for English-language assistance or travel information) is available from 9 to 5, seven days a week. Dial toll-free 0088/22–2800 or 0120/222–800 for information on eastern Japan. When using a yellow, blue, or green public phone (do not use the red phones), insert a 10-yen coin, which will be returned. There are different numbers for callers in Tokyo (3503–4400) and Kyoto (371–5649); in those cities, the service costs ¥10 per three minutes.

15 Portraits of Japan

JAPAN AT A GLANCE: A CHRONOLOGY

10,000–300 BC Neolithic Jomon hunting and fishing culture leaves richly decorated pottery.

AD 300 Yayoi culture displays knowledge of farming and metallurgy imported from Korea.

after 300 The Yamato tribe consolidates power in the rich Kansai plain and expands westward, forming the kind of military aristocratic society that was to dominate Japan's history.

c 500 Yamato leaders, claiming to be descended from the sun goddess, Amaterasu, take the title of emperor.

552 Buddhism, introduced to the Yamato court from China by way of Korea, complements rather than replaces the indigenous Shinto religion. Horyuji, a Buddhist temple built at Nara in 607, includes the oldest surviving wooden building in the world.

593–622 Prince Shotoku encourages the Japanese to embrace Chinese culture.

Nara Period

710–784 Japan has first permanent capital (at Nara); great age of Buddhist sculpture, piety, and poetry.

The Fujiwara or Heian Period

794–1160 The capital is moved from Nara to Heiankyo (Kyoto), where the imperial court is dominated by the Fujiwara family. Lady Murasaki's novel *The Tale of Genji,* written c. 1020, describes the elegant, ceremonious court life.

The Kamakura Period

1185–1335 Feudalism enters, with military and economic power in the provinces and the emperor a powerless, ceremonial figurehead in Kyoto. Samurai warriors welcome Zen, a new sect of Buddhism from China.

1192 After a war with the Taira family, Yoritomo of the Minamoto family becomes the first shogun; he places his capital in Kamakura.

1274, 1281 The fleets sent by Chinese emperor Kublai Khan to invade Japan are destroyed by typhoons, praised in Japanese history as *kamikaze,* or divine wind.

Ashikaga Period

1336–1568 The Ashikaga family assumes the title of shogun and settles in Kyoto. The Zen aesthetic flourishes in painting, landscape gardening, and tea ceremony. The Silver Pavilion on Ginkakuji in Kyoto, built in 1483, is the quintessential example of Zen-inspired architecture. The period is marked by constant warfare but also by increased trade with the mainland. Osaka develops into an important commercial city, and trade guilds appear.

1543 Portuguese sailors, the first Europeans to reach Japan, initiate trade relations with the lords of western Japan and introduce the musket, which changes Japanese warfare.

1549–1551   St. Francis Xavier, the first Jesuit missionary, introduces Christianity.

The Momoyama Period of National Unification

1568–1600   Two generals, Nobunga Oda and Hideyoshi Toyotomi, are the central figures of this period.

1592, 1597   Hideyoshi invades Korea. He brings back Korean potters, who rapidly develop a Japanese ceramic industry.

The Tokugawa Period

1600–1868   Ieyasu Tokugawa becomes shogun after the battle of Sekigahara. The military capital is established at Edo (Tokyo), which shows phenomenal economic and cultural growth. A hierarchy of four social classes—warriors, farmers, artisans, and merchants—is rigorously enforced. The merchant class, however, is increasingly prosperous and effects a transition from a rice to a money economy. Also, merchants patronize new, popular forms of art: kabuki, haiku, and the ukiyo-e school of painting. The life of the latter part of this era is beautifully illustrated in the wood-block prints of the artist Hokusai (1760–1849).

1618   Persecution of Christians who refuse to recant.

1637–1638   Japanese Christians massacred in the Shimabara uprising. Japan is closed to the outside world except for a Dutch trading post in Nagasaki harbor.

1853   The American commodore Matthew Perry reopens Japan to foreign trade.

The Meiji Restoration

1868–1912   Supporters of Emperor Meiji, calling for direct imperial rule, depose the shogun and move the capital to Edo, renaming it Tokyo. Japan is modernized along Western lines with a constitution proclaimed in 1889; a system of compulsory education and a surge of industrialization follow.

1902–1905   Japan defeats Russia in the Russo-Japanese War and achieves world-power status.

1910   Japan annexes Korea.

1914–1918   Japan joins the Allies in World War I.

1923   A catastrophic earthquake shakes Tokyo and Yokohama.

1931   Japan seizes the Chinese province of Manchuria.

1937   Following years of increasing military and diplomatic activity in northern China, open warfare breaks out (and lasts until 1945); it is resisted by both Nationalists and Communists.

1939–1945   Japan, having signed anti-Communist treaties with Nazi Germany and Italy (1936 and 1937), invades and occupies French Indochina.

1941   The Japanese attack on Pearl Harbor on December 7 brings the United States into war against Japan in the Pacific.

1942   Japan's empire extends to Indochina, Burma, Malaya, the Philippines, and Indonesia. Defeat by U.S. forces at Midway in June turns the tide of Japanese military success.

1945   Tokyo and 50 other Japanese cities are devastated by U.S. bombing raids. The United States drops atomic bombs on Hiroshima and Nagasaki, precipitating Japanese surrender.

1945–1952   The American occupation under General Douglas MacArthur disarms Japan and encourages the establishment of a democratic government. Emperor Hirohito retains his position.

1953   After the Korean War, Japan begins a period of great economic growth.

1964   Tokyo hosts the Summer Olympic games.

late 1960s   Japan develops into one of the major industrial nations in the world.

mid-1970s   Production of electronics, cars, cameras, and computers places Japan at the heart of the emerging "Pacific Rim" economic sphere and threatens to spark a trade war with the industrial nations of Europe and the United States.

1989   Emperor Hirohito dies.

1990   Coronation of Emperor Akihito. Prince Fumihito marries Kiko Kawashima.

1992   The Diet approves use of Japanese military forces under United Nations auspices.

1993   Crown Prince Naruhito marries Masako Owada.

1995   A massive earthquake strikes Kobe and environs. Approximately 5,500 people are killed and 35,000 injured; more than 100,000 buildings are destroyed.

Members of a fringe religious organization carry out a series of poison-gas attacks on the transportation networks of Toyko and Yokohama, undermining the confidence of the Japanese in their personal safety.

THE DISCREET CHARM OF JAPANESE CUISINE

LEAVE BEHIND THE HUMIDITY of Japan in summer and part the crisp linen curtain of the neighborhood *sushi-ya* some hot night in mid-July. Enter a world of white cypress and chilled sea urchin, where a welcome *oshibori* (hot towel) awaits your damp forehead, and a master chef stands at your beck and call. A cup of tea to begin. A tiny mound of ginger to freshen the palate, and you're ready to choose from the colorful array of fresh seafood on ice inside a glass case before you. Bite-size morsels arrive in friendly pairs. A glass of ice-cold beer. The young apprentice runs up and down making sure everyone has tea—and anything else that might be needed. The chef has trained for years in his art, and he's proud, in his stoic way, to demonstrate it. The *o-tsukuri* (sashimi) you've ordered arrives; today the thinly sliced raw tuna comes in the shape of a rose (Is it really your birthday?). The fourth round you order brings with it an unexpected ribbon of cucumber, sliced with a razor-sharp sushi knife into sections that expand like an accordion. The chef's made your day. . . .

Red paper lanterns dangling in the dark above a thousand tiny food stalls on the back streets of Tokyo. To the weary Japanese salaried man on his way home from the office, these *akachochin* lanterns are a prescription for the best kind of therapy known for the "subterranean homesick blues," Japanese style: one last belly-warming bottle of sake, a nerve-soothing platter of grilled chicken wings, and perhaps a few words of wisdom for the road. Without these comforting nocturnal way stations, many a fuzzy-eyed urban refugee would never survive that rumbling, fluorescent nightmare known as the last train home.

And where would half of Japan's night-owl college students be, if not for the local *shokudo,* as the neighborhood not-so-greasy spoon is known? Separated at last from mother's protective guidance (and therefore without a clue as to how an egg is boiled or a bowl of soup is heated), the male contingent of young lodging-house boarders put their lives in the hands of the old couple who runs the neighborhood café. Bent furtively over a platter of *kare-raisu* (curry and rice) or *tonkatsu teishoku* (pork cutlet set meal), these ravenous young men thumb through their baseball comics each night, still on the road to recovery from a childhood spent memorizing mathematical formulas and English phrases they hope they'll never have to use.

Down a dimly lit back street not two blocks away, a geisha in all her elaborate finery walks her last silk-suited customer out to his chauffeur-driven limousine. He has spent the evening being pampered, feasted, and fan-danced in the rarefied air of one of Tokyo's finest *ryotei*. (You must be invited to these exclusive eateries—or be a regular patron, introduced years earlier by another regular patron who vouched for your reputation with his own.) There has been the most restrained of traditional dances, some samisen playing—an oh-so-tastefully suggestive tête-à-tête. The customer has been drinking the very finest sake, accompanied by a succession of exquisitely presented hors d'oeuvres—what amounts to a seven-course meal in the end is the formal Japanese *haute cuisine* known as *kaiseki*. His grapes have all been peeled. If it were not for his company's expense account, by now he would have spent the average man's monthly salary. Lucky for him, he's not the average man.

On a stool, now, under the flimsy awning of a street stall, shielded from the wind and rain by flapping tarps, heated only by a portable kerosene stove and the steam from a vat of boiling noodles, you'll find neither tourist nor ptomaine. Here sits the everyday workingman, glass of *shochu* (a strong liquor made from sweet potatoes) in sunbaked hand, arguing over the Tigers' chances of winning the Japan Series, as he zealously slurps down a bowl of hot noodle soup sprinkled with red-pepper sauce—more atmosphere, and livelier company than you're likely to find anywhere else in

Japan. The *yatai-san,* as these inimitable street vendors are known, are an amiable, if disappearing, breed.

Somewhere between the street stalls and the exclusive ryotei, a vast culinary world exists in Japan. Tiny, over-the-counter restaurants, each with its own specialty—from familiar favorites, such as tempura, sukiyaki, or sushi, to exotic delicacies like *unagi* (eel) or *fugu* (blowfish)—inhabit every city side street. Comfortable, country-style restaurants abound, serving a variety of different *nabemono,* the one-pot stew dishes cooked right at your table. There are also lively neighborhood *robatayaki* grills, where cooks in *happi* coats wield skewered bits of meat, seafood, and vegetables over a hot charcoal grill as you watch.

A dozen years ago, sukiyaki and tempura were exotic enough for most Western travelers. Those were the days when raw fish was still something a traveler needed fortitude to try. But with *soba* (noodle) shops and sushi bars popping up everywhere from Los Angeles to Paris, it seems that—at long last—the joy of Japanese cooking has found its way westward . . . and it's about time.

There *is* something special, however, about visiting the tiger in his lair. Something no tame circus cat could ever match. Although tours to famous temples and scenic places can provide important historical and cultural background material, there is nothing like a meal in a local restaurant—be it under the tarps of the liveliest street stall, or within the quiet recesses of an elegant Japanese inn—for a taste of the real Japan. Approaching a platter of fresh sashimi in Tokyo is like devouring a hot dog smothered in mustard and onions in Yankee Stadium. There's nothing like it in the world.

The Essentials of a Japanese Meal

As exotic as it might seem, the basic formula for a traditional Japanese meal is simple. It starts with soup, followed by raw fish, then the entrée (grilled, steamed, simmered or fried fish, chicken, or vegetables), and ends with rice and pickles, with perhaps some fresh fruit for dessert, and a cup of green tea. As simple as that, almost.

An exploration of any cuisine should begin at the beginning, with a basic knowledge of what it is you're eating. Rice, of course, the traditional staple. And seafood—grilled, steamed, fried, stewed, or raw. Chicken, pork, or beef, at times—in that order of frequency. A wide variety of vegetables (wild and cultivated), steamed, sautéed, blanched, or pickled, perhaps—but never overcooked. Soybeans in every form imaginable, from tofu to soy sauce. Seaweed, in and around lots of things.

The basics are just that. But there are, admittedly, a few twists to the story, as could be expected. Beyond the raw fish, it's the incredible variety of vegetation used in Japanese cooking that still surprises the Western palate: *take-no-ko* (bamboo shoots); *renkon* (lotus root); and the treasured *matsutake* mushrooms (which grow wild in jealously guarded forest hideaways and sometimes sell for more than $60 apiece), to name but a few.

Tangy garnishes, both wild and domestic, such as *kinome* (leaves of the Japanese prickly ash pepper tree), *mitsuba* (trefoil, of the parsley family), and *shiso* (a member of the mint family) are used as a foil for oily foods. The more familiar sounding ingredients, such as sesame and ginger, appear in abundance, as do the unfamiliar—*wasabi* (Japanese horseradish), *uri-ne* (lily bulbs), *ginnan* (ginko nuts), and *daikon* (gigantic white radishes). Exotic? Perhaps, but delicious, and nothing here bites back. Simple? Yes, if you understand a few of the ground rules.

Absolute freshness is first. According to world-renowned Japanese chef Shizuo Tsuji, soup and raw fish are the two test pieces of Japanese cuisine. Freshness is the criterion for both: "I can tell at a glance by the texture of their skins—like the bloom of youth on a young girl—whether the fish is really fresh," Tsuji says in *The Art of Japanese Cooking.* A comparison as startling, perhaps, as it is revealing. To a Japanese chef, freshness is an unparalleled virtue, and much of his reputation relies on his ability to obtain the finest ingredients at the peak of season: fish brought in from the sea this morning (not yesterday), and vegetables from the earth (not the hothouse), if at all possible.

Simplicity is next. Rather than embellishing foods with heavy spices and rich sauces, the Japanese chef prefers his flavors *au naturel*. Flavors are enhanced, not elaborated; accented rather than concealed. Without a heavy dill sauce, fish is permitted a degree of natural fishiness—a garnish of fresh red ginger will be provided to offset the flavor rather than to disguise it.

The third prerequisite is beauty. Simple, natural foods must appeal to the eye as well as to the palate. Green peppers on a vermilion dish, perhaps, or an egg custard in a blue bowl. Rectangular dishes for a round eggplant. So important is the seasonal element in Japanese cooking that maple leaves and pine needles will be used to accent an autumn dish. Or two small summer delicacies, a pair of freshwater *ayu* fish, will be grilled with a purposeful twist to their tails to make them "swim" across a crystal platter to suggest the coolness of a mountain stream on a hot August night.

That's next: the mood. It can make or break the entire meal, and the Japanese connoisseur will go to great lengths to find the perfect yakitori stand—a smoky, lively place—an environment appropriate to the occasion, offering a night of grilled chicken, cold beer, and camaraderie. To a place like this, he'll take only friends he knows will appreciate the gesture.

Atmosphere depends as much on the company as it does on the lighting or the color of the drapes. In Japan, this seems to hold particularly true. The popularity of a particular *nomiya*, or bar, depends entirely on the affability of the *mama-san*, that long-suffering lady who's been listening to your troubles for years. In fancier places, mood becomes a fancier problem, to the point of quibbling over the proper amount of "water music" trickling in the basin outside your private room.

Culture: The Main Course

Sipping coffee at a sidewalk café on the Left Bank, you begin to feel what it means to be a Parisian. Slurping noodles on tatami in a neighborhood soba shop overlooking a tiny interior garden, you start to understand what it's like to live in Japan. Food, no matter which country you're in, has much to say about the culture as a whole.

Beyond the natural dictates of climate and geography, Japanese food has its roots in the centuries-old cuisine of the Imperial Court, which was imported from China—a religiously formal style of meal called *yusoku ryori*. It was prepared only by specially appointed chefs, who had the status of priests in the service of the emperor, in a culinary ritual that is now nearly a lost art. Although it was never popularly served in centuries past (a modified version can still be found in Kyoto), much of the ceremony and careful attention to detail of yusoku ryori is reflected today in the formal kaiseki meal.

Kaiseki Ryori: Japanese Haute Cuisine

Kaiseki refers to the most elegant of all styles of Japanese food available today, and *ryori* means cuisine. With its roots in the banquet feasts of the aristocracy, by the late 16th century it had developed into a meal to accompany ceremonial tea. The word kaiseki refers to a heated stone (*seki*) that Buddhist monks placed inside the folds (*kai*) of their kimonos to keep off the biting cold in the unheated temple halls where they slept and meditated.

Cha-kaiseki, as the formal meal served with tea (*cha*) is called, is intended to take the edge off your hunger at the beginning of a formal tea ceremony and to counterbalance the astringent character of the thick green tea. In the tea ceremony, balance—and the sense of calmness and well-being it inspires—is the keynote.

The formula for the basic Japanese meal derived originally from the rules governing formal kaiseki—not too large a portion, just enough; not too spicy, but perhaps with a savory sprig of trefoil to offset the bland tofu. A grilled dish is served before a steamed one, a steamed dish before a simmered one; a square plate is used for a round food; a bright green maple leaf is placed to one side to herald the arrival of spring.

Kaiseki ryori appeals to all the senses at once. An atmosphere is created in which the meal is to be experienced. The poem in calligraphy on a hanging scroll and the flowers in the alcove set the seasonal theme, a motif picked up in the pattern of the dishware chosen for the evening. The colors and shapes of the vessels complement the foods served on them. The visual harmony presented is as vital as the balance and variety of flavors of the foods themselves, for which the ultimate criterion is freshness. The finest ryotei will never serve a fish or vegetable out of its proper season—no matter how marvelous a winter melon today's modern greenhouses can guarantee. Melons are for rejoicing in the summer's bounty . . . period.

Kaiseki ryori found its way out of the formal tearooms and into a much earthier realm of the senses when it became the fashionable snack with sake in the teahouses of the geisha quarters during the 17th and 18th centuries. Not only the atmosphere, but the Chinese characters used to write the word *kaiseki* are different in this context; they refer to aristocratic "banquet seats." And banquets they are. To partake in the most exclusive of these evenings in a teahouse in Kyoto still requires a personal introduction and a great deal of money, though these days many traditional restaurants offer elegant kaiseki meals (without the geisha) at much more reasonable prices.

One excellent way to experience this incomparable cuisine on a budget is to visit a kaiseki restaurant at lunchtime. Many of them offer *kaiseki bento* lunches at a fraction of the dinner price, exquisitely presented in lacquered boxes, as a sampler of their full-course evening meal.

Shojin Ryori: Zen-Style Vegetarian Cuisine

Like an overnight stay in a Buddhist temple, *shojin ryori*, the Zen-style vegetarian cuisine, is another experience you shouldn't pass up. In traditional Japanese cuisine, the emphasis is on the natural flavor of the freshest ingredients in season, without the embellishment of heavy spices and rich sauces. This probably developed out of the Zen belief in the importance of simplicity and austerity as paths to enlightenment. Protein is provided by an almost limitless number of dishes made from soybeans—such as *yudofu*, or boiled bean curd, and *yuba*, sheets of pure protein skimmed from vats of steaming soy milk. The variety and visual beauty of a full-course shojin ryori meal offers new dimensions in dining to the vegetarian gourmet. *Gomadofu*, or sesame-flavored

bean curd, for example, is a delicious taste treat, as is *nasu-dengaku*, grilled eggplant covered with a sweet *miso* sauce.

There are many fine restaurants (particularly in the Kyoto area) that specialize in shojin ryori, but it's best to seek out one of the many temples throughout Japan that open their doors to visitors; here you can try these special meals within the actual temple halls, which often overlook a traditional garden.

Sushi, Sukiyaki, Tempura, and Nabemono: A Comfortable Middle Ground

Leaving the rarefied atmosphere of teahouses and temples behind, an entire realm of more down-to-earth gastronomic pleasures waits to be explored.

Sushi, sukiyaki, and tempura are probably the three most commonly known Japanese dishes in the Western world. Restaurants serving these dishes are to be found in abundance in every major hotel in Japan. It is best, however, to try each of these in a place that specializes in just one.

An old Japanese proverb says *"Mochi wa mochi-ya e"*—if you want rice cakes, go to a rice-cake shop. The same goes for sushi. Sushi chefs undergo a lengthy apprenticeship, and the trade is considered an art form. Possessing the discipline of a judo player, the *itamae-san* (or "man before . . . or behind . . . the counter," depending on your point of view) at a sushi-ya is a real master. Every neighborhood has its own sushi shop, and everyone you meet has his own secret little place to go for sushi.

The Tsukiji Fish Market district in Tokyo is so popular for its sushi shops that you usually have to wait in line for a seat at the counter. Some are quite expensive, some are relatively cheap. "Know before you go" is the best policy; "ask before you eat" is next.

Among the dozens of kinds of sushi available, some of the most popular are *maguro* (tuna), *ebi* (shrimp), *hamachi* (yellowtail), *uni* (sea urchin), *anago* (conger eel), *tako* (octopus), and *awabi* (abalone). The day's selection is usually displayed in a glass case at the counter, which enables you to point at whatever catches your eye. (Try the *ak-agai*, or red shellfish. The word is a euphemistic expression for the female organ, for reasons blushingly recognizable.)

Tempura, the battered and deep-fried fish and vegetable dish, is almost certain to taste better at a small shop that serves nothing else. The difficulties of preparing this seemingly simple dish lie in achieving the proper consistency of the batter and the right temperature and freshness of the oil in which it is fried.

Sukiyaki is the popular beef dish that is sautéed with vegetables in an iron skillet at the table. The tenderness of the beef is the determining factor here, and many of the best sukiyaki houses also run their own butcher shops so that they can control the quality of the beef they serve. Although beef did not become a part of the Japanese diet until the turn of the century, the Japanese are justifiably proud of their notorious beer-fed and hand-massaged beef (e.g., the famous Matsuzaka beef from Kobe, and the equally delicious Omi beef from Shiga Prefecture). Though certainly a splurge, no one should pass up an opportunity to try a beef dinner in Japan.

Apart from sukiyaki and beef, *shabu-shabu* is another possibility, though this dish has become more popular with tourists than with the Japanese. It is similar to sukiyaki in that it is prepared at the table with a combination of vegetables, but it differs in that shabu-shabu is swished briefly in boiling water, while sukiyaki is sautéed in oil and, usually, a slightly sweetened soy sauce. The word *shabu-shabu* actually refers to this swishing sound.

Nabemono, or one-pot dishes, are not as familiar to Westerners as the three mentioned above, but the variety of possibilities is endless, and nothing tastes better on a cold winter's night. Simmered in a light, fish-base broth, these stews can be made of almost anything: chicken (*tori-nabe*), oysters (*kaki-nabe*), or the sumo wrestler's favorite, the hearty *chanko-nabe* . . . with something in it for everyone. Nabemono is a popular family or party dish. The restaurants specializing in nabemono often have a casual, country atmosphere.

Bento, Soba, Udon, and Robatayaki: Feasting on a Budget

Tales of unsuspecting tourists swallowed up by money-gobbling monsters disguised as quaint little restaurants on the back streets of Japan's major cities abound in these days of the high yen. There are, however, many wonderful little places that offer excellent meals and thoughtful service—and have no intention of straining anyone's budget. To find them, you must not be afraid to venture outside your hotel lobby or worry about the fact that the dining spot has no menu in English. Many restaurants have menus posted out front that clearly state the full price you can expect to pay. (Some do add on a 10% tax, and possibly a service charge, so ask in advance.)

Here are a few suggestions for Japanese meals that do not cost a fortune and are usually a lot more fun than relying on the familiar but unexciting international fast-food chains for quick meals on a budget: *bento* lunches, *soba* or *udon* noodle dishes, and the faithful neighborhood *robatayaki* grills, ad infinitum.

The Bento. This is the traditional Japanese box lunch, available for take-out everywhere, and usually comparatively inexpensive. It can be purchased in the morning to be taken along and eaten later, either outdoors or on the train as you travel between cities. The bento consists of rice, pickles, grilled fish or meat, and vegetables, in an almost limitless variety of combinations to suit the season.

The basement level of most major department stores sell beautifully prepared bento lunches to go. In fact, a department store basement is a great place to sample and purchase the whole range of foods offered in Japan: among the things available are French bread, imported cheeses, traditional bean cakes, chocolate bonbons, barbecued chicken, grilled eel, roasted peanuts, fresh vegetables, potato salads, pickled bamboo shoots, and smoked salmon.

The *o-bento* (the "o" is honorific) in its most elaborate incarnation is served in gorgeous multilayered lacquered boxes as an accompaniment to outdoor tea ceremonies or for flower-viewing parties held in spring. Exquisite *bento-bako* (lunch boxes) made in the Edo period (1603–1868) can be found in museums and antiques shops. They are inlaid with mother-of-pearl and delicately hand-painted in gold. A wide variety of sizes and shapes of bento boxes are still handmade in major cities and small villages throughout Japan in both formal and informal styles. They make excellent souvenirs.

A major benefit to the bento lunch is its portability. Sightseeing can take you down many an unexpected path, and you need not worry about finding an appropriate place to stop for a bite to eat—if you bring your own bento. No Japanese family would ever be without one tucked carefully inside their rucksacks right beside the thermos bottle of tea on a cross-country train trip. If they do somehow run out of time to prepare one in advance—no problem—there are hundreds of wonderful options in the form of the beloved *eki-ben* ("train-station box lunch").

Each whistle-stop in Japan takes great pride in the uniqueness and flavor of the special box lunches, featuring the local delicacy, sold right at the station or from vendors inside the trains. The pursuit of the eki-ben has become a national pastime in this nation in love with its trains. Entire books have been written in Japanese explaining the features of every different eki-ben available along the 16,120 miles (26,000 kilometers) of railways in the country. This is one of the best ways to sample the different styles of regional cooking in Japan, and is highly recommended to any traveler who plans to spend time on the Japan Railway trains (*see* Regional Differences, *below*).

Soba and Udon Noodles. Soba and udon noodle dishes are another life-saving treat for stomachs (and wallets) unaccustomed to exotic flavors (and prices). Small shops serving soba (thin, brown, buckwheat noodle) and udon (thick, white, wheat noodle) dishes in a variety of combinations can be found in every neighborhood in the country. Both can be ordered plain (ask for *o-soba* or *o-udon*), in a lightly seasoned broth flavored with bonito and soy sauce, or in combination with things like tempura shrimp (*tempura soba* or *udon*), or chicken (*tori-namba soba* or *udon*). For a refreshing change in summer, try *zaru soba*, cold noodles to be dipped in a tangy soy sauce. *Nabeyaki-udon* is a hearty winter dish of udon noodles, assorted vegetables, and egg served in the pot in which it was cooked.

Robatayaki Grill. Perhaps the most exuberant of inexpensive options is the robatayaki. Beer mug in hand, elbow-to-elbow at the counter of one of these popular neighborhood grills—that is the best way to relax and join in with the local fun. You'll find no pretenses here, just a wide variety of plain good food (as much or as little as you want) with the proper amount of alcohol to get things rolling.

Robata means fireside, and the style of cooking is reminiscent of old-fashioned Japanese farmhouse meals cooked over a charcoal fire in an open hearth. It's easy to order at a robatayaki shop, because the selection of food to be grilled is lined up behind glass at the counter. Fish, meat, vegetables, tofu—take your pick. Some popular choices are *yaki-zakana* (grilled fish), particularly *kare-shio-yaki* (salted and grilled flounder) and *asari saka-mushi* (clams simmered in sake, Japanese rice wine). Try the grilled Japanese *shiitake* (mushrooms), *ao-to* (green peppers), and the *hiyayakko* (chilled tofu sprinkled with bonito flakes, diced green onions, and soy sauce). Yakitori can be ordered in most robatayaki shops, though many inexpensive drinking places specialize in this popular barbecued chicken dish.

The budget dining possibilities in Japan don't stop there. **Okonomiyaki** is another choice. Somewhat misleadingly called the Japanese pancake, it is actually a mixture of vegetables, meat, and seafood in an egg-and-flour batter grilled at your table, much better with beer than with butter. It's most popular for lunch or as an after-movie snack.

Another is **kushi-age,** skewered bits of meat, seafood, and vegetables battered, dipped in bread crumbs, and deep-fried. There are many small restaurants serving only kushi-age at a counter, and many of the robatayaki grills serve it as a sideline. It's also a popular drinking snack.

Oden, a winter favorite, is another inexpensive meal. A variety of meats and vegetables slowly simmered in vats, it goes well with beer or sake. This, too, you may order piece by piece (*ippin*) from the assortment you see steaming away behind the counter, or *moriawase*, in which case the cook will serve you up an assortment.

Sake: The Samurai Beverage

With all this talk about eating and drinking, it would be an unforgivable transgression to overlook Japan's number one alcoholic beverage, sake (pronounced *sakay*), the "beverage of the samurai," as one brewery puts it. The ancient myths call this rice wine the "drink of the gods," and there are over 2,000 different brands produced throughout Japan. A lifetime of serious scene-of-the-crime research would be necessary to explore all the possibilities and complexities of this interesting drink.

Like other kinds of wine, sake comes in sweet (*amakuchi*) and dry (*karakuchi*) varieties; these are graded *tokkyu* (superior class), *ikkyu* (first class), and *nikkyu* (second class) and are priced accordingly. (Connoisseurs say this ranking is for tax purposes and is not necessarily a true indication of quality.)

Best drunk at room temperature (*nurukan*) so as not to alter the flavor, sake is also served heated (*atsukan*) or with ice (*rokku de*). It is poured from *tokkuri* (small ceramic vessels) into tiny cups called *choko*. The diminutive size of these cups shouldn't mislead you into thinking you can't drink too much. The custom of making sure that your drinking companion's cup never runs dry often leads the novice astray.

Junmaishu is the term for pure rice wine, a blend of rice, yeast, and water to which no extra alcohol has been added. Junmaishu has the strongest and most distinctive flavor, compared with various other methods of brewing, and is preferred by the sake *tsu*, as connoisseurs are known.

Apart from the *nomiya* (bars) and restaurants, the place to sample sake is the *izakaya*, a drinking establishment that serves only sake, usually dozens of different kinds, including a selection of *jizake*, the kind produced in limited quantities by small regional breweries throughout the country.

In the words of Ikkyu, one of Japan's most revered and notorious 15th-century imbibers (and one of its "highest" Buddhist priests):

> *I have been ten days in this temple*
> *and my heart is restless.*
> *The scarlet thread of lust at my feet*
> *has reached up long.*
> *If someday you come looking for me,*
> *I will be in a shop that sells fine seafood,*
> *a good drinking place,*
> *or a brothel.*

Regional Differences

Tokyo people are known for their candor and vigor, as compared with the refined restraint of people in the older, more provincial Kyoto. This applies as much to food as it does to language, art, and fashion. Foods in the Kansai district (including Kyoto, Nara, Osaka, and Kobe) tend to be lighter, the sauces less spicy, the soups not as hardy as those of the Kanto district, of which Tokyo is the center. How many Tokyoites have been heard to grumble about the "weak" soba broth on their visits to Kyoto? You go to Kyoto for the delicate and formal kaiseki; to Tokyo for sushi.

Nigiri-sushi, with pieces of raw fish on bite-size balls of rice (the form with which most Westerners are familiar), originated in the Kanto district, where there is a bounty of fresh fish. *Saba-sushi* is the specialty of landlocked Kyoto. Actually the forerunner of nigiri-sushi, it is made by pressing salt-preserved mackerel onto a bed of rice in a mold.

Every island in the Japanese archipelago has its specialty, and, within each island, every province has its own *meibutsu ryori*, or specialty dish. In Kyushu, try *shippoku-ryori*, a banquet-style feast of different dishes in which you eat your way up to a large fish mousse topped with shrimp. This dish is the local specialty in Nagasaki, for centuries the only port through which Japan had contact with the West.

On the island of Shikoku, try *sawachi-ryori*, an extravaganza of elaborately prepared platters of fresh fish dishes, the specialty of Kochi, the main city on the Pacific Ocean side of the island. In Hokkaido, where salmon dishes are the local specialty, try *ishikari-nabe,* a hearty salmon-and-vegetable stew.

The Bottom Line

There are a couple of things that take some getting used to. Things will be easier for you in Japan if you've had some experience with chopsticks. Some of the tourist-oriented restaurants (and of course all those serving Western food) provide silverware, but most traditional restaurants in Japan offer only chopsticks. It's a good idea to practice. The secret is to learn to move only the chopstick on top, rather than to try to move both chopsticks at once.

Sitting on the floor is another obstacle for many, including the younger generation of Japanese to whom the prospect of sitting on a cushion on tatami mats for an hour or so means nothing but stiff knees and numb feet. Because of this, many restaurants now have rooms with tables and chairs. The most traditional restaurants, however, have kept to the customary style of dining in tatami rooms. Give it a try. Nothing can compare with a full-course kaiseki meal brought to your room at a traditional inn. Fresh from the bath, robed in a cotton kimono, you are free to relax and enjoy it all, including the view. After all, the carefully landscaped garden outside your door was designed specifically to be seen from this position.

The service in Japan is usually superb, particularly at a *ryori-ryokan,* as restaurant/inns are called. A maid is assigned to anticipate your every need (even a few you didn't know you had). *"O-kyakusan wa kamisama desu"* (the customer is god), as the old Japanese proverb goes. People who prefer to dine in privacy have been known to say the service is too much.

Other problems? "The portions are too small" is a common complaint. The solution is an adjustment in perspective. In the world of Japanese cuisine, there are colors to delight in and shapes, textures, and flavors are balanced for your pleasure. Naturally, the aroma, flavor, and freshness of the foods have importance, but so do the dishware, the design of the room, the sound of water in a stone basin outside. You are meant to leave the table delighted—not stuffed. An appeal is made to all the senses through the food itself, the atmosphere, and appreciation for a carefully orchestrated feast in every sense of the word—these, and the luxury of time spent in the company of friends.

This is not to say that every Japanese restaurant offers aesthetic perfection. Your basic train-platform, stand-up, gulp-it-down noodle stall ("eat-and-out" in under six minutes) should leave no doubts as to the truth of the old saying that "all feet tread not in one shoe."

In the end, you'll discover that the joy of eating in Japan lies in the adventure of exploring the possibilities. Along every city street, you'll find countless little eateries specializing in anything you can name—and some you can't. In the major cities, you'll find French restaurants, British pubs, and little places serving Italian, Chinese, Indian, and American food, if you need a change of pace. In country towns, you can explore a world of regional delicacies found nowhere else.

There is something for everyone and every budget—from the most exquisitely prepared and presented formal kaiseki meal to a delicately sculpted salmon mousse à la nouvelle cuisine, from skewers of grilled chicken in barbecue sauce to a steaming bowl of noodle soup at an outdoor stall. And much to the chagrin of culinary purists, Japan has no dearth of international fast-food chains—from burgers to spareribs to fried chicken to doughnuts to 31 flavors of American ice cream.

Sometimes the contradictions of this intriguing culture— as seen in the startling contrast between ancient traditions and modern industrial life—seem almost overwhelming. Who would ever have thought you could face salad with lettuce, tomatoes, and seaweed . . . or green-tea ice cream? As the famous potter, Kawai Kanjiro, once said, "Sometimes it's better if you don't understand everything. . . . It makes life so much more exciting."

Manners

• Don't point or gesture with chopsticks. Licking the ends of your chopsticks is rude, as is taking food from a common serving plate with the end of the chopstick you've had in your mouth.

• There is no taboo against slurping your noodle soup, though women are generally less boisterous about it than men.

• Pick up the soup bowl and drink directly from it, rather than lean over the table to sip it. Take the fish or vegetables from it with your chopsticks. Return the lid to the soup bowl when you are finished. The rice bowl, too, is to be picked up and held in one hand while you eat from it.

• When drinking with a friend, don't pour your own. Take the bottle and pour for the other person. He will in turn reach for the bottle and pour for you. Japanese will attempt to top your drink off after every few sips.

• Japanese don't pour sauces on their rice in a traditional meal. Sauces are intended for dipping foods lightly, not for dunking or soaking.

• Among faux pas that are considered nearly unpardonable, the worst perhaps is blowing your nose. Excuse yourself and leave the room if this becomes necessary.

• Although McDonald's and Häagen-Dazs have made great inroads on the custom of never eating in public, it is still considered gauche to munch on a hamburger (or an ice-cream cone) as you walk along a public street.

—By Diane Durston

A resident of Kyoto for more than 10 years, Diane Durston is the author of *Old Kyoto: A Guide to Traditional Shops, Restaurants and Inns* and *Kyoto: Seven Paths to the Heart of the City.*

THE SPRINGS OF ECSTASY

OF ALL THE MANY and varied degrees of the sublime to which the modern Japanese may aspire, none quite compares with that known as *yudedako*. The word means, quite simply, boiled octopus, and Japanese of all ages and both sexes will journey for miles and search for days for the perfect place to become one.

They do so for the simple reason that the attainment of yudedako is, so everyone from Hokkaido to Okinawa is led to believe from birth, a triumphal final step on the road to perfect physical health. It is an absolute essential for anyone ever hoping to achieve personal sobriety and mental serenity. It helps if you want marital harmony, to enjoy lifelong freedom from constipation and boils, to secure happiness, a clear skin, the faultless functioning of your sexual equipment, and to be rewarded with whatever else constitutes the Shinto equivalent of earthly Nirvana.

And the best, indeed the only place in which to become like a boiled octopus, where yudedako is to be found (in exchange for a paltry sum in folding money), is that most hallowed of Japanese institutions, the hot spring, the *onsen*. Of which, a cursory look at a good Japanese map will display, there are very, very many. The country, fissured from end to end with the cracks and crannies that are the geophysical consequence of being sited on a line of volcanoes, positively wheezes with steam and water. It gushes and sprays almost everywhere, in forest and glade, on meadowland and mountaintop. There are hot springs up in the snowfields. There are others on which float bananas and melon-size oranges. A mad-Ludwig look-alike has channeled one into a mountainside cable car, so you can steam as you fly. Monkeys will chatter and steal your towel from springs down south, while melting icicles will drip into boiling waterfalls up in Hokkaido. Some waters are naturally bloodred and scented with hibiscus, others are milky white with suspended sulfur—and smell understandably vile.

There are hundreds of them, in every prefecture, on every offshore island, even (hidden in office buildings and beside cinemas) in cities that have been built, incautiously, above the very fault lines themselves. And to all these superheated hollows flock the inhabitants of the empire in a ceaseless stream of enthusiasm. Small industries—in some towns, very large industries indeed—have sprung up around the onsen to cater to the needs of those who would plunge and soak and steam themselves in the *ofuro,* the baths. Some bath lovers confess to being ofuro-holics, and it's said that there are clinics set up to cater to their excess. "Their passion for hot bathing is proverbial, and no other people in the world take such pride in their sanitary arrangements," as a Government Railway Guide put it, 50 years ago.

Modern lyricists go further. To understand the Japanese, they chorus, there is only one True Way: You must bathe with them. Go on in, they urge—the water's fine. Become a boiled octopus, and discern in your personal conversion alongside them their true nature, their inner soul— the *kokoro,* as the language has it, of the mysterious people of Nippon.

Why not indeed? Well, one reason many Westerners—*gaijin,* as the Japanese rather smoothly call everyone who is not one of them—prefer not to take time out to go bathing in Japan is the understanding that you have to, er, take all your clothes off. *In front of them.* And you *know* they will stare at your body, quite probably finding it a good deal less lovely than their own. They may even laugh or snigger behind their hands.

Furthermore, there are stories of terrible Asian protocols involved in bathing—a series of unwritten and unspoken rules known by every Japanese from conception, the careless breaking of any of which would result in the most frightful retribution. What if I drop the soap in the ofuro? is a typical fear. And so most innocent wanderers through Japan, invited to go bathing, prefer to stay snug inside their Hiltons and their Tokyus, mumbling excuses about the nearest onsen being too far, their schedule being too tight, or that they are quite clean enough anyway, and thanks very much for asking.

I am not an ofuroholic, nor do I entirely hold to the view that the Japanese are an enigmatic master race knowable only by those who watch them wash. But on the other hand, hot-spring bathing, I have discovered, is enormous fun, and in certain places at certain times it can be truly memorable, the stuff that dreams are made on. So, in the fond hope that others may share the enthusiasm, what follows is a brief illustration of what to do and how to do it and, to a very limited extent, where.

In my case, my first bath was taken at a place in eastern Kyushu called Yufu-in; and while there are scores of other springs well within the purview of Tokyo and Osaka and Kyoto, readily accessible to the timorous or the city-bound, it is to Yufu-in I will journey, since its memory lingers most poignant.

It was an autumn morning. I caught the Shinkansen from Tokyo westward to Hakata and was thus hurled in hyperdrive between Honshu and Kyushu, arriving at the vast station of Shin-Hakata at the predicted split second. A quick scurry along platforms, down flights of granite stairs, along passageways bright with colored neon and robotic salesgirls and the *Blade Runner* twitterings of computer-generated messages, then up more granite stairways to where, slightly dusty and forlorn, stood a country train!

This was an antique that had old leather and fur where the Shinkansen had polished steel and ripstop nylon, and it creaked and swayed as it moved out over the switches. And while the bullet train had vanished bloodlessly into tunnels and darted through arrow-straight cuttings, this old dear rumbled arthritically around curves and over trestle bridges, up and ever upward until it was in the heart of the hills, where the maple trees brushed the windows and the waterfalls splashed the carriage walls. The divine wind—the infamous kamikaze that had once scattered Kubla Khan's fleet in Hakata Bay—may have blown stiffly down at sea level: Up

here it was still, and clouds stood unmoving by the mountaintops.

The stations slipped by. Moderate-size cities such as Futsukaichi and Kurume, where they make patterned cloths and rubberware. Small towns beside river crossings, with pottery factories and paper mills. And then little clusters of houses—Era and Bungomori and Bungo-Nakamura—where I first spied the telltale signs of seismic waters. In the pine forests behind each hamlet there were wisps of steam rising into the still air, like New York avenues at night and when Con Edison is at work, so rural Japan is a place of steam, hissing and bubbling out of the very earth.

AND THEN THE TRAIN eased into Yufu-in and creaked to a halt on a curve. It was warm, and there was a smell of creosote and pine tar, and a hint of sulfur in the air. After a few moments the train pulled away, and the station yard fell silent but for the cawing of a pair of crows high up in a tree. An old lady stepped from the shade, nudged me, and pointed to a crowd of bicycles for rent; 500 yen until nightfall, she suggested. I handed over the notes, she handed me a map, and on a cycle frame 10 sizes too small I wobbled off into town.

The woman had drawn crosses on the chart to indicate the best baths, but I had a guide with me, a young secretary from Fukuoka who hadn't been to an onsen for weeks and had said she was happy to swap her linguistic expertise for an hour or two of soaking. And so the pair of us headed south along a country lane, bound for a *ryokan*—a Japanese inn—called Kozenin.

There seemed to be no one about. The small dining room stood quite empty except for a stuffed boar standing by a table. But a wood fire smoldered quietly in an open grate, and a discreet cough brought an ancient attendant from behind a screen. She bowed low many times, and there was some conversation from which I caught only the word *furo*, then many *dōmo arigato gozaimashita* and much more low bowing and smiling. Then the two of us were handed *yukata*—cotton dressing gowns—and a pair of tiny squares of tie-dyed cloth called *furoshiki*. We walked outside again, down a graveled path through a small grove of pines, before coming to a pair of doors set in a plane-tree palisade. "A *rotemburo*," Yoko whispered. "Open-air pool. We're lucky."

My *kanji* is poor at the best of times, but I have become accustomed to the fact that the ideograph of "men" looks a sight more complicated than that for "women." So I pointed at what I thought was my door, Yoko grinned her assent, and we went our separate ways.

INSIDE WAS A CHANGING room: flagstones worn smooth by centuries of use, stripped-oak walls, a few old iron hooks, a hand pump, some bamboo hand-dippers, half a dozen tiny stools with commodelike openings on top, and a wooden box filled with bars of industrial-strength soap. Beyond, all I could see was steam rising from the surface of what seemed a long and pretty lake that reached deep into the forest. This was the *rotemburo* itself; other springs at Yufu-in might be indoors, but this one was in as natural a setting as its Shinto gods had decreed. I could hear the gurgling of water running into it along bamboo gutters. It was all very peaceful and—mercifully—there seemed to be no one around.

I slipped off my yukata and put it on a hook. For a few seconds, and lest anyone should be lurking, I held my furoshiki, with studied casualness, in the approximate area that is always fuzzed-out in Japanese sex films. Then I pumped water into the hand-dipper, took a bar of Lifebuoy, carried my stool down to the edge of the lake, and began to scrub.

This, I had been told, was crucial. Wash and scrub and soap and scrape every square millimeter of your body until not one molecule of grubbiness remains. And this I did, pummeling myself ruthlessly, determined to get it right. "How you doing?" shouted Yoko from behind her bamboo curtain. I replied, breathlessly, that I was doing all I should be doing, and it seemed to be going well.

"Not a drop of soapy water in the bath!" she warned, and I baled and sluiced frantically as one small trickle of foaming liquid seemed to course its errant way toward the steam. But most onsen seem to have been designed by hydraulic architects of some skill: It would take a clumsy fellow indeed to get soapy water into the ofuro, so many and so effective are the little dams of stone erected everywhere as a precaution. The only way to pollute the bath is to get into it unbathed, unrinsed, or, heaven forfend, while holding and planning to use the soap itself. And that you never, never do. As Yoko, in one final reminder, called out.

"Ready?" she then asked. And I heard a splash and a sudden gasp of pleasure. She was in.

Now came the difficult bit. I was clean as a new pin, my skin tingled from the spring-water, every atom of saponified glycerin long gone. I dropped my furoshiki completely and walked across smooth humps of granite to the edge. I dipped my toe into the steaming bath. The water was hot, indeed, but at the same time so extraordinarily soft that there seemed no pain in going farther. I stepped onto a rock slab, gasped at the slight shock, then walked forward to a deeper slab. The water rose steadily about me until it was waist-deep.

Come on!" urged Yoko, who was, quite unashamedly, watching the entire performance. I could see her now through the mist, her head and shoulders just above the water that beached and lapped against the swell of her breasts. The outline of her body below was refracted out of any recognition too precise for decency.

The only way to retain my own dignity as she watched was to submerge, and so I pitched forward and down and sat as gently as I could on a convenient boulder. Yoko was a few feet away. I smiled at her and she smiled back. She touched my toe with one of hers, then moved toward me slightly and began to massage my foot with both of her naked legs. I closed my eyes and, content and warm and blanketed in the pleasing softness of the water, began to think of paradise.

When I opened my eyes—perhaps five or 10 minutes later—I was looking up at the deep blue sky. It was framed by dozens of maple trees, their leaves brilliant red and yellow after the first frosts of autumn.

Once in a while one would dislodge, then drop and float, curling in the heat, on the surface of the bath. The air above the pool was cooler now—it was late afternoon, the sun was dipping behind Mount Yufu, and flocks of birds were flying back to their nests.

THE BATH STEAMED EVEN more vigorously in the cool of the gloaming, and the bamboo runnels carrying the source water from the springs seemed to froth with new energy. Sitting beneath one of these proved a scalding reminder of what high temperature is all about: Yoko sat gaily beneath one for a good minute and then shouted triumphantly: *"Yudedako!"* I looked over at her; she had turned a bright red, like—well, just like a boiled octopus, though minus half a dozen arms. And as I looked down I seemed to be going the same way.

So out we climbed, she careless of the looks, me still taking care to avoid the gazes of the few children who had come in while I dozed. But none of them seemed more than mildly curious; no one seemed to mind, let alone to giggle. *"Hadaka to hadaka no tsukiai"* ("Relationships between naked people are honest relationships"), they say—bathing friends are the best of friends, the bath becomes a great equalizer, no one is more curious than he should be, no one ever behaves such as to spoil the enjoyment of any other bather, no one is embarrassed nor causes embarrassment.

And in that particular sense the bath is Japan, and the lyricists are right. For the manners of the Japanese, lately so corrupted in the cities and by the boardrooms, seem to revert to their impeccable type in the unalloyed egalitarianism of the onsen. Here, rank and title, riches and power, are stripped away with the clothes: There is no way to tell if the body lolling beside you belongs to the boss of Mitsubishi, to an ambassador, to a pauper, to a mendicant priest. With rank neither claimed nor recognized, each bather offers to the other an equal degree of respect and regard.

Then again, a man is well aware in a mixed-sex bath—like this one in Yufu-in—that naked women are all about him, yet the eroticism this induces is only of the mildest form, and all is diminished by the perfect decorum. For above all, decorum and studied delight rule the protocols of bathing—you seek pleasure from the waters, and you ensure that those about you are allowed to seek it too. Small wonder so few psychiatrists find employment in Japan. The onsen to which the Japanese repair each week or each month or every six months seem marvelous devices for purging the soul of envy and anxiety and stress, as well (it is claimed) as for curing all known ills, cleansing the liver and the brain, ensuring potency and attractiveness, long life—and wealth of spirit, if not necessarily of pocket.

And thus we spent the remainder of that autumn evening. We emerged from the first bath, toweled ourselves briskly dry, and cycled to another, and another, until it got too dark to see and we feared we might miss the last train. We sampled iron springs with red water; we found silky-smooth alkali springs that gushed forth *unagi,* or "eel water"; and Yoko knew of a tiny *harinoyu,* or "needle bath," which felt like immersing into a tub filled with small and very hot hedgehogs, and yet was much more pleasant than it sounds.

But in Yufu-in there were no mud baths nor radioactive sand baths, no seaside baths, not a single bath in a cable car, nor any of the astonishingly hot *atsu-yu,* where men with paddles slap at the water to try to keep it from boiling, and where there are Bath Masters to make sure you stay only for the three minutes needed to attain yudedako, and not a fatal second longer. For all these delights I had to wait for other places, other springs.

We caught the train at 10, having dined before a log fire and drunk deep of hot sake and Sapporo beer. The cycle lady was still there, waiting in the starlight, and she smiled as we climbed aboard the old train. She said something to Yoko as we left, and both women laughed. I asked what it was. "The *gaijin* looks younger," said Yoko. "A very young boiled octopus. Very good, don't you think? Very good."

—By Simon Winchester

Asia-Pacific editor of Condé Nast Traveler *and Pacific region correspondent of* The Guardian *of London, Simon Winchester has reached yudedako more than once.*

MORE PORTRAITS

History

Fourteen hundred years of history is rather a lot to take in when going on a vacation, but two good surveys make the task much easier: Richard Storry's *A History of Modern Japan* (by modern, he means everything post-prehistoric) and George Sansom's *Japan: A Short Cultural History.* Sansom's three-volume *History of Japan* is a more exhaustive treatment.

For those interested in earlier times, Ivan Morris's *The World of the Shining Prince* uses diaries and literature of the time to reconstruct life in the ancient city of Heian (Kyoto) from 794 to 1192. It should be required reading for anyone wishing to tour old Kyoto. *The Culture of the Meiji Period,* by Irokawa Daikichi, covers Japan's 19th-century encounters with the West. Oliver Statler's *Japanese Inn* deals with 400 years of Japanese social history.

Religion

Anyone wanting to read a Zen Buddhist text should try *The Platform Sutra of the Sixth Patriarch,* one of the Zen classics, written by an ancient Chinese head of the sect and translated by Philip B. Yampolsky. Another Zen text of high importance is the Lotus Sutra; it has been translated by Leon Hurvitz as *The Scripture of the Lotus Blossom of the Fine Dharma: The Lotus Sutra.* Stuart D. Picken has written books on both major Japanese religions: *Shinto: Japan's Spiritual Roots* and *Buddhism: Japan's Cultural Identity.* William R. LaFleur's recommended *Karma of Words: Buddhism and the Literary Arts in Medieval Japan* traces how Buddhism affected medieval Japanese mentality and behavior.

Literature

The great classic of all Japanese fiction is the *Tale of Genji;* Genji, or the Shining Prince, has long been taken as the archetype of ideal male behavior. The novel was written by a woman of the court, Murasaki Shikibu, around the year 1000; two translations are available, one by Arthur Waley and another by Edward Seidensticker. Of the same period, Japan's "Golden Age," is *The Pillow Book of Sei Shonagon,* the diary of a woman's courtly life, eloquently translated by Ivan Morris.

The Edo period is well covered by literary translations. Howard Hibbett's *Floating World in Japanese Fiction* gives an excellent selection with commentaries. The racy prose of Saikaku Ihara, who lived at the end of the 17th century and embodied the rough bravura of the growing merchant class, is translated in various books, including *Some Final Words of Advice, Life of an Amorous Man,* and *Five Women Who Loved Love.* More serious literature of the same period are *haikai* poems. Basho produced great examples of these 17-syllable verses; his *Narrow Road to the Deep North and Other Travel Sketches* is available in translation. A general overview of Japanese poetry may be found in the *Penguin Book of Japanese Verse.*

Several modern Japanese novelists have been translated into English. One of the best-known writers among Westerners is Yukio Mishima, author of *The Sea of Fertility* trilogy, among many other works. His books often deal with the effects of postwar Westernization on Japanese culture. Two superb prose stylists are Junchiro Tanizaki, author of *The Makioka Sisters, Some Prefer Nettles,* and *Seven Japanese Tales,* and Nobel Prize winner Yasunari Kawabata, whose novels include *Snow Country, Beauty and Sadness,* and *The Sound of the Mountain.*

Sociology

The Japanese have a genre they refer to as *nihonjin-ron,* or studies of "Japaneseness." Western-style studies of the Japanese way of life in relation to the West also abound. Perhaps the best is Ezra Vogel's *Japan As Number One: Lessons for America.* A fine study of the Japanese mind is found in Takeo Doi's *The Anatomy of Dependence* and Chie Nakane's *Japanese Society.* Edwin O. Reischauer's *The Japanese* and his more recent *The Japanese*

Today are general overviews of Japanese society.

An exceptionally enlightening book on the Japanese sociopolitical system, especially for diplomats and business people intending to work with the Japanese, is *The Enigma of Japanese Power* by Harel van Wolferen.

Art/Architecture

A wealth of literature exists on Japanese art. Much of the early writing has not withstood the test of time, but R. Paine and Alexander Soper's *Art and Architecture of Japan* remains a good place to start. A more recent survey, though narrower in scope, is Joan Stanley-Smith's *Japanese Art*.

The *Japan Arts Library,* a multivolume survey published by Kodansha, covers most of the styles and personalities of Japanese art, including architecture. The series has volumes on castles, teahouses, screen painting, and wood-block prints. A more detailed look at the architecture of Tokyo is Edward Seidensticker's *Low City, High City. What is Japanese Architecture?,* by Kazuo Nishi and Kazuo Hozumi, is full of information on the history of Japanese architecture, with examples of buildings you will actually see on your travels.

English-Japanese Tourist Vocabulary

Basics 基本的表現

Pronunciation key: a-ah, e-hey, i-we, o-so, u-true, g-go, kyu-cue. In Japanese, all syllables receive equal stress.

Yes/No	hai/i-e	はい／いいえ
Please	o-ne-gai shi-ma-su	お願いします
Thank you (very much)	(do-mo)a-ri-ga-to go-zai-ma-su	（どうも）ありがとうございます
You're welcome	do i-ta-shi-mash-te	どういたしまして
Excuse me	su-mi-ma-sen.	すみません
Sorry	go-men na-sai	ごめんなさい
Good morning	o-ha-yo go-zai-ma-su	お早うございます
Good day/afternoon	kon-ni-chi-wa	こんにちは
Good evening	kom-ban-wa	こんばんは
Good night	o-ya-su-mi na-sai	おやすみなさい
Goodbye	sa-yo-na-ra	さようなら
Mr./Mrs./Miss	-san	一さん
Pleased to meet you	ha-ji-me-mash-te	はじめまして
How do you do?	do-zo yo-rosh-ku	どうぞよろしく

Numbers 数

The first reading is used for reading numbers, as in telephone numbers, and the second is often used for counting things.

1	i-chi / hi-to-tsu	一／一つ		17	ju-shi-chi	十七
2	ni / fu-ta-tsu	二／二つ		18	ju-ha-chi	十八
3	san / mit-su	三／三つ		19	ju-kyu	十九
4	shi / yot-tsu	四／四つ		20	ni-ju	二十
5	go / i-tsu-tsu	五／五つ		21	ni-ju-i-chi	二十一
6	ro-ku / mut-tsu	六／六つ		30	san-ju	三十
7	na-na / na-na-tsu	七／七つ		40	yon-ju	四十
8	ha-chi / yat-tsu	八／八つ		50	go-ju	五十
9	kyu / kokonotsu	九／九つ		60	ro-ku-ju	六十
10	ju / to	十／十		70	na-na-ju	七十
11	ju-i-chi	十一		80	ha-chi-ju	八十
12	ju-ni	十二		90	kyu-ju	九十
13	ju-san	十三		100	hya-ku	百
14	ju-yon	十四		1000	sen	千
15	ju-go	十五		10,000	i-chi-man	一万
16	ju-ro-ku	十六		100,000	ju-man	十万

Days of the Week 曜日

Sunday	ni-chi-yo-bi	日曜日
Monday	ge-tsu-yo-bi	月曜日
Tuesday	ka-yo-bi	火曜日
Wednesday	su-i-yo-bi	水曜日
Thursday	mo-ku-yo-bi	木曜日
Friday	kin-yo-bi	金曜日
Saturday	do-yo-bi	土曜日

Months 月

January	i-chi-ga-tsu	一月	July	shi-chi-ga-tsu	七月
February	ni-ga-tsu	二月	August	ha-chi-ga-tsu	八月
March	san-ga-tsu	三月	September	ku-ga-tsu	九月
April	shi-ga-tsu	四月	October	ju-ga-tsu	十月
May	go-ga-tsu	五月	November	ju-i-chi-ga-tsu	十一月
June	ro-ku-ga-tsu	六月	December	ju-ni-ga-tsu	十二月

Useful Expressions, Questions, and Answers よく使われる表現

Do you speak English?	ei-go ga wa-ka-ri-ma-ska	英語がわかりますか。
I don't speak Japanese.	ni-hon-go ga wa-ka-ri-ma-sen	日本語がわかりません。
I don't understand.	wa-ka-ri-ma-sen	わかりません。
I understand.	wa-ka-ri-mash-ta	わかりました。
I don't know.	shi-ri-ma-sen	知りません。
I'm American/British.	wa-ta-shi wa a-me-ri-ka/ i-gi-ri-su jin desu	私はアメリカ／イギリス人です。
What's your name?	o-na-mae wa nan deska	お名前は何ですか。
My name is . . .	. . . to mo-shi-ma-su	……と申します。
What time is it?	i-ma nan-ji deska	今何時ですか。
How?	do yat-te	どうやって。
When?	i-tsu	いつ。
Yesterday/today/ tomorrow	ki-no/kyo/ash-ta	きのう／きょう／あした
This morning	kesa	けさ
This afternoon	kyo no go-go	きょうの午後
Tonight	kom-ban	こんばん
Excuse me, what?	su-mi-ma-sen, nan de-ska	すみません、何ですか。
What is this/that?	ko-re/so-re wa nan de-ska	これ／それは何ですか。
Why?	na-ze de-ska	なぜですか。
Who?	dare desu ka	だれですか。
I am lost.	mi-chi ni ma-yo-i-mash-ta	道に迷いました。
Where is . . .	. . . wa do-ko de-ska	……はどこですか。
the train station?	e-ki	駅
the subway station?	chi-ka-te-tsu-no-eki	地下鉄の駅

the bus stop?	ba-su tei	バス停
the taxi stand?	tak-shi-i no-ri-ba	タクシー乗り場
the airport?	ku-ko	空港
the post office?	yu-bin-kyo-ku	郵便局
the bank?	gin-ko	銀行
the . . . hotel?	. . . ho-te-ru	…..ホテル
the elevator?	e-re-be-ta	エレベーター
Where are the restrooms?	toi-re wa do-ko de-ska	トイレはどこですか。
Here/there/over there	ko-ko/so-ko/a-so-ko	ここ／そこ／あそこ
Left/right	hi-da-ri/mi-gi	左／右
Straight ahead	mas-su-gu	まっすぐ
Is it near/far?	chi-kai/to-i de-ska	近い／遠いですか。
Are there any rooms?	he-ya ga a-ri-ma-ska	部屋がありますか。
I'd like . . .	. . . ga ho-shi-i no desu ga	….がほしいのですが。
a newspaper	shim-bun	新聞
a stamp	kit-te	切手
the key	ka-gi	鍵
I'd like to buy . . .	. . . o kai-tai no de-ske do	……を買いたいのですけど。
a ticket to . . .	. . . ma-de no kip-pu	……までの切符
a map	chi-zu	地図
How much is it?	i-ku-ra de-ska	いくらですか。
It's expensive/cheap.	ta-kai/ya-su-i de-su ne	高い／安いですね。
A little/a lot	sko-shi/tak-san	少し／たくさん
More/less	mot-to o-ku/sku-na-ku	もっと多く／少なく
Enough/too much	ju-bun/o-su-gi-ru	十分／多すぎる
I'd like to exchange . . .	. . . ryo-gae shi-te i-ta-da-ke-ma-ska.	……両替して頂けますか。
dollars to yen	do-ru o en ni	ドルを円に
pounds to yen	pon-do o en ni	ポンドを円に
How do you say . . . in Japanese?	ni-hon-go de . . . wa do i-i-ma-ska	日本語で……はどう言いますか。
I am ill/sick.	wa-ta-shi wa byo-ki de-su	私は病気です。
Please call a doctor.	i-sha o yon-de ku-da-sai	医者を呼んで下さい。
Please call the police.	kei-sa-tsu o yon-de ku-da-sai	警察を呼んで下さい。
Help!	tas-ke-te	助けて！

Restaurants レストラン

Basics and Useful Expressions よく使われる表現

A bottle of . . .	. . . ip-pon	…..一本
A glass/cup of . . .	. . . ip-pai	…..一杯
Ashtray	hai-za-ra	灰皿
Plate	sa-ra	皿
Bill/check	kan-jo	かんじょう
Bread	pan	パン
Breakfast	cho-sho-ku	朝食
Butter	ba-ta	バター

Cheers!	kam-pai	乾杯！
Chopsticks	ha-shi	箸
Cocktail	kak-te-ru	カクテル
Dinner	yu-sho-ku	夕食
Excuse me!	su-mi-ma-sen	すみません
Fork	fo-ku	フォーク
I am diabetic.	wa-ta-shi wa to-nyo-byo de-su	私は糖尿病です。
I am dieting.	dai-et-to chu de-su	ダイエット中です。
I am a vegetarian.	sai-sho-ku shu-gi-sha de-su	菜食主義者です。
I cannot eat . . .	. . . wa ta-be-ra-re-ma-sen	……は食べられません。
I'd like to order.	chu-mon o shi-tai desu	注文をしたいです。
I'd like . . .	. . . o o-ne-gai-shi-ma-su	……をお願いします。
I'm hungry.	o-na-ka ga su-i-te i-ma-su	お腹が空いています。
I'm thirsty.	no-do ga ka-wai-te i-ma-su	喉が渇いています。
It's good/bad.	oi-shi-i/ma-zu-i de-su	おいしい／まずいです。
Knife	nai-fu	ナイフ
Lunch	chu-sho-ku	昼食
Menu	men-yu	メニュー
Napkin	nap-kin	ナプキン
Pepper	ko-sho	こしょう
Please give me . . .	. . . o ku-da-sai.	……を下さい。
Salt	shi-o	塩
Set menu	tei-sho-ku	定食
Spoon	su-pun	スプーン
Sugar	sa-to	砂糖
Wine list	wain ris-to	ワインリスト
What do you recommend?	o-su-su-me ryo-ri wa nan de-ska	お勧め料理は何ですか。

Meat Dishes 肉料理

焼き肉	yakiniku	Thinly sliced beef and liver are marinated then barbecued over an open fire at the table.
すき焼き	sukiyaki	Thinly sliced beef, green onions, mushrooms, thin noodles, and cubes of tofu are simmered in a large iron pan in front of you. These ingredients are cooked in a mixture of soy sauce, mirin (cooking wine), and a little sugar. You are given a saucer of raw egg to cool the sukiyaki morsels before eating. Using chopsticks, you help yourself to anything on your side of the pan and dip it into the egg and then eat. Best enjoyed in a group.
しゃぶしゃぶ	shabu-shabu	Extremely thin slices of beef are plunged for an instant into boiling water flavored with soup stock and then dipped into a thin sauce and eaten.
肉じゃが	niku-jaga	Beef and potatoes stewed together with soy sauce.
ステーキ	suteki	steak
ハンバーグ	hambagu	Hamburger pattie served with sauce.

トンカツ	tonkatsu	Breaded deep fried pork cutlets.
しょうが焼	shoga-yaki	Pork cooked with ginger.
酢豚	subuta	Sweet and sour pork, originally a Chinese dish.
からあげ	kara-age	fried chicken
焼き鳥	yakitori	Pieces of chicken, white meat, liver, skin, etc. threaded on skewers with green onions and marinated in sweet soy sauce and grilled.
親子どんぶり	oyako-domburi	Literally, "mother and child bowl"—chicken and egg in broth over rice.
他人どんぶり	tanin-domburi	Literally, "strangers in a bowl"—similar to oyako domburi, but with beef instead of chicken.
ロール・キャベツ	roru kyabetsu	Rolled cabbage; beef or pork rolled in cabbage and cooked.
はやしライス	hayashi raisu	Beef flavored with tomato and soy sauce with onions and peas over rice.
カレーライス	kare-raisu	Curried rice. A thick curry gravy typically containing beef is poured over white rice.
カツカレー	katsu-kare	Curried rice with tonkatsu.
お好み焼き	okonomiyaki	Sometimes called a Japanese pancake, this is made from a batter of flour, egg, cabbage, and meat or seafood, grilled then covered with green onions and a special sauce.
シューマイ	shumai	Shrimp or pork wrapped in a light dough and steamed.
ギョーザ	gyoza	Pork spiced with ginger and garlic in a Chinese wrapper and fried or steamed.

Seafood Dishes 魚貝類料理

焼き魚	yakizakana	broiled fish
塩焼	shio yaki	Fish sprinkled with salt and broiled until crisp.
さんま	samma	saury pike
いわし	iwashi	sardines
しゃけ	shake	salmon
照り焼き	teriyaki	Fish basted in soy sauce and broiled.
ぶり	buri	yellowtail
煮魚	nizakana	stewed fish
さばのみそ煮	saba no miso ni	Mackerel stewed with soy-bean paste.
揚げ魚	agezakana	fried fish
かれいフライ	kare furai	fried halibut
刺身	sashimi	Very fresh raw fish. Served sliced thin on a bed of white radish with a saucer of soy sauce and horseradish. Eaten by dipping fish into soy sauce mixed with horseradish.
まぐろ	maguro	tuna
あまえび	amaebi	sweet shrimp

いか	ika	squid
たこ	tako	octopus
あじ	aji	horse mackerel
さわら	sawara	Spanish mackerel
しめさば	shimesaba	Mackerel marinated in vinegar.
かつおたたき	katsuo no tataki	Bonito cooked just slightly on the surface. Eaten with cut green onions and thin soy sauce.
どじょうの柳川なべ	dojo no yanagawa nabe	Loach cooked with burdock root and egg in an earthen dish. Considered a delicacy.
うな重	una-ju	Eel marinated in a slightly sweet soy sauce is charcoal-broiled and served over rice. Considered a delicacy.
天重	ten-ju	Deep fried prawns served over rice with sauce.
海老フライ	ebi furai	Deep fried breaded prawns.
あさりの酒蒸し	asari no sakamushi	Clams steamed with rice wine.

Sushi 寿司

寿司	sushi	Basically, sushi is rice, fish, and vegetables. The rice is delicately seasoned with vinegar, salt, and sugar. There are basically three types of sushi: nigiri, chirashi, and maki.
にぎり寿司	nigiri zushi	The rice is formed into a bite-sized cake and topped with various raw or cooked fish. The various types are usually named after the fish, but not all are fish. Nigiri zushi is eaten by picking up the cakes with chopsticks or the fingers, dipping the fish side in soy sauce, and eating.
まぐろ	maguro	tuna
とろ	toro	fatty tuna
たい	tai	red snapper
さば	saba	mackerel
こはだ	kohada	gizzard shad
さけ	sake	salmon
はまち	hamachi	yellowtail
ひらめ	hirame	flounder
あじ	aji	horse mackerel
たこ	tako	octopus
あなご	anago	sea eel
えび	ebi	shrimp
甘えび	ama-ebi	sweet shrimp
いか	ika	squid
みる貝	miru-gai	giant clam
あおやぎ	aoyagi	round clam
卵	tamago	egg

かずのこ	kazunoko	herring roe
かに	kani	crab
ほたて貝	hotate-gai	scallop
うに	uni	sea urchin
いくら	ikura	salmon roe
ちらしずし	chirashi sushi	In chirashi sushi, a variety of seafood is arranged on the top of the rice and served in a bowl.
巻き寿司	maki sushi	Raw fish and vegetables or other morsels are rolled in sushi rice and wrapped in dried seaweed. Some popular varieties are listed here.
鉄火巻	tekka-maki	tuna roll
かっぱ巻	kappa-maki	cucumber roll
新香巻	shinko-maki	shinko roll (shinko is a type of pickle)
カリフォルニア巻	kariforunia-maki	California roll, containing crabmeat and avocado. This was invented in the U.S. but was re-exported to Japan and is gaining popularity there.
うに	uni	Sea urchin on rice wrapped with seaweed.
いくら	ikura	Salmon roe on rice wrapped with seaweed.
太巻	futomaki	Big roll with egg and pickled vegetables.

Vegetable Dishes 野菜料理

おでん	oden	Often sold by street vendors at festivals and in parks, etc., this is vegetables, octopus, or egg in a thick batter and boiled.
天ぷら	tempura	Vegetables, shrimp, or fish deep fried in a light batter. Eaten by dipping into a thin sauce containing grated white radish.
野菜サラダ	yasai sarada	vegetable salad
大学いも	daigaku imo	fried yams in a sweet syrup
野菜いため	yasai itame	"stir-fried" vegetables
きんぴらごぼう	kimpira gobo	Carrots and burdock root, fried with soy sauce.
煮もの	nimono	stewed vegetables
かぼちゃ	kabocha	pumpkin
さといも	satoimo	taro root
たけのこ	takenoko	bamboo shoots
ごぼう	gobo	burdock root
れんこん	renkon	lotus root
酢のもの	sumono	Vegetables seasoned with vinegar.
きゅうり	kyuri	cucumber
和えもの	aemono	Vegetables and fish mixed with miso or vinegar.
ねぎ	tamanegi	onions
おひたし	ohitashi	Boiled vegetables with soy sauce and dried shaved bonito or sesame seeds.

ほうれん草	horenso	spinach
漬物	tsukemono	Japanese pickles. Made from white radish, eggplant or other vegetables. Considered essential to the Japanese meal.

Egg Dishes 卵料理

ベーコン・エッグ	bekon-eggu	bacon and eggs
ハム・エッグ	hamu-eggu	ham and eggs
スクランブルエッグ	sukuramburu eggu	scrambled eggs
ゆで卵	yude tamago	boiled eggs
目玉焼	medama-yaki	fried eggs, sunny-side up
オムレツ	omuretsu	omelet
オムライス	omuraisu	Omelet with rice inside, often eaten with ketchup.
茶わんむし	chawan mushi	Vegetables, shrimp, etc., steamed in egg custard.

Tofu Dishes 豆腐料理

Tofu, also called bean curd, is a white, high-protein food with the consistency of soft gelatin.

冷やっこ	hiya-yakko	Cold tofu with soy sauce and grated ginger.
湯どうふ	yudofu	boiled tofu
あげだしどうふ	agedashi dofu	Lightly fried plain tofu dipped in soy sauce and grated ginger.
マーボーどうふ	mabo dofu	Tofu and ground pork in a spicy red sauce. Originally a Chinese dish.
とうふの田楽	tofu no dengaku	Tofu broiled on skewers and flavored with miso.

Rice Dishes ごはん料理

ごはん	gohan	steamed white rice
おにぎり	onigiri	Triangular balls of rice with fish or vegetables inside and wrapped in a type of seaweed.
おかゆ	okayu	rice porridge
チャーハン	chahan	Fried rice; includes vegetables and pork.
ちまき	chimaki	A type of onigiri made with sweet rice.
パン	pan	Bread, but usually rolls with a meal.

Soups 汁もの

みそ汁	miso shiru	Miso soup. A thin broth containing tofu, mushrooms, or other morsels in a soup flavored with miso or soy-bean paste. The morsels are taken out of the bowl and the soup is drunk straight from the bowl without a spoon.
すいもの	suimono	Soy sauce flavored soup, often including fish and tofu.
とん汁	tonjiru	Pork soup with vegetables.

Noodles 麺類

うどん	udon	Wide flour noodles in broth. Can be lunch in a light broth or a full dinner called "nabeyaki udon" when meat, chicken, egg, and vegetables are added.
そば	soba	Buckwheat noodles. Served in a broth like udon or, during the summer, cold on a bamboo mesh and called "zaru soba."
ラーメン	ramen	Chinese noodles in broth, often with "chashu" or roast pork. Broth is soy sauce or miso flavored.
そう麺	somen	Very thin noodles, usually served cold with a tsuyu or thin sauce. Eaten during the summer.
ひやむぎ	hiyamugi	Similar to somen, but made from wheat.
やきそば	yakisoba	Noodles fried with beef and cabbage, garnished with pickled ginger and flavored with Worcestershire sauce.
スパゲッティ	supagetti	Spaghetti. There are many interesting variations on this dish, notably spaghetti in soup, often with seafood.

Fruit 果物

アーモンド	amondo	almonds
あんず	anzu	apricot
バナナ	banana	banana
ぶどう	budo	grapes
グレープフルーツ	gurepufurutsu	grapefruit
干しぶどう	hoshibudo	raisins
いちご	ichigo	strawberries
いちじく	ichijiku	figs
かき	kaki	persimmons
キーウイ	kiiui	kiwi
ココナツ	kokonatsu	coconut
くり	kuri	chestnuts
くるみ	kurumi	walnuts
マンゴ	mango	mango
メロン	meron	melon
みかん	mikan	tangerine (mandarin orange)
桃	momo	peach
梨	nashi	pear
オレンジ	orenji	orange
パイナップル	painappuru	pineapple
パパイヤ	papaiya	papaya
ピーナッツ	piinattsu	peanuts
プルーン	purun	prunes
レモン	remon	lemon
りんご	ringo	apple
さくらんぼ	sakurambo	cherry
西瓜	suika	watermelon

Dessert デザート類

アイスクリーム	aisukuriimu	ice cream
プリン	purin	caramel pudding
クレープ	kurepu	crêpes
ケーキ	keki	cake
シャーベット	shabetto	sherbet
アップルパイ	appuru pai	apple pie
ようかん	yokan	sweet bean paste jelly
コーヒーゼリ	kohii zeri	coffee-flavored gelatin
和菓子	wagashi	Japanese sweets

Drinks 飲物

Alcoholic 酒類

ビール	biiru	beer
生ビール	nama biiru	draft beer
カクテル	kakuteru	cocktail
ウィスキー	uisukii	whisky
スコッチ	sukotchi	scotch
バーボン	babon	bourbon
日本酒（酒）	nihonshu (sake)	Sake, a wine brewed from rice.
あつかん	atsukan	warmed sake
ひや	hiya	cold sake
焼酎	shochu	Spirit distilled from potatoes.
チューハイ	chuhai	Shochu mixed with soda water and flavored with lemon juice or other flavors.
ワイン	wain	wine
赤	aka	red
白	shiro	white
ロゼ	roze	rose
シャンペン	shampen	champagne
ブランデー	burande	brandy

Non-alcoholic その他の飲物

コーヒー	kohii	coffee
アイスコーヒー	aisu kohii	iced coffee
日本茶	nihon cha	Japanese green tea
紅茶	kocha	tea
レモンティー	remon tii	tea with lemon
ミルクティー	miruku tii	tea with milk
アイスティー	aisu tii	iced tea
ウーロン茶	uron cha	oolong tea
ジャスミン茶	jasumin cha	jasmine tea
牛乳／ミルク	gyunyu/miruku	milk
ココア	kokoa	hot chocolate
レモンスカッシュ	remon sukasshu	carbonated lemon soft drink
ミルクセーキ	miruku seki	milk shake
ジュース	jusu	juice, but can also mean any soft drink
レモネード	remonedo	lemonade

More Useful Phrases よく使われる表現

Temple	otera/odera/-ji/-in/-do	堂
Shrine	jinja/jingu/-gu/-do/taisha	神社
Castle	-jo	城
Park	koen	公園
River	kawa/gawa	川
Bridge	hashi/bashi	橋
Museum	hakubutsukan	博物館
Zoo	dobutsuen	動物園
Botanical gardens	shokubutsuen	植物園
Island	shima/jima/to	島
Slope	saka/zaka	坂
Hill	oka	丘
Lake	-ko	湖
Bay	-wan	湾
Plain	hara/bara/taira/daira	平
Peninsula	hanto	半島
Mountain	yama/-san/-take	山
Cape	misaki/saki	岬
Sea	kai/nada	海
Gorge	kyo	峡
Plateau	kogen	高原
Train line	sen	線
Prefecture	-ken/-fu	県
Ward	-ku	区
Exit	deguchi/-guchi	出口
Street, avenue	dori/-do/michi	道
Highway, main road	kaido	公道
In front of	mae	前
North	kita	北
South	minami	南
East	higashi	東
West	nishi	西
Shop, store	mise/-ya	店
Hot-spring spa	onsen	温泉

INDEX

NOTES

NOTES

Fodor's Travel Publications

Available at bookstores everywhere, or call 1–800–533–6478, 24 hours a day.

Gold Guides

U.S.

Alaska

Arizona

Boston

California

Cape Cod, Martha's
Vineyard, Nantucket

The Carolinas & the
Georgia Coast

Chicago

Colorado

Florida

Hawaii

Las Vegas, Reno,
Tahoe

Los Angeles

Maine, Vermont,
New Hampshire

Maui

Miami & the Keys

New England

New Orleans

New York City

Pacific North Coast

Philadelphia & the
Pennsylvania Dutch
Country

The Rockies

San Diego

San Francisco

Santa Fe, Taos,
Albuquerque

Seattle & Vancouver

The South

U.S. & British Virgin
Islands

USA

Virginia & Maryland

Waikiki

Washington, D.C.

Foreign

Australia &
New Zealand

Austria

The Bahamas

Bermuda

Budapest

Canada

Cancún, Cozumel,
Yucatán Peninsula

Caribbean

China

Costa Rica, Belize,
Guatemala

Cuba

The Czech Republic
& Slovakia

Eastern Europe

Egypt

Europe

Florence, Tuscany
& Umbria

France

Germany

Great Britain

Greece

Hong Kong

India

Ireland

Israel

Italy

Japan

Kenya & Tanzania

Korea

London

Madrid & Barcelona

Mexico

Montréal &
Québec City

Moscow, St.
Petersburg, Kiev

The Netherlands,
Belgium &
Luxembourg

New Zealand

Norway

Nova Scotia, New
Brunswick, Prince
Edward Island

Paris

Portugal

Provence &
the Riviera

Scandinavia

Scotland

Singapore

South America

South Pacific

Southeast Asia

Spain

Sweden

Switzerland

Thailand

Tokyo

Toronto

Turkey

Vienna &
the Danube

Fodor's Special-Interest Guides

Branson

Caribbean Ports
of Call

The Complete Guide
to America's
National Parks

Condé Nast Traveler
Caribbean Resort and
Cruise Ship Finder

Cruises and Ports
of Call

Fodor's London
Companion

France by Train

Halliday's New
England Food
Explorer

Healthy Escapes

Italy by Train

Kodak Guide to
Shooting Great
Travel Pictures

Shadow Traffic's
New York Shortcuts
and Traffic Tips

Sunday in New York

Sunday in
San Francisco

Walt Disney World,
Universal Studios
and Orlando

Walt Disney World
for Adults

Where Should We
Take the Kids?
California

Where Should We
Take the Kids?
Northeast

Special Series

Affordables

Caribbean
Europe
Florida
France
Germany
Great Britain
Italy
London
Paris

Fodor's Bed & Breakfasts and Country Inns

America's Best B&Bs
California's Best B&Bs
Canada's Great Country Inns
Cottages, B&Bs and Country Inns of England and Wales
The Mid-Atlantic's Best B&Bs
New England's Best B&Bs
The Pacific Northwest's Best B&Bs
The South's Best B&Bs
The Southwest's Best B&Bs
The Upper Great Lakes' Best B&Bs

The Berkeley Guides

California
Central America
Eastern Europe
Europe
France
Germany & Austria
Great Britain & Ireland
Italy
London
Mexico

Pacific Northwest & Alaska
Paris
San Francisco

Compass American Guides

Arizona
Chicago
Colorado
Hawaii
Hollywood
Las Vegas
Maine
Manhattan
Montana
New Mexico
New Orleans
Oregon
San Francisco
Santa Fe
South Carolina
South Dakota
Southwest
Texas
Utah
Virginia
Washington
Wine Country
Wisconsin
Wyoming

Fodor's Español

California
Caribe Occidental
Caribe Oriental
Gran Bretaña
Londres
Mexico
Nueva York
Paris

Fodor's Exploring Guides

Australia
Boston & New England
Britain
California
Caribbean
China
Egypt
Florence & Tuscany
Florida
France
Germany
Ireland
Israel
Italy
Japan
London
Mexico
Moscow & St. Petersburg
New York City
Paris
Prague
Provence
Rome
San Francisco
Scotland
Singapore & Malaysia
Spain
Thailand
Turkey
Venice

Fodor's Flashmaps

Boston
New York
San Francisco
Washington, D.C.

Fodor's Pocket Guides

Acapulco
Atlanta
Barbados

Jamaica
London
New York City
Paris
Prague
Puerto Rico
Rome
San Francisco
Washington, D.C.

Rivages Guides

Bed and Breakfasts of Character and Charm in France
Hotels and Country Inns of Character and Charm in France
Hotels and Country Inns of Character and Charm in Italy

Short Escapes

Country Getaways in Britain
Country Getaways in France
Country Getaways Near New York City

Fodor's Sports

Golf Digest's Best Places to Play
Skiing USA
USA Today The Complete Four Sport Stadium Guide

Fodor's Vacation Planners

Great American Learning Vacations
Great American Sports & Adventure Vacations
Great American Vacations
National Parks and Seashores of the East
National Parks of the West

Your guide to a picture-perfect vacation

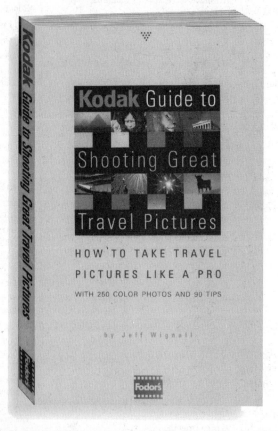

Kodak and Fodor's join together to create the guide that travelers everywhere have been asking for—one that covers the terms and techniques, the equipment and etiquette for taking first-rate travel photographs.

The most authoritative and up-to-date book of its kind, **The Kodak Guide to Shooting Great Travel Pictures** includes over 200 color photographs and spreads on 100 points of photography important to travelers, such as landscape basics, under sea shots, wildlife, city street, close-ups, photographing in museums and more.

$16.50   ($22.95 Canada)

At bookstores everywhere, or call 1-800-533-6478.

Fodor's. The name that means smart travel.™